THE
ALMANAC OF
STATE LEGISLATIVE
ELECTIONS

THE ALMANAC OF STATE LEGISLATIVE ELECTIONS

VOTING PATTERNS AND DEMOGRAPHICS 2000–2006

THIRD EDITION

WILLIAM LILLEY III • LAURENCE J. DeFRANCO • MARK F. BERNSTEIN • KARI L. RAMSBY

CQ PRESS

A Division of Congressional Quarterly Inc.

Washington, D.C.

CQ Press
1255 22nd Street, NW, Suite 400
Washington, DC 20037

Phone: 202-729-1900; toll-free, (1-866-4CQ-PRESS) 1-866-427-7737

Web: www.cqpress.com

Cover design: www.thedesignfarm.com
Compositor: Auburn Associates, Inc.

♾ The paper used in this publication exceeds the requirements of the American National Standard for Information Sciences—Permanence of Paper for Printed Library Materials, ANSI Z39.48-1992.

Printed and bound in the United States of America

11   10   09   08   07   1   2   3   4   5

ISBN: 978-0-87289-551-5

CONTENTS

PREFACE

The Almanac of State Legislative Elections: Voting Patterns and Demographics, 2000–2006, third edition, is a thorough revision, update, and expansion of the four previous books analyzing American state legislatures, all published by CQ Press, a division of Congressional Quarterly Inc. The earlier books are *The Almanac of State Legislatures* (1994), *The State Atlas of Political and Cultural Diversity* (1997), *State Legislative Elections* (1998), and *The Almanac of State Legislatures: Changing Patterns, 1990–1997* (1998). The principal authors for all of the books are Laurence J. DeFranco and William Lilley III, the founders of iMapData Inc., whose resources were extensively used in preparing this book. (iMapData is a wholly owned subsidiary of ChoicePoint Inc., a Georgia-based information, software, and analytics provider.) Prolific author and journalist Michael Barone served as a principal author for volume 3, and Mark F. Bernstein, author of several books, performed the same role in volume 4 and this volume. Kari Ramsby of iMapData managed the day-to-day process of assembling and merging the separate pieces of the books.

This volume uses a range of socioeconomic data to show how each of the nation's 6,744 state legislative districts changed during the first seven years of the twenty-first century, marking changes in population, wealth, poverty, degree of education, race, and ethnicity. Similarly, the volume uses extensive data from the fifty secretary of state offices to show voting results and voting changes in each of the districts during the new century; these changes are discussed at greater length in the introduction.

The introduction to the volume summarizes the major trends at work in all fifty states and their legislative districts. State-by-state analyses, data, and 290 maps follow. Each state profile includes an essay analyzing the major changes taking place; multicolor maps illustrating each district's gain or loss in population during the period, and statistical tables detailing each district's population change, wealth, degree of higher education, percentage of population below the poverty line, and ethnic and racial mix. So rich are the data and analysis, and so detailed and striking the maps showing population change, that the *Almanac* provides the first comprehensive look at how center-city core areas, which for decades have been losing population, are making a comeback—in some cases, relatively quickly. This important demographic shift could become one of the hallmarks of the new century.

Methodology

Four basic methodological components underlie the information in this volume, and all four reflect refinements and expansions of methodologies used in the four volumes noted above. The meshing of the four creates this book's added value.

The first component provides the boundaries for each of the 6,744 state legislative districts in a digitized (computer-readable) file. Before publication of the 1994 *Almanac,* no single volume contained all of the precise geographic boundaries of the individual state senate and state house districts. These boundaries, redrawn following the 2000 census, form the analytical spine of the volume. Because no state's redistricting process is the same, determining each state's district boundaries—some of which changed more than once during the decade—was no easy task. iMapData contacted each state legislative redistricting office following the 2000 census; whenever our researchers spotted a subsequent change, they requested shape files or census block equivalency files for digitizing new boundaries. That work—including gathering the data, digitizing the files, and creating the multicolor maps—was done by Clarence Buffalo, Peter W. Fleury, and Jeff Macintire for iMapData.

The second component is the fifty state essays introducing each chapter, written by Mark F. Bernstein (who also wrote the introduction). These essays analyze how the state's legislative profile has changed during the decade. Bernstein's essays draw from the vast range of data in components three and four described below.

The third component comprises election results for each of the state legislative districts during the twenty-first century. The initial election data were drawn from the official Web sites of the fifty secretaries of state. Further data compilation—correcting inaccuracies, discrepancies, and omissions—was done manually by Kari Ramsby and Missy Burian for iMapData. As an extremely large number of elections, election results, candidates, and parties are involved over the six-plus years (imagine approximately three times 6,744, or in excess of 20,000 elections), the task facing the secretaries of state and the iMapData team was daunting. Every effort has been made to fact-check the electoral data; no doubt, some errors exist, but they do so in the face of an exhaustive compilation and cleansing effort.

The fourth component is the *Almanac*'s district-by-district demographics. The compilation and analytical effort was done by Bamberg-Handley, a Florida-based corporation nationally known for its expertise in handling demographic data. Bamberg-Handley earned such status by means of its primary business: using demographic data to assign individual business prospects and provide an individual purchase probability metric. The Bamberg-Handley team was led by Harry Handley, who co-founded the company in 1984. For population change per district, Bamberg-Handley used the 2000 census, the census estimates for 2005 (by county), and its own projections for census block group data for 2006. The block group data were then grossed up into individual legislative district data. For average household income per district, Bamberg-Handley used 2000 census data, Bureau of Economic Analysis estimates for 2005 (all by county), and its own block-group projections for 2006. For the data on degree of college education, Bamberg-Handley used the 2000 census, the 2005 census estimates (all by county), and its own projections for block groups for 2006. For percentage below the poverty line data, Bamberg-Handley used the 2000 census, Bureau of Economic Analysis estimates for 2005 (all by county), and its own block group estimates for 2006. All the ethic and racial data came from the 2000 census, the census 2004–2005 estimates (all by county), and its own block group estimates for 2006.

William Lilley III
Laurence J. DeFranco
Mark. F. Bernstein
Kari Ramsby

INTRODUCTION

Americans have been leaving the cities for almost as long as they have been moving to them. For every Sister Carrie (Theodore Dreiser's character in the book with the same name) arriving from the farm to make a living in the heartless city of Chicago, there were Quaker families in Philadelphia moving out along the Reading and Pennsylvania Railroad lines to suburban Bryn Mawr and Chestnut Hill, abandoning the old colonial neighborhoods to immigrants and decay. As soon as advances in communication and transportation made it possible, people began moving ever farther out of town for a lot of the same reasons—for more affordable houses, bigger lots, a sense of community, and a quieter life.

The suburbs are often described as a postwar phenomenon, but as Edward Banfield showed in *The Unheavenly City Revisited*, they have been a national preoccupation for more than a century. Banfield quotes an 1857 report by a committee of the New York state legislature that observed, "As our wharves became crowded with warehouses and encompassed with bustle and noise, the wealthier citizens . . . transferred their residences to streets beyond the din; compensating for remoteness from their counting-houses by the advantages of increased luxury. Their habitations then passed into the hands, on the one side, of boarding house keepers, on the other, of real estate agents."

From a more literary perspective, William Dean Howells wrote in 1871 of his experiences in an unidentified Boston suburb he called Charlesbridge, but which might as well have been Levittown (suburb of Philadelphia) in 1955 or Rancho Cucamonga (suburb of Los Angeles) in 2007: "We were living in the country with all the conveniences and luxuries of the city about us. The house was almost new and in perfect repair; and, better than all, the kitchen had as yet given no signs of unrest in those volcanic agencies which are constantly at work there."

This has come to be called the "metropolitan doughnut," the phenomenon in which people are simultaneously pushing out from the city center and rushing in from the countryside, creating an ever-widening circle of suburbs. It has also been called the "rural rebound," but that is something of a misnomer. The rural areas growing fastest are those that are most rapidly losing their character as rural. People are not moving to places such as Roseville, California, or Schaumburg, Illinois, to live the country life, but to live the suburban life no longer possible in many crowded, older suburbs.

In region after region, a pattern repeats itself: a central city losing population (say, Washington, D.C.) is surrounded by close-in suburbs of more modest growth (Arlington, Virginia), which are themselves surrounded by more far-flung suburbs of much faster growth, often spreading into rural areas once considered outside the metropolitan area

(Leesburg, Virginia, or even Harper's Ferry, West Virginia). But that oversimplifies the progression. What one also sees, and what has become particularly apparent during the past decade, is that parts of the city rebound and grow, even if the city as a whole continues to shrink, and even as the newer suburbs expand further outward.

To be sure, downtown factories are not reopening, and the great department stores that once anchored the central shopping district are gone for good. But many cities have seen a decrease in crime and an increase in construction. In Philadelphia and St. Louis, anyone who converts old, unwanted commercial office space into residences can receive a tax abatement, and so parts of their downtowns are now filling with condominiums and restaurants. This is not exactly urban renewal—both cities, as a whole, are still losing population—but it does show that the doughnut can be filling a bit at the center even as it continues to expand at the edges.

Ten years ago, in the second edition of *The Almanac of State Legislatures,* we illustrated the changing shape of the metropolitan doughnut with examples from four cities—Philadelphia, Chicago, St. Louis, and Los Angeles—in each case tracing a line from the center of the shrinking city to their fast-growing fringes (See Tables 1–5). Our 1997 analysis supported the prevailing mood of gloom about big center cities: taking the centermost state house district in each city, we found Chicago's center city district losing 10 percent of its population, Los Angeles's, 13 percent, Philadelphia's, 7 percent, and St. Louis's, 16 percent. Revisiting those districts a decade later, we can see that while the outer suburbs have continued to expand, parts of many cities—at the center of the doughnut—have stopped losing people (or stopped losing them quite so fast) and in some cases have even begun to grow again. The Los Angeles area fits this model, too, though the extent of its increases and declines are different owing to its unique circumstances. We have added a rising Sun Belt city, Nashville, to our illustration, to show that the pattern occurs in all parts of the country.

Hence, similar state house districts in the same cities, as well as Nashville, reveal a far more stable picture than they did a decade ago. Areas that were hemorrhaging are now stable, and parts are growing. If one looks even more closely, by block group (the smallest geographic unit for which the Census Bureau collects data), the results are even more startling. Chicago's 9th house district, for example, which includes the area around the Dan Ryan and Eisenhower Expressways, had lost 13 percent of its population when we looked ten years ago. Since 2000 it has lost only 1 percent, and in some block groups population has actually risen more than 40 percent. Truly, this is a country where change is constant.

Furthermore, as the metropolitan doughnuts have expanded, they have come to cover huge amounts of territory, frequently crossing state lines. People now commute regularly to New York City from Pike County, Pennsylvania, while the Philadelphia metropolitan area reaches deep into New Jersey. One of the fastest-growing parts of the Las Vegas suburbs is in southwestern Utah, more than 100 miles away. Many of those far-flung commuters do not commute all the way to downtown, but often to other suburbs.

All these trends carry important political implications. Smaller cities have less representation in the legislatures and in Congress than they once had. Philadelphia, which once had five U.S. representatives, now has three, all of whose districts spill into the surrounding counties. Because there are fewer districts covering the same space, urban districts today are also bigger than they once were. It remains to be seen what this means politically. Inner cities are still Democratic bastions, but they carry less weight. Newer suburbs tend to attract young, white families who tend to vote Republican.

Examining these trends from the level of the state legislative district offers a ground-level view of how the country is changing—politically, racially, and demographically. It provides clues as to trends that may soon affect the national debate and explanations for changes that have already taken place.

Table 1. Chicago (State: 71% White, 15% Black, 15% Hispanic)

District	Type	Racial/Ethnic Composition 1997	Population Change 1990–1997	Racial/Ethnic Composition 2006	Population Change 2000–2006
9th	Older residential, west side	8% White 78% Black 1% Hispanic	-13%	26% White 54% Black 17% Hispanic	-1%
10th	Older residential, northwest side	5% White 80% Black 14% Hispanic	-10%	32% White 53% Black 15% Hispanic	-1%
8th	Residential urban inside South Tollway	22% White 70% Black 6% Hispanic	-6%	30% White 55% Black 15.5% Hispanic	-3%
77th	Close-in suburbs	76% White 4% Black 17% Hispanic	-1%	56% White 6% Black 30% Hispanic	-3%
46th	Close-in suburbs	80% White 1% Black 5% Asian 14% Hispanic	0	67% White 2% Black 22% Hispanic	+2%
45th	Just inside I-290	82% White 3% Black 9% Asian 6% Hispanic	+8%	67% White 4% Black 14% Hispanic	+3%
49th	Suburban Schaumburg	79% White 4% Black 9% Asian 8% Hispanic	+21%	80% White 3% Black 12% Hispanic	-1% (now the 56th district)
50th	Cook/DuPage County line	86% White 1% Black 4% Asian 8% Hispanic	+23%	85% White 2% Black 10% Hispanic	+9% (now the 55th district)
65th	Kane County	88% White 2% Black 1% Hispanic	+14%	80% White 3% Black 12% Hispanic	+32% (now the 49th district)
65th	Kane County	88% White 2% Black 1% Hispanic	+14%	85% White 2% Black 10% Hispanic	+38% (now the 50th district)

Table 2. Los Angeles (State: 56% White, 6% Black, 37% Hispanic)

District	Type	Racial/Ethnic Composition 1997	Population Change 1990–1997	Racial/Ethnic Composition 2006	Population Change 2000–2006
46th	Central Los Angeles	3% White 7% Black 75% Hispanic	-13%	6% White 7% Black 86% Hispanic	+5%
45th	Urban E. Los Angeles	8% White 3% Black 68% Hispanic	-16%	14% White 4% Black 68% Hispanic	+4%
44th	Urban San Gabriel	50% White 12% Black 13% Asian 24% Hispanic	+7%	36% White 8% Black 34% Hispanic	+4%
59th	Suburban Pasadena	54% White 6% Black 11% Asian 28% Hispanic	+11%	55% White 5% Black 28% Hispanic	+11%
36th	Suburban San Gabriel Mountains, Lancaster	65% White 5% Black 5% Asian 24% Hispanic	+29%	45% White 10% Black 35% Hispanic	+13%
34th	Rural Mojave Desert	70% White 5% Black 3% Asian 20% Hispanic	+18%	40% White 3.5% Black 44% Hispanic	+12%

Table 3. Philadelphia (State: 84% White, 10% Black, 4% Hispanic)

District	Type	Racial/Ethnic Composition 1997	Population Change 1990–1997	Racial/Ethnic Composition 2006	Population Change 2000–2006
175th	Center City, Society Hill	81% White 11% Black 2% Hispanic	-6%	50.5% White 21% Black 14% Hispanic	+1%
182nd	Center City	68% White 22% Black 5% Hispanic	-5%	57% White 25% Black 6% Hispanic	-1%
195th	Older residential, Strawberry Mansion	26% White 68% Black 3% Hispanic	-7%	27% White 62% Black 5% Hispanic	0%
197th	Older residential, Germantown	0% White 98% Black 0% Hispanic	-8%	17% White 77% Black 3.5% Hispanic	-2%
198th	Older residential, Germantown and East Mt. Airy	31% White 66% Black 1% Hispanic	-7%	21% White 66.5% Black 7% Hispanic	-6%
200th	Older residential, Chestnut Hill	26% White 71% Black	-7%	30.5% White 62% Black 3% Hispanic	-6%
154th	Close-in suburbs, Montgomery County	82% White 12% Black	-2%	68% White 22% Black 3% Hispanic	+1%
148th	Close-in suburbs, Conshohocken	93% White 3% Black	+1%	88% White 5% Black 2% Hispanic	+5%
61st	Close-in suburbs, Plymouth Meeting	88% White 4% Black 6% Asian	+10%	83.5% White 5% Black 2% Hispanic	+8%
70th	Montgomery County, Norristown	76% White 18% Black 3% Hispanic	+6%	75% White 14% Black 5% Hispanic	+5%
147th	Outer Montgomery County	96% White 1% Black 2% Hispanic	+14%	94% White 2% Black 2% Hispanic	+7%
134th	Berks County	96% White 0% Black 3% Hispanic	+5%	92% White 1% Black 3% Hispanic	+9%
130th	Berks County, Boyertown	97% White 1% Black 0% Hispanic	+6%	93% White 2% Black 2% Hispanic	+8%
128th	Berks County, Reading suburbs	96% White 1% Black 1% Hispanic	+1%	91% White 2% Black 3% Hispanic	+7%

Table 4. St. Louis (State: 84% White, 12% Black, 2% Hispanic)

District	Type	Racial/Ethnic Composition 1997	Population Change 1990–1997	Racial/Ethnic Composition 2006	Population Change 2000–2006
67th	Southern St. Louis	66% White 29% Black 3% Hispanic	-16%	49% White 40% Black 5% Hispanic	0%
65th	Urban residential	88% White 9% Black 1% Hispanic	-7%	65% White 30% Black 2% Hispanic	0%
84th	Older suburbs around Brentwood	79% White 15% Black 2% Hispanic	0	78% White 12% Black, 2% Hispanic	-1% (now the 73rd district)
87th	Middle suburbs around Clayton, Ladue	87% White 8% Black 1% Hispanic	-2%	86% White 8% Black 1.5% Hispanic	0%
86th	Middle suburbs around Chesterfield	90% White 2% Black 1% Hispanic	-2%	90.5% White 3% Black 2% Hispanic	+2% (now the 84th district)
89th	Distant suburbs	93% White 4% Black 1% Hispanic	+22%	90% White 2% Black 2% Hispanic	-1% (now in 88th district
89th	Rural St. Charles County	93% White 4% Black 1% Hispanic	+22%	92% White 3% Black 2% Hispanic	+8%
13th	Rural St. Charles County	92% White 5% Black 2% Hispanic	+21%	97% White 1% Black 1% Hispanic	+10% (now in 109th district)
13th	Warren County	92% White 5% Black 2% Hispanic	+21%	92% White 4% Black 2% Hispanic	+33%

Table 5. Nashville (State: 79% White, 16% Black, 3% Hispanic)

District	Type	Racial/Ethnic Composition 1997	Population Change 1990–1997	Racial/Ethnic Composition 2006	Population Change 2000–2006
58th	Downtown	24% White 73% Black 1% Hispanic	-3%	30% White 63% Black 4% Hispanic	+2%
54th	Downtown inside I-40	27% White 71% Black 1% Hispanic	-2%	34% White 59% Black 4% Hispanic	0%
55th	West Nashville	88% White 7% Black 4% Hispanic	+3%	75.5% White 12% Black 4% Hispanic	0%
56th	Older suburb, Belle Mead	94% White 3% Black 2% Hispanic	+14%	84% White 7% Black 3% Hispanic	+3%
61st	Inner Williamson County	93% White 4% Black 1% Hispanic	+40%	89% White 4% Black 4% Hispanic	+22%
63rd	Outer Williamson County	91% White 8% Black 0% Hispanic	+28%	86% White 8% Black 3.5% Hispanic	+25%
64th	Distant suburb, Maury County	82% White 17% Black 0% Hispanic	+26%	78% White 15% Black 4% Hispanic	+10%

About the Authors

William Lilley III, cofounder of iMapData Inc., is a former political and economic historian who was a senior corporate official of the media company CBS. He has also served as the director of the U.S. Council on Wage & Price Stability, as staff director of the Budget Committee for the U.S. House of Representatives, and as deputy assistant secretary of the U.S. Department of Housing and Urban Development. He received his Ph.D. from Yale University, taught at Yale, and has written widely on how government policies affect local economic activity, on the economics of the professional sports business, and on the socioeconomic make up of state and local constituencies.

Laurence J. DeFranco, cofounder of iMapData Inc., is an expert in geo-economics, which merges the disciplines of economics, political science, and geography with computer science. He has written, testified, and spoken widely on the effects of regulatory, economic, and legislative policies on businesses, especially in a geographic context. Previously, he ran various software and consulting firms in the political-economic and information industries and worked for CBS.

Mark F. Bernstein is a writer whose work has appeared in the *Public Interest, New Republic,* and *Wall Street Journal,* among other places. He is the author of three books, most recently, *Football: The Ivy League Origins of an American Obsession* (2001). Previously, he was a legislative aide to Rep. Richard J. Durbin, D-Ill., a research assistant to Sen. Daniel Patrick Moynihan, D-N.Y., and a law clerk to a judge on the U.S. Court of Appeals. Bernstein graduated from Princeton University and received his law degree from the University of Virginia, where he was an editor of the law review.

Kari L. Ramsby heads client services and major projects for iMapData Inc. She is an expert in political data, including elections and redistricting. Previously, she managed client projects in the telecommunications and software industries. She received her B.S. from Virginia Polytechnic Institute and State University.

ALABAMA

Two generations have passed since Alabama was a battlefield at the center of the civil rights revolution. In the early 1960s, Birmingham Public Safety Commissioner Bull Connor turned water hoses and police attack dogs on marchers while in Dallas County, Sheriff James Clark's helmeted deputies blocked Martin Luther King Jr. and other demonstrators from crossing the Edmund Pettus Bridge.

Alabama life has always been raw, befitting its beginnings on the American frontier. Though the main cleavage since the 1860s has been between white and black, Alabama was once home to one of the nation's largest populations of Creek, Cherokee, and Choctaw Indians, who were forcibly moved west in the 1830s by President Andrew Jackson. The freebooters who moved in were well described by nineteenth-century humorist James G. Baldwin, who wrote of one Alabama village that it "boasted a population of some five hundred souls; about a third of whom were single gentlemen who had come out on the vague errand of seeking their fortune, or the more definite one of seeking somebody else's."

Political radicals have also had success here, such as Jefferson Davis, who took the oath of office as president of the Confederacy on the steps of the state capitol in Montgomery. At the other end of the spectrum, in the 1960s rural Lowndes County was home to the Lowndes County Freedom Organization, organized by Stokely Carmichael, then a director of the Student Nonviolent Coordinating Committee, which took as its logo a black panther and inspired the more violent Black Panther Party.

Today, while Montgomery still boasts its beautiful antebellum mansions, it is also home to a Hyundai auto assembly plant. Birmingham is a midsized city that has had some success reinventing itself as a medical center after the decline of many of its steel mills (and having fallen hopelessly behind its one-time rival, Atlanta). Selma is now home to the National Voting Rights Museum and presidential hopefuls in 2005 joined the ceremonies to mark the fortieth anniversary of the 1965 Selma-Montgomery voting rights march. But the success of the civil rights movement can be summed up in one statistic: Alabama today has more elected African American public officials (756 out of 2004) than any other state except one—Mississippi.

Political change in Alabama was bottled up for decades, and for whites as well as blacks. In the early 1960s, Alabama still apportioned its legislative districts according to the 1900 census, despite a provision of the state constitution requiring that districts be redrawn every ten years. Some districts had forty times as many people as others. It was a challenge to those boundaries in 1964 that led the Supreme Court to issue its famous "one-man, one-vote" decision in *Reynolds v. Sims.*

African Americans gained the franchise in Alabama, but they make up a much smaller share of the state than they once did, thanks in part to the massive migrations northward after two world wars and a vicious racial climate. In 1870 blacks constituted 47 percent of the state's population. By 1910 it had dropped to 42.5 percent. Today, it is barely 26 percent.

In order to maximize black voting districts in Birmingham after the 1990 census, the state engaged in racial gerrymandering, which has had the unintended consequence (though some argue it was deliberate) of leaving the areas surrounding those black-majority districts with more white, conservative voters. If the chief beneficiaries were black Democrats, the chief casualties were white Democrats. During the 1990s, while one black Democrat was elected to Congress from a gerrymandered "majority-minority district," the party as a whole lost three U.S. House seats, as well as four in the state senate and another ten in the state house, along with the governor's mansion and both U.S. senate seats. It is emblematic that Alabama's senior U.S. senator, Richard Shelby, took office as a Democrat before switching parties, the day after the GOP won control of the Senate in the 1994 midterm landslide.

By the late 1990s, it seemed possible that Alabama could undergo a complete political transformation. Nine of the ten fastest-growing state house districts and seven of the ten fastest-growing senate districts were held by Republicans, while nine of the ten slowest-growing house and senate districts, and twenty-one of twenty-three Alabama districts that had lost population during the decade were held by Democrats. Demography, if nothing else, seemed to favor a Republican realignment.

Instead, the current decade has been a time for Alabama to catch its breath. Though still reliably Republican in presidential elections, the GOP has not made many inroads in Montgomery. Democrats, who controlled the state senate in 2000 by a margin of 24–11 controlled it by a margin of 25–10 after the 2006 elections. (Though stable, things are still rough: one state senator punched another during a floor debate in 2007.)

The state house (the only one in the country whose members serve four-year terms), which was 68–37 Democratic in 2001, was 63–42 Democratic in 2007. The areas of the state that are gaining population—the 41st house district, for example, which comprises the suburbs south of Birmingham, has grown by almost a third in the last seven years—tend to be Republican, but there are some growing Democratic areas, too, in the area around Huntsville. The GOP most likely will not take control of either chamber anytime soon.

Alabama has not gained or lost a congressional seat since 1970. Its population grew by only 1.9 percent from 2000 to 2004, less than half the national average and almost a quarter of the growth of its booming Sunbelt neighbors, Georgia and Florida.

ALABAMA
State Senate Districts

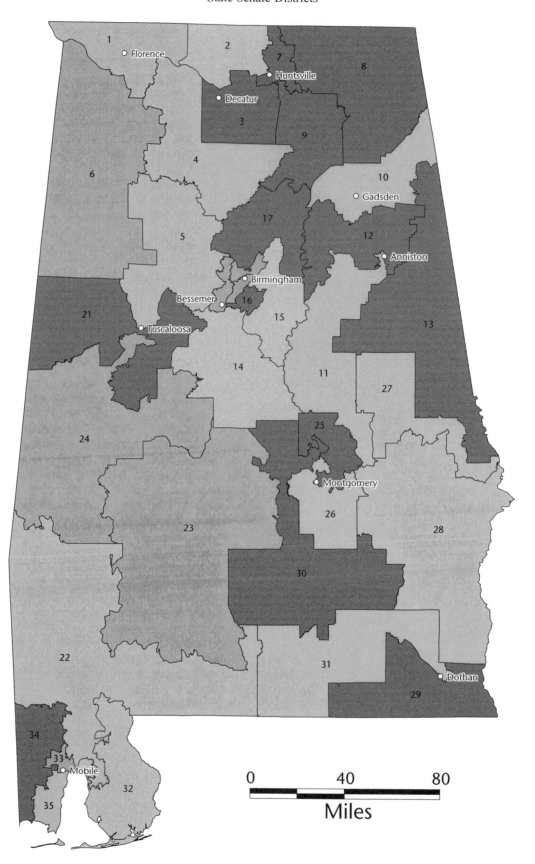

Population Growth   ▨ -5% to -1%   ▨ -1% to 3%   ▨ 3% to 10%   ▨ 10% to 19%

BIRMINGHAM

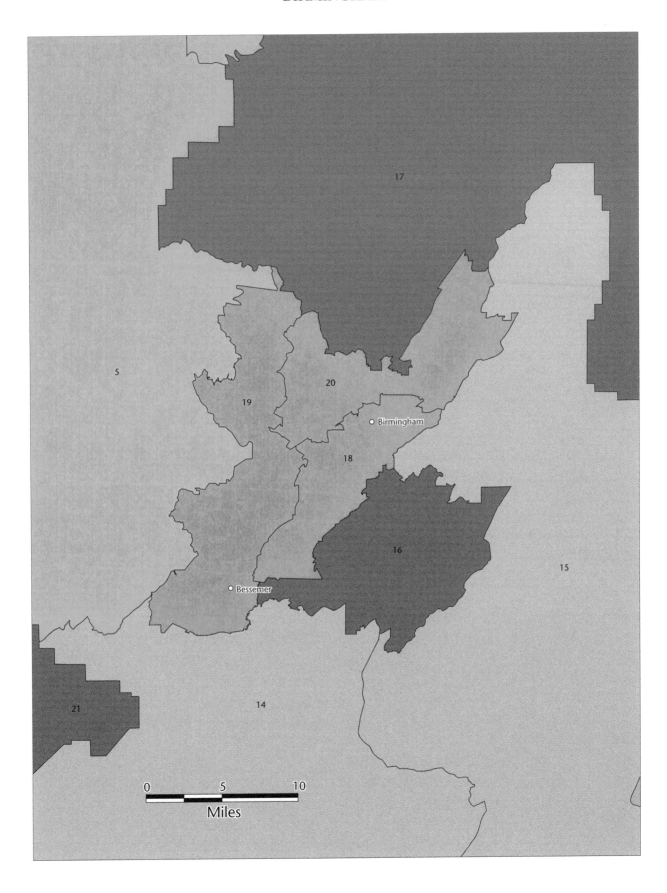

Population Growth | -5% to -1% | -1% to 3% | 3% to 10% | 10% to 19%

Alabama State Senate Districts—Election and Demographic Data

Senate Districts	General Election Results Party, Percent of Vote							Population			Avg. HH Income	2006 Pop 25+ Some College +	4-Yr Degree +	Below Poverty Line	White (Non-Hisp)	African American	American Indians, Alaska Natives	Asians, Hawaiians, Pacific Islanders	Hispanic Origin
Alabama	2000	2001	2002	2003	2004	2005	2006	2000	2006	% Change	($)	(%)	(%)	(%)	(%)	(%)	(%)	(%)	(%)
1			D, 64				D, 64	130,129	129,899	0	48,372	32.1	13.8	20.9	83.4	13.6	0.3	0.4	1.4
2			D, 58				D, 60	132,511	147,028	11	60,041	39.2	21.8	14.3	75.5	17.9	0.6	1.4	3.0
3			D, 63				R, 62	134,269	140,661	5	56,531	36.8	17.1	16.4	78.9	13.0	0.7	1.1	4.7
4			D, 62				D, 60	120,847	122,703	2	46,123	26.5	8.4	22.0	88.8	4.9	1.6	0.2	2.7
5			R, 58				R, 55	132,434	135,733	2	52,115	31.8	12.3	19.6	88.8	8.5	0.3	0.4	1.1
6			D, 61				D, 97	120,770	116,951	-3	41,513	23.9	7.4	26.2	86.4	7.1	0.4	0.2	4.1
7			D, 64				D, 65	133,002	142,677	7	59,236	42.7	24.3	17.1	61.2	32.9	0.7	1.3	2.3
8			D, 58				D, 57	133,595	140,273	5	45,301	25.5	8.8	21.8	86.0	3.8	1.2	0.3	5.8
9			D, 59				D, 53	131,910	141,679	7	56,051	35.7	18.2	17.4	85.8	2.4	0.5	1.3	7.0
10			D, 68				D, 98	122,576	123,876	1	44,215	30.2	10.1	22.3	82.0	13.7	0.3	0.4	2.3
11			D, 67				D, 64	125,486	126,555	1	43,796	26.2	8.9	25.8	63.7	33.5	0.3	0.2	1.6
12			R, 59				R, 98	128,738	134,909	5	49,528	30.9	11.5	19.1	84.7	11.6	0.4	0.5	1.7
13			D, 99				D, 50	123,831	129,977	5	44,783	26.7	8.8	21.8	76.0	21.1	0.2	0.3	1.6
14			R, 99				R, 97	133,654	153,186	15	58,966	35.3	17.4	14.4	85.0	9.5	0.3	0.6	3.3
15			R, 88				R, 99	126,869	142,134	12	82,120	44.5	24.5	10.7	86.3	9.8	0.3	0.7	2.0
16			R, 99				R, 78	130,549	138,739	6	94,788	57.0	39.4	6.7	85.0	6.6	0.2	2.7	4.2
17			R, 84				R, 99	131,095	142,505	9	50,480	31.6	10.4	16.5	88.9	6.1	0.4	0.3	3.0
18			D, 99				D, 81	124,945	121,756	-3	43,109	42.9	21.4	27.1	28.8	66.4	0.2	1.7	3.7
19			D, 77				D, 99	120,930	119,011	-2	40,392	35.1	11.8	25.6	32.9	65.5	0.2	0.2	1.2
20			D, 99				D, 80	122,985	119,442	-3	43,291	37.3	13.7	23.1	32.3	65.1	0.2	0.4	2.3
21			D, 59				D, 69	121,231	125,396	3	46,980	32.1	14.2	23.4	70.4	26.0	0.3	0.9	1.6
22			D, 51				D, 54	132,393	134,766	2	45,463	26.0	9.8	25.1	64.7	30.6	2.7	0.2	1.0
23			D, 71				D, 66	121,078	117,298	-3	37,927	23.1	8.5	36.1	36.6	62.0	0.2	0.3	0.7
24			D, 98				D, 98	120,841	117,973	-2	40,604	26.9	11.0	31.9	36.0	62.1	0.1	0.3	1.4
25			R, 78				R, 74	131,193	136,565	4	65,306	44.3	24.4	10.3	76.7	18.8	0.3	1.4	1.8
26			D, 72				D, 99	129,835	129,067	-1	42,739	30.9	13.8	26.6	28.1	69.6	0.2	0.6	1.3
27			D, 64				D, 61	129,204	129,673	0	43,022	34.2	16.9	28.3	71.8	24.2	0.3	1.5	1.5
28			D, 85				D, 99	126,991	125,891	-1	39,909	28.0	11.8	32.5	41.4	55.5	0.3	0.5	2.5
29			R, 99				R, 75	122,361	128,532	5	49,249	34.1	12.6	19.7	79.1	15.4	0.5	0.8	2.6
30			D, 99				D, 62	124,989	132,048	6	47,338	28.3	11.6	24.1	67.1	30.0	0.4	0.4	1.4
31			D, 65				D, 56	122,577	125,310	2	43,934	30.5	11.3	24.6	70.9	24.8	0.6	0.6	2.0
32			R, 90				R, 99	122,347	144,740	18	57,417	39.2	17.7	14.7	88.0	7.2	0.6	0.4	2.4
33			D, 100				D, 71	127,169	121,792	-4	39,883	30.8	16.4	30.3	34.8	62.7	0.3	0.6	1.1
34			R, 100				R, 99	129,010	136,314	6	59,825	35.2	20.7	14.2	84.0	11.3	0.5	1.5	1.5
35			D, 51				R, 51	124,369	125,208	1	49,051	31.3	15.8	22.6	62.1	32.3	0.4	2.7	1.5

Note: D=Democrat, R=Republican, R/D=Republican/Democrat (cross-filed), D/R=Democrat/Republican (cross-filed), I=Independent, C=Constitution, O=Other, GI=Green Independent, P=Progressive, P/D=Progressive/Democrat, P/D/R=Progressive/Democrat/Republican, HH=Households

ALABAMA
State House Districts

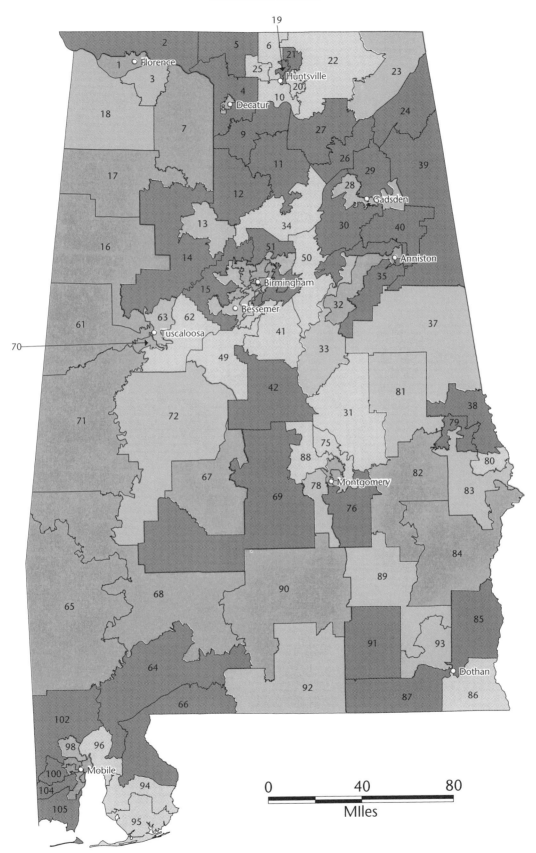

Population Growth   ☐ -7% to -2%   ☐ -2% to 1%   ☐ 1% to 8%   ☐ 8% to 32%

BIRMINGHAM

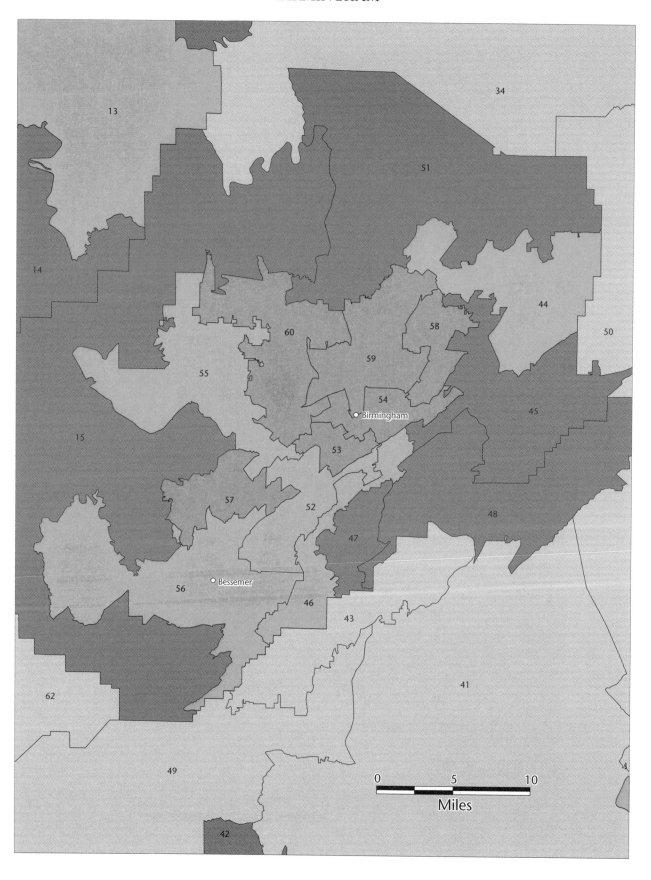

Population Growth | ▇ -7% to -2% | ▇ -2% to 1% | ▇ 1% to 8% | ▇ 8% to 32%

MONTGOMERY

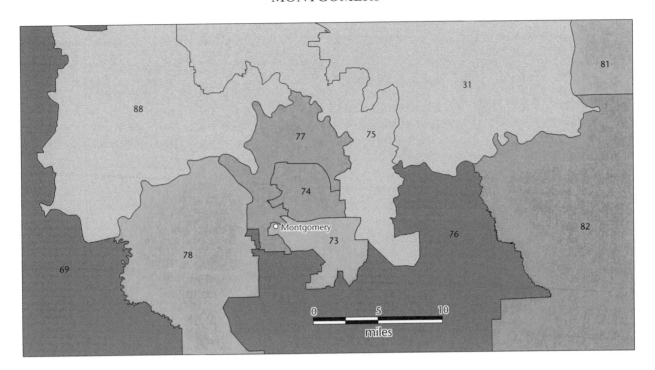

MOBILE

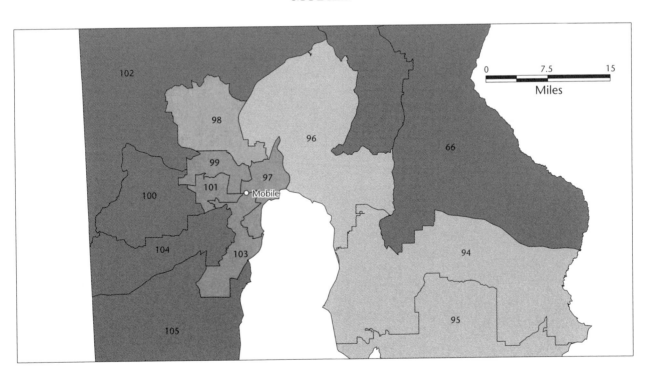

Population Growth   ▨ -7% to -2%   ▨ -2% to 1%   ■ 1% to 8%   ▨ 8% to 32%

Alabama State House Districts—Election and Demographic Data

House Districts	General Election Results Party, Percent of Vote							Population			Avg. HH Income ($)	Pop 25+ Some College + (%)	Pop 25+ 4-Yr Degree + (%)	Below Poverty Line (%)	White (Non-Hisp) (%)	African American (%)	American Indians, Alaska Natives (%)	Asians, Hawaiians, Pacific Islanders (%)	Hispanic Origin (%)
Alabama	2000	2001	2002	2003	2004	2005	2006	2000	2006	% Change	($)	(%)	(%)	(%)	(%)	(%)	(%)	(%)	(%)
1			D, 63				D, 65	43,894	41,609	-5	48,885	36.0	18.0	24.4	78.3	18.2	0.2	0.6	1.6
2			R, 52				D, 65	43,863	45,717	4	49,829	28.6	11.4	16.7	94.4	3.4	0.3	0.2	0.9
3			D, 67				D, 99	41,777	41,413	-1	46,313	31.9	12.2	21.6	76.5	20.3	0.4	0.3	1.6
4			R, 52				R, 57	85,473	88,011	3	55,086	35.2	15.2	17.8	73.8	17.0	0.6	0.6	6.5
5			D, 56				D, 57	40,309	43,428	8	49,656	30.6	13.1	20.0	82.7	11.2	0.4	0.4	3.8
6			D, 58				D, 64	42,057	46,939	12	55,759	40.6	23.2	14.5	64.3	28.4	0.8	2.1	2.5
7			D, 62				D, 68	41,022	39,768	-3	45,193	20.4	6.2	24.5	79.2	12.1	4.5	0.1	1.4
8			D, 74				D, 99	39,756	38,979	-2	46,913	34.0	13.9	20.8	61.7	25.0	0.6	0.7	11.4
9			D, 55				D, 55	41,385	43,480	5	50,653	30.3	10.9	17.8	92.2	3.5	0.7	0.2	1.8
10			R, 64				R, 98	44,323	48,183	9	65,093	52.1	33.6	10.5	75.5	14.9	0.7	3.6	3.2
11			R, 57				R, 54	43,457	45,866	6	50,312	28.6	9.3	19.4	92.2	0.4	0.4	0.2	4.9
12			D, 65				D, 63	43,607	45,183	4	42,899	28.5	8.5	22.4	92.1	2.6	0.4	0.2	3.3
13			D, 62				D, 69	40,817	40,493	-1	45,533	28.2	9.2	23.6	88.9	7.8	0.3	0.3	1.6
14			D, 64				D, 92	41,396	42,435	3	41,821	24.0	6.4	25.3	93.2	4.5	0.3	0.1	1.0
15			R, 99				R, 99	44,539	45,979	3	55,235	36.7	13.2	11.9	87.7	10.4	0.3	0.2	0.8
16			D, 55				D, 99	41,351	40,385	-2	42,633	25.8	9.0	23.7	85.8	11.9	0.2	0.2	1.3
17			D, 51				D, 64	43,244	41,003	-5	41,223	24.4	7.4	25.8	92.5	3.6	0.3	0.2	2.0
18			D, 98				D, 99	43,959	43,418	-1	43,515	24.4	7.8	26.3	82.4	5.8	0.3	0.1	8.2
19			D, 99				D, 99	41,187	42,360	3	47,133	36.9	17.7	21.1	30.7	64.9	0.4	0.9	2.2
20			R, 64				R, 99	41,516	45,131	9	97,229	60.7	45.2	5.6	89.7	3.5	0.5	3.2	1.5
21			D, 51				D, 61	42,293	45,373	7	49,654	38.6	19.9	21.5	65.6	28.2	0.8	1.1	2.6
22			D, 65				D, 98	42,587	47,404	11	52,515	32.3	15.2	15.4	88.6	5.8	1.5	0.3	1.6
23			D, 99				D, 99	43,869	43,692	0	44,254	26.2	9.1	21.9	89.2	4.8	1.6	0.3	1.9
24			R, 67				R, 99	43,661	45,125	3	46,070	24.9	7.6	22.0	84.1	2.2	0.8	0.3	8.7
25			R, 64				R, 99	41,370	46,491	12	76,722	48.0	30.7	6.8	77.3	15.6	0.7	2.1	2.5
26			D, 61				D, 59	44,328	45,848	3	44,452	24.7	8.4	24.8	77.7	1.8	0.5	0.3	15.0
27			D, 59				D, 98	43,294	45,989	6	49,395	31.6	12.3	18.9	92.3	2.2	0.6	0.3	2.9
28			D, 64				D, 66	40,366	40,195	0	42,164	29.5	8.3	23.3	77.9	17.2	0.3	0.5	3.0
29			D, 64				D, 60	42,178	44,113	5	40,455	26.7	8.1	26.0	74.8	17.9	0.5	0.3	5.5
30			R, 99				R, 99	41,981	44,008	5	51,416	33.7	12.5	17.0	90.2	5.7	0.3	0.5	2.0
31			D, 58				R, 98	41,278	45,038	9	51,928	30.1	11.2	18.7	73.6	23.0	0.3	0.4	1.8
32			D, 73				D, 74	41,723	40,691	-2	35,861	23.2	7.3	31.8	43.1	54.6	0.3	0.2	1.8
33			R, 62				R, 64	42,059	41,532	-1	44,469	26.7	8.8	25.4	74.1	23.9	0.3	0.2	0.8
34			R, 88				R, 72	43,912	49,159	12	49,360	27.2	8.1	19.0	89.1	2.3	0.4	0.1	5.5
35			D, 59				D, 70	42,080	42,759	2	49,597	30.1	10.7	19.4	78.7	16.8	0.3	0.5	2.5
36			R, 66				R, 99	41,606	43,096	4	55,492	32.3	12.2	16.0	84.0	12.1	0.4	0.7	1.8
37			D, 74				D, 70	44,201	44,405	0	38,911	22.9	7.6	25.8	73.7	23.9	0.2	0.2	1.5
38			R, 59				R, 51	44,131	44,601	1	46,550	28.2	8.7	20.6	68.5	29.2	0.2	0.3	1.2
39			D, 99				D, 99	43,819	45,237	3	40,802	22.1	7.5	23.8	88.3	5.9	0.4	0.2	3.5
40			D, 51				D, 52	42,759	44,951	5	44,821	31.0	12.4	22.1	86.3	10.3	0.4	0.6	1.4
41			R, 82				R, 99	45,177	59,519	32	68,124	37.5	19.4	13.2	87.7	7.9	0.3	0.4	2.6
42			D, 59				D, 61	43,945	47,265	8	43,475	23.2	8.3	22.6	80.9	13.0	0.3	0.2	4.1
43			R, 99				R, 99	44,519	52,401	18	96,021	55.0	36.7	4.8	89.2	4.4	0.2	1.9	3.4
44			R, 99				R, 68	42,359	42,083	-1	60,330	42.1	16.5	9.9	81.6	14.8	0.3	0.5	1.9
45			R, 83				R, 53	38,112	39,434	3	62,699	45.3	21.7	11.1	73.7	22.0	0.2	0.8	2.6
46			R, 99				R, 99	40,682	40,386	-1	105,367	57.6	41.8	6.7	87.1	6.8	0.1	2.3	2.5
47			R, 99				R, 98	43,046	44,104	2	76,270	56.0	36.7	8.1	78.6	8.6	0.2	3.5	7.5
48			R, 99				R, 99	44,479	47,152	6	124,958	58.1	42.4	6.8	88.6	5.5	0.2	1.9	2.8
49			R, 99				R, 99	43,679	52,867	21	58,918	38.6	19.5	12.1	83.8	10.9	0.3	0.7	3.1
50			R, 73				R, 99	41,496	46,568	12	56,102	29.3	9.7	17.3	87.5	9.9	0.4	0.2	1.1

Note: D=Democrat, R=Republican, R/D=Republican/Democrat (cross-filed), D/R=Democrat/Republican (cross-filed), I=Independent, C=Constitution, O=Other, GI=Green Independent, P=Progressive, P/D=Progressive/Democrat, P/D/R=Progressive/Democrat/Republican, HH=Households

Alabama State House Districts—Election and Demographic Data (cont.)

House Districts	General Election Results Party, Percent of Vote							Population			2006 Avg. HH Income ($)	Pop 25+ Some College + (%)	Pop 25+ 4-Yr Degree + (%)	Below Poverty Line (%)	White (Non-Hisp) (%)	African American (%)	American Indians, Alaska Natives (%)	Asians, Hawaiians, Pacific Islanders (%)	Hispanic Origin (%)
Alabama	2000	2001	2002	2003	2004	2005	2006	2000	2006	% Change									
51			R, 99				R, 99	43,594	45,400	4	54,660	37.1	13.5	12.8	88.9	8.5	0.2	0.4	1.2
52			D, 98				D, 98	44,083	43,466	-1	48,811	42.4	21.2	20.4	32.4	63.6	0.1	1.4	3.1
53			D, 90				D, 99	41,763	39,913	-4	39,161	45.1	23.8	30.2	29.7	63.9	0.2	3.0	3.7
54			D, 99				D, 93	40,157	38,843	-3	45,194	40.9	19.4	29.1	32.4	63.6	0.2	0.7	3.9
55			D, 99				D, 99	40,811	40,021	-2	42,475	34.3	11.2	23.9	32.3	66.0	0.2	0.2	1.2
56			D, 98				D, 99	42,884	43,080	0	40,175	35.1	12.6	28.3	38.7	58.9	0.3	0.3	1.8
57			D, 99				D, 99	39,471	38,179	-3	42,314	36.7	12.9	22.9	35.0	63.9	0.1	0.2	0.8
58			D, 99				D, 77	41,761	40,371	-3	46,063	39.2	15.1	19.3	34.7	62.5	0.2	0.5	2.1
59			D, 81				D, 99	41,032	39,908	-3	35,886	32.9	11.5	28.8	35.2	61.8	0.3	0.2	2.7
60			D, 99				D, 98	40,348	39,306	-3	44,047	37.4	13.8	24.1	32.6	65.5	0.2	0.3	1.4
61			D, 99				D, 68	39,374	38,240	-3	45,552	30.6	12.8	24.6	64.6	32.3	0.2	0.5	1.7
62			R, 54				R, 62	43,797	48,589	11	51,487	34.0	13.6	15.4	77.1	19.3	0.3	0.6	1.6
63			R, 64				R, 98	44,728	44,999	1	61,700	43.4	26.2	21.6	72.4	23.2	0.2	1.5	1.8
64			R, 55				R, 58	39,612	41,496	5	45,798	25.4	8.5	24.6	69.2	26.6	2.1	0.3	1.1
65			D, 58				D, 60	40,631	39,730	-2	42,973	23.3	7.8	26.9	66.9	28.6	3.2	0.1	0.7
66			D, 98				R, 53	40,100	41,700	4	42,465	27.0	8.8	24.4	69.6	25.7	1.6	0.3	1.5
67			D, 44				D, 79	39,586	37,633	-5	39,454	26.2	10.3	35.8	35.7	62.9	0.1	0.4	0.6
68			D, 99				D, 100	40,251	38,136	-5	39,524	22.4	8.2	32.5	38.9	59.8	0.2	0.1	0.9
69			D, 99				D, 99	41,228	42,029	2	37,191	20.9	7.3	38.2	33.9	65.0	0.2	0.2	0.7
70			D, 77				D, 99	41,887	39,751	-5	39,036	28.4	13.7	33.2	34.5	62.4	0.1	1.4	1.3
71			D, 99				D, 99	40,356	39,170	-3	38,685	24.7	9.0	35.8	34.6	64.0	0.1	0.2	1.1
72			D, 98				D, 99	41,015	41,231	1	36,818	21.1	6.6	35.3	37.9	60.8	0.1	0.1	1.1
73			R, 100				R, 62	41,032	41,251	1	69,812	52.5	33.5	9.1	64.3	30.5	0.2	2.0	2.1
74			R, 73				R, 99	40,055	37,850	-6	50,524	41.5	20.0	13.2	76.1	19.2	0.3	1.6	1.6
75			R, 99				R, 99	43,734	48,818	12	73,008	41.3	22.8	8.6	74.0	21.8	0.4	1.2	1.6
76			D, 68				D, 99	41,364	42,137	2	51,028	34.7	15.0	21.2	27.9	70.3	0.2	0.5	1.0
77			D, 100				D, 99	40,485	37,836	-7	38,581	30.3	14.7	29.9	28.6	69.5	0.2	0.4	1.1
78			D, 100				D, 98	39,921	40,181	1	36,360	25.4	10.0	32.3	27.6	70.0	0.3	0.4	1.4
79			R, 87				R, 56	44,106	45,153	2	48,841	43.8	27.8	29.6	79.9	14.6	0.2	2.6	1.7
80			D, 99				D, 62	42,710	47,209	11	48,204	32.5	11.1	18.6	76.1	19.3	0.4	0.6	2.5
81			D, 70				D, 99	42,448	41,700	-2	45,912	29.1	11.7	23.7	72.1	26.0	0.2	0.2	1.0
82			D, 99				D, 99	44,525	43,353	-3	33,795	33.1	17.0	41.1	35.3	61.4	0.2	1.6	1.1
83			D, 79				D, 98	39,793	39,409	-1	39,001	26.8	10.2	30.6	38.0	59.5	0.2	0.6	1.6
84			D, 98				D, 99	41,117	40,162	-2	38,334	23.4	7.8	33.3	43.7	51.9	0.4	0.3	4.4
85			D, 61				D, 51	40,750	42,238	4	40,198	26.9	9.6	28.6	49.3	47.7	0.2	0.4	1.8
86			D, 98				R, 50	42,048	46,399	10	45,847	31.0	10.4	19.4	80.7	15.8	0.5	0.4	1.7
87			R, 72				R, 99	40,675	41,370	2	52,726	34.0	13.9	21.1	86.1	9.6	0.6	0.6	2.1
88			R, 99				R, 76	44,391	49,715	12	57,066	33.1	13.8	14.2	80.5	15.8	0.4	0.5	1.8
89			D, 99				D, 99	43,723	43,470	-1	39,952	29.8	12.7	27.8	60.9	33.0	0.6	0.8	3.2
90			D, 99				D, 99	40,447	39,157	-3	40,807	24.1	8.4	30.7	63.1	35.3	0.3	0.2	0.8
91			D, 62				D, 51	43,688	45,996	5	49,755	34.9	14.6	19.6	74.2	18.9	0.9	1.1	3.3
92			D, 70				D, 68	40,450	39,662	-2	40,652	27.6	9.7	26.3	83.9	13.8	0.5	0.2	0.9
93			R, 99				R, 69	41,180	41,389	1	50,514	36.9	12.9	20.0	75.9	18.2	0.5	1.1	2.4
94			R, 84				R, 77	43,179	50,299	16	57,730	38.6	18.4	15.1	87.6	8.3	0.5	0.4	2.0
95			R, 99				R, 74	44,009	53,083	21	53,080	40.2	16.8	15.0	88.1	6.0	0.6	0.4	3.3
96			R, 90				R, 99	41,841	45,270	8	65,619	41.2	21.8	12.1	83.5	12.9	0.4	0.6	1.6
97			D, 100				D, 93	43,544	41,895	-4	37,905	32.1	18.1	35.4	31.2	66.5	0.2	0.5	1.3
98			D, 100				D, 98	42,178	41,659	-1	39,123	24.2	10.8	31.5	36.1	61.9	0.5	0.2	0.8
99			D, 100				D, 99	42,575	40,583	-5	42,284	33.3	18.0	26.5	33.5	64.1	0.2	0.8	1.0
100			R, 100				R, 99	42,044	44,799	7	62,545	39.6	24.3	11.0	83.5	11.0	0.4	1.8	1.9

(continued)

Note: D=Democrat, R=Republican, R/D=Republican/Democrat (cross-filed), D/R=Democrat/Republican (cross-filed), I=Independent, C=Constitution, O=Other, GI=Green Independent, P=Progressive, P/D=Progressive/Democrat, P/D/R=Progressive/Democrat/Republican, HH=Households

Alabama State House Districts—Election and Demographic Data (cont.)

House Districts	General Election Results Party, Percent of Vote							Population			Avg. HH Income	Pop 25+		Below Poverty Line	2006					
												Some College +	4-Yr Degree +		White (Non-Hisp)	African American	American Indians, Alaska Natives	Asians, Hawaiians, Pacific Islanders	Hispanic Origin
Alabama	2000	2001	2002	2003	2004	2005	2006	2000	2006	% Change	($)	(%)	(%)	(%)	(%)	(%)	(%)	(%)	(%)
101			R, 100				R, 72	39,476	38,227	-3	66,894	45.5	30.6	15.5	72.7	19.8	0.2	3.5	2.2
102			R, 78				R, 75	44,181	47,041	6	47,079	25.1	11.5	19.4	81.2	13.7	2.8	0.3	1.0
103			D, 100				D, 99	42,090	40,754	-3	39,365	28.4	12.9	29.9	35.9	60.3	0.3	1.5	1.4
104			R, 73				R, 98	44,635	45,370	2	61,731	38.0	21.3	13.6	83.6	12.1	0.4	1.3	1.4
105			R, 100				R, 98	39,834	42,586	7	49,758	26.0	11.9	20.3	80.8	11.6	0.5	4.7	1.2

Note: D=Democrat, R=Republican, R/D=Republican/Democrat (cross-filed), D/R=Democrat/Republican (cross-filed), I=Independent, C=Constitution, O=Other, GI=Green Independent, P=Progressive, P/D=Progressive/Democrat, P/D/R=Progressive/Democrat/Republican, HH=Households

ALASKA

Alaska, which became the forty-ninth state in 1959, is one of the youngest places in a young nation. Yet it remains an alien place to most Americans and one largely inaccessible even to its citizens. The state rarely makes the national news except during debates over oil drilling in the North Slope, an area above the Arctic Circle that hardly anyone visits, or perhaps during the annual running of the Iditarod, the 1,100 mile dog sled race that commemorates the delivery of diphtheria serum to Nome in 1925.

To put Alaska's age (that is, time in the Union) in some perspective, it is younger than Madonna, Matt Lauer, or Disneyland. Alaskans themselves are young; only 12 percent of the population is over age fifty-five, by far the lowest percentage in the country.

Alaska is also big. Its coastline covers 26,000 miles, longer than that of the lower forty-eight states. If superimposed on a map of those states, Alaska would stretch from Savannah, Georgia, to Los Angeles to Duluth, Minnesota. Despite the state's size, more than half of all Alaskans live in and around the city of Anchorage, which accordingly dominates the state legislature. The second largest city, Fairbanks, is connected to Anchorage by a four-lane state highway, which passes by Denali National Park with its spectacular views of Mt. McKinley, the highest peak in North America. The vast balance of the state remains sparsely populated and the capital city of Juneau is still reachable only by airplane or ship.

None of this has changed much during this decade. Although the population density of the state is just 1.1 people per square mile (by comparison, there are 9,015 people per square mile in the District of Columbia), suburban sprawl has come to Anchorage, as people have moved to outlying areas around and across Cook Inlet. All of the fastest-growing state house districts are located in and around the city—the 13th district, centered on Palmer, has increased in population by 55 percent since 2000; the 21st by 53 percent; and the 19th by 44 percent. By contrast, the 28th district, which is based on Fire Island, in the middle of Cook Inlet, has lost 10 percent of its population since 2000, as an old Air Force and Federal Aviation Administration (FAA) station located there was closed and its buildings razed. There are currently plans to construct a set of huge windmills on the island, suggesting that the state with the largest oil reserves might seek to become a pioneer in wind power, as well.

Politically, Alaska is a Republican state, yet the Democrats have made some inroads during this decade. Democrats have been competitive in gubernatorial races and have picked up seats in the state senate, having strongholds in the panhandle, the brush, and parts of downtown Anchorage. Republicans are strong almost everywhere else. As they do in the rest of the country, Democrats fare well among minority groups (here the Aleuts are the largest minority), holding all three of the Aleut-majority state house districts that run along the southwestern rim, from Nome down across the Aleutian Islands. Population trends do not clearly favor either party. Most of the fast-growing house districts are represented by Republicans, although the fastest-growing district, the 21st district (up 53 percent since 2000) is represented by a Democrat. Meanwhile, all three districts that have lost at least 10 percent of their population during the past seven years are represented in Juneau by Republicans.

With only forty state representatives and twenty state senators, Alaska has the smallest bicameral legislature in the country, a feature that owes more to the desire for economy and the difficulty of travel than to the size of the population (New Hampshire's legislature, for example, is huge).

ALASKA
State Senate Districts

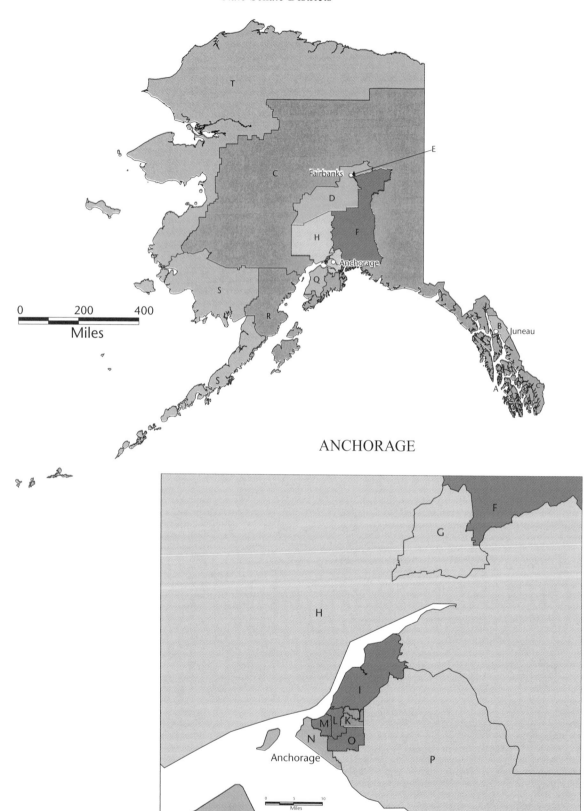

ANCHORAGE

Population Growth   ▢ -7% to 1%   ▢ 1% to 8%   ▢ 8% to 20%   ▢ 20% to 33%

Alaska State Senate Districts—Election and Demographic Data

Senate Districts	General Election Results Party, Percent of Vote							Population			Avg. HH Income	Pop 25+ Some College +	Pop 25+ 4-Yr Degree +	Below Poverty Line	White (Non-Hisp)	African American	American Indians, Alaska Natives	Asians, Hawaiians, Pacific Islanders	Hispanic Origin
Alaska	2000	2001	2002	2003	2004	2005	2006	2000	2006	% Change	($)	(%)	(%)	(%)	(%)	(%)	(%)	(%)	(%)
A	R, 54				R, 58			30,012	28,152	-6	69,298	38.6	39.3	16.1	71.7	0.3	14.5	4.3	3.5
B			D, 51				D, 65	30,714	31,177	2	79,506	42.1	46.9	12.1	72.1	0.7	11.0	5.8	4.1
C	R, 55		D, 57		R, 54			29,984	28,200	-6	51,360	32.6	29.5	27.1	49.6	0.6	41.0	1.8	2.5
D			D, 52				D, 58	32,893	34,902	6	73,868	33.1	46.2	14.7	81.2	1.7	6.2	2.2	3.7
E	R, 54		R, 70		R, 62			30,343	31,928	5	57,897	47.6	35.5	22.3	62.0	10.3	10.6	3.5	8.8
F			R, 82				R, 73	31,286	34,059	9	65,208	39.1	37.5	16.6	81.2	3.4	4.3	2.0	4.4
G	R, 53		R, 76		R, 68			31,778	42,164	33	72,576	45.8	36.5	15.5	84.0	0.7	2.1	1.1	3.5
H			R, 92				R, 69	32,769	41,094	25	67,809	39.8	36.6	20.2	85.2	0.6	2.6	0.9	3.1
I	R, 49		R, 76		R, 97			31,465	35,801	14	69,309	44.9	39.5	12.9	68.7	7.6	2.7	4.3	7.8
J			D, 50				D, 61	31,678	31,599	0	58,871	32.1	34.7	17.8	48.8	10.4	8.8	9.0	9.4
K	D, 51				D, 53			31,681	30,416	-4	73,851	40.7	42.8	13.2	58.7	8.0	6.9	7.1	7.9
L			D, 52				D, 95	30,868	34,527	12	60,509	34.3	44.0	20.1	55.4	7.2	8.2	8.1	9.9
M	R, 70		D, 57		D, 62			30,013	32,713	9	70,262	29.5	46.8	14.6	60.3	3.0	5.8	11.7	8.1
N			R, 96				R, 66	32,333	33,670	4	89,678	34.1	46.2	8.1	69.7	2.8	3.8	8.7	5.4
O	R, 65		R, 59		R, 52			31,389	35,800	14	77,636	30.2	43.4	10.9	62.6	4.6	5.0	8.1	8.0
P			R, 67				R, 53	30,301	36,484	20	112,808	43.1	52.8	7.3	81.9	1.9	2.9	3.2	3.8
Q	R, 77		M, 46		R, 77			32,865	34,580	5	64,755	23.4	35.3	21.4	85.0	0.3	6.1	1.3	3.1
R			R, 96		R, 59		R, 60	31,375	30,916	-1	65,220	31.9	36.5	19.2	69.7	0.7	12.6	8.7	4.5
S	D, 97		D, 67				D, 68	30,024	30,797	3	59,759	26.6	23.8	19.1	21.0	1.2	63.0	9.3	4.7
T					D, 65			30,151	30,780	2	60,628	32.1	18.8	19.1	14.7	0.9	77.5	3.1	3.4

Note: D=Democrat, R=Republican, R/D=Republican/Democrat (cross-filed), D/R=Democrat/Republican (cross-filed), I=Independent, C=Constitution, O=Other, GI=Green Independent, P=Progressive, P/D=Progressive/Democrat, P/D/R=Progressive/Democrat/Republican, HH=Households, M=Republican Moderate

ALASKA
State House Districts

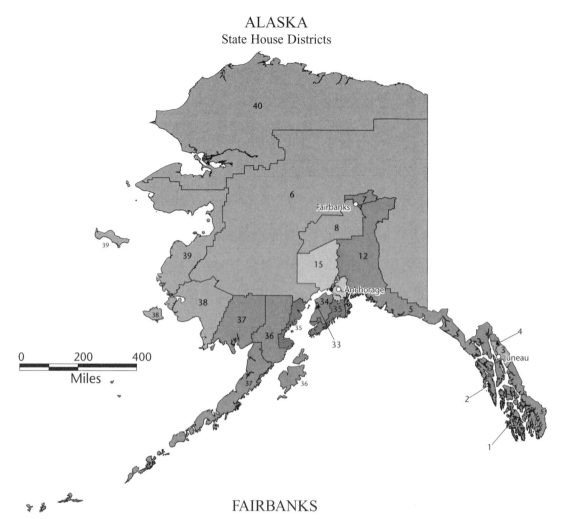

FAIRBANKS

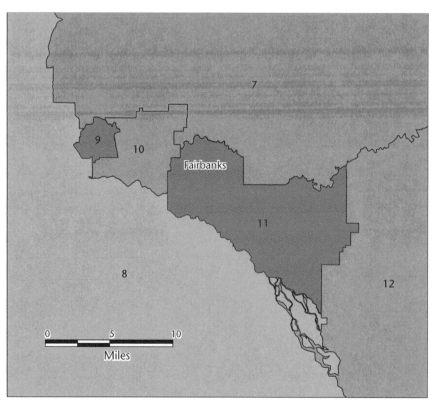

Population Growth   ▢ -11% to 0%   ▢ 0% to 9%   ▢ 9% to 23%   ▢ 23% to 56%

ANCHORAGE

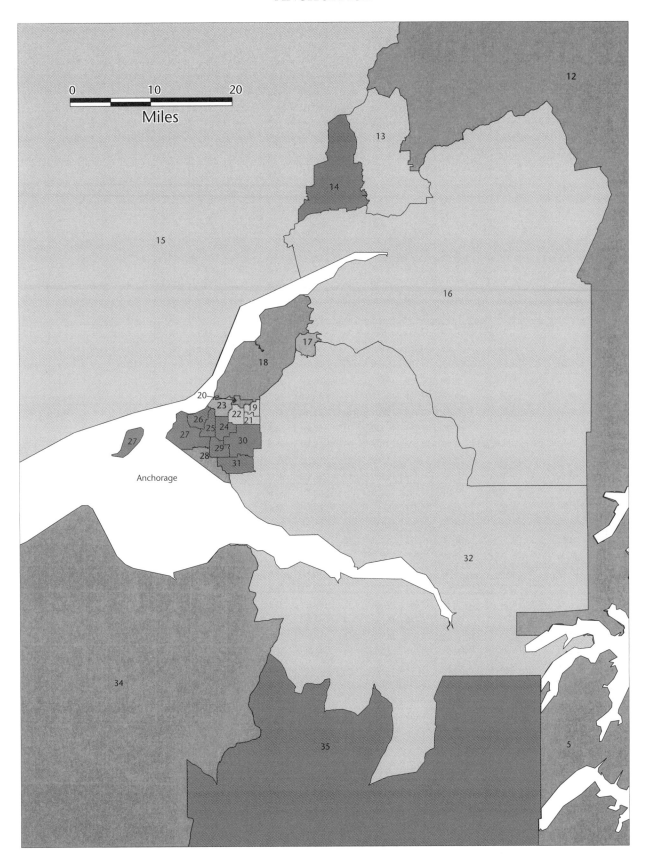

Population Growth | ■ -11% to 0% | ■ 0% to 9% | ■ 9% to 23% | □ 23% to 56%

Alaska State House Districts—Election and Demographic Data

House Districts	General Election Results Party, Percent of Vote							Population			Avg. HH Income	2006 Pop 25+ Some College +	2006 Pop 25+ 4-Yr Degree +	Below Poverty Line	White (Non-Hisp)	African American	American Indians, Alaska Natives	Asians, Hawaiians, Pacific Islanders	Hispanic Origin
Alaska	2000	2001	2002	2003	2004	2005	2006	2000	2006	% Change	($)	(%)	(%)	(%)	(%)	(%)	(%)	(%)	(%)
1	R, 95		R, 94		R, 54		R, 94	15,464	13,769	-11	69,419	39.4	13.9	13.6	71.6	0.5	11.3	5.0	3.3
2	R, 52		R, 59		R, 66		R, 56	15,439	14,589	-6	70,111	39.7	16.8	17.2	68.0	0.2	11.9	3.8	3.5
3	D, 65		D, 65		D, 71		D, 96	15,687	15,818	1	75,246	48.3	25.1	14.7	66.5	0.8	10.9	6.0	4.5
4	R, 94		R, 55		R, 65		D, 50	15,938	16,361	3	84,213	45.7	23.5	8.4	72.1	0.6	6.4	5.5	3.8
5	D, 61		D, 57		R, 50		R, 57	15,527	15,201	-2	63,641	37.3	15.5	15.1	76.2	1.3	13.6	2.7	3.3
6	R, 55		R, 97		D, 50		D, 52	15,446	16,444	6	44,704	24.8	9.7	32.0	48.8	1.0	39.3	0.9	1.7
7	R, 65		R, 57		R, 42		R, 56	16,584	15,643	-6	77,351	46.7	24.9	11.6	82.3	0.9	3.9	1.7	3.2
8	R, 63		D, 52		D, 52		D, 64	17,285	18,535	7	71,514	46.7	26.0	16.6	77.1	2.1	5.0	2.6	4.0
9	R, 51		R, 52		R, 50		D, 55	14,780	17,122	16	56,091	37.1	13.3	21.8	59.8	8.5	10.3	3.9	6.6
10	R, 77		R, 95		R, 70		R, 92	16,464	16,220	-1	59,662	34.0	10.6	22.9	58.2	12.2	4.5	3.2	10.5
11	R, 73		R, 97		R, 97		R, 70	15,374	17,781	16	71,673	38.5	12.6	13.4	78.3	2.7	3.8	1.9	4.2
12	R, 96		R, 94		R, 96		R, 71	16,840	16,616	-1	59,832	37.2	10.7	17.7	77.1	4.2	3.9	2.1	4.9
13	D, 61		R, 56		R, 67		R, 73	16,621	25,839	55	70,494	37.6	14.0	15.1	83.0	0.8	3.8	1.1	3.2
14	R, 96		R, 64		R, 62		R, 61	16,100	17,722	10	74,509	34.8	9.7	16.2	80.5	0.5	3.8	1.1	4.5
15	D, 64		R, 60		R, 49		R, 58	16,509	22,520	36	54,787	32.9	10.8	26.0	82.9	0.4	4.5	0.7	3.4
16	D, 61		R, 74		R, 72		R, 71	17,233	21,743	26	82,201	40.8	17.2	11.9	84.0	0.7	3.4	1.2	3.2
17	R, 64		R, 81		R, 64		R, 71	14,742	14,895	1	84,358	45.5	23.1	6.7	79.4	2.3	2.9	3.0	4.9
18	R, 52		R, 93		R, 98		R, 96	17,657	15,926	-10	49,035	32.7	11.1	18.8	60.6	13.2	1.3	4.7	11.3
19	R, 65		R, 62		R, 56		R, 55	12,978	18,673	44	66,537	37.9	15.2	13.8	56.2	9.7	8.0	6.1	7.9
20	R, 57		D, 48		D, 52		D, 58	13,791	13,373	-3	46,016	28.9	9.7	23.6	37.6	11.5	9.7	14.1	11.9
21	D, 54		D, 48		D, 51		D, 55	12,195	18,601	53	90,768	48.0	24.5	8.9	65.6	7.9	4.7	6.0	6.2
22	D, 55		D, 54		D, 57		D, 94	12,757	15,720	23	58,681	40.0	18.6	15.5	56.3	8.0	8.0	6.9	9.4
23	R, 61		D, 94		D, 69		D, 96	15,230	15,927	5	56,381	45.1	22.2	22.8	48.5	9.1	10.9	8.3	11.5
24	R, 73		R, 49		D, 52		D, 60	15,755	17,562	11	65,728	41.9	19.5	17.5	60.2	5.9	5.8	7.8	9.8
25	R, 60		D, 56		D, 95		D, 70	14,172	15,895	12	55,410	41.4	18.2	19.2	53.3	3.5	7.4	12.6	11.0
26	R, 92		D, 56		D, 62		D, 61	16,042	17,809	11	81,731	51.6	30.5	10.3	65.7	2.5	4.6	11.4	6.4
27	R, 62		R, 96		R, 59		D, 57	16,427	18,097	10	87,246	44.2	21.6	8.8	67.0	3.0	4.2	10.0	6.2
28	R, 79		R, 76		R, 69		R, 51	16,866	15,206	-10	93,353	49.0	25.3	7.6	71.8	2.5	3.3	7.8	5.4
29	R, 64		R, 61		R, 61		R, 56	16,278	18,155	12	68,618	41.4	17.4	12.7	58.9	5.0	5.6	8.7	9.6
30	D, 62		R, 96		R, 71		R, 95	16,042	17,979	12	87,685	45.1	21.6	7.7	66.9	4.1	4.0	7.7	6.7
31	R, 70		R, 61		R, 66		R, 96	15,247	18,127	19	109,971	50.4	30.4	5.9	80.3	1.5	2.9	3.9	4.6
32	R, 68		R, 50		R, 56		R, 53	15,954	20,214	27	122,244	56.3	37.0	5.2	85.0	1.2	2.1	2.1	3.6
33	R, 68		R, 52		R, 58		R, 56	17,061	19,088	12	66,688	35.9	12.2	20.0	81.2	0.3	4.9	1.7	4.0
34	R, 96		R, 71		R, 72		R, 94	16,780	16,098	-4	62,763	35.8	11.7	19.6	85.7	0.4	5.0	1.0	2.0
35	R, 68		R, 94		R, 48		R, 68	16,935	18,599	10	59,344	39.1	16.6	20.5	81.3	0.6	6.7	1.2	2.8
36	R, 50		R, 97		R, 79		R, 59	15,371	14,080	-8	73,811	33.1	12.1	15.1	51.4	0.8	13.5	18.3	6.7
37	D, 98		D, 96		D, 63		D, 53	15,551	15,161	-3	66,667	29.6	9.2	16.9	29.5	1.6	34.7	17.1	8.6
38	D, 98		D, 97		D, 98		D, 97	15,364	16,134	5	53,632	18.6	7.6	20.7	9.9	0.9	70.6	1.0	0.7
39	D, 97		D, 98		D, 64		D, 97	15,441	15,963	3	52,327	18.0	7.3	22.2	24.6	0.8	65.0	1.5	0.9
40	D, 94		D, 98		D, 98		D, 98	15,605	15,808	1	68,885	19.7	8.2	15.9	22.3	0.9	60.8	4.7	5.2

Note: D=Democrat, R=Republican, R/D=Republican/Democrat (cross-filed), D/R=Democrat/Republican (cross-filed), I=Independent, C=Constitution, O=Other, GI=Green Independent, P=Progressive, P/D=Progressive/Democrat, P/D/R=Progressive/Democrat/Republican, HH=Households

ARIZONA

The most enduring American myth is of taming the frontier, and although historian Frederick Jackson Turner famously declared the American frontier closed in 1890, he was mistaken. The country continues to move west, as people leave the crowded cities along the Eastern Seaboard and the Upper Midwest for new lives in western states. What Ohio was in Daniel Boone's time, and Illinois was in Lincoln's time, Arizona is today—a place where a person can make a fresh start.

Arizona entered the Union only in 1912, the last of the lower forty-eight states to do so. As recently as the 1930s, it had only one at-large congressional district. It now has eight and will add perhaps two more after the 2010 census. The twenty-ninth largest state in 1980, it is expected to become the tenth largest by 2030, with a corresponding increase in importance for national politics. Phoenix recently passed Philadelphia to become the country's fifth largest city. This sort of social dynamism is unique in the world and too little appreciated. If one compared lists of the ten largest cities in Great Britain or France a century ago and today, they would be almost identical. But several major American cities at the turn of the twentieth century—St. Louis, Cleveland, Cincinnati, Buffalo—have withered while new ones, such as San Antonio, Jacksonville, San Jose, and Phoenix, have arisen to take their place, changing the character of the country as they do so.

The old slogan that Arizonans made the desert bloom is only partly true. Almost three-quarters of the state's population is centered around Phoenix and the next largest city Tucson. Phoenix not only has more people than Atlanta, but is growing at a much faster rate. That growth has continued as Arizona's population soared by 12 percent from 2000–2004, second only to another desert wonder, Nevada. Every one of Arizona's sixty state house districts has gained population during this decade, and in only eight have the gains been less than 10 percent. The 22nd district, outside Chandler, has grown by 56 percent since 2000, and the 12th, west of Phoenix, has grown by 54 percent.

That population surge has come from two groups, the very old and the very young. Arizona exceeds the national growth rate both for persons under age fourteen and over age sixty-five. It is paradoxical that the nation's third-youngest state (by time in the Union) has one of its oldest populations. As it does in many places, this produces some political friction. Retirees, jealous of Social Security, tend to vote Democratic in national elections (though, curiously, they have elected Republicans to the legislature), while younger voters are more likely to vote for the GOP. How-ever, while senior citizens continue to make up a greater than average percentage of its population, rapid growth is also making Arizona somewhat younger.

Race, at least in the old sense of black versus white, matters relatively little in Arizona, but race in the newer sense of Anglo versus Hispanic matters much more. The 16th house district, on the western edge of Phoenix, is the only area with a significant African American population (11.7 percent), but twenty-eight of thirty house districts have a greater percentage of Hispanics. In twenty-four of sixty house districts, Hispanics constitute an absolute majority, the heaviest concentrations in the 13th, 14th, and 16th districts, forming a U around western Phoenix and stretching out toward Glendale. Native Americans, the original Arizonans, make up more than three-quarters of the population in appropriately named Apache County, in the northeastern corner of the state.

Illegal immigration is a problem here—Arizona has a long border with Mexico—yet the state's political leaders have not been as vocal about the issue as those in some other western states. In 2007 its two Republican U.S. senators supported the compromise immigration reform bill, while Republican representative John Shadegg vehemently opposed it. Former representative J. D. Hayworth, who was highly critical of illegal immigration, lost his seat in the 2006 elections. Governor Janet Napolitano, a Democrat, pungently expressed skepticism about proposals to build a wall along the border saying, "You show me a 50-foot fence and I'll show you a 51-foot ladder."

Republicans have dominated state politics for years, such as during the era of former senator and presidential candidate Barry Goldwater. However, some have suggested that rapid population growth will change Arizona's political character, making it less reliably Republican. There was some evidence for this when Bill Clinton in 1996 became the first Democrat to carry the state in a presidential election since Harry S. Truman in 1948, but George W. Bush's percentage of the state vote in both 2000 and 2004 exceeded his percentage nationally. If Arizona senator John McCain is on the GOP ticket in 2008, the Republicans are likely to do at least as well.

There is no evidence to support a Democratic emergence in the Arizona legislature. They have lost two seats, net, in the state senate since 2000 and gained only one in the state house. Republicans continue to control both chambers: the senate by a margin of 18–12 and the house by 39–21. Furthermore, the eight fastest-growing state house districts are all represented by Republicans, two of which have switched from Democrats during this decade.

ARIZONA
State Legislative Districts

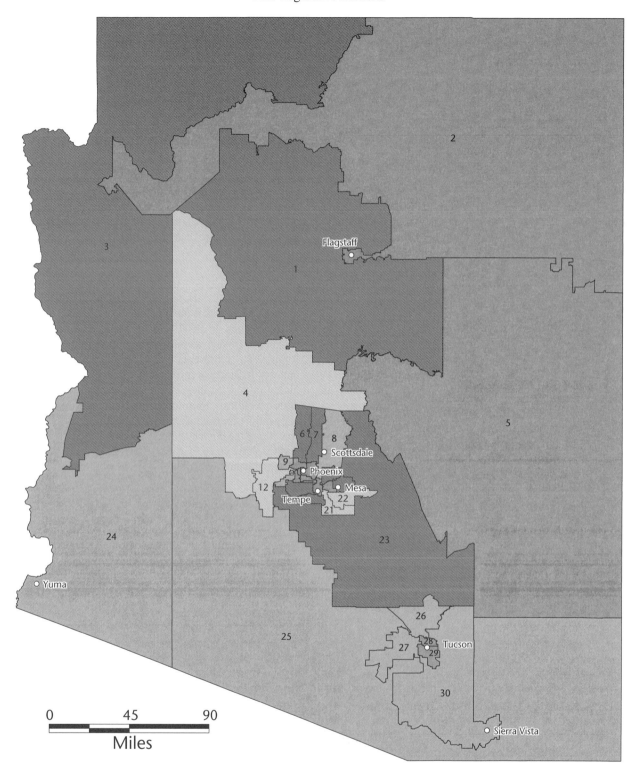

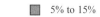

Population Growth ⬛ 5% to 15%　⬛ 15% to 21%　⬛ 21% to 37%　⬜ 37% to 58%

PHOENIX

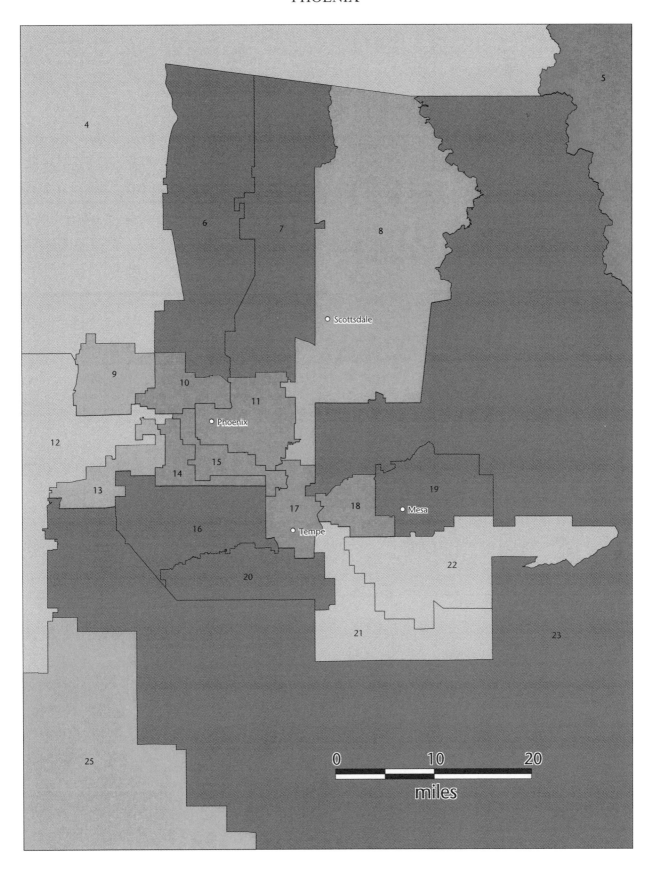

Arizona Legislative Districts—Election and Demographic Data

Senate Districts	General Election Results Party, Percent of Vote							Population			Avg. HH Income	2006 Pop 25+		Below Poverty Line	White (Non-Hisp)	African American	American Indians, Alaska Natives	Asians, Hawaiians, Pacific Islanders	Hispanic Origin
												Some College +	4-Yr Degree +						
Arizona	2000	2001	2002	2003	2004	2005	2006	2000	2006	% Change	($)	(%)	(%)	(%)	(%)	(%)	(%)	(%)	(%)
1	R, 59		R, 58		R, 60		R, 61	175,736	212,814	21	52,701	41.1	16.3	14.4	80.0	0.4	2.5	0.8	12.7
2	R, 53		D, 100		D, 100		D, 71	166,407	181,463	9	40,854	24.5	10.1	32.5	26.0	0.6	68.0	0.6	6.6
3	D, 100		R, 63		R, 100		R, 62	167,580	209,381	25	45,011	29.6	6.8	16.9	80.0	0.5	2.7	1.1	12.3
4	D, 100		R, 100		R, 100		R, 59	159,233	218,505	37	67,401	44.0	19.6	8.6	77.2	1.7	0.7	2.2	14.8
5	D, 100		D, 100		R, 55		R, 61	171,391	181,074	6	44,487	30.1	8.3	21.9	60.3	1.0	16.7	0.6	18.3
6	R, 57		R, 67		R, 66		R, 58	168,858	209,504	24	67,326	40.0	17.0	7.9	75.0	2.1	1.0	2.6	15.7
7	D, 100		R, 66		R, 67		R, 57	170,795	211,388	0	85,627	46.4	24.8	6.9	74.9	1.4	0.7	2.6	16.6
8	D, 54		R, 85		R, 66		R, 65	171,181	201,953	18	100,818	55.9	33.4	6.4	82.7	1.2	0.5	2.6	10.9
9	R, 57		R, 64		R, 60		R, 54	169,294	195,337	15	59,837	39.8	16.5	10.3	70.8	2.5	0.8	2.9	18.7
10	D, 84		R, 53		R, 55		R, 57	168,881	185,051	10	55,127	34.9	13.7	12.2	60.2	3.4	1.8	4.1	26.0
11	D, 80		R, 64		R, 58		R, 55	175,776	191,960	9	103,008	50.7	29.6	8.9	73.0	2.4	1.6	2.5	16.7
12	R, 52		R, 54		R, 54		R, 100	174,438	270,762	55	58,780	32.0	11.7	10.6	48.9	5.0	1.4	2.7	36.0
13	D, 50		D, 100		D, 100		D, 100	166,169	198,151	19	43,826	20.1	6.3	18.6	22.0	6.2	2.0	2.1	64.1
14	D, 77		D, 81		D, 100		D, 100	170,866	188,959	11	38,144	19.4	6.8	28.1	19.4	5.0	3.2	2.8	68.3
15	R, 100		D, 63		D, 65		D, 70	165,115	183,420	11	45,887	31.4	13.3	18.3	37.6	5.1	4.3	2.6	46.0
16	R, 54		D, 100		D, 100		D, 73	170,177	211,949	25	43,116	20.6	7.8	25.7	17.8	11.7	3.4	1.5	67.7
17	R, 100		D, 53		D, 61		D, 63	171,831	188,314	10	53,752	40.4	21.4	14.5	58.9	3.3	2.3	5.2	25.2
18	R, 100		R, 100		R, 100		R, 70	178,485	194,938	9	49,860	30.9	12.0	14.0	48.9	3.2	2.4	2.2	36.1
19	R, 60		R, 65		R, 100		R, 61	171,651	208,818	22	58,759	39.1	16.1	11.3	76.7	1.5	0.9	1.6	15.5
20	D, 62		R, 100		R, 76		R, 53	173,243	214,398	24	88,284	47.9	27.8	5.1	68.0	3.6	1.0	6.9	17.4
21	R, 56		R, 100		R, 100		R, 100	170,585	245,340	44	69,702	40.4	18.5	8.1	59.0	2.7	1.4	3.4	27.4
22	D, 100		R, 61		R, 100		R, 59	176,094	277,144	57	71,816	40.7	17.9	6.6	72.1	2.0	0.8	3.2	17.5
23	D, 100		D, 100		D, 100		D, 54	174,569	223,892	28	47,931	24.7	6.5	19.8	44.2	2.9	10.9	1.0	35.3
24	R, 59		D, 100		D, 83		D, 49	171,892	199,743	16	46,167	23.8	6.9	19.9	32.1	2.1	2.9	1.4	55.6
25	D, 66		D, 61		D, 56		D, 58	168,313	199,428	18	43,792	28.2	9.5	22.6	41.5	1.2	7.3	1.1	45.1
26	R, 57		R, 100		R, 100		D, 50	170,856	197,804	16	69,953	49.6	26.6	9.6	73.7	1.3	0.9	2.6	17.4
27	D, 56		D, 76		D, 100		D, 100	168,499	194,266	15	42,685	30.7	12.8	22.6	31.2	3.1	4.9	2.9	53.2
28	R, 83		D, 74		D, 64		D, 100	172,452	183,117	6	44,715	45.9	24.1	18.3	63.7	3.4	1.5	3.8	22.5
29	R, 63		D, 100		D, 63		D, 100	165,996	181,593	9	39,215	28.1	9.4	22.1	30.3	5.3	2.8	2.5	54.2
30	D, 66		R, 100		R, 100		R, 62	170,701	199,217	17	73,032	50.4	26.1	8.0	71.8	3.5	0.8	3.2	16.9

Note: D=Democrat, R=Republican, R/D=Republican/Democrat (cross-filed), D/R=Democrat/Republican (cross-filed), I=Independent, C=Constitution, O=Other, GI=Green Independent, P=Progressive, P/D=Progressive/Democrat, P/D/R=Progressive/Democrat/Republican, HH=Households

Arizona Legislative Districts—Election and Demographic Data

House Districts	General Election Results Party, Percent of Vote							Population			Avg. HH Income	Pop 25+		Below Poverty Line	White (Non-Hisp)	African American	American Indians, Alaska Natives	Asians, Hawaiians, Pacific Islanders	Hispanic Origin
												Some College +	4-Yr Degree +						
Arizona	2000	2001	2002	2003	2004	2005	2006	2000	2006	% Change	($)	(%)	(%)	(%)	(%)	(%)	(%)	(%)	(%)
1	R, 41		R, 37		R, 33		R, 35	175,736	212,814	21	52,701	41.1	16.3	14.4	80.0	0.4	2.5	0.8	12.7
1	D, 31		R, 36		R, 32		R, 30	175,736	212,814	21	52,701	41.1	16.3	14.4	80.0	0.4	2.5	0.8	12.7
2	D, 26		D, 51		D, 39		D, 45	166,407	181,463	9	40,854	24.5	10.1	32.5	26.0	0.6	68.0	0.6	6.6
2	R, 26		D, 49		D, 33		D, 39	166,407	181,463	9	40,854	24.5	10.1	32.5	26.0	0.6	68.0	0.6	6.6
3	D, 61		R, 33		R, 32		R, 37	167,580	209,381	25	45,011	29.6	6.8	16.9	80.0	0.5	2.7	1.1	12.3
3	D, 39		R, 30		R, 30		R, 37	167,580	209,381	25	45,011	29.6	6.8	16.9	80.0	0.5	2.7	1.1	12.3
4	R, 30		R, 38		R, 50		R, 31	159,233	218,505	37	67,401	44.0	19.6	8.6	77.2	1.7	0.7	2.2	14.8
4	R, 30		R, 38		R, 50		R, 30	159,233	218,505	37	67,401	44.0	19.6	8.6	77.2	1.7	0.7	2.2	14.8
5	D, 38		R, 32		R, 38		R, 54	171,391	181,074	6	44,487	30.1	8.3	21.9	60.3	1.0	16.7	0.6	18.3
5	R, 32		R, 26		D, 31		D, 46	171,391	181,074	6	44,487	30.1	8.3	21.9	60.3	1.0	16.7	0.6	18.3
6	R, 38		R, 33		R, 38		R, 51	168,858	209,504	24	67,326	40.0	17.0	7.9	75.0	2.1	1.0	2.6	15.7
6	R, 33		R, 29		R, 36		R, 49	168,858	209,504	24	67,326	40.0	17.0	7.9	75.0	2.1	1.0	2.6	15.7
7	D, 31		R, 39		R, 33		R, 30	170,795	211,388	0	85,627	46.4	24.8	6.9	74.9	1.4	0.7	2.6	16.6
7	D, 27		R, 35		R, 31		R, 28	170,795	211,388	0	85,627	46.4	24.8	6.9	74.9	1.4	0.7	2.6	16.6
8	D, 30		R, 40		R, 34		R, 33	171,181	201,953	18	100,818	55.9	33.4	6.4	82.7	1.2	0.5	2.6	10.9
8	D, 28		R, 31		R, 28		R, 29	171,181	201,953	18	100,818	55.9	33.4	6.4	82.7	1.2	0.5	2.6	10.9
9	R, 34		R, 34		R, 50		R, 37	169,294	195,337	15	59,837	39.8	16.5	10.3	70.8	2.5	0.8	2.9	18.7
9	R, 32		R, 29		R, 50		R, 32	169,294	195,337	15	59,837	39.8	16.5	10.3	70.8	2.5	0.8	2.9	18.7
10	D, 46		R, 32		R, 27		R, 27	168,881	185,051	10	55,127	34.9	13.7	12.2	60.2	3.4	1.8	4.1	26.0
10	D, 41		R, 27		R, 28		D, 27	168,881	185,051	10	55,127	34.9	13.7	12.2	60.2	3.4	1.8	4.1	26.0
11	D, 46		R, 33		R, 39		R, 35	175,776	191,960	9	103,008	50.7	29.6	8.9	73.0	2.4	1.6	2.5	16.7
11	D, 40		R, 30		R, 38		D, 33	175,776	191,960	9	103,008	50.7	29.6	8.9	73.0	2.4	1.6	2.5	16.7
12	R, 31		R, 32		R, 30		R, 52	174,438	270,762	55	58,780	32.0	11.7	10.6	48.9	5.0	1.4	2.7	36.0
12	R, 28		R, 30		R, 29		R, 48	174,438	270,762	55	58,780	32.0	11.7	10.6	48.9	5.0	1.4	2.7	36.0
13	D, 28		D, 53		D, 39		D, 52	166,169	198,151	19	43,826	20.1	6.3	18.6	22.0	6.2	2.0	2.1	64.1
13	R, 25		D, 47		D, 34		D, 48	166,169	198,151	19	43,826	20.1	6.3	18.6	22.0	6.2	2.0	2.1	64.1
14	D, 32		D, 33		D, 51		D, 38	170,866	188,959	11	38,144	19.4	6.8	28.1	19.4	5.0	3.2	2.8	68.3
14	R, 27		D, 33		D, 49		D, 35	170,866	188,959	11	38,144	19.4	6.8	28.1	19.4	5.0	3.2	2.8	68.3
15	R, 38		D, 30		D, 31		D, 33	165,115	183,420	11	45,887	31.4	13.3	18.3	37.6	5.1	4.3	2.6	46.0
15	R, 34		D, 23		D, 30		D, 33	165,115	183,420	11	45,887	31.4	13.3	18.3	37.6	5.1	4.3	2.6	46.0
16	R, 60		D, 50		D, 51		D, 41	170,177	211,949	25	43,116	20.6	7.8	25.7	17.8	11.7	3.4	1.5	67.7
16	R, 40		D, 50		D, 49		D, 39	170,177	211,949	25	43,116	20.6	7.8	25.7	17.8	11.7	3.4	1.5	67.7
17	R, 31		D, 26		D, 27		D, 28	171,831	188,314	10	53,752	40.4	21.4	14.5	58.9	3.3	2.3	5.2	25.2
17	R, 30		R, 24		R, 25		D, 28	171,831	188,314	10	53,752	40.4	21.4	14.5	58.9	3.3	2.3	5.2	25.2
18	R, 37		R, 52		R, 38		R, 36	178,485	194,938	9	49,860	30.9	12.0	14.0	48.9	3.2	2.4	2.2	36.1
18	R, 33		R, 48		R, 37		R, 34	178,485	194,938	9	49,860	30.9	12.0	14.0	48.9	3.2	2.4	2.2	36.1
19	R, 55		R, 55		R, 52		R, 35	171,651	208,818	22	58,759	39.1	16.1	11.3	76.7	1.5	0.9	1.6	15.5
19	R, 45		R, 45		R, 48		R, 37	171,651	208,818	22	58,759	39.1	16.1	11.3	76.7	1.5	0.9	1.6	15.5
20	D, 40		R, 40		R, 34		R, 43	173,243	214,398	24	88,284	47.9	27.8	5.1	68.0	3.6	1.0	6.9	17.4
20	D, 33		R, 34		R, 33		R, 39	173,243	214,398	24	88,284	47.9	27.8	5.1	68.0	3.6	1.0	6.9	17.4
21	R, 53		R, 40		R, 53		R, 38	170,585	245,340	44	69,702	40.4	18.5	8.1	59.0	2.7	1.4	3.4	27.4
21	R, 47		R, 32		R, 47		R, 31	170,585	245,340	44	69,702	40.4	18.5	8.1	59.0	2.7	1.4	3.4	27.4
22	D, 44		R, 54		R, 45		R, 41	176,094	277,144	57	71,816	40.7	17.9	6.6	72.1	2.0	0.8	3.2	17.5
22	D, 35		R, 46		R, 42		R, 40	176,094	277,144	57	71,816	40.7	17.9	6.6	72.1	2.0	0.8	3.2	17.5
23	D, 46		D, 37		D, 33		D, 29	174,569	223,892	28	47,931	24.7	6.5	19.8	44.2	2.9	10.9	1.0	35.3
23	D, 44		D, 32		D, 31		D, 24	174,569	223,892	28	47,931	24.7	6.5	19.8	44.2	2.9	10.9	1.0	35.3
24	R, 38		D, 45		R, 34		D, 29	171,892	199,743	16	46,167	23.8	6.9	19.9	32.1	2.1	2.9	1.4	55.6
24	R, 31		R, 43		D, 31		D, 23	171,892	199,743	16	46,167	23.8	6.9	19.9	32.1	2.1	2.9	1.4	55.6
25	D, 35		D, 28		D, 27		D, 27	168,313	199,428	18	43,792	28.2	9.5	22.6	41.5	1.2	7.3	1.1	45.1
25	D, 34		R, 25		R, 27		R, 24	168,313	199,428	18	43,792	28.2	9.5	22.6	41.5	1.2	7.3	1.1	45.1

(continued)

Note: D=Democrat, R=Republican, R/D=Republican/Democrat (cross-filed), D/R=Democrat/Republican (cross-filed), I=Independent, C=Constitution, O=Other, GI=Green Independent, P=Progressive, P/D=Progressive/Democrat, P/D/R=Progressive/Democrat/Republican, HH=Households

Arizona Legislative Districts—Election and Demographic Data (cont.)

House Districts	General Election Results Party, Percent of Vote							Population			Avg. HH Income	Pop 25+		Below Poverty Line	2006 White (Non-Hisp)	African American	American Indians, Alaska Natives	Asians, Hawaiians, Pacific Islanders	Hispanic Origin
												Some College +	4-Yr Degree +						
Arizona	2000	2001	2002	2003	2004	2005	2006	2000	2006	% Change	($)	(%)	(%)	(%)	(%)	(%)	(%)	(%)	(%)
26	R, 31		R, 46		R, 32		R, 38	170,856	197,804	16	69,953	49.6	26.6	9.6	73.7	1.3	0.9	2.6	17.4
26	R, 31		R, 45		R, 28		D, 33	170,856	197,804	16	69,953	49.6	26.6	9.6	73.7	1.3	0.9	2.6	17.4
27	R, 35		D, 54		D, 54		D, 43	168,499	194,266	15	42,685	30.7	12.8	22.6	31.2	3.1	4.9	2.9	53.2
27	D, 32		D, 46		D, 46		D, 38	168,499	194,266	15	42,685	30.7	12.8	22.6	31.2	3.1	4.9	2.9	53.2
28	R, 39		D, 36		D, 32		D, 39	172,452	183,117	6	44,715	45.9	24.1	18.3	63.7	3.4	1.5	3.8	22.5
28	R, 33		D, 35		D, 31		D, 39	172,452	183,117	6	44,715	45.9	24.1	18.3	63.7	3.4	1.5	3.8	22.5
29	R, 57		D, 39		D, 60		D, 43	165,996	181,593	9	39,215	28.1	9.4	22.1	30.3	5.3	2.8	2.5	54.2
29	R, 43		D, 33		D, 40		D, 33	165,996	181,593	9	39,215	28.1	9.4	22.1	30.3	5.3	2.8	2.5	54.2
30	R, 33		R, 30		R, 37		R, 36	170,701	199,217	17	73,032	50.4	26.1	8.0	71.8	3.5	0.8	3.2	16.9
30	R, 30		R, 29		R, 35		R, 34	170,701	199,217	17	73,032	50.4	26.1	8.0	71.8	3.5	0.8	3.2	16.9

Note: D=Democrat, R=Republican, R/D=Republican/Democrat (cross-filed), D/R=Democrat/Republican (cross-filed), I=Independent, C=Constitution, O=Other, GI=Green Independent, P=Progressive, P/D=Progressive/Democrat, P/D/R=Progressive/Democrat/Republican, HH=Households

ARKANSAS

Since Bill Clinton's retirement in 2001, Arkansas has again faded from national attention. An argument can be made that, for most of its history, Arkansas has been the country's most obscure state. Occasionally an Arkansan pierces the national consciousness—politicians such as Senate Majority Leader and Democratic vice-presidential candidate Joseph Robinson, Senator J. William Fulbright, and segregationist Governor Orval Faubus; business geniuses such as Sam Walton; or literary figures such as poet Maya Angelou or pot-boiler novelist John Grisham—but for the most part the state has remained a little-understood and much-denigrated land of hillbillies, hog farmers, and cypress swamps.

Sadly, the stereotype was not without basis. Overall, Arkansas remains poor and poorly educated. It has the third-lowest average household income (ahead of only Mississippi and West Virginia) and, Clinton's twelve years as governor notwithstanding, only West Virginia has a lower college graduation rate (16 percent). It also has one of the oldest populations of any state and is growing older.

Arkansas is the only state with a significant frontage on the Mississippi River not to have developed a significant port there. A place of wrenching poverty, it is also, like West Virginia, a place of great natural beauty—home to twenty-seven species of orchids and, at one time, considerable quantities of both diamonds and freshwater pearls. For many years Arkansas also produced almost all the country's bauxite, an essential ingredient in making aluminum, and still produces half the world's supply of bromine, a flame retardant and gasoline additive.

There are stark demographic and political contrasts here as well. State population hardly grew at all in the 1980s, slightly exceeded the national average in the 1990s, and has been close to, though a bit below, the national average since 2000. The Little Rock suburbs have grown, but the northwestern corner of the state has grown faster. This is the home of the University of Arkansas, of Tyson Foods, and most famously of Wal-Mart, one of the great American success stories. Sam Walton founded the company in 1962 in the little town of Bentonville (it still is headquartered there). From those beginnings, Wal-Mart has grown to become the largest company in the United States with worldwide sales

of $312 billion in 2005. Five of Walton's heirs regularly top the *Forbes* magazine list of the wealthiest Americans.

At the other end of the state, and the other extreme of circumstance, population loss has been steepest in the Mississippi delta districts across the river from Memphis. One of these house districts, the 55th, which is centered around the town of Blytheville, just below the Missouri boot heel, was hit hard when the U.S. Air Force base closed in the early 1990s. At about the same time, though, a Japanese steel manufacturer moved in, offering much higher wages than military pay, and the Delta area is now home to several plants that manufacture auto parts. If those plants are attracting workers, they are not attracting residents, as the 55th district has lost 10 percent of its population since 2000. The state worked hard to lure a Toyota assembly plant to nearby Marion, but in February 2007 the company announced that it was locating the plant in Tupelo, Mississippi.

African Americans are a significant minority in Arkansas, but as in Alabama, they are not evenly distributed around the state. The districts along the western and northern tiers bordering Oklahoma and Missouri are almost entirely white. On the other hand, districts in cotton and rice country along the Mississippi, in downtown Little Rock, and in Pine Bluff, are almost 70 percent black. The 65th house district, which includes Ft. Smith, is more than one quarter Hispanic and 10 percent Asian. Hispanics also comprise more than a quarter of the population in the Ozarks, many of them immigrants who have been attracted by good-paying jobs at the Tyson poultry processing plants.

Showing a contrary streak, for a while during Clinton's presidency Arkansas seemed to flirt with the Republicans. The GOP won a U.S. Senate seat (which they have since lost) and the governorship after Clinton's Democratic successor was convicted in the Whitewater scandal. The state legislature is oddly split. Democrats have a solid, 72–28 majority in the state house, a number that has fluctuated only slightly during this decade. The state senate, on the other hand, was evenly split between the parties after the 2002 elections but the GOP now controls it, 18–12. George W. Bush carried Arkansas twice, the first time costing Clinton's vice president, Al Gore, the White House.

ARKANSAS
State Senate Districts

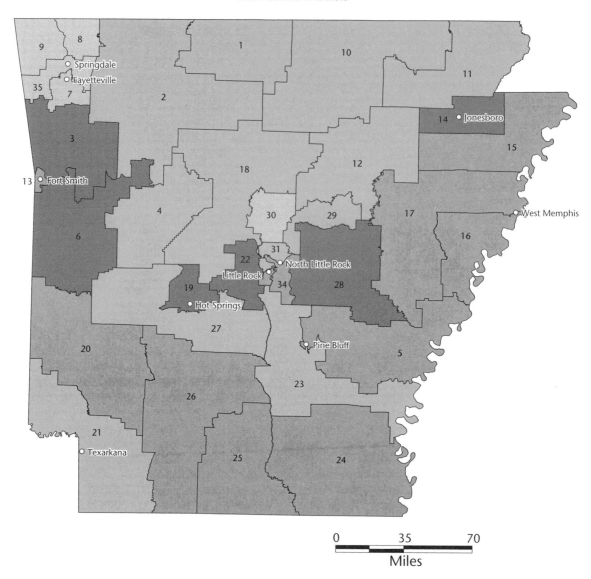

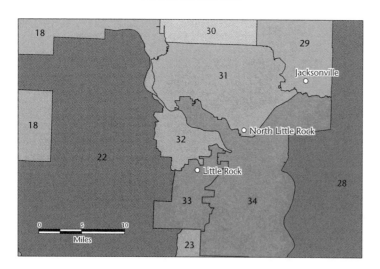

LITTLE ROCK

Population Growth   ■ -7% to 1%   ■ 1% to 6%   ■ 6% to 15%   ■ 15% to 29%

Arkansas State Senate Districts—Election and Demographic Data

Senate Districts	General Election Results Party, Percent of Vote							Population			Avg. HH Income	Pop 25+		Below Poverty Line	2006 White (Non-Hisp)	African American	American Indians, Alaska Natives	Asians, Hawaiians, Pacific Islanders	Hispanic Origin
												Some College +	4-Yr Degree +						
Arkansas	2000	2001	2002	2003	2004	2005	2006	2000	2006	% Change	($)	(%)	(%)	(%)	(%)	(%)	(%)	(%)	(%)
1	D, 100		R, 53		R, 100			79,110	83,411	5	41,247	31.8	9.7	20.6	95.5	0.4	0.7	0.5	1.3
2			D, 57		D, 100			78,290	81,801	4	41,785	25.4	9.0	24.1	88.5	0.3	0.9	0.4	6.4
3	D, 100		R, 100		R, 100			77,968	85,240	9	43,348	25.9	7.6	20.2	87.6	0.9	1.9	1.3	4.2
4	D, 100		R, 58		R, 100			75,003	78,274	4	45,384	28.8	12.3	20.5	82.8	2.5	0.7	0.9	7.9
5	D, 100		D, 78				D, 100	74,037	71,802	-3	38,266	24.5	9.1	30.4	33.2	63.7	0.2	0.4	1.8
6	D, 100		D, 100				D, 100	80,845	87,719	9	45,411	27.1	8.9	19.4	86.9	1.4	1.1	1.4	5.2
7			D, 50		D, 52			74,959	87,858	17	48,324	37.8	21.5	20.5	80.3	3.5	1.3	2.9	7.0
8	D, 100		R, 100		R, 100			77,356	96,093	24	56,354	33.0	13.7	13.1	71.2	0.4	1.2	1.9	18.1
9	D, 100		R, 100		R, 100			72,810	93,533	28	55,231	33.5	14.9	12.5	81.8	0.4	2.4	1.3	8.8
10	D, 97		D, 100				D, 100	77,940	80,285	3	38,590	25.6	8.3	24.7	94.8	1.0	0.7	0.2	1.3
11			D, 100				D, 72	76,531	78,276	2	42,237	21.9	7.4	22.8	95.3	0.6	0.5	0.2	1.4
12	R, 56		D, 100		D, 100			81,056	84,351	4	44,362	24.7	9.4	21.6	89.5	5.1	0.4	0.6	2.3
13	D, 100		R, 50				R, 100	78,389	78,208	0	50,928	33.5	13.0	19.4	62.5	8.5	1.8	6.1	14.3
14			D, 100				D, 100	77,988	83,313	7	47,050	32.3	15.6	20.2	84.5	8.5	0.4	0.9	3.4
15	D, 55		D, 100				D, 100	77,562	72,441	-7	39,243	21.2	7.0	27.2	70.6	24.2	0.3	0.5	2.5
16			D, 90				D, 100	74,427	69,410	-7	36,828	22.7	7.2	33.7	34.6	61.7	0.2	0.6	3.1
17			D, 100		D, 100			78,019	76,759	-2	43,504	23.6	8.4	24.9	64.5	32.1	0.3	0.5	1.6
18			D, 100				D, 100	78,854	83,151	5	45,634	29.2	11.0	20.4	90.6	4.6	0.6	0.4	1.8
19			D, 100				D, 60	73,307	78,727	7	46,193	35.4	14.0	18.4	82.6	9.5	0.7	0.8	3.8
20	R, 51		D, 100		D, 100			73,122	73,144	0	41,233	23.3	7.9	25.1	65.8	14.6	1.0	0.4	13.1
21			D, 60				D, 100	73,465	75,954	3	44,862	26.6	8.6	23.6	70.5	23.0	0.8	0.4	2.9
22	D, 65		D, 59				D, 100	81,653	91,516	12	65,555	37.5	16.7	10.7	89.5	5.0	0.5	1.2	2.0
23			D, 100		D, 100			73,407	74,780	2	50,521	27.6	10.5	16.6	82.2	13.2	0.4	1.0	1.7
24			D, 100		D, 100			75,686	72,876	-4	42,159	23.5	9.5	27.4	58.5	33.7	0.2	0.4	4.9
25	D, 100		D, 100		D, 54			73,805	70,739	-4	42,760	28.0	10.2	23.9	63.0	33.5	0.2	0.5	1.7
26			D, 100		D, 100			73,129	70,448	-4	41,959	26.7	11.5	27.1	62.3	32.8	0.4	0.5	2.6
27	R, 58		D, 100				D, 100	73,396	76,981	5	46,441	27.2	9.6	18.2	89.3	5.4	0.6	0.4	2.2
28	D, 100		D, 54				D, 100	76,569	84,858	11	50,977	28.2	10.0	17.3	84.2	11.2	0.5	0.6	1.9
29	D, 65		D, 59				D, 100	78,254	82,799	6	45,886	30.5	11.0	17.8	78.7	12.8	0.5	1.4	3.4
30			R, 100		R, 100			78,566	91,414	16	53,383	35.9	18.1	16.9	84.6	8.9	0.5	1.1	2.6
31			D, 53		D, 100			80,094	83,106	4	59,364	43.1	19.4	9.4	79.2	13.3	0.5	1.2	3.3
32			D, 69		D, 100			73,782	74,854	1	76,257	56.6	35.2	9.4	74.7	16.7	0.3	3.6	2.6
33			D, 73		D, 78			72,583	72,455	0	43,624	33.9	13.2	19.7	35.3	56.9	0.3	1.2	5.0
34			D, 100				D, 100	73,471	73,067	-1	38,698	29.2	10.0	28.4	35.9	59.0	0.4	0.6	2.8
35			R, 52				R, 54	78,936	91,545	16	51,836	30.5	13.3	14.9	66.9	0.8	1.2	3.3	19.6

Note: D=Democrat, R=Republican, R/D=Republican/Democrat (cross-filed), D/R=Democrat/Republican (cross-filed), I=Independent, C=Constitution, O=Other, GI=Green Independent, P=Progressive, P/D=Progressive/Democrat, P/D/R=Progressive/Democrat/Republican, HH=Households

ARKANSAS
State House Districts

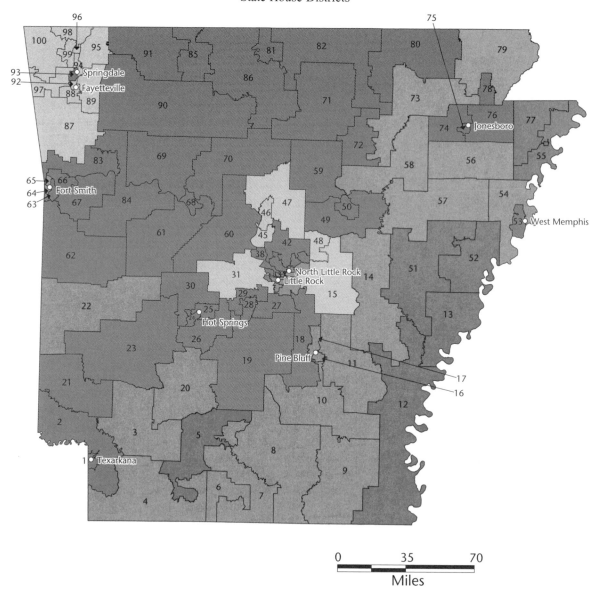

0   35   70
Miles

LITTLE ROCK

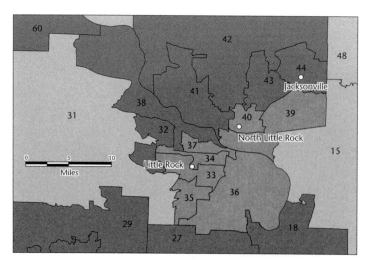

Population Growth   ▨ -11% to -5%   ▨ -5% to 1%   ▨ 1% to 12%   ▢ 12% to 33%

Arkansas State House Districts—Election and Demographic Data

House Districts	General Election Results Party, Percent of Vote							Population			Avg. HH Income	Pop 25+ Some College +	Pop 25+ 4-Yr Degree +	Below Poverty Line	2006 White (Non-Hisp)	African American	American Indians, Alaska Natives	Asians, Hawaiians, Pacific Islanders	Hispanic Origin
Arkansas	2000	2001	2002	2003	2004	2005	2006	2000	2006	% Change	($)	(%)	(%)	(%)	(%)	(%)	(%)	(%)	(%)
1	R, 69		R, 100		D, 57			26,325	26,690	1	47,258	29.3	10.4	24.2	61.6	33.0	0.5	0.8	2.1
2	R, 100		D, 100		D, 100		D, 56	25,913	28,131	9	44,752	26.5	7.5	21.7	80.1	13.9	1.2	0.3	1.9
3	R, 61		D, 100		D, 100		D, 78	27,095	26,845	-1	40,833	21.8	7.7	25.8	55.3	29.8	0.4	0.2	11.8
4	R, 100		R, 56		D, 100			25,543	24,789	-3	45,351	27.5	11.6	24.5	70.6	26.0	0.3	0.5	1.6
5	R, 100		D, 100		D, 100			26,291	24,551	-7	36,948	23.9	8.6	31.7	40.7	56.7	0.2	0.3	1.0
6	R, 62		D, 100		D, 100		D, 76	28,186	26,923	-4	46,225	31.0	13.0	24.9	58.9	37.5	0.2	0.8	1.8
7	D, 65		D, 100		D, 100			28,288	27,499	-3	43,057	28.8	9.2	19.9	75.2	21.8	0.3	0.3	1.5
8	R, 54		D, 100		D, 100			27,794	26,752	-4	39,489	20.9	7.8	28.4	56.9	32.9	0.2	0.2	6.3
9	R, 63		D, 100		D, 100			27,813	27,113	-3	44,689	22.4	8.0	23.3	68.3	24.5	0.2	0.4	4.2
10	D, 100		D, 100		D, 100			26,977	26,182	-3	46,608	26.6	11.5	22.4	73.4	22.2	0.4	0.6	2.1
11	R, 100		D, 100		D, 79			24,970	24,343	-3	38,156	22.3	6.7	29.6	38.8	56.9	0.2	0.3	2.7
12	R, 100		D, 100		D, 100			28,061	26,061	-7	37,999	21.9	8.8	31.5	49.5	45.1	0.3	0.4	3.8
13	D, 56		D, 100		D, 100			26,426	23,598	-11	36,017	23.9	8.3	34.3	37.4	59.7	0.2	0.4	1.6
14	R, 100		D, 100		D, 100			27,915	26,707	-4	43,743	23.7	8.5	23.4	75.3	21.9	0.3	0.5	1.1
15	R, 57		D, 58		D, 100			26,294	29,568	12	47,227	25.0	8.2	19.4	81.5	13.9	0.5	0.3	2.1
16	D, 100		D, 100		D, 100			25,213	24,156	-4	49,467	32.0	16.0	25.8	28.5	68.5	0.2	1.5	1.0
17	D, 100		D, 100		D, 100			25,761	24,836	-4	38,847	26.1	10.2	28.5	34.5	63.1	0.2	0.5	1.1
18	D, 100		D, 100		D, 100		D, 69	26,611	27,197	2	51,393	29.2	10.6	15.0	81.9	14.3	0.4	0.8	1.4
19	D, 100		D, 100		D, 100		D, 58	25,993	27,668	6	48,157	25.0	7.7	18.1	89.2	6.3	0.5	0.2	2.0
20	D, 100		D, 100		D, 100			27,727	26,988	-3	40,252	29.7	13.7	27.1	67.2	25.8	0.4	0.8	3.8
21	R, 53		D, 77		D, 100			26,211	27,103	3	41,838	22.6	7.4	23.4	55.8	14.3	1.3	0.5	21.3
22	R, 59		D, 100		D, 100			26,123	25,304	-3	39,877	26.2	7.9	25.5	90.3	0.3	1.5	0.4	3.6
23	R, 100		D, 100		D, 100		D, 72	25,448	26,378	4	42,816	23.0	7.4	22.8	87.7	2.4	0.8	0.3	5.1
24	D, 100		D, 100		D, 100			26,001	27,994	8	46,739	37.1	14.4	15.9	83.4	7.1	0.6	0.9	5.4
25	D, 100		D, 100		D, 100		D, 65	27,749	29,003	5	46,368	32.7	13.1	25.4	75.2	16.5	0.7	1.1	3.6
26	D, 100		D, 100		D, 100			26,648	27,414	3	43,911	28.2	10.7	18.9	83.6	11.8	0.5	0.4	1.8
27	D, 100		D, 100		D, 58		D, 70	25,578	28,304	11	50,975	26.5	7.7	11.1	88.5	5.8	0.6	1.0	2.0
28	D, 100		D, 73		D, 67		D, 52	25,905	27,989	8	57,311	31.8	12.2	13.5	89.6	4.7	0.4	0.6	2.5
29	R, 100		D, 48		D, 46			28,111	31,214	11	56,368	34.7	12.4	11.0	92.9	2.3	0.5	0.9	1.8
30	D, 57		R, 66		R, 59		R, 57	26,863	29,376	9	47,976	36.6	14.8	13.0	92.0	2.6	0.7	0.4	2.2
31	D, 100		R, 100				R, 100	28,230	32,075	14	69,004	44.4	22.8	9.9	85.3	9.5	0.6	1.2	1.9
32	R, 100		R, 56				R, 100	27,480	29,427	7	89,785	57.0	37.3	7.3	77.4	11.9	0.2	5.3	2.9
33	D, 54		D, 100		D, 100		D, 100	26,468	25,933	-2	47,117	36.1	15.0	20.7	32.0	60.5	0.2	1.8	4.4
34	D, 61		D, 100		D, 100		D, 100	25,459	25,269	-1	40,718	36.8	15.9	23.2	26.7	68.5	0.3	1.5	2.8
35	D, 59		D, 71		D, 100		D, 100	25,596	24,923	-3	39,875	29.8	9.0	18.5	30.9	59.2	0.3	1.0	6.9
36	D, 65		D, 100		D, 100		D, 100	25,571	25,352	-1	39,491	29.4	10.3	28.5	31.1	63.0	0.4	0.6	3.6
37	D, 100		D, 100		D, 100		D, 100	25,309	25,348	0	56,029	53.9	31.2	15.1	73.2	20.2	0.3	2.1	2.2
38	D, 58		D, 61		D, 52		D, 100	27,859	28,278	2	86,550	58.5	37.2	8.2	81.8	11.2	0.3	2.3	2.4
39	D, 100		D, 100		D, 100		D, 100	26,960	26,964	0	35,550	25.1	7.2	31.3	32.1	63.1	0.4	0.5	2.4
40	R, 54		D, 51		D, 100		D, 58	26,514	26,380	-1	60,853	47.8	23.6	8.2	79.1	13.8	0.4	1.4	3.1
41	R, 100		R, 100				R, 58	26,204	27,103	3	59,996	40.8	18.6	13.0	76.0	16.2	0.6	0.9	3.7
42	D, 67		D, 53		D, 100		D, 100	29,052	31,818	10	52,977	34.4	13.1	11.9	86.5	7.2	0.7	0.6	2.4
43	D, 48		D, 56		D, 100		D, 100	26,483	27,696	5	54,691	40.7	15.6	9.6	79.7	12.6	0.6	1.4	3.2
44	R, 53		D, 56		D, 100		D, 100	27,889	28,638	3	41,779	32.6	9.1	17.0	61.9	26.8	0.5	2.8	4.7
45	R, 100		D, 55		D, 65		D, 100	25,695	29,366	14	45,240	34.6	17.2	23.4	73.5	17.5	0.5	1.4	4.4
46	D, 100		R, 100		D, 53		D, 100	26,702	32,437	21	62,303	40.8	23.6	13.6	87.1	7.4	0.4	1.6	1.8
47	D, 55		D, 100		D, 100		D, 52	26,892	30,613	14	48,126	28.2	10.5	16.8	93.0	2.3	0.7	0.3	1.7
48	D, 100		R, 52		R, 72		R, 100	27,739	33,686	21	57,106	33.3	12.0	11.8	93.2	0.9	0.5	0.9	2.3
49	R, 100		D, 52		D, 100		D, 63	27,970	31,049	11	44,683	26.0	9.2	20.2	91.2	2.5	0.6	0.5	2.6
50	D, 62		D, 100		D, 100		D, 100	27,564	28,817	5	48,838	30.0	15.1	18.9	86.1	6.8	0.3	0.7	3.1

(continued)

Note: D=Democrat, R=Republican, R/D=Republican/Democrat (cross-filed), D/R=Democrat/Republican (cross-filed), I=Independent, C=Constitution, O=Other, GI=Green Independent, P=Progressive, P/D=Progressive/Democrat, P/D/R=Progressive/Democrat/Republican, HH=Households

Arkansas State House Districts—Election and Demographic Data (cont.)

House Districts	General Election Results Party, Percent of Vote							Population			Avg. HH Income	Pop 25+		Below Poverty Line	White (Non-Hisp)	African American	American Indians, Alaska Natives	Asians, Hawaiians, Pacific Islanders	Hispanic Origin
												Some College +	4-Yr Degree +						
Arkansas	2000	2001	2002	2003	2004	2005	2006	2000	2006	% Change	($)	(%)	(%)	(%)	(%)	(%)	(%)	(%)	(%)
51	D, 59		D, 100		D, 100		D, 100	26,958	25,013	-7	39,990	22.2	7.4	29.1	58.6	38.1	0.3	0.6	1.6
52	D, 53		D, 100		D, 100		D, 100	26,499	24,416	-8	33,010	22.0	6.1	37.5	32.3	62.3	0.2	0.6	6.3
53	R, 61		D, 52		D, 60		D, 59	24,991	26,093	4	49,569	31.2	12.3	16.0	69.6	26.0	0.3	0.9	1.9
54	D, 100		D, 100		D, 68		D, 100	26,101	26,301	1	38,182	17.9	5.5	35.4	28.2	68.9	0.2	0.5	1.9
55	D, 100		D, 100		D, 100		D, 100	26,497	23,779	-10	35,827	20.0	6.5	33.8	40.5	55.8	0.2	0.5	1.9
56	D, 83		D, 100		D, 100		D, 100	25,618	25,287	-1	36,761	17.8	5.2	27.2	88.1	7.5	0.2	0.3	2.1
57	D, 100		D, 72		D, 100		D, 64	27,164	25,999	-4	42,669	21.4	7.1	25.5	72.9	24.4	0.3	0.4	1.0
58	D, 100		D, 100		D, 100		D, 100	27,535	27,523	0	41,986	21.2	7.6	25.0	84.5	11.5	0.4	0.2	1.7
59	D, 100		D, 100		D, 52		D, 55	26,983	28,893	7	45,037	29.9	11.0	19.3	95.4	0.4	0.5	0.2	1.9
60	R, 54		D, 67		D, 50		D, 59	27,776	28,573	3	45,148	24.1	8.7	21.6	85.3	9.5	0.7	0.3	2.0
61	D, 100		D, 100		D, 100		D, 100	27,860	28,405	2	45,153	23.3	9.0	21.6	73.5	1.2	0.7	0.8	14.8
62	R, 100		R, 57				R, 100	25,584	26,874	5	43,822	26.0	7.3	20.0	87.8	0.8	1.4	1.4	4.4
63	R, 57		R, 59		R, 69		R, 100	27,248	28,194	3	66,706	43.1	19.9	13.1	75.8	5.0	1.4	5.4	7.2
64	D, 100		R, 56		R, 53		R, 100	26,019	25,864	-1	52,592	35.5	13.5	16.7	78.0	3.9	2.1	3.4	7.1
65	D, 100		D, 97		D, 100		D, 62	27,992	27,622	-1	34,630	22.6	6.1	28.1	40.3	15.7	1.7	9.3	26.9
66	D, 100		R, 100				R, 100	27,033	28,634	6	45,332	25.8	7.5	18.7	80.4	1.5	2.0	2.8	7.5
67	D, 100		R, 100				D, 51	26,468	29,472	11	48,571	30.3	9.9	14.2	89.0	1.0	1.4	1.7	3.4
68	R, 100		R, 57				R, 100	27,514	28,921	5	45,626	34.0	16.1	19.8	84.2	5.0	0.8	1.5	5.2
69	R, 100		D, 100		D, 100		D, 100	28,111	30,073	7	43,366	24.5	10.1	22.5	85.2	1.3	0.7	0.4	8.3
70	D, 100		R, 53				R, 100	28,182	29,393	4	44,455	27.9	10.5	22.4	93.9	0.7	0.7	0.4	1.9
71	D, 100		D, 100		D, 100		D, 100	25,406	26,173	3	37,273	26.4	8.4	25.8	94.7	1.1	0.8	0.2	1.2
72	D, 100		R, 55		D, 100		D, 100	26,428	26,786	1	46,124	27.6	11.1	20.0	90.3	2.7	0.4	1.1	2.9
73	D, 100		D, 66		D, 59		D, 72	25,625	25,659	0	38,039	20.8	6.6	24.2	95.9	0.7	0.5	0.1	1.0
74	D, 100		D, 100		D, 100		D, 100	28,216	30,297	7	41,795	27.4	11.6	26.6	77.3	14.2	0.4	1.1	4.7
75	D, 100		D, 100		D, 53		D, 53	26,384	27,707	5	55,749	43.1	24.5	15.7	87.5	6.3	0.3	1.1	2.5
76	D, 100		D, 100		D, 50		D, 54	27,700	30,236	9	43,885	26.1	10.3	18.4	90.8	3.6	0.4	0.4	2.8
77	D, 100		R, 100				D, 57	25,570	23,379	-9	45,446	26.0	9.5	20.5	82.2	10.1	0.3	0.7	3.7
78	D, 100		D, 100		D, 100		D, 100	26,230	28,279	8	46,756	25.4	9.5	19.8	94.7	0.5	0.4	0.3	1.9
79	D, 100		D, 100		D, 100		D, 100	26,103	25,223	-3	39,858	18.5	5.8	24.9	95.4	0.4	0.7	0.1	1.2
80	D, 100		D, 100		D, 56		D, 100	28,240	28,866	2	39,310	26.0	8.6	24.3	94.7	0.9	0.7	0.2	1.4
81	D, 100		R, 59				R, 100	27,786	29,175	5	41,619	33.5	11.1	17.5	95.7	0.4	0.5	0.5	1.2
82	D, 100		D, 100		D, 47		D, 100	27,557	29,143	6	40,003	26.6	7.8	23.2	95.9	0.8	0.6	0.3	0.9
83	D, 100		D, 100		R, 58		R, 100	26,063	28,861	11	43,055	25.9	7.1	20.5	91.3	0.6	1.7	0.5	2.9
84	D, 100		D, 100		D, 100		D, 100	25,774	26,751	4	40,919	23.5	7.2	24.2	93.5	1.5	0.7	0.3	1.8
85	D, 100		R, 55				R, 100	27,464	29,015	6	44,171	32.2	10.1	21.5	95.1	0.5	0.7	0.5	1.6
86	D, 100		D, 100		D, 51		D, 52	27,973	28,421	2	37,868	28.0	7.9	24.9	95.5	0.3	0.8	0.4	1.2
87	D, 100		R, 100		R, 55		R, 61	27,217	31,324	15	41,572	26.3	8.7	20.9	89.0	0.4	2.3	0.7	3.6
88	D, 100		D, 100		D, 100		D, 100	26,836	31,834	19	49,566	37.5	20.4	18.1	80.2	3.2	1.5	1.8	5.1
89	D, 100		R, 100		R, 58		D, 51	28,587	33,381	17	63,426	39.3	22.0	11.7	87.1	1.2	1.0	1.8	5.1
90	D, 62		D, 100		R, 56		R, 62	27,789	28,430	2	38,699	22.7	7.9	27.5	92.7	0.4	0.9	0.2	2.9
91	D, 100		R, 59				R, 52	27,405	29,583	8	44,190	28.5	10.4	22.0	79.9	0.2	0.9	0.6	13.1
92	D, 57		D, 100		D, 100		D, 73	27,270	31,530	16	38,598	36.4	22.4	28.1	75.1	5.6	1.4	4.7	8.1
93	R, 100		R, 100				R, 100	26,048	28,492	9	52,385	32.6	14.1	13.3	58.9	0.7	1.0	3.7	26.3
94	D, 100		R, 63				R, 100	27,690	34,339	24	52,694	29.6	13.1	14.2	54.7	1.0	1.0	5.4	29.3
95	D, 100		R, 67		R, 63		R, 100	27,640	34,723	26	55,650	32.0	12.6	14.8	72.0	0.2	1.2	0.7	17.9
96	D, 83		R, 68				R, 100	25,644	30,270	18	54,962	31.3	13.5	14.5	60.9	0.4	1.2	2.6	26.3
97	D, 100		R, 100				R, 99	24,506	29,444	20	55,698	28.4	12.8	15.1	76.7	0.8	3.0	1.3	11.9
98	D, 100		R, 100				R, 64	26,628	34,602	30	55,203	43.7	18.5	7.8	90.1	0.2	1.0	1.2	4.6
99	D, 63		R, 100				R, 100	25,115	33,236	32	61,842	34.8	17.0	11.6	81.6	0.7	1.4	2.6	8.8
100	D, 76		R, 67				R, 100	26,110	32,980	26	47,598	26.3	9.7	16.5	82.9	0.2	3.0	0.5	7.6

Note: D=Democrat, R=Republican, R/D=Republican/Democrat (cross-filed), D/R=Democrat/Republican (cross-filed), I=Independent, C=Constitution, O=Other, GI=Green Independent, P=Progressive, P/D=Progressive/Democrat, P/D/R=Progressive/Democrat/Republican, HH=Households

CALIFORNIA

California, whose possibilities have long seemed limitless, may be reaching its limits. It is by far the most populous state—with more than 64 million people, it is almost as big as New York and Florida combined—but its growth rate has begun to slow. Gaining congressional seats has been a California birthright; it has done so after every census since joining the Union in 1850. The size of its delegation has increased almost ninefold in the last century, from eight in 1900 to fifty-three today, the largest congressional delegation any state has ever had. But the 2010 round of reapportionment is expected to be the first in which California does not gain at least one congressional seat.

Some of that is certainly because it is hard for a state already so big to continue growing, although California did grow at a rate of 6 percent from 2000 to 2004; not as good as many states but better than some. Some is due to troubles in the aerospace and defense industries in the early 1990s and the bursting of the dot-com bubble in the early 2000s, weakening three of California's economic pillars. But some of it also reveals a decision by many white Californians to leave congested and overpriced areas for a more relaxed lifestyle in places such as California inland cities such as Sacramento—or out of state cities such as Portland.

As Michael Barone has pointed out, California is part of a national trend in which native-born whites are leaving many of the big coastal cities and being replaced by newly arrived immigrants. Los Angeles, he writes, had a domestic outflow of 6 percent during this decade, which has been off-set by an immigrant inflow of 6 percent. The city is holding its own, in other words, but it is also changing as whites move eastward into the Inland Empire and Central Valley, while their place is being taken by immigrants, many from Mexico, Latin America, and Southeast Asia. The fastest growing assembly districts are in Riverside and San Bernardino Counties, east of Los Angeles (the 64th and 66th assembly districts have each grown by 27 percent since 2000). The two assembly districts that have lost population at the fastest rate are the 12th and 13th, both in San Francisco. As Barone has discovered, that city has seen a domestic outflow of 10 percent since 2000, attributable in large part to the slowing of the Internet boom but also because of high real estate prices, and that has not been offset by a 7 percent immigrant inflow.

California politics have been raucous during the decade with the usual spate of propositions on the ballot each year, the recall of Democratic governor Gray Davis in 2003, and his replacement by Republican movie star Arnold Schwarzenegger. But voter discontent has not been reflected in the composition of the state legislature, and deliberately so. California may not have invented the gerrymander, but it can be said to have perfected it under the influence of U.S. representative and political genius Phil Burton during the 1970s and 1980s. The Democrats have controlled the state senate without interruption since 1970, and the state assembly for all but two years during that period. After the 2000 census, an agreement was reached in Sacramento to draw the political boundaries to preserve the partisan status quo.

The plan certainly succeeded. Despite term limits, which were supposed to promote turnover in office, not a single one of the forty state senate seats has changed partisan hands since 2000 and only one in the eighty-seat state assembly. Most races are not even competitive. In 2006 none of the twenty contested senate races and only three of eighty assembly races were won with less than 55 percent of the vote. (California congressional races are little better: only three of the fifty-three seats were won with less than 55 percent of the vote.)

Governor Schwarzenegger took a lot of heat for proposing that reapportionment be turned over to a panel of retired judges and he succeeded in placing a referendum to do that on the 2005 ballot. It was overwhelmingly defeated by the voters.

It should be mentioned that California's legislature is small by national standards. Pennsylvania, for example, has a fifty-seat senate and a 203-seat house. A member of the California assembly can represent as many as half a million people and state senators more than 900,000, making members of the legislature as distant from their constituents as TV characters. Politics here is conducted at the wholesale, not the retail, level.

Sometime within the past decade, non-Hispanic whites became a minority in California. Hispanics are the second-largest group (and make up at least 20 percent of the population in sixty of the eighty assembly districts), but Asians are now the third-largest group, outnumbering African Americans and making up almost 11 percent of the population, more than in any state except Hawaii. While whites and Asians have tended to vote Republican, with blacks and, increasingly, Hispanics voting Democratic, California could see much more political turnover if things were ever taken out of the hands of the gerrymanderers.

CALIFORNIA
State Senate Districts

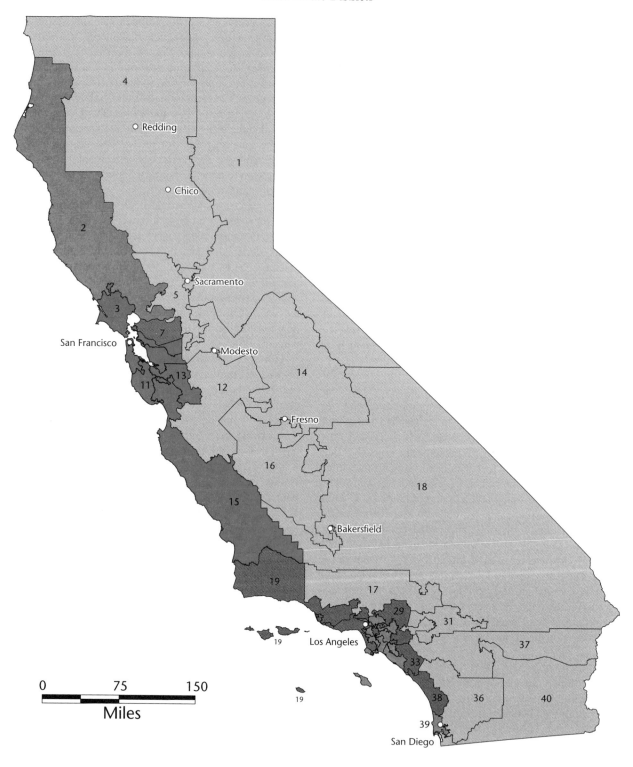

Population Growth | ■ -5% to 3% | □ 3% to 5% | ■ 5% to 10% | □ 10% to 29%

LOS ANGELES

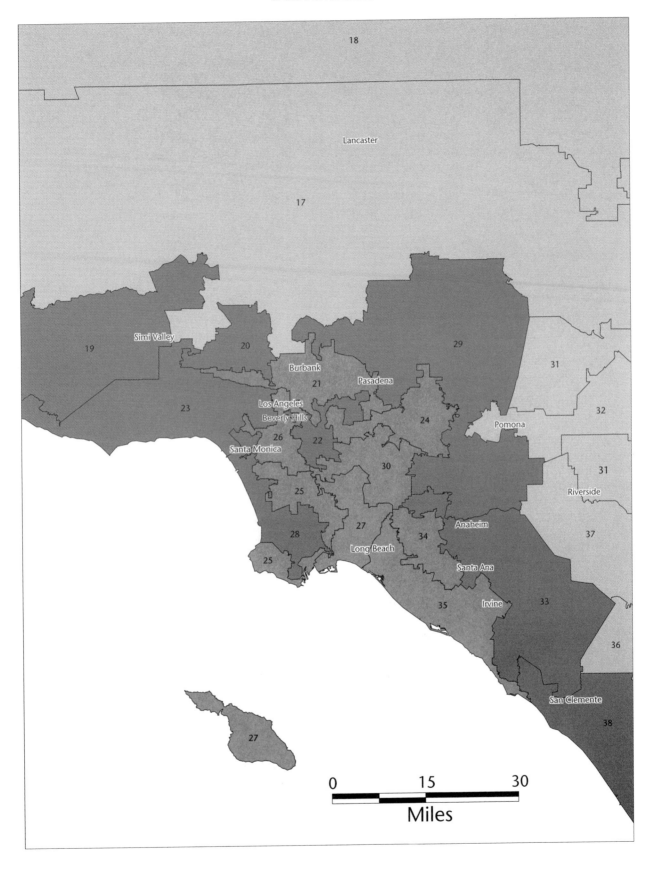

Population Growth ▪ -5% to 3%   ▪ 3% to 5%   ▪ 5% to 10%   ▢ 10% to 29%

SAN FRANCISCO

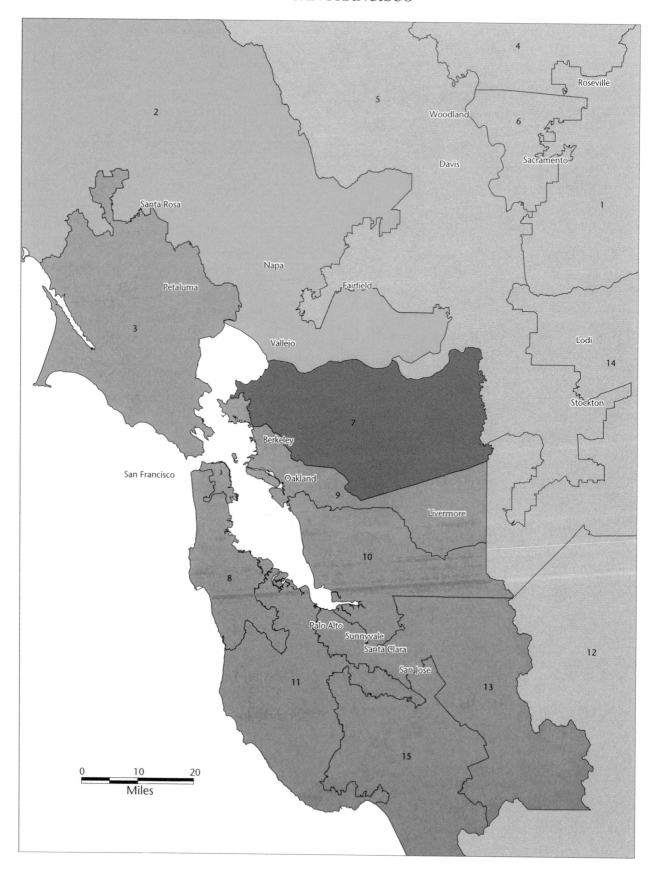

Population Growth
-5% to 3%
3% to 5%
5% to 10%
10% to 29%

California State Senate Districts—Election and Demographic Data

Senate Districts	General Election Results Party, Percent of Vote							Population			Avg. HH Income	Pop 25+ Some College +	Pop 25+ 4-Yr Degree +	Below Poverty Line	2006 White (Non-Hisp)	African American	American Indians, Alaska Natives	Asians, Hawaiians, Pacific Islanders	Hispanic Origin
California	2000	2001	2002	2003	2004	2005	2006	2000	2006	% Change	($)	(%)	(%)	(%)	(%)	(%)	(%)	(%)	(%)
1	R, 58				R, 63			857,943	1,019,627	19	77,046	45.8	22.3	10.2	76.0	2.4	0.7	5.2	11.9
2			D, 63				D, 66	853,794	887,598	4	66,636	42.2	18.2	14.0	62.7	4.1	1.4	6.9	20.4
3	D, 73				D, 68			848,923	820,506	-3	98,375	55.8	37.9	12.0	59.9	5.3	0.4	15.9	15.7
4			R, 58				R, 61	848,307	939,906	11	54,309	37.0	13.6	18.8	74.1	1.1	1.4	4.1	14.4
5	D, 48				D, 52			840,271	975,545	16	62,926	35.8	14.1	15.7	42.6	7.3	0.7	14.7	31.8
6			D, 71				D, 59	838,752	931,832	11	54,879	36.2	15.3	16.0	48.5	10.7	0.8	15.2	22.2
7	D, 54				D, 100			850,877	919,915	8	99,880	48.1	25.8	7.4	58.3	5.7	0.4	13.0	19.5
8			D, 78				D, 78	847,014	805,649	-5	102,563	52.2	35.0	8.1	44.1	2.8	0.2	36.0	16.4
9	D, 83				D, 77			842,710	847,218	1	75,328	44.7	28.4	15.9	38.7	19.9	0.4	18.9	22.3
10			D, 67				D, 73	848,208	844,556	0	92,283	44.2	26.3	7.9	37.7	5.9	0.4	33.8	23.1
11	D, 59				D, 67			843,434	820,094	-3	116,444	52.1	35.1	7.6	58.1	2.7	0.3	17.2	18.2
12			R, 48				R, 60	835,031	934,653	12	54,693	24.3	7.7	19.1	28.8	3.0	0.9	6.9	55.1
13	D, 69				D, 69			842,406	836,803	-1	91,180	42.1	26.6	9.5	31.2	2.7	0.5	31.3	36.5
14			R, 100				R, 67	846,726	979,149	16	63,207	37.1	14.3	15.1	54.0	2.7	0.9	6.6	29.7
15	R, 55				R, 53			874,853	879,197	0	93,135	45.9	25.6	11.2	56.0	2.1	0.6	9.0	27.1
16			D, 70				D, 100	849,874	956,193	13	42,061	20.5	5.8	30.1	17.5	6.4	1.2	7.9	66.2
17	R, 64				R, 60			832,008	945,467	14	68,345	34.7	14.2	14.3	48.8	6.8	0.6	6.4	32.5
18			R, 100				R, 70	850,108	966,540	14	54,721	31.0	10.1	18.7	49.7	4.0	1.1	4.4	34.2
19	R, 58				R, 61			860,531	913,284	6	90,167	45.0	23.5	9.4	61.2	1.7	0.5	6.3	25.3
20			D, 100				D, 75	836,170	879,440	5	54,714	26.9	13.1	19.2	20.1	5.3	0.6	11.6	63.5
21	D, 59				D, 78			859,198	895,677	4	72,524	43.7	25.9	15.0	42.2	5.4	0.4	18.6	31.3
22			D, 100				D, 76	825,982	868,452	5	45,314	23.1	12.3	32.9	11.2	6.1	0.8	16.7	73.8
23	D, 71				D, 66			843,788	892,883	6	112,415	49.8	32.3	11.3	54.9	3.1	0.4	9.5	26.4
24			D, 71				D, 74	848,755	886,548	4	57,033	26.1	12.2	18.8	15.8	3.6	0.8	21.5	66.6
25	D, 82				D, 74			853,909	891,509	4	62,872	29.5	14.1	21.9	21.6	25.2	0.5	12.2	45.3
26			D, 100				D, 89	863,952	902,914	5	56,796	34.6	19.5	25.4	24.4	22.1	0.5	13.8	42.3
27	D, 61				D, 63			843,931	878,297	4	62,472	32.6	16.2	17.3	27.7	9.3	0.6	15.0	48.1
28			D, 62				D, 62	834,722	877,330	5	81,776	44.0	26.9	12.1	39.9	6.3	0.4	17.3	34.3
29	R, 49				R, 62			853,076	914,337	7	85,828	42.7	22.8	9.5	43.7	3.4	0.4	21.3	30.9
30			D, 67				D, 71	842,664	877,195	4	57,129	24.0	10.6	18.7	12.9	3.4	0.8	9.1	76.9
31	R, 59				R, 60			850,985	1,017,408	20	66,691	34.7	13.9	14.7	43.9	6.1	0.7	7.2	37.6
32			D, 68				D, 100	844,467	957,017	13	52,798	23.8	7.6	21.1	19.2	10.7	0.9	6.5	64.3
33	R, 66				R, 69			850,013	927,490	9	99,545	48.8	27.4	6.9	57.8	1.6	0.3	13.5	23.3
34			D, 62				D, 50	838,024	872,235	4	56,125	25.7	10.5	16.6	20.9	2.0	0.7	19.4	60.4
35	R, 60				R, 64			850,277	890,449	5	98,295	50.5	28.8	8.1	59.4	1.2	0.3	18.0	18.3
36			R, 70				R, 63	847,503	955,969	13	75,871	42.5	20.5	9.8	64.6	2.9	0.7	6.6	21.0
37	R, 62				R, 60			850,989	1,090,744	28	63,713	33.2	13.0	15.3	46.2	6.4	0.8	5.0	36.9
38			R, 66				R, 74	846,975	902,141	7	84,264	43.1	23.6	9.7	54.4	3.0	0.5	7.7	29.1
39	D, 56				D, 60			845,343	878,754	4	68,203	46.5	27.1	13.8	51.0	7.6	0.4	15.0	23.4
40			D, 56				D, 62	859,691	966,698	12	53,220	27.3	11.2	20.8	21.5	5.5	0.7	9.9	62.6

Note: D=Democrat, R=Republican, R/D=Republican/Democrat (cross-filed), D/R=Democrat/Republican (cross-filed), I=Independent, C=Constitution, O=Other, GI=Green Independent, P=Progressive, P/D=Progressive/Democrat, P/D/R=Progressive/Democrat/Republican, HH=Households

CALIFORNIA
State Assembly Districts

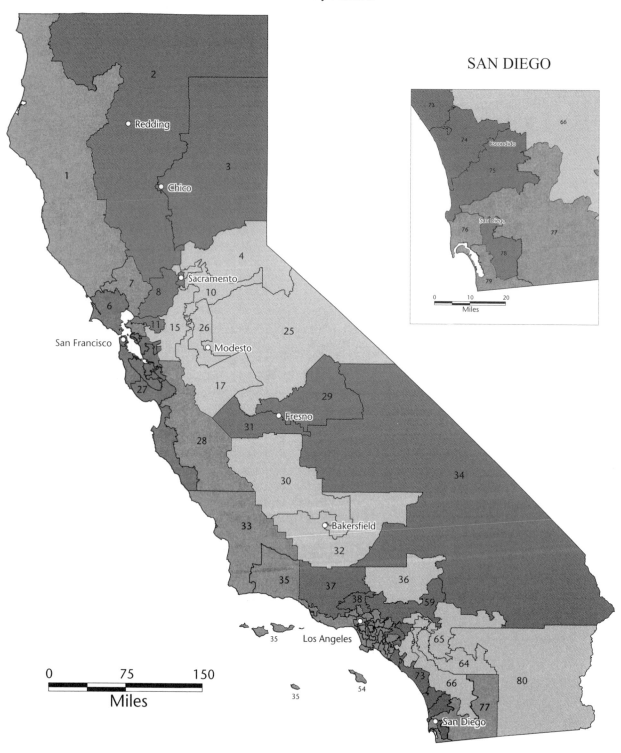

SAN DIEGO

Population Growth   ■ -8% to 1%   ■ 1% to 6%   ■ 6% to 13%   □ 13% to 27%

LOS ANGELES

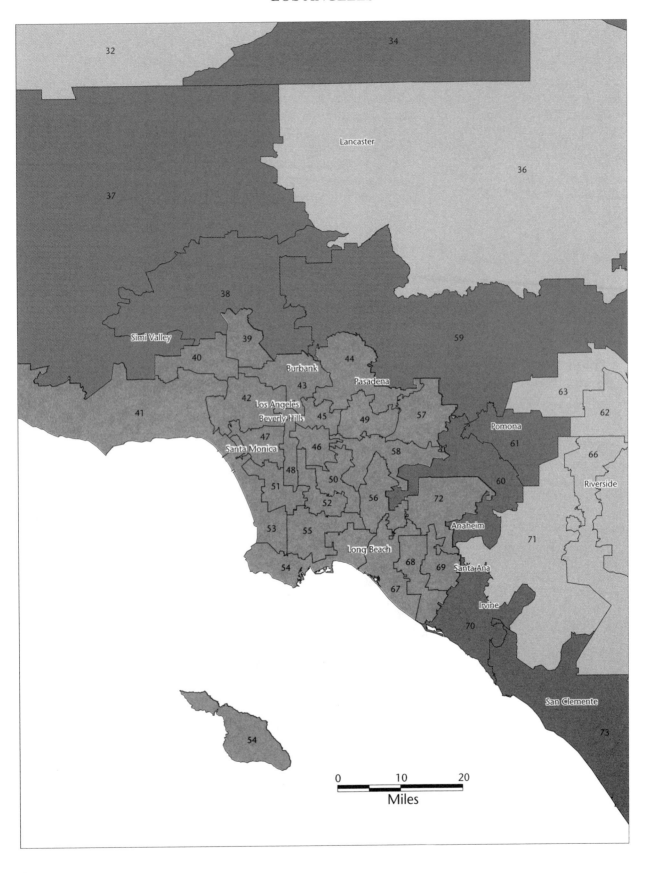

Population Growth · ▨ -8% to 1% · ▨ 1% to 6% · ▨ 6% to 13% · ▨ 13% to 27%

SAN FRANCISCO

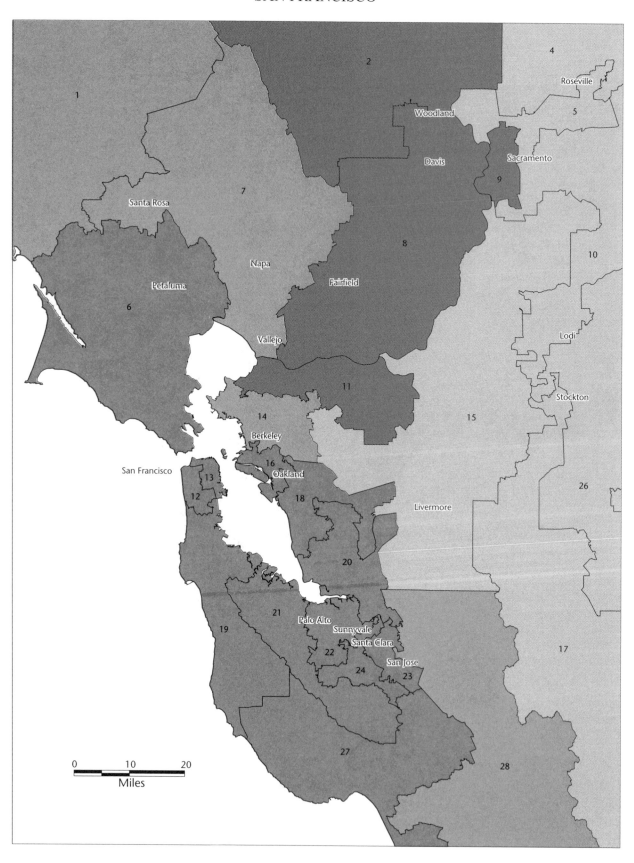

1

2

4

Roseville

5

Woodland

Davis

Sacramento

9

7

Santa Rosa

8

Napa

10

Petaluma

Fairfield

6

Vallejo

Lodi

11

Stockton

14

15

Berkeley

16

Oakland

San Francisco

13

18

26

12

Livermore

20

21

Palo Alto

Sunnyvale

19

Santa Clara

22

San Jose

17

24

23

27

28

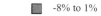

Population Growth   ▣ -8% to 1%   ▣ 1% to 6%   ▣ 6% to 13%   ▢ 13% to 27%

California State Assembly Districts—Election and Demographic Data

Assembly Districts	General Election Results Party, Percent of Vote							Population			Avg. HH Income	Pop 25+ Some College +	Pop 25+ 4-Yr Degree +	Below Poverty Line	2006 White (Non-Hisp)	African American	American Indians, Alaska Natives	Asians, Hawaiians, Pacific Islanders	Hispanic Origin
California	2000	2001	2002	2003	2004	2005	2006	2000	2006	% Change	($)	(%)	(%)	(%)	(%)	(%)	(%)	(%)	(%)
1	D, 64		D, 49		D, 61		D, 65	424,178	439,552	4	55,165	39.7	15.9	18.6	74.0	1.1	2.5	1.9	15.5
2	R, 69		R, 67		R, 65		R, 68	427,682	467,638	9	51,226	33.8	10.3	19.6	70.1	0.9	1.5	4.2	17.6
3	R, 61		R, 61		R, 59		R, 61	423,133	454,133	7	54,061	39.5	14.6	18.4	77.7	1.6	1.2	3.5	11.8
4	R, 67		R, 67		R, 67		R, 59	421,179	516,877	23	72,076	44.3	22.4	9.9	76.9	1.9	0.6	4.3	12.3
5	R, 76		R, 65		R, 60		R, 62	429,641	496,962	16	71,973	44.5	21.7	11.0	70.5	4.8	0.6	6.9	13.0
6	D, 64		D, 69		D, 73		D, 66	423,677	422,002	0	107,562	52.5	31.3	8.0	73.5	1.9	0.3	4.8	15.3
7	D, 66		D, 76		D, 60		D, 99	429,425	445,181	4	74,612	43.0	19.0	10.7	53.4	6.8	0.7	11.1	24.6
8	D, 62		D, 58		D, 63		D, 66	423,263	457,094	8	68,824	41.4	18.0	12.9	52.3	6.9	0.6	11.3	24.7
9	D, 70		D, 70		D, 67		D, 70	418,485	455,023	9	52,564	34.3	15.4	19.5	37.0	13.9	0.9	20.5	28.1
10	R, 54		R, 60		R, 76		R, 61	427,099	499,389	17	71,931	41.9	18.8	11.5	59.0	5.9	0.6	12.7	17.9
11	D, 67		D, 65		D, 67		D, 66	424,798	453,326	7	75,917	40.9	16.9	9.7	48.9	7.9	0.5	13.9	26.3
12	D, 82		D, 78		D, 78		D, 71	419,422	387,331	-8	90,198	52.0	36.2	10.1	34.7	4.2	0.2	47.3	14.6
13	D, 79		D, 81		D, 82		D, 87	434,718	405,535	-7	91,375	60.2	46.1	15.0	47.4	8.2	0.3	26.6	16.3
14	D, 84		D, 100		D, 77		D, 82	426,475	440,924	3	91,054	51.2	34.9	13.1	49.0	13.3	0.3	16.6	18.9
15	R, 61		R, 54		R, 55		R, 55	428,196	488,780	14	110,840	49.3	27.8	5.9	66.1	2.5	0.4	9.6	17.2
16	D, 67		D, 84		D, 88		D, 90	419,468	414,284	-1	67,788	41.9	26.1	18.0	30.5	24.3	0.5	23.0	24.0
17	D, 53		D, 56		D, 61		D, 60	426,628	505,817	19	53,266	25.3	7.6	21.3	29.2	5.9	0.8	12.9	49.5
18	D, 75		D, 72		D, 84		D, 68	425,716	420,756	-1	77,640	41.0	22.3	9.6	40.4	11.7	0.5	20.6	26.6
19	D, 70		D, 63		D, 71		D, 74	420,666	408,272	-3	108,012	51.0	32.0	6.6	50.4	2.1	0.3	26.6	18.7
20	D, 64		D, 67		D, 69		D, 65	429,251	425,489	-1	105,036	47.0	29.7	6.5	38.2	4.1	0.3	39.0	19.0
21	D, 55		D, 60		D, 52		D, 68	423,870	409,412	-3	153,853	55.2	41.1	6.5	59.8	3.0	0.2	14.9	18.3
22	D, 68		D, 58		D, 70		D, 69	423,696	420,629	-1	107,440	54.9	39.6	6.8	45.5	2.0	0.3	36.4	15.2
23	D, 72		D, 82		D, 67		D, 74	425,644	424,598	0	82,956	33.4	18.4	12.1	21.3	3.3	0.6	32.4	48.9
24	D, 50		D, 100		D, 59		D, 65	424,725	414,356	-2	105,023	50.3	31.3	7.2	52.9	2.4	0.4	23.2	18.7
25	R, 61		R, 62		R, 68		R, 62	423,701	484,412	14	59,972	34.7	10.1	15.1	62.7	2.4	1.0	3.9	24.1
26	D, 66		R, 57		R, 63		R, 58	424,162	500,232	18	56,991	27.8	8.6	18.1	42.2	3.6	0.8	9.2	39.2
27	D, 65		D, 61		D, 69		D, 70	425,179	418,362	-2	88,929	49.8	29.9	9.8	61.3	2.7	0.5	7.4	22.5
28	D, 53		D, 61		D, 63		D, 57	428,164	439,881	3	72,911	29.1	13.8	13.5	21.9	2.3	0.8	11.2	61.5
29	R, 70		R, 61		R, 62		R, 66	429,021	482,273	12	62,072	38.3	17.0	16.1	46.0	3.7	1.0	8.7	35.0
30	D, 66		D, 50		D, 55		D, 52	429,988	492,416	15	44,890	19.1	5.2	28.3	18.7	6.5	1.1	5.4	65.5
31	D, 63		D, 100		D, 58		D, 100	418,057	460,306	10	42,144	24.3	7.8	29.6	18.1	5.8	1.2	11.2	64.3
32	R, 70		R, 76		R, 79		R, 72	417,889	475,810	14	58,080	32.0	10.4	17.4	54.0	4.4	0.9	4.4	30.3
33	R, 64		R, 63		R, 56		R, 67	425,364	433,681	2	61,300	40.2	16.7	14.7	57.4	2.4	0.7	4.1	29.7
34	R, 66		R, 65		R, 69		R, 68	428,281	480,271	12	51,258	28.1	9.2	20.9	39.8	3.5	1.3	4.5	43.8
35	D, 62		D, 62		D, 53		D, 63	426,432	440,590	3	77,519	39.2	20.7	12.6	42.5	1.8	0.7	5.2	42.6
36	R, 63		R, 64		R, 66		R, 62	424,786	480,972	13	56,747	31.2	10.9	17.6	44.7	10.1	0.7	5.3	34.6
37	R, 51		R, 63		R, 55		R, 57	428,137	455,580	6	95,707	44.9	22.7	8.2	59.2	1.7	0.4	6.8	26.7
38	R, 51		R, 61		R, 61		R, 57	427,492	477,471	12	90,706	42.8	22.0	8.1	57.1	3.0	0.4	10.3	25.1
39	D, 78		D, 76		D, 77		D, 100	419,745	441,339	5	51,632	22.0	10.2	21.7	12.6	5.0	0.7	10.4	75.3
40	D, 70		D, 56		D, 58		D, 63	419,827	437,970	4	65,322	36.1	19.2	15.2	36.2	4.8	0.5	13.6	42.5
41	D, 60		D, 61		D, 60		D, 62	421,077	444,616	6	119,020	50.5	32.3	10.1	57.8	3.1	0.4	8.6	24.6
42	D, 67		D, 74		D, 75		D, 74	421,385	439,150	4	106,757	58.1	40.3	12.2	67.0	3.6	0.2	9.0	15.8
43	D, 59		D, 61		D, 77		D, 63	426,741	443,214	4	64,641	41.1	23.4	17.0	43.9	3.3	0.4	13.7	33.6
44	D, 62		D, 60		D, 66		D, 58	434,037	452,409	4	81,493	44.5	27.5	13.5	36.0	8.1	0.5	22.0	34.4
45	D, 100		D, 86		D, 76		D, 83	431,470	450,074	4	41,881	25.6	13.2	29.7	14.2	4.0	0.7	19.2	68.5
46	D, 84		D, 86		D, 85		D, 100	422,099	445,293	5	36,462	17.8	8.6	38.9	6.4	6.6	0.8	8.6	85.9
47	D, 83		D, 82		D, 81		D, 85	425,465	442,756	4	67,896	42.6	25.9	18.9	31.8	23.8	0.4	14.0	30.7
48	D, 94		D, 88		D, 89		D, 89	426,131	446,076	5	36,591	24.1	11.4	35.5	14.7	25.1	0.6	15.1	54.5
49	D, 100		D, 67		D, 66		D, 63	422,721	439,408	4	60,272	31.1	16.7	19.4	18.6	1.9	0.6	40.7	50.2
50	D, 85		D, 73		D, 75		D, 78	429,708	446,151	4	48,008	19.5	8.2	22.7	10.0	6.4	0.8	6.6	80.8

(continued)

Note: D=Democrat, R=Republican, R/D=Republican/Democrat (cross-filed), D/R=Democrat/Republican (cross-filed), I=Independent, C=Constitution, O=Other, GI=Green Independent, P=Progressive, P/D=Progressive/Democrat, P/D/R=Progressive/Democrat/Republican, HH=Households

California State Assembly Districts—Election and Demographic Data (cont.)

Assembly Districts	General Election Results Party, Percent of Vote							Population			Avg. HH Income	2006 Pop 25+ Some College +	2006 Pop 25+ 4-Yr Degree +	2006 Below Poverty Line	2006 White (Non-Hisp)	2006 African American	2006 American Indians, Alaska Natives	2006 Asians, Hawaiians, Pacific Islanders	2006 Hispanic Origin
California	2000	2001	2002	2003	2004	2005	2006	2000	2006	% Change	($)	(%)	(%)	(%)	(%)	(%)	(%)	(%)	(%)
51	D, 78		D, 100		D, 84		D, 74	423,126	439,526	4	53,823	29.9	13.4	20.4	20.8	24.9	0.5	12.3	47.2
52	D, 87		D, 90		D, 100		D, 100	427,551	448,368	5	43,166	18.0	7.0	33.0	11.8	24.0	0.7	6.1	66.9
53	D, 64		D, 61		D, 50		D, 58	415,530	434,478	5	95,152	53.1	34.4	9.0	55.3	3.0	0.4	17.2	21.5
54	D, 59		D, 60		D, 53		D, 61	427,858	444,816	4	82,166	43.8	25.4	14.6	43.6	7.7	0.5	14.4	30.9
55	D, 75		D, 80		D, 67		D, 68	424,808	442,975	4	56,726	29.1	13.0	20.1	23.4	12.9	0.6	19.3	47.9
56	D, 61		D, 61		D, 60		D, 58	419,587	433,268	3	64,032	30.4	14.0	13.1	23.5	4.4	0.7	20.5	54.8
57	D, 73		D, 65		D, 69		D, 63	425,559	442,553	4	62,386	27.7	12.4	14.4	18.7	4.5	0.8	15.0	65.2
58	D, 75		D, 63		D, 62		D, 69	423,920	439,168	4	63,543	29.4	14.2	16.7	17.1	2.7	0.7	14.5	69.2
59	R, 48		R, 63		R, 58		R, 56	439,685	490,037	11	74,348	39.6	18.0	12.2	55.2	4.7	0.6	7.5	27.9
60	R, 59		R, 69		R, 67		R, 70	426,413	460,924	8	98,823	44.7	24.9	7.4	43.1	2.8	0.3	26.2	28.5
61	D, 54		D, 62		D, 64		D, 63	424,374	471,401	11	59,147	25.6	9.1	16.8	20.3	7.6	0.8	8.1	63.8
62	D, 63		D, 69		D, 65		D, 68	422,074	483,527	15	50,226	22.1	6.2	23.5	17.8	12.3	0.9	5.2	66.1
63	R, 58		R, 61		R, 58		R, 60	425,469	492,923	16	67,910	36.9	14.9	13.9	42.2	8.1	0.6	8.4	37.5
64	R, 54		R, 63		R, 61		R, 61	431,140	547,400	27	70,827	35.3	15.2	14.5	46.7	7.3	0.6	6.1	34.9
65	R, 47		R, 63		R, 62		R, 60	423,332	519,595	23	50,389	30.8	10.0	19.2	50.7	5.9	0.9	3.5	33.5
66	R, 64		R, 68		R, 62		R, 62	416,994	529,343	27	69,314	32.4	12.8	12.4	45.9	3.7	1.1	4.9	38.3
67	R, 62		R, 69		R, 64		R, 60	423,596	438,221	3	82,976	46.4	23.3	8.9	57.0	1.7	0.4	16.0	21.7
68	R, 57		R, 65		R, 61		R, 62	422,584	438,210	4	68,238	37.7	17.2	12.4	39.2	1.2	0.5	27.6	31.6
69	D, 63		D, 65		D, 61		D, 66	426,631	443,229	4	56,923	22.2	9.4	16.8	13.3	1.7	0.8	13.7	75.1
70	R, 60		R, 67		R, 61		R, 60	425,995	466,282	9	111,354	54.4	34.5	7.4	61.3	1.4	0.2	17.6	16.6
71	R, 66		R, 73		R, 69		R, 72	432,980	518,176	20	99,355	43.3	22.5	6.6	54.4	3.2	0.4	9.5	28.3
72	R, 68		R, 68		R, 66		R, 59	425,115	440,999	4	72,588	38.0	18.5	11.1	39.7	1.9	0.5	13.6	41.0
73	R, 65		R, 68		R, 63		R, 73	419,446	448,095	7	90,226	44.5	23.2	8.6	58.0	3.6	0.5	7.4	25.5
74	R, 57		R, 61		R, 57		R, 58	424,241	453,756	7	86,895	45.3	25.9	9.6	56.4	2.1	0.5	5.6	29.2
75	R, 64		R, 59		R, 60		R, 58	429,941	456,722	6	100,369	51.7	34.2	7.4	59.4	2.0	0.3	19.1	16.9
76	D, 61		D, 62		D, 54		D, 64	421,466	436,363	4	59,613	48.1	27.3	14.2	56.3	5.3	0.5	9.3	24.3
77	R, 52		R, 66		R, 65		R, 61	431,648	445,478	3	68,319	41.5	18.8	11.9	68.0	3.0	0.7	4.5	19.0
78	D, 56		R, 49		R, 49		R, 51	428,409	457,033	7	65,614	39.2	19.4	13.4	37.9	10.6	0.4	18.8	32.4
79	D, 77		D, 66		D, 85		D, 63	420,736	434,374	3	49,512	28.3	11.6	21.7	22.5	7.1	0.6	11.3	59.9
80	R, 52		R, 52		R, 59		R, 52	420,195	520,333	24	54,579	26.4	9.8	20.9	24.5	3.6	1.0	3.4	62.7

Note: D=Democrat, R=Republican, R/D=Republican/Democrat (cross-filed), D/R=Democrat/Republican (cross-filed), I=Independent, C=Constitution, O=Other, GI=Green Independent, P=Progressive, P/D=Progressive/Democrat, P/D/R=Progressive/Democrat/Republican, HH=Households

COLORADO

The city of Denver sits like an island in the middle of a geographic and political ocean. It is the largest city between Kansas City and San Francisco and is also the most politically liberal spot in a sea of conservatism that spreads across the western plains and Rocky Mountains. Many of Colorado's best-known politicians in recent decades have been liberal Denver Democrats. In 2008 the city will host the Democratic presidential convention, exactly a century after it last did so.

But Republicans outnumber Democrats in the state by 170,000 and there are conservative bastions, especially Colorado Springs, center of what might be called the military-theocratic complex. Home to the U.S. Air Force Academy and the Army's huge Ft. Carson, in recent years it has also attracted more than 100 evangelical groups, including Dr. James Dobson's Focus on the Family, whose campus occupies eighty-one acres, and the recently disgraced Rev. Ted Haggard, who has said that God told him to move his New Life Church here from Baton Rouge in 1996. *Time* magazine has dubbed the city "the Vatican of evangelical Christianity."

Liberals and conservatives have been battling it out in Colorado during the past two decades like nowhere else in the country, and they are fighting over a rich prize. The 1990s were a boom time, as they were throughout the region, and that has continued in this decade. Five of the seven fastest-growing states in the country are located in the Mountain Time Zone. Rapid growth earned Colorado a new congressional seat in 2002.

The state's growth, however, has not been so much in Denver as in its less-crowded, less-polluted suburbs, particularly to the north and west. Suburban sprawl has boosted the population of 30th house district, in Aurora County, northeast of the city, by 48 percent since 2000 and by 30 percent in the 27th district (Jefferson County) to the northwest. These are not especially wealthy areas. New residents tend to be middle-class families who want a bigger yard and a safer neighborhood.

Race plays a role in state politics, but it does not seem to be a dominant one. As they do everywhere, Democrats hold the districts, centered in Denver, with the largest concentrations of African American residents, although the 17th house district, south of Colorado Springs, which is 20 percent black is represented by a Republican. Hispanics are a more politically influential group in Colorado and here they lean toward the Democrats, a situation that should be a cause of great concern for the state GOP. Hispanics make up 13 percent of the state, the fifth-highest rate in the country. But again the state is split. Denver has elected a Hispanic mayor and its junior U.S. senator, Ken Salazar, is of Hispanic ancestry, but former representative Tom Tancredo (who lost his seat in 2006) has been one of the loudest voices against illegal immigration and launched his 2008 presidential bid on that platform.

So it should not be surprising that the state legislature, the most evenly split in the nation, has been a free-for-all.

Republicans controlled both houses of the legislature rather comfortably through the 1990s but things have changed. They controlled the senate, 20–15, in 2000; lost control to the Democrats in 2002 (for the first time in forty years) by a single seat; regained it by a single seat in 2004; then lost it again by a single seat in 2006. In the house, Democrats slowly chipped away at a 40–25 Republican majority in 2000 before picking up a net gain of seven seats in 2006 to win control, 35–30.

What happened? Under state law, legislative redistricting is done by an eleven-member commission. Democrats, who controlled the commission, pushed through a redistricting plan that was tossed out by the state supreme court. A new Democratic plan passed muster and enabled the party to win control of the state house in 2004 despite receiving 60,000 fewer total votes than Republican candidates. Tim Gill, a gay activist who made millions from a desktop publishing company during the dot-come boom, also donated more than $20 million to help win legislative seats for the Democrats.

(There was a similar fight over congressional redistricting, which in Colorado is done by the legislature. Because each party controlled one chamber after the 2000 elections, the legislature was unable to come up with a plan. A state court adopted the Democratic plan, but when Republicans retook the state senate in 2002, they tried to enact a new redistricting plan. The case went to the state supreme court, which struck it down on the grounds that the state constitution allows reapportionment only once per decade).

The 2006 elections were nearly a clean sweep for the Democrats, who won races for governor, attorney general, treasurer, and secretary of state, and retook both chambers of the legislature. This is the first time Democrats have controlled the state's executive and legislative branches since 1962.

As often happens, the election was close and could have gone either way. Republicans, for example, had held the 27th state house district by narrow margins for several years before losing it in 2006 by 109 votes. Control of the state senate turned on the outcome in the 5th senate district southwest of Denver, where a Republican who had won with a comfortable 58 percent of the vote in 2002 was replaced by a Democrat who squeaked in with 51 percent.

So it would probably be wrong to read too much into recent election results. Democrats currently represent all five of the fastest-growing state house districts, but also three of the five that are losing population fastest. The most politically competitive legislative districts over the last several years show no clear population trend; some are growing and some are shrinking. Things rest on a knife's edge. The state voted for Bill Clinton in 1992 but switched to Bob Dole in 1996. Notwithstanding the recent Democratic surge, Colorado voted for George W. Bush twice and by a slightly wider margin in 2004. It will surely be an electoral prize in 2008, as well, and could go either way.

COLORADO
State Senate Districts

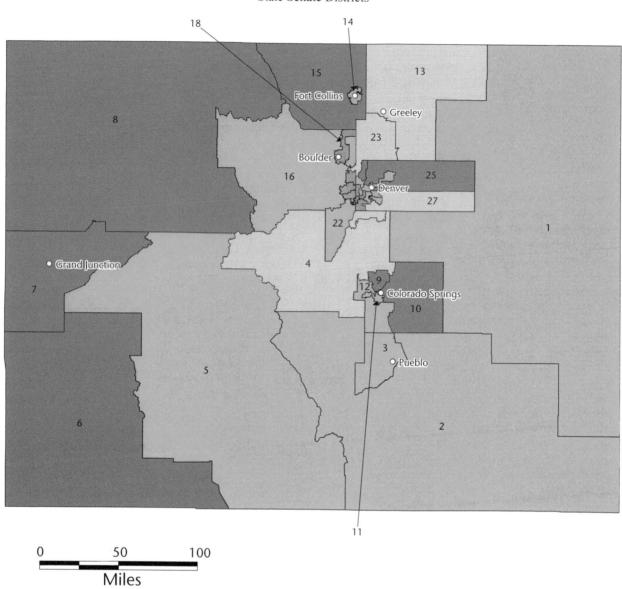

0   50   100

Miles

Population Growth   ▢ -7% to -2%   ▢ -2% to 7%   ▢ 7% to 23%   ▢ 23% to 49%

DENVER

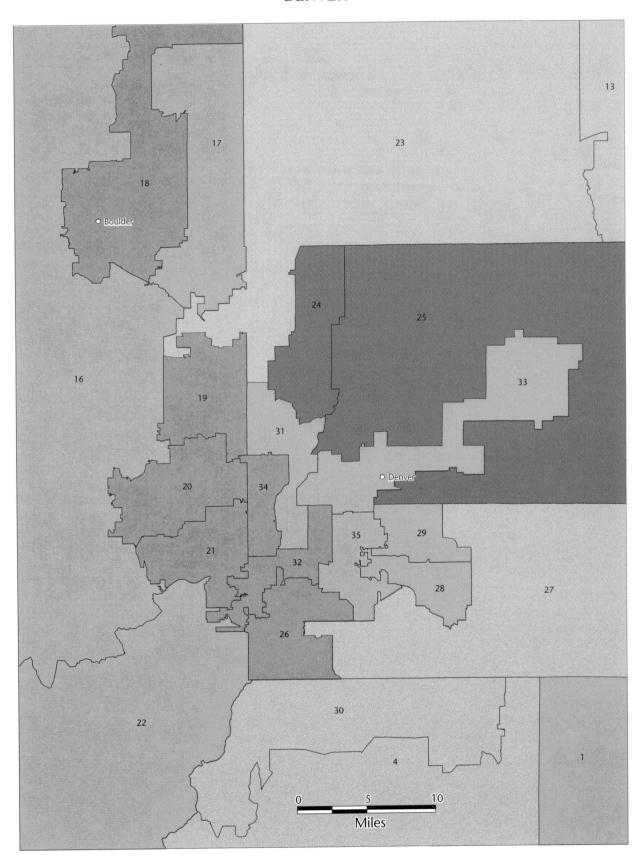

Population Growth   ☐ -7% to -2%   ☐ -2% to 7%   ■ 7% to 23%   ☐ 23% to 49%

Colorado State Senate Districts—Election and Demographic Data

Senate Districts	General Election Results Party, Percent of Vote							Population			Avg. HH Income	Pop 25+		2006					
												Some College +	4-Yr Degree +	Below Poverty Line	White (Non-Hisp)	African American	American Indians, Alaska Natives	Asians, Hawaiians, Pacific Islanders	Hispanic Origin
Colorado	2000	2001	2002	2003	2004	2005	2006	2000	2006	% Change	($)	(%)	(%)	(%)	(%)	(%)	(%)	(%)	(%)
1			R, 73				R, 71	121,994	121,486	0	52,416	29.0	9.8	16.5	72.1	1.1	0.4	0.5	19.3
2			R, 57				R, 61	125,853	124,432	-1	46,297	30.1	10.1	19.7	66.7	3.1	0.9	0.7	23.6
3			D, 62				D, 100	124,741	132,113	6	47,108	31.4	11.4	18.4	47.3	2.4	0.9	1.0	41.3
4	R, 59				R, 69			122,100	155,903	28	101,593	49.1	27.5	5.2	87.6	0.6	0.3	1.2	7.4
5			R, 58				D, 51	120,053	122,761	2	53,557	37.4	18.5	17.9	66.5	0.8	0.6	0.8	23.2
6			D, 54				D, 60	123,790	133,897	8	55,535	38.3	19.0	15.4	79.3	0.4	2.4	0.6	12.2
7			R, 100				R, 70	120,418	133,349	11	51,194	35.0	14.2	14.5	82.5	0.5	0.5	0.8	11.4
8	R, 49				R, 51			121,596	133,274	10	76,787	41.3	21.0	8.1	72.6	0.4	0.4	0.8	20.3
9			R, 83				R, 69	126,257	142,762	13	75,682	46.6	26.0	5.8	79.6	3.6	0.4	3.8	8.9
10	R, 65				R, 100			122,927	141,853	15	60,049	40.4	16.6	8.3	74.0	5.8	0.4	3.1	11.7
11			R, 47				D, 61	120,223	120,461	0	45,466	33.3	12.4	15.8	54.7	12.4	0.7	3.4	22.8
12	R, 76				R, 78			122,192	126,270	3	70,497	40.7	19.1	8.5	69.0	8.4	0.5	4.0	13.1
13	D, 52		R, 83				R, 60	125,341	155,222	24	56,585	32.1	14.2	15.4	60.6	0.8	0.5	1.3	27.6
14	D, 52				R, 56			126,981	133,322	5	64,856	46.7	29.2	12.6	80.7	1.1	0.3	3.1	10.4
15			R, 62				R, 61	251,159	269,347	7	67,787	46.1	26.0	10.2	83.0	0.7	0.3	2.0	9.8
16			D, 52				D, 60	118,463	125,383	6	104,499	55.7	37.4	5.6	88.3	0.5	0.2	1.9	6.6
17	D, 54				D, 54			122,821	130,270	6	79,390	50.1	32.2	7.6	71.0	0.7	0.4	3.1	18.8
18	D, 72				D, 78			119,630	114,848	-4	78,115	57.7	45.6	12.4	81.0	1.2	0.2	4.2	9.6
19	D, 49				D, 54			122,561	118,308	-3	74,310	44.8	22.7	4.8	78.6	0.8	0.3	3.8	13.0
20			R, 50				D, 57	119,302	113,035	-5	62,446	42.4	22.3	10.3	75.6	1.1	0.5	2.4	15.9
21	D, 54				D, 59		D, 56	121,574	113,634	-7	66,575	44.2	23.6	7.2	69.0	1.5	0.6	3.7	21.0
22			R, 65				R, 53	121,234	125,585	4	95,614	50.4	29.5	2.7	85.4	0.7	0.3	2.2	8.9
23	R, 49				R, 58			126,577	157,653	25	78,283	37.9	18.9	7.1	66.9	0.8	0.4	3.2	21.8
24			D, 58				D, 60	126,884	149,539	18	61,273	30.4	12.7	8.3	55.8	1.8	0.6	3.9	31.5
25	D, 55				D, 57			129,946	147,041	13	56,638	23.2	8.5	12.8	40.7	7.1	0.7	2.4	43.9
26	R, 75				R, 51			119,740	115,217	-4	80,447	44.2	28.2	8.6	77.7	1.6	0.4	2.4	14.4
27	R, 52				R, 62			120,295	155,829	30	119,816	49.5	34.6	3.4	78.5	3.9	0.2	5.3	9.7
28	R, 53				D, 55			125,153	129,993	4	67,033	44.4	25.2	5.0	65.8	9.9	0.3	6.3	14.6
29	D, 54				D, 63			119,409	118,875	0	51,388	33.0	15.8	10.2	42.5	18.9	0.5	5.6	32.0
30			R, 71				R, 63	122,517	181,415	48	107,302	51.1	32.6	2.8	85.1	1.2	0.2	3.9	7.2
31	D, 71				D, 100			124,671	126,040	1	53,976	34.8	19.0	15.1	45.4	3.1	0.7	5.1	39.8
32			D, 81				D, 71	120,142	115,348	-4	75,305	46.3	30.1	9.7	59.6	2.6	0.6	4.2	26.9
33	D, 87				D, 100			125,468	125,243	0	53,429	33.4	17.7	18.2	28.3	35.4	0.6	2.7	34.8
34			D, 85				D, 100	125,627	119,390	-5	46,189	23.3	11.9	19.5	18.9	2.8	1.2	3.0	69.1
35	D, 54				D, 63			120,949	120,200	-1	68,629	53.3	35.1	9.2	67.3	8.2	0.4	4.7	15.5

Note: D=Democrat, R=Republican, R/D=Republican/Democrat (cross-filed), D/R=Democrat/Republican (cross-filed), I=Independent, C=Constitution, O=Other, GI=Green Independent, P=Progressive, P/D=Progressive/Democrat, P/D/R=Progressive/Democrat/Republican, HH=Households

COLORADO
State House Districts

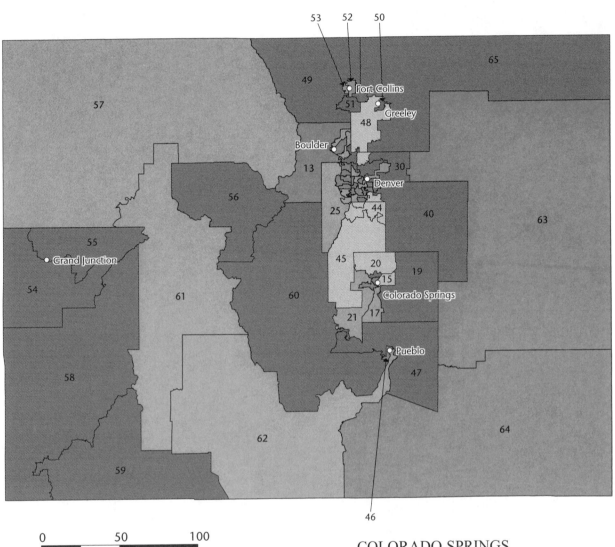

53 52 50

65

49

57

Fort Collins

51

Greeley

48

Boulder

13

30

Denver

56

25

44

40

63

55

45

Grand Junction

20

19

54

15

Colorado Springs

61

60

21

17

58

Pueblo

47

62

64

59

46

0   50   100

Miles

COLORADO SPRINGS

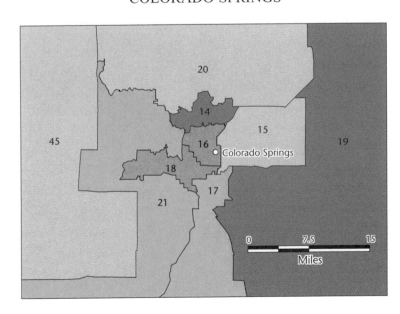

20

45

14

15

19

16

Colorado Springs

18

17

21

0   7.5   15

Miles

Population Growth   ☐ -6% to 2%   ☐ 2% to 10%   ☐ 10% to 24%   ☐ 24% to 52%

DENVER

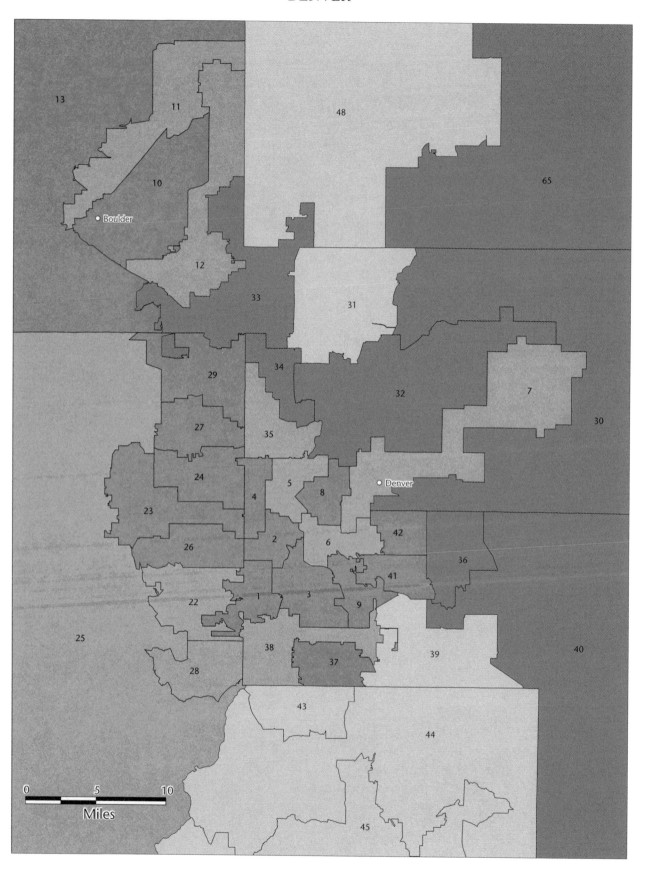

Population Growth   ▨ -6% to 2%   ▨ 2% to 10%   ▨ 10% to 24%   ▨ 24% to 52%

Colorado State House Districts—Election and Demographic Data

House Districts	General Election Results Party, Percent of Vote							Population			Avg. HH Income	2006 Pop 25+ Some College +	2006 Pop 25+ 4-Yr Degree +	Below Poverty Line	White (Non-Hisp)	African American	American Indians, Alaska Natives	Asians, Hawaiians, Pacific Islanders	Hispanic Origin
Colorado	2000	2001	2002	2003	2004	2005	2006	2000	2006	% Change	($)	(%)	(%)	(%)	(%)	(%)	(%)	(%)	(%)
1	D, 59		D, 100		D, 61		D, 55	63,828	63,725	0	59,267	33.9	16.5	10.1	46.5	2.3	0.8	5.4	38.7
2	D, 73		D, 72		D, 83		D, 100	63,806	61,570	-4	44,859	24.0	12.9	20.3	21.3	3.5	1.1	4.4	65.6
3	D, 81		D, 56		D, 61		D, 100	68,633	66,895	-3	78,988	48.7	33.2	9.9	75.6	2.0	0.5	2.9	14.5
4	D, 67		D, 70		D, 76		D, 82	68,321	66,104	-3	49,035	28.3	14.9	16.5	25.4	2.6	1.1	2.3	61.5
5	D, 81		D, 72		D, 79		D, 100	62,220	64,999	4	47,520	33.7	19.8	23.3	27.8	6.6	1.0	2.6	55.6
6	D, 64		D, 84		D, 70		D, 76	71,412	73,842	3	81,312	57.3	40.6	9.9	69.4	7.3	0.4	3.9	15.0
7	D, 77		D, 75		D, 86		D, 100	64,507	67,068	4	65,669	34.4	17.9	10.4	30.7	35.8	0.5	3.3	31.0
8	D, 89		D, 83		D, 100		D, 100	67,590	66,159	-2	55,593	40.8	25.7	18.7	37.1	31.9	0.6	2.3	27.9
9	D, 61		D, 50		D, 61		D, 100	59,014	59,075	0	66,412	54.5	34.8	8.0	69.3	7.4	0.3	4.9	14.2
10	D, 50		D, 83		D, 100		D, 100	69,446	68,037	-2	69,281	55.1	42.8	13.9	78.2	1.5	0.3	5.2	10.9
11	D, 83		D, 49		D, 100		D, 64	65,949	71,647	9	82,323	53.1	35.4	7.3	77.1	0.6	0.4	2.7	14.1
12	R, 77		D, 61		D, 67		D, 100	68,547	71,294	4	80,097	50.5	34.1	7.8	67.9	0.9	0.4	3.4	21.3
13	D, 57		D, 67		D, 84		D, 83	66,972	66,838	0	85,636	58.5	43.0	9.4	87.8	0.6	0.3	2.1	6.2
14	D, 69		R, 85		R, 100		R, 69	63,967	74,863	17	75,556	49.4	27.5	4.3	79.6	3.9	0.3	4.3	8.3
15	R, 68		R, 71		R, 68		R, 67	66,853	83,671	25	61,565	41.5	17.2	6.6	71.4	7.2	0.4	3.9	12.5
16	R, 58		R, 66		R, 61		R, 100	64,859	64,772	0	53,036	39.2	17.4	12.3	71.9	5.2	0.5	2.7	14.4
17	R, 49		R, 61		R, 58		R, 57	66,756	70,181	5	46,410	29.1	7.6	13.0	44.9	19.4	0.7	5.1	24.9
18	R, 68		D, 48		D, 55		D, 61	67,595	67,621	0	46,128	36.7	16.9	16.6	65.1	6.4	0.7	2.0	19.5
19	R, 61		R, 63		R, 100		R, 66	66,890	73,729	10	54,867	33.1	8.6	9.7	67.0	8.8	0.5	3.4	14.3
20	R, 85		R, 85		R, 77		R, 74	66,617	83,555	25	99,999	49.0	30.3	3.4	86.8	2.1	0.3	2.4	5.8
21	R, 56		R, 67		R, 100		R, 59	62,755	67,160	7	78,643	48.7	28.0	8.3	81.0	3.1	0.3	3.6	8.5
22	R, 49		R, 59		R, 52		R, 53	64,822	66,438	2	83,498	49.3	28.4	3.8	79.2	1.3	0.4	3.7	12.4
23	D, 51		R, 53		D, 48		D, 56	64,605	63,333	-2	69,066	43.2	23.8	10.1	74.0	1.5	0.6	2.8	16.9
24	D, 51		D, 100		D, 79		D, 99	67,359	64,337	-4	55,954	39.2	19.2	11.1	68.1	1.1	0.6	1.9	22.6
25	R, 57		R, 100		R, 59		R, 57	66,321	72,307	9	129,288	55.6	37.2	3.2	90.7	0.4	0.2	1.4	5.5
26	D, 54		D, 52		D, 57		D, 61	65,210	61,486	-6	62,174	44.9	23.5	6.6	72.7	1.2	0.4	3.7	18.2
27	R, 55		R, 51		R, 52		D, 50	66,907	65,221	-3	71,798	44.8	21.8	7.4	81.2	0.6	0.3	2.3	12.0
28	R, 77		R, 60		R, 58		R, 56	65,129	66,940	3	93,453	49.8	28.8	2.6	85.8	0.6	0.2	2.2	8.7
29	R, 52		R, 49		D, 51		D, 53	66,762	67,436	1	75,664	44.7	23.2	3.3	77.2	1.0	0.3	5.1	13.3
30	R, 57		D, 51		D, 54		D, 60	70,231	80,303	14	53,039	23.2	8.6	14.0	36.9	11.1	0.7	2.8	45.6
31	R, 50		R, 52		D, 52		D, 58	65,881	82,310	25	74,251	36.2	17.0	4.7	65.9	1.4	0.5	3.4	23.8
32	D, 76		D, 58		D, 62		D, 57	71,127	83,978	18	53,572	21.4	6.8	12.4	40.1	2.8	0.8	2.1	46.2
33	R, 53		R, 53		R, 53		D, 51	66,451	79,761	20	89,171	48.0	29.4	5.2	77.5	1.1	0.3	5.3	12.2
34	D, 78		D, 100		D, 100		D, 100	66,641	77,699	17	63,385	30.7	13.8	9.1	54.0	1.8	0.6	5.0	32.8
35	D, 65		D, 79		D, 65		D, 67	66,808	70,893	6	57,088	26.1	10.8	10.9	45.5	1.5	0.6	7.1	40.6
36	D, 53		D, 54		D, 55		D, 62	65,478	72,295	10	63,040	37.5	18.0	5.1	56.8	13.8	0.4	6.2	19.9
37	R, 55		R, 65		R, 58		R, 51	65,774	64,098	-3	100,929	53.4	37.9	3.8	87.1	1.2	0.2	2.7	7.0
38	R, 80		R, 62		R, 59		D, 53	70,200	72,874	4	96,718	47.1	31.7	7.4	79.8	1.8	0.3	2.7	12.5
39	R, 65		R, 65		R, 55		R, 52	66,435	95,555	44	114,880	48.6	33.7	2.8	74.6	4.9	0.2	6.8	10.9
40	R, 59		R, 80		R, 63		R, 60	67,958	81,655	20	76,793	41.0	20.3	4.2	76.8	4.9	0.3	3.9	10.8
41	D, 56		D, 56		D, 61		D, 65	71,305	72,213	1	61,333	46.5	27.8	7.3	61.6	13.1	0.3	6.7	15.6
42	D, 59		D, 61		D, 66		D, 81	66,923	67,221	0	46,627	29.3	13.6	12.4	35.2	20.6	0.5	4.8	40.6
43	D, 52		R, 100		R, 64		R, 61	64,591	95,767	48	106,813	52.3	35.2	2.2	84.1	1.3	0.2	4.7	7.3
44	R, 68		R, 72		R, 100		R, 64	68,056	103,230	52	109,061	50.2	30.1	3.4	86.6	1.1	0.2	2.8	6.7
45	R, 52		R, 82		R, 67		R, 65	66,142	92,295	40	110,000	49.6	27.7	4.5	90.0	0.6	0.3	1.2	5.7
46	D, 100		D, 100		D, 100		D, 76	63,922	64,701	1	43,834	31.1	11.0	20.6	46.0	2.8	0.8	0.8	42.7
47	R, 76		D, 51		D, 52		D, 63	67,124	77,448	15	56,639	32.2	12.3	12.1	63.6	4.1	0.8	1.3	25.7
48	R, 84		R, 57		R, 63		R, 58	66,035	93,119	41	71,448	36.1	15.9	8.6	68.2	0.5	0.4	1.2	21.7
49	R, 83		R, 100		R, 54		R, 55	65,801	75,553	15	76,648	48.1	25.0	6.8	87.0	0.4	0.4	0.8	7.8
50	R, 75		R, 78		D, 53		D, 59	68,122	83,930	23	45,941	25.8	10.6	19.9	47.6	1.2	0.6	1.6	38.7

(continued)

Note: D=Democrat, R=Republican, R/D=Republican/Democrat (cross-filed), D/R=Democrat/Republican (cross-filed), I=Independent, C=Constitution, O=Other, GI=Green Independent, P=Progressive, P/D=Progressive/Democrat, P/D/R=Progressive/Democrat/Republican, HH=Households

Colorado State House Districts—Election and Demographic Data (cont.)

House Districts	General Election Results Party, Percent of Vote							Population			Avg. HH Income	Pop 25+		2006					
												Some College +	4-Yr Degree +	Below Poverty Line	White (Non-Hisp)	African American	American Indians, Alaska Natives	Asians, Hawaiians, Pacific Islanders	Hispanic Origin
Colorado	2000	2001	2002	2003	2004	2005	2006	2000	2006	% Change	($)	(%)	(%)	(%)	(%)	(%)	(%)	(%)	(%)
51	R, 58		R, 52		R, 87		R, 56	64,344	71,829	12	64,266	42.9	20.1	8.8	84.6	0.4	0.4	1.0	9.8
52	D, 50		R, 52		R, 49		D, 53	68,274	73,021	7	71,181	49.0	30.9	10.7	79.0	0.8	0.3	2.5	12.3
53	D, 52		D, 52		D, 59		D, 59	64,323	69,771	8	57,076	43.5	26.5	14.7	81.0	1.3	0.3	3.6	9.8
54	R, 82		R, 85		R, 67		R, 62	65,518	73,776	13	51,538	34.4	14.0	14.0	80.9	0.5	0.5	0.7	12.9
55	R, 83		R, 100		D, 55		D, 55	67,825	76,703	13	49,794	34.0	13.6	15.5	82.6	0.6	0.5	0.9	11.1
56	R, 49		R, 51		D, 55		D, 67	65,944	73,304	11	88,926	48.1	29.6	6.2	66.1	0.6	0.4	1.1	24.6
57	R, 79		R, 64		R, 68		R, 63	68,591	74,553	9	62,704	40.1	17.9	10.1	85.5	0.4	0.3	0.6	10.0
58	R, 79		R, 52		R, 100		R, 62	68,859	76,923	12	52,947	33.9	15.7	16.2	80.6	0.3	1.6	0.6	12.4
59	R, 65		R, 100		R, 100		R, 52	67,234	73,970	10	56,904	41.7	21.5	15.0	87.2	0.4	5.1	0.6	11.6
60	R, 48		R, 66		R, 54		R, 60	64,191	71,054	11	52,808	40.4	16.7	14.4	86.7	1.1	0.5	0.5	7.9
61	D, 54		R, 52		D, 61		D, 100	65,856	71,064	8	76,332	47.0	26.1	8.6	76.1	0.4	0.3	1.0	17.6
62	R, 51		D, 61		D, 59		D, 55	70,112	72,008	3	39,088	25.3	9.5	26.3	34.1	1.3	1.2	0.8	53.1
63	R, 87		R, 86		R, 74		R, 73	67,887	67,454	-1	47,976	25.5	8.2	18.3	67.5	1.5	0.5	0.5	22.7
64	R, 67		R, 50		D, 54		D, 55	67,980	65,035	-4	42,169	27.6	8.9	23.3	52.8	1.2	1.0	0.8	36.5
65	R, 90		R, 71		R, 73		R, 100	65,813	77,914	18	54,799	29.0	9.9	15.7	68.0	0.8	0.4	0.8	22.2

Note: D=Democrat, R=Republican, R/D=Republican/Democrat (cross-filed), D/R=Democrat/Republican (cross-filed), I=Independent, C=Constitution, O=Other, GI=Green Independent, P=Progressive, P/D=Progressive/Democrat, P/D/R=Progressive/Democrat/Republican, HH=Households

CONNECTICUT

"I am an American," declares Hank Morgan, the protagonist in Mark Twain's 1889 satire, *A Connecticut Yankee in King Arthur's Court.* "I was born and reared in Hartford, in the State of Connecticut—anyway, just over the river, in the country. So I am a Yankee of the Yankees—and practical; yes, and nearly barren of sentiment, I suppose—or poetry, in other words."

Twain was also barren of sentiment, so it was not he who romanticized Hank, but for generations a Connecticut Yankee was an American archetype: white, Protestant, practical, thrifty, stubborn, a lowercase democrat, a mechanic, and born inventor. Connecticut was the nation's workshop and Connecticut residents held more patents per capita than residents of any other state. They produced everything: tools in New Britain, guns in Norwich and Middletown, axes in Collinsville, bicycles in Hartford, clocks in New Haven—even submarines in Groton and helicopters in Stratford.

Manufacturing is not what it was a hundred years ago and neither are Connecticut Yankees. Though John Cheever stories and *New Yorker* cartoons set them as madras-clad preppies, the archetypal Connecticut resident today might well be an Italian Catholic from West Haven. Hispanics have become the state's largest ethnic group, so tomorrow's archetype might well be a Dominican from Bridgeport.

When it was founded in 1682, the western boundary of Connecticut stretched all the way to the Pacific Ocean. Now it is the third-smallest state by land area, although one of the most populous. Connecticut's southwestern border on its nubby panhandle is only twelve miles from a more modern Valhalla—New York City—which accounts for its popularity as a place to live for the many wealthy professionals who crowd the morning and evening commuter trains.

Connecticut grew more slowly than any other state in New England during the 1990s and is projected to grow more slowly than any of them over the next thirty years as well. Buoyed by some of those Wall Street bond traders who live across the border in Greenwich and Stamford, however, Connecticut has the highest median household income level in the country: $66,000. The five wealthiest state house districts in the country are located here—led by the 125th (New Canaan) where it is more than $250,000, the richest district in the United States—and eight of the top eleven. In Hartford's 5th district, where blacks and Hispanics make up more than 87 percent of the population, household income is less than $34,000.

The presence of so many prominent colleges and universities—Yale, Wesleyan, and Trinity, among others—helps to account for the high number of college graduates here.

Almost one-third of Connecticut residents have completed a bachelor's degree, the fourth-highest rate in the country (behind Massachusetts, Colorado, and Maryland). In the 19th state house district (West Hartford), almost 62 percent of the people have at least attended college. But in the 4th district (downtown Hartford), fewer than 22 percent have done so.

Given that income distribution is so uneven, it is not surprising that racial distribution is uneven, too. Four house districts have an African American majority—three in Hartford and one in New Haven—while the 94th house district, encompassing Yale University, is almost 13 percent Asian. Hispanics have also joined the Connecticut melting pot. Seven state house districts have Hispanic majorities, in Bridgeport, New Haven, and Hartford.

Immigration, in fact, is accounting for much of the state's growth. There are no boom areas here, as there are in most of the western states, but although Connecticut is one of the most suburban states, it is interesting that two of the three state house districts that are growing fastest are located in downtown New Haven and downtown Bridgeport. Both are heavily Hispanic. Hartford, interestingly, is what Michael Barone characterizes as one of the country's "static cities," meaning that immigrants are arriving at about the same rate that Americans are leaving, keeping the city's overall population fairly even.

On the other hand, few parts of Connecticut are shrinking to any great extent. Stagnating might be a more descriptive term. Of 141 state house districts, twenty-three have experienced no growth in this decade.

Like other New England states, Connecticut once had separate representatives for each town, which explains why a place covering such a small land area has such a big house of representatives. Democrats control that house by a large and growing margin. For much of the 1990s, control of the state senate, whose members serve two-year terms, swung between the parties. But Democrats regained the edge in 1996 and have not lost it since, in fact adding a few seats along the way so that they now outnumber GOP member two-to-one.

Nationally, Connecticut has been one of the party's best states nationally, voting Democratic by large margins in every presidential race since 1984. In more than 200 years of statehood, however, it has produced only one president of its own: George W. Bush, born in New Haven in 1946 while his father was still at Yale. Democrats have not won a gubernatorial election since 1978, failing even after John Rowland was forced to resign in 2004 before going to prison for corruption.

CONNECTICUT
State Senate Districts

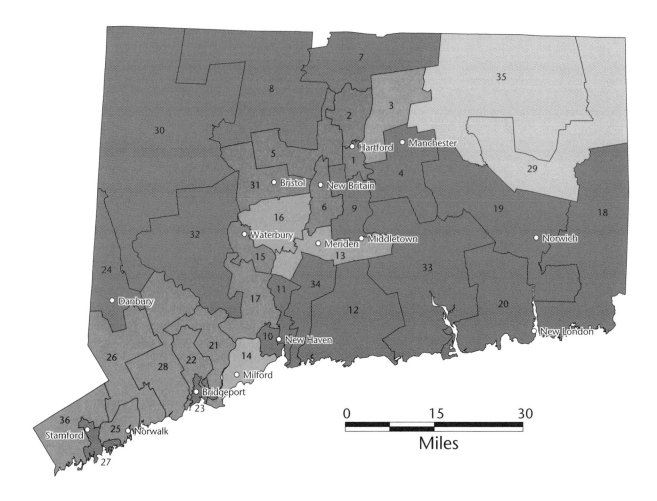

Population Growth ▢ 0% to 2%   ▢ 2% to 3%   ▢ 3% to 7%   ▢ 7% to 9%

Connecticut State Senate Districts—Election and Demographic Data

Senate Districts	General Election Results Party, Percent of Vote							Population			Avg. HH Income	2006 Pop 25+		Below Poverty Line	White (Non-Hisp)	African American	American Indians, Alaska Natives	Asians, Hawaiians, Pacific Islanders	Hispanic Origin
												Some College +	4-Yr Degree +						
Connecticut	2000	2001	2002	2003	2004	2005	2006	2000	2006	% Change	($)	(%)	(%)	(%)	(%)	(%)	(%)	(%)	(%)
1	D, 89		D, 71		D, 86		D, 88	90,444	91,337	1	45,390	29.4	14.4	25.7	21.7	15.1	0.3	2.7	51.0
2	D, 100		D, 77		D, 94		D, 79	92,363	93,219	1	58,428	33.3	16.5	22.3	29.9	50.8	0.2	2.3	14.4
3	D, 60		D, 59		D, 67		D, 70	95,033	96,947	2	69,128	39.3	19.1	10.1	67.8	11.4	0.1	4.5	10.2
4	D, 58		D, 64		D, 66		D, 58	97,414	100,489	3	85,390	48.4	28.2	7.8	79.8	6.4	0.1	3.9	5.5
5	D, 72		D, 69		D, 57		D, 68	94,780	96,008	1	104,706	53.3	37.5	7.8	79.3	5.5	0.1	5.3	5.9
6	D, 68		D, 54		D, 95		D, 93	92,878	93,688	1	57,195	34.0	17.0	15.8	55.3	9.2	0.2	3.1	23.8
7	R, 100		R, 63		R, 51		R, 53	95,224	98,683	4	76,487	41.6	19.6	7.8	82.3	6.7	0.1	2.0	4.8
8	R, 100		R, 65		R, 61		R, 50	92,820	96,235	4	101,253	47.2	29.9	7.6	89.5	2.3	0.1	2.5	3.0
9	D, 73		D, 70		D, 61		D, 58	95,887	100,113	4	72,895	44.6	25.4	8.4	80.4	6.7	0.1	3.8	5.3
10	D, 86		D, 100		D, 100		D, 88	92,220	96,198	4	50,913	31.7	17.2	23.3	31.5	42.6	0.2	4.0	20.4
11	D, 82		D, 76		D, 100		D, 100	91,371	94,818	4	60,341	39.0	25.9	20.2	52.9	15.0	0.2	6.0	20.5
12	R, 100		R, 60		D, 52		D, 64	94,254	97,675	4	99,938	50.5	32.7	6.1	90.2	2.2	0.0	2.5	2.7
13	D, 78		D, 60		D, 70		D, 72	97,585	99,983	2	69,355	38.3	20.6	12.0	68.3	6.7	0.1	2.4	16.5
14	R, 55		R, 60		D, 52		D, 64	92,258	94,694	3	78,338	42.4	23.3	8.4	84.8	4.2	0.1	3.3	4.6
15	D, 64		D, 91		D, 90		D, 88	92,407	93,219	1	52,262	31.6	14.3	19.6	51.5	14.0	0.2	2.0	25.0
16	R, 54		D, 53		D, 60		R, 55	100,157	102,440	2	68,985	38.0	18.5	10.4	77.0	7.5	0.1	2.1	8.4
17	D, 70		D, 100		D, 94		D, 72	90,954	92,254	1	74,444	38.1	20.7	10.7	75.3	10.9	0.1	3.1	6.9
18	R, 63		R, 58		R, 54		D, 51	98,483	101,808	3	67,759	36.1	18.1	9.4	85.7	3.7	0.5	2.6	4.0
19	D, 71		D, 54		D, 62		D, 70	93,047	95,914	3	68,962	37.6	19.9	10.6	83.0	4.3	0.7	2.2	5.1
20	D, 68		D, 62		D, 61		D, 61	91,674	95,383	4	74,735	39.4	22.5	10.2	74.0	7.7	0.3	2.9	9.8
21	R, 62		R, 62		R, 91		R, 52	93,235	93,803	1	84,515	44.0	26.0	7.5	85.3	3.7	0.1	2.5	5.5
22	D, 59		D, 55		D, 54		D, 54	96,947	97,469	1	78,260	40.8	24.6	11.3	61.4	12.7	0.1	3.9	16.4
23	D, 81		D, 75		D, 73		D, 82	91,907	95,634	4	43,049	25.5	12.5	27.0	20.1	34.9	0.3	4.2	43.5
24	R, 92		R, 100		R, 65		R, 100	97,616	101,812	4	82,005	40.8	25.7	9.0	65.6	6.0	0.1	5.9	15.3
25	R, 55		R, 59		D, 58		D, 63	95,696	96,752	1	114,989	46.9	31.7	8.4	62.0	13.4	0.1	4.3	16.9
26	R, 100		R, 100		R, 60		R, 56	98,683	99,906	1	199,718	56.8	45.2	4.4	88.7	2.2	0.1	3.6	3.1
27	D, 67		D, 53		D, 61		D, 62	96,778	100,266	4	95,903	43.7	30.4	11.8	50.5	16.5	0.1	6.4	22.5
28	R, 64		R, 100		R, 65		R, 100	100,652	102,286	2	149,463	51.4	38.3	5.2	88.9	2.5	0.0	2.9	3.3
29	D, 100		R, 90		D, 100		D, 76	91,603	99,755	9	60,934	29.1	15.2	14.9	77.5	3.3	0.2	3.3	9.5
30	R, 65		R, 71		R, 93		R, 67	97,671	102,209	5	89,336	42.1	23.5	8.0	90.5	1.5	0.1	2.0	3.7
31	R, 72		D, 65		D, 53		D, 59	90,114	91,161	1	62,647	35.8	15.0	10.3	84.7	3.7	0.1	2.0	5.3
32	R, 93		R, 64		R, 100		R, 89	94,801	98,372	4	87,567	43.8	24.5	7.1	91.4	1.7	0.1	1.8	3.0
33	D, 64		D, 62		D, 70		D, 72	91,991	96,023	4	88,150	43.0	24.7	6.7	92.1	1.6	0.1	1.6	2.6
34	D, 61		R, 50		R, 88		R, 86	94,307	97,622	4	73,660	38.7	21.5	8.8	85.8	3.0	0.1	3.0	5.2
35	R, 100		R, 65		R, 67		R, 87	94,389	101,298	7	73,768	41.3	22.1	8.4	91.0	1.8	0.1	2.1	2.6
36	R, 100		R, 100		R, 92		R, 59	97,803	99,729	2	200,864	55.4	44.5	6.3	78.9	4.1	0.0	6.1	7.5

Note: D=Democrat, R=Republican, R/D=Republican/Democrat (cross-filed), D/R=Democrat/Republican (cross-filed), I=Independent, C=Constitution, O=Other, GI=Green Independent, P=Progressive, P/D=Progressive/Democrat, P/D/R=Progressive/Democrat/Republican, HH=Households

CONNECTICUT
State Assembly Districts

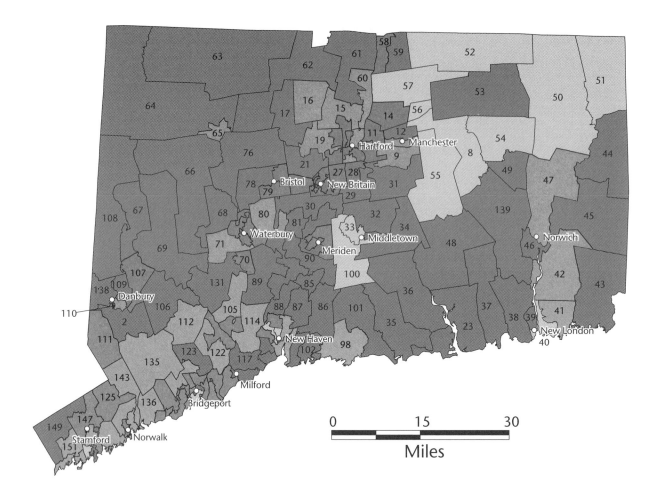

Population Growth   ☐ -2% to 1%   ☐ 1% to 2%   ☐ 2% to 6%   ☐ 6% to 17%

HARTFORD

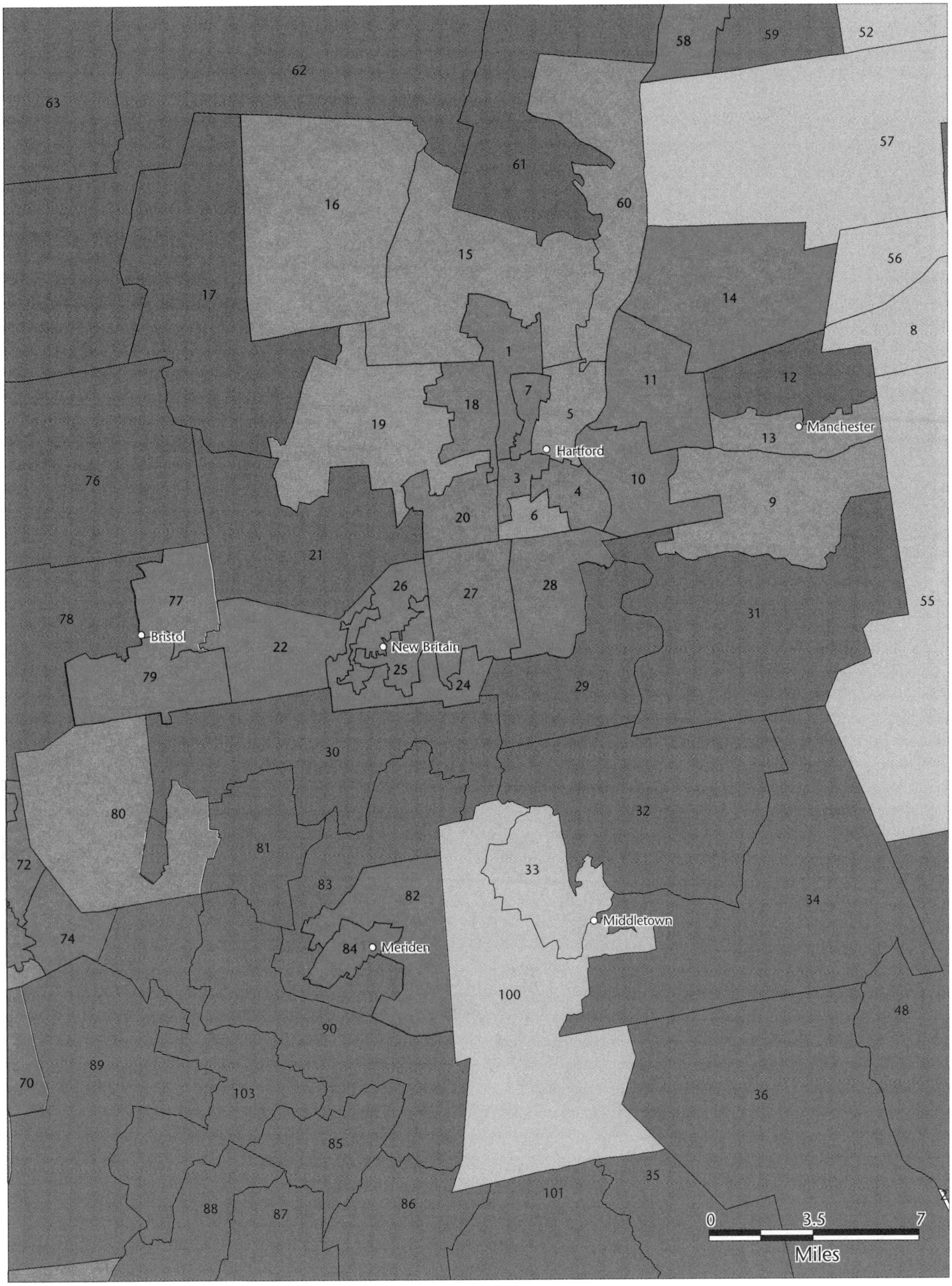

Population Growth -2% to 1% 1% to 2% 2% to 6% 6% to 17%

BRIDGEPORT/NEW HAVEN

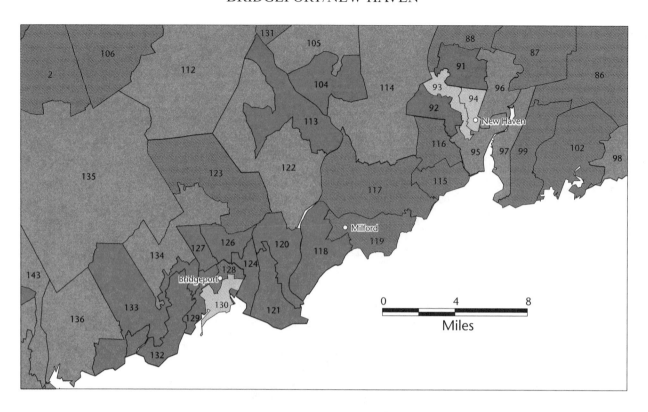

STAMFORD/NORWALK

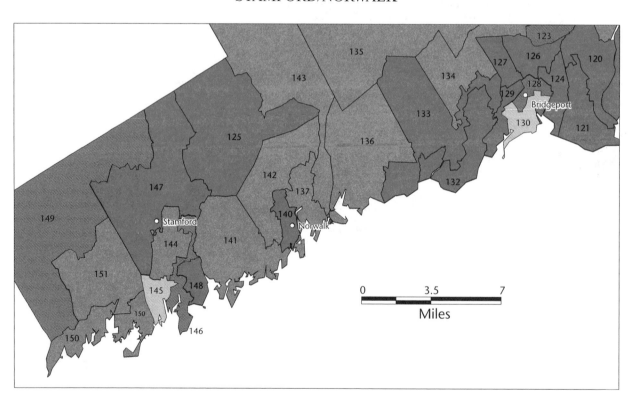

Population Growth   ▮ -2% to 1%   ▮ 1% to 2%   ▮ 2% to 6%   ▮ 6% to 17%

Connecticut State Assembly Districts—Election and Demographic Data

Assembly Districts	General Election Results Party, Percent of Vote							Population			Avg. HH Income	Pop 25+		Below Poverty Line	White (Non-Hisp)	African American	American Indians, Alaska Natives	Asians, Hawaiians, Pacific Islanders	Hispanic Origin
												Some College +	4-Yr Degree +					2006	
Connecticut	2000	2001	2002	2003	2004	2005	2006	2000	2006	% Change	($)	(%)	(%)	(%)	(%)	(%)	(%)	(%)	(%)
1	D, 100		D, 100		D, 100		D, 100	21,919	21,996	0	58,772	34.0	17.0	21.7	29.4	53.0	0.1	2.5	12.9
2	D, 100		R, 52		D, 50		D, 54	22,682	23,417	3	97,410	45.1	30.1	6.8	78.1	3.8	0.2	5.6	7.9
3	D, 100		D, 100		D, 95		D, 92	19,923	20,121	1	35,729	23.5	10.4	35.4	8.0	15.7	0.3	3.5	72.5
4	D, 100		D, 88		D, 86		D, 100	22,046	22,260	1	34,050	21.7	9.4	33.3	10.2	16.1	0.3	2.5	65.9
5	D, 100		D, 91		D, 97		D, 96	22,131	22,525	2	33,675	22.1	10.1	40.1	9.7	54.4	0.3	1.1	39.0
6	D, 100		D, 80		D, 80		D, 94	22,566	22,911	2	45,873	29.9	13.0	20.9	21.9	15.5	0.3	2.3	50.9
7	D, 100		D, 92		D, 100		D, 93	21,215	21,143	0	36,473	26.0	11.3	33.3	11.8	67.7	0.3	1.5	20.2
8	D, 63		D, 55		D, 90		D, 57	23,283	24,843	7	85,509	45.2	24.0	6.3	92.4	1.2	0.1	1.3	2.6
9	D, 64		D, 63		D, 95		D, 69	24,188	24,434	1	91,943	49.3	28.0	5.6	82.1	5.4	0.0	4.1	4.7
10	D, 75		D, 71		D, 74		D, 74	23,376	23,373	0	51,099	32.2	12.5	16.5	51.7	18.9	0.2	4.3	17.4
11	D, 67		D, 62		D, 71		D, 74	21,334	21,141	-1	57,750	32.2	12.3	13.2	45.7	21.0	0.2	6.4	19.9
12	R, 100		D, 59		D, 65		D, 76	23,472	24,476	4	67,180	44.7	21.9	7.4	75.8	8.0	0.1	4.3	6.8
13	D, 65		D, 60		D, 72		D, 65	22,351	22,705	2	58,295	40.2	19.4	12.4	67.7	11.7	0.1	4.4	10.0
14	D, 57		D, 62		R, 56		R, 57	23,120	23,344	1	96,609	49.6	30.1	4.0	84.2	4.4	0.1	5.4	3.0
15	D, 100		D, 71		D, 75		D, 96	23,924	24,170	1	86,653	47.9	27.1	8.6	51.8	37.2	0.1	2.3	5.0
16	R, 100		R, 100		R, 65		D, 49	22,407	22,736	1	126,670	57.0	41.7	4.1	89.6	2.7	0.0	3.0	2.0
17	D, 55		R, 50		R, 60		R, 100	22,153	23,269	5	129,471	56.2	38.4	4.6	90.2	2.5	0.0	2.7	2.0
18	D, 77		D, 74		D, 100		D, 74	22,128	22,179	0	98,113	51.6	39.4	9.4	77.9	6.4	0.1	5.3	6.2
19	R, 50		R, 59		R, 57		D, 57	22,192	22,463	1	139,594	61.7	48.4	6.3	85.6	3.2	0.1	4.7	3.3
20	D, 66		D, 51		D, 72		D, 100	21,598	21,593	0	72,468	45.5	27.8	9.1	65.4	8.0	0.1	8.3	12.8
21	D, 100		D, 59		D, 63		D, 71	23,463	23,989	2	107,309	51.7	34.1	7.7	84.5	3.5	0.1	4.8	3.9
22	D, 100		D, 74		D, 77		R, 95	22,978	23,126	1	58,165	37.2	16.3	10.7	73.2	5.9	0.2	3.1	11.5
23	D, 74		R, 57		R, 62		R, 87	22,261	22,826	3	97,943	50.6	31.8	7.0	93.2	1.0	0.1	2.1	2.0
24	D, 100		D, 68		D, 75		D, 75	21,670	21,647	0	57,705	34.4	16.7	12.5	56.3	10.1	0.1	3.1	22.9
25	D, 100		D, 70		D, 100		D, 78	23,978	23,975	0	40,592	25.8	11.7	26.2	33.1	13.6	0.3	2.4	42.6
26	R, 100		R, 54		D, 100		D, 80	23,085	23,088	0	52,815	32.6	17.0	14.4	59.6	8.5	0.1	3.8	19.8
27	D, 77		D, 75		D, 95		D, 94	23,015	23,178	1	70,941	44.1	23.1	8.4	83.8	3.8	0.1	3.5	5.1
28	D, 100		D, 95		D, 100		D, 60	24,154	24,301	1	73,421	47.2	27.2	8.8	84.5	3.7	0.0	2.3	5.3
29	D, 68		D, 51		D, 65		D, 94	22,794	23,947	5	77,164	49.2	28.9	6.3	82.6	4.6	0.1	5.0	4.3
30	R, 55		R, 50		D, 53		D, 59	24,264	25,158	4	79,752	44.2	22.9	7.2	89.1	2.6	0.1	2.5	2.9
31	R, 100		R, 65		R, 59		D, 50	22,994	23,705	3	119,528	57.0	40.5	5.3	87.3	2.9	0.1	3.8	2.9
32	D, 63		D, 63		D, 100		D, 69	22,817	23,550	3	77,805	43.3	24.6	7.2	88.9	3.5	0.0	1.5	3.4
33	D, 94		D, 57		D, 67		D, 64	21,841	23,278	7	63,736	37.9	22.3	12.9	69.3	14.4	0.2	4.3	7.5
34	D, 57		D, 62		D, 55		D, 51	22,041	23,202	5	74,932	34.1	17.6	7.9	83.6	6.4	0.1	3.0	3.7
35	D, 55		D, 55		D, 100		D, 70	23,744	24,803	4	82,637	46.9	27.3	7.0	91.8	0.8	0.1	1.7	3.5
36	D, 54		D, 54		D, 100		D, 66	21,553	22,755	6	105,351	47.7	29.4	5.7	93.7	1.4	0.1	1.1	2.1
37	D, 58		D, 69		D, 54		D, 56	22,048	22,820	4	87,009	45.2	27.6	6.4	82.0	5.9	0.3	3.4	5.4
38	D, 69		D, 69		D, 52		D, 69	23,817	24,308	2	76,623	38.4	21.8	7.6	84.0	3.8	0.3	3.3	5.0
39	D, 91		D, 63		D, 67		D, 65	21,486	21,932	2	45,405	26.8	12.4	19.5	43.2	19.5	0.5	2.8	27.1
40	D, 100		D, 54		D, 63		D, 100	21,268	22,918	8	57,785	34.3	16.3	9.9	71.0	9.5	0.5	4.8	8.3
41	R, 70		R, 100		R, 100		D, 52	21,861	22,131	1	74,224	42.6	24.5	7.4	82.7	4.9	0.3	3.7	4.5
42	D, 52		R, 50		D, 59		D, 100	23,638	24,095	2	73,597	38.8	21.2	7.6	83.9	3.6	1.5	2.7	4.2
43	R, 37		R, 100		R, 100		R, 100	23,527	24,193	3	81,005	43.1	26.2	8.8	92.3	1.2	0.5	1.7	1.8
44	R, 94		R, 58		R, 55		R, 65	22,986	24,143	5	56,166	27.7	9.2	13.4	91.0	1.2	0.3	1.5	2.9
45	D, 100		D, 64		D, 74		D, 75	22,773	23,752	4	62,564	30.8	12.7	9.7	91.7	1.6	0.5	1.1	2.4
46	R, 54		D, 100		D, 93		D, 100	21,302	21,734	2	53,147	33.1	16.1	17.3	71.5	8.6	0.8	3.3	9.0
47	D, 100		D, 68		D, 100		D, 61	23,296	23,737	2	60,597	33.7	16.1	12.8	86.2	3.2	0.4	1.7	4.2
48	D, 62		D, 57		D, 100		D, 100	22,532	23,310	3	83,788	41.7	22.7	6.0	92.9	1.6	0.2	0.9	2.1
49	D, 79		D, 64		D, 81		D, 54	22,107	23,309	5	51,215	26.0	13.2	19.7	50.7	5.0	0.3	2.2	29.3
50	D, 100		D, 53		R, 50		R, 51	21,814	23,583	8	72,074	39.4	21.0	9.2	92.8	1.6	0.2	0.9	2.0

(continued)

Note: D=Democrat, R=Republican, R/D=Republican/Democrat (cross-filed), D/R=Democrat/Republican (cross-filed), I=Independent, C=Constitution, O=Other, GI=Green Independent, P=Progressive, P/D=Progressive/Democrat, P/D/R=Progressive/Democrat/Republican, HH=Households

Connecticut State Assembly Districts—Election and Demographic Data (cont.)

Assembly Districts	General Election Results Party, Percent of Vote							Population			Avg. HH Income	Pop 25+ Some College +	Pop 25+ 4-Yr Degree +	Below Poverty Line	2006 White (Non-Hisp)	African American	American Indians, Alaska Natives	Asians, Hawaiians, Pacific Islanders	Hispanic Origin
Connecticut	2000	2001	2002	2003	2004	2005	2006	2000	2006	% Change	($)	(%)	(%)	(%)	(%)	(%)	(%)	(%)	(%)
51	D, 100		D, 100		D, 56		D, 100	24,413	26,051	7	60,565	29.7	12.6	12.9	93.4	1.1	0.3	1.0	1.7
52	D, 52		R, 59		R, 67		R, 94	22,012	23,650	7	76,650	36.0	15.6	8.3	85.5	5.0	0.2	1.2	4.9
53	D, 100		D, 93		D, 93		D, 53	23,158	24,522	6	86,023	43.9	27.2	7.5	92.8	1.1	0.1	2.3	1.9
54	D, 100		D, 77		D, 95		D, 94	22,951	26,832	17	74,182	29.7	22.0	14.5	77.6	4.7	0.1	8.0	5.8
55	R, 100		R, 100		R, 69		R, 65	22,304	23,895	7	98,451	49.8	29.4	4.8	94.2	1.4	0.1	1.1	1.6
56	D, 55		D, 55		D, 68		D, 77	21,054	22,551	7	57,932	40.0	19.3	9.7	82.7	4.7	0.1	4.1	5.0
57	D, 100		D, 92		D, 91		D, 87	24,581	26,785	9	73,411	42.2	21.4	7.0	90.0	3.0	0.1	2.4	2.1
58	D, 100		D, 100		D, 67		D, 67	22,821	22,876	0	62,777	37.3	16.4	9.8	86.9	4.1	0.1	2.1	3.4
59	D, 100		D, 94		D, 65		D, 67	21,934	22,662	3	71,820	39.4	14.7	6.8	75.6	10.1	0.2	1.9	7.3
60	D, 62		D, 55		D, 66		D, 78	22,154	22,589	2	66,929	40.0	17.6	9.1	70.8	16.1	0.1	3.7	5.3
61	R, 100		R, 94		R, 91		R, 51	22,497	23,323	4	94,991	47.6	27.5	7.1	80.0	9.0	0.1	3.3	4.2
62	R, 100		R, 94		R, 91		R, 92	22,396	23,688	6	99,770	50.6	31.9	4.3	92.2	2.1	0.1	1.4	2.0
63	R, 100		D, 50		D, 54		D, 67	22,641	23,720	5	69,179	37.3	18.1	10.0	91.3	1.3	0.1	1.1	3.6
64	D, 53		D, 56		D, 59		D, 68	23,629	24,546	4	81,315	42.2	22.4	9.0	92.2	1.4	0.1	1.6	3.1
65	D, 47		R, 50		R, 53		R, 50	22,320	22,761	2	51,307	27.0	10.2	15.2	83.9	3.1	0.1	2.7	6.4
66	R, 58		R, 93		R, 60		R, 85	22,327	23,439	5	96,876	47.1	27.7	7.5	94.3	0.7	0.1	1.3	2.1
67	R, 55		R, 69		R, 68		R, 100	22,236	23,347	5	90,247	40.6	21.6	5.9	88.4	1.7	0.1	2.7	4.6
68	R, 77		R, 69		R, 73		R, 100	23,566	24,154	2	76,824	36.8	18.2	8.5	89.9	1.7	0.1	1.7	4.4
69	R, 100		R, 64		R, 100		R, 100	22,996	23,825	4	105,931	52.4	33.5	6.5	92.3	1.6	0.0	1.7	2.5
70	R, 70		R, 80		R, 92		R, 74	21,016	21,092	0	64,198	34.7	15.7	9.9	84.1	3.8	0.1	2.5	5.4
71	R, 58		R, 70		R, 82		R, 80	23,815	24,234	2	67,489	39.1	21.1	11.1	80.4	4.9	0.1	2.3	7.7
72	D, 79		D, 73		D, 84		D, 56	21,944	22,022	0	41,431	25.5	10.1	27.8	30.3	30.5	0.3	1.5	34.8
73	D, 61		D, 62		D, 82		D, 85	22,171	22,168	0	57,955	36.8	16.7	15.6	59.6	14.0	0.2	2.1	17.9
74	D, 100		R, 64		R, 60		R, 94	21,257	21,279	0	50,563	33.0	14.5	14.3	65.9	10.5	0.1	2.7	14.9
75	D, 76		D, 71		D, 64		D, 58	22,509	22,565	0	34,892	24.0	9.8	31.1	24.1	17.1	0.3	1.9	52.2
76	R, 68		R, 70		R, 69		R, 89	24,019	25,275	5	93,891	42.3	22.5	6.1	94.0	1.2	0.1	1.2	1.8
77	D, 74		D, 73		D, 64		R, 51	22,323	22,318	0	62,385	36.6	14.6	11.5	82.3	4.0	0.1	2.6	5.9
78	R, 100		R, 100		R, 92		R, 93	23,653	24,274	3	66,519	32.7	12.9	10.1	89.3	2.6	0.1	1.2	3.7
79	D, 70		D, 68		D, 100		D, 68	23,311	23,281	0	57,422	34.1	13.9	10.1	80.7	4.6	0.1	2.0	7.5
80	R, 100		D, 55		D, 62		D, 67	22,429	22,824	2	73,145	38.2	17.6	7.1	89.0	3.5	0.1	1.4	3.2
81	D, 68		D, 52		D, 100		D, 68	21,545	22,358	4	70,175	41.3	19.7	7.6	89.7	2.5	0.0	1.7	2.7
82	D, 66		D, 63		D, 90		D, 72	21,659	21,863	1	65,496	37.2	17.3	9.0	67.8	6.2	0.1	2.2	17.7
83	D, 62		D, 65		D, 100		D, 71	21,589	22,354	4	70,243	40.3	19.9	9.3	79.1	4.3	0.1	2.6	9.5
84	D, 74		D, 75		D, 100		D, 100	21,113	20,896	-1	41,537	26.8	11.1	23.5	37.3	9.6	0.3	1.4	44.1
85	D, 57		D, 100		D, 95		D, 86	21,587	22,313	3	73,501	40.1	22.1	8.4	83.9	2.4	0.1	2.7	7.5
86	R, 100		R, 100		R, 57		R, 51	21,010	21,677	3	79,987	39.3	20.7	6.6	89.7	2.9	0.1	2.0	3.0
87	D, 63		D, 58		D, 64		D, 67	22,897	23,357	2	85,543	41.2	25.4	7.0	86.3	3.8	0.1	4.4	3.1
88	D, 100		D, 100		D, 96		D, 95	23,407	24,498	5	72,254	44.9	30.1	10.0	78.1	8.1	0.1	6.7	4.1
89	D, 62		D, 100		D, 56		D, 55	22,173	22,827	3	96,784	47.4	29.0	4.2	90.0	2.7	0.1	2.5	2.6
90	D, 67		D, 100		D, 100		D, 69	23,645	24,450	3	96,390	41.8	24.9	7.2	79.3	6.6	0.2	2.4	7.4
91	D, 100		D, 82		D, 81		D, 100	22,176	22,344	1	65,754	36.8	19.9	14.4	57.6	29.0	0.1	2.8	7.3
92	D, 85		D, 100		D, 96		D, 85	22,867	22,940	0	56,627	38.5	23.7	21.5	34.2	44.3	0.3	2.5	16.2
93	D, 91		D, 100		D, 73		D, 100	20,653	23,372	13	53,821	30.0	17.2	29.3	26.1	50.0	0.3	3.8	20.0
94	D, 91		D, 100		D, 100		D, 100	22,233	23,615	6	46,177	33.3	23.4	28.4	35.0	40.7	0.2	12.9	9.5
95	D, 90		D, 78		D, 100		D, 100	21,796	22,016	1	40,886	23.1	11.5	34.8	13.9	29.9	0.3	0.9	59.9
96	D, 100		D, 74		D, 80		D, 100	21,627	21,978	2	64,667	46.5	34.6	18.1	52.5	16.3	0.1	5.7	20.4
97	D, 53		D, 100		D, 100		D, 73	21,779	22,177	2	46,767	29.9	14.4	22.6	47.3	19.7	0.2	3.7	24.0
98	D, 95		D, 100		D, 67		D, 100	22,443	22,805	2	119,180	54.5	38.3	5.6	90.2	2.3	0.0	2.4	2.9
99	D, 72		D, 61		D, 74		D, 54	22,510	23,443	4	59,387	33.1	16.1	12.4	85.4	2.7	0.1	2.7	5.7
100	D, 56		R, 52		R, 51		R, 60	23,428	25,036	7	80,923	43.6	25.6	6.4	85.9	5.7	0.1	2.3	3.3

(continued)

Note: D=Democrat, R=Republican, R/D=Republican/Democrat (cross-filed), D/R=Democrat/Republican (cross-filed), I=Independent, C=Constitution, O=Other, GI=Green Independent, P=Progressive, P/D=Progressive/Democrat, P/D/R=Progressive/Democrat/Republican, HH=Households

Connecticut State Assembly Districts—Election and Demographic Data (cont.)

Assembly Districts	General Election Results Party, Percent of Vote							Population			Avg. HH Income	Pop 25+		Below Poverty Line	2006 White (Non-Hisp)	African American	American Indians, Alaska Natives	Asians, Hawaiians, Pacific Islanders	Hispanic Origin
												Some College +	4-Yr Degree +						
Connecticut	2000	2001	2002	2003	2004	2005	2006	2000	2006	% Change	($)	(%)	(%)	(%)	(%)	(%)	(%)	(%)	(%)
101	R, 100		R, 100		D, 53		D, 60	22,215	23,018	4	125,593	55.8	39.1	4.4	91.4	2.0	0.0	2.4	2.1
102	D, 61		D, 68		D, 100		D, 64	23,893	24,726	3	74,100	47.4	28.3	8.1	86.5	2.9	0.1	4.0	4.0
103	D, 51		R, 51		R, 56		R, 60	23,223	23,754	2	94,656	49.4	32.3	6.1	87.6	3.6	0.0	3.3	3.1
104	D, 76		D, 73		D, 52		D, 57	22,879	23,035	1	53,637	31.6	14.0	14.8	74.0	8.7	0.2	1.9	10.9
105	R, 59		R, 65		R, 62		R, 100	21,952	22,185	1	65,875	38.6	17.8	8.2	86.8	3.2	0.1	2.5	4.4
106	R, 90		R, 89		R, 85		R, 75	22,152	22,942	4	128,187	50.6	36.0	4.6	88.6	3.1	0.1	2.4	3.3
107	R, 62		R, 100		R, 93		R, 93	22,136	22,299	1	100,887	47.5	31.4	4.8	86.7	2.3	0.1	4.2	4.0
108	R, 72		R, 100		R, 100		R, 100	23,487	24,533	4	111,531	45.8	29.0	5.3	90.4	1.7	0.1	2.1	3.5
109	D, 67		D, 61		D, 56		D, 58	22,623	23,927	6	73,432	39.4	24.2	7.3	64.8	7.4	0.1	6.9	14.4
110	D, 65		D, 60		D, 60		D, 67	22,221	22,560	2	54,379	32.7	18.4	16.4	43.4	7.5	0.2	6.4	32.5
111	R, 100		R, 100		R, 66		R, 100	23,693	23,866	1	177,352	57.3	45.7	5.2	90.0	1.9	0.1	3.1	2.9
112	R, 63		R, 67		R, 65		R, 100	22,734	23,168	2	113,809	48.2	31.6	4.4	89.7	2.4	0.0	2.3	3.3
113	R, 57		R, 64		R, 57		R, 90	21,843	22,007	1	83,319	42.7	23.5	7.9	85.0	2.7	0.1	3.5	5.6
114	R, 57		R, 100		R, 100		R, 67	22,208	22,512	1	125,255	49.8	33.6	5.9	85.9	3.3	0.0	4.8	3.2
115	D, 78		D, 100		D, 96		D, 70	21,225	22,045	4	56,575	34.7	17.0	13.6	75.5	8.9	0.1	3.7	7.9
116	D, 74		D, 87		D, 89		D, 69	21,830	22,421	3	51,115	32.6	15.2	15.3	46.0	27.8	0.2	4.7	17.6
117	R, 54		R, 100		D, 52		D, 61	23,239	23,813	2	84,020	42.8	23.7	7.0	87.0	4.0	0.1	3.1	3.3
118	D, 62		D, 100		D, 100		D, 100	22,063	22,132	0	77,801	41.6	22.9	7.8	84.6	3.4	0.1	4.3	5.0
119	D, 61		D, 64		D, 57		D, 71	22,332	23,033	3	79,067	45.8	24.4	6.8	87.3	3.0	0.1	2.4	4.4
120	R, 62		R, 68		R, 53		R, 54	20,802	20,491	-1	75,756	42.7	25.4	8.3	86.6	3.5	0.0	1.7	5.4
121	D, 76		D, 60		D, 75		D, 76	22,566	22,303	-1	59,026	34.3	18.0	12.2	61.4	19.1	0.1	2.6	13.1
122	R, 100		R, 57		R, 100		R, 100	22,669	22,937	1	97,383	49.3	30.4	6.1	89.8	2.2	0.1	2.4	3.2
123	R, 59		R, 65		R, 63		R, 63	23,939	24,594	3	113,536	48.6	33.6	5.9	86.2	3.6	0.0	3.6	4.0
124	D, 85		D, 73		D, 81		D, 83	23,897	24,106	1	38,974	26.7	11.9	25.4	22.1	42.2	0.2	1.7	37.2
125	D, 80		R, 97		R, 100		R, 100	21,805	21,897	0	250,617	59.4	49.0	3.6	89.6	2.2	0.0	3.4	2.4
126	D, 86		D, 84		D, 83		D, 80	22,251	22,435	1	59,423	30.8	14.1	14.3	30.9	37.6	0.3	2.6	28.5
127	D, 73		D, 77		D, 63		D, 94	23,911	23,616	-1	53,459	35.0	18.3	13.5	51.9	15.0	0.1	4.1	22.1
128	D, 86		D, 83		D, 80		D, 86	21,119	21,706	3	39,529	21.8	11.1	32.6	12.2	26.6	0.3	4.2	63.3
129	D, 76		D, 58		D, 75		D, 93	22,260	22,075	-1	56,274	35.0	19.5	18.4	36.4	23.9	0.3	5.2	30.6
130	D, 84		D, 78		D, 79		D, 82	23,348	25,998	11	39,869	23.6	12.7	34.6	16.0	30.2	0.4	8.2	50.3
131	R, 87		R, 57		R, 68		R, 91	22,785	23,770	4	85,327	41.5	23.0	6.9	88.1	2.9	0.1	1.8	4.2
132	R, 95		R, 58		D, 52		D, 58	23,797	23,683	0	115,250	50.3	36.4	7.5	86.1	2.7	0.1	3.7	4.3
133	R, 84		R, 100		R, 100		D, 53	24,914	25,139	1	169,831	50.5	38.6	4.9	88.1	3.0	0.0	2.9	3.5
134	R, 55		R, 53		R, 54		D, 50	24,347	24,762	2	125,586	48.9	34.3	5.1	87.7	3.3	0.1	2.8	3.8
135	R, 100		R, 100		R, 82		R, 88	23,460	23,820	2	205,730	57.6	46.3	3.0	90.3	2.0	0.0	2.9	2.7
136	R, 56		R, 52		D, 51		D, 66	22,751	23,000	1	240,513	60.6	49.8	3.6	88.9	2.3	0.0	3.4	3.2
137	D, 71		D, 61		D, 64		D, 65	24,024	24,265	1	78,440	44.5	27.7	10.5	58.9	13.5	0.1	5.3	19.3
138	R, 63		R, 50		R, 60		R, 52	22,950	24,124	5	93,956	43.4	28.8	7.4	69.2	6.7	0.1	6.9	11.8
139	D, 100		D, 57		D, 64		D, 65	23,531	24,205	3	72,904	34.1	16.9	6.9	85.1	3.7	0.4	1.8	5.0
140	D, 76		D, 56		D, 75		D, 71	21,810	21,873	0	65,913	34.6	19.4	13.0	33.0	30.0	0.2	3.6	35.5
141	R, 75		R, 77		R, 58		R, 100	23,759	24,015	1	247,958	58.4	48.2	3.8	88.8	2.4	0.0	3.4	3.3
142	R, 89		R, 65		R, 92		R, 54	24,291	24,758	2	115,753	51.3	34.4	5.2	73.4	8.4	0.1	4.4	10.1
143	R, 100		R, 100		R, 61		R, 100	21,884	22,219	2	193,854	54.6	42.4	5.2	84.5	3.6	0.0	4.3	5.0
144	D, 100		D, 100		D, 55		D, 70	21,972	22,236	1	100,180	48.1	35.8	9.7	66.1	8.4	0.1	9.1	12.0
145	D, 75		D, 100		D, 100		D, 100	22,236	24,126	8	62,963	30.2	17.8	19.6	24.3	35.4	0.2	3.4	39.3
146	D, 100		D, 100		D, 69		D, 94	23,238	24,468	5	84,379	49.2	35.4	12.6	53.5	12.0	0.1	8.2	21.7
147	R, 100		R, 52		R, 60		D, 53	24,011	24,121	0	188,930	54.5	43.5	6.2	82.0	4.6	0.0	5.1	5.2
148	D, 71		D, 53		D, 62		D, 69	22,407	22,412	0	75,590	42.0	26.4	8.1	48.1	16.8	0.1	6.8	25.2
149	R, 100		R, 100		R, 61		R, 100	23,025	23,535	2	228,067	55.8	45.1	4.9	82.9	2.9	0.0	5.4	6.0
150	R, 100		R, 100		R, 100		R, 100	20,623	20,909	1	178,409	54.3	43.0	8.7	75.2	3.7	0.1	6.1	11.1
151	R, 100		R, 100		R, 100		R, 51	22,524	22,855	1	202,637	57.3	46.1	5.8	79.9	2.8	0.0	8.3	6.4

Note: D=Democrat, R=Republican, R/D=Repunlican/Democrat (cross-filed), D/R=Democrat/Republican (cross-filed), I=Independent, C=Constitution, O=Other, GI=Green Independent, P=Progressive, P/D=Progressive/Democrat, P/D/R=Progressive/Democrat/Republican, HH=Households

DELAWARE

The only part of Delaware that most Americans ever see is the busy part of Interstate 95 that cuts through Wilmington (and even that may be bypassed) on the route between New York and Washington, D.C., slicing off the northwestern corner of the state. Indeed, if one goes by population, Wilmington more or less is Delaware; nearly two-thirds of its citizens live in the city or its suburbs. Yet the city has no network television stations and no significant airport; it relies on Philadelphia, about twenty miles away, for both. Squeezed in between the Atlantic Ocean and the Chesapeake Bay, low-lying, coastal Delaware is only 448 feet above sea level at its highest point.

Looking at Delaware on a map will reveal two geographic curiosities. For one, it has only three counties, fewest of any state (and only two at high tide, so the old joke goes). Second, Delaware's boundary with Pennsylvania is the only state boundary, perhaps the only one in the world, to be defined by the arc of a circle. This is the Twelve Mile Arc, whose center is the courthouse dome in New Castle, a few miles south of Wilmington. (The center point was described as "ye end of ye Horse Dyke at New Castle" in a 1701 survey made for William Penn.) The Mason-Dixon Line, which separates Pennsylvania from Maryland (and in national mythology, North from South), originates at the point where Delaware's western boundary connects with that arc. Delaware is also unique in that it was first settled by Dutch and Swedes.

South of Wilmington, along that Route 13 that leads to Maryland's Eastern Shore and the Delmarva Peninsula, one finds low, rural country filled with crossroads towns and small farms. Tyson has a large poultry processing plant along this route, the odor of which announces its approach almost before it can be seen. Southern Delaware also has Rehoboth, Dewey, and Bethany beaches, increasingly popular weekend destinations for people from Baltimore and Washington.

Once a slave-holding territory before the Civil War, today Delaware is 19 percent African American, the ninth-highest percentage in the country, almost the same as Virginia and ranked squarely in the middle of the southern states. It also has one of the fastest rates of black population growth.

Delaware's African American population is concentrated in downtown Wilmington and its eastern edge. The 1st house district is 71 percent African American; the 2nd, 66 percent; the 3rd, 58.9 percent; and the 16th, 50.2 percent. The 3rd district is also 30 percent Hispanic, the only large concentration of Hispanics in the state. Curiously, however, the district has been represented in Dover by a white woman, Helene Keeley, first elected in 1996; she serves as the minority whip and has run unopposed in three of the past four general elections.

Illustrating the sharp racial divides that characterize many U.S. cities, however, the 4th house district, just west of Wilmington, is only 18 percent African American, and average household income there jumps from $41,000 to more than $93,000. Continue just slightly west, into the 12th district, home to many DuPonts, and average household income is more than $124,000. Both districts are represented by Republicans.

Though still one of the least populous states (because it is one of the smallest), Delaware has grown at a faster rate than the national average during the past twenty-five years. The fastest-growing areas during this decade have been downstate, running along the Delaware Bay down to the beach, as people commute further from Wilmington and even Annapolis, Maryland.

Historically, neither political party has dominated Delaware. It has elected both Democrats and Republicans to statewide office and voted for the winner in every presidential election from 1952 to 1996. But like much of the rest of the Northeast corridor, it has moved toward the Democrats in this decade, voting decisively for Al Gore in 2000 and John Kerry in 2004. The current governor and both U.S. senators are now Democrats, although the lone U.S. representative (a former governor himself) is a Republican. Democrats control the state senate, Republicans the house, and the partisan breakdown in both chambers is exactly the same as it was seven years ago.

DELAWARE
State Senate Districts

Population Growth ☐ 1% to 3% ☐ 3% to 11% ☐ 11% to 14% ☐ 14% to 20%

Delaware State Senate Districts—Election and Demographic Data

Senate Districts	General Election Results Party, Percent of Vote							Population			Avg. HH Income	Pop 25+		2006					
														Below Poverty Line	White (Non-Hisp)	African American	American Indians, Alaska Natives	Asians, Hawaiians, Pacific Islanders	Hispanic Origin
												Some College +	4-Yr Degree +						
Delaware	2000	2001	2002	2003	2004	2005	2006	2000	2006	% Change	($)	(%)	(%)	(%)	(%)	(%)	(%)	(%)	(%)
1	D, 64		D, 64				D, 65	37,313	38,322	3	72,370	48.1	29.9	12.3	61.4	30.8	0.1	2.5	5.1
2			D, 100		D, 100			35,604	36,476	2	51,505	30.3	14.5	20.3	28.5	66.0	0.1	1.1	6.6
3			D, 75		D, 100			34,601	35,877	4	47,639	30.1	14.6	24.2	32.3	47.5	0.2	1.4	25.4
4			R, 72		R, 100			36,209	37,799	4	136,541	60.7	44.7	4.3	87.2	4.2	0.0	5.7	2.3
5	R, 52		R, 100				R, 53	34,126	35,055	3	80,267	48.9	31.1	6.9	76.9	14.9	0.1	4.4	3.1
6			R, 55		R, 100			34,346	35,758	4	90,097	39.8	29.5	14.1	83.1	6.0	0.1	6.7	3.2
7	D, 68		D, 100				D, 72	34,629	36,168	4	76,002	40.4	21.7	8.2	79.4	7.4	0.1	3.5	8.3
8	D, 56		D, 51				D, 58	35,631	37,430	5	86,664	51.6	32.8	4.8	82.7	4.7	0.1	6.7	5.0
9	D, 100		D, 58				D, 100	39,541	40,281	2	66,880	40.3	20.5	8.1	71.8	11.6	0.1	5.3	10.2
10			R, 59		R, 55			37,858	43,689	15	78,877	41.5	22.3	5.0	76.6	14.4	0.1	3.7	4.3
11			D, 100		D, 100			39,084	42,239	8	64,719	37.0	19.1	8.4	64.9	22.1	0.1	5.1	7.3
12	R, 56		R, 100				R, 100	39,068	43,858	12	71,626	38.4	19.7	7.5	69.1	21.8	0.1	3.4	5.1
13	D, 100		D, 100				D, 100	33,833	35,688	5	59,740	34.4	16.5	11.3	54.4	32.6	0.1	2.7	11.3
14	D, 100		D, 59				D, 59	37,208	42,971	15	62,576	32.8	14.2	12.0	75.4	18.4	0.2	1.3	3.9
15	D, 56		D, 100				D, 100	35,480	40,780	15	55,546	25.1	8.5	13.0	84.1	10.9	0.4	1.2	2.2
16			R, 67		R, 69			39,488	45,543	15	55,640	30.4	11.9	14.3	74.4	17.8	0.2	2.0	4.2
17			R, 100		R, 51			39,204	45,285	16	57,144	36.7	18.2	15.0	57.3	33.2	0.2	4.2	4.5
18			R, 57		R, 63			39,004	45,907	18	60,969	37.0	17.2	12.7	82.7	11.0	0.2	1.3	3.8
19	D, 100		D, 64				D, 78	38,479	43,410	13	50,842	22.9	8.4	16.9	62.0	24.7	0.3	0.8	12.0
20	D, 56		D, 59				D, 100	39,669	47,399	19	58,386	35.4	15.6	13.0	81.2	11.0	0.4	1.2	5.3
21			D, 100		D, 60			39,282	43,862	12	50,484	24.5	9.2	17.7	75.5	18.2	0.1	1.4	3.8

Note: D=Democrat, R=Republican, R/D=Republican/Democrat (cross-filed), D/R=Democrat/Republican (cross-filed), I=Independent, C=Constitution, O=Other, GI=Green Independent, P=Progressive, P/D=Progressive/Democrat, P/D/R=Progressive/Democrat/Republican, HH=Households

DELAWARE
State House Districts

Population Growth   ▨ 0% to 2%   ▨ 2% to 5%   ▨ 5% to 13%   ▨ 13% to 24%

Delaware State House Districts—Election and Demographic Data

House Districts	General Election Results Party, Percent of Vote							Population			Avg. HH Income	Pop 25+ Some College +	Pop 25+ 4-Yr Degree +	Below Poverty Line	2006 White (Non-Hisp)	African American	Indians, Alaska Natives	American Hawaiians, Pacific Islanders	Asians, Hispanic Origin
Delaware	2000	2001	2002	2003	2004	2005	2006	2000	2006	% Change	($)	(%)	(%)	(%)	(%)	(%)	(%)	(%)	(%)
1	D, 100		D, 100		D, 100		D, 100	18,189	18,605	2	54,982	37.0	18.6	19.0	24.1	71.6	0.2	1.1	4.2
2	D, 100		D, 100		D, 100		D, 100	20,951	21,521	3	47,162	28.1	12.9	25.3	26.3	66.7	0.1	0.8	9.8
3	D, 100		D, 74		D, 100		D, 100	18,864	19,500	3	41,012	27.3	13.0	30.4	21.5	58.9	0.1	1.2	29.8
4	R, 59		R, 100		R, 58		D, 55	18,530	18,821	2	93,170	56.8	40.3	10.7	71.9	18.3	0.1	2.2	7.1
5	D, 100		D, 100		D, 100		D, 100	19,680	21,347	8	59,631	38.4	19.4	10.9	52.1	36.6	0.1	3.7	8.1
6	R, 61		R, 63		D, 52		D, 61	19,990	20,387	2	79,684	50.9	31.7	7.5	75.9	17.4	0.1	2.9	3.1
7	R, 100		R, 52		R, 61		R, 55	18,444	18,621	1	92,540	53.7	36.8	5.3	84.2	8.8	0.0	4.0	2.3
8	D, 71		D, 61		D, 100		D, 77	19,086	21,080	10	64,433	30.3	12.9	11.5	76.2	17.8	0.1	0.9	4.4
9	R, 51		R, 100		R, 64		R, 53	18,697	23,007	23	85,431	39.4	19.1	6.5	86.5	8.8	0.0	1.5	2.4
10	R, 68		R, 92		R, 57		R, 57	19,983	20,648	3	96,362	49.9	32.6	7.5	75.2	14.5	0.0	6.2	3.3
11	R, 64		R, 66		R, 100		R, 58	19,219	19,582	2	89,877	52.9	35.1	5.4	83.8	7.8	0.1	4.8	3.0
12	R, 100		R, 100		R, 65		R, 65	18,475	19,194	4	124,604	51.2	33.7	6.8	81.7	6.9	0.0	4.4	6.0
13	D, 100		D, 100		D, 100		D, 60	19,735	19,937	1	53,777	31.9	13.8	11.8	67.9	12.4	0.1	1.6	16.3
14	D, 100		D, 53		D, 68		D, 69	18,598	21,954	18	68,877	42.2	21.5	10.5	88.0	7.1	0.2	1.3	2.6
15	R, 100		R, 55		D, 50		D, 74	22,105	26,235	19	76,911	38.4	19.7	6.0	70.2	21.1	0.1	3.4	4.7
16	D, 95		D, 100		D, 82		D, 100	20,432	20,760	2	52,903	27.5	11.4	15.9	41.3	50.2	0.1	0.9	10.2
17	D, 74		D, 100		D, 82		D, 84	18,346	18,964	3	61,017	34.3	16.8	10.3	69.9	15.4	0.1	2.4	11.1
18	R, 58		R, 100		R, 100		R, 56	20,961	21,572	3	69,480	39.4	19.8	7.3	63.7	20.7	0.1	7.4	7.9
19	D, 100		D, 100		D, 100		D, 100	19,490	20,032	3	59,378	36.9	17.0	9.4	79.0	8.5	0.1	2.1	8.8
20	R, 100		R, 100		R, 100		R, 56	20,375	21,647	6	107,250	53.1	36.4	3.5	83.9	3.9	0.0	8.0	3.7
21	R, 100		R, 100		R, 69		R, 100	19,654	20,286	3	78,539	49.5	30.2	5.6	82.2	5.7	0.1	5.9	5.2
22	R, 100		R, 100		R, 100		R, 89	19,387	20,501	6	108,658	57.3	40.2	3.7	83.9	4.4	0.0	8.4	2.6
23	R, 54		R, 53		D, 54		D, 100	19,128	19,425	2	73,543	40.7	29.5	16.9	81.4	7.2	0.0	7.0	3.4
24	R, 100		R, 100		R, 100		R, 100	19,065	19,545	3	68,677	35.8	18.3	9.5	64.0	17.0	0.1	4.2	13.8
25	R, 64		R, 60		R, 58		D, 52	20,572	21,699	5	61,561	31.9	18.2	11.6	78.8	10.5	0.1	4.1	5.4
26	D, 74		D, 96		D, 100		D, 100	19,316	21,253	10	65,871	37.8	20.1	6.8	63.9	23.0	0.1	5.8	6.9
27	R, 100		R, 100		R, 100		R, 51	16,524	17,720	7	75,782	41.9	22.8	3.8	72.8	17.9	0.1	4.2	4.2
28	D, 96		D, 60		D, 100		D, 100	18,240	20,699	13	52,891	31.7	11.8	15.3	65.8	25.9	0.5	2.8	4.0
29	R, 56		R, 71		R, 59		R, 100	17,169	19,804	15	58,745	25.2	9.5	12.3	87.0	7.9	0.5	1.4	2.1
30	R, 70		R, 66		R, 59		R, 63	18,257	21,213	16	52,485	23.3	7.0	14.4	82.8	12.9	0.1	0.8	2.2
31	R, 100		R, 63		R, 100		R, 55	17,668	20,691	17	58,841	39.5	21.1	15.7	54.1	36.8	0.2	4.8	4.0
32	R, 52		R, 56		R, 62		R, 100	17,964	19,666	9	52,689	34.8	14.9	15.0	56.9	31.9	0.2	3.8	6.2
33	R, 62		R, 62		R, 100		D, 51	18,886	21,600	14	55,262	30.6	12.0	14.5	75.2	16.5	0.2	1.7	4.8
34	R, 66		R, 100		R, 100		R, 56	19,050	21,716	14	59,786	32.7	14.8	12.2	73.3	18.8	0.2	2.7	3.8
35	R, 58		R, 93		R, 92		R, 100	18,515	21,441	16	50,853	21.4	7.6	16.3	65.0	25.3	0.2	0.9	8.3
36	R, 64		R, 67		R, 60		R, 62	18,739	21,220	13	51,579	30.1	11.3	15.0	71.8	18.6	0.2	0.9	7.8
37	D, 66		D, 50		R, 73		R, 100	19,179	21,213	11	57,564	30.0	13.6	15.1	66.2	19.0	0.4	0.7	12.5
38	D, 64		R, 50		R, 61		R, 72	20,083	24,755	23	62,788	40.5	18.2	10.5	88.3	4.9	0.1	1.0	4.9
39	R, 67		R, 67		R, 58		R, 69	18,555	19,331	4	49,749	26.1	11.0	19.6	68.1	24.0	0.1	1.8	5.3
40	R, 100		R, 100		R, 100		R, 100	19,989	22,027	10	50,858	24.2	8.5	18.0	79.3	15.6	0.1	1.4	2.6
41	D, 60		R, 60		R, 70		R, 63	20,414	24,529	20	48,861	24.9	9.1	16.1	74.7	16.7	0.7	1.2	5.7

Note: D=Democrat, R=Republican, R/D=Republican/Democrat (cross-filed), D/R=Democrat/Republican (cross-filed), I=Independent, C=Constitution, O=Other, GI=Green Independent, P=Progressive, P/D=Progressive/Democrat, P/D/R=Progressive/Democrat/Republican, HH=Households

FLORIDA

Fifty years ago, before the Castro revolution in Cuba, before the surge in new arrivals from the Caribbean and Latin America spurred by the 1965 Immigration and Nationality Act, Florida was home to relatively few Hispanics and proportionately many more African Americans. It also had just begun to welcome retirees (the concept of moving to a different part of the country after retirement—indeed, the concept of retirement itself—was not much older). Miami Beach was a ritzy vacation spot and Orlando was a sleepy town amid the orange groves. No state has changed more during the past half-century, and few have a better claim to national importance in the next fifty years.

Florida is now a mega-state, the fourth largest behind California, Texas, and New York. Having grown at twice the national average since 2000, it will overtake New York to become the third-largest state sometime in the next decade. Growth has been general around the state, the fastest-growing districts being the 61st (suburban Tampa), which has grown by 46 percent since 2000; the 74th (Cape Coral and Sanibel), which has grown by 37 percent; and the 12th (along the so-called Space Coast south of Jacksonville), which has grown by 36 percent. The 3rd house district, encompassing downtown Pensacola, is the only one to have lost population in this decade, and that only slightly.

As is true elsewhere, general population trends obscure much more interesting details. As Michael Barone has pointed out, for example, although the overall population of Miami has grown by 9.1 percent during this decade, whites have been leaving and Hispanic immigrants have been taking their place. Growth in Tampa and Jacksonville, on the other hand, has been primarily among whites.

Florida has the smallest percentage of African Americans of any southern state and about the same percentage as New Jersey and they are concentrated into a relatively small geographic area. Only twelve of the 120 Florida house districts have a black majority, most running in a strip of districts in Dade and Broward Counties just off the ocean (with its much more valuable real estate), running with a few interruptions from Pompano Beach to Hialeah.

Hispanics are now the second-largest racial group in Florida and the Hispanic population has been growing almost half again as quickly as the black population, largely thanks to immigration. That has also made it more diverse, as second- or third-generation Cubans have pushed over to make room for new arrivals from the Caribbean and South America. Twelve house districts have a Hispanic majority, all located in a quadrant of southeast Florida, starting at Miami Beach and Hialeah, then running down toward Homestead.

Hispanics here are, as a whole, wealthier than blacks, and almost all the Hispanic-majority house districts are represented by Republicans. Every black-majority district in the state is represented by a Democrat. There is considerable friction between the two groups, which has bubbled over more than once into riots.

Of course, Florida also leads the nation in senior citizens. Eighteen percent of its population is over age sixty-five, although in only two house districts do they constitute a majority: one north (the 46th) and one south (the 17th) of Tampa. The newer Florida retirees are culturally, religiously, and economically different than the generation that settled in Miami Beach in the 1960s and 1970s. To seize on but one small example, many early retirees, having come from crowded northeastern cities where they had never learned to drive, rode the Miami Beach busses. More recent retirees came from the suburbs and have settled in Broward County where one needs a car.

Florida's senior citizens are also overwhelmingly white, a characteristic that is not often mentioned. The 17th district south of Sarasota, home to many recent retirees, has a higher percentage of white residents (almost 94 percent) than any other district in the state.

Florida is extremely competitive in national elections, as the 2000 presidential race acutely demonstrated, one of the most competitive of the big states. But at the same time the legislature has become decidedly more Republican. In 1990 Democrats controlled both houses of the legislature; by 1996 they controlled neither. Democrats, in fact, have not added to their number of seats in the state house since 1982 and are now outnumbered in that body by a margin of more than two to one.

Demographic trends are strongly against the Democrats. The number of Hispanics is growing and most of the state house districts with heavily Hispanic populations elect Republicans. Furthermore, all twenty of the fastest-growing house districts in terms of population also have Republican representatives.

Florida seems still to be adjusting to its political prominence. It has not yet produced a national political figure of note, nor has a Floridian ever served on a major party presidential ticket. By contrast, a New Yorker appeared on at least one of the major party's tickets in seventeen of the twenty presidential elections between 1880 and 1960. For decades, the governor of New York was almost a de facto presidential contender, simply by virtue of the office. That has yet to happen to Florida. Given its rich, and soon to be richer, pot of electoral votes and the key constituencies that both parties find here, someone in the current generation of Florida politicians will surely change that.

FLORIDA
State Senate Districts

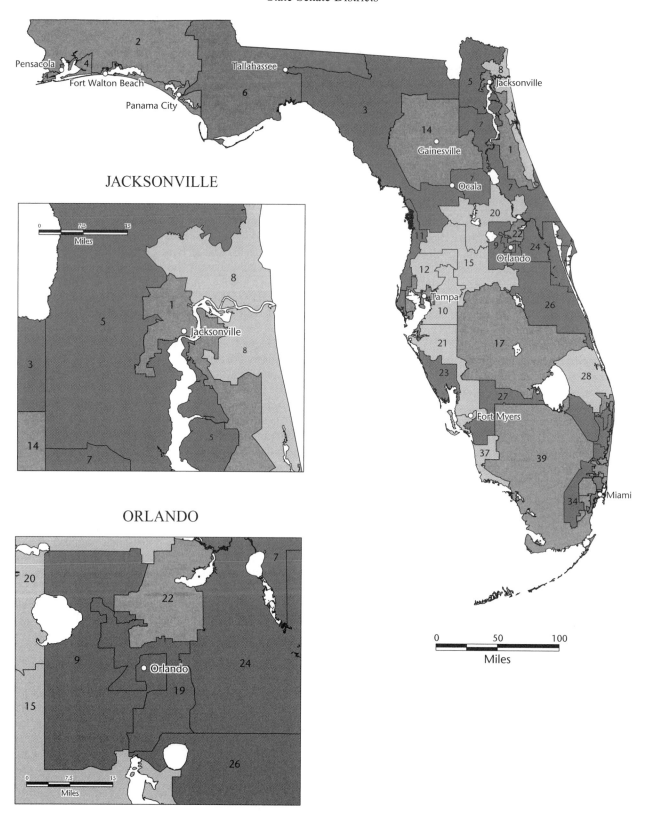

Population Growth   ▮ 0% to 6%   ▮ 6% to 12%   ▮ 12% to 19%   ▮ 19% to 30%

MIAMI

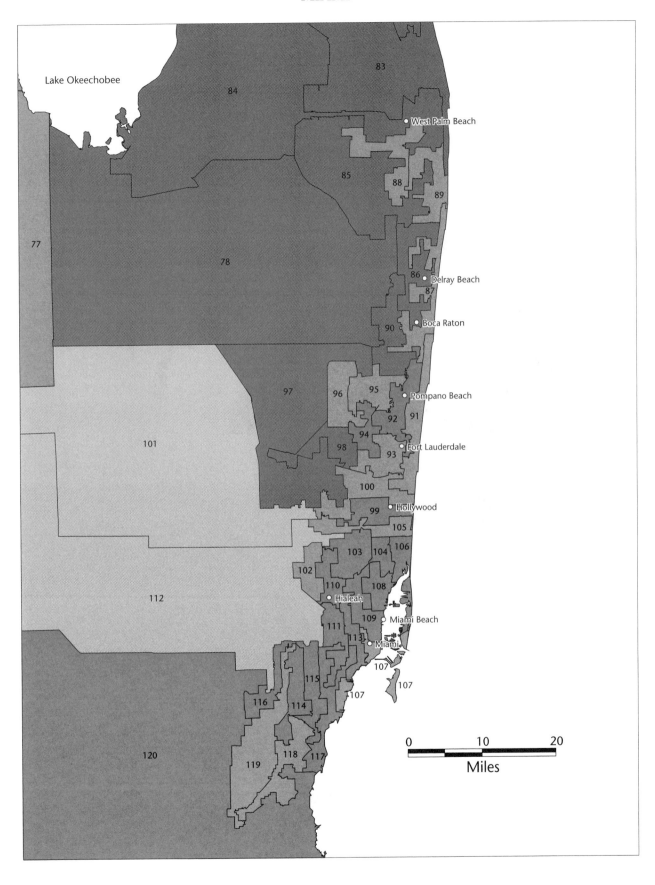

Lake Okeechobee

West Palm Beach

Delray Beach

Boca Raton

Pompano Beach

Fort Lauderdale

Hollywood

Hialeah

Miami Beach

Miami

Population Growth | 0% to 6% | 6% to 12% | 12% to 19% | 19% to 30%

TAMPA

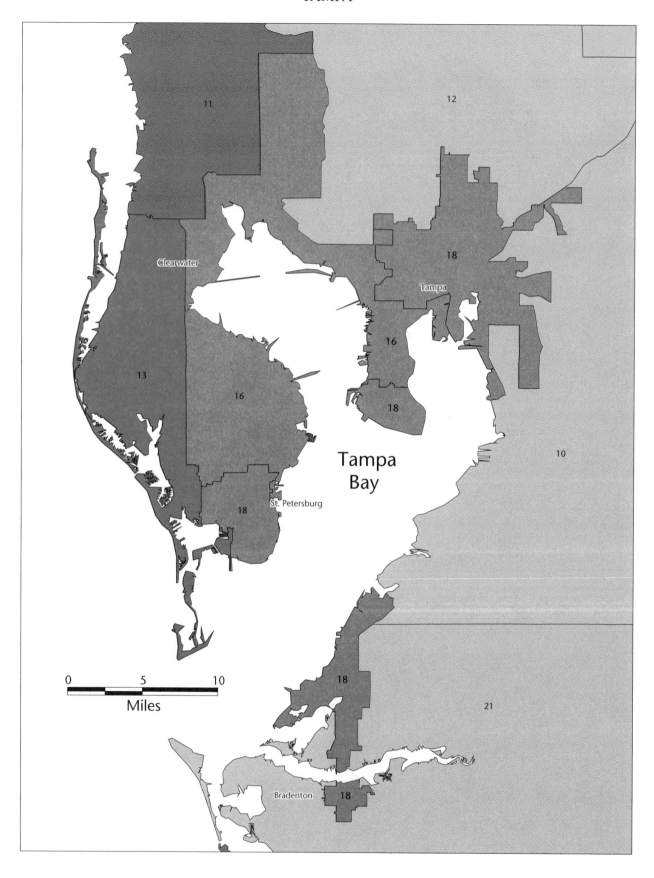

Clearwater

Tampa

Tampa
Bay

St. Petersburg

Bradenton

11

12

18

16

13

16

18

18

10

21

18

18

0   5   10
Miles

Population Growth   0% to 6%   6% to 12%   12% to 19%   19% to 30%

Florida State Senate Districts—Election and Demographic Data

Senate Districts	General Election Results Party, Percent of Vote							Population			Avg. HH Income ($)	Pop 25+ Some College + (%)	Pop 25+ 4-Yr Degree + (%)	Below Poverty Line (%)	White (Non-Hisp) (%)	African American (%)	American Indians, Alaska Natives (%)	Asians, Hawaiians, Pacific Islanders (%)	Hispanic Origin (%)
Florida	2000	2001	2002	2003	2004	2005	2006	2000	2006	% Change	($)	(%)	(%)	(%)	(%)	(%)	(%)	(%)	(%)
1	R, 58							398,534	425,090	7	45,135	31.1	12.5	21.7	43.4	49.2	0.2	2.5	4.7
2								395,318	431,676	9	48,359	32.0	11.0	19.2	76.2	16.5	0.8	1.9	2.8
3	D, 65		R, 54		R, 66			399,042	450,537	13	46,208	30.9	11.5	18.2	78.7	12.7	0.3	1.1	6.0
4								405,604	445,312	10	58,362	42.5	18.3	13.0	79.4	10.0	0.5	3.2	4.4
5	D, 57				R, 100			402,323	466,605	16	66,559	38.4	17.1	9.6	78.9	10.8	0.3	3.0	5.2
6								399,122	417,407	5	50,102	35.6	18.3	22.5	60.9	32.5	0.3	1.5	4.2
7			R, 57					400,158	450,238	13	50,712	36.4	14.2	15.5	83.3	6.8	0.3	1.1	6.7
8			R, 66				R, 100	397,920	481,200	21	70,721	43.3	21.7	10.0	78.8	10.2	0.2	3.3	5.8
9	R, 60							407,119	478,495	18	71,927	42.8	24.3	10.1	60.6	10.1	0.3	5.1	21.4
10							R, 52	402,349	480,004	19	55,651	33.8	15.7	13.3	68.3	10.1	0.3	1.7	16.5
11	R, 57		R, 63		R, 65			401,410	451,384	12	53,051	40.5	16.6	13.9	89.1	1.8	0.2	1.4	6.0
12							R, 71	402,707	493,717	23	63,318	42.0	22.8	11.7	67.3	7.5	0.3	3.6	19.2
13	R, 52		R, 60					399,386	402,163	1	58,047	43.9	20.4	13.3	84.2	5.0	0.2	2.1	6.8
14							R, 54	398,305	429,517	8	47,088	36.7	17.7	23.1	69.9	19.9	0.3	2.8	6.0
15	R, 52				R, 61			395,631	488,098	23	48,560	29.2	9.8	15.2	69.8	9.5	0.3	1.2	16.5
16			R, 64				D, 51	398,216	426,398	7	65,218	43.8	23.7	11.7	75.8	5.4	0.2	4.4	12.1
17					R, 100			399,253	435,513	9	50,492	28.0	10.4	17.9	64.1	13.0	0.5	1.3	18.0
18							D, 100	397,458	422,033	6	40,521	28.9	12.8	24.6	37.8	42.1	0.3	1.8	22.5
19			D, 51		D, 65			393,822	448,970	14	47,949	32.5	14.7	17.6	34.9	31.3	0.3	3.9	33.7
20			R, 100					399,713	516,787	29	52,636	35.6	15.2	14.2	77.0	9.3	0.2	1.1	10.7
21	D, 70		R, 66					400,958	490,219	22	58,881	40.7	18.3	11.3	82.3	4.8	0.2	1.2	9.5
22							R, 60	398,150	432,442	9	66,947	44.7	24.4	11.1	67.6	10.5	0.2	3.6	15.8
23			R, 67		R, 78			398,171	455,846	14	63,143	44.0	21.7	11.1	85.2	4.2	0.5	1.1	6.1
24			R, 100					398,744	467,787	17	56,251	39.5	19.3	13.3	72.8	10.5	0.3	2.9	11.3
25			R, 55		R, 99			399,490	440,853	10	90,649	51.4	30.7	10.4	77.2	6.3	0.2	2.1	12.3
26								399,688	466,208	17	56,444	36.9	16.1	13.7	74.0	11.3	0.2	1.6	10.9
27	R, 83		D, 54		D, 79			398,596	468,643	18	63,125	39.9	19.8	11.5	66.2	8.0	0.2	1.8	21.4
28							R, 62	399,653	490,739	23	75,007	41.4	19.3	9.5	80.0	6.5	0.2	1.4	10.0
29			D, 88					396,932	433,691	9	43,528	27.5	12.6	23.6	27.2	59.0	0.2	1.3	15.3
30			D, 68				D, 88	402,832	466,658	16	76,885	45.7	26.1	10.7	73.9	6.6	0.1	2.3	14.9
31	R, 53							402,669	445,700	11	61,762	40.7	21.1	14.5	56.8	14.1	0.3	3.2	26.1
32	D, 66						D, 100	402,321	451,279	12	61,547	39.7	19.9	12.3	59.6	15.8	0.2	3.6	20.4
33			D, 100					400,153	418,180	5	41,868	25.9	11.3	28.2	19.1	60.2	0.2	1.3	36.9
34			D, 64		D, 62			395,744	466,988	18	77,420	41.3	22.1	9.7	43.1	14.3	0.1	4.0	42.5
35	D, 61							389,281	416,364	7	71,123	42.5	24.8	19.6	41.2	19.0	0.2	2.7	42.3
36			R, 100				R, 100	398,998	414,504	4	56,679	36.4	20.3	25.0	21.0	8.6	0.2	1.6	74.3
37								398,796	496,284	24	75,600	42.6	20.8	10.4	71.7	7.4	0.2	1.0	17.2
38							R, 78	403,343	435,093	8	62,932	38.6	20.0	13.7	21.9	6.0	0.1	2.5	74.1
39	R, 100		D, 68		D, 62			425,787	457,280	7	53,803	27.6	13.1	24.7	31.7	34.7	0.3	1.2	40.9
40								402,641	440,294	9	51,834	32.0	16.3	20.9	12.7	5.8	0.1	1.5	85.0

Note: D=Democrat, R=Republican, R/D=Republican/Democrat (cross-filed), D/R=Democrat/Republican (cross-filed), I=Independent, C=Constitution, O=Other, GI=Green Independent, P=Progressive, P/D=Progressive/Democrat, P/D/R=Progressive/Democrat/Republican, HH=Households

FLORIDA
State House Districts

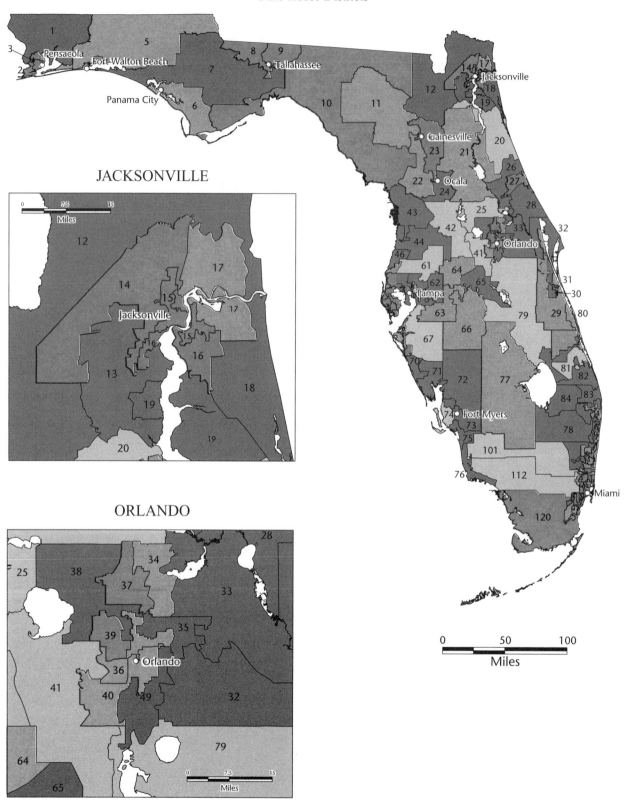

JACKSONVILLE

ORLANDO

Pensacola
Fort Walton Beach
Panama City
Tallahassee
Gainesville
Ocala
Orlando
Jacksonville
Tampa
Fort Myers
Miami

Population Growth   -2% to 7%   7% to 13%   13% to 27%   27% to 46%

MIAMI

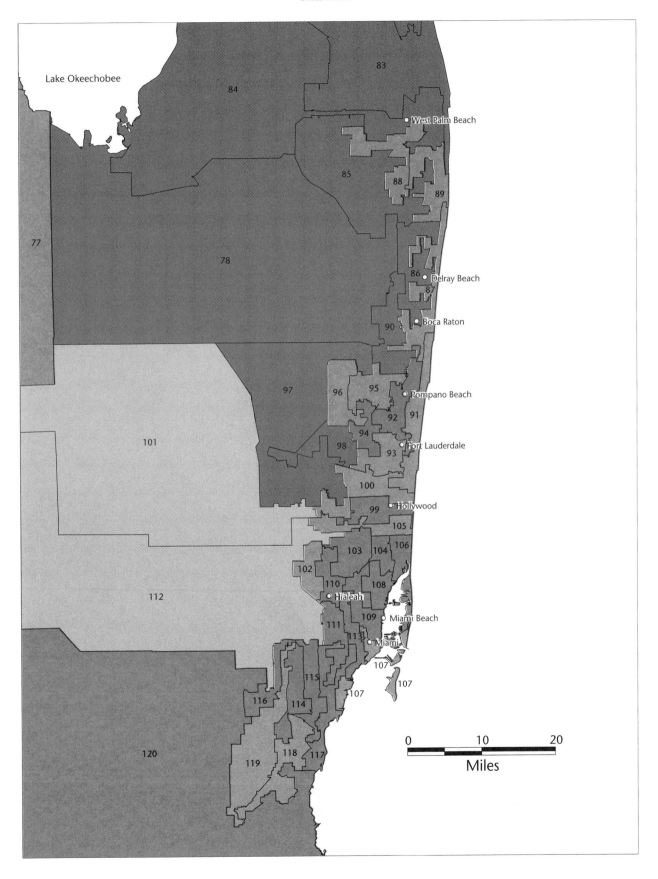

Population Growth | -2% to 7% | 7% to 13% | 13% to 27% | 27% to 46%

TAMPA

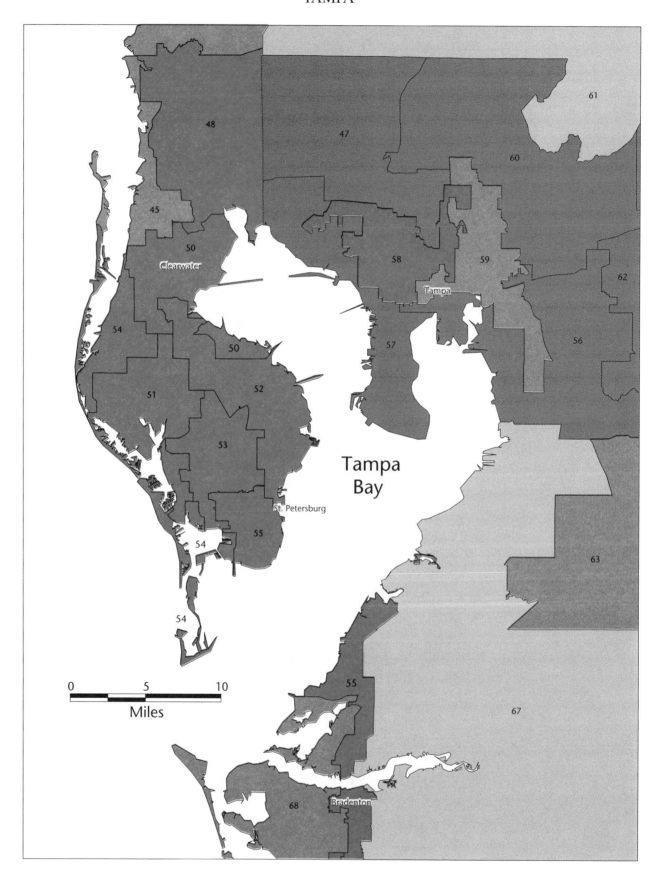

Population Growth   ▮ -2% to 7%   ▮ 7% to 13%   ▮ 13% to 27%   ▯ 27% to 46%

Florida State House Districts—Election and Demographic Data

House Districts	General Election Results Party, Percent of Vote							Population			Avg. HH Income ($)	Pop 25+ Some College + (%)	Pop 25+ 4-Yr Degree + (%)	Below Poverty Line (%)	White (Non-Hisp) (%)	African American (%)	American Indians, Alaska Natives (%)	Asians, Hawaiians, Pacific Islanders (%)	Hispanic Origin (%)
										2006									
Florida	2000	2001	2002	2003	2004	2005	2006	2000	2006	% Change	($)	(%)	(%)	(%)	(%)	(%)	(%)	(%)	(%)
1			R, 100		R, 99			136,447	159,975	17	55,497	34.7	12.7	15.9	85.2	8.0	0.9	1.4	2.6
2	R, 75		R, 80		R, 100			132,788	136,615	3	54,875	42.0	16.9	13.1	75.8	14.1	0.6	3.3	3.7
3	R, 53		R, 82		R, 100		R, 62	133,807	132,177	-1	50,078	37.0	15.6	21.2	60.1	32.1	0.6	3.2	2.6
4			R, 85					129,927	145,153	12	58,643	42.9	18.3	10.5	78.2	8.4	0.5	3.6	6.2
5	R, 67		R, 81		R, 74		R, 100	136,800	149,605	9	44,466	28.0	8.9	21.3	77.1	14.8	0.8	1.4	3.7
6	R, 79						R, 67	132,693	142,439	7	48,882	35.0	12.9	17.9	77.4	14.6	0.5	2.5	3.2
7	R, 53		R, 59		R, 71			136,943	157,685	15	54,615	32.8	13.2	16.6	80.7	12.7	0.6	0.7	3.6
8	D, 78				D, 100			130,533	134,630	3	38,855	34.2	16.7	28.0	39.8	53.9	0.2	1.6	5.0
9	D, 56		D, 83		D, 85			135,049	136,824	1	70,114	54.3	35.6	14.0	72.6	19.2	0.2	3.0	4.2
10	D, 61		D, 85					132,646	141,791	7	40,704	23.6	7.7	25.9	68.7	26.0	0.4	0.5	3.9
11	D, 62		D, 80		D, 61		D, 51	134,309	151,710	13	47,873	31.9	12.1	18.9	80.1	11.6	0.3	1.4	5.4
12	R, 58		R, 84					133,300	150,911	13	57,708	27.1	9.1	15.5	81.9	13.4	0.4	0.6	2.6
13	R, 79		R, 85					133,790	158,529	18	61,693	34.6	13.2	9.9	73.0	14.5	0.3	3.8	6.4
14							D, 67	134,322	139,610	4	43,578	27.8	9.7	22.1	37.6	56.8	0.2	2.2	3.0
15			D, 81				D, 100	130,397	135,777	4	41,666	29.8	11.8	25.4	34.9	59.1	0.2	1.5	4.6
16			R, 78					133,727	141,138	6	57,484	41.3	20.2	12.7	69.7	17.2	0.3	4.3	6.9
17			R, 79					130,367	144,026	10	64,030	38.5	17.3	8.6	68.3	17.4	0.3	5.6	7.0
18	R, 69		R, 83		R, 80			131,269	151,961	16	88,969	49.9	29.7	7.9	78.9	9.7	0.2	3.6	5.8
19			R, 84					135,543	165,774	22	77,222	45.4	22.8	6.1	81.7	7.6	0.2	3.4	5.3
20	D, 52		D, 81		R, 56			133,504	181,713	36	56,877	37.7	15.6	13.0	82.1	10.0	0.2	1.3	5.1
21	R, 56		R, 65					135,158	148,044	10	45,346	25.1	7.6	22.0	77.8	11.2	0.4	0.5	8.2
22	R, 54		R, 48				R, 56	136,102	152,109	12	49,387	43.3	23.0	20.0	77.4	9.3	0.2	3.9	7.4
23	D, 76		D, 78		D, 81		D, 64	134,544	137,124	2	42,616	38.2	19.8	27.5	55.4	34.3	0.2	3.1	6.4
24	R, 58		R, 77				R, 56	134,611	155,733	16	49,455	32.1	11.2	16.4	76.5	9.9	0.4	1.3	10.0
25	R, 62				R, 99			134,464	178,207	33	54,762	36.0	15.8	14.8	77.5	8.6	0.3	1.2	10.7
26	D, 51		R, 52		R, 55		R, 55	135,294	154,817	14	56,087	41.6	19.1	12.2	82.4	4.5	0.2	1.3	9.5
27	R, 52				D, 94		D, 61	133,115	138,995	4	41,525	34.8	13.2	21.4	68.2	23.2	0.2	1.6	5.9
28	D, 57		D, 55		R, 50		R, 57	134,014	157,436	17	56,147	42.1	18.0	11.7	85.1	4.8	0.2	1.3	6.8
29	R, 100		R, 54					136,656	152,639	12	51,258	34.7	13.5	14.8	77.4	11.7	0.3	1.1	7.6
30	R, 65		R, 79		R, 63			133,726	161,965	21	60,815	42.5	20.4	10.1	78.3	8.1	0.3	2.6	8.6
31	R, 55		R, 67		R, 68		R, 60	131,609	143,552	9	55,755	42.0	20.3	13.3	81.3	7.8	0.2	2.3	6.5
32	R, 58		R, 67		D, 100		R, 100	133,436	157,502	18	60,857	41.9	20.4	12.3	76.0	8.4	0.3	2.3	10.7
33	R, 59		R, 79				R, 62	134,245	161,620	20	67,900	40.8	22.1	11.0	68.2	12.6	0.3	3.0	14.2
34	R, 60		R, 76		R, 61			134,641	146,795	9	65,844	43.2	21.2	10.0	69.9	7.6	0.2	3.7	15.7
35	R, 55		R, 63		R, 57		R, 100	131,059	149,275	14	64,520	42.2	25.5	12.2	57.7	8.3	0.2	5.5	25.2
36	R, 51		D, 50				D, 61	143,056	159,986	12	49,509	39.4	20.8	16.3	43.7	25.9	0.3	4.7	26.2
37	R, 70		R, 76					132,592	138,613	5	78,425	48.9	27.6	8.3	70.9	7.9	0.2	3.6	15.0
38	R, 51		R, 63		R, 59			135,685	155,236	14	62,985	37.6	19.4	12.8	61.4	16.0	0.3	2.7	17.7
39	D, 77		D, 75		D, 90		D, 100	126,300	134,783	7	44,449	29.3	13.1	21.4	25.7	58.7	0.2	3.1	14.7
40	R, 55		R, 77				R, 63	130,302	142,403	9	67,063	44.7	25.9	10.5	60.7	7.9	0.2	5.2	23.2
41	R, 68		R, 79		R, 100		R, 58	135,641	192,802	42	72,756	40.0	21.7	10.3	60.7	9.8	0.3	4.4	22.5
42	R, 55		R, 82		R, 75		R, 58	134,034	179,384	34	49,348	33.9	13.9	14.1	77.4	11.2	0.2	0.9	8.9
43			R, 64		R, 63			133,132	153,726	15	45,143	31.6	10.5	16.5	91.5	2.4	0.3	1.0	3.6
44	R, 55		R, 58		R, 60		R, 51	133,701	164,204	23	47,252	30.9	10.1	15.0	84.5	5.4	0.3	0.9	7.6
45	R, 99		R, 62		R, 62		R, 59	131,830	145,206	10	51,520	42.4	17.4	13.3	90.0	1.6	0.2	1.4	5.3
46	R, 63		R, 61		R, 56			133,856	155,839	16	41,248	35.2	11.4	17.5	90.2	1.0	0.3	1.0	5.8
47	R, 64		R, 58		R, 69		R, 60	135,131	155,404	15	68,298	44.9	25.5	10.1	64.3	8.2	0.2	4.1	21.6
48	R, 80		R, 85				R, 52	135,882	142,910	5	68,768	46.3	23.4	10.1	87.3	2.8	0.2	2.4	5.9
49	R, 52		R, 54		R, 52		R, 54	134,217	158,920	18	51,774	34.2	14.9	13.2	32.3	12.2	0.3	5.3	51.3
50	R, 54		R, 64				R, 55	132,162	135,029	2	52,993	41.9	19.4	13.7	75.8	8.9	0.2	2.5	10.9

(continued)

Note: D=Democrat, R=Republican, R/D=Republican/Democrat (cross-filed), D/R=Democrat/Republican (cross-filed), I=Independent, C=Constitution, O=Other, GI=Green Independent, P=Progressive, P/D=Progressive/Democrat, P/D/R=Progressive/Democrat/Republican, HH=Households

Florida State House Districts—Election and Demographic Data (cont.)

House Districts	General Election Results Party, Percent of Vote							Population			Avg. HH Income ($)	Pop 25+ Some College + (%)	Pop 25+ 4-Yr Degree + (%)	2006 Below Poverty Line (%)	White (Non-Hisp) (%)	African American (%)	American Indians, Alaska Natives (%)	Asians, Hawaiians, Pacific Islanders (%)	Hispanic Origin (%)
Florida	2000	2001	2002	2003	2004	2005	2006	2000	2006	% Change	($)	(%)	(%)	(%)	(%)	(%)	(%)	(%)	(%)
51	R, 54		R, 60		R, 62		D, 51	135,105	135,071	0	55,496	41.0	17.8	12.7	88.4	2.0	0.2	2.7	5.0
52	R, 56		R, 53		R, 53		D, 54	133,550	134,008	0	56,531	44.2	22.4	13.1	82.0	5.3	0.2	3.6	6.9
53	D, 56		D, 53				D, 60	135,030	132,347	-2	42,512	33.7	12.5	17.0	77.9	5.8	0.3	5.7	7.9
54			R, 77				R, 53	133,914	135,807	1	68,988	49.8	25.8	12.8	85.7	5.6	0.2	1.5	5.6
55			D, 78					132,929	137,008	3	40,292	27.9	11.4	24.9	34.5	52.6	0.3	0.9	15.2
56	R, 60		R, 77		R, 100		R, 58	134,904	165,482	23	67,429	39.8	21.7	10.0	67.5	10.4	0.3	2.6	17.1
57	R, 100		R, 53		R, 59		R, 55	136,061	156,799	15	78,011	47.7	29.0	9.8	66.6	8.0	0.2	4.2	19.1
58	D, 62		D, 63		D, 70		D, 69	133,275	140,406	5	43,376	30.7	14.0	18.9	38.5	18.9	0.4	2.9	42.9
59			D, 89				D, 84	129,358	142,230	10	35,882	25.4	11.2	30.2	27.5	56.9	0.3	1.6	20.1
60	D, 50		R, 55		R, 58		R, 57	136,134	155,613	14	64,545	41.2	24.7	12.7	67.7	10.6	0.3	4.2	15.5
61	R, 58		R, 59				R, 60	131,840	192,104	46	56,373	39.5	18.5	13.2	77.7	4.5	0.3	2.1	12.9
62	R, 66		R, 78		R, 64		R, 68	132,712	151,908	14	62,264	32.5	15.8	12.2	66.2	8.9	0.3	1.6	19.1
63	R, 65						R, 60	134,650	147,573	10	55,413	31.9	13.5	13.5	69.1	11.9	0.3	1.4	14.4
64	R, 100		R, 75		R, 59			131,228	147,599	12	48,660	29.3	10.3	16.4	72.1	15.7	0.3	1.2	9.1
65	R, 54		R, 74		R, 61			134,114	158,022	18	49,539	28.8	10.0	16.2	65.7	14.2	0.3	1.1	16.4
66	R, 100		R, 100		R, 60			135,278	146,659	8	51,433	26.3	9.9	18.8	57.9	13.0	0.4	1.6	23.4
67			R, 80					133,278	175,783	32	69,251	43.0	21.4	9.0	81.5	3.2	0.2	1.4	11.0
68	R, 55		R, 62		R, 100			132,764	142,807	8	53,745	41.6	18.8	12.8	82.4	4.3	0.2	1.3	9.5
69	R, 52		R, 57		R, 73		D, 51	135,541	143,723	6	66,959	45.7	24.3	10.2	81.1	4.0	0.2	1.4	11.2
70	R, 72		R, 82		R, 79		R, 51	133,138	151,831	14	71,407	51.8	28.4	8.9	93.8	1.3	0.1	1.0	2.9
71	R, 100				R, 56		R, 100	133,405	164,500	23	50,261	36.9	14.1	11.7	89.5	3.6	0.2	1.0	4.3
72	R, 77		R, 80		R, 100			133,463	157,759	18	54,258	32.2	12.3	13.6	72.2	8.2	0.5	1.1	15.3
73	R, 62		R, 63				R, 53	134,784	157,882	17	51,681	35.1	15.8	16.5	63.3	16.9	0.3	1.3	16.9
74	R, 100		R, 69					133,147	181,840	37	67,740	42.3	18.4	9.6	81.5	2.7	0.2	1.2	12.0
75	R, 100		R, 82					133,105	156,945	18	72,443	49.0	24.5	8.9	78.8	2.3	0.1	0.8	14.8
76			R, 88				R, 78	135,699	165,209	22	94,941	50.8	27.5	7.7	78.6	3.2	0.1	0.9	14.5
77	R, 55		R, 80		R, 67		R, 60	131,715	143,968	9	44,444	24.2	8.3	20.4	55.1	11.8	0.7	0.8	27.8
78								136,555	158,881	16	74,540	38.0	21.2	13.8	61.6	18.6	0.2	2.3	16.7
79	R, 50		R, 76				R, 65	135,139	173,979	29	50,686	28.7	9.7	15.1	57.9	6.1	0.4	2.2	29.4
80	R, 64		R, 79					133,686	151,025	13	66,673	40.0	17.9	12.9	80.9	9.4	0.2	1.1	6.9
81	R, 59		R, 76		R, 100		R, 54	133,712	169,874	27	62,796	38.3	15.2	10.5	78.5	7.4	0.2	1.4	10.4
82	R, 100						R, 54	133,032	158,460	19	74,244	42.4	20.1	9.9	82.2	5.8	0.2	1.1	8.9
83	R, 58				R, 58		R, 51	134,635	161,432	20	105,123	50.2	30.1	7.2	83.7	4.2	0.1	2.1	8.5
84	D, 70							132,743	152,386	15	47,045	27.0	13.3	24.8	28.5	55.9	0.2	1.4	18.5
85	D, 63		D, 51		D, 51		D, 58	132,365	150,742	14	78,181	40.1	21.3	8.2	67.3	7.0	0.2	2.3	20.7
86					D, 100		D, 100	132,711	152,504	15	63,708	41.7	22.8	11.5	64.7	21.5	0.1	1.8	10.6
87	R, 52		R, 55		R, 58		R, 55	135,364	152,564	13	92,888	52.0	31.9	9.7	78.7	6.4	0.1	2.2	10.7
88	D, 85							133,415	148,786	12	52,835	37.8	18.9	14.1	62.7	11.8	0.2	2.5	21.3
89	D, 100		D, 60					134,237	147,956	10	54,347	33.4	16.3	16.0	44.6	14.4	0.4	1.8	39.1
90			D, 84					135,800	155,328	14	78,290	47.9	28.0	12.1	78.9	5.2	0.1	2.3	11.3
91	R, 56		R, 79				R, 55	131,840	142,092	8	89,284	56.5	33.6	10.7	82.5	3.7	0.1	1.6	10.4
92	D, 61		D, 85					135,030	144,062	7	47,749	32.9	14.9	18.2	46.2	32.0	0.3	1.8	20.5
93					D, 99		D, 82	129,501	142,326	10	48,175	29.1	13.6	23.1	32.0	55.2	0.2	1.4	13.5
94					D, 99			134,067	141,845	6	42,929	29.3	11.8	20.0	28.2	57.3	0.1	2.4	15.8
95			D, 81					135,838	148,041	9	53,298	39.1	18.5	12.5	62.2	12.9	0.2	3.2	20.4
96	D, 68		D, 84		D, 77			133,115	148,850	12	67,816	41.2	21.6	12.4	63.9	11.7	0.1	3.9	19.5
97	D, 62		D, 51		R, 51		D, 53	136,049	163,289	20	111,438	45.0	27.7	5.9	64.8	6.5	0.1	3.9	24.1
98	D, 67		D, 100		D, 68			134,945	154,268	14	67,350	43.8	24.1	11.8	58.3	12.3	0.1	4.0	25.7
99							D, 75	131,268	140,156	7	54,941	37.6	18.1	15.8	52.7	12.1	0.5	3.2	31.9
100	D, 73							133,773	147,353	10	60,052	39.0	19.2	13.7	58.0	12.8	0.2	3.4	25.9

(continued)

Note: D=Democrat, R=Republican, R/D=Republican/Democrat (cross-filed), D/R=Democrat/Republican (cross-filed), I=Independent, C=Constitution, O=Other, GI=Green Independent, P=Progressive, P/D=Progressive/Democrat, P/D/R=Progressive/Democrat/Republican, HH=Households

Florida State House Districts—Election and Demographic Data (cont.)

House Districts	General Election Results Party, Percent of Vote							Population			Avg. HH Income	Pop 25+		2006 Below Poverty Line	2006 White (Non-Hisp)	2006 African American	2006 American Indians, Alaska Natives	2006 Asians, Hawaiians, Pacific Islanders	2006 Hispanic Origin
												Some College +	4-Yr Degree +						
Florida	2000	2001	2002	2003	2004	2005	2006	2000	2006	% Change	($)	(%)	(%)	(%)	(%)	(%)	(%)	(%)	(%)
101			R, 58					133,078	177,596	33	78,744	35.9	18.4	8.7	46.5	10.4	0.3	3.1	39.5
102							R, 100	130,754	145,813	12	54,597	30.9	15.1	17.8	12.5	7.3	0.1	1.5	84.7
103					D, 100			133,378	138,046	3	48,023	26.2	10.6	20.7	15.2	71.8	0.2	1.0	28.8
104			D, 85				D, 100	135,014	140,216	4	41,174	27.9	12.2	26.7	21.9	57.9	0.2	2.8	31.1
105			D, 89					136,196	150,020	10	49,312	36.3	17.1	18.2	42.8	30.3	0.2	2.7	28.7
106	D, 85							136,082	144,316	6	66,899	46.4	27.4	18.7	45.7	7.7	0.1	2.1	45.6
107			R, 66				D, 52	126,729	139,900	10	68,483	41.7	26.4	29.9	23.2	6.9	0.2	1.5	71.9
108	D, 82		D, 76				D, 81	130,384	133,475	2	47,295	30.0	14.7	25.8	23.8	54.9	0.2	2.1	30.1
109	D, 100		D, 100		D, 100		D, 100	136,881	142,650	4	47,355	27.8	14.6	36.3	21.5	59.3	0.2	1.0	34.1
110			R, 100				R, 100	135,420	143,073	6	49,140	31.0	14.9	20.5	15.5	10.8	0.1	1.4	80.5
111					R, 66		R, 100	131,238	135,905	4	56,937	36.4	20.5	23.3	18.2	6.7	0.1	1.0	78.9
112			R, 100				R, 100	127,681	162,446	27	66,336	36.9	19.3	11.7	23.7	10.1	0.1	3.1	69.6
113			R, 74		R, 100		R, 100	130,789	136,370	4	50,900	31.2	16.8	28.0	14.6	10.8	0.1	0.9	81.5
114			R, 100		R, 64			135,247	139,621	3	65,761	39.6	21.4	14.4	25.5	7.2	0.1	2.6	69.6
115	R, 100		R, 74		R, 100			136,521	143,177	5	75,056	42.7	24.7	13.8	25.9	4.9	0.1	2.7	69.9
116	D, 58		R, 64					134,514	142,384	6	56,669	36.9	18.3	13.6	18.0	6.2	0.1	2.7	78.0
117	R, 100		R, 87					137,702	143,784	4	78,760	39.6	23.4	18.7	26.3	5.4	0.1	2.2	69.6
118	D, 100		D, 74					132,636	145,086	9	44,020	25.8	11.0	26.8	24.3	43.1	0.2	1.9	46.0
119	D, 51		R, 72		R, 100		R, 100	136,179	148,780	9	61,003	35.4	17.1	14.1	25.8	9.4	0.2	2.3	67.6
120	R, 50		R, 62		R, 60		D, 57	136,445	143,541	5	63,609	38.7	18.1	13.6	49.4	8.3	0.2	1.5	41.4

Note: D=Democrat, R=Republican, R/D=Republican/Democrat (cross-filed), D/R=Democrat/Republican (cross-filed), I=Independent, C=Constitution, O=Other, GI=Green Independent, P=Progressive, P/D=Progressive/Democrat, P/D/R=Progressive/Democrat/Republican, HH=Households

GEORGIA

As computers have made gerrymandering more of a science, it has also become a more effective tool for rewarding the party that draws the lines and punishing the party that does not. Rather than engage in the long, often litigious, and always acrimonious exercise every decade, legislators in some states, such as California, band together to declare a truce and produce a reapportionment plan that protects incumbents of both parties. Georgia is not one of those states.

For almost a decade and a half, there has been partisan blood on the marble floors of the state capitol as legislators have tried and retried to draw borders that maximize their advantage. Cases have gone up to the U.S. Supreme Court and back. There has been greater opportunity for mischief because Georgia has more counties (159) than any other state, and as a consequence, its house of representatives is unusually large, at 180 members.

In 1991 Georgia's congressional delegation included nine Democrats and one Republican (Newt Gingrich). In an attempt to comply with the Voting Rights Act and maximize black voting strength, districts were drawn by black Democrats and white Republicans. Within four years, Georgia had eight Republican representatives and only three Democrats, and Gingrich was Speaker of the House. The lines were redrawn in 1995 by court order, but the partisan composition remained unchanged.

The effects were not so extreme in the state legislature, although the Republicans doubled their strength in the senate between 1990 and 1996 and picked up forty seats in the house. Nevertheless, Democrats set new districts after the 2000 census with the now-familiar tortured boundaries drawn to extract the maximum amount of partisan advantage. They placed more Democratic voters in fast-growing suburban districts, hoping to dilute Republican strength there, and fewer in reliably Democratic urban districts. The plan achieved its aim, as Democrats gained four seats in the state house in the 2002 elections (while losing two in the state senate). Republicans sued, claiming that the new districts were numerically unbalanced, violating the constitutional requirement of one-man, one-vote. A lower court agreed and the U.S. Supreme Court upheld the decision by an 8–1 margin.

A judge redrew the legislative districts in 2004 and Democrats lost six seats in the senate (giving Republicans control) and three more in the house. In 2005 the legislature took another stab at reapportionment, over Democratic objections that it was unfair to redraw the lines in mid-decade. Under the new plan, which took effect in 2006, Republicans picked up four more seats in the senate to gain a 34–22 margin. In the state house, however, the GOP picked up twenty-six seats, taking control of that chamber for the first time since Reconstruction. Although Democrats have fared better in congressional races, now holding six of thirteen districts, Georgia currently has a Republican governor (the first one ever to be reelected) and two Republican U.S. senators.

It should be noted that, while most states either slowly gain congressional seats or slowly lose them, Georgia is one of the few that has lost representation in Congress then gained it back again. Georgia had twelve congressional districts throughout the 1910s and 1920s. It lost two seats in the 1930 census but now has thirteen and should gain another after the 2010 census. That might seem to provide ample room in which to devise reapportionment plans that would satisfy all sides, but so far it has not.

All the partisan wrangling takes place against a backdrop of continuing growth. Georgia's population is now the ninth largest in the country and is expected to become the eighth within the next few decades. It is yet another state in which population shifts have created what might be called the urban doughnut, an increasingly hollow urban core surrounded by growing suburbs that are pushing into previously rural areas. Atlanta, for example, which hosted the 1996 Summer Olympics and is home to corporate giants Coca Cola and CNN, is only the forty-second largest city in the country, smaller than Mesa, Arizona, and Virginia Beach, Virginia. But the Atlanta metro area is the ninth largest, on a par with Washington, D.C., and Detroit.

Atlanta residents continue to move further away from downtown, accepting longer commutes in exchange for more space and more affordable real estate. The 109th house district, in Henry County south of the city, has grown by 51 percent in this decade, while the 23rd and 24th districts, in Forsyth County northeast of Atlanta, have grown by 49 and 48 percent, respectively. Early in 2007, a proposal was introduced that would allow some of Atlanta's white suburban neighborhoods to secede from black-majority Fulton County and form their own county. Though it seems unlikely that the plan will ever be enacted, it does speak to what is likely to be continuing racial friction. The only areas of the state that are losing population are some of the rural counties in the northwestern and southwestern corners of the state.

Metro Atlanta, which is home to several black universities and has long had a large African American middle class, also has some of the wealthiest black-majority districts. Average household income in the 89th house district (centered on suburban DeKalb County), which is almost 82 percent black, is more than $60,000, well above the state or national averages. However, just twelve miles away, the 61st district (downtown Atlanta), which is three-quarters African American, it is only $36,000.

Perhaps mercifully, Gov. Sonny Perdue has introduced a constitutional amendment that would take reapportionment away from the legislature and entrust it to an independent commission. Several other states, including Montana, Idaho, Washington, and New Jersey, have similar measures but it does not seem to have become a trend. California voters rejected such a proposal in 2005.

GEORGIA
State Senate Districts

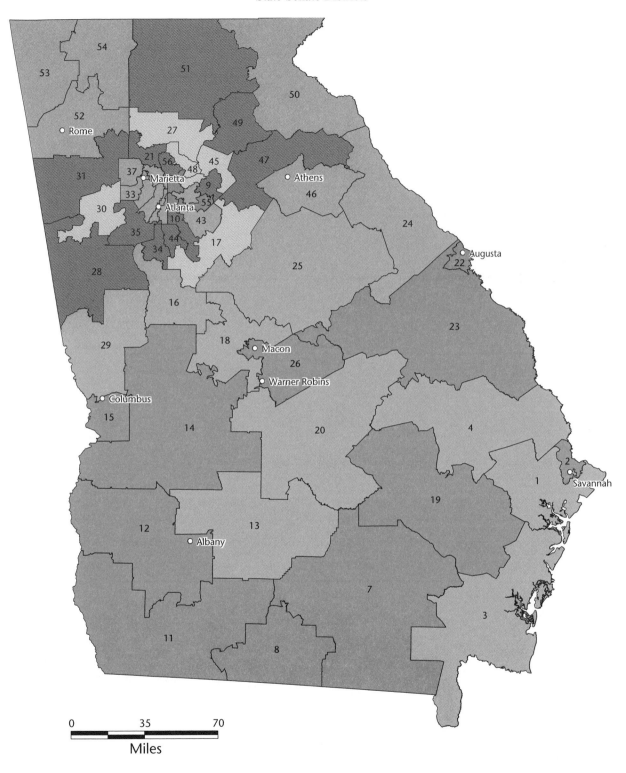

Population Growth   ■ -2% to 7%   ■ 7% to 18%   ■ 18% to 28%   ■ 28% to 47%

ATLANTA

Population Growth ▮ -2% to 7% ▮ 7% to 18% ▮ 18% to 28% ▯ 28% to 47%

Georgia State Senate Districts—Election and Demographic Data

Senate Districts	General Election Results Party, Percent of Vote							Population			Avg. HH Income	Pop 25+ Some College +	Pop 25+ 4-Yr Degree +	Below Poverty Line	White (Non-Hisp)	African American	American Indians, Alaska Natives	2006 Asians, Hawaiians, Pacific Islanders	Hispanic Origin
Georgia	2000	2001	2002	2003	2004	2005	2006	2000	2006	% Change	($)	(%)	(%)	(%)	(%)	(%)	(%)	(%)	(%)
1	R, 100		R, 100		R, 72		R, 100	146,268	157,613	8	70,083	38.9	18.6	12.1	69.4	21.2	0.1	2.6	3.5
2	D, 78		D, 100		D, 100		D, 100	145,136	149,804	3	45,855	28.5	11.0	24.1	35.4	58.2	0.1	2.1	3.1
3	D, 60		D, 53		R, 67		R, 100	147,172	158,530	8	52,415	29.7	11.3	17.7	68.7	24.8	0.2	1.0	3.2
4	D, 100		D, 56		R, 73		R, 100	147,646	168,368	14	47,711	24.4	10.5	24.8	65.6	26.5	0.1	0.9	4.7
5	R, 100		D, 58		D, 100		D, 100	145,953	187,642	29	59,019	33.2	16.9	8.8	27.0	24.9	0.2	15.1	37.6
6	R, 73		R, 52		D, 54		D, 61	145,234	162,613	12	65,085	44.2	25.4	9.6	41.9	33.1	0.1	4.3	18.5
7	D, 53		D, 59		R, 62		R, 100	146,089	152,287	4	42,502	19.8	6.5	25.5	67.0	22.7	0.1	0.7	6.5
8	D, 100		D, 100		D, 56		D, 58	146,534	154,482	5	46,046	27.9	11.3	23.3	55.2	38.5	0.1	1.4	3.1
9	R, 100		R, 100		R, 75		R, 100	144,944	182,672	26	85,040	39.3	20.9	5.8	69.4	10.4	0.1	6.4	10.4
10	D, 85		D, 100		D, 100		D, 100	145,892	173,473	19	62,736	32.9	14.2	11.3	37.4	57.3	0.1	1.3	3.0
11	D, 100		R, 50		R, 53		R, 60	147,850	153,497	4	42,211	20.9	7.3	27.3	55.8	33.4	0.2	0.5	7.6
12	D, 100		D, 100		D, 73		D, 78	145,580	144,811	-1	45,853	26.0	9.7	27.1	37.0	59.9	0.1	0.7	1.7
13	D, 100		D, 52		R, 59		R, 100	144,668	156,041	8	49,339	22.8	8.4	23.4	61.6	30.7	0.1	1.0	4.7
14	D, 100		D, 65		D, 100		D, 100	147,903	151,408	2	44,253	22.0	8.8	25.7	48.7	45.9	0.1	0.6	3.6
15	D, 100		D, 100		D, 100		D, 100	146,026	144,534	-1	43,820	27.9	9.1	23.1	35.6	54.6	0.2	1.7	4.7
16	R, 58		R, 70		R, 100		R, 100	143,684	161,530	12	70,555	32.5	15.5	13.3	71.1	22.5	0.1	2.1	2.8
17	R, 100		R, 100		R, 100		R, 69	146,665	207,984	42	67,373	27.8	10.1	10.1	77.9	16.2	0.1	1.2	2.9
18	R, 69		R, 51		R, 62		R, 100	145,984	164,875	13	64,279	34.0	14.6	10.8	72.2	20.8	0.1	2.1	2.7
19	D, 100		R, 65		R, 63		R, 100	145,498	155,423	7	42,659	21.6	6.6	24.9	58.7	29.1	0.1	1.0	7.6
20	D, 71		D, 66		R, 56		R, 100	146,615	164,077	12	49,477	23.8	9.3	21.9	63.4	32.2	0.1	1.1	2.2
21	R, 74		R, 100		R, 100		R, 100	147,399	179,106	22	92,500	44.1	23.5	4.5	80.9	5.6	0.1	2.5	7.1
22	D, 75		R, 50		D, 57		D, 100	144,343	141,720	-2	46,886	29.4	10.8	23.8	33.2	59.3	0.3	1.9	2.3
23	D, 100		D, 100		D, 50		D, 51	147,003	148,704	1	45,997	24.1	9.2	24.3	52.4	42.0	0.1	1.3	2.4
24	R, 100		R, 73		R, 70		R, 100	147,026	165,780	13	63,480	33.3	15.6	15.1	70.5	21.4	0.1	3.3	2.8
25	D, 52		D, 55		R, 52		R, 57	146,992	158,702	8	53,632	23.4	9.5	20.5	55.1	40.8	0.1	0.8	2.3
26	D, 80		D, 70		D, 66		D, 100	145,508	147,769	2	43,162	23.7	9.1	26.5	37.8	58.0	0.1	1.1	2.2
27	R, 63		R, 100		R, 100		R, 100	145,688	213,818	47	87,436	37.9	19.7	8.7	83.3	3.0	0.1	1.2	8.4
28	R, 100		R, 100		R, 100		R, 100	145,439	180,199	24	63,163	28.7	12.0	14.0	75.5	17.5	0.1	0.9	4.2
29	D, 51		D, 100		R, 60		R, 67	147,579	159,974	8	60,034	32.9	15.0	15.3	65.9	28.0	0.1	1.8	2.3
30	R, 64		R, 100		R, 100		R, 69	147,775	194,264	31	62,114	26.8	10.8	12.3	69.1	15.1	0.4	1.2	4.7
31	D, 63		D, 50		R, 65		R, 68	146,992	180,187	23	54,408	23.7	8.5	15.9	79.3	10.3	0.1	0.8	6.2
32	R, 62		R, 100		R, 74		R, 68	146,875	164,183	12	117,792	59.1	41.1	5.2	75.1	10.0	0.1	6.1	5.7
33	D, 68		D, 100		D, 60		D, 60	145,629	165,280	13	63,548	37.0	17.2	10.9	48.1	29.6	0.1	3.3	16.0
34	D, 62		D, 59		D, 70		D, 100	143,940	173,084	20	63,407	34.1	16.0	9.0	34.1	53.7	0.1	4.7	6.6
35	D, 100		D, 100		D, 100		D, 100	147,574	176,212	19	54,355	33.5	15.7	14.2	34.8	56.3	0.1	1.7	6.1
36	D, 100		D, 100		D, 100		D, 100	147,022	170,980	16	52,543	37.5	24.7	25.9	27.9	59.6	0.1	3.1	8.6
37	D, 100		R, 100		R, 100		R, 100	146,635	170,269	16	86,389	46.3	25.3	5.3	75.6	10.8	0.1	3.6	6.3
38	D, 100		D, 100		D, 100		D, 100	148,496	170,490	15	92,042	42.6	29.5	18.6	30.6	61.2	0.1	1.6	5.8
39	D, 100		D, 100		D, 100		D, 100	143,867	167,989	17	67,117	42.0	28.7	19.6	35.2	55.5	0.1	3.9	4.6
40	R, 100		D, 54		R, 63		R, 64	147,454	153,953	4	98,954	53.1	38.6	7.6	48.5	15.4	0.2	11.3	20.4
41	R, 100		D, 59		D, 59		D, 57	148,628	161,636	9	72,608	44.4	26.0	7.9	42.6	34.0	0.1	9.0	12.6
42	D, 65		D, 60		D, 78		D, 79	141,575	144,369	2	70,409	48.2	35.7	12.9	42.9	39.4	0.1	5.5	10.3
43	D, 100		D, 100		D, 75		D, 78	144,535	163,524	13	64,200	36.1	17.2	9.5	33.1	58.8	0.1	1.8	5.6
44	D, 100		D, 80		D, 100		D, 100	145,167	178,510	23	60,671	27.9	12.6	11.5	40.5	38.3	0.1	7.2	13.3
45	R, 100		R, 100		R, 100		R, 100	148,250	196,048	32	86,609	39.1	21.4	5.3	72.4	8.2	0.1	6.8	9.3
46	D, 51		R, 51		R, 52		R, 56	145,072	156,435	8	52,435	37.8	24.0	23.5	63.1	23.3	0.1	3.5	7.4
47	R, 52		R, 52		R, 71		R, 65	146,934	186,061	27	55,294	23.4	7.8	16.0	78.1	13.6	0.1	1.8	4.0
48	R, 100		R, 100		R, 100		R, 100	147,958	191,689	30	113,828	52.2	37.1	4.1	63.5	12.1	0.1	12.9	8.4
49	R, 67		R, 80		R, 100		R, 81	147,589	184,150	25	63,618	26.3	11.7	14.2	58.0	7.8	0.2	2.0	25.1
50	D, 51		D, 55		R, 58		R, 53	145,566	158,590	9	47,684	24.7	9.7	19.4	81.7	9.3	0.1	1.3	5.0

(continued)

Note: D=Democrat, R=Republican, R/D=Republican/Democrat (cross-filed), D/R=Democrat/Republican (cross-filed), I=Independent, C=Constitution, O=Other, GI=Green Independent, P=Progressive, P/D=Progressive/Democrat, P/D/R=Progressive/Democrat/Republican, HH=Households

Georgia State Senate Districts—Election and Demographic Data (cont.)

Senate Districts	General Election Results Party, Percent of Vote							Population			Avg. HH Income	Pop 25+		Below Poverty Line	White (Non-Hisp)	African American	American Indians, Alaska Natives	Asians, Hawaiians, Pacific Islanders	Hispanic Origin
												Some College +	4-Yr Degree +						
Georgia	2000	2001	2002	2003	2004	2005	2006	2000	2006	% Change	($)	(%)	(%)	(%)	(%)	(%)	(%)	(%)	(%)
51	R, 100		R, 100		R, 67		R, 100	144,784	180,644	25	52,541	27.3	10.5	16.6	89.7	2.6	0.2	0.6	3.8
52	D, 54		R, 54		R, 64		R, 64	145,576	161,651	11	52,910	24.2	9.2	17.4	73.9	11.6	0.1	1.2	9.0
53	R, 55		R, 100		R, 100		R, 63	147,156	162,151	10	46,809	24.6	8.1	18.4	89.6	5.8	0.1	0.8	1.7
54	R, 100		R, 69		R, 100		R, 100	146,083	165,865	14	53,758	20.8	7.1	16.0	65.7	3.5	0.1	1.0	21.3
55	D, 100		D, 100		D, 76		D, 100	146,753	155,407	6	67,788	39.9	21.5	8.9	30.5	57.4	0.1	4.7	5.0
56	R, 100		R, 100		R, 100		R, 100	146,021	174,157	19	105,279	56.2	40.1	5.6	62.9	17.5	0.1	5.4	10.3

Note: D=Democrat, R=Republican, R/D=Republican/Democrat (cross-filed), D/R=Democrat/Republican (cross-filed), I=Independent, C=Constitution, O=Other, GI=Green Independent, P=Progressive, P/D=Progressive/Democrat, P/D/R=Progressive/Democrat/Republican, HH=Households

GEORGIA
State House Districts

SAVANNAH

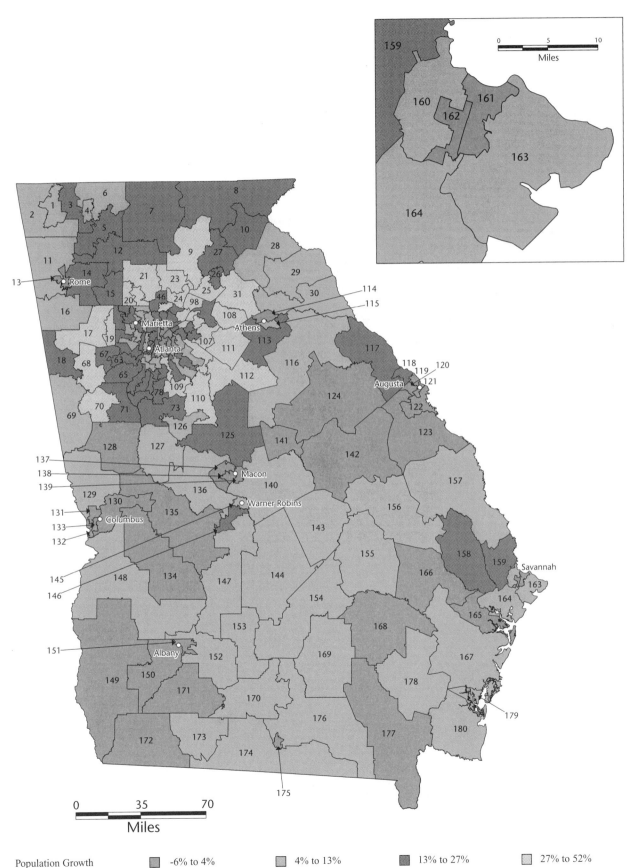

Population Growth   ▢ -6% to 4%   ▢ 4% to 13%   ▢ 13% to 27%   ▢ 27% to 52%

ATLANTA

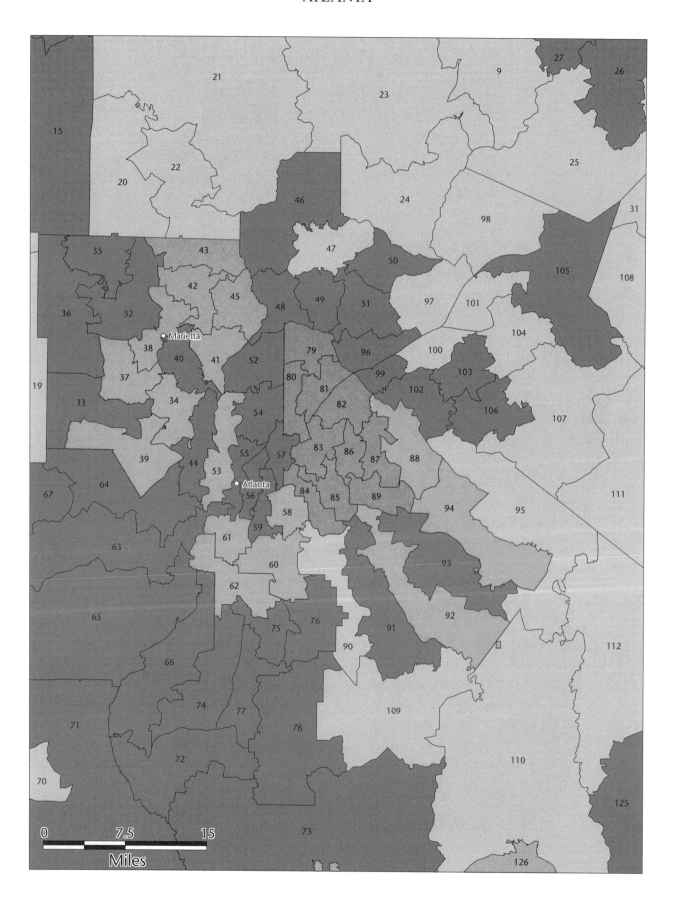

Population Growth   ■ -6% to 4%   ■ 4% to 13%   ■ 13% to 27%   □ 27% to 52%

Georgia State House Districts—Election and Demographic Data

House Districts	General Election Results Party, Percent of Vote							Population			2006 Avg. HH Income ($)	Pop 25+ Some College + (%)	Pop 25+ 4-Yr Degree + (%)	Below Poverty Line (%)	White (Non-Hisp) (%)	African American (%)	American Indians, Alaska Natives (%)	Asians, Hawaiians, Pacific Islanders (%)	Hispanic Origin (%)
Georgia	2000	2001	2002	2003	2004	2005	2006	2000	2006	% Change	($)	(%)	(%)	(%)	(%)	(%)	(%)	(%)	(%)
1	R, 58		R, 51		R, 54		R, 100	46,423	50,465	9	41,964	23.6	6.9	20.4	89.8	5.9	0.1	1.1	1.2
2	D, 60		R, 100		R, 69		R, 67	46,230	49,031	6	47,054	24.0	7.9	18.8	92.2	3.9	0.2	0.6	1.4
3	R, 65				R, 100		R, 71	46,623	54,446	17	56,031	28.3	10.2	13.1	89.4	2.8	0.2	1.0	3.8
3P1			R, 100					46,623	54,446	17	56,031	28.3	10.2	13.1	89.4	2.8	0.2	1.0	3.8
3P2			R, 100					46,623	54,446	17	56,031	28.3	10.2	13.1	89.4	2.8	0.2	1.0	3.8
4	R, 100		R, 74		R, 62		R, 100	44,942	50,116	12	59,785	22.5	9.5	17.4	38.4	5.7	0.2	1.8	42.9
5	R, 59		R, 56		R, 100		R, 100	46,286	53,874	16	49,172	20.2	6.2	18.8	70.2	4.2	0.1	0.9	18.7
6	D, 51		R, 75		R, 100		R, 100	45,677	51,560	13	53,572	20.1	5.9	14.7	76.0	2.7	0.1	0.6	14.3
7	R, 52		R, 62		R, 100		R, 100	45,401	53,593	18	46,261	24.3	9.2	19.5	87.8	1.9	0.2	0.6	5.5
8	D, 60		D, 53		D, 100		D, 51	46,126	53,212	15	48,940	30.3	11.6	18.8	90.9	2.7	0.1	0.8	3.2
9	R, 60		R, 100		R, 100		R, 100	46,402	61,676	33	62,846	30.1	12.6	13.6	89.3	2.1	0.3	0.6	4.6
10	D, 100		R, 60		R, 73		R, 100	45,151	52,134	15	51,161	26.1	10.6	16.5	79.8	5.2	0.1	2.3	8.6
11	D, 100		D, 100		D, 58		D, 100	45,687	49,028	7	47,353	22.6	8.3	18.5	83.3	9.6	0.1	0.8	3.7
12	D, 63		R, 100		R, 100		R, 100	45,282	55,524	23	54,071	23.8	9.0	12.9	89.6	3.1	0.1	0.5	3.8
13	D, 59				D, 100		R, 51	44,189	45,712	3	46,323	24.7	10.8	21.9	57.5	24.0	0.2	2.0	12.4
13P1			D, 59					44,189	45,712	3	46,323	24.7	10.8	21.9	57.5	24.0	0.2	2.0	12.4
13P2			D, 55					44,189	45,712	3	46,323	24.7	10.8	21.9	57.5	24.0	0.2	2.0	12.4
14	R, 61				R, 62		R, 100	46,907	54,750	17	57,654	24.2	8.5	14.1	84.5	8.9	0.1	0.8	3.5
14P1			R, 100					46,907	54,750	17	57,654	24.2	8.5	14.1	84.5	8.9	0.1	0.8	3.5
14P2			R, 100					46,907	54,750	17	57,654	24.2	8.5	14.1	84.5	8.9	0.1	0.8	3.5
15	R, 100		R, 81		R, 66		R, 100	46,566	56,639	22	58,846	26.2	10.3	12.9	76.7	11.4	0.1	1.0	7.6
16	R, 100		R, 100		D, 59		D, 53	46,042	50,003	9	47,301	20.1	5.8	20.4	72.7	12.9	0.1	0.5	9.1
17	R, 100		R, 100		R, 100		R, 100	46,672	64,002	37	57,044	21.7	7.0	13.2	86.3	8.0	0.1	0.5	3.2
18	D, 52		R, 54		R, 70		R, 67	45,631	55,121	21	46,886	22.4	10.5	22.9	70.1	20.1	0.1	1.2	5.9
19	R, 69		D, 61		R, 100		R, 100	44,524	64,264	44	69,006	29.2	11.3	7.5	83.5	9.2	0.2	1.0	4.1
20	D, 100		D, 100		R, 100		R, 100	46,340	60,234	30	81,368	38.9	18.5	6.1	78.5	4.9	0.2	1.9	9.7
21	R, 100		R, 77		R, 100		R, 100	46,818	63,373	35	74,540	33.1	14.6	10.8	80.6	3.8	0.2	0.7	9.9
22	D, 63		D, 100		R, 100		R, 76	45,849	62,294	36	83,829	39.9	19.3	5.3	83.4	4.3	0.2	1.6	6.9
23	D, 100		D, 60		R, 85		R, 100	45,989	68,564	49	76,450	35.8	17.2	9.7	84.9	2.3	0.1	0.7	8.2
24	R, 52		R, 100		R, 100		R, 100	46,038	68,129	48	116,887	46.9	28.8	5.0	83.5	3.1	0.1	2.3	7.5
25	D, 50		R, 50		R, 100		R, 100	44,789	58,294	30	67,228	31.1	13.2	9.6	70.9	5.7	0.1	1.7	15.8
26	R, 100		R, 100		R, 63		R, 58	47,124	56,170	19	56,264	21.3	10.2	20.8	30.4	14.3	0.2	3.3	48.3
27	D, 67		R, 100		R, 100		R, 100	45,776	54,889	20	66,096	29.8	13.6	12.7	81.2	2.8	0.1	0.7	10.5
28	R, 100		R, 100		D, 54		D, 53	45,848	48,869	7	45,839	22.3	8.2	20.2	83.8	9.9	0.1	0.9	3.2
29	D, 42		R, 75		D, 100		D, 66	45,883	48,436	6	44,856	21.6	7.8	21.2	81.1	15.0	0.1	0.8	1.5
30	R, 100		R, 100		R, 100		R, 100	45,814	48,853	7	46,151	20.4	7.2	21.1	73.2	20.8	0.1	0.5	3.4
31	R, 100		R, 100		R, 100		R, 77	45,706	58,733	29	54,159	21.0	7.7	17.4	74.0	10.6	0.1	1.8	9.5
32	R, 50		R, 100		R, 100		R, 100	47,218	56,934	21	86,014	47.8	27.1	6.0	72.8	10.4	0.1	4.6	8.0
33	D, 100				D, 59		D, 100	44,477	50,607	14	65,396	38.3	16.7	7.9	58.8	29.9	0.1	2.2	6.6
33P1			D, 60					44,477	50,607	14	65,396	38.3	16.7	7.9	58.8	29.9	0.1	2.2	6.6
33P2			D, 54					44,477	50,607	14	65,396	38.3	16.7	7.9	58.8	29.9	0.1	2.2	6.6
33P3			D, 58					44,477	50,607	14	65,396	38.3	16.7	7.9	58.8	29.9	0.1	2.2	6.6
34	R, 70				R, 59		R, 58	45,227	50,550	12	72,296	47.4	27.9	8.3	52.4	23.6	0.1	4.4	16.3
34P1			D, 56					45,227	50,550	12	72,296	47.4	27.9	8.3	52.4	23.6	0.1	4.4	16.3
34P2			D, 52					45,227	50,550	12	72,296	47.4	27.9	8.3	52.4	23.6	0.1	4.4	16.3
34P3			R, 53					45,227	50,550	12	72,296	47.4	27.9	8.3	52.4	23.6	0.1	4.4	16.3
35	D, 51		R, 100		R, 100		R, 100	44,032	50,154	14	72,097	44.8	22.6	6.5	71.2	13.1	0.1	3.9	7.5
36	R, 58		R, 100		R, 75		R, 100	46,609	53,066	14	100,712	45.2	25.0	3.7	83.5	8.4	0.1	1.9	3.6
37	R, 100		R, 100		D, 51		D, 52	48,768	53,632	10	71,686	39.9	19.4	8.1	49.0	29.3	0.1	3.8	14.9
38	R, 100		R, 100		R, 53		R, 100	43,712	48,957	12	65,303	39.1	20.1	12.7	43.6	27.4	0.2	4.1	22.1

(continued)

Note: D=Democrat, R=Republican, R/D=Republican/Democrat (cross-filed), D/R=Democrat/Republican (cross-filed), I=Independent, C=Constitution, O=Other, GI=Green Independent, P=Progressive, P/D=Progressive/Democrat, P/D/R=Progressive/Democrat/Republican, HH=Households

Georgia State House Districts—Election and Demographic Data (cont.)

House Districts	General Election Results Party, Percent of Vote							Population			Avg. HH Income ($)	Pop 25+ Some College + (%)	Pop 25+ 4-Yr Degree + (%)	2006 Below Poverty Line (%)	2006 White (Non-Hisp) (%)	2006 African American (%)	2006 American Indians, Alaska Natives (%)	2006 Asians, Hawaiians, Pacific Islanders (%)	2006 Hispanic Origin (%)
Georgia	2000	2001	2002	2003	2004	2005	2006	2000	2006	% Change									
39	R, 100		R, 100		D, 65		D, 100	46,008	50,121	9	57,068	32.2	14.1	12.0	40.9	40.6	0.1	1.6	14.8
40	R, 73		R, 100		D, 100		D, 100	43,465	50,329	16	50,587	38.7	21.1	13.1	29.4	34.0	0.2	5.5	31.2
41	R, 100		R, 100		R, 100		R, 67	46,813	51,453	10	88,061	57.6	37.8	6.1	61.3	17.9	0.1	7.8	8.7
42	R, 100				R, 100		R, 100	45,514	49,203	8	94,612	52.5	30.7	4.3	76.2	8.7	0.1	6.6	5.3
42P1			D, 52					45,514	49,203	8	94,612	52.5	30.7	4.3	76.2	8.7	0.1	6.6	5.3
42P2			D, 56					45,514	49,203	8	94,612	52.5	30.7	4.3	76.2	8.7	0.1	6.6	5.3
42P3			D, 53					45,514	49,203	8	94,612	52.5	30.7	4.3	76.2	8.7	0.1	6.6	5.3
42P4			D, 56					45,514	49,203	8	94,612	52.5	30.7	4.3	76.2	8.7	0.1	6.6	5.3
43	R, 100				R, 74		R, 100	45,580	47,971	5	103,288	51.3	30.5	2.4	80.3	7.6	0.1	4.0	5.2
43P1			D, 100					45,580	47,971	5	103,288	51.3	30.5	2.4	80.3	7.6	0.1	4.0	5.2
43P2			D, 65					45,580	47,971	5	103,288	51.3	30.5	2.4	80.3	7.6	0.1	4.0	5.2
44	R, 100		D, 100		D, 100		D, 100	45,533	51,662	13	62,519	39.7	24.8	20.1	29.6	62.9	0.1	2.2	5.2
45	R, 75		D, 79		R, 100		R, 72	45,774	50,212	10	159,622	59.2	43.3	2.6	83.8	5.0	0.0	5.6	3.5
46	R, 100		R, 72		R, 100		R, 76	47,688	58,359	22	123,405	56.9	40.4	4.8	76.6	12.7	0.1	4.2	3.9
47	D, 100		D, 100		R, 100		R, 100	46,102	59,438	29	94,323	52.5	37.2	5.9	60.2	15.5	0.1	7.7	12.1
48	D, 85				R, 53		R, 59	47,064	55,751	18	85,435	58.2	41.2	6.5	57.2	22.1	0.1	5.2	11.4
48P1			D, 100					47,064	55,751	18	85,435	58.2	41.2	6.5	57.2	22.1	0.1	5.2	11.4
48P2			D, 100					47,064	55,751	18	85,435	58.2	41.2	6.5	57.2	22.1	0.1	5.2	11.4
48P3			D, 100					47,064	55,751	18	85,435	58.2	41.2	6.5	57.2	22.1	0.1	5.2	11.4
48P4			D, 100					47,064	55,751	18	85,435	58.2	41.2	6.5	57.2	22.1	0.1	5.2	11.4
49	D, 100		D, 100		R, 100		R, 100	43,570	49,746	14	122,922	56.5	41.0	3.7	64.4	16.6	0.1	6.1	9.3
50	D, 100		D, 100		R, 100		R, 100	44,684	54,490	22	140,582	54.1	42.1	3.0	65.4	13.3	0.1	14.5	4.1
51	D, 100		D, 100		R, 76		R, 100	47,113	57,873	23	138,322	54.1	38.6	4.5	62.9	11.1	0.1	12.8	10.2
52	D, 100		R, 76		R, 69		R, 100	45,296	52,525	16	131,456	60.5	47.1	6.9	61.8	15.6	0.1	3.8	13.2
53	D, 100		R, 54		D, 100		D, 100	47,820	53,776	12	84,126	37.7	25.6	23.2	27.2	66.5	0.1	1.4	4.2
54	D, 100		D, 100		R, 100		R, 100	45,060	55,562	23	139,529	67.5	55.5	7.9	73.5	14.1	0.1	3.3	6.0
55	D, 100		D, 79		D, 100		D, 100	44,957	51,699	15	57,751	40.1	27.9	22.0	30.8	63.0	0.1	2.4	2.7
56	D, 100				D, 100		D, 100	45,677	53,242	17	49,888	33.0	22.7	32.8	32.3	54.7	0.1	8.9	3.0
56P1			D, 100					45,677	53,242	17	49,888	33.0	22.7	32.8	32.3	54.7	0.1	8.9	3.0
56P2			D, 57					45,677	53,242	17	49,888	33.0	22.7	32.8	32.3	54.7	0.1	8.9	3.0
57	D, 100		D, 100		D, 100		D, 100	46,644	53,351	14	86,137	64.8	52.9	9.3	60.2	16.3	0.1	5.0	12.2
58	D, 100		D, 100		D, 100		D, 100	45,114	47,609	6	42,454	29.8	16.4	25.6	20.2	71.5	0.1	1.3	7.3
59	R, 100				D, 100		D, 100	46,267	56,021	21	44,370	37.5	24.2	29.3	25.6	66.0	0.1	2.3	5.3
59P1			D, 100					46,267	56,021	21	44,370	37.5	24.2	29.3	25.6	66.0	0.1	2.3	5.3
59P2			D, 100					46,267	56,021	21	44,370	37.5	24.2	29.3	25.6	66.0	0.1	2.3	5.3
59P3			D, 71					46,267	56,021	21	44,370	37.5	24.2	29.3	25.6	66.0	0.1	2.3	5.3
60	R, 63				D, 81		D, 100	45,720	51,146	12	41,863	22.1	8.9	25.7	20.3	62.0	0.1	4.8	15.5
60P1			D, 100					45,720	51,146	12	41,863	22.1	8.9	25.7	20.3	62.0	0.1	4.8	15.5
60P2			D, 100					45,720	51,146	12	41,863	22.1	8.9	25.7	20.3	62.0	0.1	4.8	15.5
60P3			D, 100					45,720	51,146	12	41,863	22.1	8.9	25.7	20.3	62.0	0.1	4.8	15.5
61	D, 57				D, 100		D, 100	46,215	51,025	10	36,594	28.2	13.2	28.4	15.2	76.0	0.1	1.6	8.1
61P1			D, 100					46,215	51,025	10	36,594	28.2	13.2	28.4	15.2	76.0	0.1	1.6	8.1
61P2			D, 68					46,215	51,025	10	36,594	28.2	13.2	28.4	15.2	76.0	0.1	1.6	8.1
61P3			D, 69					46,215	51,025	10	36,594	28.2	13.2	28.4	15.2	76.0	0.1	1.6	8.1
62	D, 62		D, 100		D, 100		D, 100	47,195	53,309	13	48,070	30.1	14.6	16.7	17.5	67.5	0.1	4.6	14.3
63	R, 62		R, 100		D, 100		D, 100	45,399	52,265	15	66,055	36.8	18.7	13.5	38.3	57.2	0.1	1.2	2.1
64	D, 63		R, 100		D, 100		D, 100	45,101	54,482	21	62,816	36.3	18.5	13.1	39.3	53.7	0.1	1.6	4.6
65	D, 100		R, 100		D, 100		D, 100	44,189	50,692	15	49,741	33.3	15.4	15.2	28.1	64.0	0.1	1.3	5.5
66	D, 100		D, 100		D, 66		D, 100	46,834	54,833	17	64,940	39.0	19.2	11.5	32.8	60.8	0.1	1.6	3.3
67	D, 100				R, 66		R, 64	46,852	58,534	25	63,983	28.4	11.1	10.7	70.9	19.9	0.2	1.6	5.1

(continued)

Note: D=Democrat, R=Republican, R/D=Republican/Democrat (cross-filed), D/R=Democrat/Republican (cross-filed), I=Independent, C=Constitution, O=Other, GI=Green Independent, P=Progressive, P/D=Progressive/Democrat, P/D/R=Progressive/Democrat/Republican, HH=Households

Georgia State House Districts—Election and Demographic Data (cont.)

House Districts	General Election Results Party, Percent of Vote							Population			Avg. HH Income ($)	Pop 25+ Some College + (%)	Pop 25+ 4-Yr Degree + (%)	Below Poverty Line (%)	White (Non-Hisp) (%)	African American (%)	American Indians, Alaska Natives (%)	Asians, Hawaiians, Pacific Islanders (%)	Hispanic Origin (%)
															2006				
Georgia	2000	2001	2002	2003	2004	2005	2006	2000	2006	% Change	($)	(%)	(%)	(%)	(%)	(%)	(%)	(%)	(%)
67P1			R, 100					46,852	58,534	25	63,983	28.4	11.1	10.7	70.9	19.9	0.2	1.6	5.1
67P2			R, 100					46,852	58,534	25	63,983	28.4	11.1	10.7	70.9	19.9	0.2	1.6	5.1
68	D, 100		R, 69		R, 100		R, 72	45,599	58,071	27	56,720	24.7	9.6	15.7	81.8	13.4	0.1	1.0	2.1
69	D, 100				R, 69		R, 65	45,024	50,401	12	55,647	26.9	13.2	17.4	79.6	15.3	0.1	0.8	2.3
69P1			D, 100					45,024	50,401	12	55,647	26.9	13.2	17.4	79.6	15.3	0.1	0.8	2.3
69P2			D, 54					45,024	50,401	12	55,647	26.9	13.2	17.4	79.6	15.3	0.1	0.8	2.3
70	D, 100				R, 100		R, 100	45,749	59,276	30	60,686	27.4	11.2	16.1	64.2	27.7	0.1	1.0	5.7
70P1			R, 76					45,749	59,276	30	60,686	27.4	11.2	16.1	64.2	27.7	0.1	1.0	5.7
70P2			R, 100					45,749	59,276	30	60,686	27.4	11.2	16.1	64.2	27.7	0.1	1.0	5.7
70P3			R, 100					45,749	59,276	30	60,686	27.4	11.2	16.1	64.2	27.7	0.1	1.0	5.7
71	D, 93				R, 100		R, 100	45,467	56,395	24	78,051	35.6	14.9	6.4	80.1	11.2	0.1	1.2	5.1
71P1			R, 100					45,467	56,395	24	78,051	35.6	14.9	6.4	80.1	11.2	0.1	1.2	5.1
71P2			R, 100					45,467	56,395	24	78,051	35.6	14.9	6.4	80.1	11.2	0.1	1.2	5.1
72	D, 100		D, 51		R, 100		R, 72	45,586	53,664	18	95,270	47.5	25.2	4.7	79.8	9.4	0.1	4.3	4.2
73	D, 100		R, 100		R, 100		R, 100	47,305	55,500	17	65,743	27.3	10.3	12.3	79.6	15.5	0.1	1.1	2.1
74	R, 69		D, 100		D, 61		D, 100	43,597	51,379	18	70,835	38.0	18.8	8.2	31.6	57.3	0.1	4.0	5.9
75	D, 67		D, 100		D, 100		D, 100	47,757	55,523	16	49,813	27.2	11.6	12.2	26.9	50.6	0.1	7.8	15.8
76	R, 100		R, 100		D, 91		D, 100	45,287	53,409	18	58,177	29.4	13.7	10.6	39.5	43.8	0.1	7.2	7.9
77	D, 100		D, 54		D, 100		D, 100	45,337	52,806	16	57,276	28.9	12.3	10.5	32.2	54.6	0.1	5.3	7.1
78	D, 58		D, 73		D, 100		D, 100	45,608	57,201	25	75,372	33.0	16.7	8.2	51.5	37.4	0.2	4.3	5.1
79	R, 100		R, 71		R, 100		R, 72	44,840	46,326	3	108,319	60.0	45.9	5.8	57.8	16.5	0.1	10.3	11.0
80	R, 100		R, 100		D, 51		D, 66	44,397	45,843	3	91,045	52.9	40.2	9.0	43.6	19.5	0.2	6.8	25.9
81	R, 100		D, 100		R, 55		R, 59	46,508	46,375	0	59,238	37.0	23.2	13.0	21.5	15.1	0.3	13.1	51.0
82	R, 100		D, 82		R, 50		D, 53	47,038	46,916	0	80,501	54.8	38.6	6.9	48.2	21.6	0.1	11.7	15.5
83	R, 76		D, 100		D, 100		D, 100	44,487	45,311	2	81,208	58.9	46.7	10.0	69.2	14.8	0.1	9.1	3.9
84	R, 100				D, 100		D, 100	43,758	42,979	-2	60,133	37.1	22.7	16.0	20.9	74.2	0.1	1.2	2.4
84P1			D, 57					43,758	42,979	-2	60,133	37.1	22.7	16.0	20.9	74.2	0.1	1.2	2.4
84P2			D, 64					43,758	42,979	-2	60,133	37.1	22.7	16.0	20.9	74.2	0.1	1.2	2.4
85	R, 69				D, 85		R, 100	45,757	44,823	-2	57,851	40.5	25.3	15.0	27.6	65.4	0.1	2.6	2.7
85P1			R, 100					45,757	44,823	-2	57,851	40.5	25.3	15.0	27.6	65.4	0.1	2.6	2.7
85P2			R, 100					45,757	44,823	-2	57,851	40.5	25.3	15.0	27.6	65.4	0.1	2.6	2.7
86	R, 100		R, 100		D, 100		D, 100	48,033	46,965	-2	49,000	34.8	18.2	15.8	19.2	60.4	0.1	9.9	5.4
87	R, 69		R, 100		D, 100		D, 100	46,278	45,228	-2	62,770	42.2	22.1	7.8	19.3	68.2	0.1	5.3	5.8
88	D, 100				D, 100		D, 100	44,897	47,826	7	74,911	45.6	26.6	7.3	30.2	58.1	0.1	4.8	5.4
88P1			R, 55					44,897	47,826	7	74,911	45.6	26.6	7.3	30.2	58.1	0.1	4.8	5.4
88P2			R, 56					44,897	47,826	7	74,911	45.6	26.6	7.3	30.2	58.1	0.1	4.8	5.4
89	D, 100		R, 100		D, 100		D, 100	43,746	42,962	-2	60,233	37.9	19.4	8.7	10.8	81.8	0.0	2.9	3.4
90	D, 100		D, 100		D, 100		D, 100	45,671	58,899	29	62,195	33.6	14.6	8.9	37.1	56.0	0.1	2.2	3.9
91	R, 64		R, 68		D, 100		D, 100	44,372	55,366	25	73,200	36.5	16.7	5.3	45.9	49.2	0.1	1.2	2.5
92	D, 52		D, 50		D, 70		D, 100	46,281	51,094	10	75,366	39.2	18.9	6.3	38.2	57.0	0.1	1.5	1.9
93	D, 100		D, 55		D, 100		D, 100	46,256	54,494	18	63,703	38.1	18.5	8.3	32.1	61.8	0.1	1.7	3.1
94	D, 70		D, 100		D, 100		D, 100	43,719	48,550	11	60,782	33.6	16.1	12.3	35.0	51.5	0.1	2.1	11.7
95	D, 100		D, 100		R, 100		R, 52	46,491	60,508	30	72,893	36.3	17.2	7.7	68.0	20.3	0.1	3.0	6.1
96	D, 78		R, 58		D, 54		D, 100	46,302	57,993	25	58,088	30.9	15.8	10.3	23.9	24.1	0.2	12.6	45.5
97	D, 62		D, 64		R, 71		R, 100	46,409	64,578	39	89,986	47.3	29.9	4.3	58.9	10.7	0.1	14.8	12.8
98	R, 100		D, 69		R, 100		R, 100	45,947	58,989	28	79,963	37.2	20.0	7.5	69.8	7.9	0.1	4.9	13.2
99	R, 100		D, 53		D, 67		D, 100	44,138	54,402	23	56,895	29.7	14.9	9.8	19.6	25.2	0.2	17.6	47.3
100	D, 100		D, 57		D, 59		D, 100	46,179	62,612	36	62,197	37.0	18.7	6.4	37.0	23.0	0.1	15.4	25.1
101	D, 52		D, 54		R, 70		R, 100	45,601	65,458	44	86,711	41.6	24.2	4.5	65.2	11.0	0.1	11.3	9.8
102	R, 100		D, 100		R, 69		R, 100	45,590	56,010	23	83,730	43.1	25.0	5.8	59.4	11.2	0.1	13.0	13.8

(continued)

Note: D=Democrat, R=Republican, R/D=Republican/Democrat (cross-filed), D/R=Democrat/Republican (cross-filed), I=Independent, C=Constitution, O=Other, GI=Green Independent, P=Progressive, P/D=Progressive/Democrat, P/D/R=Progressive/Democrat/Republican, HH=Households

Georgia State House Districts—Election and Demographic Data (cont.)

House Districts	General Election Results Party, Percent of Vote							Population			Avg. HH Income	2006 Pop 25+ Some College +	2006 Pop 25+ 4-Yr Degree +	Below Poverty Line	White (Non-Hisp)	African American	American Indians, Alaska Natives	Asians, Hawaiians, Pacific Islanders	Hispanic Origin
Georgia	2000	2001	2002	2003	2004	2005	2006	2000	2006	% Change	($)	(%)	(%)	(%)	(%)	(%)	(%)	(%)	(%)
103	R, 100		D, 100		R, 100		R, 100	44,417	54,771	23	86,611	42.1	23.4	4.3	63.4	12.2	0.1	9.7	11.7
104	R, 100		D, 64		R, 61		R, 100	45,001	60,669	35	72,745	34.6	17.6	8.6	62.9	12.9	0.1	6.2	14.6
105	R, 100		D, 69		R, 78		R, 100	46,130	57,074	24	87,988	36.1	18.0	4.7	79.2	7.3	0.1	4.0	6.5
106	R, 68		R, 73		R, 100		R, 67	46,011	55,249	20	89,848	40.6	20.8	4.9	74.2	9.8	0.1	4.4	8.0
107	R, 100		D, 100		R, 100		R, 100	45,442	58,875	30	78,977	35.4	15.7	6.0	82.6	6.3	0.1	2.7	5.3
108	R, 100		D, 100		R, 100		R, 100	45,558	61,158	34	57,697	24.5	7.1	13.8	76.1	11.2	0.1	3.2	6.5
109	R, 52		D, 52		R, 62		R, 100	46,081	69,702	51	77,442	35.5	14.9	7.2	72.9	17.4	0.1	3.3	4.7
110	D, 100		R, 100		R, 73		R, 100	47,408	68,966	45	66,914	26.3	8.3	8.8	79.5	15.4	0.1	0.7	2.9
111	D, 100		D, 100		R, 79		R, 100	46,257	59,254	28	59,015	23.8	8.2	14.9	74.6	20.2	0.1	1.1	2.3
112	R, 71		D, 100		R, 59		R, 100	45,846	60,770	33	57,504	23.4	9.8	16.3	65.4	29.3	0.1	1.0	3.0
113	R, 100		D, 100		R, 100		R, 61	45,193	51,154	13	70,331	40.6	25.5	11.8	79.7	12.3	0.1	2.2	3.4
114	R, 100		D, 58		D, 100		D, 100	45,079	45,953	2	45,233	32.1	18.4	26.5	41.5	39.8	0.1	2.3	15.3
115	D, 63		D, 100		D, 56		D, 52	45,714	49,239	8	42,594	43.4	30.9	32.2	66.8	19.5	0.1	6.5	4.7
116	D, 100		D, 100		D, 57		R, 64	45,502	48,913	7	55,199	23.4	10.0	23.1	54.1	40.5	0.1	0.7	3.7
117	D, 100		R, 100		R, 100		R, 100	46,202	55,183	19	56,536	30.6	11.1	14.5	72.3	19.9	0.2	1.9	3.1
118	D, 100		D, 100		R, 100		R, 100	45,380	52,429	16	82,364	45.0	25.3	5.2	78.4	10.6	0.1	5.9	2.6
119	R, 54		D, 100		R, 100		R, 100	45,798	46,548	2	75,552	49.0	28.1	11.9	69.6	20.7	0.1	4.8	2.2
120	D, 100		D, 100		D, 100		D, 67	45,822	44,873	-2	45,573	29.6	10.9	20.1	34.9	58.9	0.1	2.0	2.4
121	D, 100				D, 73		D, 70	44,267	41,973	-5	33,484	20.6	6.4	34.9	32.7	62.9	0.1	1.3	1.6
121P1			R, 100					44,267	41,973	-5	33,484	20.6	6.4	34.9	32.7	62.9	0.1	1.3	1.6
121P2			D, 51					44,267	41,973	-5	33,484	20.6	6.4	34.9	32.7	62.9	0.1	1.3	1.6
122	D, 100		D, 74		D, 100		D, 100	45,446	45,853	1	46,123	27.1	6.5	19.4	41.1	51.6	0.1	2.0	2.6
123	D, 100		R, 100		D, 59		D, 100	47,927	48,843	2	44,120	24.8	7.3	23.7	39.6	52.8	0.2	1.7	3.5
124	D, 100				D, 100		D, 100	45,867	46,071	0	46,570	20.4	7.5	26.0	50.4	47.0	0.1	0.4	1.4
124P1			D, 100					45,867	46,071	0	46,570	20.4	7.5	26.0	50.4	47.0	0.1	0.4	1.4
124P2			D, 100					45,867	46,071	0	46,570	20.4	7.5	26.0	50.4	47.0	0.1	0.4	1.4
125	R, 100		D, 100		R, 53		R, 59	44,977	50,829	13	55,973	23.9	9.3	18.0	64.2	32.0	0.1	0.6	2.0
126	D, 100		R, 100		R, 54		R, 59	43,499	45,359	4	49,489	21.3	8.0	20.8	54.2	40.9	0.1	1.0	2.6
127	D, 100				R, 100		R, 100	46,540	49,743	7	50,605	22.4	8.7	19.1	72.5	24.0	0.1	0.7	1.7
128	D, 100		D, 65		D, 100		D, 100	45,473	47,064	3	41,610	19.0	6.7	25.6	48.4	48.0	0.1	0.6	2.0
129	R, 100				R, 100		R, 100	45,823	51,088	11	69,660	34.0	15.9	13.9	73.5	21.6	0.1	1.3	1.8
129P1			D, 55					45,823	51,088	11	69,660	34.0	15.9	13.9	73.5	21.6	0.1	1.3	1.8
129P2			D, 100					45,823	51,088	11	69,660	34.0	15.9	13.9	73.5	21.6	0.1	1.3	1.8
130	R, 100		D, 100		D, 67		D, 100	44,363	45,851	3	54,522	29.7	10.7	14.8	41.6	48.0	0.2	2.3	4.5
131	D, 54		R, 52		R, 100		R, 100	46,676	48,383	4	61,329	40.9	18.5	10.2	73.4	17.5	0.2	3.0	2.9
132	R, 100		D, 68		D, 100		D, 100	45,102	43,698	-3	34,493	22.8	7.4	32.3	30.9	60.4	0.2	1.3	4.5
133	D, 100		D, 100		D, 100		D, 100	45,739	44,750	-2	47,826	31.2	9.7	19.0	31.1	61.6	0.2	1.8	3.1
134	D, 100		D, 100		D, 51		D, 56	45,560	46,010	1	43,661	23.7	10.7	25.2	47.5	46.6	0.1	0.7	4.0
135	D, 62		D, 100		D, 58		D, 65	45,801	46,557	2	39,244	19.8	7.3	30.8	34.5	59.8	0.1	0.6	4.6
136	D, 100		D, 100		D, 56		R, 68	46,478	51,619	11	59,790	30.0	11.8	13.9	72.9	20.9	0.1	1.3	2.4
137	D, 100		R, 61		R, 100		R, 100	45,565	47,238	4	77,735	44.6	25.1	8.0	75.9	18.3	0.1	2.9	1.5
138	D, 100		R, 100		D, 100		D, 100	45,913	45,967	0	37,381	19.7	6.0	27.7	27.4	69.3	0.1	0.8	1.7
139	R, 64		D, 100		D, 100		D, 100	44,679	43,995	-2	39,350	22.1	8.9	34.2	27.8	69.4	0.1	0.8	1.5
140	D, 100		D, 75		R, 50		R, 54	46,426	48,863	5	51,032	21.6	7.4	19.4	62.3	34.4	0.1	0.5	1.5
141	D, 100				D, 65		D, 100	45,473	46,524	2	51,538	25.8	11.0	19.8	51.6	44.4	0.1	1.4	1.5
141P1			D, 55					45,473	46,524	2	51,538	25.8	11.0	19.8	51.6	44.4	0.1	1.4	1.5
141P2			D, 55					45,473	46,524	2	51,538	25.8	11.0	19.8	51.6	44.4	0.1	1.4	1.5
142	D, 100		D, 67		D, 72		D, 67	45,542	46,127	1	41,218	17.1	6.2	30.7	42.3	55.6	0.1	0.4	1.2
143	D, 100		D, 100		D, 76		D, 100	45,563	48,297	6	47,011	22.0	9.4	23.7	60.5	35.8	0.1	1.2	1.6
144	D, 100		D, 100		D, 100		R, 60	46,223	48,743	5	43,362	21.0	7.0	24.3	65.0	31.1	0.1	0.7	2.0

(continued)

Note: D=Democrat, R=Republican, R/D=Republican/Democrat (cross-filed), D/R=Democrat/Republican (cross-filed), I=Independent, C=Constitution, O=Other, GI=Green Independent, P=Progressive, P/D=Progressive/Democrat, P/D/R=Progressive/Democrat/Republican, HH=Households

Georgia State House Districts—Election and Demographic Data (cont.)

House Districts	General Election Results Party, Percent of Vote							Population			Avg. HH Income	Pop 25+ Some College +	Pop 25+ 4-Yr Degree +	Below Poverty Line	2006 White (Non-Hisp)	African American	American Indians, Alaska Natives	Asians, Hawaiians, Pacific Islanders	Hispanic Origin
Georgia	2000	2001	2002	2003	2004	2005	2006	2000	2006	% Change	($)	(%)	(%)	(%)	(%)	(%)	(%)	(%)	(%)
145	R, 57		D, 100		R, 100		R, 70	46,410	50,391	9	47,767	30.3	9.2	16.3	54.7	34.9	0.2	2.5	5.2
146	D, 100		R, 100		R, 100		R, 70	44,809	56,238	26	65,455	37.4	15.8	9.1	70.9	20.8	0.1	2.5	3.6
147	D, 100		R, 60		D, 67		R, 66	45,383	48,183	6	48,099	22.3	8.6	26.0	55.3	39.3	0.1	0.9	3.1
148	D, 100				D, 100		D, 100	46,088	50,035	9	46,662	24.5	8.4	23.5	48.9	42.8	0.2	1.2	4.0
149	D, 100				D, 100		D, 100	45,772	44,153	-4	40,448	21.6	7.1	30.6	47.9	48.7	0.1	0.3	2.1
150	R, 100				D, 100		D, 100	45,722	45,716	0	56,995	31.4	14.5	23.9	34.0	63.5	0.1	0.9	1.1
151	D, 100				D, 100		D, 100	45,477	45,199	-1	38,631	25.3	8.4	28.8	34.8	61.6	0.1	0.8	1.8
152	R, 100				R, 65		R, 100	46,419	51,098	10	57,625	27.0	9.1	17.1	71.2	24.6	0.1	1.0	1.7
153	R, 100				R, 100		R, 55	45,332	47,688	5	47,736	22.5	8.7	24.3	53.7	33.1	0.1	1.3	9.2
154	R, 75				R, 58		R, 100	45,044	48,172	7	42,354	19.6	6.9	27.4	60.1	33.3	0.0	0.5	4.5
155	D, 100				D, 53		R, 100	45,567	47,857	5	40,778	19.8	7.6	28.7	60.6	26.9	0.1	0.6	8.7
156	D, 100				D, 100		R, 100	45,312	48,458	7	42,222	22.2	9.9	30.8	57.5	34.0	0.1	0.7	5.9
157	D, 100				R, 65		R, 100	45,781	50,748	11	47,373	21.0	8.1	25.0	60.8	35.5	0.1	0.4	2.2
158	D, 100				R, 100		R, 100	46,403	52,869	14	45,892	27.6	13.0	26.3	68.6	26.5	0.1	1.2	2.0
159	D, 100				R, 100		R, 100	46,763	56,769	21	60,517	27.1	9.4	11.6	78.6	14.5	0.2	1.6	2.8
160	D, 100				D, 100		D, 100	46,059	49,502	7	39,246	24.7	9.2	30.1	33.5	59.6	0.1	1.6	4.2
161	D, 100				D, 100		D, 100	44,155	44,892	2	47,416	28.0	11.2	23.7	33.3	61.8	0.1	2.4	1.4
162	D, 100				D, 100		D, 100	46,242	45,691	-1	50,177	34.0	14.6	21.6	37.4	56.2	0.1	1.8	3.2
163	R, 68				R, 100		R, 100	46,207	49,154	6	94,831	52.9	30.4	6.9	81.1	12.1	0.1	3.3	1.7
164	D, 100				R, 100		R, 100	44,840	49,435	10	64,486	39.2	18.2	10.5	69.5	20.7	0.1	3.0	4.1
165	R, 100				D, 54		D, 67	46,793	47,107	1	44,602	28.5	8.0	19.2	37.6	47.1	0.2	2.8	6.4
166	D, 100				R, 100		R, 100	44,871	45,611	2	39,377	19.6	5.3	27.1	49.1	34.0	0.1	1.0	11.1
167	D, 100				R, 63		R, 100	46,040	51,354	12	57,628	30.3	12.3	16.9	71.0	21.4	0.2	0.8	4.2
168	D, 57				R, 100		R, 100	45,612	47,182	3	42,185	19.0	5.6	26.3	73.3	17.9	0.1	0.6	5.6
169	D, 100				D, 100		R, 70	45,924	49,229	7	44,837	19.4	6.1	25.0	57.8	25.7	0.1	0.8	11.3
170	D, 100				D, 79		R, 100	47,398	49,855	5	43,426	19.8	6.8	24.0	62.6	19.2	0.1	0.5	12.3
171	D, 56				D, 100		R, 64	44,579	44,872	1	40,280	19.3	6.5	29.8	48.3	43.8	0.1	0.5	5.6
172					R, 51		R, 53	46,219	47,747	3	41,640	22.1	7.5	28.1	51.6	40.4	0.2	0.6	6.1
173	D, 52				R, 64		R, 100	45,566	47,512	4	46,917	26.0	10.7	22.9	59.5	35.4	0.2	0.6	2.9
174	R, 100				D, 53		D, 100	45,623	48,264	6	44,064	21.1	7.8	24.0	60.8	30.0	0.2	0.5	6.0
175	D, 100				D, 65		D, 70	44,575	45,865	3	46,788	30.6	14.8	25.6	47.3	46.5	0.1	2.1	2.4
176	D, 100				D, 61		D, 100	46,384	49,908	8	45,452	29.4	9.2	21.1	66.3	26.7	0.2	1.5	3.0
177	D, 100				R, 57		R, 64	46,351	45,852	-1	40,376	20.0	6.8	25.0	65.5	29.7	0.1	0.8	2.6
178	D, 59				D, 51		R, 100	44,581	48,899	10	42,784	19.8	6.5	24.4	77.4	16.5	0.1	0.6	3.5
179	D, 100				R, 100		R, 68	45,299	48,124	6	50,673	33.3	14.0	19.0	57.1	35.4	0.1	1.0	5.4
180	R, 52				R, 100		R, 100	46,150	48,588	5	51,360	29.3	9.0	15.2	70.3	21.5	0.2	1.5	2.9

Note: D=Democrat, R=Republican, R/D=Republican/Democrat (cross-filed), D/R=Democrat/Republican (cross-filed), I=Independent, C=Constitution, O=Other, GI=Green Independent, P=Progressive, P/D=Progressive/Democrat, P/D/R=Progressive/Democrat/Republican, HH=Households

HAWAII

Hawaii, the most geographically remote state, is also the most different from the rest of the country in terms of history, culture, and ethnicity. It is one of three U.S. states to have once been an independent country (Vermont and Texas are the others). The Hawaii state senate claims descent from the House of Nobles, which before annexation by the United States governed the Kingdom of Hawaii, an elected monarchy. In 1993 Congress unanimously passed a resolution apologizing for the overthrow of the Kingdom after the Spanish-American War.

Native Hawaiians retain certain privileges under law here. The 1978 state constitutional convention required the teaching of native island culture in the public schools and created an Office of Hawaiian Affairs (OHA), which was given control of certain public lands and charged with improving the lives of native Hawaiian peoples. The OHA is run by an elected board of directors and, at first, only people who could prove Hawaiian ancestry were eligible to vote in board elections. This restriction was challenged as a form of racial discrimination and in 2000 the U.S. Supreme Court extended suffrage to all state residents, regardless of ancestry. Recently Democratic senator Daniel Akaka has been pushing a bill that would create a native Hawaiian government and empower it to deal with the federal government, a proposal the Bush administration and many others have strongly opposed.

Nowhere else in the United States do Pacific Islanders exert as much influence as they do in Hawaii, where they make up more than 9 percent of the state population (not surprising, perhaps, since Hawaii is a Pacific island). But by far the largest ethnic group in the state are Asians, who make up more than 41 percent of the population, four times more than in the state with the second-highest concentration (California) and seven times more than in the state with the third-largest (New Jersey). The percentage of Asians and Pacific Islanders in Hawaii is roughly the same as the percentage of whites in Texas.

The Asian population is ethnically diverse, fairly wealthy, and includes a mixture of Japanese (Hawaii is also a popular tourist destination on both sides of the Pacific), Chinese, and Filipinos, who are by far the state's largest immigrant group. Former governor Ben Cayetano was the only governor of predominantly Filipino extraction in American history and both of Hawaii's U.S. senators are of Japanese ancestry.

The flip side is that Hawaii has the smallest percentage of whites, and one of the smallest percentages of African Americans. Only 23 percent of Hawaii's residents are white and in only one of its fifty-one house districts do they constitute a majority. The 29th house district in Honolulu, which is 80 percent Asian (the highest Asian percentage of any district in the country), is only 4 percent white. The only significant concentration of African Americans on the islands is in the 46th house district, which takes in the large western end of Oahu, and is 9 percent black.

Population has been growing rapidly on the big island of Hawaii and on the western edge of Oahu around Ewa Beach. The only district in which population has fallen slightly in this decade is the overwhelmingly white 51st district. Hawaii is the third-wealthiest state after Connecticut and New Jersey, has one of the highest percentages of college graduates, and a very low rate of unemployment. The wealthiest districts are located on the eastern end of the big island (the 17th, 18th, and 19th house districts) and Kaneohe (the 49th district). The 4th house district on the eastern edge of Hawaii, which also has the largest concentration of Hispanics, is the state's poorest.

Although it has had a Republican governor since 2002, the first ever elected here, Hawaii is perhaps the country's most Democratic, and liberal, state; the party holds both senate seats and all four seats in Congress. It has voted Democratic in every presidential election since statehood, with the exception of the Richard Nixon landslide of 1972 and the Ronald Reagan landslide in 1984. Republicans made some gains in the state house of representatives, holding nineteen out of fifty-one seats following the 2002 elections, but the GOP have seen those gains wiped out in the last two election cycles, and Democrats now control the chamber, 41–10. Republican state senators, who could caucus in a phone booth in 2000 (when Democrats held a 23–2 edge) now count five members. The situation seems unlikely to change in Hawaii anytime soon.

Finally, it is worth pointing out that, although Hawaii has cast a small shadow over national politics, that may change if Illinois senator Barak Obama, born in Honolulu two years after statehood, is on the Democratic presidential ticket in 2008.

HAWAII
State Senate Districts

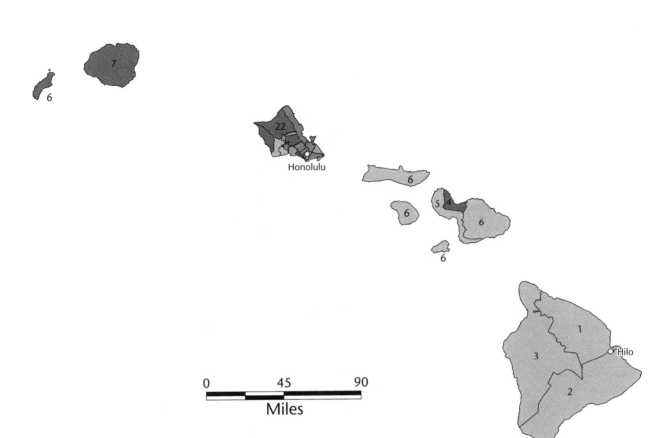

Honolulu

Hilo

0   45   90
Miles

Population Growth   ■ -2% to 2%   ■ 2% to 4%   ■ 4% to 10%   ■ 10% to 18%

OAHU

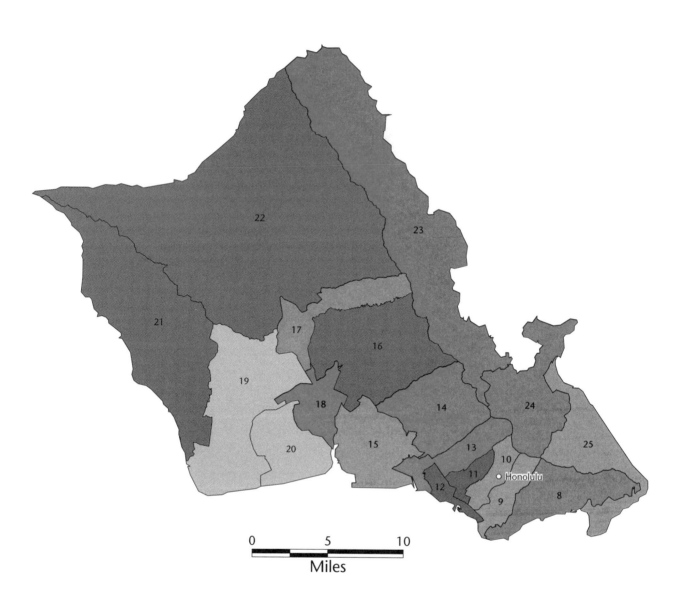

Population Growth ▮ -2% to 2% ▮ 2% to 4% ▮ 4% to 10% ▯ 10% to 18%

Hawaii State Senate Districts—Election and Demographic Data

Senate Districts	General Election Results Party, Percent of Vote							Population			Avg. HH Income	Pop 25+		Below Poverty Line	2006 White (Non-Hisp)	African American	American Indians, Alaska Natives	Asians, Hawaiians, Pacific Islanders	Hispanic Origin
												Some College +	4-Yr Degree +						
Hawaii	2000	2001	2002	2003	2004	2005	2006	2000	2006	% Change	($)	(%)	(%)	(%)	(%)	(%)	(%)	(%)	(%)
1			D, 76					49,325	55,255	12	57,992	32.1	14.8	19.2	23.9	0.4	0.1	38.0	11.8
2	D, 61		D, 62					50,428	57,563	14	46,950	33.3	13.3	23.0	29.0	0.6	0.1	31.3	13.5
3	D, 72		R, 55		R, 52			48,938	56,206	15	69,422	36.5	16.6	11.7	42.7	0.4	0.1	23.1	10.8
4								42,500	46,100	8	69,905	29.6	12.2	13.9	18.0	0.2	0.4	57.4	9.4
5	D, 56		D, 51		D, 59			40,760	46,600	14	75,079	40.3	17.8	10.3	48.4	0.6	0.5	32.0	8.6
6					D, 71			44,974	49,832	11	70,998	37.4	17.1	13.7	40.3	0.3	0.5	33.0	8.7
7			D, 73		D, 66			58,456	63,405	8	65,780	35.3	13.6	13.9	27.3	0.3	0.4	44.3	9.5
8	R, 59		R, 63					45,927	46,192	1	127,001	56.1	39.0	4.7	24.4	0.3	0.1	58.9	3.2
9	D, 61		D, 68				D, 77	49,068	50,242	2	76,070	45.5	26.9	11.4	17.6	0.5	0.2	64.3	4.3
10								46,289	47,578	3	66,053	48.3	32.2	14.6	18.0	0.9	0.2	64.8	4.2
11	D, 76		D, 61				D, 73	44,203	46,260	5	56,609	46.9	28.4	16.6	15.5	1.0	0.2	65.3	5.0
12	D, 60		R, 58		R, 57			41,956	44,594	6	52,945	46.7	27.8	21.5	24.3	1.4	0.2	61.1	4.2
13							D, 76	47,672	47,635	0	74,011	39.6	22.6	16.6	7.9	0.4	0.1	76.5	4.4
14								49,197	48,354	-2	76,889	32.9	16.2	13.8	10.1	1.6	0.1	70.0	6.1
15	D, 77							70,346	72,353	3	65,123	38.4	19.2	8.0	26.7	5.8	0.3	47.3	7.9
16								45,890	48,834	6	86,250	45.6	24.8	4.6	11.6	1.3	0.2	67.3	6.2
17			D, 73		D, 69			44,406	45,577	3	78,982	44.9	23.8	4.7	17.1	2.9	0.2	53.3	8.3
18								46,393	45,943	-1	72,012	32.0	14.0	14.4	11.7	2.0	0.2	68.2	7.1
19			D, 65				R, 56	47,511	53,679	13	79,951	39.5	19.8	4.1	15.6	2.0	0.2	56.1	8.9
20	D, 50						D, 63	45,268	53,207	18	69,486	34.3	15.9	8.1	12.7	1.9	0.2	61.2	9.1
21			D, 71		D, 73			42,691	45,525	7	58,213	22.1	8.7	20.8	10.1	1.1	0.3	46.8	14.8
22								65,360	68,894	5	57,314	33.4	15.9	13.3	26.6	6.9	0.5	37.8	12.3
23			D, 52		D, 54			44,423	44,968	1	78,011	40.3	23.3	9.6	21.9	0.8	0.2	45.1	7.6
24	R, 73		R, 65				D, 57	54,926	55,425	1	86,500	40.6	23.9	6.5	30.3	2.8	0.4	39.0	9.1
25	R, 70		R, 57				R, 68	43,627	44,629	2	97,399	44.0	27.3	7.8	31.5	0.6	0.2	41.7	6.0

Note: D=Democrat, R=Republican, R/D=Republican/Democrat (cross-filed), D/R=Democrat/Republican (cross-filed), I=Independent, C=Constitution, O=Other, GI=Green Independent, P=Progressive, P/D=Progressive/Democrat, P/D/R=Progressive/Democrat/Republican, HH=Households

HAWAII
State House Districts

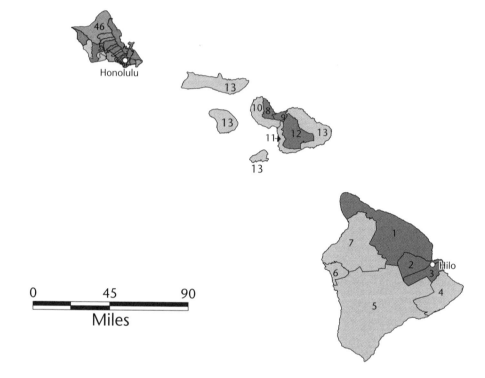

Honolulu

Hilo

0   45   90

Miles

Population Growth   ◼ -3% to 5%   ◼ 5% to 10%   ◼ 10% to 14%   ◻ 14% to 22%

OAHU

Population Growth ■ -3% to 5%   ■ 5% to 10%   ■ 10% to 14%   □ 14% to 22%

Hawaii State House Districts—Election and Demographic Data

House Districts	General Election Results Party, Percent of Vote							Population			Avg. HH Income	Pop 25+ Some College +	Pop 25+ 4-Yr Degree +	Below Poverty Line	White (Non-Hisp)	African American	American Indians, Alaska Natives	Asians, Hawaiians, Pacific Islanders	Hispanic Origin
Hawaii	2000	2001	2002	2003	2004	2005	2006	2000	2006	% Change	($)	(%)	(%)	(%)	(%)	(%)	(%)	(%)	(%)
1								23,024	25,692	12	58,508	29.9	12.8	18.7	27.3	0.3	0.1	33.9	13.6
2			D, 75		D, 75		D, 76	21,635	24,257	12	51,554	31.5	14.7	31.4	21.2	0.5	0.1	39.5	12.7
3			D, 55		D, 62		D, 85	20,944	23,378	12	60,941	37.2	16.8	19.6	15.9	0.2	0.0	48.3	9.3
4	D, 39		D, 55		D, 59		D, 50	22,378	27,205	22	42,141	30.8	11.5	34.2	33.4	0.7	0.1	24.3	16.8
5	R, 53		D, 48		D, 65		D, 74	21,563	25,172	17	50,294	33.7	14.0	27.7	35.9	0.5	0.1	26.3	11.2
6			R, 61		D, 54			20,324	24,284	19	68,195	37.1	17.3	16.1	46.2	0.4	0.1	21.9	10.8
7	R, 55		D, 51		D, 57		D, 62	19,689	23,108	17	78,404	38.8	17.9	11.5	42.9	0.3	0.0	22.1	9.2
8	D, 54		D, 63		D, 58		D, 66	20,763	23,220	12	68,094	31.2	13.4	16.9	19.8	0.3	0.4	53.8	9.6
9	D, 81		D, 63		D, 63		D, 81	21,984	24,293	11	71,909	28.3	11.1	18.0	16.3	0.2	0.3	60.6	9.2
10	R, 46		R, 62		D, 50		D, 56	20,334	23,359	15	77,417	35.7	15.9	13.6	41.8	0.5	0.5	37.4	9.5
11	R, 56		R, 64		R, 63		D, 60	20,664	24,003	16	72,837	44.7	19.6	13.9	56.0	0.7	0.6	25.9	7.5
12	D, 85		R, 58		D, 53		D, 83	22,634	25,256	12	82,994	42.7	20.8	14.9	44.3	0.3	0.5	28.9	9.6
13	D, 80		D, 59		D, 72		D, 72	22,602	25,834	14	59,042	32.3	13.5	22.1	36.5	0.3	0.6	36.7	7.9
14	D, 67		D, 62		D, 59			19,677	21,995	12	65,610	35.3	14.3	21.2	35.8	0.4	0.5	35.4	8.7
15	R, 54		D, 81		D, 71		D, 60	20,704	22,542	9	67,657	37.3	14.4	16.7	23.0	0.3	0.4	49.5	9.4
16			D, 71		D, 72		D, 71	18,416	20,396	11	63,947	33.0	12.0	18.7	23.1	0.2	0.2	48.3	10.5
17					R, 53		R, 57	22,452	24,136	8	112,128	55.9	37.7	7.4	28.6	0.4	0.1	53.2	3.6
18	D, 83				D, 54		D, 72	22,331	23,051	3	117,874	53.7	35.9	7.8	23.4	0.3	0.1	59.8	3.1
19	R, 51		R, 66		R, 55		R, 57	22,056	22,935	4	121,378	52.3	35.6	10.1	19.0	0.2	0.1	64.4	3.4
20	D, 63		D, 78		D, 75		D, 75	20,930	21,499	3	89,897	45.5	28.5	14.5	15.3	0.3	0.1	66.9	4.2
21	R, 75		D, 54		D, 78		D, 80	27,713	28,400	2	57,221	48.2	27.8	19.4	22.7	1.0	0.2	59.0	4.9
22	D, 67		D, 76		D, 78		D, 79	21,902	22,502	3	44,606	42.1	24.1	27.9	11.5	1.0	0.2	72.3	4.2
23			R, 76		R, 61		D, 52	18,545	20,765	12	55,495	54.1	32.5	24.3	34.2	1.7	0.2	51.7	3.7
24	D, 57		D, 59		D, 62		D, 82	21,569	22,256	3	94,928	50.5	37.5	15.3	20.6	0.6	0.2	63.1	3.8
25	D, 65		D, 69		D, 64		D, 60	25,104	26,686	6	63,187	50.1	32.1	18.3	17.9	1.0	0.2	62.1	5.0
26	D, 57		D, 62		D, 65		D, 62	25,798	26,385	2	70,991	47.7	28.7	19.8	14.5	0.7	0.1	67.0	4.5
27	D, 73		R, 57		R, 52		R, 58	22,633	23,469	4	69,115	39.8	23.1	21.8	6.5	0.3	0.1	77.7	4.3
28					D, 51		D, 52	23,090	24,490	6	51,024	39.8	23.1	32.0	13.3	1.2	0.2	70.9	4.7
29	D, 75		D, 80		D, 73		D, 79	18,584	19,218	3	59,697	27.4	12.1	25.6	4.4	0.4	0.1	79.7	5.4
30	D, 66		D, 87		D, 83		D, 63	24,602	24,893	1	80,949	31.2	15.2	14.7	8.8	1.2	0.1	73.4	6.0
31			D, 62		D, 61		D, 80	22,863	24,531	7	72,002	42.7	24.0	11.3	13.3	2.8	0.2	66.7	5.8
32	R, 59		R, 64				R, 60	51,285	54,778	7	62,416	37.6	17.8	12.0	30.0	7.1	0.4	42.2	8.4
33			D, 72		D, 50		D, 72	24,192	24,778	2	80,932	41.5	21.5	9.3	14.3	1.9	0.2	61.7	6.7
34								26,224	27,407	5	86,373	42.2	22.8	10.2	17.8	2.7	0.3	61.2	6.7
35	D, 77		D, 82		D, 80		D, 66	21,836	22,430	3	75,712	32.4	14.6	15.4	7.2	0.8	0.1	75.7	6.0
36	D, 80		D, 71		D, 80		D, 81	22,240	22,386	1	81,228	41.6	19.9	10.1	10.6	1.3	0.1	65.3	7.8
37			R, 51		D, 52		D, 74	23,546	23,844	1	81,348	46.2	23.7	5.7	17.2	3.0	0.2	54.3	8.0
38	D, 66		D, 53		D, 62		D, 67	27,827	29,767	7	78,898	45.2	26.2	8.3	14.7	2.2	0.2	56.2	7.9
39	R, 57		D, 73		D, 75		D, 75	21,975	23,150	5	54,331	32.8	15.2	22.6	14.8	2.5	0.3	53.1	11.4
40	D, 59		R, 61		R, 72		D, 52	25,857	29,275	13	77,557	38.2	18.6	6.2	18.8	2.2	0.2	50.2	9.7
41	D, 55				D, 57		D, 59	24,327	26,892	11	80,012	38.8	19.8	6.2	9.3	1.6	0.2	67.0	7.4
42	R, 56		D, 65		D, 76		D, 69	22,579	25,942	15	67,507	34.4	16.0	12.5	7.0	1.8	0.2	69.9	8.8
43	D, 68		D, 52		R, 60		R, 64	27,210	31,563	16	71,814	33.7	15.4	9.2	15.3	1.8	0.2	58.6	8.6
44	R, 45		D, 54		D, 50		R, 53	23,077	26,583	15	63,735	23.0	9.4	16.1	9.0	1.1	0.2	50.4	12.8
45	D, 59		D, 61		D, 74		D, 78	21,206	21,975	4	55,033	22.6	8.8	25.5	12.0	1.2	0.4	42.4	17.1
46	R, 70		D, 52		D, 52		D, 52	43,148	47,063	9	53,204	31.2	13.9	20.5	34.1	9.3	0.6	27.9	12.4
47	R, 54		R, 62		R, 75			24,603	25,214	2	80,977	40.5	23.7	11.4	22.0	0.7	0.2	43.2	7.9
48	D, 54		D, 59		D, 56		D, 78	23,243	24,066	4	79,356	41.2	22.0	10.2	15.3	0.8	0.2	55.6	7.4
49			R, 53		D, 51		D, 74	22,022	22,562	2	96,973	45.2	28.5	8.5	25.7	0.8	0.1	44.1	7.3
50	R, 60		R, 78		R, 78			36,201	36,648	1	82,940	39.2	23.4	12.0	46.2	4.0	0.6	21.0	10.3
51	R, 52		D, 52		D, 64		D, 74	22,009	21,525	-2	81,983	38.8	25.1	7.1	27.7	1.1	0.2	38.7	8.9

Note: D=Democrat, R=Republican, R/D=Republican/Democrat (cross-filed), D/R=Democrat/Republican (cross-filed), I=Independent, C=Constitution, O=Other, GI=Green Independent, P=Progressive, P/D=Progressive/Democrat, P/D/R=Progressive/Democrat/Republican, HH=Households

IDAHO

There is irony in the fact that Idaho, now regarded as one of the most Republican and conservative states in the country, has produced three notable U.S. senators, with very different styles and viewpoints, from three different political parties. Republican William E. Borah was a national figure in the 1910s and 1920s, a brilliant orator, staunch opponent of the League of Nations, and advocate for recognizing the Soviet Union after the 1917 revolution. More recently, Democrat Frank Church chaired hearings into misconduct by the Central Intelligence Agency (CIA) and made a respectable though too-late run for the presidential nomination in 1976. In between was Glen Taylor, who became an early critic of nuclear proliferation and served as Henry Wallace's running mate on the Progressive Party ticket in 1948 (and gained some notoriety at the time for singing his acceptance speech to the convention). Clearly, Idaho appreciates mavericks.

Indeed, there are many unconventional corners here and those who try to characterize it too quickly are often wrong. The state, which made its reputation by pulling gold and silver from the ground, and still has some of the nation's largest reserves of both, now has a reputation for pulling something decidedly less glamorous—potatoes. One of its largest ethnic groups is Basques. On a more ominous note, Idaho was, until just a few years ago, home to the Aryan Nations, a white supremacist group. In 1992 it was the site of the infamous FBI shoot-out at Ruby Ridge. A century ago, however, Idaho was the site of left-wing violence, when Gov. Frank Steunenberg was assassinated by a bomb planted in his mailbox, and "Big Bill" Haywood, general secretary of the Western Federation of Miners, was tried for his murder and ultimately acquitted.

Long isolated from the rest of the country, Idaho has for the past two decades been very much a part of the Rocky Mountain surge. Its population soared by 28.5 percent during the 1990s, faster than Florida or Texas and the fifth-fastest rate in the country (the four states with faster growth were also located in the Mountain West). It has been the fourth-fastest growing state in this decade. Four state house districts around Caldwell and Boise (the 12th, 13th, 14th, and 21st) have grown by more than 25 percent during that time. The Boise metropolitan area, in fact, grew by more than 45 percent during the 1990s and by almost 13 percent from 2000 to 2004, in both cases among the fastest rates of growth in the country.

The state has no great extremes of wealth and poverty as do many states on the East Coast and Midwest. The wealthiest sections include all the districts in and around Boise. The poorest sections include the 12th house district, which takes in much of the sheep-grazing and fruit-growing region in the far southwest, and the logging areas in the mid-panhandle.

Race is not an issue in Idaho politics. Twenty-three of its thirty-five senate districts and forty of its seventy house districts are at least 85 percent white. Although Idaho has one of the fastest-growing African American populations, that merely shows the mirage of small numbers; according to the Census Bureau, there are still fewer than 3,400 African Americans in the entire state and they do not make up more than 1.5 percent of the population in any state house district. Two districts are at least a quarter Hispanic, many of them migrant farm workers.

Idaho has thirty-five legislative districts and elects one senator and two representatives from each, a practice used in three other western states, Oregon, Washington, and Arizona. Although Democrats have been able to win elections here (the state had Democratic governors continuously from 1970 to 1994), the many new arrivals, if anything, have made the state more conservative, as the governor, all the congressional representatives, and almost all statewide elected officials are now Republicans. Republicans also outnumber Democrats heavily in both chambers of the state legislature, although Democrats have made some modest gains during this decade. In 2004, however, the party failed to recruit a candidate for a U.S. senate race for the first time in state history.

Although essential to American democracy, state legislatures are generally not stepping stones to statewide office. Only twenty of the current governors, for example, ever served in the legislature, and only thirty-five of the current U.S. senators. Idaho, however, is an exception. Its governor and both senators are all veterans of the legislature. In no other state is this currently the case.

IDAHO
State Legislative Districts

NAMPA/BOISE

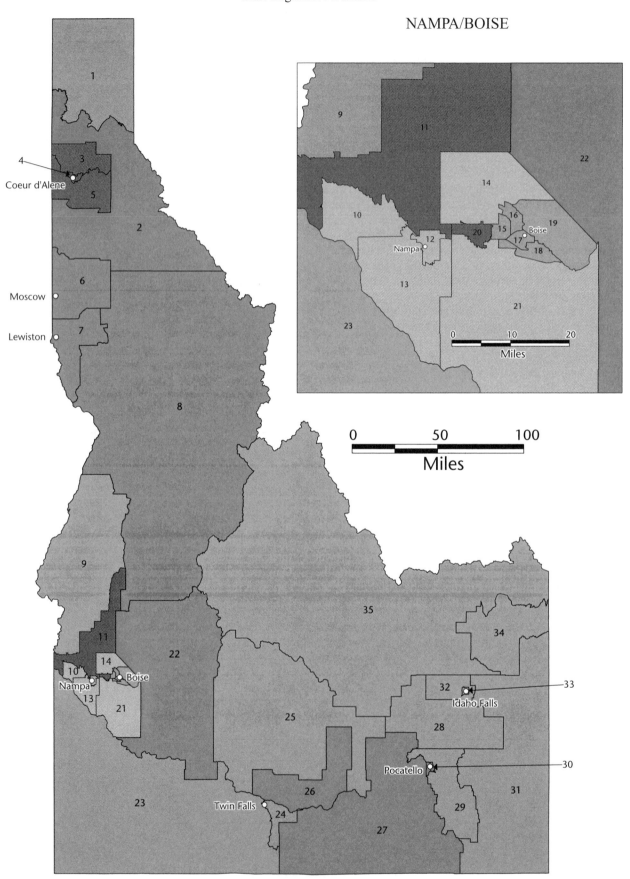

Population Growth   ■ -2% to 4%   ■ 4% to 14%   ■ 14% to 23%   ■ 23% to 35%

Idaho Legislative Districts—Election and Demographic Data

Senate Districts	General Election Results Party, Percent of Vote							Population			Avg. HH Income ($)	Pop 25+ Some College + (%)	Pop 25+ 4-Yr Degree + (%)	2006 Below Poverty Line (%)	2006 White (Non-Hisp) (%)	2006 African American (%)	2006 American Indians, Alaska Natives (%)	2006 Asians, Hawaiians, Pacific Islanders (%)	2006 Hispanic Origin (%)
Idaho	2000	2001	2002	2003	2004	2005	2006	2000	2006	% Change	($)	(%)	(%)	(%)	(%)	(%)	(%)	(%)	(%)
1	R, 73		R, 72		R, 75		R, 69	36,171	39,076	8	46,774	37.1	13.3	19.6	94.6	0.1	1.4	0.6	2.2
2	R, 69		D, 51		R, 53		R, 59	35,890	36,224	1	42,079	30.6	8.3	21.4	94.2	0.1	3.5	0.3	2.2
3	R, 82		R, 56		R, 100		R, 100	34,983	41,861	20	55,902	39.9	13.1	12.8	94.1	0.1	1.0	0.6	3.0
4	R, 100		R, 60		R, 100		R, 49	35,736	40,771	14	45,652	39.1	13.6	17.4	93.2	0.1	1.0	0.9	3.5
5	R, 82		R, 52		R, 71		R, 67	36,001	42,323	18	55,326	38.6	12.4	12.8	94.2	0.1	0.9	0.7	2.9
6	R, 100		R, 60		R, 100		R, 100	34,657	34,475	-1	46,554	45.9	27.5	21.5	91.8	0.4	0.9	2.9	2.6
7	R, 58		R, 53		R, 52		R, 51	37,712	37,761	0	49,383	38.5	13.6	16.7	89.2	0.2	6.6	0.9	2.1
8	R, 100		R, 61		R, 100		R, 52	35,866	35,264	0	42,822	35.2	12.4	19.1	93.0	0.1	2.8	0.5	2.2
9	R, 100		R, 68		R, 59		R, 61	35,776	37,483	5	44,505	29.0	8.1	19.9	79.6	0.1	1.1	1.2	14.0
10	R, 100		R, 100		R, 100		R, 100	35,169	43,597	24	47,504	26.5	8.5	18.7	57.8	0.2	1.1	1.4	30.5
11	R, 72		R, 76		R, 100		R, 77	36,584	43,046	18	46,186	29.7	7.9	17.2	80.1	0.1	1.0	0.7	13.5
12	R, 83		R, 61		R, 100		R, 66	36,133	45,746	27	43,030	28.0	9.4	17.0	67.4	0.2	1.5	1.5	22.4
13	R, 100		R, 70		R, 100		R, 71	37,222	49,886	34	53,755	33.8	12.3	12.7	78.7	0.2	1.0	1.3	13.7
14	R, 67		R, 79		R, 70		R, 68	39,550	50,407	27	84,457	47.9	28.0	6.0	91.7	0.3	0.6	2.0	3.9
15	R, 69		R, 59		R, 66		R, 62	36,494	39,761	9	59,715	46.0	22.5	9.1	87.9	0.4	0.8	3.7	5.2
16	R, 61		R, 54		D, 54		D, 100	37,211	39,947	7	59,470	46.3	24.1	11.5	85.4	0.3	1.1	2.3	8.2
17	R, 56		D, 54		D, 56		D, 67	36,522	38,383	5	47,723	41.8	19.6	14.7	83.7	0.6	1.3	3.0	8.6
18	R, 80		R, 68		D, 55		D, 63	36,767	38,866	6	64,420	48.4	26.9	8.8	87.3	0.5	0.8	3.6	5.6
19	D, 68		D, 71		D, 71		D, 75	39,077	42,783	9	71,432	56.0	37.1	12.0	89.8	0.4	0.8	2.2	4.9
20	R, 100		R, 65		R, 70		R, 64	34,930	42,198	21	65,569	42.3	20.6	8.7	90.4	0.3	0.6	1.9	4.9
21	D, 100		R, 58		R, 100		R, 100	40,363	50,977	26	71,188	42.4	19.9	6.6	89.0	0.2	1.1	1.9	6.0
22	R, 69		D, 49		R, 55		R, 68	35,979	36,169	1	47,137	39.3	11.6	14.5	80.1	1.5	1.2	2.1	11.6
23	R, 100		R, 56		R, 65		R, 63	36,455	39,299	8	44,210	30.0	8.7	19.4	74.7	0.1	1.9	0.8	17.3
24	R, 100		R, 100		R, 77		R, 100	36,682	39,159	7	51,436	35.0	11.8	16.2	85.4	0.1	0.8	1.4	9.8
25	R, 100		D, 64		D, 100		D, 100	38,224	41,533	9	67,599	40.4	20.2	13.5	75.9	0.1	0.8	0.8	17.9
26	R, 100		R, 71		R, 100		R, 100	38,518	38,047	-1	46,219	28.6	7.8	19.1	64.8	0.2	1.1	0.6	26.4
27	R, 79		R, 100		R, 100		R, 100	37,092	36,961	0	45,157	28.3	8.5	20.0	70.6	0.1	1.8	0.5	21.0
28	R, 100		R, 100		R, 68		R, 62	37,827	39,468	4	49,990	30.3	8.9	17.0	73.8	0.1	8.7	0.9	12.8
29	R, 74		D, 53		D, 51		D, 51	37,414	39,289	5	61,039	40.2	17.4	13.2	92.9	0.2	3.1	1.4	4.4
30	R, 100		D, 65		D, 100		D, 100	38,285	39,040	2	43,207	38.5	14.4	21.1	87.1	0.5	2.1	1.6	6.2
31	R, 100		R, 76		R, 100		R, 100	38,554	42,582	10	51,753	32.7	10.7	14.8	90.4	0.1	0.5	0.3	6.5
32	R, 100		R, 69		R, 72		R, 69	75,492	83,111	10	58,002	38.2	16.6	14.7	85.3	0.3	0.9	1.3	9.4
33	D, 63		R, 59		R, 100		R, 60	38,048	40,659	7	51,349	37.3	16.4	15.8	82.9	0.4	1.1	1.4	11.0
34	R, 63		R, 100		R, 100		R, 93	38,484	42,842	11	45,302	33.6	11.5	20.8	89.2	0.1	0.5	0.9	6.8
35	R, 100		R, 76		R, 77		R, 69	35,976	37,725	5	46,170	33.3	10.0	18.7	87.1	0.1	0.7	0.3	8.3

Note: D=Democrat, R=Republican, R/D=Republican/Democrat (cross-filed), D/R=Democrat/Republican (cross-filed), I=Independent, C=Constitution, O=Other, GI=Green Independent, P=Progressive, P/D=Progressive/Democrat, P/D/R=Progressive/Democrat/Republican, HH=Households

Idaho Legislative Districts—Election and Demographic Data

House Districts	General Election Results Party, Percent of Vote							Population			Avg. HH Income	Pop 25+		Below Poverty Line	2006 White (Non-Hisp)	African American	American Indians, Alaska Natives	Asians, Hawaiians, Pacific Islanders	Hispanic Origin
Idaho	2000	2001	2002	2003	2004	2005	2006	2000	2006	% Change	($)	Some College + (%)	4-Yr Degree + (%)	(%)	(%)	(%)	(%)	(%)	(%)
1A	R, 61		R, 55		R, 50		R, 51	36,171	39,076	8	46,774	37.1	13.3	19.6	94.6	0.1	1.4	0.6	2.2
1B	R, 53		R, 65		R, 100		R, 63	36,171	39,076	8	46,774	37.1	13.3	19.6	94.6	0.1	1.4	0.6	2.2
2A	R, 65		D, 57		D, 74		D, 100	35,890	36,224	1	42,079	30.6	8.3	21.4	94.2	0.1	3.5	0.3	2.2
2B	R, 100		R, 51		R, 58		R, 56	35,890	36,224	1	42,079	30.6	8.3	21.4	94.2	0.1	3.5	0.3	2.2
3A	R, 100		R, 100		R, 100		R, 100	34,983	41,861	20	55,902	39.9	13.1	12.8	94.1	0.1	1.0	0.6	3.0
3B	R, 57		R, 68		R, 91		R, 100	34,983	41,861	20	55,902	39.9	13.1	12.8	94.1	0.1	1.0	0.6	3.0
4A	D, 51		D, 48		R, 54		R, 54	35,736	40,771	14	45,652	39.1	13.6	17.4	93.2	0.1	1.0	0.9	3.5
4B	R, 83		D, 49		D, 51		D, 57	35,736	40,771	14	45,652	39.1	13.6	17.4	93.2	0.1	1.0	0.9	3.5
5A	R, 66		R, 56		R, 64		R, 64	36,001	42,323	18	55,326	38.6	12.4	12.8	94.2	0.1	0.9	0.7	2.9
5B	R, 51		R, 54		R, 69		R, 66	36,001	42,323	18	55,326	38.6	12.4	12.8	94.2	0.1	0.9	0.7	2.9
6A	R, 100		R, 100		R, 61		R, 100	34,657	34,475	-1	46,554	45.9	27.5	21.5	91.8	0.4	0.9	2.9	2.6
6B	R, 66		D, 53		D, 55		D, 62	34,657	34,475	-1	46,554	45.9	27.5	21.5	91.8	0.4	0.9	2.9	2.6
7A	D, 100		D, 52		D, 57		D, 55	37,712	37,761	0	49,383	38.5	13.6	16.7	89.2	0.2	6.6	0.9	2.1
7B	R, 54		D, 60		D, 51		D, 100	37,712	37,761	0	49,383	38.5	13.6	16.7	89.2	0.2	6.6	0.9	2.1
8A	R, 70		R, 60		R, 57		R, 53	35,866	35,264	0	42,822	35.2	12.4	19.1	93.0	0.1	2.8	0.5	2.2
8B	R, 100		D, 52		R, 50		R, 61	35,866	35,264	0	42,822	35.2	12.4	19.1	93.0	0.1	2.8	0.5	2.2
9A	R, 100		R, 62		R, 100		R, 100	35,776	37,483	5	44,505	29.0	8.1	19.9	79.6	0.1	1.1	1.2	14.0
9B	R, 58		R, 80		R, 100		R, 100	35,776	37,483	5	44,505	29.0	8.1	19.9	79.6	0.1	1.1	1.2	14.0
10A	R, 100		R, 70		R, 100		R, 100	35,169	43,597	24	47,504	26.5	8.5	18.7	57.8	0.2	1.1	1.4	30.5
10B	R, 100		R, 100		R, 100		R, 66	35,169	43,597	24	47,504	26.5	8.5	18.7	57.8	0.2	1.1	1.4	30.5
11A	R, 100		R, 100		R, 78		R, 75	36,584	43,046	18	46,186	29.7	7.9	17.2	80.1	0.1	1.0	0.7	13.5
11B	R, 74		R, 100		R, 70		R, 100	36,584	43,046	18	46,186	29.7	7.9	17.2	80.1	0.1	1.0	0.7	13.5
12A	R, 100		R, 77		R, 100		R, 63	36,133	45,746	27	43,030	28.0	9.4	17.0	67.4	0.2	1.5	1.5	22.4
12B	R, 100		R, 65		R, 70		R, 68	36,133	45,746	27	43,030	28.0	9.4	17.0	67.4	0.2	1.5	1.5	22.4
13A	R, 100		R, 67		R, 100		R, 69	37,222	49,886	34	53,755	33.8	12.3	12.7	78.7	0.2	1.0	1.3	13.7
13B	R, 57		R, 80		R, 81		R, 100	37,222	49,886	34	53,755	33.8	12.3	12.7	78.7	0.2	1.0	1.3	13.7
14A	R, 69		R, 65		R, 100		R, 100	39,550	50,407	27	84,457	47.9	28.0	6.0	91.7	0.3	0.6	2.0	3.9
14B	R, 61		R, 59		R, 70		R, 66	39,550	50,407	27	84,457	47.9	28.0	6.0	91.7	0.3	0.6	2.0	3.9
15A	R, 72		R, 63		R, 80		R, 55	36,494	39,761	9	59,715	46.0	22.5	9.1	87.9	0.4	0.8	3.7	5.2
15B	R, 63		R, 53		R, 77		R, 74	36,494	39,761	9	59,715	46.0	22.5	9.1	87.9	0.4	0.8	3.7	5.2
16A	D, 57		R, 79		D, 57		D, 100	37,211	39,947	7	59,470	46.3	24.1	11.5	85.4	0.3	1.1	2.3	8.2
16B	R, 58		D, 54		R, 51		D, 53	37,211	39,947	7	59,470	46.3	24.1	11.5	85.4	0.3	1.1	2.3	8.2
17A	R, 51		R, 51		R, 50		D, 57	36,522	38,383	5	47,723	41.8	19.6	14.7	83.7	0.6	1.3	3.0	8.6
17B	R, 100		R, 48		R, 52		D, 58	36,522	38,383	5	47,723	41.8	19.6	14.7	83.7	0.6	1.3	3.0	8.6
18A	R, 65		R, 60		R, 59		D, 49	36,767	38,866	6	64,420	48.4	26.9	8.8	87.3	0.5	0.8	3.6	5.6
18B	R, 72		R, 56		R, 55		D, 53	36,767	38,866	6	64,420	48.4	26.9	8.8	87.3	0.5	0.8	3.6	5.6
19A	D, 67		D, 86		R, 71		D, 100	39,077	42,783	9	71,432	56.0	37.1	12.0	89.8	0.4	0.8	2.2	4.9
19B	D, 75		D, 83		D, 67		D, 100	39,077	42,783	9	71,432	56.0	37.1	12.0	89.8	0.4	0.8	2.2	4.9
20A	R, 73		R, 68		R, 85		R, 81	34,930	42,198	21	65,569	42.3	20.6	8.7	90.4	0.3	0.6	1.9	4.9
20B	R, 100		R, 64		R, 66		R, 66	34,930	42,198	21	65,569	42.3	20.6	8.7	90.4	0.3	0.6	1.9	4.9
21A	D, 100		R, 62		R, 70		R, 100	40,363	50,977	26	71,188	42.4	19.9	6.6	89.0	0.2	1.1	1.9	6.0
21B	R, 61		R, 65		R, 100		R, 100	40,363	50,977	26	71,188	42.4	19.9	6.6	89.0	0.2	1.1	1.9	6.0
22A	R, 85		R, 100		R, 72		R, 61	35,979	36,169	1	47,137	39.3	11.6	14.5	80.1	1.5	1.2	2.1	11.6
22B	R, 100		R, 54		R, 55		R, 56	35,979	36,169	1	47,137	39.3	11.6	14.5	80.1	1.5	1.2	2.1	11.6
23A	R, 100		R, 60		R, 71		R, 68	36,455	39,299	8	44,210	30.0	8.7	19.4	74.7	0.1	1.9	0.8	17.3
23B	R, 84		R, 67		R, 100		R, 100	36,455	39,299	8	44,210	30.0	8.7	19.4	74.7	0.1	1.9	0.8	17.3
24A	R, 76		R, 100		R, 100		R, 100	36,682	39,159	7	51,436	35.0	11.8	16.2	85.4	0.1	0.8	1.4	9.8
24B	R, 80		R, 67		R, 66		R, 100	36,682	39,159	7	51,436	35.0	11.8	16.2	85.4	0.1	0.8	1.4	9.8
25A	R, 100		D, 100		D, 100		D, 100	38,224	41,533	9	67,599	40.4	20.2	13.5	75.9	0.1	0.8	0.8	17.9
25B	R, 100		R, 51		D, 51		D, 100	38,224	41,533	9	67,599	40.4	20.2	13.5	75.9	0.1	0.8	0.8	17.9

(continued)

Note: D=Democrat, R=Republican, R/D=Republican/Democrat (cross-filed), D/R=Democrat/Republican (cross-filed), I=Independent, C=Constitution, O=Other, GI=Green Independent, P=Progressive, P/D=Progressive/Democrat, P/D/R=Progressive/Democrat/Republican, HH=Households

Idaho Legislative Districts—Election and Demographic Data (cont.)

House Districts	General Election Results Party, Percent of Vote							Population			Avg. HH Income	Pop 25+		Below Poverty Line	2006 White (Non-Hisp)	African American	American Indians, Alaska Natives	Asians, Hawaiians, Pacific Islanders	Hispanic Origin
												Some College +	4-Yr Degree +						
Idaho	2000	2001	2002	2003	2004	2005	2006	2000	2006	% Change	($)	(%)	(%)	(%)	(%)	(%)	(%)	(%)	(%)
26A	R, 100		R, 100		R, 78		R, 67	38,518	38,047	-1	46,219	28.6	7.8	19.1	64.8	0.2	1.1	0.6	26.4
26B	R, 74		R, 100		R, 100		R, 100	38,518	38,047	-1	46,219	28.6	7.8	19.1	64.8	0.2	1.1	0.6	26.4
27A	R, 73		R, 66		R, 100		R, 100	37,092	36,961	0	45,157	28.3	8.5	20.0	70.6	0.1	1.8	0.5	21.0
27B	R, 77		R, 100		R, 83		R, 100	37,092	36,961	0	45,157	28.3	8.5	20.0	70.6	0.1	1.8	0.5	21.0
28A	R, 100		R, 59		R, 55		R, 55	37,827	39,468	4	49,990	30.3	8.9	17.0	73.8	0.1	8.7	0.9	12.8
28B	R, 100		R, 73		R, 100		R, 63	37,827	39,468	4	49,990	30.3	8.9	17.0	73.8	0.1	8.7	0.9	12.8
29A	R, 100		D, 50		R, 52		R, 51	37,414	39,289	5	61,039	40.2	17.4	13.2	92.9	0.2	3.1	1.4	4.4
29B	R, 100		D, 53		D, 51		D, 51	37,414	39,289	5	61,039	40.2	17.4	13.2	92.9	0.2	3.1	1.4	4.4
30A	R, 100		D, 60		D, 60		D, 100	38,285	39,040	2	43,207	38.5	14.4	21.1	87.1	0.5	2.1	1.6	6.2
30B	R, 62		D, 53		D, 53		D, 62	38,285	39,040	2	43,207	38.5	14.4	21.1	87.1	0.5	2.1	1.6	6.2
31A	R, 100		R, 70		R, 100		R, 100	38,554	42,582	10	51,753	32.7	10.7	14.8	90.4	0.1	0.5	0.3	6.5
31B	R, 100		R, 61		R, 100		R, 100	38,554	42,582	10	51,753	32.7	10.7	14.8	90.4	0.1	0.5	0.3	6.5
32A	R, 100		R, 100		R, 100		R, 71	75,492	83,111	10	58,002	38.2	16.6	14.7	85.3	0.3	0.9	1.3	9.4
32B	R, 80		R, 65		R, 100		R, 100	75,492	83,111	10	58,002	38.2	16.6	14.7	85.3	0.3	0.9	1.3	9.4
33A	D, 100		R, 61		R, 64		D, 51	38,048	40,659	7	51,349	37.3	16.4	15.8	82.9	0.4	1.1	1.4	11.0
33B	D, 56		R, 45		R, 100		R, 53	38,048	40,659	7	51,349	37.3	16.4	15.8	82.9	0.4	1.1	1.4	11.0
34A	D, 52		R, 100		R, 91		R, 100	38,484	42,842	11	45,302	33.6	11.5	20.8	89.2	0.1	0.5	0.9	6.8
34B	R, 78		R, 100		R, 86		R, 100	38,484	42,842	11	45,302	33.6	11.5	20.8	89.2	0.1	0.5	0.9	6.8
35A	R, 58		R, 75		R, 100		R, 100	35,976	37,725	5	46,170	33.3	10.0	18.7	87.1	0.1	0.7	0.3	8.3
35B	R, 63		R, 100		R, 99		R, 72	35,976	37,725	5	46,170	33.3	10.0	18.7	87.1	0.1	0.7	0.3	8.3

Note: D=Democrat, R=Republican, R/D=Republican/Democrat (cross-filed), D/R=Democrat/Republican (cross-filed), I=Independent, C=Constitution, O=Other, GI=Green Independent, P=Progressive, P/D=Progressive/Democrat, P/D/R=Progressive/Democrat/Republican, HH=Households

Illinois has recuperated, or at least stabilized, after a rough twenty years, but it continues to lose prominence in a changing country. The state's population grew just 3 percent during the 1970s, and not at all during the 1980s. That has improved somewhat. It grew by 8.7 percent during the 1990s; slow but still better than other Rust Belt behemoths—New York, Pennsylvania, Ohio, and Michigan.

After slipping behind Pennsylvania in population during the 1980s, Illinois passed Pennsylvania in the 1990s to once again become the country's fifth-largest state. Illinois, however, is projected to lose a congressional district in the next round of reapportionment and as many as three during the next three decades.

Population gains have occurred almost entirely in Chicago's outer suburbs. Like many other cities, Chicago has seen a hollowing out of the urban core and a widening of the suburban doughnuts. The original ring suburbs—Cicero, Des Plaines, Skokie, Evanston—are full and many are developing urban-type problems of their own. So residents, predominantly white, have moved still further out into Kane, Kendall, and Will Counties, places as much as forty miles from the Loop. The 84th house district, in the outer part of Will County, has grown by 64 percent in the last six years. Increasingly people commute not to jobs downtown, but to other suburbs.

Sixty-nine of 118 state house districts (58 percent) have either lost population during this decade or made no gain. Losses have been sharpest in rural areas farther from the big cities, especially the 74th district, in Knox County, and the 101st, in Macon County, both of which have shrunk by about 5 percent.

As for Chicago itself, while its population has grown slightly in this decade, the city's growth has occurred almost entirely among immigrants. There has been a domestic outflow of more than 400,000 people, offset however, by an influx of more than 377,000 immigrants, from places both old and new. According to the Institute for Metropolitan Affairs at Roosevelt University, the countries that have produced the largest number of foreign-born residents in the greater Chicago area are Mexico, Poland, and India.

The racial composition of Chicago is also changing. Illinois is 15 percent African American and that is overwhelmingly centered in Chicago, which has more black residents than any other city in the country, the legacy of the great migration of southern blacks in search of industrial jobs after World War II. Today, eighteen state house districts have a black majority, many of them appallingly poor. To the extent blacks are migrating, it is to some of the older, closer-in suburbs that whites are leaving.

What is changing the face of Chicago is its Hispanic population. Illinois is 10 percent Hispanic, but as much as 92 percent of that Hispanic population lives in Chicago and the surrounding suburban counties. Its rapid rate of increase has led some to rechristen Illinois "the Land of Lincoln and Latinos." Chicago's Hispanic population, however, is not monolithic; it is roughly two-thirds Mexican and one-third Puerto Rican, and there has been some friction between the groups. There has also been friction between Hispanics and blacks in Chicago, most notably over the effect that creation of an Hispanic-majority congressional district would have on black political influence in surrounding districts.

Certainly, this is not the last struggle between Chicago's ethnic groups, but as the city comes to cast a smaller share of the state's vote, the current mayor, Richard M. Daley, will not have the same ability his father once had to influence national or even state elections. The days when Daley could hope to control the city without Hispanic support have already ended.

Historically, downstate politicians who controlled state politics kept the city of Chicago underrepresented in the legislature. They ignored a provision in the state constitution requiring reapportionment every decade, so that by the 1920s the city held only a third of the seats in the general assembly even though it accounted for half the state's population. Some Chicago state house districts had five times as many people as others.

Even today, the Illinois general assembly has several unusual characteristics. State senators run for two four-year terms and one two-year term in the course of a decade, in order to make sure that all do not come up for election in the same year. As recently as the 1960s, the state house of representatives had 177 members, three elected from each of fifty-nine legislative districts under a system of cumulative voting. Voters could cast all three of their votes for a single candidate, give one vote to each of three candidates, or even one and a half to each of two candidates. As Lord Bryce observed in *The American Commonwealth* (1888), "So far as I have been able to gather, experience has not commended the scheme, and it has not improved the quality of the legislature." In 1980 it was scrapped and the size of the house was reduced to 118 seats.

Politically, the Illinois legislature was one of the nation's battlegrounds not very long ago, but a truce has been declared. The Democrats, who controlled both chambers of the general assembly in 1990, lost both in the Republican sweep of 1994. Two years later, they retook the house by the slimmest of margins, 60–58, while the GOP held on to the senate, 31–28. Democrats retook the state senate in 2004, part of a backlash against corruption in Springfield that ultimately sent former Republican governor Jim Ryan to prison. Democrats also made small gains in the state house. The Illinois congressional delegation is almost evenly split, thanks to a reapportionment plan engineered in 2000 by then House Speaker J. Dennis Hastert that protected incumbents of both parties.

The Land of Lincoln has not produced a serious presidential contender since Adlai Stevenson half a century ago. That should change in 2008 when Illinois senator Barak Obama faces Chicago native Hillary Rodham Clinton in the Democratic primaries.

ILLINOIS
State Senate Districts

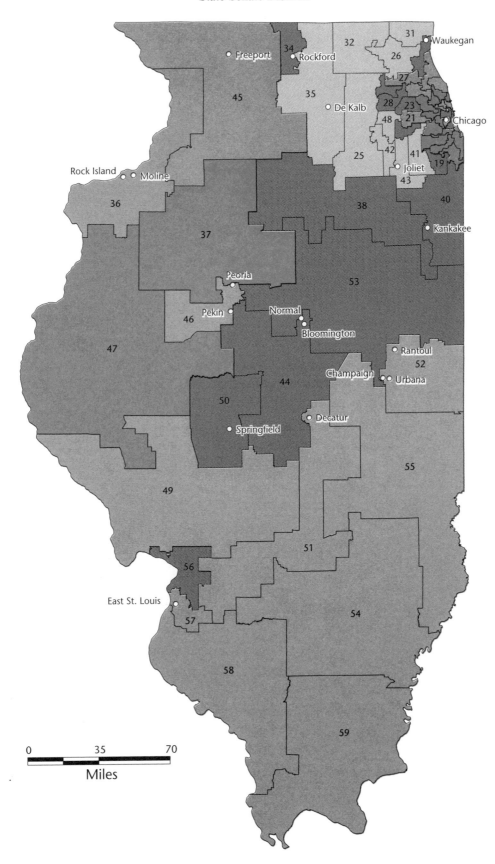

Population Growth   ▨ -4% to -2%   ▨ -2% to 2%   ■ 2% to 11%   ▨ 11% to 42%

CHICAGO

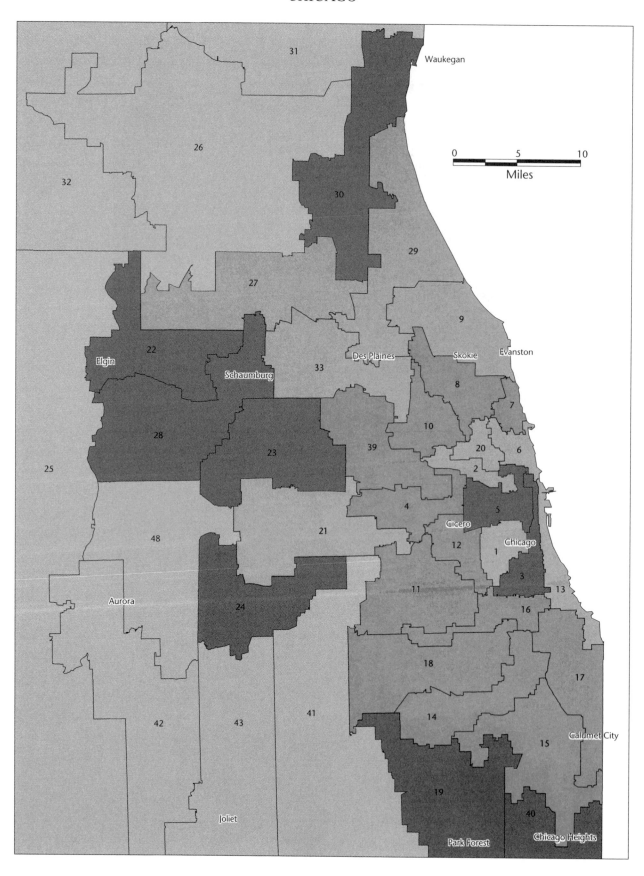

Population Growth ■ -4% to -2% ■ -2% to 2% ■ 2% to 11% □ 11% to 42%

Illinois State Senate Districts—Election and Demographic Data

Senate Districts	General Election Results Party, Percent of Vote							Population			Avg. HH Income ($)	2006 Pop 25+ Some College + (%)	4-Yr Degree + (%)	Below Poverty Line (%)	White (Non-Hisp) (%)	African American (%)	American Indians, Alaska Natives (%)	Asians, Hawaiians, Pacific Islanders (%)	Hispanic Origin (%)
Illinois	2000	2001	2002	2003	2004	2005	2006	2000	2006	% Change	($)	(%)	(%)	(%)	(%)	(%)	(%)	(%)	(%)
1			D, 100				D, 83	204,380	200,503	-2	44,612	21.5	10.3	24.6	13.7	13.0	0.4	6.1	73.7
2			D, 100		D, 100			210,976	208,967	-1	53,208	27.0	14.4	21.8	18.4	14.1	0.3	3.4	67.3
3	D, 100		D, 100		D, 100		D, 90	209,880	215,169	3	56,750	32.7	18.8	30.4	28.0	52.4	0.2	8.1	15.6
4			D, 85				D, 88	215,982	208,284	-4	60,968	34.8	17.2	16.3	31.3	54.1	0.1	3.4	14.2
5			D, 100		D, 86			215,694	229,038	6	66,246	34.5	21.0	26.8	28.6	53.7	0.2	5.2	16.2
6	D, 70		D, 100				D, 81	213,644	211,356	-1	95,841	61.4	49.5	8.6	67.5	8.2	0.2	6.4	14.9
7			D, 100				D, 87	212,754	206,814	-3	50,095	44.7	29.2	19.5	41.7	19.2	0.3	13.4	26.4
8			D, 69		D, 72			210,558	204,222	-3	73,687	44.0	27.3	12.1	55.1	7.0	0.2	20.6	16.0
9	D, 100		D, 100				D, 100	213,560	211,843	-1	125,339	52.9	39.6	8.8	65.0	13.7	0.1	10.2	9.4
10			D, 100				D, 100	211,335	204,621	-3	66,665	38.4	19.2	10.2	69.3	5.2	0.1	4.9	17.0
11			D, 100		D, 69			210,326	205,089	-2	62,048	33.3	15.2	11.4	62.4	8.4	0.1	2.6	22.5
12	D, 94		D, 64				D, 100	207,553	200,880	-3	50,930	22.7	10.3	17.6	16.6	9.4	0.4	2.7	71.8
13			D, 100				D, 90	211,566	213,335	1	65,297	44.0	27.1	24.3	28.1	58.0	0.1	5.3	10.9
14			D, 100		D, 100			207,477	201,136	-3	62,638	36.4	16.3	15.0	35.1	54.6	0.1	1.9	10.1
15	D, 100		H, 40				D, 100	208,161	203,325	-2	54,732	34.7	14.2	16.6	36.5	53.0	0.1	1.9	10.0
16			D, 89				D, 92	206,609	198,951	-4	48,626	29.7	12.1	23.1	27.8	58.4	0.2	2.0	15.1
17			D, 100		D, 100			214,641	206,702	-4	52,104	35.4	15.1	18.9	26.0	59.3	0.2	1.7	17.6
18	R, 57		D, 69				D, 100	214,251	208,251	-3	69,622	40.1	20.1	9.7	72.5	14.6	0.1	2.6	8.4
19			D, 67				D, 77	208,740	216,591	4	73,281	41.3	20.1	8.0	59.7	28.4	0.1	3.3	8.1
20	R, 100		D, 100		D, 100		0	204,137	200,477	-2	52,453	29.5	15.6	17.9	22.9	9.7	0.3	7.6	60.6
21	R, 65		R, 100				R, 100	210,096	213,765	2	94,292	49.4	31.8	6.6	79.3	3.8	0.1	7.4	7.9
22			R, 57				D, 54	209,304	225,105	8	69,566	34.4	17.1	7.7	47.2	8.0	0.2	8.4	33.9
23			R, 100		R, 100			213,603	218,505	2	83,602	41.3	23.4	6.7	67.4	2.6	0.1	10.0	18.1
24	R, 52		R, 70				R, 100	211,395	220,554	4	110,372	51.6	35.9	5.2	78.0	3.3	0.1	11.1	6.5
25			R, 100				R, 65	211,931	286,325	35	93,470	43.8	23.7	4.9	82.3	2.4	0.1	2.2	11.0
26			R, 100		R, 61			213,775	245,226	15	119,290	46.9	29.8	5.3	81.9	1.3	0.1	4.0	10.5
27	R, 51		R, 60				R, 53	209,685	207,186	-1	97,365	49.4	31.5	5.1	72.2	5.3	0.1	8.6	11.9
28	R, 61		R, 68		R, 100		R, 100	210,762	219,598	4	93,712	44.6	25.8	4.5	72.7	3.8	0.1	11.5	10.7
29			D, 56		D, 71			212,368	215,663	2	130,446	50.7	36.5	6.4	70.8	4.4	0.1	10.4	12.5
30	D, 55		D, 58				D, 63	207,076	221,074	7	89,132	37.2	23.5	10.2	44.0	14.7	0.3	7.2	33.8
31			R, 69				D, 51	209,298	235,790	13	76,140	40.3	22.3	7.3	71.7	6.0	0.2	3.9	15.2
32			R, 70		R, 62			208,799	253,501	21	83,953	41.6	20.8	6.1	83.6	0.7	0.1	2.0	11.2
33	R, 100		R, 100				D, 51	210,036	205,949	-2	77,837	44.8	26.3	7.1	68.6	5.5	0.1	9.1	14.8
34			R, 100				R, 56	210,364	216,898	3	53,749	31.0	12.1	14.6	71.2	12.8	0.2	2.1	11.7
35			R, 100		R, 66			210,103	234,657	12	68,028	35.9	16.4	12.0	81.2	3.1	0.1	2.3	10.5
36	D, 100		D, 100				D, 61	210,755	207,224	-2	54,181	32.5	11.4	13.6	82.8	5.5	0.1	1.1	8.2
37			R, 53				R, 60	211,649	207,279	-2	59,279	36.1	14.9	12.0	91.2	3.4	0.1	1.5	2.7
38			D, 58		R, 52			210,919	223,829	6	57,925	31.0	10.4	12.1	90.3	1.0	0.1	0.8	6.3
39	R, 100		D, 100				D, 77	206,180	199,519	-3	71,289	35.8	19.1	13.4	49.1	21.4	0.2	4.3	25.4
40			D, 100				D, 70	212,204	222,592	5	61,018	33.8	13.9	13.2	63.1	23.1	0.1	1.2	11.4
41			R, 72		R, 100			209,666	245,316	17	105,677	46.5	27.0	4.3	84.7	3.0	0.1	4.3	6.8
42	R, 64		R, 63				D, 52	209,585	295,770	41	77,651	36.6	19.2	7.4	57.4	7.8	0.2	2.6	28.4
43			D, 100				D, 70	211,571	259,692	23	65,200	36.9	16.3	10.0	58.4	17.9	0.2	2.9	19.4
44			R, 63		R, 100			212,085	217,257	2	62,850	37.3	19.3	11.1	90.0	4.4	0.1	1.9	2.5
45	R, 100		R, 100				R, 100	210,707	211,996	1	56,119	31.1	10.6	12.7	90.0	3.0	0.1	0.6	4.6
46			D, 100				D, 58	208,064	203,968	-2	49,256	30.8	10.4	17.7	81.5	13.6	0.2	1.1	2.5
47			D, 52		D, 62			210,300	203,403	-3	46,842	29.6	11.4	17.3	93.5	2.3	0.1	0.7	2.4
48	R, 100		R, 100				R, 100	209,891	235,137	12	103,124	49.2	33.5	4.5	74.9	3.6	0.1	7.4	12.6
49			D, 100		D, 100		D, 60	211,044	210,477	0	47,983	27.4	9.1	16.6	95.5	2.3	0.1	0.4	1.0
50			R, 71		R, 100			210,151	214,500	2	60,540	38.1	19.0	11.9	86.8	9.4	0.1	1.4	1.4

(continued)

Note: D=Democrat, R=Republican, R/D=Republican/Democrat (cross-filed), D/R=Democrat/Republican (cross-filed), I=Independent, C=Constitution, O=Other, GI=Green Independent, P=Progressive, P/D=Progressive/Democrat, P/D/R=Progressive/Democrat/Republican, HH=Households

Illinois State Senate Districts—Election and Demographic Data (cont.)

Senate Districts	General Election Results Party, Percent of Vote							Population			Avg. HH Income	Pop 25+		Below Poverty Line	2006 White (Non-Hisp)	African American	American Indians, Alaska Natives	Asians, Hawaiians, Pacific Islanders	Hispanic Origin
												Some College +	4-Yr Degree +						
Illinois	2000	2001	2002	2003	2004	2005	2006	2000	2006	% Change	($)	(%)	(%)	(%)	(%)	(%)	(%)	(%)	(%)
51	R, 71		R, 59				R, 100	210,927	208,540	-1	53,945	30.9	11.9	15.7	88.2	8.8	0.1	0.6	1.4
52			R, 51				D, 49	211,862	214,196	1	45,409	37.3	19.3	19.8	75.5	12.4	0.1	6.4	4.1
53			R, 100		R, 100			208,520	216,536	4	64,862	35.4	16.4	10.6	92.2	2.5	0.1	1.6	2.5
54	D, 100		R, 54				R, 65	210,357	206,666	-2	46,614	29.5	8.6	18.2	94.5	3.0	0.1	0.6	1.2
55			R, 68				R, 100	210,264	207,982	-1	49,633	31.5	11.5	16.8	95.5	1.4	0.1	0.6	1.6
56			D, 100		D, 66			212,393	217,229	2	57,393	38.7	15.3	13.2	88.7	7.2	0.1	1.0	2.0
57	D, 75		D, 67				D, 100	208,704	210,047	1	50,878	36.1	14.7	19.8	61.6	33.5	0.2	1.1	3.0
58			R, 63				R, 100	210,635	212,230	1	51,137	33.3	13.2	19.9	87.8	7.5	0.1	1.3	2.1
59	D, 59		D, 70		D, 53			210,134	211,070	0	42,800	30.7	9.4	22.5	92.1	5.2	0.2	0.4	1.4

Note: D=Democrat, R=Republican, R/D=Republican/Democrat (cross-filed), D/R=Democrat/Republican (cross-filed), I=Independent, C=Constitution, O=Other, GI=Green Independent, P=Progressive, P/D=Progressive/Democrat, P/D/R=Progressive/Democrat/Republican, HH=Households

ILLINOIS
State House Districts

EAST ST. LOUIS

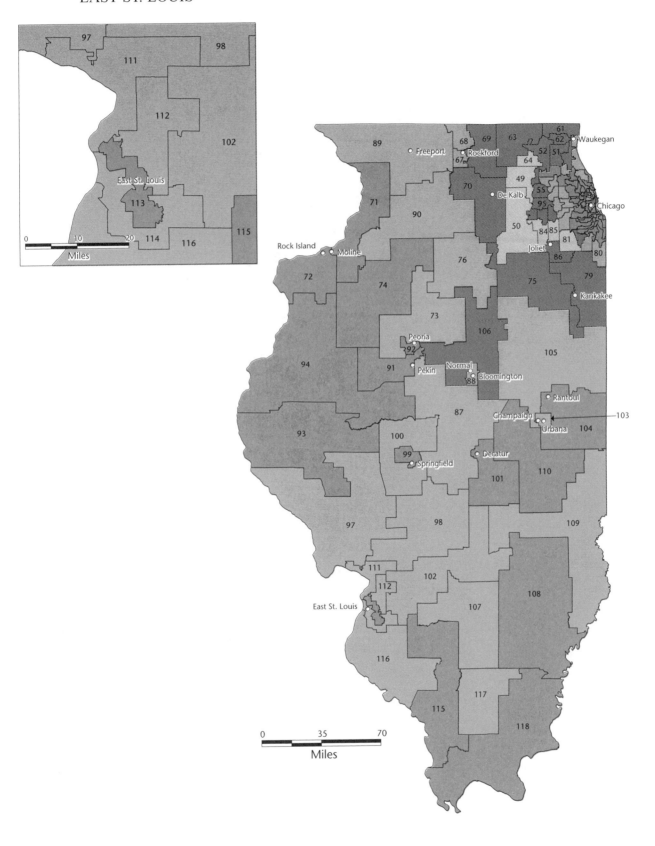

Population Growth ▦ -6% to -1% ▦ -1% to 6% ▦ 6% to 27% ▦ 27% to 65%

CHICAGO

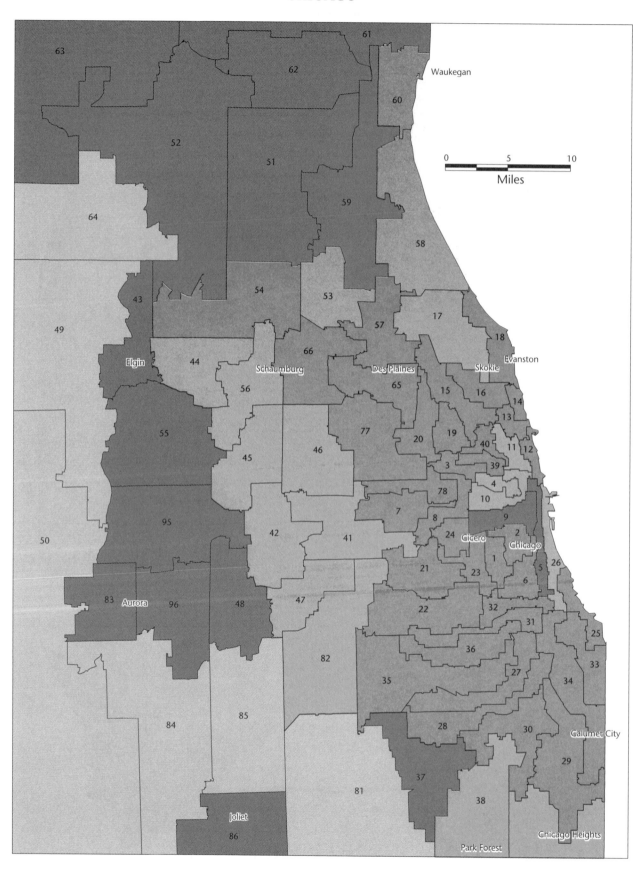

Population Growth   ■ -6% to -1%   ■ -1% to 6%   ■ 6% to 27%   ■ 27% to 65%

Illinois State House Districts—Election and Demographic Data

House Districts	General Election Results Party, Percent of Vote							Population			Avg. HH Income ($)	Pop 25+ Some College + (%)	Pop 25+ 4-Yr Degree + (%)	Below Poverty Line (%)	2006 White (Non-Hisp) (%)	African American (%)	American Indians, Alaska Natives (%)	Asians, Hawaiians, Pacific Islanders (%)	Hispanic Origin (%)
Illinois	2000	2001	2002	2003	2004	2005	2006	2000	2006	% Change	($)	(%)	(%)	(%)	(%)	(%)	(%)	(%)	(%)
1	D, 100		D, 100		D, 100		D, 91	98,142	96,177	-2	45,690	19.8	9.2	23.5	12.2	14.1	0.4	3.4	76.8
2	D, 100		D, 83		D, 100		D, 100	106,723	104,465	-2	43,746	23.0	11.3	25.4	14.9	12.0	0.4	8.3	71.1
3	D, 100		D, 100		D, 100		D, 100	108,141	105,992	-2	55,211	24.2	11.3	18.5	17.1	10.9	0.3	3.7	70.8
4	D, 100		D, 100		D, 100		D, 100	103,695	103,464	0	51,576	29.8	17.6	24.2	19.6	17.3	0.4	3.0	63.4
5	D, 100		D, 83		D, 82		D, 86	98,183	107,218	9	68,002	41.5	27.3	28.3	34.0	50.2	0.1	9.9	7.0
6	D, 100		D, 100		D, 100		D, 100	110,557	106,373	-4	39,645	23.6	10.0	34.5	22.3	54.7	0.2	6.3	24.4
7	D, 100		D, 85		D, 100		D, 100	102,579	98,430	-4	66,062	37.6	18.9	13.4	32.7	53.4	0.1	3.7	12.8
8	D, 100		D, 76		D, 79		D, 84	114,466	110,512	-3	55,905	32.3	15.7	19.4	30.2	54.7	0.1	3.1	15.5
9	D, 100		D, 93		D, 100		D, 89	112,588	124,680	11	60,828	34.1	20.7	29.1	25.8	54.3	0.2	7.5	16.6
10	D, 100		D, 100		D, 87		D, 100	102,859	103,669	1	72,686	35.0	21.5	23.9	32.1	53.2	0.1	2.4	15.3
11	D, 68		D, 87		D, 72		D, 83	107,852	108,427	1	101,104	55.2	43.3	8.9	62.8	7.5	0.2	6.0	20.0
12	D, 75		D, 74		D, 76		D, 81	106,403	103,156	-3	91,803	67.8	55.8	8.3	72.4	8.9	0.1	6.9	9.7
13	D, 100		D, 82		D, 100		D, 100	107,197	105,269	-2	53,683	46.1	30.5	19.7	43.0	16.3	0.3	14.9	26.0
14	R, 62		D, 80		D, 100		D, 90	105,533	101,183	-4	46,259	43.1	27.8	19.2	40.3	22.3	0.3	11.8	26.9
15	D, 78		D, 68		D, 67		D, 100	108,144	105,373	-3	77,705	44.1	26.6	10.9	58.4	5.4	0.2	17.7	16.8
16	D, 100		D, 76		D, 77		D, 100	103,282	99,335	-4	69,177	44.0	28.1	13.4	51.3	8.7	0.2	23.8	15.1
17	D, 87		R, 51		R, 54		R, 59	105,574	105,065	0	133,882	54.0	39.1	5.6	69.6	6.8	0.1	13.8	8.4
18	D, 100		D, 71		D, 75		D, 100	108,439	106,863	-1	117,395	51.8	40.1	11.5	60.6	20.4	0.1	6.7	10.4
19	D, 100		D, 100		D, 78		D, 100	105,943	102,956	-3	64,798	37.5	18.8	11.0	64.3	5.4	0.2	5.6	20.6
20	D, 78		R, 54		R, 59		R, 60	105,485	101,400	-4	68,625	39.3	19.6	9.3	74.7	5.1	0.1	4.2	13.3
21	D, 100		D, 66		D, 68		D, 75	103,280	100,325	-3	64,033	35.5	17.1	11.4	65.2	8.6	0.1	2.4	20.4
22	D, 83		D, 72		D, 78		D, 83	107,675	105,021	-2	60,031	31.2	13.4	11.5	59.7	8.1	0.2	2.7	24.6
23	D, 100		D, 100		D, 100		D, 100	103,963	101,262	-3	52,235	22.4	10.2	18.0	16.5	10.4	0.3	2.5	71.4
24	D, 100		R, 54		D, 53		D, 78	103,798	99,474	-4	49,655	23.0	10.3	17.1	16.6	8.3	0.5	3.0	72.2
25	D, 100		D, 95		D, 100		D, 96	104,859	101,760	-3	48,805	41.5	24.6	24.8	25.4	57.3	0.2	5.2	16.0
26	D, 100		D, 100		D, 100		D, 85	109,066	113,718	4	78,489	46.2	29.4	24.0	31.0	58.1	0.1	5.6	6.2
27	D, 100		D, 82		D, 100		D, 100	102,899	99,338	-3	64,218	39.0	18.3	14.1	34.9	55.3	0.1	1.8	9.6
28	D, 93		D, 80		D, 85		D, 85	104,239	101,137	-3	60,965	33.9	14.4	16.0	35.4	53.9	0.1	2.0	10.7
29	D, 100		D, 76		D, 100		D, 86	104,410	101,492	-3	57,571	36.4	15.3	15.8	37.1	53.4	0.1	1.9	8.8
30	D, 88		D, 80		D, 100		D, 100	104,630	102,323	-2	51,691	33.0	13.0	17.4	35.8	52.8	0.1	1.9	11.1
31	D, 100		D, 88		D, 100		D, 100	101,639	97,860	-4	52,212	31.8	13.3	20.0	35.4	55.7	0.1	2.1	7.6
32	D, 100		D, 93		D, 100		D, 95	104,110	99,924	-4	44,700	27.5	10.9	26.6	21.1	61.3	0.2	2.0	22.5
33	D, 100		D, 92		D, 100		D, 94	104,879	100,871	-4	53,741	34.2	15.0	19.5	22.4	58.1	0.2	1.7	25.2
34	D, 79		D, 88		D, 100		D, 93	110,172	105,871	-4	50,709	36.5	15.1	18.4	29.7	60.5	0.1	1.6	10.4
35	D, 67		D, 63		D, 76		D, 100	106,541	104,638	-2	75,468	41.7	21.6	8.1	77.3	9.8	0.1	2.6	8.2
36	D, 72		D, 100		D, 78		D, 100	109,129	104,625	-4	63,726	38.4	18.6	11.3	67.4	19.8	0.1	2.6	8.6
37	D, 65		D, 69		D, 100		D, 100	103,202	110,429	7	74,919	40.3	19.4	6.4	79.4	6.3	0.1	3.8	8.5
38	R, 50		D, 81		D, 86		D, 100	105,947	106,187	0	71,564	42.3	20.7	9.8	39.0	51.2	0.1	2.7	7.7
39	R, 74		D, 100		D, 100		D, 100	105,961	104,832	-1	50,959	28.9	15.4	19.1	19.4	10.4	0.3	3.6	66.5
40	R, 100		D, 100		D, 82		D, 100	98,146	95,278	-3	54,171	30.2	15.9	16.5	26.8	9.0	0.3	11.9	54.1
41	R, 70		R, 67		R, 100		R, 100	107,118	107,111	0	94,817	48.1	29.5	6.3	79.7	4.6	0.1	6.0	8.1
42	R, 62		R, 63		R, 100		R, 62	103,262	106,590	3	93,799	50.7	34.1	6.9	78.9	3.0	0.1	8.8	7.8
43	R, 54		R, 59		R, 51		R, 54	102,966	118,134	15	64,299	29.1	12.7	10.1	38.8	7.5	0.3	3.8	46.0
44	R, 100		R, 61		R, 100		D, 52	106,488	106,787	0	74,879	40.4	22.0	5.4	56.3	8.5	0.1	13.3	20.6
45	R, 100		R, 69		R, 100		R, 57	105,930	108,643	3	86,264	42.8	25.0	6.6	67.2	3.6	0.1	13.3	14.4
46	R, 71		R, 100		R, 63		R, 51	107,806	109,636	2	80,971	39.8	21.7	6.9	67.4	1.6	0.1	6.7	21.7
47	R, 57		R, 71		R, 66		R, 63	105,631	107,376	2	102,618	50.2	33.7	5.7	76.9	3.3	0.1	11.0	7.5
48	R, 71		R, 89		R, 62		R, 100	106,127	113,179	7	118,208	53.0	38.0	4.6	79.1	3.3	0.1	11.1	5.5
49	R, 100		R, 100		R, 100		R, 60	106,268	139,961	32	94,847	45.4	25.3	4.9	79.6	2.8	0.1	3.4	12.0
50	R, 68		R, 100		R, 70		R, 67	105,463	145,748	38	92,159	42.3	22.3	4.9	84.9	2.0	0.1	1.1	9.9

(continued)

Note: D=Democrat, R=Republican, R/D=Republican/Democrat (cross-filed), D/R=Democrat/Republican (cross-filed), I=Independent, C=Constitution, O=Other, GI=Green Independent, P=Progressive, P/D=Progressive/Democrat, P/D/R=Progressive/Democrat/Republican, HH=Households

Illinois State House Districts—Election and Demographic Data (cont.)

House Districts	General Election Results Party, Percent of Vote							Population			Avg. HH Income	Pop 25+ Some College +	Pop 25+ 4-Yr Degree +	2006 Below Poverty Line	White (Non-Hisp)	African American	American Indians, Alaska Natives	Asians, Hawaiians, Pacific Islanders	Hispanic Origin
Illinois	2000	2001	2002	2003	2004	2005	2006	2000	2006	% Change	($)	(%)	(%)	(%)	(%)	(%)	(%)	(%)	(%)
51	R, 64		R, 66		R, 59		R, 58	106,563	119,886	13	138,258	49.5	34.7	4.2	79.0	1.5	0.1	6.2	11.1
52	R, 100		R, 69		R, 70		R, 100	107,509	125,232	16	102,254	44.4	25.0	6.2	84.6	1.0	0.1	1.9	9.9
53	R, 60		R, 67		R, 59		R, 60	103,753	102,858	-1	87,573	50.6	32.5	4.8	76.1	4.7	0.1	7.8	9.5
54	R, 100		R, 100		R, 100		R, 67	106,262	104,301	-2	107,683	48.1	30.6	5.4	68.5	5.8	0.1	9.5	14.2
55	R, 52		R, 69		R, 100		R, 100	104,644	113,994	9	103,298	43.8	25.6	4.0	75.3	2.5	0.1	9.6	11.3
56	R, 69		R, 100		R, 100		R, 100	106,955	106,101	-1	84,634	45.3	26.0	4.9	69.8	5.2	0.1	13.7	10.1
57	R, 58		D, 55		D, 69		D, 100	104,196	102,296	-2	82,726	45.6	28.2	8.0	59.9	5.8	0.1	17.2	15.8
58	D, 100		D, 62		D, 66		D, 69	108,595	113,422	4	178,088	55.2	44.0	4.7	81.2	3.1	0.1	4.2	9.6
59	D, 64		D, 50		D, 60		D, 100	105,738	116,083	10	117,626	48.6	34.2	5.8	66.6	4.3	0.1	10.5	16.4
60	D, 61		D, 66		D, 72		D, 100	101,703	105,042	3	50,806	24.7	11.7	16.7	24.4	26.1	0.4	3.6	52.9
61	R, 67		R, 63		R, 63		R, 100	105,352	117,445	11	70,730	38.1	19.0	8.4	72.1	8.9	0.2	2.5	13.6
62	R, 67		R, 61		R, 54		R, 52	104,296	118,336	13	81,904	42.5	25.6	6.1	71.3	3.1	0.2	5.3	16.7
63	D, 52		D, 69		D, 65		D, 100	105,038	120,780	15	72,105	36.9	16.1	8.0	80.4	0.5	0.1	1.1	14.7
64	R, 73		R, 66		R, 61		R, 100	104,114	132,714	27	95,314	46.0	25.1	4.2	86.5	0.9	0.1	2.8	8.1
65	R, 100		R, 61		R, 66		R, 100	105,089	103,071	-2	79,435	43.6	25.1	7.8	69.1	5.2	0.1	8.8	14.7
66	R, 100		R, 100		R, 100		R, 100	105,073	102,649	-2	76,240	46.0	27.4	6.5	68.0	5.8	0.1	9.5	14.9
67	D, 100		D, 58		D, 100		D, 100	103,627	104,095	0	44,451	26.4	9.5	19.8	57.3	21.0	0.3	2.4	18.1
68	R, 100		R, 100		R, 61		R, 100	106,760	112,469	5	62,557	35.2	14.5	9.7	85.3	5.3	0.2	1.8	5.8
69	R, 65		R, 100		R, 100		R, 52	105,468	119,372	13	76,916	36.8	16.6	8.4	81.6	2.3	0.1	2.0	11.2
70	R, 100		R, 100		R, 57		R, 60	105,354	115,639	10	58,627	35.1	16.2	15.6	80.9	4.0	0.1	2.7	9.8
71	D, 100		D, 100		D, 55		D, 53	106,277	104,564	-2	54,082	32.6	11.3	12.8	85.5	2.8	0.2	1.4	7.7
72	D, 100		D, 100		D, 69		D, 100	104,774	102,596	-2	54,284	32.3	11.5	14.4	79.9	8.2	0.1	0.7	8.7
73	R, 100		R, 100		R, 100		R, 100	106,542	106,909	0	69,900	40.8	19.3	8.8	92.2	2.9	0.1	2.2	1.8
74	R, 66		R, 69		R, 69		R, 100	105,487	100,390	-5	48,211	31.1	10.3	15.2	90.1	3.9	0.1	0.7	3.6
75	D, 100		D, 71		D, 52		D, 66	105,709	118,410	12	63,634	32.1	11.2	10.0	92.0	1.1	0.1	0.8	4.8
76	D, 65		D, 68		D, 100		D, 72	105,432	105,282	0	52,146	29.7	9.5	13.9	88.3	0.9	0.1	0.8	8.1
77	R, 100		R, 100		R, 100		R, 100	103,334	100,168	-3	58,308	32.8	15.3	11.6	55.6	5.9	0.2	5.2	30.1
78	R, 100		D, 80		D, 100		D, 100	102,888	99,051	-4	84,692	38.8	23.0	15.0	41.4	36.8	0.1	3.5	20.8
79	D, 63		D, 100		D, 53		D, 66	105,774	114,221	8	58,554	31.1	11.3	14.0	69.4	21.1	0.1	0.6	7.9
80	D, 70		D, 100		D, 100		D, 73	107,083	108,674	1	63,706	36.6	16.6	12.4	56.9	25.1	0.2	1.8	15.0
81	R, 100		R, 100		R, 100		R, 100	104,942	138,214	32	96,283	43.4	22.2	4.0	87.4	2.3	0.1	1.8	7.4
82	R, 59		R, 71		R, 66		R, 65	105,007	107,027	2	116,341	50.4	33.2	4.7	81.1	4.0	0.1	7.5	6.1
83	R, 64		D, 54		D, 100		D, 70	106,678	126,012	18	56,583	25.5	11.4	13.0	33.1	13.2	0.3	1.6	51.0
84	R, 100		R, 100		R, 100		R, 100	103,198	169,670	64	92,843	44.8	25.0	3.3	79.2	3.8	0.1	3.4	11.6
85	D, 71		R, 80		R, 80		R, 54	106,840	138,371	30	73,585	39.7	18.4	6.0	63.9	14.9	0.2	4.6	15.3
86	D, 75		D, 100		D, 100		D, 100	105,284	121,556	15	56,325	33.7	14.0	14.1	52.5	21.2	0.2	1.1	24.0
87	R, 75		R, 100		R, 100		R, 100	107,180	107,509	0	62,387	32.8	13.0	9.5	96.6	1.2	0.1	0.5	1.0
88	R, 71		R, 100		R, 84		R, 81	105,331	109,808	4	63,269	41.7	25.5	12.7	83.7	7.5	0.1	3.2	4.0
89	R, 100		R, 64		R, 100		R, 100	105,161	106,186	1	57,377	31.6	11.4	12.5	92.5	3.7	0.1	0.6	2.1
90	R, 100		R, 65		R, 100		R, 63	105,925	105,824	0	54,819	30.6	9.8	12.9	87.5	2.3	0.1	0.6	7.2
91	D, 100		D, 100		D, 100		D, 61	104,217	102,300	-2	51,701	30.6	8.8	14.2	94.8	2.3	0.2	0.5	1.5
92	D, 100		D, 100		R, 50		R, 59	104,123	101,575	-2	46,767	30.9	11.9	21.2	68.2	25.1	0.2	1.6	3.4
93	R, 100		R, 100		R, 100		R, 67	105,546	102,788	-3	47,324	29.2	10.8	17.1	92.2	3.2	0.1	0.4	3.1
94	R, 58		R, 54		R, 100		R, 61	105,126	100,624	-4	46,346	30.0	11.9	17.6	94.9	1.4	0.1	1.0	1.7
95	R, 58		R, 85		R, 61		R, 61	103,099	113,244	10	98,273	45.5	29.1	5.5	72.2	2.5	0.1	4.1	18.8
96	R, 100		R, 70		R, 100		R, 100	107,273	121,998	14	107,345	52.7	37.6	3.7	77.1	4.6	0.1	10.5	6.8
97	R, 100		R, 59		R, 100		R, 100	106,257	106,211	0	49,976	28.5	10.4	15.8	95.3	2.4	0.1	0.4	1.0
98	D, 100		D, 100		D, 100		D, 100	105,352	104,452	-1	45,960	26.2	7.9	17.4	95.8	2.1	0.1	0.3	1.0
99	R, 75		R, 60		R, 64		R, 57	105,840	104,123	-2	49,915	34.8	16.4	15.3	80.1	15.7	0.2	1.3	1.5
100	R, 100		R, 63		R, 100		R, 100	104,647	110,355	5	71,967	41.2	21.6	7.9	93.1	3.4	0.1	1.5	1.3

(continued)

Note: D=Democrat, R=Republican, R/D=Republican/Democrat (cross-filed), D/R=Democrat/Republican (cross-filed), I=Independent, C=Constitution, O=Other, GI=Green Independent, P=Progressive, P/D=Progressive/Democrat, P/D/R=Progressive/Democrat/Republican, HH=Households

Illinois State House Districts—Election and Demographic Data (cont.)

House Districts	General Election Results Party, Percent of Vote							Population			Avg. HH Income	Pop 25+		Below Poverty Line	2006 White (Non-Hisp)	African American	American Indians, Alaska Natives	Asians, Hawaiians, Pacific Islanders	Hispanic Origin
												Some College +	4-Yr Degree +						
Illinois	2000	2001	2002	2003	2004	2005	2006	2000	2006	% Change	($)	(%)	(%)	(%)	(%)	(%)	(%)	(%)	(%)
101	D, 100		D, 100		D, 53		D, 55	105,818	100,352	-5	49,357	28.7	10.2	17.8	83.0	13.9	0.1	0.6	1.2
102	R, 71		R, 59		R, 100		R, 100	105,071	107,793	3	58,677	32.9	13.4	13.5	93.0	4.0	0.1	0.7	1.5
103	R, 56		D, 53		D, 62		D, 59	106,429	110,241	4	43,791	43.6	27.9	23.3	67.6	14.4	0.1	11.2	5.3
104	R, 53		R, 77		R, 100		R, 100	105,879	104,034	-2	47,138	30.7	10.3	16.0	84.0	10.4	0.1	1.2	2.8
105	R, 100		R, 100		R, 100		R, 100	103,757	104,573	1	62,974	33.2	15.0	11.7	90.3	2.5	0.1	2.1	3.4
106	R, 100		R, 100		R, 72		R, 69	105,083	111,937	7	66,669	37.4	17.6	9.5	94.0	2.5	0.1	1.0	1.6
107	R, 74		D, 55		D, 68		D, 50	105,742	105,039	-1	48,271	29.5	8.8	17.6	91.3	5.6	0.1	0.6	1.4
108	D, 100		D, 54		R, 62		R, 69	105,009	101,652	-3	45,003	29.6	8.4	18.8	97.8	0.2	0.1	0.5	0.9
109	D, 69		R, 57		R, 67		R, 100	105,563	104,887	-1	46,923	29.0	8.7	17.0	96.4	1.4	0.1	0.3	1.2
110	R, 66		R, 67		R, 100		R, 100	105,037	103,073	-2	52,370	34.1	14.3	16.6	94.5	1.5	0.1	0.9	2.1
111	D, 100		D, 67		D, 68		D, 100	105,377	105,308	0	50,725	35.9	11.4	16.0	88.8	8.0	0.2	0.5	1.6
112	D, 59		D, 69		D, 100		D, 60	107,625	112,168	4	63,814	41.3	18.9	10.4	88.6	6.5	0.1	1.5	2.3
113	D, 100		D, 100		D, 100		D, 100	103,241	101,531	-2	51,691	37.3	14.5	15.9	80.9	12.4	0.2	1.0	4.1
114	D, 100		D, 62		D, 66		D, 62	106,037	108,719	3	50,027	35.0	14.8	23.9	43.2	53.1	0.2	1.3	2.0
115	R, 63		R, 61		R, 60		R, 78	105,494	102,719	-3	44,274	35.8	16.4	26.4	84.5	8.9	0.2	2.3	2.8
116	D, 61		D, 100		D, 100		D, 100	105,505	109,515	4	58,117	30.9	10.1	13.0	91.0	6.2	0.1	0.4	1.5
117	D, 51		D, 63		D, 72		D, 100	105,344	108,658	3	43,459	32.4	10.8	21.3	95.8	1.5	0.1	0.5	1.3
118	D, 56		D, 63		D, 100		D, 66	105,157	102,416	-3	42,075	28.9	8.0	23.8	88.1	9.0	0.2	0.4	1.4

Note: D=Democrat, R=Republican, R/D=Republican/Democrat (cross-filed), D/R=Democrat/Republican (cross-filed), I=Independent, C=Constitution, O=Other, GI=Green Independent, P=Progressive, P/D=Progressive/Democrat, P/D/R=Progressive/Democrat/Republican, HH=Households

Indiana is a land of rather unflattering nicknames. Indianans are known as "Hoosiers," which the *Oxford English Dictionary* defines as "an inexperienced, awkward, or unsophisticated person." Residents of southern Indiana, along the Wabash River are sometimes called "Butternuts." Nevertheless, no less jaded an observer than Theodore Dreiser once gushed about his home state, "There is about it a charm I shall not be able to express. . . . This is a region not unlike those which produce gold or fleet horses or oranges or adventurers." It has been a land of literature, producing not only Dreiser but also Booth Tarkington, James Whitcomb Riley, and Kurt Vonnegut.

Taking a much less romantic view, John Gunther, in his book *Inside USA,* declared Indiana the national capital of joiners. "You do not meet three neighbors to play bridge," he wrote in the 1940s; "you organize the Upper Tenth Avenue Bridge Club, with a membership of four, and choose your president and secretary-treasurer."

Indiana stretches between north and south. Gary, which is heavily African American, abuts Chicago. New Albany, which lies across from Louisville, has few blacks. Southern Indiana is rural and agricultural, while in the cities of Gary, Hammond, and Fort Wayne, northern Indiana has (or in many cases, had) some of the heaviest industry in the United States.

In between sits Indianapolis, a city planned for the center of the state, and in many ways still the pin on which it revolves. It is the twelfth-largest city in the country and second-largest capital city, after Phoenix. It is also one of the largest cities in the United States that is not on a navigable body of water. Despite being situated between two important waterways, Lake Michigan and the Ohio River, Indiana seems to have been directed toward overland travel, a tradition nicely reflected in the state's most important annual sporting event, the Indianapolis 500.

Indiana grew by almost 10 percent in the 1990s, below the national average but much faster than it did in the 1980s, when it grew by just 1 percent. Growth has remained below the national average in this decade as well, although Indiana has grown faster than other states in the region, which is certainly faint praise. It lost a congressional seat in 2000 and is expected to lose another in the coming decades.

The fastest-growing areas of the state almost perfectly surround the city of Indianapolis. The two fastest-growing, the 29th district in Hamilton County northeast of the city, and the Fortieth in Hendricks County, west of the city, have grown by 52 and 33 percent, respectively,

in this decade. They are good examples of what has been called the metropolitan doughnut, as outer ring suburbs grow while older suburbs closer to the central city stagnate or decline. The two districts that have lost population at the greatest rate, the 100th and the 96th, are located in east and northeast Indianapolis. Nevertheless, population loss has been widespread—fully a third of the state house districts have either lost population or posted no gain since 2000.

Although Indiana was the strongest northern outpost of the Ku Klux Klan during World War I, it has long had a significant black population, almost entirely concentrated in Gary and downtown Indianapolis, the product of the great migration of African Americans around the middle of the twentieth century to seek work in northern factories. In the 1990s seven of the one hundred state house districts were more than 60 percent black, but now none is, and only two even have a black majority.

Northwest Indiana is also home to the state's only significant Hispanic neighborhoods. The 1st, 2nd, and 12th districts, in the old industrial northwestern corner of the state around Hammond, are all more than 20 percent Hispanic. The only concentration of Asians is in West Lafayette, home of Purdue University, the 26th district, which is 8 percent Asian.

Indiana has a reputation as being a staunchly Republican state, as exemplified by its voting in presidential elections. But in statewide contests, the state does elect Democrats. Though its two most famous U.S. senators recently have been Richard Lugar and Dan Quayle, they won their seats by defeating liberal Democrats Vance Hartke and Birch Bayh, respectively. Bayh's son, Evan, now holds one of the U.S. Senate seats, was a popular governor before that, and would be an attractive addition to a Democratic ticket in 2008.

In the legislature, Democrats were close to a majority in the senate as recently as 1990, but now trail, 33–17. The state house of representatives, on the other hand, has been one of the most closely contested in the country for more than a decade. It was deadlocked, 50–50, following the 1996 elections. Democrats won a narrow majority in 2000 and 2002 but Republicans chipped away in the last two election cycles and regained the chamber in 2006. Indiana's congressional races have also been among the hottest in the country. Republicans held seven of the nine seats as recently as 2004 but now hold only four. Indiana may be feeling some of the tide that seems to be pulling much of the rest of the industrial Midwest toward the Democrats.

INDIANA
State Senate Districts

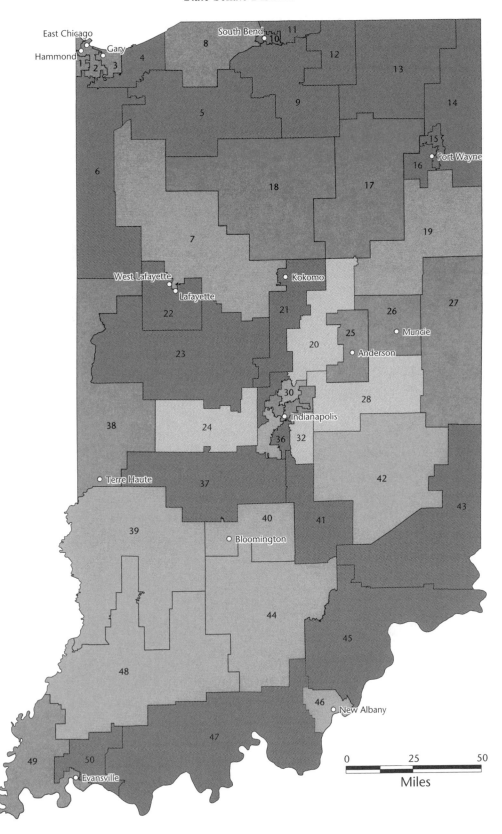

Population Growth | ☐ -6% to 0% | ☐ 0% to 3% | ☐ 3% to 13% | ☐ 13% to 24%

INDIANAPOLIS

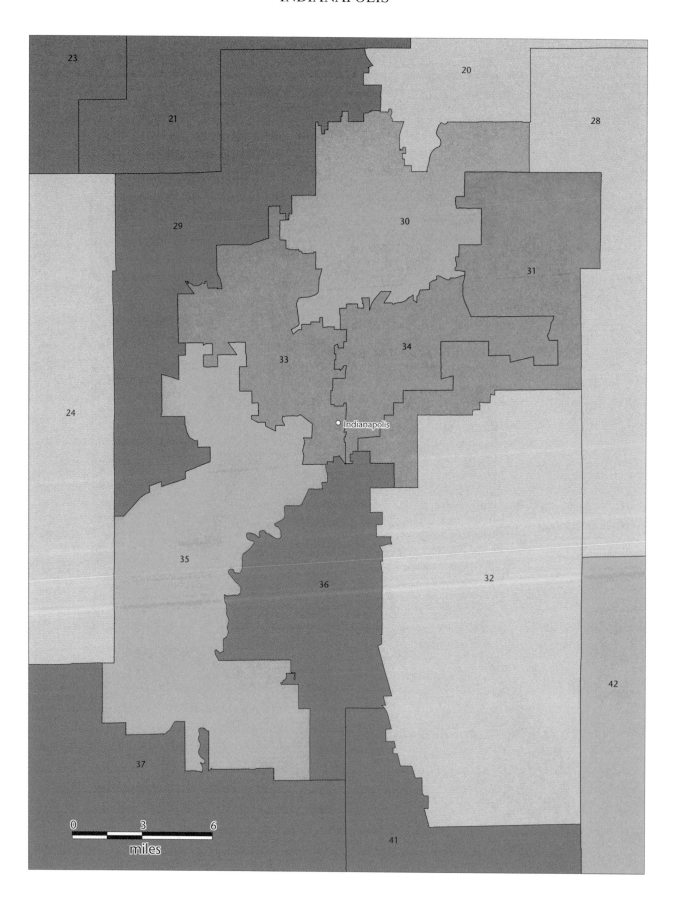

Population Growth   ▨ -6% to 0%   ▨ 0% to 3%   ▨ 3% to 13%   ▨ 13% to 24%

INDIANA

Indiana State Senate Districts—Election and Demographic Data

Senate Districts	General Election Results Party, Percent of Vote							Population			Avg. HH Income ($)	Pop 25+ Some College + (%)	Pop 25+ 4-Yr Degree + (%)	Below Poverty Line (%)	White (Non-Hisp) (%)	African American (%)	American Indians, Alaska Natives (%)	Asians, Hawaiians, Pacific Islanders (%)	Hispanic Origin (%)
Indiana	2000	2001	2002	2003	2004	2005	2006	2000	2006	% Change									
1			D, 100				D, 62	122,687	124,101	1	61,428	33.2	14.5	12.5	65.2	8.4	0.2	1.6	17.1
2	D, 100				D, 92			121,978	122,437	0	50,073	25.3	8.0	20.4	37.4	33.4	0.3	0.7	25.1
3	D, 100				D, 100			116,834	118,888	2	46,799	27.1	8.1	23.0	39.3	49.0	0.2	0.5	8.5
4			D, 56				D, 63	123,407	132,517	7	70,214	34.2	15.1	8.9	80.8	5.0	0.2	1.2	8.4
5	D, 100				R, 50			120,680	126,247	5	60,878	30.3	13.8	12.0	89.5	1.7	0.2	0.8	4.7
6			R, 89				R, 63	119,842	124,524	4	68,370	32.8	13.7	8.6	86.0	4.6	0.2	0.9	4.6
7	R, 54				R, 100			120,876	123,234	2	58,144	28.3	12.0	11.6	89.9	0.8	0.2	0.7	4.9
8	D, 100				D, 55			120,222	120,592	0	54,553	29.6	11.3	12.8	82.7	8.9	0.2	0.6	4.0
9	R, 100				R, 100			126,356	131,228	4	60,113	29.2	12.0	10.9	84.4	2.6	0.2	0.8	6.6
10	D, 96				D, 100			118,151	116,410	-1	43,795	29.1	10.9	18.8	62.8	18.9	0.4	1.5	9.8
11			R, 100				R, 57	119,722	125,272	5	68,709	35.8	16.9	8.4	85.2	4.2	0.2	2.0	4.2
12	R, 100				R, 77			121,568	131,105	8	59,971	24.3	10.6	11.6	67.7	5.5	0.2	1.1	16.3
13	R, 100				R, 100			119,895	124,410	4	56,929	22.9	8.8	11.2	88.7	0.3	0.2	0.4	5.8
14			R, 100				R, 100	123,966	132,506	7	64,356	32.7	13.2	8.8	92.2	2.4	0.2	0.8	2.1
15			R, 67				R, 57	121,212	125,709	4	56,134	35.5	14.8	14.1	65.6	21.0	0.3	2.0	6.5
16	R, 68				R, 100			124,082	128,336	3	61,507	38.0	17.6	12.3	78.8	6.4	0.3	1.9	7.1
17			R, 100				R, 100	122,972	122,613	0	57,519	28.0	11.0	11.0	95.4	0.6	0.4	0.6	1.3
18	R, 93				R, 100			119,878	119,439	0	51,522	24.0	8.1	12.9	89.1	1.5	0.4	0.5	5.0
19			R, 68				R, 100	118,208	118,564	0	51,803	25.0	9.1	12.8	93.3	1.3	0.2	0.4	2.3
20	R, 100				R, 76			125,653	154,716	23	86,898	41.4	26.0	8.5	90.0	3.1	0.2	2.0	2.6
21			R, 65				R, 62	121,455	134,342	11	69,215	34.9	18.4	11.7	89.2	4.2	0.2	1.3	2.3
22			R, 66				R, 61	122,517	127,272	4	55,403	38.9	24.5	17.0	80.3	2.4	0.2	6.0	6.6
23			R, 100				R, 100	122,862	129,117	5	53,623	25.1	9.9	12.9	91.2	0.4	0.2	0.4	4.7
24	R, 100				R, 100			121,429	149,554	23	67,275	33.5	15.9	8.9	93.8	1.3	0.2	0.9	2.0
25			D, 54				D, 61	122,679	119,228	-3	54,536	29.3	11.3	13.7	86.6	8.3	0.2	0.5	2.2
26			D, 51				D, 54	121,210	119,885	-1	52,160	31.1	15.0	17.9	89.1	6.4	0.2	0.9	1.2
27			R, 100				R, 60	120,152	117,256	-2	47,554	25.3	9.3	16.1	91.7	3.1	0.1	0.5	2.0
28	R, 89				R, 89			120,679	145,368	20	74,154	36.3	19.3	8.7	94.9	1.3	0.1	0.9	1.4
29			R, 92				R, 100	121,273	132,899	10	84,542	47.4	30.5	7.6	75.8	11.7	0.1	3.7	5.3
30	R, 65				R, 89			120,028	120,945	1	81,886	55.1	38.5	6.2	81.5	9.0	0.1	2.5	3.9
31			R, 93				R, 54	120,257	119,576	-1	60,929	37.5	19.9	11.4	73.2	14.9	0.2	1.8	5.9
32	R, 65				R, 68			122,518	139,442	14	62,091	35.7	17.0	7.7	88.6	4.5	0.2	1.5	2.8
33	D, 77				D, 93			121,975	119,276	-2	50,425	35.7	18.8	18.5	34.0	53.4	0.2	2.2	8.4
34	D, 83				D, 100			123,371	116,512	-6	43,617	27.1	10.8	22.9	28.8	61.9	0.2	0.8	7.5
35	R, 60				R, 62			123,979	126,511	2	53,737	29.6	13.1	13.2	77.1	9.2	0.2	1.4	7.7
36	R, 65				R, 62			123,976	129,354	4	56,313	33.3	16.2	12.1	84.5	4.7	0.2	1.3	5.7
37	R, 68				R, 73			121,038	126,698	5	58,038	25.6	9.9	12.5	96.4	0.8	0.2	0.3	0.9
38			D, 60				D, 100	123,148	120,476	-2	47,094	29.3	12.8	19.0	91.3	4.5	0.2	0.8	1.0
39			R, 64				R, 53	122,176	123,538	1	47,548	28.5	10.8	17.1	94.2	2.2	0.2	0.8	1.1
40	D, 100				D, 64			123,855	125,270	1	50,609	42.6	27.9	20.1	87.7	2.8	0.2	3.8	2.2
41			R, 87				R, 51	118,948	129,586	9	59,772	30.7	14.4	11.4	91.6	1.6	0.1	1.6	2.8
42	R, 90				R, 70			121,139	121,618	0	54,991	22.7	8.7	13.3	95.7	0.8	0.1	0.6	1.4
43			R, 90				R, 69	121,085	128,371	6	56,035	24.3	9.1	12.6	96.9	0.5	0.2	0.4	0.8
44	R, 91				R, 100			120,534	122,943	2	49,609	23.9	9.5	15.4	94.5	0.4	0.2	0.6	2.2
45			D, 85				D, 59	123,892	131,088	6	51,779	26.4	9.8	14.1	94.7	1.4	0.2	0.4	1.5
46			D, 61				D, 64	121,431	124,925	3	57,251	33.2	13.3	13.6	87.0	6.8	0.2	0.8	2.3
47			D, 57				D, 64	121,787	128,430	5	52,242	25.2	9.1	14.4	95.5	0.5	0.2	0.3	2.0
48			D, 100				D, 100	119,059	120,369	1	50,112	25.6	8.6	16.2	95.0	0.9	0.1	0.4	1.9
49			D, 97				D, 62	119,933	118,841	-1	44,945	27.5	9.3	18.9	86.6	9.6	0.2	0.5	1.0
50	R, 100				R, 91			117,997	125,048	6	70,359	40.4	20.1	8.6	93.1	2.6	0.1	1.3	1.3

Note: D=Democrat, R=Republican, R/D=Republican/Democrat (cross-filed), D/R=Democrat/Republican (cross-filed), I=Independent, C=Constitution, O=Other, GI=Green Independent, P=Progressive, P/D=Progressive/Democrat, P/D/R=Progressive/Democrat/Republican, HH=Households

INDIANA
State House Districts

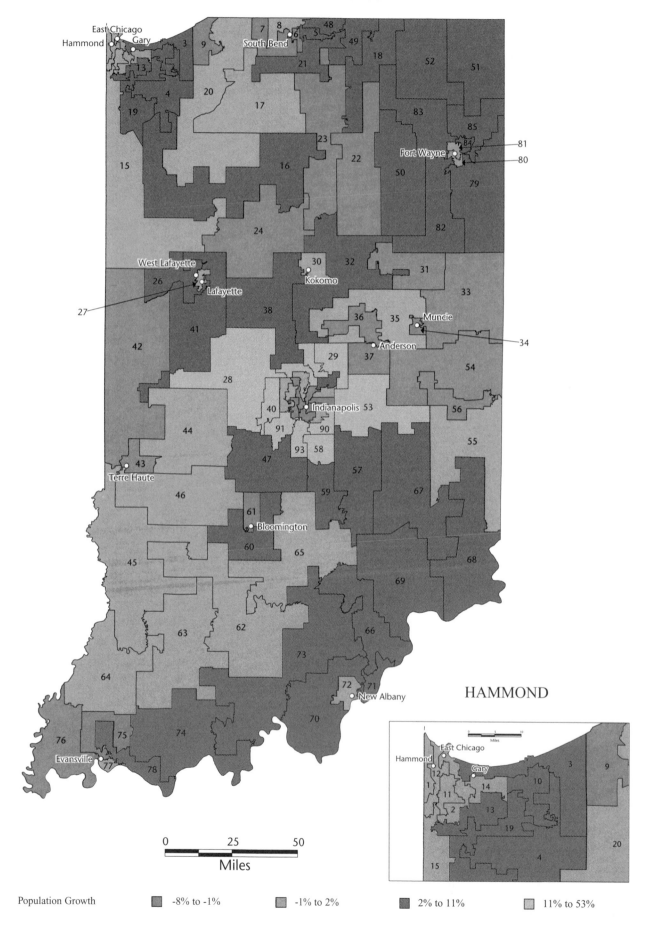

HAMMOND

Population Growth ▨ -8% to -1% ▨ -1% to 2% ▨ 2% to 11% ▢ 11% to 53%

INDIANAPOLIS

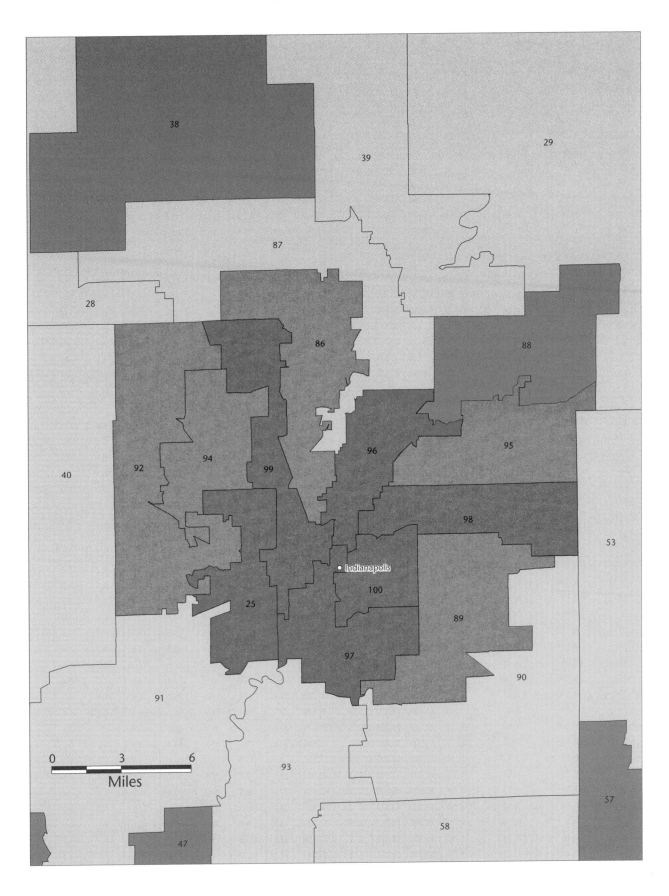

Population Growth ▨ -8% to -1% ▨ -1% to 2% ▨ 2% to 11% ☐ 11% to 53%

Indiana State House Districts—Election and Demographic Data

House Districts	General Election Results Party, Percent of Vote							Population			Avg. HH Income ($)	Pop 25+ Some College + (%)	Pop 25+ 4-Yr Degree + (%)	Below Poverty Line (%)	White (Non-Hisp) (%)	African American (%)	American Indians, Alaska Natives (%)	Asians, Hawaiians, Pacific Islanders (%)	Hispanic Origin (%)
Indiana	2000	2001	2002	2003	2004	2005	2006	2000	2006	% Change	($)	(%)	(%)	(%)	(%)	(%)	(%)	(%)	(%)
1	D, 100		D, 66		D, 60		D, 55	61,811	61,607	0	51,515	29.8	12.1	18.0	55.2	15.1	0.2	1.0	20.7
2	D, 100		D, 78		D, 100		D, 100	61,466	61,864	1	52,841	27.4	9.7	21.2	38.9	37.4	0.2	0.9	20.0
3	D, 100		D, 100		D, 69		D, 73	61,400	63,459	3	59,306	34.3	14.9	17.9	50.6	41.4	0.2	0.6	4.8
4	R, 70		R, 100		R, 70		R, 53	58,661	64,523	10	82,314	40.0	20.8	8.2	90.6	1.7	0.1	1.4	3.7
5	D, 61		D, 60		D, 51		D, 57	59,377	61,035	3	50,451	28.7	10.8	14.5	74.0	9.0	0.3	1.5	8.6
6	D, 66		D, 63		D, 100		D, 68	59,601	58,453	-2	48,332	30.4	13.1	16.6	70.4	13.5	0.3	2.1	7.7
7	D, 68		D, 100		D, 60		D, 100	60,662	60,028	-1	50,369	30.5	10.7	16.7	61.3	19.7	0.3	0.8	11.0
8	D, 61		D, 55		D, 100		D, 100	58,864	59,577	1	65,546	39.1	19.2	11.6	77.8	11.0	0.3	2.0	4.4
9	D, 100		D, 86		D, 89		D, 100	59,603	58,778	-1	53,314	29.5	11.7	13.9	77.1	14.8	0.2	0.7	3.8
10	D, 58		D, 100		D, 100		D, 62	60,560	64,278	6	63,041	30.6	12.5	10.4	84.6	1.2	0.2	0.9	8.8
11	D, 100		D, 100		D, 59		D, 100	59,907	60,564	1	57,963	30.9	10.8	10.7	68.9	12.2	0.2	1.1	12.2
12	D, 100		D, 100		D, 53		D, 62	61,482	62,275	1	64,496	31.9	14.5	14.4	49.1	10.1	0.3	2.0	29.8
13	D, 72		D, 68		D, 61		D, 100	61,906	63,767	3	63,077	33.3	12.6	8.3	68.6	14.5	0.2	1.2	10.1
14	D, 100		D, 100		D, 86		D, 87	63,618	64,440	1	44,752	23.1	5.9	26.5	34.6	52.3	0.2	0.4	10.2
15	R, 63		R, 64		R, 66		R, 50	59,146	59,467	1	59,044	28.1	10.5	10.6	87.7	2.7	0.2	0.6	4.9
16	R, 100		R, 100		R, 100		R, 100	61,645	63,110	2	54,245	23.7	8.9	12.9	92.4	0.5	0.2	0.3	3.7
17	D, 69		R, 58		R, 61		D, 52	60,365	60,569	0	52,964	24.5	9.4	13.6	89.4	0.6	0.2	0.4	5.7
18	R, 100		R, 91		R, 100		R, 100	62,536	67,828	8	61,751	23.9	10.4	10.3	86.8	0.6	0.2	0.7	6.4
19	D, 54		D, 55		D, 58		D, 64	59,985	63,239	5	65,505	32.8	13.1	9.3	83.0	5.8	0.2	1.0	5.8
20	R, 100		R, 83		R, 54		R, 49	62,860	63,791	1	55,765	26.7	9.5	12.3	88.8	3.2	0.3	0.4	4.2
21	R, 100		R, 100		R, 64		R, 53	62,310	65,984	6	56,970	27.0	10.5	11.6	74.6	5.2	0.2	1.0	11.3
22	R, 69		R, 100		R, 100		R, 58	60,059	58,439	-3	55,028	25.8	10.1	11.0	94.5	0.4	0.4	0.5	1.9
23	R, 100		R, 90		R, 100		R, 65	60,128	58,716	-2	53,465	21.4	7.2	12.3	89.3	1.6	0.5	0.4	4.4
24	R, 58		R, 100		R, 68		R, 100	60,870	59,781	-2	54,003	25.4	9.3	11.9	85.4	1.0	0.2	0.5	8.4
25	D, 50		D, 62		D, 66		D, 87	59,299	56,427	-5	43,572	24.5	9.5	15.5	60.0	23.9	0.3	1.3	10.5
26	R, 64		R, 54		D, 52		D, 58	58,518	60,877	4	57,450	40.0	26.6	16.4	79.8	2.6	0.2	8.0	5.4
27	D, 61		D, 60		D, 66		D, 61	61,626	62,560	2	46,319	36.0	20.9	19.8	77.8	2.7	0.2	4.2	9.3
28	R, 100		R, 100		R, 100		R, 100	62,390	72,132	16	62,452	29.4	12.6	10.0	96.2	0.4	0.2	0.3	1.6
29	R, 92		R, 82		R, 100		R, 71	61,435	93,610	52	92,342	46.9	31.2	5.6	92.3	1.5	0.1	1.9	2.4
30	D, 55		D, 55		R, 52		D, 56	60,945	60,618	-1	54,828	29.8	12.0	13.9	84.2	8.2	0.3	1.2	2.3
31	R, 100		R, 71		R, 50		R, 50	60,758	57,840	-5	46,173	24.2	9.2	17.0	85.2	7.7	0.3	0.5	2.8
32	R, 54		R, 100		R, 71		R, 100	61,774	65,431	6	62,374	29.6	12.1	10.6	94.4	1.1	0.3	0.7	1.6
33	D, 54		D, 57		R, 55		R, 53	60,637	59,323	-2	47,358	23.4	8.2	15.9	93.9	1.7	0.2	0.3	1.9
34	D, 60		D, 60		D, 85		D, 62	61,210	59,950	-2	41,903	27.6	13.6	23.6	84.4	10.0	0.2	1.0	1.6
35	R, 57		R, 100		R, 60		R, 54	64,088	64,902	1	67,849	35.3	17.5	9.5	94.8	1.7	0.1	0.7	1.1
36	R, 52		D, 52		D, 62		D, 63	58,976	58,206	-1	52,986	27.2	11.0	14.5	90.2	4.4	0.2	0.4	2.4
37	D, 100		D, 51		D, 63		D, 100	61,252	58,729	-4	54,788	30.5	11.1	13.3	83.0	12.2	0.2	0.5	2.0
38	R, 100		R, 100		R, 100		R, 100	60,828	65,024	7	66,305	28.7	13.4	11.1	87.1	0.7	0.2	0.8	7.1
39	R, 100		R, 100		R, 77		R, 72	61,463	78,042	27	107,889	50.8	36.8	4.5	89.0	1.6	0.1	3.9	3.1
40	R, 74		R, 91		R, 91		R, 100	61,429	81,500	33	73,141	38.1	19.4	6.8	93.7	0.7	0.2	1.1	2.4
41	R, 100		R, 100		R, 60		R, 67	62,198	64,037	3	61,099	32.8	16.0	11.1	91.1	1.0	0.2	1.2	3.4
42	D, 62		D, 61		D, 63		D, 70	62,009	61,242	-1	49,684	25.8	9.5	15.7	96.4	0.9	0.2	0.3	1.1
43	D, 89		D, 87		D, 100		D, 64	59,062	56,420	-4	47,597	31.7	15.4	20.1	88.2	6.5	0.2	1.3	1.2
44	D, 100		R, 58		R, 67		R, 53	61,300	62,204	1	49,567	24.1	9.7	15.0	94.7	2.0	0.2	0.5	0.9
45	D, 76		D, 51		R, 57		R, 58	60,671	60,545	0	46,029	27.2	8.5	18.3	95.4	1.7	0.2	0.4	0.9
46	D, 58		R, 53		D, 52		D, 58	61,569	62,671	2	49,462	30.2	12.9	15.3	91.5	3.6	0.3	1.2	1.3
47	R, 74		R, 87		R, 100		R, 100	61,018	64,831	6	62,530	24.9	9.4	11.8	97.3	0.1	0.2	0.3	0.8
48	R, 69		R, 66		R, 100		R, 55	60,847	64,395	6	67,128	32.7	14.8	8.5	81.2	4.0	0.2	1.6	7.3
49	R, 100		R, 100		R, 100		R, 54	60,618	64,231	6	64,041	27.1	12.7	10.1	72.4	1.5	0.2	1.3	15.7
50	R, 100		R, 100		R, 72		R, 85	60,634	61,997	2	57,478	27.2	10.3	11.0	96.7	0.3	0.3	0.4	1.0

(continued)

Note: D=Democrat, R=Republican, R/D=Republican/Democrat (cross-filed), D/R=Democrat/Republican (cross-filed), I=Independent, C=Constitution, O=Other, GI=Green Independent, P=Progressive, P/D=Progressive/Democrat, P/D/R=Progressive/Democrat/Republican, HH=Households

Indiana State House Districts—Election and Demographic Data (cont.)

House Districts	General Election Results Party, Percent of Vote							Population			Avg. HH Income ($)	Pop 25+ Some College + (%)	Pop 25+ 4-Yr Degree + (%)	Below Poverty Line (%)	2006 White (Non-Hisp) (%)	African American (%)	American Indians, Alaska Natives (%)	Asians, Hawaiians, Pacific Islanders (%)	Hispanic Origin (%)
Indiana	2000	2001	2002	2003	2004	2005	2006	2000	2006	% Change									
51	R, 100		R, 79		R, 64		R, 56	60,535	62,425	3	58,607	27.9	10.8	10.4	94.2	0.4	0.2	0.5	2.5
52	D, 55		R, 51		R, 66		R, 55	60,313	62,731	4	53,266	22.2	7.8	12.1	92.1	0.3	0.1	0.5	3.5
53	R, 86		R, 86		R, 87		R, 100	61,136	68,971	13	72,304	34.0	15.4	7.6	96.3	0.5	0.1	0.5	1.3
54	R, 65		R, 80		R, 67		R, 47	63,392	62,419	-2	53,753	28.6	11.0	12.2	96.1	1.1	0.1	0.4	0.9
55	R, 66		R, 69		R, 69		R, 58	62,399	63,142	1	59,574	25.3	10.0	12.0	96.7	1.1	0.1	0.4	0.6
56	D, 52		D, 52		D, 51		D, 60	59,716	57,271	-4	44,413	23.8	7.9	18.4	88.9	5.4	0.2	0.5	2.0
57	R, 53		R, 59		R, 100		R, 53	61,460	62,879	2	56,969	27.0	11.2	12.1	92.5	1.2	0.1	1.3	2.9
58	R, 81		R, 72		R, 72		R, 65	62,097	72,998	18	62,594	34.6	16.4	9.1	94.2	0.6	0.1	1.2	2.0
59	R, 100		R, 75		R, 100		R, 61	60,443	62,864	4	58,054	30.2	14.6	12.2	90.6	2.3	0.1	1.5	3.1
60	D, 57		D, 59		D, 65		D, 100	61,268	63,861	4	59,302	42.5	25.4	11.6	91.5	1.9	0.2	2.2	1.6
61	D, 100		D, 75		D, 88		D, 75	60,514	58,654	-3	39,605	43.7	32.2	29.5	83.1	3.8	0.2	5.9	2.9
62	D, 100		D, 62		D, 57		D, 62	60,345	61,521	2	44,844	21.5	7.3	18.6	96.8	0.4	0.2	0.3	1.0
63	D, 100		D, 100		D, 51		D, 62	60,342	61,383	2	54,310	23.4	8.6	14.6	94.3	0.4	0.1	0.3	3.0
64	D, 55		D, 55		R, 50		D, 54	60,212	60,228	0	44,585	29.0	10.1	18.8	94.5	2.2	0.2	0.7	1.0
65	R, 68		R, 64		R, 90		R, 100	61,852	63,023	2	56,889	28.4	12.3	12.4	95.4	0.5	0.2	0.9	1.3
66	D, 56		D, 100		D, 60		D, 100	59,314	61,676	4	50,332	23.6	8.4	15.6	91.4	0.7	0.2	0.8	4.0
67	R, 100		R, 85		R, 71		R, 73	60,963	62,310	2	53,301	22.7	9.3	13.9	96.6	0.3	0.2	0.7	1.0
68	D, 50		D, 61		D, 87		D, 64	61,119	64,902	6	53,367	23.4	8.4	14.1	97.2	0.6	0.1	0.3	0.7
69	D, 57		D, 56		R, 53		D, 54	60,581	62,471	3	49,460	24.5	9.4	14.4	95.1	1.1	0.2	0.5	1.0
70	D, 57		D, 57		D, 53		D, 56	62,105	66,536	7	60,415	30.4	11.4	11.0	96.0	0.7	0.2	0.4	1.4
71	D, 67		D, 64		D, 100		D, 64	61,626	64,423	5	52,883	32.4	11.7	13.0	83.2	9.4	0.2	1.0	2.9
72	D, 59		D, 55		D, 55		D, 59	60,869	61,827	2	60,124	34.2	15.0	13.8	90.0	5.0	0.2	0.7	1.6
73	D, 100		D, 100		D, 100		D, 100	60,987	63,696	4	48,190	20.8	7.0	17.0	96.8	0.6	0.1	0.2	1.0
74	D, 100		D, 100		D, 92		D, 69	60,485	63,005	4	50,729	25.9	9.5	14.5	94.6	0.3	0.1	0.3	2.8
75	D, 100		D, 60		D, 100		D, 100	59,304	58,282	-2	48,934	29.3	10.8	14.8	92.2	3.6	0.1	0.8	1.2
76	D, 64		D, 96		D, 55		D, 100	60,997	60,283	-1	53,295	28.3	11.2	16.3	95.5	1.9	0.2	0.5	0.6
77	D, 100		D, 100		D, 50		D, 56	59,830	59,769	0	50,312	34.5	14.4	17.5	77.3	17.4	0.2	0.8	1.5
78	R, 100		R, 100		R, 100		R, 100	62,038	68,003	10	77,134	42.9	21.7	6.7	94.4	1.6	0.1	1.3	1.3
79	R, 100		R, 100		R, 100		R, 100	64,475	66,513	3	53,870	25.6	8.3	11.8	90.3	2.6	0.2	0.4	3.4
80	D, 100		D, 58		D, 64		D, 65	59,005	59,232	0	42,408	28.7	10.0	19.9	52.8	25.7	0.4	1.6	12.8
81	D, 64		D, 50		D, 100		D, 100	60,235	60,394	0	43,660	31.3	11.3	17.4	60.0	23.9	0.3	2.1	9.0
82	R, 100		R, 73		R, 100		R, 100	60,175	62,915	5	76,531	37.6	18.3	8.7	91.7	1.7	0.2	1.0	2.7
83	R, 70		R, 100		R, 100		R, 100	62,294	65,749	6	64,558	33.2	14.7	8.8	83.4	1.9	0.3	1.6	7.6
84	R, 74		R, 100		R, 100		R, 64	59,948	61,633	3	64,811	43.1	20.2	8.7	85.9	5.1	0.2	2.0	3.1
85	R, 73		R, 100		R, 100		R, 100	61,550	67,962	10	75,006	38.2	17.4	6.3	92.9	1.9	0.1	1.1	1.7
86	R, 62		D, 50		D, 52		D, 56	60,952	61,220	0	92,977	50.2	34.8	10.0	68.3	22.4	0.1	2.4	4.2
87	R, 66		R, 72		R, 100		R, 68	62,973	71,647	14	99,646	56.0	40.8	5.7	89.2	2.8	0.1	3.0	2.8
88	R, 66		R, 100		R, 92		R, 65	60,582	63,365	5	93,185	51.5	35.3	5.3	81.4	9.1	0.1	2.7	3.7
89	R, 54		R, 91		R, 100		R, 52	60,983	61,931	2	51,706	32.8	15.1	10.4	85.1	6.3	0.2	1.2	4.1
90	R, 95		R, 72		R, 92		R, 67	60,505	70,710	17	66,396	37.3	17.8	7.2	88.7	4.3	0.1	1.7	2.7
91	R, 64		R, 89		R, 100		R, 62	60,506	67,726	12	60,748	28.5	11.2	9.8	90.5	3.5	0.2	0.9	2.6
92	R, 60		R, 92		R, 63		R, 59	60,393	61,488	2	65,414	41.5	21.9	8.5	78.7	10.6	0.2	2.8	4.2
93	R, 91		R, 92		R, 100		R, 100	62,543	71,796	15	76,435	40.9	21.7	5.8	91.7	1.8	0.1	1.4	2.8
94	D, 60		D, 64		D, 71		D, 100	62,794	63,179	1	56,212	40.8	23.0	10.2	42.0	36.5	0.2	3.8	13.9
95	D, 100		D, 94		D, 71		D, 70	59,105	59,618	1	53,162	31.9	13.8	14.9	43.4	46.5	0.2	1.4	6.9
96	D, 76		D, 92		D, 69		D, 100	60,038	56,679	-6	54,028	39.8	22.4	17.7	42.7	50.6	0.2	1.1	3.4
97	D, 55		D, 90		D, 54		R, 50	59,559	57,566	-3	42,442	27.5	13.4	19.3	72.3	15.1	0.3	1.0	7.5
98	D, 78		D, 67		D, 100		D, 100	60,859	59,056	-3	44,573	28.5	10.6	16.7	43.2	48.6	0.2	1.3	4.5
99	D, 80		D, 69		D, 70		D, 100	60,356	58,589	-3	52,043	37.9	21.6	19.3	44.0	43.6	0.2	2.6	7.7
100	D, 60		D, 60		D, 100		D, 70	60,924	56,644	-7	38,080	23.3	9.3	23.9	61.0	17.8	0.4	0.6	14.4

Note: D=Democrat, R=Republican, R/D=Republican/Democrat (cross-filed), D/R=Democrat/Republican (cross-filed), I=Independent, C=Constitution, O=Other, GI=Green Independent, P=Progressive, P/D=Progressive/Democrat, P/D/R=Progressive/Democrat/Republican, HH=Households

IOWA

Iowa, land of hogs, corn, and insurance companies, is the slowest-growing state in the farm belt and the ninth slowest in the nation. During the 1990s Iowa's population grew by just 5.4 percent, a figure that nevertheless represented a dramatic improvement over the 1980s, when in the midst of a deep agricultural recession, it fell by almost 5 percent. It has grown by only 1 percent in this decade, less than a quarter of the national rate. More people are moving into Iowa than are leaving it for the first time since the 1910s, but the Census Bureau still projects Iowa to be the third slowest-growing state over the next generation.

Two important reasons for Iowa's sluggishness are its economy, which is based on agriculture, and its population, which is old. Iowa is the third oldest state in the country, trailing only Florida and virtually tied with Pennsylvania; more than 15 percent of its population is age sixty-five or older. Almost all of the state house districts that have lost population since 2000 are rural, in sharp contrast to many other states, where urban areas are the ones losing people. Nowhere was the loss severe, just steady and widespread, although the 49th house district, centered on Ft. Dodge, shrank by 9 percent from 2000 to 2007, the fastest rate in the state. In all, forty-six of one hundred state house districts have either lost population or posted no gain during this decade. On the other hand, the 47th district, centered on Dallas County west of Des Moines, has grown by 36 percent in that period. The adjacent 69th district, covering Polk County north of Des Moines, grew by a quarter.

The state's wealth is centered around Des Moines, which is home to several large insurance companies, including the Principal Financial Group. In the 69th district, in the city's southwestern suburbs, average household income is $92,000, by far the highest in the state. The poorest sections are in downtown Des Moines, the old shipping center of Davenport, Waterloo, and one rural district (the 94th) down by the Missouri border. (Iowa's counties are stacked neatly, like blocks and are named after presidents and important historical figures from the time when the state was settled—hence, Polk, Dallas, Madison, DeWitt, Clinton, and Marshall Counties, among others.)

Although it has had some industry, fewer than 2 percent of the state's residents are black and it has the highest percentage of white residents (96.6 percent) of any state outside New England. The only two districts with a significant share of African Americans, the 22nd and the 66th, are also two of the state's poorest. The state's Hispanic population is growing rapidly. Ten years ago, only one house district was 10 percent Hispanic; now eight are, with the highest concentration in the 2nd house district, which takes in the packing houses of Sioux City.

Iowa lost one congressional district after the 2000 census and is expected to lose another after the 2010 reapportionment. This is uncharted territory here. Iowa was a boom state once, and the size of its congressional delegation exploded from two seats in 1850 to six in 1860 to nine in 1870, at which time it was more populous than Michigan. From there, however, it has been a steady, though gentle, decline.

The state legislature is organized around legislative districts, with one senator and two representatives elected from each. It has become extremely competitive in presidential elections, narrowly backing Al Gore in 2000 and George W. Bush in 2004. It has been equally competitive in legislative races. This has happened after some rolling around. In 1990 the state house had fifty-five Democrats and forty-five Republicans; in 1996 it had forty-six Democrats and fifty-four Republicans. During this decade, however, Democrats have picked up a few more seats and Republicans control the chamber only by a 51–49 margin.

The state senate saw a similar flip in the past decade, going from a 29–21 Democratic majority in 1990 to a 29–21 Republican majority just six years later. The chamber was tied at twenty-five seats apiece after the 2004 elections; each party appointed a co-leader and the two alternated weeks running the senate. Democrats, however, broke the tie in 2006 by gaining seats. They now control both chambers of the legislature and the governor's mansion for the first time in four decades. Back in the 1940s, John Gunther suggested an explanation for this partisan shift. "When the farmer is rich," he wrote in *Inside U.S.A.,* "he placidly votes Republican by and large. When poor, his vote will be a protest vote."

IOWA
State Senate Districts

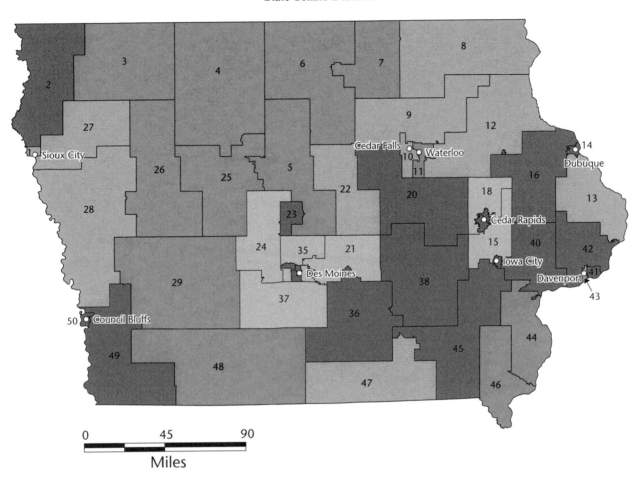

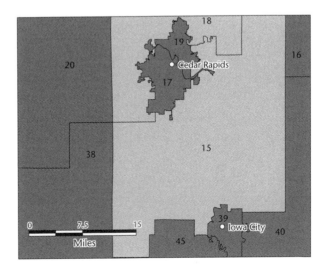

DES MOINES

CEDAR RAPIDS/IOWA CITY

Population Growth ■ -7% to -2%   ■ -2% to 0%   ■ 0% to 6%   □ 6% to 22%

Iowa State Senate Districts—Election and Demographic Data

Senate Districts	General Election Results Party, Percent of Vote							Population			Avg. HH Income ($)	Pop 25+ Some College + (%)	Pop 25+ 4-Yr Degree + (%)	Below Poverty Line (%)	2006 White (Non-Hisp) (%)	African American (%)	American Indians, Alaska Natives (%)	Asians, Hawaiians, Pacific Islanders (%)	Hispanic Origin (%)
Iowa	2000	2001	2002	2003	2004	2005	2006	2000	2006	% Change	($)	(%)	(%)	(%)	(%)	(%)	(%)	(%)	(%)
1			D, 64				D, 67	58,181	57,130	-2	54,338	30.4	13.0	16.3	66.4	3.2	3.8	3.5	18.2
2	R, 99		R, 100		R, 100			58,786	60,053	2	53,565	31.0	13.6	13.0	94.2	0.2	0.2	0.5	3.7
3			R, 61				R, 57	58,627	57,225	-2	49,862	35.6	13.2	14.0	96.6	0.2	0.3	0.5	1.8
4	D, 61				D, 60			58,734	55,200	-6	46,455	33.6	10.8	15.8	96.4	0.2	0.3	0.3	2.0
5			R, 57				D, 50	58,093	56,528	-3	51,740	37.1	15.2	12.5	94.3	0.3	0.3	0.7	2.9
6	R, 70				R, 58			58,836	57,379	-2	48,963	35.8	12.5	13.3	93.5	0.2	0.2	0.4	3.9
7			D, 61				D, 70	58,483	56,766	-3	47,571	35.1	13.1	16.1	94.7	0.7	0.2	0.6	2.4
8	R, 57		R, 57		R, 55			58,386	57,382	-2	48,641	29.0	11.9	15.7	95.4	0.3	0.2	0.4	2.5
9			R, 60				D, 52	59,064	58,472	-1	50,188	33.0	12.9	14.0	97.4	0.4	0.1	0.4	1.0
10	R, 65				D, 54			58,263	57,644	-1	61,435	45.4	26.4	13.7	93.0	2.6	0.2	1.4	1.6
11			D, 66				D, 70	57,910	55,969	-3	42,843	36.6	16.0	18.7	76.1	16.2	0.4	0.8	4.2
12	R, 59				D, 53			60,034	59,221	-1	50,793	28.6	10.2	15.5	97.3	0.4	0.3	0.3	1.1
13			D, 55				D, 65	58,441	58,267	0	48,368	30.0	10.8	15.6	95.0	1.7	0.3	0.5	1.5
14	R, 60				D, 99			59,116	60,602	3	53,842	34.1	18.0	13.2	94.0	1.3	0.3	0.8	2.2
15			D, 60				D, 78	59,533	65,637	10	69,470	51.0	31.6	10.8	89.8	2.4	0.4	3.6	2.2
16	R, 56		R, 51		D, 50			56,861	58,258	2	53,035	29.9	11.3	13.6	97.1	0.8	0.2	0.3	1.0
17			D, 99				D, 99	57,560	60,472	5	52,091	37.3	14.9	12.4	90.5	3.3	0.5	1.9	1.9
18	D, 57				R, 60			61,575	65,758	7	70,552	43.2	21.0	7.2	95.5	1.0	0.3	1.0	1.2
19			R, 57				D, 59	55,857	56,171	1	67,207	47.9	26.1	9.5	89.1	5.0	0.3	1.6	2.0
20	D, 51		R, 61		R, 99			58,343	60,288	3	50,927	31.6	10.7	13.2	94.0	0.2	2.8	0.2	1.8
21			D, 62				D, 56	58,948	62,819	7	56,173	35.7	14.5	10.8	94.9	1.1	0.4	0.8	1.8
22	D, 58				R, 51			58,232	57,707	-1	48,924	33.5	13.1	13.9	83.1	0.9	0.4	0.7	10.5
23			D, 54				D, 57	58,575	59,966	2	58,090	52.3	36.1	16.1	86.9	2.5	0.2	6.4	2.4
24	R, 55				R, 57			60,179	73,116	21	62,957	39.0	18.3	11.1	91.2	0.7	0.2	0.6	4.8
25			D, 58				D, 66	58,602	55,820	-5	46,343	33.7	12.5	16.3	92.3	2.7	0.4	0.5	2.6
26	R, 65				R, 99			58,392	56,649	-3	47,440	30.9	12.2	15.8	86.8	0.3	0.2	1.7	8.7
27			R, 52				R, 99	58,528	58,291	0	53,365	34.2	14.4	11.8	91.4	0.7	0.8	0.9	4.1
28	R, 57		R, 49		R, 99			58,620	58,148	-1	49,338	29.5	10.7	15.8	91.7	0.3	0.5	0.3	5.5
29			R, 61				R, 78	58,636	57,026	-3	47,546	30.2	11.3	15.1	97.7	0.2	0.2	0.2	1.1
30	R, 55		R, 89		R, 62			56,746	60,874	7	86,924	53.4	32.1	5.2	88.7	2.0	0.2	2.7	4.2
31			D, 56				D, 66	55,600	57,475	3	60,537	45.1	22.8	11.7	82.5	4.8	0.5	2.1	7.0
32	R, 59				R, 58			60,851	64,020	5	71,195	51.9	28.6	6.2	90.5	2.7	0.2	2.1	2.7
33			D, 99				D, 99	57,799	59,152	2	40,958	37.6	16.4	19.7	58.3	17.4	0.8	5.6	14.2
34	D, 99		D, 98		D, 99			58,795	63,214	8	48,891	37.1	14.7	14.3	77.6	6.2	0.5	3.2	9.3
35			R, 98				R, 52	58,500	69,958	20	81,627	47.8	24.9	6.9	94.9	1.1	0.3	1.0	1.7
36	D, 60				R, 60			59,974	62,089	4	50,080	29.1	12.0	15.3	96.9	0.3	0.3	0.7	1.0
37			R, 49				D, 50	59,854	64,956	9	59,848	35.0	14.1	10.7	96.6	0.3	0.3	0.4	1.5
38	R, 65				D, 52			58,022	58,786	1	49,997	30.6	12.4	14.9	95.7	0.5	0.3	0.7	1.7
39			D, 98				D, 69	57,288	59,317	4	53,536	51.7	36.4	19.7	86.5	3.4	0.4	3.9	3.6
40	R, 58		R, 51		R, 54			59,355	61,041	3	55,848	33.9	13.8	12.4	84.8	0.7	0.4	0.7	9.2
41			R, 85				R, 49	58,221	59,261	2	69,665	47.9	27.2	11.3	86.3	6.1	0.3	1.5	3.7
42	D, 54		R, 53		D, 51			58,700	61,601	5	59,607	34.8	13.1	11.4	93.7	1.6	0.3	0.6	2.2
43			D, 68				D, 77	58,988	58,519	-1	47,402	33.8	13.1	16.9	76.0	10.4	0.7	2.1	7.4
44	R, 65		D, 69		D, 99			58,079	56,132	-3	52,428	32.8	11.8	14.0	88.0	2.8	0.4	0.6	6.1
45			R, 53				D, 50	59,722	62,026	4	49,224	34.4	15.9	15.6	94.3	0.5	0.3	0.8	2.8
46	R, 53				D, 53			58,332	56,504	-3	50,220	31.7	11.0	15.4	92.2	2.5	0.4	1.0	2.3
47			D, 57				D, 64	57,763	57,029	-1	41,188	30.0	10.7	20.4	91.8	0.7	0.4	0.5	5.3
48	R, 70				R, 54			58,839	57,126	-3	41,911	30.0	10.4	18.8	94.8	0.3	0.4	0.4	3.0
49			R, 99				R, 82	59,096	59,678	1	56,674	35.6	13.8	13.2	95.7	0.7	0.4	0.4	2.0
50	D, 99				D, 54			57,893	59,069	2	48,951	29.0	9.6	15.1	88.7	1.1	0.7	0.6	6.3

Note: D=Democrat, R=Republican, R/D=Republican/Democrat (cross-filed), D/R=Democrat/Republican (cross-filed), I=Independent, C=Constitution, O=Other, GI=Green Independent, P=Progressive, P/D=Progressive/Democrat, P/D/R=Progressive/Democrat/Republican, HH=Households

IOWA
State House Districts

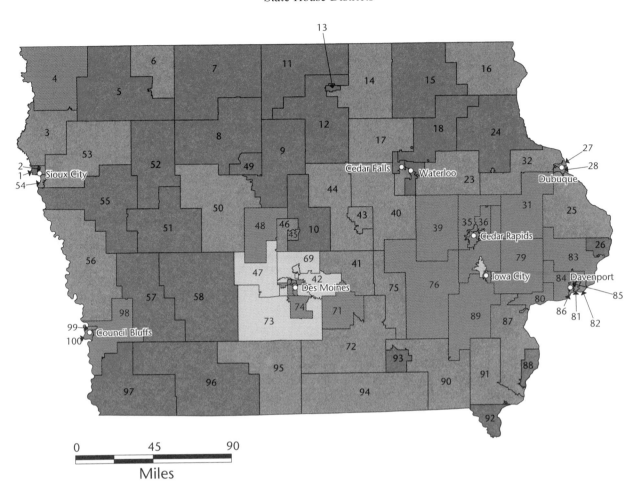

0   45   90

Miles

DES MOINES

CEDAR RAPIDS/IOWA CITY

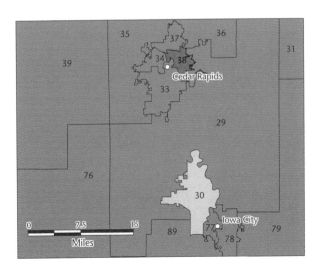

Population Growth ▮ -9% to -2%   ▮ -2% to 2%   ▮ 2% to 9%   ▯ 9% to 37%

Iowa State House Districts—Election and Demographic Data

House Districts	General Election Results Party, Percent of Vote							Population			Avg. HH Income	2006 Pop 25+		Below Poverty Line	White (Non-Hisp)	African American	American Indians, Alaska Natives	Asians, Hawaiians, Pacific Islanders	Hispanic Origin
												Some College +	4-Yr Degree +						
Iowa	2000	2001	2002	2003	2004	2005	2006	2000	2006	% Change	($)	(%)	(%)	(%)	(%)	(%)	(%)	(%)	(%)
1	R, 54		D, 60		D, 56		D, 63	28,580	27,913	-2	62,972	32.1	14.4	14.2	83.4	3.3	0.9	2.6	13.1
2	D, 68		D, 61		D, 99		D, 99	29,563	29,149	-1	46,226	28.7	11.7	18.3	75.2	3.1	1.2	4.3	23.3
3	R, 67		R, 100		R, 100		R, 100	28,794	29,250	2	55,626	33.1	14.9	12.4	93.9	0.4	0.3	0.5	3.7
4	R, 100		R, 100		R, 100		R, 100	29,997	30,796	3	51,491	29.1	12.4	13.7	94.5	0.1	0.1	0.4	3.8
5	R, 100		R, 100		R, 69		R, 82	29,856	28,524	-4	46,423	31.4	10.9	14.8	96.3	0.3	0.3	0.4	1.9
6	R, 100		D, 49		R, 53		R, 73	28,760	28,675	0	53,015	39.7	15.4	13.3	96.8	0.2	0.3	0.5	1.6
7	D, 64		D, 99		D, 57		D, 74	28,988	27,598	-5	45,120	32.7	9.7	16.4	95.7	0.2	0.3	0.3	2.5
8	D, 58		D, 67		D, 99		D, 76	29,772	27,604	-7	47,779	34.6	11.8	15.3	97.1	0.1	0.2	0.4	1.5
9	R, 100		R, 59		R, 58		D, 55	29,324	28,534	-3	47,929	32.8	11.6	13.7	92.2	0.3	0.3	0.8	4.4
10	R, 60		R, 57		R, 59		R, 53	28,830	28,040	-3	55,856	41.5	18.9	10.9	96.4	0.4	0.3	0.6	1.4
11	R, 100		R, 99		R, 99		R, 55	29,167	28,322	-3	48,699	34.4	11.5	13.1	95.2	0.2	0.2	0.4	2.6
12	R, 100		R, 61		R, 69		R, 80	29,689	29,060	-2	49,219	37.1	13.6	13.5	91.9	0.2	0.3	0.4	5.1
13	R, 53		R, 52		R, 53		R, 51	28,400	26,753	-6	49,299	39.5	15.7	16.1	92.0	1.3	0.3	0.8	3.6
14	R, 53		D, 99		D, 99		D, 75	30,103	30,016	0	45,935	31.2	10.8	16.1	97.1	0.2	0.1	0.4	1.4
15	D, 99		D, 99		D, 59		D, 68	29,300	27,863	-5	49,258	27.5	9.6	16.1	98.0	0.1	0.1	0.3	0.9
16	R, 99		R, 99		R, 97		R, 59	29,104	29,519	1	48,019	30.5	14.0	15.2	92.9	0.4	0.2	0.6	4.1
17	R, 91		R, 99		R, 95		R, 56	29,884	30,026	0	50,889	34.1	14.1	12.9	97.7	0.4	0.1	0.4	0.7
18	R, 63		R, 52		R, 55		D, 56	29,196	28,445	-3	49,477	31.7	11.6	15.1	97.0	0.3	0.2	0.4	1.2
19	R, 54		R, 54		D, 51		D, 50	30,000	29,213	-3	58,958	42.6	26.1	14.4	93.7	2.2	0.2	1.2	1.5
20	D, 69		R, 53		R, 57		D, 52	28,243	28,393	1	63,716	48.2	26.7	13.1	92.2	3.0	0.2	1.5	1.7
21	R, 100		D, 61		D, 61		R, 52	28,737	27,823	-3	45,711	41.5	20.2	15.8	86.9	5.8	0.3	0.9	3.4
22	R, 53		D, 66		D, 99		D, 77	29,268	28,220	-4	39,810	31.8	11.9	21.7	65.5	26.4	0.5	0.6	4.9
23	D, 60		R, 51		R, 54		R, 51	29,361	29,153	-1	55,249	30.4	10.4	13.9	97.5	0.5	0.3	0.4	0.7
24	R, 59		D, 55		D, 55		D, 100	30,643	30,022	-2	46,551	26.8	10.0	17.1	97.1	0.4	0.3	0.2	1.4
25	D, 71		D, 99		D, 55		D, 60	29,173	29,749	2	51,341	27.8	9.9	14.7	98.3	0.1	0.2	0.3	0.6
26	D, 99		D, 98		D, 99		D, 60	29,271	28,503	-3	45,442	32.2	11.8	16.5	91.6	3.3	0.5	0.7	2.4
27	D, 58		D, 99		D, 99		D, 71	29,736	30,431	2	49,599	30.6	14.7	11.8	95.4	1.0	0.2	0.6	1.6
28	D, 68		D, 98		D, 66		D, 72	29,386	30,161	3	57,940	37.6	21.3	14.5	92.6	1.6	0.3	1.0	2.8
29	D, 76		D, 98		D, 98		D, 60	30,787	32,891	7	72,065	43.1	23.0	8.6	97.0	0.4	0.3	0.5	1.0
30	D, 56		D, 65		D, 83		D, 74	28,519	32,499	14	67,402	58.8	40.2	12.4	82.8	4.4	0.4	6.8	3.5
31	R, 99		R, 52		D, 54		D, 74	29,668	30,880	4	50,857	30.9	10.7	14.5	96.0	1.3	0.4	0.4	1.2
32	R, 51		R, 65		R, 62		R, 66	27,213	27,381	1	55,485	28.8	12.1	12.6	98.4	0.2	0.1	0.2	0.7
33	D, 99		D, 61		D, 99		D, 99	29,701	31,714	7	47,797	34.0	12.5	14.1	88.5	4.4	0.6	2.2	2.1
34	D, 100		D, 57		D, 99		D, 67	27,765	28,646	3	57,091	40.9	17.6	10.2	92.7	2.2	0.4	1.6	1.7
35	D, 99		R, 53		R, 52		R, 54	30,835	33,412	8	70,989	41.2	19.8	6.6	95.5	1.2	0.3	0.9	1.1
36	D, 99		D, 57		D, 54		D, 53	30,930	32,542	5	70,228	45.4	22.3	7.8	95.5	0.7	0.3	1.2	1.2
37	R, 54		R, 57		R, 56		D, 51	26,649	27,194	2	68,352	49.9	27.4	7.3	92.1	2.7	0.2	2.0	1.6
38	D, 53		D, 53		D, 57		D, 65	29,126	28,854	-1	65,913	46.0	24.8	11.8	86.3	7.2	0.3	1.2	2.4
39	R, 59		R, 52		D, 54		D, 56	29,189	31,483	8	52,511	30.7	10.1	13.0	98.1	0.2	0.2	0.2	0.7
40	R, 53		R, 98		R, 67		R, 55	29,166	28,796	-1	49,230	32.7	11.4	13.4	94.7	0.2	2.8	0.2	2.6
41	R, 62		D, 61		D, 85		D, 63	29,284	29,252	0	53,600	31.6	13.0	12.0	95.9	1.1	0.3	0.6	1.4
42	R, 54		D, 63		D, 63		D, 98	29,657	33,537	13	58,589	39.2	15.8	9.6	94.0	1.1	0.5	1.0	2.1
43	D, 56		D, 57		D, 99		D, 73	28,317	28,323	0	48,815	32.2	13.4	15.1	72.9	1.3	0.6	1.0	17.6
44	D, 53		R, 51		R, 98		R, 50	29,933	29,383	-2	49,028	34.7	12.8	12.7	93.4	0.5	0.2	0.4	3.7
45	D, 64		D, 60		D, 56		D, 99	29,319	30,238	3	45,947	48.3	32.5	21.9	87.1	2.7	0.2	5.8	2.5
46	D, 78		D, 55		D, 86		D, 63	29,315	29,765	2	67,901	56.3	39.7	11.3	86.8	2.3	0.2	7.1	2.2
47	R, 56		R, 56		R, 58		R, 52	29,546	40,209	36	72,702	43.3	23.0	8.6	95.8	0.8	0.1	0.7	1.4
48	R, 60		D, 51		D, 56		D, 61	29,648	31,828	7	50,442	33.1	11.9	14.1	85.5	0.5	0.4	0.4	9.3
49	D, 85		D, 60		D, 99		D, 79	29,158	26,550	-9	46,502	35.5	14.4	15.7	89.9	3.6	0.3	0.8	3.4
50	D, 79		R, 53		R, 99		R, 55	29,487	29,293	-1	46,185	32.1	10.7	16.9	94.5	1.8	0.4	0.3	1.9

(continued)

Note: D=Democrat, R=Republican, R/D=Republican/Democrat (cross-filed), D/R=Democrat/Republican (cross-filed), I=Independent, C=Constitution, O=Other, GI=Green Independent, P=Progressive, P/D=Progressive/Democrat, P/D/R=Progressive/Democrat/Republican, HH=Households

Iowa State House Districts—Election and Demographic Data (cont.)

House Districts	General Election Results Party, Percent of Vote							Population			Avg. HH Income ($)	Pop 25+		Below Poverty Line	2006 White (Non-Hisp)	African American	American Indians, Alaska Natives	Asians, Hawaiians, Pacific Islanders	Hispanic Origin
Iowa	2000	2001	2002	2003	2004	2005	2006	2000	2006	% Change	($)	Some College + (%)	4-Yr Degree + (%)	Line (%)	Hisp) (%)	American (%)	Natives (%)	Islanders (%)	Origin (%)
51	R, 58		R, 99		R, 99		R, 92	29,533	28,738	-3	49,085	30.5	11.2	15.5	96.5	0.2	0.2	0.3	2.2
52	R, 60		R, 100		R, 99			28,882	27,919	-3	45,679	31.2	13.1	16.2	77.4	0.4	0.2	3.1	15.4
53	D, 99		R, 69		R, 60		R, 100	31,011	31,247	1	52,555	33.4	13.2	12.9	95.7	0.4	0.4	0.6	2.0
54	D, 99		R, 98		R, 58		R, 97	27,618	27,138	-2	54,303	35.2	15.8	10.5	86.5	1.1	1.2	1.3	6.5
55	R, 62		R, 100		R, 99		R, 77	29,622	28,912	-2	47,313	28.5	10.7	16.8	86.2	0.5	0.5	0.4	9.8
56	R, 52		R, 61		R, 56		R, 51	28,987	29,206	1	51,362	30.6	10.7	14.9	97.2	0.1	0.6	0.2	1.2
57	D, 99		R, 63		R, 99		R, 74	29,421	28,450	-3	46,982	31.7	12.7	14.1	97.7	0.2	0.3	0.2	1.0
58	R, 58		R, 51		R, 60		R, 86	29,377	28,715	-2	48,104	28.8	9.9	16.0	97.8	0.1	0.1	0.2	1.1
59	R, 60		R, 98		R, 60		R, 58	28,599	29,752	4	88,109	55.0	33.5	5.4	88.8	2.1	0.2	2.5	4.2
60	R, 59		R, 99		R, 99		R, 98	29,127	32,162	10	85,895	51.9	30.7	5.0	88.7	2.0	0.2	2.9	4.1
61	D, 54		D, 53		D, 59		D, 67	26,626	27,448	3	76,693	53.1	31.8	10.3	85.7	5.6	0.4	1.7	4.3
62	R, 55		D, 67		D, 99		D, 99	28,140	29,194	4	44,690	37.9	14.6	13.0	80.7	3.8	0.6	2.4	9.1
63	R, 66		R, 99		R, 65		R, 98	30,878	33,848	10	84,440	52.4	30.2	5.3	92.1	1.9	0.2	2.1	2.4
64	D, 51		D, 98		D, 63		D, 99	30,006	30,196	1	58,148	51.4	26.9	6.9	88.7	3.5	0.3	2.1	3.1
65	R, 99		D, 98		D, 98		D, 98	27,847	27,976	0	45,136	39.2	16.9	14.3	71.2	11.0	0.6	4.6	8.5
66	D, 57		D, 99		D, 89		D, 61	30,202	31,399	4	37,283	36.0	16.0	24.4	47.6	23.3	0.9	6.5	19.1
67	D, 67		D, 63		D, 65		D, 61	30,566	33,974	11	52,287	37.4	15.4	14.1	76.5	4.6	0.5	3.3	11.3
68	D, 89		D, 99		D, 68		D, 98	28,897	29,887	3	45,028	36.6	13.8	14.5	78.3	8.0	0.5	3.0	7.6
69	D, 99		R, 54		R, 53		R, 55	30,052	37,403	24	92,300	47.8	25.2	6.6	94.9	0.9	0.3	1.0	1.8
70	D, 98		R, 98		R, 60		R, 98	28,453	32,533	14	69,805	48.0	24.6	7.1	94.8	1.2	0.2	1.0	1.6
71	D, 98		R, 62		R, 99		R, 57	29,538	31,349	6	54,910	32.8	15.2	12.8	96.1	0.4	0.3	1.1	1.3
72	D, 65		R, 59		R, 56		R, 60	30,423	30,706	1	45,398	25.2	8.7	17.7	97.7	0.2	0.2	0.4	0.7
73	R, 61		R, 56		R, 63		R, 58	29,363	33,120	13	58,674	33.2	11.7	11.2	97.3	0.1	0.4	0.3	1.1
74	R, 99		D, 99		D, 99		D, 51	30,505	31,832	4	61,105	37.0	16.6	10.2	95.8	0.4	0.2	0.5	1.8
75	R, 67		R, 98		R, 51		D, 53	28,835	28,867	0	50,307	31.7	14.3	16.0	94.7	0.9	0.4	1.3	1.6
76	R, 59		R, 55		R, 65		R, 54	29,207	29,924	2	49,718	29.6	10.7	13.8	96.7	0.1	0.3	0.2	1.8
77	R, 54		D, 98		D, 84		D, 80	27,334	28,046	3	46,995	49.1	37.6	26.4	86.5	2.8	0.4	5.2	3.1
78	R, 53		D, 99		D, 99		D, 80	30,241	31,521	4	59,305	54.2	35.6	13.6	86.4	4.1	0.5	2.8	4.0
79	D, 99		R, 53		R, 54		R, 62	29,799	30,597	3	53,883	34.2	13.9	11.4	88.1	0.4	0.4	0.9	6.7
80	R, 54		R, 98		D, 52		D, 60	29,610	30,508	3	57,828	33.7	13.7	13.4	81.6	0.9	0.5	0.6	11.6
81	R, 64		R, 58		R, 55		R, 51	29,207	29,663	2	62,731	45.4	25.4	13.9	80.2	10.6	0.4	1.6	4.6
82	R, 65		R, 62		R, 99		R, 54	29,317	29,871	2	76,537	50.2	28.9	8.7	92.2	1.7	0.3	1.4	2.9
83	R, 98		R, 57		R, 61		R, 57	29,939	30,829	3	60,064	35.4	13.1	11.7	96.7	0.4	0.3	0.4	1.3
84	R, 63		R, 54		R, 56		D, 50	28,684	30,675	7	59,188	34.3	13.1	11.1	90.9	2.7	0.4	0.9	3.2
85	R, 65		D, 58		D, 58		D, 54	28,730	28,691	0	54,390	37.4	14.9	12.0	81.7	8.8	0.3	2.1	4.6
86	R, 99		D, 63		D, 64		D, 69	30,078	29,642	-1	40,697	30.3	11.4	21.4	70.8	11.8	1.0	2.2	10.1
87	R, 60		R, 57		R, 60		R, 55	29,181	28,942	-1	54,008	31.5	11.4	12.3	86.4	0.7	0.2	0.5	9.3
88	R, 56		D, 99		D, 99		D, 99	28,919	27,192	-6	50,885	34.1	12.3	15.5	89.5	5.1	0.5	0.6	2.6
89	D, 93		R, 61		R, 56		R, 55	30,437	32,316	6	50,623	34.2	15.4	13.5	93.7	0.6	0.3	0.5	3.2
90	D, 60		D, 50		D, 54		D, 79	29,324	29,729	1	47,803	34.7	16.5	17.6	94.9	0.5	0.2	1.0	2.4
91	R, 67		R, 71		R, 99		R, 72	30,387	29,962	-1	53,081	33.0	11.7	14.1	93.4	1.9	0.4	1.3	1.7
92	D, 99		D, 77		D, 55		D, 75	27,951	26,527	-5	47,237	30.3	10.1	16.7	90.9	3.2	0.4	0.5	2.9
93	D, 58		D, 99		D, 99		D, 99	28,903	28,117	-3	42,253	31.6	12.2	18.8	86.5	1.2	0.5	0.8	9.5
94	D, 58		D, 52		D, 59		D, 64	28,871	28,904	0	40,130	28.5	9.3	22.0	97.1	0.3	0.3	0.3	1.2
95	R, 100		D, 52		D, 99		D, 64	29,447	29,055	-1	42,574	30.3	10.8	18.9	93.7	0.4	0.4	0.5	3.6
96	R, 61		R, 99		R, 61		R, 99	29,413	28,074	-5	41,246	29.7	10.0	18.6	96.0	0.1	0.4	0.3	2.3
97	R, 99		R, 59		R, 62		R, 95	29,245	28,126	-4	47,477	33.4	12.3	17.2	94.8	1.0	0.6	0.4	2.2
98	D, 56		R, 62		R, 64		R, 61	29,800	31,491	6	65,530	37.6	15.2	9.2	96.4	0.3	0.3	0.4	1.8
99	D, 99		D, 52		R, 56		R, 53	28,197	28,362	1	50,695	30.7	11.6	15.3	88.2	1.1	0.9	0.7	6.5
100	D, 65		R, 98		D, 60		D, 52	29,636	30,627	3	47,299	27.3	7.7	14.9	89.1	1.1	0.6	0.5	6.0

Note: D=Democrat, R=Republican, R/D=Republican/Democrat (cross-filed), D/R=Democrat/Republican (cross-filed), I=Independent, C=Constitution, O=Other, GI=Green Independent, P=Progressive, P/D=Progressive/Democrat, P/D/R=Progressive/Democrat/Republican, HH=Households

KANSAS

In the 1930s Walter Prescott Webb, a professor at the University of Texas, popularized the theory that the Great Plains begin at the 100th meridian, for it is there that the annual rainfall drops below twenty inches. To the east of that line, there is enough rain to grow crops without irrigation. To the west, the land is drier and better suited to grazing. Kansas sits squarely astride the 100th meridian, which passes almost exactly through Dodge City, perhaps the most notorious town on the frontier in the 1880s. It is the gateway to the Plains and to the West.

The 100th meridian is not a bad dividing line for Kansas. The eastern part of the state is hilly and green. As the plains roll west past the two university towns of Lawrence and Manhattan on Interstate 70, the landscape turns yellow, the trees give way to wheat fields, oil wells, and cattle. Table-flat plains roll out interminably until they meet the foothills of the Rockies. (The land may be flat, but it is not level. Kansas, like the continent, slopes upward, rising 3,000 feet in elevation from the eastern border with Missouri to the western border with Colorado. The highest point in Kansas, Mt. Sunflower, is at a higher elevation than the Alleghenies in Pennsylvania.)

Coronado passed through here in the sixteenth century, searching for the City of Gold. Outsiders tore the state apart in the 1850s over slavery, earning it the name "Bleeding Kansas." More recently, it has produced Bob Dole, who is laconic, and hatchet-wielding Carrie Nation, scourge of saloons, who was not. Those who have not spent much time there depict it as bland and monochromatic. When Dorothy, perhaps the state's most famous fictional resident, emerges from her twister-tossed house, she steps out of sepia into brilliant Technicolor and tells her dog, "I don't think we're in Kansas anymore."

The state motto is "Ad astra per aspera"—"To the stars by hard ways"—and an economy built on wheat, corn, cattle, oil, and gas is bound to have its hard ways. Its rate of growth has been well below the national average for decades and half the state house districts have lost population, some dramatically. Four districts have lost more than ten percent of their population since 2000; the 65th district, in Geary County, has shrunk by 17 percent. Simply put, parts of Kansas are shrinking because young people are not moving in and old people are dying off. More than half of the state's counties experienced more deaths than births during the 1990s.

The Kansas suburbs of Kansas City, Missouri, are wealthy and gaining population. (John Gunther, in his *Inside U.S.A.*, noted that while Kansas City is not capital of its own state, it is effectively the capital of another, a unique situation in America.) While the rest of Kansas is growing at a rate less than half the national average, the 48th house district, which includes the fancy suburb of Overland Park, has grown by 61 percent since 2000. That is more than twice as fast as any other district in the state, although other parts of the Kansas City suburbs are also growing.

What accounts for the growth? Kansas City is headquarters to a surprising number of midsized and growing companies: Hallmark greeting cards, Sprint, and Russell Stover candies. Pizza Hut and Payless Shoes are also not far away. Also, much suburban growth has been the result of flight from the disastrous Kansas City, Missouri, school system. So a lot of people were not moving very far, just a few miles across the state line.

Those suburbs are also the wealthiest part of the state. In four districts, average household income exceeds $100,000, all of them surrounding Kansas City. Average income in the 28th district around Overland Park is more than $166,000—higher than the Rhode Island district that includes Newport. But only a few miles from the 100th district, which includes Wichita (average income $89,000), is the 102nd district, one of the state's poorest, where average income is less than $34,000.

Only 87 percent of Kansans are white, one of the lowest percentages in the Farm Belt. The state is 6 percent African American, greater than Massachusetts. That is not surprising, if one thinks about it. The state was home to John Brown and was born amid a bloody feud over whether it would permit slavery. After the Civil War, a few groups of ex-slaves homesteaded in the northwest part of the state. Everyone knows *Brown v. Board of Education,* the 1954 Supreme Court decision outlawing segregation in public schools, but not as many realize that the board of education in question was located in Topeka. The state house district that includes Topeka is about 12 percent African American today, but in two districts just north of Kansas City, the 34th and 35th, it is more than 45 percent.

In western Kansas, which is geographically and cuturally similar to West Texas and Oklahoma, there are sizable Hispanic communities, comprised in large measure of oil field workers who have traveled up Highway 83, which runs from Canada to Mexico. Five districts in this area are more than 45 percent Hispanic: the 125th (Liberal), 119th (Dodge City), 103rd (Wichita), and also the 37th and 32nd (both Kansas City). One district in Wichita, the 88th, is almost 11 percent Asian.

Unlike most other states in the region, Kansas has a large state house of representatives, with 125 members. Hard as it may be to remember in a place known as a bastion of the Republican Party, Kansas just reelected a Democratic governor and as recently as 1990 Democrats controlled the state house of representatives. Since 2000 the GOP has added to its already large majorities in both chambers of the legislature.

KANSAS
State Senate Districts

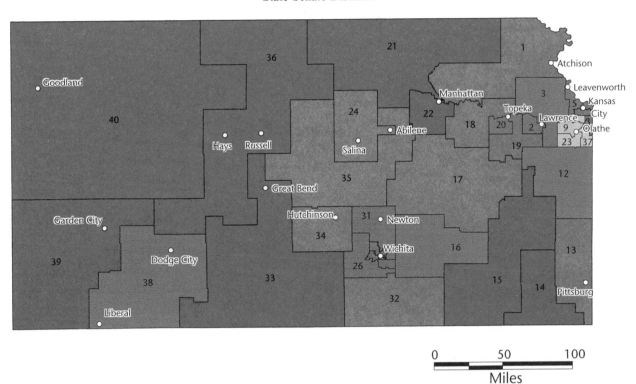

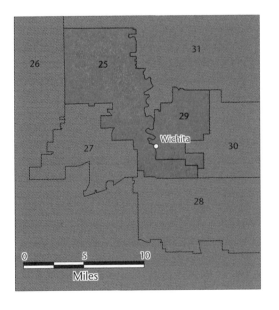

WICHITA

KANSAS CITY

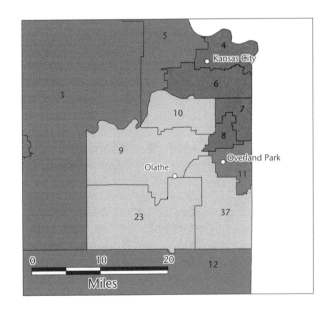

Population Growth ■ -10% to -3% ■ -3% to 3% ■ 3% to 14% □ 14% to 37%

Kansas State Senate Districts—Election and Demographic Data

Senate Districts	General Election Results Party, Percent of Vote							Population			Avg. HH Income	Pop 25+ Some College +	Pop 25+ 4-Yr Degree +	2006 Below Poverty Line	2006 White (Non-Hisp)	2006 African American	2006 American Indians, Alaska Natives	2006 Asians, Hawaiians, Pacific Islanders	2006 Hispanic Origin
Kansas	2000	2001	2002	2003	2004	2005	2006	2000	2006	% Change	($)	(%)	(%)	(%)	(%)	(%)	(%)	(%)	(%)
1	R, 60				R, 55			66,873	68,057	2	46,633	30.3	12.8	17.0	90.5	1.8	3.5	0.4	2.3
2	R, 65				D, 51			67,607	70,571	4	51,400	47.8	31.2	19.6	81.1	3.7	3.3	5.3	4.1
3	R, 54				R, 52			72,221	77,815	8	61,814	38.5	18.7	11.1	91.5	1.8	1.4	1.1	2.5
4	D, 86				D, 100			65,759	63,984	-3	41,918	26.4	7.5	23.0	37.5	42.9	0.8	2.3	18.2
5	D, 66				D, 52			67,940	70,847	4	59,737	37.7	17.1	10.7	76.9	12.4	0.9	1.9	5.6
6	D, 100				D, 79			69,954	69,412	-1	44,102	25.9	9.1	18.2	51.2	9.8	1.0	3.0	31.7
7	R, 100				R, 56			68,154	69,041	1	85,200	60.0	39.8	5.9	88.3	1.7	0.3	2.2	5.6
8	R, 68				R, 60			64,898	65,734	1	65,091	56.6	33.3	6.3	85.1	2.2	0.4	4.0	6.4
9	R, 71				R, 60			62,674	76,251	22	77,103	50.4	29.2	5.8	84.7	2.8	0.5	3.6	6.2
10	R, 59				R, 61			63,919	73,441	15	83,790	53.2	31.8	5.6	85.6	2.4	0.4	3.8	5.6
11	R, 73				R, 100			63,985	71,046	11	121,745	59.5	42.4	4.1	87.2	1.8	0.3	5.8	3.8
12	R, 57				R, 65			66,563	70,976	7	53,728	31.7	12.0	14.2	94.3	1.0	0.8	0.3	2.2
13	D, 50				D, 50			65,766	64,971	-1	42,114	35.1	14.3	22.2	91.6	1.6	1.5	1.2	2.4
14	R, 72				R, 65			64,600	61,874	-4	41,321	34.1	10.8	19.5	87.3	3.4	3.0	0.6	2.8
15	R, 73				R, 100			66,732	63,260	-5	42,141	32.7	10.7	19.6	92.5	1.5	1.6	0.4	2.2
16	R, 71				R, 70			64,840	67,935	5	58,306	36.4	14.0	12.6	92.9	1.1	1.0	0.6	2.8
17	R, 59				R, 62			66,384	65,321	-2	45,151	32.3	14.5	18.1	79.6	1.3	0.6	1.6	12.4
18	R, 50				D, 50			64,983	65,933	1	53,121	35.1	16.2	13.8	83.7	5.1	1.3	0.9	6.3
19	D, 66				D, 61			63,573	63,388	0	48,223	29.5	11.7	16.7	69.5	10.9	1.6	0.8	13.2
20	R, 67				R, 63			63,626	66,075	4	62,245	45.8	25.8	8.7	85.3	4.3	0.8	2.2	5.0
21	R, 71				R, 100			63,450	59,840	-6	45,373	32.6	13.0	16.8	96.5	0.5	0.4	0.4	1.3
22	R, 100				R, 62			82,055	78,510	-4	45,497	42.3	22.5	19.9	74.8	10.0	0.7	5.2	5.7
23	R, 73				R, 100			63,277	76,737	21	76,171	46.7	25.7	5.5	85.2	2.1	0.5	2.5	7.1
24	R, 55				R, 59			68,953	69,606	1	49,837	35.3	14.0	14.0	85.4	2.1	0.6	1.9	6.9
25	R, 50				R, 66			70,004	68,609	-2	47,747	34.9	15.3	13.5	74.2	4.1	1.7	3.0	12.6
26	R, 73				R, 58			67,999	73,800	9	65,029	35.4	15.4	7.3	89.5	1.2	1.0	1.8	4.2
27	R, 71				R, 64			66,438	70,357	6	68,276	42.5	21.8	7.8	84.1	2.2	1.1	3.2	6.6
28	D, 52				R, 58			67,532	71,863	6	50,033	28.3	9.1	13.0	69.6	5.9	1.8	7.2	11.3
29	D, 100				D, 70			69,675	68,611	-2	38,575	30.6	12.7	25.0	41.8	29.6	1.3	5.9	20.9
30	R, 55				R, 60			69,856	72,722	4	76,113	49.5	29.5	8.9	77.8	6.3	0.8	7.3	5.4
31	D, 52				R, 64			69,644	73,684	6	58,350	37.8	18.0	10.9	78.6	2.6	0.8	1.8	11.8
32	D, 100				D, 49			67,164	65,504	-2	50,267	35.0	12.4	15.6	87.7	1.5	1.7	1.3	5.5
33	R, 100				R, 100			67,972	65,149	-4	44,693	36.2	13.0	16.9	88.7	0.6	0.6	0.4	7.1
34	R, 59				R, 59			64,818	63,277	-2	48,811	36.9	13.0	15.6	86.7	2.4	0.7	0.7	6.5
35	R, 71				R, 72			68,000	67,957	0	48,684	35.0	13.5	14.4	93.3	0.8	0.5	0.5	3.3
36	D, 71				D, 56			71,024	66,848	-6	45,243	37.7	16.5	17.6	94.6	0.8	0.4	0.7	2.3
37	R, 67				R, 71			62,979	86,181	37	106,441	53.6	37.1	3.2	88.4	2.0	0.2	4.3	3.7
38	R, 66				R, 100			68,715	71,455	4	50,662	29.2	11.2	16.0	44.8	1.9	0.8	2.9	43.1
39	R, 100				R, 100			69,010	66,455	-4	51,817	28.7	10.5	14.5	49.9	1.0	1.1	2.6	36.2
40	R, 83				R, 67			67,977	61,331	-10	45,641	35.8	13.0	16.5	92.4	0.7	0.4	0.4	4.3

Note: D=Democrat, R=Republican, R/D=Republican/Democrat (cross-filed), D/R=Democrat/Republican (cross-filed), I=Independent, C=Constitution, O=Other, GI=Green Independent, P=Progressive, P/D=Progressive/Democrat, P/D/R=Progressive/Democrat/Republican, HH=Households

KANSAS
State House Districts

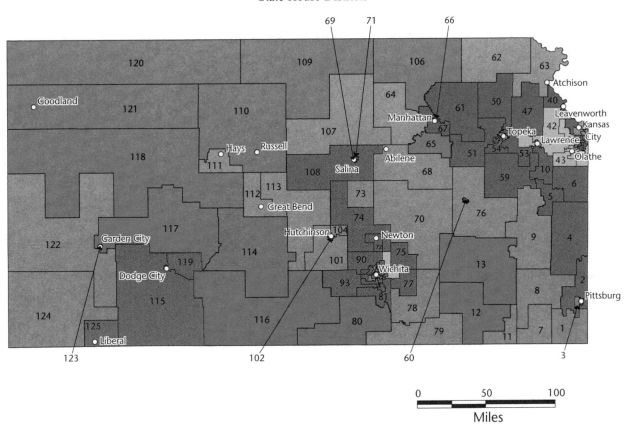

TOPEKA

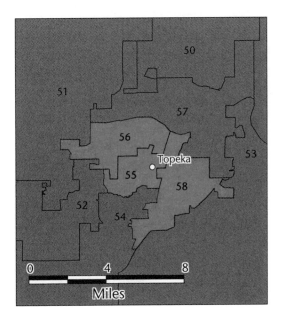

Population Growth ■ -18% to -5% ■ -5% to 0% ■ 0% to 12% □ 12% to 62%

WICHITA

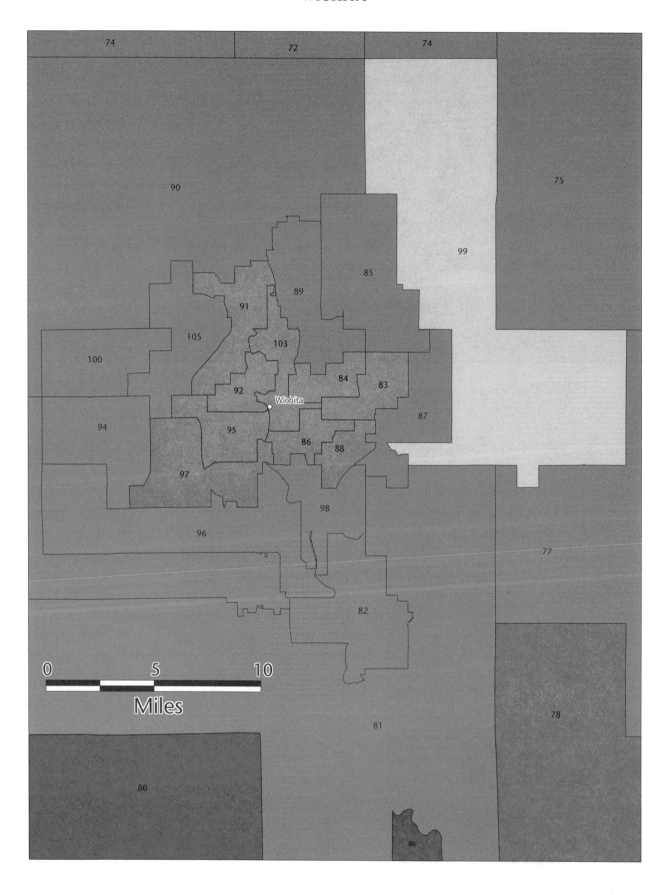

Population Growth ▉ -18% to -5% ▉ -5% to 0% ▉ 0% to 12% ☐ 12% to 62%

KANSAS CITY

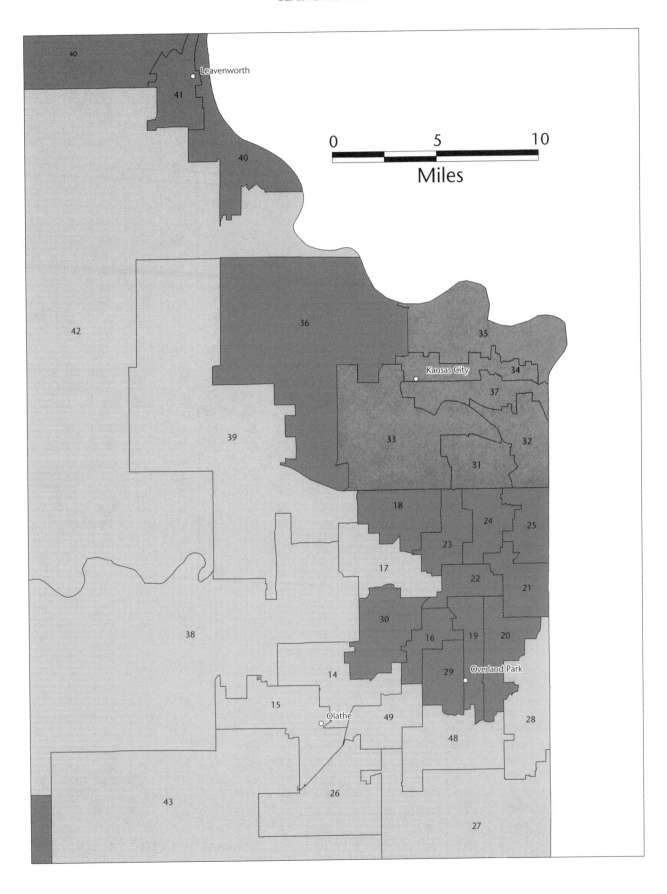

Population Growth

- ■ -18% to -5%
- ■ -5% to 0%
- ■ 0% to 12%
- □ 12% to 62%

Kansas State House Districts—Election and Demographic Data

House Districts	General Election Results Party, Percent of Vote							Population			Avg. HH Income	2006 Pop 25+		Below Poverty Line	White (Non-Hisp)	African American	American Indians, Alaska Natives	Asians, Hawaiians, Pacific Islanders	Hispanic Origin
												Some College +	4-Yr Degree +						
Kansas	2000	2001	2002	2003	2004	2005	2006	2000	2006	% Change	($)	(%)	(%)	(%)	(%)	(%)	(%)	(%)	(%)
1	D, 100		D, 100		D, 86		D, 100	20,514	19,508	-5	40,069	29.1	8.6	22.1	91.2	0.5	4.1	0.4	1.1
2	D, 100		D, 86		D, 84		D, 84	21,106	21,124	0	43,507	35.5	14.0	19.1	94.8	1.3	1.0	0.4	1.4
3	D, 62		D, 74		D, 59		D, 71	19,981	19,864	-1	40,430	37.9	18.7	26.0	86.1	2.3	1.2	2.8	5.0
4	R, 100		R, 62		R, 52		D, 51	19,606	19,611	0	44,187	32.7	11.6	19.4	95.6	1.3	0.8	0.5	0.9
5	D, 64		D, 64		D, 63		D, 66	21,056	21,892	4	46,649	31.2	12.1	16.6	92.0	1.8	0.9	0.5	3.0
6	R, 100		R, 100		R, 73		R, 70	21,660	23,529	9	66,863	35.5	14.6	10.0	95.4	0.9	0.6	0.3	1.7
7	D, 75		R, 56		R, 100		R, 58	20,704	19,832	-4	40,612	35.9	11.7	18.9	87.3	4.2	2.2	0.5	3.1
8	D, 50		D, 100		D, 100		D, 100	20,222	19,481	-4	44,300	32.8	10.5	18.5	93.1	0.6	1.1	0.4	2.8
9	R, 100		R, 100		R, 100		R, 52	21,937	21,588	-2	43,425	30.6	9.8	19.1	94.4	0.9	0.8	0.3	1.9
10	R, 100		D, 54		D, 51		D, 64	23,993	25,212	5	52,072	39.4	20.4	15.5	87.0	2.1	2.6	2.8	3.4
11	D, 100		D, 56		R, 51		R, 60	21,526	20,485	-5	40,924	35.3	10.6	19.8	82.7	5.2	5.0	0.7	2.8
12	R, 75		R, 100		R, 100		R, 75	19,861	18,550	-7	43,799	34.7	12.4	19.1	89.0	3.4	1.8	0.6	2.8
13	R, 100		R, 100		R, 66		R, 100	19,571	18,493	-6	38,619	31.5	9.5	20.5	95.1	0.3	1.0	0.3	1.9
14	R, 100		R, 61		R, 100		R, 60	20,296	25,959	28	71,245	47.5	28.3	6.8	84.9	3.1	0.4	4.0	5.4
15	R, 65		R, 60		R, 100		R, 55	22,453	25,472	13	64,954	44.3	22.0	8.3	74.5	3.6	0.7	3.1	13.9
16	R, 100		R, 100		R, 52		D, 50	19,335	20,151	4	75,262	60.7	39.5	4.0	86.8	2.2	0.3	4.7	4.5
17	R, 73		R, 81		R, 66		R, 66	21,459	25,448	19	90,210	56.3	37.5	4.5	85.6	2.4	0.3	5.0	4.7
18	R, 54		R, 56		R, 100		D, 49	19,073	19,469	2	77,834	51.4	28.2	6.0	86.7	2.6	0.4	3.3	5.1
19	R, 100		R, 100		R, 100		R, 57	21,590	22,555	4	76,702	57.8	36.6	6.1	81.4	2.3	0.3	7.8	6.7
20	R, 100		R, 55		R, 67		R, 58	20,801	22,180	7	98,122	62.7	41.3	4.7	89.5	1.3	0.2	3.6	4.0
21	R, 67		R, 100		R, 100		R, 74	22,498	22,838	2	84,549	64.6	44.2	4.4	92.7	0.7	0.2	1.7	3.3
22	D, 59		D, 100		D, 61		D, 100	20,567	20,843	1	54,156	52.6	28.0	8.5	81.0	3.1	0.6	3.9	8.9
23	R, 56		R, 53		R, 53		R, 52	19,618	19,699	0	54,286	51.3	26.8	7.9	79.6	3.7	0.5	4.0	9.0
24	R, 100		R, 100		R, 100		R, 52	21,459	21,649	1	61,892	54.1	32.2	7.1	84.2	2.6	0.4	2.7	7.5
25	R, 66		R, 57		R, 57		R, 54	19,499	19,721	1	120,766	62.6	45.5	5.7	89.7	1.0	0.3	1.7	5.5
26	R, 100		R, 100		R, 71		R, 64	21,813	27,285	25	83,287	50.8	30.2	2.7	89.3	2.3	0.3	2.8	3.7
27	R, 100		R, 82		R, 82		R, 100	20,330	25,793	27	108,117	54.3	36.4	2.2	91.7	1.1	0.2	2.9	2.8
28	R, 73		R, 100		R, 100		R, 100	21,389	24,704	15	166,109	58.8	43.9	2.4	92.2	1.5	0.3	3.4	2.0
29	R, 100		R, 100		R, 66		R, 59	19,969	21,569	8	93,471	59.3	41.3	3.9	86.0	2.2	0.3	6.5	3.9
30	R, 100		R, 100		R, 79		R, 54	21,853	23,713	9	70,403	52.9	31.4	5.3	83.3	2.9	0.4	4.6	6.6
31	D, 100		D, 100		D, 100		D, 68	19,151	18,726	-2	44,599	22.6	7.1	17.3	53.2	8.5	1.1	2.2	31.0
32	D, 100		D, 100		D, 82		D, 100	21,394	20,894	-2	37,078	25.7	10.9	24.7	33.4	10.8	1.2	5.1	49.0
33	D, 69		D, 100		D, 100		D, 100	22,885	22,884	0	51,186	29.3	9.4	12.6	64.6	17.8	0.9	1.6	12.9
34	D, 100		D, 100		D, 100		D, 100	20,968	20,631	-2	40,490	26.1	6.9	23.0	31.8	54.4	0.7	1.8	12.3
35	D, 100		D, 100		D, 100		D, 100	21,446	20,579	-4	43,410	27.0	7.7	23.9	40.3	48.5	0.7	2.1	8.7
36	D, 100		D, 100		D, 67		D, 68	21,670	22,262	3	62,395	38.5	14.4	9.1	75.4	14.0	0.6	0.8	7.4
37	D, 78		D, 100		D, 100		D, 100	20,051	19,325	-4	38,526	22.0	6.8	25.2	33.9	17.1	1.2	3.8	45.4
38	D, 71		R, 55		R, 100		R, 56	24,348	30,908	27	87,951	48.3	27.2	7.1	89.1	1.7	1.3	1.7	4.4
39	R, 71		R, 100		R, 100		R, 52	20,300	25,320	25	81,717	43.0	21.9	6.7	89.1	1.8	0.5	1.1	5.5
40	D, 60		D, 56		D, 100		D, 100	21,146	22,415	6	55,004	34.8	16.4	14.0	77.1	13.0	1.0	2.1	4.2
41	D, 62		D, 100		D, 55		D, 100	19,565	20,385	4	53,290	36.6	16.3	11.1	75.4	13.9	1.0	2.3	4.9
42	R, 61		R, 100		R, 100		R, 100	20,721	23,357	13	69,001	37.6	17.5	7.1	91.8	2.3	0.6	1.4	2.2
43	R, 100		R, 100		R, 100		R, 57	21,194	24,206	14	65,339	40.8	18.6	6.8	90.1	1.1	0.7	1.4	4.6
44	D, 69		D, 100		D, 100		D, 79	21,685	21,659	0	51,731	49.1	35.6	21.1	80.0	4.0	1.9	7.8	4.0
45	R, 64		R, 81		R, 79		R, 77	20,852	24,301	17	69,167	54.6	36.1	11.3	86.1	3.2	1.8	3.2	3.3
46	D, 71		D, 100		D, 100		D, 87	22,672	22,450	-1	40,576	45.6	27.6	23.9	82.7	4.9	2.6	4.0	5.1
47	R, 56		R, 56		R, 100		R, 65	19,872	20,700	4	56,071	30.7	12.4	12.8	95.6	0.3	1.0	0.2	1.6
48	D, 100		R, 100		R, 69		R, 62	20,331	32,736	61	136,143	54.7	40.9	1.5	88.4	2.0	0.1	5.0	3.3
49	R, 51		R, 100		R, 100		R, 55	21,845	27,172	24	89,559	51.0	32.2	4.8	84.3	2.9	0.4	4.9	5.5
50	R, 75		R, 100		R, 60		R, 61	19,936	20,798	4	60,009	31.1	12.4	10.6	89.6	0.4	5.2	0.3	3.1

(continued)

Note: D=Democrat, R=Republican, R/D=Republican/Democrat (cross-filed), D/R=Democrat/Republican (cross-filed), I=Independent, C=Constitution, O=Other, GI=Green Independent, P=Progressive, P/D=Progressive/Democrat, P/D/R=Progressive/Democrat/Republican, HH=Households

Kansas State House Districts—Election and Demographic Data (cont.)

House Districts	General Election Results Party, Percent of Vote							Population			Avg. HH Income ($)	Pop 25+		Below Poverty Line (%)	2006 White (Non-Hisp) (%)	African American (%)	American Indians, Alaska Natives (%)	Asians, Hawaiians, Pacific Islanders (%)	Hispanic Origin (%)
Kansas	2000	2001	2002	2003	2004	2005	2006	2000	2006	% Change	($)	Some College + (%)	4-Yr Degree + (%)	(%)	(%)	(%)	(%)	(%)	(%)
51	R, 70		R, 62		R, 73		R, 100	20,502	22,136	8	66,429	39.6	20.3	6.7	91.7	1.8	0.7	1.2	3.1
52	R, 57		R, 75		R, 74		R, 72	18,966	19,870	5	71,225	50.0	30.4	7.3	85.8	3.8	0.6	3.0	4.7
53	D, 61		D, 55		D, 51		D, 64	22,180	23,005	4	60,862	37.3	16.7	8.3	84.3	4.7	1.0	0.7	6.9
54	R, 50		R, 53		R, 64		R, 51	20,968	21,682	3	60,665	46.1	25.6	9.0	85.2	4.9	0.9	1.8	4.8
55	D, 68		D, 100		D, 100		D, 100	20,878	20,401	-2	48,651	37.9	19.8	18.0	71.2	11.8	1.5	1.6	10.2
56	D, 70		D, 62		D, 57		D, 59	19,995	19,434	-3	44,678	39.8	19.5	15.7	80.3	6.6	1.5	1.0	7.4
57	D, 100		D, 61		D, 100		D, 100	19,314	19,371	0	43,015	21.6	7.0	18.4	63.9	7.3	2.4	0.5	20.5
58	D, 100		D, 100		D, 100		D, 76	19,702	19,270	-2	39,668	26.0	9.7	20.5	54.8	22.4	2.3	1.4	15.8
59	R, 100		R, 100		R, 100		R, 51	21,597	22,552	4	50,698	29.5	11.0	14.8	95.8	0.2	0.8	0.4	1.4
60	R, 100		R, 55		R, 66		R, 69	20,277	20,293	0	42,554	33.9	17.1	22.4	63.3	2.7	0.6	3.1	23.7
61	R, 100		R, 100		R, 78		R, 79	20,619	21,675	5	51,163	33.3	14.8	13.9	93.9	0.7	0.7	0.4	2.7
62	R, 100		D, 58		D, 54		D, 53	20,643	19,792	-4	43,899	28.6	12.0	19.0	91.5	0.8	4.8	0.3	1.4
63	D, 61		D, 100		D, 80		D, 79	22,153	21,921	-1	42,077	29.2	12.0	19.3	91.4	3.7	1.0	0.5	1.9
64	R, 100		R, 100		R, 100		R, 73	26,137	25,154	-4	45,769	34.7	11.0	14.6	74.9	10.2	0.8	2.9	7.1
65	D, 52		R, 65		R, 65		R, 52	19,727	16,290	-17	44,300	33.0	10.1	17.0	63.2	19.2	0.9	5.6	5.9
66	R, 57		D, 50		D, 54		D, 58	30,013	30,495	2	36,444	44.2	28.2	26.9	84.2	3.7	0.5	5.4	4.0
67	R, 63		R, 52		D, 50		D, 58	20,713	20,958	1	59,789	52.6	32.9	13.5	84.6	4.8	0.7	3.9	3.8
68	R, 100		R, 53		R, 100		R, 57	19,837	19,453	-2	46,292	32.0	11.1	16.3	93.8	0.5	0.6	0.4	3.4
69	R, 59		R, 100		R, 50		R, 51	19,214	18,845	-2	42,538	32.0	12.0	15.7	76.0	2.9	0.7	2.7	12.8
70	R, 63		R, 100		R, 100		R, 100	20,049	19,623	-2	46,280	32.8	12.6	15.1	92.6	2.1	0.8	0.3	3.1
71	R, 100		R, 55		R, 100		R, 60	18,494	19,080	3	51,944	37.6	15.8	14.1	85.6	3.2	0.7	1.8	5.9
72	R, 100		D, 53		D, 100		R, 50	20,216	20,884	3	51,539	38.3	17.5	13.4	78.3	1.8	0.5	0.9	13.0
73	R, 100		R, 100		R, 100		R, 100	20,456	20,076	-2	53,283	37.4	16.8	13.2	93.9	0.9	0.4	0.7	2.5
74	R, 100		R, 100		R, 100		R, 100	19,670	20,542	4	53,786	35.7	13.8	10.6	94.7	0.4	0.5	0.4	2.4
75	R, 100		R, 56		R, 54		R, 54	20,862	21,460	3	55,102	35.8	12.2	13.7	93.0	1.2	1.0	0.5	2.7
76	R, 100		R, 100		R, 69		R, 64	44,023	43,828	0	45,216	33.0	15.6	18.8	73.2	1.6	0.6	2.2	16.7
77	R, 100		R, 100		R, 56		R, 61	20,792	21,945	6	59,039	36.6	14.1	10.5	93.8	0.3	1.1	0.5	2.8
78	D, 73		D, 65		D, 100		D, 52	19,736	19,655	0	51,205	36.5	14.4	15.9	85.7	1.7	1.4	2.9	6.4
79	D, 68		D, 100		R, 55		R, 100	20,798	20,244	-3	45,585	35.0	10.7	18.0	85.4	2.3	2.8	0.7	6.4
80	R, 59		R, 100		R, 100		D, 57	21,663	20,413	-6	48,424	32.2	11.3	16.8	91.8	0.7	1.1	0.5	3.8
81	R, 54		R, 61		R, 65		R, 51	23,045	24,383	6	64,229	35.2	13.4	8.3	90.4	1.4	1.4	1.5	3.3
82	R, 62		R, 80		R, 64		R, 61	20,346	22,349	10	68,194	41.7	20.6	6.9	89.3	1.4	1.0	1.8	4.3
83	R, 100		R, 72		R, 84		R, 68	20,368	19,843	-3	88,010	56.5	37.3	8.3	85.6	4.2	0.6	3.7	4.1
84	D, 73		D, 100		D, 73		D, 100	19,124	18,436	-4	38,006	31.1	12.1	27.2	38.4	43.1	1.0	7.4	9.0
85	R, 64		R, 68		R, 65		R, 62	21,349	23,810	12	81,143	51.8	33.1	5.4	79.0	6.9	0.6	7.0	4.5
86	D, 52		D, 100		D, 52		D, 57	20,041	19,297	-4	42,095	31.8	11.8	17.1	66.3	7.6	1.8	3.8	15.8
87	R, 51		R, 56		R, 57		D, 57	22,394	23,499	5	65,307	42.9	21.2	8.5	71.9	8.4	1.0	9.3	6.7
88	D, 62		D, 50		D, 63		D, 59	21,190	20,747	-2	38,241	31.2	12.8	20.5	52.1	10.7	1.7	10.9	21.0
89	D, 72		D, 100		D, 67		D, 100	18,777	19,962	6	43,920	31.2	13.1	24.4	44.7	40.8	1.0	6.3	5.6
90	R, 62		R, 100		R, 100		R, 69	22,659	23,334	3	66,135	35.6	15.3	6.6	91.6	1.0	0.9	0.7	3.8
91	R, 56		R, 55		R, 64		R, 53	20,348	19,740	-3	53,072	40.3	18.1	9.6	78.9	2.9	1.2	2.5	10.4
92	D, 54		D, 61		D, 100		D, 62	20,120	19,229	-4	42,091	33.3	15.9	14.0	62.1	4.1	1.6	1.8	23.8
93	D, 100		D, 100		R, 58		R, 55	20,865	22,191	6	60,652	30.8	12.3	9.6	91.5	0.8	1.1	0.9	3.4
94	R, 100		R, 67		R, 74		R, 100	19,318	21,397	11	74,922	44.0	21.5	3.8	86.6	1.7	1.0	2.9	5.3
95	D, 100		D, 79		D, 58		D, 62	20,187	19,606	-3	40,518	28.2	10.1	16.8	72.4	4.3	2.3	2.7	13.6
96	R, 53		R, 50		R, 60		D, 51	20,825	22,689	9	50,225	29.4	9.2	10.7	79.0	2.9	1.8	4.9	7.8
97	R, 66		R, 100		R, 100		R, 64	20,419	20,249	-1	50,008	29.1	10.0	11.6	74.7	4.8	1.8	5.0	9.9
98	D, 63		D, 100		D, 62		D, 100	21,396	23,060	8	44,067	25.9	6.8	16.6	64.7	8.2	2.0	7.7	13.0
99	R, 67		R, 71		R, 100		R, 68	21,459	24,538	14	85,971	47.1	27.7	6.8	86.9	2.3	0.8	4.9	3.2
100	R, 71		R, 66		R, 100		R, 69	20,826	22,995	10	89,197	46.0	26.6	3.0	88.1	1.4	0.6	3.2	4.7

(continued)

Note: D=Democrat, R=Republican, R/D=Republican/Democrat (cross-filed), D/R=Democrat/Republican (cross-filed), I=Independent, C=Constitution, O=Other, GI=Green Independent, P=Progressive, P/D=Progressive/Democrat, P/D/R=Progressive/Democrat/Republican, HH=Households

Kansas State House Districts—Election and Demographic Data (cont.)

House Districts	General Election Results Party, Percent of Vote							Population			Avg. HH Income	Pop 25+		Below Poverty Line	2006 White (Non-Hisp)	African American	American Indians, Alaska Natives	Asians, Hawaiians, Pacific Islanders	Hispanic Origin
Kansas	2000	2001	2002	2003	2004	2005	2006	2000	2006	% Change	($)	Some College + (%)	4-Yr Degree + (%)	(%)	(%)	(%)	(%)	(%)	(%)
101	R, 53		R, 53		D, 51		D, 100	21,510	21,185	-2	52,217	36.0	11.9	13.3	92.3	1.1	0.6	0.4	3.6
102	D, 100		D, 72		D, 100		D, 100	19,761	19,032	-4	33,489	28.8	6.6	22.6	74.4	5.6	1.1	0.9	13.1
103	D, 100		D, 100		D, 100		D, 100	22,348	21,818	-2	36,463	24.9	10.1	25.3	34.6	9.9	1.8	3.8	46.5
104	R, 69		R, 100		R, 100		R, 78	19,536	19,098	-2	60,764	46.5	21.0	11.0	92.5	1.0	0.3	1.0	3.5
105	D, 100		R, 69		R, 66		R, 60	20,304	21,771	7	64,200	43.4	22.3	8.5	84.9	2.2	1.2	3.7	5.6
106	R, 100		R, 59		R, 100		R, 78	20,021	18,643	-7	44,277	30.5	11.8	17.7	97.0	0.2	0.5	0.3	1.2
107	R, 100		R, 100		R, 100		R, 71	20,599	19,612	-5	45,535	33.6	12.6	15.9	96.7	0.3	0.4	0.3	1.6
108	D, 79		D, 66		D, 60		D, 100	60,148	60,523	1	50,274	35.8	14.3	13.9	84.2	2.6	0.6	2.1	7.4
109	R, 100		R, 100		R, 100		R, 100	20,584	18,144	-12	41,775	35.7	12.1	16.5	97.4	0.2	0.3	0.4	1.0
110	R, 58		R, 100		R, 100		R, 100	21,597	20,009	-7	40,382	33.7	13.1	18.5	96.9	0.4	0.4	0.3	1.2
111	D, 73		D, 100		D, 100		D, 100	22,290	21,856	-2	50,228	40.9	22.2	19.3	92.8	0.6	0.3	1.3	3.2
112	R, 100		R, 100		R, 54		R, 50	20,126	19,984	-1	44,188	35.1	12.3	17.5	80.3	1.2	0.6	0.4	13.6
113	R, 100		R, 69		R, 72		R, 100	20,034	19,553	-2	43,955	33.8	11.4	16.9	91.1	0.7	0.6	0.4	5.3
114	D, 68		D, 55		R, 56		R, 51	21,744	20,364	-6	45,845	38.8	14.7	15.7	88.1	1.7	0.6	0.6	6.5
115	R, 100		R, 73		R, 100		R, 100	21,756	22,433	3	48,901	30.4	10.9	15.8	61.5	0.6	0.6	2.6	28.4
116	D, 63		D, 76		D, 100		D, 100	21,521	20,159	-6	46,049	35.9	12.9	15.7	95.0	0.2	0.6	0.3	2.6
117	R, 100		R, 100		R, 100		R, 74	41,593	39,163	-6	50,180	28.8	10.7	15.7	47.7	1.2	1.0	3.8	37.3
118	R, 68		R, 64		R, 66		R, 100	20,296	18,250	-10	45,320	34.9	12.7	17.0	92.4	0.2	0.4	0.3	4.4
119	D, 57		D, 55		R, 68		R, 85	21,576	22,318	3	52,915	32.3	12.8	15.1	40.3	1.8	0.8	2.1	48.9
120	R, 100		R, 66		R, 65		R, 62	21,049	19,350	-8	42,081	35.4	12.3	16.6	95.0	1.1	0.3	0.5	2.2
121	R, 100		R, 100		R, 92		R, 89	20,163	18,264	-9	47,467	37.6	13.7	16.7	92.5	0.6	0.3	0.6	4.1
122	R, 82		R, 80		R, 100		R, 100	20,670	19,912	-4	52,499	32.8	12.0	13.8	69.6	0.4	0.9	0.6	20.9
123	R, 100		R, 83		R, 100		R, 100	18,600	16,517	-11	53,525	31.7	11.5	15.9	49.8	1.5	1.2	2.9	35.6
124	R, 100		R, 100		R, 100		R, 100	20,485	19,754	-4	53,459	30.3	11.6	13.0	58.8	0.5	1.1	0.6	30.7
125	R, 100		R, 100		R, 100		R, 100	21,615	22,734	5	48,913	24.9	9.9	17.7	33.1	3.4	0.9	4.0	52.9

Note: D=Democrat, R=Republican, R/D=Republican/Democrat (cross-filed), D/R=Democrat/Republican (cross-filed), I=Independent, C=Constitution, O=Other, GI=Green Independent, P=Progressive, P/D=Progressive/Democrat, P/D/R=Progressive/Democrat/Republican, HH=Households

KENTUCKY

This is how Ben Lucien Burman in 1923 described Kentucky in *The Nation*. "Is not Kentucky the land of grizzled feudists and defiant moonshiners; of soft-hatted politicians who recite poetry and tote pistols; is it not the land of dashing Night Riders and tobacco-chewing Methuselahs; is it not Wild West on Main Street? It is. All of these. But it is not savage; merely romantic. Therefore let a mechanized world be grateful."

Kentucky, as one can see, is a state that defies easy classification. Although it sits along some of the most important transportation routes in America, both water (the Mississippi River, the Ohio, the Cumberland, the Tennessee) and land (the National Road), it is not a popular destination, except for passengers changing planes at Cincinnati's airport, which is located in Covington. When it was admitted to the Union in 1792, during George Washington's administration (the first state off the eastern seaboard), it certainly was a romantic place, where rich bottom land was tilled, one imagines, to the tune of a Stephen Foster ballad.

All that stopped with the Civil War, as Kentucky, though it remained in the Union, served as an entry point for attacks on the South by Ulysses S. Grant and the Army of the Tennessee. Politically, the home of Henry Clay has produced few leaders of note since 1860, when it was the birthplace of three major presidential candidates, Abraham Lincoln, Stephen Douglas, and John Breckenridge. Alben Barkeley, vice president under Harry Truman, was the last Kentuckian to hold national office, unless one calls the commissioner of Major League Baseball a national officeholder, in which case include former governor and Senator Albert "Happy" Chandler, who held the job from 1945 to 1951.

The Kentucky most Americans see on television each May, and the part that is foremost in national mythology, is bluegrass horse country, home to the Kentucky Derby and mint juleps. It is a land of surpassing beauty, one not even exceeded by an area most of the country does not see, the wrenching poverty of the mountains. Kentucky is the sixth-poorest state in terms of average household income, and only Nevada, Mississippi, and West Virginia have a lower percentage of college graduates. The unemployment rate in some parts of the mountains—mining country—is 14 percent. Nearly one state resident in six lives below the poverty line.

An economy so reliant on coal, tobacco, and (in this abstemious age) whiskey would be precarious at any time but is particularly so today. The state's overall rate of growth is below the national average, though it has improved from the 1980s when it grew at less than 1 percent. Population is falling sharply in downtown Coving-

ton, in Paducah, the 8th house district outside Hopkinsville in the southwest, and to a lesser extent in the eastern coal counties, which have already lost many of their residents. On the other hand, the Louisville and Cincinnati suburbs around Covington are growing, and spreading into outlying rural areas, a process seen around the nation. The 60th house district has swelled by 30 percent since 2000.

The wealthiest Kentucky districts are not so wealthy by the standards of other states. There is only one $100,000 district here, the 48th in suburban Louisville (the Pendennis Club set), which has the highest average household income. At the other extreme, Kentucky has two of the twenty poorest state house districts in the United States, both of which, not surprisingly, are located in the eastern mountains. In the 90th district, the third-poorest in the country, average household income is just $27,784, only 6 percent have earned a college degree, and more than four in ten live below the poverty line.

Kentucky is one of the least racially diverse states, though slavery was once permitted here. Fifty-eight of the one hundred districts in the state house of representatives are more than 90 percent white. African Americans are found in significant numbers in only three house districts in downtown Louisville. The 77th house district, centered just outside of Lexington, is 11 percent Hispanic. Many work in the tobacco and horse farms.

The Republican tide that has been rising through the South and the more rural interior of the country has reached Kentucky after some delay. For the first time the state has a Republican governor and two Republican U.S. senators (one of whom, Mitch McConnell, is the Senate minority leader), and the GOP holds five of six congressional seats. Republicans won control of the state senate in 2000 and have added to their majority there. Democrats had a cushion of thirty-two seats in the state house until 2004, but Republicans have picked up ten seats in the last two election cycles.

A few final notes about the Bluegrass State. Technically, Kentucky is not a "state" but a "commonwealth, one of four in the country (Massachusetts, Pennsylvania, and Virginia are the others), although the designation, which was popular in the eighteenth century, is a mere choice of words and has no legal significance. Kentucky also remains one of four states (Mississippi, New Jersey, and Virginia are the others) that holds its gubernatorial elections in odd-numbered years. Finally, it is also, as John Gunther pointed out in his book, *Inside U.S.A.,* home to a geographic oddity: Kentucky's little peninsula sticking out from Tennessee into the Mississippi River is not territorially adjacent to the rest of the state.

KENTUCKY
State Senate Districts

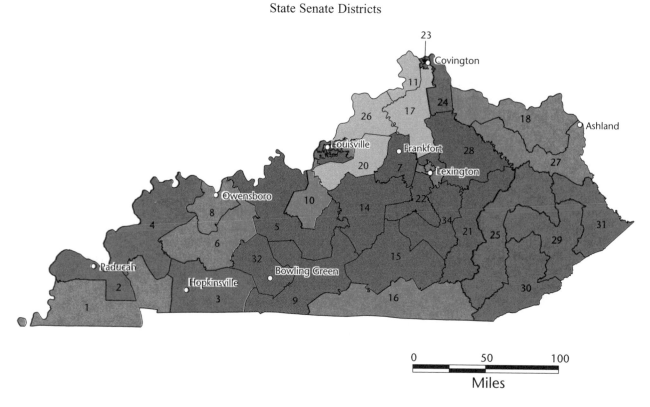

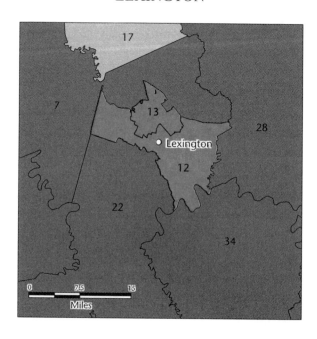

LOUISVILLE

LEXINGTON

Population Growth   ■ -3% to 1%   ■ 1% to 4%   ■ 4% to 11%   ■ 11% to 22%

Kentucky State Senate Districts—Election and Demographic Data

Senate Districts	General Election Results Party, Percent of Vote							Population			Avg. HH Income	Pop 25+ 2006		Below Poverty Line	White (Non-Hisp)	African American	American Indians, Alaska Natives	Asians, Hawaiians, Pacific Islanders	Hispanic Origin
	2000	2001	2002	2003	2004	2005	2006	2000	2006	% Change	($)	Some College + (%)	4-Yr Degree + (%)	(%)	(%)	(%)	(%)	(%)	(%)
Kentucky																			
1	D, 100				R, 51			110,695	112,713	2	44,205	27.5	11.8	23.1	89.2	5.8	0.2	0.7	2.4
2			R, 51				D, 41	103,896	103,694	0	49,755	31.8	12.3	19.0	90.2	6.4	0.2	0.6	1.2
3	D, 53				D, 54			109,563	107,835	-2	43,609	24.3	7.7	21.2	75.6	16.4	0.4	1.3	3.4
4			D, 56				D, 100	107,827	108,036	0	47,130	24.8	8.1	20.1	90.9	5.6	0.2	0.3	1.7
5	R, 56				R, 55			108,828	115,245	6	43,632	20.9	6.7	22.5	93.5	3.0	0.3	0.4	1.5
6			D, 62				D, 70	100,892	102,228	1	44,150	21.2	7.0	23.4	93.0	4.1	0.2	0.3	1.2
7	R, 58				D, 63			112,501	117,259	4	59,069	34.3	17.5	13.3	85.5	7.8	0.2	0.7	4.0
8			D, 54				D, 100	101,515	103,431	2	51,145	29.0	11.7	18.0	93.0	3.6	0.1	0.5	1.3
9	R, 100				R, 100			105,479	110,641	5	43,312	19.9	7.4	24.0	94.0	3.4	0.2	0.4	1.0
10			R, 64				R, 57	107,689	110,977	3	50,289	30.6	10.1	15.0	81.0	9.8	0.4	2.4	3.0
11	R, 74				R, 100			105,128	128,254	22	70,522	34.2	15.6	9.4	92.6	1.4	0.2	1.5	2.5
12			R, 57				R, 57	105,187	107,886	3	68,957	48.7	34.0	11.1	83.8	7.2	0.2	3.3	3.4
13	D, 100				D, 100			110,625	114,117	3	47,581	39.3	26.2	21.0	69.0	18.6	0.2	3.2	7.0
14			R, 100				R, 100	110,249	118,015	7	47,370	23.0	9.1	21.0	91.4	5.4	0.1	0.5	1.3
15	R, 68				R, 100			105,221	111,477	6	39,014	21.5	7.9	28.7	96.2	1.0	0.2	0.4	1.3
16			R, 100				R, 72	101,837	105,016	3	34,106	18.6	7.6	34.5	96.0	1.0	0.3	0.2	1.5
17	D, 70				R, 55			104,794	118,203	13	59,082	27.1	11.6	13.5	94.3	2.0	0.2	0.5	1.5
18			R, 62				R, 53	106,113	107,757	2	42,310	23.4	8.0	24.2	96.6	1.3	0.2	0.3	0.7
19	D, 61				D, 62			111,521	111,367	0	66,119	50.6	30.2	9.6	87.8	6.0	0.2	1.8	2.3
20			R, 56				R, 100	105,877	124,532	18	58,831	26.6	9.2	13.2	91.0	2.9	0.3	0.5	3.5
21	R, 58				R, 100			101,651	107,219	5	36,908	18.6	7.2	29.6	97.3	0.5	0.3	0.3	0.7
22			R, 100				R, 100	105,014	114,917	9	59,712	35.1	19.2	14.7	90.4	4.6	0.2	1.5	1.7
23	R, 53				R, 53			102,256	103,025	1	61,614	34.5	16.9	14.6	90.7	4.8	0.2	0.9	1.7
24			R, 100				R, 100	102,826	102,232	-1	57,048	30.0	13.8	13.8	95.8	1.2	0.2	0.6	1.0
25	R, 69				R, 87			103,279	103,743	0	30,923	16.9	6.7	40.0	95.9	2.1	0.2	0.2	0.8
26			R, 100				R, 100	111,841	124,686	11	86,490	40.3	23.0	10.6	90.3	4.2	0.2	1.3	2.2
27	D, 58				D, 58			107,807	109,928	2	43,006	26.8	10.3	25.5	95.6	1.5	0.2	0.4	1.2
28			D, 100				D, 100	110,353	116,195	5	48,908	24.2	9.8	20.1	92.8	3.7	0.2	0.2	1.7
29	D, 100				D, 100			101,040	99,681	-1	33,143	21.8	7.6	36.0	97.6	0.8	0.1	0.4	0.6
30			D, 66				D, 100	105,048	102,711	-2	31,882	19.1	7.0	37.3	95.8	1.8	0.3	0.5	0.8
31	D, 53				D, 61			105,989	104,171	-2	37,489	21.0	7.8	31.5	97.6	0.4	0.1	0.5	0.7
32			R, 100				R, 100	105,585	113,390	7	51,965	31.6	16.2	19.6	86.9	6.9	0.8	1.7	3.3
33	D, 100				D, 100			102,751	103,718	1	36,691	27.6	10.3	31.0	43.7	52.3	0.3	0.8	1.6
34			D, 54				D, 56	111,037	121,340	9	43,574	26.6	12.7	23.5	93.4	3.2	0.3	0.7	1.2
35	D, 70				D, 78			107,449	107,152	0	37,938	30.7	12.8	25.5	57.7	34.9	0.3	1.6	3.6
36			R, 58				R, 100	107,707	110,714	3	88,466	53.5	34.0	6.9	86.3	6.6	0.2	2.5	2.7
37	D, 68				D, 100			108,381	108,423	0	47,001	29.8	10.7	14.9	84.9	6.8	0.3	2.4	3.5
38			R, 58				R, 57	111,025	115,610	4	58,042	33.9	13.3	10.0	89.3	5.0	0.3	1.5	2.1

Note: D=Democrat, R=Republican, R/D=Republican/Democrat (cross-filed), D/R=Democrat/Republican (cross-filed), I=Independent, C=Constitution, O=Other, GI=Green Independent, P=Progressive, P/D=Progressive/Democrat, P/D/R=Progressive/Democrat/Republican, HH=Households

KENTUCKY
State House Districts

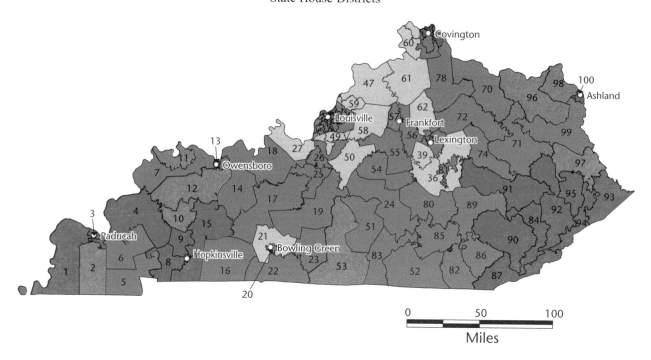

COVINGTON

LEXINGTON

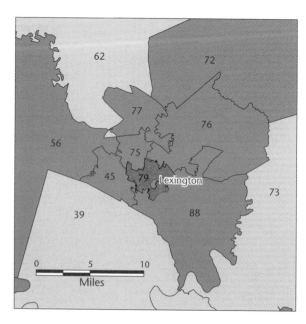

Population Growth   ■ -7% to 0%   ■ 0% to 2%   ■ 2% to 9%   □ 9% to 30%

LOUISVILLE

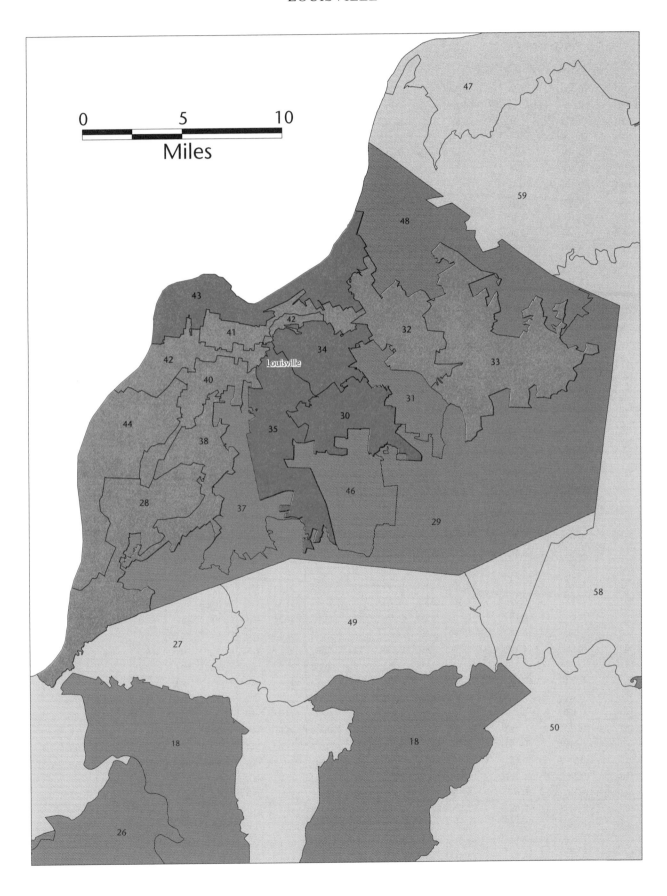

Population Growth    -7% to 0%   ☐ 0% to 2%   ■ 2% to 9%   ☐ 9% to 30%

Kentucky State House Districts—Election and Demographic Data

House Districts	General Election Results Party, Percent of Vote							Population			Avg. HH Income	Pop 25+		2006					
												Some College +	4-Yr Degree +	Below Poverty Line	White (Non-Hisp)	African American	American Indians, Alaska Natives	Asians, Hawaiians, Pacific Islanders	Hispanic Origin
Kentucky	2000	2001	2002	2003	2004	2005	2006	2000	2006	% Change	($)	(%)	(%)	(%)	(%)	(%)	(%)	(%)	(%)
1	D, 100		D, 100		R, 55		R, 58	39,635	39,109	-1	50,489	27.3	10.3	20.1	90.4	6.8	0.2	0.3	1.0
2	D, 100		D, 72		D, 63		D, 100	42,278	43,012	2	46,559	25.9	10.1	22.9	89.5	3.7	0.2	0.3	4.2
3	D, 100		D, 100		D, 100		D, 66	37,831	36,287	-4	44,607	32.5	13.3	24.2	78.8	16.4	0.3	0.9	1.7
4	D, 100		D, 100		D, 61		D, 100	40,370	39,278	-3	44,777	24.9	7.8	21.3	95.9	1.9	0.2	0.3	0.7
5	D, 100		D, 100		R, 52		R, 58	38,509	39,820	3	44,434	33.5	17.1	21.6	91.9	3.4	0.2	1.6	1.6
6	D, 100		D, 100		D, 51		D, 59	40,420	41,495	3	48,257	29.2	10.5	17.0	96.4	1.3	0.2	0.2	0.9
7	D, 100		D, 100		D, 54		D, 100	39,030	40,022	3	50,081	24.8	8.6	17.0	88.3	7.8	0.1	0.4	1.7
8	D, 100		D, 100		D, 51		D, 52	36,286	34,709	-4	44,178	29.0	10.7	23.0	71.8	23.9	0.2	0.9	1.5
9	D, 100		D, 100		D, 100		R, 54	39,427	38,914	-1	42,519	24.7	6.1	17.5	66.0	19.0	0.8	2.4	6.4
10	D, 62		D, 100		D, 100		D, 100	38,091	38,198	0	45,901	23.9	8.1	22.1	89.9	6.7	0.2	0.5	1.4
11	D, 100		D, 100		D, 100		D, 100	38,816	39,473	2	48,928	29.0	10.5	18.6	89.0	7.4	0.2	0.5	1.7
12	D, 100		D, 100		D, 100		D, 100	39,536	40,206	2	50,140	24.5	8.1	18.8	94.3	2.0	0.2	0.3	2.3
13	R, 61		R, 100		R, 57		D, 52	40,616	39,810	-2	45,063	31.1	13.3	21.7	90.4	5.8	0.2	0.6	1.3
14	R, 60		D, 57		D, 56		D, 100	42,524	44,644	5	53,466	24.6	9.4	18.7	96.6	0.7	0.2	0.4	1.2
15	D, 100		D, 100		D, 100		D, 72	38,640	38,569	0	41,325	19.2	6.1	25.1	93.8	4.0	0.2	0.2	1.0
16	R, 100		R, 100		R, 55		R, 53	38,064	38,920	2	44,289	20.5	7.2	22.8	89.2	7.1	0.2	0.3	1.8
17	R, 100		R, 66		R, 69		R, 100	41,320	43,582	5	41,427	18.0	5.8	24.4	96.9	0.4	0.2	0.2	1.3
18	R, 100		R, 100		R, 69		R, 100	41,457	43,552	5	46,495	20.4	6.2	19.5	94.6	2.4	0.3	0.3	1.2
19	D, 54		D, 61		R, 53		D, 54	42,327	43,813	4	40,896	18.6	6.1	26.5	94.0	3.6	0.3	0.2	1.0
20	D, 100		D, 100		D, 100		D, 100	41,750	44,431	6	55,855	37.3	21.2	20.5	80.1	9.3	0.2	2.7	4.7
21	D, 100		D, 100		R, 51		R, 51	42,879	47,077	10	50,064	29.7	14.0	18.4	85.9	7.4	0.3	1.3	2.9
22	D, 100		D, 100		D, 58		D, 100	41,881	43,986	5	47,451	23.9	10.2	19.8	92.8	4.4	0.2	0.5	1.0
23	R, 100		R, 100		R, 100		D, 53	38,364	40,676	6	45,079	21.4	8.6	22.1	93.4	3.8	0.2	0.6	1.1
24	D, 100		R, 51		R, 100		R, 100	38,852	41,705	7	38,073	17.0	6.1	28.9	92.8	3.9	0.2	0.4	1.8
25	D, 58		D, 100		D, 100		D, 100	40,909	42,313	3	53,935	32.2	12.0	15.3	89.6	5.3	0.3	1.7	1.3
26	D, 56		D, 53		D, 53		R, 53	39,372	40,413	3	49,360	33.0	10.0	14.5	70.1	16.2	0.6	4.1	4.4
27	D, 100		D, 100		R, 55		D, 53	42,293	47,044	11	48,455	24.6	7.2	15.8	87.2	5.2	0.6	1.1	3.3
28	D, 67		D, 100		D, 53		D, 64	38,126	38,886	2	51,386	29.0	10.1	12.2	92.4	3.7	0.3	0.7	1.3
29	R, 57		R, 100		R, 63		R, 100	44,285	46,226	4	68,715	38.9	17.7	6.6	90.8	4.7	0.2	1.1	1.5
30	D, 100		D, 100		D, 70		D, 74	41,408	41,040	-1	47,030	36.6	15.6	15.5	60.5	30.2	0.2	2.4	4.7
31	D, 54		D, 61		D, 58		D, 100	42,475	43,724	3	62,266	46.8	24.2	8.3	83.7	8.9	0.2	1.8	3.3
32	D, 54		R, 64		R, 63		R, 100	42,191	42,781	1	75,896	55.2	34.6	8.1	85.6	6.1	0.2	3.3	2.9
33	R, 68		R, 100		R, 70		R, 100	39,282	39,995	2	91,990	52.6	33.6	5.6	87.8	5.5	0.2	2.5	2.5
34	D, 100		D, 67		D, 66		D, 100	43,555	42,420	-3	73,426	58.0	39.1	9.4	91.4	3.8	0.2	1.5	1.7
35	D, 68		D, 66		D, 64		D, 100	40,168	39,562	-2	50,059	33.8	15.2	15.4	88.2	5.8	0.3	1.2	2.5
36	R, 92		R, 72		R, 100		R, 100	41,336	47,130	14	46,657	27.1	11.4	19.4	94.9	2.1	0.2	0.4	1.3
37	D, 63		D, 100		D, 100		D, 100	38,118	38,952	2	40,163	26.8	9.7	19.0	79.6	7.4	0.3	4.8	5.5
38	D, 70		D, 100		D, 59		D, 56	38,506	38,524	0	46,034	29.4	10.9	18.3	83.5	9.9	0.3	1.9	2.3
39	D, 57		D, 100		D, 58		D, 73	40,132	45,056	12	59,097	32.7	16.2	14.6	92.8	2.9	0.2	0.9	1.5
40	D, 100		D, 100		D, 100		D, 100	39,850	40,378	1	36,620	27.0	9.8	27.9	59.1	34.0	0.3	1.6	3.1
41	D, 100		D, 100		D, 100		D, 78	36,981	37,394	1	41,870	34.3	18.1	33.2	49.0	45.5	0.2	1.8	2.3
42	D, 100		D, 100		D, 100		D, 100	39,578	40,151	1	38,606	31.7	14.1	28.3	45.8	49.8	0.3	0.7	1.7
43	D, 92		D, 53		D, 63		D, 72	40,993	40,857	0	55,541	31.7	15.3	29.2	48.5	48.0	0.2	0.6	1.2
44	D, 100		D, 100		D, 100		D, 100	38,219	38,609	1	48,672	27.7	8.8	14.2	82.3	14.1	0.2	0.6	1.3
45	R, 61		R, 100		R, 66		R, 100	40,648	42,238	4	75,180	50.1	35.0	6.4	89.5	3.4	0.1	3.3	2.1
46	D, 62		D, 62		D, 53		D, 100	40,952	42,156	3	51,798	33.0	11.1	12.4	79.3	13.4	0.3	1.5	3.5
47	R, 100		D, 58		D, 100		D, 100	44,214	49,317	12	54,305	25.8	10.0	18.0	91.7	2.6	0.3	0.4	2.8
48	R, 100		R, 100		R, 100		R, 57	45,442	47,612	5	111,524	54.8	37.2	5.3	85.1	7.7	0.2	3.2	2.2
49	D, 54		R, 56		R, 56		D, 53	41,071	45,788	11	57,356	24.8	6.8	11.7	96.8	0.4	0.4	0.4	1.0
50	D, 100		D, 69		R, 54		R, 100	42,056	47,511	13	54,869	25.3	9.7	16.7	92.6	4.4	0.1	0.6	1.1

(continued)

Note: D=Democrat, R=Republican, R/D=Republican/Democrat (cross-filed), D/R=Democrat/Republican (cross-filed), I=Independent, C=Constitution, O=Other, GI=Green Independent, P=Progressive, P/D=Progressive/Democrat, P/D/R=Progressive/Democrat/Republican, HH=Households

Kentucky State House Districts—Election and Demographic Data (cont.)

House Districts	General Election Results Party, Percent of Vote							Population			Avg. HH Income	Pop 25+ Some College +	Pop 25+ 4-Yr Degree +	Below Poverty Line	2006 White (Non-Hisp)	African American	American Indians, Alaska Natives	Asians, Hawaiians, Pacific Islanders	Hispanic Origin
Kentucky	2000	2001	2002	2003	2004	2005	2006	2000	2006	% Change	($)	(%)	(%)	(%)	(%)	(%)	(%)	(%)	(%)
51	R, 54		R, 59		R, 100		R, 53	40,180	41,458	3	41,421	22.5	8.9	28.2	94.0	3.6	0.1	0.3	1.0
52	R, 100		R, 100		R, 72		R, 100	41,778	42,721	2	32,397	17.7	6.0	34.8	95.7	1.0	0.3	0.1	1.8
53	R, 100		R, 100		R, 100		R, 100	40,529	40,861	1	38,336	17.3	6.5	31.3	95.0	2.3	0.1	0.1	1.4
54	D, 51		R, 58		R, 56		R, 50	38,105	39,450	4	49,727	27.6	13.0	19.5	87.4	8.4	0.2	0.6	1.7
55	D, 100		D, 65		R, 51		R, 51	42,128	45,805	9	51,884	24.9	9.2	15.1	94.1	2.6	0.2	0.4	1.4
56	D, 53		D, 100		D, 54		D, 56	41,961	43,612	4	64,497	39.9	22.4	11.5	86.8	4.7	0.1	0.8	5.7
57	D, 72		D, 62		D, 100		D, 100	38,413	38,581	0	54,476	33.8	17.7	15.9	85.3	9.6	0.1	0.9	2.3
58	R, 100		R, 52		R, 55		R, 55	42,324	50,833	20	61,765	30.0	12.5	13.9	82.8	6.5	0.3	0.6	7.2
59	R, 100		R, 100		R, 100		R, 100	39,357	45,583	16	89,905	43.4	23.6	5.8	89.5	5.7	0.2	0.8	2.3
60	R, 100		R, 64		R, 100		R, 68	43,340	56,264	30	72,993	33.8	15.5	8.3	93.2	1.1	0.3	1.8	2.0
61	D, 100		D, 100		D, 58		D, 69	40,505	44,620	10	48,557	18.5	6.4	18.6	96.4	0.7	0.3	0.4	1.2
62	D, 53		D, 69		D, 54		D, 63	39,951	47,175	18	62,945	32.0	15.2	13.6	84.5	6.6	0.3	0.7	5.5
63	R, 77		R, 100		R, 100		R, 100	41,690	41,383	-1	87,900	47.8	27.3	6.8	95.3	1.0	0.1	1.4	1.2
64	D, 100		D, 100		R, 100		R, 100	39,270	41,164	5	61,085	30.6	13.7	10.7	96.2	0.7	0.2	0.6	1.2
65	D, 100		D, 100		D, 100		D, 66	38,612	37,782	-2	42,783	26.7	11.3	22.6	84.6	10.4	0.3	0.5	2.1
66	R, 100		R, 100		R, 100		R, 100	41,494	50,630	22	68,424	34.9	15.7	9.3	91.1	1.8	0.2	1.6	3.4
67	D, 100		D, 100		D, 51		D, 100	39,148	36,661	-6	47,968	27.3	12.3	17.7	93.0	2.7	0.3	0.8	1.5
68	R, 100		R, 100		R, 100		R, 53	39,608	38,742	-2	66,113	38.2	19.2	9.6	97.1	0.5	0.1	0.7	0.8
69	R, 100		R, 100		R, 100		R, 51	39,131	42,066	8	62,852	29.9	12.3	9.5	93.9	2.0	0.1	0.7	1.9
70	D, 99		D, 100		D, 65		D, 100	39,045	40,881	5	42,983	23.6	8.5	22.7	94.2	3.4	0.2	0.3	0.8
71	D, 100		D, 100		D, 100		D, 100	38,847	40,097	3	38,630	22.0	10.4	31.0	95.0	2.3	0.2	0.5	1.0
72	D, 100		D, 100		D, 55		D, 76	40,180	41,683	4	48,628	23.4	9.5	23.5	89.8	5.0	0.2	0.2	3.0
73	D, 100		D, 100		D, 53		D, 57	39,608	43,252	9	54,316	29.2	12.4	15.2	93.0	3.8	0.2	0.3	1.3
74	D, 100		D, 100		D, 100		D, 73	40,009	42,194	5	41,334	19.8	8.4	25.8	95.8	2.0	0.1	0.1	0.9
75	D, 100		D, 65		D, 100		D, 100	40,479	41,763	3	47,608	42.2	31.0	23.9	80.4	7.7	0.2	6.3	3.5
76	D, 100		D, 100		D, 51		D, 100	42,178	43,497	3	59,125	43.4	28.8	12.9	81.0	10.7	0.2	2.1	3.8
77	D, 100		D, 100		D, 100		D, 100	40,123	42,361	6	42,619	32.4	18.7	24.1	51.0	36.1	0.3	1.1	11.2
78	D, 100		D, 100		D, 57		D, 100	39,588	42,536	7	52,038	21.5	7.9	16.6	96.2	1.2	0.2	0.2	1.1
79	D, 100		D, 100		D, 56		D, 54	43,826	44,238	1	58,573	48.4	33.2	14.2	80.8	9.9	0.2	3.1	3.5
80	R, 100		R, 67		R, 100		R, 100	42,190	44,809	6	36,508	16.9	6.5	28.6	96.0	1.4	0.2	0.2	1.3
81	D, 100		D, 100		D, 56		D, 100	38,325	40,717	6	46,602	34.0	18.2	23.9	88.7	6.4	0.3	1.4	1.4
82	R, 59		R, 66		R, 100		R, 100	42,837	46,397	8	35,626	21.3	9.6	32.1	97.3	0.3	0.3	0.3	0.8
83	R, 100		R, 100		R, 100		R, 100	41,545	42,718	3	36,413	22.8	8.4	29.9	96.4	0.8	0.2	0.4	1.4
84	R, 54		R, 55		R, 100		R, 50	42,034	41,681	-1	34,425	21.3	8.0	34.4	95.8	1.7	0.3	0.6	0.8
85	R, 100		R, 100		R, 100		R, 100	42,604	45,554	7	42,062	22.7	8.6	25.6	96.4	0.8	0.3	0.5	1.0
86	R, 68		R, 60		R, 100		R, 72	41,943	43,315	3	32,363	17.2	7.0	36.9	97.2	0.6	0.3	0.2	0.7
87	D, 52		D, 67		D, 100		D, 78	42,424	41,346	-3	30,735	17.5	6.8	39.2	94.9	2.5	0.3	0.5	0.9
88	R, 100		R, 52		R, 67		R, 60	36,901	39,059	6	77,427	48.9	35.0	9.4	84.1	7.0	0.2	4.1	2.5
89	R, 55		R, 100		R, 100		R, 100	40,533	41,826	3	35,990	19.3	7.9	32.7	97.3	0.6	0.3	0.4	0.7
90	R, 100		R, 100		R, 100		R, 100	42,349	41,277	-3	27,784	16.7	6.2	42.2	95.0	2.6	0.2	0.2	1.1
91	R, 51		D, 54		D, 100		D, 100	39,197	38,656	-1	33,555	17.9	6.6	36.3	97.5	0.9	0.2	0.2	0.7
92	D, 100		D, 100		D, 62		D, 100	42,712	42,415	-1	31,869	19.2	6.7	37.1	98.4	0.3	0.1	0.2	0.5
93	D, 100		D, 100		D, 100		D, 100	42,707	40,924	-4	34,193	18.1	5.8	31.6	97.7	0.5	0.1	0.4	0.6
94	D, 100		R, 56		R, 53		D, 60	41,461	40,075	-3	40,765	24.8	10.1	30.9	96.8	1.0	0.1	0.7	0.8
95	D, 100		D, 100		D, 77		D, 100	39,587	39,280	-1	33,978	23.3	7.8	36.0	96.9	1.3	0.1	0.5	0.7
96	D, 100		D, 100		D, 55		D, 67	41,001	41,191	0	36,507	19.1	6.4	29.5	98.4	0.1	0.3	0.1	0.5
97	D, 71		D, 100		D, 100		D, 66	40,684	41,036	1	36,110	21.2	7.5	33.1	98.0	0.1	0.1	0.3	0.7
98	D, 57		D, 57		D, 100		D, 100	39,787	40,237	1	47,361	27.3	8.7	20.5	97.1	0.6	0.2	0.5	0.7
99	D, 100		D, 100		D, 100		D, 100	38,677	40,158	4	37,835	22.4	7.9	29.7	97.6	0.5	0.2	0.3	0.6
100	R, 100		R, 100		R, 100		R, 100	37,291	36,421	-2	48,808	32.7	11.9	21.3	93.6	2.8	0.2	0.5	1.8

Note: D=Democrat, R=Republican, R/D=Republican/Democrat (cross-filed), D/R=Democrat/Republican (cross-filed), I=Independent, C=Constitution, O=Other, GI=Green Independent, P=Progressive, P/D=Progressive/Democrat, P/D/R=Progressive/Democrat/Republican, HH=Households

LOUISIANA

Any discussion of Louisiana politics must now begin with Hurricane Katrina, which devastated New Orleans economically, socially, and ultimately politically. Eighty percent of the city was under water at one time and even today large sections have been abandoned and may never be rebuilt. Nineteen state house districts, most in Orleans Parish but some further west along the Gulf Coast, lost more than a fifth of their population. Nine lost more than 75 percent, effectively ceasing to exist. No other place in the country has seen this level of disruption since the Dust Bowl.

With so many people still in flux accurate numbers are hard to come by, but Baton Rouge is now the state's largest city for the first time ever, perhaps twice as big as New Orleans, swelled over the last three years by thousands of refugees. Depending on the count, New Orleans may even have fallen behind Shreveport in population.

Louisiana's population had been stagnant for some time. From 1980 to 1990, it grew by just 14,000 people—four-tenths of a percent. It fared somewhat better in the 1990s, as the petrochemical industry recovered but has grown scarcely at all since 2000 or, to put it better, almost any gains it had made were wiped out once the storms came in August 2005. Projected to lose a congressional seat even before Katrina, this is now a certainty.

Notwithstanding Huey Long's legacy of wealth redistribution, Louisiana has had extremes of wealth and poverty, often within walking distance of each other. The wealthiest house district in the state is still the 89th, which takes in the Garden District of New Orleans, and where the average income is $104,000. (Nature, though, is a leveler both of rich and poor; with the city's economy in a shambles, this district has lost almost a third of its population.) Scarcely more than a mile away is the 96th district, 87 percent African American, where the average household income is $28,000. It has lost 83 percent of its population.

Five of the ten poorest state house districts in the United States, in fact, are located in Louisiana but only so much of this can be blamed on Katrina. Although two of the districts are in central New Orleans, which had an unemployment rate of close to 20 percent before the hurricane and one of the highest murder rates, the other three are distributed around the state, located in the downtown areas of Monroe, Baton Rouge, and Shreveport.

Before the storms, Louisiana had the second-highest percentage of African Americans of any state in the coun-try, more than Michigan or Ohio. The Census Bureau had projected that whites would become a minority in Louisiana within the next two decades, as they have in California, Texas, and other states, but because many of those who lost everything in Katrina were African American, that process will be delayed for a long time.

The political consequences of their out-migration, though, could be profound. According to the traditional configuration, there are two Louisianas: the northern half, which is Protestant and grows cotton, and the southern half, which is Catholic and grows rice and sugar. Given that New Orleans is now grossly overrepresented, both in the legislature and in Congress, there have been suggestions to reapportion in mid-decade. That is not all grave robbing; tens of thousands of New Orleans residents have moved to the northern part of the state, overburdening roads and schools. It is estimated that the 5th and 6th congressional districts, centered on Baton Rouge and Alexandria, currently have almost twice as many residents as any other district in the country.

Like two other southern states, Georgia and North Carolina, Louisiana's attempts at playing racial politics in reapportionment have proved a nightmare. The state redrew its congressional districts four times during the 1990s. In 2001 the state's congressional representatives drew up a redistricting plan that, although opposed by black lawmakers, passed the legislature with only minor changes. Democrats still control the state house by a margin of 61–41 but have lost ten seats in the last four years. Republicans have made smaller gains in the state senate. When the day of reckoning does come, after the 2010 census, power is certain to shift dramatically from the more ethnically and racially diverse, Democratic-leaning south to the more native, conservative, Republican-leaning northern part of the state and Republicans could well take control of the legislature.

Louisiana is unique for its open primary system of voting, which is only thirty years old. Candidates for state offices run in a unified September primary, one of the latest primaries in the nation. If no candidate wins a majority of the vote, a runoff between the top two candidates is held in December, which depresses turnout. Because federal courts have ruled that all federal elections must be held on the same date throughout the country, the open primary for congressional races is held in November on the same day the rest of the country votes, with a December runoff, if needed.

LOUISIANA
State Senate Districts

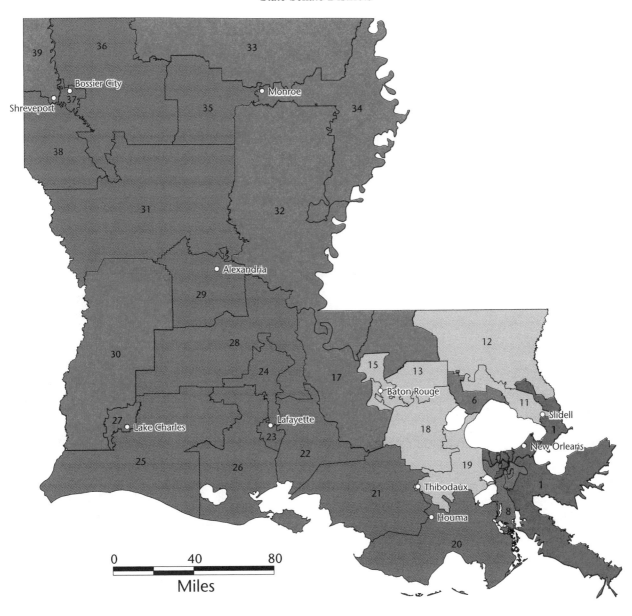

Population Growth   ■ -83% to -8%   ■ -8% to 3%   ■ 3% to 9%   □ 9% to 24%

BATON ROUGE/NEW ORLEANS

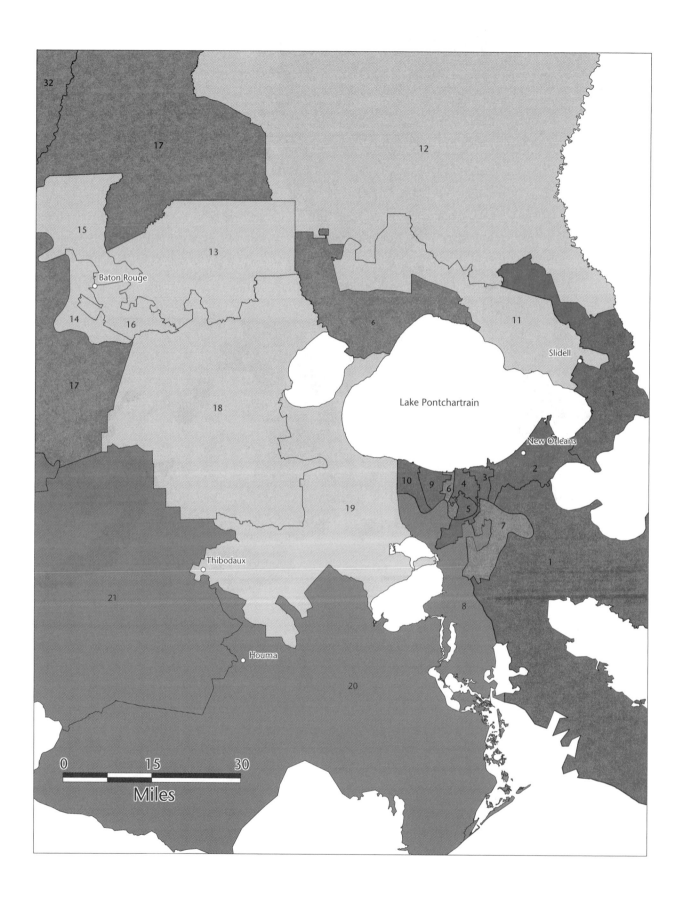

Population Growth   ▆ -83% to -8%   ▆ -8% to 3%   ▆ 3% to 9%   ▢ 9% to 24%

Louisiana State Senate Districts—Election and Demographic Data

Senate Districts	General Election Results Party, Percent of Vote							Population			2006 Avg. HH Income ($)	Pop 25+ Some College + (%)	Pop 25+ 4-Yr Degree + (%)	Below Poverty Line (%)	White (Non-Hisp) (%)	African American (%)	American Indians, Alaska Natives (%)	Asians, Hawaiians, Pacific Islanders (%)	Hispanic Origin (%)
Louisiana	2000	2001	2002	2003	2004	2005	2006	2000	2006	% Change	($)	(%)	(%)	(%)	(%)	(%)	(%)	(%)	(%)
1				R, 61				120,326	56,815	-53	55,248	29.8	11.9	19.0	77.9	14.3	0.9	1.2	4.2
2				D, 53				109,124	21,997	-80	41,387	31.3	18.9	23.6	11.8	80.2	0.1	5.9	1.8
3				D, 72		D, 51		109,698	47,317	-57	42,088	30.2	14.0	24.9	35.2	59.5	0.3	1.8	3.3
4				D, 68	D, 86			110,354	19,516	-82	45,173	35.6	24.4	28.7	31.5	63.8	0.1	1.0	3.9
5				D, 82				109,760	57,903	-47	47,441	39.0	28.8	30.8	34.8	59.8	0.2	1.3	4.1
6						R, 51		118,957	109,455	-8	74,266	41.5	26.7	18.6	77.2	17.0	0.2	1.3	3.2
7								118,241	119,637	1	49,309	32.9	16.7	22.3	39.6	50.1	0.4	4.0	6.0
8				D, 56				113,524	117,836	4	52,392	33.1	13.7	17.5	61.1	26.1	0.7	4.5	6.6
9				D, 61				114,213	74,913	-34	57,052	46.8	24.3	13.1	77.3	8.2	0.3	3.1	8.7
10				R, 71				112,140	84,536	-25	58,713	40.0	19.3	14.9	65.1	21.0	0.3	2.1	10.4
11				R, 65				118,978	131,911	11	66,944	39.4	20.1	13.9	81.6	12.7	0.4	0.9	3.1
12								120,183	133,968	11	44,218	24.5	10.6	26.4	70.8	26.5	0.2	0.2	1.
13								117,945	145,243	23	56,055	30.1	12.4	13.2	88.9	6.9	0.3	0.8	2.0
14				D, 53				119,996	132,295	10	42,030	33.9	18.0	31.8	33.6	61.0	0.2	2.6	2.8
15		D, 51		D, 79				114,929	128,274	12	43,594	32.6	13.2	22.3	33.4	63.0	0.1	1.9	1.5
16				R, 78			R, 58	119,979	136,222	14	79,119	52.6	31.4	9.7	79.5	13.6	0.2	2.9	2.8
17				D, 62				119,785	123,144	3	47,625	22.9	8.8	23.0	57.9	40.0	0.2	0.3	1.3
18				D, 52				119,808	147,979	24	53,639	23.7	9.3	18.3	70.2	25.9	0.2	0.3	2.7
19								119,721	131,049	9	55,767	27.2	11.5	17.9	65.4	29.8	0.3	0.7	3.3
20	D, 52			D, 83				118,082	126,142	7	46,765	19.2	7.5	22.3	76.3	13.5	5.2	1.0	2.2
21				D, 88				120,560	124,597	3	47,213	21.5	8.7	24.0	67.8	26.8	1.1	1.1	2.3
22								119,648	128,066	7	43,468	19.5	7.8	26.4	63.3	32.3	0.3	1.7	1.5
23				R, 88				117,776	128,136	9	61,950	41.0	22.9	15.2	82.2	11.9	0.3	1.8	2.7
24				D, 67				111,341	116,590	5	38,082	23.6	9.8	32.8	43.3	54.6	0.2	0.3	1.1
25								114,638	119,917	5	47,760	24.8	10.5	22.4	80.7	16.1	0.3	0.6	1.5
26				D, 54				113,542	121,906	7	42,943	19.9	7.7	26.4	78.2	18.1	0.2	1.1	1.6
27								112,908	114,539	1	49,538	29.8	12.2	22.0	63.8	32.6	0.3	0.7	1.8
28								118,738	124,082	5	36,390	18.3	7.1	33.4	69.3	27.4	0.7	0.3	1.9
29				D, 79				109,400	114,823	5	46,107	28.3	12.0	25.2	60.2	35.4	0.6	1.1	2.0
30				R, 72				112,546	114,669	2	44,702	25.4	9.0	20.6	76.9	14.5	0.9	1.1	4.2
31								113,295	116,895	3	41,923	23.6	9.8	28.3	68.9	25.6	2.1	0.3	1.9
32				D, 80				109,059	111,626	2	41,892	21.5	8.2	27.9	71.9	25.8	0.3	0.2	1.2
33								109,235	112,117	3	46,572	27.0	12.3	24.4	67.8	29.7	0.1	0.4	1.6
34								108,878	107,986	-1	34,424	23.0	10.1	36.2	32.4	65.4	0.1	0.6	1.5
35				R, 52				110,063	114,700	4	49,564	35.0	18.6	23.4	72.9	23.7	0.2	0.9	1.6
36				D, 68				109,531	116,838	7	48,274	28.5	10.8	23.1	67.0	29.8	0.3	0.5	1.8
37				R, 60				109,080	115,998	6	52,827	38.3	20.2	17.2	65.7	26.7	0.4	1.7	4.1
38								109,822	116,804	6	54,458	31.2	16.5	18.7	64.5	31.4	0.5	0.9	2.2
39				D, 71				113,064	114,141	1	37,661	23.3	11.1	31.3	31.5	66.5	0.3	0.3	1.4

Note: D=Democrat, R=Republican, R/D=Republican/Democrat (cross-filed), D/R=Democrat/Republican (cross-filed), I=Independent, C=Constitution, O=Other, GI=Green Independent, P=Progressive, P/D=Progressive/Democrat, P/D/R=Progressive/Democrat/Republican, HH=Households

LOUISIANA
State House Districts

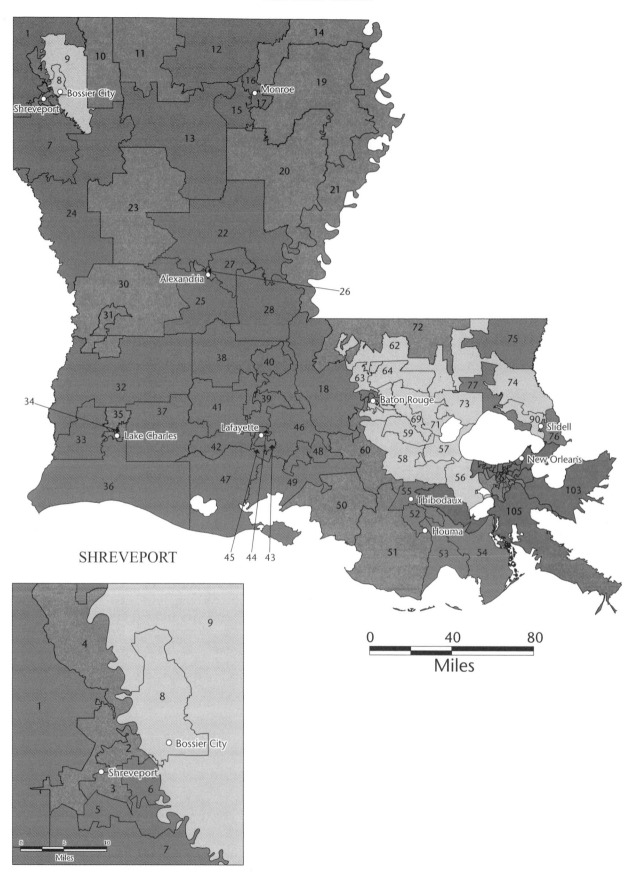

SHREVEPORT

Population Growth   ■ -86% to -4%   ■ -4% to 2%   ■ 2% to 10%   □ 10% to 31%

BATON ROUGE

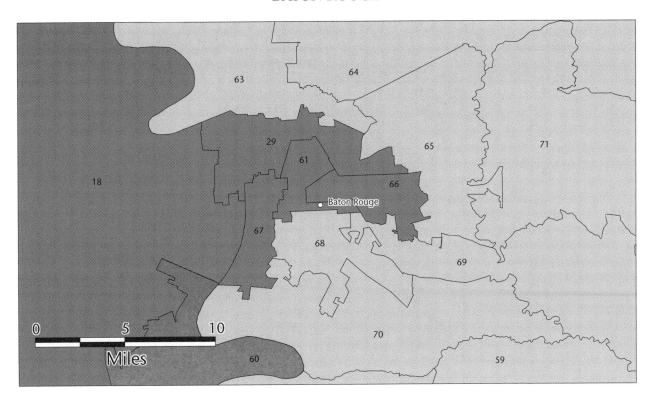

NEW ORLEANS

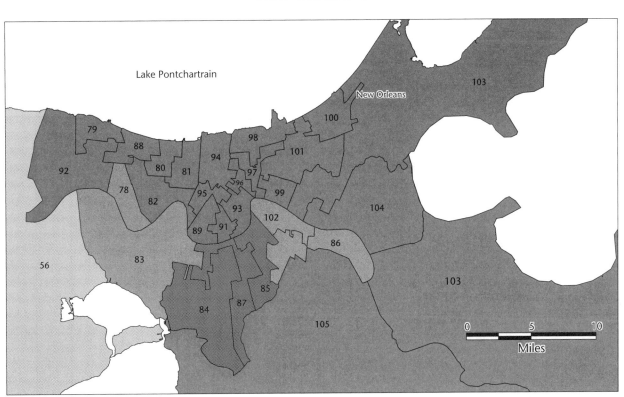

Population Growth   ▨ -86% to -4%   ▨ -4% to 2%   ▨ 2% to 10%   ▢ 10% to 31%

Louisiana State House Districts—Election and Demographic Data

House Districts	General Election Results Party, Percent of Vote							Population			Avg. HH Income ($)	Pop 25+ Some College + (%)	Pop 25+ 4-Yr Degree + (%)	Below Poverty Line (%)	2006 White (Non-Hisp) (%)	African American (%)	American Indians, Alaska Natives (%)	Asians, Hawaiians, Pacific Islanders (%)	Hispanic Origin (%)
Louisiana	2000	2001	2002	2003	2004	2005	2006	2000	2006	% Change	($)	(%)	(%)	(%)	(%)	(%)	(%)	(%)	(%)
1				D, 70				43,354	46,402	7	48,292	28.4	13.9	20.7	67.7	29.4	0.4	0.3	1.5
2				D, 81				33,278	33,294	0	31,183	22.9	11.1	40.4	17.1	80.3	0.3	0.3	2.5
3				D, 52				39,559	39,103	-1	30,139	19.3	8.6	36.2	15.5	82.8	0.2	0.4	1.2
4				D, 62				37,934	38,267	1	40,346	26.2	12.8	26.5	27.1	70.4	0.2	0.4	2.1
5								38,100	39,654	4	57,760	38.4	22.5	13.7	71.8	22.9	0.4	1.5	2.5
6				R, 69				43,361	44,820	3	64,003	47.3	32.3	13.2	75.9	18.1	0.4	1.7	2.9
7								45,114	49,418	10	55,916	27.4	13.5	21.1	66.8	29.4	0.6	0.5	2.1
8				R, 67				45,374	51,416	13	52,741	34.9	13.6	16.7	69.5	21.4	0.5	1.9	4.9
9								45,954	51,088	11	56,684	35.1	12.4	13.9	76.0	17.8	0.4	1.1	3.1
10								41,750	42,460	2	42,075	25.6	9.7	24.4	64.1	33.6	0.3	0.2	1.1
11	D, 58							39,897	40,273	1	35,458	26.9	13.5	35.2	37.8	59.9	0.1	0.5	1.6
12				R, 50				44,543	46,110	4	46,991	31.7	16.9	24.7	73.4	22.1	0.2	1.1	2.3
13				D, 56				40,624	41,755	3	40,614	24.5	10.0	27.3	70.3	27.6	0.3	0.2	1.2
14								41,669	42,320	2	42,768	24.0	10.4	27.1	65.3	32.8	0.2	0.3	1.1
15								46,889	49,433	5	48,567	30.9	13.8	18.9	84.9	11.8	0.3	0.4	1.8
16								43,196	44,493	3	64,285	44.5	25.9	17.2	74.8	21.0	0.1	1.7	1.6
17								38,037	39,099	3	29,140	21.2	7.9	41.9	10.1	88.8	0.1	0.3	1.0
18								43,450	44,658	3	47,489	21.3	8.1	22.3	60.8	37.2	0.2	0.3	1.3
19								43,163	43,124	0	38,441	21.9	9.5	30.4	61.6	35.9	0.2	0.2	1.8
20				D, 63				41,836	42,113	1	38,021	18.6	7.3	32.1	71.2	26.8	0.3	0.2	1.1
21							D, 60	40,069	38,656	-4	33,451	20.2	7.7	36.5	40.9	57.2	0.1	0.2	1.5
22				D, 52			D, 54	43,065	45,003	5	42,723	22.4	8.4	26.3	81.3	15.3	0.7	0.2	1.4
23				D, 83				45,534	45,761	0	41,082	25.4	11.8	31.1	57.5	38.4	0.9	0.5	1.3
24				D, 76				42,870	44,292	3	39,340	19.7	7.4	30.9	65.3	27.0	4.0	0.2	2.7
25								43,290	47,228	9	54,829	32.4	14.7	19.7	71.3	23.0	0.8	1.2	2.7
26				D, 53				32,656	32,673	0	33,519	21.9	8.5	36.3	27.5	69.8	0.3	0.8	1.3
27				D, 61				38,736	41,022	6	49,150	30.7	12.5	19.5	80.9	14.9	0.7	1.0	1.5
28				D, 51				41,498	43,801	6	36,781	17.3	6.7	33.5	67.1	30.2	0.9	0.2	1.1
29				D, 80		D, 59		36,886	40,286	9	38,342	28.5	11.0	28.1	17.5	79.9	0.1	1.3	1.5
30								41,180	39,614	-4	42,808	25.9	9.4	21.6	76.5	13.2	1.5	1.4	4.4
31				R, 50				31,569	31,904	1	45,413	28.6	10.2	19.3	62.8	23.8	0.7	1.8	8.0
32								49,435	52,080	5	41,322	19.8	7.1	25.1	79.0	16.0	1.1	0.5	2.8
33								45,643	48,261	6	49,350	27.3	10.2	18.5	87.0	9.6	0.3	0.3	1.7
34				D, 70				36,928	37,140	1	37,894	23.6	8.2	31.6	23.5	73.6	0.2	0.6	1.4
35				R, 54				42,388	43,191	2	55,744	33.0	14.0	18.0	79.4	16.6	0.3	0.7	2.0
36				R, 81				50,805	52,163	3	62,140	34.6	16.7	14.2	84.0	11.0	0.3	1.4	2.2
37								45,027	47,563	6	41,433	19.5	6.9	26.2	80.1	17.3	0.3	0.3	1.2
38				D, 81				44,054	46,605	6	35,124	19.0	7.5	36.3	70.6	27.6	0.2	0.2	1.1
39				D, 59				51,081	55,994	10	46,903	25.9	10.8	21.0	73.0	23.9	0.2	0.5	1.5
40				D, 75	D, 53			45,238	47,748	6	32,934	20.6	8.4	38.9	39.0	59.2	0.1	0.3	0.9
41				D, 58				44,036	45,883	4	38,675	19.6	6.9	31.2	76.3	21.6	0.2	0.2	1.2
42								44,883	47,392	6	42,040	20.4	8.3	27.2	74.9	22.5	0.2	0.3	1.4
43								50,666	55,295	9	71,919	46.4	27.8	11.9	85.5	9.3	0.3	1.4	2.5
44								39,857	40,677	2	37,731	25.1	10.9	32.5	31.7	65.4	0.2	0.9	1.7
45					O, 55			49,710	54,209	9	57,024	39.3	21.2	16.1	83.0	10.6	0.3	2.0	2.8
46				D, 80				46,542	50,622	9	42,099	18.7	7.1	27.1	63.0	34.0	0.2	1.1	1.2
47				D, 64				43,601	46,077	6	41,699	20.1	8.2	27.0	78.2	16.6	0.2	2.3	2.0
48								41,212	43,559	6	42,672	21.2	9.5	27.3	61.6	33.5	0.2	2.2	1.5
49								44,158	46,849	6	45,883	18.9	7.1	23.9	71.3	23.1	0.6	1.7	1.9
50				D, 73				37,906	38,374	1	40,833	19.0	6.6	27.2	60.6	34.4	1.1	0.6	1.9

(continued)

Note: D=Democrat, R=Republican, R/D=Republican/Democrat (cross-filed), D/R=Democrat/Republican (cross-filed), I=Independent, C=Constitution, O=Other, GI=Green Independent, P=Progressive, P/D=Progressive/Democrat, P/D/R=Progressive/Democrat/Republican, HH=Households

Louisiana State House Districts—Election and Demographic Data (cont.)

House Districts	General Election Results Party, Percent of Vote							Population			Avg. HH Income ($)	Pop 25+ Some College + (%)	Pop 25+ 4-Yr Degree + (%)	Below Poverty Line (%)	White (Non-Hisp) (%)	African American (%)	American Indians, Alaska Natives (%)	Asians, Hawaiians, Pacific Islanders (%)	Hispanic Origin (%)
Louisiana	2000	2001	2002	2003	2004	2005	2006	2000	2006	% Change									
51				D, 80				39,584	40,197	2	41,480	17.8	6.5	26.9	62.3	24.0	6.4	2.5	3.4
52				R, 50				47,007	50,874	8	56,817	25.9	11.4	18.1	76.5	17.1	2.3	0.6	2.2
53		D, 51		D, 54				41,312	43,930	6	46,349	20.1	8.0	23.0	74.6	16.4	4.4	1.2	1.9
54				D, 52				40,062	42,972	7	46,730	18.9	7.7	21.0	87.0	4.3	3.5	0.9	2.5
55								39,547	41,775	6	49,385	25.0	12.5	22.3	72.7	24.0	0.6	0.7	1.3
56								45,051	49,876	11	63,230	29.8	12.6	15.0	70.5	24.7	0.2	0.6	3.3
57								46,669	51,543	10	52,384	25.1	9.3	18.6	55.1	40.4	0.2	0.6	3.5
58				D, 85				42,417	48,968	15	47,339	20.1	7.4	28.3	33.7	64.5	0.1	0.2	1.7
59				R, 58				59,467	77,612	31	59,743	26.9	11.1	12.6	84.7	9.6	0.3	0.5	3.7
60				D, 52				39,305	39,411	0	45,233	19.5	7.2	25.7	60.7	37.2	0.2	0.2	1.6
61								40,458	43,246	7	34,255	31.0	13.4	32.5	19.3	78.4	0.1	0.9	1.4
62	R, 52							48,061	52,983	10	49,627	25.8	11.3	21.9	66.6	30.3	0.2	0.4	1.8
63			D, 60	D, 74				38,971	44,274	14	42,801	29.2	12.4	26.8	23.5	75.1	0.1	0.3	1.1
64								48,437	56,968	18	51,044	28.3	10.2	15.2	73.7	23.9	0.3	0.3	1.1
65				R, 73				39,304	44,070	12	59,784	38.9	17.0	8.4	77.3	17.2	0.3	1.7	2.6
66						R, 53		44,781	48,230	8	49,006	41.8	19.5	18.3	53.2	38.7	0.2	4.9	2.6
67				D, 60				36,338	39,597	9	29,469	32.2	18.8	41.0	41.4	48.8	0.3	5.5	3.7
68								43,626	48,838	12	82,362	55.3	35.1	11.9	72.9	21.9	0.2	1.9	2.4
69		R, 60		R, 71				49,853	58,831	18	71,510	44.1	23.4	9.0	84.3	9.7	0.3	2.1	2.8
70				R, 74				56,682	67,250	19	75,776	47.9	29.4	13.1	70.3	21.5	0.1	3.3	3.9
71								54,281	68,754	27	52,500	24.7	8.6	16.2	91.3	5.6	0.3	0.3	1.7
72				D, 82				40,318	40,612	1	38,614	21.9	8.7	33.1	41.8	56.5	0.1	0.3	1.3
73				R, 75				49,853	55,832	12	44,867	27.7	12.9	25.0	74.2	22.9	0.2	0.5	1.6
74								59,031	73,187	24	55,063	31.2	14.4	18.7	84.4	11.6	0.3	0.3	2.4
75				D, 51				42,771	44,708	5	36,471	20.2	8.5	30.1	65.4	32.8	0.2	0.2	1.1
76				R, 78				46,406	47,650	3	63,404	38.3	18.4	13.9	80.1	12.7	0.4	1.4	3.9
77								53,067	56,299	6	70,956	40.6	23.0	15.1	83.1	11.9	0.3	0.6	3.0
78				R, 69				37,263	35,843	-4	61,718	42.9	21.4	13.6	77.0	16.2	0.2	0.9	4.6
79								38,220	21,665	-43	70,945	42.7	21.9	9.8	65.3	12.7	0.4	3.9	15.8
80				R, 71				39,733	25,394	-36	57,759	47.3	25.2	13.8	72.6	9.4	0.3	4.0	10.9
81				R, 57				36,313	20,637	-43	74,846	53.8	33.0	11.3	87.8	3.4	0.3	2.1	5.0
82								39,845	31,189	-22	52,291	44.8	23.4	15.2	76.5	12.7	0.3	1.9	6.8
83								38,889	39,624	2	38,257	27.1	9.2	24.2	54.2	35.6	0.6	4.3	4.9
84				D, 80				42,859	44,139	3	54,190	32.1	12.8	15.6	66.7	21.0	0.6	4.0	6.6
85								45,726	47,319	3	53,513	36.7	16.2	19.4	50.6	35.8	0.5	5.0	7.3
86		R, 58						43,674	43,391	-1	58,498	38.2	21.0	16.8	46.8	39.3	0.4	5.7	7.4
87				D, 60		D, 67		38,650	39,876	3	41,929	28.8	10.7	26.7	24.2	67.6	0.2	3.8	5.1
88		R, 51		R, 54				37,478	21,517	-43	65,041	47.7	25.3	11.9	76.1	6.7	0.2	4.3	10.1
89								36,951	25,539	-31	104,128	49.8	42.2	19.8	65.2	27.5	0.2	1.8	4.1
90								60,502	67,191	11	71,721	40.7	20.5	12.6	82.2	11.4	0.5	0.9	3.3
91			D, 51	D, 58				36,161	26,886	-26	52,982	44.0	33.5	28.1	41.2	53.3	0.2	1.2	3.9
92								37,348	29,117	-22	44,057	31.1	12.4	20.6	47.6	38.8	0.4	1.7	12.1
93				D, 89				35,648	18,311	-49	38,971	31.6	22.3	37.1	26.4	68.9	0.2	1.3	3.6
94								40,365	7,417	-82	66,113	50.0	37.5	15.3	66.0	23.2	0.2	2.1	7.0
95								39,606	8,474	-79	39,928	34.2	23.9	32.5	26.1	68.5	0.2	1.4	4.6
96				D, 57		D, 57		36,274	6,273	-83	28,454	24.8	14.4	42.3	10.2	87.6	0.1	0.3	2.2
97				D, 65			D, 51	35,435	6,241	-82	34,333	29.7	18.5	29.9	12.5	84.1	0.1	0.6	2.8
98				D, 60				39,482	6,855	-83	51,328	39.6	26.4	16.7	26.5	68.1	0.1	1.7	3.6
99				D, 69				35,402	6,306	-82	28,967	24.0	13.2	38.0	7.7	90.7	0.1	0.2	1.6
100		D, 55		D, 53				40,364	7,930	-80	48,319	34.4	21.8	18.7	9.4	82.9	0.1	5.5	2.0

(continued)

Note: D=Democrat, R=Republican, R/D=Republican/Democrat (cross-filed), D/R=Democrat/Republican (cross-filed), I=Independent, C=Constitution, O=Other, GI=Green Independent, P=Progressive, P/D=Progressive/Democrat, P/D/R=Progressive/Democrat/Republican, HH=Households

Louisiana State House Districts—Election and Demographic Data (cont.)

House Districts	General Election Results Party, Percent of Vote							Population			Avg. HH Income	2006							
												Pop 25+		Below Poverty Line	White (Non-Hisp)	African American	American Indians, Alaska Natives	Asians, Hawaiians, Pacific Islanders	Hispanic Origin
												Some College +	4-Yr Degree +						
Louisiana	2000	2001	2002	2003	2004	2005	2006	2000	2006	% Change	($)	(%)	(%)	(%)	(%)	(%)	(%)	(%)	(%)
101				D, 78				38,197	6,694	-82	35,021	28.2	16.5	28.6	7.1	90.4	0.1	0.7	1.5
102			D, 66	D, 63				36,466	35,452	-3	44,015	31.1	19.7	25.4	29.8	63.8	0.2	1.8	4.7
103				D, 62				38,703	11,121	-71	45,655	24.1	10.4	22.7	64.1	21.7	0.3	7.6	6.3
104	R, 51			R, 61				39,807	5,871	-85	50,442	26.6	7.1	17.7	81.5	9.8	0.4	1.9	5.0
105				D, 64				43,897	36,670	-16	54,434	25.5	9.9	18.9	77.8	14.6	1.7	1.5	3.0

Note: D=Democrat, R=Republican, R/D=Republican/Democrat (cross-filed), D/R=Democrat/Republican (cross-filed), I=Independent, C=Constitution, O=Other, GI=Green Independent, P=Progressive, P/D=Progressive/Democrat, P/D/R=Progressive/Democrat/Republican, HH=Households

MAINE

Stuck in a far corner of the nation, Maine's position has always been precarious. Perhaps because it was settled later than the others (the only state, as has been pointed out, to be settled from southwest to northeast), it never developed the manufacturing base that helped Connecticut and Massachusetts thrive, did not receive as many immigrants as, say, Rhode Island, and more recently has been too far from the Boston sprawl to lure as many transplants as tax-free New Hampshire. It did not become a state until 1820, when it was broken off from Massachusetts and brought into the Union to offset slave-holding Missouri as part of the Missouri Compromise. For a time it was a frontier, and by 1830, it had as many congressional representatives (eight) as Arizona and Maryland do now. But it has been a long and pretty much uninterrupted decline from there.

That sort of slide is not going to be reversed, but while Maine cannot be said to be booming, it is at least doing better. Its chief products are agricultural and agriculture is no longer a labor intensive occupation. Of course most of the nation's lobsters come from here, but so does much of its maple syrup, potatoes, brown eggs, and blueberries. A growth field lately has been call centers. Customer service calls to companies including MBNA and T-Mobile are answered in Maine. Those operations rarely employ more than a few hundred people but they are something.

That is not to say that there have not been pockets of growth here. Eighteen state house districts have enjoyed double digit growth since 2000, scattered in Waldo County, around the town of Auburn, and along the New Hampshire border. No area is experiencing dramatic population losses, but almost a third of the state house districts have posted either zero or negative growth in this decade.

Income growth has also been slow, leaving Maine's average household income just 70 percent of that in Massachusetts. The wealthiest areas are four suburban house districts along the waterfront above Portland; the poorest are scattered among downtown Portland, Lewiston, and the frontier. The house district that includes Kennebunkport (the 65th), summer home of the Bush family, is the eighth-wealthiest district, but average household income there is less than two-thirds of what it is in the very wealthiest district.

As might be expected in a state that is experiencing little growth and a lot of emigration, Maine is one of the older states; 13 percent of its population is over age sixty-five. Its unemployment rate is right at the national average, though there are pockets of deep poverty.

According to the Census Bureau, there are only 5,100 African Americans in the entire state; Maine is more than 98 percent white, second only (and barely) to Vermont. It has its ethnic minorities, including the Greeks and Poles who immigrated to much of the rest of New England. One of the state's most famous politicians of recent years was former governor and U.S. senator Edmund Muskie, whose father anglicized the family name from Marciszewski when he arrived in this country. But more prevalent here are French Canadians and Native Americans, ethnic and racial groups not found in many other places.

Unique among the states, Maine makes special provision for its Native Americans, providing for two nonvoting representatives from the Penobscot Nation and the Passamaquoddy Tribes in the state house of representatives, a practice that dates to 1823. Like other New England states, Maine has a huge house—151 members—and the effect has been to give rural interests great influence. Maine's state senate is unusual in that the state constitution requires only that there be an odd number of members and that the number be between thirty-one and thirty-five. Currently there are thirty-five senators, but that could be cut by statute. State elections were held in September until 1958.

In 1946 John Gunther wrote in *Inside U.S.A.,* "The trend—in Maine as elsewhere in New England—is all toward urbanization, industrialization, which, as we know, usually means more Democrats." Gunther was right about the trend, if not the cause; he did not foresee environmentalists or the cultural liberalism that have made Maine more Democratic. Once the most rock-ribbed of Republican states, Maine is now politically unpredictable. It has two Republican U.S. senators, both women, and has elected two Independent governors in the last thirty years. It is also one of only seven states that does not have an office of lieutenant governor.

In recent presidential races (as it was in 1936, when it was one of only two states that supported Alf Landon over Franklin D. Roosevelt), Maine has been the country's worst bellwether in predicting the eventual presidential victor. It voted for the losing candidate in 1948, 1960, 1968, 1976, 2000, 2004, and came close to doing so in 1980. Twice it was Ross Perot's best state; in 1992, he actually finished ahead of George H. W. Bush, who more or less lived there.

Democrats control both houses of the general assembly, although the margins have swung widely. There has been a huge amount of turnover—not necessarily a bad thing in this over-gerrymandered political age. In the past two elections, more than one-third of the seats in Maine's legislature have changed partisan hands. Democrats in the state house gained seven seats in 2002, lost them again in 2004, and now control the chamber by a single vote. Eccentricity should not be unexpected in the only one of the mainland states that is not on the way to anywhere else.

MAINE
State Senate Districts

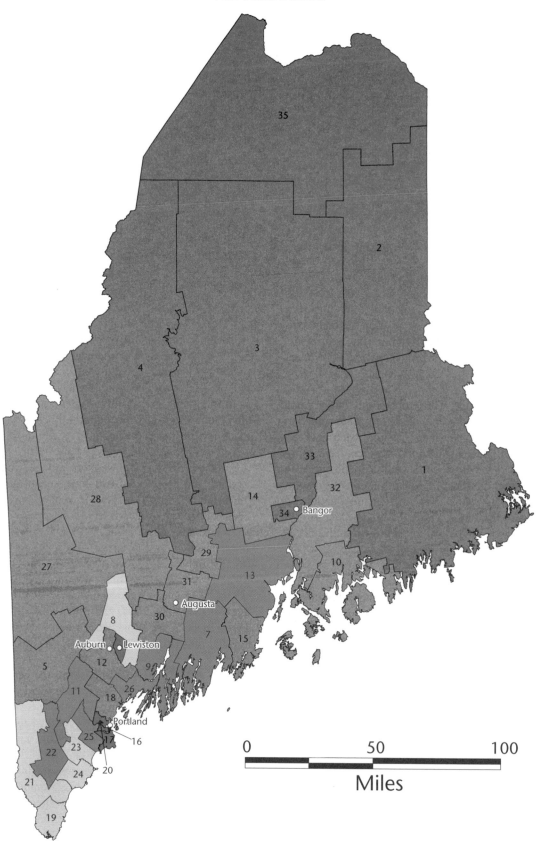

Population Growth   ▮ -3% to 1%   ▮ 1% to 5%   ▮ 5% to 8%   ▯ 8% to 13%

Maine State Senate Districts—Election and Demographic Data

Senate Districts	General Election Results Party, Percent of Vote							Population			Avg. HH Income	Pop 25+ Some College +	Pop 25+ 4-Yr Degree +	2006 Below Poverty Line	2006 White (Non-Hisp)	2006 African American	2006 American Indians, Alaska Natives	2006 Asians, Hawaiians, Pacific Islanders	2006 Hispanic Origin
Maine	2000	2001	2002	2003	2004	2005	2006	2000	2006	% Change	($)	(%)	(%)	(%)	(%)	(%)	(%)	(%)	(%)
1	D, 69		D, 73		R, 57		D, 55	36,552	35,661	-2	36,879	28.4	11.6	27.4	93.2	0.3	2.2	0.3	1.1
2	R, 54		R, 64		R, 54		R, 55	37,178	36,165	-3	38,692	29.7	12.1	24.9	95.6	0.3	1.0	0.4	0.9
3	D, 69		D, 52		R, 54		R, 52	36,240	36,384	0	38,457	27.3	10.1	23.0	97.1	0.2	0.2	0.3	0.5
4	R, 54		R, 58		D, 49		D, 60	36,173	36,297	0	42,392	26.9	9.6	21.2	96.9	0.2	0.2	0.2	0.5
5	I, 67		D, 50		D, 57		D, 62	36,126	37,257	3	48,160	34.6	17.0	16.5	96.3	0.4	0.1	0.4	0.8
6	R, 58		R, 52		D, 53		D, 57	35,094	34,960	0	42,789	26.2	10.3	22.2	92.5	1.2	0.1	0.8	1.6
7	D, 69		D, 100		D, 62		D, 55	36,711	38,606	5	53,221	39.2	20.4	14.4	97.4	0.2	0.1	0.3	0.6
8	R, 64		R, 100		D, 76		D, 67	36,036	39,077	8	51,176	28.3	9.1	12.9	95.2	0.5	0.1	0.3	1.4
9	R, 59		R, 55		D, 100		D, 68	37,034	39,256	6	55,783	37.7	18.9	13.4	93.6	1.0	0.1	0.6	1.7
10	R, 67		D, 100		D, 59		D, 67	36,618	37,997	4	52,071	41.8	23.0	16.8	95.6	0.3	0.2	0.4	0.9
11	D, 50		R, 48		R, 57		R, 57	36,228	38,688	7	59,378	41.7	23.4	8.4	96.4	0.5	0.1	0.4	0.7
12	R, 53		R, 58		D, 55		D, 64	37,420	38,928	4	56,442	35.4	16.8	14.0	95.6	0.5	0.1	0.6	0.8
13	R, 55		D, 52		R, 51		R, 47	36,146	38,755	7	46,814	33.9	17.3	19.3	96.2	0.2	0.2	0.2	0.7
14	D, 54		D, 65		D, 52		D, 63	36,862	37,902	3	50,011	33.5	13.3	17.2	96.8	0.3	0.2	0.3	0.6
15	D, 63		D, 54		R, 53		R, 51	36,960	38,496	4	51,948	39.0	21.0	15.6	96.8	0.3	0.1	0.4	0.7
16	D, 67		D, 50		D, 70		D, 70	35,633	35,952	1	48,303	50.0	35.1	19.2	84.4	3.5	0.3	3.3	3.2
17	R, 60		R, 64		D, 55		D, 57	35,762	35,975	1	74,266	53.3	35.5	9.4	94.1	0.6	0.1	1.4	1.4
18	D, 65		D, 56		R, 55		R, 56	36,472	37,487	3	94,655	55.5	40.8	7.0	96.5	0.4	0.1	0.7	0.9
19	R, 61		R, 55		R, 54		R, 52	35,994	39,656	10	73,523	46.3	25.1	8.7	95.4	0.8	0.1	0.6	1.4
20	D, 69		R, 52		R, 56		R, 58	35,565	35,661	0	58,217	48.9	32.0	11.9	91.1	1.8	0.1	2.3	1.4
21	D, 69		D, 70		D, 51		R, 52	37,899	42,799	13	56,410	35.6	15.0	13.0	96.1	0.4	0.1	0.6	1.0
22	D, 62		D, 56		R, 55		R, 53	36,998	39,612	7	51,062	29.8	11.2	15.4	95.0	0.4	0.2	1.3	1.1
23	D, 46		D, 53		R, 55		R, 55	37,288	40,632	9	55,216	38.9	16.8	13.5	95.9	0.4	0.1	0.6	1.0
24	R, 54		D, 50		D, 52		D, 63	35,925	38,851	8	59,544	40.4	21.3	13.6	95.6	0.5	0.1	0.9	1.0
25	R, 100		R, 100		D, 54		D, 57	36,203	38,677	7	62,140	45.0	28.2	11.3	95.0	0.7	0.1	1.0	1.0
26	R, 53		R, 57		R, 54		R, 63	35,592	37,442	5	68,124	48.0	33.5	12.3	92.2	1.3	0.1	1.3	2.1
27	R, 64		D, 53		R, 59		R, 54	37,264	38,474	3	44,694	29.2	12.0	18.2	97.1	0.1	0.1	0.3	0.7
28	D, 79		D, 74		D, 64		D, 64	36,829	37,875	3	46,777	35.6	18.1	18.5	96.5	0.2	0.2	0.4	0.8
29	D, 53		R, 51		R, 100		R, 59	37,083	37,805	2	45,406	31.2	13.5	19.1	94.8	0.5	0.2	0.7	1.2
30	D, 61		D, 55		D, 59		D, 57	36,903	37,997	3	51,834	37.0	17.1	14.4	96.0	0.4	0.2	0.4	0.9
31	D, 66		D, 58		R, 58		R, 57	35,721	36,535	2	47,395	34.0	15.0	17.8	95.4	0.4	0.2	0.8	1.0
32	D, 59		D, 52		D, 51		D, 54	36,042	36,979	3	49,876	37.6	17.6	15.2	96.6	0.2	0.4	0.4	0.6
33	R, 51		R, 63		R, 61		R, 59	36,933	36,778	0	43,979	29.9	14.6	21.9	93.9	0.7	1.0	1.1	0.9
34	R, 58		R, 55		R, 51		R, 54	36,133	35,917	-1	50,319	39.6	18.9	20.1	92.8	1.0	0.5	1.1	1.4
35	R, 55		R, 64		D, 57		D, 63	36,626	35,797	-2	40,757	30.0	12.4	22.7	95.4	0.6	0.4	0.6	1.1

Note: D=Democrat, R=Republican, R/D=Republican/Democrat (cross-filed), D/R=Democrat/Republican (cross-filed), I=Independent, C=Constitution, O=Other, GI=Green Independent, P=Progressive, P/D=Progressive/Democrat, P/D/R=Progressive/Democrat/Republican, HH=Households

MAINE
State House Districts

BANGOR

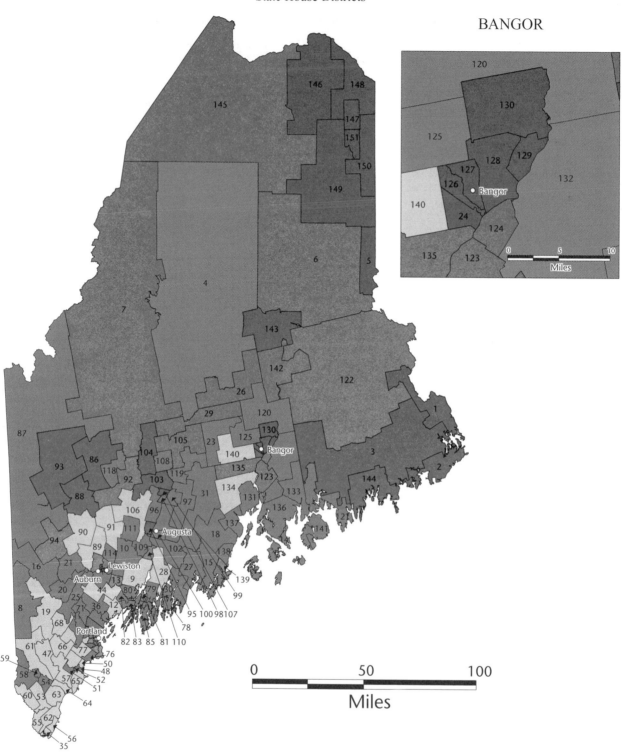

Population Growth ■ -5% to -1%   ■ -1% to 2%   ■ 2% to 7%   □ 7% to 22%

LEWISTON

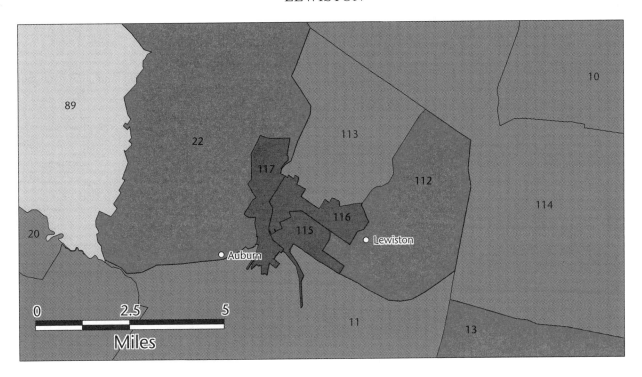

PORTLAND

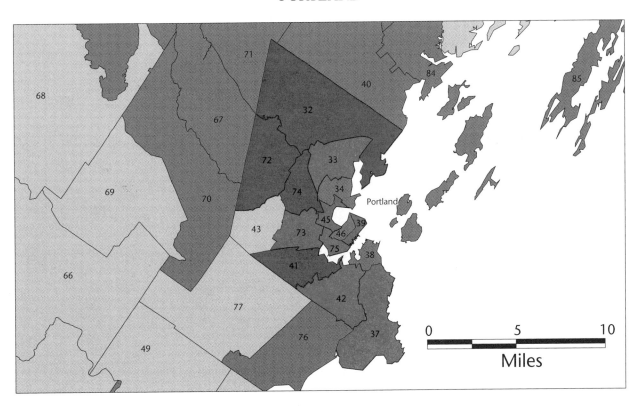

Population Growth ▮ -5% to -1%   ▮ -1% to 2%   ▮ 2% to 7%   ▢ 7% to 22%

Maine State House Districts—Election and Demographic Data

House Districts	General Election Results Party, Percent of Vote							Population			2006 Avg. HH Income ($)	Pop 25+ Some College + (%)	Pop 25+ 4-Yr Degree + (%)	Below Poverty Line (%)	White (Non-Hisp) (%)	African American (%)	American Indians, Alaska Natives (%)	Asians, Hawaiians, Pacific Islanders (%)	Hispanic Origin (%)
Maine	2000	2001	2002	2003	2004	2005	2006	2000	2006	% Change	($)	(%)	(%)	(%)	(%)	(%)	(%)	(%)	(%)
1	D, 65		D, 57		D, 74		D, 100	8,382	8,086	-4	42,819	28.5	9.7	27.6	81.4	0.2	16.3	0.4	0.9
2	R, 57		R, 100		D, 79		D, 100	8,332	8,032	-4	33,039	31.3	14.3	28.2	94.9	0.5	0.7	0.5	0.9
3	D, 100		R, 49		D, 55		R, 59	8,448	8,357	-1	37,973	28.3	12.2	23.9	96.4	0.1	0.4	0.2	0.5
4	R, 53		R, 53		R, 54		R, 70	8,664	8,842	2	37,759	27.9	11.1	23.5	96.6	0.2	0.3	0.2	0.4
5	R, 63		R, 53		D, 69		D, 75	8,298	7,963	-4	36,297	31.1	12.7	28.0	94.7	0.4	3.8	0.4	0.9
6	R, 60		R, 61		D, 63		D, 63	9,003	9,044	0	36,483	24.5	8.0	25.1	97.2	0.1	0.4	0.1	0.6
7	R, 55		R, 53		D, 53		D, 50	8,813	8,941	1	36,964	26.5	9.4	22.4	97.4	0.1	0.3	0.1	0.6
8	R, 73		R, 100		R, 70		D, 52	8,839	9,192	4	45,457	31.8	13.9	18.4	96.0	0.2	0.1	0.3	1.1
9	R, 53		R, 69		R, 66		R, 64	8,806	9,482	8	53,569	34.5	15.5	15.3	95.7	0.4	0.1	0.3	1.1
10	D, 71		D, 66		D, 69		D, 81	8,065	8,434	5	49,416	32.6	13.9	13.5	96.8	0.3	0.2	0.4	0.9
11	R, 63		R, 60		R, 48		R, 59	8,861	9,056	2	58,597	30.6	12.5	9.5	96.3	0.5	0.1	0.5	0.5
12	D, 51		R, 52		R, 71		R, 63	8,200	8,945	9	92,358	52.3	36.0	9.9	95.2	0.5	0.2	1.1	1.1
13	R, 63		R, 61		D, 59		D, 52	8,609	8,699	1	45,460	29.4	8.8	12.1	95.4	0.7	0.1	0.5	1.0
14	D, 61		D, 54		D, 66		D, 69	8,282	8,583	4	49,228	37.3	21.2	18.4	96.6	0.2	0.2	0.2	0.6
15	D, 100		D, 100		D, 57		D, 62	8,486	9,036	6	45,450	30.2	14.5	13.1	97.3	0.2	0.2	0.2	0.6
16	D, 82		D, 100		D, 59		D, 66	8,708	9,180	5	51,649	40.2	22.6	16.7	95.7	0.5	0.1	0.2	1.1
17	D, 54		D, 100		D, 60		D, 59	8,651	9,001	4	54,028	37.2	19.1	15.7	97.0	0.4	0.1	0.4	0.5
18	D, 77		D, 100		D, 52		D, 52	8,029	8,331	4	50,926	37.5	19.6	15.8	96.8	0.1	0.1	0.1	0.9
19	D, 100		D, 65		D, 62		D, 78	8,391	9,069	8	50,896	34.0	16.8	14.6	96.9	0.4	0.1	0.3	0.7
20	D, 100		D, 100		R, 100		D, 50	8,463	8,789	4	56,650	39.4	21.1	13.4	96.8	0.4	0.1	0.4	0.6
21	R, 68		R, 100		D, 57		D, 59	8,613	9,064	5	46,671	28.0	11.0	15.7	96.4	0.4	0.2	0.4	0.6
22	R, 59		R, 67		D, 68		R, 70	9,877	9,851	0	61,062	39.9	21.2	13.2	95.4	0.6	0.1	1.0	1.0
23	R, 100		D, 55		D, 60		R, 60	8,698	8,918	3	43,703	29.5	11.2	21.1	96.6	0.2	0.1	0.2	0.8
24	D, 58		D, 54		R, 57		R, 63	9,287	9,015	-3	48,277	42.4	20.3	21.1	93.3	1.1	0.6	0.8	1.3
25	D, 59		D, 55		R, 100		R, 77	8,992	9,620	7	71,436	42.9	24.1	7.2	96.8	0.5	0.1	0.3	0.5
26	D, 66		R, 88		R, 68		R, 66	8,822	8,828	0	37,504	28.6	10.7	24.1	96.3	0.3	0.3	0.3	0.7
27	R, 56		R, 54		R, 51		R, 66	8,184	8,538	4	53,823	34.2	17.2	17.5	97.7	0.2	0.1	0.4	0.5
28	D, 75		D, 58		R, 62		R, 59	8,474	9,079	7	49,047	34.6	15.8	13.0	96.4	0.3	0.2	0.3	0.7
29	D, 55		D, 60		R, 56		R, 60	8,620	8,553	-1	38,597	25.7	9.1	23.8	97.3	0.4	0.2	0.2	0.6
30	D, 100		D, 80		D, 61		R, 60	8,603	8,914	4	56,584	46.4	26.3	12.7	98.0	0.1	0.1	0.3	0.5
31	D, 65		GI, 65		D, 68		D, 53	8,250	8,457	3	40,924	28.3	12.7	22.8	96.0	0.2	0.2	0.2	0.7
32	D, 72		D, 59		R, 59		R, 51	7,774	7,675	-1	121,671	59.5	45.7	6.5	96.4	0.3	0.1	1.1	0.7
33	D, 100		D, 75		D, 65		R, 53	8,700	8,842	2	75,160	51.1	35.7	10.1	93.2	1.3	0.1	1.5	1.4
34	D, 100		D, 100		R, 61		D, 54	7,958	8,323	5	56,490	52.5	34.8	12.9	91.4	1.7	0.1	3.0	1.0
35	D, 83		D, 72		D, 66		D, 68	8,532	9,390	10	61,881	44.0	23.5	10.6	92.1	2.0	0.1	0.7	2.5
36	D, 74		R, 65		D, 70		D, 68	8,509	8,760	3	70,006	48.0	31.2	5.8	95.9	0.6	0.1	0.5	1.0
37	D, 72		D, 74		D, 47		D, 52	7,637	7,628	0	121,397	63.2	49.4	5.8	96.3	0.3	0.0	1.2	0.8
38	R, 100		R, 58		R, 58		R, 53	8,321	8,488	2	58,231	54.0	35.2	11.1	94.2	0.5	0.2	0.9	1.4
39	R, 100		D, 100		R, 53		R, 50	9,254	9,295	0	41,468	49.3	34.2	19.3	84.7	3.4	0.3	2.3	3.7
40	R, 61		R, 66		R, 54		R, 58	8,679	9,052	4	102,918	55.4	40.9	7.2	97.0	0.2	0.1	0.5	1.0
41	R, 66		R, 63		R, 51		D, 55	8,300	8,129	-2	45,856	40.7	21.3	12.6	90.2	1.2	0.1	2.4	2.4
42	R, 56		R, 100		R, 50		R, 54	8,073	8,052	0	68,588	53.0	32.9	8.3	94.8	0.5	0.1	1.3	1.2
43	D, 55		R, 56		R, 50		R, 50	7,346	7,897	8	42,621	40.7	22.4	16.9	93.3	1.0	0.1	1.2	1.5
44	R, 100		I, 62		D, 60		R, 50	8,991	9,948	11	62,178	40.3	21.3	8.6	96.7	0.3	0.1	0.4	0.9
45	R, 100		R, 58		D, 63		D, 63	8,047	8,155	1	62,225	56.8	41.7	9.9	91.5	1.2	0.2	1.7	1.6
46	R, 100		R, 50		R, 49		D, 51	7,102	7,296	3	33,971	40.9	26.5	30.7	72.1	7.6	0.5	5.2	6.2
47	R, 53		R, 54		D, 52		D, 68	8,812	9,600	9	55,494	32.9	12.0	9.5	97.1	0.2	0.2	0.2	0.9
48	D, 66		D, 53		R, 60		R, 56	8,235	8,584	4	51,499	40.3	19.7	18.0	94.9	0.5	0.1	0.7	1.1
49	D, 66		D, 63		R, 51		R, 51	8,988	9,933	11	59,874	37.4	15.8	9.1	96.9	0.3	0.1	0.5	0.8
50	D, 58		D, 70		R, 64		D, 53	8,675	9,365	8	50,062	43.9	18.6	15.0	95.0	0.6	0.2	0.5	1.5

(continued)

Note: D=Democrat, R=Republican, R/D=Republican/Democrat (cross-filed), D/R=Democrat/Republican (cross-filed), I=Independent, C=Constitution, O=Other, GI=Green Independent, P=Progressive, P/D=Progressive/Democrat, P/D/R=Progressive/Democrat/Republican, HH=Households

Maine State House Districts—Election and Demographic Data (cont.)

House Districts	General Election Results Party, Percent of Vote							Population			Avg. HH Income ($)	Pop 25+ Some College + (%)	4-Yr Degree + (%)	Below Poverty Line (%)	2006 White (Non-Hisp) (%)	African American (%)	American Indians, Alaska Natives (%)	Asians, Hawaiians, Pacific Islanders (%)	Hispanic Origin (%)
Maine	2000	2001	2002	2003	2004	2005	2006	2000	2006	% Change	($)	(%)	(%)	(%)	(%)	(%)	(%)	(%)	(%)
51	D, 100		D, 58		R, 53		R, 53	9,264	9,809	6	46,605	31.8	12.3	17.8	94.7	0.7	0.2	1.2	0.8
52	D, 57		D, 58		D, 56		D, 57	6,987	7,165	3	36,780	25.9	10.3	24.1	92.9	1.0	0.3	1.1	1.4
53	D, 53		D, 51		D, 58		D, 54	7,500	8,188	9	61,648	36.8	15.2	9.0	95.5	0.5	0.1	0.9	1.0
54	R, 70		D, 55		R, 55		R, 63	8,739	9,158	5	49,120	27.1	9.9	17.7	93.3	0.4	0.2	2.2	1.5
55	R, 70		D, 52		D, 40		R, 50	8,888	10,026	13	73,731	41.6	22.7	8.3	96.4	0.4	0.1	0.4	0.9
56	D, 50		D, 53		R, 50		D, 61	7,953	8,826	11	88,544	52.8	30.8	8.5	96.3	0.2	0.0	0.6	1.1
57	D, 51		D, 54		D, 56		D, 58	8,570	9,736	14	62,194	39.3	17.6	9.0	96.7	0.2	0.2	0.5	0.8
58	R, 74		R, 74		R, 58		R, 68	8,920	9,441	6	51,800	31.8	12.2	15.3	95.4	0.3	0.1	0.9	1.2
59	R, 54		R, 100		D, 63		D, 67	8,578	8,810	3	44,378	27.3	9.6	19.4	92.6	0.6	0.2	2.0	1.5
60	R, 59		I, 44		D, 54		R, 53	9,848	11,924	21	54,377	29.2	10.8	14.8	96.0	0.4	0.1	0.9	0.8
61	D, 56		R, 56		R, 53		D, 57	8,445	9,266	10	51,444	34.9	13.7	12.8	96.7	0.3	0.1	0.3	0.8
62	R, 55		R, 66		D, 54		D, 62	8,672	9,386	8	72,780	52.4	28.1	8.0	96.8	0.6	0.1	0.4	0.9
63	D, 100		R, 51		D, 62		D, 60	8,054	9,026	12	66,847	44.9	22.3	9.9	96.3	0.3	0.1	0.5	1.0
64	R, 62		R, 69		D, 55		D, 62	8,284	9,244	12	73,477	53.1	33.0	7.4	96.7	0.2	0.0	0.9	0.7
65	R, 100		R, 51		D, 61		D, 57	8,279	8,983	9	77,894	46.2	26.6	8.4	97.1	0.3	0.1	0.5	0.9
66	D, 57		D, 58		D, 67		D, 62	8,736	9,812	12	59,886	32.9	14.4	9.8	96.8	0.3	0.1	0.4	0.9
67	D, 68		R, 52		D, 50		D, 58	7,965	8,432	6	58,554	41.4	23.6	7.4	96.0	0.6	0.2	0.5	0.8
68	R, 52		R, 58		R, 52		R, 55	8,009	8,666	8	56,130	41.4	22.4	6.8	96.5	0.4	0.1	0.3	0.8
69	D, 69		D, 62		D, 43		D, 60	8,156	8,950	10	65,780	36.5	20.0	10.9	95.7	0.5	0.2	0.7	1.0
70	D, 63		D, 76		D, 56		D, 52	9,166	9,473	3	59,506	45.7	28.8	11.7	95.4	0.8	0.1	0.7	0.8
71	R, 100		R, 62		D, 63		D, 66	8,557	8,955	5	56,363	45.2	26.1	8.3	96.0	0.5	0.2	0.4	0.4
72	R, 51		R, 57		D, 66		D, 60	7,848	7,741	-1	58,868	43.1	23.8	10.9	93.9	1.1	0.2	0.9	1.4
73	D, 55		D, 52		D, 68		D, 62	8,297	8,236	-1	67,047	52.7	36.9	9.1	91.7	1.1	0.1	3.0	1.1
74	I, 60		D, 52		D, 68		D, 73	9,126	9,018	-1	48,672	44.7	27.4	16.5	85.7	3.1	0.2	4.9	1.7
75	D, 66		R, 54		R, 52		R, 54	8,205	8,124	-1	51,459	54.9	41.7	17.5	87.7	2.9	0.3	2.1	2.5
76	D, 64		D, 54		D, 67		D, 69	8,190	8,612	5	89,648	56.0	40.2	6.2	95.8	0.4	0.1	1.1	0.9
77	D, 68		D, 100		D, 65		D, 67	9,138	10,023	10	68,841	48.7	31.0	8.6	95.2	0.5	0.1	1.4	0.8
78	R, 54		D, 53		R, 45		D, 57	8,147	8,487	4	60,458	46.0	26.2	12.6	97.4	0.1	0.1	0.4	0.7
79	D, 61		D, 63		R, 55		D, 62	9,429	9,799	4	57,599	39.3	22.1	10.5	91.9	1.8	0.1	0.7	2.1
80	D, 100		R, 50		D, 54		D, 53	8,643	9,215	7	56,458	39.8	21.4	9.6	91.3	1.6	0.1	1.3	2.1
81	D, 100		R, 50		D, 52		R, 50	8,372	8,478	1	49,102	35.1	16.3	16.4	90.0	1.9	0.3	0.6	2.8
82	D, 53		R, 44		R, 51		R, 70	8,371	8,541	2	50,139	46.5	32.0	16.7	90.8	1.5	0.1	1.7	2.4
83	D, 58		D, 60		D, 56		R, 56	8,136	8,589	6	66,603	45.1	32.8	10.2	90.6	1.6	0.1	1.9	2.5
84	D, 100		R, 56		D, 62		D, 52	8,145	8,353	3	89,403	60.6	47.7	8.4	96.7	0.5	0.0	0.4	0.9
85	R, 62		R, 51		R, 56		R, 55	8,552	9,115	7	68,784	49.7	33.2	13.2	95.8	0.3	0.2	0.5	1.6
86	D, 71		D, 100		R, 52		R, 52	8,609	8,481	-1	43,240	33.6	16.3	19.0	96.8	0.3	0.2	0.4	0.8
87	D, 62		D, 58		D, 62		D, 57	8,822	9,197	4	46,559	34.8	17.1	17.5	97.0	0.2	0.2	0.3	0.5
88	R, 57		D, 58		R, 58		R, 55	8,259	8,117	-2	41,420	25.7	9.1	19.4	97.1	0.1	0.1	0.5	0.7
89	D, 68		D, 65		D, 51		D, 56	7,949	9,341	18	64,904	32.1	13.3	10.2	92.0	0.2	0.1	0.3	3.0
90	D, 56		D, 63		D, 51		I, 75	8,935	10,081	13	47,491	30.3	12.2	16.0	96.7	0.2	0.1	0.5	0.7
91	D, 74		D, 64		R, 51		D, 51	8,425	9,560	13	46,358	28.8	10.3	17.6	96.6	0.4	0.1	0.1	0.8
92	D, 100		D, 61		D, 65		D, 67	8,933	8,959	0	45,563	31.8	12.8	18.6	96.7	0.3	0.2	0.4	0.7
93	D, 76		D, 59		R, 51		R, 57	8,973	8,682	-3	40,391	25.8	10.4	21.8	97.5	0.1	0.1	0.3	0.7
94	D, 100		R, 51		R, 52		D, 50	8,340	8,419	1	45,109	28.5	12.4	19.7	97.3	0.2	0.2	0.2	0.5
95	R, 57		D, 57		R, 51		R, 52	8,228	8,059	-2	41,640	31.9	15.2	23.0	93.8	0.6	0.2	1.3	1.2
96	R, 61		R, 65		R, 54		D, 55	8,568	8,992	5	49,351	32.2	13.5	14.1	97.1	0.1	0.1	0.4	0.7
97	D, 65		D, 100		R, 57		R, 56	8,434	8,909	6	52,182	32.7	13.4	14.5	96.8	0.1	0.1	0.4	0.8
98	D, 37		D, 37		R, 57		R, 56	8,433	8,435	0	43,149	33.8	16.4	23.1	94.2	0.6	0.3	0.7	1.2
99	D, 53		D, 65		R, 58		R, 52	8,623	8,895	3	45,740	36.5	15.9	15.1	96.1	0.2	0.1	0.4	1.0
100	D, 100		D, 72		R, 59		R, 63	7,844	7,789	-1	42,835	37.6	17.0	21.0	93.2	0.6	0.2	1.6	1.4

(continued)

Note: D=Democrat, R=Republican, R/D=Republican/Democrat (cross-filed), D/R=Democrat/Republican (cross-filed), I=Independent, C=Constitution, O=Other, GI=Green Independent, P=Progressive, P/D=Progressive/Democrat, P/D/R=Progressive/Democrat/Republican, HH=Households

Maine State House Districts—Election and Demographic Data (cont.)

House Districts	General Election Results Party, Percent of Vote							Population			Avg. HH Income	Pop 25+ Some College +	Pop 25+ 4-Yr Degree +	Below Poverty Line	White (Non-Hisp)	African American	American Indians, Alaska Natives	Asians, Hawaiians, Pacific Islanders	Hispanic Origin
															2006				
Maine	2000	2001	2002	2003	2004	2005	2006	2000	2006	% Change	($)	(%)	(%)	(%)	(%)	(%)	(%)	(%)	(%)
101	D, 100		D, 51		R, 51		R, 56	8,268	8,656	5	50,055	33.0	13.9	13.9	96.8	0.2	0.2	0.2	0.7
102	D, 77		R, 59		R, 55		D, 50	8,679	9,286	7	46,634	32.1	13.8	17.2	96.5	0.2	0.4	0.4	0.8
103	R, 55		R, 55		R, 52		R, 54	8,276	7,923	-4	48,459	30.0	11.7	17.9	96.8	0.3	0.2	0.3	0.5
104	D, 55		D, 64		R, 52		R, 53	8,743	8,471	-3	44,207	27.3	9.2	21.7	97.3	0.2	0.1	0.1	0.3
105	D, 55		D, 55		R, 54		R, 56	8,674	8,734	1	38,640	23.9	8.5	21.9	97.4	0.1	0.1	0.3	0.4
106	R, 72		D, 51		D, 51		D, 59	8,422	9,017	7	61,108	41.9	20.2	12.1	96.7	0.1	0.1	0.3	0.6
107	D, 55		R, 54		I, 61		I, 65	8,206	7,862	-4	47,082	27.7	13.0	22.0	92.2	1.1	0.3	1.4	1.8
108	R, 60		R, 52		R, 54		R, 54	8,786	9,327	6	43,509	27.5	10.3	21.4	95.9	0.3	0.2	0.5	0.8
109	R, 60		R, 61		R, 61		R, 53	8,485	8,731	3	46,362	41.1	19.8	14.4	95.5	0.6	0.2	0.6	1.0
110	R, 64		D, 52		D, 55		D, 57	7,399	7,395	0	55,295	33.3	13.7	16.5	94.6	0.5	0.3	0.4	1.1
111	D, 51		R, 50		R, 63		R, 66	8,815	9,057	3	54,486	44.6	23.9	13.6	96.8	0.3	0.2	0.4	0.9
112	R, 53		R, 64		R, 59		R, 52	7,899	8,031	2	47,877	27.9	10.5	15.1	93.9	0.9	0.1	0.6	1.1
113	R, 71		R, 68		D, 51		D, 54	8,368	8,550	2	57,811	32.8	14.4	11.8	94.2	0.8	0.1	1.5	1.1
114	R, 46		D, 54		D, 69		D, 73	8,435	8,777	4	52,716	27.7	8.3	8.6	96.8	0.3	0.1	0.3	0.8
115	D, 100		R, 53		D, 74		D, 71	8,339	8,075	-3	29,236	20.7	7.4	33.6	89.2	2.1	0.3	0.4	2.8
116	R, 59		R, 61		D, 44		D, 74	8,208	7,967	-3	38,232	22.8	9.0	25.6	92.0	1.2	0.2	0.9	1.7
117	D, 58		D, 61		D, 77		D, 69	7,789	7,590	-3	35,238	25.9	8.9	25.4	92.6	1.0	0.2	0.7	1.3
118	D, 54		D, 63		I, 51		D, 52	8,275	8,566	4	41,187	30.1	17.5	23.7	95.4	0.3	0.1	0.6	1.1
119	D, 56		D, 53		D, 49		D, 50	8,456	9,015	7	46,542	27.7	10.3	16.8	95.2	0.6	0.2	0.6	1.0
120	D, 64		D, 64		D, 50		D, 57	8,597	8,921	4	44,627	28.3	10.6	17.7	95.4	0.4	0.9	0.3	0.6
121	D, 68		D, 100		D, 56		D, 52	8,539	8,831	3	45,308	35.8	17.3	15.9	93.7	0.6	0.3	0.5	1.5
122	R, 50		R, 53		D, 67		D, 61	8,088	8,237	2	39,163	23.5	8.0	25.0	96.8	0.2	0.5	0.1	0.6
123	D, 100		D, 100		D, 63		D, 64	8,552	8,666	1	47,831	34.7	14.8	15.0	97.0	0.2	0.1	0.2	0.7
124	R, 57		R, 62		R, 55		D, 64	8,817	8,885	1	48,642	43.4	20.4	17.4	96.2	0.4	0.3	0.6	0.9
125	R, 51		R, 58		D, 53		D, 55	8,629	9,089	5	53,421	33.1	10.9	15.1	96.4	0.3	0.3	0.2	0.5
126	R, 77		R, 68		D, 55		D, 62	8,124	7,919	-3	44,759	32.7	14.8	28.2	88.8	1.6	0.7	1.4	2.5
127	D, 59		R, 63		R, 62		R, 51	8,297	8,099	-2	53,148	41.5	21.3	18.1	93.5	0.9	0.4	1.5	1.2
128	R, 61		R, 44		R, 62		D, 48	8,436	8,292	-2	51,694	43.4	23.3	16.3	94.0	0.7	0.3	1.2	0.9
129	D, 55		D, 62		D, 59		D, 66	7,915	7,645	-3	44,739	30.8	20.9	23.7	90.5	1.6	0.5	2.6	1.8
130	D, 48		D, 56		D, 54		D, 59	9,568	9,366	-2	43,135	31.0	14.9	24.8	90.3	0.8	5.7	1.6	0.9
131	D, 53		D, 60		R, 53		R, 58	8,478	8,733	3	46,503	32.8	15.0	16.7	96.7	0.1	0.2	0.1	0.4
132	R, 64		R, 54		D, 61		D, 70	8,006	8,177	2	56,115	38.9	18.7	11.9	97.1	0.2	0.3	0.3	0.5
133	D, 100		D, 37		D, 56		D, 100	8,305	8,690	5	53,193	42.4	20.4	16.4	95.7	0.2	0.3	0.4	0.8
134	D, 100		D, 100		D, 61		D, 66	8,177	9,957	22	47,203	31.9	16.7	19.9	96.2	0.2	0.2	0.2	0.8
135	R, 59		D, 53		D, 59		D, 80	8,784	8,864	1	65,430	43.6	21.7	10.8	96.8	0.4	0.1	0.5	0.6
136	D, 52		D, 54		D, 74		D, 100	8,511	8,785	3	53,512	43.5	25.3	15.9	95.9	0.3	0.2	0.3	0.6
137	D, 50		R, 54		R, 52		D, 53	8,426	8,768	4	50,297	40.4	22.5	18.4	95.9	0.3	0.1	0.3	0.7
138	R, 73		R, 78		R, 53		R, 56	8,488	8,899	5	67,358	54.8	34.5	13.1	96.7	0.3	0.0	0.4	1.0
139	D, 61		D, 62		D, 50		R, 52	8,410	8,392	0	39,568	35.3	17.2	20.0	96.5	0.2	0.1	0.5	0.7
140	D, 61		D, 67		R, 100		D, 51	8,878	9,731	10	50,770	34.6	12.7	14.2	96.9	0.2	0.1	0.4	0.6
141	D, 53		R, 53		D, 57		D, 58	8,213	8,455	3	59,286	46.2	29.3	16.8	96.6	0.2	0.1	0.6	0.8
142	R, 71		R, 67		R, 51		D, 60	8,464	8,481	0	41,986	28.5	11.8	21.1	97.3	0.2	0.2	0.3	0.4
143	R, 100		D, 51		D, 57		D, 69	8,458	8,262	-2	41,413	30.0	11.3	20.8	97.8	0.1	0.2	0.4	0.3
144	D, 50		D, 61		R, 56		R, 60	8,740	8,625	-1	34,629	27.8	12.1	28.8	93.5	0.3	0.3	0.2	2.0
145	R, 100		D, 55		D, 54		D, 60	8,433	8,480	1	42,028	29.1	12.2	25.0	97.0	0.3	0.3	0.5	0.6
146	D, 100		R, 55		R, 51		R, 41	8,662	8,548	-1	40,990	28.4	11.3	20.2	97.6	0.2	0.2	0.3	0.4
147	R, 60		D, 53		R, 58		R, 48	8,343	8,010	-4	44,032	33.6	15.3	21.6	94.8	0.4	0.8	1.0	0.9
148	R, 46		R, 100		R, 58		R, 52	8,536	8,130	-5	34,528	27.3	10.5	26.4	91.7	1.7	0.3	0.6	2.8
149	D, 79		D, 58		R, 52		D, 63	8,431	8,148	-3	40,740	29.7	11.1	20.7	96.4	0.1	0.7	0.3	0.7
150	D, 100		D, 81		R, 64		R, 53	8,285	8,100	-2	37,704	29.1	12.6	24.6	96.4	0.3	0.4	0.1	0.9
151	R, 52		I, 65		D, 69		D, 74	8,142	7,813	-4	44,676	36.3	16.4	23.3	93.8	0.4	1.3	0.8	1.1

Note: D=Democrat, R=Republican, R/D=Republican/Democrat (cross-filed), D/R=Democrat/Republican (cross-filed), I=Independent, C=Constitution, O=Other, GI=Green Independent, P=Progressive, P/D=Progressive/Democrat, P/D/R=Progressive/Democrat/Republican, HH=Households

MARYLAND

H. L. Mencken usually had a sharp word for everything, and he did not spare his home state. "Maryland," he wrote in the 1920s, "bulges with normalcy. . . . Here, it appears, is the dream paradise of every true Americano, the heaven imagined by the Rotary Club, the Knights of Pythias, and the American Legion. Here is the goal whither all the rest of the Republic is striving and pining to drift."

In some respects, Mencken was right, though he would not have been pleased about it. If the United States is an increasingly suburban country, Maryland is its most suburban state. With the single exception of Baltimore, almost two-thirds of its people live in a huge suburban "Y" running from the edge of Cumberland in the west and the Interstate 95 corridor in the northeast, through the Annapolis and Washington suburbs, and down the west bank of the Chesapeake almost to its mouth.

Suburban areas tend to be wealthy, and so is Maryland—the second wealthiest state overall in terms of median household income, just a few dollars behind New Jersey. It also has one of the highest percentages of college graduates (in the 16th house district, around Chevy Chase in the Washington, D.C., suburbs, almost 60 percent of the residents have completed college—the fifth-highest rate in the nation). As is true in so many places, the fastest growing parts of the state are the outer suburbs—around Washington, Baltimore, and Annapolis—another example of the so-called urban doughnut, in which the older inner suburbs are losing groups to faster-growing suburbs farther from the city center. Population is falling in poorer parts of Baltimore.

But geography tells something about a state as well as residential patterns, and so there is more to Maryland than its malls and soccer moms. The Mason-Dixon Line, which forms the state's border with Pennsylvania, is supposed to divide North from South, although as Mencken also observed, this is untrue geographically, culturally, and historically. If the divide is not there, though, it is someplace close, for Maryland has characteristics of both regions.

It is a northern state, hence its wealth, but also its slow rate of economic growth—third-slowest in the nation since 1990 and much more in line with New England than with the New South. It is southern in its atmosphere along the sleepy Eastern Shore, and also in the state's high percentage of African Americans—27 percent, higher than Alabama. In keeping with its air of cross-pollination of north and south, though, black districts in Maryland are among the wealthiest black districts in the United States.

Prince George's County in the Washington, D.C., suburbs boasts one of the strongest and broadest black middle classes anywhere. The county's 24th house district is 91 percent African American, the second-greatest concentration of any state house district in the country. Average household income is more than $59,000, close to the state average. The extremely wealthy districts in Maryland, though, are in Montgomery County, on the other side of Washington, where the percentage of African Americans is much lower. In the 15th and 16th house districts, around Bethesda and Potomac, average household income is $117,000. It is also high slightly farther out in Silver Spring and Wheaton, and in the Baltimore suburbs.

Poverty in Maryland is also much more integrated than it is elsewhere. The poorest and third-poorest districts are heavily black neighborhoods in downtown Baltimore. But the second and fourth-poorest are in Cumberland, in the far western counties where there are hardly any blacks at all.

In addition to being one of the most oddly shaped states (at the town of Hancock on Interstate 70, it is barely two miles wide), Maryland has an odd way of numbering the districts in its legislature. The state is divided into forty-seven legislative districts, each of which elects one member of the senate and three members of the House of Delegates, most of whom are elected at large by block voting. In some parts of the state, though, delegates are elected individually from subdistricts, which vary in number.

Redistricting was ugly after the last census, both in terms of the wrangling needed to achieve it and in the shape of the districts achieved. The congressional redistricting plan, devised by the general assembly, succeeded in protecting incumbents. The legislative redistricting plan, drawn up by the governor (then a Democrat), was tossed out by the state court of appeals, which then substituted its own plan. From a partisan standpoint, almost nothing has changed. Democrats control the senate by the same two-to-one margin they did six years ago and have lost only a few seats in the house of delegates. Members of both chambers, incidentally, serve four-year terms. Politically this is one of the most Democratic states, one of only six to vote for Jimmy Carter's reelection in 1980. Though one of the original thirteen states, Maryland has never played much of a role on the national stage, with the possible exception of 1972 when the country was treated to the prospect of not one, but two Marylanders (Spiro Agnew and Sargent Shriver) running for vice president. Mencken would have smiled at that.

MARYLAND
State Senate Districts

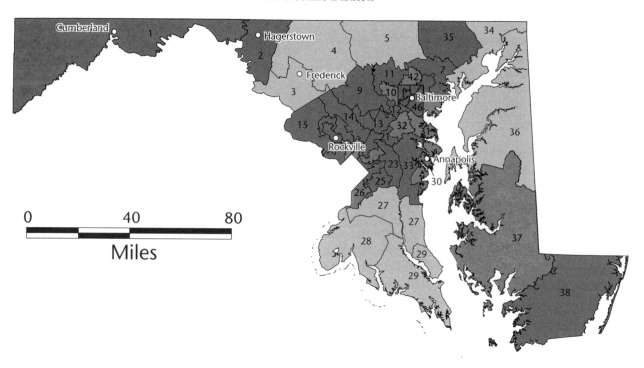

WASHINGTON, D.C. SUBURBS

BALTIMORE

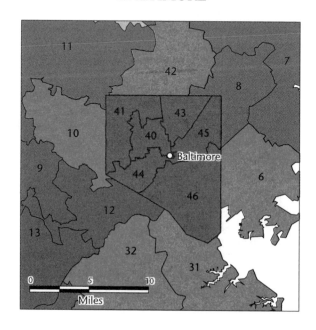

Population Growth ▪ -5% to 0% ▪ 0% to 5% ▪ 5% to 10% ▪ 10% to 18%

Maryland State Senate Districts—Election and Demographic Data

Senate Districts	General Election Results Party, Percent of Vote							Population			Avg. HH Income ($)	Pop 25+ Some College + (%)	Pop 25+ 4-Yr Degree + (%)	Below Poverty Line (%)	2006 White (Non-Hisp) (%)	African American (%)	American Indians, Alaska Natives (%)	Asians, Hawaiians, Pacific Islanders (%)	Hispanic Origin (%)
Maryland	2000	2001	2002	2003	2004	2005	2006	2000	2006	% Change	($)	(%)	(%)	(%)	(%)	(%)	(%)	(%)	(%)
1			R, 99				R, 73	117,389	115,782	-1	45,025	25.1	9.7	20.4	93.3	4.5	0.1	0.6	0.8
2			R, 71				R, 99	117,807	125,969	7	54,756	28.3	11.3	14.8	85.9	9.6	0.1	1.2	2.1
3			R, 55				R, 52	118,228	138,760	17	75,972	38.2	20.7	7.7	74.6	10.4	0.4	3.0	6.7
4			R, 76				R, 99	111,904	126,942	13	82,316	33.4	17.0	6.7	90.5	2.6	0.3	0.9	2.5
5			R, 74				R, 98	117,317	130,381	11	86,138	38.3	21.6	7.0	93.0	2.9	0.1	1.7	1.4
6			D, 98				D, 70	108,926	109,233	0	50,291	26.1	9.7	14.8	81.7	13.3	0.2	1.3	2.2
7			R, 58				R, 57	113,407	121,516	7	73,094	37.2	19.9	8.6	83.9	9.4	0.1	2.9	2.4
8			D, 58				D, 58	114,568	123,553	8	62,547	38.5	19.8	7.9	77.4	14.5	0.1	4.8	2.2
9			R, 98				R, 62	118,527	130,200	10	105,139	47.3	33.2	5.0	78.9	5.9	0.2	8.1	2.4
10			D, 81				D, 99	119,997	122,130	2	59,986	40.7	21.2	9.5	29.3	63.8	0.1	3.8	2.6
11			D, 63				D, 71	114,995	122,741	7	95,145	50.9	34.9	6.6	67.1	23.8	0.1	4.6	3.4
12			D, 63				D, 62	116,528	124,047	6	77,458	45.0	30.4	8.2	71.7	16.1	0.1	6.6	3.8
13			R, 51				D, 56	115,739	125,708	9	95,079	48.6	35.6	4.7	60.2	19.4	0.4	8.9	5.1
14			D, 61				D, 68	112,593	121,750	8	109,384	50.9	36.6	3.8	58.9	19.6	0.1	13.6	6.2
15			D, 51				D, 66	109,255	119,016	9	146,417	56.2	44.3	3.7	65.0	8.5	0.1	18.0	7.0
16			D, 72				D, 76	105,851	112,937	7	163,032	67.0	58.3	4.2	75.8	4.4	0.1	10.9	7.0
17			D, 71				D, 99	112,135	122,251	9	85,767	51.1	37.6	7.2	49.2	12.8	0.2	17.7	19.0
18			D, 97				D, 76	112,900	117,664	4	104,646	51.7	39.1	7.0	50.5	14.3	0.1	10.8	21.9
19			D, 70				D, 68	109,829	115,666	5	91,149	51.4	36.1	7.2	51.2	18.2	0.1	13.6	15.3
20			D, 82				D, 99	109,027	114,253	5	73,145	47.5	34.5	10.1	32.7	33.5	0.2	11.8	23.1
21			D, 97				D, 68	111,807	118,212	6	71,092	41.1	25.4	8.1	45.9	35.2	0.1	9.4	9.4
22			D, 99				D, 99	112,486	116,119	3	66,697	38.5	23.7	8.8	19.3	50.9	0.5	8.1	20.2
23			D, 80				D, 99	106,861	113,711	6	95,870	48.5	31.0	3.3	30.5	49.6	0.4	4.5	7.4
24			D, 100				D, 100	110,939	120,287	8	59,009	32.2	14.6	12.0	6.7	91.2	0.3	1.2	6.0
25			D, 100				D, 100	104,308	111,576	7	75,087	38.3	19.3	6.6	11.2	82.7	0.5	1.8	6.5
26			D, 99				D, 99	107,453	111,188	3	77,420	39.1	19.7	7.1	10.2	81.4	0.4	5.1	6.4
27			D, 72				D, 70	114,998	128,087	11	88,292	39.1	20.4	5.6	52.5	40.8	0.2	2.5	3.7
28			D, 64				D, 65	116,316	135,455	16	77,642	33.6	13.2	7.2	64.8	27.9	0.3	2.4	3.3
29			D, 58				D, 64	117,216	138,151	18	72,806	33.7	16.3	8.4	78.8	15.1	0.5	2.0	2.5
30			D, 55				D, 53	117,017	121,842	4	92,156	49.5	31.0	7.2	76.3	15.7	0.1	1.9	4.8
31			D, 62				R, 51	114,396	116,492	2	69,218	37.8	17.0	8.1	83.7	10.0	0.2	2.3	2.4
32			D, 59				D, 61	115,805	120,617	4	66,835	40.6	18.6	7.9	67.0	21.4	0.2	4.8	4.9
33			R, 54				R, 56	115,458	122,587	6	106,796	52.4	32.6	3.9	87.0	7.0	0.1	2.5	2.3
34			R, 60				R, 57	115,727	128,261	11	62,365	32.0	12.0	10.2	75.9	15.1	0.8	1.7	3.1
35			R, 98				R, 68	117,145	128,122	9	83,932	41.0	21.6	5.8	89.5	3.9	0.6	1.8	1.5
36			R, 62				R, 64	118,462	132,202	12	67,237	31.3	14.5	11.7	84.9	9.9	0.1	1.0	2.7
37			R, 69				R, 56	117,470	122,043	4	58,246	29.2	13.9	16.8	67.9	27.4	0.1	1.3	2.5
38			R, 69				R, 99	119,041	125,921	6	55,494	31.5	14.5	15.1	74.1	21.6	0.1	1.5	2.0
39			D, 66				D, 98	107,004	112,680	5	87,431	49.2	33.7	4.7	50.4	17.2	0.1	16.3	14.2
40			D, 100				D, 90	104,946	101,026	-4	40,856	28.6	17.6	28.8	23.0	72.8	0.3	2.7	1.8
41			D, 97				D, 99	109,612	105,647	-4	57,378	35.0	22.7	20.3	25.4	72.6	0.3	1.0	1.7
42			D, 51				D, 56	106,549	108,348	2	86,027	50.2	36.3	8.9	81.6	8.4	0.1	6.3	2.6
43			D, 99				D, 89	109,357	107,188	-2	58,431	33.6	22.0	18.0	28.1	67.5	0.3	2.6	2.1
44			D, 100				D, 90	111,319	108,870	-2	34,602	23.3	12.7	35.2	20.8	76.7	0.3	1.9	1.5
45			D, 84				D, 86	111,405	106,246	-5	42,212	25.0	13.0	23.1	25.6	72.2	0.4	0.9	1.7
46			D, 99				D, 73	107,362	104,281	-3	47,300	29.7	19.4	24.1	55.0	37.0	1.1	2.0	6.1
47			D, 99				D, 99	104,028	110,852	7	56,519	31.2	17.0	13.1	14.9	62.2	0.2	4.5	29.4

Note: D=Democrat, R=Republican, R/D=Republican/Democrat (cross-filed), D/R=Democrat/Republican (cross-filed), I=Independent, C=Constitution, O=Other, GI=Green Independent, P=Progressive, P/D=Progressive/Democrat, P/D/R=Progressive/Democrat/Republican, HH=Households

MARYLAND
State House Districts

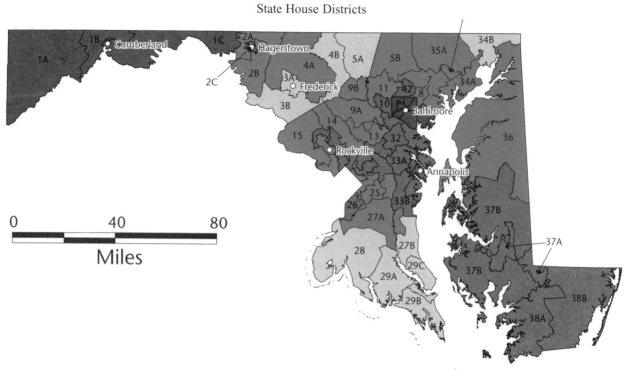

WASHINGTON, D.C., SUBURBS

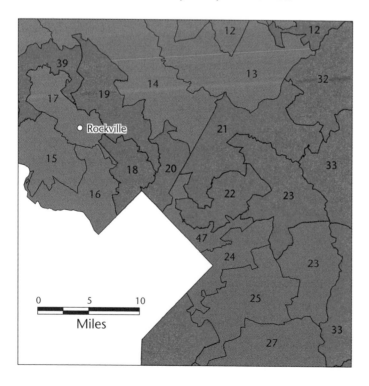

Population Growth   ■ -5% to 1%   ■ 1% to 6%   ■ 6% to 12%   □ 12% to 23%

BALTIMORE

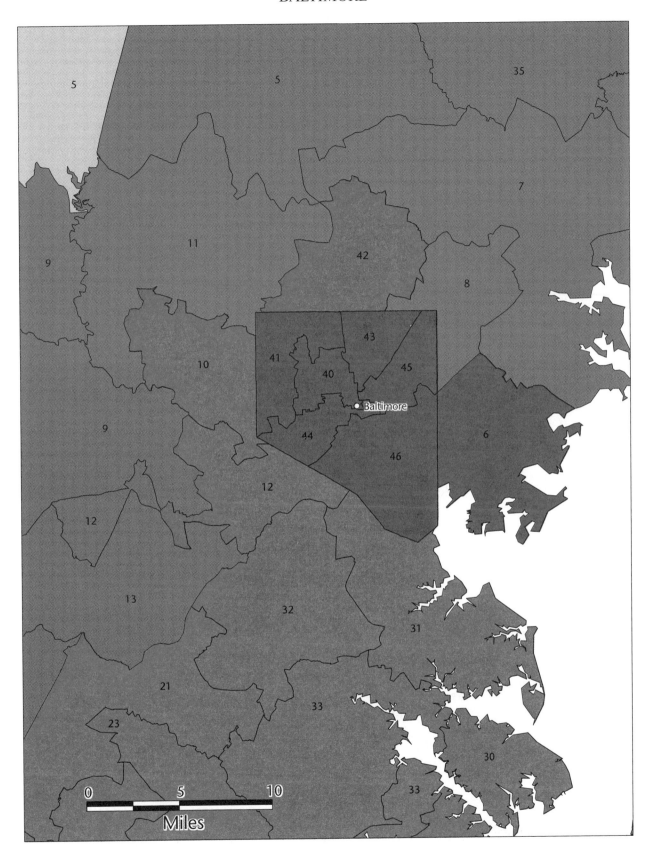

Population Growth   ■ -5% to 1%   ■ 1% to 6%   ■ 6% to 12%   □ 12% to 23%

Maryland State House Districts—Election and Demographic Data

House Districts	General Election Results Party, Percent of Vote							Population			Avg. HH Income ($)	Pop 25+ Some College + (%)	Pop 25+ 4-Yr Degree + (%)	Below Poverty Line (%)	White (Non-Hisp) (%)	African American (%)	American Indians, Alaska Natives (%)	Asians, Hawaiians, Pacific Islanders (%)	Hispanic Origin (%)
Maryland	2000	2001	2002	2003	2004	2005	2006	2000	2006	% Change	($)	(%)	(%)	(%)	(%)	(%)	(%)	(%)	(%)
1A			R, 99				R, 56	39,481	38,926	-1	44,027	23.4	8.8	21.7	97.5	1.2	0.0	0.4	0.4
1B			D, 56				D, 56	38,613	37,568	-3	46,280	29.0	12.4	19.3	91.1	6.3	0.1	1.0	0.8
1C			R, 50				R, 57	39,277	38,965	-1	44,875	23.0	7.8	20.2	91.2	6.0	0.1	0.6	1.3
2A			R, 75				R, 99	39,416	42,963	9	61,223	29.6	12.2	11.3	92.0	3.9	0.1	1.2	1.9
2B			R, 72				R, 99	39,284	42,231	8	62,579	31.5	12.9	10.9	82.7	14.0	0.0	1.1	1.4
2C			D, 59				D, 56	39,050	40,378	3	42,404	23.6	8.6	20.7	82.9	11.1	0.1	1.3	2.8
3A			D, 25				D, 26	78,798	91,294	16	72,245	39.4	21.8	8.1	74.0	13.0	0.1	3.8	7.4
3A			R, 26				D, 29	78,798	91,294	16	72,245	39.4	21.8	8.1	74.0	13.0	0.1	3.8	7.4
3B			R, 62				R, 61	39,414	47,078	19	83,901	35.9	18.6	6.8	89.2	5.3	0.1	1.4	2.8
4A			R, 32				R, 40	73,432	81,621	11	82,821	34.9	18.1	6.7	93.1	2.4	0.1	1.0	2.5
4A			R, 36				R, 37	73,432	81,621	11	82,821	34.9	18.1	6.7	93.1	2.4	0.1	1.0	2.5
4B			R, 76				R, 70	38,401	44,907	17	81,426	30.7	14.9	6.7	93.6	2.9	0.1	0.8	1.7
5A			R, 34				R, 36	78,204	88,364	13	71,628	33.5	16.1	8.2	93.6	2.7	0.1	1.1	1.5
5A			R, 76				R, 33	78,204	88,364	13	71,628	33.5	16.1	8.2	93.6	2.7	0.1	1.1	1.5
5B			R, 71				R, 99	38,789	41,311	7	115,422	48.4	33.3	4.5	91.8	3.3	0.0	2.9	1.1
6			D, 21				D, 23	108,883	108,902	0	50,290	26.1	9.7	14.8	81.7	13.3	0.2	1.3	2.2
6			D, 21				D, 21	108,883	108,902	0	50,290	26.1	9.7	14.8	81.7	13.3	0.2	1.3	2.2
6			D, 21				D, 21	108,883	108,902	0	50,290	26.1	9.7	14.8	81.7	13.3	0.2	1.3	2.2
7			R, 17				R, 20	113,164	120,979	7	73,216	37.2	19.9	8.6	84.0	9.4	0.1	2.8	2.3
7			R, 20				R, 19	113,164	120,979	7	73,216	37.2	19.9	8.6	84.0	9.4	0.1	2.8	2.3
7			R, 19				R, 19	113,164	120,979	7	73,216	37.2	19.9	8.6	84.0	9.4	0.1	2.8	2.3
8			D, 17				D, 18	114,731	123,380	8	62,535	38.5	19.8	7.9	77.3	14.5	0.1	4.8	2.2
8			R, 17				D, 17	114,731	123,380	8	62,535	38.5	19.8	7.9	77.3	14.5	0.1	4.8	2.2
8			R, 20				D, 17	114,731	123,380	8	62,535	38.5	19.8	7.9	77.3	14.5	0.1	4.8	2.2
9A			R, 33				R, 40	79,983	86,827	9	114,828	50.5	38.9	4.8	77.8	6.9	0.1	11.5	2.6
9A			R, 67				R, 32	79,983	86,827	9	114,828	50.5	38.9	4.8	77.8	6.9	0.1	11.5	2.6
9B			R, 62				R, 72	38,715	43,236	12	84,957	40.8	21.7	5.4	91.9	3.9	0.1	1.3	1.9
10			D, 23				D, 34	119,979	121,792	2	59,979	40.7	21.2	9.6	29.1	64.1	0.1	3.8	2.6
10			D, 22				D, 34	119,979	121,792	2	59,979	40.7	21.2	9.6	29.1	64.1	0.1	3.8	2.6
10			D, 24				D, 32	119,979	121,792	2	59,979	40.7	21.2	9.6	29.1	64.1	0.1	3.8	2.6
11			D, 23				D, 26	116,024	123,426	6	94,941	50.9	34.9	6.6	67.0	23.9	0.1	4.6	3.4
11			D, 22				D, 25	116,024	123,426	6	94,941	50.9	34.9	6.6	67.0	23.9	0.1	4.6	3.4
11			D, 24				D, 24	116,024	123,426	6	94,941	50.9	34.9	6.6	67.0	23.9	0.1	4.6	3.4
12A			D, 25				D, 31	78,541	81,284	3	67,528	38.8	23.4	9.4	77.1	12.8	0.1	5.5	3.0
12A			D, 32				D, 28	78,541	81,284	3	67,528	38.8	23.4	9.4	77.1	12.8	0.1	5.5	3.0
12B			D, 97				D, 75	38,106	42,452	11	94,471	56.7	43.7	6.2	61.6	22.6	0.1	8.7	5.4
13			D, 21				D, 22	115,913	125,609	8	95,077	48.6	35.6	4.7	64.9	19.4	0.1	8.9	5.0
13			D, 17				D, 22	115,913	125,609	8	95,077	48.6	35.6	4.7	64.9	19.4	0.1	8.9	5.0
13			D, 19				D, 20	115,913	125,609	8	95,077	48.6	35.6	4.7	64.9	19.4	0.1	8.9	5.0
14			D, 19				D, 22	112,181	121,020	8	109,228	50.9	36.6	3.8	58.9	19.6	0.1	13.6	6.2
14			D, 19				D, 22	112,181	121,020	8	109,228	50.9	36.6	3.8	58.9	19.6	0.1	13.6	6.2
14			D, 20				D, 22	112,181	121,020	8	109,228	50.9	36.6	3.8	58.9	19.6	0.1	13.6	6.2
15			D, 17				D, 22	109,883	119,413	9	146,048	56.2	44.3	3.7	64.9	8.5	0.1	18.0	7.0
15			D, 18				D, 22	109,883	119,413	9	146,048	56.2	44.3	3.7	64.9	8.5	0.1	18.0	7.0
15			R, 19				D, 17	109,883	119,413	9	146,048	56.2	44.3	3.7	64.9	8.5	0.1	18.0	7.0
16			D, 24				D, 25	106,722	113,824	7	162,501	67.1	58.3	4.3	75.8	4.4	0.1	10.8	7.0
16			D, 26				D, 25	106,722	113,824	7	162,501	67.1	58.3	4.3	75.8	4.4	0.1	10.8	7.0
16			D, 25				D, 25	106,722	113,824	7	162,501	67.1	58.3	4.3	75.8	4.4	0.1	10.8	7.0
17			D, 25				D, 25	112,540	122,331	9	85,392	51.1	37.6	7.2	49.2	12.9	0.2	17.7	19.1
17			D, 26				D, 24	112,540	122,331	9	85,392	51.1	37.6	7.2	49.2	12.9	0.2	17.7	19.1

(continued)

Note: D=Democrat, R=Republican, R/D=Republican/Democrat (cross-filed), D/R=Democrat/Republican (cross-filed), I=Independent, C=Constitution, O=Other, GI=Green Independent, P=Progressive, P/D=Progressive/Democrat, P/D/R=Progressive/Democrat/Republican, HH=Households

Maryland State House Districts—Election and Demographic Data (cont.)

House Districts	General Election Results Party, Percent of Vote							Population			Avg. HH Income	Pop 25+		Below Poverty Line	2006 White (Non-Hisp)	African American	American Indians, Alaska Natives	Asians, Hawaiians, Pacific Islanders	Hispanic Origin
												Some College +	4-Yr Degree +						
Maryland	2000	2001	2002	2003	2004	2005	2006	2000	2006	% Change	($)	(%)	(%)	(%)	(%)	(%)	(%)	(%)	(%)
17			D, 25				D, 24	112,540	122,331	9	85,392	51.1	37.6	7.2	49.2	12.9	0.2	17.7	19.1
18			D, 34				D, 24	111,632	115,741	4	104,803	51.4	38.8	7.0	50.3	14.2	0.1	10.9	22.1
18			D, 33				D, 23	111,632	115,741	4	104,803	51.4	38.8	7.0	50.3	14.2	0.1	10.9	22.1
18			D, 32				D, 23	111,632	115,741	4	104,803	51.4	38.8	7.0	50.3	14.2	0.1	10.9	22.1
19			D, 34				D, 24	109,437	114,928	5	91,475	51.4	36.2	7.1	51.3	18.1	0.1	13.5	15.3
19			D, 33				D, 23	109,437	114,928	5	91,475	51.4	36.2	7.1	51.3	18.1	0.1	13.5	15.3
19			D, 33				D, 23	109,437	114,928	5	91,475	51.4	36.2	7.1	51.3	18.1	0.1	13.5	15.3
20			D, 25				D, 32	110,415	115,455	5	72,755	47.3	34.3	10.1	32.4	33.5	0.2	11.8	23.6
20			D, 27				D, 30	110,415	115,455	5	72,755	47.3	34.3	10.1	32.4	33.5	0.2	11.8	23.6
20			D, 21				D, 31	110,415	115,455	5	72,755	47.3	34.3	10.1	32.4	33.5	0.2	11.8	23.6
21			D, 25				D, 30	111,177	117,224	5	71,115	41.1	25.4	8.0	45.9	35.1	0.1	9.4	9.4
21			D, 24				D, 29	111,177	117,224	5	71,115	41.1	25.4	8.0	45.9	35.1	0.1	9.4	9.4
21			D, 25				D, 29	111,177	117,224	5	71,115	41.1	25.4	8.0	45.9	35.1	0.1	9.4	9.4
22			D, 29				D, 34	112,039	115,355	3	66,916	38.6	23.8	8.8	25.8	51.0	0.2	8.1	19.1
22			D, 31				D, 33	112,039	115,355	3	66,916	38.6	23.8	8.8	25.8	51.0	0.2	8.1	19.1
22			D, 30				D, 32	112,039	115,355	3	66,916	38.6	23.8	8.8	25.8	51.0	0.2	8.1	19.1
23A			D, 37				D, 48	68,118	70,686	4	96,837	48.1	31.3	3.6	45.0	42.8	0.1	5.5	6.8
23A			D, 33				D, 43	68,118	70,686	4	96,837	48.1	31.3	3.6	45.0	42.8	0.1	5.5	6.8
23B			D, 99				D, 99	38,240	42,257	11	94,217	49.3	30.7	2.8	32.1	60.4	0.1	2.8	5.8
24			D, 34				D, 34	110,729	119,711	8	59,186	32.1	14.6	12.0	5.3	91.2	0.1	1.2	4.9
24			D, 33				D, 33	110,729	119,711	8	59,186	32.1	14.6	12.0	5.3	91.2	0.1	1.2	4.9
24			D, 33				D, 33	110,729	119,711	8	59,186	32.1	14.6	12.0	5.3	91.2	0.1	1.2	4.9
25			D, 35				D, 33	104,170	111,141	7	75,144	38.3	19.3	6.6	12.3	82.6	0.1	1.8	5.6
25			D, 32				D, 31	104,170	111,141	7	75,144	38.3	19.3	6.6	12.3	82.6	0.1	1.8	5.6
25			D, 33				D, 31	104,170	111,141	7	75,144	38.3	19.3	6.6	12.3	82.6	0.1	1.8	5.6
26			D, 28				D, 34	108,883	112,402	3	77,113	39.0	19.7	7.2	10.6	81.4	0.1	5.0	5.4
26			D, 29				D, 31	108,883	112,402	3	77,113	39.0	19.7	7.2	10.6	81.4	0.1	5.0	5.4
26			D, 30				D, 30	108,883	112,402	3	77,113	39.0	19.7	7.2	10.6	81.4	0.1	5.0	5.4
27A			D, 38				D, 40	78,569	84,903	8	90,702	40.5	21.3	4.9	39.2	53.3	0.2	3.0	4.7
27A			D, 36				D, 38	78,569	84,903	8	90,702	40.5	21.3	4.9	39.2	53.3	0.2	3.0	4.7
27B			D, 98				D, 57	35,938	42,333	18	83,507	36.3	18.6	7.0	80.4	15.5	0.1	1.2	1.7
28			R, 20				D, 25	116,230	135,013	16	77,670	33.6	13.2	7.2	64.8	28.0	0.3	2.4	3.3
28			D, 20				D, 24	116,230	135,013	16	77,670	33.6	13.2	7.2	64.8	28.0	0.3	2.4	3.3
28			D, 19				D, 22	116,230	135,013	16	77,670	33.6	13.2	7.2	64.8	28.0	0.3	2.4	3.3
29A			D, 98				D, 65	39,557	45,594	15	76,280	28.6	11.8	8.6	84.2	11.9	0.1	1.3	1.3
29B			D, 59				D, 64	37,457	42,979	15	65,288	33.7	16.7	10.2	72.4	19.5	0.1	3.3	2.9
29C			R, 52				R, 60	40,149	49,149	22	76,546	38.5	20.2	6.5	79.7	14.1	0.1	1.6	3.0
30			D, 18				R, 17	116,611	121,102	4	92,146	49.5	31.0	7.3	76.3	15.6	0.1	1.9	4.8
30			D, 17				D, 17	116,611	121,102	4	92,146	49.5	31.0	7.3	76.3	15.6	0.1	1.9	4.8
30			R, 17				D, 17	116,611	121,102	4	92,146	49.5	31.0	7.3	76.3	15.6	0.1	1.9	4.8
31			R, 24				R, 18	114,634	116,385	2	69,127	37.7	17.0	8.1	83.7	10.1	0.2	2.3	2.4
31			R, 16				R, 18	114,634	116,385	2	69,127	37.7	17.0	8.1	83.7	10.1	0.2	2.3	2.4
31			D, 16				R, 17	114,634	116,385	2	69,127	37.7	17.0	8.1	83.7	10.1	0.2	2.3	2.4
32			D, 18				D, 19	116,219	120,696	4	66,792	40.6	18.6	7.9	67.0	21.4	0.2	4.8	4.9
32			D, 18				D, 18	116,219	120,696	4	66,792	40.6	18.6	7.9	67.0	21.4	0.2	4.8	4.9
32			R, 20				D, 18	116,219	120,696	4	66,792	40.6	18.6	7.9	67.0	21.4	0.2	4.8	4.9
33A			R, 33				R, 29	77,479	81,953	6	110,367	53.7	34.1	3.1	86.4	6.7	0.1	3.0	2.5
33A			R, 26				R, 26	77,479	81,953	6	110,367	53.7	34.1	3.1	86.4	6.7	0.1	3.0	2.5
33B			R, 55				R, 58	38,404	40,689	6	100,295	49.6	29.6	5.2	88.2	7.5	0.1	1.4	1.9
34A			R, 35				D, 32	75,431	82,078	9	60,485	33.2	12.4	10.6	69.8	21.8	0.1	2.2	4.1

(continued)

Note: D=Democrat, R=Republican, R/D=Republican/Democrat (cross-filed), D/R=Democrat/Republican (cross-filed), I=Independent, C=Constitution, O=Other, GI=Green Independent, P=Progressive, P/D=Progressive/Democrat, P/D/R=Progressive/Democrat/Republican, HH=Households

Maryland State House Districts—Election and Demographic Data (cont.)

House Districts	General Election Results Party, Percent of Vote							Population			Avg. HH Income	Pop 25+		Below Poverty Line	2006 White (Non-Hisp)	African American	American Indians, Alaska Natives	Asians, Hawaiians, Pacific Islanders	Hispanic Origin
												Some College +	4-Yr Degree +						
Maryland	2000	2001	2002	2003	2004	2005	2006	2000	2006	% Change	($)	(%)	(%)	(%)	(%)	(%)	(%)	(%)	(%)
34A			D, 34				D, 27	75,431	82,078	9	60,485	33.2	12.4	10.6	69.8	21.8	0.1	2.2	4.1
34B			D, 56				D, 55	42,074	47,901	14	65,325	29.3	11.1	9.4	93.1	3.4	0.1	0.9	1.5
35A			R, 50				R, 40	79,318	86,437	9	84,399	39.5	20.4	5.8	92.8	3.6	0.1	1.4	1.3
35A			R, 49				R, 35	79,318	86,437	9	84,399	39.5	20.4	5.8	92.8	3.6	0.1	1.4	1.3
35B			R, 61				R, 63	37,587	41,091	9	82,997	44.2	24.2	5.7	89.8	4.5	0.1	2.7	1.8
36			R, 28				R, 53	118,564	131,974	11	67,251	31.3	14.5	11.7	84.9	9.9	0.1	1.0	2.7
36			R, 19				R, 53	118,564	131,974	11	67,251	31.3	14.5	11.7	84.9	9.9	0.1	1.0	2.7
36			R, 19				R, 59	118,564	131,974	11	67,251	31.3	14.5	11.7	84.9	9.9	0.1	1.0	2.7
37A			D, 56				D, 99	38,215	39,057	2	44,872	23.9	10.3	21.9	44.9	49.4	0.1	1.6	3.7
37B			R, 50				R, 35	89,274	92,416	4	61,800	30.2	14.5	15.7	74.5	21.6	0.1	1.1	2.0
37B			R, 50				R, 32	89,274	92,416	4	61,800	30.2	14.5	15.7	74.5	21.6	0.1	1.1	2.0
38A			R, 56				R, 63	39,921	42,049	5	54,281	28.8	13.2	19.3	63.3	33.0	0.1	1.1	1.7
38B			D, 30				D, 27	79,258	83,671	6	56,001	32.9	15.2	13.2	79.4	15.8	0.1	1.6	2.1
38B			D, 28				D, 25	79,258	83,671	6	56,001	32.9	15.2	13.2	79.4	15.8	0.1	1.6	2.1
39			D, 20				D, 24	106,614	111,908	5	87,856	49.2	33.8	4.6	50.5	17.1	0.1	16.3	14.2
39			D, 20				D, 23	106,614	111,908	5	87,856	49.2	33.8	4.6	50.5	17.1	0.1	16.3	14.2
39			D, 19				D, 21	106,614	111,908	5	87,856	49.2	33.8	4.6	50.5	17.1	0.1	16.3	14.2
40			D, 35				D, 32	105,254	101,005	-4	41,325	28.3	17.6	29.0	23.3	71.5	0.1	3.3	1.8
40			D, 33				D, 32	105,254	101,005	-4	41,325	28.3	17.6	29.0	23.3	71.5	0.1	3.3	1.8
40			D, 32				D, 28	105,254	101,005	-4	41,325	28.3	17.6	29.0	23.3	71.5	0.1	3.3	1.8
41			D, 35				D, 34	109,165	104,923	-4	57,328	35.0	22.7	20.4	24.5	72.7	0.1	1.0	1.6
41			D, 33				D, 30	109,165	104,923	-4	57,328	35.0	22.7	20.4	24.5	72.7	0.1	1.0	1.6
41			D, 32				D, 29	109,165	104,923	-4	57,328	35.0	22.7	20.4	24.5	72.7	0.1	1.0	1.6
42			R, 17				R, 18	106,625	108,134	1	85,969	50.2	36.3	8.9	81.6	8.4	0.1	6.3	2.6
42			R, 17				D, 18	106,625	108,134	1	85,969	50.2	36.3	8.9	81.6	8.4	0.1	6.3	2.6
42			R, 17				R, 17	106,625	108,134	1	85,969	50.2	36.3	8.9	81.6	8.4	0.1	6.3	2.6
43			D, 32				D, 29	105,021	102,552	-2	58,745	33.9	22.1	17.4	27.0	68.6	0.1	2.1	2.0
43			D, 31				D, 29	105,021	102,552	-2	58,745	33.9	22.1	17.4	27.0	68.6	0.1	2.1	2.0
43			D, 29				D, 28	105,021	102,552	-2	58,745	33.9	22.1	17.4	27.0	68.6	0.1	2.1	2.0
44			D, 33				D, 34	114,370	111,676	-2	34,531	23.5	12.8	35.1	19.6	76.9	0.1	1.9	1.4
44			D, 30				D, 33	114,370	111,676	-2	34,531	23.5	12.8	35.1	19.6	76.9	0.1	1.9	1.4
44			D, 28				D, 32	114,370	111,676	-2	34,531	23.5	12.8	35.1	19.6	76.9	0.1	1.9	1.4
45			D, 31				D, 33	108,951	103,623	-5	42,434	25.2	13.2	22.9	25.5	71.7	0.1	0.9	1.6
45			D, 31				D, 31	108,951	103,623	-5	42,434	25.2	13.2	22.9	25.5	71.7	0.1	0.9	1.6
45			D, 30				D, 31	108,951	103,623	-5	42,434	25.2	13.2	22.9	25.5	71.7	0.1	0.9	1.6
46			D, 29				D, 30	108,755	105,387	-3	47,054	29.5	19.3	24.3	53.0	38.2	0.3	1.9	5.8
46			D, 30				D, 30	108,755	105,387	-3	47,054	29.5	19.3	24.3	53.0	38.2	0.3	1.9	5.8
46			D, 29				D, 29	108,755	105,387	-3	47,054	29.5	19.3	24.3	53.0	38.2	0.3	1.9	5.8
47			D, 35				D, 35	103,687	110,164	6	56,440	31.2	17.0	13.0	14.8	62.5	0.2	4.4	29.2
47			D, 33				D, 34	103,687	110,164	6	56,440	31.2	17.0	13.0	14.8	62.5	0.2	4.4	29.2
47			D, 32				D, 31	103,687	110,164	6	56,440	31.2	17.0	13.0	14.8	62.5	0.2	4.4	29.2

Note: D=Democrat, R=Republican, R/D=Republican/Democrat (cross-filed), D/R=Democrat/Republican (cross-filed), I=Independent, C=Constitution, O=Other, GI=Green Independent, P=Progressive, P/D=Progressive/Democrat, P/D/R=Progressive/Democrat/Republican, HH=Households

MASSACHUSETTS

The role a state plays in national life tells mysterious yet revealing things about its character. Virginia has produced a host of major political figures; North Carolina hardly any. New Yorkers have been much more prominent in government than have Pennsylvanians. Another of the original thirteen states, Connecticut, did not put anyone on a major party political ticket until 2000. Massachusetts, on the other hand, never seems to stop. Ignoring the Adamses and the Kennedys, serious attempts have been mounted within the past three decades by Michael Dukakis, John Kerry, Paul Tsongas, and, in the 2008 election cycle, former governor Mitt Romney.

Some of the Massachusetts proclivity for political leaders might be attributed to the many renowned colleges and universities in the state, but while that might account for Oliver Wendell Holmes and Henry Cabot Lodge, former House Speaker Tip O'Neill was no scholar and his predecessor, John McCormick, never even finished high school. Nor is it necessarily due to a widespread public spiritedness, notwithstanding the Puritan imperative to do good in the world. Massachusetts politics, from at least the time of James Michael Curley, has been as baroque as anywhere in the country and Boston, the home of blue-nosed censors and deep racial tensions, has been as much noted for its narrow-mindedness.

Yet Massachusetts continues to exercise an influence over national life greater than its size would seem to accord it, and that size has been shrinking. The state had sixteen congressional districts in 1920 and only ten today. Massachusetts enjoyed the dot-com boom of the late 1990s, which was centered as much along the Route 128 high-tech corridor as it was in Redmond, Washington, or Silicon Valley, California, but even so the state grew at less than half the national rate. Since 2000, with the decline and slow recovery of the tech industry, Massachusetts's rate of growth has been the slowest in New England and the sixth slowest in the country. What growth there has been has occurred primarily in Worcester County in the middle of the state, which actually forms the middle arc of a much larger crescent of newer, outer Boston suburbs that spills into New Hampshire (long favored by Boston expatriates because of its low taxes) down into Rhode Island and eastern Connecticut. The areas that have lost population fastest are all in Suffolk County, which includes Boston and its older, close-in suburbs, and in the Berkshires.

The wealthiest parts of Massachusetts are the outer suburbs of Boston in Middlesex County: Weston, Newton, Brookline, and Concord. In twenty-four state house dis-

tricts, average annual household income exceeds $100,000. Small cities that depended most on manufacturing have fared worst, especially Springfield and Lawrence.

A hotbed of abolitionism before the Civil War and the first state after Reconstruction to elect an African American to the U.S. Senate (Republican Edward Brooke in 1972), Massachusetts has earned a reputation for racial tolerance, although Boston has a reputation for being inhospitable to blacks. In 2007 it was the only state with an African American governor, Deval Patrick.

It is somewhat unexpected, then, to find the state so racially homogeneous. Massachusetts is only 5 percent black; by percentages, that puts it just a shade behind Kansas and Wisconsin. Ninety-seven of its 160 state house districts are 80 percent white or more. All three of the state house districts with an African American majority are located in Boston.

Massachusetts may be a predominantly white state, but it is not really a Yankee state anymore and has not been for many years. Much of it is now rich with persons of Irish, Italian, Greek, and Portuguese ancestry. It also has two pockets of Hispanics: the district in downtown Lawrence (81 percent—it is also the poorest district in the state); the district on the west side of Springfield (53 percent). Three more districts, in Boston, Middlesex County, and Quincy, are more than 20 percent Asian.

The state legislature is known as the General Court (formerly The Great and General Court of the Commonwealth of Massachusetts). The name is not the only thing that is big. The Massachusetts House of Representatives has 160 districts, second in size only to New Hampshire's and Pennsylvania's. However, the legislature was even larger up until 1978 when it had 240 members. In Massachusetts, as in only a few other states, members of both chambers serve two-year terms.

Republicans held the governor's mansion continuously from 1991 to 2007, but Democrats dominate the General Court and, if anything, their lead is growing. Republican legislators must have a hard time finding reasons to come to work. The state house, which was 118–37 Democratic in 1990 was 131–24–1 Democratic in 2000 and 140–19 (with one vacancy) in 2007. The party's edge in the senate grew from 25–15 to 34–6 during the same period. Given that there was little partisan gerrymandering to be done after the 2000 census, the big fight came between the politicians, who wanted to draw lines that would protect incumbents, and African Americans, who alleged that the proposed maps unfairly minimized their voting strength.

MASSACHUSETTS
State Senate Districts

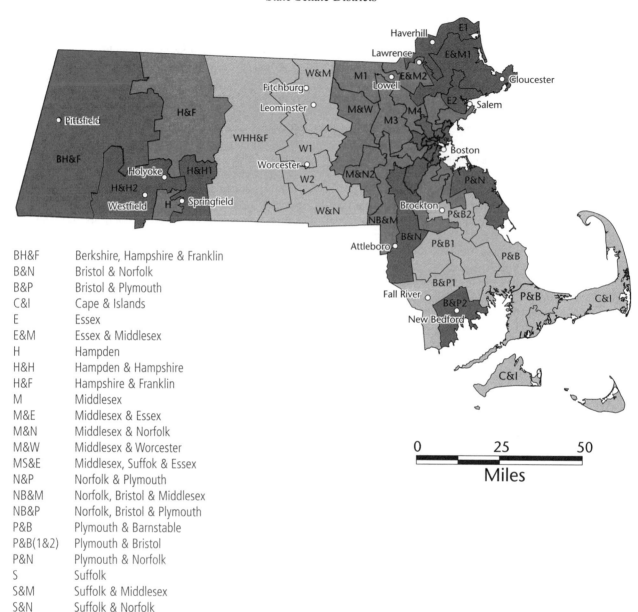

BH&F	Berkshire, Hampshire & Franklin
B&N	Bristol & Norfolk
B&P	Bristol & Plymouth
C&I	Cape & Islands
E	Essex
E&M	Essex & Middlesex
H	Hampden
H&H	Hampden & Hampshire
H&F	Hampshire & Franklin
M	Middlesex
M&E	Middlesex & Essex
M&N	Middlesex & Norfolk
M&W	Middlesex & Worcester
MS&E	Middlesex, Suffok & Essex
N&P	Norfolk & Plymouth
NB&M	Norfolk, Bristol & Middlesex
NB&P	Norfolk, Bristol & Plymouth
P&B	Plymouth & Barnstable
P&B(1&2)	Plymouth & Bristol
P&N	Plymouth & Norfolk
S	Suffolk
S&M	Suffolk & Middlesex
S&N	Suffolk & Norfolk
W	Worcester
W&M	Worcester & Middlesex
W&N	Worcester & Norfolk
WHH&F	Worcester, Hampden, Hampshire & Franklin

Population Growth   ■ -6% to -1%   ■ -1% to 2%   ■ 2% to 4%   □ 4% to 7%

BOSTON

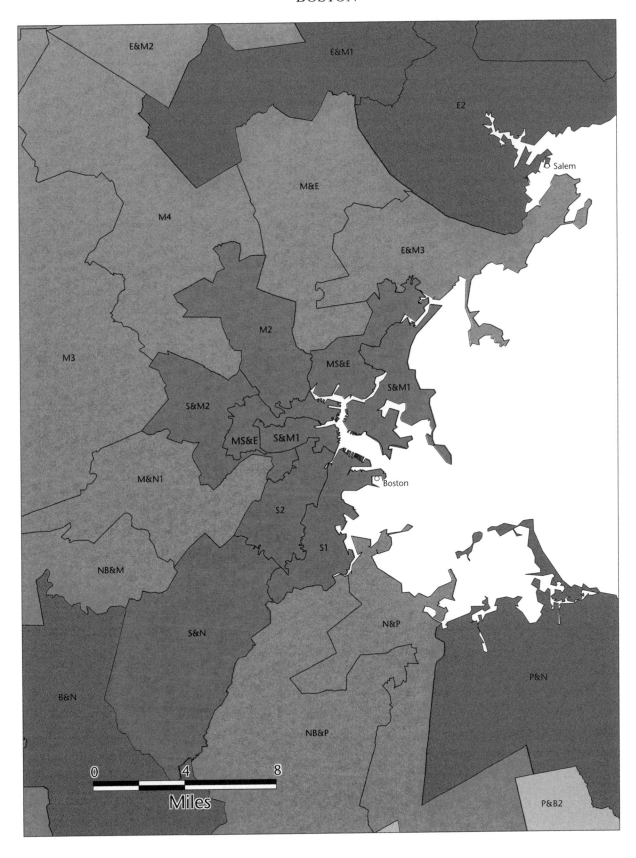

Population Growth   ■ -14% to -3%   ■ 0% to 9%   ■ 10% to 16%   □ 18% to 24%

Massachusetts State Senate Districts—Election and Demographic Data

Senate Districts	General Election Results Party, Percent of Vote							Population			Avg. HH Income	Pop 25+		Below Poverty Line	2006 White (Non-Hisp)	African American	American Indians, Alaska Natives	Asians, Hawaiians, Pacific Islanders	Hispanic Origin
												Some College +	4-Yr Degree +						
Mass.	2000	2001	2002	2003	2004	2005	2006	2000	2006	% Change	($)	(%)	(%)	(%)	(%)	(%)	(%)	(%)	(%)
BH&F**			D, 83		D, 78		D, 71	152,986	149,596	-2	58,561	37.1	19.3	14.9	92.8	2.2	0.2	1.3	2.3
BHH&F*	D, 100																		
B1*	D, 100																		
B2*	D, 100																		
B&N**			R, 100		D, 57		D, 60	157,547	161,632	3	96,899	44.4	28.7	7.7	90.6	1.9	0.2	3.0	2.5
B&P1**			D, 100		D, 100		D, 100	163,892	170,946	4	54,784	31.1	14.9	19.2	90.5	2.0	0.2	2.0	3.0
B&P2**			D, 100		D, 100		D, 82	155,933	160,307	3	52,905	29.4	14.5	21.3	78.8	3.5	0.5	1.1	9.0
C&I	D, 57		D, 60		D, 57		D, 63	164,403	171,328	4	65,287	48.8	26.1	11.3	91.1	3.0	0.8	0.8	2.0
E1	D, 100		D, 100		D, 69		D, 100	164,850	170,523	3	72,017	42.2	25.4	12.0	81.9	1.8	0.2	2.1	10.9
E2	D, 100		D, 100		D, 100		D, 100	158,291	162,907	3	72,151	44.2	27.6	11.4	83.9	1.9	0.2	2.1	9.2
E3*	D, 100																		
E&M1	R, 100		R, 72		R, 65		R, 100	167,225	173,072	3	95,112	47.7	32.3	9.4	90.8	0.8	0.1	2.3	5.0
E&M2	D, 100		D, 63		D, 72		D, 100	162,500	163,731	1	73,546	36.8	23.5	16.8	52.4	3.4	0.5	4.6	31.3
E&M3**			D, 100		D, 100		D, 100	153,893	156,271	2	73,379	41.1	25.9	15.4	66.9	7.7	0.3	5.7	15.7
H	D, 86		D, 100		D, 74		D, 100	153,415	154,072	0	47,232	30.5	14.1	23.5	51.7	16.8	0.4	2.5	24.2
H&H1	R, 100		R, 100		R, 100		D, 60	155,695	158,980	2	67,393	38.4	20.3	12.7	73.5	8.9	0.2	1.9	11.9
H&H2	R, 100		R, 70		R, 100		R, 100	154,118	158,280	3	53,923	33.2	15.5	17.2	71.8	3.3	0.3	1.4	17.2
H&F	D, 89		D, 100		D, 84		D, 85	153,084	155,150	1	61,483	43.5	26.9	14.3	86.0	2.5	0.3	4.6	4.2
M1	D, 84		D, 72		D, 76		D, 76	159,038	160,383	1	72,568	36.7	24.5	15.0	68.4	3.4	0.2	14.5	10.9
M2	D, 100		D, 100		D, 100		D, 100	150,761	148,773	-1	76,583	46.0	34.7	11.9	77.6	6.1	0.2	7.0	5.9
M3	R, 73		D, 100		D, 60		D, 64	164,447	165,256	0	117,485	52.4	40.8	7.6	81.5	3.2	0.1	8.2	5.1
M4	D, 75		D, 100		D, 66		D, 100	157,485	157,674	0	93,060	49.9	36.1	7.3	86.4	2.1	0.1	7.9	2.1
M5*	D, 70																		
M&E**			R, 100		R, 57		R, 100	157,986	156,723	-1	80,146	46.9	31.8	10.3	82.9	3.8	0.1	8.3	3.1
M&N1	D, 100		D, 100		D, 77		D, 100	154,761	156,279	1	134,928	59.6	52.0	9.0	80.1	2.9	0.1	11.8	3.7
M&N2**			D, 100		D, 57		D, 100	157,732	156,685	-1	88,863	49.5	36.0	8.3	81.9	3.5	0.1	5.2	6.3
MN&W*	D, 100																		
M&S*	D, 100																		
MS&E	D, 100		D, 100		D, 100		D, 100	165,285	160,322	-3	65,284	41.3	30.3	17.2	58.4	8.9	0.3	9.0	19.6
M&W	D, 83		D, 60		D, 60		D, 100	163,234	166,186	2	105,530	50.7	38.1	7.9	85.3	2.3	0.2	6.1	4.0
NB&M	D, 70		D, 60		R, 51		R, 100	165,264	167,298	1	111,575	48.2	34.0	7.7	89.9	1.9	0.1	4.2	2.5
NB&P	R, 54		D, 100		D, 100		D, 75	154,382	155,435	1	88,372	44.6	28.2	8.9	81.6	8.8	0.1	5.2	2.5
N&P	D, 100		D, 100		D, 100		D, 100	155,388	158,491	2	68,122	41.0	23.6	10.7	81.8	2.7	0.2	11.7	2.4
N&S*	D, 100																		
P&B	D, 65		D, 58		D, 58		D, 100	165,401	173,937	5	74,398	42.1	21.6	9.9	93.6	1.9	0.4	0.9	1.5
P&B1	D, 74		D, 100		D, 74		D, 100	160,044	167,852	5	65,243	33.0	15.3	12.2	89.3	3.0	0.3	0.9	3.0
P&B2	D, 100		D, 100		D, 68		D, 100	154,103	160,726	4	65,146	29.7	12.9	15.1	70.9	12.9	0.3	2.1	6.3
P&N	R, 52		R, 63		R, 100		R, 64	156,979	162,435	3	94,217	47.5	29.4	8.8	94.4	1.3	0.1	1.7	1.2
S1	D, 100		D, 86		D, 82		D, 100	164,970	155,850	-6	54,806	33.9	19.8	20.8	32.0	44.4	0.5	8.7	13.2
S2	D, 100		D, 100		D, 100		D, 72	162,521	157,114	-3	68,412	43.5	31.9	23.2	32.7	36.5	0.5	10.4	22.2
S&M*	D, 83																		
S&M1**			D, 78		D, 80		D, 100	166,236	159,495	-4	65,147	42.0	30.4	17.2	57.2	11.3	0.4	9.9	18.1
S&M2**			D, 100		D, 83		D, 100	156,026	151,799	-3	77,405	53.6	44.1	15.5	70.2	8.2	0.2	12.0	6.7
S&N	D, 100		D, 100		D, 64		D, 69	151,077	144,158	-5	76,262	45.5	30.4	11.6	68.4	13.7	0.3	5.0	9.7
W1	D, 71		D, 61		D, 67		D, 73	157,191	165,126	5	67,515	42.4	27.5	16.7	71.7	6.1	0.4	4.3	13.8
W2	D, 79		D, 100		D, 61		D, 68	161,793	169,839	5	65,571	39.6	24.0	14.2	78.6	4.1	0.3	6.1	8.1
WHH&F	D, 100		D, 83		D, 75		D, 100	153,281	162,106	6	59,681	36.2	18.5	12.8	94.2	1.0	0.3	0.8	2.3
W&M	D, 100		D, 100		D, 62		D, 100	156,484	162,800	4	61,959	38.7	21.9	14.1	79.9	3.6	0.3	3.1	10.0
W&N	D, 100		D, 74		D, 71		D, 100	160,825	170,523	6	65,532	38.4	21.3	12.7	89.8	1.2	0.2	1.6	4.9

*Applies to 2000 District only.

**Applies to 2002–2006 Districts.

Note: D=Democrat, R=Republican, R/D=Republican/Democrat (cross-filed), D/R=Democrat/Republican (cross-filed), I=Independent, C=Constitution, O=Other, GI=Green Independent, P=Progressive, P/D=Progressive/Democrat, P/D/R=Progressive/Democrat/Republican, HH=Households

MASSACHUSETTS
State House Districts

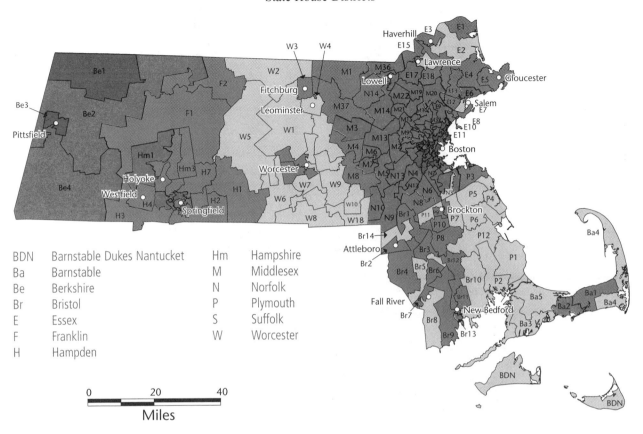

BDN — Barnstable Dukes Nantucket
Ba — Barnstable
Be — Berkshire
Br — Bristol
E — Essex
F — Franklin
H — Hampden

Hm — Hampshire
M — Middlesex
N — Norfolk
P — Plymouth
S — Suffolk
W — Worcester

0   20   40
Miles

WORCESTER

LOWELL/LAWRENCE

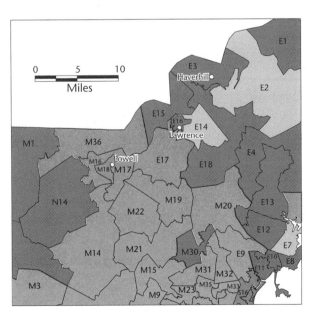

Population Growth   -8% to -3%   -3% to 1%   1% to 4%   4% to 9%

BOSTON

Population Growth   ■ -8% to -3%   ■ -3% to 1%   ■ 1% to 4%   ■ 4% to 9%

SPRINGFIELD

Be2

F1

Hm1

Hm2

Hm3

Be4

Holyoke

H5

H8

H7

H1

H4

Westfield

H6

H9

H12

Springfield

H10

H11

H3

H2

0 5 10

Miles

Population Growth   -8% to -3%   -3% to 1%   1% to 4%   4% to 9%

Massachusetts State House Districts—Election and Demographic Data

House Districts	General Election Results Party, Percent of Vote							Population			Avg. HH Income	Pop 25+		Below Poverty Line	White (Non-Hisp)	African American	American Indians, Alaska Natives	Asians, Hawaiians, Pacific Islanders	Hispanic Origin
												Some College +	4-Yr Degree +					2006	
Mass.	2000	2001	2002	2003	2004	2005	2006	2000	2006	% Change	($)	(%)	(%)	(%)	(%)	(%)	(%)	(%)	(%)
Ba1	R, 100		R, 62		D, 51		D, 52	40,746	42,371	4	61,336	50.3	25.9	9.8	94.6	1.5	0.3	0.7	1.7
Ba2	D, 73		D, 50		D, 59		D, 56	39,749	40,010	1	58,561	42.9	19.7	14.1	87.3	4.3	0.7	1.4	2.6
Ba3	D, 56		D, 50		D, 53		D, 100	40,291	42,242	5	71,680	47.8	25.2	9.4	92.0	2.2	1.0	0.9	1.7
Ba4	R, 100		R, 100		R, 57		D, 56	39,117	40,724	4	64,271	52.5	30.6	12.2	94.1	2.0	0.2	0.5	1.3
Ba5**			R, 51		R, 66		R, 100	39,243	41,114	5	73,129	47.3	23.9	8.4	94.0	1.4	0.9	0.8	1.4
BDN	D, 69		D, 100		D, 70		D, 70	38,893	40,842	5	76,744	50.1	30.5	10.0	89.0	4.3	0.9	1.1	2.1
Be1	D, 100		D, 100		D, 82		D, 100	37,981	36,709	-3	52,550	28.7	15.6	19.5	92.5	1.7	0.2	1.6	2.4
Be2	R, 65		R, 77		D, 70		D, 77	40,580	40,378	0	59,995	40.5	20.1	11.2	96.3	0.8	0.2	0.8	1.1
Be3	D, 100		D, 100		D, 100		D, 100	39,191	37,413	-5	52,116	34.9	15.1	17.0	89.2	4.4	0.2	1.6	3.0
Be4	D, 100		D, 50		D, 73		D, 100	39,318	39,033	-1	67,753	42.4	24.6	12.2	92.9	1.9	0.2	1.1	2.8
Br1	R, 58		R, 100		R, 100		R, 51	38,097	38,863	2	91,777	43.5	27.0	7.3	91.2	2.0	0.2	2.5	1.7
Br2	R, 100		R, 100		R, 100		R, 54	38,472	39,493	3	63,390	35.7	18.4	11.8	84.5	2.2	0.2	4.2	6.2
Br3	D, 100		D, 100		D, 100		D, 100	37,231	38,630	4	54,918	31.2	14.3	14.3	87.3	3.0	0.2	1.0	5.2
Br4	D, 100		D, 100		D, 63		D, 57	42,592	44,160	4	75,612	37.6	20.9	9.0	95.1	1.1	0.2	1.1	1.0
Br5	D, 67		D, 100		D, 80		D, 100	39,222	40,879	4	63,056	33.5	15.9	12.8	91.5	1.9	0.2	0.9	3.2
Br6	D, 100		D, 100		D, 100		D, 100	38,139	39,512	4	54,215	33.7	15.7	20.4	88.7	3.0	0.2	1.9	3.8
Br7	D, 100		D, 85		D, 85		D, 87	38,682	39,658	3	38,801	23.5	9.3	26.3	85.1	3.1	0.3	2.6	5.5
Br8	D, 100		D, 100		D, 100		D, 100	38,264	40,023	5	53,063	30.1	15.1	20.3	90.7	1.6	0.2	2.9	2.5
Br9	D, 100		D, 100		D, 100		D, 100	41,090	42,295	3	68,823	34.2	19.3	13.9	86.5	2.0	0.3	1.5	4.4
Br10	D, 76		D, 100		D, 65		D, 71	38,915	41,363	6	73,314	38.4	20.9	11.2	94.5	1.3	0.2	0.7	0.9
Br11	D, 100		D, 100		D, 100		D, 64	37,600	39,037	4	53,221	26.9	11.7	20.9	84.4	2.2	0.4	0.8	7.6
Br12	D, 100		D, 100		D, 100		D, 69	39,643	41,084	4	52,663	29.3	13.2	20.9	78.6	3.7	0.6	1.1	10.0
Br13	D, 100		D, 100		D, 100		D, 79	41,368	41,640	1	42,743	25.9	12.4	26.2	67.7	6.3	0.7	1.0	13.5
Br14	R, 65		R, 100		R, 65		R, 100	43,788	46,293	6	76,425	42.9	25.3	8.4	92.1	1.6	0.2	2.3	2.4
E1	D, 52		D, 100		D, 66		D, 100	41,526	43,179	4	76,952	46.1	28.7	10.0	92.0	0.7	0.2	0.9	5.2
E2	D, 63		D, 60		D, 63		D, 62	40,110	42,030	5	92,194	46.6	30.0	7.5	92.2	0.7	0.2	0.9	5.1
E3	D, 100		D, 100		D, 68		D, 100	39,827	40,969	3	61,573	37.7	20.8	15.2	74.3	3.5	0.3	1.8	15.7
E4	R, 85		R, 100		R, 62		R, 100	41,842	43,062	3	117,219	51.1	36.9	8.9	89.8	0.8	0.1	2.2	6.3
E5	D, 100		D, 76		D, 100		D, 100	41,305	42,144	2	69,636	46.4	29.1	13.4	91.2	0.8	0.1	1.0	5.6
E6	D, 60		D, 62		D, 67		D, 81	38,521	38,830	1	76,779	46.2	30.5	11.0	89.2	1.4	0.2	1.9	6.2
E7	D, 100		D, 100		D, 74		D, 100	40,766	42,532	4	61,620	43.4	27.6	13.8	71.6	3.9	0.3	2.7	16.4
E8	D, 81		D, 100		D, 65		D, 100	40,192	40,611	1	107,948	57.1	43.1	9.2	86.7	2.5	0.1	1.6	7.3
E9	D, 63		D, 100		D, 66		D, 100	41,370	41,767	1	80,115	44.4	26.4	8.6	91.6	1.0	0.1	2.1	4.3
E10	D, 100		D, 100		D, 100		D, 100	40,861	41,389	1	49,778	32.3	17.4	21.2	50.3	12.9	0.4	8.0	24.7
E11	D, 100		D, 100		D, 100		D, 100	39,939	40,695	2	55,241	31.9	17.9	21.7	49.1	12.8	0.5	10.5	24.3
E12	D, 100		D, 60		D, 66		D, 69	40,155	41,158	2	65,706	40.4	22.5	12.4	84.9	1.4	0.2	2.0	8.6
E13	D, 66		D, 53		D, 58		D, 100	38,849	40,039	3	87,844	47.1	30.2	7.1	91.6	0.7	0.1	1.7	5.2
E14	D, 100		D, 55		D, 66		D, 100	41,716	43,550	4	71,316	39.3	25.5	14.2	57.8	3.1	0.4	5.0	27.5
E15	D, 100		D, 62		D, 100		D, 61	40,871	42,126	3	64,730	38.2	22.1	14.1	72.7	2.0	0.3	3.0	17.3
E16	D, 64		D, 48		D, 43		D, 80	37,800	38,240	1	36,631	23.2	12.4	37.3	9.3	7.0	1.2	2.7	81.1
E17	D, 100		D, 100		D, 62		D, 100	41,740	42,038	1	97,839	46.1	33.3	12.0	66.3	2.3	0.3	6.3	19.2
E18**			D, 51		D, 58		D, 59	39,062	40,167	3	110,930	49.5	35.5	8.9	86.1	1.2	0.1	4.5	6.8
F1	D, 100		D, 79		D, 71		D, 100	42,016	42,499	1	63,063	44.3	26.0	11.9	92.7	1.2	0.3	2.1	2.2
F2	D, 100		D, 100		D, 76		D, 100	40,204	41,189	2	47,768	35.2	15.7	17.7	92.0	1.4	0.3	1.1	3.1
H1	R, 100		R, 100		R, 63		R, 100	38,666	39,971	3	57,094	35.3	16.9	12.4	92.7	1.3	0.3	0.9	3.2
H2	R, 81		R, 57		R, 100		R, 100	41,870	43,195	3	88,190	48.1	31.0	10.1	86.6	2.9	0.2	2.4	6.0
H3	D, 100		D, 100		D, 72		D, 50	40,670	41,714	3	63,699	37.6	18.1	10.5	89.2	2.1	0.2	1.2	5.4
H4	R, 100		R, 63		R, 100		R, 100	39,632	40,418	2	59,579	35.9	18.2	15.0	84.9	2.2	0.2	1.2	8.4
H5	D, 58		D, 73		D, 100		D, 100	40,272	41,159	2	43,187	28.7	13.5	26.9	39.8	5.7	0.4	1.4	43.8
H6	D, 62		D, 100		D, 64		D, 100	41,104	41,097	0	52,459	35.5	16.9	15.9	79.0	3.8	0.2	2.1	10.8

(continued)

Note: D=Democrat, R=Republican, R/D=Republican/Democrat (cross-filed), D/R=Democrat/Republican (cross-filed), I=Independent, C=Constitution, O=Other, GI=Green Independent, P=Progressive, P/D=Progressive/Democrat, P/D/R=Progressive/Democrat/Republican, HH=Households

Massachusetts State House Districts—Election and Demographic Data (cont.)

House Districts	General Election Results Party, Percent of Vote							Population			Avg. HH Income	Pop 25+ Some College +	Pop 25+ 4-Yr Degree +	Below Poverty Line	2006 White (Non-Hisp)	African American	American Indians, Alaska Natives	Asians, Hawaiians, Pacific Islanders	Hispanic Origin
Mass.	2000	2001	2002	2003	2004	2005	2006	2000	2006	% Change	($)	(%)	(%)	(%)	(%)	(%)	(%)	(%)	(%)
H7	D, 63		D, 100		D, 100		D, 100	38,778	39,302	1	57,427	33.1	14.2	13.1	81.7	5.4	0.2	1.1	9.3
H8	D, 100		D, 100		D, 82		D, 81	37,916	38,572	2	46,857	28.7	10.8	16.8	76.4	4.0	0.3	1.5	13.0
H9	D, 85		D, 100		D, 100		D, 77	39,448	39,472	0	48,862	28.6	12.0	17.9	54.9	14.7	0.3	1.6	23.2
H10	D, 100		D, 100		D, 72		D, 79	37,108	37,237	0	32,233	23.6	10.4	39.4	23.1	18.1	0.5	3.8	53.4
H11	D, 100		D, 100		D, 79		D, 100	40,453	41,027	1	43,430	24.1	9.6	27.8	27.3	46.3	0.5	2.2	27.5
H12	D, 100		D, 60		D, 63		D, 59	43,451	44,420	2	70,892	43.4	24.0	10.8	80.4	6.8	0.2	2.3	8.0
H13*	D, 100																		
Hm1	D, 100		D, 66		D, 80		D, 82	42,012	41,931	0	63,523	47.9	30.1	12.8	87.8	1.9	0.3	3.2	4.5
Hm2	D, 100		D, 55		D, 100		D, 100	38,878	39,498	2	62,545	42.5	22.5	11.8	90.7	1.5	0.2	3.3	2.7
Hm3	D, 85		D, 100		D, 78		D, 100	38,299	39,413	3	71,501	40.2	29.3	15.3	75.4	5.0	0.2	10.3	6.1
M1	R, 55		R, 64		R, 99		R, 60	40,449	41,847	3	86,143	44.9	29.5	7.8	92.5	1.7	0.2	2.5	1.7
M2	D, 80		D, 100		D, 55		D, 100	41,485	41,192	-1	203,081	57.0	49.0	5.5	86.0	1.9	0.1	8.1	2.7
M3	D, 79		D, 100		D, 74		D, 100	39,262	39,198	0	89,535	47.6	34.4	8.0	90.5	1.4	0.2	3.0	2.9
M4	D, 100		D, 71		D, 71		D, 100	42,398	42,927	1	82,064	47.4	32.7	9.4	82.5	2.5	0.2	5.3	6.2
M5	D, 100		D, 64		D, 68		D, 65	38,965	38,526	-1	107,232	54.3	41.1	7.0	88.7	2.1	0.1	5.1	2.3
M6	D, 72		D, 75		D, 62		D, 24	40,254	39,352	-2	83,378	50.4	37.2	9.4	73.7	5.1	0.1	7.1	10.2
M7	D, 70		D, 76		D, 63		D, 100	40,610	40,003	-1	77,372	47.4	34.5	10.0	72.4	5.1	0.2	6.5	11.2
M8	R, 53		R, 70		R, 100		R, 100	39,341	40,002	2	125,138	52.4	39.9	6.1	91.2	1.4	0.1	4.4	1.8
M9	D, 53		D, 100		D, 60		D, 100	41,615	40,953	-2	102,113	48.8	37.4	6.9	81.0	3.3	0.1	10.9	3.3
M10	D, 100		D, 100		D, 100		D, 82	39,150	39,923	2	68,601	46.2	33.8	12.5	70.2	5.2	0.2	8.9	13.1
M11	D, 100		D, 81		D, 73		D, 100	39,221	38,839	-1	143,992	59.6	51.2	6.2	84.5	2.5	0.1	8.5	3.0
M12	D, 84		D, 100		D, 100		D, 100	36,263	36,621	1	159,189	58.6	51.5	6.6	81.5	2.8	0.1	11.1	3.0
M13	R, 62		R, 100		R, 52		D, 52	38,361	38,042	-1	177,276	58.7	49.3	4.9	88.1	2.3	0.1	6.2	1.9
M14	D, 100		D, 59		D, 60		D, 100	39,503	39,828	1	155,352	59.2	49.0	5.5	86.2	2.0	0.1	7.3	2.6
M15	D, 100		D, 69		D, 70		D, 100	40,030	39,720	-1	112,017	56.8	45.4	7.0	84.3	1.9	0.1	10.4	1.9
M16	R, 80		D, 72		D, 100		D, 77	39,057	38,894	0	61,648	37.1	23.2	12.8	74.6	3.7	0.2	9.3	9.3
M17	D, 100		D, 72		D, 78		D, 100	40,886	40,392	-1	55,629	32.2	20.1	20.3	59.6	4.2	0.2	16.2	16.6
M18	D, 100		D, 77		D, 100		D, 100	37,598	37,376	-1	51,772	28.7	18.4	21.6	46.1	5.2	0.3	31.0	17.7
M19	D, 100		D, 70		D, 100		D, 100	38,603	38,753	0	79,446	40.8	24.7	6.2	92.5	1.2	0.1	3.7	1.4
M20	D, 100		R, 100		R, 66		R, 100	40,367	40,225	0	113,553	50.1	36.3	5.3	93.4	0.8	0.1	2.8	2.0
21	R, 100		D, 65		D, 65		D, 100	40,802	40,261	-1	100,538	51.7	37.7	5.1	85.0	1.8	0.1	10.3	1.7
M22	R, 100		D, 100		D, 62		D, 100	39,831	40,110	1	83,573	39.7	23.5	6.1	90.6	1.7	0.1	4.6	1.8
M23	D, 100		D, 100		D, 74		D, 100	41,041	40,193	-2	86,973	55.4	42.8	9.0	84.6	5.1	0.2	5.8	2.4
M24	D, 81		D, 100		D, 75		D, 69	40,891	40,476	-1	101,382	56.9	47.1	8.6	74.9	9.3	0.2	9.7	3.8
M25	D, 100		D, 100		D, 82		D, 89	40,626	40,044	-1	80,934	57.6	52.8	12.4	67.7	7.7	0.2	15.4	6.7
M26	D, 100		D, 63		D, 86		D, 100	39,425	39,796	1	60,296	41.9	32.4	18.9	58.2	11.1	0.3	10.2	14.9
M27	D, 100		D, 81		D, 81		D, 100	40,318	39,779	-1	64,699	48.4	38.6	12.1	74.8	6.0	0.2	8.5	6.7
M28	D, 100		D, 72		D, 100		D, 60	40,809	40,247	-1	52,654	32.1	18.8	16.6	69.7	7.9	0.3	6.3	10.8
M29	D, 100		D, 100		D, 100		D, 72	38,733	38,228	-1	98,401	58.5	47.2	8.3	84.8	3.2	0.2	6.5	3.3
M30	D, 86		D, 100		D, 62		D, 100	39,023	39,660	2	75,470	44.7	29.7	9.3	86.2	2.1	0.1	6.6	3.3
M31	D, 100		D, 100		D, 62		D, 100	38,838	38,073	-2	111,698	53.6	40.4	7.6	90.2	1.4	0.1	5.3	1.7
M32	D, 100		D, 65		D, 67		D, 100	42,241	41,607	-2	86,782	50.7	35.1	9.3	92.1	1.5	0.1	3.6	1.2
M33	D, 68		D, 100		D, 100		D, 100	38,017	37,924	0	59,081	40.7	26.2	14.7	68.6	7.5	0.2	16.4	5.0
M34	D, 61		D, 100		D, 68		D, 100	37,961	37,235	-2	64,734	39.1	28.0	14.4	72.9	9.0	0.2	7.1	7.1
35	D, 100		D, 100		D, 66		D, 100	39,728	39,406	-1	64,122	43.0	28.3	11.6	77.7	6.0	0.1	10.1	3.9
M36	D, 100		D, 57		D, 100		D, 100	40,647	40,352	-1	75,370	38.5	22.7	8.1	90.2	1.5	0.1	4.7	2.2
M37	D, 100		D, 52		D, 63		D, 64	42,423	43,538	3	108,965	50.4	36.9	6.5	84.5	3.9	0.2	5.0	4.5
M38*	D, 67																		
M39*	D, 78																		
N1	D, 100		D, 100		D, 78		D, 100	40,475	40,220	-1	68,959	43.3	27.2	8.3	69.5	4.7	0.2	22.2	2.4

(continued)

Note: D=Democrat, R=Republican, R/D=Republican/Democrat (cross-filed), D/R=Democrat/Republican (cross-filed), I=Independent, C=Constitution, O=Other, GI=Green Independent, P=Progressive, P/D=Progressive/Democrat, P/D/R=Progressive/Democrat/Republican, HH=Households

Massachusetts State House Districts—Election and Demographic Data (cont.)

House Districts	General Election Results Party, Percent of Vote							Population			Avg. HH Income	Pop 25+ Some College +	Pop 25+ 4-Yr Degree +	Below Poverty Line	2006 White (Non-Hisp)	African American	American Indians, Alaska Natives	Asians, Hawaiians, Pacific Islanders	Hispanic Origin
Mass.	2000	2001	2002	2003	2004	2005	2006	2000	2006	% Change	($)	(%)	(%)	(%)	(%)	(%)	(%)	(%)	(%)
N2	D, 100		D, 100		D, 100		D, 100	38,308	38,508	1	63,476	43.6	27.1	12.3	77.5	3.1	0.2	15.0	3.0
N3	D, 100		D, 100		D, 100		D, 100	39,834	41,597	4	64,900	40.9	22.7	12.4	83.9	3.2	0.2	8.5	2.8
N4	D, 100		D, 100		D, 68		D, 71	40,911	41,230	1	103,438	47.9	32.7	8.8	90.1	2.4	0.2	3.6	2.6
N5	D, 100		D, 100		D, 72		D, 100	42,063	41,832	-1	77,376	42.4	25.0	9.4	87.7	3.7	0.1	5.0	2.1
N6	D, 89		D, 70		D, 67		D, 100	39,884	39,943	0	80,993	44.0	27.9	10.2	87.1	4.9	0.1	4.0	2.2
N7	D, 100		D, 64		D, 100		D, 100	38,718	37,967	-2	92,051	45.6	29.5	9.3	67.2	18.9	0.1	7.8	3.9
N8	D, 100		D, 100		D, 100		D, 73	41,596	42,474	2	105,617	49.7	34.8	7.9	87.3	4.8	0.1	4.4	1.8
N9	R, 69		R, 100		R, 56		R, 100	40,587	40,921	1	106,130	45.1	29.8	6.4	89.7	2.9	0.2	2.5	3.3
N10	D, 100		D, 100		D, 100		D, 100	38,535	38,720	0	89,829	44.8	29.6	7.2	93.3	1.5	0.1	2.8	1.4
N11	D, 100		D, 63		D, 100		D, 100	37,541	37,328	-1	63,811	41.5	22.6	10.4	90.9	2.3	0.2	3.0	2.1
N12	D, 100		D, 100		D, 100		D, 100	39,507	39,085	-1	85,134	47.8	31.7	7.8	88.9	2.3	0.1	5.5	2.0
N13	D, 73		D, 100		D, 100		D, 100	41,641	41,486	0	152,323	57.0	45.8	5.8	91.3	1.2	0.1	5.0	1.6
N14	R, 55		D, 56		D, 62		D, 100	40,498	41,225	2	116,344	52.9	40.1	5.4	90.6	0.9	0.1	6.0	1.3
N15	D, 100		D, 100		D, 100		D, 100	40,300	40,967	2	98,860	62.0	55.0	13.1	73.0	3.6	0.1	16.4	5.5
P1	R, 65		R, 67		R, 62		R, 100	39,874	42,592	7	74,138	38.2	18.6	9.1	91.9	2.8	0.3	0.9	2.2
P2	D, 60		R, 52		R, 52		R, 57	40,768	43,227	6	60,988	32.4	12.3	14.8	90.2	2.8	0.5	0.7	1.5
P3	D, 58		D, 68		D, 94		D, 100	42,175	43,762	4	108,193	51.2	34.7	8.3	95.3	0.9	0.1	1.4	1.1
P4	D, 76		D, 100		D, 100		D, 100	39,104	41,125	5	97,740	47.7	27.5	8.4	95.8	1.0	0.1	0.7	0.9
P5	D, 100		D, 63		D, 100		D, 63	40,820	42,508	4	96,244	40.6	21.9	8.8	94.5	1.6	0.1	1.4	1.0
P6	R, 65		R, 54		R, 100		R, 52	39,737	42,082	6	95,041	41.9	22.9	7.6	95.9	1.2	0.1	0.8	0.8
P7	D, 100		D, 59		D, 65		D, 52	41,594	43,727	5	70,839	33.6	14.9	9.5	95.1	1.6	0.2	0.8	1.0
P8	D, 100		D, 79		D, 58		D, 100	39,702	40,912	3	80,792	36.4	19.3	8.1	88.4	3.6	0.2	1.4	2.5
P9	D, 100		D, 100		D, 100		D, 100	40,163	41,493	3	53,624	25.4	10.3	20.3	54.4	19.8	0.4	2.9	10.5
P10	D, 67		D, 100		D, 71		D, 100	40,455	41,873	4	64,633	28.2	11.1	13.0	71.6	14.1	0.4	1.9	6.3
P11	D, 100		D, 100		D, 69		D, 100	37,796	39,387	4	68,014	32.8	17.2	16.5	64.6	15.9	0.3	3.3	7.1
P12	D, 76		D, 100		D, 69		D, 51	42,971	45,580	6	80,489	37.9	19.8	9.7	95.2	1.6	0.2	0.6	0.9
S1	D, 100		D, 100		D, 88		D, 100	39,670	37,353	-6	42,997	27.6	15.7	24.1	35.5	11.3	0.5	6.7	45.2
S2	D, 100		D, 100		D, 100		D, 100	43,576	41,208	-5	64,851	36.9	25.0	22.3	35.5	13.0	0.5	7.4	43.6
S3	D, 100		D, 100		D, 100		D, 79	35,570	34,879	-2	83,991	54.1	44.0	17.7	49.9	14.2	0.4	23.3	10.8
S4	D, 100		D, 100		D, 100		D, 100	39,572	38,088	-4	57,942	39.7	26.6	20.4	62.0	13.4	0.4	9.0	11.4
S5	D, 74		D, 89		D, 100		D, 84	37,025	35,163	-5	46,779	26.0	13.8	27.6	14.6	54.6	0.6	6.6	24.0
S6	D, 100		D, 100		D, 100		D, 100	38,827	36,532	-6	45,158	26.7	13.1	27.8	8.1	78.6	0.6	1.9	18.1
S7	D, 100		D, 100		D, 100		D, 100	41,423	40,448	-2	42,841	33.1	21.6	30.4	26.5	48.8	0.5	7.2	20.3
S8	D, 72		D, 100		D, 75		D, 100	40,386	39,139	-3	107,104	63.1	55.7	11.8	64.8	12.5	0.3	12.7	7.1
S9	D, 79		D, 100		D, 100		D, 100	36,962	35,503	-4	68,398	51.2	42.6	23.9	49.8	18.8	0.4	15.1	14.3
S10	D, 100		D, 65		D, 81		D, 100	40,918	38,769	-5	89,113	53.5	40.3	8.6	74.3	9.0	0.3	7.8	5.6
S11	D, 87		D, 100		D, 100		D, 100	37,915	35,522	-6	52,767	40.7	27.3	19.6	32.4	32.7	0.6	5.5	31.6
S12	D, 100		D, 100		D, 100		D, 100	37,939	35,801	-6	69,358	40.4	24.1	14.9	37.0	50.5	0.4	4.3	6.7
S13	D, 100		D, 100		D, 89		D, 100	36,563	34,172	-7	58,726	35.4	20.6	17.2	38.1	31.0	0.5	18.2	10.1
S14	D, 100		D, 100		D, 81		D, 100	36,971	34,034	-8	55,946	37.5	21.6	18.2	41.7	34.5	0.4	4.0	19.0
S15	D, 100		D, 76		D, 100		D, 100	38,226	36,845	-4	82,347	49.7	38.8	18.3	45.0	21.0	0.5	9.9	23.0
S16	D, 100		D, 100		D, 100		D, 100	39,517	37,752	-4	56,950	33.2	17.4	17.9	68.1	8.9	0.3	5.0	14.0
S17	D, 100		D, 100		D, 100		D, 100	39,004	37,527	-4	52,831	50.3	41.6	22.3	58.4	10.4	0.3	16.8	11.5
S18	D, 100		D, 100		D, 100		D, 81	39,447	37,114	-6	65,636	48.8	40.7	19.6	62.2	9.0	0.3	16.0	9.6
S19	D, 83		D, 75		D, 78		D, 100	37,601	34,765	-8	60,484	38.9	21.9	16.0	69.1	9.0	0.4	6.9	10.3
W1	D, 52		R, 58		R, 100		R, 69	43,532	47,056	8	83,448	48.0	31.3	7.9	94.6	1.1	0.2	1.4	1.7
W2	D, 100		D, 65		D, 100		D, 100	39,513	41,239	4	54,908	35.9	18.2	15.2	91.4	1.7	0.3	1.6	3.4
3	D, 100		D, 100		D, 100		D, 77	39,726	40,494	2	49,583	31.8	16.5	19.0	67.4	4.5	0.4	5.6	17.9
W4	D, 100		D, 100		D, 69		D, 62	39,465	41,398	5	58,523	38.4	21.5	14.6	75.3	4.5	0.2	3.2	13.4
W5	R, 100		D, 56		D, 69		D, 69	39,101	41,291	6	58,276	36.3	18.7	13.1	95.5	0.8	0.3	0.7	1.5

(continued)

Note: D=Democrat, R=Republican, R/D=Republican/Democrat (cross-filed), D/R=Democrat/Republican (cross-filed), I=Independent, C=Constitution, O=Other, GI=Green Independent, P=Progressive, P/D=Progressive/Democrat, P/D/R=Progressive/Democrat/Republican, HH=Households

Massachusetts State House Districts—Election and Demographic Data (cont.)

House Districts	General Election Results Party, Percent of Vote							Population			Avg. HH Income	Pop 25+		Below Poverty Line	2006 White (Non-Hisp)	African American	American Indians, Alaska Natives	Asians, Hawaiians, Pacific Islanders	Hispanic Origin
												Some College +	4-Yr Degree +						
Mass.	2000	2001	2002	2003	2004	2005	2006	2000	2006	% Change	($)	(%)	(%)	(%)	(%)	(%)	(%)	(%)	(%)
W6	D, 55		D, 51		D, 65		D, 55	39,314	41,613	6	58,350	35.3	18.7	14.7	82.4	1.3	0.3	1.5	11.1
W7	R, 56		R, 65		R, 100		R, 100	38,971	41,391	6	66,777	40.1	21.9	11.0	94.9	1.0	0.2	1.5	1.5
W8	D, 100		D, 100		D, 59		D, 100	39,010	41,637	7	60,672	36.6	19.6	14.6	92.3	1.2	0.3	1.2	3.3
W9	R, 100		R, 100		R, 65		R, 100	40,958	43,550	6	86,596	45.1	30.0	9.8	93.0	1.2	0.2	2.1	2.1
W10	D, 66		D, 100		D, 100		D, 65	37,484	39,329	5	69,632	43.5	25.5	12.1	89.8	1.5	0.1	2.1	4.2
W11	R, 100		R, 100		R, 100		R, 100	39,221	42,286	8	89,027	52.2	37.9	9.3	81.5	2.2	0.2	10.4	4.3
W12	D, 73		D, 80		D, 65		D, 100	39,269	41,331	5	84,550	46.5	31.2	9.8	84.6	2.8	0.2	3.5	6.5
W13	D, 70		D, 100		D, 100		D, 100	37,850	39,116	3	76,207	46.3	31.7	12.5	80.3	4.1	0.3	3.4	8.5
W14	D, 71		D, 100		D, 100		D, 74	38,147	40,435	6	59,779	41.2	23.9	16.5	69.8	8.5	0.4	3.6	14.9
W15	D, 82		D, 100		D, 100		D, 100	39,247	41,004	4	42,263	30.8	17.7	28.8	48.8	11.0	0.7	7.4	28.8
W16	D, 100		D, 84		D, 76		D, 100	38,865	39,683	2	48,563	30.8	16.6	18.3	67.8	7.1	0.5	7.0	13.4
W17	D, 100		D, 100		D, 100		D, 100	38,883	40,378	4	51,941	33.1	17.8	19.6	66.4	6.6	0.5	8.0	15.3
W18**			D, 45		D, 73		D, 100	41,166	43,399	5	73,968	38.9	21.3	9.2	95.0	0.9	0.2	1.5	1.4

* Applies to 2000 District Only

** Applies to 2002-2006 Districts

Note: D=Democrat, R=Republican, R/D=Republican/Democrat (cross-filed), D/R=Democrat/Republican (cross-filed), I=Independent, C=Constitution, O=Other, GI=Green Independent, P=Progressive, P/D=Progressive/Democrat, P/D/R=Progressive/Democrat/Republican, HH=Households

MICHIGAN

Michigan in the 1980s was in some ways reminiscent of Oklahoma in the 1930s. The oil shock of 1979 and the ensuing depression (for that is what it was here) crushed an economy built on automobile manufacturing and other heavy industry. Thousands of unemployed Michigan families, camping in their cars, fled south to Texas where they were known disparagingly as "Black Tag people" for the color of their license plates. The number of workers in Michigan's auto industry shrank from 437,000 in October 1978 to 289,000 in October 1982, and those new assembly plants that are still being built are being built in the South, where wages and taxes are lower. Despite a recovery in the 1990s, a more mechanized assembly line means those jobs are not coming back. Even so, the state's population grew at a little more than half the national rate, and it has been a little less than half the national rate in this decade.

"Sustainability" has become a byword of the spreading environmental movement, but sustainability has never characterized Michigan's economy. It grew on the strength of timber and its huge stands of hard wood trees were strip-cut in the nineteenth century to help build houses around the country. In his terrific history of Chicago, *Nature's Metropolis*, William Cronon tells the story of James S. Little, a Canadian businessman, who warned as early as 1876 that the supply was limited. Loggers in Michigan and elsewhere, Little wrote, were "not only burning the candle at both ends . . . but cutting it in two, and setting the match to the four ends to enable them to double the process of exhaustion." He was right, more literally than he had intended, for a huge fire in 1881 destroyed much of what was left.

Michigan rose to its greatest heights as the center of the U.S. auto industry, but by the 1970s, "Made in Detroit" had not become an indicator of quality. The Big Three automakers rebounded for a time by capitalizing on the popularity of gas-guzzling SUVs, but they have been hit again by high gasoline prices and a growing fear of global warming. Michigan was the capital of the UAW and the Teamsters, but union membership peaked at about one-third of the workforce in the 1950s and is now closer to one-eighth.

Detroit, buckle on the Rust Belt, has been losing population for decades. The country's fifth-largest city in 1980, it has fallen to eleventh today, surpassed by the Sun Belt giants Dallas, Phoenix, San Antonio, San Diego, and San Jose. Urban parts of Wayne County continue to empty out, despite efforts to revitalize downtown by the building of new stadiums for the Detroit Tigers and Lions. As Michael Barone, a Detroit native, has pointed out from census data, almost 200,000 people have moved out of Detroit since 2000, but only about 89,000 immigrants have moved in to take their place. Many residents are leaving the state altogether but those who are staying are moving to the outer suburbs. The 47th state house district, in Livingston County, has grown by 18 percent over the last six years, and the adjacent 66th district has grown by 14 percent. Heavily rural districts on the Upper Peninsula, on the other hand, have held even.

Thanks to its glory days at the center of the American economy, Michigan remains one of the wealthier states, and its wealthiest sections are in Detroit's newer suburbs north of the city—Birmingham (average household income over $173,000 in the 40th house district), Bloomfield Hills, and Auburn Hills—as well as its older, eastern suburbs such as Grosse Pointe. Not surprisingly, downtown Detroit remains desperately poor, one of the poorest parts of the United States. Unemployment is up again and Michigan now has the second-highest rate in the country.

Racially, Michigan ranks about in the middle: it is twenty-eighth in percentage of white residents, tied for twenty-fifth in percentage of Hispanics. Although it ranks fifteenth overall in percentage of African Americans (the state is 14 percent black), that fits in with other northern industrial states. Blacks migrated to Michigan to find work; hence, the black population is concentrated in the old industrial base and is largely absent elsewhere. Twelve house districts, all but one of them in Detroit, have a black majority. Although Michigan has a very small percentage of Hispanics, they now constitute a majority of residents in the 12th district along the Detroit River near River Rouge.

A fact of particular interest since September 11, 2001, is that Michigan has a larger percentage of Arab residents than any other state. Most are immigrants from Lebanon, Syria, and Egypt, but there is a large number of Palestinians, as well. Almost 30 percent of Dearborn's population is Arab. It is home to the Arab American National Museum as well as the largest mosque in the United States, and many street signs are in both English and Arabic.

The state legislature, which was one of the most closely contested in the country during the 1990s, is less so today. Republicans have controlled both chambers throughout the decade by small but steady margins. An effort was made in 2005 to put a referendum on the ballot to convert the state to a unicameral legislature, but it failed to gain enough support to be placed on the ballot.

It is the eighth-largest state today and is projected to be the eleventh largest still in 2025. At its peak, as recently as the 1970s—before the oil shock kicked it—it had nineteen congressional districts. It has lost four in the last two rounds of reapportionment and by 2030 is expected to have only thirteen.

MICHIGAN
State Senate Districts

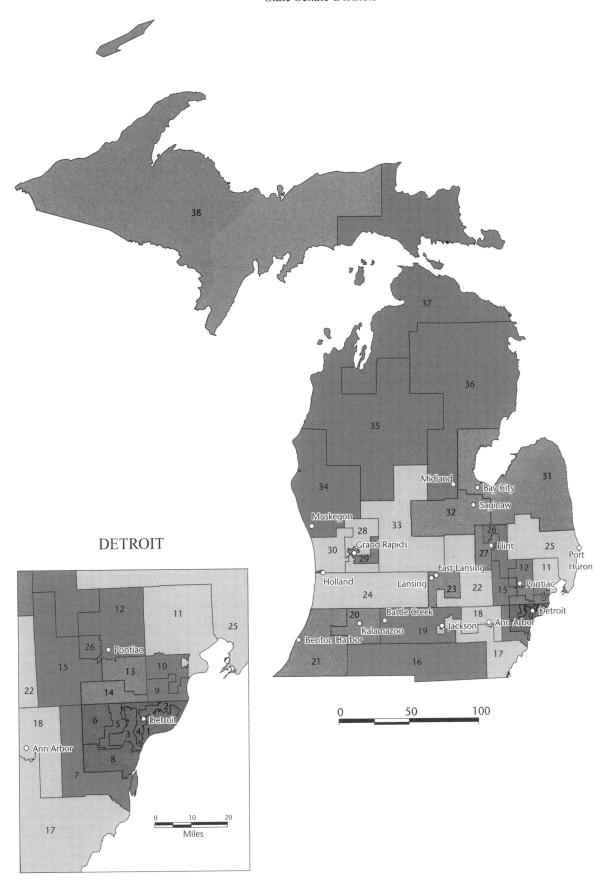

DETROIT

Population Growth ▮ -7% to -2%   ▮ -2% to 1%   ▮ 1% to 5%   ▯ 5% to 12%

Michigan State Senate Districts—Election and Demographic Data

Senate Districts	General Election Results Party, Percent of Vote							Population			Avg. HH Income	Pop 25+		Below Poverty Line	White (Non-Hisp)	African American	American Indians, Alaska Natives	Asians, Hawaiians, Pacific Islanders	Hispanic Origin
												Some College +	4-Yr Degree +		2006				
	2000	2001	2002	2003	2004	2005	2006	2000	2006	% Change	($)	(%)	(%)	(%)	(%)	(%)	(%)	(%)	(%)
Michigan																			
1			D, 94				D, 96	248,679	237,113	-5	40,912	30.1	11.7	31.3	16.0	75.6	0.3	1.5	7.
2			D, 68				D, 73	251,498	236,256	-6	64,457	32.3	15.1	22.4	33.2	59.1	0.2	3.8	1.5
3			D, 81				D, 82	253,540	239,493	-6	53,328	32.7	13.3	20.4	38.2	53.9	0.2	1.1	3.04
4			D, 96				D, 96	247,866	232,550	-6	47,589	29.5	10.6	26.6	15.5	72.9	0.4	0.9	13.
5			D, 83				D, 85	246,029	231,529	-6	52,651	32.1	11.7	17.7	34.9	58.5	0.3	1.9	3.0
6			R, 54				D, 52	269,849	258,113	-4	67,264	39.3	17.2	8.2	82.9	9.4	0.3	2.6	2.9
7			R, 56				R, 52	270,845	276,694	2	85,760	43.8	23.3	6.6	80.6	8.8	0.3	5.1	3.1
8			D, 66				D, 71	268,714	257,049	-4	58,153	31.4	10.7	12.0	77.6	12.7	0.5	1.6	5.4
9			D, 62				D, 66	258,466	263,031	2	61,111	35.7	13.0	10.4	90.6	2.6	0.3	2.9	1.
10			D, 54				D, 66	273,525	284,869	4	68,551	38.4	15.3	9.4	88.6	2.7	0.2	4.2	2.0
11			R, 68				R, 59	254,372	281,562	11	82,378	40.2	16.2	7.5	90.7	3.0	0.3	1.7	2.5
12			R, 63				R, 56	275,214	282,905	3	88,506	46.2	27.5	9.7	73.7	13.0	0.3	4.8	5.9
13			R, 63				R, 49	265,893	261,951	-1	106,557	55.3	37.8	6.4	84.8	3.1	0.2	8.4	1.7
14			D, 70				D, 73	276,549	272,136	-2	83,052	52.0	32.9	9.1	64.9	25.0	0.2	5.7	1.7
15			R, 62				R, 58	273,789	284,781	4	101,555	49.8	30.6	5.2	87.4	3.0	0.2	5.5	2.0
16			R, 61				R, 65	253,193	258,107	2	56,624	28.7	9.6	12.6	88.4	2.1	0.3	0.7	5.5
17			R, 60				R, 53	252,283	267,538	6	72,235	38.7	17.6	9.9	88.2	4.1	0.3	2.6	2.8
18			D, 66				D, 71	264,264	279,699	6	76,301	53.5	38.3	12.1	72.2	12.7	0.3	8.8	3.1
19			D, 55				D, 61	255,144	259,872	2	55,396	33.1	10.9	14.2	81.9	10.5	0.5	1.1	3.5
20			R, 57				R, 52	256,124	256,509	0	61,285	41.7	20.7	13.2	81.7	9.3	0.4	2.4	3.4
21			R, 65				R, 58	276,134	277,733	1	55,736	32.1	11.9	15.7	78.5	12.0	0.5	1.2	5.0
22			R, 68				R, 59	247,374	276,978	12	79,546	39.3	16.3	7.9	95.0	0.6	0.4	0.7	1.8
23			D, 53				D, 70	256,529	254,936	-1	59,713	43.8	23.5	15.5	72.1	11.4	0.5	5.3	6.5
24			R, 64				R, 58	267,864	282,984	6	63,110	34.1	12.5	10.0	88.5	2.7	0.4	1.0	4.6
25			R, 56				R, 51	251,910	266,101	6	65,707	31.5	8.9	11.1	92.2	1.8	0.4	0.6	3.1
26			D, 56				D, 61	269,853	279,752	4	69,451	39.8	17.4	9.3	85.5	7.3	0.4	1.6	3.0
27			D, 66				D, 76	272,631	273,740	0	56,711	35.1	12.8	17.1	66.5	27.0	0.5	1.0	2.6
28			R, 74				R, 64	273,132	288,855	6	71,363	39.0	20.3	8.7	85.8	2.7	0.4	2.1	6.0
29			R, 54				R, 52	275,942	281,415	2	59,785	38.4	21.5	14.1	62.5	16.2	0.5	3.2	13.3
30			R, 75				R, 71	263,243	283,089	8	69,532	35.0	17.6	8.1	84.2	1.1	0.3	2.7	7.6
31			D, 61				D, 76	265,991	260,952	-2	52,234	28.5	8.6	15.4	92.7	1.1	0.4	0.5	3.1
32			R, 55				D, 49	252,500	249,333	-1	55,347	30.6	10.8	16.0	72.5	16.3	0.4	1.0	6.8
33			R, 63				R, 54	252,749	266,533	5	56,946	32.3	11.5	14.0	90.7	2.5	0.9	1.0	2.8
34			R, 51				R, 51	273,354	282,470	3	51,221	30.4	9.3	16.3	81.3	9.2	0.7	0.5	5.3
35			R, 61				R, 59	254,084	265,862	5	48,292	30.0	10.6	17.5	93.8	1.6	0.9	0.5	1.6
36			R, 51				R, 62	258,269	260,944	1	53,302	32.9	12.4	16.0	95.4	0.7	0.4	1.0	1.3
37			R, 60				R, 59	249,590	261,267	5	55,047	36.8	14.7	14.0	91.3	1.3	3.3	0.5	1.4
38			D, 61				D, 70	267,138	261,868	-2	46,290	33.2	13.0	18.2	93.5	1.5	1.8	0.8	0.9

Note: D=Democrat, R=Republican, R/D=Republican/Democrat (cross-filed), D/R=Democrat/Republican (cross-filed), I=Independent, C=Constitution, O=Other, GI=Green Independent, P=Progressive, P/D=Progressive/Democrat, P/D/R=Progressive/Democrat/Republican, HH=Households

MICHIGAN
State House Districts

GRAND RAPIDS

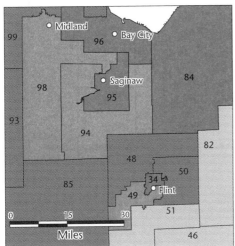

BAY CITY/FLINT

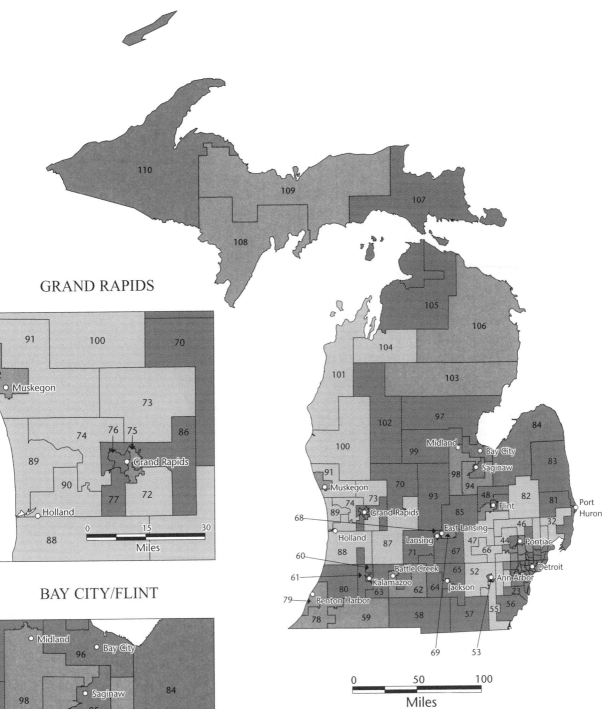

Population Growth   ▓ -7% to -2%   ▓ -2% to 1%   ▓ 1% to 5%   ░ 5% to 18%

DETROIT

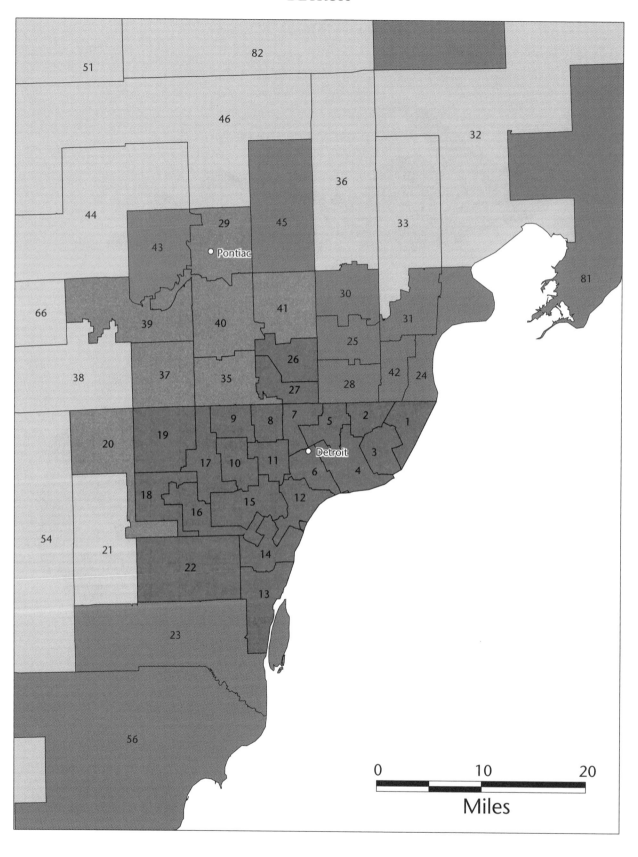

Population Growth   ■ -14% to -3%   ■ 0% to 9%   ■ 10% to 16%   □ 18% to 24%

Michigan State House Districts—Election and Demographic Data

House Districts	General Election Results Party, Percent of Vote							Population			Avg. HH Income ($)	Pop 25+ Some College + (%)	4-Yr Degree + (%)	Below Poverty Line (%)	White (Non-Hisp) (%)	African American (%)	American Indians, Alaska Natives (%)	Asians, Hawaiians, Pacific Islanders (%)	Hispanic Origin (%)
Michigan	2000	2001	2002	2003	2004	2005	2006	2000	2006	% Change	($)	(%)	(%)	(%)	(%)	(%)	(%)	(%)	(%)
1	R, 62		R, 56		R, 57		R, 52	88,836	83,288	-6	102,151	49.5	30.7	8.2	68.7	25.4	0.2	2.1	2.0
2	D, 92		D, 95		D, 95		D, 96	88,040	82,205	-7	45,417	23.2	6.3	25.6	12.3	81.6	0.2	3.6	1.3
3	D, 95		D, 96		D, 96		D, 94	87,425	82,208	-6	43,376	26.1	8.3	29.7	9.3	88.0	0.2	0.5	1.2
4	D, 96		D, 96		D, 96		D, 94	88,472	84,746	-4	37,846	31.7	12.7	33.4	11.7	84.3	0.2	1.0	1.5
5	D, 96		D, 93		D, 100		D, 100	89,350	84,352	-6	40,151	26.0	8.7	30.0	23.9	64.0	0.3	5.9	1.5
6	D, 93		D, 94		D, 92		D, 95	88,952	84,426	-5	37,017	30.5	11.7	36.2	10.2	84.6	0.3	2.2	2.2
7	D, 95		D, 96		D, 96		D, 97	89,487	83,355	-7	47,572	31.7	12.4	27.9	10.8	85.5	0.2	0.7	1.4
8	D, 91		D, 97		D, 96		D, 97	88,753	83,445	-6	54,710	35.1	12.1	19.1	5.5	92.2	0.2	0.4	1.2
9	D, 96		D, 94		D, 95		D, 94	88,573	83,315	-6	54,656	33.9	12.1	19.3	13.9	82.5	0.3	0.8	1.5
10	D, 97		D, 89		D, 91		D, 94	87,333	81,867	-6	45,605	28.7	9.4	22.4	24.4	68.1	0.3	1.3	3.9
11	D, 94		D, 95		D, 96		D, 100	88,256	82,460	-7	45,213	28.1	8.9	25.7	13.5	82.0	0.2	0.5	1.5
12	D, 96		D, 90		D, 87		D, 96	87,816	82,940	-6	41,084	21.1	7.6	31.1	20.6	28.4	0.8	1.2	52.5
13	D, 92		D, 65		D, 64		D, 69	89,854	86,038	-4	61,723	36.1	13.9	9.7	85.6	6.5	0.4	1.6	4.0
14	D, 93		D, 74		D, 73		D, 78	91,443	86,144	-6	54,226	30.6	10.3	13.6	73.3	15.0	0.5	0.9	7.9
15	R, 54		R, 100		D, 65		D, 76	90,557	86,819	-4	64,252	39.1	20.3	13.8	78.6	6.8	0.3	2.2	4.4
16	D, 67		D, 75		D, 70		D, 73	94,334	89,243	-5	56,928	32.4	11.1	12.3	65.9	25.3	0.4	2.8	3.8
17	D, 77		D, 50		D, 59		D, 77	93,394	88,130	-6	62,599	37.8	15.7	8.2	81.3	10.6	0.3	1.9	3.4
17*			D, 61																
18	D, 63		D, 70		D, 68		D, 73	86,382	82,760	-4	58,429	35.5	13.9	10.1	79.0	11.7	0.4	3.4	3.2
19	R, 61		R, 63		R, 53		R, 55	93,472	90,061	-4	81,218	46.2	24.4	6.0	87.0	6.1	0.2	2.8	2.4
20	R, 64		R, 61		R, 60		D, 51	91,494	91,204	0	95,242	47.8	28.4	6.7	81.4	9.5	0.3	4.3	2.6
21	R, 59		R, 54		R, 58		R, 56	91,614	96,590	5	84,885	44.9	25.2	6.4	75.6	10.4	0.3	8.6	3.1
22	D, 74		D, 69		D, 70		D, 72	88,330	84,858	-4	57,680	28.4	8.4	13.8	73.0	18.4	0.5	1.9	3.9
23	D, 51		D, 49		D, 55		D, 63	87,242	88,467	1	75,766	36.6	14.8	7.7	83.2	8.4	0.4	2.4	3.6
24	D, 71		R, 54		R, 63		R, 59	87,891	90,564	3	68,696	41.4	16.4	8.4	94.0	1.4	0.2	1.3	1.6
25	D, 75		D, 57		D, 61		D, 67	89,969	91,873	2	68,352	40.5	17.0	8.4	89.7	1.5	0.2	5.0	1.5
26	D, 59		D, 61		D, 49		D, 62	91,269	88,930	-3	68,459	50.0	30.0	8.4	89.0	2.7	0.3	4.1	1.7
27	D, 73		D, 71		D, 73		D, 79	92,677	89,698	-3	64,531	45.4	26.0	10.7	77.2	14.9	0.3	2.7	1.9
28	D, 73		D, 67		D, 70		D, 75	93,662	95,632	2	53,736	30.2	9.6	13.0	86.9	3.8	0.4	4.3	2.0
29	R, 52		D, 76		D, 75		D, 76	86,695	86,141	-1	52,514	35.6	17.8	19.2	44.3	36.2	0.4	4.7	12.9
29*							D, 77												
30	R, 61		R, 62		R, 54		R, 60	91,499	94,496	3	76,876	40.7	18.3	8.0	88.3	1.2	0.2	6.0	1.8
31	D, 61		D, 60		D, 55		D, 63	89,151	93,292	5	64,798	37.3	13.0	11.4	84.6	8.2	0.3	2.1	2.6
32	R, 67		R, 56		R, 66		R, 59	90,889	100,480	11	73,528	35.3	11.0	8.2	91.0	3.0	0.4	0.8	2.8
33	R, 58		R, 60		R, 61		R, 54	88,110	99,523	13	83,572	41.0	16.9	6.0	93.3	1.2	0.2	2.0	1.9
34	D, 65		D, 88		D, 89		D, 90	85,988	83,329	-3	42,438	27.6	7.7	29.0	30.5	63.5	0.5	0.5	3.1
35	D, 75		D, 80		D, 87		D, 89	92,026	91,010	-1	71,555	52.1	30.7	10.4	39.3	52.5	0.2	4.0	1.5
36	D, 85		R, 67		R, 65		R, 61	93,022	100,832	8	89,109	42.8	19.6	6.2	92.3	1.0	0.2	2.4	2.4
37	R, 50		D, 52		D, 57		D, 62	91,852	90,966	-1	99,729	56.2	38.7	6.5	78.9	7.0	0.1	10.2	1.7
38	R, 64		R, 65		R, 61		R, 60	90,245	96,657	7	89,646	50.3	31.8	5.1	85.8	2.5	0.2	7.3	2.4
39	R, 58		R, 61		R, 52		R, 50	87,344	87,814	1	126,331	54.3	36.6	4.4	84.5	4.2	0.1	7.5	1.6
40	R, 73		R, 62		R, 100		R, 65	87,892	86,687	-1	173,568	65.0	50.7	3.8	86.2	4.6	0.1	6.0	1.7
41	R, 60		R, 69		R, 58		R, 58	93,953	93,352	-1	98,752	53.3	36.1	6.0	79.1	2.6	0.2	14.6	1.7
42	R, 67		D, 65		D, 72		D, 73	86,910	88,789	2	56,123	31.7	9.3	12.0	90.7	3.4	0.3	2.0	1.8
43	D, 73		R, 53		R, 57		R, 59	86,095	88,217	2	79,254	46.3	25.2	6.5	86.3	3.8	0.3	2.9	4.4
44	R, 62		R, 70		R, 68		R, 67	96,066	101,631	6	91,916	45.6	24.0	4.9	92.0	1.9	0.3	1.7	2.4
45	R, 70		R, 69		R, 63		R, 60	94,122	96,117	2	115,853	53.8	36.4	5.6	84.8	3.3	0.2	7.7	2.6
46	R, 64		R, 71		R, 63		R, 61	93,067	99,181	7	84,209	45.0	23.2	6.0	91.4	2.4	0.2	1.6	2.7
47	D, 59		R, 69		R, 71		R, 62	83,887	98,951	18	83,772	40.5	17.2	5.6	95.4	0.5	0.4	0.7	1.6
48	D, 91		D, 69		D, 73		D, 67	87,156	88,697	2	61,110	34.0	11.4	11.7	81.1	13.2	0.5	0.5	2.4

(continued)

Note: D=Democrat, R=Republican, R/D=Republican/Democrat (cross-filed), D/R=Democrat/Republican (cross-filed), I=Independent, C=Constitution, O=Other, GI=Green Independent, P=Progressive, P/D=Progressive/Democrat, P/D/R=Progressive/Democrat/Republican, HH=Households

Michigan State House Districts—Election and Demographic Data (cont.)

House Districts	General Election Results Party, Percent of Vote							Population			Avg. HH Income ($)	Pop 25+ Some College + (%)	Pop 25+ 4-Yr Degree + (%)	Below Poverty Line (%)	White (Non-Hisp) (%)	African American (%)	American Indians, Alaska Natives (%)	Asians, Hawaiians, Pacific Islanders (%)	Hispanic Origin (%)
										2006									
Michigan	2000	2001	2002	2003	2004	2005	2006	2000	2006	% Change	($)	(%)	(%)	(%)	(%)	(%)	(%)	(%)	(%)
49	D, 79		D, 69		D, 70		D, 75	86,745	85,955	-1	56,811	38.0	14.7	15.5	72.1	19.7	0.6	1.7	2.9
50	D, 62		D, 68		D, 65		D, 65	86,753	90,400	4	58,709	33.4	11.2	12.4	87.2	6.5	0.5	0.8	2.5
51	D, 64		R, 50		R, 55		R, 51	90,443	95,003	5	77,507	44.5	21.0	7.2	90.0	4.1	0.3	2.0	1.8
52	D, 65		R, 53		D, 55		D, 63	97,521	105,900	9	98,104	58.2	42.1	6.7	81.2	4.9	0.2	9.4	2.2
53	D, 71		D, 78		D, 80		D, 80	91,396	93,475	2	67,650	55.2	45.1	14.3	71.4	9.4	0.3	11.7	4.1
54	D, 70		D, 69		D, 68		D, 68	95,035	101,386	7	64,929	47.3	27.4	14.2	67.0	22.2	0.4	4.5	2.9
55	R, 61		R, 53		D, 50		D, 64	97,072	104,816	8	75,890	44.6	24.3	8.8	83.5	5.9	0.3	4.6	3.4
56	R, 50		R, 66		D, 49		D, 53	94,821	99,312	5	67,232	29.4	8.8	11.7	91.6	2.8	0.3	0.7	2.6
56*							D, 54												
57	D, 74		D, 69		D, 59		D, 67	92,740	95,820	3	60,639	30.6	11.5	10.9	84.5	2.4	0.4	0.7	8.0
58	R, 66		R, 67		R, 73		R, 73	92,528	93,881	1	53,110	27.3	8.0	13.6	92.8	1.6	0.3	0.5	2.6
59	R, 69		R, 67		R, 71		R, 66	99,444	100,241	1	56,847	28.8	9.5	13.6	87.5	3.9	0.4	0.9	4.6
60	D, 66		D, 64		D, 68		D, 71	95,239	91,887	-4	49,206	37.0	18.8	19.4	71.2	17.1	0.4	2.8	4.8
61	R, 54		R, 57		R, 55		R, 51	93,614	95,031	2	68,161	47.8	25.9	10.1	85.5	6.4	0.3	3.0	2.4
62	D, 67		R, 53		R, 53		R, 54	95,095	95,482	0	50,256	29.9	9.9	16.6	76.6	13.7	0.6	1.7	4.3
63	R, 55		R, 57		R, 59		R, 55	93,475	95,227	2	65,759	39.4	15.4	9.6	90.0	4.1	0.4	1.2	2.1
64	R, 60		R, 64		R, 50		D, 53	86,380	88,405	2	58,399	35.0	12.4	14.4	83.3	9.3	0.4	1.0	3.3
65	R, 62		R, 56		R, 51		D, 53	87,047	90,456	4	63,333	35.4	10.3	10.0	89.6	5.5	0.3	0.5	2.3
66	R, 72		R, 73		R, 71		R, 66	87,803	100,409	14	98,607	45.3	22.3	5.6	94.9	0.8	0.3	1.0	1.5
67	R, 58		D, 59		D, 55		D, 60	94,150	95,601	2	59,656	40.2	15.0	11.0	79.4	9.3	0.4	2.4	4.9
68	D, 60		D, 68		D, 69		D, 74	92,643	89,407	-3	48,057	41.8	18.3	16.9	62.0	17.1	0.7	3.6	11.1
69	D, 68		D, 63		D, 66		D, 67	90,054	90,346	0	73,317	48.2	35.4	17.3	79.3	5.8	0.3	9.2	2.9
70	D, 57		R, 66		R, 66		R, 63	86,399	89,953	4	50,179	27.5	7.1	15.0	89.3	4.3	0.5	0.5	3.1
71	R, 61		R, 56		R, 59		R, 58	96,154	99,179	3	64,595	41.1	15.5	9.4	84.9	6.3	0.4	1.8	4.1
72	R, 74		R, 73		R, 68		R, 66	90,479	96,103	6	76,291	43.7	25.7	7.9	81.1	6.2	0.3	5.2	4.7
73	R, 71		R, 70		R, 65		R, 65	93,635	99,806	7	68,810	38.3	18.5	9.2	92.4	1.0	0.3	0.8	3.6
74	R, 68		R, 78		R, 75		R, 70	94,301	102,601	9	67,544	35.6	16.4	8.4	90.8	1.4	0.3	1.4	3.8
75	R, 53		R, 54		R, 52		D, 51	92,037	92,913	1	60,195	41.4	24.4	13.5	60.9	24.6	0.3	3.3	8.0
76	D, 66		D, 61		D, 67		D, 73	91,916	92,973	1	46,532	30.3	14.7	20.5	46.6	18.7	0.9	1.6	27.0
77	R, 60		R, 71		R, 66		R, 67	85,993	88,266	3	58,499	34.5	16.0	9.6	76.6	4.4	0.4	3.4	10.5
78	R, 70		R, 58		R, 59		R, 52	90,013	89,449	-1	54,715	33.7	12.5	14.3	83.2	6.8	0.5	1.7	4.6
79	R, 63		R, 69		R, 63		R, 65	91,146	90,374	-1	56,860	34.2	13.8	17.9	70.8	23.2	0.3	1.3	3.1
80	R, 63		R, 68		R, 58		R, 61	86,775	90,391	4	54,338	28.8	9.6	14.3	81.6	4.7	0.7	0.5	8.3
81	R, 53		R, 66		R, 56		R, 60	95,090	99,151	4	67,109	32.2	9.0	10.1	94.7	0.8	0.4	0.4	2.2
82	R, 60		R, 59		R, 58		R, 53	87,779	93,314	6	68,966	31.4	8.9	9.0	92.4	0.9	0.3	0.6	3.7
83	R, 66		R, 64		D, 56		D, 73	90,018	92,198	2	53,085	27.8	8.5	17.0	89.5	3.2	0.5	0.7	3.6
84	R, 64		R, 55		R, 64		D, 51	94,434	91,945	-3	51,956	26.5	7.7	14.5	94.4	0.9	0.4	0.5	2.3
85	R, 61		R, 61		R, 53		R, 55	85,327	88,224	3	60,180	32.6	10.5	11.9	94.8	0.4	0.4	0.5	2.2
86	R, 64		R, 69		R, 67		R, 64	90,866	93,606	3	82,918	43.8	26.2	8.1	89.9	1.8	0.3	1.5	4.2
87	R, 67		R, 64		R, 63		R, 56	92,534	97,955	6	60,962	31.3	9.4	10.3	94.5	0.9	0.4	0.4	2.1
88	R, 87		R, 69		R, 67		R, 60	96,082	103,501	8	62,319	29.3	11.3	11.1	86.2	1.6	0.5	0.8	7.0
89	R, 75		R, 73		R, 72		R, 61	85,963	93,079	8	75,851	38.6	20.5	7.2	89.7	0.8	0.3	1.6	4.7
90	R, 77		R, 82		R, 79		R, 78	85,880	91,697	7	64,155	31.2	16.0	8.9	70.3	1.7	0.3	5.7	15.5
91	R, 54		R, 51		R, 52		D, 56	86,710	91,526	6	58,078	34.2	10.9	11.5	90.3	2.9	0.7	0.6	3.3
92	D, 70		D, 67		D, 66		D, 71	85,536	84,921	-1	46,586	29.3	8.1	19.8	64.3	26.5	0.7	0.6	5.4
93	R, 66		R, 67		R, 67		R, 56	94,930	98,215	3	62,354	33.9	12.1	11.5	90.4	2.3	0.4	0.8	3.7
94	R, 58		R, 58		R, 59		R, 53	89,270	88,970	0	66,555	37.2	15.7	10.2	88.5	3.4	0.3	1.8	3.8
95	D, 100		D, 74		D, 77		D, 81	85,638	82,190	-4	43,228	24.6	6.7	24.3	43.5	41.4	0.4	0.4	12.1
96	D, 68		D, 64		D, 64		D, 73	92,594	90,027	-3	54,147	33.4	11.1	15.3	89.9	1.6	0.5	0.7	4.6
97	D, 66		D, 51		R, 52		R, 54	91,611	93,100	2	46,544	26.3	6.7	19.0	95.5	0.7	0.6	0.4	1.5

(continued)

Note: D=Democrat, R=Republican, R/D=Republican/Democrat (cross-filed), D/R=Democrat/Republican (cross-filed), I=Independent, C=Constitution, O=Other, GI=Green Independent, P=Progressive, P/D=Progressive/Democrat, P/D/R=Progressive/Democrat/Republican, HH=Households

Michigan State House Districts—Election and Demographic Data (cont.)

House Districts	General Election Results Party, Percent of Vote							Population			Avg. HH Income	Pop 25+		Below Poverty Line	2006 White (Non-Hisp)	African American	American Indians, Alaska Natives	Asians, Hawaiians, Pacific Islanders	Hispanic Origin
												Some College +	4-Yr Degree +						
Michigan	2000	2001	2002	2003	2004	2005	2006	2000	2006	% Change	($)	(%)	(%)	(%)	(%)	(%)	(%)	(%)	(%)
98	R, 66		R, 64		R, 65		R, 61	86,389	86,421	0	67,590	39.2	19.0	11.9	89.4	3.1	0.3	2.1	3.1
99	R, 51		R, 62		R, 57		R, 58	95,503	99,624	4	53,281	33.5	14.6	17.7	91.3	1.5	1.7	1.5	2.0
100	R, 63		R, 65		R, 61		R, 58	86,454	91,388	6	48,156	25.6	7.7	19.0	85.1	2.3	0.7	0.4	7.5
101	R, 57		R, 54		R, 56		R, 52	90,184	94,792	5	53,165	35.8	14.4	14.4	92.2	0.9	1.5	0.4	2.9
102	R, 62		R, 67		R, 64		R, 62	94,482	98,306	4	47,806	29.1	10.8	18.1	93.9	1.8	0.5	0.8	1.3
103	D, 68		D, 58		D, 57		D, 69	89,243	89,932	1	44,522	27.8	8.0	18.3	96.1	0.4	0.5	0.5	1.2
104	R, 72		R, 65		R, 67		R, 58	94,002	101,775	8	60,198	39.6	16.4	10.8	94.9	0.5	0.8	0.6	1.7
105	R, 67		R, 64		R, 62		R, 64	94,901	99,321	5	54,008	32.9	12.5	14.2	95.4	0.3	1.3	0.4	1.1
106	D, 68		D, 51		D, 58		D, 65	91,297	90,489	-1	45,394	30.4	8.7	18.1	96.9	0.6	0.4	0.3	0.9
107	R, 71		R, 69		D, 54		D, 59	86,300	87,945	2	51,165	35.8	13.9	16.3	84.1	2.9	7.7	0.6	1.3
108	D, 75		R, 52		R, 69		R, 55	91,934	90,648	-1	48,076	31.7	10.9	17.3	95.8	0.2	1.5	0.5	0.8
109	D, 68		D, 69		D, 67		D, 67	89,774	88,649	-1	48,455	35.3	15.1	16.8	91.8	2.5	2.1	0.7	1.0
110	D, 51		D, 70		D, 68		D, 63	86,269	83,102	-4	42,036	32.6	12.9	20.5	92.8	1.6	1.9	1.2	0.8

* Partial Term Ending

Note: D=Democrat, R=Republican, R/D=Republican/Democrat (cross-filed), D/R=Democrat/Republican (cross-filed), I=Independent, C=Constitution, O=Other, GI=Green Independent, P=Progressive, P/D=Progressive/Democrat, P/D/R=Progressive/Democrat/Republican, HH=Households

MINNESOTA

The state of Minnesota has been depicted both as a place of oppressive conformity, by Sinclair Lewis, and of gentle eccentricity, by Garrison Keillor. It has been a place for hearty pioneers to build a better life, as in Laura Ingalls Wilder's *Little House on the Prairie,* and a place from which jaded sophisticates flee, such as St. Paul's F. Scott Fitzgerald and Sauk Center's Sinclair Lewis. All, though, recognized in Minnesotans an earnestness, a dogged sincerity, which may be said to characterize the state's politics, as well. Three of its most famous political leaders of recent generations—Harold Stassen, Hubert Humphrey, and Walter Mondale—were tribunes, if nothing else, of the virtues of plugging away. And so does Minnesota.

Although Keillor would say that the children of Lake Wobegon are all above average, Minnesota has been just below it in terms of population growth over the past three decades. The state's two metropolitan areas, Minneapolis and St. Paul, long linked rhetorically as the "Twin Cities," are more and more becoming Siamese twins, blending into each other ever more seamlessly, though the two are vastly different in history, outlook, and ethnic composition. Historically, they dominated the wheat belt that extended west through the Dakotas, and General Mills, Pillsbury, and other St. Paul millers were vilified in the radical press for oppressing the farmers.

The fastest-growing parts of Minnesota are the outer Twin City suburbs, and the fastest-shrinking are the Twin City centers. For the most part, growth has occurred to the south and west, if only because the eastern St. Paul suburbs quickly run out of room at the St. Croix River. State house district 35A, in Scott County west of Minneapolis, has grown by 42 percent since 2000. (Minnesota, like several other states, is divided into legislative districts, each of which elects one state senator and two representatives from an "A" and "B" district). Just to the north of it, the district that contains Eden Prairie, one of the nicer older suburbs, have grown by just nine percent.

Wealth and poverty for the most part follow the same divisions. Minneapolis is wealthier than St. Paul, and so are its suburbs. Average household income in district 33B, which includes the town of Wayzata and Lake Minnetonka, is $145,000. Other wealthy areas include the Hennepin County suburbs of Edina and Eden Prairie. The poorest sections of the state are in downtown Minneapolis and downtown Duluth, the Mesabi Iron Range, and the Sioux Indian reservations in north-central Minnesota, where unemployment runs in the double digits.

Elsewhere, little of Minnesota is growing rapidly. Indeed, the Census Bureau estimates that most of the state's counties will lose population between now and 2020, by which time as much as 68 percent of the state's population will live in the greater Twin Cities area. With a few exceptions of some high-tech growth, Minnesota's economy is mostly rural, based on mining and logging in the Iron Range, or else on wheat and dairy farming. Between an urban core pushing out and a hinterland migrating in, the Twin City suburbs have become a magnet drawing from both ends.

Minnesota is homogeneous, though it does have some racial and ethnic minorities—Chippewa, Sioux, Norwegians—one does not find in many other places. It has the smallest percentage of African Americans (2.2 percent) of any state with even a modicum of heavy industry. The only black neighborhoods are in downtown Minneapolis, which also has some Hispanic enclaves. On the other hand, all but nine of its sixty-seven legislative districts are at least three-quarters white. In this respect, Minnesota is much more akin to the Dakotas than it is to Illinois or the industrial giants to the southeast. Asians, however, now make up the largest minority group in St. Paul, many of them Thais and Hmong refugees from Laos.

The dominant political party for decades was the Democratic-Farmer-Labor Party, an amalgamation created in 1944 by Hubert Humphrey between the state's Democratic Party and the Farmer-Labor Party formed during World War I in imitation of the Socialist Nonpartisan League. For twenty years, incidentally, the Republican Party here was known as the Independent-Republican Party—the name was changed in 1975 to distance the state's GOP from the stain of Watergate—but it was changed back in 1995.

Between Stassen, Humphrey, and Mondale, a Minnesotan either appeared on a national ticket or made a serious bid for a place on it in every presidential election between 1948 and 1984, a feat unparalleled for a state of its size. Though it was the only state to vote for Mondale (and that barely), it seemed for a while to be growing more competitive; George W. Bush lost the state twice but not as badly as a social and economic conservative might have done in Humphrey's day. Republicans have won gubernatorial and senatorial elections recently, and of course, former pro wrestler Jesse Ventura, riding a protest vote, was elected governor as an Independent in 1998—defeating Hubert Humphrey's son, Skip, in doing so.

The 2006 legislative elections, however, were a disaster for Minnesota Republicans, something the state party blamed on the unpopularity of President Bush and the Iraq war. Though the lost the gubernatorial election narrowly, Democrats gained six seats in the state senate, which they now control by a margin of 44–23. (Minnesota state senators serve four-year terms except at the start of each decade, when they are elected for two-year terms.) In the house, it was even worse—Democrats picked up nineteen seats, defeating a dozen Republican incumbents along the way, and now hold a commanding 85–49 majority.

Republicans are holding their national convention in Minneapolis in 2008. The last time they did so, in 1892, they nominated Benjamin Harrison for reelection. They will hope to do better this time, not only nationally but statewide.

MINNESOTA
State Senate Districts

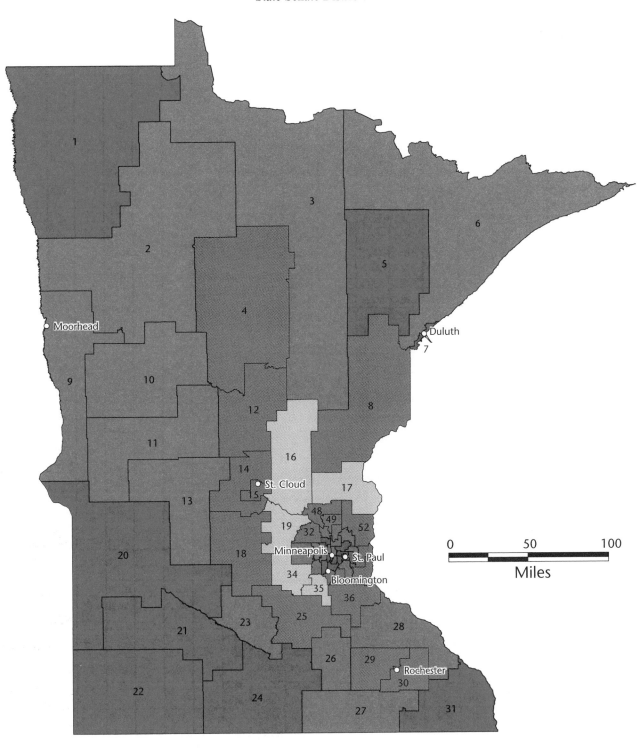

Population Growth ■ -6% to -1% ■ -1% to 6% ■ 6% to 24% □ 24% to 41%

MINNEAPOLIS/ST. PAUL

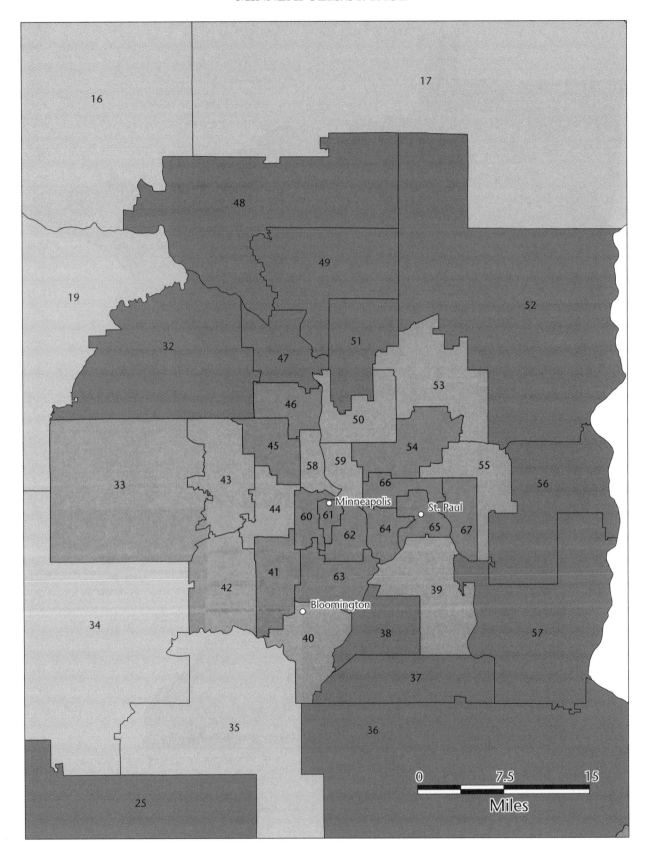

Population Growth   ⬛ -6% to -1%   ⬜ -1% to 6%   ⬛ 6% to 24%   ⬜ 24% to 41%

Minnesota State Senate Districts—Election and Demographic Data

Senate Districts	General Election Results Party, Percent of Vote							Population			Avg. HH Income ($)	Pop 25+ Some College + (%)	Pop 25+ 4-Yr Degree + (%)	Below Poverty Line (%)	2006 White (Non-Hisp) (%)	African American (%)	American Indians, Alaska Natives (%)	Asians, Hawaiians, Pacific Islanders (%)	Hispanic Origin (%)
Minnesota	2000	2001	2002	2003	2004	2005	2006	2000	2006	% Change	($)	(%)	(%)	(%)	(%)	(%)	(%)	(%)	(%)
1	D, 60		D, 64				D, 96	74,075	72,343	-2	48,179	33.2	11.2	16.6	92.1	0.4	1.0	1.0	3.0
2	D, 64		D, 58				D, 61	73,039	74,825	2	44,848	30.5	10.0	21.3	83.7	0.3	11.5	0.4	1.4
3	D, 46		D, 60				D, 65	73,155	73,475	0	47,980	35.2	11.7	17.0	95.8	0.3	1.3	0.4	0.7
4	D, 61		R, 54				D, 52	73,355	80,255	9	47,843	35.9	14.2	18.7	87.6	0.5	8.2	0.7	1.0
5	D, 75		D, 77				D, 78	73,224	70,806	-3	47,494	38.6	11.8	17.0	96.1	0.4	1.0	0.5	0.7
6	D, 70		D, 72				D, 71	73,117	74,348	2	54,806	39.0	15.5	12.9	94.5	0.9	1.7	0.7	0.8
7	D, 88		D, 73				D, 75	72,230	69,938	-3	48,684	40.5	19.5	18.5	90.4	2.1	2.2	1.6	1.1
8	D, 67		D, 55				D, 57	73,657	81,125	10	50,190	29.1	8.5	16.0	92.0	1.3	3.1	0.5	1.4
9	D, 64		D, 62				D, 70	73,991	76,972	4	51,549	38.5	15.8	16.6	91.2	0.6	1.4	1.1	2.8
10	R, 58		R, 60				D, 55	73,184	73,959	1	48,005	32.4	11.3	19.4	95.2	0.5	0.4	0.6	1.5
11	D, 58		D, 54				R, 51	73,587	75,774	3	48,646	33.0	10.7	17.9	95.5	0.4	0.3	0.6	1.9
12	D, 51		R, 50				R, 55	73,236	78,687	7	50,239	33.2	11.2	16.8	96.4	0.5	0.6	0.5	1.0
13	R, 46		D, 54				R, 51	73,667	75,255	2	53,095	32.9	11.2	15.6	89.4	0.5	0.2	0.5	6.0
14	R, 65		R, 57				R, 58	75,141	85,057	13	61,069	34.8	13.5	10.2	95.8	0.5	0.1	1.0	1.5
15	D, 58		R, 51				D, 56	72,367	78,301	8	57,822	38.1	17.1	12.8	88.3	2.9	0.6	4.1	2.1
16	R, 54		R, 61				R, 57	74,548	93,867	26	62,498	32.2	9.5	10.6	95.1	0.4	1.3	0.5	1.4
17	R, 51		R, 52				D, 47	73,972	91,836	24	65,414	33.4	10.1	8.5	95.2	0.6	0.4	0.9	1.6
18	D, 50		R, 69				R, 62	72,596	78,638	8	57,538	30.9	10.2	12.1	93.0	0.4	0.2	0.7	3.6
19	R, 57		R, 62				R, 61	72,588	93,120	28	71,463	33.8	11.9	7.2	95.5	0.5	0.2	0.7	1.8
20	R, 65		D, 63				D, 67	73,969	69,776	-6	46,153	31.3	9.8	15.9	92.3	0.8	0.7	0.8	3.2
21	R, 48		R, 99				R, 60	73,008	70,006	-4	52,119	31.3	12.2	14.2	90.9	0.9	0.7	1.3	3.6
22	D, 65		D, 50				D, 58	73,541	71,414	-3	46,597	30.2	9.9	15.9	87.2	0.7	0.4	2.5	5.8
23	R, 61		D, 47				D, 57	74,625	76,438	2	55,994	39.8	18.8	12.9	90.4	1.6	0.3	2.5	3.0
24	D, 59		R, 47				R, 62	73,382	71,506	-3	49,869	32.7	11.3	13.7	92.0	0.5	0.2	0.6	4.1
25	R, 53		R, 53				R, 52	71,831	83,332	16	63,729	32.7	14.1	10.8	92.5	0.5	0.2	1.1	3.4
26	D, 51		R, 60				R, 54	73,073	77,219	6	58,366	33.5	12.3	10.7	86.2	2.3	0.3	1.5	6.5
27	R, 53		D, 46				D, 68	73,527	72,974	-1	51,905	32.3	10.0	13.9	87.8	0.6	0.2	1.5	6.5
28	R, 64		D, 52				D, 54	70,877	73,845	4	59,580	35.0	13.2	11.2	94.5	0.8	0.6	1.1	1.7
29	D, 56		R, 57				R, 55	72,956	82,643	13	69,569	44.1	22.0	7.9	87.8	2.2	0.2	5.0	2.5
30	R, 62		R, 39				D, 52	75,417	80,821	7	69,530	42.5	20.5	10.2	85.0	3.7	0.2	5.1	3.5
31	R, 64		R, 53				D, 47	74,407	73,011	-2	50,350	35.5	14.7	14.8	95.6	0.8	0.1	1.6	0.8
32	R, 56		R, 65				R, 58	72,056	82,692	15	96,395	48.6	26.7	2.4	88.0	3.7	0.4	3.8	1.7
33	R, 60		R, 65				R, 59	73,584	74,583	1	126,950	55.6	35.3	4.7	88.5	3.6	0.3	3.4	1.9
34	R, 65		R, 61				R, 60	75,584	94,761	25	90,906	41.1	21.4	6.4	90.3	0.9	0.2	2.3	4.2
35	R, 67		R, 68				D, 47	70,597	99,132	40	90,820	42.0	20.3	4.7	88.9	1.4	0.7	3.4	3.2
36	R, 62		R, 66				R, 57	75,653	86,751	15	87,249	43.1	21.6	4.1	90.9	1.3	0.3	2.3	3.0
37	R, 63		R, 64				R, 54	74,138	81,492	10	88,453	49.4	28.4	4.1	86.8	2.8	0.3	4.3	2.9
38	D, 51		R, 50				D, 54	72,951	77,444	6	87,992	52.3	33.0	3.9	82.0	4.6	0.2	7.0	3.3
39	D, 65		D, 58				D, 64	71,920	76,001	6	77,675	47.3	26.4	7.2	82.3	2.6	0.4	2.7	7.9
40	D, 62		R, 57				D, 52	74,218	76,509	3	71,159	50.5	27.1	6.8	80.2	5.8	0.4	6.2	3.9
41	R, 59		R, 56				R, 56	72,965	70,981	-3	112,445	62.6	43.3	5.3	85.3	4.3	0.3	5.4	2.2
42	R, 66		R, 49				R, 52	74,124	77,374	4	111,739	57.3	38.8	4.1	83.3	4.9	0.3	6.1	2.6
43	R, 63		R, 54				D, 52	75,617	77,332	2	108,784	57.8	37.8	4.0	83.7	5.6	0.4	5.2	2.5
44	D, 65		D, 59				D, 68	72,717	72,706	0	67,692	56.0	33.9	7.2	78.2	7.3	0.5	5.6	5.0
45	R, 54		D, 60				D, 64	73,801	73,040	-1	65,305	50.2	26.5	6.8	79.4	8.0	0.5	4.8	3.9
46	D, 60		D, 60				D, 67	73,830	71,187	-4	59,434	41.7	17.3	9.0	60.9	19.1	0.6	10.8	5.0
47	D, 64		D, 46				D, 51	74,337	79,090	6	76,986	44.0	21.2	4.7	83.5	5.4	0.5	5.6	2.3
48	D, 57		R, 54				R, 51	72,797	82,286	13	74,131	38.2	15.7	6.7	93.2	1.2	0.5	1.1	2.1
49	D, 53		R, 62				R, 52	73,500	81,057	10	83,278	41.0	19.5	4.0	92.2	1.6	0.4	1.8	1.9
50	R, 52		D, 55				D, 63	75,253	76,481	2	67,142	44.9	25.3	8.3	81.2	4.9	0.8	5.9	3.4

(continued)

Note: D=Democrat, R=Republican, R/D=Republican/Democrat (cross-filed), D/R=Democrat/Republican (cross-filed), I=Independent, C=Constitution, O=Other, GI=Green Independent, P=Progressive, P/D=Progressive/Democrat, P/D/R=Progressive/Democrat/Republican, HH=Households

Minnesota State Senate Districts—Election and Demographic Data (cont.)

Senate Districts	General Election Results Party, Percent of Vote							Population			Avg. HH Income	Pop 25+		Below Poverty Line	White (Non-Hisp)	African American	American Indians, Alaska Natives	Asians, Hawaiians, Pacific Islanders	Hispanic Origin
												Some College +	4-Yr Degree +		2006				
Minnesota	2000	2001	2002	2003	2004	2005	2006	2000	2006	% Change	($)	(%)	(%)	(%)	(%)	(%)	(%)	(%)	(%)
51	D, 54		D, 53				D, 54	74,733	83,186	11	68,568	39.0	18.4	5.8	86.6	2.4	0.6	4.1	3.1
52	D, 57		R, 54				R, 52	73,300	80,986	10	91,181	43.6	21.7	5.1	94.5	0.9	0.3	1.3	1.5
53	R, 56		R, 52				D, 53	71,176	72,163	1	91,685	49.1	29.3	4.9	88.2	2.6	0.3	4.5	1.9
54	D, 65		D, 57				D, 62	73,343	70,884	-3	72,592	52.0	31.3	6.8	80.8	5.0	0.4	8.3	2.4
55	D, 57		D, 60				D, 67	73,901	74,340	1	67,188	42.0	18.6	7.5	82.7	4.7	0.4	5.9	3.3
56	R, 52		R, 53				D, 53	73,216	83,188	14	97,746	49.5	28.0	3.4	86.7	3.3	0.4	4.8	2.7
57	D, 58		D, 50				D, 65	72,785	78,437	8	71,725	39.0	16.1	6.6	89.5	2.0	0.4	1.6	3.9
58	D, 67		D, 66				D, 79	72,857	72,205	-1	49,640	34.6	16.2	19.7	32.6	41.8	1.2	14.8	6.8
59	D, 69		D, 76				D, 76	73,219	73,155	0	45,779	41.1	24.6	20.1	64.5	12.2	1.3	8.8	8.5
60	D, 76		D, 79				D, 83	74,089	71,991	-3	80,972	64.8	46.6	9.5	76.8	9.4	0.7	4.3	5.0
61	D, 87		D, 75				D, 84	71,974	69,902	-3	41,736	39.3	21.4	21.4	30.6	29.6	3.1	6.9	29.7
62	D, 73		D, 63				D, 81	73,829	70,835	-4	62,397	52.2	31.3	8.1	68.3	11.0	1.9	4.4	9.2
63	D, 67		D, 48				D, 69	73,806	72,102	-2	65,114	50.8	27.6	7.6	71.8	9.0	0.6	6.9	7.7
64	D, 72		D, 72				D, 76	75,290	71,799	-5	75,459	54.5	39.0	9.7	76.6	8.2	0.4	6.2	4.4
65	D, 76		D, 96				D, 76	73,385	70,277	-4	46,327	35.7	17.8	19.8	40.8	20.2	1.1	19.1	15.8
66	D, 75		D, 73				D, 78	71,534	69,036	-3	54,363	41.1	24.9	14.8	57.1	12.4	0.8	18.2	7.8
67	D, 100		D, 60				D, 69	72,806	69,168	-5	51,009	33.6	14.4	14.3	52.7	12.8	1.0	18.6	10.7

Note: D=Democrat, R=Republican, R/D=Republican/Democrat (cross-filed), D/R=Democrat/Republican (cross-filed), I=Independent, C=Constitution, O=Other, GI=Green Independent, P=Progressive, P/D=Progressive/Democrat, P/D/R=Progressive/Democrat/Republican, HH=Households

MINNESOTA
State House Districts

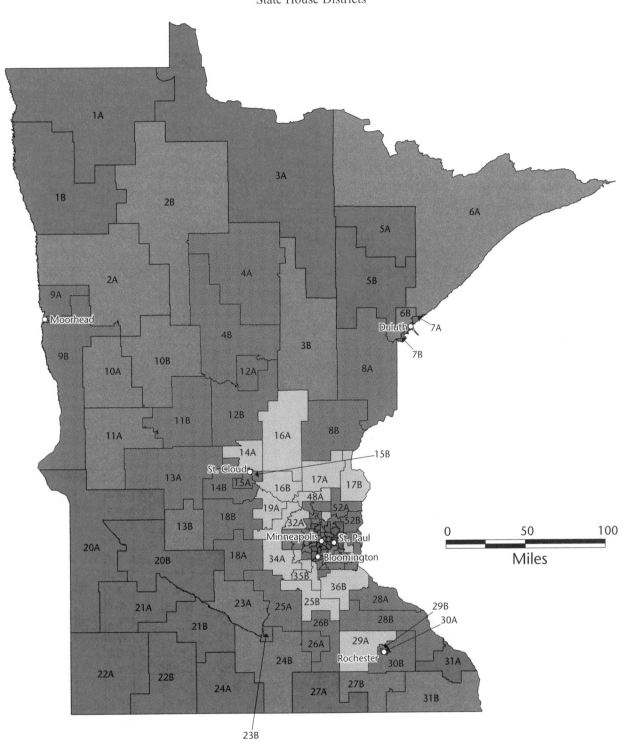

Population Growth — -7% to -1% — -1% to 3% — 3% to 14% — 14% to 43%

MINNEAPOLIS/ST. PAUL

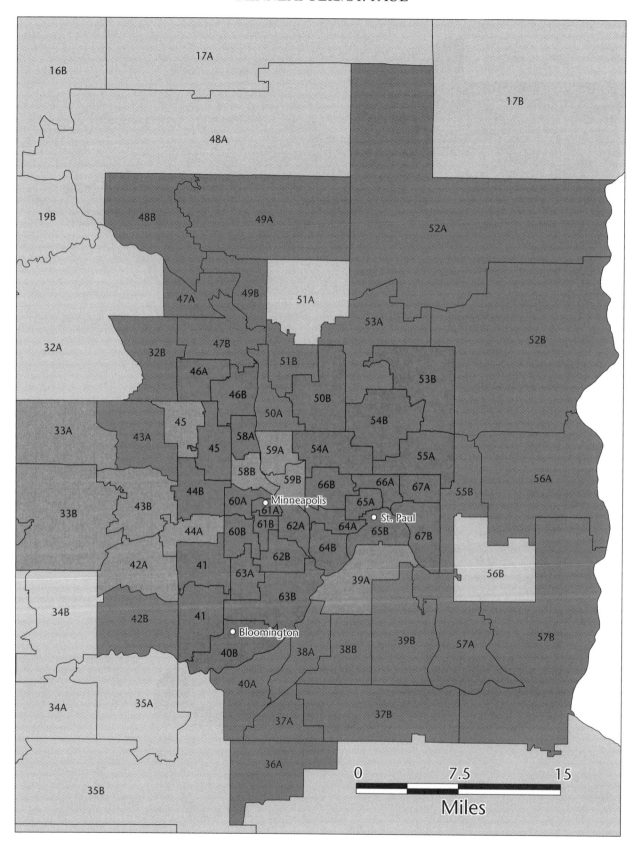

Population Growth ■ -7% to -1%   ■ -1% to 3%   ■ 3% to 14%   □ 14% to 43%

Minnesota State House Districts—Election and Demographic Data

House Districts	General Election Results Party, Percent of Vote							Population			Avg. HH Income ($)	Pop 25+ Some College + (%)	Pop 25+ 4-Yr Degree + (%)	Below Poverty Line (%)	2006 White (Non-Hisp) (%)	African American (%)	American Indians, Alaska Natives (%)	Asians, Hawaiians, Pacific Islanders (%)	Hispanic Origin (%)
Minnesota	2000	2001	2002	2003	2004	2005	2006	2000	2006	% Change									
1A	R, 52		R, 66		R, 62		D, 54	36,823	35,943	-2	46,326	31.4	10.1	16.7	95.0	0.3	0.8	1.5	1.2
1B	R, 54		D, 55		D, 53		D, 57	37,830	36,793	-3	49,986	35.0	12.3	16.6	89.4	0.5	1.1	0.4	4.8
2A	D, 59		D, 54		D, 59		D, 69	36,910	37,626	2	43,361	29.9	9.0	20.7	84.8	0.3	9.0	0.5	1.8
2B	D, 58		R, 51		D, 51		D, 54	36,607	37,487	2	46,407	31.2	11.2	21.8	81.7	0.4	16.6	0.4	1.1
3A	D, 100		D, 99		D, 77		D, 60	36,652	35,722	-3	47,386	34.2	10.9	17.7	95.9	0.3	1.3	0.3	0.8
3B	D, 60		D, 53		D, 55		D, 97	36,687	37,758	3	48,536	36.1	12.4	16.4	95.8	0.4	1.4	0.6	0.6
4A	R, 59		R, 56		D, 52		D, 65	36,964	40,288	9	44,193	35.3	14.8	21.3	79.2	0.6	17.3	1.0	1.4
4B	R, 52		R, 58		R, 57		R, 52	36,544	39,951	9	51,223	36.6	13.6	16.2	95.8	0.4	1.5	0.4	0.8
5A	D, 77		D, 80		D, 76		D, 80	36,805	35,520	-3	44,933	39.5	12.1	17.3	96.1	0.4	1.1	0.5	0.6
5B	D, 65		D, 75		D, 73		D, 76	36,609	35,299	-4	50,201	37.7	11.6	16.7	96.1	0.5	0.8	0.4	0.8
6A	D, 100		D, 56		D, 69		D, 97	36,664	36,670	0	51,451	40.3	16.2	14.4	94.5	0.4	2.6	0.4	0.7
6B	D, 70		D, 72		D, 71		D, 72	38,118	39,103	3	58,712	38.3	15.2	11.1	94.5	1.3	0.9	1.0	0.9
7A	D, 75		D, 62		D, 66		D, 69	36,210	35,032	-3	60,708	46.3	27.1	12.9	92.3	1.4	1.2	2.0	1.0
7B	D, 73		D, 55		D, 77		D, 97	36,328	35,051	-4	38,694	34.6	12.0	22.8	88.5	2.7	3.3	1.2	1.2
8A	D, 70		D, 67		D, 68		D, 68	36,756	39,992	9	49,471	30.6	9.3	16.7	89.9	1.4	4.9	0.5	1.1
8B	D, 59		R, 50		R, 50		D, 52	37,084	41,144	11	50,904	27.7	7.8	15.3	94.1	1.1	1.3	0.6	1.6
9A	R, 72		R, 60		R, 55		R, 59	35,945	37,097	3	52,284	38.5	17.6	16.9	88.5	1.0	1.5	1.7	3.7
9B	D, 54		D, 68		D, 71		D, 77	38,362	40,007	4	51,001	38.4	14.1	16.3	93.8	0.4	1.3	0.5	1.9
10A	R, 100		R, 60		R, 60		R, 56	36,705	37,014	1	50,906	35.3	13.2	17.4	93.6	0.6	0.5	0.9	2.2
10B	R, 100		R, 98		R, 64		R, 61	36,656	36,948	1	44,993	29.5	9.3	21.5	96.9	0.4	0.4	0.4	0.9
11A	R, 72		R, 67		R, 59		R, 63	36,272	37,009	2	47,888	36.0	12.5	17.5	96.4	0.6	0.3	0.7	0.9
11B	D, 67		D, 56		D, 62		D, 61	37,496	38,769	3	49,406	30.1	8.9	18.3	94.7	0.2	0.3	0.5	2.8
12A	R, 55		R, 57		R, 50		D, 55	36,750	40,073	9	50,653	36.7	12.9	15.6	95.7	0.5	0.7	0.5	1.1
12B	D, 70		R, 57		R, 50		D, 52	36,665	38,618	5	49,796	29.5	9.4	18.2	97.0	0.4	0.4	0.5	0.8
13A	R, 60		R, 55		R, 67		R, 69	36,933	38,605	5	51,681	30.1	9.7	16.9	96.3	0.3	0.1	0.3	2.0
13B	D, 67		D, 57		D, 53		D, 54	36,890	36,632	-1	54,541	35.9	12.8	14.2	82.5	0.8	0.3	0.6	10.2
14A	R, 100		R, 48		R, 62		R, 54	38,516	44,983	17	62,320	37.8	14.8	9.6	95.9	0.5	0.2	1.1	1.3
14B	R, 74		R, 67		D, 52		D, 57	36,926	40,213	9	59,539	31.4	12.2	11.0	95.7	0.5	0.1	0.9	1.7
15A	D, 57		R, 57		R, 63		R, 55	36,409	39,548	9	64,948	40.1	17.7	10.2	89.4	2.1	0.4	3.9	2.3
15B	D, 58		D, 56		D, 64		D, 65	36,017	38,622	7	50,485	36.1	16.3	15.3	87.1	3.7	0.7	4.3	1.9
16A	D, 52		R, 57		R, 54		R, 51	36,590	43,094	18	53,598	28.3	8.2	15.6	94.4	0.5	2.5	0.4	1.1
16B	R, 62		R, 58		R, 62		R, 58	38,168	50,814	33	70,992	35.5	10.6	5.3	95.8	0.3	0.3	0.5	1.7
17A	R, 58		R, 53		R, 53		R, 51	37,243	45,171	21	64,164	32.6	9.8	8.5	95.8	0.4	0.5	0.6	1.4
17B	D, 46		R, 55		R, 52		D, 50	36,896	46,654	26	66,685	34.2	10.3	8.6	94.6	0.8	0.4	1.1	1.8
18A	R, 45		R, 62		R, 57		R, 57	36,462	38,317	5	58,172	32.5	10.6	10.4	91.3	0.3	0.2	0.8	4.8
18B	D, 49		R, 53		R, 56		R, 53	36,321	40,363	11	56,906	29.3	9.8	13.8	94.5	0.4	0.2	0.5	2.5
19A	R, 63		R, 61		R, 58		R, 58	35,324	45,343	28	66,523	33.5	12.3	8.2	95.3	0.5	0.3	0.8	1.8
19B	R, 57		R, 46		R, 60		R, 61	37,383	47,675	28	76,409	34.0	11.5	6.1	95.6	0.5	0.2	0.7	1.8
20A	R, 80		D, 53		D, 55		D, 57	36,880	34,428	-7	44,040	31.9	10.2	17.8	94.2	1.3	0.4	1.1	1.4
20B	R, 100		D, 51		D, 53		D, 57	37,191	35,292	-5	48,179	30.7	9.5	14.0	90.5	0.2	1.0	0.4	5.0
21A	R, 70		R, 69		R, 61		R, 61	37,136	35,204	-5	52,289	32.9	13.2	14.2	89.6	1.4	1.2	1.8	3.3
21B	R, 65		R, 60		R, 60		R, 55	35,979	34,736	-3	51,953	29.8	11.3	14.2	92.3	0.2	0.2	0.7	4.0
22A	D, 54		R, 54		R, 57		R, 56	36,754	35,173	-4	46,148	29.7	9.3	15.9	95.1	0.4	0.5	0.8	1.7
22B	R, 70		R, 58		R, 51		R, 52	36,962	36,242	-2	47,035	30.7	10.6	15.9	79.8	0.9	0.2	4.3	9.8
23A	R, 66		R, 52		D, 50		D, 52	37,657	38,040	1	59,888	37.7	16.8	11.1	91.3	1.0	0.3	1.5	3.7
23B	R, 57		D, 58		D, 56		D, 61	37,188	38,445	3	52,292	41.9	20.7	14.5	89.3	2.2	0.3	3.6	2.3
24A	D, 64		R, 72		R, 63		R, 66	37,075	35,087	-5	47,588	30.7	10.9	15.1	88.3	0.4	0.1	0.7	6.3
24B	D, 51		R, 52		R, 60		R, 54	36,479	36,416	0	52,254	34.7	11.7	12.2	95.6	0.5	0.2	0.5	2.0
25A	R, 51		R, 46		R, 61		R, 57	36,213	40,878	13	58,730	30.8	11.3	12.2	92.4	0.3	0.2	0.5	3.8
25B	R, 65		R, 50		R, 51		D, 50	35,811	42,469	19	69,338	34.5	16.8	9.1	92.5	0.7	0.3	1.7	3.0

(continued)

Note: D=Democrat, R=Republican, R/D=Republican/Democrat (cross-filed), D/R=Democrat/Republican (cross-filed), I=Independent, C=Constitution, O=Other, GI=Green Independent, P=Progressive, P/D=Progressive/Democrat, P/D/R=Progressive/Democrat/Republican, HH=Households

Minnesota State House Districts—Election and Demographic Data (cont.)

House Districts	General Election Results Party, Percent of Vote							Population			Avg. HH Income	Pop 25+ Some College +	Pop 25+ 4-Yr Degree +	Below Poverty Line	2006 White (Non-Hisp)	African American	American Indians, Alaska Natives	Asians, Hawaiians, Pacific Islanders	Hispanic Origin
Minnesota	2000	2001	2002	2003	2004	2005	2006	2000	2006	% Change	($)	(%)	(%)	(%)	(%)	(%)	(%)	(%)	(%)
26A	R, 100		R, 69		R, 54		R, 56	36,622	38,028	4	58,598	34.6	14.2	10.1	88.4	2.6	0.3	1.3	4.4
26B	D, 67		R, 52		D, 49		D, 52	36,621	39,189	7	58,132	32.5	10.5	11.4	84.2	2.1	0.4	1.7	8.5
27A	R, 64		R, 57		R, 56		D, 51	36,564	35,489	-3	49,558	31.4	9.3	13.8	89.4	0.4	0.2	0.8	5.6
27B	D, 52		R, 51		D, 52		D, 56	37,138	37,483	1	54,126	33.1	10.7	13.9	86.4	0.8	0.2	2.1	7.3
28A	R, 54		R, 57		R, 54		D, 51	36,780	38,422	4	60,991	34.8	13.5	11.2	93.8	1.1	1.0	1.0	1.9
28B	R, 100		R, 66		R, 64		R, 61	34,205	35,367	3	57,971	35.3	12.9	11.3	95.3	0.5	0.2	1.2	1.4
29A	R, 66		R, 53		R, 60		R, 58	37,671	43,702	16	69,240	39.4	17.1	8.5	91.3	1.1	0.2	2.8	2.4
29B	R, 64		R, 68		R, 51		D, 50	35,483	38,970	10	70,083	49.5	27.6	7.2	83.9	3.5	0.2	7.4	2.5
30A	R, 65		R, 40		D, 51		D, 53	37,060	38,574	4	66,661	44.3	23.2	12.5	77.3	6.1	0.3	7.9	5.3
30B	R, 52		R, 71		D, 51		D, 52	38,511	42,216	10	72,426	40.7	18.0	7.2	92.1	1.5	0.1	2.6	1.9
31A	R, 100		D, 65		D, 66		D, 70	38,173	36,498	-4	50,412	37.0	16.7	15.2	93.7	1.2	0.2	2.7	0.9
31B	R, 59		R, 53		R, 52		D, 50	36,456	36,557	0	50,296	34.0	12.8	14.4	97.5	0.4	0.1	0.5	0.8
32A	D, 65		R, 61		R, 54		R, 65	37,504	46,649	24	105,010	47.7	27.1	2.6	88.6	3.6	0.3	3.4	1.7
32B	R, 53		R, 98		R, 53		R, 49	34,555	35,882	4	86,563	49.7	26.1	2.0	87.2	3.9	0.4	4.2	1.8
33A	R, 58		R, 62		R, 64		R, 97	36,147	37,050	2	107,316	52.1	30.7	4.7	88.1	3.7	0.3	3.7	1.8
33B	R, 60		R, 98		R, 62		R, 55	37,319	37,254	0	145,254	59.0	39.8	4.7	88.9	3.5	0.3	3.0	1.9
34A	R, 100		R, 68		R, 69		R, 66	39,163	49,697	27	80,455	36.1	16.1	7.5	92.5	0.5	0.2	1.3	3.4
34B	R, 63		R, 60		R, 60		R, 61	36,256	44,658	23	102,369	46.5	27.2	5.3	87.8	1.3	0.2	3.3	5.1
35A	R, 100		R, 53		R, 59		R, 54	34,235	48,752	42	85,923	40.9	18.9	5.3	87.8	1.5	1.2	2.6	4.0
35B	R, 58		R, 66		R, 63		R, 62	36,617	50,526	38	96,059	43.0	21.7	3.9	89.9	1.2	0.3	4.1	2.5
36A	R, 62		R, 70		R, 62		R, 61	37,736	41,539	10	98,575	46.8	25.9	2.3	90.0	1.8	0.3	3.1	2.6
36B	R, 100		R, 59		R, 62		R, 56	38,101	45,220	19	77,547	39.7	17.7	5.5	91.7	0.8	0.3	1.6	3.4
37A	R, 68		R, 61		R, 51		D, 51	36,988	41,017	11	88,164	50.6	29.1	4.3	86.6	3.1	0.3	4.5	2.6
37B	R, 63		R, 67		R, 65		R, 97	37,327	40,474	8	88,766	48.1	27.6	3.9	87.1	2.5	0.3	4.0	3.3
38A	R, 54		R, 54		R, 52		D, 50	37,194	39,703	7	79,676	52.1	30.8	4.3	79.8	5.2	0.2	8.0	3.5
38B	R, 66		R, 53		R, 54		R, 50	36,173	37,988	5	98,012	52.4	35.3	3.4	84.3	4.0	0.2	5.9	3.1
39A	D, 68		D, 54		D, 55		D, 65	35,342	36,389	3	77,423	49.9	29.0	8.7	79.6	2.7	0.4	2.8	9.7
39B	D, 62		D, 65		D, 68		D, 72	36,611	39,464	8	78,063	45.0	24.0	5.4	84.9	2.6	0.4	2.6	6.2
40A	D, 57		R, 59		R, 50		D, 53	38,069	40,793	7	71,983	47.8	26.5	7.3	79.2	5.6	0.4	6.2	4.7
40B	D, 67		D, 59		D, 66		D, 68	36,202	35,590	-2	70,209	53.6	27.8	6.1	81.4	5.9	0.4	6.3	3.0
41A	R, 68		R, 65		R, 57		R, 60	37,669	36,737	-2	118,640	63.5	45.8	5.7	87.6	3.9	0.3	4.0	1.9
41B	R, 65		R, 64		R, 53		R, 53	35,442	34,232	-3	106,349	61.6	40.5	4.9	82.8	4.8	0.3	7.0	2.5
42A	R, 61		R, 52		D, 51		D, 55	36,918	36,797	0	105,340	58.0	37.9	4.5	85.3	4.5	0.3	5.0	2.3
42B	R, 70		R, 72		R, 60		R, 64	37,205	40,418	9	117,684	56.6	39.7	3.7	81.6	5.3	0.3	7.2	2.8
43A	R, 63		R, 62		R, 56		R, 53	38,318	39,849	4	109,454	56.8	37.3	3.5	82.5	5.7	0.4	6.1	2.6
43B	R, 100		R, 60		R, 52		D, 54	37,746	37,739	0	108,247	58.8	38.4	4.5	85.1	5.4	0.4	4.2	2.3
44A	D, 56		R, 49		D, 56		D, 70	36,403	37,290	2	62,741	54.7	32.3	7.8	76.2	7.6	0.5	6.0	6.0
44B	R, 59		D, 55		D, 67		D, 69	36,363	35,273	-3	73,546	57.5	35.8	6.3	80.6	7.0	0.5	5.1	3.9
45A	R, 100		R, 54		D, 50		D, 57	35,540	35,554	0	64,173	50.0	26.8	7.6	79.0	7.6	0.5	5.1	4.4
45B	R, 61		D, 58		D, 56		D, 65	38,749	37,799	-2	66,475	50.3	26.2	6.1	79.6	8.4	0.6	4.6	3.4
46A	D, 48		D, 55		D, 62		D, 64	35,857	34,731	-3	61,983	41.9	17.8	9.4	57.9	22.1	0.6	9.8	6.0
46B	D, 61		D, 52		D, 63		D, 66	38,310	36,617	-4	57,055	41.5	16.8	8.6	63.8	16.2	0.7	11.7	4.0
47A	D, 56		R, 61		D, 52		D, 54	35,126	36,511	4	76,466	41.8	19.2	4.2	87.7	4.2	0.5	3.0	2.1
47B	D, 56		R, 52		D, 51		D, 56	38,979	42,148	8	77,744	46.0	23.1	5.1	79.8	6.4	0.5	7.9	2.4
48A	R, 58		R, 59		R, 58		R, 56	36,667	43,553	19	75,845	36.9	14.2	6.2	94.8	0.6	0.4	0.9	1.7
48B	D, 52		R, 56		R, 63		R, 61	36,125	38,545	7	72,321	39.6	17.3	7.2	91.5	1.9	0.6	1.4	2.4
49A	R, 55		R, 64		R, 63		R, 60	38,609	42,491	10	96,319	41.6	20.3	3.0	94.0	0.8	0.3	1.5	1.7
49B	D, 55		R, 58		R, 56		R, 54	36,434	40,050	10	70,770	40.2	18.5	4.9	90.4	2.5	0.6	2.1	2.1
50A	R, 57		D, 60		D, 64		D, 62	36,821	39,044	6	55,735	40.0	20.0	9.6	80.2	5.1	1.1	4.7	4.7
50B	R, 62		R, 55		R, 52		D, 54	38,610	37,408	-3	81,016	49.8	30.7	6.4	82.1	4.7	0.5	7.2	2.2

(continued)

Note: D=Democrat, R=Republican, R/D=Republican/Democrat (cross-filed), D/R=Democrat/Republican (cross-filed), I=Independent, C=Constitution, O=Other, GI=Green Independent, P=Progressive, P/D=Progressive/Democrat, P/D/R=Progressive/Democrat/Republican, HH=Households

Minnesota State House Districts—Election and Demographic Data (cont.)

House Districts	General Election Results Party, Percent of Vote							Population			Avg. HH Income ($)	Pop 25+ Some College + (%)	Pop 25+ 4-Yr Degree + (%)	Below Poverty Line (%)	2006 White (Non-Hisp) (%)	African American (%)	American Indians, Alaska Natives (%)	Asians, Hawaiians, Pacific Islanders (%)	Hispanic Origin (%)
Minnesota	2000	2001	2002	2003	2004	2005	2006	2000	2006	% Change									
51A	R, 50		R, 55		R, 55		D, 53	36,890	42,851	16	73,116	38.4	17.4	4.8	88.5	1.6	0.6	3.5	2.9
51B	R, 60		D, 61		D, 55		D, 60	36,759	39,026	6	63,889	39.8	19.5	6.8	84.7	3.2	0.6	4.8	3.4
52A	D, 53		R, 61		R, 59		R, 55	35,537	38,638	9	80,445	38.8	16.4	5.2	94.1	1.1	0.4	1.0	1.7
52B	D, 51		R, 59		R, 52		R, 52	38,308	42,746	12	100,845	48.0	26.4	5.0	94.6	0.8	0.2	1.5	1.4
53A	R, 57		R, 55		R, 54		D, 50	35,209	36,739	4	102,384	48.9	31.5	3.8	89.6	1.9	0.3	4.1	1.9
53B	R, 49		R, 55		R, 58		R, 54	36,338	35,620	-2	81,712	49.2	27.0	5.9	86.7	3.4	0.4	4.9	2.0
54A	D, 58		D, 53		D, 59		D, 65	36,374	34,680	-5	67,542	54.4	34.1	7.5	80.3	5.3	0.4	8.3	2.6
54B	D, 65		R, 51		D, 52		D, 54	37,104	36,150	-3	77,756	49.8	28.6	5.9	81.3	4.6	0.4	8.4	2.1
55A	R, 69		D, 59		D, 55		D, 67	37,789	36,793	-3	63,096	41.9	19.3	8.7	80.3	5.5	0.5	7.5	2.9
55B	D, 59		D, 59		D, 56		D, 66	36,270	37,542	4	71,204	42.0	17.8	6.3	84.9	3.9	0.4	4.2	3.7
56A	R, 58		R, 52		R, 53		D, 51	37,935	42,451	12	96,097	47.6	25.8	4.6	88.5	3.4	0.5	3.2	2.3
56B	R, 51		R, 59		R, 55		D, 51	35,454	40,718	15	99,465	51.5	30.5	2.3	84.8	3.2	0.2	6.4	3.1
57A	D, 50		D, 57		D, 68		D, 61	37,301	38,698	4	63,924	35.7	12.8	7.5	86.0	3.0	0.5	1.7	5.6
57B	D, 64		R, 54		R, 59		R, 55	35,801	39,885	11	79,832	42.2	19.4	5.5	92.9	1.2	0.3	1.5	2.2
58A	D, 71		D, 68		D, 80		D, 76	36,846	35,358	-4	50,240	34.9	15.0	15.4	42.1	33.1	1.2	13.9	5.9
58B	D, 87		D, 67		D, 84		D, 73	36,180	36,842	2	49,222	34.5	17.3	23.7	23.7	50.1	1.2	15.6	7.6
59A	D, 74		D, 96		D, 61		D, 82	36,753	36,655	0	48,889	44.7	23.5	14.2	67.0	9.3	1.7	5.3	11.2
59B	D, 63		D, 95		D, 59		D, 73	36,781	36,635	0	42,139	37.4	25.7	26.6	61.6	15.2	0.8	12.4	5.9
60A	D, 70		D, 76		D, 74		D, 81	36,811	36,132	-2	75,056	63.1	44.1	13.1	71.7	12.6	0.8	4.5	6.4
60B	D, 71		D, 98		D, 79		D, 82	37,056	35,478	-4	88,596	66.7	49.4	4.7	82.5	6.0	0.5	4.0	3.4
61A	D, 78		D, 85		D, 88		D, 88	36,599	35,733	-2	34,810	38.1	20.4	24.6	31.4	27.0	4.2	7.0	29.3
61B	D, 80		D, 80		D, 87		D, 89	35,968	34,574	-4	49,742	40.6	22.6	17.1	29.8	32.0	1.8	6.8	30.0
62A	D, 69		D, 73		D, 75		D, 84	37,871	36,230	-4	57,037	49.6	28.6	10.2	63.7	11.8	2.7	4.5	11.5
62B	D, 62		D, 70		D, 75		D, 80	36,134	34,604	-4	67,962	54.9	34.2	5.8	73.3	10.2	1.0	4.3	6.9
63A	D, 68		D, 57		D, 66		D, 75	35,943	35,322	-2	70,187	55.8	33.5	7.2	75.2	8.6	0.5	5.3	6.8
63B	D, 63		D, 58		D, 62		D, 58	37,994	36,737	-3	59,666	46.0	21.9	8.1	68.6	9.5	0.7	8.5	8.6
64A	D, 75		D, 76		D, 77		D, 66	37,486	35,192	-6	71,501	51.5	36.9	10.1	75.6	9.8	0.5	6.2	3.7
64B	D, 63		D, 69		D, 70		D, 71	36,128	34,861	-4	79,706	57.7	41.5	9.3	78.3	6.1	0.4	6.3	5.1
65A	D, 64		D, 79		D, 76		D, 80	37,806	35,463	-6	44,389	29.3	13.2	22.0	30.3	28.2	1.0	28.7	9.2
65B	D, 64		D, 73		D, 70		D, 78	37,918	36,837	-3	48,535	42.6	23.0	18.0	50.2	12.3	1.1	9.3	21.6
66A	D, 75		D, 72		D, 75		D, 77	36,539	34,808	-5	46,037	31.5	15.3	18.5	42.8	15.8	0.9	26.4	11.3
66B	D, 75		D, 72		D, 75		D, 78	34,856	33,952	-3	61,534	50.9	34.8	11.9	72.8	9.0	0.6	9.7	4.2
67A	D, 77		D, 69		D, 73		D, 78	37,141	35,108	-5	46,773	32.6	13.2	14.5	52.1	10.7	0.9	20.7	11.5
67B	D, 66		D, 67		D, 59		D, 72	35,839	34,061	-5	55,407	34.5	15.7	14.1	53.4	14.9	1.0	16.4	9.9

Note: D=Democrat, R=Republican, R/D=Republican/Democrat (cross-filed), D/R=Democrat/Republican (cross-filed), I=Independent, C=Constitution, O=Other, GI=Green Independent, P=Progressive, P/D=Progressive/Democrat, P/D/R=Progressive/Democrat/Republican, HH=Households

MISSISSIPPI

Perhaps no part of Mississippi better exemplifies the progress the state has made in the past thirty years, as well as the limits of that progress, as the town of Tunica. Less than two decades ago it was a rundown Delta crossroads thirty-five miles south of Memphis, surrounded by cotton fields and catfish farms. In 1991 the state approved riverboat gambling here. Just a year later, 1.7 million people visited and spent $140 million. Today, the riverbank is lined with nine casinos and scores of hotels, conference centers, driving ranges, and restaurants that employ more than 15,000 people. Tunica is the fifth-largest casino market in the country, with more square footage than Atlantic City's.

As Atlantic City has demonstrated, gambling will not necessarily lift a place out of poverty, but it has done a good job in Mississippi. But Mississippi may be forgiven for embracing economic development wherever it can find it. At the other end of the state, along the Gulf Coast, casinos have reopened and even expanded after the destruction of Hurricane Katrina. Here the problem is a labor shortage caused by soaring real estate prices that have made it hard to find workers for places such as the Oreck vacuum cleaner plant in Long Beach and the Northrop Grumman shipyard in Pascagoula.

Notwithstanding the casino glitz, Mississippi remains one of the nation's poorest and worst-educated states. Like the rest of the South, it has been growing during the past two decades, but there are really two Souths. States in the eastern South—Virginia, the Carolinas, Georgia, and Florida—have been growing rapidly, being annexed, to a large extent, into the wealthy economy of the eastern seaboard. States in the western South—Alabama, Mississippi, Louisiana, and Arkansas—never developed major cities (with the exception of New Orleans, which was already there) or (with the exception of Birmingham) major industry. So Mississippi's growth rate, which was a notch below the national average in the 1990s, has been less than half of it in this decade.

Mississippi has only one large city, Jackson, but its fastest-growing area is the suburbs of a city in another state—Memphis, Tennessee—which has been called the capital of the Mississippi Delta. This is another manifestation of the metropolitan doughnut phenomenon seen around the country, in which Memphis residents move further and further out of town into new suburbs, such as Hernando, Olive Branch, and Holly Springs. The areas that are losing population fastest are the poor Delta districts north of Vicksburg but too far from Memphis. The Gulf Coast is doing well, much better than areas not far away in Louisiana. Population in the 93rd house district, which encompasses almost the entire coast, has grown by 9 percent since 2000.

The wealthiest housing district in the state is the 64th, encompassing the suburbs northeast of Jackson along the Ross Barnett Reservoir, where average household income is $88,000 a year. The poorest district, the 70th, is in downtown Jackson, about three miles away, where average household income is $32,000. As for Tunica County, prosperity clings to the shoreline by its fingernails. The 25th house district, along the river where all the casinos are located, has grown by 19 percent and household income is 50 percent above the state average. But the 9th district, just inland, has lost population and is one of the dozen poorest districts in the state.

Mississippi has the highest percentage of black residents of any state in the country (36 percent) and only Hawaii has a lower percentage of whites. The districts with the greatest concentrations of African Americans are along the Delta, where blacks often make up more than three-quarters of the population. Underscoring the progress that has been made during the past two generations, Mississippi has more elected black officials than any other state.

Although Mississippi has the second-smallest percentage of college graduates (leading only West Virginia), that is in line with other states in the cotton South. It is worth tweaking Yankee notions of superiority, though, to observe that the rate of college graduation in the worst Mississippi district (the 40th, where it is 6 percent) is much better than in dozens of northern inner-city districts.

Mississippi began severing its allegiance to the national Democratic Party in 1964, though it had given notice as early as 1948, when Gov. Fielding Wright served as Strom Thurmond's running mate on the Dixiecrat ticket. Today, it has a Republican governor and two Republican U.S. senators and is one of the party's most reliable states in presidential elections. The latest round of congressional redistricting was a fiasco that went up to the U.S. Supreme Court before a lower court plan was imposed that splits the four-member delegation evenly between the parties.

The legislature has been a different story. Republicans have made some gains in the Mississippi house of representatives, but the Democrats still have an almost thirty-seat majority. The state senate, though, switched hands for the first time in 2007 amid charges of betrayal. Although Democrats held a 34–18 majority at the beginning of the decade, Republicans picked up seats and trailed only 27–23 going into 2006. One Democrat died and was replaced by a Republican in a special election. Then, in early January, a Democratic state senator announced that he was switching parties (his younger brother still serves in the state house as a Democrat). This put the senate at a 26–26 tie. Because the Republican lieutenant governor breaks all ties, the GOP gained control of the chamber for the first time since Reconstruction. A few weeks later, another Democratic senator, a forty-year veteran, switched parties as well, giving the GOP an outright majority of 27–25.

MISSISSIPPI
State Senate Districts

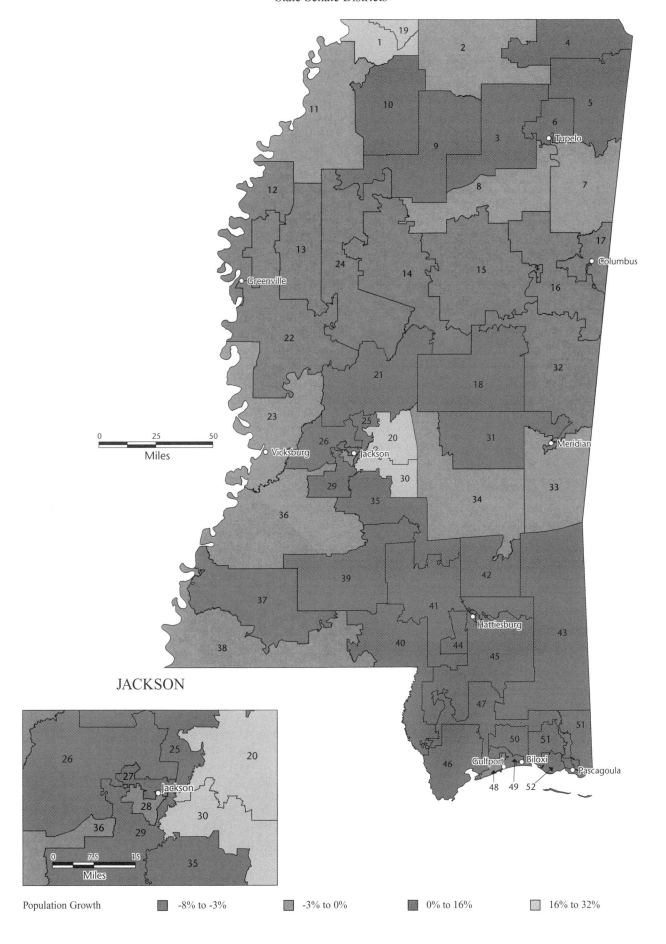

JACKSON

Population Growth ▨ -8% to -3% ▨ -3% to 0% ▨ 0% to 16% ▨ 16% to 32%

Mississippi State Senate Districts—Election and Demographic Data

Senate Districts	General Election Results Party, Percent of Vote							Population			Avg. HH Income	Pop 25+		Below Poverty Line	2006 White (Non-Hisp)	African American	American Indians, Alaska Natives	Asians, Hawaiians, Pacific Islanders	Hispanic Origin
Miss.	2000	2001	2002	2003	2004	2005	2006	2000	2006	% Change	($)	Some College + (%)	4-Yr Degree + (%)	(%)	(%)	(%)	(%)	(%)	(%)
1				D, 83				52,085	68,350	31	59,913	29.8	8.4	11.8	72.4	16.0	0.6	0.3	4.5
2				D, 75				53,135	53,047	0	42,058	20.5	7.0	27.5	54.4	43.6	0.1	0.0	1.6
3				D, 61				55,075	57,537	4	44,739	24.0	9.4	22.5	78.9	17.1	0.1	0.1	3.1
4				R, 52				53,549	54,255	1	40,493	23.7	8.6	25.5	83.3	13.1	0.1	0.1	2.5
5				D, 57				54,949	55,240	1	40,798	24.0	7.4	24.9	87.1	10.5	0.1	0.1	1.4
6				R, 69				52,650	55,248	5	57,310	34.9	15.5	16.0	79.7	17.9	0.0	0.3	1.3
7				D, 58				53,568	53,471	0	41,206	24.2	8.4	24.8	65.2	33.2	0.0	0.1	1.2
8				D, 100				55,332	54,387	-2	39,528	22.7	7.8	26.4	55.5	41.6	0.1	0.1	2.5
9				D, 60				57,206	58,914	3	43,356	33.2	17.9	27.4	64.8	32.7	0.1	0.5	1.4
10				D, 100				57,386	59,855	4	43,820	24.4	8.4	26.4	54.4	43.9	0.1	0.1	1.4
11				D, 71				52,307	50,900	-3	37,788	23.3	9.1	35.1	30.1	68.3	0.0	0.2	1.5
12				D, 100				55,597	51,402	-8	36,896	23.0	9.8	37.0	21.8	77.3	0.1	0.2	1.1
13				D, 69				53,912	49,679	-8	37,781	23.8	9.5	33.7	25.5	73.1	0.0	0.2	1.7
14				R, 65				57,521	54,628	-5	42,135	26.7	11.3	28.3	54.1	44.2	0.1	0.2	1.1
15				R, 56				55,016	53,052	-4	41,286	32.0	17.2	28.6	68.4	28.9	0.1	0.7	1.3
16				D, 100				51,975	49,711	-4	40,891	26.6	13.5	33.2	34.7	64.8	0.1	0.2	1.1
17				R, 49				52,375	50,219	-4	50,176	32.4	15.6	22.1	61.3	36.3	0.1	0.3	1.2
18				D, 54				57,404	60,563	6	40,994	23.4	8.4	27.9	61.5	32.5	3.3	0.1	2.1
19				R, 100				54,429	71,381	31	65,168	33.8	12.3	8.7	76.8	13.1	0.5	0.3	2.9
20				R, 100				53,635	62,218	16	75,673	48.9	29.5	8.2	83.3	14.4	0.2	0.4	1.4
21				D, 70				53,604	56,677	6	42,832	24.5	11.6	32.5	29.6	69.4	0.7	0.1	3.2
22				R, 56				52,684	48,485	-8	44,998	27.4	13.7	28.2	47.3	50.6	0.1	0.3	1.8
23				R, 57				53,646	52,411	-2	49,774	33.1	14.2	21.0	53.1	44.9	0.1	0.3	1.3
24				D, 100				51,859	49,528	-4	33,692	20.0	8.2	42.1	19.0	79.4	0.0	0.1	1.8
25				R, 100				55,673	60,979	10	89,006	55.7	39.6	8.4	67.5	23.1	0.6	0.9	1.5
26				D, 100				53,447	53,794	1	50,021	37.8	18.4	21.1	21.4	74.1	0.1	0.2	0.7
27				D, 100				54,880	52,478	-4	39,809	33.4	15.9	29.5	17.4	78.2	0.2	0.2	0.9
28				D, 100				54,902	53,845	-2	37,219	29.8	11.2	31.0	21.2	77.5	0.1	0.1	1.2
29				R, 50				57,605	58,676	2	55,330	42.4	20.1	14.0	46.6	42.4	0.2	0.4	0.9
30				R, 100				56,512	65,604	16	55,515	34.2	14.1	13.9	75.5	21.6	0.1	0.3	1.9
31				R, 62				56,034	56,516	1	47,620	28.7	10.5	24.0	61.5	33.5	1.9	0.2	3.2
32				D, 62				52,966	51,086	-4	35,768	23.3	8.5	36.5	34.2	64.4	0.8	0.1	1.3
33				R, 61				55,414	54,207	-2	44,319	30.3	10.7	22.1	64.3	32.8	0.6	0.2	1.0
34				D, 100				55,137	54,416	-1	39,487	22.1	6.8	28.2	54.5	42.6	0.1	0.1	2.7
35				R, 58				53,031	56,779	7	46,468	26.0	8.7	23.8	63.9	34.4	0.0	0.1	1.2
36				D, 83				53,079	52,439	-1	37,492	27.1	9.8	31.5	32.0	66.8	0.0	0.1	1.2
37				D, 100				56,920	54,472	-4	42,428	29.2	11.8	28.2	57.5	41.0	0.1	0.1	1.0
38				D, 100				52,928	51,934	-2	37,649	21.4	7.6	35.1	36.0	63.0	0.1	0.1	0.8
39				D, 100				54,893	55,482	1	41,205	27.0	8.9	27.5	65.4	33.0	0.1	0.1	1.1
40				R, 58				57,102	59,402	4	39,816	26.5	9.5	27.4	73.2	24.3	0.1	0.1	1.5
41				D, 71				55,817	56,145	1	38,395	25.4	9.2	30.5	57.0	41.5	0.1	0.1	1.2
42				R, 59				55,146	56,099	2	44,521	30.0	11.2	22.0	72.1	22.7	0.1	0.1	4.1
43				D, 53				57,109	59,167	4	41,141	21.0	6.6	27.4	72.7	25.1	0.1	0.1	1.6
44				R, 100				55,570	60,979	10	51,410	35.7	16.8	20.3	78.2	19.3	0.1	0.3	1.5
45				R, 61				54,302	57,088	5	44,903	35.3	17.0	24.9	73.4	23.7	0.1	0.4	1.6
46				D, 54				56,115	60,533	8	49,937	34.6	13.1	19.4	85.1	10.8	0.2	0.5	2.3
47				D, 65				53,084	54,281	2	46,168	29.0	9.1	23.3	57.5	39.2	0.1	0.2	2.3
48				D, 58				54,633	53,477	-2	49,920	32.4	12.1	20.2	57.7	37.6	0.1	0.8	2.5
49				R, 100				56,119	58,087	4	53,593	41.6	18.3	15.2	74.5	19.8	0.2	0.8	3.0
50				D, 100				53,991	55,659	3	46,412	32.0	9.9	17.9	73.1	19.0	0.2	2.0	3.3

(continued)

Note: D=Democrat, R=Republican, R/D=Republican/Democrat (cross-filed), D/R=Democrat/Republican (cross-filed), I=Independent, C=Constitution, O=Other, GI=Green Independent, P=Progressive, P/D=Progressive/Democrat, P/D/R=Progressive/Democrat/Republican, HH=Households

Mississippi State Senate Districts—Election and Demographic Data (cont.)

Senate Districts	General Election Results Party, Percent of Vote							Population			Avg. HH Income	Pop 25+		Below Poverty Line	2006 White (Non-Hisp)	African American	American Indians, Alaska Natives	Asians, Hawaiians, Pacific Islanders	Hispanic Origin
												Some College +	4-Yr Degree +						
Miss.	2000	2001	2002	2003	2004	2005	2006	2000	2006	% Change	($)	(%)	(%)	(%)	(%)	(%)	(%)	(%)	(%)
51				R, 65				56,738	58,966	4	51,231	29.8	9.4	14.8	81.9	14.2	0.1	0.8	1.9
52				R, 73				53,849	55,912	4	56,590	39.1	16.0	14.4	76.5	17.7	0.1	0.7	3.5

Note: D=Democrat, R=Republican, R/D=Republican/Democrat (cross-filed), D/R=Democrat/Republican (cross-filed), I=Independent, C=Constitution, O=Other, GI=Green Independent, P=Progressive, P/D=Progressive/Democrat, P/D/R=Progressive/Democrat/Republican, HH=Households

MISSISSIPPI
State House Districts

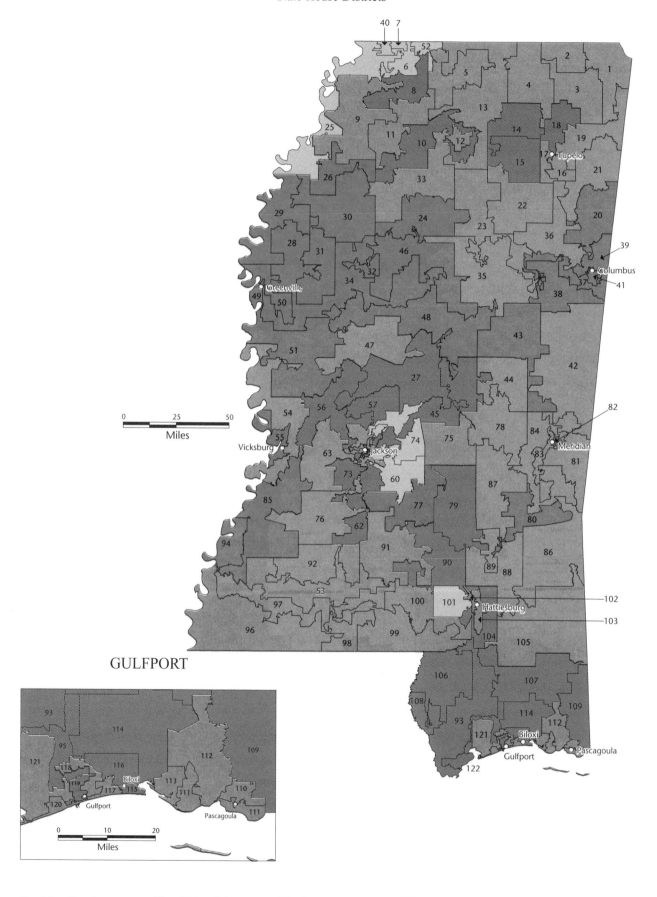

GULFPORT

Population Growth ■ -12% to -3% ■ -3% to 4% ■ 4% to 13% □ 13% to 39%

JACKSON

Population Growth   ▇ -12% to -3%   ▇ -3% to 4%   ▇ 4% to 13%   ▢ 13% to 39%

Mississippi State House Districts—Election and Demographic Data

House Districts	General Election Results Party, Percent of Vote							Population			Avg. HH Income	Pop 25+		Below Poverty Line	2006 White (Non-Hisp)	African American	American Indians, Alaska Natives	Asians, Hawaiians, Pacific Islanders	Hispanic Origin
Miss.	2000	2001	2002	2003	2004	2005	2006	2000	2006	% Change	($)	Some College + (%)	4-Yr Degree + (%)	(%)	(%)	(%)	(%)	(%)	(%)
1				D, 100				23,096	23,443	2	42,902	23.0	7.7	22.5	92.8	4.4	0.1	0.1	1.7
2				D, 66				23,145	23,014	-1	39,917	25.5	10.3	27.8	79.2	17.5	0.0	0.1	2.3
3				D, 65				23,615	23,414	-1	40,787	23.7	7.6	25.2	87.0	11.2	0.1	0.1	0.9
4				D, 84				22,383	22,538	1	38,664	21.1	7.0	25.5	78.0	17.2	0.1	0.1	3.6
5				D, 100				22,035	21,765	-1	41,088	20.0	7.8	30.4	31.8	67.0	0.1	0.1	1.2
6				R, 82				25,126	34,815	39	65,296	34.4	12.8	10.9	82.8	13.9	0.1	0.3	2.1
7				R, 83				22,930	28,011	22	61,183	32.3	10.8	9.8	85.0	9.8	0.1	0.4	3.3
8				R, 100				22,297	24,561	10	52,161	25.3	8.0	17.9	72.5	25.2	0.1	0.1	1.7
9				D, 100				21,823	21,408	-2	35,887	19.2	6.6	35.6	26.7	72.0	0.0	0.1	1.6
10				D, 73				23,413	24,661	5	46,398	31.0	13.5	24.4	70.2	27.8	0.1	0.2	1.4
11				D, 100				21,942	22,614	3	39,452	21.9	7.4	31.4	35.9	62.7	0.0	0.1	1.5
12				R, 53				21,323	21,833	2	47,002	40.7	26.8	28.6	70.4	25.7	0.1	1.2	1.6
13				D, 100				22,610	22,837	1	40,129	22.4	7.3	27.4	69.4	28.8	0.1	0.0	1.3
14				D, 100				23,388	24,366	4	46,106	24.8	10.2	21.2	77.4	18.6	0.0	0.1	3.2
15				D, 54				24,503	26,033	6	45,305	23.9	9.1	22.8	78.6	17.5	0.1	0.1	3.2
16				D, 100				22,120	22,526	2	45,255	27.8	9.7	21.1	60.3	36.7	0.1	0.3	1.9
17				R, 56				24,286	24,760	2	62,035	37.9	17.2	14.6	69.0	28.7	0.1	0.3	1.3
18				R, 53				23,752	25,262	6	48,409	30.3	13.2	21.9	72.4	25.8	0.1	0.2	0.9
19				D, 54				24,421	25,250	3	44,202	24.4	7.3	21.2	91.6	5.4	0.1	0.1	1.7
20				D, 56				25,512	24,201	-5	39,910	26.9	10.2	23.4	75.0	22.8	0.0	0.2	1.4
21				D, 100				23,445	23,623	1	42,736	24.5	8.1	24.2	78.6	19.9	0.0	0.1	0.9
22				D, 77				23,339	23,099	-1	38,994	19.5	6.7	27.6	56.9	38.5	0.1	0.1	4.5
23				R, 58				21,804	21,321	-2	40,769	27.4	12.1	28.2	60.6	36.9	0.1	0.2	1.8
24				D, 100				21,813	20,989	-4	38,751	25.0	9.8	27.6	55.1	43.7	0.1	0.1	0.7
25				D, 57				22,262	26,461	19	55,153	29.3	9.6	18.7	60.9	33.7	0.1	0.3	4.6
26				D, 100				21,655	19,939	-8	33,153	23.5	9.2	41.3	19.9	78.9	0.0	0.2	0.9
27				D, 100				21,307	23,046	8	38,430	21.4	8.5	32.3	31.1	67.7	0.1	0.1	1.2
28				D, 100				24,664	23,045	-7	43,197	28.9	15.3	28.1	49.2	48.8	0.1	0.3	1.6
29				D, 100				21,591	20,161	-7	35,815	26.7	11.7	35.5	22.9	75.5	0.0	0.2	1.4
30				D, 100				23,196	21,484	-7	34,838	19.4	7.5	38.7	21.9	76.8	0.0	0.2	1.3
31				D, 100				21,397	19,560	-9	40,389	24.8	9.7	32.5	23.7	74.9	0.0	0.1	2.2
32				D, 100				24,346	22,729	-7	34,163	21.2	9.2	40.6	21.0	77.1	0.0	0.3	1.7
33				D, 100				22,802	23,006	1	38,939	26.2	11.0	28.2	53.9	44.7	0.1	0.1	1.3
34				D, 100				24,381	23,142	-5	42,220	24.2	11.1	29.0	40.7	56.6	0.0	0.2	2.5
35				R, 60				22,573	22,334	-1	39,608	27.7	12.0	27.3	73.4	24.6	0.1	0.2	1.1
36				D, 78				21,909	22,302	2	42,029	22.4	8.8	30.6	34.0	64.8	0.0	0.1	1.1
37				R, 66				25,195	23,177	-8	47,907	37.5	22.5	27.1	70.4	27.0	0.0	0.9	1.0
38				D, 100				21,442	20,561	-4	43,066	32.7	20.1	33.7	36.3	61.4	0.0	0.9	0.9
39				D, 58				24,390	23,326	-4	56,380	36.2	18.4	16.2	73.2	24.5	0.1	0.3	1.1
40				R, 73				24,251	31,079	28	54,074	27.0	6.0	11.7	80.5	11.8	0.2	0.3	5.4
41				D, 100				23,548	21,996	-7	37,406	26.0	11.9	33.5	32.5	65.8	0.0	0.1	1.1
42				D, 66				22,792	22,345	-2	36,145	21.2	8.0	35.1	30.0	68.6	0.1	0.1	1.2
43				D, 74				22,424	21,640	-3	41,651	24.6	10.1	27.6	54.2	43.6	0.5	0.1	1.7
44				D, 53				22,514	23,091	3	43,729	25.4	8.7	26.2	66.5	26.3	9.9	0.1	1.7
45				D, 100				22,314	24,811	11	40,306	21.8	8.0	29.1	54.8	36.5	10.8	0.1	2.9
46				R, 74				23,965	22,667	-5	46,732	28.3	12.1	24.1	68.5	29.9	0.0	0.2	0.9
47				D, 100				22,785	22,111	-3	33,754	21.5	7.9	42.9	24.6	73.6	0.1	0.2	3.7
48				D, 100				23,266	22,323	-4	38,502	24.0	9.0	33.6	48.5	49.2	0.1	0.1	1.8
49				D, 100				23,254	20,569	-12	41,708	24.2	11.1	34.7	25.1	73.8	0.0	0.3	0.9
50				D, 100				24,379	22,781	-7	38,788	23.1	9.8	34.2	23.4	75.3	0.0	0.1	1.1

(continued)

Note: D=Democrat, R=Republican, R/D=Republican/Democrat (cross-filed), D/R=Democrat/Republican (cross-filed), I=Independent, C=Constitution, O=Other, GI=Green Independent, P=Progressive, P/D=Progressive/Democrat, P/D/R=Progressive/Democrat/Republican, HH=Households

Mississippi State House Districts—Election and Demographic Data (cont.)

House Districts	General Election Results Party, Percent of Vote							Population			Avg. HH Income ($)	Pop 25+ Some College + (%)	Pop 25+ 4-Yr Degree + (%)	Below Poverty Line (%)	White (Non-Hisp) (%)	African American (%)	American Indians, Alaska Natives (%)	Asians, Hawaiians, Pacific Islanders (%)	Hispanic Origin (%)
Miss.	2000	2001	2002	2003	2004	2005	2006	2000	2006	% Change									
51				D, 100				23,930	21,874	-9	33,929	20.6	7.6	37.6	26.2	71.9	0.1	0.1	4.0
52				R, 100				23,231	30,251	30	68,460	34.6	13.4	8.6	77.7	18.5	0.1	0.3	2.5
53				D, 57				21,760	21,655	0	37,817	24.4	7.4	30.0	56.0	42.8	0.1	0.1	0.8
54				R, 100				24,426	24,488	0	55,574	36.8	17.6	16.1	68.4	29.0	0.1	0.4	1.6
55				D, 100				24,425	22,817	-7	44,170	30.1	11.7	25.2	32.8	65.8	0.0	0.2	1.1
56				R, 79				27,128	28,739	6	66,840	40.7	23.3	16.4	73.7	24.6	0.0	0.3	0.9
57				D, 67				23,096	24,788	7	54,127	29.6	17.6	29.0	25.9	73.0	0.0	0.1	1.3
58				R, 100				22,983	26,161	14	74,893	53.2	38.0	5.2	85.7	11.7	0.1	0.8	1.0
59				R, 100				23,432	26,256	12	78,631	54.6	32.6	7.2	85.8	11.7	0.1	0.4	1.3
60				R, 85				23,206	27,412	18	57,569	33.0	13.0	14.3	74.1	23.5	0.1	0.2	1.6
61				R, 87				25,784	29,489	14	53,258	35.9	14.9	14.1	77.3	18.9	0.1	0.4	2.4
62				R, 87				26,078	28,625	10	48,478	28.8	9.2	19.4	77.9	19.9	0.0	0.2	1.3
63				D, 100				21,982	22,012	0	50,028	35.0	13.6	19.5	29.0	69.9	0.0	0.1	1.1
64				R, 100				25,236	26,375	5	88,624	60.3	41.6	8.8	74.2	22.2	0.0	0.8	2.1
65								23,451	23,411	0	43,655	40.2	21.0	22.1	22.1	76.5	0.0	0.4	0.9
66				D, 100				21,798	21,209	-3	61,599	47.7	28.8	19.5	40.0	57.9	0.1	0.5	1.0
67				D, 100				24,224	24,242	0	39,026	31.3	13.8	29.3	18.4	80.3	0.1	0.3	1.2
68				D, 70				20,381	19,954	-2	37,640	29.9	13.1	31.7	16.2	82.6	0.1	0.1	1.3
69				D, 100				22,357	21,098	-6	39,754	31.9	13.4	28.0	19.7	79.1	0.1	0.2	1.0
70				D, 100				23,011	21,674	-6	32,447	28.6	12.1	36.0	17.7	81.0	0.1	0.2	1.1
71				R, 69				24,084	24,995	4	43,692	31.7	11.1	18.9	48.8	49.4	0.1	0.2	1.1
72				D, 100				25,847	25,611	-1	59,932	39.0	20.3	18.5	24.9	74.0	0.0	0.2	0.8
73				R, 68				23,093	24,695	7	60,115	41.9	17.9	10.3	69.9	28.8	0.1	0.2	0.8
74				R, 100				24,553	29,503	20	79,384	43.4	25.2	10.8	80.0	17.8	0.0	0.4	1.4
75				D, 76				22,024	21,993	0	43,029	21.6	7.1	27.8	50.9	40.1	0.1	0.1	8.7
76				D, 75				22,254	22,534	1	37,559	26.3	8.6	31.9	30.9	67.8	0.0	0.1	1.3
77				R, 56				24,441	23,293	-5	40,203	23.2	8.4	27.0	69.1	28.6	0.1	0.1	1.6
78				D, 60				22,335	23,127	4	40,856	25.0	8.5	26.6	71.3	26.6	4.0	0.1	1.3
79				D, 55				22,853	24,385	7	42,356	23.5	7.6	26.3	61.6	36.9	0.1	0.1	1.3
80				D, 100				21,786	20,663	-5	36,944	21.7	6.8	33.1	27.7	68.7	0.2	0.1	4.4
81				R, 100				22,045	22,246	1	49,293	30.3	10.2	19.2	74.2	23.0	0.1	0.2	1.7
82				D, 100				21,462	19,925	-7	37,798	29.4	12.4	35.7	31.7	66.9	0.1	0.2	1.1
83				R, 66				21,805	21,210	-3	40,149	30.0	10.3	27.8	51.7	46.5	0.1	0.2	1.2
84				R, 100				25,361	25,314	0	49,711	33.6	12.1	20.6	78.8	19.3	0.1	0.2	1.1
85				D, 100				24,696	22,751	-8	38,113	27.7	11.5	33.0	29.0	70.0	0.0	0.1	0.8
86				D, 100				22,705	22,221	-2	39,135	21.2	7.1	30.5	64.2	34.9	0.0	0.1	0.7
87				D, 100				22,132	22,313	1	39,830	24.4	8.0	26.7	53.4	45.2	0.0	0.1	1.1
88				R, 53				23,488	24,105	3	42,090	26.2	7.7	22.5	85.7	11.2	0.1	0.1	2.1
89				D, 100				22,584	21,973	-3	47,687	34.0	14.4	20.5	71.7	22.0	0.1	0.2	5.0
90				D, 60				23,972	25,071	5	41,270	24.5	8.4	29.1	65.1	33.4	0.1	0.1	1.1
91				D, 100				22,509	21,998	-2	38,926	24.0	8.2	30.8	43.5	55.4	0.1	0.1	1.0
92				R, 72				24,512	25,109	2	42,751	29.5	10.4	24.9	76.6	22.2	0.1	0.1	0.7
93				D, 62				24,180	26,354	9	45,851	28.0	7.7	23.7	83.9	13.4	0.2	0.1	1.6
94				D, 100				21,613	20,378	-6	37,466	26.1	10.9	32.7	29.7	69.1	0.1	0.1	0.9
95				R, 60				24,419	26,147	7	56,272	38.2	15.2	14.1	79.0	16.0	0.2	0.6	2.7
96				D, 100				23,828	23,160	-3	36,986	20.9	8.3	36.2	36.6	62.4	0.0	0.0	1.0
97				R, 60				25,095	24,688	-2	46,354	30.7	12.0	26.0	70.4	28.1	0.1	0.1	0.9
98				D, 100				23,342	22,755	-3	34,798	22.5	7.5	33.8	35.4	63.4	0.1	0.1	0.9
99				D, 64				24,737	25,258	2	36,522	21.4	7.2	32.0	63.5	34.8	0.1	0.1	1.1
100				R, 52				24,488	24,480	0	38,715	26.9	10.2	28.8	68.0	30.3	0.1	0.1	1.0

(continued)

Note: D=Democrat, R=Republican, R/D=Republican/Democrat (cross-filed), D/R=Democrat/Republican (cross-filed), I=Independent, C=Constitution, O=Other, GI=Green Independent, P=Progressive, P/D=Progressive/Democrat, P/D/R=Progressive/Democrat/Republican, HH=Households

Mississippi State House Districts—Election and Demographic Data (cont.)

House Districts	General Election Results Party, Percent of Vote							Population			Avg. HH Income	Pop 25+		2006					
												Some College +	4-Yr Degree +	Below Poverty Line	White (Non-Hisp)	African American	American Indians, Alaska Natives	Asians, Hawaiians, Pacific Islanders	Hispanic Origin
Miss.	2000	2001	2002	2003	2004	2005	2006	2000	2006	% Change	($)	(%)	(%)	(%)	(%)	(%)	(%)	(%)	(%)
101				R, 100				24,176	27,937	16	64,122	40.7	22.7	15.7	83.5	13.9	0.0	0.4	1.4
102				R, 72				25,031	25,789	3	46,029	43.8	25.1	24.1	66.8	29.6	0.1	0.8	2.0
103				D, 100				24,090	24,808	3	35,042	27.5	11.2	35.2	33.3	65.1	0.1	0.1	1.4
104				R, 100				24,574	26,089	6	48,345	33.8	14.3	18.1	86.2	11.3	0.1	0.1	1.4
105				D, 100				23,550	23,651	0	38,710	20.8	6.1	29.9	67.2	30.6	0.1	0.1	1.6
106				R, 61				23,877	25,796	8	41,997	28.4	9.4	24.9	76.7	20.5	0.2	0.1	1.6
107				D, 58				24,903	27,479	10	43,780	24.0	7.0	24.1	81.8	15.7	0.1	0.1	1.6
108				R, 100				24,021	26,296	9	45,918	31.6	11.1	22.1	86.2	10.1	0.2	0.2	2.0
109				R, 100				24,110	26,157	8	48,782	23.5	6.4	17.0	87.3	10.0	0.1	0.2	1.6
110				D, 100				22,062	21,537	-2	44,611	27.7	8.6	26.1	29.5	67.6	0.1	0.2	3.2
111				R, 100				23,871	24,530	3	54,161	36.1	13.7	17.5	74.7	19.4	0.1	0.6	3.9
112				R, 100				24,181	24,977	3	50,870	33.0	10.3	15.9	72.7	22.5	0.2	0.4	3.0
113				R, 100				22,778	23,520	3	62,293	44.1	19.7	9.2	82.9	10.8	0.1	1.3	3.2
114				R, 100				23,124	24,211	5	52,721	32.8	11.5	13.4	86.4	9.0	0.2	1.3	1.9
115				D, 100				22,362	21,227	-5	42,804	31.7	11.1	23.2	60.4	29.5	0.2	3.2	4.4
116				R, 73				24,025	26,158	9	50,781	34.6	10.8	12.2	82.1	11.6	0.2	1.6	2.5
117				R, 100				24,504	24,951	2	51,003	42.6	17.7	15.5	70.8	21.4	0.1	1.2	4.0
118				R, 100				24,780	25,663	4	56,273	40.8	18.5	15.7	72.5	22.3	0.2	0.6	2.9
119				D, 100				20,001	18,871	-6	35,645	26.2	8.2	27.4	36.9	59.6	0.1	0.4	2.2
120				R, 100				24,021	23,696	-1	58,137	41.5	18.2	14.1	80.2	14.5	0.2	1.0	2.4
121				D, 68				24,118	24,864	3	53,258	30.6	10.7	19.1	69.7	26.0	0.2	0.8	2.0
122				D, 100				23,591	24,767	5	44,034	33.3	12.9	21.6	82.3	13.0	0.3	0.5	2.6

Note: D=Democrat, R=Republican, R/D=Republican/Democrat (cross-filed), D/R=Democrat/Republican (cross-filed), I=Independent, C=Constitution, O=Other, GI=Green Independent, P=Progressive, P/D=Progressive/Democrat, P/D/R=Progressive/Democrat/Republican, HH=Households

MISSOURI

St. Louis proclaims itself the "Gateway to the West"—from a time when the West began on the far bank of the Mississippi River)—but that of course depends on the direction from which one approaches it. No state borders more states than Missouri, so it is more accurately a gateway to many regions: across Interstate 70, it is indeed a gateway to the West (though Kansas City is a better one). Down the river, it is a gateway to the cotton South. Through Branson, it is a gateway to the Ozarks. Up the Missouri River, it is a gateway to the Rockies. Overland toward Chicago, it is a gateway to the Great Lakes. Across the Mississippi at the Cairo, Illinois, junction with the Ohio River, it is a gateway to the Appalachians. Finally, for Mormons, who believe that the Resurrection will occur near Independence—it is a gateway to heaven.

The geographic center of the country, Missouri is also its statistical center. The mean center of population—the place where an imaginary, flat map of the United States would balance if everyone in the country weighed the same—has been located here since 1980. Illustrating how much the country has pushed west during its history, in 1790 that point was located twenty-three miles west of Baltimore. In 2000 it was located in Phelps County, Missouri, about one hundred miles southwest of St. Louis.

Missouri's two great cities, located about as far apart from one another as geographically possible, are very different. In 1904 St. Louis was the fourth-largest city in the country, a place capable of hosting the World's Fair, the Democratic national convention, and the Summer Olympics in the same year. Today it is the fifty-second largest city, having lost more than 12 percent of its population during the 1990s. Kansas City is now the larger of the two (though the St. Louis metro area is still larger), and ranks thirty-ninth in population, slightly more populous than Atlanta.

Like the rest of the region, Missouri has grown at a slower rate than the rest of the country. Agricultural areas across the country have been losing population, and urban centers are seeing a shift to newer, more distant but less-crowded suburbs. This has been true in Missouri as well. The fastest-growing state house districts are located primarily north and northwest of St. Louis, in St. Louis and St. Charles Counties, pushing further out along Interstate 70 toward Columbia, in some cases sixty miles from the Gateway Arch. The 13th state house district, located in the middle of this area, has grown by a third since 2000. Out west, the 123rd and 124th districts south of Kansas City have also grown rapidly. In both cities, suburban growth has pushed across state boundaries into Kansas and Illinois. East St. Louis, Illinois, may be one of the most notorious slums in America, but the districts south of it are growing rapidly.

Another growing part of Missouri is Christian County, located between Springfield and Branson, home to a grow-ing number of retirees and the area where most of the country's stretch limos are built. Branson itself—the country music wonder and retirement mecca that bills itself as the "Family Friendly Las Vegas"—is now one of the country's most popular tourist destinations, drawing nearly eight million visitors a year, a particularly remarkable feat because it is not served by a large airport or an interstate highway.

No part of the state is experiencing rapid population loss, but the sections that are losing the most residents are located in the Bootheel—known as "Little Dixie"—as well as districts in downtown St. Joseph and in St. Louis, including sections of that city that were long represented in Congress by former House majority leader Richard Gephardt.

The greater St. Louis area has huge disparities of wealth. In its older suburbs, especially leafy Frontenac and Chesterfield, average household income exceeds $120,000, but average income in some of the downtown St. Louis districts is not much more than $35,000. In the state's poorest district, the 137th in downtown Springfield, it is less than $32,000, making it one of the poorest districts in the country.

Both St. Louis and Kansas City have had large and vibrant African American communities, and each has developed its own style of blues. Eleven percent of Missouri residents are African American, which places the state about midway between its neighbors Kansas, Illinois, and Arkansas. The state has seventeen black-majority house districts, but five that are more than 70 percent black. Tellingly, three are located within the St. Louis city limits, but two others are located in older suburbs just west of the city, in Bellerive and Northwoods. The 40th house district, in Jackson County just outside Kansas City, is more than 30 percent Hispanic. Of 163 state house districts, 126 are at least 80 percent white. Most of those districts are in the vast middle of the state, although the areas just outside heavily black St. Louis are just as heavily white.

Democrats controlled both chambers of the legislature throughout the 1990s but lost control in this decade because of term limits, which both parties agree enabled the Republicans to pick up many rural districts previously held by longtime Democratic incumbents. In 2002, the first year in which term limits became effective, Republicans reversed an 18–16 Democratic majority in the state senate and have since added to it, now controlling the chamber 21–13. In 2004 the GOP picked up fifteen seats in the state house to win control there and currently enjoys a 92–71 majority. Term limits cut both ways, so the 2008 and 2010 election cycles will force the retirement of many Republican legislators, giving the Democrats hope for a resurgence.

MISSOURI
State Senate Districts

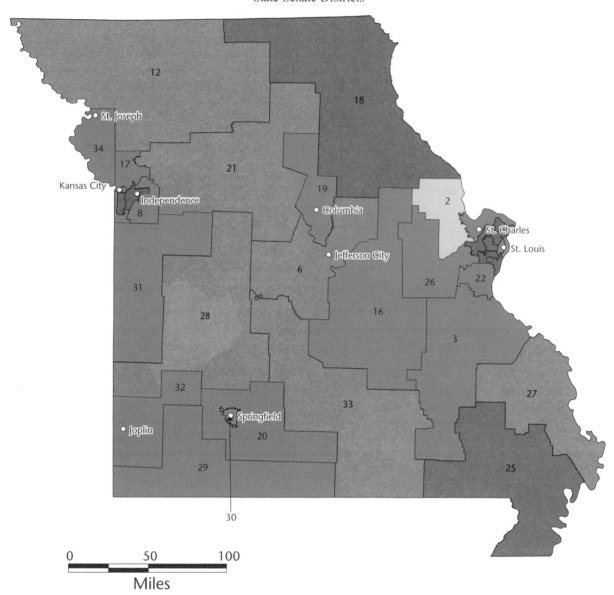

0   50   100

Miles

KANSAS CITY

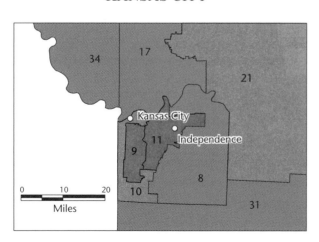

0   10   20

Miles

Population Growth   ■ -6% to -3%   ■ -3% to 2%   ■ 2% to 22%   □ 22% to 23%

ST. LOUIS

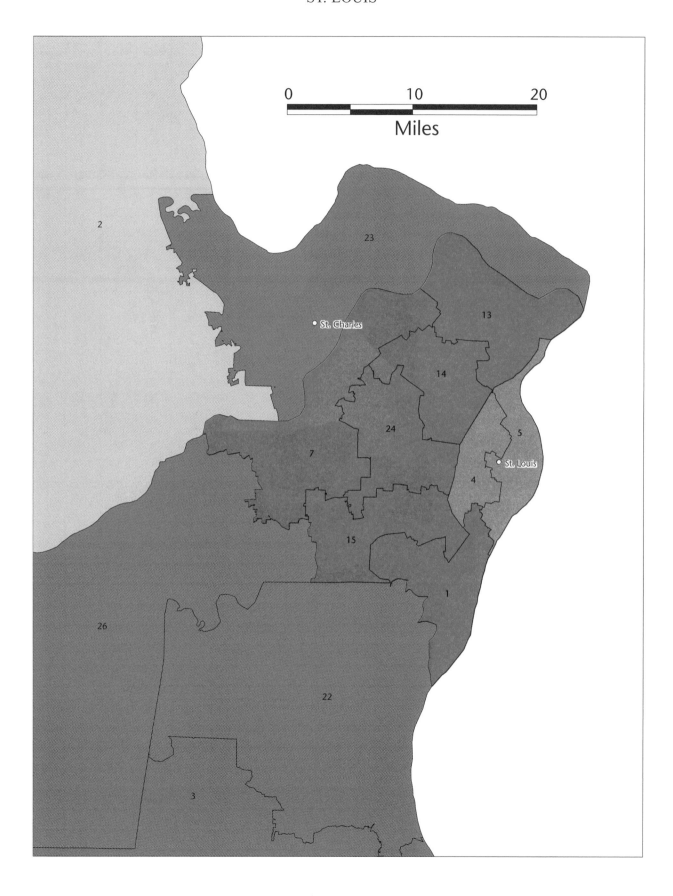

Population Growth　　■ -6% to -3%　　■ -3% to 2%　　■ 2% to 22%　　□ 22% to 23%

Missouri State Senate Districts—Election and Demographic Data

Senate Districts	General Election Results Party, Percent of Vote							Population			Avg. HH Income	Pop 25+ 2006		Below Poverty Line	White (Non-Hisp)	African American	American Indians, Alaska Natives	Asians, Hawaiians, Pacific Islanders	Hispanic Origin
												Some College +	4-Yr Degree +						
Missouri	2000	2001	2002	2003	2004	2005	2006	2000	2006	% Change	($)	(%)	(%)	(%)	(%)	(%)	(%)	(%)	(%)
1	R, 62				D, 50			155,645	150,099	-4	62,278	44.7	22.3	9.3	88.1	6.9	0.1	1.5	1.9
2			R, 59				R, 54	160,894	197,844	23	72,506	39.2	19.0	7.5	93.5	2.4	0.1	0.7	1.8
3	D, 64				R, 51			159,926	168,135	5	46,069	26.6	7.5	19.5	95.7	1.6	0.2	0.3	0.9
4			D, 100				D, 100	160,622	157,568	-2	43,174	41.2	23.6	23.1	43.1	53.1	0.4	2.3	2.1
5	D, 91				D, 91			159,026	158,186	-1	38,736	35.7	19.8	29.6	37.7	54.9	0.6	2.5	3.0
6			R, 59				R, 68	169,708	171,075	1	52,057	31.7	14.2	14.7	89.9	6.0	0.2	0.7	1.6
7	R, 100				R, 61			165,627	159,206	-4	107,425	54.4	35.0	5.2	87.9	4.0	0.1	4.6	2.1
8			R, 61				R, 58	163,998	173,800	6	74,700	44.7	21.3	6.5	87.8	4.7	0.2	1.3	3.9
9	D, 100				D, 100			163,932	157,443	-4	39,764	32.3	10.9	25.4	25.7	64.6	0.2	1.4	8.0
10			D, 100				D, 72	164,001	159,841	-3	58,412	47.8	26.1	14.8	60.6	19.8	0.3	3.2	12.0
11	D, 87				D, 63			163,528	158,026	-3	50,840	38.6	14.5	11.8	81.9	7.6	0.3	1.7	5.3
12			R, 100				R, 59	164,978	161,601	-2	44,595	27.4	10.4	19.8	95.2	1.5	0.2	0.4	1.6
13	D, 100				D, 81			164,599	156,617	-5	56,391	40.8	17.0	11.1	49.7	46.9	0.1	0.8	1.4
14			D, 100				D, 100	162,706	153,477	-6	47,269	38.9	16.8	16.7	41.6	53.7	0.1	1.3	2.0
15	R, 59				R, 52			165,291	160,153	-3	76,543	52.8	32.2	7.0	90.4	4.1	0.1	2.5	1.7
16			R, 71				D, 52	168,181	173,286	3	43,498	27.8	10.5	19.6	88.8	3.8	0.3	1.7	2.8
17	D, 62				R, 53			164,611	177,843	8	65,494	40.3	18.1	7.4	87.3	2.8	0.3	1.9	4.9
18			R, 56				D, 52	159,910	154,481	-3	43,356	26.4	10.8	20.9	93.0	3.9	0.1	0.5	1.3
19	D, 58				D, 53			160,098	165,066	3	53,102	42.6	26.0	16.8	83.8	8.5	0.2	3.0	2.2
20			R, 57				R, 64	338,850	360,301	6	50,255	36.5	15.9	16.0	92.5	1.8	0.4	1.1	2.1
21	D, 100				R, 52			161,540	158,712	-2	49,222	26.6	10.4	16.3	92.0	3.7	0.2	0.4	2.0
22			D, 60				D, 60	172,638	181,665	5	62,034	32.9	10.9	9.4	96.0	0.8	0.2	0.6	1.3
23	R, 54				R, 58			161,908	178,845	10	69,455	44.2	22.2	6.6	91.9	2.9	0.1	1.2	2.3
24			D, 52				D, 61	167,733	161,241	-4	88,362	53.5	35.3	9.6	79.8	10.6	0.1	4.8	2.6
25	R, 53				R, 57			170,676	163,470	-4	38,189	22.9	8.1	27.4	88.2	8.1	0.3	0.3	1.6
26			R, 70				R, 63	167,126	177,225	6	75,934	36.5	16.6	10.1	94.5	1.8	0.1	1.0	1.4
27	R, 100				R, 66			164,194	164,697	0	45,667	27.1	11.9	20.1	89.8	6.6	0.6	0.6	1.2
28			R, 65				R, 57	165,923	168,759	2	40,719	26.6	9.0	21.5	93.4	1.1	0.4	0.4	2.7
29	R, 100				R, 69			168,830	175,364	4	43,476	27.9	9.2	19.7	90.1	0.3	0.6	0.4	5.4
30			R, 51				R, 57	150,664	148,524	-1	44,674	37.8	17.0	18.2	88.6	3.4	0.4	1.8	3.0
31	D, 52				R, 63			166,917	180,573	8	54,713	32.3	12.6	14.0	91.7	2.2	0.4	0.9	2.7
32			R, 100				R, 64	165,348	170,688	3	45,789	31.2	11.6	18.3	88.7	1.2	1.0	0.9	4.7
33	R, 62				R, 65			166,821	170,146	2	41,420	26.5	9.5	23.3	95.6	0.4	0.5	0.4	1.3
34			R, 52				R, 59	159,786	163,969	3	61,412	38.6	18.0	12.2	88.6	4.0	0.3	1.4	3.5

Note: D=Democrat, R=Republican, R/D=Republican/Democrat (cross-filed), D/R=Democrat/Republican (cross-filed), I=Independent, C=Constitution, O=Other, GI=Green Independent, P=Progressive, P/D=Progressive/Democrat, P/D/R=Progressive/Democrat/Republican, HH=Households

MISSOURI
State House Districts

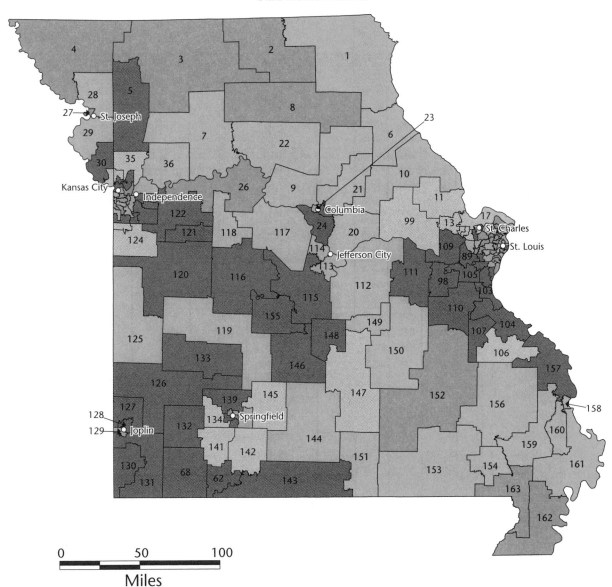

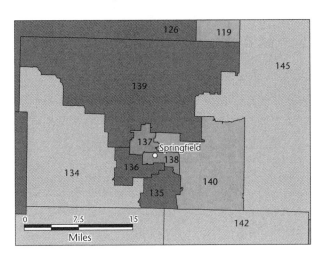

SPRINGFIELD

Population Growth ▢ -6% to -1%   ▢ -1% to 4%   ▢ 4% to 12%   ▢ 12% to 34%

KANSAS CITY

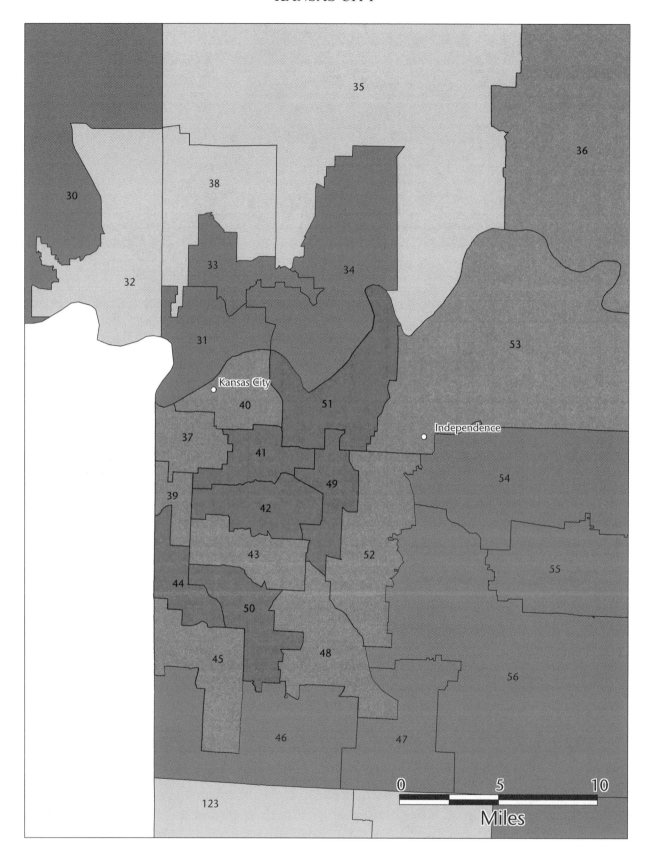

Population Growth   ■ -6% to -1%   ■ -1% to 4%   ■ 4% to 12%   □ 12% to 34%

ST. LOUIS

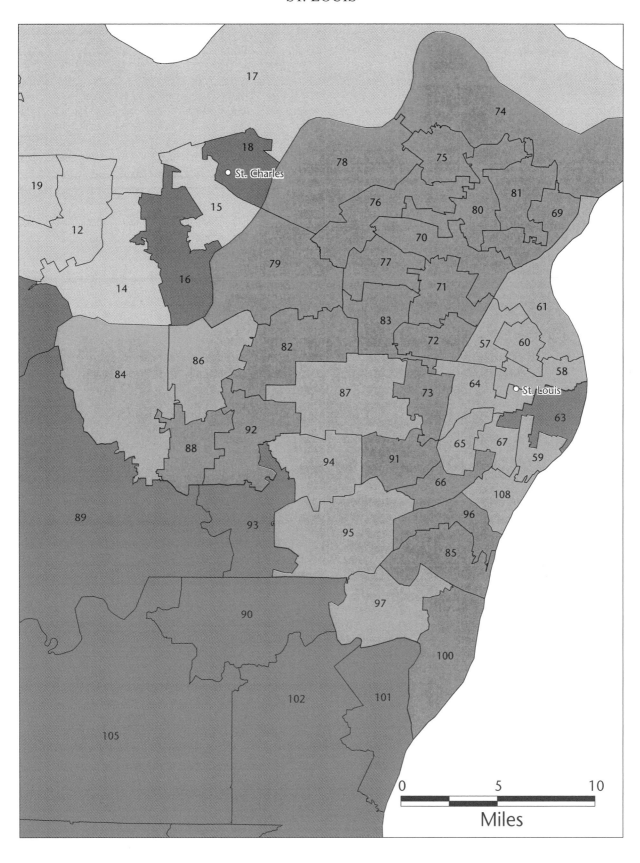

St. Charles

St. Louis

Population Growth -6% to -1%   -1% to 4%   4% to 12%   12% to 34%

Missouri State House Districts—Election and Demographic Data

House Districts	General Election Results Party, Percent of Vote							Population			Avg. HH Income	Pop 25+		2006 Below Poverty Line	White (Non-Hisp)	African American	American Indians, Alaska Natives	Asians, Hawaiians, Pacific Islanders	Hispanic Origin
												Some College +	4-Yr Degree +						
Missouri	2000	2001	2002	2003	2004	2005	2006	2000	2006	% Change	($)	(%)	(%)	(%)	(%)	(%)	(%)	(%)	(%)
1	D, 100		R, 56		R, 58		R, 54	34,446	34,106	-1	41,286	24.8	8.7	21.6	96.9	0.9	0.1	0.2	0.8
2	R, 55		R, 67		R, 64		D, 51	35,397	34,315	-3	40,466	31.3	16.0	26.2	92.3	0.9	0.1	1.3	3.5
3	R, 100		D, 55		D, 66		D, 53	36,773	36,023	-2	40,254	25.9	8.4	21.4	96.6	0.2	0.2	0.3	1.6
4	R, 73		R, 53		R, 100		R, 64	35,551	34,602	-3	42,757	29.6	14.2	21.6	96.0	1.3	0.2	0.7	0.9
5	R, 100		R, 51		R, 55		R, 51	33,997	36,392	7	50,031	29.5	9.9	16.2	93.0	3.9	0.3	0.2	1.3
6	D, 100		D, 54		D, 100		D, 83	36,270	36,080	-1	46,256	26.6	10.7	18.3	91.9	5.0	0.2	0.4	1.2
7	R, 69		R, 80		R, 73		R, 65	34,568	34,649	0	43,614	25.2	9.6	20.3	96.1	1.6	0.2	0.2	0.9
8	D, 55		R, 58		R, 52		D, 51	34,989	33,776	-3	40,864	23.7	9.0	21.2	96.3	1.5	0.2	0.2	0.8
9	D, 63		D, 59		D, 58		D, 57	35,108	36,017	3	47,513	30.2	13.7	17.3	92.8	4.0	0.3	0.5	1.1
10	D, 59		D, 52		D, 51		D, 62	34,598	35,766	3	42,813	22.7	7.1	19.9	88.6	7.2	0.2	0.2	2.1
11	D, 60		D, 60		D, 62		D, 52	34,862	44,424	27	54,442	24.0	7.3	13.2	94.8	1.7	0.2	0.3	1.5
12	D, 100		R, 100		R, 73		R, 58	35,691	44,420	24	82,474	46.0	24.6	2.9	93.5	2.1	0.1	1.0	2.0
13	R, 100		R, 66		R, 65		R, 100	34,486	45,931	33	74,257	42.0	20.5	7.5	91.9	4.0	0.1	0.6	1.8
14	R, 67		R, 59		R, 100		R, 60	34,423	39,638	15	84,424	47.2	25.5	3.8	92.9	2.6	0.1	1.2	1.8
15	D, 50		D, 53		R, 51		R, 50	34,558	40,460	17	66,396	45.0	21.9	6.7	90.6	3.6	0.1	1.6	2.2
16	R, 57		R, 100		R, 54		R, 55	34,920	38,754	11	79,069	47.1	24.5	3.9	93.1	2.5	0.1	1.3	1.7
17	D, 52		R, 50		R, 57		R, 51	35,586	41,319	16	64,910	40.6	18.5	7.9	92.9	2.3	0.1	0.9	2.1
18	R, 57		R, 86		R, 82		R, 53	33,008	36,066	9	60,810	41.7	22.2	10.2	90.2	3.3	0.2	0.8	3.3
19	R, 84		R, 100		R, 60		R, 58	32,891	41,128	25	75,234	43.7	22.3	4.3	93.4	2.1	0.1	1.0	2.0
20	R, 53		R, 66		R, 61		R, 61	35,259	36,254	3	51,529	30.0	12.3	13.4	90.0	6.4	0.3	0.7	1.1
21	D, 100		R, 56		R, 61		R, 52	35,638	36,050	1	51,473	33.3	16.3	13.8	89.3	6.3	0.3	0.8	1.5
22	D, 52		R, 50		R, 54		R, 54	34,488	34,842	1	42,498	27.7	9.0	18.2	90.6	6.0	0.2	0.4	1.6
23	D, 100		D, 66		D, 71		D, 73	34,875	35,489	2	53,907	50.7	34.4	17.2	74.7	14.7	0.2	4.5	3.0
24	D, 64		D, 52		R, 56		R, 51	34,999	38,175	9	66,826	48.8	33.4	12.9	87.2	5.4	0.2	3.2	2.0
25	D, 78		D, 54		D, 66		D, 100	34,752	37,546	8	43,747	41.2	27.4	23.0	80.3	9.6	0.2	5.1	2.4
26	D, 100		D, 100		D, 64		D, 100	34,379	32,984	-4	46,762	27.3	12.1	16.5	87.3	4.7	0.2	0.7	4.4
27	D, 100		D, 56		D, 100		D, 68	35,308	33,439	-5	43,186	29.5	11.4	20.0	88.5	5.7	0.3	0.4	2.8
28	R, 69		R, 64		R, 100		R, 98	35,749	36,435	2	55,981	35.9	16.3	14.4	92.0	4.1	0.2	0.8	1.8
29	D, 61		D, 68		D, 56		D, 76	35,461	35,581	0	51,223	28.7	10.1	15.1	93.9	1.4	0.2	0.3	2.5
30	D, 51		R, 51		R, 52		R, 56	34,424	38,438	12	75,832	43.7	21.8	6.3	88.6	2.4	0.3	1.9	4.2
31	D, 75		D, 63		D, 69		D, 100	34,909	36,428	4	56,687	36.5	15.9	10.9	80.5	4.5	0.3	3.7	7.1
32	R, 100		R, 61		R, 51		D, 60	35,964	41,808	16	73,649	48.6	26.1	7.5	84.7	5.0	0.2	2.6	4.7
33	D, 58		D, 59		R, 52		R, 51	33,823	35,497	5	63,947	43.7	19.0	6.4	89.8	1.8	0.2	1.6	4.3
34	R, 65		R, 54		R, 56		R, 59	34,196	37,713	10	66,615	38.7	18.2	8.2	89.4	2.6	0.2	1.1	3.9
35	R, 62		R, 55		R, 57		R, 58	35,640	43,645	22	74,824	40.1	18.0	5.4	93.2	1.2	0.2	0.7	2.7
36	D, 71		D, 100		R, 51		R, 61	35,001	36,317	4	55,162	25.0	8.3	14.1	93.8	2.1	0.2	0.3	1.7
37	D, 92		D, 100		D, 91		D, 100	34,008	35,235	4	38,102	37.7	16.0	27.8	25.2	59.1	0.3	1.4	15.1
38	D, 88		D, 53		D, 52		R, 56	34,297	38,903	13	66,585	42.1	19.1	5.4	84.8	3.6	0.3	2.3	5.9
39	D, 68		D, 100		D, 100		D, 82	34,129	33,963	0	57,575	57.0	37.1	16.4	67.9	13.5	0.4	3.3	11.0
40	D, 100		D, 100		D, 100		D, 100	35,098	35,075	0	36,768	27.8	10.3	28.3	37.0	17.9	0.5	7.8	30.6
41	D, 100		D, 100		D, 100		D, 100	33,971	33,136	-2	36,973	27.4	8.6	31.6	25.6	60.9	0.3	1.4	12.0
42	D, 100		D, 100		D, 100		D, 100	33,741	32,661	-3	41,567	33.3	11.4	22.7	31.0	63.1	0.2	1.0	4.6
43	D, 100		D, 100		D, 100		D, 100	35,548	35,231	-1	40,611	33.1	11.0	23.2	27.8	67.4	0.2	0.6	3.4
44	D, 73		D, 100		D, 100		D, 100	35,318	34,165	-3	76,530	55.3	34.6	10.1	69.1	21.7	0.2	1.8	5.1
45	D, 61		D, 71		D, 72		D, 87	34,071	34,283	1	52,136	47.7	21.6	10.7	68.6	20.8	0.2	2.1	5.8
46	D, 86		D, 61		D, 63		D, 58	35,237	38,083	8	69,262	45.8	22.2	9.4	64.1	27.5	0.2	1.7	4.6
47	R, 63		R, 54		R, 100		R, 51	34,996	38,459	10	68,328	46.0	20.6	6.8	87.4	4.8	0.3	1.1	4.1
48	D, 89		D, 51		R, 53		R, 52	32,803	33,187	1	63,592	47.6	22.0	8.5	78.0	14.8	0.2	1.3	3.8
49	D, 100		D, 56		D, 100		D, 100	34,604	33,852	-2	52,700	41.3	15.3	9.1	84.0	6.2	0.3	1.3	5.1
50	D, 100		D, 82		D, 100		D, 100	34,550	33,478	-3	45,456	37.0	13.1	14.4	38.4	53.7	0.2	1.3	5.0

(continued)

Note: D=Democrat, R=Republican, R/D=Republican/Democrat (cross-filed), D/R=Democrat/Republican (cross-filed), I=Independent, C=Constitution, O=Other, GI=Green Independent, P=Progressive, P/D=Progressive/Democrat, P/D/R=Progressive/Democrat/Republican, HH=Households

Missouri State House Districts—Election and Demographic Data (cont.)

House Districts	General Election Results Party, Percent of Vote							Population			Avg. HH Income	Pop 25+ Some College +	2006 Pop 25+ 4-Yr Degree +	Below Poverty Line	White (Non-Hisp)	African American	American Indians, Alaska Natives	Asians, Hawaiians, Pacific Islanders	Hispanic Origin
Missouri	2000	2001	2002	2003	2004	2005	2006	2000	2006	% Change	($)	(%)	(%)	(%)	(%)	(%)	(%)	(%)	(%)
51	D, 100		D, 62		D, 67		D, 100	34,946	33,713	-4	40,255	31.5	10.0	18.6	82.1	4.5	0.5	2.3	6.4
52	R, 100		D, 51		D, 52		D, 66	35,540	36,849	4	61,249	44.7	19.6	8.7	86.7	4.8	0.2	1.5	4.6
53	D, 65		D, 60		D, 70		D, 65	34,835	34,751	0	49,441	31.7	10.2	13.0	84.5	4.3	0.4	2.0	5.2
54	R, 61		R, 58		R, 100		R, 60	34,334	36,039	5	73,328	43.7	20.5	5.3	87.4	4.4	0.2	1.4	4.4
55	R, 65		R, 55		R, 63		R, 62	32,691	34,954	7	65,108	38.2	14.9	7.7	88.4	3.7	0.2	1.2	4.2
56	R, 100		R, 64		R, 100		R, 100	36,838	39,979	9	91,222	49.1	26.6	4.2	88.1	5.1	0.2	1.3	3.5
57	D, 100		D, 100		D, 100		D, 100	33,299	33,651	1	32,901	32.5	15.2	37.4	22.8	73.5	0.1	1.3	0.8
58	D, 100		D, 89		D, 100		D, 100	31,732	32,875	4	39,768	40.6	26.3	37.6	35.9	58.3	0.1	2.7	1.8
59	D, 85		D, 88		D, 89		D, 89	34,456	34,279	-1	39,162	33.8	18.7	27.7	40.7	50.5	0.2	3.3	3.9
60	D, 100		D, 100		D, 100		D, 100	33,776	34,287	2	34,594	34.6	16.3	32.2	22.8	73.7	0.1	1.3	0.6
61	D, 100		D, 100		D, 100		D, 100	36,259	36,421	0	34,473	30.9	13.9	30.5	25.2	71.2	0.1	1.3	0.7
62	D, 100		R, 67		R, 67		R, 71	33,351	35,647	7	48,523	35.6	13.0	16.1	93.3	0.4	0.5	0.5	3.4
63	D, 100		D, 82		D, 85		D, 90	33,616	35,561	6	43,450	40.5	24.2	27.3	37.9	55.9	0.2	1.9	2.8
64	D, 100		D, 100		D, 80		D, 100	34,635	34,776	0	58,854	46.1	33.0	22.0	54.5	36.6	0.1	3.6	2.5
65	D, 73		D, 66		D, 69		D, 100	32,353	32,392	0	52,851	50.2	30.3	9.3	65.1	29.1	0.2	2.0	2.0
66	D, 87		D, 59		D, 68		D, 100	33,857	33,252	-2	48,816	43.6	22.7	11.7	75.7	16.7	0.1	2.6	2.6
67	D, 91		D, 100		D, 91		D, 90	34,268	34,117	0	37,839	38.2	20.3	20.8	49.0	39.7	0.2	4.7	4.8
68	D, 60		R, 61		R, 100		R, 71	34,551	36,403	5	41,613	25.8	8.4	20.4	86.8	0.2	0.5	0.4	7.7
69	D, 100		D, 94		D, 97		D, 95	34,480	33,210	-4	46,560	34.3	12.0	16.2	32.7	64.5	0.1	0.5	1.2
70	D, 100		D, 100		D, 96		D, 100	34,697	33,256	-4	42,224	33.4	11.7	20.4	24.5	72.7	0.1	0.6	0.9
71	D, 100		D, 93		D, 100		D, 100	34,386	33,571	-2	41,973	37.1	14.8	21.3	22.0	74.3	0.1	0.9	2.0
72	D, 100		D, 100		D, 100		D, 100	32,717	31,614	-3	53,678	45.6	25.2	18.2	31.0	63.8	0.1	2.1	1.7
73	D, 84		D, 65		D, 69		D, 70	35,090	34,693	-1	85,917	54.0	37.5	11.6	77.7	12.2	0.1	4.9	2.4
74	D, 100		D, 100		D, 100		D, 100	36,301	35,724	-2	70,658	45.4	21.6	6.4	63.9	31.6	0.1	1.4	1.6
75	D, 83		D, 60		D, 83		D, 100	34,460	33,289	-3	57,649	42.9	17.3	6.5	79.8	15.7	0.1	1.0	1.8
76	D, 100		D, 64		D, 65		D, 100	32,391	31,837	-2	53,143	42.2	17.9	9.7	74.4	19.3	0.1	1.8	2.4
77	D, 73		D, 71		D, 100		D, 100	33,662	32,606	-3	43,492	35.8	13.5	14.4	74.5	16.8	0.1	1.9	4.3
78	R, 51		D, 50		D, 70		D, 100	34,360	33,121	-4	57,763	42.5	18.7	7.2	86.1	8.6	0.1	1.3	2.1
79	D, 100		D, 56		D, 59		D, 69	35,564	34,982	-2	66,136	53.1	32.7	6.2	81.7	5.9	0.1	8.0	2.9
80	D, 68		D, 100		D, 94		D, 100	34,393	33,296	-3	51,716	40.9	17.9	12.7	37.9	59.1	0.1	0.7	1.1
81	D, 100		D, 100		D, 100		D, 100	34,006	33,342	-2	56,164	39.1	15.5	12.7	27.9	69.6	0.1	0.5	1.0
82	R, 100		D, 51		D, 57		D, 64	34,394	34,032	-1	110,308	61.2	43.1	6.8	84.2	5.7	0.1	6.5	2.1
83	D, 67		D, 100		D, 100		D, 100	34,731	33,737	-3	68,882	47.7	27.5	11.1	73.9	17.2	0.1	3.6	2.8
84	D, 65		R, 76		R, 100		R, 100	33,754	34,404	2	153,190	56.1	39.7	4.8	90.5	2.8	0.0	3.6	2.0
85	D, 65		R, 52		R, 50		R, 52	35,327	34,786	-2	54,495	44.1	20.2	9.5	93.4	2.0	0.1	1.5	1.8
86	R, 100		R, 70		R, 100		R, 56	33,474	33,310	0	122,713	61.5	44.4	4.4	87.7	2.5	0.1	6.9	1.9
87	R, 85		R, 67		R, 60		R, 55	36,547	36,402	0	147,118	63.2	46.4	5.9	86.2	8.0	0.1	3.0	1.5
88	R, 100		R, 68		R, 100		R, 100	33,962	33,502	-1	84,872	53.1	32.7	5.6	90.1	2.3	0.1	3.7	2.4
89	R, 100		R, 73		R, 100		R, 100	34,321	37,035	8	110,787	51.5	32.6	3.3	91.6	3.3	0.1	2.2	1.7
90	D, 52		D, 57		D, 54		D, 56	33,640	36,946	10	57,962	32.2	9.3	9.6	96.0	0.5	0.2	0.6	1.4
91	R, 54		R, 58		R, 83		R, 51	34,865	34,156	-2	85,222	57.9	40.4	7.3	92.3	3.0	0.1	1.7	1.7
92	R, 100		R, 65		R, 100		R, 56	34,650	33,840	-2	107,201	56.1	38.0	4.6	87.3	3.2	0.1	6.0	1.9
93	R, 100		R, 59		R, 60		R, 52	34,341	35,959	5	80,846	49.7	28.7	5.4	91.3	2.5	0.1	3.0	1.9
94	R, 100		R, 100		R, 54		R, 51	32,957	32,639	-1	98,331	58.6	39.5	7.1	89.1	6.8	0.1	1.6	1.3
95	R, 100		R, 57		R, 100		R, 60	33,592	33,352	-1	77,265	52.9	28.4	5.9	93.7	2.2	0.1	1.7	1.2
96	D, 74		D, 55		D, 60		D, 69	32,748	31,579	-4	51,379	41.1	17.7	9.9	93.5	1.7	0.1	1.2	2.0
97	R, 61		R, 57		R, 59		R, 62	35,168	35,375	1	76,662	48.3	25.9	5.4	93.9	1.7	0.1	1.8	1.5
98	D, 53		R, 54		R, 62		R, 57	33,940	36,033	6	57,074	28.6	7.8	12.3	95.9	1.4	0.2	0.2	1.0
99	R, 59		R, 67		R, 100		R, 64	34,735	39,534	14	53,812	26.9	8.2	14.6	94.2	2.0	0.2	0.3	1.9
100	D, 65		D, 51		D, 57		D, 100	33,036	32,680	-1	75,313	44.9	22.9	4.9	95.7	1.1	0.0	1.1	1.2

(continued)

Note: D=Democrat, R=Republican, R/D=Republican/Democrat (cross-filed), D/R=Democrat/Republican (cross-filed), I=Independent, C=Constitution, O=Other, GI=Green Independent, P=Progressive, P/D=Progressive/Democrat, P/D/R=Progressive/Democrat/Republican, HH=Households

Missouri State House Districts—Election and Demographic Data (cont.)

House Districts	General Election Results Party, Percent of Vote							Population			Avg. HH Income ($)	Pop 25+ Some College + (%)	Pop 25+ 4-Yr Degree + (%)	Below Poverty Line (%)	2006 White (Non-Hisp) (%)	African American (%)	American Indians, Alaska Natives (%)	Asians, Hawaiians, Pacific Islanders (%)	Hispanic Origin (%)
Missouri	2000	2001	2002	2003	2004	2005	2006	2000	2006	% Change	($)	(%)	(%)	(%)	(%)	(%)	(%)	(%)	(%)
101	D, 59		D, 54		D, 56		D, 67	32,928	34,982	6	61,848	32.7	10.0	8.0	96.5	0.3	0.1	0.5	1.4
102	D, 66		D, 100		D, 51		D, 60	33,988	37,260	10	63,801	32.6	9.8	7.1	96.4	0.3	0.2	0.5	1.4
103	D, 61		D, 63		D, 60		D, 100	34,322	36,839	7	55,187	29.8	9.1	14.5	94.7	2.5	0.2	0.6	0.9
104	D, 100		D, 100		D, 70		D, 66	33,915	35,872	6	51,884	25.7	6.3	14.1	96.6	0.9	0.2	0.3	1.0
105	D, 69		D, 100		D, 100		D, 56	34,021	37,244	9	61,731	29.1	8.5	10.7	96.3	0.7	0.2	0.3	1.2
106	R, 57		R, 57		R, 54		R, 100	34,886	39,723	14	47,319	28.9	9.5	18.9	93.5	3.3	0.2	0.7	1.1
107	D, 100		D, 71		D, 53		D, 88	33,929	36,906	9	40,268	27.1	7.0	20.9	97.6	0.2	0.2	0.3	0.8
108	D, 80		D, 100		D, 100		D, 82	34,367	34,238	0	42,382	37.5	19.7	19.0	58.4	33.2	0.2	2.1	4.3
109	R, 70		R, 62		R, 100		R, 100	34,985	38,370	10	70,877	38.2	16.1	8.6	96.7	1.1	0.1	0.4	0.8
110	D, 66		D, 56		D, 69		D, 100	34,138	37,125	9	52,388	26.2	7.4	18.1	95.6	1.9	0.2	0.2	1.0
111	R, 67		R, 62		R, 100		R, 57	34,110	36,019	6	51,650	27.5	7.9	14.8	97.6	0.2	0.1	0.4	1.1
112	R, 100		R, 59		R, 74		R, 60	32,860	33,538	2	46,579	24.5	8.3	17.1	97.3	0.3	0.2	0.4	1.0
113	D, 100		R, 52		R, 68		R, 56	33,715	33,477	-1	55,817	35.4	17.1	14.0	81.9	14.0	0.2	0.7	1.6
114	R, 67		R, 75		R, 68		R, 72	33,689	34,452	2	63,612	43.1	24.1	9.7	86.7	7.6	0.2	1.5	2.3
115	R, 100		R, 75		R, 100		R, 70	34,963	37,327	7	44,871	25.3	8.7	19.1	97.1	0.3	0.2	0.2	1.0
116	R, 53		R, 62		R, 100		R, 100	35,085	37,570	7	39,904	27.7	8.5	20.2	95.9	0.6	0.3	0.2	1.4
117	R, 100		R, 79		R, 100		R, 70	33,813	35,003	4	46,498	25.0	9.5	16.1	89.2	6.2	0.2	0.3	2.1
118	R, 100		R, 60		R, 100		R, 61	34,417	34,597	1	44,338	31.3	10.9	17.8	84.4	3.4	0.2	0.6	7.4
119	R, 100		R, 65		R, 100		R, 75	34,295	35,556	4	38,716	23.7	7.2	25.0	96.2	0.2	0.4	0.4	1.4
120	R, 56		R, 100		R, 71		R, 56	34,126	36,024	6	45,015	25.8	8.9	18.3	95.8	0.9	0.4	0.3	1.3
121	D, 56		R, 60		R, 86		R, 67	35,217	37,637	7	44,271	36.8	17.1	19.2	83.9	5.8	0.4	2.5	3.6
122	D, 100		D, 62		R, 57		R, 56	35,298	37,240	6	58,967	29.5	11.0	11.3	94.8	1.5	0.2	0.4	1.4
123	R, 100		R, 52		R, 63		R, 100	34,378	40,682	18	63,511	35.0	12.7	9.2	89.0	2.5	0.3	0.9	5.0
124	R, 54		R, 62		R, 64		D, 50	35,364	41,603	18	65,206	33.4	12.3	9.4	95.0	0.9	0.4	0.5	1.7
125	R, 55		R, 52		R, 54		R, 60	34,572	35,015	1	42,023	25.1	9.3	20.6	95.5	0.7	0.4	0.4	1.7
126	R, 100		R, 67		R, 74		R, 70	35,370	37,563	6	40,482	25.3	8.3	20.2	95.4	0.3	0.4	0.3	1.7
127	R, 67		R, 74		R, 100		R, 69	33,700	35,949	7	45,576	29.4	10.8	18.5	83.2	0.9	0.7	1.1	9.6
128	R, 100		R, 100		R, 100		R, 100	34,766	37,734	9	44,878	34.0	13.8	17.3	90.4	1.5	0.8	1.1	3.2
129	R, 69		R, 69		R, 100		R, 100	34,557	34,952	1	46,852	33.0	13.1	19.7	87.2	2.7	1.0	0.9	4.6
130	R, 73		R, 100		R, 69		R, 72	34,201	36,401	6	42,896	28.6	9.3	20.4	85.5	0.6	1.8	1.3	5.9
131	R, 100		R, 100		R, 73		R, 69	33,382	35,191	5	46,122	27.6	8.4	18.8	87.0	0.4	1.2	0.3	7.2
132	R, 100		R, 63		R, 100		R, 52	33,273	35,080	5	43,193	25.7	8.9	20.2	90.7	0.3	0.5	0.3	5.1
133	R, 100		R, 72		R, 75		R, 100	34,692	36,373	5	38,724	25.6	9.8	23.7	95.2	0.5	0.4	0.4	1.8
134	R, 70		R, 71		R, 70		R, 63	34,246	38,452	12	53,029	39.0	16.6	11.1	94.9	0.7	0.3	1.0	1.4
135	R, 70		R, 74		R, 67		R, 56	33,779	35,607	5	68,746	52.1	28.5	8.3	92.9	1.1	0.2	2.1	1.9
136	R, 53		R, 100		R, 100		R, 56	33,900	36,681	8	44,451	40.8	17.3	13.4	88.8	3.3	0.3	2.1	3.1
137	R, 56		R, 61		R, 53		D, 56	34,623	34,160	-1	31,845	25.0	7.3	28.9	86.1	4.4	0.7	1.2	3.9
138	D, 60		R, 51		D, 53		D, 58	33,646	32,700	-3	42,729	40.4	19.5	18.0	88.9	3.0	0.5	2.2	2.6
139	R, 58		R, 62		R, 68		R, 54	33,909	36,378	7	48,264	34.9	14.0	15.0	95.3	0.9	0.4	0.4	1.4
140	R, 69		R, 64		R, 100		R, 63	34,427	35,372	3	65,320	40.3	21.0	16.1	90.2	3.4	0.4	1.3	2.4
141	R, 100		R, 66		R, 75		R, 69	34,687	40,690	17	50,235	33.6	12.3	15.7	96.0	0.4	0.3	0.4	1.5
142	D, 60		R, 63		R, 89		R, 100	34,692	44,506	28	52,873	34.0	14.1	14.9	95.5	0.2	0.3	0.3	1.9
143	R, 100		R, 100		R, 70		R, 67	34,186	36,757	8	43,200	28.3	9.3	19.3	95.2	0.3	0.4	0.3	1.9
144	R, 100		R, 72		R, 100		R, 100	33,629	34,785	3	36,894	23.5	7.9	27.3	96.2	0.3	0.4	0.2	1.3
145	R, 72		R, 72		R, 100		R, 100	33,587	38,285	14	43,859	25.3	8.4	18.5	95.2	1.2	0.4	0.3	1.3
146	R, 75		R, 71		R, 74		R, 74	34,234	35,855	5	43,874	23.4	8.5	22.0	95.6	0.5	0.3	0.4	1.5
147	D, 100		D, 83		R, 58		R, 62	33,035	37,906	15	36,572	24.4	7.9	25.9	86.0	5.1	0.6	1.2	3.9
148	D, 66		D, 87		R, 63		R, 68	33,793	36,752	9	45,452	32.2	12.7	15.8	75.7	10.0	0.6	3.3	5.9
149	R, 51		R, 61		R, 56		R, 57	33,454	34,781	4	43,846	34.1	16.1	22.6	90.2	1.8	0.3	3.4	1.9
150	D, 51		D, 56		D, 60		R, 64	34,072	35,331	4	40,908	23.6	7.7	23.0	96.4	0.3	0.4	0.3	1.2

(continued)

Note: D=Democrat, R=Republican, R/D=Republican/Democrat (cross-filed), D/R=Democrat/Republican (cross-filed), I=Independent, C=Constitution, O=Other, GI=Green Independent, P=Progressive, P/D=Progressive/Democrat, P/D/R=Progressive/Democrat/Republican, HH=Households

Missouri State House Districts—Election and Demographic Data (cont.)

House Districts	General Election Results Party, Percent of Vote							Population			Avg. HH Income	Pop 25+		Below Poverty Line	White (Non-Hisp)	African American	American Indians, Alaska Natives	Asians, Hawaiians, Pacific Islanders	Hispanic Origin
												Some College +	4-Yr Degree +						
Missouri	2000	2001	2002	2003	2004	2005	2006	2000	2006	% Change	($)	(%)	(%)	(%)	(%)	(%)	(%)	(%)	(%)
151	R, 75		R, 100		R, 59		R, 71	34,246	35,001	2	38,276	26.2	8.7	25.0	95.4	0.4	0.6	0.6	1.3
152	D, 100		D, 56		D, 66		D, 100	34,036	33,641	-1	36,784	22.4	7.1	26.5	95.4	0.8	0.6	0.2	1.0
153	D, 100		R, 61		R, 64		R, 53	34,383	35,242	2	35,748	23.5	7.8	28.3	95.6	0.3	1.0	0.2	1.2
154	R, 100		R, 68		R, 100		R, 74	34,390	34,180	-1	42,730	29.0	10.0	23.4	90.2	5.9	0.3	0.6	1.3
155	R, 60		R, 66		R, 69		R, 100	35,413	37,882	7	51,793	36.3	14.4	13.9	96.3	0.3	0.3	0.4	1.4
156	R, 58		R, 100		R, 65		R, 57	33,913	34,538	2	36,453	21.6	6.5	25.6	97.3	0.3	0.3	0.3	0.6
157	R, 100		R, 67		R, 100		R, 100	33,278	34,882	5	52,501	29.5	13.5	13.3	96.1	1.2	0.2	0.5	0.9
158	R, 58		R, 89		R, 100		R, 62	33,897	33,935	0	49,305	37.0	20.0	19.4	85.1	10.0	0.2	1.4	1.6
159	R, 55		R, 100		R, 55		R, 57	34,912	35,706	2	42,240	24.9	10.3	21.4	97.0	0.5	0.2	0.2	0.8
160	R, 60		R, 52		R, 68		R, 58	34,224	34,591	1	43,127	24.4	9.6	22.2	84.1	12.7	0.2	0.4	1.5
161	R, 57		R, 62		R, 67		D, 51	34,581	34,729	0	39,307	19.1	7.2	26.8	83.4	14.3	0.1	0.1	1.1
162	D, 100		D, 100		D, 68		D, 100	34,556	32,777	-5	35,796	19.1	7.0	32.2	76.3	19.4	0.1	0.3	2.6
163	D, 100		R, 51		R, 56		D, 59	34,095	33,019	-3	36,656	21.6	7.3	29.5	86.9	8.5	0.2	0.3	2.5

Note: D=Democrat, R=Republican, R/D=Republican/Democrat (cross-filed), D/R=Democrat/Republican (cross-filed), I=Independent, C=Constitution, O=Other, GI=Green Independent, P=Progressive, P/D=Progressive/Democrat, P/D/R=Progressive/Democrat/Republican, HH=Households

MONTANA

There are few sights in North America more impressive than a Montana wheat field in August. Vast rolling hills stretch out endlessly under an overwhelming blue sky, the only sound the hum of a thresher. Despite its nickname, "Big Sky Country," few people appreciate how big the fourth-largest state is. As John Gunther described it in his book, *Inside U.S.A.,* one of every twenty-five American square miles is Montanan.

Montana straddles two regions, just as it does the Continental Divide, and this has defined its history. Eastern Montana, like eastern Colorado, is a land of wheat fields. In the west, Butte was once the wildest town in America. Built on huge copper mines (Butte was "a mile high and a mile deep"), it was run by the Anaconda Copper Company, widely reviled and known simply as "The Company." For a time Butte was also home to the International Workers of the World (or "Wobblies," as they were called), who tried to organize the miners. Given that explosive combination, it is not surprising that Butte was also the scene of some of the worst labor violence in U.S. history. "What the Harvard-Yale game is to intercollegiate football," wrote Arthur Fisher in *The Nation* in 1923, "all this and more the battles with the Company are to Montana." Fisher quoted an old rancher who observed that the state's real trouble "is that her graveyards aren't big enough."

In many ways, Montana is emptier now than it once was. Lewis and Clark crossed it in 1805 and within twenty-five years Fort Union on the Missouri River had grown to become, in Ian Frazier's phrase, "the Times Square of the Plains," the intersection of continental fur-trading network. Native Americans stopped roaming not long after they defeated Custer at Little Big Horn in 1876. Montana still does not have a city with 100,000 people.

The Montana straddle still defines the state. Counties east of the divide have much in common with the Dakotas; they are poor and are losing people. Seventeen state house districts have lost at least 5 percent of their population since 2000, led by the 36th district, near the Saskatchewan border, which has lost 11 percent. The parts of Montana on or to the west of the Continental Divide have more in common with Idaho and have grown. Twenty-six state house districts have grown by 10 percent or more since 2000, almost all of them in and around Bozeman or Missoula. That is where the two state universities are located, but the real driving force behind growth in this area seems to be recreation—skiing, whitewater rafting, and hiking in nearby Yellowstone National Park. This part of the state is welcoming more young families as well as celebrities such as Ted Turner and Jane Fonda, who get all the attention.

Increased demand for cleaner burning low-sulfur coal has also helped raise Montana's economy. Ten years ago, average household income in the state was less than in Maine and Louisiana. Now it is closer to the Carolinas. The wealthiest districts are in Billings and Bozeman; the poorest districts are in the Blackfeet and Flathead Indian reservations. Nevertheless, though conditions on the reservations are typically grim, Montana as a whole has the nation's lowest rate of unemployment.

Native Americans make up about 6 percent of the population, but otherwise Montana is one of the least diverse states in the country. Ninety-one of one hundred house districts are more than 80 percent white. None is more than 5 percent African American or 11 percent Hispanic. Montana is also one of the older states in terms of median age, much closer in that respect to West Virginia than to Idaho.

Given its strong labor background, and the orneriness of farmers in bad times, Montana is a Republican state that can go Democratic. It was the home of Mike Mansfield, former Senate majority leader and ambassador to Japan, although the state's heyday may have come in the mid-1920s, when Democratic senator Burton Wheeler, virulent isolationist and Nazi apologist, ran for vice president with Robert LaFollette on the Progressive Party ticket while his colleague, Democrat Thomas Walsh, led the congressional investigation of the Teapot Dome scandal. Though the Mountain West is sometimes viewed as an area of complacent small-town conservatism, it is striking that most of the political figures it has produced have been radicals.

In recent years, Montana's geographic split has influenced its political split. During the past half-century, Montana has had six Republican governors and four Democrats, and it currently has two Democratic U.S. senators. Since a new state constitution was adopted in the early 1970s, Democrats have controlled the state house of representatives for ten sessions and the Republicans have controlled it for ten. Democrats have controlled the state senate for eleven sessions, the Republicans for nine. It remains the most evenly divided legislature in the country: Republicans hold the house, 50–49, with one independent; Democrats hold the senate, 26–24.

MONTANA
State Senate Districts

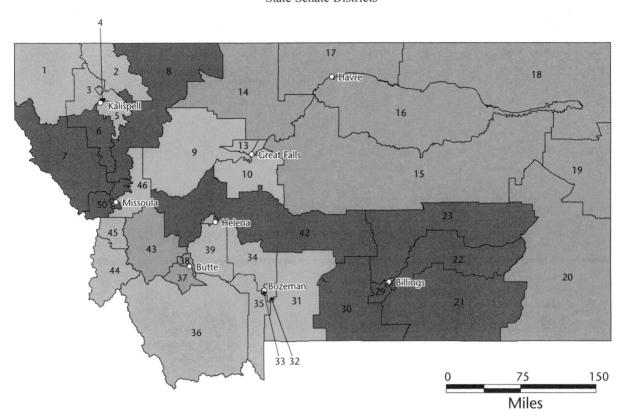

GREAT FALLS

HELENA

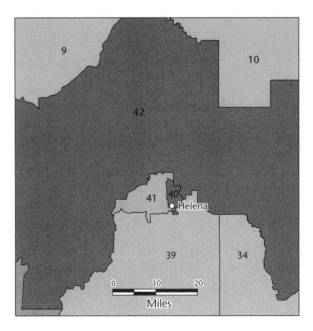

Population Growth ▨ -10% to -1%   ▨ -1% to 3%   ■ 3% to 11%   ▢ 11% to 22%

MISSOULA

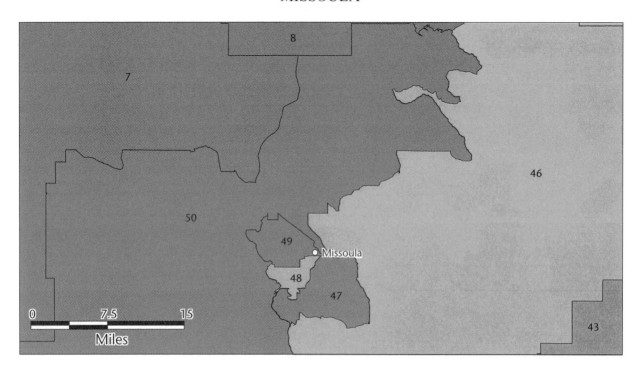

BILLINGS

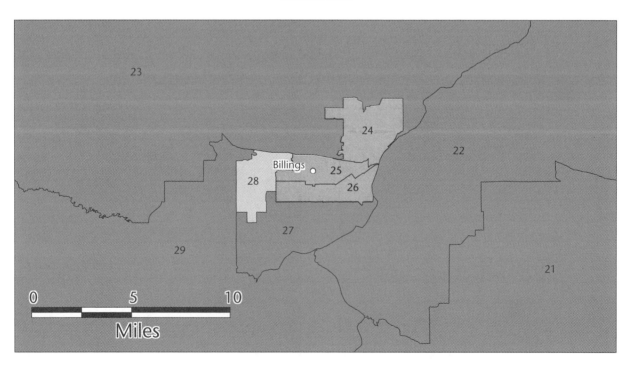

Population Growth   ▨ -10% to -1%   ▨ -1% to 3%   ▨ 3% to 11%   ▨ 11% to 22%

Montana State Senate Districts—Election and Demographic Data

Senate Districts	General Election Results Party, Percent of Vote							Population			Avg. HH Income	Pop 25+ Some College +	Pop 25+ 4-Yr Degree +	Below Poverty Line	White (Non-Hisp)	African American	American Indians, Alaska Natives	Asians, Hawaiians, Pacific Islanders	Hispanic Origin
														2006					
Montana	2000	2001	2002	2003	2004	2005	2006	2000	2006	% Change	($)	(%)	(%)	(%)	(%)	(%)	(%)	(%)	(%)
1			R, 54				R, 55	18,840	19,310	2	37,082	31.2	11.4	25.8	93.9	0.1	1.4	0.3	1.9
2	R, 68				D, 50			18,288	20,913	14	46,682	37.0	18.6	18.5	93.3	0.1	1.8	0.5	2.2
3	D, 52				R, 70			19,708	22,304	13	56,943	39.5	20.9	14.5	94.9	0.1	1.1	0.4	1.7
4			R, 100				R, 62	18,024	19,760	10	45,858	36.1	17.6	18.7	92.9	0.3	1.8	0.4	2.4
5	R, 71						R, 60	19,468	22,811	17	50,180	42.4	23.1	16.5	93.5	0.1	1.6	0.4	2.3
6	R, 57				R, 57			19,176	21,080	10	42,210	35.1	16.1	22.8	72.8	0.1	20.3	0.3	3.1
7			R, 62		D, 62			18,669	20,366	9	43,520	33.9	14.2	22.4	89.6	0.1	4.6	0.3	2.6
8	R, 57						D, 71	19,176	20,100	5	40,249	30.0	11.2	30.0	35.2	0.1	60.0	0.1	3.2
9			D, 54		R, 100			18,096	18,230	1	56,812	39.5	19.9	16.0	93.4	0.2	2.4	0.3	1.7
10	R, 51				D, 52			18,077	18,433	2	47,528	37.4	15.6	20.6	89.9	0.9	3.7	0.4	2.6
11			R, 61				D, 74	18,035	17,428	-3	40,557	38.3	16.7	22.0	83.9	1.2	7.2	0.9	3.7
12			R, 100				D, 57	16,547	16,466	0	39,806	35.3	14.7	19.1	83.7	2.4	4.3	1.0	4.7
13			R, 57				D, 100	18,301	18,432	1	45,664	34.6	13.3	16.1	89.5	0.5	4.3	0.5	2.1
14			D, 51				R, 70	17,453	16,611	-5	42,478	35.7	15.6	19.1	91.5	0.1	4.9	0.3	1.2
15	D, 60						R, 69	19,261	18,234	-5	41,561	36.3	15.5	21.7	95.8	0.1	1.7	0.1	0.9
16			R, 66		D, 100			21,023	20,260	-4	36,299	30.1	10.7	29.0	39.2	0.1	57.5	0.3	2.4
17	R, 74						D, 62	15,354	14,984	-2	41,933	36.7	15.2	21.3	84.1	0.1	10.9	0.2	2.0
18	D, 69				R, 68			17,761	15,991	-10	42,820	35.1	13.4	20.9	90.4	0.1	5.3	0.3	1.4
19	D, 81				R, 57			18,418	17,025	-8	42,515	36.0	13.1	20.7	94.7	0.2	1.6	0.1	1.9
20			R, 100				R, 100	17,854	17,141	-4	40,463	37.0	13.3	20.6	95.9	0.2	1.3	0.2	1.3
21			D, 64		D, 100			17,157	17,840	4	36,890	27.8	9.9	28.4	31.4	0.0	63.6	0.1	4.3
22	D, 57				D, 53			17,793	19,385	9	51,344	35.4	14.5	14.8	88.8	0.3	4.1	0.4	3.6
23			D, 100				R, 69	21,158	22,109	4	60,128	40.3	20.1	15.3	93.9	0.2	1.4	0.3	2.3
24			D, 71		D, 57			17,307	17,643	2	52,230	39.5	18.0	14.6	88.8	0.4	3.6	0.5	3.7
25	R, 100						R, 51	16,711	17,131	3	48,344	46.1	27.2	17.2	88.4	0.5	3.9	0.5	3.8
26			D, 68		D, 50			16,621	17,038	3	34,142	36.4	15.3	22.3	79.5	0.8	5.4	0.6	9.0
27	D, 51				R, 57			18,107	18,896	4	38,216	33.2	13.2	19.1	81.2	0.9	5.7	0.4	7.2
28			R, 53				R, 71	17,165	19,095	11	65,087	49.8	29.7	10.2	93.6	0.2	1.7	0.4	2.2
29	D, 100						R, 59	18,427	20,066	9	66,022	38.4	19.7	14.5	93.5	0.2	1.6	0.4	2.5
30	R, 67		D, 100				R, 61	17,860	18,660	4	47,921	36.4	16.4	16.9	94.5	0.2	0.9	0.2	2.3
31	R, 58						R, 59	18,423	18,735	2	44,782	40.3	18.8	18.3	93.9	0.3	1.1	0.3	2.6
32	D, 60						D, 56	18,209	21,429	18	58,469	54.2	36.1	14.5	94.1	0.3	1.1	0.6	1.9
33			D, 100		D, 67			16,301	18,944	16	42,761	49.6	33.5	18.7	92.2	0.4	1.8	1.4	2.3
34			D, 68		R, 100			17,677	20,272	15	53,360	47.1	24.8	11.7	94.8	0.2	0.9	0.4	2.0
35	R, 59						R, 62	18,519	22,419	21	56,904	48.8	26.6	10.9	94.5	0.1	0.8	0.4	2.5
36	D, 50				R, 100			18,124	18,274	1	42,613	41.3	19.7	20.7	93.5	0.1	1.3	0.2	2.6
37	R, 100				D, 100			16,196	15,603	-4	49,639	38.3	18.8	17.8	94.2	0.1	1.4	0.4	2.4
38			R, 100		D, 76			18,409	16,988	-8	39,525	35.5	15.5	20.7	89.9	0.2	3.1	0.4	3.9
39			R, 62				R, 51	18,365	20,527	12	52,268	41.8	21.9	12.8	93.1	0.2	2.2	0.3	1.8
40	R, 100						D, 68	17,662	18,493	5	52,581	44.4	24.6	15.3	93.0	0.2	2.3	0.5	2.0
41			R, 69		D, 67			15,921	16,190	2	50,129	48.0	30.0	16.6	92.7	0.3	2.2	0.6	2.2
42	R, 100						R, 69	18,638	19,614	5	45,911	37.1	16.8	16.1	94.5	0.1	1.7	0.3	1.8
43			D, 59		D, 100			17,171	16,407	-4	40,412	32.5	12.5	21.3	92.2	0.3	2.8	0.2	2.0
44			R, 58				R, 62	18,091	20,452	13	48,593	39.5	18.1	19.8	93.5	0.1	1.2	0.4	2.6
45			D, 71		R, 67			17,905	20,784	16	51,178	40.0	17.2	14.4	94.5	0.2	0.9	0.4	2.1
46			D, 62		D, 55			17,859	18,176	2	54,856	47.7	26.5	16.1	93.6	0.2	1.6	0.4	1.9
47	R, 100				D, 100			20,265	21,060	4	56,090	49.2	33.2	18.2	91.8	0.4	2.3	1.1	2.1
48	R, 100						D, 67	17,391	17,517	1	42,334	47.7	24.4	16.7	92.4	0.4	2.4	0.7	2.0
49	D, 100						D, 64	17,646	19,492	10	38,087	41.5	19.7	19.7	90.7	0.3	2.6	1.3	2.6
50	R, 100				D, 59			18,011	19,757	10	50,280	43.7	22.6	21.3	91.0	0.2	3.3	0.6	2.1

Note: D=Democrat, R=Republican, R/D=Republican/Democrat (cross-filed), D/R=Democrat/Republican (cross-filed), I=Independent, C=Constitution, O=Other, GI=Green Independent, P=Progressive, P/D=Progressive/Democrat, P/D/R=Progressive/Democrat/Republican, HH=Households

MONTANA
State House Districts

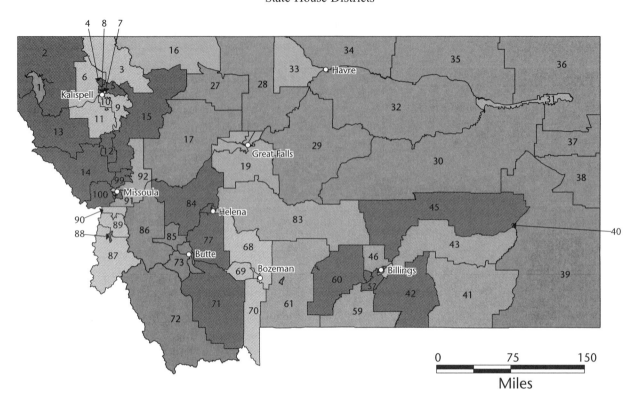

Miles

0   75   150

BOZEMAN

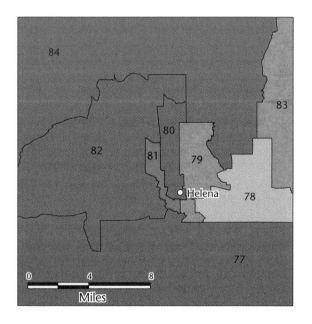

HELENA

Population Growth   ■ -11% to -1%   ■ -1% to 4%   ■ 4% to 12%   ■ 12% to 25%

GREAT FALLS

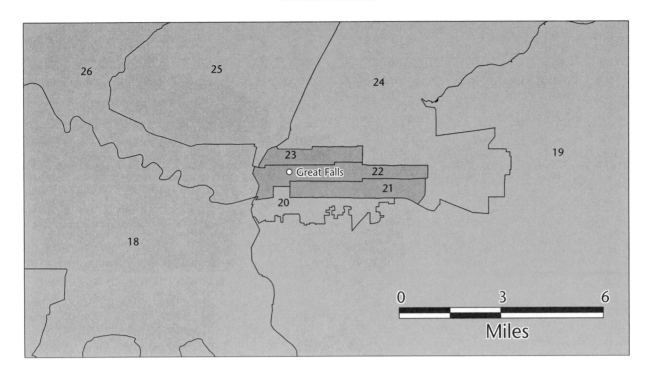

BILLINGS

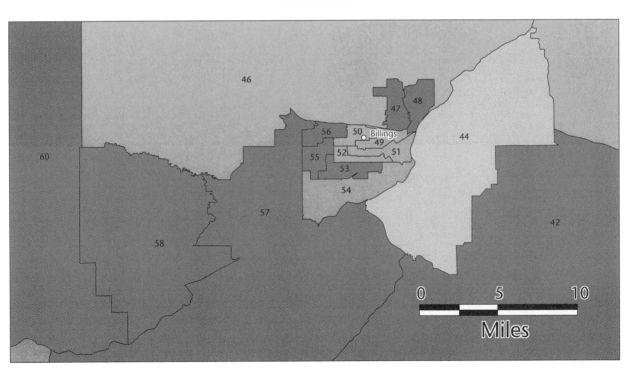

Population Growth | ▨ -11% to -1% | ▨ -1% to 4% | ▨ 4% to 12% | ▨ 12% to 25%

MISSOULA

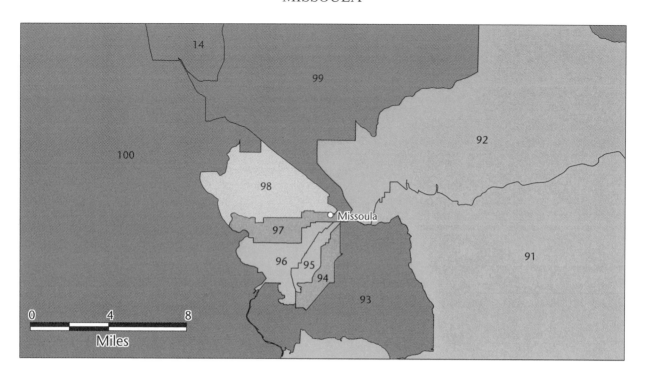

BUTTE

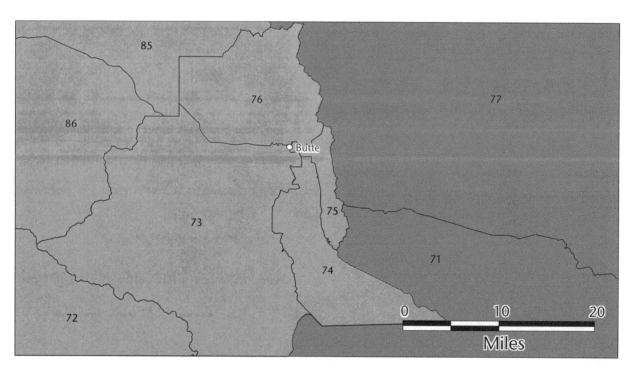

Population Growth   -11% to -1%   -1% to 4%   4% to 12%   12% to 25%

Montana State House Districts—Election and Demographic Data

House Districts	General Election Results Party, Percent of Vote							Population			Avg. HH Income	Pop 25+		2006 Below Poverty Line	White (Non-Hisp)	African American	American Indians, Alaska Natives	Asians, Hawaiians, Pacific Islanders	Hispanic Origin
												Some College +	4-Yr Degree +						
Montana	2000	2001	2002	2003	2004	2005	2006	2000	2006	% Change	($)	(%)	(%)	(%)	(%)	(%)	(%)	(%)	(%)
1	R, 77		R, 72		R, 49		R, 48	8,918	8,684	-3	36,724	30.6	10.5	25.2	93.4	0.1	1.5	0.3	2.0
2	D, 100		D, 100		R, 58		R, 55	9,761	10,435	7	37,384	31.8	12.1	26.2	94.3	0.1	1.3	0.3	1.9
3	R, 56		R, 100		R, 63		D, 51	9,188	10,761	17	42,054	30.5	12.5	21.0	92.6	0.1	2.2	0.5	2.2
4	D, 62		D, 100		D, 55		D, 62	8,873	9,858	11	51,367	44.0	25.1	16.0	94.1	0.1	1.3	0.6	2.1
5	D, 51		D, 57		R, 68		R, 68	10,229	11,383	11	55,766	36.7	18.4	11.5	95.6	0.1	1.1	0.3	1.4
6	D, 57		D, 60		R, 65		R, 48	9,168	10,567	15	58,479	42.6	23.7	17.3	94.2	0.1	1.1	0.5	2.0
7	D, 58		D, 55		R, 67		R, 67	9,565	10,813	13	48,267	35.3	17.3	15.7	93.0	0.2	1.7	0.4	2.3
8	R, 68		R, 100		D, 52		R, 51	8,476	8,922	5	42,571	36.8	17.8	22.4	92.8	0.3	1.8	0.4	2.5
9	R, 100		R, 69		R, 100		R, 61	9,555	11,149	17	50,897	45.5	24.8	15.1	92.8	0.1	2.2	0.3	2.4
10	R, 66		R, 62		R, 76		R, 74	9,772	11,460	17	50,043	39.6	21.5	17.5	94.2	0.1	1.1	0.4	2.1
11	D, 63		D, 61		R, 59		R, 60	8,722	9,772	12	41,115	38.7	18.0	21.3	82.1	0.2	11.9	0.4	2.2
12	R, 53		R, 55		C, 37		C, 56	10,095	10,895	8	43,067	32.0	14.5	24.2	65.4	0.1	27.0	0.3	3.8
13	D, 55		D, 50		D, 50		R, 54	9,151	10,108	10	38,054	32.4	12.5	25.6	91.2	0.1	3.4	0.2	2.4
14	R, 61		R, 58		R, 58		R, 62	9,323	10,013	7	49,440	35.5	15.9	18.6	88.2	0.1	5.7	0.5	2.7
15	R, 55		R, 55		D, 100		D, 100	9,398	10,021	7	42,376	30.2	12.9	28.2	42.9	0.1	52.5	0.1	3.7
16	D, 50		D, 56		D, 100		D, 100	9,415	9,702	3	38,872	29.9	9.5	31.0	37.6	0.1	59.6	0.1	2.5
17	R, 62		D, 65		R, 100		R, 67	8,780	8,663	-1	40,120	34.9	14.5	21.6	94.6	0.2	1.7	0.0	1.4
18	R, 60		D, 53		R, 59		R, 61	9,203	9,374	2	75,356	44.4	25.6	9.5	92.4	0.3	3.0	0.7	2.1
19	D, 52		R, 58		R, 53		R, 53	10,355	10,571	2	48,299	36.8	15.3	19.9	93.1	0.7	2.0	0.2	1.9
20	R, 51		D, 53		D, 58		D, 50	7,523	7,635	1	46,799	38.2	16.1	21.3	85.6	1.2	6.0	0.8	3.4
21	R, 67		R, 60		D, 78		D, 56	8,110	7,740	-5	43,316	40.0	17.7	18.1	84.8	1.2	7.1	0.9	3.3
22	R, 57		R, 54		D, 60		D, 58	9,816	9,557	-3	38,343	36.9	15.7	24.9	83.0	1.1	7.3	0.9	3.9
23	R, 56		R, 52		D, 72		D, 73	7,135	6,915	-3	38,446	36.8	16.3	22.3	86.1	1.0	5.9	0.7	3.3
24	R, 77		R, 52		D, 69		D, 56	9,369	9,480	1	41,029	34.1	13.4	16.0	81.9	3.5	3.1	1.3	5.7
25	R, 64		R, 66		D, 100		D, 67	8,918	8,934	0	52,852	39.0	15.8	12.1	92.2	0.4	2.6	0.5	1.8
26	D, 52		R, 54		D, 52		D, 56	9,215	9,305	1	39,190	30.4	11.0	19.4	87.0	0.6	5.8	0.5	2.5
27	R, 53		R, 54		R, 52		R, 100	8,317	7,902	-5	42,703	34.8	16.4	19.1	88.0	0.1	7.9	0.3	1.4
28	R, 72		R, 51		R, 67		R, 61	9,061	8,600	-5	42,264	36.6	14.8	19.2	94.8	0.1	2.1	0.3	1.0
29	D, 66		D, 69		R, 69		R, 58	8,487	7,858	-7	41,528	36.5	15.3	21.3	95.7	0.1	1.4	0.1	1.1
30	D, 57		D, 79		R, 100		R, 66	10,515	10,107	-4	41,652	36.2	15.6	22.0	96.4	0.1	1.5	0.2	0.8
31	R, 66		R, 62		D, 63		D, 100	9,272	9,244	0	33,714	27.3	9.9	32.2	34.5	0.0	62.7	0.4	2.3
32	R, 72		R, 80		D, 59		D, 100	11,757	10,990	-7	38,436	32.6	11.3	26.4	51.1	0.1	46.7	0.2	1.8
33	R, 67		R, 69		D, 69		D, 58	7,106	7,125	0	41,002	37.6	15.6	18.5	87.9	0.1	7.3	0.2	2.0
34	R, 53		R, 76		D, 60		D, 100	8,638	8,178	-5	43,354	36.0	15.1	23.0	84.8	0.1	11.4	0.2	1.9
35	D, 62		D, 60		R, 56		R, 83	8,423	7,623	-9	43,571	33.2	12.8	20.3	91.1	0.1	5.2	0.3	1.0
36	D, 100		D, 100		R, 100		D, 53	9,197	8,219	-11	42,150	37.0	14.0	21.4	89.7	0.1	5.6	0.3	1.7
37	D, 66		D, 100		R, 100		R, 100	9,189	8,435	-8	44,196	34.8	13.9	19.0	93.5	0.1	1.7	0.2	2.7
38	D, 77		D, 79		D, 51		R, 57	9,078	8,428	-7	40,822	37.3	12.2	22.3	96.0	0.3	1.4	0.1	1.1
39	R, 51		R, 54		R, 100		R, 75	9,566	9,263	-3	40,067	35.0	12.5	20.8	96.8	0.1	1.1	0.2	0.8
40	R, 70		R, 100		D, 100		D, 53	8,547	8,088	-5	41,296	39.3	14.5	19.9	94.7	0.1	1.6	0.3	1.8
41	R, 45		D, 46		D, 100		D, 63	8,304	8,525	3	33,553	27.6	9.1	31.0	34.3	0.0	62.4	0.1	3.8
42	D, 78		D, 60		D, 100		D, 100	8,706	9,139	5	40,059	28.0	10.6	25.9	39.6	0.0	56.5	0.2	4.6
43	D, 56		D, 56		D, 59		R, 50	9,374	9,501	1	51,458	33.8	13.2	16.7	88.4	0.3	4.8	0.2	3.5
44	D, 69		D, 100		R, 51		R, 56	8,323	9,751	17	51,181	37.0	15.7	12.8	89.1	0.3	3.4	0.5	3.7
45	D, 51		D, 53		R, 100		R, 73	9,646	10,214	6	44,456	35.4	14.2	20.4	93.9	0.1	1.5	0.2	2.5
46	D, 60		D, 69		R, 67		R, 66	10,814	11,109	3	76,017	44.5	25.4	9.9	93.9	0.3	1.2	0.4	2.1
47	D, 57		D, 68		R, 59		R, 67	8,655	9,143	6	64,622	43.9	23.2	8.9	89.8	0.5	3.1	0.6	3.1
48	D, 60		D, 100		D, 51		D, 56	8,148	8,770	8	41,130	35.2	12.8	19.2	87.9	0.3	4.0	0.4	4.3
49	R, 52		R, 59		R, 57		D, 59	8,592	8,695	1	35,273	42.6	22.4	21.8	84.9	0.6	5.2	0.5	5.3
50	R, 100		R, 54		R, 56		R, 62	8,181	8,482	4	65,703	50.0	32.5	10.4	92.3	0.4	2.5	0.4	2.0

(continued)

Note: D=Democrat, R=Republican, R/D=Republican/Democrat (cross-filed), D/R=Democrat/Republican (cross-filed), I=Independent, C=Constitution, O=Other, GI=Green Independent, P=Progressive, P/D=Progressive/Democrat, P/D/R=Progressive/Democrat/Republican, HH=Households

Montana State House Districts—Election and Demographic Data (cont.)

House Districts	General Election Results Party, Percent of Vote							Population			Avg. HH Income	Pop 25+ Some College +	Pop 25+ 4-Yr Degree +	Below Poverty Line	2006 White (Non-Hisp)	African American	American Indians, Alaska Natives	Asians, Hawaiians, Pacific Islanders	Hispanic Origin
Montana	2000	2001	2002	2003	2004	2005	2006	2000	2006	% Change	($)	(%)	(%)	(%)	(%)	(%)	(%)	(%)	(%)
51	R, 52		D, 57		D, 51		D, 59	9,106	9,365	3	32,858	35.7	15.9	24.1	75.4	0.8	6.7	0.6	10.9
52	D, 53		D, 68		D, 56		D, 61	7,285	7,415	2	35,674	37.2	14.4	19.9	84.9	0.7	3.6	0.5	6.5
53	D, 69		D, 64		R, 55		R, 65	8,674	9,266	7	40,302	36.5	15.0	19.0	84.4	0.8	4.7	0.2	5.8
54	D, 61		D, 74		D, 54		D, 59	8,795	8,999	2	36,303	29.5	10.9	19.3	77.5	1.0	6.8	0.5	8.9
55	R, 56		R, 60		R, 64		R, 57	9,284	10,166	10	56,639	45.2	24.0	10.1	93.0	0.3	1.9	0.4	2.5
56	R, 54		R, 64		R, 62		R, 100	8,242	9,209	12	74,094	54.2	35.6	10.6	94.0	0.2	1.4	0.4	2.2
57	D, 100		D, 100		R, 61		R, 62	9,653	10,509	9	77,002	41.6	24.3	12.7	93.3	0.2	1.7	0.5	2.3
58	R, 58		R, 59		D, 51		R, 50	8,403	9,108	8	53,576	34.5	14.2	16.3	93.7	0.2	1.5	0.3	2.7
59	R, 68		R, 63		R, 52		R, 50	8,621	8,948	4	44,584	38.1	18.9	18.6	94.9	0.2	0.9	0.2	2.0
60	R, 64		R, 60		R, 65		R, 100	9,105	9,544	5	51,338	34.8	14.2	15.1	94.1	0.1	0.9	0.2	2.5
61	R, 69		R, 100		R, 58		R, 62	18,249	18,531	2	44,777	40.3	18.8	18.3	93.9	0.3	1.1	0.3	2.6
62	R, 49		R, 50		R, 57		D, 53	8,495	7,976	-6	41,747	38.2	15.8	20.5	93.3	0.3	1.2	0.3	3.1
63	R, 53		R, 51		R, 51		D, 50	9,866	11,281	14	76,636	58.3	40.9	12.0	95.6	0.1	0.7	0.6	1.5
64	D, 54		D, 61		D, 56		D, 57	8,452	10,224	21	40,594	49.8	30.9	16.5	92.6	0.4	1.5	0.6	2.4
65	D, 100		D, 100		D, 61		D, 66	7,367	7,956	8	44,801	47.6	31.5	21.8	90.4	0.6	2.3	2.0	2.5
66	D, 80		D, 85		D, 63		D, 66	8,628	10,618	23	41,117	50.9	34.9	17.2	93.4	0.2	1.5	0.9	2.2
67	D, 80		D, 100		R, 70		R, 71	9,524	10,892	14	48,235	46.7	24.1	11.1	94.3	0.1	1.0	0.4	2.4
68	D, 48		D, 64		R, 65		R, 60	7,950	9,124	15	59,157	47.4	25.6	12.3	95.5	0.2	0.9	0.3	1.4
69	D, 59		D, 55		R, 69		R, 65	9,127	11,407	25	48,802	42.5	21.0	11.9	95.3	0.1	0.8	0.4	1.9
70	D, 47		D, 54		R, 60		R, 53	9,179	10,732	17	65,071	55.4	32.5	10.0	93.6	0.2	0.7	0.4	3.2
71	D, 50		R, 64		R, 73		R, 61	8,988	9,624	7	42,555	40.9	19.3	19.9	94.6	0.1	0.9	0.2	2.0
72	D, 55		D, 100		R, 100		R, 76	9,130	8,623	-6	42,637	41.7	20.0	21.7	92.2	0.2	1.7	0.2	3.3
73	D, 51		D, 49		D, 100		D, 100	7,688	7,242	-6	45,362	35.8	15.4	19.1	93.2	0.1	1.8	0.4	2.8
74	R, 50		R, 60		D, 57		D, 100	8,284	8,125	-2	53,613	40.5	21.8	16.5	95.0	0.1	1.1	0.5	2.0
75	R, 65		R, 62		D, 88		D, 100	9,611	8,971	-7	43,536	36.2	16.3	17.5	91.9	0.2	2.2	0.3	3.3
76	R, 100		R, 100		D, 72		D, 82	8,725	7,927	-9	35,234	34.8	14.8	24.0	87.8	0.2	4.0	0.5	4.5
77	R, 75		R, 58		R, 57		R, 50	9,622	10,641	11	57,694	44.5	24.9	13.5	94.3	0.1	1.4	0.5	1.6
78	R, 56		D, 51		D, 51		D, 53	8,755	9,861	13	46,886	39.0	19.0	11.9	91.9	0.3	3.1	0.2	2.0
79	R, 100		R, 100		D, 62		D, 65	8,929	9,021	1	58,058	47.2	29.1	12.3	93.5	0.1	2.3	0.6	1.7
80	R, 100		R, 49		D, 58		D, 62	8,600	9,298	8	46,681	41.6	20.0	18.4	92.4	0.2	2.4	0.5	2.3
81	R, 83		R, 62		D, 71		D, 73	8,079	7,895	-2	46,315	49.5	31.9	18.8	92.4	0.3	2.2	0.7	2.2
82	D, 50		D, 55		D, 62		D, 71	7,513	7,942	6	54,681	46.6	28.1	13.7	92.9	0.2	2.2	0.5	2.2
83	R, 67		R, 62		R, 100		R, 69	9,581	9,915	3	43,613	34.6	16.0	18.0	95.3	0.1	1.3	0.3	1.6
84	R, 64		R, 70		R, 64		R, 68	9,125	9,778	7	47,933	39.2	17.3	14.2	93.4	0.1	2.2	0.3	2.1
85	D, 100		D, 100		D, 51		D, 100	8,967	8,413	-6	40,869	31.5	11.4	18.0	90.2	0.4	4.0	0.2	2.3
86	R, 57		D, 55		D, 100		D, 100	7,892	7,678	-3	40,099	33.6	13.9	24.0	94.4	0.1	1.5	0.2	1.7
87	R, 53		R, 58		R, 66		R, 65	9,390	10,880	16	57,938	41.0	18.4	17.8	93.4	0.1	1.4	0.3	2.6
88	R, 100		R, 100		R, 53		R, 54	8,461	9,261	9	39,105	37.8	17.8	21.6	93.6	0.1	1.0	0.5	2.6
89	R, 100		R, 58		R, 67		R, 68	9,200	10,696	16	52,401	39.1	16.6	15.0	94.1	0.1	0.9	0.5	2.3
90	R, 53		D, 51		R, 58		R, 59	8,637	9,990	16	49,761	40.9	17.8	13.8	94.9	0.2	1.0	0.2	2.0
91	D, 96		D, 69		D, 52		D, 58	8,560	8,594	0	48,871	40.7	18.3	15.4	92.7	0.2	1.8	0.3	2.1
92	D, 100		D, 62		D, 55		D, 60	9,268	9,532	3	59,381	54.1	33.9	16.9	94.3	0.1	1.4	0.5	1.7
93	R, 61		R, 61		D, 100		D, 64	10,054	10,915	9	61,396	47.4	33.1	19.8	91.2	0.4	2.7	1.4	2.1
94	R, 100		R, 56		D, 63		D, 60	10,078	9,926	-2	50,960	51.1	33.4	17.3	92.6	0.4	1.8	0.8	2.2
95	R, 65		R, 66		D, 60		D, 60	8,690	8,662	0	44,593	49.6	26.4	14.5	92.8	0.3	2.0	0.7	2.0
96	R, 54		R, 58		D, 62		D, 56	8,613	8,783	2	40,726	45.8	22.4	18.5	91.8	0.4	2.8	0.8	2.0
97	R, 55		R, 100		D, 65		D, 71	8,038	7,846	-2	39,190	45.7	23.8	18.8	90.9	0.3	2.4	1.5	2.5
98	D, 100		D, 100		D, 55		D, 58	8,952	10,910	22	37,678	38.3	16.6	20.0	90.7	0.3	2.8	1.1	2.6
99	R, 65		R, 100		D, 64		D, 70	9,688	10,767	11	38,840	44.5	22.5	27.7	87.6	0.3	5.2	0.9	2.8
100	R, 70		R, 100		R, 49		R, 55	8,481	9,149	8	65,543	42.7	22.5	10.6	94.7	0.1	1.4	0.2	1.5

Note: D=Democrat, R=Republican, R/D=Republican/Democrat (cross-filed), D/R=Democrat/Republican (cross-filed), I=Independent, C=Constitution, O=Other, GI=Green Independent, P=Progressive, P/D=Progressive/Democrat, P/D/R=Progressive/Democrat/Republican, HH=Households

NEBRASKA

As the United States was being settled before the Civil War, pioneers moved through Nebraska and kept on going. The vast, treeless prairies reminded many of an ocean, and it intimidated them. There was no wood for shelter, little water for stock or farming, no hills to break the ceaseless wind. Whether Mormons seeking the Kingdom of God or pioneers on the Oregon Trail seeking more hospitable land in the Willamette Valley, they left Nebraska to the grasshoppers. "I do not remember crossing the Missouri River, or anything about the long day's journey through Nebraska," says Jim Burden, the narrator in Willa Cather's novel *My Antonia*. "The only thing very noticeable about Nebraska was that it was still, all day long, Nebraska."

In the 1880s the eastern fringe of Nebraska became a stop for cattle drives moving east toward Chicago and market. Omaha, like Kansas City 200 miles south, filled with stockyards and slaughterhouses. Eastern Nebraska is famous for corn, but west of the 100th meridian, there is not enough rain for agriculture, so it is grazing land. Over the years, Nebraska produced some radicals, most famously William Jennings Bryan and George Norris, but never much industry. Little of the state west of Lincoln has been developed.

Demographically, Nebraska can be separated into Omaha, Lincoln, and everywhere else. Population growth, though slow over the past few decades, is almost identical to the rate of growth in South Dakota and Kansas, the states immediately to the north and south, but slower than in Missouri and Colorado, the states immediately to the east and west. There are few extremes at either end of the growth scale; the fast are not very fast nor the slow very slow. Growth has occurred mostly in the Omaha suburbs, with one startling exception: the 34th district, a rural area near Grand Island that has more than doubled in size since 2000. Other rural districts, however, particularly in the northeast corner of the state and the Sand Hills near the South Dakota line, have continued to lose people.

Omaha and Lincoln contain just about the only high-income areas of the state. The suburbs are wealthy, the city districts poorer. Nebraska has two districts that are much wealthier than the rest. These are the 39th district, in Douglas County northwest of Omaha (average household income, $108,000) and the 4th district, on the western edge of Omaha (average household income, $100,000). Here is the home of investor Warren Buffett, founder of Berkshire Hathaway, the massive holding company. *Forbes* magazine lists Buffett as the third-richest person in the world, with an estimated net worth of $52 billion. By far the poorest district in Nebraska is the 11th, across town and along the river, where average income is only $30,000.

Nebraska, of course, is the Cornhusker State, and there is now a record demand for corn, much of it because of the growing use of ethanol in gasoline. Most Nebraska corn is grown for animal feed, but it is estimated that by 2011 as much as two-thirds of it will be destined not for the table or the feed lot, but for the fuel tank. It has been many years since agriculture was a labor-intensive industry, so it is unlikely that the increased value of corn will bring many people back to the farms.

Nebraska is overwhelmingly white; in thirty-three of its forty-nine districts, the population is at least 80 percent white. This is not to say that it lacks all ethnic diversity. Many Scandinavian families followed the land speculators to Nebraska, and perhaps a tenth of the state is of Czech extraction. The heroine in *My Antonia*, recall, was Bohemian. The state is less than 4 percent African American (about the same percentage as Rhode Island), most of whom are drawn into Omaha's 11th senate district, the only black-majority district in the state. The 7th district, just south of it, is 46 percent Hispanic. Another district, in Grand Island, is one-quarter Hispanic.

Nebraska's legislature is unicameral and nonpartisan, the only one of either in the country. The single legislative chamber is called the Senate. This system was adopted as an experiment, pushed through in 1934 by U.S. senator George Norris, who thought the bicameral system produced too much stalemate. In the United States, unicameral legislatures, although uncommon, were not unprecedented. Pennsylvania and Georgia had unicameral legislatures before 1789, and Minnesota's legislature was nonpartisan (though bicameral) until 1972. Candidates may not run with party designations, but that does not stop them from declaring an affiliation or receiving a party endorsement. In the current Nebraska Senate, avowed Republicans outnumber avowed Democrats, 31–15, with three Independents in the mix.

When Nebraska switched to its unicameral government, it cut the size of its legislature from 133 to 43, putting 90 politicians out of work, which probably explains why it has not been tried elsewhere. This is the only way in which supposedly bland Nebraska has shown itself unafraid to do things differently. It is also one of three states—Louisiana and North Dakota are the others—whose capitol is a skyscraper.

NEBRASKA
State Legislative Districts

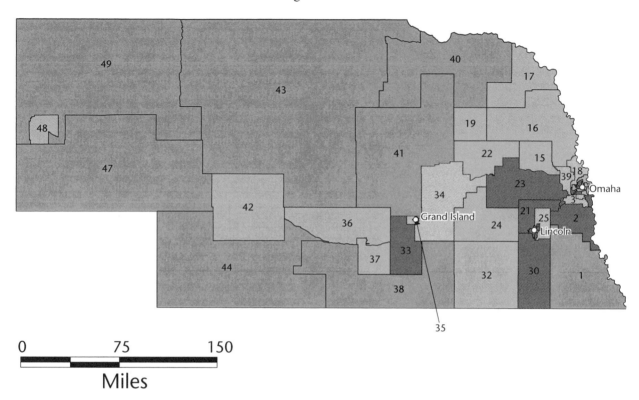

35

0   75   150

Miles

LINCOLN

OMAHA

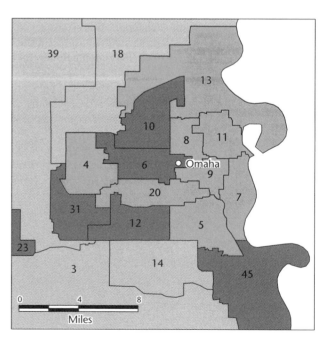

Population Growth   ■ -9% to -5%   ■ -5% to 1%   ■ 1% to 4%   ■ 14% to 25%

Nebraska Legislative Districts—Election and Demographic Data

Senate Districts	General Election Results Party, Percent of Vote							Population			Avg. HH Income	Pop 25+ Some College +	Pop 25+ 4-Yr Degree +	Below Poverty Line	White (Non-Hisp)	African American	American Indians, Alaska Natives	Asians, Hawaiians, Pacific Islanders	Hispanic Origin
Nebraska	2000	2001	2002	2003	2004	2005	2006	2000	2006	% Change	($)	(%)	(%)	(%)	(%)	(%)	(%)	(%)	(%)
1	79				51			34,321	32,423	-6	45,940	32.1	12.9	16.4	94.0	0.3	0.5	0.8	2.0
2			63				69	33,456	34,552	3	57,860	34.1	13.7	10.8	93.9	0.4	0.2	0.5	2.5
3	99				62			36,298	43,485	20	74,972	45.3	22.6	4.8	84.0	3.8	0.2	2.0	4.9
4			100				57	33,944	34,011	0	100,998	52.7	34.5	3.8	88.7	2.9	0.1	2.2	2.8
5	60				100			35,191	34,788	-1	44,710	31.2	11.1	16.1	60.9	5.1	0.4	1.2	22.3
6			58				61	34,719	35,508	2	74,022	52.3	32.8	8.4	84.3	4.1	0.2	3.8	3.8
7	97		100		100			33,960	33,572	-1	36,097	28.8	12.8	23.2	34.0	4.8	0.7	1.4	46.2
8			100				52	33,886	33,203	-2	44,363	40.6	20.9	13.9	73.1	13.7	0.4	1.6	6.0
9	55				57			36,317	35,446	-2	43,742	40.1	23.0	19.0	63.7	6.6	0.5	3.0	18.8
10			51				77	35,732	37,309	4	56,020	45.5	23.2	8.8	81.8	7.7	0.2	2.4	3.8
11	96				100			33,397	32,907	-1	30,546	26.7	10.0	32.5	37.7	50.3	0.5	1.0	6.0
12			78				50	33,607	34,224	2	65,000	44.2	23.3	6.0	83.2	2.9	0.2	2.7	6.4
13	52				69			34,841	35,143	1	51,580	36.1	16.1	15.7	68.5	19.5	0.4	1.0	5.4
14			68				75	35,629	41,534	17	72,889	43.6	20.9	5.2	86.6	2.0	0.2	2.2	4.6
15	100				100			36,121	35,236	-2	48,038	30.2	11.2	14.4	87.5	0.5	0.2	0.7	7.3
16			100				67	34,479	33,172	-4	44,904	28.0	9.2	16.8	86.5	0.5	5.3	0.3	4.0
17	99				60			35,944	34,414	-4	47,226	28.0	11.6	16.6	65.7	0.5	0.6	2.1	20.3
18	57		61				56	36,481	43,972	21	82,858	45.4	25.2	6.7	90.0	2.7	0.2	1.9	2.3
19	98				100			35,127	35,174	0	46,981	32.3	11.9	16.6	76.9	0.9	0.6	0.5	13.7
20			100				58	33,814	33,412	-1	64,293	48.1	27.2	9.5	86.7	3.1	0.2	1.7	4.5
21	99				100			34,924	38,171	9	54,165	38.7	17.1	11.2	84.9	2.1	0.4	3.0	4.6
22			53				100	35,085	33,967	-3	50,288	31.9	11.6	14.7	83.2	0.4	0.1	0.5	9.8
23	99				53			34,571	35,090	2	53,606	30.5	12.4	13.4	80.7	0.5	0.1	0.3	10.8
24			100				51	35,027	34,089	-3	51,510	35.0	13.6	13.7	94.6	0.6	0.1	0.5	2.1
25	99				100			36,282	41,624	15	83,131	53.7	34.4	5.4	92.8	0.8	0.1	1.8	1.9
26			61				59	35,091	35,518	1	51,011	44.9	22.2	11.9	88.3	1.6	0.2	2.5	3.4
27	57				100			33,494	34,670	4	57,505	47.8	25.3	12.1	79.7	3.4	0.4	3.3	7.0
28			100				57	35,922	35,119	-2	44,469	48.9	28.1	16.8	79.5	3.1	0.4	3.9	6.5
29	56				70			34,812	35,900	3	69,025	51.1	31.6	6.1	89.8	1.6	0.1	2.6	2.8
30			100				58	36,353	38,035	5	53,105	35.9	15.2	13.0	94.4	0.8	0.3	0.6	1.7
31	99				50			35,220	37,198	6	81,142	47.8	27.7	4.2	89.3	2.4	0.1	1.7	3.2
32			53				59	34,833	33,234	-5	45,882	30.1	10.7	16.6	86.4	0.4	0.2	1.0	8.6
33	63				55			35,663	37,864	6	49,718	35.5	13.8	14.6	87.8	0.6	0.2	1.6	5.9
34			66				51	34,807	43,267	24	48,324	31.7	11.3	15.7	74.3	0.4	0.1	1.0	15.3
35	73				100			33,476	33,443	0	44,894	30.4	10.7	17.7	59.5	0.4	0.2	1.6	25.7
36			100				55	36,725	36,862	0	47,780	29.8	12.6	15.6	63.3	0.2	0.2	0.6	22.9
37	100		100		68			35,146	35,482	1	49,647	40.4	21.0	15.3	89.6	0.7	0.2	0.9	4.6
38			64				54	35,439	32,888	-7	45,169	34.6	12.5	16.3	95.0	0.3	0.1	0.4	2.3
39	64				100			36,003	44,325	23	108,229	45.8	26.8	3.7	91.4	1.8	0.1	1.4	2.5
40			67				67	34,575	31,677	-8	42,193	29.2	10.0	19.6	95.9	0.3	1.0	0.2	1.1
41	50		63		100			36,119	33,856	-6	40,694	30.7	10.4	20.1	96.0	0.3	0.1	0.2	1.7
42			69				57	34,639	34,703	0	49,819	35.6	11.6	16.8	87.4	0.6	0.2	0.5	5.9
43	52				50			34,194	31,615	-8	40,031	33.9	12.1	19.6	96.2	0.3	0.4	0.4	1.1
44			100				58	35,091	32,669	-7	43,484	35.3	11.8	17.5	93.9	0.3	0.2	0.3	2.8
45	57				56			35,584	38,433	8	59,738	41.9	17.5	7.8	78.0	5.5	0.2	2.9	6.8
46			70				55	32,542	33,190	2	39,484	33.4	15.9	21.5	74.8	4.5	0.5	6.5	6.6
47	54				100			34,062	31,624	-7	43,961	34.0	11.7	17.1	90.0	0.3	0.3	0.4	5.2
48			100				58	33,209	32,225	-3	46,703	34.6	12.8	18.2	66.9	0.3	0.9	0.6	20.3
49	80		57		100			33,930	31,003	-9	45,922	35.5	13.8	19.0	85.4	0.5	1.6	0.5	6.2

Note: D=Democrat, R=Republican, R/D=Republican/Democrat (cross-filed), D/R=Democrat/Republican (cross-filed), I=Independent, C=Constitution, O=Other, GI=Green Independent, P=Progressive, P/D=Progressive/Democrat, P/D/R=Progressive/Democrat/Republican, HH=Households

NEVADA

Nevada, a state built on silver mining, is no stranger to boom and bust. It was born on a boom, with the discovery of the Comstock Lode in 1859, and was admitted to the Union six years later, with only about ten thousand inhabitants, in order to provide Abraham Lincoln with enough votes in the Senate to pass the Thirteenth Amendment. By the end of the century, many of the mines had been played out.

James Bryce, an English lord, liked most things he saw in the United States but served scorn on Nevada in his landmark book, *The American Commonwealth,* which nevertheless nailed the state's political history pretty well. "Its population is obviously unworthy of the privilege of sending two men to the Senate," Bryce wrote, "and it did in fact allow itself to sink forthwith . . . into a sort of rotten borough which could be controlled or purchased by the leaders of a Silver Ring. It would evidently have been better to allow Nevada to remain in the condition of a Territory till a large settled and orderly community had occupied her surface, which is at present a parched and dismal desert, where the streams that descend from the eastern slope of the Sierra Nevada soon lose themselves in lakes or marshes."

One shudders to think of what Bryce would have had to say about Las Vegas, but it took a while for Nevada to settle on sin as an economic base. Slot machines were banned in 1901 and a quickie, six-month divorce law repealed in 1913. Nevada soon reversed itself, lowering the wait for a divorce to three months in 1927, then knocked it down again to six weeks in 1931, when it also legalized gambling.

As late as the 1960s, when the Rat Pack played the Sands Hotel, Las Vegas was still more a tourist destination than a city, and Reno remained a rival. The real Las Vegas boom, and hence the Nevada boom, has come more recently, when the city stopped being a resort and started becoming a new home for young families fed up with the congestion of southern California or for northeasterners seeking a warmer climate.

Nevada swelled by 50 percent during the 1980s, a rate of 6,000 new residents each week, and by 66 percent in the 1990s. It has grown by another 17 percent in this decade, four times the national average and a rate only Arizona comes close to matching. As recently as 1980, it had only one seat in Congress. It now has three and will have five by 2030.

A map of Nevada's population, though, resembles a large funnel, with everything squeezed down into the lower tip, which is Clark County and its two big cities, Las Vegas and Henderson. Everything turns on Clark County and, to a much lesser extent, Reno. Take them away, and the state becomes Wyoming. The Las Vegas metro area, which grew by more than 85 percent during the 1990s, is now the thirty-second largest and is about the same size as the Providence, Columbus, and Virginia Beach metro areas. But Henderson, which had 24,000 residents in 1980, has 225,000 now and is bigger than Orlando or Durham, North Carolina.

This area is expanding at a breathtaking rate. The 22nd state house district, just southwest of Henderson, has grown by 157 percent just since 2000; the 13th district, just west of that, by 122 percent. The only part of the state to have lost people in this decade is the sheep-grazing country near the Utah and Idaho borders.

Nevada does not show the extreme aggregations of wealth suggestive of a boom, of persons making their fortunes overnight. The wealthy districts are not that wealthy, and average income figures quickly level off from both ends of the scale into a broad middle that suggests stable and sustainable growth. Furthermore, three of the six wealthiest districts are not in Las Vegas at all, but in Reno and Carson City. The poorest districts are located in North Las Vegas and the southern part of the city, areas in which Hispanics make up three-quarters of the population. This shows how the composition of the state is changing. In 1990 Hispanics made up 10 percent of Nevada's population, in 2000 they made up 20 percent.

There are currently sixty-three members of the state legislature (forty-two members of the assembly and twenty-one senators), although the state constitution authorizes a legislature of up to seventy-five members. Given that Las Vegas, Henderson, and Reno account for thirty-two of those assembly seats and seventeen of the senate seats, it is, if anything, surprising that the influx of huge numbers of new residents has not shaken up the state's political system even more.

Nevada has been a Republican state but there is evidence that rapid growth will also make it more politically competitive. George W. Bush carried the state twice but received only 50 percent of the vote each time, his worst showing in the Mountain West. The 1998 U.S. Senate race between Democrat Harry Reid and Republican John Ensign, now colleagues, was won by Reid with a 428-vote margin. The U.S. representative for the rapidly growing Las Vegas district is also a Democrat. A Republican won the governor's race in 2006, but Democrats won races for attorney general, treasurer, and secretary of state.

Democrats control the state assembly and their margin there has hardly budged since 2000. Republicans have controlled the state senate through the decade but do so now only by a single seat. Although Republicans hold some Las Vegas senatorial districts, their strength tends to be in other parts of the state. Given the rate at which Las Vegas is booming, the GOP's hold on the chamber may be in jeopardy.

NEVADA
State Senate Districts

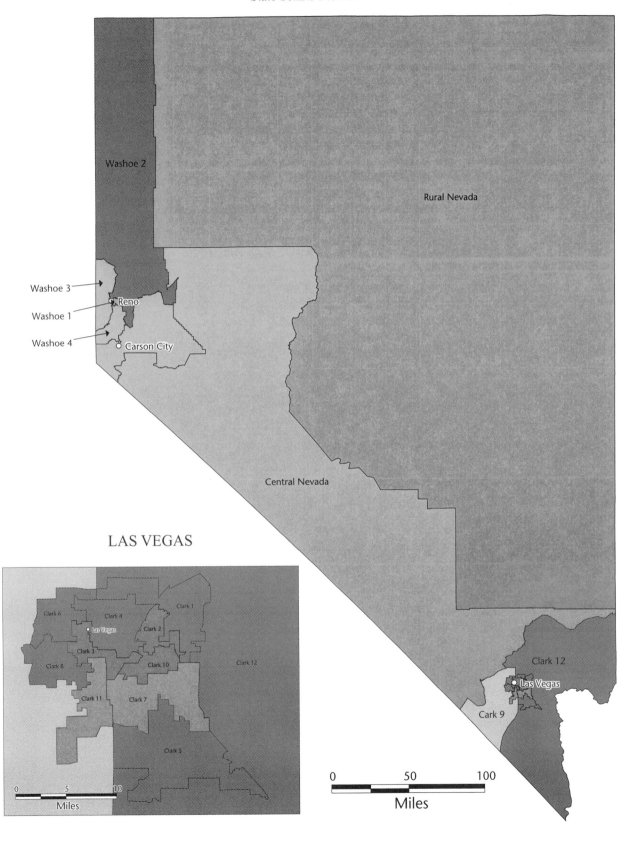

Washoe 2

Rural Nevada

Washoe 3

Reno

Washoe 1

Washoe 4   Carson City

Central Nevada

Clark 12

Las Vegas

Cark 9

LAS VEGAS

Clark 6   Clark 4   Clark 1

Las Vegas   Clark 2

Clark 3

Clark 8   Clark 10   Clark 12

Clark 11   Clark 7

Clark 5

0   5   10
Miles

0   50   100
Miles

Population Growth   -2% to 15%   15% to 24%   24% to 105%   105% to 106%

Nevada State Senate Districts—Election and Demographic Data

Senate Districts	General Election Results Party, Percent of Vote							Population			Avg. HH Income	Pop 25+		Below Poverty Line	White (Non-Hisp)	African American	American Indians, Alaska Natives	Asians, Hawaiians, Pacific Islanders	Hispanic Origin
												Some College +	4-Yr Degree +		2006				
Nevada	2000	2001	2002	2003	2004	2005	2006	2000	2006	% Change	($)	(%)	(%)	(%)	(%)	(%)	(%)	(%)	(%)
Clark-1					D, 61			99,421	129,204	29.96	55,157	27.1	7.9	11.0	51.2	14.8	1.0	7.1	26.2
Clark-2	D, 61		D, 67				D, 73	95,529	107,506	12.54	44,538	13.1	3.6	24.0	18.4	16.3	1.2	4.3	69.6
Clark-3	D, 62				D, 61			99,712	110,134	10.45	53,325	28.8	10.1	15.6	53.3	10.7	0.9	7.1	27.6
Clark-4	D, 100				D, 72			106,461	135,739	27.50	57,164	26.0	7.9	14.7	42.1	25.7	1.0	5.4	29.6
Clark-5	R, 56		R, 57		R, 55		D, 48	193,683	258,663	33.55	79,519	39.4	16.5	6.1	70.5	3.9	0.6	7.6	15.9
Clark-6	R, 54				R, 68			91,341	117,049	28.15	81,919	42.3	18.4	5.5	72.7	6.2	0.5	6.8	12.7
Clark-7	D, 68		D, 100		D, 64		D, 100	191,203	223,299	16.79	49,359	28.9	10.0	14.6	51.1	8.3	0.9	8.2	31.5
Clark-8	D, 62		R, 63				R, 55	93,651	118,770	26.82	92,480	41.2	18.8	6.3	69.1	6.2	0.6	8.7	14.3
Clark-9			R, 54				R, 66	97,556	200,408	105.43	82,161	38.7	16.1	6.3	67.2	4.5	0.6	11.8	14.8
Clark-10			D, 67				D, 100	100,240	110,883	10.62	43,043	20.3	6.5	22.1	30.6	10.1	1.1	8.5	54.0
Clark-11					D, 54			98,189	112,967	15.05	50,309	29.5	10.0	12.8	49.0	7.0	0.9	10.5	32.5
Clark-12			R, 63				R, 67	98,886	145,300	46.94	67,865	34.1	12.4	9.7	69.9	4.0	1.0	5.3	17.7
Washoe-1							D, 100	90,386	102,214	13.09	44,849	27.8	10.9	19.4	48.1	3.4	2.2	9.0	36.0
Washoe-2			R, 57				R, 55	84,875	105,282	24.04	66,234	34.7	13.8	7.6	72.4	1.5	3.2	4.7	15.6
Washoe-3	R, 76				R, 68			90,788	107,721	18.65	81,127	45.5	24.9	7.0	78.6	1.3	1.0	6.2	10.7
Washoe-4			R, 76				R, 100	89,131	105,554	18.43	81,512	43.0	21.9	10.0	68.5	1.4	1.2	4.5	21.2
Capital			R, 82				R, 78	93,035	110,803	19.10	64,287	39.5	13.0	12.0	79.0	1.0	2.3	2.0	13.2
Central Nevada	R, 68				R, 71			91,324	105,090	15.07	56,297	32.0	9.4	14.5	78.3	1.8	3.2	2.0	12.5
Rural Nevada	R, 83				R, 79			91,376	89,808	-1.72	56,922	28.9	8.4	13.6	70.3	1.3	4.8	1.0	19.2

Note: D=Democrat, R=Republican, R/D=Republican/Democrat (cross-filed), D/R=Democrat/Republican (cross-filed), I=Independent, C=Constitution, O=Other, GI=Green Independent, P=Progressive, P/D=Progressive/Democrat, P/D/R=Progressive/Democrat/Republican, HH=Households

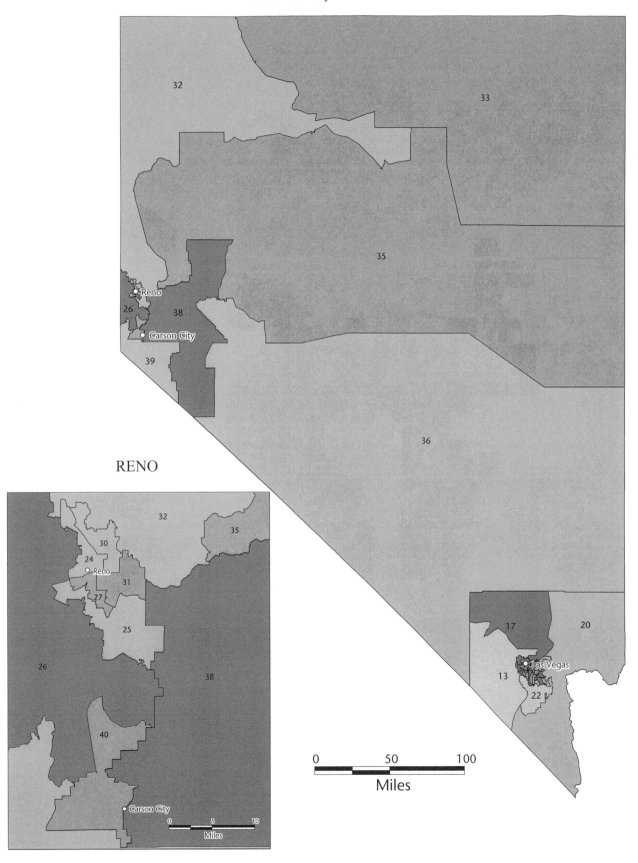

NEVADA
State Assembly Districts

RENO

Population Growth   -4% to 13%   13% to 25%   25% to 121%   121% to 158%

LAS VEGAS

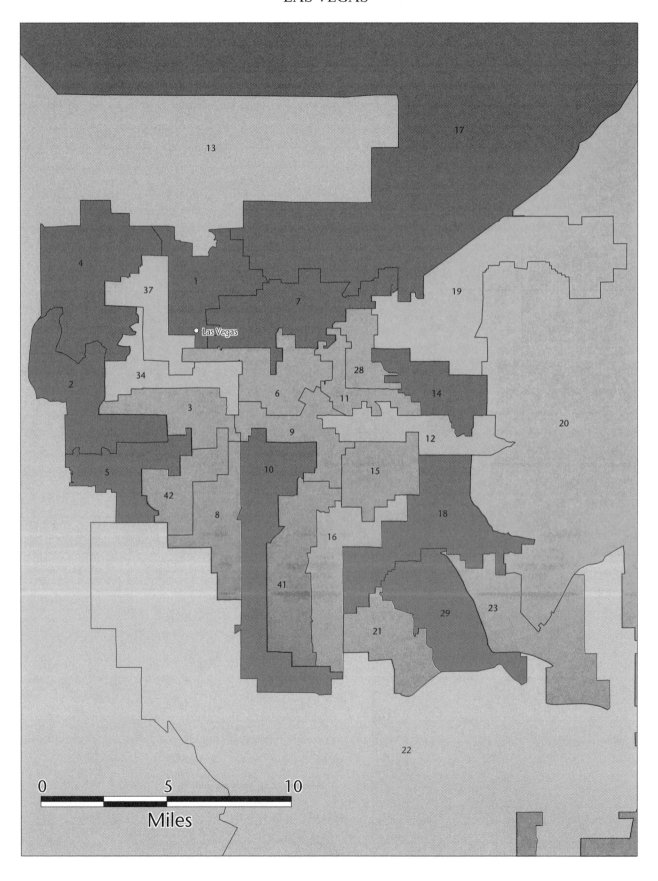

Population Growth ■ -4% to 13% ■ 13% to 25% ■ 25% to 121% □ 121% to 158%

Nevada State Assembly Districts—Election and Demographic Data

Assembly Districts	General Election Results Party, Percent of Vote							Population			Avg. HH Income	Pop 25+		Below Poverty Line	White (Non-Hisp)	African American	American Indians, Alaska Natives	Asians, Hawaiians, Pacific Islanders	Hispanic Origin
										2006									
												Some College +	4-Yr Degree +						
Nevada	2000	2001	2002	2003	2004	2005	2006	2000	2006	% Change	($)	(%)	(%)	(%)	(%)	(%)	(%)	(%)	(%)
1	D, 65		D, 64		D, 54		D, 58	49,187	62,750	27.57	67,604	32.5	10.7	6.5	65.3	8.9	0.9	5.1	18.4
2	R, 73		R, 77		R, 58		R, 52	48,980	66,895	36.58	102,356	45.6	23.3	5.4	73.0	4.9	0.4	8.8	11.7
3	D, 67		D, 49		D, 60		D, 51	46,949	50,234	7.00	57,574	30.0	10.0	12.2	57.8	7.0	0.9	6.6	26.0
4	R, 77		R, 65		R, 63		R, 56	45,412	62,397	37.40	92,289	44.8	20.3	5.4	76.2	4.7	0.5	6.4	11.1
5	R, 55		R, 55		R, 51		R, 51	45,792	58,136	26.96	78,091	38.7	16.1	7.2	61.1	5.4	0.4	18.0	15.1
6	D, 66		D, 70		D, 74		D, 100	49,149	54,474	10.83	47,438	20.6	6.6	24.5	31.6	32.1	1.0	4.6	39.1
7	D, 77		D, 61		D, 70		D, 61	47,672	62,701	31.53	54,450	22.9	6.6	14.9	32.3	30.3	0.9	6.2	37.5
8	D, 65		D, 65		D, 67		D, 68	50,331	55,396	10.06	45,372	28.4	9.8	14.1	45.1	7.8	1.0	11.5	35.8
9	D, 66		D, 100		D, 79		D, 75	45,956	48,128	4.73	46,611	27.1	10.3	22.5	41.3	9.0	0.9	8.1	42.3
10	D, 67		D, 100		D, 55		D, 53	46,620	63,798	36.85	53,526	33.4	12.7	14.0	53.4	6.6	0.8	11.9	27.8
11	D, 63		D, 68		D, 73		D, 100	47,286	50,205	6.17	43,021	13.3	4.0	26.6	15.5	11.4	1.3	5.6	74.9
12	D, 54		D, 100		D, 68		D, 71	48,530	56,396	16.21	48,483	24.0	7.4	15.6	44.9	9.0	1.0	11.2	36.1
13	R, 51		R, 55		R, 55		R, 52	48,302	107,211	121.96	81,602	39.5	16.2	4.5	67.6	5.9	0.7	9.2	15.3
14	D, 56		D, 58		D, 61		D, 75	52,375	66,019	26.05	55,655	23.1	7.1	13.6	42.3	13.9	1.0	9.0	36.7
15	D, 52		D, 52		D, 60		D, 100	45,343	48,648	7.29	53,513	32.8	11.7	12.6	60.1	6.6	1.0	5.9	25.2
16	D, 58		D, 58		D, 62		D, 76	49,615	56,372	13.62	60,851	34.6	13.4	10.6	57.8	6.1	0.8	8.4	26.4
17	D, 58		D, 52		D, 57		D, 54	46,755	66,093	41.36	59,332	30.1	9.0	8.6	52.1	16.4	0.9	7.1	23.7
18	D, 100		D, 65		D, 62		D, 66	51,841	68,393	31.93	56,713	29.7	9.9	11.7	59.2	6.7	1.0	5.8	25.5
19	D, 58		D, 57		D, 68		D, 70	50,854	58,340	14.72	49,222	23.1	6.0	15.0	46.1	14.9	1.3	5.8	33.3
20	R, 63		R, 59		R, 71		R, 69	51,657	61,840	19.71	62,764	32.8	11.3	11.1	71.2	2.7	1.2	2.5	19.2
21	R, 59		R, 55		R, 56		R, 51	46,052	55,716	20.98	95,936	42.7	19.5	5.5	74.4	3.6	0.5	7.2	13.0
22	R, 50		R, 64		R, 56		R, 56	47,245	121,480	157.13	88,077	41.3	17.6	6.6	73.7	3.1	0.6	7.7	13.4
23	D, 63		D, 100		D, 58		D, 51	46,698	55,984	19.89	57,098	28.4	8.3	11.8	70.6	4.0	1.1	3.4	18.9
24	D, 54		R, 52		R, 48		D, 55	45,529	52,528	15.37	51,649	33.2	15.0	14.5	59.9	3.0	1.7	8.8	24.7
25	R, 82		R, 84		R, 67		R, 100	46,557	54,910	17.94	95,439	52.2	30.6	6.0	82.4	1.2	0.7	4.9	9.1
26	R, 67		R, 61		R, 61		R, 64	49,948	62,639	25.41	98,645	48.7	27.9	5.8	82.4	0.9	0.7	6.1	8.2
27	D, 100		D, 53		D, 63		D, 76	47,954	53,268	11.08	50,014	36.2	17.7	17.2	56.5	2.7	1.6	7.5	28.9
28	D, 55		D, 65		D, 76		D, 100	45,747	48,683	6.42	45,536	11.8	3.2	24.3	14.8	13.4	1.1	4.2	76.3
29	D, 79		R, 55		D, 54		D, 58	49,025	63,096	28.70	75,616	38.4	16.7	6.1	69.2	4.6	0.7	6.8	16.9
30	D, 53		R, 50		D, 59		D, 100	48,777	57,616	18.12	49,443	25.6	7.7	15.0	54.1	3.1	2.1	6.7	31.9
31	D, 51		D, 55		D, 59		D, 58	50,305	54,526	8.39	53,373	30.3	11.2	13.0	52.5	2.3	2.2	6.5	33.5
32	R, 58		R, 65		R, 66		R, 59	46,645	55,848	19.73	76,563	37.4	15.9	5.2	76.7	1.4	2.4	4.1	12.8
33	R, 100		R, 74		R, 100		R, 100	47,597	46,058	-3.23	59,112	29.1	8.7	12.0	67.1	0.6	6.0	1.0	21.8
34	R, 76		D, 52		D, 100		D, 100	49,666	56,577	13.91	64,562	34.1	13.0	8.3	60.0	8.0	0.8	7.2	22.8
35	D, 81		R, 52		R, 56		R, 100	48,151	46,842	-2.72	54,663	30.2	8.7	15.0	72.6	1.9	7.0	1.9	14.2
36	D, 54		R, 62		R, 73		R, 53	49,338	56,452	14.42	47,967	27.9	7.7	17.2	81.3	1.6	3.3	1.6	10.0
37	R, 78		D, 51		D, 54		D, 100	45,429	55,789	22.80	64,269	34.6	13.0	7.9	61.3	10.2	0.7	8.2	18.8
38	D, 65		R, 53		R, 60		R, 62	50,883	65,490	28.71	56,691	34.0	8.9	12.6	80.3	0.7	2.4	1.2	12.6
39	R, 71		R, 84		R, 63		R, 65	49,228	56,616	15.01	82,929	46.2	18.0	9.5	83.0	0.2	1.6	2.3	10.7
40	D, 53		R, 50		D, 51		D, 56	45,210	49,206	8.84	58,247	37.1	12.8	13.5	71.0	1.7	2.6	2.5	19.8
41	D, 65		D, 54		D, 59		D, 60	47,671	50,755	6.47	48,053	29.2	10.7	17.1	47.3	7.8	0.9	10.2	34.4
42	D, 100		D, 65		D, 59		D, 100	46,196	50,094	8.44	59,853	30.4	10.8	9.9	53.3	6.1	0.7	10.8	27.9

Note: D=Democrat, R=Republican, R/D=Republican/Democrat (cross-filed), D/R=Democrat/Republican (cross-filed), I=Independent, C=Constitution, O=Other, GI=Green Independent, P=Progressive, P/D=Progressive/Democrat, P/D/R=Progressive/Democrat/Republican, HH=Households

NEW HAMPSHIRE

New Hampshire's has a very unusual legislature. Its upper chamber has only twenty-four members, making it the second-smallest state senate in the country. Its lower chamber has 400 members, making it the third-largest deliberative body in the world, behind the House of Commons in London and the House of Representatives in Washington. If the U.S. House were apportioned at the same rate, it would have almost 100,000 members.

Representatives in the New Hampshire house may have as few as 3,000 constituents. Many of the districts are small enough that it is possible to know a large share of the voters personally, to keep one's telephone number listed, and to campaign on foot, practicing the sort of retail politics that New Hampshire voters require of aspiring presidential candidates who visit every four years. Contrast that with California, where members of the state assembly represent more than 420,000 people and TV or radio advertising is the only effective way to communicate. Such are the quirks of democracy in different corners of the United States.

Small, however, is not necessarily beautiful. "As a body it mills about with a vast deal of waste motion because of its unwieldy size," wrote journalist Ralph D. Paine of the New Hampshire house in the *Atlantic Monthly* more than eighty years ago. "It grinds a small amount of grist for the number of hands employed. Every attempt to decrease its numbers by the enactment of a constitutional amendment has been pugnaciously defeated. The men of the farms and villages refuse to be robbed of the prize of going to the legislature. It is an honor which custom decrees should pass in rotation from one substantial citizen to another. As a rule it shows a greedy spirit to expect more than one term at Concord."

In addition to keeping the size of its legislature sacrosanct, New Hampshire is also famous for its refusal to enact an income or sales tax. That parsimony has made it a haven for the overtaxed from other parts of New England. The state has also become a high-tech center and claims to have the nation's highest rate of Internet access. New Hampshire has grown faster than any other state in the region, more than twice as fast as Massachusetts during the 1990s and more than four times as fast since 2000.

The New Hampshire that has embraced high tech is doing quite well, especially parts of Merrimac County south of Concord and Belknap County in the Lakes Region. Few places are now losing population; the shakeout in the manufacturing, logging, and shipbuilding industries that made the early 1990s traumatic seems complete.

New Hampshire is a fairly wealthy state: median household income is almost $57,000, about what it is in Hawaii. The wealthiest district, in fact the only one in which household income exceeds $100,000, is in Hillsboro County, where many Massachusetts tax refugees live (Boston is less than an hour's drive away) and home to a number of high-tech businesses. The poorest district is in Coos (the name has two syllables) County up by the Quebec, Canada, border, where more than one person in eight speaks French at home.

Racially, New Hampshire is one of the most homogeneous states. It is 96.0 percent white (just behind Vermont, which is 96.8 percent, according to recent Census Bureau calculations) and although some of its house districts are as small as neighborhoods, it has only one (in Manchester) where African Americans make up less than 5 percent of the population. Hispanics make up less than 2 percent of the state's population, although more than a quarter of part of Nashua.

Notwithstanding some glacial demographic changes, colonial traditions live on. One tradition is that that New Hampshire's governor is the last in the country to serve a two-year term. Another is that he or she is officially known as "Your Excellency." A third is that the legislature is officially known as the General Court, as it is in Massachusetts and as it once was in Vermont.

Republicans controlled the General Court for decades but the Democratic governor vetoed their redistricting plan in 2002, sending the matter to the state supreme court, which made some radical changes. While keeping the number of representatives at 400 (it was trimmed from 432 back in 1942), the court consolidated more than half of the legislative districts, creating many more multimember districts and replacing much of the old system, which gave each small town its own seat, with a number of at-large seats.

Those changes, combined with the state's general drift to the left (though less pronounced than in Vermont) have created much more unpredictability. New Hampshire was the only state to vote for George W. Bush in 2000 but abandon him in 2004. Democrats made big gains in the house in the first election under the new plan, picking up twenty-two seats only to lose them and more in the next election. But they gained ninety-two seats in 2006 and now enjoy a 239–161 majority. For good measure, they picked up five senate seats to win a majority in that body, as well, and now control both the governor's mansion and the legislature for the first time since 1874.

NEW HAMPSHIRE
State Senate Districts

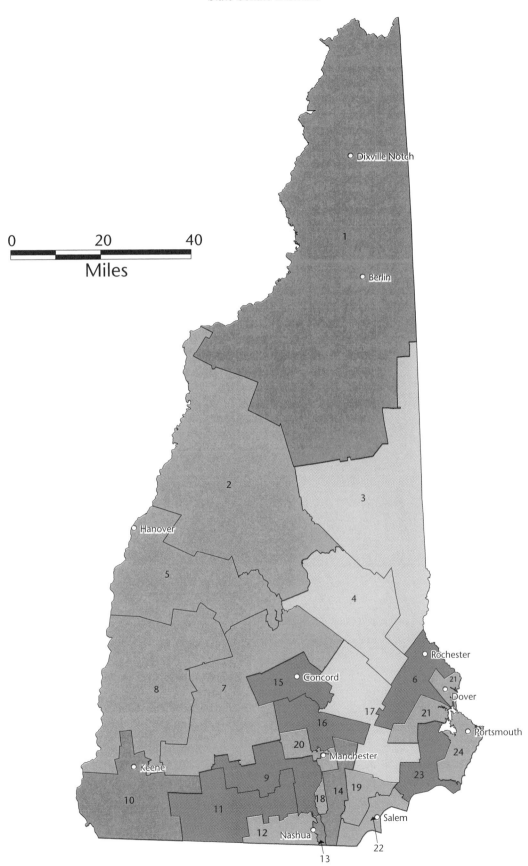

Population Growth   ☐ 1% to 5%   ☐ 5% to 7%   ☐ 7% to 9%   ☐ 9% to 11%

New Hampshire State Senate Districts—Election and Demographic Data

| Senate Districts | General Election Results Party, Percent of Vote | | | | | | | Population | | | Avg. HH Income | Pop 25+ | | 2006 Below Poverty Line | White (Non-Hisp) | African American | American Indians, Alaska Natives | Asians, Hawaiians, Pacific Islanders | Hispanic Origin |
| | | | | | | | | | | | | Some College + | 4-Yr Degree + | | | | | | |
New Hamp.	2000	2001	2002	2003	2004	2005	2006	2000	2006	% Change	($)	(%)	(%)	(%)	(%)	(%)	(%)	(%)	(%)
1	R, 51		R, 68		R, 60		R, 58	50,510	51,518	2.00	47,267	32.2	14.5	17.5	96.8	0.2	0.5	0.7	0.9
2	R, 72		R, 58		R, 54		D, 55	51,353	54,206	5.56	59,307	38.6	20.9	12.5	96.8	0.3	0.3	0.8	0.8
3	R, 54		R, 66		R, 60		R, 51	50,214	55,116	9.76	56,956	37.8	17.6	13.0	97.1	0.2	0.5	0.6	0.9
4	R, 54		R, 58		R, 53		D, 52	51,054	56,276	10.23	61,901	38.1	17.4	10.7	96.6	0.4	0.5	0.8	0.9
5	D, 52		D, 53		D, 58		D, 71	49,148	51,992	5.79	67,717	41.4	26.0	11.2	92.8	0.8	0.5	3.1	1.6
6	D, 51		R, 55		R, 59		D, 59	52,659	56,778	7.82	57,092	37.0	16.3	11.6	95.3	0.6	0.3	1.3	1.5
7	R, 50		R, 56		R, 52		D, 58	49,344	52,707	6.82	64,266	38.4	20.5	9.6	96.8	0.3	0.4	0.7	1.0
8	D, 100		R, 52		R, 62		R, 58	51,070	54,080	5.89	60,580	35.2	18.1	12.1	97.0	0.3	0.5	0.6	0.9
9	R, 62		R, 67		R, 64		R, 53	53,296	57,378	7.66	100,087	46.4	30.1	4.0	94.7	0.7	0.3	1.9	1.6
10	R, 58		R/D, 99	R, 52		D, 63	50,826	52,812		3.91	56,904	35.7	19.4	13.4	96.4	0.4	0.4	0.8	1.1
11	D, 49		R, 60		R, 51		R, 54	53,253	57,633	8.22	80,170	41.2	25.4	8.1	95.4	0.8	0.3	1.4	1.4
12	R, 55		R, 61		R, 50		D, 58	50,119	52,773	5.30	90,956	48.1	31.6	5.3	89.0	1.4	0.2	5.1	3.1
13	D, 62		D, 50		D/R, 99	D, 59	48,176	49,850		3.47	60,881	36.7	21.2	13.2	74.8	3.0	0.7	5.5	13.0
14	R, 56		R, 66		R, 61		R, 55	53,720	56,108	4.45	87,260	42.1	23.9	5.1	94.0	0.8	0.3	1.7	2.3
15	D, 62		D, 60		D, 67		D, 71	53,520	57,849	8.09	64,752	43.1	23.4	11.4	94.0	1.0	0.5	1.8	1.7
16	R, 51		R, 64		R, 62		R, 51	52,460	56,644	7.98	76,013	44.3	27.0	7.7	91.6	1.4	0.4	3.1	2.5
17	R, 63		R, 61		R, 61		R, 59	51,437	56,557	9.95	68,435	38.0	18.1	8.3	96.6	0.4	0.4	0.5	1.2
18	D, 54		R, 53		R, 50		D, 56	47,154	49,797	5.61	59,320	33.9	17.1	11.4	87.7	1.8	0.5	2.8	5.6
19	R, 58		R, 69		R, 60		R/D, 100	52,445	55,645	6.10	83,061	44.6	26.2	6.4	93.9	0.8	0.3	1.7	2.4
20	D, 56		D, 53		D, 54		D, 62	54,443	57,393	5.42	54,296	31.9	16.5	16.2	85.4	2.5	0.6	2.5	6.7
21	D, 66		D, 54		D, 54		R/D, 100	50,873	53,812	5.78	64,594	42.1	25.1	11.3	92.5	1.1	0.3	3.3	1.6
22	R, 59		R, 67		R, 62		R, 53	52,363	55,401	5.80	82,090	42.4	23.7	7.0	93.2	0.5	0.3	2.5	2.5
23	D, 53		R, 54		D, 52		D, 60	52,838	57,291	8.43	76,383	45.3	27.3	8.9	95.4	0.5	0.2	1.5	1.5
24	D, 51		D, 56		D, 52		D, 59	51,974	55,444	6.68	79,783	53.8	36.5	9.8	93.7	1.3	0.2	2.3	1.7

Note: D=Democrat, R=Republican, R/D=Republican/Democrat (cross-filed), D/R=Democrat/Republican (cross-filed), I=Independent, C=Constitution, O=Other, GI=Green Independent, P=Progressive, P/D=Progressive/Democrat, P/D/R=Progressive/Democrat/Republican, HH=Households

NEW HAMPSHIRE
State House Districts

Be — Belknap
Ca — Carroll
Ch — Cheshire
Co — Coos
Gr — Grafton
Hi — Hillsborough
Me — Merrimack
Ro — Rockingham
St — Strafford
Su — Sullivan

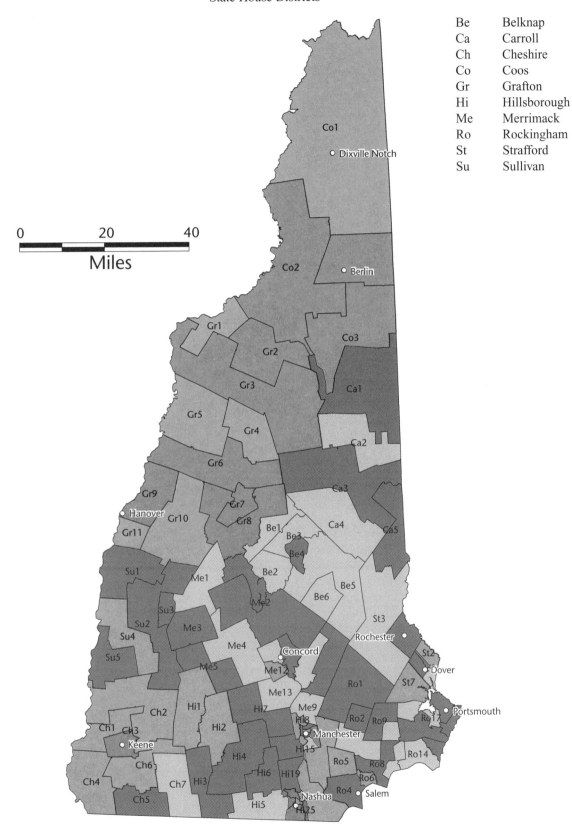

Population Growth — -4% to 3%   — 3% to 5%   — 5% to 8%   — 8% to 17%

CONCORD/MANCHESTER

Be6

Be5

Me6

Me11

Me10

○ Concord

Me4

Me12

Me7

Me8

Ro1

Me13

Hi7

Me9

Ro2

Hi8

Hi17

Hi9

Hi
10

Hi11

Hi12

Manchester ○

Hi4

Hi14

Hi13

Ro7

Hi16

Hi18

Hi15

Ro3

Ro5

Hi19

0   4   8

Miles

Population Growth   ■ -4% to 3%   ■ 3% to 5%   ■ 5% to 8%   ■ 8% to 17%

PORTSMOUTH/ROCHESTER

Population Growth ▢ -4% to 3% ▢ 3% to 5% ▢ 5% to 8% ▢ 8% to 17%

KEENE

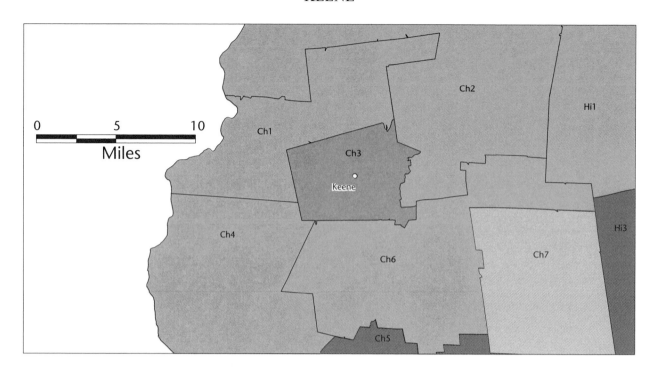

NASHUA

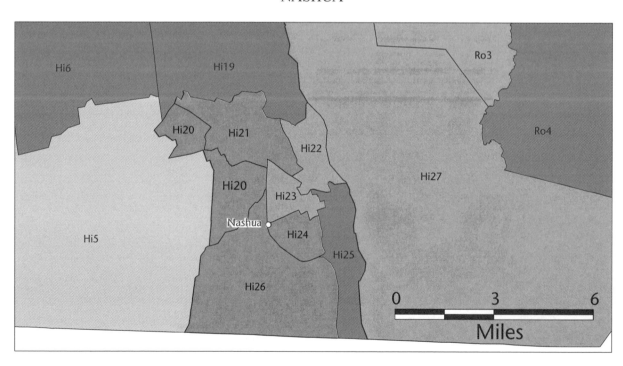

Population Growth ▨ -4% to 3%   ▨ 3% to 5%   ▨ 5% to 8%   ▨ 8% to 17%

New Hampshire State House Districts—Election and Demographic Data

| House Districts | General Election Results Party, Percent of Vote | | | | | | | Population | | | Avg. HH Income | Pop 25+ | | 2006 | | | | | |
| | | | | | | | | | | | | Some College + | 4-Yr Degree + | Below Poverty Line | White (Non-Hisp) | African American | American Indians, Alaska Natives | Asians, Hawaiians, Pacific Islanders | Hispanic Origin |
New Hamp.	2000	2001	2002	2003	2004	2005	2006	2000	2006	% Change	($)	(%)	(%)	(%)	(%)	(%)	(%)	(%)	(%)
Be1****	R, 36				R, 54		R, 54	3,198	3,636	14	57,932	41.5	22.5	10.9	97.0	0.4	0.2	0.5	0.7
Be1****	R, 35							3,198	3,636	14	57,932	41.5	22.5	10.9	97.0	0.4	0.2	0.5	0.7
Be2****	R, 27				R, 27		D, 30	6,197	6,783	9	56,765	34.7	15.1	9.0	96.2	0.1	0.6	1.0	0.9
Be2****	D, 23				D, 26		R, 25	6,197	6,783	9	56,765	34.7	15.1	9.0	96.2	0.1	0.6	1.0	0.9
Be3****	R, 40				R, 35		R, 32	5,976	6,791	14	78,175	44.0	24.1	10.5	97.5	0.2	0.3	0.8	0.5
Be3****	R, 34				R, 33		R, 30	5,976	6,791	14	78,175	44.0	24.1	10.5	97.5	0.2	0.3	0.8	0.5
Be4****	R, 36				R, 14		D, 11	16,365	17,514	7	48,393	34.5	15.6	14.6	95.3	0.7	0.7	1.1	1.1
Be4****	D, 33				R, 12		R, 11	16,365	17,514	7	48,393	34.5	15.6	14.6	95.3	0.7	0.7	1.1	1.1
Be4****					R, 11		D, 11	16,365	17,514	7	48,393	34.5	15.6	14.6	95.3	0.7	0.7	1.1	1.1
Be4****					R, 11		D, 10	16,365	17,514	7	48,393	34.5	15.6	14.6	95.3	0.7	0.7	1.1	1.1
Be4****					R, 10		R, 10	16,365	17,514	7	48,393	34.5	15.6	14.6	95.3	0.7	0.7	1.1	1.1
Be5****	R, 23				R/D, 11		R, 9	22,371	25,040	12	71,671	39.9	18.2	9.2	97.1	0.3	0.4	0.7	
Be5****	R, 23				R, 10		R, 8	22,371	25,040	12	71,671	39.9	18.2	9.2	97.1	0.3	0.4	0.7	0.8
Be5****	R, 20				R, 10		R, 8	22,371	25,040	12	71,671	39.9	18.2	9.2	97.1	0.3	0.4	0.7	0.8
Be5****					R, 9		R, 8	22,371	25,040	12	71,671	39.9	18.2	9.2	97.1	0.3	0.4	0.7	0.8
Be5****					R, 9		R, 8	22,371	25,040	12	71,671	39.9	18.2	9.2	97.1	0.3	0.4	0.7	0.8
Be5****					R, 9		R, 8	22,371	25,040	12	71,671	39.9	18.2	9.2	97.1	0.3	0.4	0.7	0.8
Be5****					R, 9		R, 7	22,371	25,040	12	71,671	39.9	18.2	9.2	97.1	0.3	0.4	0.7	0.8
Be6****	R, 65				R, 68		R, 100	3,063	3,403	11	63,356	41.5	19.8	8.1	98.4	0.1	0.3	0.2	0.3
Be7*	R, 10																		
Be7*	R, 10																		
Be7*	R, 9																		
Be7*	R, 9																		
Be7*	R, 9																		
Be7*	D, 9																		
Be29**			R, 21																
Be29**			R, 20																
Be29**			R, 20																
Be30**			R, 10																
Be30**			R, 10																
Be30**			R, 10																
Be30**			R, 10																
Be30**			R, 10																
Be30**			R, 9																
Be30**			R, 9																
Be31**			R, 9																
Be31**			R, 9																
Be31**			R, 9																
Be31**			R, 8																
Be31**			R, 8																
Be31**			R, 8																
Be31**			R, 8																
Be31**			R, 8																
Ca1****	R, 99				R, 17		D, 15	12,434	13,310	7	51,814	41.0	20.8	13.7	96.8	0.3	0.5	1.0	0.7
Ca1****					R, 15		D, 13	12,434	13,310	7	51,814	41.0	20.8	13.7	96.8	0.3	0.5	1.0	0.7
Ca1****					R, 14		R, 13	12,434	13,310	7	51,814	41.0	20.8	13.7	96.8	0.3	0.5	1.0	0.7
Ca1****					D, 13		R, 13	12,434	13,310	7	51,814	41.0	20.8	13.7	96.8	0.3	0.5	1.0	0.7
Ca2****	R, 37				R, 54		D, 56	3,128	3,458	11	52,341	38.6	19.6	12.8	97.0	0.1	0.7	0.2	1.2
Ca2****	R, 35							3,128	3,458	11	52,341	38.6	19.6	12.8	97.0	0.1	0.7	0.2	1.2
Ca3****	R, 99				R, 20		R, 20	9,285	10,022	8	47,932	36.6	18.1	15.4	97.3	0.3	0.5	0.3	0.8

(continued)

Note: D=Democrat, R=Republican, R/D=Republican/Democrat (cross-filed), D/R=Democrat/Republican (cross-filed), I=Independent, C=Constitution, O=Other, GI=Green Independent, P=Progressive, P/D=Progressive/Democrat, P/D/R=Progressive/Democrat/Republican, HH=Households

New Hampshire State House Districts—Election and Demographic Data (cont.)

House Districts	General Election Results Party, Percent of Vote							Population			Avg. HH Income	Pop 25+		Below Poverty Line	2006 White (Non-Hisp)	African American	American Indians, Alaska Natives	Asians, Hawaiians, Pacific Islanders	Hispanic Origin
												Some College +	4-Yr Degree +						
New Hamp.	2000	2001	2002	2003	2004	2005	2006	2000	2006	% Change	($)	(%)	(%)	(%)	(%)	(%)	(%)	(%)	(%)
Ca3****					R, 20		D, 20	9,285	10,022	8	47,932	36.6	18.1	15.4	97.3	0.3	0.5	0.3	0.8
Ca3****					R, 19		D, 20	9,285	10,022	8	47,932	36.6	18.1	15.4	97.3	0.3	0.5	0.3	0.8
Ca4	R, 59		R/D, 22		R, 17		R, 16	12,920	14,558	13	69,078	48.3	25.8	10.4	97.6	0.1	0.2	0.6	1.0
Ca4			R/D, 21		R, 17		R, 16	12,920	14,558	13	69,078	48.3	25.8	10.4	97.6	0.1	0.2	0.6	1.0
Ca4			R, 18		R, 16		R, 15	12,920	14,558	13	69,078	48.3	25.8	10.4	97.6	0.1	0.2	0.6	1.0
Ca4			R, 18		R, 16		R, 14	12,920	14,558	13	69,078	48.3	25.8	10.4	97.6	0.1	0.2	0.6	1.0
Ca5	R, 51		R, 59		R, 30		R, 31	5,953	6,419	8	59,806	34.9	14.8	13.2	97.3	0.2	0.6	0.3	0.9
Ca5	R, 48				R, 28		R, 28	5,953	6,419	8	59,806	34.9	14.8	13.2	97.3	0.2	0.6	0.3	0.9
Ca6***	R, 94		R, 20																
Ca6***			R, 19																
Ca6***			R, 19																
Ca7***	R, 60		R/D, 24																
Ca7***			R, 22																
Ca7***			R, 22																
Ca7***			R, 22																
Ca8***	R, 100		R/D, 55																
Ca8***			R, 44																
Ca9*	R, 99																		
Ca10*	R, 42																		
Ca10*	R, 33																		
Ch1****	D, 65				D, 53		D, 54	3,155	3,307	5	67,797	44.4	25.4	7.3	96.5	0.2	0.5	0.7	1.4
Ch2****	D, 29				D, 20		D, 19	9,031	9,334	3	61,242	40.8	23.3	11.4	96.8	0.2	0.8	0.4	1.1
Ch2****	D, 25				D, 19		D, 19	9,031	9,334	3	61,242	40.8	23.3	11.4	96.8	0.2	0.8	0.4	1.1
Ch2****					R, 17		D, 18	9,031	9,334	3	61,242	40.8	23.3	11.4	96.8	0.2	0.8	0.4	1.1
Ch3****	D, 60				D, 10		D, 12	22,618	23,002	2	56,635	37.2	22.1	15.4	96.2	0.5	0.3	1.0	1.2
Ch3****					D, 10		D, 12	22,618	23,002	2	56,635	37.2	22.1	15.4	96.2	0.5	0.3	1.0	1.2
Ch3****					D, 10		D, 12	22,618	23,002	2	56,635	37.2	22.1	15.4	96.2	0.5	0.3	1.0	1.2
Ch3****					D, 10		D, 12	22,618	23,002	2	56,635	37.2	22.1	15.4	96.2	0.5	0.3	1.0	1.2
Ch3****					D, 9		D, 12	22,618	23,002	2	56,635	37.2	22.1	15.4	96.2	0.5	0.3	1.0	1.2
Ch3****					D, 9		D, 12	22,618	23,002	2	56,635	37.2	22.1	15.4	96.2	0.5	0.3	1.0	1.2
Ch3****					D, 9		D, 10	22,618	23,002	2	56,635	37.2	22.1	15.4	96.2	0.5	0.3	1.0	1.2
Ch4****	R, 99				D, 15		D, 18	11,992	12,534	5	51,993	31.3	14.5	13.6	96.4	0.4	0.6	0.5	1.0
Ch4****					D, 14		D, 17	11,992	12,534	5	51,993	31.3	14.5	13.6	96.4	0.4	0.6	0.5	1.0
Ch4****					D, 14		D, 17	11,992	12,534	5	51,993	31.3	14.5	13.6	96.4	0.4	0.6	0.5	1.0
Ch4****					R, 13		D, 15	11,992	12,534	5	51,993	31.3	14.5	13.6	96.4	0.4	0.6	0.5	1.0
Ch5****	D, 98				D, 56		D, 63	3,264	3,488	7	63,090	38.4	19.7	9.1	96.6	0.4	0.6	0.3	1.1
Ch6****	R, 54				D, 15		D, 18	11,894	12,342	4	58,864	34.9	18.0	10.6	97.0	0.2	0.4	0.7	1.1
Ch6****					D, 14		D, 15	11,894	12,342	4	58,864	34.9	18.0	10.6	97.0	0.2	0.4	0.7	1.1
Ch6****					R, 13		D, 13	11,894	12,342	4	58,864	34.9	18.0	10.6	97.0	0.2	0.4	0.7	1.1
Ch6****					R, 12		R, 12	11,894	12,342	4	58,864	34.9	18.0	10.6	97.0	0.2	0.4	0.7	1.1
Ch7****	D, 55				R, 15		D, 14	12,580	13,757	9	65,152	34.0	18.7	9.4	95.9	0.9	0.4	0.8	1.2
Ch7****					R, 15		R, 14	12,580	13,757	9	65,152	34.0	18.7	9.4	95.9	0.9	0.4	0.8	1.2
Ch7****					R, 14		R, 14	12,580	13,757	9	65,152	34.0	18.7	9.4	95.9	0.9	0.4	0.8	1.2
Ch7****					D, 12		R, 13	12,580	13,757	9	65,152	34.0	18.7	9.4	95.9	0.9	0.4	0.8	1.2
Ch8*	D, 30																		
Ch8*	R, 28																		
Ch9*	R, 50																		
Ch9*	R, 49																		
Ch10*	R, 60																		
Ch11*	D, 34																		

(continued)

Note: D=Democrat, R=Republican, R/D=Republican/Democrat (cross-filed), D/R=Democrat/Republican (cross-filed), I=Independent, C=Constitution, O=Other, GI=Green Independent, P=Progressive, P/D=Progressive/Democrat, P/D/R=Progressive/Democrat/Republican, HH=Households

New Hampshire State House Districts—Election and Demographic Data (cont.)

House Districts	General Election Results Party, Percent of Vote							Population			Avg. HH Income	Pop 25+		2006					
												Some College +	4-Yr Degree +	Below Poverty Line	White (Non-Hisp)	African American	American Indians, Alaska Natives	Asians, Hawaiians, Pacific Islanders	Hispanic Origin
New Hamp.	2000	2001	2002	2003	2004	2005	2006	2000	2006	% Change	($)	(%)	(%)	(%)	(%)	(%)	(%)	(%)	(%)
Ch11*	R, 34																		
Ch12*	D, 97																		
Ch13*	R, 64																		
Ch14*	D, 48																		
Ch15*	D, 61																		
Ch16*	D, 53																		
Ch17*	D, 64																		
Ch18*	R, 51																		
Ch19*	D, 20																		
Ch19*	R, 20																		
Ch19*	D, 18																		
Ch24**			D, 14																
Ch24**			D, 13																
Ch24**			R, 13																
Ch24**			D, 13																
Ch25**			D, 9																
Ch25**			D, 9																
Ch25**			D, 9																
Ch25**			D, 9																
Ch25**			D, 9																
Ch25**			D, 8																
Ch25**			R, 7																
Ch26**			R, 11																
Ch26**			D, 11																
Ch26**			D, 11																
Ch26**			D, 11																
Ch26**			D, 10																
Ch27**			D, 15																
Ch27**			D, 14																
Ch27**			R, 13																
Ch27**			R, 13																
Ch28**			R, 20																
Ch28**			R, 20																
Ch28**			R, 19																
Ch28**			D, 13																
Co1	R, 49		R/D, 48		R/D, 52		R/D, 51	5,931	6,217	5	45,594	22.5	8.5	18.6	97.8	0.0	0.4	0.2	0.6
Co1	R, 38		R/D, 45		R/D, 48		R/D, 49	5,931	6,217	5	45,594	22.5	8.5	18.6	97.8	0.0	0.4	0.2	0.6
Co2	D, 99		R/D, 14		R, 15		D, 15	12,138	12,312	1	47,133	27.8	12.8	17.6	96.7	0.2	0.5	0.5	1.1
Co2			R, 13		R, 14		R, 13	12,138	12,312	1	47,133	27.8	12.8	17.6	96.7	0.2	0.5	0.5	1.1
Co2			R, 13		R, 14		D, 13	12,138	12,312	1	47,133	27.8	12.8	17.6	96.7	0.2	0.5	0.5	1.1
Co2			R, 12		D, 14		R, 13	12,138	12,312	1	47,133	27.8	12.8	17.6	96.7	0.2	0.5	0.5	1.1
Co2			R, 11					12,138	12,312	1	47,133	27.8	12.8	17.6	96.7	0.2	0.5	0.5	1.1
Co3	R, 99		D, 17		R, 99		D, 54	3,357	3,351	0	43,188	34.3	13.1	16.7	96.4	0.1	0.4	1.5	0.7
Co3			R. 16					3,357	3,351	0	43,188	34.3	13.1	16.7	96.4	0.1	0.4	1.5	0.7
Co3			D, 15					3,357	3,351	0	43,188	34.3	13.1	16.7	96.4	0.1	0.4	1.5	0.7
Co3			D, 14					3,357	3,351	0	43,188	34.3	13.1	16.7	96.4	0.1	0.4	1.5	0.7
Co4****	R, 100				D, 25		D/R, 25	11,664	11,268	-3	41,042	25.5	6.7	20.7	97.4	0.2	0.4	0.5	0.8
Co4****					D, 23		D/R, 25	11,664	11,268	-3	41,042	25.5	6.7	20.7	97.4	0.2	0.4	0.5	0.8
Co4****					R, 20		D/R, 24	11,664	11,268	-3	41,042	25.5	6.7	20.7	97.4	0.2	0.4	0.5	0.8
Co4****					D, 18		D, 16	11,664	11,268	-3	41,042	25.5	6.7	20.7	97.4	0.2	0.4	0.5	0.8

(continued)

Note: D=Democrat, R=Republican, R/D=Republican/Democrat (cross-filed), D/R=Democrat/Republican (cross-filed), I=Independent, C=Constitution, O=Other, GI=Green Independent, P=Progressive, P/D=Progressive/Democrat, P/D/R=Progressive/Democrat/Republican, HH=Households

New Hampshire State House Districts—Election and Demographic Data (cont.)

House Districts	General Election Results Party, Percent of Vote							Population			Avg. HH Income ($)	Pop 25+ Some College + (%)	Pop 25+ 4-Yr Degree + (%)	Below Poverty Line (%)	2006 White (Non-Hisp) (%)	African American (%)	American Indians, Alaska Natives (%)	Asians, Hawaiians, Pacific Islanders (%)	Hispanic Origin (%)
New Hamp.	2000	2001	2002	2003	2004	2005	2006	2000	2006	% Change									
Co5*	R, 99																		
Co6*	R, 29																		
Co6*	D, 28																		
Co7*	R, 17																		
Co7*	D, 15																		
Co7*	D, 15																		
Co7*	R, 15																		
Co7*	R, 13																		
Gr1****	R, 29				R, 32		R, 28	6,246	6,459	3	52,735	37.3	18.5	17.4	94.7	0.4	0.9	1.2	1.7
Gr1****	R, 28				R, 31		R, 27	6,246	6,459	3	52,735	37.3	18.5	17.4	94.7	0.4	0.9	1.2	1.7
Gr1****	R, 24							6,246	6,459	3	52,735	37.3	18.5	17.4	94.7	0.4	0.9	1.2	1.7
Gr2****	R, 96				D, 62		D, 71	3,336	3,434	3	54,011	45.4	26.4	15.4	96.1	0.1	1.0	0.7	0.9
Gr3****	R, 56				R, 30		R/D, 47	6,437	6,517	1	50,942	37.8	19.3	13.7	97.4	0.1	0.5	0.6	0.5
Gr3****					R, 29		R, 27	6,437	6,517	1	50,942	37.8	19.3	13.7	97.4	0.1	0.5	0.6	0.5
Gr4****	R, 59				R/D, 100		D, 39	3,107	3,234	4	51,857	39.5	21.5	13.8	97.1	0.2	0.2	0.4	0.8
Gr5****	R, 43				R/D, 55		R, 55	6,045	6,294	4	47,960	34.0	17.2	13.7	97.1	0.4	0.3	0.6	0.8
Gr5****	R, 35				R, 45		R, 44	6,045	6,294	4	47,960	34.0	17.2	13.7	97.1	0.4	0.3	0.6	0.8
Gr6****	R, 31				R, 31		D, 30	6,003	6,145	2	58,333	40.1	21.0	13.2	96.9	0.2	0.4	0.8	0.7
Gr6****	D, 28				R, 28		D, 26	6,003	6,145	2	58,333	40.1	21.0	13.2	96.9	0.2	0.4	0.8	0.7
Gr7****	D, 31				R, 44		D, 32	6,428	6,553	2	49,756	29.7	18.7	19.6	94.8	0.5	0.2	1.2	1.7
Gr7****	D, 25				D, 35		D, 31	6,428	6,553	2	49,756	29.7	18.7	19.6	94.8	0.5	0.2	1.2	1.7
Gr8****	R, 40				R/D, 33		D, 18	9,454	9,623	2	57,467	40.3	21.0	12.4	96.4	0.3	0.4	1.2	0.8
Gr8****	R, 37				R, 24		R, 18	9,454	9,623	2	57,467	40.3	21.0	12.4	96.4	0.3	0.4	1.2	0.8
Gr8****					R, 24		D, 17	9,454	9,623	2	57,467	40.3	21.0	12.4	96.4	0.3	0.4	1.2	0.8
Gr9	R, 77		R/D, 54		D, 20		D, 25	11,306	11,633	3	109,795	49.3	42.0	8.0	85.2	1.7	0.6	8.2	2.8
Gr9			R/D, 44		D, 20		D, 25	11,306	11,633	3	109,795	49.3	42.0	8.0	85.2	1.7	0.6	8.2	2.8
Gr9					D, 19		D, 25	11,306	11,633	3	109,795	49.3	42.0	8.0	85.2	1.7	0.6	8.2	2.8
Gr9					D, 19		D, 25	11,306	11,633	3	109,795	49.3	42.0	8.0	85.2	1.7	0.6	8.2	2.8
Gr10	D, 17		D/R, 99		R, 18		D, 19	9,662	10,017	4	52,795	36.5	19.1	10.4	97.2	0.2	0.2	0.8	0.8
Gr10	D, 16				D, 17		D, 19	9,662	10,017	4	52,795	36.5	19.1	10.4	97.2	0.2	0.2	0.8	0.8
Gr10	D, 15				D, 17		D, 18	9,662	10,017	4	52,795	36.5	19.1	10.4	97.2	0.2	0.2	0.8	0.8
Gr10	D, 15							9,662	10,017	4	52,795	36.5	19.1	10.4	97.2	0.2	0.2	0.8	0.8
Gr11	R, 36		R/D, 53		D, 16		D, 19	12,764	13,281	4	62,745	43.2	27.4	12.3	91.6	0.9	0.6	3.9	1.9
Gr11	R, 27		R, 47		D, 15		D, 19	12,764	13,281	4	62,745	43.2	27.4	12.3	91.6	0.9	0.6	3.9	1.9
Gr11					D, 15		D, 19	12,764	13,281	4	62,745	43.2	27.4	12.3	91.6	0.9	0.6	3.9	1.9
Gr11					D, 14		D, 18	12,764	13,281	4	62,745	43.2	27.4	12.3	91.6	0.9	0.6	3.9	1.9
Gr12***	R, 61		R, 98																
Gr13***	D, 57		R/D, 42																
Gr13***			R, 36																
Gr14***	R, 20		R/D, 47																
Gr14***	D, 19		R, 34																
Gr14***	R, 18																		
Gr14***	D, 16																		
Gr15**			D, 30																
Gr15**			D, 27																
Gr16**			R, 25																
Gr16**			R, 22																
Gr16**			R, 22																
Gr17**			D, 9																
Gr17**			D, 9																

(continued)

Note: D=Democrat, R=Republican, R/D=Republican/Democrat (cross-filed), D/R=Democrat/Republican (cross-filed), I=Independent, C=Constitution, O=Other, GI=Green Independent, P=Progressive, P/D=Progressive/Democrat, P/D/R=Progressive/Democrat/Republican, HH=Households

New Hampshire State House Districts—Election and Demographic Data (cont.)

House Districts	General Election Results Party, Percent of Vote							Population			Avg. HH Income	Pop 25+		Below Poverty Line	2006 White (Non-Hisp)	African American	American Indians, Alaska Natives	Asians, Hawaiians, Pacific Islanders	Hispanic Origin
												Some College +	4-Yr Degree +						
New Hamp.	2000	2001	2002	2003	2004	2005	2006	2000	2006	% Change	($)	(%)	(%)	(%)	(%)	(%)	(%)	(%)	(%)
Gr17**			D, 9																
Gr17**			D, 9																
Gr17**			D, 8																
Gr17**			D, 8																
Gr17**			D, 8																
Gr18**			D, 14																
Gr18**			D, 14																
Gr18**			R, 14																
Gr18**			R, 13																
Hi1****	R, 48				R, 21		D/R, 29	9,169	9,599	5	61,287	38.8	21.4	12.5	96.6	0.3	0.5	1.0	0.9
Hi1****					R, 20		D, 21	9,169	9,599	5	61,287	38.8	21.4	12.5	96.6	0.3	0.5	1.0	0.9
Hi1****					D, 17		D, 18	9,169	9,599	5	61,287	38.8	21.4	12.5	96.6	0.3	0.5	1.0	0.9
Hi2****	R, 63				R, 28		D, 26	6,556	6,865	5	62,784	38.7	23.2	9.2	96.6	0.4	0.6	0.5	0.9
Hi2****					D, 24		D, 26	6,556	6,865	5	62,784	38.7	23.2	9.2	96.6	0.4	0.6	0.5	0.9
Hi3****	R, 100				D, 16		D, 17	12,673	13,621	7	65,210	40.5	24.3	9.7	96.0	0.5	0.2	1.4	1.2
Hi3****					R, 14		D, 14	12,673	13,621	7	65,210	40.5	24.3	9.7	96.0	0.5	0.2	1.4	1.2
Hi3****					R, 12		R, 14	12,673	13,621	7	65,210	40.5	24.3	9.7	96.0	0.5	0.2	1.4	1.2
Hi3****					R, 12		D, 12	12,673	13,621	7	65,210	40.5	24.3	9.7	96.0	0.5	0.2	1.4	1.2
Hi4****	R, 64				R, 15		D, 14	12,892	13,821	7	81,882	44.4	27.7	6.0	96.8	0.4	0.2	0.7	1.1
Hi4****					D, 14		R, 13	12,892	13,821	7	81,882	44.4	27.7	6.0	96.8	0.4	0.2	0.7	1.1
Hi4****					R, 13		D, 13	12,892	13,821	7	81,882	44.4	27.7	6.0	96.8	0.4	0.2	0.7	1.1
Hi4****					R, 13		D, 13	12,892	13,821	7	81,882	44.4	27.7	6.0	96.8	0.4	0.2	0.7	1.1
Hi5****	R, 37				R, 17		R, 15	13,663	15,086	10	113,935	50.6	35.2	4.8	95.1	0.5	0.2	2.1	1.3
Hi5****	R, 29				R, 17		R, 15	13,663	15,086	10	113,935	50.6	35.2	4.8	95.1	0.5	0.2	2.1	1.3
Hi5****					R, 14		D, 13	13,663	15,086	10	113,935	50.6	35.2	4.8	95.1	0.5	0.2	2.1	1.3
Hi5****					D, 13		D, 13	13,663	15,086	10	113,935	50.6	35.2	4.8	95.1	0.5	0.2	2.1	1.3
Hi6****	R, 99				R/D, 11		R, 8	24,990	26,789	7	94,802	45.3	29.8	6.5	94.7	0.9	0.2	1.7	1.6
Hi6****					R/D, 11		R, 8	24,990	26,789	7	94,802	45.3	29.8	6.5	94.7	0.9	0.2	1.7	1.6
Hi6****					R/D, 11		R, 7	24,990	26,789	7	94,802	45.3	29.8	6.5	94.7	0.9	0.2	1.7	1.6
Hi6****					R/D, 10		R, 7	24,990	26,789	7	94,802	45.3	29.8	6.5	94.7	0.9	0.2	1.7	1.6
Hi6****					R, 8		R, 7	24,990	26,789	7	94,802	45.3	29.8	6.5	94.7	0.9	0.2	1.7	1.6
Hi6****					R, 8		D, 7	24,990	26,789	7	94,802	45.3	29.8	6.5	94.7	0.9	0.2	1.7	1.6
Hi6****					R, 8		R, 7	24,990	26,789	7	94,802	45.3	29.8	6.5	94.7	0.9	0.2	1.7	1.6
Hi6****					R, 7		R, 6	24,990	26,789	7	94,802	45.3	29.8	6.5	94.7	0.9	0.2	1.7	1.6
Hi7****	R, 15				R/D, 11		R, 7	24,886	26,427	6	70,970	36.1	19.7	8.1	96.8	0.3	0.3	0.6	1.1
Hi7****	R, 14				R/D, 10		R, 7	24,886	26,427	6	70,970	36.1	19.7	8.1	96.8	0.3	0.3	0.6	1.1
Hi7****	R, 14				R/D, 10		R, 7	24,886	26,427	6	70,970	36.1	19.7	8.1	96.8	0.3	0.3	0.6	1.1
Hi7****	R, 13				R/D, 10		R, 7	24,886	26,427	6	70,970	36.1	19.7	8.1	96.8	0.3	0.3	0.6	1.1
Hi7****	R, 13				R, 9		R, 7	24,886	26,427	6	70,970	36.1	19.7	8.1	96.8	0.3	0.3	0.6	1.1
Hi7****					R, 9		R, 6	24,886	26,427	6	70,970	36.1	19.7	8.1	96.8	0.3	0.3	0.6	1.1
Hi7****					R, 8		R, 6	24,886	26,427	6	70,970	36.1	19.7	8.1	96.8	0.3	0.3	0.6	1.1
Hi8****	R, 52				D, 20		D, 20	7,576	7,825	3	107,686	47.3	33.2	4.6	94.0	0.8	0.1	2.3	1.9
Hi8****	R, 46				R, 18		D, 18	7,576	7,825	3	107,686	47.3	33.2	4.6	94.0	0.8	0.1	2.3	1.9
Hi8****					D, 18		R, 17	7,576	7,825	3	107,686	47.3	33.2	4.6	94.0	0.8	0.1	2.3	1.9
Hi9****	R, 98				R, 20		R, 19	9,157	9,757	7	65,060	44.9	27.5	8.5	87.5	2.5	0.4	3.5	4.3
Hi9****					D, 19		D, 18	9,157	9,757	7	65,060	44.9	27.5	8.5	87.5	2.5	0.4	3.5	4.3
Hi9****					R, 17		D, 17	9,157	9,757	7	65,060	44.9	27.5	8.5	87.5	2.5	0.4	3.5	4.3
Hi10****	D, 53				D, 28		D, 21	11,547	12,218	6	46,678	32.4	18.5	24.3	70.7	5.2	0.8	5.1	15.2
Hi10****					D, 27		D, 20	11,547	12,218	6	46,678	32.4	18.5	24.3	70.7	5.2	0.8	5.1	15.2

(continued)

Note: D=Democrat, R=Republican, R/D=Republican/Democrat (cross-filed), D/R=Democrat/Republican (cross-filed), I=Independent, C=Constitution, O=Other, GI=Green Independent, P=Progressive, P/D=Progressive/Democrat, P/D/R=Progressive/Democrat/Republican, HH=Households

New Hampshire State House Districts—Election and Demographic Data (cont.)

House Districts	General Election Results Party, Percent of Vote							Population			Avg. HH Income ($)	Pop 25+ Some College + (%)	Pop 25+ 4-Yr Degree + (%)	Below Poverty Line (%)	White (Non-Hisp) (%)	African American (%)	American Indians, Alaska Natives (%)	Asians, Hawaiians, Pacific Islanders (%)	Hispanic Origin (%)
New Hamp.	2000	2001	2002	2003	2004	2005	2006	2000	2006	% Change									
Hi10****					D, 24		D, 19	11,547	12,218	6	46,678	32.4	18.5	24.3	70.7	5.2	0.8	5.1	15.2
Hi11****	D, 59				R, 20		D, 22	8,034	8,301	3	49,000	31.3	15.0	15.4	82.8	2.8	0.5	4.1	7.4
Hi11****					D, 19		D, 17	8,034	8,301	3	49,000	31.3	15.0	15.4	82.8	2.8	0.5	4.1	7.4
Hi11****					R, 18		D, 17	8,034	8,301	3	49,000	31.3	15.0	15.4	82.8	2.8	0.5	4.1	7.4
Hi12****	R, 52				D/R, 29		D, 24	8,963	9,116	2	46,226	27.2	12.3	17.5	75.8	3.1	0.7	5.0	12.5
Hi12****					D/R, 27		D, 21	8,963	9,116	2	46,226	27.2	12.3	17.5	75.8	3.1	0.7	5.0	12.5
Hi12****					D, 23		D, 20	8,963	9,116	2	46,226	27.2	12.3	17.5	75.8	3.1	0.7	5.0	12.5
Hi13****	R, 20				R, 20		D, 20	8,917	9,162	3	61,823	39.3	20.8	7.5	93.0	1.2	0.3	2.3	2.0
Hi13****	R, 18				D, 18		R, 18	8,917	9,162	3	61,823	39.3	20.8	7.5	93.0	1.2	0.3	2.3	2.0
Hi13****	R, 18				R, 17		D, 17	8,917	9,162	3	61,823	39.3	20.8	7.5	93.0	1.2	0.3	2.3	2.0
Hi13****	R, 17							8,917	9,162	3	61,823	39.3	20.8	7.5	93.0	1.2	0.3	2.3	2.0
Hi14****	R, 26				R, 22		D, 22	7,467	7,929	6	50,317	29.0	13.4	13.8	84.9	1.6	0.5	3.0	8.5
Hi14****	R, 23				D, 21		D, 19	7,467	7,929	6	50,317	29.0	13.4	13.8	84.9	1.6	0.5	3.0	8.5
Hi14****	R, 22				D, 21		D, 18	7,467	7,929	6	50,317	29.0	13.4	13.8	84.9	1.6	0.5	3.0	8.5
Hi15****	R, 20				R, 25		R, 19	7,412	8,023	8	64,442	37.6	19.2	8.7	91.8	0.9	0.3	3.2	2.8
Hi15****	R, 18				D, 22		D, 18	7,412	8,023	8	64,442	37.6	19.2	8.7	91.8	0.9	0.3	3.2	2.8
Hi15****	R, 18				R, 21		D, 17	7,412	8,023	8	64,442	37.6	19.2	8.7	91.8	0.9	0.3	3.2	2.8
Hi15****	R, 18							7,412	8,023	8	64,442	37.6	19.2	8.7	91.8	0.9	0.3	3.2	2.8
Hi16****	R, 99				D/R, 30		D, 21	8,501	8,826	4	54,857	28.1	12.9	14.4	83.7	3.5	0.5	2.2	7.7
Hi16****					D, 26		D, 21	8,501	8,826	4	54,857	28.1	12.9	14.4	83.7	3.5	0.5	2.2	7.7
Hi16****					R, 24		D, 20	8,501	8,826	4	54,857	28.1	12.9	14.4	83.7	3.5	0.5	2.2	7.7
Hi17****	R, 38				R, 8		D, 8	26,815	27,804	4	51,203	33.1	17.6	14.1	86.3	2.7	0.6	3.6	4.9
Hi17****	R, 36				R, 7		D, 7	26,815	27,804	4	51,203	33.1	17.6	14.1	86.3	2.7	0.6	3.6	4.9
Hi17****					R, 7		D, 7	26,815	27,804	4	51,203	33.1	17.6	14.1	86.3	2.7	0.6	3.6	4.9
Hi17****					R, 7		D, 7	26,815	27,804	4	51,203	33.1	17.6	14.1	86.3	2.7	0.6	3.6	4.9
Hi17****					R, 7		R, 7	26,815	27,804	4	51,203	33.1	17.6	14.1	86.3	2.7	0.6	3.6	4.9
Hi17****					R, 7		D, 6	26,815	27,804	4	51,203	33.1	17.6	14.1	86.3	2.7	0.6	3.6	4.9
Hi17****					R, 6		D, 6	26,815	27,804	4	51,203	33.1	17.6	14.1	86.3	2.7	0.6	3.6	4.9
Hi17****					D, 6		R, 6	26,815	27,804	4	51,203	33.1	17.6	14.1	86.3	2.7	0.6	3.6	4.9
Hi18****	R, 10				R, 11		R, 11	19,176	20,694	8	124,907	50.5	35.9	4.1	95.2	0.5	0.1	2.0	1.5
Hi18****	R, 10				R, 11		R, 11	19,176	20,694	8	124,907	50.5	35.9	4.1	95.2	0.5	0.1	2.0	1.5
Hi18****	R, 9				R, 11		R, 11	19,176	20,694	8	124,907	50.5	35.9	4.1	95.2	0.5	0.1	2.0	1.5
Hi18****	R, 9				R, 11		R, 10	19,176	20,694	8	124,907	50.5	35.9	4.1	95.2	0.5	0.1	2.0	1.5
Hi18****	R, 9				R, 11		R, 10	19,176	20,694	8	124,907	50.5	35.9	4.1	95.2	0.5	0.1	2.0	1.5
Hi18****	R, 9				R, 10		R, 10	19,176	20,694	8	124,907	50.5	35.9	4.1	95.2	0.5	0.1	2.0	1.5
Hi18****	R, 8							19,176	20,694	8	124,907	50.5	35.9	4.1	95.2	0.5	0.1	2.0	1.5
Hi18****	R, 8							19,176	20,694	8	124,907	50.5	35.9	4.1	95.2	0.5	0.1	2.0	1.5
Hi19****	R, 100				R, 9		R, 8	24,736	26,264	6	88,994	44.4	26.6	3.7	93.6	0.9	0.3	2.4	1.9
Hi19****					R, 9		R, 8	24,736	26,264	6	88,994	44.4	26.6	3.7	93.6	0.9	0.3	2.4	1.9
Hi19****					R, 8		R, 7	24,736	26,264	6	88,994	44.4	26.6	3.7	93.6	0.9	0.3	2.4	1.9
Hi19****					R, 8		R, 7	24,736	26,264	6	88,994	44.4	26.6	3.7	93.6	0.9	0.3	2.4	1.9
Hi19****					R, 7		D, 7	24,736	26,264	6	88,994	44.4	26.6	3.7	93.6	0.9	0.3	2.4	1.9
Hi19****					R, 7		R, 7	24,736	26,264	6	88,994	44.4	26.6	3.7	93.6	0.9	0.3	2.4	1.9
Hi19****					R, 7		R, 7	24,736	26,264	6	88,994	44.4	26.6	3.7	93.6	0.9	0.3	2.4	1.9
Hi19****					R, 7		R, 6	24,736	26,264	6	88,994	44.4	26.6	3.7	93.6	0.9	0.3	2.4	1.9
Hi20****	R, 51				D, 18		D, 20	7,601	7,684	1	77,546	50.5	32.5	6.5	90.4	1.6	0.3	4.1	2.6
Hi20****	D, 48				D, 18		D, 20	7,601	7,684	1	77,546	50.5	32.5	6.5	90.4	1.6	0.3	4.1	2.6
Hi20****					R, 17		D, 18	7,601	7,684	1	77,546	50.5	32.5	6.5	90.4	1.6	0.3	4.1	2.6
Hi21****	R, 100				R, 20		D, 21	10,998	11,162	1	78,672	48.2	32.6	6.0	82.4	2.3	0.3	7.7	5.7
Hi21****					D, 18		R, 17	10,998	11,162	1	78,672	48.2	32.6	6.0	82.4	2.3	0.3	7.7	5.7

(continued)

Note: D=Democrat, R=Republican, R/D=Republican/Democrat (cross-filed), D/R=Democrat/Republican (cross-filed), I=Independent, C=Constitution, O=Other, GI=Green Independent, P=Progressive, P/D=Progressive/Democrat, P/D/R=Progressive/Democrat/Republican, HH=Households

New Hampshire State House Districts—Election and Demographic Data (cont.)

House Districts	General Election Results Party, Percent of Vote							Population			Avg. HH Income ($)	Pop 25+ Some College + (%)	Pop 25+ 4-Yr Degree + (%)	Below Poverty Line (%)	White (Non-Hisp) (%)	African American (%)	American Indians, Alaska Natives (%)	Asians, Hawaiians, Pacific Islanders (%)	Hispanic Origin (%)
New Hamp.	2000	2001	2002	2003	2004	2005	2006	2000	2006	% Change									
Hi21****					R, 18		D, 17	10,998	11,162	1	78,672	48.2	32.6	6.0	82.4	2.3	0.3	7.7	5.7
Hi22****	R, 35				D, 19		D, 22	9,127	9,479	4	62,929	38.3	23.5	12.2	79.2	2.4	0.9	2.2	12.8
Hi22****	R, 34				D, 19		D, 21	9,127	9,479	4	62,929	38.3	23.5	12.2	79.2	2.4	0.9	2.2	12.8
Hi22****					D, 17		D, 21	9,127	9,479	4	62,929	38.3	23.5	12.2	79.2	2.4	0.9	2.2	12.8
Hi23****	R, 14				D, 25		D, 34	9,573	10,034	5	46,695	26.5	12.6	21.7	58.5	4.7	1.1	3.0	27.5
Hi23****	R, 13				D, 24		D, 34	9,573	10,034	5	46,695	26.5	12.6	21.7	58.5	4.7	1.1	3.0	27.5
Hi23****	R, 12				D, 20		D, 32	9,573	10,034	5	46,695	26.5	12.6	21.7	58.5	4.7	1.1	3.0	27.5
Hi23****	R, 12							9,573	10,034	5	46,695	26.5	12.6	21.7	58.5	4.7	1.1	3.0	27.5
Hi23****	R, 12							9,573	10,034	5	46,695	26.5	12.6	21.7	58.5	4.7	1.1	3.0	27.5
Hi23****	R, 12							9,573	10,034	5	46,695	26.5	12.6	21.7	58.5	4.7	1.1	3.0	27.5
Hi24****	R, 29				D/R, 31		D, 26	9,679	9,832	2	61,694	32.5	14.8	11.4	83.8	2.1	0.5	2.2	8.7
Hi24****	R, 25				D, 27		D, 25	9,679	9,832	2	61,694	32.5	14.8	11.4	83.8	2.1	0.5	2.2	8.7
Hi24****	D, 24				D, 22		D, 22	9,679	9,832	2	61,694	32.5	14.8	11.4	83.8	2.1	0.5	2.2	8.7
Hi25****	R, 99				D, 36		D, 25	12,503	13,331	7	56,811	38.1	21.4	12.7	76.4	2.4	0.6	8.8	9.5
Hi25****					D, 34		D, 24	12,503	13,331	7	56,811	38.1	21.4	12.7	76.4	2.4	0.6	8.8	9.5
Hi25****					D, 28		R, 20	12,503	13,331	7	56,811	38.1	21.4	12.7	76.4	2.4	0.6	8.8	9.5
Hi26****	R, 19				D, 6		D, 6	25,828	26,195	1	86,959	46.8	30.7	4.8	84.9	2.1	0.3	7.8	3.7
Hi26****	D, 18				D, 6		D, 6	25,828	26,195	1	86,959	46.8	30.7	4.8	84.9	2.1	0.3	7.8	3.7
Hi26****	D, 18				D, 5		D, 6	25,828	26,195	1	86,959	46.8	30.7	4.8	84.9	2.1	0.3	7.8	3.7
Hi26****					R, 5		D, 6	25,828	26,195	1	86,959	46.8	30.7	4.8	84.9	2.1	0.3	7.8	3.7
Hi26****					R, 5		D, 6	25,828	26,195	1	86,959	46.8	30.7	4.8	84.9	2.1	0.3	7.8	3.7
Hi26****					R, 5		D, 5	25,828	26,195	1	86,959	46.8	30.7	4.8	84.9	2.1	0.3	7.8	3.7
Hi26****					D, 5		D, 5	25,828	26,195	1	86,959	46.8	30.7	4.8	84.9	2.1	0.3	7.8	3.7
Hi26****					D, 5		D, 5	25,828	26,195	1	86,959	46.8	30.7	4.8	84.9	2.1	0.3	7.8	3.7
Hi26****					R, 5		R, 5	25,828	26,195	1	86,959	46.8	30.7	4.8	84.9	2.1	0.3	7.8	3.7
Hi26****					D, 5		D, 5	25,828	26,195	1	86,959	46.8	30.7	4.8	84.9	2.1	0.3	7.8	3.7
Hi27****	R, 21				R, 6		R, 5	42,163	44,267	5	83,031	39.5	21.5	4.8	94.4	0.8	0.3	1.6	1.9
Hi27****	R, 20				R, 5		R, 5	42,163	44,267	5	83,031	39.5	21.5	4.8	94.4	0.8	0.3	1.6	1.9
Hi27****	R, 19				R, 5		R, 5	42,163	44,267	5	83,031	39.5	21.5	4.8	94.4	0.8	0.3	1.6	1.9
Hi27****					R, 5		R, 4	42,163	44,267	5	83,031	39.5	21.5	4.8	94.4	0.8	0.3	1.6	1.9
Hi27****					R, 5		R, 4	42,163	44,267	5	83,031	39.5	21.5	4.8	94.4	0.8	0.3	1.6	1.9
Hi27****					R, 5		R, 4	42,163	44,267	5	83,031	39.5	21.5	4.8	94.4	0.8	0.3	1.6	1.9
Hi27****					R, 4		R, 4	42,163	44,267	5	83,031	39.5	21.5	4.8	94.4	0.8	0.3	1.6	1.9
Hi27****					R, 4		R, 4	42,163	44,267	5	83,031	39.5	21.5	4.8	94.4	0.8	0.3	1.6	1.9
Hi27****					R, 4		D, 4	42,163	44,267	5	83,031	39.5	21.5	4.8	94.4	0.8	0.3	1.6	1.9
Hi27****					R, 4		D, 4	42,163	44,267	5	83,031	39.5	21.5	4.8	94.4	0.8	0.3	1.6	1.9
Hi27****					R, 4		R, 4	42,163	44,267	5	83,031	39.5	21.5	4.8	94.4	0.8	0.3	1.6	1.9
Hi27****					R, 4		R, 4	42,163	44,267	5	83,031	39.5	21.5	4.8	94.4	0.8	0.3	1.6	1.9
Hi27****					R, 4		R, 4	42,163	44,267	5	83,031	39.5	21.5	4.8	94.4	0.8	0.3	1.6	1.9
Hi28*	D, 23																		
Hi28*	R, 20																		
Hi28*	D, 19																		
Hi29	D, 34																		
Hi29*	D, 26																		
Hi29*	R, 21																		
Hi30*	D, 22																		
Hi30*	D, 21																		
Hi30*	R, 19																		
Hi31*	D, 34																		
Hi31*	D, 33																		

(continued)

Note: D=Democrat, R=Republican, R/D=Republican/Democrat (cross-filed), D/R=Democrat/Republican (cross-filed), I=Independent, C=Constitution, O=Other, GI=Green Independent, P=Progressive, P/D=Progressive/Democrat, P/D/R=Progressive/Democrat/Republican, HH=Households

New Hampshire State House Districts—Election and Demographic Data (cont.)

House Districts	General Election Results Party, Percent of Vote							Population			Avg. HH Income	Pop 25+		Below Poverty Line	2006 White (Non-Hisp)	African American	American Indians, Alaska Natives	Asians, Hawaiians, Pacific Islanders	Hispanic Origin
												Some College +	4-Yr Degree +						
New Hamp.	2000	2001	2002	2003	2004	2005	2006	2000	2006	% Change	($)	(%)	(%)	(%)	(%)	(%)	(%)	(%)	(%)
Hi31*	D, 32																		
Hi32*	D, 36																		
Hi32*	D, 33																		
Hi32*	D, 31																		
Hi33*	D, 24																		
Hi33*	D, 22																		
Hi33*	D, 19																		
Hi34*	D, 23																		
Hi34*	R, 23																		
Hi34*	R, 20																		
Hi35*	R, 52																		
Hi36*	D, 99																		
Hi37*	D, 19																		
Hi37*	D, 18																		
Hi37*	R, 17																		
Hi38*	R, 19																		
Hi38*	D, 19																		
Hi38*	R, 16																		
Hi39*	D, 22																		
H\i39*	R, 22																		
Hi39*	D, 19																		
Hi40	R, 24																		
Hi40*	D, 23																		
Hi40*	R, 20																		
Hi41*	D, 22																		
Hi41*	R, 22																		
Hi41*	D, 19																		
Hi42***	D, 19		R/D, 30																
Hi42***	D, 17		R/D, 29																
Hi42***	R, 17		R, 23																
Hi43***	D, 23		R, 29																
Hi43***	D, 20		R, 25																
Hi43***	D, 19																		
Hi44***	D, 20		D, 17																
Hi44***	R, 19		R, 17																
Hi44***	L, 18		R, 15																
Hi44***			R, 15																
Hi45***	R, 20		R, 15																
Hi45***	R, 19		R, 15																
Hi45***	D, 18		R, 14																
Hi45***			R, 14																
Hi46***	R, 21		R, 16																
Hi46***	R, 17		R, 16																
Hi46***	D, 16		R, 16																
Hi46***			R, 15																
Hi47***	D, 24		R, 10																
Hi47***	D, 23		R, 9																
Hi47***	R, 23		R, 9																
Hi47***			R, 9																
Hi47***			R, 8																

(continued)

Note: D=Democrat, R=Republican, R/D=Republican/Democrat (cross-filed), D/R=Democrat/Republican (cross-filed), I=Independent, C=Constitution, O=Other, GI=Green Independent, P=Progressive, P/D=Progressive/Democrat, P/D/R=Progressive/Democrat/Republican, HH=Households

New Hampshire State House Districts—Election and Demographic Data (cont.)

House Districts	General Election Results Party, Percent of Vote							Population			Avg. HH Income	Pop 25+		2006					
												Some College +	4-Yr Degree +	Below Poverty Line	White (Non-Hisp)	African American	American Indians, Alaska Natives	Asians, Hawaiians, Pacific Islanders	Hispanic Origin
New Hamp.	2000	2001	2002	2003	2004	2005	2006	2000	2006	% Change	($)	(%)	(%)	(%)	(%)	(%)	(%)	(%)	(%)
Hi47***			R, 8																
Hi47***			R, 7																
Hi47***			R, 7																
Hi48***	R, 20		R/D, 11																
Hi48***	R, 20		R/D, 11																
Hi48***	R, 18		R/D, 10																
Hi48***			R/D, 10																
Hi48***			R/D, 10																
Hi48***			R, 9																
Hi48***			R, 9																
Hi48***			R, 9																
Hi49**			R, 10																
Hi49**			R, 10																
Hi49**			R, 10																
Hi49**			R, 9																
Hi49**			R, 9																
Hi49**			D, 9																
Hi50**			R, 5																
Hi50**			R, 5																
Hi50**			R, 5																
Hi50**			D, 5																
Hi50**			R, 5																
Hi50**			D, 5																
Hi50**			R, 5																
Hi50**			R, 4																
Hi50**			D, 4																
Hi50**			D, 4																
Hi50**			R, 4																
Hi51**			R, 22																
Hi51**			R, 18																
Hi51**			D, 18																
Hi52**			D, 19																
Hi52**			D, 18																
Hi52**			D, 18																
Hi53**			R, 18																
Hi53**			R, 18																
Hi53**			D, 17																
Hi54**			R, 20																
Hi54**			D, 18																
Hi54**			R, 16																
Hi55**			D, 20																
Hi55**			R, 18																
Hi55**			D, 17																
Hi56**			R, 21																
Hi56**			R, 19																
Hi56**			D, 17																
Hi57**			R, 15																
Hi57**			R, 15																
Hi57**			R, 15																
Hi57**			R, 14																

(continued)

Note: D=Democrat, R=Republican, R/D=Republican/Democrat (cross-filed), D/R=Democrat/Republican (cross-filed), I=Independent, C=Constitution, O=Other, GI=Green Independent, P=Progressive, P/D=Progressive/Democrat, P/D/R=Progressive/Democrat/Republican, HH=Households

New Hampshire State House Districts—Election and Demographic Data (cont.)

House Districts	General Election Results Party, Percent of Vote							Population			Avg. HH Income	Pop 25+ Some College +	Pop 25+ 4-Yr Degree +	Below Poverty Line	2006 White (Non-Hisp)	African American	American Indians, Alaska Natives	Asians, Hawaiians, Pacific Islanders	Hispanic Origin
New Hamp.	2000	2001	2002	2003	2004	2005	2006	2000	2006	% Change	($)	(%)	(%)	(%)	(%)	(%)	(%)	(%)	(%)
Hi57**			R, 14																
Hi57**			R, 14																
Hi58**			R/D, 9																
Hi58**			R/D, 8																
Hi58**			R/D, 8																
Hi58**			R/D, 8																
Hi58**			R/D, 8																
Hi58**			R/D, 8																
Hi58**			R/D, 7																
Hi58**			R, 7																
Hi58**			R, 6																
Hi58**			R, 6																
Hi58**			R, 6																
Hi59**			R, 27																
Hi59**			R, 27																
Hi59**			R, 25																
Hi60**			R, 19																
Hi60**			R, 18																
Hi60**			D, 18																
Hi61**			R, 19																
Hi61**			R, 19																
Hi61**			R, 17																
Hi62**			D, 10																
Hi62**			D, 10																
Hi62**			D, 10																
Hi62**			D, 9																
Hi62**			D, 9																
Hi62**			D, 9																
Hi63**			R, 18																
Hi63**			R, 18																
Hi63**			D, 18																
Hi64**			R, 21																
Hi64**			R, 19																
Hi64**			R, 18																
Hi65**			D, 12																
Hi65**			D, 10																
Hi65**			D, 10																
Hi65**			D, 10																
Hi65**			D, 10																
Hi65**			R, 10																
Hi66**			R/D, 8																
Hi66**			R, 6																
Hi66**			R, 6																
Hi66**			R, 6																
Hi66**			R, 6																
Hi66**			R, 6																
Hi66**			R, 6																
Hi66**			D, 5																
Hi66**			R, 5																
Hi66**			R, 5																

(continued)

Note: D=Democrat, R=Republican, R/D=Republican/Democrat (cross-filed), D/R=Democrat/Republican (cross-filed), I=Independent, C=Constitution, O=Other, GI=Green Independent, P=Progressive, P/D=Progressive/Democrat, P/D/R=Progressive/Democrat/Republican, HH=Households

New Hampshire State House Districts—Election and Demographic Data (cont.)

House Districts	General Election Results Party, Percent of Vote							Population			Avg. HH Income ($)	Pop 25+ Some College + (%)	Pop 25+ 4-Yr Degree + (%)	Below Poverty Line (%)	White (Non-Hisp) (%)	African American (%)	American Indians, Alaska Natives (%)	Asians, Hawaiians, Pacific Islanders (%)	Hispanic Origin (%)
New Hamp.	2000	2001	2002	2003	2004	2005	2006	2000	2006	% Change	($)	(%)	(%)	(%)	(%)		(%)	(%)	(%)
Hi66**			R, 5																
Me1****	R, 31				R, 30		D, 29	6,123	6,663	9	88,333	52.0	35.3	7.2	97.7	0.2	0.1	0.8	0.8
Me1****	R, 27				D, 26		R, 28	6,123	6,663	9	88,333	52.0	35.3	7.2	97.7	0.2	0.1	0.8	0.8
Me2****	R, 22				R, 29		D, 19	9,250	9,928	7	50,020	30.1	10.8	17.3	95.8	0.4	0.4	0.8	1.4
Me2****	R, 20				R, 25		R, 17	9,250	9,928	7	50,020	30.1	10.8	17.3	95.8	0.4	0.4	0.8	1.4
Me2****	R, 18				D, 25		D, 17	9,250	9,928	7	50,020	30.1	10.8	17.3	95.8	0.4	0.4	0.8	1.4
Me3****	D, 30				D, 51		D/R, 99	3,576	3,828	7	74,183	50.2	29.8	6.3	96.4	0.3	0.3	0.5	1.5
Me3****	D, 25							3,576	3,828	7	74,183	50.2	29.8	6.3	96.4	0.3	0.3	0.5	1.5
Me4****	D, 62				D, 22		D, 23	10,157	11,099	9	80,485	47.6	29.1	7.5	97.7	0.1	0.3	0.5	0.7
Me4****					D, 19		D, 21	10,157	11,099	9	80,485	47.6	29.1	7.5	97.7	0.1	0.3	0.5	0.7
Me4****					R, 16		D, 20	10,157	11,099	9	80,485	47.6	29.1	7.5	97.7	0.1	0.3	0.5	0.7
Me5****	R, 65				D, 31		D, 32	5,679	6,022	6	69,464	41.7	25.5	11.8	95.7	0.5	0.3	1.1	1.2
Me5****					R, 26		D, 26	5,679	6,022	6	69,464	41.7	25.5	11.8	95.7	0.5	0.3	1.1	1.2
Me6****	D, 65				D, 11		D/R, 16	18,356	19,715	7	62,685	36.7	17.0	8.6	97.1	0.4	0.3	0.6	0.9
Me6****					R, 10		D/R, 15	18,356	19,715	7	62,685	36.7	17.0	8.6	97.1	0.4	0.3	0.6	0.9
Me6****					R, 10		D, 10	18,356	19,715	7	62,685	36.7	17.0	8.6	97.1	0.4	0.3	0.6	0.9
Me6****					D, 10		D, 10	18,356	19,715	7	62,685	36.7	17.0	8.6	97.1	0.4	0.3	0.6	0.9
Me6****					D, 9		D, 10	18,356	19,715	7	62,685	36.7	17.0	8.6	97.1	0.4	0.3	0.6	0.9
Me6****					R, 9		R, 8	18,356	19,715	7	62,685	36.7	17.0	8.6	97.1	0.4	0.3	0.6	0.9
Me7****	R, 20				D/R, 28		D, 21	9,183	9,972	9	60,494	36.6	16.2	9.9	97.0	0.4	0.5	0.5	0.7
Me7****	R, 18				D, 20		D, 20	9,183	9,972	9	60,494	36.6	16.2	9.9	97.0	0.4	0.5	0.5	0.7
Me7****	R, 16				R, 18		D, 19	9,183	9,972	9	60,494	36.6	16.2	9.9	97.0	0.4	0.5	0.5	0.7
Me8****	R, 53				D, 14		D, 15	12,687	13,491	6	56,260	32.5	12.3	11.0	96.8	0.4	0.2	0.4	1.2
Me8****					R, 13		D, 14	12,687	13,491	6	56,260	32.5	12.3	11.0	96.8	0.4	0.2	0.4	1.2
Me8****					R, 13		D, 13	12,687	13,491	6	56,260	32.5	12.3	11.0	96.8	0.4	0.2	0.4	1.2
Me8****					R, 13		D, 13	12,687	13,491	6	56,260	32.5	12.3	11.0	96.8	0.4	0.2	0.4	1.2
Me9****	R, 16				R, 20		R, 19	12,232	13,512	10	74,918	41.3	22.4	6.6	93.7	0.8	0.4	2.5	2.0
Me9****	R, 14				R, 18		R, 17	12,232	13,512	10	74,918	41.3	22.4	6.6	93.7	0.8	0.4	2.5	2.0
Me9****	R, 14				R, 16		D, 17	12,232	13,512	10	74,918	41.3	22.4	6.6	93.7	0.8	0.4	2.5	2.0
Me9****	R, 14				R, 15		R, 17	12,232	13,512	10	74,918	41.3	22.4	6.6	93.7	0.8	0.4	2.5	2.0
Me10****	R, 31				D, 16		D/R, 25	12,766	13,924	9	58,457	39.7	17.7	9.9	92.6	1.4	0.6	1.7	2.6
Me10****	D, 27				D, 15		D/R, 25	12,766	13,924	9	58,457	39.7	17.7	9.9	92.6	1.4	0.6	1.7	2.6
Me10****					D, 14		D/R, 25	12,766	13,924	9	58,457	39.7	17.7	9.9	92.6	1.4	0.6	1.7	2.6
Me10****					R, 14		D/R, 25	12,766	13,924	9	58,457	39.7	17.7	9.9	92.6	1.4	0.6	1.7	2.6
Me11****	R, 27				R, 14		D, 15	16,157	17,390	8	58,485	44.2	24.6	13.5	92.8	1.5	0.4	2.4	1.7
Me11****	R, 25				D, 12		D, 14	16,157	17,390	8	58,485	44.2	24.6	13.5	92.8	1.5	0.4	2.4	1.7
Me11****	R, 20				D, 11		D, 13	16,157	17,390	8	58,485	44.2	24.6	13.5	92.8	1.5	0.4	2.4	1.7
Me11****					R, 11		D, 13	16,157	17,390	8	58,485	44.2	24.6	13.5	92.8	1.5	0.4	2.4	1.7
Me11****					D, 11		R, 10	16,157	17,390	8	58,485	44.2	24.6	13.5	92.8	1.5	0.4	2.4	1.7
Me12****	R, 18				D, 18		D, 20	11,866	12,458	5	70,340	44.9	27.7	11.5	93.6	0.8	0.5	2.7	1.5
Me12****	D, 17				R, 16		D, 18	11,866	12,458	5	70,340	44.9	27.7	11.5	93.6	0.8	0.5	2.7	1.5
Me12****	D, 15				D, 15		D, 18	11,866	12,458	5	70,340	44.9	27.7	11.5	93.6	0.8	0.5	2.7	1.5
Me12****	D, 14				D, 15		R, 15	11,866	12,458	5	70,340	44.9	27.7	11.5	93.6	0.8	0.5	2.7	1.5
Me13****	D, 27				D, 21		D, 21	9,556	11,120	16	93,720	48.4	29.9	5.0	96.7	0.2	0.3	1.4	0.7
Me13****	R, 25				R, 20		R, 19	9,556	11,120	16	93,720	48.4	29.9	5.0	96.7	0.2	0.3	1.4	0.7
Me13****	R, 24				D, 17		D, 18	9,556	11,120	16	93,720	48.4	29.9	5.0	96.7	0.2	0.3	1.4	0.7
Me14*	R, 62																		
Me15*	R, 51																		
Me16*	D, 99																		
Me17*	D, 63																		

(continued)

Note: D=Democrat, R=Republican, R/D=Republican/Democrat (cross-filed), D/R=Democrat/Republican (cross-filed), I=Independent, C=Constitution, O=Other, GI=Green Independent, P=Progressive, P/D=Progressive/Democrat, P/D/R=Progressive/Democrat/Republican, HH=Households

New Hampshire State House Districts—Election and Demographic Data (cont.)

House Districts	General Election Results Party, Percent of Vote							Population			Avg. HH Income	Pop 25+		Below Poverty Line	2006 White (Non-Hisp)	African American	American Indians, Alaska Natives	Asians, Hawaiians, Pacific Islanders	Hispanic Origin
												Some College +	4-Yr Degree +						
New Hamp.	2000	2001	2002	2003	2004	2005	2006	2000	2006	% Change	($)	(%)	(%)	(%)	(%)	(%)	(%)	(%)	(%)
Me18*	R, 60																		
Me19*	D, 65																		
Me20*	D, 66																		
Me21*	D, 100																		
Me22*	D, 57																		
Me23*	D, 99																		
Me24*	D, 22																		
Me24*	D, 20																		
Me24*	R, 19																		
Me32**			R, 32																
Me32**			R, 26																
Me33**			D, 21																
Me33**			R, 20																
Me33**			R, 19																
Me34**			D, 9																
Me34**			R, 9																
Me34**			D, 9																
Me34**			R, 9																
Me34**			D, 8																
Me34**			R, 8																
Me35**			R, 10																
Me35**			R, 10																
Me35**			R, 9																
Me35**			R, 9																
Me35**			D, 9																
Me35**			R, 9																
Me36**			R, 19																
Me36**			D, 18																
Me36**			D, 17																
Me37**			R, 9																
Me37**			R, 9																
Me37**			R, 8																
Me37**			R, 8																
Me37**			R, 7																
Me37**			R, 7																
Me37**			R, 7																
Me37**			R, 7																
Me38**			D, 15																
Me38**			D, 14																
Me38**			R, 14																
Me38**			R, 13																
Me39**			D, 13																
Me39**			D, 11																
Me39**			R, 11																
Me39**			D, 11																
Me39**			D, 11																
Me40**			R, 18																
Me40**			D, 17																
Me40**			D, 13																
Me40**			D, 12																

(continued)

Note: D=Democrat, R=Republican, R/D=Republican/Democrat (cross-filed), D/R=Democrat/Republican (cross-filed), I=Independent, C=Constitution, O=Other, GI=Green Independent, P=Progressive, P/D=Progressive/Democrat, P/D/R=Progressive/Democrat/Republican, HH=Households

New Hampshire State House Districts—Election and Demographic Data (cont.)

House Districts	General Election Results Party, Percent of Vote							Population			Avg. HH Income	Pop 25+ Some College +	Pop 25+ 4-Yr Degree +	Below Poverty Line	2006 White (Non-Hisp)	African American	American Indians, Alaska Natives	Asians, Hawaiians, Pacific Islanders	Hispanic Origin
New Hamp.	2000	2001	2002	2003	2004	2005	2006	2000	2006	% Change	($)	(%)	(%)	(%)	(%)	(%)	(%)	(%)	(%)
Me41**		R, 22																	
Me41**		R, 20																	
Me41**			D, 20																
Ro1****	R, 62				R, 12		D, 11	15,060	16,024	6	74,537	42.9	23.9	6.1	96.9	0.4	0.4	0.7	1.0
Ro1****					R, 12		R, 11	15,060	16,024	6	74,537	42.9	23.9	6.1	96.9	0.4	0.4	0.7	1.0
Ro1****					R, 12		R, 11	15,060	16,024	6	74,537	42.9	23.9	6.1	96.9	0.4	0.4	0.7	1.0
Ro1****					R, 11		D, 10	15,060	16,024	6	74,537	42.9	23.9	6.1	96.9	0.4	0.4	0.7	1.0
Ro1****					R, 11		R, 10	15,060	16,024	6	74,537	42.9	23.9	6.1	96.9	0.4	0.4	0.7	1.0
Ro2****	R, 100				R, 38		R, 35	9,408	9,971	6	56,640	33.6	14.2	10.4	96.5	0.6	0.5	0.3	1.3
Ro2****					R, 31		R, 33	9,408	9,971	6	56,640	33.6	14.2	10.4	96.5	0.6	0.5	0.3	1.3
Ro2****					R, 30		R, 32	9,408	9,971	6	56,640	33.6	14.2	10.4	96.5	0.6	0.5	0.3	1.3
Ro3****	R, 65				R, 9		R, 7	30,935	32,231	4	90,539	43.9	25.7	5.4	94.1	0.7	0.3	1.7	2.4
Ro3****					R, 8		R, 6	30,935	32,231	4	90,539	43.9	25.7	5.4	94.1	0.7	0.3	1.7	2.4
Ro3****					R, 8		R, 6	30,935	32,231	4	90,539	43.9	25.7	5.4	94.1	0.7	0.3	1.7	2.4
Ro3****					R, 7		R, 6	30,935	32,231	4	90,539	43.9	25.7	5.4	94.1	0.7	0.3	1.7	2.4
Ro3****					R, 7		R, 6	30,935	32,231	4	90,539	43.9	25.7	5.4	94.1	0.7	0.3	1.7	2.4
Ro3****					R, 7		R, 6	30,935	32,231	4	90,539	43.9	25.7	5.4	94.1	0.7	0.3	1.7	2.4
Ro3****					R, 7		R, 6	30,935	32,231	4	90,539	43.9	25.7	5.4	94.1	0.7	0.3	1.7	2.4
Ro3****					R, 7		R, 6	30,935	32,231	4	90,539	43.9	25.7	5.4	94.1	0.7	0.3	1.7	2.4
Ro4****	R, 39				R, 5		R, 5	39,090	41,465	6	93,505	44.5	26.9	6.4	92.2	0.6	0.3	3.0	2.8
Ro4****					R, 5		R, 5	39,090	41,465	6	93,505	44.5	26.9	6.4	92.2	0.6	0.3	3.0	2.8
Ro4****					R, 5		R, 5	39,090	41,465	6	93,505	44.5	26.9	6.4	92.2	0.6	0.3	3.0	2.8
Ro4****					R, 5		R, 5	39,090	41,465	6	93,505	44.5	26.9	6.4	92.2	0.6	0.3	3.0	2.8
Ro4****					R, 5		R, 5	39,090	41,465	6	93,505	44.5	26.9	6.4	92.2	0.6	0.3	3.0	2.8
Ro4****					R, 5		R, 5	39,090	41,465	6	93,505	44.5	26.9	6.4	92.2	0.6	0.3	3.0	2.8
Ro4****					R, 5		R, 4	39,090	41,465	6	93,505	44.5	26.9	6.4	92.2	0.6	0.3	3.0	2.8
Ro4****					R, 4		R, 4	39,090	41,465	6	93,505	44.5	26.9	6.4	92.2	0.6	0.3	3.0	2.8
Ro4****					R, 4		R, 4	39,090	41,465	6	93,505	44.5	26.9	6.4	92.2	0.6	0.3	3.0	2.8
Ro4****					R, 4		R, 4	39,090	41,465	6	93,505	44.5	26.9	6.4	92.2	0.6	0.3	3.0	2.8
Ro4****					R, 4		R, 4	39,090	41,465	6	93,505	44.5	26.9	6.4	92.2	0.6	0.3	3.0	2.8
Ro4****					R, 4		R, 4	39,090	41,465	6	93,505	44.5	26.9	6.4	92.2	0.6	0.3	3.0	2.8
Ro5****	R, 100				R, 6		R/D, 11	32,517	33,857	4	68,313	41.3	22.1	7.4	92.8	1.1	0.3	1.7	3.0
Ro5****					R, 6		R, 7	32,517	33,857	4	68,313	41.3	22.1	7.4	92.8	1.1	0.3	1.7	3.0
Ro5****					R, 6		R, 7	32,517	33,857	4	68,313	41.3	22.1	7.4	92.8	1.1	0.3	1.7	3.0
Ro5****					R, 5		R, 7	32,517	33,857	4	68,313	41.3	22.1	7.4	92.8	1.1	0.3	1.7	3.0
Ro5****					R, 5		D, 6	32,517	33,857	4	68,313	41.3	22.1	7.4	92.8	1.1	0.3	1.7	3.0
Ro5****					R, 5		R, 6	32,517	33,857	4	68,313	41.3	22.1	7.4	92.8	1.1	0.3	1.7	3.0
Ro5****					R, 5		R, 6	32,517	33,857	4	68,313	41.3	22.1	7.4	92.8	1.1	0.3	1.7	3.0
Ro5****					R, 5		R, 6	32,517	33,857	4	68,313	41.3	22.1	7.4	92.8	1.1	0.3	1.7	3.0
Ro5****					R, 5		D, 6	32,517	33,857	4	68,313	41.3	22.1	7.4	92.8	1.1	0.3	1.7	3.0
Ro6****	R, 100				R/D, 54		R/D, 50	6,354	6,603	4	92,169	52.4	32.4	6.2	95.5	0.4	0.2	2.0	1.4
Ro6****					R/D, 46		R/D, 50	6,354	6,603	4	92,169	52.4	32.4	6.2	95.5	0.4	0.2	2.0	1.4
Ro7****	R, 65				R/D, 20		D/R, 30	13,468	15,246	13	80,487	41.6	20.9	5.7	96.7	0.4	0.4	0.5	1.3
Ro7****					R, 17		D/R, 29	13,468	15,246	13	80,487	41.6	20.9	5.7	96.7	0.4	0.4	0.5	1.3
Ro7****					R, 17		R, 21	13,468	15,246	13	80,487	41.6	20.9	5.7	96.7	0.4	0.4	0.5	1.3
Ro7****					R, 16		R, 20	13,468	15,246	13	80,487	41.6	20.9	5.7	96.7	0.4	0.4	0.5	1.3

(continued)

Note: D=Democrat, R=Republican, R/D=Republican/Democrat (cross-filed), D/R=Democrat/Republican (cross-filed), I=Independent, C=Constitution, O=Other, GI=Green Independent, P=Progressive, P/D=Progressive/Democrat, P/D/R=Progressive/Democrat/Republican, HH=Households

New Hampshire State House Districts—Election and Demographic Data (cont.)

House Districts	General Election Results Party, Percent of Vote							Population			Avg. HH Income	Pop 25+		Below Poverty Line	2006 White (Non-Hisp)	African American	American Indians, Alaska Natives	Asians, Hawaiians, Pacific Islanders	Hispanic Origin
New Hamp.	2000	2001	2002	2003	2004	2005	2006	2000	2006	% Change	($)	Some College + (%)	4-Yr Degree + (%)	(%)	(%)	(%)	(%)	(%)	(%)
Ro8****	R, 52				R/D, 15		R/D, 17	22,038	23,544	7	83,401	45.1	24.8	6.7	96.5	0.3	0.2	0.8	1.6
Ro8****					R/D, 14		R/D, 16	22,038	23,544	7	83,401	45.1	24.8	6.7	96.5	0.3	0.2	0.8	1.6
Ro8****					R/D, 14		R/D, 16	22,038	23,544	7	83,401	45.1	24.8	6.7	96.5	0.3	0.2	0.8	1.6
Ro8****					R, 12		R/D, 16	22,038	23,544	7	83,401	45.1	24.8	6.7	96.5	0.3	0.2	0.8	1.6
Ro8****					R, 12		R/D, 16	22,038	23,544	7	83,401	45.1	24.8	6.7	96.5	0.3	0.2	0.8	1.6
Ro8****					R, 12		R, 10	22,038	23,544	7	83,401	45.1	24.8	6.7	96.5	0.3	0.2	0.8	1.6
Ro8****					R, 11		R, 10	22,038	23,544	7	83,401	45.1	24.8	6.7	96.5	0.3	0.2	0.8	1.6
Ro9****	R, 47				R, 27		R, 18	8,946	9,433	5	66,451	38.3	17.1	7.6	96.3	0.3	0.3	0.6	1.3
Ro9****	R, 36				R, 26		R, 17	8,946	9,433	5	66,451	38.3	17.1	7.6	96.3	0.3	0.3	0.6	1.3
Ro9****					R, 25		D, 17	8,946	9,433	5	66,451	38.3	17.1	7.6	96.3	0.3	0.3	0.6	1.3
Ro10****	R, 100				R, 64		R/D,	3,179	3,697	16	88,649	43.5	25.1	6.8	93.1	1.0	0.5	1.4	2.8
Ro11****	R, 100				R, 28		D, 27	6,018	6,662	11	75,318	43.5	22.9	6.0	96.4	0.5	0.2	0.3	1.7
Ro11****					D, 25		R, 25	6,018	6,662	11	75,318	43.5	22.9	6.0	96.4	0.5	0.2	0.3	1.7
Ro12****	R, 31				D/R, 30		D/R, 36	9,262	10,216	10	64,029	43.5	26.9	10.5	91.7	0.6	0.2	3.9	2.3
Ro12****	R, 30				D, 25		D, 26	9,262	10,216	10	64,029	43.5	26.9	10.5	91.7	0.6	0.2	3.9	2.3
Ro12****	R, 25				R, 23		D, 24	9,262	10,216	10	64,029	43.5	26.9	10.5	91.7	0.6	0.2	3.9	2.3
Ro13****	R, 9				R/D, 9		R/D, 12	24,953	26,310	5	87,930	51.3	34.6	7.9	96.1	0.4	0.2	1.3	1.2
Ro13****	R, 8				R, 8		D, 8	24,953	26,310	5	87,930	51.3	34.6	7.9	96.1	0.4	0.2	1.3	1.2
Ro13****	R, 8				R, 8		D, 7	24,953	26,310	5	87,930	51.3	34.6	7.9	96.1	0.4	0.2	1.3	1.2
Ro13****	R, 8				D, 7		D, 7	24,953	26,310	5	87,930	51.3	34.6	7.9	96.1	0.4	0.2	1.3	1.2
Ro13****	R, 7				R, 7		D, 7	24,953	26,310	5	87,930	51.3	34.6	7.9	96.1	0.4	0.2	1.3	1.2
Ro13****	R, 7				R, 7		D, 7	24,953	26,310	5	87,930	51.3	34.6	7.9	96.1	0.4	0.2	1.3	1.2
Ro13****	R, 7				R, 7		R, 6	24,953	26,310	5	87,930	51.3	34.6	7.9	96.1	0.4	0.2	1.3	1.2
Ro13****	R, 7				R, 7		R, 6	24,953	26,310	5	87,930	51.3	34.6	7.9	96.1	0.4	0.2	1.3	1.2
Ro13****	R, 7							24,953	26,310	5	87,930	51.3	34.6	7.9	96.1	0.4	0.2	1.3	1.2
Ro13****	R, 7							24,953	26,310	5	87,930	51.3	34.6	7.9	96.1	0.4	0.2	1.3	1.2
Ro13****	R, 6							24,953	26,310	5	87,930	51.3	34.6	7.9	96.1	0.4	0.2	1.3	1.2
Ro14****	R, 100				R, 16		D, 14	13,321	14,545	9	71,014	42.0	23.6	10.5	96.1	0.4	0.3	0.9	1.4
Ro14****					R, 14		R, 13	13,321	14,545	9	71,014	42.0	23.6	10.5	96.1	0.4	0.3	0.9	1.4
Ro14****					R, 14		R, 13	13,321	14,545	9	71,014	42.0	23.6	10.5	96.1	0.4	0.3	0.9	1.4
Ro14****					R, 13		D, 13	13,321	14,545	9	71,014	42.0	23.6	10.5	96.1	0.4	0.3	0.9	1.4
Ro15****	R, 52				R, 13		R, 24	14,453	15,194	5	79,361	51.0	33.0	8.6	95.7	0.5	0.3	1.3	1.5
Ro15****	R, 48				R, 12		R, 20	14,453	15,194	5	79,361	51.0	33.0	8.6	95.7	0.5	0.3	1.3	1.5
Ro15****					R, 11		R, 20	14,453	15,194	5	79,361	51.0	33.0	8.6	95.7	0.5	0.3	1.3	1.5
Ro15****					R, 11		R, 20	14,453	15,194	5	79,361	51.0	33.0	8.6	95.7	0.5	0.3	1.3	1.5
Ro15****					R, 11		R, 16	14,453	15,194	5	79,361	51.0	33.0	8.6	95.7	0.5	0.3	1.3	1.5
Ro16****	R, 45				D, 11		D, 13	21,431	22,746	6	66,188	53.6	36.9	12.5	90.2	2.6	0.3	3.7	2.2
Ro16****	R, 32				D, 11		D, 13	21,431	22,746	6	66,188	53.6	36.9	12.5	90.2	2.6	0.3	3.7	2.2
Ro16****					D, 11		D, 13	21,431	22,746	6	66,188	53.6	36.9	12.5	90.2	2.6	0.3	3.7	2.2
Ro16****					D, 10		D, 12	21,431	22,746	6	66,188	53.6	36.9	12.5	90.2	2.6	0.3	3.7	2.2
Ro16****					D, 10		D, 12	21,431	22,746	6	66,188	53.6	36.9	12.5	90.2	2.6	0.3	3.7	2.2
Ro16****					D, 9		D, 12	21,431	22,746	6	66,188	53.6	36.9	12.5	90.2	2.6	0.3	3.7	2.2
Ro16****					D, 8		D, 11	21,431	22,746	6	66,188	53.6	36.9	12.5	90.2	2.6	0.3	3.7	2.2
Ro17****	R, 34				R, 54		D, 52	3,383	3,748	11	86,599	51.3	32.9	6.4	95.8	0.4	0.1	2.1	1.2
Ro17****	R, 29							3,383	3,748	11	86,599	51.3	32.9	6.4	95.8	0.4	0.1	2.1	1.2
Ro18****	R, 26				R, 31		D, 28	5,931	6,251	5	109,502	62.9	46.8	5.7	97.2	0.3	0.1	0.9	1.0
Ro18****	R, 25				R, 29		D, 25	5,931	6,251	5	109,502	62.9	46.8	5.7	97.2	0.3	0.1	0.9	1.0
Ro18****	R, 24							5,931	6,251	5	109,502	62.9	46.8	5.7	97.2	0.3	0.1	0.9	1.0
Ro18****	R, 24							5,931	6,251	5	109,502	62.9	46.8	5.7	97.2	0.3	0.1	0.9	1.0
Ro19*	D, 23																		

(continued)

Note: D=Democrat, R=Republican, R/D=Republican/Democrat (cross-filed), D/R=Democrat/Republican (cross-filed), I=Independent, C=Constitution, O=Other, GI=Green Independent, P=Progressive, P/D=Progressive/Democrat, P/D/R=Progressive/Democrat/Republican, HH=Households

New Hampshire State House Districts—Election and Demographic Data (cont.)

House Districts	General Election Results Party, Percent of Vote							Population			Avg. HH Income	Pop 25+		Below Poverty Line	2006 White (Non-Hisp)	African American	American Indians, Alaska Natives	Asians, Hawaiians, Pacific Islanders	Hispanic Origin
												Some College +	4-Yr Degree +						
New Hamp.	2000	2001	2002	2003	2004	2005	2006	2000	2006	% Change	($)	(%)	(%)	(%)	(%)	(%)	(%)	(%)	(%)
Ro19*	R, 19																		
Ro19*	D, 16																		
Ro20*	R, 14																		
Ro20*	R, 14																		
Ro20*	R, 14																		
Ro20*	D, 13																		
Ro20*	R, 13																		
Ro21*	R, 23																		
Ro21*	R, 22																		
Ro21*	D, 20																		
Ro22*	R, 12																		
Ro22*	D, 12																		
Ro22*	R, 11																		
Ro22*	R, 10																		
Ro22*	R, 10																		
Ro23*	R, 100																		
Ro24*	R, 31																		
Ro24*	R, 25																		
Ro25*	R, 24																		
Ro25*	R, 22																		
Ro25*	R, 22																		
Ro26*	R, 8																		
Ro26*	R, 7																		
Ro26*	R, 7																		
Ro26*	D, 7																		
Ro26*	D, 7																		
Ro26*	R, 6																		
Ro26*	R, 6																		
Ro26*	R, 6																		
Ro26*	D, 6																		
Ro27*	R, 36																		
Ro27*	R, 34																		
Ro27*	R, 30																		
Ro28*	R, 100																		
Ro29*	R, 10																		
Ro29*	R, 9																		
Ro29*	R, 9																		
Ro29*	R, 8																		
Ro29*	R, 8																		
Ro29*	R, 8																		
Ro29*	R, 8																		
Ro30*	D, 81																		
Ro31*	D, 99																		
Ro32*	D, 99																		
Ro33*	D, 41																		
Ro33*	D, 33																		
Ro34*	D, 99																		
Ro35*	D, 42																		
Ro35*	R, 29																		
Ro36*	D, 72																		

(continued)

Note: D=Democrat, R=Republican, R/D=Republican/Democrat (cross-filed), D/R=Democrat/Republican (cross-filed), I=Independent, C=Constitution, O=Other, GI=Green Independent, P=Progressive, P/D=Progressive/Democrat, P/D/R=Progressive/Democrat/Republican, HH=Households

New Hampshire State House Districts—Election and Demographic Data (cont.)

House Districts	General Election Results Party, Percent of Vote							Population			Avg. HH Income	Pop 25+		Below Poverty Line	White (Non-Hisp)	African American	American Indians, Alaska Natives	Asians, Hawaiians, Pacific Islanders	Hispanic Origin
												Some College +	4-Yr Degree +						
New Hamp.	2000	2001	2002	2003	2004	2005	2006	2000	2006	% Change	($)	(%)	(%)	(%)	(%)	(%)	(%)	(%)	(%)
Ro73**			R/D, 14																
Ro73**			R, 12																
Ro73**			R, 12																
Ro73**			R, 12																
Ro73**			R, 11																
Ro74**			R/D, 33																
Ro74**			R/D, 33																
Ro74**			R/D, 32																
Ro75**			R, 8																
Ro75**			R, 8																
Ro75**			R, 8																
Ro75**			R, 8																
Ro75**			R, 8																
Ro75**			R, 7																
Ro75**			R, 7																
Ro75**			R, 7																
Ro75**			R, 7																
Ro76**			R, 6																
Ro76**			R, 6																
Ro76**			R, 6																
Ro76**			R, 5																
Ro76**			R, 5																
Ro76**			R, 5																
Ro76**			R, 5																
Ro76**			R, 5																
Ro76**			R, 5																
Ro76**			R, 5																
Ro76**			R, 5																
Ro76**			R, 5																
Ro76**			R, 5																
Ro77**			R, 7																
Ro77**			R, 7																
Ro77**			R, 7																
Ro77**			R, 7																
Ro77**			R/D, 7																
Ro77**			R/D, 7																
Ro77**			R, 7																
Ro77**			R, 7																
Ro77**			R, 6																
Ro77**			R, 6																
Ro77**			R, 6																
Ro78**			R, 41																
Ro78**			R, 35																
Ro79**			R/D, 10																
Ro79**			R/D, 9																
Ro79**			R/D, 9																
Ro79**			R/D, 9																
Ro79**			R/D, 8																
Ro79**			R/D, 8																
Ro79**			R/D, 8																

(continued)

Note: D=Democrat, R=Republican, R/D=Republican/Democrat (cross-filed), D/R=Democrat/Republican (cross-filed), I=Independent, C=Constitution, O=Other, GI=Green Independent, P=Progressive, P/D=Progressive/Democrat, P/D/R=Progressive/Democrat/Republican, HH=Households

New Hampshire State House Districts—Election and Demographic Data (cont.)

House Districts	General Election Results Party, Percent of Vote							Population			Avg. HH Income	Pop 25+		Below Poverty Line	White (Non-Hisp)	African American	American Indians, Alaska Natives	Asians, Hawaiians, Pacific Islanders	Hispanic Origin
												Some College +	4-Yr Degree +						
															2006				
New Hamp.	2000	2001	2002	2003	2004	2005	2006	2000	2006	% Change	($)	(%)	(%)	(%)	(%)	(%)	(%)	(%)	(%)
Ro79**			R/D, 8																
Ro79**			R/D, 8																
Ro79**			R, 8																
Ro79**			R, 8																
Ro80**			R/D, 21																
Ro80**			R, 21																
Ro80**			D, 20																
Ro80**			R, 20																
Ro81**			R, 40																
Ro81**			D, 31																
Ro82**			R, 29																
Ro82**			D, 28																
Ro82**			D, 23																
Ro83**			R, 9																
Ro83**			R, 8																
Ro83**			R, 7																
Ro83**			R, 7																
Ro83**			R, 7																
Ro83**			R, 7																
Ro83**			R, 7																
Ro83**			R, 7																
Ro84**			R, 16																
Ro84**			R, 16																
Ro84**			R, 16																
Ro84**			R, 14																
Ro85**			R, 14																
Ro85**			R, 14																
Ro85**			R, 13																
Ro85**			R, 13																
Ro85**			R, 13																
Ro86**			D, 10																
Ro86**			D, 9																
Ro86**			D, 9																
Ro86**			D, 9																
Ro86**			D, 8																
Ro86**			D, 8																
Ro86**			D, 8																
Ro87**			R, 100																
Ro88**			R, 29																
Ro88**			R, 26																
St1****	R, 99				R, 7		D, 7	28,256	30,073	6	53,266	33.5	12.9	13.1	95.5	0.6	0.4	1.3	1.3
St1****					R, 6		D, 7	28,256	30,073	6	53,266	33.5	12.9	13.1	95.5	0.6	0.4	1.3	1.3
St1****					R, 6		D, 7	28,256	30,073	6	53,266	33.5	12.9	13.1	95.5	0.6	0.4	1.3	1.3
St1****					D, 6		D, 6	28,256	30,073	6	53,266	33.5	12.9	13.1	95.5	0.6	0.4	1.3	1.3
St1****					D, 6		D, 6	28,256	30,073	6	53,266	33.5	12.9	13.1	95.5	0.6	0.4	1.3	1.3
St1****					R, 6		D, 6	28,256	30,073	6	53,266	33.5	12.9	13.1	95.5	0.6	0.4	1.3	1.3
St1****					D, 6		R, 6	28,256	30,073	6	53,266	33.5	12.9	13.1	95.5	0.6	0.4	1.3	1.3
St1****					R, 6		D, 6	28,256	30,073	6	53,266	33.5	12.9	13.1	95.5	0.6	0.4	1.3	1.3
St1****					R, 6		D, 6	28,256	30,073	6	53,266	33.5	12.9	13.1	95.5	0.6	0.4	1.3	1.3
St1****					R, 6		D, 6	28,256	30,073	6	53,266	33.5	12.9	13.1	95.5	0.6	0.4	1.3	1.3
St2****	D, 53				D/R, 21		D, 19	14,547	15,117	4	55,260	36.6	16.4	13.0	93.8	0.8	0.3	1.7	2.0

(continued)

Note: D=Democrat, R=Republican, R/D=Republican/Democrat (cross-filed), D/R=Democrat/Republican (cross-filed), I=Independent, C=Constitution, O=Other, GI=Green Independent, P=Progressive, P/D=Progressive/Democrat, P/D/R=Progressive/Democrat/Republican, HH=Households

New Hampshire State House Districts—Election and Demographic Data (cont.)

House Districts	General Election Results Party, Percent of Vote							Population			Avg. HH Income	2006 Pop 25+ Some College +	2006 Pop 25+ 4-Yr Degree +	Below Poverty Line	White (Non-Hisp)	African American	American Indians, Alaska Natives	Asians, Hawaiians, Pacific Islanders	Hispanic Origin
New Hamp.	2000	2001	2002	2003	2004	2005	2006	2000	2006	% Change	($)	(%)	(%)	(%)	(%)	(%)	(%)	(%)	(%)
St2****					D/R, 19		D, 19	14,547	15,117	4	55,260	36.6	16.4	13.0	93.8	0.8	0.3	1.7	2.0
St2****					D, 17		D, 19	14,547	15,117	4	55,260	36.6	16.4	13.0	93.8	0.8	0.3	1.7	2.0
St2****					D, 17		D, 17	14,547	15,117	4	55,260	36.6	16.4	13.0	93.8	0.8	0.3	1.7	2.0
St2****					D, 14		D, 17	14,547	15,117	4	55,260	36.6	16.4	13.0	93.8	0.8	0.3	1.7	2.0
St3****	R, 27				R, 7		D, 7	24,709	27,072	10	61,384	36.9	15.4	8.9	97.0	0.2	0.4	0.6	1.0
St3****	D, 26				R, 7		D, 7	24,709	27,072	10	61,384	36.9	15.4	8.9	97.0	0.2	0.4	0.6	1.0
St3****					R, 7		D, 7	24,709	27,072	10	61,384	36.9	15.4	8.9	97.0	0.2	0.4	0.6	1.0
St3****					R, 7		D, 7	24,709	27,072	10	61,384	36.9	15.4	8.9	97.0	0.2	0.4	0.6	1.0
St3****					R, 7		D, 7	24,709	27,072	10	61,384	36.9	15.4	8.9	97.0	0.2	0.4	0.6	1.0
St3****					D, 7		D, 7	24,709	27,072	10	61,384	36.9	15.4	8.9	97.0	0.2	0.4	0.6	1.0
St3****					D, 7		D, 7	24,709	27,072	10	61,384	36.9	15.4	8.9	97.0	0.2	0.4	0.6	1.0
St3****					R, 7		D, 6	24,709	27,072	10	61,384	36.9	15.4	8.9	97.0	0.2	0.4	0.6	1.0
St4****	R, 52				D, 24		D, 29	7,936	8,405	6	52,572	41.8	23.2	11.1	89.2	1.4	0.3	5.8	1.9
St4****					D, 24		D, 29	7,936	8,405	6	52,572	41.8	23.2	11.1	89.2	1.4	0.3	5.8	1.9
St4****					D, 24		D, 28	7,936	8,405	6	52,572	41.8	23.2	11.1	89.2	1.4	0.3	5.8	1.9
St5****	D, 56				D, 18		D, 19	8,252	8,992	9	68,722	53.1	29.4	8.7	94.2	0.6	0.2	2.9	1.2
St5****					D, 18		D, 19	8,252	8,992	9	68,722	53.1	29.4	8.7	94.2	0.6	0.2	2.9	1.2
St5****					R, 17		D, 18	8,252	8,992	9	68,722	53.1	29.4	8.7	94.2	0.6	0.2	2.9	1.2
St6****	R, 51				D, 19		D, 22	9,828	10,340	5	55,232	42.5	21.9	12.5	92.2	1.9	0.4	2.1	1.9
St6****	D, 49				D, 19		D, 21	9,828	10,340	5	55,232	42.5	21.9	12.5	92.2	1.9	0.4	2.1	1.9
St6****					D, 19		D, 20	9,828	10,340	5	55,232	42.5	21.9	12.5	92.2	1.9	0.4	2.1	1.9
St7****	D, 100				D/R, 14		D/R, 17	19,025	19,904	5	79,120	39.4	29.6	13.1	92.3	0.9	0.3	3.9	1.7
St7****					D, 11		D/R, 17	19,025	19,904	5	79,120	39.4	29.6	13.1	92.3	0.9	0.3	3.9	1.7
St7****					D, 11		D/R, 17	19,025	19,904	5	79,120	39.4	29.6	13.1	92.3	0.9	0.3	3.9	1.7
St7****					D, 11		D, 13	19,025	19,904	5	79,120	39.4	29.6	13.1	92.3	0.9	0.3	3.9	1.7
St7****					D, 11		D, 13	19,025	19,904	5	79,120	39.4	29.6	13.1	92.3	0.9	0.3	3.9	1.7
St7****					D, 11		D, 12	19,025	19,904	5	79,120	39.4	29.6	13.1	92.3	0.9	0.3	3.9	1.7
St8*	D, 26																		
St8*	D, 25																		
St8*	D, 24																		
St8*	D, 24																		
St9*	D, 63																		
St10*	D, 61																		
St11*	D, 17																		
St11*	D, 14																		
St11*	D, 14																		
St11*	R, 13																		
St12*	D, 14																		
St12*	D, 13																		
St12*	R, 13																		
St12*	D, 13																		
St13*	D, 57																		
St14*	D, 27																		
St14*	D, 25																		
St14*	D, 24																		
St14*	D, 23																		
St15*	D, 26																		
St15*	R, 25																		
St16*	R, 33																		
St16*	D, 33																		

(continued)

Note: D=Democrat, R=Republican, R/D=Republican/Democrat (cross-filed), D/R=Democrat/Republican (cross-filed), I=Independent, C=Constitution, O=Other, GI=Green Independent, P=Progressive, P/D=Progressive/Democrat, P/D/R=Progressive/Democrat/Republican, HH=Households

New Hampshire State House Districts—Election and Demographic Data (cont.)

House Districts	General Election Results Party, Percent of Vote							Population			Avg. HH Income ($)	Pop 25+ Some College + (%)	Pop 25+ 4-Yr Degree + (%)	Below Poverty Line (%)	White (Non-Hisp) (%)	African American (%)	American Indians, Alaska Natives (%)	Asians, Hawaiians, Pacific Islanders (%)	Hispanic Origin (%)
New Hamp.	2000	2001	2002	2003	2004	2005	2006	2000	2006	% Change									
St17*	R, 35																		
St17*	R, 29																		
St18*	R, 36																		
St18*	D, 32																		
St19*	D, 38																		
St19*	R, 31																		
St67**			D/R, 6																
St67**			D/R, 5																
St67**			D/R, 5																
St67**			R, 5																
St67**			R, 5																
St67**			R, 4																
St67**			R, 4																
St67**			D/R, 4																
St67**			R, 4																
St67**			R, 4																
St67**			D, 4																
St67**			D, 4																
St67**			D, 4																
St67**			R, 4																
St68**			R, 8																
St68**			R, 8																
St68**			R, 7																
St68**			R, 7																
St68**			R, 7																
St68**			R, 7																
St68**			D, 6																
St68**			D, 6																
St69**			R, 20																
St69**			D, 18																
St69**			D, 17																
St70**			D, 21																
St70**			D, 20																
St70**			D, 20																
St71**			D/R, 23																
St71**			R, 21																
St71**			R, 21																
St72**			D/R, 16																
St72**			D/R, 15																
St72**			D/R, 14																
St72**			D, 12																
St72**			D, 11																
St72**			D, 11																
Su1****	D, 66			D, 30		D/R, 50	6,172	6,524	6	77,925	49.5	31.0	7.0	97.4	0.3	0.5	0.5	0.6
Su1****				D, 26		D/R, 50	6,172	6,524	6	77,925	49.5	31.0	7.0	97.4	0.3	0.5	0.5	0.6
Su2****	R, 99			D/R, 26		R, 18	10,025	10,712	7	53,063	29.3	12.8	13.4	97.2	0.1	0.5	0.5	0.8
Su2****				R, 21		D, 17	10,025	10,712	7	53,063	29.3	12.8	13.4	97.2	0.1	0.5	0.5	0.8
Su2****				D, 19		D, 17	10,025	10,712	7	53,063	29.3	12.8	13.4	97.2	0.1	0.5	0.5	0.8
Su3****	R, 100			R, 58		D, 54	2,840	3,022	6	79,478	47.0	28.3	7.2	97.4	0.2	0.4	0.6	0.6
Su4****	R, 24			D/R, 20		D/R, 20	15,624	16,275	4	50,147	26.6	10.3	15.9	96.9	0.3	0.4	0.8	0.7

(continued)

Note: D=Democrat, R=Republican, R/D=Republican/Democrat (cross-filed), D/R=Democrat/Republican (cross-filed), I=Independent, C=Constitution, O=Other, GI=Green Independent, P=Progressive, P/D=Progressive/Democrat, P/D/R=Progressive/Democrat/Republican, HH=Households

New Hampshire State House Districts—Election and Demographic Data (cont.)

House Districts	General Election Results Party, Percent of Vote							Population			Avg. HH Income	Pop 25+ Some College +	4-Yr Degree +	Below Poverty Line	2006 White (Non-Hisp)	African American	American Indians, Alaska Natives	Asians, Hawaiians, Pacific Islanders	Hispanic Origin
New Hamp.	2000	2001	2002	2003	2004	2005	2006	2000	2006	% Change	($)	(%)	(%)	(%)	(%)	(%)	(%)	(%)	(%)
Su4****	R, 23				D/R, 18		D/R, 19	15,624	16,275	4	50,147	26.6	10.3	15.9	96.9	0.3	0.4	0.8	0.7
Su4****	D, 20				D/R, 18		D/R, 19	15,624	16,275	4	50,147	26.6	10.3	15.9	96.9	0.3	0.4	0.8	0.7
Su4****					D/R, 17		D/R, 18	15,624	16,275	4	50,147	26.6	10.3	15.9	96.9	0.3	0.4	0.8	0.7
Su4****					R, 14		D, 12	15,624	16,275	4	50,147	26.6	10.3	15.9	96.9	0.3	0.4	0.8	0.7
Su5****	R, 53				D/R, 46		D/R, 62	6,212	6,696	8	52,610	27.3	10.9	11.4	97.5	0.4	0.5	0.2	0.9
Su5****					D, 36		D, 38	6,212	6,696	8	52,610	27.3	10.9	11.4	97.5	0.4	0.5	0.2	0.9
Su6*	D, 54																		
Su7*	D, 100																		
Su8*	D, 99																		
Su9*	D, 99																		
Su10*	D, 100																		
Su11*	D, 55																		
Su11*	D, 44																		
Su19**			D, 31																
Su19**			R, 25																
Su20**			R, 22																
Su20**			R, 21																
Su20**			D, 17																
Su21**			R/D, 100																
Su22**			D/R, 22																
Su22**			D/R, 20																
Su22**			D/R, 20																
Su22**			D/R, 19																
Su22**			D/R, 18																
Su23**			D/R, 57																
Su23**			D, 43																

* Applies to 2000 only

** Applies to 2002 only

*** Applies only to 2000 and 2002

**** Applies only to 2000, 2004, and 2006

Note: D=Democrat, R=Republican, R/D=Republican/Democrat (cross-filed), D/R=Democrat/Republican (cross-filed), I=Independent, C=Constitution, O=Other, GI=Green Independent, P=Progressive, P/D=Progressive/Democrat, P/D/R=Progressive/Democrat/Republican, HH=Households

NEW JERSEY

The old line about North Carolina being "a vale of humility between two mountains of conceit" could just as easily be applied to New Jersey. To New Yorkers or Philadelphians, the state can seem like one vast expanse of exit signs along the Turnpike or Garden State Parkway. On weekday mornings, the Lincoln Tunnel is jammed with commuters trying to get into Manhattan, just as the Walt Whitman Bridge is likely to be backed up with people from the Gloucester County subdivisions crossing the Delaware River into Philadelphia.

As Edmund Wilson wrote in the 1920s, "Almost every characteristic phase of New Jersey takes its function from the nearness of the cities." The dividing line is roughly at Trenton; to the north, people get New York TV and read the New York papers; to the south, it is Philadelphia and the *Inquirer.* The state's largest city, Newark, though part of a mighty manufacturing and transportation strip running from Elizabeth to Paramus, is about the same size as St. Paul, Minnesota, and as thoroughly overshadowed by its cross-river neighbor.

That is, of course, unfair to New Jersey. With the exception of the Pine Barrens and the shore communities, it is essentially a suburban state in one long "S" running from the George Washington Bridge to Atlantic City. As those suburban areas have grown more established, they have developed their own identities. New Jersey now roots for particularly New Jersey sports teams as well as those from New York and Philadelphia. It has also developed an independent pride at being a safer, saner place to live.

This suburban agglomeration has made New Jersey the tenth most-populous state and given it a steady, if unremarkable rate of growth. Though it is growing faster than either Pennsylvania or New York that is not surprising considering that it draws many commuters from both. Few places are either expanding or shrinking very quickly, but the fastest-growing areas are in Burlington County (a suburb of Philadelphia), Warren County (a suburb of New York), the area along Route 1 north of Princeton, and Ocean County, a popular retirement destination that Michael Barone calls "a kind of Frost Belt Florida." The 32nd assembly district, which encompasses Secaucus, has been the greatest population-loser during this decade, although the neighboring 33rd district, which includes Hoboken and the Hudson riverfront, has grown slightly.

The development of the metropolitan doughnut, the phenomenon seen in Chicago, St. Louis, and elsewhere, in which people are moving out of both the cities and the rural areas for the suburbs, is taking place here, as well, though it is masked by the fact that the two big cities are in other states. But people are also moving out of Camden and Newark, and the ring of suburbs has crept out to Morristown and Glassboro and beyond, with more suburb to suburb commuting.

Because large parts of the state are suburbs of two wealthy cities, New Jersey is the county's wealthiest state, with average household income almost $62,000 a year. (By comparison, it is less than $50,000 in New York State and less than $45,000 in Pennsylvania). The wealthiest neighborhoods are all in the New York half, in Morris and Passaic Counties, but eight state senate districts boast average household income of more than $100,000 a year. The poorest part of the state is still downtown Newark, despite that city's modest revival of recent years.

New Jersey is more than 70 percent white, but as in much of the rest of the county, its racial mix is developing beyond the traditional black-and-white. It is surprising that there are no black-majority state assembly districts, although African Americans comprise 49.3 percent of the 28th district, which lies west of Newark. Four districts around Newark are more that one-third Hispanic, including the 33rd district, which is almost 60 percent Hispanic and is home to the largest concentration of Cuban-Americans outside Miami. New Jersey also has the third-highest percentage of Asian residents, after (but far after) only Hawaii and California. The number of Asians in the state doubled during the 1990s, driven, according to the *New York Times*, by well-educated professionals moving in to take advantage of high-tech and scientific jobs.

For a generation, New Jersey alternated between Democratic and Republican governors but it now seems as solidly a Democratic state as its neighbors. Democrats have controlled the state assembly for almost a decade, adding to their majority over the last several elections. Democrats also captured control of the state senate in 2004 and currently hold a 22–18 majority there. As in only a few other places, the length of terms in the state senate varies. Ordinarily, state senators serve for four years but for only two years in the first election held in each decade, in order to ensure that any changes made in district boundaries are reflected quickly. Redistricting is handled by an appointed commission, rather than the legislature. New Jersey is also one of the few states that holds its gubernatorial and legislative elections in odd-numbered years.

Finally, New Jersey was also one of the few states that did not have an office of lieutenant governor. In case of the governor's death or incapacitation, the president of the state senate would take over. But having exercised this provision three times in the space of a decade, the state has thought better of it and voters in 2005 approved a referendum to change the constitution and elect New Jersey's first lieutenant governor in 2009.

NEW JERSEY
State Legislative Districts

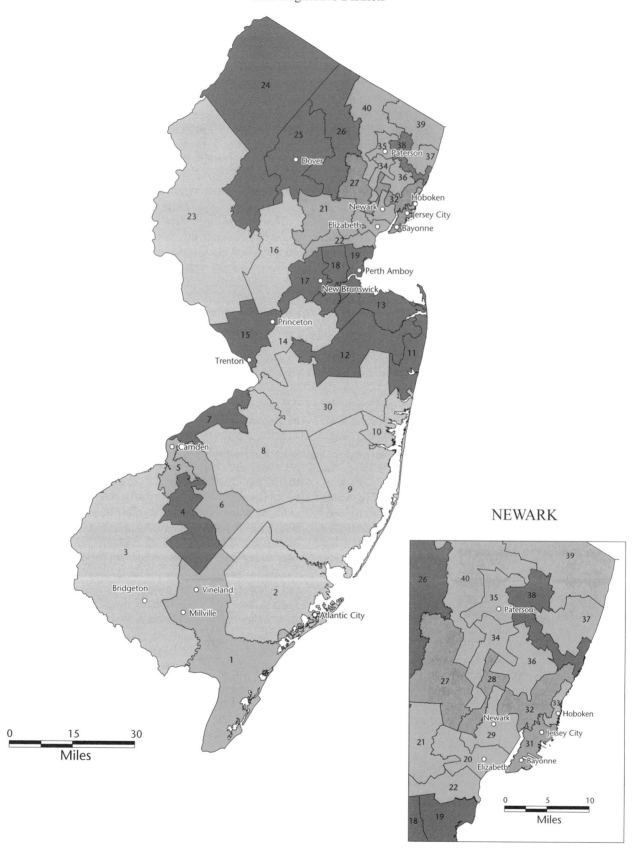

NEWARK

Population Growth   ▨ -4% to 0%   ▢ 0% to 2%   ▨ 2% to 7%   ▢ 7% to 13%

New Jersey Legislative Districts—Election and Demographic Data

Senate Districts	General Election Results Party, Percent of Vote							Population			Avg. HH Income ($)	Pop 25+		Below Poverty Line (%)	White (Non-Hisp) (%)	African American (%)	American Indians, Alaska Natives (%)	Asians, Hawaiians, Pacific Islanders (%)	Hispanic Origin (%)
												Some College + (%)	4-Yr Degree + (%)						
New Jersey	2000	2001	2002	2003	2004	2005	2006	2000	2006	% Change	($)	(%)	(%)	(%)	(%)	(%)	(%)	(%)	(%)
1		R, 50		R, 81				214,218	216,180	1	60,832	28.0	12.4	14.1	70.3	10.2	1.2	1.5	15.3
2		R, 87		R, 60				215,414	233,360	8	62,747	30.2	13.8	13.9	53.7	18.5	0.1	7.6	14.7
3		D, 51		D, 54				209,886	225,591	7	64,673	30.0	13.1	12.9	74.4	14.9	1.7	1.3	7.1
4		R, 58		D, 50				210,920	222,753	6	68,994	35.3	16.6	10.0	77.7	11.5	0.1	3.5	4.1
5		D, 69		D, 65				208,901	210,751	1	52,146	27.1	11.0	19.6	47.4	24.2	0.2	2.9	20.0
6		D, 67		D, 61				214,451	218,216	2	85,523	43.0	24.8	9.1	75.7	10.6	0.1	6.9	3.9
7		R, 54		R, 60				209,871	218,837	4	68,853	37.5	18.2	9.2	60.2	23.4	0.1	4.1	7.9
8		R, 61		R, 67				214,946	234,714	9	91,038	45.4	27.2	6.5	81.6	7.5	0.1	4.3	
9		R, 59		R, 66				211,511	237,037	12	59,515	31.6	16.4	11.4	89.2	2.1	0.1	1.4	4.7
10		R, 57		R, 65				208,589	225,215	8	73,148	36.6	21.1	9.7	87.6	2.0	0.1	2.5	5.5
11		R, 62		R, 59				211,678	217,759	3	82,057	41.9	24.0	11.9	68.6	14.4	0.1	3.5	9.7
12		R, 59		D, 52				212,366	225,221	6	110,117	45.7	29.4	6.8	73.3	6.5	0.1	8.1	9.3
13		R, 64		R, 54				218,182	224,178	3	95,337	39.7	22.6	8.0	76.0	4.3	0.1	9.2	7.8
14		R, 52		R, 59				207,681	225,974	9	95,274	45.0	29.7	6.4	68.3	7.5	0.1	14.0	6.9
15		D, 69		D, 67				199,590	207,080	4	82,930	37.9	25.0	14.8	49.0	27.3	0.4	5.2	15.1
16		R, 67		R, 100				200,664	216,216	8	125,873	48.0	36.1	5.2	71.6	3.2	0.3	10.2	9.5
17		D, 69		D, 61				210,826	221,172	5	80,956	39.9	27.1	9.1	43.5	16.7	0.1	18.3	19.3
18		D, 65		D, 58				204,215	213,424	5	94,318	43.5	29.2	7.2	57.9	6.3	0.1	24.1	9.0
19		D, 77		D, 65				211,001	221,048	5	71,228	31.9	17.7	11.2	44.9	8.1	0.1	14.1	28.3
20		D, 80		D, 62				202,444	206,370	2	60,545	31.9	18.1	16.7	31.4	21.4	0.8	5.2	41.7
21		R, 59		R, 67				225,784	229,642	2	150,589	52.5	40.6	5.3	77.0	4.1	0.2	7.5	7.4
22		D, 59		D, 55				204,136	208,092	2	79,055	38.0	22.6	10.1	45.0	23.4	0.5	5.6	20.7
23		R, 69		R, 68				220,560	239,719	9	94,233	39.5	22.8	7.5	87.7	2.6	0.1	2.5	4.8
24		R, 74		R, 68				205,648	218,753	6	97,457	40.8	22.6	6.6	87.6	1.7	0.1	2.9	5.5
25		R, 66		R, 55				212,162	222,404	5	111,115	47.4	32.0	6.0	70.7	4.1	0.1	6.5	15.0
26		R, 66		R, 66				197,200	204,549	4	102,742	46.5	31.1	5.4	76.7	2.0	0.1	11.2	7.3
27		D, 65		D, 66				212,818	212,092	0	106,889	43.0	30.5	10.8	49.6	31.4	0.1	7.5	8.2
28		D, 69		D, 73				212,400	208,715	-2	55,631	28.3	15.3	18.8	26.6	49.3	0.1	5.6	17.7
29		D, 100		D, 83				202,696	206,066	2	43,857	22.3	11.2	31.2	20.6	39.5	0.2	2.2	40.1
30		R, 62		R, 63				216,158	237,735	10	74,335	34.9	19.2	11.1	73.5	8.5	0.1	3.2	11.0
31		D, 74		D, 79				202,386	197,724	-2	57,410	33.1	21.2	21.0	30.7	23.9	0.2	14.4	24.6
32		D, 69		D, 77				220,551	212,178	-4	59,375	31.1	19.3	16.6	30.4	6.9	0.2	12.7	44.5
33		D, 75		D, 81				199,576	201,568	1	66,790	37.2	27.2	17.7	22.5	6.3	0.3	9.9	58.6
34		D, 65		D, 70				209,107	209,506	0	79,099	34.9	21.1	14.5	40.4	34.5	0.1	4.9	15.4
35		D, 100		D, 69				211,667	215,403	2	64,580	22.0	10.4	19.1	26.0	21.3	0.2	3.4	42.8
36		D, 51		D, 53				211,319	212,145	0	64,603	30.4	18.4	13.3	45.5	6.0	0.2	8.7	30.3
37		D, 66		D, 62				215,644	219,699	2	91,911	43.7	30.3	9.6	45.8	13.2	0.1	17.6	22.1
38		D, 53		D, 56				214,204	221,304	3	84,173	43.7	29.9	9.8	62.5	2.5	0.1	17.7	14.7
39		R, 63		R, 62				214,258	216,630	1	125,556	48.9	35.7	5.2	75.8	2.0	0.0	13.6	6.4
40		R, 62		R, 64				208,762	211,653	1	130,041	46.9	33.5	5.5	77.7	3.2	0.1	7.5	8.0

Note: D=Democrat, R=Republican, R/D=Republican/Democrat (cross-filed), D/R=Democrat/Republican (cross-filed), I=Independent, C=Constitution, O=Other, GI=Green Independent, P=Progressive, P/D=Progressive/Democrat, P/D/R=Progressive/Democrat/Republican, HH=Households

New Jersey Legislative Districts—Election and Demographic Data

House Districts	General Election Results Party, Percent of Vote							Population			Avg. HH Income	Pop 25+		2006					
												Some College +	4-Yr Degree +	Below Poverty Line	White (Non-Hisp)	African American	American Indians, Alaska Natives	Asians, Hawaiians, Pacific Islanders	Hispanic Origin
New Jersey	2000	2001	2002	2003	2004	2005	2006	2000	2006	% Change	($)	(%)	(%)	(%)	(%)	(%)	(%)	(%)	(%)
1		R, 30		D, 27		D, 36		214,218	216,180	1	60,832	28.0	12.4	14.1	70.3	10.2	1.2	1.5	15.3
1		D, 26		R, 26		D, 28		214,218	216,180	1	60,832	28.0	12.4	14.1	70.3	10.2	1.2	1.5	15.3
2		R, 28		D, 31		D, 28		215,414	233,360	8	62,747	30.2	13.8	13.9	53.7	18.5	0.1	7.6	14.7
2		R, 28		D, 30		R, 26		215,414	233,360	8	62,747	30.2	13.8	13.9	53.7	18.5	0.1	7.6	14.7
3		D, 28		D, 25		D, 30		209,886	225,591	7	64,673	30.0	13.1	12.9	74.4	14.9	1.7	1.3	7.1
3		D, 27		D, 25		D, 30		209,886	225,591	7	64,673	30.0	13.1	12.9	74.4	14.9	1.7	1.3	7.1
4		R, 28		D, 27		D, 30		210,920	222,753	6	68,994	35.3	16.6	10.0	77.7	11.5	0.1	3.5	4.1
4		D, 25		D, 27		D, 32		210,920	222,753	6	68,994	35.3	16.6	10.0	77.7	11.5	0.1	3.5	4.1
5		D, 43		D, 32		D, 45		208,901	210,751	1	52,146	27.1	11.0	19.6	47.4	24.2	0.2	2.9	20.0
5		D, 40		D, 30		D, 42		208,901	210,751	1	52,146	27.1	11.0	19.6	47.4	24.2	0.2	2.9	20.0
6		D, 33		D, 29		D, 31		214,451	218,216	2	85,523	43.0	24.8	9.1	75.7	10.6	0.1	6.9	3.9
6		D, 32		D, 28		D, 29		214,451	218,216	2	85,523	43.0	24.8	9.1	75.7	10.6	0.1	6.9	3.9
7		D, 30		D, 26		D, 33		209,871	218,837	4	68,853	37.5	18.2	9.2	60.2	23.4	0.1	4.1	7.9
7		D, 28		D, 26		D, 33		209,871	218,837	4	68,853	37.5	18.2	9.2	60.2	23.4	0.1	4.1	7.9
8		R, 30		D, 34		D, 32		214,946	234,714	9	91,038	45.4	27.2	6.5	81.6	7.5	0.1	4.3	3.8
8		R, 30		D, 33		D, 28		214,946	234,714	9	91,038	45.4	27.2	6.5	81.6	7.5	0.1	4.3	3.8
9		R, 30		R, 29		R, 32		211,511	237,037	12	59,515	31.6	16.4	11.4	89.2	2.1	0.1	1.4	4.7
9		R, 30		D, 33		R, 36		211,511	237,037	12	59,515	31.6	16.4	11.4	89.2	2.1	0.1	1.4	4.7
10		R, 29		D, 30		R, 32		208,589	225,215	8	73,148	36.6	21.1	9.7	87.6	2.0	0.1	2.5	5.5
10		R, 30		D, 32		R, 32		208,589	225,215	8	73,148	36.6	21.1	9.7	87.6	2.0	0.1	2.5	5.5
11		R, 30		D, 30		R, 26		211,678	217,759	3	82,057	41.9	24.0	11.9	68.6	14.4	0.1	3.5	9.7
11		R, 27		D, 30		R, 26		211,678	217,759	3	82,057	41.9	24.0	11.9	68.6	14.4	0.1	3.5	9.7
12		R, 27		D, 27		R. 25		212,366	225,221	6	110,117	45.7	29.4	6.8	73.3	6.5	0.1	8.1	9.3
12		R, 26		D, 26		D, 24		212,366	225,221	6	110,117	45.7	29.4	6.8	73.3	6.5	0.1	8.1	9.3
13		R, 29		R, 24		R. 26		218,182	224,178	3	95,337	39.7	22.6	8.0	76.0	4.3	0.1	9.2	7.8
13		R, 28		R, 24		R, 26		218,182	224,178	3	95,337	39.7	22.6	8.0	76.0	4.3	0.1	9.2	7.8
14		D, 27		R, 25		R, 28		207,681	225,974	9	95,274	45.0	29.7	6.4	68.3	7.5	0.1	14.0	6.9
14		D, 26		D, 25		D, 27		207,681	225,974	9	95,274	45.0	29.7	6.4	68.3	7.5	0.1	14.0	6.9
15		D, 34		D, 28		D, 35		199,590	207,080	4	82,930	37.9	25.0	14.8	49.0	27.3	0.4	5.2	15.1
15		D, 34		D, 31		D, 33		199,590	207,080	4	82,930	37.9	25.0	14.8	49.0	27.3	0.4	5.2	15.1
16		R, 34		R, 38		R, 32		200,664	216,216	8	125,873	48.0	36.1	5.2	71.6	3.2	0.3	10.2	9.5
16		R, 33		R, 39		D, 32		200,664	216,216	8	125,873	48.0	36.1	5.2	71.6	3.2	0.3	10.2	9.5
17		D, 34		D, 38		D, 34		210,826	221,172	5	80,956	39.9	27.1	9.1	43.5	16.7	0.1	18.3	19.3
17		D, 32		D, 28		D, 32		210,826	221,172	5	80,956	39.9	27.1	9.1	43.5	16.7	0.1	18.3	19.3
18		D, 33		D, 29		D, 30		204,215	213,424	5	94,318	43.5	29.2	7.2	57.9	6.3	0.1	24.1	9.0
18		D, 31		D, 30		D, 32		204,215	213,424	5	94,318	43.5	29.2	7.2	57.9	6.3	0.1	24.1	9.0
19		D, 37		D, 30		D, 35		211,001	221,048	5	71,228	31.9	17.7	11.2	44.9	8.1	0.1	14.1	28.3
19		D, 36		D, 27		D, 32		211,001	221,048	5	71,228	31.9	17.7	11.2	44.9	8.1	0.1	14.1	28.3
20		D, 41		D, 31		D, 50		202,444	206,370	2	60,545	31.9	18.1	16.7	31.4	21.4	0.8	5.2	41.7
20		D, 41		D, 31		D, 50		202,444	206,370	2	60,545	31.9	18.1	16.7	31.4	21.4	0.8	5.2	41.7
21		R, 32		D, 29		R, 30		225,784	229,642	2	150,589	52.5	40.6	5.3	77.0	4.1	0.2	7.5	7.4
21		R, 28		R, 30		R, 30		225,784	229,642	2	150,589	52.5	40.6	5.3	77.0	4.1	0.2	7.5	7.4
22		D, 31		R, 27		D, 32		204,136	208,092	2	79,055	38.0	22.6	10.1	45.0	23.4	0.5	5.6	20.7
22		D, 30		D, 29		D, 30		204,136	208,092	2	79,055	38.0	22.6	10.1	45.0	23.4	0.5	5.6	20.7
23		R, 32		R, 30		R, 32		220,560	239,719	9	94,233	39.5	22.8	7.5	87.7	2.6	0.1	2.5	4.8
23		R, 29		R, 31		R, 30		220,560	239,719	9	94,233	39.5	22.8	7.5	87.7	2.6	0.1	2.5	4.8
24		R, 36		R, 39		R, 34		205,648	218,753	6	97,457	40.8	22.6	6.6	87.6	1.7	0.1	2.9	5.5
24		R, 34		R, 41		R, 33		205,648	218,753	6	97,457	40.8	22.6	6.6	87.6	1.7	0.1	2.9	5.5
25		R, 30		R, 37		R, 28		212,162	222,404	5	111,115	47.4	32.0	6.0	70.7	4.1	0.1	6.5	15.0
25		R, 30		R, 38		R, 27		212,162	222,404	5	111,115	47.4	32.0	6.0	70.7	4.1	0.1	6.5	15.0

(continued)

Note: D=Democrat, R=Republican, R/D=Republican/Democrat (cross-filed), D/R=Democrat/Republican (cross-filed), I=Independent, C=Constitution, O=Other, GI=Green Independent, P=Progressive, P/D=Progressive/Democrat, P/D/R=Progressive/Democrat/Republican, HH=Households

New Jersey Legislative Districts—Election and Demographic Data (cont.)

House Districts	General Election Results Party, Percent of Vote							Population			Avg. HH Income	Pop 25+ Some College +	Pop 25+ 4-Yr Degree +	Below Poverty Line	White (Non-Hisp)	African American	American Indians, Alaska Natives	Asians, Hawaiians, Pacific Islanders	Hispanic Origin
New Jersey	2000	2001	2002	2003	2004	2005	2006	2000	2006	% Change	($)	(%)	(%)	(%)	(%)	(%)	(%)	(%)	(%)
26		R, 34		R, 32		R, 30		197,200	204,549	4	102,742	46.5	31.1	5.4	76.7	2.0	0.1	11.2	7.3
26		R, 32		R, 33		R, 29		197,200	204,549	4	102,742	46.5	31.1	5.4	76.7	2.0	0.1	11.2	7.3
27		D, 31		D, 31		D, 35		212,818	212,092	0	106,889	43.0	30.5	10.8	49.6	31.4	0.1	7.5	8.2
27		D, 29		D, 33		D, 32		212,818	212,092	0	106,889	43.0	30.5	10.8	49.6	31.4	0.1	7.5	8.2
28		D, 37		D, 36		D. 40		212,400	208,715	-2	55,631	28.3	15.3	18.8	26.6	49.3	0.1	5.6	17.7
28		D, 37		D, 37		D, 40		212,400	208,715	-2	55,631	28.3	15.3	18.8	26.6	49.3	0.1	5.6	17.7
29		D, 45		D, 41		D, 45		202,696	206,066	2	43,857	22.3	11.2	31.2	20.6	39.5	0.2	2.2	40.1
29		D, 43		D, 43		D, 44		202,696	206,066	2	43,857	22.3	11.2	31.2	20.6	39.5	0.2	2.2	40.1
30		R, 31		D, 32		R, 33		216,158	237,735	10	74,335	34.9	19.2	11.1	73.5	8.5	0.1	3.2	11.0
30		R, 30		D, 33		R, 32		216,158	237,735	10	74,335	34.9	19.2	11.1	73.5	8.5	0.1	3.2	11.0
31		D, 38		D, 39		D, 41		202,386	197,724	-2	57,410	33.1	21.2	21.0	30.7	23.9	0.2	14.4	24.6
31		D, 36		D, 40		D, 39		202,386	197,724	-2	57,410	33.1	21.2	21.0	30.7	23.9	0.2	14.4	24.6
32		D, 37		D, 39		D, 39		220,551	212,178	-4	59,375	31.1	19.3	16.6	30.4	6.9	0.2	12.7	44.5
32		D, 36		D, 48		D, 38		220,551	212,178	-4	59,375	31.1	19.3	16.6	30.4	6.9	0.2	12.7	44.5
33		D, 38		D, 40		D, 41		199,576	201,568	1	66,790	37.2	27.2	17.7	22.5	6.3	0.3	9.9	58.6
33		D, 38		D, 42		D, 40		199,576	201,568	1	66,790	37.2	27.2	17.7	22.5	6.3	0.3	9.9	58.6
34		D, 34		D, 31		D, 51		209,107	209,506	0	79,099	34.9	21.1	14.5	40.4	34.5	0.1	4.9	15.4
34		D, 32		D, 33		D, 50		209,107	209,506	0	79,099	34.9	21.1	14.5	40.4	34.5	0.1	4.9	15.4
35		D, 51		D, 39		D, 35		211,667	215,403	2	64,580	22.0	10.4	19.1	26.0	21.3	0.2	3.4	42.8
35		D, 49		D, 40		D, 28		211,667	215,403	2	64,580	22.0	10.4	19.1	26.0	21.3	0.2	3.4	42.8
36		R, 27		D, 26		D, 32		211,319	212,145	0	64,603	30.4	18.4	13.3	45.5	6.0	0.2	8.7	30.3
36		D, 25		D, 25		D, 30		211,319	212,145	0	64,603	30.4	18.4	13.3	45.5	6.0	0.2	8.7	30.3
37		D, 34		D, 33		D, 36		215,644	219,699	2	91,911	43.7	30.3	9.6	45.8	13.2	0.1	17.6	22.1
37		D, 33		D, 31		D, 35		215,644	219,699	2	91,911	43.7	30.3	9.6	45.8	13.2	0.1	17.6	22.1
38		R, 25		R, 27		D, 30		214,204	221,304	3	84,173	43.7	29.9	9.8	62.5	2.5	0.1	17.7	14.7
38		D, 25		R, 25		D, 30		214,204	221,304	3	84,173	43.7	29.9	9.8	62.5	2.5	0.1	17.7	14.7
39		R, 31		R, 33		R, 28		214,258	216,630	1	125,556	48.9	35.7	5.2	75.8	2.0	0.0	13.6	6.4
39		R, 30		R, 33		R, 26		214,258	216,630	1	125,556	48.9	35.7	5.2	75.8	2.0	0.0	13.6	6.4
40		R, 31		R, 32		R, 31		208,762	211,653	1	130,041	46.9	33.5	5.5	77.7	3.2	0.1	7.5	8.0
40		R, 30		R, 32		R, 31		208,762	211,653	1	130,041	46.9	33.5	5.5	77.7	3.2	0.1	7.5	8.0

Note: D=Democrat, R=Republican, R/D=Republican/Democrat (cross-filed), D/R=Democrat/Republican (cross-filed), I=Independent, C=Constitution, O=Other, GI=Green Independent, P=Progressive, P/D=Progressive/Democrat, P/D/R=Progressive/Democrat/Republican, HH=Households

NEW MEXICO

The United States took the territory that is now New Mexico as one of the spoils of the Mexican War, although New Mexico was never considered as attractive as the real prizes, Texas and California. Its southern quarter (as well as the southern quarter of Arizona) was not annexed until 1853, as part of the Gadsden Purchase, and New Mexico itself was the next to last of the lower forty-eight states to be admitted to the Union. In some respects, it has also been the last part of the contiguous United States to join the American commonwealth.

Settlement in much of the West is measured in decades, but Santa Fe was founded in 1610, three years after Jamestown on the other side of the continent, and the Spanish had been there for seventy years before that. "For almost three centuries preceding the American occupation," writes the author of the *WPA Guide to New Mexico,* "the trend of settlement here was all from the south. Contact with the outside world was not from the east or from the Atlantic seaboard, but from Mexico City, and through Mexico from Spain." Thus, the nation to the south is still referred to locally, as it is throughout the region, as "Old Mexico."

During the past two decades, New Mexico has shared in the Mountain Time Zone but not nearly to the same extent as Colorado, Arizona, Nevada, Texas, or even Utah, the states that border it. Its rate of growth has only been a shade above the national average since 2000, though it grew rapidly during the 1980s and 1990s, filling with people attracted to a cleaner, quieter way of life and year-round sunshine. Think how much greater that growth could have been had Harvard dropout Bill Gates and Washington State dropout Paul Allen not decided to move the computer company they then called "Micro-soft" from Albuquerque to Bellevue in 1979.

Albuquerque is New Mexico's largest city, but by national standards it is not all that big; its metropolitan area contains three-quarters of a million people—about as many as Omaha or the Allentown-Bethlehem region in Pennsylvania. Still, as Michael Barone has observed, that is more than the population of the entire state of New Mexico seventy years ago. Recent growth has been primarily in Albuquerque suburbs, especially the area of Rio Rancho in San-doval County, which has grown by 36 percent, and parts of Bernalillo County southeast of the city. The 28th house district, also located in Bernalillo County but closer in, has lost population to some of the outer suburbs.

New Mexico is a poor state, particularly in rural areas. Average household income on the Navajo and Zuni Indian reservations is less than $34,000 a year, and the unemployment rate is as high as 60 percent. Income levels are also depressed in the eastern grazing lands as well as near the border in Las Cruces. There are, however, pockets of considerable wealth, almost all in the residential neighborhoods and older suburbs of Albuquerque.

Although a minority, whites predominate in those wealthier parts of Albuquerque as well as in the rural east (spiritually more a part of the Texas panhandle, which it borders). Five New Mexico house districts are more than 75 percent Hispanic, including districts in central Albuquerque (85 percent), along the Mexican border (85 percent), rural Mora County (78 percent), and Las Vegas (75 percent). Not surprisingly, Native Americans make up more than 70 percent of the population in the three districts where the biggest reservations are located. The 63rd house district, which includes Guadalupe County stretching from Santa Rosa to Portales, is 9 percent black, the only sizable concentration of African Americans in the state.

Its high Hispanic and Native American populations make New Mexico one of the most Democratic states in a heavily Republican region. Al Gore won it in 2000 by 365 votes but John Kerry lost it by 6,000 in 2004. The incumbent Democratic governor, Bill Richardson, is the first New Mexican to make a legitimate run for the presidency. His party holds both chambers of the legislature and the margins have barely changed in this decade.

Finally, New Mexico has one of the strongest Green Parties in the nation (this was Ralph Nader's third-best state in 2000). If the Greens do not hold any seats in the legislature, they do sometimes make a difference in close races. There have been reports of appeals by both of the major parties for the Greens to enter or stay out of particular races here in order to hurt the opposition.

NEW MEXICO
State Senate Districts

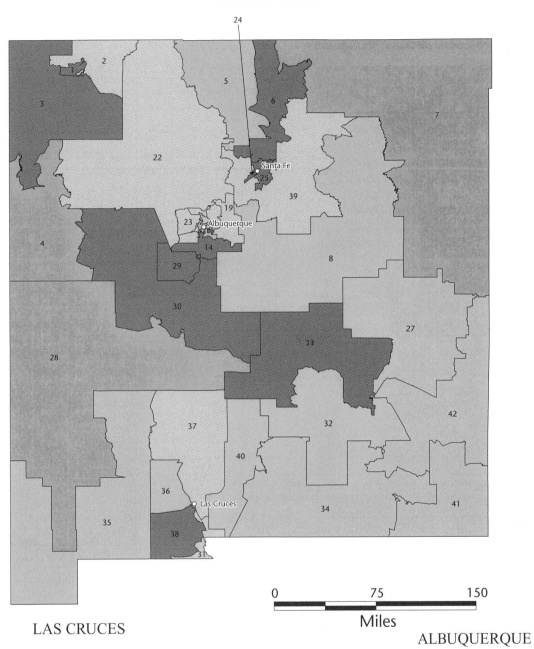

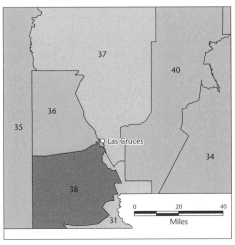

LAS CRUCES

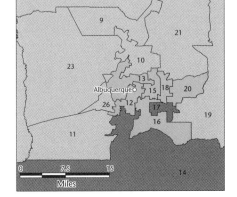

ALBUQUERQUE

Population Growth   ▨ -6% to -1%   ▨ -1% to 4%   ▨ 4% to 13%   ▨ 13% to 37%

New Mexico State Senate Districts—Election and Demographic Data

Senate Districts	General Election Results Party, Percent of Vote							Population			Avg. HH Income ($)	Pop 25+ Some College + (%)	Pop 25+ 4-Yr Degree + (%)	Below Poverty Line (%)	2006 White (Non-Hisp) (%)	African American (%)	American Indians, Alaska Natives (%)	Asians, Hawaiians, Pacific Islanders (%)	Hispanic Origin (%)
New Mexico	2000	2001	2002	2003	2004	2005	2006	2000	2006	% Change	($)	(%)	(%)	(%)	(%)	(%)	(%)	(%)	(%)
1	R, 82				R, 64			43,920	47,656	9	50,324	31.2	10.7	19.0	53.8	1.1	23.9	0.6	19.5
2	R, 65				R, 100			45,137	53,560	19	52,240	29.4	8.4	16.7	57.6	0.4	16.4	0.3	22.1
3	D, 78				D, 100			43,094	45,834	6	32,694	18.6	4.2	39.3	12.2	0.4	81.4	0.3	8.7
4	D, 100				D, 100			44,373	43,103	-3	39,604	22.9	8.0	32.9	22.1	0.7	67.5	0.8	11.4
5	D, 100				D, 100			45,362	45,275	0	54,734	33.0	16.1	19.6	24.8	0.6	7.5	1.1	65.8
6	D, 100				D, 100			44,353	47,470	7	49,295	38.6	19.6	22.1	32.6	0.6	8.2	0.9	54.3
7	R, 69				R, 50			40,771	39,362	-3	45,315	32.5	13.1	19.6	54.7	1.7	1.1	1.4	36.4
8	D, 100				D, 63			41,393	41,772	1	40,977	31.1	12.4	24.8	30.0	1.8	2.4	0.6	58.9
9	R, 55				R, 100			41,930	49,041	17	62,220	38.6	16.4	9.2	52.0	3.2	2.9	1.4	36.1
10	R, 54				R, 54			43,009	52,053	21	67,217	44.7	21.6	12.0	52.3	2.3	2.7	2.5	36.5
11	D, 68				D, 64			41,062	49,392	20	46,855	23.2	6.9	17.0	13.1	3.5	3.7	0.8	79.7
12	D, 74				D, 74			43,551	44,435	2	38,582	34.2	15.9	27.3	27.2	4.4	4.9	2.1	60.5
13	D, 100				D, 100			44,345	45,641	3	54,946	38.9	18.9	17.9	32.3	2.4	4.9	1.3	56.6
14	D, 55				D, 54			40,514	43,180	7	43,534	26.3	10.1	23.7	24.0	3.4	8.8	1.6	62.5
15	R, 53				R, 53			45,016	45,855	2	51,204	47.2	22.2	12.6	53.2	3.4	3.7	2.9	33.6
16	D, 100				D, 100			42,155	42,612	1	49,908	48.6	26.7	19.4	56.9	4.9	4.2	3.5	27.7
17	D, 59				D, 56			41,418	43,975	6	36,934	32.0	11.0	24.3	34.4	5.8	6.3	4.4	50.2
18	R, 100				R, 100			43,102	44,721	4	55,857	50.4	24.1	10.9	62.7	3.0	2.3	3.1	26.0
19	R, 100				R, 100			40,912	47,273	16	72,336	48.6	23.8	9.8	63.5	2.2	2.6	2.2	25.2
20	R, 100				R, 100			42,542	43,745	3	63,410	49.7	23.7	10.7	61.2	3.4	2.5	3.5	26.4
21	R, 100				R, 100			41,169	47,794	16	96,093	56.2	35.5	5.9	66.1	1.5	2.4	3.2	22.9
22	D, 100				D, 66			43,890	49,744	13	41,034	23.2	8.6	30.8	25.8	0.8	60.4	0.7	16.6
23	R, 83				R, 100			44,491	60,508	36	67,103	45.7	20.3	6.0	47.4	3.7	3.1	2.2	39.6
24	D, 100				D, 100			43,248	47,178	9	48,724	35.4	17.2	16.5	25.7	1.0	2.8	1.4	66.1
25	D, 62				D, 79			44,752	47,961	7	81,449	59.9	40.9	11.2	59.0	0.7	1.7	1.6	32.0
26	D, 64				D, 100			42,937	49,198	15	48,826	32.6	11.3	15.0	20.4	4.7	4.1	1.5	69.4
27	R, 100				D, 100			43,363	44,053	2	38,122	29.2	9.5	26.4	47.9	7.4	1.1	1.8	36.8
28	D, 61				D, 100			44,605	42,043	-6	38,737	33.4	14.2	25.3	41.9	0.8	2.1	0.8	48.1
29	D, 51				D, 63			42,928	44,917	5	45,884	28.7	10.1	18.5	31.1	1.7	2.8	0.6	58.2
30	D, 100				D, 62			44,054	48,428	10	40,826	24.7	8.2	24.5	33.4	1.6	22.4	0.7	43.6
31	D, 59				D, 100			42,573	48,116	13	41,871	19.4	8.0	31.1	12.2	1.0	1.2	0.4	84.1
32	D, 59				D, 100			42,040	42,292	1	39,198	21.4	6.4	29.9	29.4	2.7	7.9	0.5	56.9
33	R, 100				R, 100			43,254	45,579	5	49,682	37.3	14.8	18.1	58.2	1.5	1.5	0.7	31.9
34	R, 100				R, 59			47,877	49,606	4	47,844	33.4	11.8	18.1	57.9	3.0	1.2	1.2	31.4
35	D, 100				D, 100			40,072	40,418	1	32,815	21.5	7.2	32.0	38.4	1.1	1.2	0.4	54.1
36	D, 59				D, 59			43,765	45,086	3	45,205	29.1	12.7	24.3	25.3	2.3	2.1	0.7	65.0
37	R, 71				R, 100			46,281	53,421	15	49,893	38.2	19.7	18.1	39.8	2.3	1.7	1.5	49.2
38	D, 59				D, 68			44,314	46,985	6	40,840	29.6	14.7	28.1	25.7	2.5	2.4	1.5	65.2
39	D, 56				D, 72			43,741	49,447	13	57,583	38.4	21.5	18.4	31.8	1.0	2.4	1.4	57.7
40	R, 69				R, 100			44,340	44,987	1	40,212	32.0	9.2	20.6	51.4	5.8	1.5	1.7	35.4
41	R, 100				R, 100			44,822	45,105	1	41,072	19.6	5.8	27.2	31.5	5.8	1.4	0.5	55.3
42	R, 93				R, 100			43,554	44,871	3	44,937	27.6	8.5	22.4	48.7	4.1	1.2	0.6	38.7

Note: D=Democrat, R=Republican, R/D=Republican/Democrat (cross-filed), D/R=Democrat/Republican (cross-filed), I=Independent, C=Constitution, O=Other, GI=Green Independent, P=Progressive, P/D=Progressive/Democrat, P/D/R=Progressive/Democrat/Republican, HH=Households

NEW MEXICO
State House Districts

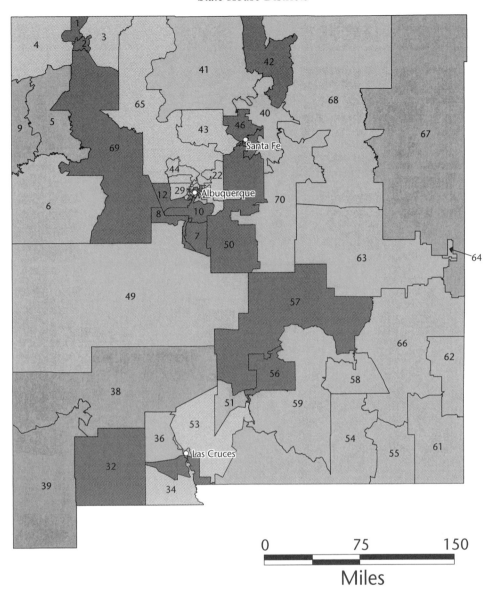

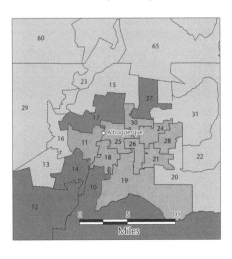

LAS CRUCES

ALBUQUERQUE

Population Growth ▣ -10% to -2%   ▢ -2% to 4%   ▣ 4% to 13%   ▢ 13% to 41%

New Mexico State House Districts—Election and Demographic Data

House Districts	General Election Results Party, Percent of Vote							Population			Avg. HH Income	2006 Pop 25+ Some College +	Pop 25+ 4-Yr Degree +	Below Poverty Line	White (Non-Hisp)	African American	American Indians, Alaska Natives	Asians, Hawaiians, Pacific Islanders	Hispanic Origin
New Mexico	2000	2001	2002	2003	2004	2005	2006	2000	2006	% Change	($)	(%)	(%)	(%)	(%)	(%)	(%)	(%)	(%)
1	R, 57		R, 100		R, 100		R, 69	25,138	27,539	10	60,603	36.5	13.4	14.4	66.0	0.8	25.1	0.6	14.3
2	R, 98		R, 100		R, 100		R, 63	26,490	29,776	12	45,513	27.5	8.0	19.9	63.5	1.1	22.6	0.5	25.4
3	R, 76		R, 100		R, 100		R, 100	26,484	31,164	18	51,625	29.1	8.7	17.2	72.6	0.4	13.9	0.3	25.3
4	D, 69		D, 100		D, 62		D, 100	26,983	31,143	15	35,360	21.5	4.6	31.6	16.4	0.4	79.8	0.3	5.8
5	D, 67		D, 100		D, 100		D, 100	24,817	24,191	-3	36,823	22.5	8.2	35.4	19.5	0.6	75.0	0.9	10.9
6	D, 100		D, 100		D, 100		D, 72	29,089	29,615	2	36,219	21.6	6.5	32.8	28.1	0.6	61.5	0.4	17.2
7	D, 50		D, 100		D, 55		D, 54	26,841	28,107	5	45,974	28.4	10.1	17.9	33.7	1.7	2.1	0.6	55.3
8	D, 49		D, 51		D, 52		D, 53	25,711	27,499	7	44,720	27.3	9.2	19.7	30.5	1.9	3.0	0.4	59.4
9	D, 100		D, 100		D, 79		D, 100	26,596	25,396	-5	40,322	20.7	6.2	34.1	20.6	0.9	71.7	0.7	16.9
10	D, 72		D, 100		D, 100		D, 100	25,622	27,529	7	41,365	24.0	8.4	23.8	23.6	4.5	12.4	0.8	60.9
11	D, 79		D, 79		D, 100		D, 100	26,404	27,212	3	44,199	34.3	16.8	26.1	24.3	3.0	4.7	1.0	66.4
12	D, 67		D, 100		D, 100		D, 100	25,235	27,588	9	43,114	22.8	6.8	22.0	16.4	2.5	8.8	0.8	73.9
13	D, 68		D, 100		D, 68		D, 100	27,514	35,629	29	45,602	23.2	6.3	17.1	12.3	5.3	4.9	1.1	79.6
14	D, 78		D, 76		D, 73		D, 77	26,526	27,893	5	42,328	24.1	8.5	25.6	9.5	2.2	2.7	0.9	85.1
15	R, 51		R, 51		R, 53		R, 54	26,969	31,722	18	67,606	42.1	19.1	13.3	46.1	2.0	4.6	2.5	41.9
16	D, 100		D, 100		D, 60		D, 69	26,028	30,448	17	53,711	38.0	14.8	10.6	25.4	4.6	3.6	1.5	64.2
17	D, 69		D, 100		D, 100		D, 100	25,127	27,081	8	53,542	38.5	18.1	17.3	32.2	2.3	3.5	1.2	57.6
18	D, 100		D, 100		D, 100		D, 83	24,783	24,986	1	44,550	45.8	27.6	26.8	51.1	4.0	4.1	5.5	32.1
19	D, 100		D, 71		D, 100		D, 76	27,504	28,057	2	43,043	43.9	20.2	21.3	49.5	6.7	5.6	3.4	33.3
20	R, 100		R, 66		R, 100		R, 100	27,361	31,303	14	67,726	49.6	25.0	10.1	59.1	3.4	2.9	4.6	26.6
21	D, 54		D, 60		D, 100		D, 100	26,282	27,079	3	41,414	35.5	11.6	20.1	41.6	6.1	5.1	3.7	42.2
22	R, 100		R, 65		R, 100		R, 58	27,041	32,929	22	83,381	52.6	28.6	6.5	70.5	0.8	1.4	0.9	21.6
23	R, 100		R, 56		R, 53		R, 53	27,451	33,467	22	77,046	49.0	26.1	6.5	53.2	2.9	2.5	2.1	35.4
24	R, 100		R, 59		R, 100		R, 55	27,775	27,681	0	52,334	48.4	21.3	11.1	61.8	3.1	2.2	3.7	26.5
25	D, 69		D, 100		D, 100		D, 100	26,376	26,317	0	48,557	44.1	21.0	14.9	45.9	3.5	4.8	2.7	40.4
26	D, 52		D, 100		D, 61		D, 100	23,926	24,055	1	35,869	32.2	12.4	26.1	32.6	5.1	6.3	3.5	53.6
27	R, 100		R, 66		R, 100		R, 100	26,403	28,000	6	86,301	57.1	34.8	6.3	69.7	1.9	1.4	4.9	19.5
28	R, 59		R, 62		R, 100		R, 56	26,898	27,077	1	61,593	48.8	22.4	10.6	60.9	3.3	2.4	2.9	27.3
29	R, 60		R, 60		R, 55		R, 53	26,390	37,166	41	65,663	45.7	19.8	6.1	46.7	4.2	3.4	2.2	39.7
30	R, 54		R, 64		R, 100		R, 56	27,029	27,360	1	51,542	49.0	23.3	12.5	56.7	3.6	4.0	2.8	29.6
31	R, 100		R, 63		R, 57		R, 59	25,865	30,406	18	88,426	59.5	35.6	6.7	73.3	2.2	1.4	3.0	17.6
32	D, 59		D, 100		D, 54		D, 62	25,057	26,792	7	32,031	18.8	6.8	33.3	31.6	1.3	1.3	0.5	60.8
33	D, 69		D, 100		D, 60		D, 100	24,854	26,420	6	45,023	35.3	18.3	24.1	30.3	2.3	2.4	1.6	60.5
34	D, 100		D, 64		D, 100		D, 100	27,564	32,424	18	45,327	20.8	9.0	29.8	12.1	0.9	1.2	0.3	84.6
35	D, 65		D, 62		D, 62		D, 67	24,512	25,451	4	35,629	28.3	11.6	31.3	27.0	4.3	2.9	1.7	60.8
36	D, 50		D, 51		D, 52		D, 56	24,543	24,817	1	48,631	28.9	13.3	23.8	26.0	1.6	1.8	0.5	64.7
37	R, 66		R, 59		R, 51		D, 52	24,765	27,989	13	50,724	40.2	21.4	16.2	41.1	2.3	1.5	1.6	48.4
38	R, 100		R, 52		R, 100		D, 100	23,966	22,660	-5	38,856	35.9	13.3	23.5	62.1	0.6	1.2	0.3	30.4
39	D, 66		D, 100		D, 100		D, 100	25,496	23,154	-9	37,847	28.4	10.8	25.6	34.5	0.7	1.6	0.4	57.4
40	D, 100		D, 100		D, 100		D, 100	25,435	25,483	0	42,123	28.7	11.1	24.0	14.8	0.7	7.5	0.4	77.9
41	D, 66		D, 100		D, 100		D, 100	25,081	25,143	0	42,639	27.9	11.5	24.6	18.7	0.6	8.7	0.3	73.0
42	D, 100		D, 56		D, 100		D, 100	24,737	26,911	9	42,712	37.3	18.9	25.4	34.9	0.6	7.2	0.6	52.3
43	R, 84		R, 100		R, 100		R, 100	27,215	31,000	14	79,965	48.2	31.8	8.5	55.0	0.5	1.6	3.3	33.4
44	R, 56		R, 64		R, 100		R, 59	26,779	32,724	22	64,798	43.9	19.4	7.9	58.6	3.3	2.6	2.0	29.3
45	D, 100		D, 100		D, 100		D, 100	24,046	26,501	10	48,467	33.8	15.7	15.3	23.9	1.1	2.7	1.6	68.4
46	D, 63		D, 100		D, 100		D, 100	27,157	29,582	9	67,232	45.3	25.8	16.2	33.4	0.7	7.1	0.8	54.8
47	D, 71		D, 68		D, 76		D, 100	26,438	28,610	8	91,496	62.2	43.0	8.1	65.4	0.6	1.4	1.4	26.3
48	D, 100		D, 67		D, 100		D, 100	25,685	27,000	5	53,693	46.5	27.8	17.0	38.7	0.9	2.7	1.7	51.5
49	R, 61		R, 66		R, 61		R, 100	26,820	26,932	0	40,080	29.7	12.7	28.3	39.7	1.1	8.0	1.3	45.9
50	D, 60		D, 100		D, 100		D, 100	26,946	29,983	11	51,655	35.2	15.7	18.6	45.5	1.3	2.3	0.6	43.4

(continued)

Note: D=Democrat, R=Republican, R/D=Republican/Democrat (cross-filed), D/R=Democrat/Republican (cross-filed), I=Independent, C=Constitution, O=Other, GI=Green Independent, P=Progressive, P/D=Progressive/Democrat, P/D/R=Progressive/Democrat/Republican, HH=Households

New Mexico State House Districts—Election and Demographic Data (cont.)

House Districts	General Election Results Party, Percent of Vote							Population			Avg. HH Income ($)	Pop 25+ Some College + (%)	Pop 25+ 4-Yr Degree + (%)	Below Poverty Line (%)	White (Non-Hisp) (%)	African American (%)	American Indians, Alaska Natives (%)	Asians, Hawaiians, Pacific Islanders (%)	Hispanic Origin (%)
New Mexico	2000	2001	2002	2003	2004	2005	2006	2000	2006	% Change									
51	R, 55		R, 60		R, 67		R, 100	23,925	24,446	2	38,233	29.8	7.7	22.3	51.5	7.7	1.2	2.1	33.6
52	D, 50		D, 62		D, 63		D, 100	27,311	29,843	9	46,092	26.6	13.8	25.5	20.2	1.3	1.5	1.1	73.2
53	R, 98		R, 61		R, 58		D, 52	28,568	32,581	14	42,589	27.8	11.2	21.9	30.2	3.0	1.6	1.1	59.2
54	D, 100		D, 100		D, 100		R, 55	25,704	25,791	0	39,389	19.7	5.8	26.7	34.1	2.9	1.6	0.4	56.1
55	D, 59		D, 100		D, 100		D, 100	25,701	25,634	0	50,242	29.6	11.0	18.9	53.8	1.5	1.2	0.9	36.5
56	R, 71		R, 86		R, 88		R, 65	26,092	27,391	5	49,363	37.8	12.9	16.6	57.8	3.4	11.5	1.2	23.9
57	R, 100		R, 67		R, 68		R, 74	22,660	24,035	6	49,853	40.3	15.9	15.6	64.5	0.7	1.6	0.7	27.3
58	D, 50		D, 52		R, 55		R, 54	25,209	25,150	0	37,386	19.4	5.0	30.2	24.5	3.1	1.6	0.5	65.2
59	R, 70		R, 100		R, 100		R, 59	24,780	25,275	2	48,110	33.9	12.7	21.9	50.6	2.5	1.4	0.7	38.5
60	R, 57		D, 50		D, 52		D, 57	27,317	32,063	17	54,338	37.6	13.6	8.7	54.3	3.3	2.8	1.8	33.0
61	D, 65		D, 58		D, 100		R, 51	24,686	25,190	2	39,065	18.1	5.1	29.6	28.4	7.6	1.4	0.5	57.2
62	R, 66		R, 100		R, 100		R, 100	26,173	26,894	3	48,634	30.7	10.0	18.7	54.2	4.4	1.2	0.7	32.9
63	D, 54		D, 89		D, 57		D, 100	28,155	28,450	1	33,935	23.1	6.0	29.9	35.4	9.0	1.3	1.7	49.7
64	R, 100		R, 100		R, 100		R, 100	23,950	24,064	0	50,616	36.4	12.5	17.7	58.8	7.0	0.8	2.6	27.2
65	D, 77		D, 100		D, 100		D, 100	26,806	32,176	20	45,671	20.9	7.6	30.0	23.7	0.6	55.6	0.5	28.5
66	R, 100		R, 100		R, 100		R, 100	27,002	27,552	2	40,863	29.4	11.4	24.3	51.6	2.2	1.3	0.8	36.7
67	R, 65		R, 100		R, 100		R, 100	24,302	23,070	-5	40,956	27.0	10.2	25.2	54.8	1.3	1.1	0.7	35.6
68	D, 58		D, 100		D, 62			24,978	24,577	-2	40,399	31.3	12.9	22.7	32.1	0.5	1.7	0.6	58.9
69	D, 100		D, 100		D, 100		D, 100	27,285	29,886	10	34,488	20.4	6.3	33.1	23.8	1.1	65.1	0.5	19.2
70	D, 100		D, 100		D, 100		D, 100	25,296	24,982	-1	38,019	30.7	13.0	28.0	16.6	2.2	2.7	0.7	75.0

Note: D=Democrat, R=Republican, R/D=Republican/Democrat (cross-filed), D/R=Democrat/Republican (cross-filed), I=Independent, C=Constitution, O=Other, GI=Green Independent, P=Progressive, P/D=Progressive/Democrat, P/D/R=Progressive/Democrat/Republican, HH=Households

NEW YORK

New York City's history is inseparable from its geography. Manhattan, of course, is an island, and a narrow one at that. With little room to grow to the south or west before the bridges and tunnels were built, the city built vertically, stacking office workers in skyscrapers and erecting apartments instead of row houses. Given an opportunity to do so, the city also expanded outward. The population of Brooklyn increased 40 percent in the decade after the Brooklyn Bridge was opened in 1883. Automobiles made it possible for Queens to grow by 177 percent between 1920 and 1940. More recently, with the opening of the Verrazano Narrows Bridge in 1964, Staten Island's population grew by one-third.

The city also spilled beyond its borders. Commuting out across Long Island and up the Hudson on freeways built by Parks Commissioner Robert Moses, New York began to sprawl. Canarsie gave way to Levittown, which gave way to West Babylon, just as Mount Vernon gave way to White Plains. Brooklyn and the Bronx are less crowded today than they were in the 1920s, while Manhattan has fewer people than it did in 1900. Queens, on the other hand, has three times as many people as it did eighty years ago.

Outward expansion of the city continues but for the first time in decades, there are signs of a slight reversal. The 97th assembly district, in Orange County near the Delaware River, is the fastest-growing part of the state (and growth continues beyond it, in Pennsylvania). But the second-fastest growing district is the 64th, which covers the Financial District and most of the Lower East Side of Manhattan, while the third fastest is the 50th, which runs along the East River in Brooklyn both above and below the Williamsburg Bridge.

Some of the increase in population may be due to the young traders and lawyers who have moved into lofts and co-ops, but this is mainly the product of immigration. New York is still the second most-popular destination for new arrivals to this country and it is filling up with Chinese, Dominicans, Russians, and thousands of others, just as the same areas once did with Irish, Eastern Europeans, Italians, and Russian Jews. The 64th district, which includes Chinatown, is half Asian and 17 percent Hispanic (its representative in Albany is the Jewish speaker of the assembly). Brooklyn now is home to great numbers of Pakistanis and Haitians. According to Census Bureau data, whites are pouring out of New York but immigrants are pouring in at a rate that has not been seen in nearly a century.

The part of New York that is losing population fastest is Buffalo and neighboring Niagara County, which raises some uncomfortable questions. Cities develop because they serve a need. Upstate, for example, Utica thrived in the early nineteenth century because it was located at a convenient pass through the Mohawk Valley. Buffalo became one of the biggest American cities because its port provided the perfect reloading point between the Erie Canal (later the railroads) and the Great Lakes. That location soon made it a natural place for steel and flour mills. But those reasons for Buffalo's existence no longer exist, and so the city's decline seems irreversible no matter what steps government takes to stop it.

So notwithstanding pockets of growth and Manhattan's continuing importance as a financial and cultural center, New York State as a whole has continued to decline and this will have important political implications. The country's most populous state until 1970, when California overtook it, New York has now fallen behind Texas and, according to the Census Bureau, its fall has not ended. Where New York had forty-five congressional seats during the 1940s, it now has twenty-nine, and it is expected to have only twenty-three by the year 2030, diminishing its political importance dramatically.

A shrinking state, perhaps, but still a wealthy one. Nevertheless, the juxtaposition of wealth and poverty in New York can be striking. Given that the people moving into the city seem increasingly to fall into two groups, well-educated professionals and new immigrants, this should not be surprising. Income, of course, is highest in the Upper East Side of Manhattan (the 73rd assembly district) and in the expensive older suburbs of White Plains and Oyster Bay, where the fruits of the stock market and law firm booms have been reaped. In the 73rd district, average income is almost $177,000 a year. This district is 75 percent white and 64 percent of its residents have a college degree. Less than two miles away, though, is the South Bronx, and the 84th assembly district, the state's poorest. Average income there is barely $30,000. It is 71 percent Hispanic, 27 percent African American, and only 11 percent have finished college.

Politically, Democrats control the state assembly and Republicans control the state senate, an arrangement that has lasted for four decades and which is perpetuated by careful gerrymandering. As Michael Barone wrote in the 1998 edition of *The Almanac of State Legislative Elections,* "Republicans make no serious effort to win the assembly and Democrats would not know what to do with the senate if it fell into their hands." According to the Brennan Center for Justice at New York University Law School, during the past decade as many New York state legislators have died in office as have been defeated for reelection. Since 2000 Democrats have widened their majority in the assembly, though, and cut the GOP majority in the senate to only four seats, so things could change no matter what the gerrymanderers intended.

NEW YORK
State Senate Districts

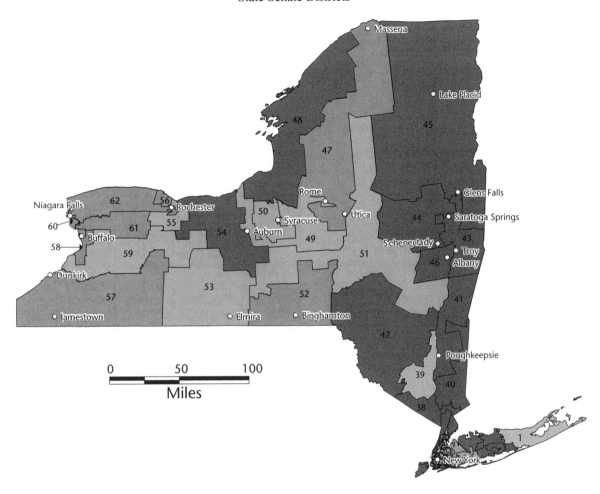

LONG ISLAND

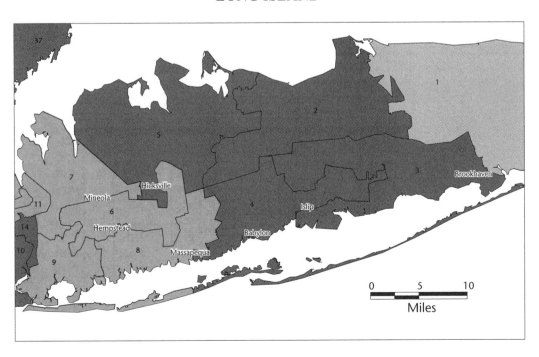

Population Growth ■ -4% to -1%　■ -1% to 1%　■ 1% to 7%　■ 7% to 10%

NEW YORK CITY

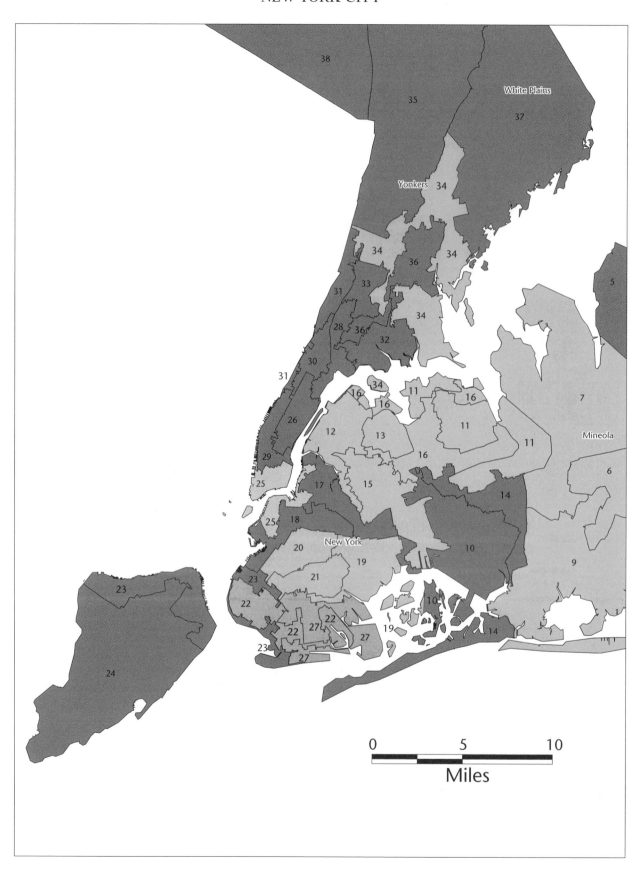

Population Growth   ▨ -4% to -1%   ▨ -1% to 1%   ▨ 1% to 7%   ▨ 7% to 10%

New York State Senate Districts—Election and Demographic Data

Senate Districts	General Election Results Party, Percent of Vote							Population			Avg. HH Income ($)	Pop 25+ Some College + (%)	Pop 25+ 4-Yr Degree + (%)	2006 Below Poverty Line (%)	2006 White (Non-Hisp) (%)	2006 African American (%)	2006 American Indians, Alaska Natives (%)	2006 Asians, Hawaiians, Pacific Islanders (%)	2006 Hispanic Origin (%)
New York	2000	2001	2002	2003	2004	2005	2006	2000	2006	% Change									
1	R, 50		R, 55		R, 50		R, 47	306,484	329,992	8	78,796	38.6	21.1	9.9	79.6	5.7	0.3	1.9	9.9
2	R, 44		R, 48		R, 44		R, 46	306,847	323,066	5	104,082	42.1	25.8	6.4	84.7	2.1	0.1	5.3	6.3
3	R, 43		R, 47		R, 42		D, 41	304,662	316,826	4	79,967	32.6	16.1	8.9	63.8	7.9	0.2	2.7	21.3
4	R, 43		R, 50		R, 42		R, 46	304,929	316,094	4	82,055	33.1	16.3	9.0	67.9	9.7	0.1	2.5	16.4
5	R, 42		R, 51		R, 44		R, 43	307,058	311,856	2	132,600	47.6	33.0	6.8	77.9	3.9	0.1	6.1	9.7
6	R, 40		R, 47		R, 43		R, 43	309,487	308,658	0	93,231	39.1	23.4	9.0	62.9	16.0	0.1	4.3	14.5
7	R, 42		R, 49		R, 45		R, 44	303,881	305,551	1	125,718	45.8	32.1	7.6	66.6	8.7	0.1	10.4	12.1
8	R, 44		R, 52		R, 48		R, 47	304,642	303,453	0	94,333	39.8	23.3	7.7	65.0	15.4	0.1	2.8	13.8
9	R, 48		R, 55		R, 53		R, 51	305,795	304,002	-1	99,457	44.9	29.2	9.0	74.1	6.9	0.1	4.7	11.3
10	D, 66		D, 59		D, 65		D, 67	314,233	322,318	3	61,600	32.1	18.1	16.9	20.6	47.6	0.4	12.8	16.1
11	R, 44		R, 44		R, 36		R, 41	324,184	323,459	0	75,825	40.7	27.5	11.5	42.9	8.5	0.2	30.0	15.8
12	R, 67		D, 49		D, 59		D, 66	320,114	319,309	0	51,946	34.3	22.5	20.4	32.3	7.7	0.3	22.0	35.5
13	D, 60		D, 50		D, 60		D, 66	319,415	319,073	0	52,730	29.5	17.7	20.4	15.6	11.8	0.4	24.9	58.2
14	D, 55		D, 58		D, 63		D, 67	318,008	324,994	2	62,212	34.1	19.9	18.3	23.3	47.6	0.3	11.4	16.8
15	R, 35		R, 44		R, 35		D, 42	310,575	312,588	1	61,047	30.2	17.6	16.4	42.2	6.1	0.3	16.5	28.4
16	D, 58		D, 49		D, 56		D, 65	324,080	323,777	0	62,616	43.1	30.4	15.8	39.0	6.3	0.1	37.7	16.8
17	D, 66		D, 51		D, 59		D, 62	322,543	340,184	5	39,398	23.4	12.6	34.8	15.9	28.0	0.5	6.3	54.0
18	D, 64		D, 61		D, 67		D, 64	310,294	322,908	4	50,595	31.9	19.7	29.2	19.7	54.9	0.4	4.8	24.2
19	D, 66		D, 60		D, 67		D, 66	299,373	300,592	0	43,193	26.6	13.5	31.4	17.2	65.5	0.2	4.1	15.0
20	D, 71		D, 56		D, 65		D, 59	322,544	325,053	1	51,628	32.1	19.2	24.4	22.7	55.6	0.3	6.8	15.4
21	D, 54		D, 52		D, 63		D, 63	302,647	303,246	0	50,752	30.1	16.3	24.8	26.2	54.9	0.2	7.1	10.1
22	D, 53		R, 44		R, 44		R, 43	304,254	297,779	-2	58,628	34.9	21.6	20.0	62.4	6.3	0.1	18.4	8.8
23	D, 49		D, 43		D, 50		D, 55	316,862	324,797	3	51,456	28.0	15.4	26.1	38.7	18.4	0.3	16.3	25.4
24	R, 41		R, 52		R, 48		R, 49	312,301	328,173	5	83,617	32.9	17.6	10.4	78.7	2.4	0.1	7.2	9.7
25	D, 53		D, 49		D, 59		D, 63	316,732	345,824	9	78,588	44.3	34.5	21.9	41.8	10.2	0.2	25.1	19.5
26	D, 41		D, 50		D, 62		D, 70	314,235	324,875	3	151,828	73.5	63.7	7.9	73.5	5.7	0.1	10.6	6.0
27	D, 63		D, 46		D, 47		D, 62	301,474	295,659	-2	55,283	37.8	24.2	24.2	64.4	9.7	0.1	14.1	7.9
28	D, 66		D, 53		D, 63		D, 68	325,184	338,830	4	52,830	29.2	17.3	34.2	14.3	32.1	0.6	4.4	56.3
29	D, 76		D, 60		D, 66		D, 69	297,554	305,827	3	115,774	69.2	58.6	10.3	64.2	8.0	0.2	10.6	11.9
30	D, 64		D, 63		D, 70		D, 70	305,086	317,482	4	51,074	38.8	26.8	31.9	21.0	45.5	0.4	5.4	30.3
31	D, 70		D, 58		D, 66		D, 66	317,840	329,684	4	75,327	43.4	32.1	21.6	21.4	13.6	0.5	6.0	54.6
32	D, 65		D, 52		D, 69		D, 70	300,224	309,910	3	37,053	22.9	8.5	34.9	10.1	35.0	0.6	3.9	65.0
33	D, 68		D, 56		D, 67		D, 67	298,335	305,050	2	38,267	23.9	9.9	35.0	10.3	29.0	0.7	5.9	65.2
34	R, 39		R, 46		D, 44		D, 53	336,855	339,623	1	71,264	34.6	19.4	17.0	43.5	18.2	0.2	5.7	29.5
35	D, 40		R, 45		R, 50		D, 49	312,128	317,618	2	92,946	41.4	27.8	13.3	50.2	14.5	0.2	7.4	24.0
36	D, 56		D, 65		D, 70		D, 74	308,971	317,834	3	46,025	27.7	11.4	29.0	11.8	61.0	0.4	2.1	35.2
37	R, 51		D, 56		D, 57		D, 64	308,819	316,537	2	139,213	46.5	34.8	10.1	59.6	10.1	0.1	5.8	20.9
38	R, 44		R, 49		R, 43		R, 45	321,184	332,620	4	96,714	42.7	27.6	9.9	68.5	10.1	0.2	6.4	12.3
39	R, 51		R, 59		R, 51		R, 51	306,692	336,356	10	68,867	37.9	17.7	12.5	71.7	8.3	0.2	2.0	14.7
40	R, 47		R, 54		R, 47		R, 43	304,517	319,798	5	110,037	43.9	27.4	7.2	79.4	5.1	0.1	2.6	10.2
41	R, 55		R, 59		R, 50		R, 44	301,912	315,096	4	71,638	38.5	18.7	11.5	78.1	8.8	0.1	3.0	7.6
42	D, 59		R, 49		R, 42		R, 43	301,000	312,508	4	57,244	33.8	14.9	15.8	79.5	6.0	0.2	1.5	10.0
43	R, 55		R, 54		R, 52		R, 45	300,962	314,989	5	65,243	39.1	19.4	11.3	91.0	3.1	0.1	1.9	2.4
44	R, 47		R, 55		R, 50		R, 47	303,847	307,998	1	55,328	33.9	15.3	14.9	88.5	3.9	0.1	1.6	4.0
45	R, 62		R, 57		R, 56		R, 55	300,274	305,505	2	50,748	30.2	12.5	16.9	91.2	3.3	0.8	0.7	2.6
46	R, 57		D, 57		D, 50		D, 63	294,495	297,457	1	63,196	41.6	22.4	13.8	79.8	11.0	0.1	3.5	3.7
47	R, 56		R, 58		R, 53		R, 43	290,777	285,079	-2	50,223	31.4	12.8	18.2	89.4	4.2	0.3	1.4	2.9
48	R, 53		R, 61		R, 55		R, 52	292,175	296,707	2	47,652	27.7	9.9	18.8	91.0	3.4	0.3	0.8	2.5
49	R, 54		R, 61		R, 41		D, 53	290,513	292,654	1	57,825	36.0	17.3	18.0	81.5	11.1	0.3	2.2	3.0
50	R, 52		R, 58		R, 46		R, 47	291,424	289,472	-1	59,213	42.5	19.3	13.5	88.0	4.5	0.6	2.3	2.4

(continued)

Note: D=Democrat, R=Republican, R/D=Republican/Democrat (cross-filed), D/R=Democrat/Republican (cross-filed), I=Independent, C=Constitution, O=Other, GI=Green Independent, P=Progressive, P/D=Progressive/Democrat, P/D/R=Progressive/Democrat/Republican, HH=Households

New York State Senate Districts—Election and Demographic Data (cont.)

Senate Districts	General Election Results Party, Percent of Vote							Population			Avg. HH Income	Pop 25+		Below Poverty Line	2006 White (Non-Hisp)	African American	American Indians, Alaska Natives	Asians, Hawaiians, Pacific Islanders	Hispanic Origin
												Some College +	4-Yr Degree +						
New York	2000	2001	2002	2003	2004	2005	2006	2000	2006	% Change	($)	(%)	(%)	(%)	(%)	(%)	(%)	(%)	(%)
51	R, 62		R, 57		R, 51		R, 48	293,082	295,443	1	48,984	31.7	13.3	17.9	93.3	2.0	0.2	0.8	2.4
52	R, 60		R, 61		R, 51		R, 50	291,127	285,089	-2	51,675	33.7	14.5	16.8	91.1	2.4	0.1	2.6	2.1
53	R, 60		R, 61		R, 46		R, 49	293,414	294,169	0	50,789	33.7	16.7	18.2	89.5	3.3	0.2	3.3	2.1
54	D, 60		R, 55		R, 54		R, 51	289,959	293,895	1	60,024	34.9	15.5	12.7	90.3	3.4	0.1	1.3	3.0
55	R, 56		R, 54		R, 49		R, 47	300,968	301,419	0	76,304	45.2	26.1	9.9	83.7	6.8	0.1	3.3	3.8
56	R, 56		R, 43		R, 44		R, 46	304,135	298,759	-2	55,623	36.8	19.2	18.5	61.2	23.7	0.2	3.2	8.8
57	D, 48		R, 63		R, 57		R, 53	294,951	289,031	-2	46,388	28.4	10.7	18.6	91.7	2.0	0.6	0.6	3.2
58	D, 49		D, 48		D, 48		D, 54	297,653	287,070	-4	50,187	34.8	16.3	15.9	86.2	4.6	0.2	1.1	5.1
59	R, 53		R, 56		R, 49		R, 44	299,314	299,487	0	61,979	36.5	17.4	10.8	93.2	2.6	0.6	0.7	1.8
60	R, 53		D, 52		D, 58		D, 52	296,941	285,896	-4	42,284	32.5	15.4	27.0	54.6	36.7	0.5	1.7	4.9
61	R, 52		R, 56		R, 49		R, 49	298,827	290,226	-3	67,342	42.2	24.6	11.1	91.1	2.8	0.2	3.2	1.5
62			R, 53		R, 50		R, 50	302,337	298,400	-1	56,775	32.6	13.2	13.2	88.9	4.9	0.3	1.2	2.8

Note: D=Democrat, R=Republican, R/D=Republican/Democrat (cross-filed), D/R=Democrat/Republican (cross-filed), I=Independent, C=Constitution, O=Other, GI=Green Independent, P=Progressive, P/D=Progressive/Democrat, P/D/R=Progressive/Democrat/Republican, HH=Households

NEW YORK
State Assembly Districts

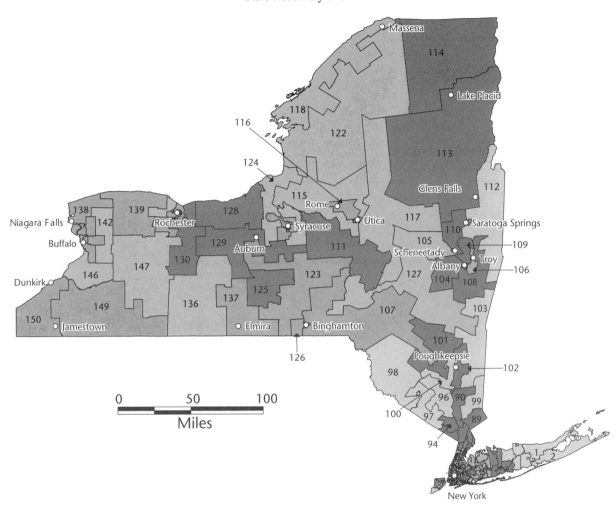

Massena
114
Lake Placid
118
116
122
124
113
115
Glens Falls
112
Rome
Syracuse
Utica
117
110
Saratoga Springs
105
109
128
139
138
142
Rochester
Niagara Falls
Schenectady
Troy
111
106
Buffalo
129
Auburn
104
108
Albany
147
130
127
103
146
123
Dunkirk
136
137
125
107
149
126
101
150
Elmira
Binghamton
Poughkeepsie
Jamestown
102
98
96
90
99
100
97
89
94

New York

0   50   100
Miles

ROCHESTER

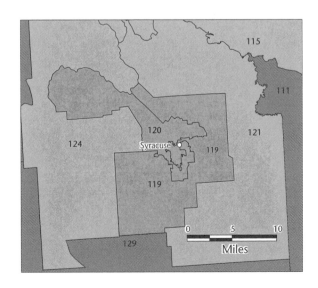

139
134
132
135
128
Rochester
133
131
130

0   5   10
Miles

SYRACUSE

115
111
124
120
121
Syracuse
119
119
129

0   5   10
Miles

Population Growth   -5% to -1%   -1% to 1%   1% to 5%   5% to 12%

NEW YORK CITY

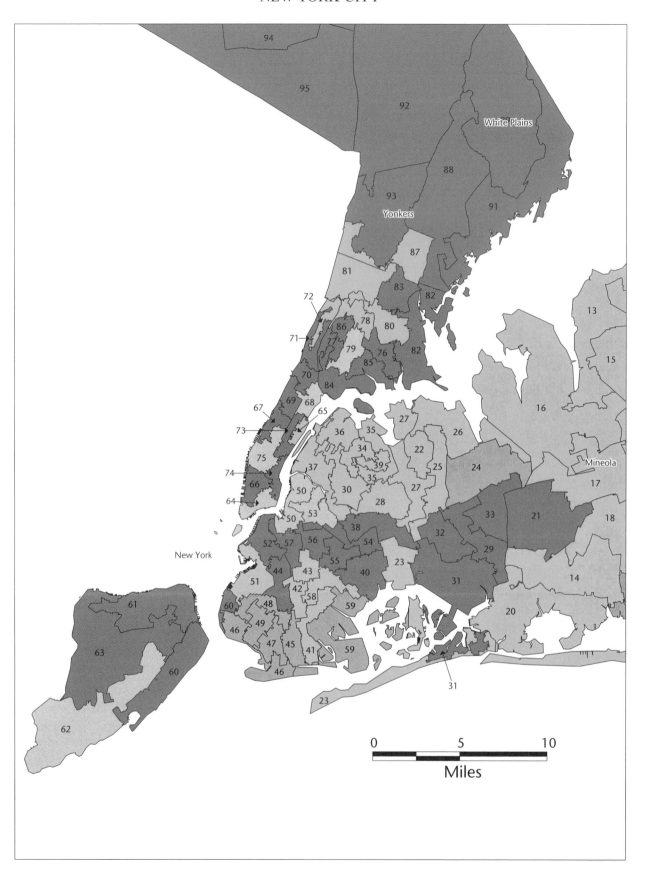

Population Growth ▨ -5% to -1%   ▨ -1% to 1%   ▨ 1% to 5%   ▨ 5% to 12%

BUFFALO

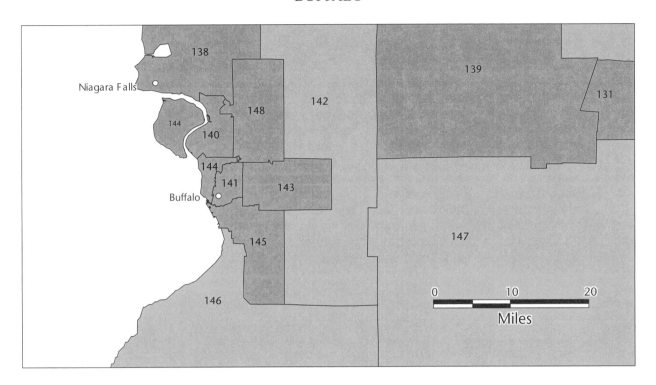

LONG ISLAND

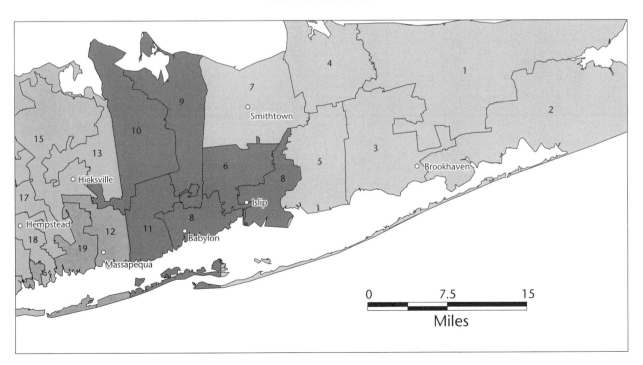

Population Growth ■ -5% to -1% ■ -1% to 1% ■ 1% to 5% ■ 5% to 12%

New York State Assembly Districts—Election and Demographic Data

Assembly Districts	General Election Results Party, Percent of Vote							Population			Avg. HH Income	Pop 25+		Below Poverty Line	2006 White (Non-Hisp)	African American	American Indians, Alaska Natives	Asians, Hawaiians, Pacific Islanders	Hispanic Origin
	2000	2001	2002	2003	2004	2005	2006	2000	2006	% Change	($)	Some College + (%)	4-Yr Degree + (%)	(%)	(%)	(%)	(%)	(%)	(%)
New York	2000	2001	2002	2003	2004	2005	2006	2000	2006	% Change	($)	(%)	(%)	(%)	(%)	(%)	(%)	(%)	(%)
1	R, 52		R, 57		R, 51		D, 50	130,597	140,254	7	75,750	38.1	20.0	10.2	85.1	4.4	0.1	1.4	7.0
2	R, 50		R, 54		R, 46		R, 44	130,677	140,388	7	78,515	36.7	20.4	10.9	77.3	5.4	0.6	1.4	12.4
3	D, 39		D, 42		D, 49		D, 52	131,618	139,122	6	74,714	33.5	15.9	9.0	71.9	7.8	0.2	2.4	14.5
4	D, 51		D, 48		D, 49		D, 58	131,398	139,481	6	94,643	39.8	24.2	6.7	79.0	3.2	0.1	7.5	8.3
5	D, 57		D, 53		D, 44		D, 47	129,151	136,090	5	85,787	36.5	18.5	8.3	87.3	1.3	0.1	2.8	6.9
6	R, 44		D, 46		D, 50		D, 55	132,141	136,993	4	72,754	26.6	12.1	11.5	27.7	19.2	0.3	3.2	51.0
7	R, 39		R, 49		R, 45		R, 44	133,587	140,588	5	104,448	44.2	26.8	6.0	88.8	1.2	0.0	3.3	5.3
8	R, 43		R, 51		R, 44		R, 43	130,573	134,965	3	89,133	37.1	19.7	7.2	85.4	2.3	0.1	2.2	7.8
9	R, 46		R, 41		R, 45		R, 44	130,818	133,196	2	116,297	44.5	28.4	6.0	86.6	1.9	0.1	3.8	5.9
10	R, 42		R, 48		R, 40		D, 43	130,047	134,664	4	120,915	44.5	29.9	6.8	74.4	5.9	0.1	4.6	11.8
11	D, 49		D, 48		D, 49		D, 54	132,172	137,217	4	75,247	30.0	13.6	10.5	58.1	22.8	0.2	2.1	15.1
12	R, 50		R, 58		R, 53		R, 51	130,050	128,015	-2	95,545	41.5	23.6	6.0	86.5	2.9	0.0	2.9	6.0
13	D, 52		D, 52		D, 52		D, 56	131,911	132,126	0	136,518	48.9	35.3	7.1	74.5	6.4	0.1	6.8	10.2
14	R, 45		R, 48		R, 45		R, 45	127,552	126,319	-1	96,230	43.9	27.7	8.7	74.7	5.9	0.1	4.8	11.7
15	R, 48		R, 54		R, 47		R, 44	132,461	132,148	0	116,806	43.4	28.2	7.1	70.4	5.3	0.1	9.0	13.1
16	D, 57		R, 46		D, 57		D, 63	134,564	134,001	0	161,645	53.7	41.6	6.4	74.5	2.9	0.1	12.6	8.0
17	R, 46		R, 54		R, 47		R, 40	132,651	131,498	-1	107,151	44.1	28.7	7.4	75.0	6.1	0.1	7.1	9.4
18	D, 66		D, 61		D, 65		D, 68	126,267	127,263	1	74,210	31.9	17.3	14.7	23.1	49.2	0.3	2.4	31.1
19	R, 39		R, 47		R, 44		R, 44	131,068	128,502	-2	101,755	42.9	26.1	5.7	79.9	3.8	0.1	3.1	10.2
20	D, 59		D, 57		D, 54		D, 60	134,749	134,421	0	104,501	46.9	31.8	9.9	76.0	6.0	0.1	3.8	11.1
21	R, 41		R, 54		R, 47		R, 49	131,614	133,684	2	87,056	39.7	23.9	8.9	63.7	14.7	0.1	7.5	11.8
22	R, 46		D, 38		D, 54		D, 60	123,736	123,843	0	51,271	37.0	25.0	20.9	20.4	5.5	0.2	57.4	21.9
23	D, 57		D, 51		D, 55		D, 63	121,880	122,697	1	62,046	31.6	18.8	19.0	49.1	14.6	0.3	9.8	20.6
24	D, 58		D, 60		D, 63		D, 67	131,225	128,913	-2	78,629	45.7	32.2	9.7	43.2	10.5	0.2	32.3	11.4
25	D, 55		D, 53		D, 60		D, 59	131,121	131,887	1	65,989	36.1	23.9	15.3	30.0	10.5	0.4	33.1	23.3
26	D, 55		D, 57		D, 52		D, 62	122,931	122,513	0	78,595	44.9	31.0	10.0	59.8	4.1	0.1	23.6	9.7
27	D, 59		D, 53		D, 58		D, 62	135,457	136,658	1	60,926	38.7	25.5	15.8	41.3	9.6	0.3	21.6	23.8
28	D, 55		D, 48		D, 53		D, 58	124,105	125,205	1	73,220	49.4	36.4	13.0	59.9	4.5	0.1	19.8	12.3
29	D, 71		D, 68		D, 73		D, 72	114,672	117,814	3	66,282	33.6	18.2	14.7	12.9	62.9	0.3	10.0	12.1
30	D, 50		D, 45		D, 55		D, 60	122,970	122,303	-1	57,130	34.1	21.6	16.9	43.3	4.6	0.2	21.8	26.5
31	D, 68		D, 60		D, 65		D, 65	118,277	120,353	2	55,220	28.0	14.6	22.1	17.0	52.2	0.4	9.6	20.0
32	D, 72		D, 68		D, 75		D, 72	119,814	123,592	3	53,016	27.4	13.5	21.9	11.1	63.0	0.4	9.2	15.6
33	D, 70		D, 64		D, 71		D, 71	120,396	124,388	3	74,950	34.5	19.0	11.3	17.3	57.2	0.3	12.1	11.7
34	D, 64		D, 52		D, 59		D, 64	130,570	130,785	0	54,271	32.9	20.4	18.1	19.2	5.7	0.4	28.9	53.6
35	D, 64		D, 55		D, 60		D, 64	120,165	120,586	0	51,874	32.3	19.7	20.4	19.1	19.4	0.4	28.0	41.7
36	D, 58		D, 51		D, 61		D, 66	125,143	125,635	0	54,736	37.3	25.1	17.9	44.3	4.8	0.2	18.4	25.7
37	D, 60		D, 54		D, 63		D, 69	128,123	127,538	0	48,325	30.1	18.7	23.8	26.6	11.3	0.4	18.2	43.7
38	D, 51		D, 45		D, 47		D, 52	115,529	117,042	1	56,244	26.7	14.7	17.8	30.0	8.1	0.5	17.3	38.4
39	D, 62		D, 51		D, 63		D, 65	121,227	120,416	-1	52,106	26.4	16.1	22.5	12.1	7.3	0.5	26.6	67.3
40	D, 67		D, 61		D, 70		D, 66	117,305	118,772	1	36,955	24.7	12.0	35.9	13.3	65.6	0.3	3.3	22.4
41	D, 67		D, 61		D, 63		D, 68	116,155	115,042	-1	58,703	36.7	21.8	19.3	44.4	37.5	0.1	9.1	6.7
42	D, 62		D, 59		D, 70		D, 67	114,091	113,795	0	47,811	28.9	15.5	25.8	18.5	64.3	0.2	4.8	12.8
43	D, 74		D, 61		D, 69		D, 57	113,882	114,487	1	45,515	29.1	14.8	26.3	15.8	73.1	0.2	2.9	7.0
44	D, 60		D, 51		D, 55		D, 56	132,059	133,934	1	60,726	38.1	26.4	20.8	44.7	19.2	0.3	14.6	16.7
45	D, 56		D, 55		D, 53		D, 57	117,479	115,000	-2	54,941	38.4	25.2	25.0	67.9	6.9	0.1	15.0	6.1
46	D, 49		D, 39		D, 45		D, 53	130,460	127,791	-2	46,807	36.8	23.0	28.5	52.4	17.0	0.2	11.3	14.8
47	D, 52		D, 45		D, 53		D, 65	114,357	111,325	-3	48,728	33.3	20.1	25.3	58.9	6.4	0.1	22.5	9.2
48	D, 40		R, 36		R, 41		D, 40	123,635	121,061	-2	52,730	27.3	16.9	27.9	61.1	6.2	0.1	18.5	9.3
49	D, 56		D, 46		D, 54		D, 62	117,735	115,795	-2	51,078	29.2	17.4	24.4	57.6	5.0	0.1	25.1	8.6
50	D, 47		D, 61		D, 64		D, 70	129,954	143,689	11	43,762	26.8	16.6	30.3	44.2	18.4	0.3	4.8	25.3

(continued)

Note: D=Democrat, R=Republican, R/D=Republican/Democrat (cross-filed), D/R=Democrat/Republican (cross-filed), I=Independent, C=Constitution, O=Other, GI=Green Independent, P=Progressive, P/D=Progressive/Democrat, P/D/R=Progressive/Democrat/Republican, HH=Households

New York State Assembly Districts—Election and Demographic Data (cont.)

Assembly Districts	General Election Results Party, Percent of Vote							Population			Avg. HH Income ($)	Pop 25+ Some College + (%)	Pop 25+ 4-Yr Degree + (%)	Below Poverty Line (%)	White (Non-Hisp) (%)	African American (%)	American Indians, Alaska Natives (%)	Asians, Hawaiians, Pacific Islanders (%)	Hispanic Origin (%)
New York	2000	2001	2002	2003	2004	2005	2006	2000	2006	% Change	($)	(%)	(%)	(%)	(%)	(%)	(%)	(%)	(%)
51	D, 61		D, 46		D, 62		D, 66	128,607	128,708	0	43,190	25.0	14.0	29.8	18.3	12.3	0.6	20.6	53.4
52	D, 58		D, 57		D, 66		D, 62	119,525	125,169	5	95,874	54.0	43.7	12.7	49.3	18.0	0.2	7.3	20.5
53	D, 63		D, 60		D, 64		D, 69	119,465	125,884	5	34,799	22.3	12.2	38.1	10.4	19.2	0.6	7.3	70.8
54	D, 61		D, 54		D, 63		D, 63	121,155	124,438	3	41,843	21.3	10.2	37.5	10.1	38.3	0.5	6.9	53.8
55	D, 73		D, 66		D, 74		D, 65	117,715	121,666	3	33,379	21.5	9.9	42.4	10.0	72.8	0.3	2.5	19.9
56	D, 72		D, 65		D, 74		D, 73	128,624	132,914	3	39,508	24.8	12.0	36.4	9.6	77.1	0.3	2.6	12.4
57	D, 68		D, 64		D, 70		D, 65	123,200	126,897	3	51,767	35.2	22.0	25.0	16.5	66.0	0.3	4.7	14.0
58	D, 59		D, 63		D, 75		D, 71	119,710	120,000	0	50,745	30.3	15.1	22.3	11.0	78.3	0.2	3.5	5.9
59	D, 44		D, 52		D, 53		D, 62	121,000	119,589	-1	67,423	35.1	19.7	14.6	48.1	36.2	0.1	5.9	7.5
60	D, 53		R, 42		R, 42		D, 41	119,322	124,620	4	70,513	33.7	19.2	15.3	70.4	4.1	0.1	8.5	13.3
61	R, 51		D, 45		D, 49		D, 56	120,295	125,592	4	64,964	30.2	16.0	18.5	41.7	25.3	0.3	6.0	26.3
62	D, 56		R, 54		R, 55		R, 53	125,213	134,822	8	87,414	31.9	16.5	8.9	85.1	1.6	0.1	4.3	7.5
63	D, 61		D, 40		D, 44		D, 51	120,926	126,005	4	80,000	33.4	18.4	11.9	65.3	6.8	0.1	12.0	13.9
64	D, 62		D, 54		D, 61		D, 68	130,383	144,921	11	64,507	42.5	32.5	25.2	29.1	6.8	0.2	47.6	17.3
65	D, 59		D, 53		D, 61		D, 70	132,061	132,882	1	128,021	71.4	62.0	8.1	72.4	6.9	0.1	9.5	6.6
66	D, 66		D, 66		D, 71		D, 72	129,793	134,324	3	124,542	69.8	60.0	9.5	69.6	6.2	0.1	11.7	7.3
67	D, 65		D, 65		D, 68		D, 70	134,710	139,844	4	136,289	70.1	60.7	10.2	64.6	8.6	0.2	8.8	12.5
68	D, 73		D, 53		D, 64		D, 68	124,758	133,651	7	45,147	31.9	20.7	38.1	17.1	36.0	0.5	5.5	48.8
69	D, 69		D, 53		D, 68		D, 75	141,720	148,187	5	94,474	55.7	46.2	17.8	43.4	20.1	0.3	9.5	22.8
70	D, 79		D, 61		D, 70		D, 74	121,255	126,544	4	36,875	33.0	19.5	36.6	12.6	56.8	0.5	3.5	32.0
71	D, 72		D, 56		D, 68		D, 73	149,270	154,569	4	42,172	35.4	23.2	31.3	14.6	30.3	0.6	4.9	53.7
72	D, 71		D, 47		D, 67		D, 76	120,348	120,751	0	40,668	31.4	20.0	31.9	7.3	13.2	0.8	4.5	78.7
73	R, 38		D, 41		D, 59		D, 66	117,107	119,347	2	176,997	73.3	64.0	6.9	75.3	5.4	0.1	8.8	6.1
74	D, 65		D, 55		D, 66		D, 65	122,753	126,268	3	91,303	60.1	48.7	14.3	49.3	10.4	0.3	13.6	21.6
75	D, 66		D, 54		D, 65		D, 70	128,555	140,409	9	122,238	69.4	58.1	11.6	62.1	8.0	0.2	12.2	12.8
76	D, 63		D, 52		D, 65		D, 67	115,883	117,646	2	40,972	25.9	10.1	28.5	11.2	34.1	0.5	6.2	61.7
77	D, 71		D, 61		D, 68		D, 70	122,300	126,315	3	33,588	19.2	6.1	43.5	6.9	43.0	0.7	1.9	63.4
78	D, 67		D, 56		D, 67		D, 69	120,983	121,928	1	38,115	23.2	9.8	34.7	11.3	25.5	0.7	6.6	65.3
79	D, 66		D, 61		D, 64		D, 68	123,262	131,616	7	32,398	19.2	6.3	45.3	8.2	44.1	0.7	1.3	62.7
80	D, 58		D, 53		D, 55		D, 59	129,227	128,939	0	47,748	31.4	15.4	22.5	29.5	22.0	0.4	7.7	41.1
81	D, 61		D, 57		D, 65		D, 67	125,978	126,780	1	65,006	39.3	23.2	18.0	33.7	23.0	0.3	7.5	35.0
82	D, 52		D, 51		D, 54		D, 61	119,824	121,040	1	57,688	33.6	15.3	16.5	39.7	23.3	0.2	3.9	32.6
83	D, 60		D, 64		D, 70		D, 72	112,578	117,189	4	54,731	30.7	12.9	23.0	10.3	72.0	0.3	2.1	23.3
84	D, 63		D, 50		D, 68		D, 67	123,421	128,097	4	30,573	18.6	5.8	43.6	6.8	35.0	0.8	2.0	72.7
85	D, 53		D, 55		D, 68		D, 71	118,852	122,907	3	34,261	19.8	6.3	40.3	9.1	39.5	0.6	2.0	65.1
86	D, 56		D, 57		D, 67		D, 67	115,131	119,190	4	34,152	19.5	6.6	41.1	6.5	34.4	0.8	3.7	70.4
87	R, 45		D, 57		D, 60		D, 64	133,059	134,145	1	54,306	31.7	17.7	22.6	25.4	40.4	0.3	4.2	32.3
88	D, 52		D, 49		D, 54		D, 60	121,567	125,723	3	144,306	47.8	36.0	10.2	59.6	12.7	0.1	7.0	17.8
89	D, 49		D, 46		D, 48		D, 57	125,911	128,156	2	174,121	51.3	39.8	6.3	77.0	4.8	0.1	5.2	10.3
90	D, 53		D, 46		D, 45		D, 53	131,234	135,175	3	99,719	43.2	27.7	8.8	67.0	10.1	0.2	3.5	15.9
91	R, 53		D, 42		D, 53		D, 59	122,215	124,217	2	118,888	43.7	31.6	11.3	56.9	8.1	0.1	4.5	25.8
92	D, 50		D, 51		D, 53		D, 59	133,724	137,267	3	133,082	49.5	36.9	6.1	64.7	10.7	0.1	8.7	13.5
93	D, 51		R, 46		D, 36		D, 42	130,751	132,282	1	72,279	39.5	24.2	13.4	56.4	13.0	0.2	6.7	19.8
94	R, 50		D, 51		D, 47		D, 52	129,947	131,908	2	101,826	45.4	30.7	7.7	62.5	9.2	0.1	8.2	17.0
95	R, 50		D, 43		D, 47		D, 50	128,593	133,130	4	92,670	39.2	26.0	12.3	67.9	14.2	0.1	6.8	9.0
96	R, 44		R, 53		R, 48		R, 43	129,403	141,853	10	79,083	41.5	20.4	8.3	78.8	4.6	0.2	2.1	11.7
97	R, 46		R, 54		D, 40		R, 43	131,662	147,388	12	79,952	40.0	20.2	11.9	78.0	5.5	0.2	2.2	11.7
98	D, 56		D, 53		D, 54		D, 57	127,583	136,307	7	56,429	31.7	12.5	17.0	71.8	8.3	0.2	1.5	14.9
99	R, 57		R, 54		R, 47		R, 46	130,116	138,174	6	107,129	44.7	27.6	6.0	84.7	2.4	0.1	2.6	8.3
100	R, 58		R, 51		R, 44		R, 41	130,564	138,343	6	59,029	33.8	14.8	17.1	54.5	20.1	0.2	1.8	20.6

(continued)

Note: D=Democrat, R=Republican, R/D=Republican/Democrat (cross-filed), D/R=Democrat/Republican (cross-filed), I=Independent, C=Constitution, O=Other, GI=Green Independent, P=Progressive, P/D=Progressive/Democrat, P/D/R=Progressive/Democrat/Republican, HH=Households

New York State Asssembly Districts—Election and Demographic Data (cont.)

Asssembly Districts	General Election Results Party, Percent of Vote							Population			Avg. HH Income	Pop 25+ Some College +	Pop 25+ 4-Yr Degree +	Below Poverty Line	White (Non-Hisp)	African American	American Indians, Alaska Natives	Asians, Hawaiians, Pacific Islanders	Hispanic Origin
New York	2000	2001	2002	2003	2004	2005	2006	2000	2006	% Change	($)	(%)	(%)	(%)	(%)	(%)	(%)	(%)	(%)
101	D, 56		D, 51		D, 53		D, 55	127,233	131,091	3	59,924	38.2	19.5	15.0	81.6	5.7	0.2	1.9	7.5
102	R, 53		R, 56		R, 47		R, 44	129,045	135,234	5	76,329	40.4	19.6	8.4	78.0	7.1	0.1	4.5	8.0
103	R, 58		R, 62		R, 52		R, 42	128,095	134,814	5	76,112	37.1	17.7	10.6	85.6	4.8	0.1	1.9	5.5
104	D, 62		D, 59		D, 57		D, 66	130,066	132,048	2	60,045	42.3	24.1	15.2	77.4	11.9	0.1	4.1	4.3
105	D, 56		D, 53		D, 54		D, 59	130,836	130,445	0	49,312	29.8	11.5	17.6	82.9	6.6	0.2	1.3	6.4
106	D, 62		D, 56		D, 55		D, 65	124,133	124,775	1	50,149	33.3	14.3	18.8	76.1	14.8	0.1	2.5	4.4
107	R, 45		R, 61		R, 55		R, 53	127,435	125,069	-2	51,977	32.1	12.5	15.7	94.6	1.3	0.2	0.7	2.0
108	R, 52		R, 41		R, 44		D, 40	128,817	131,637	2	72,134	40.7	20.8	9.2	90.9	3.3	0.1	1.5	2.7
109	R, 62		R, 51		D, 45		D, 52	133,905	140,412	5	74,989	45.7	25.6	7.3	89.6	3.1	0.1	3.8	2.2
110	R, 56		R, 56		R, 51		R, 49	133,671	138,308	3	68,056	42.5	23.2	10.7	91.3	2.3	0.1	2.2	2.6
111	D, 47		D, 50		D, 48		D, 59	127,577	132,279	4	53,852	32.8	14.3	15.7	94.8	1.5	0.2	0.8	1.6
112	R, 56		R, 53		R, 52		R, 46	128,918	136,181	6	57,983	32.2	13.8	12.6	94.5	1.8	0.1	0.6	1.9
113	R, 58		R, 47		R, 51		R, 55	132,309	135,249	2	52,965	33.1	14.1	14.8	94.7	1.6	0.1	0.6	1.9
114	R, 51		R, 57		D, 46		R, 44	132,634	134,082	1	47,825	28.5	11.4	19.5	87.6	4.9	1.6	0.8	3.2
115	R, 57		R, 42		R, 50		R, 50	129,754	130,227	0	57,981	32.6	13.2	12.5	96.3	0.8	0.2	0.9	0.9
116	D, 51		D, 52		D, 53		D, 53	127,439	121,995	-4	44,651	30.3	11.4	21.7	78.6	10.1	0.2	1.8	6.5
117	R, 55		R, 59		R, 53		R, 53	128,579	127,424	-1	44,910	29.3	10.5	18.6	95.6	1.1	0.1	0.6	1.5
118	D, 60		R, 44		D, 58		D, 55	126,984	126,993	0	45,843	29.8	11.8	21.2	91.1	3.3	0.5	1.1	2.2
119	D, 57		D, 53		D, 56		D, 63	130,841	129,089	-1	57,802	39.8	19.5	18.9	69.8	20.2	0.9	2.3	4.4
120	D, 48		D, 58		D, 55		D, 59	127,598	125,130	-2	45,017	36.5	16.5	23.2	78.0	10.1	0.7	4.3	4.0
121	R, 48		R, 53		R, 47		D, 45	127,096	128,000	1	71,887	46.1	22.6	8.1	92.0	2.6	0.3	2.4	1.3
122	R, 71		R, 50		R, 57		R, 55	129,631	130,733	1	45,754	26.3	8.9	18.7	89.4	4.2	0.3	0.9	2.7
123	R, 62		R, 55		R, 45		R, 47	125,267	123,469	-1	51,398	30.9	11.9	15.7	93.7	2.3	0.2	0.6	1.9
124	R, 55		R, 44		R, 50		R, 42	129,337	129,757	0	58,156	36.2	16.3	14.9	95.3	0.9	0.2	0.9	1.5
125	D, 55		D, 48		D, 53		D, 55	125,986	130,652	4	53,864	42.1	27.0	19.5	84.4	2.9	0.2	7.2	3.1
126	R, 54		R, 36		D, 45		D, 59	129,361	125,634	-3	51,079	36.5	17.6	19.7	85.0	4.4	0.1	5.1	3.2
127	R, 57		R, 51		R, 45		R, 40	128,466	129,532	1	52,607	31.0	12.6	15.8	92.9	1.9	0.2	0.6	2.9
128	R, 62		R, 66		R, 55		R, 55	126,921	128,479	1	56,631	29.1	10.8	13.4	92.3	2.6	0.2	0.6	2.6
129	R, 48		R, 49		R, 43		R, 47	128,426	132,119	3	57,083	34.2	14.2	13.1	91.4	2.9	0.2	0.8	3.1
130	R, 64		R, 50		R, 45		R, 44	124,365	127,829	3	84,407	44.9	25.3	7.9	90.2	3.0	0.1	3.5	1.9
131	D, 49		D, 47		D, 43		D, 51	127,009	124,951	-2	50,678	37.5	19.7	19.4	66.3	17.7	0.3	3.5	8.7
132	D, 59		D, 58		D, 54		D, 64	128,180	125,684	-2	67,129	45.7	26.7	11.4	82.0	7.0	0.1	4.0	4.5
133	D, 61		D, 58		D, 56		D, 63	126,128	123,277	-2	41,567	26.1	10.2	28.4	34.6	47.1	0.2	2.3	15.1
134	D, 60		R, 41		R, 45		R, 45	126,605	126,122	0	64,873	38.9	18.1	8.8	90.3	3.3	0.1	1.8	2.7
135	D, 50		D, 49		D, 49		D, 52	125,015	127,549	2	84,748	50.8	31.2	6.8	91.5	2.3	0.1	3.2	1.7
136	R, 44		R, 67		R, 62		R, 58	123,248	122,722	0	50,492	30.5	12.2	17.0	95.6	1.2	0.2	1.0	1.1
137	R, 57		R, 65		R, 47		R, 51	126,513	124,225	-2	49,895	30.3	12.0	16.7	91.0	4.5	0.2	0.8	1.9
138	D, 51		D, 51		D, 50		D, 49	127,788	125,186	-2	51,340	30.7	11.5	17.6	86.6	8.8	0.8	0.7	1.6
139	R, 49		R, 58		R, 56		R, 50	127,881	125,162	-2	54,848	30.4	11.4	12.5	90.4	4.1	0.3	0.6	2.8
140	D, 58		D, 53		D, 55		D, 56	126,740	121,033	-5	51,852	37.8	18.8	13.5	94.2	1.9	0.2	1.2	1.4
141	D, 63		D, 68		D, 73		D, 76	131,957	127,261	-4	35,816	29.6	12.7	33.5	27.9	66.6	0.2	1.5	3.1
142	R, 43		R, 55		R, 50		R, 41	127,557	126,331	-1	68,810	38.6	19.2	10.7	93.5	2.9	0.2	0.9	1.4
143	D, 54		D, 50		D, 48		D, 53	131,414	127,797	-3	53,377	35.7	16.3	11.8	94.2	2.9	0.1	1.0	1.0
144	D, 59		D, 53		D, 55		D, 57	132,048	127,089	-4	47,448	37.2	20.7	24.6	64.6	13.2	0.7	2.6	14.0
145	D, 47		D, 53		D, 49		D, 55	133,521	128,690	-4	55,635	36.6	18.4	13.6	93.6	1.4	0.2	0.8	2.5
146	D, 44		D, 42		R, 47		R, 46	132,320	131,207	-1	57,715	35.8	17.6	11.9	90.4	3.7	1.2	0.5	2.7
147	R, 53		R, 52		R, 56		R, 51	127,117	126,920	0	52,841	28.5	10.9	14.4	91.3	3.6	0.2	0.9	2.6
148	R, 45		R, 47		R, 46		R, 51	125,325	122,532	-2	79,332	48.2	32.3	9.7	87.7	3.7	0.1	5.9	1.5
149	R, 59		R, 63		R, 59		R, 48	125,510	122,862	-2	45,601	27.3	9.9	18.7	95.1	1.0	1.1	0.6	1.1
150	D, 53		D, 43		D, 52		D, 55	126,173	121,869	-3	46,900	30.6	11.9	18.6	88.9	2.5	0.3	0.5	5.3

Note: D=Democrat, R=Republican, R/D=Republican/Democrat (cross-filed), D/R=Democrat/Republican (cross-filed), I=Independent, C=Constitution, O=Other, GI=Green Independent, P=Progressive, P/D=Progressive/Democrat, P/D/R=Progressive/Democrat/Republican, HH=Households

NORTH CAROLINA

North Carolina has never received the attention it deserves. Unlike Virginia and South Carolina, its neighbors to the north and south, it never developed a great port on the Atlantic Ocean and did not pursue a plantation economy. It initially declined to ratify the Constitution and later voted against secession, relenting only after Ft. Sumpter had fallen. As one writer put it, North Carolina "got into the Union too late to vote for George Washington and got out of it too late to vote for Jefferson Davis."

It still does not receive its just due. Charlotte is a major banking center and now one of the twenty biggest cities in the country, the center of a region stretching from Washington to Atlanta. Just behind it are the Raleigh and Durham metro areas, the so-called Research Triangle, home of several major universities and more than 1.3 million people. As a whole, North Carolina was the second fastest-growing state in the South during the 1990s and has been so during this decade, as well. Yet it has slipped from being the tenth-biggest state in 1990 to eleventh biggest today because Georgia has grown even faster. Indeed, North Carolina may be as much overshadowed by Georgia today as it has traditionally been by Virginia.

North Carolina is yet another state where one finds growth concentrated toward the outer suburbs, in this case in a ring around Raleigh. Many of these new arrivals are young whites from the Northeast and they tend to be more Republican than the state as a whole. George W. Bush carried North Carolina twice by comfortable margins, even with a favorite son, John Edwards, on the Democratic ticket in 2004.

The state's population is 72 percent white, almost exactly the regional average. Districts in the mountains toward Tennessee and north along the Virginia border in the Appalachians are almost entirely white. There are eleven black-majority house districts, all but evenly split between downtown urban areas (Greensboro, Winston-Salem, Charlotte), and rural areas (tobacco country around Rocky Mount). Charlotte and Winston-Salem now have significant Hispanic neighborhoods. The 48th house district, in Robeson County, is more than 20 percent Native American, most of them are members of the Lumbee tribe, the largest Indian nation east of the Mississippi River.

No state in the country has had as much trouble redrawing its electoral boundaries. Volumes have been written about attempts to redraw North Carolina's congressional districts in the 1990s, a dispute that went up to the U.S. Supreme Court four times before it was finally resolved. It gained another congressional seat in 2000, though it did not engender as much legal wrangling, and is projected to gain two more by 2030.

Legislative reapportionment after the 2000 census has been only slightly less convoluted. In 2001 the Democratic-controlled legislature drew new lines for general assembly and state senate districts and, predictably, the Republicans challenged them in court. In May 2002 the North Carolina

Supreme Court sided with the Republicans, invalidating the legislative reapportionment plan on the grounds that it improperly split counties between districts. The court also ruled that all legislators must be elected in single-member districts, invalidating the long-standing state practice of creating some multimember districts and dissolving the districts held by eight state senators and seventeen members of the assembly.

Because the decision was handed down in May, the upcoming 2002 primary was postponed until later in the summer. The legislature redrew maps but this time a lower state court struck them down and imposed its own map to be used provisionally for the 2002 elections only, until a third set of maps could be drawn. These districts helped the Republicans immensely. They picked up seven seats in the state senate and took control of the general assembly by one seat, 61–59. A few weeks after the elections, however, Democrats persuaded a longtime Republican lawmaker to switch parties, creating a 60–60 tie. The assembly then elected co-speakers who took turns running the chamber.

The state assembly waited until November 2003 before attempting to fix the legislative boundaries. Republicans challenged them again and the courts postponed the primary again. Ultimately, maps favorable to the Democrats were approved and the party recaptured the general assembly in 2004, at which point the Republican who had defected to their side two years earlier switched back to the GOP. Democrats gained another five seats in 2006 and now control the assembly, 68–52. They currently control the senate, as well, by a margin of 31–19.

An excellent organization called North Carolina Data-Net has compiled data that yield fascinating insights into the changing landscape of North Carolina's legislature over the past quarter-century and provides a glimpse into trends that are reshaping other states, as well. Prompted in part, no doubt, by all the legal battling, spending on North Carolina legislative races has increased more than fourfold in just ten years, from $7.9 million to $26.2 million. In North Carolina, however, Democrats spend twice as much as Republicans. The group has also found that the candidate that spends more money wins more than 85 percent of the time, something that is surely true elsewhere.

The composition of North Carolina's legislature has also changed over the last three decades. (Incidentally, the lower chamber was officially known as the North Carolina House of Commons until 1868). There are more women serving and more minorities. Legislators now come from different walks of life, too. In 1971, 79 percent listed their principal occupation as business, law, or sales. By 2005 only 52 percent did, but 36 percent listed themselves as either retired or self-employed. In 1971, just as tellingly, 14 percent of the state's legislators were farmers and only 5 percent were educators. By 2005 those numbers had been reversed: only 3 percent now are farmers, but 13 percent are educators.

NORTH CAROLINA
State Senate Districts

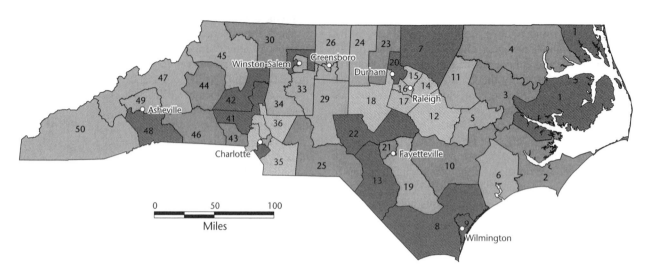

CHARLOTTE

WINSTON-SALEM/GREENSBORO

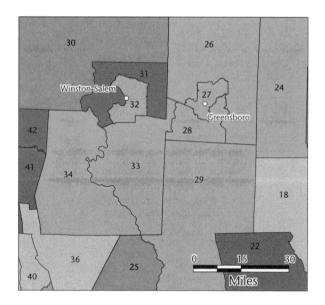

Population Growth   ▨ 0% to 4%   ▨ 4% to 9%   ▨ 9% to 18%   ▨ 18% to 32%

North Carolina State Senate Districts—Election and Demographic Data

Senate Districts	General Election Results Party, Percent of Vote							Population			Avg. HH Income	2006 Pop 25+		Below Poverty	White (Non-Hisp)	African American	American Indians, Alaska Natives	Asians, Hawaiians, Pacific Islanders	Hispanic Origin
												Some College +	4-Yr Degree +						
N. Carolina	2000	2001	2002	2003	2004	2005	2006	2000	2006	% Change	($)	(%)	(%)	(%)	(%)	(%)	(%)	(%)	(%)
1	D, 70		D, 67		D, 65		D, 69	158,310	176,588	12	49,518	31.9	12.5	19.2	71.5	24.0	0.2	0.6	2.7
2	D, 100		D, 52		D, 54		R, 57	163,560	167,571	2	51,568	35.5	13.6	16.4	76.3	17.9	0.3	1.0	2.6
3	D, 54		D, 67		D, 66		D, 100	152,386	156,873	3	43,748	26.1	9.7	23.9	46.3	48.3	0.2	0.5	4.6
4	R, 65		D, 84		D, 100		D, 70	158,052	158,729	0	40,777	23.3	8.2	27.1	46.2	50.6	1.2	0.5	1.2
5	D, 60		D, 51		D, 57		D, 58	159,939	167,110	4	49,859	33.6	15.1	20.8	58.6	31.7	0.3	1.6	6.5
6	D, 100		D, 52		R, 52		R, 65	160,870	168,885	5	44,661	27.7	8.2	16.9	67.7	19.2	0.6	2.2	6.1
7	D, 69		D, 54		D, 57		D, 61	158,480	176,806	12	48,572	25.8	8.9	19.9	54.7	38.0	0.7	0.4	5.8
8	D, 61		D, 55		D, 54		D, 53	168,191	192,735	15	47,975	29.8	10.2	20.2	72.6	20.9	1.0	0.3	3.7
9	D, 62		R, 65		D, 51		D, 63	160,376	182,099	14	58,736	43.7	22.3	15.1	78.1	16.6	0.3	1.1	2.7
10	D, 55		D, 55		D, 62		D, 64	168,553	175,220	4	43,781	24.8	8.3	23.2	51.8	32.6	0.6	0.4	13.1
11	D, 54		D, 60		D, 60		D, 62	161,177	170,515	6	50,487	27.3	11.5	20.3	52.4	35.8	1.0	0.7	6.5
12	R, 29		R, 58		R, 100		R, 65	157,028	188,948	20	52,929	29.7	10.9	16.0	71.2	16.0	0.3	0.5	9.5
12	R, 32							157,028	188,948	20	52,929	29.7	10.9	16.0	71.2	16.0	0.3	0.5	9.5
13	D, 38		D, 100		D, 100		D, 100	157,460	171,720	9	40,948	23.1	7.8	26.1	37.8	29.0	25.0	0.8	8.5
13	D, 35							157,460	171,720	9	40,948	23.1	7.8	26.1	37.8	29.0	25.0	0.8	8.5
14	D, 32		D, 65		D, 64		D, 66	152,871	190,057	24	58,209	43.5	24.4	11.3	46.6	39.5	0.3	2.5	10.9
14	D, 39							152,871	190,057	24	58,209	43.5	24.4	11.3	46.6	39.5	0.3	2.5	10.9
15	D, 61		R, 57		R, 85		R, 55	151,711	188,323	24	94,154	57.7	41.4	5.8	77.6	10.8	0.2	3.7	6.2
16	D, 27		D, 49		D, 59		D, 100	152,318	183,642	21	72,421	51.5	38.1	10.9	67.5	15.2	0.3	6.7	8.4
16	D, 26							152,318	183,642	21	72,421	51.5	38.1	10.9	67.5	15.2	0.3	6.7	8.4
17	D, 55		R, 62		R, 59		R, 100	170,373	208,121	22	83,103	51.6	35.0	6.1	75.8	12.0	0.3	4.2	6.0
17	D, 51							170,373	208,121	22	83,103	51.6	35.0	6.1	75.8	12.0	0.3	4.2	6.0
18	D, 80		D, 56		D, 58		D, 100	168,555	200,012	19	65,492	42.4	26.5	13.2	61.2	20.2	0.3	3.9	11.7
19	R, 100		D, 63		D, 100		D, 100	167,592	177,972	6	51,401	31.3	10.6	18.5	62.0	28.0	1.9	1.5	4.3
20	D, 36		D, 89		D, 90		D, 100	153,300	168,227	10	57,519	37.5	20.8	16.1	40.1	46.5	0.2	2.1	12.4
20	R, 36							153,300	168,227	10	57,519	37.5	20.8	16.1	40.1	46.5	0.2	2.1	12.4
21	R, 56		D, 67		D, 61		D, 62	167,612	167,958	0	47,574	34.9	12.0	15.8	43.7	41.4	0.7	3.5	7.8
22	R, 100		R, 54		R, 52		R, 63	165,221	190,165	15	54,082	33.4	13.5	16.9	70.4	19.1	0.6	0.8	7.2
23	D, 53		D, 66		D, 65		D, 74	155,193	158,511	2	65,755	43.4	28.8	16.2	72.3	16.8	0.3	3.9	4.9
24	D, 59		R, 58		R, 58		D, 51	154,094	167,033	8	52,164	30.0	12.4	15.9	66.9	20.9	0.3	1.0	9.8
25	D, 100		D, 58		D, 82		D, 63	165,770	170,789	3	45,389	24.7	8.5	22.1	65.4	27.8	2.1	1.3	2.7
26	R, 100		R, 85		R, 100		R, 62	168,899	178,958	6	58,853	32.9	15.3	14.1	76.1	14.6	1.5	0.8	4.0
27	R, 48		D, 56		D, 66		D, 100	164,316	173,443	6	65,683	43.5	26.1	12.2	61.1	26.2	0.4	4.0	7.1
27	R, 52							164,316	173,443	6	65,683	43.5	26.1	12.2	61.1	26.2	0.4	4.0	7.1
28	D, 26		D, 64		D, 100		D, 100	157,715	166,706	6	54,884	33.4	16.9	17.0	47.2	43.6	0.4	3.1	5.5
28	D, 27							157,715	166,706	6	54,884	33.4	16.9	17.0	47.2	43.6	0.4	3.1	5.5
29	D, 51		R, 65		R, 71		R, 100	156,834	167,611	7	50,703	23.9	8.0	15.9	73.3	8.3	1.0	1.0	11.2
30	D, 79		R, 61		R, 65		R, 100	162,274	168,298	4	48,652	25.8	8.2	17.9	86.0	3.9	0.2	0.5	7.0
31	D, 100		R, 88		R, 100		R, 100	154,245	168,952	10	75,556	47.8	30.9	8.3	83.2	7.5	0.2	1.5	6.2
32	D, 62		D, 100		D, 70		D, 100	152,931	163,060	7	47,836	35.8	20.5	19.7	42.0	43.3	0.3	1.2	14.4
33	D, 100		R, 100		R, 100		R, 100	168,768	181,971	8	54,793	30.1	12.1	14.0	82.1	9.1	0.3	1.3	5.5
34	D, 56		R, 60		R, 63		R, 61	164,836	176,649	7	52,589	28.8	10.8	15.4	77.8	13.6	0.2	0.9	6.0
35	R, 67		R, 67		R, 100		R, 100	158,426	207,816	31	69,301	34.3	15.5	9.9	76.2	12.1	0.3	1.1	8.7
36	R, 56		R, 66		R, 81		R, 63	154,550	184,859	20	60,511	32.0	13.0	11.1	77.3	12.2	0.3	1.3	7.5
37	D, 55		D, 100		D, 100		D, 100	162,933	171,797	5	65,530	45.1	26.0	9.9	52.7	28.4	0.3	3.8	14.3
38	R, 89		D, 100		D, 100		D, 100	163,090	197,575	21	56,829	35.3	16.6	14.2	41.9	46.0	0.3	3.5	9.5
39	R, 100		R, 65		R, 89		R, 100	168,031	194,221	16	108,568	55.9	38.3	4.6	81.4	7.1	0.2	4.2	5.6
40	D, 64		R, 55		D, 58		D, 61	165,074	210,025	27	74,927	41.9	25.6	9.7	53.5	30.4	0.2	4.7	10.4
41	D, 100		R, 68		R, 69		R, 100	166,511	188,358	13	59,339	31.0	11.7	13.2	80.3	10.8	0.2	1.2	6.1
42	R, 90		R, 100		R, 100		R, 56	167,747	184,163	10	55,183	29.5	11.3	13.2	78.5	8.0	0.2	3.3	8.3

(continued)

Note: D=Democrat, R=Republican, R/D=Republican/Democrat (cross-filed), D/R=Democrat/Republican (cross-filed), I=Independent, C=Constitution, O=Other, GI=Green Independent, P=Progressive, P/D=Progressive/Democrat, P/D/R=Progressive/Democrat/Republican, HH=Households

North Carolina State Senate Districts—Election and Demographic Data (cont.)

Senate Districts	General Election Results Party, Percent of Vote							Population			Avg. HH Income	Pop 25+		Below Poverty ine	2006 White (Non-Hisp)	African American	American Indians, Alaska Natives	Asians, Hawaiians, Pacific Islanders	Hispanic Origin
												Some College +	4-Yr Degree +						
N. Carolina	2000	2001	2002	2003	2004	2005	2006	2000	2006	% Change	($)	(%)	(%)	(%)	(%)	(%)	(%)	(%)	(%)
43			D, 53		D, 54		D, 100	163,671	169,746	4	53,896	29.2	10.6	15.9	72.0	14.5	0.7	1.2	6.1
44			R, 100		R, 62		R, 100	166,990	171,108	2	47,790	26.0	8.9	16.4	84.7	5.9	0.2	2.7	4.6
45			R, 62		R, 62		D, 50	165,769	172,891	4	47,105	28.9	12.1	19.6	91.0	3.1	0.1	0.7	3.6
46			D, 52		D, 53		D, 54	158,696	164,045	3	46,895	26.4	9.4	19.3	79.6	16.9	0.1	0.7	1.8
47			D, 49		R, 53		D, 51	159,491	167,330	5	44,009	28.8	10.3	19.7	92.9	2.0	0.3	0.5	3.0
48			R, 67		R, 62		R, 100	160,952	178,196	11	55,686	39.9	18.9	13.1	87.9	3.3	0.2	0.8	5.8
49			D, 56		D, 61		D, 66	152,368	162,330	7	49,580	37.0	17.7	16.7	83.4	9.0	0.3	0.8	4.6
50			R, 56		D, 49		D, 60	153,619	164,611	7	45,889	33.1	13.4	19.3	90.3	2.0	4.2	0.4	1.7

*After 2000, NC went from 42 districts to 50 districts due to redistricting.

Note: D=Democrat, R=Republican, R/D=Republican/Democrat (cross-filed), D/R=Democrat/Republican (cross-filed), I=Independent, C=Constitution, O=Other, GI=Green Independent, P=Progressive, P/D=Progressive/Democrat, P/D/R=Progressive/Democrat/Republican, HH=Households

NORTH CAROLINA
State House Districts

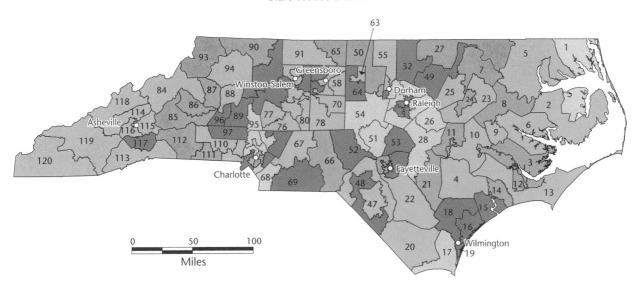

RALEIGH

FAYETTEVILLE

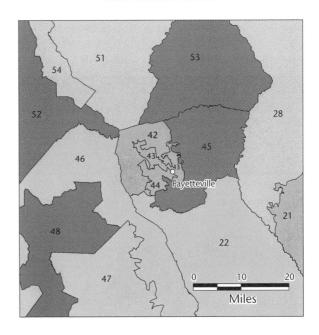

Population Growth | -5% to 3% | 3% to 9% | 9% to 18% | 18% to 45%

WINSTON-SALEM/GREENSBORO

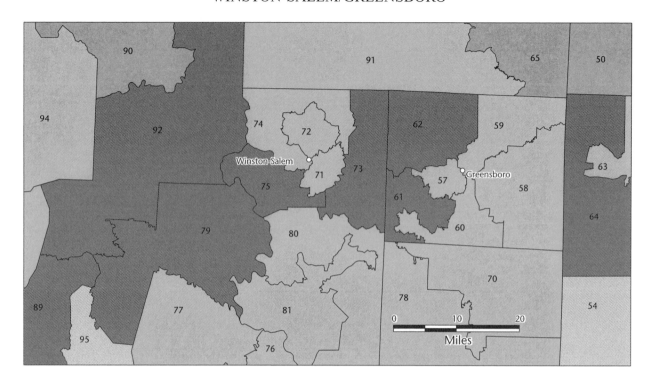

CHARLOTTE

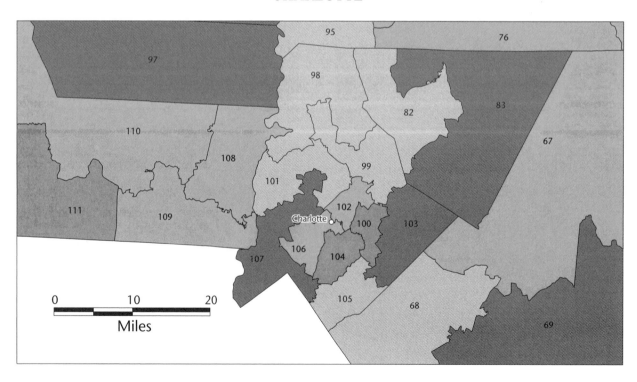

Population Growth · -5% to 3% · 3% to 9% · 9% to 18% · 18% to 45%

North Carolina State House Districts—Election and Demographic Data

House Districts	General Election Results Party, Percent of Vote							Population			Avg. HH Income	Pop 25+		Below Poverty ine	2006 White (Non-Hisp)	African American	American Indians, Alaska Natives	Asians, Hawaiians, Pacific Islanders	Hispanic Origin
												Some College +	4-Yr Degree +						
N. Carolina	2000	2001	2002	2003	2004	2005	2006	2000	2006	% Change	($)	(%)	(%)	(%)	(%)	(%)	(%)	(%)	(%)
1	D, 100		D, 100		D, 100		D, 100	64,325	76,179	18	48,629	30.3	10.5	19.3	69.6	26.4	0.3	0.9	2.0
2	D, 55		D, 63		D, 62		D, 69	64,188	68,900	7	52,056	34.6	15.3	16.6	74.6	21.1	0.2	0.5	2.6
3	D, 46		R, 50		D, 51		D, 56	64,518	64,723	0	51,900	35.4	13.4	15.1	76.7	17.3	0.4	1.2	2.5
4	D, 35		D, 52		D, 100		D, 63	64,751	68,654	6	41,652	24.3	7.5	23.8	54.2	25.7	0.2	0.4	15.9
4	R, 40							64,751	68,654	6	41,652	24.3	7.5	23.8	54.2	25.7	0.2	0.4	15.9
5	D, 100		D, 84		D, 83		D, 64	64,291	66,510	3	41,896	23.6	7.7	26.4	47.3	50.3	0.5	0.3	1.2
6	D, 64		D, 54		D, 55		D, 63	71,193	75,179	6	46,574	31.7	14.3	23.3	67.8	26.5	0.1	0.7	3.9
7	D, 100		D, 100		D, 100		D, 100	62,683	62,397	0	40,122	23.0	8.7	27.7	38.4	57.9	0.6	0.9	1.9
8	D, 100		D, 100		D, 74		D, 100	66,966	68,651	3	41,173	26.8	9.9	26.9	42.5	51.9	0.2	0.6	4.8
9	D, 55		D, 65		D, 100		D, 57	66,849	71,990	8	55,659	41.1	21.6	19.3	70.2	22.8	0.2	1.8	3.5
10	D, 52		R, 51		R, 57		D, 55	70,321	73,291	4	48,162	26.4	8.6	18.6	58.2	29.2	0.2	0.5	10.1
11	D, 60		R, 51		R, 100		R, 65	70,987	72,867	3	50,534	31.7	11.3	15.0	69.5	22.4	0.3	1.5	4.9
12	D, 55		D, 87		D, 64		D, 66	62,788	60,133	-4	42,699	29.0	10.6	24.5	47.5	46.8	0.3	1.0	3.2
13	R, 100		R, 56		R, 71		R, 58	70,224	74,082	5	52,951	36.9	14.1	16.0	84.5	10.8	0.3	0.7	2.4
14	D, 30		R, 54		R, 61		R, 58	66,582	64,573	-3	46,575	31.7	10.2	15.5	65.1	22.3	0.5	3.0	5.2
14	D, 27							66,582	64,573	-3	46,575	31.7	10.2	15.5	65.1	22.3	0.5	3.0	5.2
15	R, 59		R, 71		R, 100		R, 62	69,025	78,665	14	43,611	24.8	6.7	16.4	68.8	15.5	0.7	2.0	7.7
16	D, 64		R, 56		R, 100		R, 100	68,827	79,038	15	62,030	43.7	21.7	13.3	85.4	9.1	0.3	1.0	2.9
17	D, 42		R, 49		R, 50		R, 62	64,008	79,209	24	52,711	33.8	12.8	15.7	83.6	12.2	3.2	0.4	3.2
17	D, 41							64,008	79,209	24	52,711	33.8	12.8	15.7	83.6	12.2	3.2	0.4	3.2
18	D, 50		D, 74		D, 64		D, 64	64,677	72,764	13	41,374	30.5	11.2	24.5	54.1	40.0	0.4	0.5	4.4
18	R, 44							64,677	72,764	13	41,374	30.5	11.2	24.5	54.1	40.0	0.4	0.5	4.4
19	D, 28		R, 89		R, 100		R, 100	68,870	77,760	13	65,904	48.4	26.0	10.6	88.4	6.4	0.3	1.3	2.4
19	R, 27							68,870	77,760	13	65,904	48.4	26.0	10.6	88.4	6.4	0.3	1.3	2.4
20	R, 60		D, 82		D, 100		D, 63	63,459	66,054	4	40,889	24.4	7.2	27.0	63.3	29.8	2.0	0.3	3.6
21	D, 91		D, 100		D, 100		D, 100	69,323	70,333	1	42,143	24.5	8.2	25.9	39.0	47.4	1.0	0.6	12.7
22	D, 39		D, 62		D, 100		D, 100	71,705	76,764	7	47,844	28.4	9.4	20.5	63.6	27.7	2.1	0.8	4.2
22	D, 35							71,705	76,764	7	47,844	28.4	9.4	20.5	63.6	27.7	2.1	0.8	4.2
23	D, 34		D, 53		D, 66		D, 71	65,938	68,266	4	45,903	23.5	8.5	20.1	56.6	36.5	0.2	0.3	6.0
23	D, 30							65,938	68,266	4	45,903	23.5	8.5	20.1	56.6	36.5	0.2	0.3	6.0
23	D, 26							65,938	68,266	4	45,903	23.5	8.5	20.1	56.6	36.5	0.2	0.3	6.0
24	D, 34		D, 100		D, 100		D, 100	63,850	63,596	0	45,440	23.4	9.3	26.1	37.4	55.5	0.2	0.5	7.5
24	D, 32							63,850	63,596	0	45,440	23.4	9.3	26.1	37.4	55.5	0.2	0.5	7.5
25	D, 18		R, 59		R, 100		R, 62	65,046	69,869	7	54,557	28.7	12.0	17.2	65.6	27.3	0.3	0.6	4.8
25	R, 19							65,046	69,869	7	54,557	28.7	12.0	17.2	65.6	27.3	0.3	0.6	4.8
25	R, 18							65,046	69,869	7	54,557	28.7	12.0	17.2	65.6	27.3	0.3	0.6	4.8
26	D, 74		R, 100		R, 100		R, 100	69,586	85,196	22	54,098	30.1	11.7	17.0	66.0	19.3	0.3	0.5	11.5
27	R, 84		D, 100		D, 100		D, 100	66,836	66,678	0	42,812	24.4	8.7	26.4	40.9	54.6	1.3	0.4	2.7
28	D, 100		R, 100		R, 100		R, 100	72,039	87,954	22	50,344	27.4	9.3	16.5	74.2	11.6	0.6	0.3	10.4
29	R, 100		D, 100		D, 100		D, 100	65,090	71,541	10	67,123	47.3	33.8	15.5	40.8	45.2	0.2	4.3	10.6
30	R, 62		D, 85		D, 88		D, 100	65,931	70,260	7	61,840	44.9	29.8	13.7	55.0	23.6	0.2	5.6	14.0
31	R, 55		D, 81		D, 86		D, 100	64,033	76,945	20	58,826	38.6	22.1	13.4	39.2	45.5	0.3	3.7	12.8
32	D, 100		D, 58		D, 88		D, 100	66,694	74,111	11	50,837	25.2	8.4	18.5	56.5	35.9	0.3	0.4	6.3
33	D, 100		D, 66		D, 92		D, 100	69,284	82,471	19	55,011	44.8	25.9	11.3	35.4	48.5	0.3	3.6	13.7
34	R, 54		R, 58		D, 51		D, 59	69,740	77,151	11	80,108	58.5	41.7	5.9	70.5	14.1	0.2	3.6	9.8
35	D, 52		D, 53		D, 89		D, 100	68,868	79,037	15	70,348	52.9	39.6	9.7	68.0	11.1	0.3	7.7	10.6
36	D, 64		R, 86		R, 83		R, 51	70,560	81,099	15	92,113	56.7	41.7	4.6	80.2	6.1	0.2	6.4	5.3
37	D, 57		R, 59		R, 85		R, 57	71,278	93,750	32	74,313	48.8	30.9	7.5	74.4	14.8	0.3	2.1	6.6
38	R, 70		D, 90		D, 67		D, 100	71,233	78,576	10	52,746	42.4	27.1	17.4	52.9	33.7	0.4	2.6	9.6
39	R, 100		R, 57		D, 54		D, 59	69,767	87,500	25	60,662	42.7	23.1	10.4	59.4	28.9	0.3	1.6	8.5

(continued)

Note: D=Democrat, R=Republican, R/D=Republican/Democrat (cross-filed), D/R=Democrat/Republican (cross-filed), I=Independent, C=Constitution, O=Other, GI=Green Independent, P=Progressive, P/D=Progressive/Democrat, P/D/R=Progressive/Democrat/Republican, HH=Households

North Carolina State House Districts—Election and Demographic Data (cont.)

House Districts	General Election Results Party, Percent of Vote							Population			Avg. HH Income	2006 Pop 25+ Some College +	2006 Pop 25+ 4-Yr Degree +	Below Poverty ine	White (Non-Hisp)	African American	American Indians, Alaska Natives	Asians, Hawaiians, Pacific Islanders	Hispanic Origin
N. Carolina	2000	2001	2002	2003	2004	2005	2006	2000	2006	% Change	($)	(%)	(%)	(%)	(%)	(%)	(%)	(%)	(%)
40	R, 24		R, 85		R, 62		R, 100	70,624	99,864	41	105,216	54.0	37.8	6.3	81.8	10.5	0.2	2.9	3.4
40	R, 23							70,624	99,864	41	105,216	54.0	37.8	6.3	81.8	10.5	0.2	2.9	3.4
40	R, 23							70,624	99,864	41	105,216	54.0	37.8	6.3	81.8	10.5	0.2	2.9	3.4
41	R, 51		D, 51		R, 100		D, 52	68,541	90,922	33	97,727	58.3	44.5	4.5	77.1	8.2	0.2	8.4	4.8
41	R, 49							68,541	90,922	33	97,727	58.3	44.5	4.5	77.1	8.2	0.2	8.4	4.8
42	R, 63		D, 100		D, 66		D, 100	68,188	67,736	-1	45,326	32.9	9.3	16.0	39.4	43.9	0.7	3.7	9.0
43	R, 100		D, 100		D, 100		D, 100	60,990	60,470	-1	41,075	31.3	10.7	22.7	38.8	48.7	0.7	2.6	7.2
44	D, 62		D, 53		D, 58		D, 100	66,007	64,543	-2	56,367	39.9	15.1	11.7	55.4	29.8	1.0	3.9	6.7
45	R, 33		D, 62		D, 60		D, 52	69,492	76,274	10	54,139	33.5	12.2	16.4	64.3	25.8	1.8	1.7	3.8
45	R, 32							69,492	76,274	10	54,139	33.5	12.2	16.4	64.3	25.8	1.8	1.7	3.8
46	R, 40		D, 63		D, 100		D, 100	65,706	70,275	7	42,827	26.2	8.4	22.5	59.5	25.3	9.9	0.9	8.0
46	R, 38							65,706	70,275	7	42,827	26.2	8.4	22.5	59.5	25.3	9.9	0.9	8.0
47	D, 59		D, 73		D, 100		D, 100	65,636	69,401	6	43,098	23.8	9.7	26.0	26.4	20.6	53.1	0.8	9.5
48	D, 18		D, 100		D, 100		D, 100	63,107	70,235	11	39,311	21.5	6.7	28.7	31.7	45.4	21.1	0.6	5.2
48	R, 20							63,107	70,235	11	39,311	21.5	6.7	28.7	31.7	45.4	21.1	0.6	5.2
48	R, 17							63,107	70,235	11	39,311	21.5	6.7	28.7	31.7	45.4	21.1	0.6	5.2
49	R, 60		D, 52		D, 57		D, 59	65,456	74,289	13	49,001	27.0	9.8	18.9	61.9	29.5	1.8	0.5	5.6
50	R, 100		R, 81		D, 100		D, 100	65,840	67,639	3	60,614	35.6	17.1	13.9	70.2	23.9	0.2	0.7	3.5
51	D, 18		R, 51		R, 51		D, 54	70,296	87,968	25	52,839	30.6	10.2	15.8	64.1	19.9	0.4	1.0	11.1
51	R, 20							70,296	87,968	25	52,839	30.6	10.2	15.8	64.1	19.9	0.4	1.0	11.1
51	R, 18							70,296	87,968	25	52,839	30.6	10.2	15.8	64.1	19.9	0.4	1.0	11.1
52	D, 28		R, 86		R, 100		R, 43	70,238	77,891	11	62,172	41.4	20.4	14.0	76.5	15.3	0.5	0.6	5.2
52	R, 26							70,238	77,891	11	62,172	41.4	20.4	14.0	76.5	15.3	0.5	0.6	5.2
53	R, 61		R, 62		R, 59		R, 53	69,917	76,491	9	47,147	27.1	9.2	21.0	64.7	23.4	0.7	0.9	8.7
54	D, 55		D, 86		D, 100		D, 70	68,945	82,201	19	65,820	40.0	24.1	14.2	69.4	15.4	0.3	1.6	10.2
55	R, 100		D, 55		D, 89		D, 100	64,623	68,106	5	57,401	32.3	13.8	16.4	59.0	33.8	0.4	0.8	5.0
56	D, 100		D, 80		D, 100		D, 100	63,608	61,860	-3	70,324	51.4	42.0	19.4	71.0	11.7	0.3	7.9	7.0
57	R, 100		R, 84		D, 57		D, 63	70,443	72,925	4	65,483	44.2	26.2	10.6	60.5	22.2	0.4	6.3	9.0
58	D, 100		D, 86		D, 66		D, 66	70,796	74,379	5	51,701	30.4	13.9	17.1	43.5	51.0	0.3	0.8	4.0
59	D, 100		D, 54		D, 57		D, 59	70,778	74,411	5	64,943	39.3	23.1	14.5	64.6	25.9	0.3	2.3	5.7
60	D, 57		D, 84		D, 100		D, 60	69,289	72,582	5	44,805	28.7	11.9	20.1	40.3	50.3	0.6	3.0	6.0
61	R, 51		R, 79		R, 100		R, 100	69,841	76,989	10	70,231	42.4	24.8	10.3	73.4	14.6	0.3	4.1	6.0
62	R, 59		R, 62		R, 100		R, 100	71,283	78,727	10	81,674	50.5	32.6	7.0	84.1	9.4	0.2	2.1	3.0
63	D, 55		D, 50		D, 55		D, 100	63,948	68,459	7	46,628	27.8	11.2	18.5	53.4	28.4	0.3	1.4	16.5
64	D, 61		R, 100		R, 100		R, 100	66,833	74,387	11	59,325	34.2	15.5	12.1	82.3	9.1	0.2	0.9	5.9
65	R, 100		D, 100		D, 53		D, 67	66,981	66,587	-1	45,068	26.0	8.3	20.1	73.9	23.0	2.2	0.4	5.2
66	D, 85		R, 100		D, 95		D, 71	70,598	71,435	1	42,385	22.0	6.9	25.0	60.4	28.1	1.0	1.3	8.3
67	D, 100		R, 68		R, 66		R, 100	69,716	74,317	7	53,641	26.9	9.7	16.1	84.1	9.5	0.2	2.0	3.2
68	R, 100		D, 56		R, 100		R, 100	70,796	101,969	44	74,206	37.0	17.4	7.3	85.8	6.8	0.3	1.0	4.5
69	R, 91		D, 65		D, 63		D, 67	69,381	80,667	16	53,525	22.8	7.9	19.7	53.8	32.3	0.3	0.5	13.9
70	D, 100		R, 51		R, 92		R, 65	64,162	69,102	8	49,641	24.0	7.9	14.8	77.2	7.7	0.4	0.8	11.6
71	D, 63		D, 66		D, 87		D, 100	62,855	65,711	5	41,479	31.1	17.6	24.8	30.0	53.4	0.3	0.9	18.7
72	R, 57		D, 55		D, 100		D, 100	62,585	66,843	7	48,542	35.8	20.4	19.1	42.0	45.5	0.3	1.1	12.9
73	R, 67		R, 100		R, 86		R, 100	65,984	72,699	10	61,903	39.7	20.8	9.7	82.2	7.1	0.3	1.1	7.1
74	R, 100		R, 65		R, 63		R, 100	64,895	68,658	6	84,642	50.5	35.2	9.6	82.7	9.1	0.2	1.4	5.5
75	D, 61		R, 59		R, 100		R, 100	65,683	72,698	11	70,286	49.7	32.0	7.6	80.8	9.4	0.2	2.1	6.3
76	R, 56		R, 100		R, 100		R, 100	66,913	70,087	5	49,399	25.8	7.3	14.5	84.8	6.7	0.2	0.9	5.6
77	R, 100		D, 55		D, 61		D, 62	63,579	66,758	5	52,127	30.8	13.4	17.0	65.9	24.9	0.3	1.3	6.5
78	D, 100		R, 91		R, 100		R, 100	66,544	70,923	7	52,554	24.4	8.3	14.5	83.4	3.7	0.3	0.8	8.9
79	D, 100		R, 87		R, 100		R, 100	64,114	72,394	13	57,884	29.5	11.5	14.3	78.1	12.6	0.2	1.2	6.6

(continued)

Note: D=Democrat, R=Republican, R/D=Republican/Democrat (cross-filed), D/R=Democrat/Republican (cross-filed), I=Independent, C=Constitution, O=Other, GI=Green Independent, P=Progressive, P/D=Progressive/Democrat, P/D/R=Progressive/Democrat/Republican, HH=Households

North Carolina State House Districts—Election and Demographic Data (cont.)

House Districts	General Election Results Party, Percent of Vote							Population			Avg. HH Income	Pop 25+ Some College +	Pop 25+ 4-Yr Degree +	Below Poverty ine	White (Non-Hisp)	African American	American Indians, Alaska Natives	Asians, Hawaiians, Pacific Islanders	Hispanic Origin
	2000	2001	2002	2003	2004	2005	2006	2000	2006	% Change	($)	(%)	(%)	(%)	(%)	(%)	(%)	(%)	(%)
N. Carolina																			
80	R, 62		R, 100		R, 100		R, 100	71,805	77,461	8	52,684	28.2	9.5	13.3	91.2	4.1	0.3	0.6	2.8
81	R, 63		D, 53		D, 100		D, 100	62,789	66,332	6	47,524	25.3	8.7	17.5	70.4	16.2	0.3	1.7	9.6
82	R, 100		R, 58		R, 85		R, 100	65,437	80,335	23	65,371	34.8	15.4	10.5	72.7	13.4	0.2	1.5	10.7
83	R, 100		R, 65		R, 87		R, 100	67,349	76,145	13	58,110	29.9	11.3	11.5	81.1	10.6	0.3	0.9	5.6
84	R, 64		R, 84		R, 87		R, 100	64,426	67,170	4	41,690	25.6	9.1	21.2	91.4	3.1	0.3	0.2	3.8
85	D, 100		R, 58		R, 66		R, 54	68,068	70,105	3	43,952	23.5	6.4	17.7	88.2	3.9	0.2	2.7	3.4
86	D, 59		D, 59		D, 100		D, 51	63,905	64,340	1	50,271	29.0	11.1	16.6	78.9	7.6	0.2	4.3	6.3
87	D, 100		R, 51		R, 60		R, 100	63,891	65,378	2	48,595	26.3	8.9	15.7	88.8	4.6	0.2	0.6	4.3
88	R, 100		R, 100		R, 56		D, 53	64,440	68,542	6	57,776	30.0	12.8	14.7	78.7	9.2	0.1	2.6	7.5
89	D, 30		R, 86		R, 100		R, 100	63,970	70,426	10	54,569	27.9	9.4	12.3	83.6	7.1	0.2	2.2	5.4
89	D, 28							63,970	70,426	10	54,569	27.9	9.4	12.3	83.6	7.1	0.2	2.2	5.4
90	R, 54		D, 53		D, 58		D, 61	64,128	63,832	0	46,635	27.2	9.5	20.8	81.4	4.0	0.2	0.8	10.1
91	R, 86		R, 57		R, 57		R, 62	69,031	71,815	4	49,612	24.6	7.5	15.3	88.9	6.5	0.2	0.3	2.8
92	R, 57		R, 87		R, 100		R, 100	63,694	69,575	9	49,449	25.5	7.2	16.9	86.7	3.4	0.1	0.3	7.1
93	R, 90		R, 63		R, 52		D, 55	66,935	68,287	2	44,770	35.1	18.1	21.8	94.6	1.2	0.2	0.6	2.4
94	R, 89		R, 85		R, 100		R, 56	66,216	68,602	4	47,114	25.4	8.7	19.6	88.6	4.1	0.1	0.4	4.9
95	R, 61		R, 100		R, 100		R, 100	66,965	82,102	23	65,042	34.9	14.8	12.3	79.3	13.4	0.2	1.5	4.2
96	D, 53		R, 58		R, 100		R, 100	64,818	71,071	10	53,004	28.8	10.8	12.5	77.7	6.1	0.2	4.5	9.7
97	D, 73		R, 59		R, 61		R, 100	64,890	71,645	10	54,264	27.9	9.5	13.8	82.8	6.5	0.2	0.4	8.5
98	D, 100		R, 58		R, 100		R, 100	69,750	101,063	45	99,180	50.9	34.2	5.0	80.6	11.1	0.2	2.7	4.4
99			D, 100		D, 100		D, 100	70,962	92,022	30	64,293	42.0	24.5	8.2	52.6	30.0	0.3	6.5	10.1
100			D, 61		D, 100		D, 50	70,640	72,118	2	50,513	40.8	20.7	10.0	44.8	33.6	0.3	4.6	17.9
101			D, 100		D, 100		D, 100	67,986	80,657	19	53,381	32.5	13.9	15.5	39.3	50.7	0.3	3.3	7.5
102			D, 91		D, 100		D, 100	70,727	73,303	4	54,159	33.3	17.5	17.3	30.4	50.1	0.3	3.5	17.9
103			R, 90		R, 57		R, 58	70,744	79,917	13	70,001	45.4	23.3	6.0	73.4	15.3	0.4	3.0	6.5
104			R, 90		R, 100		R, 67	70,100	71,965	3	119,349	62.0	45.1	5.1	84.8	6.1	0.1	3.7	4.1
105			R, 90		R, 100		R, 100	70,111	91,410	30	111,778	54.6	37.6	3.2	83.1	6.2	0.2	4.5	4.7
106			D, 100		D, 100		D, 100	68,400	73,294	7	74,331	44.9	27.1	11.0	48.4	28.5	0.4	4.0	19.1
107			D, 100		D, 68		D, 100	67,682	77,647	15	55,183	35.5	16.5	15.9	40.2	48.8	0.3	3.8	7.7
108			R, 84		R, 69		R, 59	70,406	73,663	5	53,719	32.4	12.5	13.4	82.6	8.5	0.2	2.0	5.4
109			R, 54		R, 61		R, 100	70,536	73,367	4	57,129	29.4	11.0	17.5	71.3	20.7	0.2	1.0	6.4
110			R, 100		R, 63		R, 62	71,868	75,812	5	49,166	24.6	6.9	15.9	84.1	11.5	0.2	0.4	3.0
111			R, 53		R, 55		R, 61	67,876	68,294	1	49,362	27.2	10.1	18.8	73.0	23.5	0.1	1.1	1.4
112			D, 58		D, 61		D, 71	70,561	72,137	2	43,836	26.2	9.1	20.6	84.7	11.5	0.1	0.4	2.2
113			R, 84		R, 100		R, 100	66,975	71,098	6	54,688	39.3	19.0	13.5	90.5	3.7	0.2	0.4	3.7
114			D, 61		D, 62		D, 64	66,224	71,173	7	48,738	35.8	17.4	17.9	84.6	8.3	0.3	0.8	4.3
115			D, 51		D, 60		D, 68	70,759	74,840	6	51,788	40.5	20.1	15.1	83.1	10.5	0.3	1.0	3.5
116			R, 100		R, 62		R, 51	70,283	76,366	9	57,103	38.1	17.5	13.6	89.4	3.3	0.3	0.9	4.2
117			R, 89		R, 68		R, 67	69,729	76,840	10	51,421	38.8	17.4	13.9	84.1	3.5	0.2	0.9	8.6
118			D, 53		D, 100		D, 69	63,926	67,700	6	45,569	31.8	12.1	19.0	95.5	1.3	0.3	0.3	1.7
119			D, 55		D, 52		D, 59	64,377	69,399	8	45,393	34.2	14.7	19.5	85.5	1.8	10.9	0.5	1.9
120			R, 100		R, 100		R, 100	63,979	69,199	8	43,153	30.2	10.4	21.2	94.5	1.2	1.2	0.4	1.7

*After 2000, NC went from 98 districts to 120 districts due to redistricting.

Note: D=Democrat, R=Republican, R/D=Republican/Democrat (cross-filed), D/R=Democrat/Republican (cross-filed), I=Independent, C=Constitution, O=Other, GI=Green Independent, P=Progressive, P/D=Progressive/Democrat, P/D/R=Progressive/Democrat/Republican, HH=Households

NORTH DAKOTA

North Dakota was founded and settled by optimists. It took optimism to come here at all, to look across the lonely plains and imagine something grander. The first white explorers to cross it were Lewis and Clark, who spent the winter of 1804–1805 near Mandan before continuing on in search of a water route across the continent. Theodore Roosevelt fancied himself a cowboy and built a ranch in the Bad Lands before blizzard and drought drove him out. In *The American Commonwealth,* Lord Bryce describes attending a ceremony laying the cornerstone for the old territorial capitol in Bismarck in 1883. The lot was a mile or so outside of town and he asked whether a park was planned around it. No, he was told; this is where the center of city is destined to be someday. When a later generation built a bigger capitol, they put up a skyscraper.

Optimism also infected the Nonpartisan League, which dominated North Dakota politics from 1915 to 1922. The League was built by the generation of northern European farmers who had been conned into moving to North Dakota in the first place by railroad speculators (Bismarck was given its name to help sell the place to Germans). They advocated socialism, whipped up a frenzy of enthusiasm for cooperative agriculture, and railed against the Minnesota mill owners. "Albeit Bismarck is the capital where the Governor resides and the legislature convenes," one North Dakota radical wrote at the time, "the actual seat of the State government always has been in St. Paul and Minneapolis, homes of the overlords who played with its destinies." When World War I came, many North Dakotans sided with the Kaiser and their plans for state-owned grain elevators and mills collapsed along with wheat prices after the war ended. Governor Lynn Frazier, a League member, was recalled in 1921, the only American governor to be recalled until California's Gray Davis in 2003.

Economic radicalism came back into fashion during the 1930s and so did the Nonpartisan League, in the person of "Wild Bill" Langer. Langer started his education at the University of North Dakota and finished it at Columbia, passing up job offers from Manhattan law firms to return home and enter politics. He was elected governor in 1932 and during the worst months of the Depression he declared a state moratorium on foreclosures for debt, called out the National Guard to stop sheriff sales of farm property, and used state troopers to protect strikes rather than break them. The state supreme court ordered him removed from office after he was convicted of fraud in 1934 but Langer later got his conviction reversed, was reelected governor in 1936, and went on to serve in the U.S. Senate for nineteen years as one of the country's leading isolationists.

Although its politics have become tamer, North Dakota's commercial outline would still be familiar to an earlier generation. The western part of the state is better suited to grazing; the eastern part is where much of the country's durum (pasta) wheat is grown. It remains a state of small farmers and ranchers. Fargo and Grand Forks, the only cities of any size (though neither has more than 100,000 residents), hug Interstate 29 and the Red River on the state's eastern border, as if people were too intimidated by the vast, flat land behind them to venture any further.

North Dakota is the only state in the Union to have lost population in this decade, but the trend has been downward for much longer. Periodic farm crises during the past seventy-five years have thrown ever more people off the land. Michael Barone wrote that the counties containing Fargo, Grand Forks, Minot, and Bismarck grew in population from 134,000 in 1930 to 317,000 in 2000, while the population of the remaining forty-nine counties fell from 546,000 to 325,000. Much of North Dakota, in other words, is emptier today than at any time since the Native Americans roamed there. Some have proposed shortening the state's name to "Dakota" to evoke more of an image of the Wild West and less of cold, snowy plains.

Fargo, which has a thriving partnership with its sister city, Moorhead, Minnesota, across the Red River, is the only place in the state to have grown at all this decade. Several rural districts, many along the Canadian border, have lost as much as 10 percent of their populations. The cities are also the only places of real wealth, though even that is modest by national standards. Average household income is $73,000 in Fargo's 41st house district, where large homes can be bought for less than $150,000.

Native Americans, mostly Sioux, make up about 5 percent of the state's population, and are the only large minority group. Unemployment on the reservations still runs as high as 65 percent, but ironically income is rising there thanks to gambling. Casinos at the Turtle Mountain, Standing Rock, and Fort Berthold reservations are now among the state's biggest private employers.

The spirit of the old Nonpartisan League is still strong enough that North Dakota's two U.S. senators and lone representative are Democrats. (The Nonpartisan League, though historically a wild offshoot of the GOP, eventually merged with the Democrats). Republicans, however, have captured the governorship and hold both houses of the legislative assembly by comfortable margins. The state is divided into legislative districts, each of which elects one senator and two representatives. A constitution amendment reduced the number of districts from forty-nine to forty-seven in 2002.

NORTH DAKOTA
State Legislative Districts

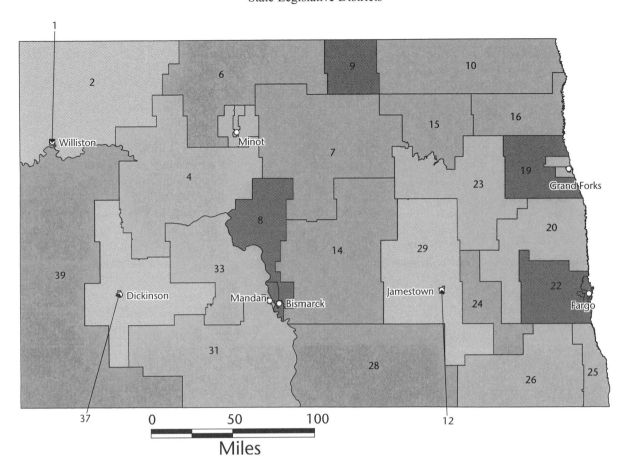

MINOT

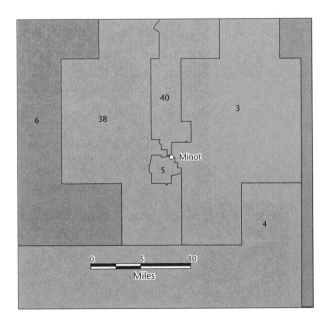

GRAND FORKS

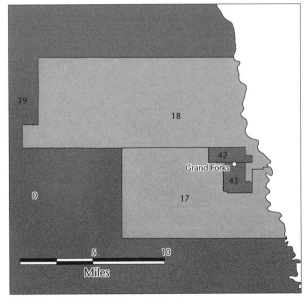

Population Growth   ▓ -17% to -12%   ▓ -12% to -5%   ▓ -5% to 76%   ▓ 76% to 81%

FARGO

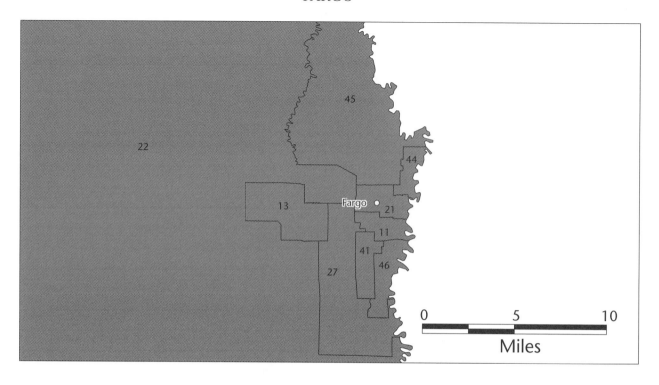

BISMARCK

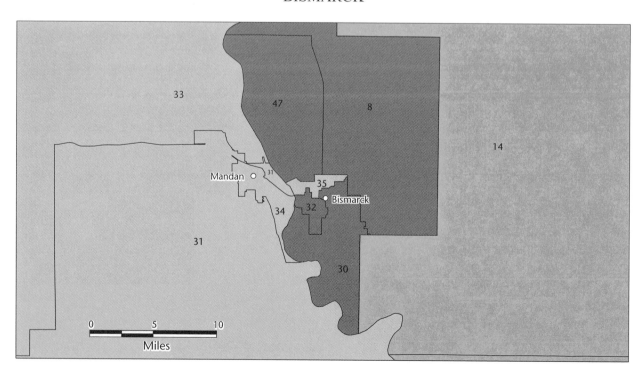

Population Growth   ▢ -17% to -12%   ▢ -12% to -5%   ▢ -5% to 76%   ▢ 76% to 81%

North Dakota Legislative Districts—Election and Demographic Data

Senate Districts	General Election Results Party, Percent of Vote							Population			Avg. HH Income	Pop 25+ Some College +	Pop 25+ 4-Yr Degree +	Below Poverty Line	White (Non-Hisp)	African American	American Indians, Alaska Natives	Asians, Hawaiians, Pacific Islanders	Hispanic Origin
															2006				
N. Dakota	2000	2001	2002	2003	2004	2005	2006	2000	2006	% Change	($)	(%)	(%)	(%)	(%)	(%)	(%)	(%)	(%)
1			R, 66				R, 59	13,096	11,758	-10	43,458	36.8	13.0	18.3	91.5	0.3	4.4	0.4	1.7
2	R, 55				R, 56			13,175	23,775	80	42,334	35.7	11.7	20.1	92.5	0.2	4.3	0.3	1.2
3			R, 59				D, 55	13,675	12,184	-11	42,587	35.5	12.6	18.9	90.9	0.8	4.4	0.5	2.0
4	D, 54				D, 58			13,049	11,993	-8	39,049	32.2	10.4	24.1	62.5	0.1	32.7	0.4	2.9
5			D, 52				D, 56	13,099	11,601	-11	50,551	42.7	19.8	15.4	92.1	1.1	2.8	0.9	1.9
6	D, 62				D, 62			13,057	11,378	-13	42,398	35.9	10.7	19.5	96.1	0.2	1.7	0.3	0.8
7			D, 56				D, 66	14,186	12,401	-13	39,291	32.7	10.5	23.3	96.7	0.2	1.5	0.2	0.9
8	R, 58				R, 60			14,209	14,056	-1	51,327	39.1	13.6	13.0	96.1	0.1	2.2	0.2	0.6
9			D, 100				D, 54	13,674	13,104	-4	35,874	29.0	9.4	32.1	26.1	0.1	71.4	0.1	1.0
10	R, 46				R, 59			13,661	11,670	-15	46,506	35.4	11.7	17.3	92.7	0.2	2.2	0.3	3.0
11			D, 63				D, 68	14,199	13,553	-5	53,123	48.9	23.5	11.3	92.0	1.2	2.0	1.2	1.9
12	D, 50				R, 52			13,059	11,410	-13	41,831	36.6	17.6	18.4	94.2	0.4	2.2	0.7	1.6
13			R, 72				R, 63	13,069	13,729	5	54,119	44.0	16.3	10.4	93.7	0.5	1.9	0.4	1.9
14	R, 70				R, 69			12,987	11,285	-13	44,147	32.3	10.7	21.9	96.8	0.2	1.5	0.3	0.8
15			R, 56				R, 55	13,749	11,929	-13	47,303	38.1	13.5	17.3	91.3	0.3	5.9	0.4	0.8
16	D, 52				D, 53			13,243	11,385	-14	44,176	32.6	10.5	16.8	88.0	0.4	1.8	0.3	7.1
17			R, 58				R, 61	13,086	11,653	-11	62,862	49.8	25.7	11.4	94.0	0.5	2.0	0.8	1.8
18	D, 56				D, 54			14,221	12,861	-10	41,396	40.2	14.5	16.7	86.9	2.3	3.5	0.8	4.3
19			R, 59				D, 50	13,093	12,461	-5	50,486	41.7	14.7	11.4	90.8	1.7	1.3	1.1	3.1
20	D, 56				D, 100			13,126	11,911	-9	49,730	40.0	14.9	14.4	95.1	0.1	1.5	0.3	2.0
21			D, 58				D, 64	13,194	12,875	-2	33,076	42.1	17.5	23.9	86.6	1.8	4.5	2.2	2.6
22	R, 62		R, 60		R, 62			13,655	14,028	3	60,725	44.0	16.0	9.9	96.8	0.2	0.8	0.4	1.1
23			D, 55				D, 62	13,957	12,398	-11	39,619	30.7	10.0	23.2	69.7	0.1	27.9	0.2	1.8
24	D, 100				D, 100			14,119	12,377	-12	43,952	36.6	15.6	18.4	96.0	0.4	1.3	0.4	0.9
25			R, 52				D, 54	14,096	12,756	-10	46,948	38.1	11.1	17.6	94.2	0.5	2.8	0.4	1.3
26	D, 51		D, 61		D, 100			14,775	13,266	-10	46,976	31.1	9.1	17.0	96.2	0.1	1.2	0.3	1.3
27			R, 55				D, 56	13,543	14,819	9	47,253	44.7	19.9	12.3	92.7	0.7	1.9	1.4	1.7
28	R, 63				R, 69			14,099	11,790	-16	39,626	30.8	11.3	25.7	96.7	0.1	1.0	0.3	1.2
29			D, 51				R, 54	13,941	24,542	76	46,003	33.6	14.3	17.2	95.8	0.3	1.6	0.5	1.1
30	R, 60				R, 71			15,315	15,344	0	59,037	43.5	19.1	12.5	90.6	0.4	6.5	0.3	1.2
31			D, 52				D, 56	14,725	13,694	-7	45,108	31.3	10.5	25.2	70.8	0.1	27.1	0.2	1.3
32	R, 51				R, 58			14,415	14,253	-1	51,882	43.5	18.9	16.1	90.8	0.3	6.5	0.5	1.1
33			R, 62				R, 57	14,397	13,207	-8	53,727	34.5	10.6	16.0	95.8	0.1	1.9	0.4	0.7
34	R, 66				R, 64			13,351	12,479	-7	43,622	36.1	13.5	17.6	93.0	0.3	4.0	0.5	1.1
35			R, 63				D, 50	14,285	12,723	-11	52,927	50.7	25.8	13.4	94.7	0.3	2.8	0.7	0.8
36	R, 65				R, 56			14,203	25,475	79	42,875	36.1	15.4	21.1	95.4	0.2	1.8	0.4	1.2
37			R, 71				R, 66	12,923	11,750	-9	43,239	40.6	18.8	19.7	94.8	0.3	2.3	0.3	1.2
38	R, 62				R, 63			12,966	11,653	-10	51,713	38.9	16.8	12.3	88.1	3.2	1.7	1.2	3.6
39			R, 100				R, 100	14,494	12,584	-13	43,257	35.3	12.7	19.7	96.3	0.2	1.6	0.2	0.8
40	R, 63				R, 68			13,237	11,899	-10	44,203	40.2	14.1	14.8	84.1	3.8	3.6	1.9	4.3
41			R, 70				R, 100	13,663	14,493	6	72,827	53.3	29.1	7.8	94.1	0.7	1.3	1.8	1.2
42	D, 52				R, 50			13,199	12,734	-4	35,616	36.4	18.7	23.6	85.6	1.1	6.4	1.8	3.2
43			R, 53				D, 52	13,204	12,696	-4	53,101	45.2	21.3	17.3	91.8	0.8	2.6	1.5	2.0
44	R, 54				R, 57			12,637	12,042	-5	53,139	51.7	27.4	13.2	94.2	0.4	1.6	1.3	1.3
45			R, 51				D, 53	14,069	14,628	4	52,595	41.0	22.1	16.0	90.9	0.7	1.8	3.7	1.6
46	R, 61				R, 64			13,077	12,753	-2	68,976	52.8	29.7	10.7	93.2	1.1	1.5	1.2	1.5
47			R, 63				R, 68	13,988	14,318	2	63,999	52.5	28.4	10.2	94.6	0.3	2.2	1.0	0.9
48*	R, 57																		

Note: D=Democrat, R=Republican, R/D=Republican/Democrat (cross-filed), D/R=Democrat/Republican (cross-filed), I=Independent, C=Constitution, O=Other, GI=Green Independent, P=Progressive, P/D=Progressive/Democrat, P/D/R=Progressive/Democrat/Republican, HH=Households

North Dakota Legislative Districts—Election and Demographic Data

House Districts	General Election Results Party, Percent of Vote							Population			Avg. HH Income	Pop 25+		Below Poverty Line	White (Non-Hisp)	African American	American Indians, Alaska Natives	Asians, Hawaiians, Pacific Islanders	Hispanic Origin
												Some College +	4-Yr Degree +						
N. Dakota	2000	2001	2002	2003	2004	2005	2006	2000	2006	% Change	($)	(%)	(%)	(%)	(%)	(%)	(%)	(%)	(%)
1			R, 30				R, 38	13,096	11,758	-10	43,458	36.8	13.0	18.3	91.5	0.3	4.4	0.4	1.7
1			R, 28				R, 37	13,096	11,758	-10	43,458	36.8	13.0	18.3	91.5	0.3	4.4	0.4	1.7
2	R, 26				R, 27			13,175	23,775	80	42,334	35.7	11.7	20.1	92.5	0.2	4.3	0.3	1.2
2	D, 25				D, 26			13,175	23,775	80	42,334	35.7	11.7	20.1	92.5	0.2	4.3	0.3	1.2
3			R, 29		D, 50		D, 28	13,675	12,184	-11	42,587	35.5	12.6	18.9	90.9	0.8	4.4	0.5	2.0
3			R, 27				D, 27	13,675	12,184	-11	42,587	35.5	12.6	18.9	90.9	0.8	4.4	0.5	2.0
4	D, 29				R, 34			13,049	11,993	-8	39,049	32.2	10.4	24.1	62.5	0.1	32.7	0.4	2.9
4	D, 27				D, 34			13,049	11,993	-8	39,049	32.2	10.4	24.1	62.5	0.1	32.7	0.4	2.9
5			R, 27				D, 29	13,099	11,601	-11	50,551	42.7	19.8	15.4	92.1	1.1	2.8	0.9	1.9
5			D, 27				D, 26	13,099	11,601	-11	50,551	42.7	19.8	15.4	92.1	1.1	2.8	0.9	1.9
6	R, 28				D, 31			13,057	11,378	-13	42,398	35.9	10.7	19.5	96.1	0.2	1.7	0.3	0.8
6	D, 27				R, 30			13,057	11,378	-13	42,398	35.9	10.7	19.5	96.1	0.2	1.7	0.3	0.8
7			R, 27				D, 28	14,186	12,401	-13	39,291	32.7	10.5	23.3	96.7	0.2	1.5	0.2	0.9
7			D, 26				R, 26	14,186	12,401	-13	39,291	32.7	10.5	23.3	96.7	0.2	1.5	0.2	0.9
8	R, 32				R, 32			14,209	14,056	-1	51,327	39.1	13.6	13.0	96.1	0.1	2.2	0.2	0.6
8	R, 27				R, 29			14,209	14,056	-1	51,327	39.1	13.6	13.0	96.1	0.1	2.2	0.2	0.6
9			D, 58				D, 58	13,674	13,104	-4	35,874	29.0	9.4	32.1	26.1	0.1	71.4	0.1	1.0
9			D, 42				D, 42	13,674	13,104	-4	35,874	29.0	9.4	32.1	26.1	0.1	71.4	0.1	1.0
10	R, 26				R, 29			13,661	11,670	-15	46,506	35.4	11.7	17.3	92.7	0.2	2.2	0.3	3.0
10	R, 25				R, 28			13,661	11,670	-15	46,506	35.4	11.7	17.3	92.7	0.2	2.2	0.3	3.0
11			D, 28				D, 32	14,199	13,553	-5	53,123	48.9	23.5	11.3	92.0	1.2	2.0	1.2	1.9
11			D, 27				D, 31	14,199	13,553	-5	53,123	48.9	23.5	11.3	92.0	1.2	2.0	1.2	1.9
12	D, 33				D, 29			13,059	11,410	-13	41,831	36.6	17.6	18.4	94.2	0.4	2.2	0.7	1.6
12	R, 29				D, 27			13,059	11,410	-13	41,831	36.6	17.6	18.4	94.2	0.4	2.2	0.7	1.6
13			R, 35				R, 29	13,069	13,729	5	54,119	44.0	16.3	10.4	93.7	0.5	1.9	0.4	1.9
13			R, 32				R, 27	13,069	13,729	5	54,119	44.0	16.3	10.4	93.7	0.5	1.9	0.4	1.9
14	R, 30				R, 29			12,987	11,285	-13	44,147	32.3	10.7	21.9	96.8	0.2	1.5	0.3	0.8
14	R, 29				R, 27			12,987	11,285	-13	44,147	32.3	10.7	21.9	96.8	0.2	1.5	0.3	0.8
15			R, 31				R, 28	13,749	11,929	-13	47,303	38.1	13.5	17.3	91.3	0.3	5.9	0.4	0.8
15			R, 28				R, 27	13,749	11,929	-13	47,303	38.1	13.5	17.3	91.3	0.3	5.9	0.4	0.8
16	R, 30				R, 37			13,243	11,385	-14	44,176	32.6	10.5	16.8	88.0	0.4	1.8	0.3	7.1
16	R, 28				R, 35			13,243	11,385	-14	44,176	32.6	10.5	16.8	88.0	0.4	1.8	0.3	7.1
17			R, 29				D, 28	13,086	11,653	-11	62,862	49.8	25.7	11.4	94.0	0.5	2.0	0.8	1.8
17			D, 25				R, 26	13,086	11,653	-11	62,862	49.8	25.7	11.4	94.0	0.5	2.0	0.8	1.8
18	D, 34				D, 39			14,221	12,861	-10	41,396	40.2	14.5	16.7	86.9	2.3	3.5	0.8	4.3
18	D, 34				R, 31			14,221	12,861	-10	41,396	40.2	14.5	16.7	86.9	2.3	3.5	0.8	4.3
19			R, 32				D, 30	13,093	12,461	-5	50,486	41.7	14.7	11.4	90.8	1.7	1.3	1.1	3.1
19			R, 30				R, 26	13,093	12,461	-5	50,486	41.7	14.7	11.4	90.8	1.7	1.3	1.1	3.1
20	D, 30				D, 51			13,126	11,911	-9	49,730	40.0	14.9	14.4	95.1	0.1	1.5	0.3	2.0
20	D, 26				D, 49			13,126	11,911	-9	49,730	40.0	14.9	14.4	95.1	0.1	1.5	0.3	2.0
21			D, 29				D, 31	13,194	12,875	-2	33,076	42.1	17.5	23.9	86.6	1.8	4.5	2.2	2.6
21			D, 25				D, 29	13,194	12,875	-2	33,076	42.1	17.5	23.9	86.6	1.8	4.5	2.2	2.6
22	R, 29				R, 32			13,655	14,028	3	60,725	44.0	16.0	9.9	96.8	0.2	0.8	0.4	1.1
22	R, 27				R, 29			13,655	14,028	3	60,725	44.0	16.0	9.9	96.8	0.2	0.8	0.4	1.1
23			R, 28		R, 51		R, 27	13,957	12,398	-11	39,619	30.7	10.0	23.2	69.7	0.1	27.9	0.2	1.8
23			R, 28				D, 25	13,957	12,398	-11	39,619	30.7	10.0	23.2	69.7	0.1	27.9	0.2	1.8
24	D, 28				D, 30			14,119	12,377	-12	43,952	36.6	15.6	18.4	96.0	0.4	1.3	0.4	0.9
24	D, 27				D, 30			14,119	12,377	-12	43,952	36.6	15.6	18.4	96.0	0.4	1.3	0.4	0.9
25			D, 30		R, 58		R, 38	14,096	12,756	-10	46,948	38.1	11.1	17.6	94.2	0.5	2.8	0.4	1.3
25			D, 28				D, 38	14,096	12,756	-10	46,948	38.1	11.1	17.6	94.2	0.5	2.8	0.4	1.3

(continued)

Note: D=Democrat, R=Republican, R/D=Republican/Democrat (cross-filed), D/R=Democrat/Republican (cross-filed), I=Independent, C=Constitution, O=Other, GI=Green Independent, P=Progressive, P/D=Progressive/Democrat, P/D/R=Progressive/Democrat/Republican, HH=Households

North Dakota Legislative Districts—Election and Demographic Data (cont.)

House Districts	General Election Results Party, Percent of Vote							Population			Avg. HH Income	Pop 25+		Below Poverty Line	2006 White (Non-Hisp)	African American	American Indians, Alaska Natives	Asians, Hawaiians, Pacific Islanders	Hispanic Origin
N. Dakota	2000	2001	2002	2003	2004	2005	2006	2000	2006	% Change	($)	Some College + (%)	4-Yr Degree + (%)	(%)	(%)	(%)	(%)	(%)	(%)
26	D, 28		D, 54		D, 53			14,775	13,266	-10	46,976	31.1	9.1	17.0	96.2	0.1	1.2	0.3	1.3
26	R, 25				D, 47			14,775	13,266	-10	46,976	31.1	9.1	17.0	96.2	0.1	1.2	0.3	1.3
27			R, 29				D, 31	13,543	14,819	9	47,253	44.7	19.9	12.3	92.7	0.7	1.9	1.4	1.7
27			R, 27				R, 27	13,543	14,819	9	47,253	44.7	19.9	12.3	92.7	0.7	1.9	1.4	1.7
28	R, 31				R, 32			14,099	11,790	-16	39,626	30.8	11.3	25.7	96.7	0.1	1.0	0.3	1.2
28	R, 27				R, 31			14,099	11,790	-16	39,626	30.8	11.3	25.7	96.7	0.1	1.0	0.3	1.2
29			R, 31				R, 29	13,941	24,542	76	46,003	33.6	14.3	17.2	95.8	0.3	1.6	0.5	1.1
29			R, 28				R, 26	13,941	24,542	76	46,003	33.6	14.3	17.2	95.8	0.3	1.6	0.5	1.1
30	R, 31				R, 33			15,315	15,344	0	59,037	43.5	19.1	12.5	90.6	0.4	6.5	0.3	1.2
30	R, 26				R, 31			15,315	15,344	0	59,037	43.5	19.1	12.5	90.6	0.4	6.5	0.3	1.2
31			D, 29				D, 29	14,725	13,694	-7	45,108	31.3	10.5	25.2	70.8	0.1	27.1	0.2	1.3
31			D, 28				D, 28	14,725	13,694	-7	45,108	31.3	10.5	25.2	70.8	0.1	27.1	0.2	1.3
32	R, 27				R, 30			14,415	14,253	-1	51,882	43.5	18.9	16.1	90.8	0.3	6.5	0.5	1.1
32	R, 26				R, 29			14,415	14,253	-1	51,882	43.5	18.9	16.1	90.8	0.3	6.5	0.5	1.1
33			R, 29				R, 30	14,397	13,207	-8	53,727	34.5	10.6	16.0	95.8	0.1	1.9	0.4	0.7
33			R, 28				R, 29	14,397	13,207	-8	53,727	34.5	10.6	16.0	95.8	0.1	1.9	0.4	0.7
34	R, 31				R, 39			13,351	12,479	-7	43,622	36.1	13.5	17.6	93.0	0.3	4.0	0.5	1.1
34	R, 31				R, 39			13,351	12,479	-7	43,622	36.1	13.5	17.6	93.0	0.3	4.0	0.5	1.1
35			R, 29				R, 30	14,285	12,723	-11	52,927	50.7	25.8	13.4	94.7	0.3	2.8	0.7	0.8
35			R, 27				R, 26	14,285	12,723	-11	52,927	50.7	25.8	13.4	94.7	0.3	2.8	0.7	0.8
36	R, 33				D, 26			14,203	25,475	79	42,875	36.1	15.4	21.1	95.4	0.2	1.8	0.4	1.2
36	R, 27				R, 26			14,203	25,475	79	42,875	36.1	15.4	21.1	95.4	0.2	1.8	0.4	1.2
37			R, 32				R, 29	12,923	11,750	-9	43,239	40.6	18.8	19.7	94.8	0.3	2.3	0.3	1.2
37			R, 25				R, 26	12,923	11,750	-9	43,239	40.6	18.8	19.7	94.8	0.3	2.3	0.3	1.2
38	R, 28				R, 32			12,923	11,750	-9	43,239	40.6	18.8	19.7	94.8	0.3	2.3	0.3	1.2
38	R, 27				R, 31			12,923	11,750	-9	43,239	40.6	18.8	19.7	94.8	0.3	2.3	0.3	1.2
39			R, 50				R, 50	14,494	12,584	-13	43,257	35.3	12.7	19.7	96.3	0.2	1.6	0.2	0.8
39			R, 50				R, 50	14,494	12,584	-13	43,257	35.3	12.7	19.7	96.3	0.2	1.6	0.2	0.8
40	R, 32				R, 33			13,237	11,899	-10	44,203	40.2	14.1	14.8	84.1	3.8	3.6	1.9	4.3
40	R, 29				R, 33			13,237	11,899	-10	44,203	40.2	14.1	14.8	84.1	3.8	3.6	1.9	4.3
41			R, 34				R, 52	13,663	14,493	6	72,827	53.3	29.1	7.8	94.1	0.7	1.3	1.8	1.2
41			R, 32				R, 48	13,663	14,493	6	72,827	53.3	29.1	7.8	94.1	0.7	1.3	1.8	1.2
42	R, 30				R, 30			13,199	12,734	-4	35,616	36.4	18.7	23.6	85.6	1.1	6.4	1.8	3.2
42	R, 27				R, 27			13,199	12,734	-4	35,616	36.4	18.7	23.6	85.6	1.1	6.4	1.8	3.2
43			R, 26				D, 30	13,204	12,696	-4	53,101	45.2	21.3	17.3	91.8	0.8	2.6	1.5	2.0
43			D, 25				R, 24	13,204	12,696	-4	53,101	45.2	21.3	17.3	91.8	0.8	2.6	1.5	2.0
44	R, 30				R, 28			12,637	12,042	-5	53,139	51.7	27.4	13.2	94.2	0.4	1.6	1.3	1.3
44	R, 28				R, 28			12,637	12,042	-5	53,139	51.7	27.4	13.2	94.2	0.4	1.6	1.3	1.3
45			R, 31				R, 28	14,069	14,628	4	52,595	41.0	22.1	16.0	90.9	0.7	1.8	3.7	1.6
45			R, 27				D, 26	14,069	14,628	4	52,595	41.0	22.1	16.0	90.9	0.7	1.8	3.7	1.6
46	R, 33				R, 33			13,077	12,753	-2	68,976	52.8	29.7	10.7	93.2	1.1	1.5	1.2	1.5
46	R, 31				R, 31			13,077	12,753	-2	68,976	52.8	29.7	10.7	93.2	1.1	1.5	1.2	1.5
47			R, 55				R, 36	13,988	14,318	2	63,999	52.5	28.4	10.2	94.6	0.3	2.2	1.0	0.9
47			R, 45				R, 34	13,988	14,318	2	63,999	52.5	28.4	10.2	94.6	0.3	2.2	1.0	0.9
48*	D, 29																		
48*	D, 27																		

*A constitutional amendment reduced the number of districts from forty-nine to forty-seven in 2002. District forty-nine did not have any general election results in 2000.

Note: D=Democrat, R=Republican, R/D=Republican/Democrat (cross-filed), D/R=Democrat/Republican (cross-filed), I=Independent, C=Constitution, O=Other, GI=Green Independent, P=Progressive, P/D=Progressive/Democrat, P/D/R=Progressive/Democrat/Republican, HH=Households

OHIO

Ohio, rather than Pennsylvania, might better be called the Keystone State, linking as it does the Eastern seaboard with the Midwest and the border South with the Great Lakes. It can be divided into three broad longitudinal bands, each with its representative big city. In the industrial north, Cleveland, as well as Toledo, Youngstown, and Akron, once formed the heart of the country's industrial strength. In the middle of the state is Columbus, now the state's biggest city and a growing corporate headquarters. In the South, Cincinnati looks across the Ohio River at Kentucky and down toward the Mississippi. The state is, as writer Louis Bromfield once put it, "the farthest west of the east and the farthest north of the south."

Americans today take state boundaries for granted but it is interesting to speculate how the country might have evolved had the same territory been cut up differently. In his book, *The Shaping of America,* D. W. Meinig of Syracuse University posits that if the land lying west of Georgia had been split latitudinally, thus creating two long states running east-west rather than north-south, the character of the states created would nevertheless have been the same as those that became Alabama and Mississippi because the entire area was settled by the same people from the same places. But, Meinig suggests, if the states lying west of Pennsylvania and Virginia had been drawn latitudinally and then cut into quarters, the consequences would have been great. "The resulting states would have been markedly, profoundly different in character from Ohio, Indiana, and Illinois; the southern pair created by such a division would have been two more 'Kentuckys'—heavily dominated by Uplands Southerners, with Cincinnati and the Miami Valley a somewhat greater enclave than Louisville, while the northern pair would have been almost purely Yankee and Midland in cultural character." Given Ohio's importance as a Union bulwark during the Civil War, two more states dominated by southerners might have turned U.S. history in a very different direction indeed.

During the second half of the nineteenth century, Ohio earned the nickname "Mother of Presidents" for a string of mostly unremarkable Republicans born in the state who later became chief executive. Ohio could also lay a good claim to being known as the Mother of Plutocrats, too. John D. Rockefeller of Cleveland saw the possibilities of oil shortly after the first well was struck in Pennsylvania and formed the Standard Oil Company, which became the biggest corporation in the world. Harvey Firestone built an empire of rubber in Akron. On a decidedly more modest scale, New York Yankee owner George Steinbrenner made his original fortune building ships on Lake Erie.

Ohio was the sixth-largest state in 1980 and is now the seventh largest, having been pushed aside by Florida. Population grew by less than 1 percent in the 1980s and again in this decade, in line with most of the rest of the industrial heartland of the country known unflatteringly as the Rust Belt. Although it remains an important state in presidential years, Ohio's political clout has fallen, too. It had twenty-six electoral votes in 1970 but only twenty today, and it is expected to have only sixteen by the year 2030.

With the exception of Columbus, Ohio's major cities have been shrinking; fewer people live in Cleveland and Cincinnati today than lived there in 1900. In fact, the only cities with at least 100,000 residents that are shrinking faster are Ft. Wayne, Indiana; Pittsburgh; and flood-ravaged New Orleans. But Ohio's suburbs have grown, particularly those farther from the city core. The fastest-growing suburbs are two outside Columbus—the 2nd district, in Delaware County (birthplace of President Rutherford B. Hayes), 5th district, in Fairfield County (birthplace of William Tecumseh Sherman)—and one outside Cincinnati—the 67th district, in Warren County (birthplace of Neil Armstrong). The areas losing population fastest are evenly distributed between the lakefront districts of Cleveland and the riverfront districts of Cincinnati.

Ohio's unemployment rate is now above the national average and the second highest (to Michigan) among the industrial states. Income distribution shows an interesting split. Around Cleveland, the wealthier districts are, as one would expect, in the older, closer-in suburbs. Around Columbus, on the other hand, the wealthy districts are in the newly growing suburbs, fitting for a growing city and something one finds around Atlanta, too. One thing all the wealthiest Ohio districts share in common is that they are more than 85 percent white.

Ohio is 85 percent white and 11.5 percent African American; it has fewer blacks and more whites than New York, Michigan, or Illinois, though not Pennsylvania. The percentage of whites is highest in the rural farming counties, but is 90 percent or more in forty-seven of the ninety-nine house districts. There are five black-majority districts in the state house, four of which are in Cuyahoga County, including the old Cleveland neighborhood called Slavic Village, which says much about how the city has changed. Ohio also has a smaller percentage of Hispanics than the other industrial giants, and these are concentrated in the lakeshore sections around Cleveland.

The 2006 elections were hard for Republicans statewide, owing to the almost universal unpopularity of Gov. Bob Taft, whose approval rating at one point sank to 6.5 percent, possibly an all-time American low. They lost the open governor's race and a U.S. Senate race. Republicans, however, still control both houses of the general assembly, as they have for some time. Democrats gained six seats in the state house, though, to give them more seats than they have had in almost a decade. As recently as 1990, they had a majority of twenty-three seats.

OHIO
State Senate Districts

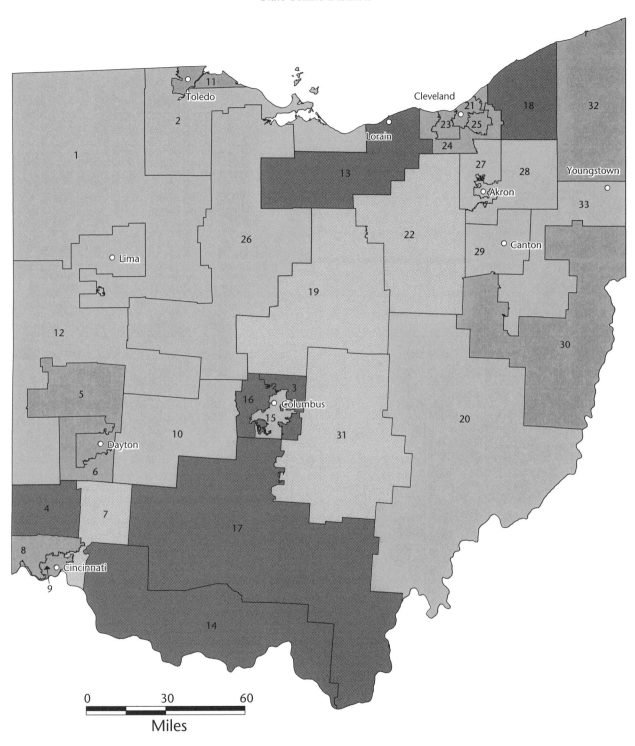

Population Growth ▨ -7% to -1% ▨ -1% to 2% ▨ 2% to 7% ▨ 7% to 17%

Ohio State Senate Districts—Election and Demographic Data

| Senate Districts | General Election Results Party, Percent of Vote | | | | | | | Population | | | Avg. HH Income | Pop 25+ | | 2006 | | | | | |
| | | | | | | | | | | | | Some College + | 4-Yr Degree + | Below Poverty Line | White (Non-Hisp) | African American | American Indians, Alaska Natives | Asians, Hawaiians, Pacific Islanders | Hispanic Origin |
Ohio	2000	2001	2002	2003	2004	2005	2006	2000	2006	% Change	($)	(%)	(%)	(%)	(%)	(%)	(%)	(%)	(%)
1			R, 68				R, 60	354,261	357,211	1	55,500	25.6	9.5	12.0	91.8	1.0	0.1	0.7	4.0
2	R, 100				R, 63			346,854	352,784	2	68,307	36.3	17.7	11.0	89.1	4.2	0.1	1.4	3.2
3			R, 58				R, 54	353,020	364,266	3	71,109	45.0	27.0	8.2	75.8	14.8	0.2	3.7	3.3
4	R, 67				R, 66			332,486	351,607	6	65,699	35.9	17.6	11.2	88.4	5.7	0.1	2.1	2.3
5			D, 52				D, 61	344,106	337,855	-2	49,447	31.7	13.1	19.1	66.4	29.6	0.2	0.9	1.6
6	R, 58				R, 64			331,327	325,673	-2	67,021	45.0	23.9	8.8	89.4	5.1	0.1	2.3	1.6
7			R, 71				R, 62	330,925	367,351	11	87,266	43.3	27.0	8.1	89.3	5.8	0.1	2.2	1.5
8	R, 63				R, 64			341,521	325,872	-5	69,627	39.9	22.8	8.8	79.9	15.4	0.1	2.0	1.4
9			D, 100				D, 72	331,929	309,799	-7	43,104	33.5	18.4	24.1	52.3	42.6	0.1	1.9	1.8
10	R, 64				R, 65			334,571	338,324	1	60,685	33.3	15.4	12.6	87.1	7.9	0.2	1.6	1.5
11			D, 72				D, 100	338,698	328,811	-3	46,421	29.8	11.8	19.8	66.6	22.9	0.2	1.3	6.4
12	R, 77				R, 79			344,653	343,021	0	54,264	24.2	8.4	13.8	92.5	4.7	0.8	0.7	1.3
13			R, 50				D, 63	355,737	369,144	4	61,045	30.6	12.3	12.2	81.7	7.5	0.6	0.7	6.9
14	R, 80				R, 67			354,702	369,467	4	55,319	26.7	10.6	17.0	95.7	1.6	0.2	0.6	0.9
15			D, 73				D, 79	362,926	367,445	1	43,860	32.6	16.5	21.7	57.2	34.4	0.2	2.8	3.2
16	R, 77				R, 58			352,015	361,517	3	71,417	48.1	31.6	9.2	80.3	7.5	0.1	5.8	4.2
17			R, 54				R, 60	343,587	353,641	3	47,404	22.8	7.9	19.2	94.1	3.3	0.2	0.4	0.9
18	R, 58				R, 60			341,907	353,031	3	73,058	38.4	18.4	8.7	93.1	2.2	0.1	1.3	2.0
19	R, 67		R, 68				R, 59	340,837	396,045	16	70,032	33.0	16.6	11.4	91.6	4.6	0.1	1.2	1.3
20	R, 64				R, 54			354,168	355,753	0	45,160	25.0	9.6	20.9	94.5	2.5	0.2	0.8	0.7
21			D, 82				D, 85	339,289	321,985	-5	41,950	32.6	16.1	29.5	38.1	52.7	0.2	2.1	6.8
22	R, 58				R, 100			342,417	369,215	8	63,609	28.5	13.5	10.7	95.9	1.2	0.1	0.8	1.0
23			D, 67				D, 68	334,512	315,398	-6	50,989	36.6	17.3	13.6	77.6	9.7	0.2	2.4	6.9
24	R, 65				R, 62			350,418	339,720	-3	83,995	46.6	27.8	6.8	87.5	6.6	0.0	3.1	1.4
25			D, 85				D, 78	345,678	326,400	-6	56,326	37.8	18.7	16.4	46.4	49.2	0.1	1.7	1.3
26	R, 63				R, 100			341,532	345,156	1	53,248	24.7	8.6	13.3	91.7	2.8	0.1	0.6	2.9
27			R, 53				R, 52	338,561	344,854	2	69,423	40.4	22.0	10.9	88.7	7.0	0.1	1.9	1.1
28	D, 62				D, 65			357,548	360,949	1	54,720	32.3	15.3	15.8	79.8	16.0	0.1	1.5	1.0
29			R, 58				R, 56	337,074	340,373	1	57,206	27.1	12.2	13.4	88.8	7.7	0.2	0.7	1.0
30	D, 100				D, 67			343,253	338,664	-1	45,771	24.3	8.6	18.3	94.5	3.2	0.1	0.4	0.9
31			R, 100				R, 57	355,092	387,144	9	59,175	29.1	12.0	12.6	94.8	2.3	0.2	0.7	0.9
32	D, 51				D, 66			328,816	322,307	-2	51,348	26.0	9.8	15.3	89.6	6.9	0.1	0.6	1.5
33			D, 68				D, 100	343,537	342,685	0	50,087	28.6	13.8	17.6	81.6	13.5	0.1	0.6	2.6

Note: D=Democrat, R=Republican, R/D=Republican/Democrat (cross-filed), D/R=Democrat/Republican (cross-filed), I=Independent, C=Constitution, O=Other, GI=Green Independent, P=Progressive, P/D=Progressive/Democrat, P/D/R=Progressive/Democrat/Republican, HH=Households

OHIO
State House Districts

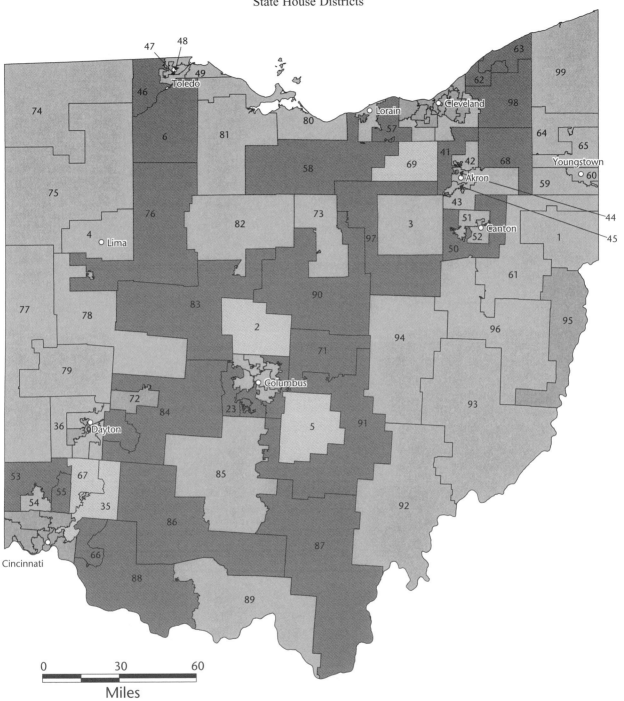

Population Growth | ■ -8% to -4% | ■ -4% to 2% | ■ 2% to 13% | □ 13% to 43%

CLEVELAND

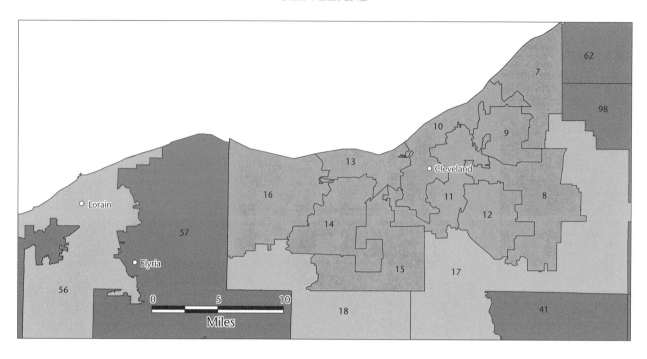

CINCINNATI

Population Growth   ▨ -8% to -4%   ▨ -4% to 2%   ▨ 2% to 13%   ▨ 13% to 43%

COLUMBUS

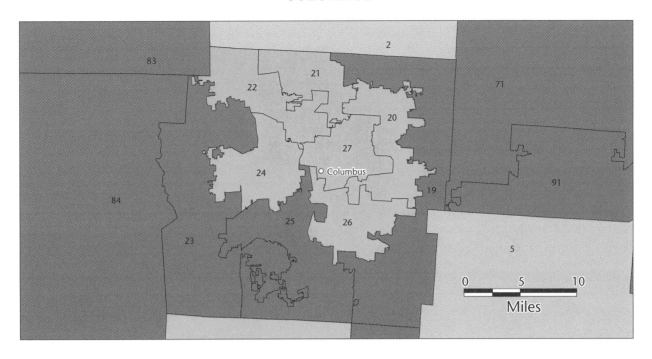

DAYTON

Population Growth   ■ -8% to -4%   ■ -4% to 2%   ■ 2% to 13%   □ 13% to 43%

Ohio State House Districts—Election and Demographic Data

House Districts	General Election Results Party, Percent of Vote							Population			Avg. HH Income	2006 Pop 25+		Below Poverty Line	White (Non-Hisp)	African American	American Indians, Alaska Natives	Asians, Hawaiians, Pacific Islanders	Hispanic Origin
												Some College +	4-Yr Degree +						
Ohio	2000	2001	2002	2003	2004	2005	2006	2000	2006	% Change	($)	(%)	(%)	(%)	(%)	(%)	(%)	(%)	(%)
1	R, 75		R, 57		R, 51		D, 56	111,375	110,057	-1	46,819	23.4	7.9	17.1	95.0	2.5	0.1	0.3	1.3
2	R, 75		R, 73		R, 69		R, 63	112,212	159,435	42	97,576	44.2	27.3	5.9	91.9	2.9	0.1	2.1	1.7
3	D, 60		R, 67		R, 66		R, 100	110,895	112,926	2	55,619	25.4	11.8	12.1	95.2	1.8	0.1	0.9	1.0
4	R, 65		R, 77		R, 100		R, 58	108,237	104,833	-3	50,207	26.7	9.2	17.1	85.1	13.0	2.3	0.7	1.7
5	D, 53		R, 100		R, 100		R, 58	122,521	141,302	15	64,654	33.1	14.3	10.1	93.7	2.8	0.1	1.0	1.2
6	R, 60		R, 68		R, 63		R, 57	120,642	123,789	3	62,604	35.8	17.8	12.9	90.6	1.5	0.2	1.4	4.1
7	R, 61		D, 79		D, 74		D, 80	110,517	103,671	-6	48,664	39.9	19.8	15.3	61.2	33.9	0.1	1.8	1.4
8	D, 87		D, 100		D, 100		D, 100	119,670	114,124	-5	73,880	42.4	24.7	15.6	42.3	52.8	0.1	2.3	1.2
9	D, 74		D, 82		D, 100		D, 84	114,748	108,497	-5	55,938	41.5	24.6	22.2	36.6	57.8	0.1	2.7	1.5
10	D, 83		D, 100		D, 100		D, 84	109,351	103,378	-5	37,467	28.8	12.2	31.1	35.5	47.7	0.3	2.2	15.2
11	D, 82		D, 78		D, 100		D, 100	114,979	109,435	-5	32,358	27.4	11.4	35.2	41.9	52.0	0.1	1.4	4.0
12	D, 100		D, 86		D, 86		D, 89	116,753	109,322	-6	44,996	30.9	11.4	18.6	36.6	60.3	0.1	1.0	1.2
13	D, 100		D, 64		D, 100		D, 77	110,427	103,746	-6	47,829	37.9	20.4	18.2	67.4	12.3	0.3	2.4	12.9
14	D, 86		D, 71		D, 76		D, 77	111,394	104,573	-6	50,448	34.3	14.7	12.9	77.5	11.2	0.2	2.4	5.9
15	R, 58		D, 100		D, 67		D, 75	113,285	107,171	-5	54,585	37.6	16.7	9.6	88.1	5.7	0.1	2.4	2.1
16	R, 61		R, 59		R, 59		D, 51	118,727	112,306	-5	83,655	49.1	30.0	6.9	88.3	5.2	0.1	3.1	1.7
17	D, 71		R, 63		R, 53		R, 67	122,867	118,664	-3	94,008	47.7	29.8	6.7	86.1	8.4	0.0	3.4	1.0
18	D, 56		R, 53		R, 67		R, 59	109,315	108,722	-1	73,223	42.9	23.4	7.0	88.1	6.1	0.1	2.7	1.5
19	D, 68		R, 65		R, 60		R, 55	121,006	132,303	9	73,153	41.9	23.3	7.9	80.4	12.5	0.2	2.5	2.4
20	D, 100		R, 61		R, 56		R, 50	114,966	117,137	2	71,478	45.3	27.8	8.9	75.2	15.8	0.2	3.7	3.1
21	D, 82		R, 55		R, 53		R, 51	117,613	114,931	-2	68,692	48.4	30.5	7.9	71.2	16.5	0.1	5.1	4.5
22	D, 80		R, 67		R, 61		R, 53	120,264	121,735	1	75,051	54.7	38.4	8.1	80.0	6.6	0.1	7.8	3.6
23	R, 100		R, 100		R, 100		R, 56	114,670	120,962	5	69,603	40.8	23.0	7.7	83.9	6.9	0.2	3.2	3.9
24	R, 63		R, 60		R, 56		D, 55	117,331	118,550	1	69,282	48.8	33.5	11.4	77.1	8.9	0.2	6.4	5.2
25	R, 59		D, 55		D, 55		D, 68	122,309	126,606	4	49,589	33.2	17.2	17.1	79.8	12.0	0.2	2.6	3.0
26	R, 58		D, 79		D, 100		D, 82	120,566	118,879	-1	44,575	35.0	17.3	20.2	45.0	47.2	0.2	2.5	3.4
27	R, 52		D, 82		D, 100		D, 87	121,010	122,401	1	36,711	29.7	15.1	28.5	46.0	45.0	0.2	3.3	3.4
28	R, 55		R, 59		R, 53		R, 52	112,384	106,778	-5	77,616	45.1	28.6	9.4	68.7	23.9	0.1	4.0	2.0
29	R, 62		R, 71		R, 56		R, 59	118,343	112,888	-5	61,452	37.4	19.6	9.2	77.6	18.4	0.1	1.2	1.4
30	D, 88		R, 76		R, 73		R, 100	110,871	105,798	-5	69,982	37.6	20.5	7.5	93.8	3.5	0.1	1.0	0.7
31	D, 68		D, 65		D, 69		D, 67	109,383	101,379	-7	40,020	30.3	15.3	22.2	66.2	28.8	0.1	1.7	1.6
32	D, 47		D, 71		D, 100		D, 66	111,834	105,735	-5	42,945	35.3	21.3	28.5	44.9	48.7	0.1	3.1	2.1
33	D, 57		D, 67		D, 74		D, 75	111,607	103,076	-8	46,347	34.7	18.5	21.1	46.3	50.0	0.1	0.9	1.6
34	R, 64		R, 63		R, 60		R, 54	110,565	104,410	-6	86,193	51.3	36.1	9.8	84.7	10.7	0.1	1.9	1.6
35	R, 63		R, 100		R, 73		R, 65	110,518	125,084	13	95,317	43.8	27.9	6.8	90.6	3.9	0.1	2.7	1.7
36	R, 67		R, 60		R, 62		R, 60	110,575	108,249	-2	65,588	40.8	18.9	8.2	89.2	6.3	0.1	1.7	1.4
37	R, 67		R, 64		R, 65		R, 100	112,188	109,693	-2	66,180	45.8	24.7	9.1	90.0	4.6	0.1	2.2	1.6
38	D, 82		R, 64		R, 61		R, 56	108,867	107,559	-1	69,317	48.4	28.0	8.8	89.0	4.5	0.1	3.1	1.8
39	D, 69		D, 77		D, 77		D, 73	111,980	107,130	-4	39,505	31.5	13.2	26.6	49.0	46.5	0.2	0.9	2.1
40	R, 55		D, 72		D, 70		D, 74	117,077	113,047	-3	47,297	35.2	15.3	20.2	53.5	42.3	0.2	0.9	1.6
41	R, 50		R, 58		D, 50		D, 58	114,516	121,095	6	87,855	46.5	27.6	6.8	88.2	7.0	0.1	2.5	1.1
42	R, 61		R, 61		R, 57		R, 51	110,928	112,284	1	77,361	44.7	26.0	9.1	92.7	3.1	0.1	2.1	1.0
43	R, 51		R, 54		R, 58		D, 60	122,401	124,073	1	62,675	34.6	15.9	9.4	95.5	2.0	0.1	0.8	0.6
44	D, 79		D, 100		D, 100		D, 81	116,731	114,484	-2	41,688	30.8	14.6	24.3	49.9	44.0	0.2	2.4	1.7
45	R, 54		D, 70		D, 74		D, 77	113,538	111,403	-2	43,042	29.3	11.8	16.6	85.1	10.9	0.2	1.1	1.1
46	R, 64		R, 70		R, 62		R, 60	115,761	118,357	2	82,675	42.1	23.1	8.5	88.8	4.5	0.1	2.4	2.5
47	D, 73		D, 68		D, 71		D, 74	109,609	106,114	-3	45,196	30.4	12.8	19.0	72.1	12.5	0.2	1.7	9.6
48	R, 56		D, 79		D, 100		D, 82	116,155	112,975	-3	39,874	27.8	11.0	27.7	42.4	49.2	0.2	1.4	5.3
49	D, 100		D, 70		D, 71		D, 70	113,028	109,293	-3	54,040	31.3	11.7	12.6	85.9	5.9	0.2	1.0	4.5
50	D, 65		R, 57		R, 58		R, 58	110,705	114,010	3	59,957	25.5	10.3	10.2	95.9	1.8	0.1	0.4	0.8

(continued)

Note: D=Democrat, R=Republican, R/D=Republican/Democrat (cross-filed), D/R=Democrat/Republican (cross-filed), I=Independent, C=Constitution, O=Other, GI=Green Independent, P=Progressive, P/D=Progressive/Democrat, P/D/R=Progressive/Democrat/Republican, HH=Households

Ohio State House Districts—Election and Demographic Data (cont.)

House Districts	General Election Results Party, Percent of Vote							Population			Avg. HH Income ($)	Pop 25+		Below Poverty Line (%)	White (Non-Hisp) (%)	African American (%)	American Indians, Alaska Natives (%)	Asians, Hawaiians, Pacific Islanders (%)	Hispanic Origin (%)
												Some College + (%)	4-Yr Degree + (%)				2006		
Ohio	2000	2001	2002	2003	2004	2005	2006	2000	2006	% Change	($)	(%)	(%)	(%)	(%)	(%)	(%)	(%)	(%)
51	R, 66		R, 70		R, 100		R, 63	118,039	119,511	1	65,697	33.2	17.3	10.4	91.4	5.0	0.1	1.3	1.0
52	D, 56		D, 65		D, 71		D, 75	109,038	107,064	-2	45,030	22.0	8.5	19.8	78.5	17.0	0.3	0.4	1.2
53	D, 61		R, 64		R, 66		R, 57	111,192	118,867	7	62,984	31.1	14.2	12.7	93.5	2.9	0.1	1.1	1.3
54	D, 58		R, 72		R, 100		R, 57	109,833	110,550	1	57,357	34.3	15.2	12.2	86.4	7.0	0.1	1.5	3.2
55	R, 65		R, 100		D, 70		R, 100	111,962	122,205	9	76,550	42.1	23.2	8.6	85.2	7.2	0.1	3.5	2.5
56	R, 49		D, 71		D, 74		D, 100	115,439	117,027	1	50,972	27.6	10.0	17.7	62.8	15.3	0.3	0.8	15.8
57	D, 52		R, 55		R, 47		D, 56	120,792	127,552	6	72,252	37.4	17.0	8.2	89.7	4.8	0.1	1.1	2.4
58	R, 67		R, 58		R, 54		D, 51	120,016	124,541	4	58,979	26.4	9.7	10.8	91.4	3.0	0.1	0.4	3.3
59	R, 69		D, 58		D, 62		D, 72	114,048	111,989	-2	62,420	39.4	22.1	10.4	93.5	2.9	0.1	0.9	1.6
60	R, 61		D, 80		D, 82		D, 100	112,322	111,362	-1	37,892	24.5	10.3	26.8	56.9	35.4	0.2	0.4	5.5
61	D, 100		D, 61		D, 66		D, 57	117,921	119,575	1	49,060	22.4	9.3	16.1	94.4	3.2	0.1	0.4	0.8
62	R, 52		R, 63		D, 53		D, 65	113,199	115,798	2	66,077	38.4	16.7	8.6	94.8	1.7	0.1	1.5	1.1
63	R, 48		R, 62		D, 50		R, 52	114,624	118,224	3	63,395	35.1	14.6	9.3	90.1	2.8	0.1	1.0	4.2
64	D, 90		D, 54		R, 54		D, 55	107,245	103,648	-3	53,009	25.8	9.8	15.5	83.4	13.7	0.1	0.7	0.9
65	D, 61		D, 70		D, 71		D, 79	112,694	109,192	-3	53,071	28.8	11.5	14.4	93.5	3.9	0.1	0.6	0.9
66	D, 60		R, 100		R, 100		R, 64	118,981	128,690	8	69,322	34.3	16.6	9.9	95.1	1.3	0.1	1.2	1.3
67	D, 67		R, 100		R, 100		R, 62	110,305	137,819	25	80,138	36.8	19.2	7.7	91.7	3.9	0.1	1.9	1.4
68	R, 59		D, 56		D, 64		D, 65	118,818	122,261	3	59,740	31.3	15.4	13.6	92.3	4.1	0.1	1.4	0.8
69	R, 52		R, 60		R, 55		R, 55	113,992	128,951	13	77,837	36.3	17.6	7.0	95.3	1.3	0.1	1.0	1.3
70	R, 54		R, 72		R, 69		R, 60	111,769	115,937	4	64,317	39.2	20.6	12.1	85.3	7.9	0.2	3.2	1.7
71	R, 70		R, 100		R, 58		R, 62	110,585	117,480	6	58,205	29.8	13.3	12.8	93.9	2.7	0.2	0.9	0.9
72	R, 58		R, 57		R, 60		R, 53	108,435	101,655	-6	51,088	28.0	10.2	15.9	82.7	12.4	0.2	0.8	1.9
73	D, 53		D, 64		D, 100		D, 63	111,779	110,477	-1	48,728	24.5	8.1	16.4	85.4	11.3	0.1	0.6	1.1
74	R, 66		R, 100		R, 100		R, 55	119,711	119,351	0	55,640	25.7	8.8	11.1	89.4	1.1	0.2	0.6	5.8
75	R, 59		R, 100		R, 69		R, 56	115,297	113,572	-1	54,661	22.9	7.6	11.7	92.4	0.7	0.1	0.3	3.9
76	R, 62		R, 69		R, 68		R, 60	119,789	124,290	4	56,137	27.9	12.0	13.0	93.6	1.1	0.1	1.2	2.4
77	R, 63		R, 75		R, 70		R, 65	119,788	120,171	0	54,166	22.2	7.5	13.2	97.0	0.4	0.1	0.4	1.2
78	R, 53		D, 58		D, 100		R, 52	117,105	117,999	1	58,015	24.2	8.6	11.4	95.3	1.6	0.1	0.8	1.0
79	D, 58		R, 69		R, 66		R, 61	115,779	117,889	2	60,713	28.7	11.0	10.9	94.8	1.9	0.1	0.9	1.1
80	R, 60		D, 57		D, 100		D, 63	111,478	111,183	0	59,690	30.6	11.9	11.7	87.8	6.8	0.1	0.5	2.9
81	R, 60		R, 54		R, 59		R, 60	118,921	117,401	-1	52,471	26.2	8.9	12.9	87.6	2.5	0.1	0.5	6.2
82	R, 63		R, 67		R, 62		R, 100	110,067	107,275	-3	47,594	22.5	7.2	15.4	94.0	2.8	0.1	0.6	1.3
83	R, 85		R, 70		R, 73		R, 64	113,066	120,491	7	59,461	25.4	9.6	11.5	93.8	3.1	0.1	0.7	1.0
84	R, 64		R, 63		R, 66		R, 61	114,884	120,755	5	65,896	32.1	14.8	9.9	92.6	4.2	0.2	0.8	1.0
85	D, 50		R, 54		R, 62		R, 51	116,945	117,977	1	51,167	23.9	8.3	16.1	90.9	6.3	0.2	0.5	1.0
86	R, 64		R, 65		R, 61		R, 53	108,398	113,908	5	48,956	23.1	7.9	18.4	95.5	1.8	0.2	0.4	0.9
87	R, 67		R, 56		R, 66		R, 58	118,827	121,840	3	42,528	21.5	7.5	22.7	96.0	1.8	0.2	0.3	0.8
88	R, 100		R, 100		R, 62		R, 100	115,574	123,547	7	55,101	22.2	7.7	15.5	97.4	0.7	0.2	0.2	0.7
89	R, 69		D, 59		D, 67		D, 68	120,486	117,049	-3	40,863	23.0	7.2	25.6	94.6	2.8	0.3	0.3	0.7
90	R, 60		R, 67		R, 63		R, 57	117,182	125,957	7	55,372	26.2	10.6	13.1	96.7	0.9	0.1	0.5	0.8
91	D, 58		R, 67		R, 53		D, 52	122,390	128,178	5	54,113	24.1	8.4	15.2	96.7	1.2	0.2	0.3	0.7
92	D, 100		R, 58		R, 59		R, 51	119,323	119,873	0	41,846	27.6	12.2	26.1	93.6	2.4	0.2	1.4	0.8
93	R, 57		R, 59		D, 52		D, 71	118,499	117,310	-1	45,344	24.3	8.5	19.5	95.9	1.8	0.2	0.5	0.7
94	D, 100		R, 100		R, 100		R, 53	116,817	118,536	1	48,265	23.1	8.2	17.2	94.0	3.5	0.1	0.4	0.7
95	R, 65		D, 60		D, 69		D, 79	112,262	107,075	-5	42,274	25.2	8.4	21.6	92.9	4.9	0.1	0.4	0.6
96	R, 59		D, 62		D, 54		D, 68	119,919	121,326	1	48,132	24.3	9.3	16.2	95.5	2.2	0.1	0.4	0.9
97	R, 70		R, 62		R, 65		R, 60	118,003	127,308	8	56,239	23.4	10.8	13.0	97.2	0.6	0.1	0.5	0.8
98	D, 53		R, 70		R, 65		R, 57	114,537	118,981	4	90,642	41.5	23.9	8.1	94.6	2.2	0.0	1.5	0.8
99	D, 68		D, 66		D, 67		D, 67	109,113	109,205	0	47,859	23.3	7.9	16.2	91.5	3.4	0.1	0.5	2.7

Note: D=Democrat, R=Republican, R/D=Republican/Democrat (cross-filed), D/R=Democrat/Republican (cross-filed), I=Independent, C=Constitution, O=Other, GI=Green Independent, P=Progressive, P/D=Progressive/Democrat, P/D/R=Progressive/Democrat/Republican, HH=Households

OKLAHOMA

Oklahomans, as everyone knows, are called "Sooners" because of the many who jumped the start of the claims period to grab homesteads (and thus got there "sooner" than they were supposed to). The fight song of the University of Oklahoma is titled "Boomer Sooner," and that too is appropriate. As Burton Rascoe wrote in *The Nation* more than sixty years ago, "Oklahoma has been, from the first, a boomer State, even before it was a State—when old Oklahoma Territory was thrown open to settlers. It was peopled by and large by land gamblers instead of home seekers."

Any state with working oil rigs on the grounds of the state capitol will likely exhibit a gambling spirit, one that thrives and fails on the boom and bust cycle of that most speculative industry. The 1980s were a time of bust in the oil business, when Oklahoma grew by just 4 percent. The 1990s were a more prosperous time, not only in oil but in wheat and livestock grazing, two of the state's other leading industries. Growth has slowed again since 2000, notwithstanding the rise in oil prices, making Oklahoma much closer to Kansas in that respect than to Texas.

The growing areas are located around the two largest metropolitan centers, Oklahoma City in the middle of the state (and planned that way) and Tulsa in the northeast. These include districts within the cities and in their suburbs. Rural areas are losing people, especially districts in Ellis County, adjacent to the Texas panhandle, and along the Red River. Median household income here is well below average, comparable to that in Alabama and New Mexico. The only really wealthy district is the 67th, in southeast Tulsa (where the average household income is $99,000); nowhere else is it more than $83,000. There are poor districts, but with the exception of one in "Little Dixie" along the Red River, all are in central Oklahoma City or Tulsa. The district that contains the Osage reservation in the northeast part of the state is neither especially poor, nor does it have an unusually high rate of unemployment.

Nearly 8 percent of Oklahoma residents are Native American, although that does not count many who are not full-blooded. (The state was only 5.3 percent Native American when it was admitted to the Union in 1907.) What is now eastern Oklahoma was originally Indian Territory, where whites were forbidden to enter. Native Americans were also relocated to the western part of the state, known as Oklahoma Territory, but whites were permitted there, too. Native American make up more than one-third of the population in only one state house district—the 86th district, which takes in Adair and Cherokee Counties along the Arkansas line. Surprisingly, the 36th district, home of the large Osage reservation is only 17 percent Native American.

In 2000 76 percent of Oklahomans were white, but a decade earlier the figure was 82 percent. Although African Americans are numerically the largest minority in the state, concentrated overwhelmingly in Oklahoma City and Tulsa, their numbers have not changed much in the past decade. The Hispanic population, on the other hand, has doubled, though it still accounts for only 5 percent.

The Oklahoma legislature has some structural curiosities. Since 1964 the state constitution has fixed the number of senatorial districts at forty-eight. Until recently, however, those districts were not numbered sequentially, although the house districts are. During parts of the 1990s, for example, there were no 25th, 27th, 28th, 30th, 36th, or 53rd senatorial districts. The official explanation was that less-populated districts were sometimes collapsed together, but numbers could disappear from the map and then reappear decades later in a different part of the state. Influential members of the senate could sometimes choose their new district number, rather like selecting a uniform number on a baseball team. The number of state house districts is fixed by a formula set forth in the constitution; there are currently 101. Reversing the national trend, 2006 was an excellent year for Oklahoma Republicans; they retook the state house and forged a 24–24 tie in the senate, which now has co-presidents *pro tempore*.

Oklahoma's capitol building has also changed. When it was built in 1919, plans called for it to have a dome, but the state ran out of money. The capitol had a flat roof for eighty-three years until the dome was finally added in 2002, with a seventeen-foot tall statue of a Native American at the peak.

OKLAHOMA
State Senate Districts

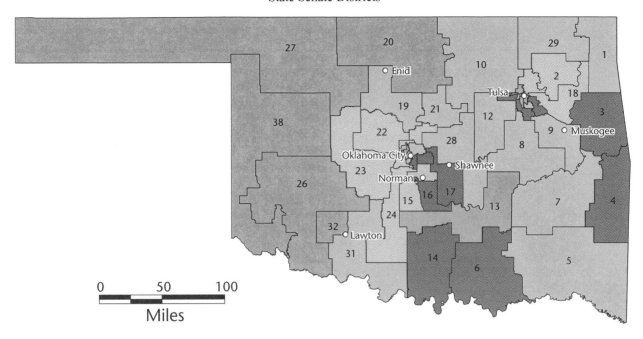

OKLAHOMA CITY

TULSA

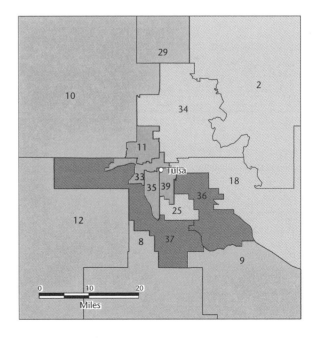

Population Growth   ▒ -6% to 0%   ▢ 0% to 4%   ▓ 4% to 7%   ▢ 7% to 15%

Oklahoma State Senate Districts—Election and Demographic Data

Senate Districts	General Election Results Party, Percent of Vote							Population			Avg. HH Income	Pop 25+		Below Poverty Line	White (Non-Hisp)	African American	American Indians, Alaska Natives	Asians, Hawaiians, Pacific Islanders	Hispanic Origin
															2006				
												Some College +	4-Yr Degree +						
Oklahoma	2000	2001	2002	2003	2004	2005	2006	2000	2006	% Change	($)	(%)	(%)	(%)	(%)	(%)	(%)	(%)	(%)
1				D, 61				72,530	75,178	4	41,595	28.1	9.2	23.0	68.5	0.4	18.9	0.4	3.2
2			D, 77				D, 58	70,719	80,381	14	53,487	32.5	10.8	15.9	74.2	0.7	13.2	0.4	2.9
3								74,307	77,679	5	37,870	26.8	11.8	28.4	51.2	0.8	33.5	0.3	4.7
4			D, 81				D, 78	72,935	76,739	5	39,041	24.6	7.9	25.5	71.8	2.0	12.5	0.3	5.2
5	D, 81							70,788	70,862	0	35,874	23.3	8.0	31.3	68.7	7.5	13.6	0.3	3.1
6			D, 58					70,643	73,790	4	38,981	28.0	11.0	26.9	73.4	1.3	12.1	0.4	5.1
7								70,007	72,077	3	39,875	28.2	9.2	26.8	72.6	2.9	14.3	0.3	2.5
8								72,733	74,328	2	41,209	27.5	9.1	25.5	68.3	6.7	14.3	0.3	2.3
9	D, 68				D, 65			73,195	75,300	3	43,004	29.9	10.9	23.7	61.1	12.0	14.4	0.7	3.8
10			D, 64				D, 58	74,193	76,513	3	46,642	29.1	9.8	19.4	75.4	1.8	12.7	0.4	2.0
11	D, 80				D, 87			70,184	68,558	-2	33,655	27.6	9.5	31.5	30.9	46.1	5.4	0.5	13.6
12							R, 53	72,208	74,156	3	47,065	26.4	8.6	20.5	77.9	3.6	9.0	0.4	2.4
13	D, 75				D, 63			70,741	70,157	-1	39,364	28.0	12.1	24.5	74.2	2.3	13.0	0.5	3.4
14			D, 73					73,123	76,276	4	43,110	27.3	10.5	22.6	75.2	5.4	8.4	0.6	4.2
15	R, 56				R, 57			69,949	77,122	10	66,161	42.9	22.7	13.3	80.3	2.5	4.5	2.5	4.4
16							D, 58	74,181	77,685	5	44,906	37.9	18.7	22.5	75.0	4.2	5.2	3.2	5.9
17	D, 58							71,422	75,665	6	47,210	30.6	11.2	19.2	78.0	2.5	9.8	0.8	2.9
18			D, 70				D, 53	71,573	77,655	8	46,881	29.3	9.9	18.1	68.1	3.9	12.5	1.1	6.1
19	R, 61				R, 68			72,285	73,860	2	47,400	31.6	13.4	17.7	80.8	3.4	2.4	1.4	6.6
20			R, 46					70,795	68,266	-4	45,053	31.8	12.6	19.6	81.7	1.8	6.2	0.6	4.2
21	D, 55				D, 60			72,261	74,776	3	43,377	38.9	22.4	25.6	77.4	7.2	4.3	3.4	2.7
22							R, 69	74,524	83,807	12	62,112	38.1	16.6	12.7	79.4	3.5	4.4	2.1	5.6
23					R, 62			71,430	79,457	11	48,851	29.6	12.0	19.3	73.7	4.1	8.7	2.0	5.8
24			D, 50				R, 51	72,437	77,950	8	52,228	34.5	13.5	14.7	81.8	2.1	4.6	1.3	5.2
25								71,370	78,116	9	82,285	49.7	28.5	6.0	80.9	3.3	3.4	2.8	4.7
26							D, 51	70,271	67,070	-5	40,719	28.0	10.7	24.6	73.4	4.0	7.5	0.4	8.7
27					R, 80			71,796	70,565	-2	47,007	29.9	12.5	18.6	71.3	0.8	1.8	0.5	16.9
28			R, 52					70,527	72,710	3	43,867	27.2	9.2	22.1	76.1	4.2	10.6	0.5	2.7
29					R, 65			72,251	72,968	1	50,712	33.3	14.9	18.6	73.5	2.5	10.9	0.7	3.3
30								72,503	74,004	2	58,916	45.2	24.9	12.4	69.6	9.3	2.8	3.6	8.7
31	D, 64				R, 53			72,223	73,803	2	43,537	29.7	10.9	22.7	69.8	10.2	5.6	1.6	6.6
32					D, 50		D, 63	71,039	68,478	-4	46,192	35.2	13.3	18.7	57.1	18.0	4.8	3.4	9.6
33	D, 54				D, 51			71,217	69,534	-2	51,320	42.6	22.6	16.6	70.0	5.9	6.2	1.4	9.3
34			R, 51				R, 61	72,454	78,148	8	53,812	34.7	13.3	14.0	74.2	3.5	7.3	1.0	6.5
35								71,477	71,196	0	77,971	53.0	33.2	11.0	74.8	7.2	3.4	2.1	7.2
36							R, 65	72,469	76,680	6	55,839	37.7	15.4	11.9	71.3	5.2	5.6	2.9	8.0
37	R, 51				R, 65			74,529	78,926	6	56,274	36.8	16.7	14.7	75.0	4.9	6.6	0.9	5.8
38							R, 64	70,477	66,454	-6	43,461	32.2	13.4	22.1	68.5	4.4	3.5	1.1	13.5
39	R, 69				R, 75			74,730	73,368	-2	53,612	46.5	23.6	12.9	65.8	7.7	3.9	3.1	12.2
40			R, 62				R, 59	72,452	72,232	0	53,350	45.6	24.1	14.2	69.2	8.5	3.1	3.8	9.6
41	R, 77				R, 69			71,366	78,738	10	79,366	47.8	31.5	11.8	80.3	4.7	2.5	3.6	4.1
42			R, 54					71,182	74,694	5	51,761	37.6	15.3	12.4	71.4	10.6	3.7	2.4	5.8
43	R, 52				R, 57			74,073	77,424	5	46,607	34.1	12.3	15.3	64.2	12.5	3.9	3.2	9.4
44								71,777	72,480	1	36,563	24.5	8.5	24.2	45.2	5.5	5.1	2.3	30.9
45	R, 72							71,188	81,284	14	57,083	37.2	13.7	12.6	73.1	4.9	3.8	4.6	7.4
46							D, 70	69,812	70,767	1	35,659	28.5	13.9	30.4	37.3	14.2	4.9	5.2	32.6
47	R, 72				R, 71			70,315	77,815	11	64,986	50.2	30.9	9.0	75.2	9.1	2.3	4.3	4.5
48			D, 75					70,420	71,691	2	45,519	34.7	16.4	24.4	37.2	49.9	2.1	1.7	5.3
49																			
50																			
51*	R, 77																		

*Note: *Districts reduced from 51 districts in 2000, to 48 districts due to redistricting.
Note: D=Democrat, R=Republican, R/D=Republican/Democrat (cross-filed), D/R=Democrat/Republican (cross-filed), I=Independent, C=Constitution, O=Other, GI=Green Independent, P=Progressive, P/D=Progressive/Democrat, P/D/R=Progressive/Democrat/Republican, HH=Households

OKLAHOMA
State House Districts

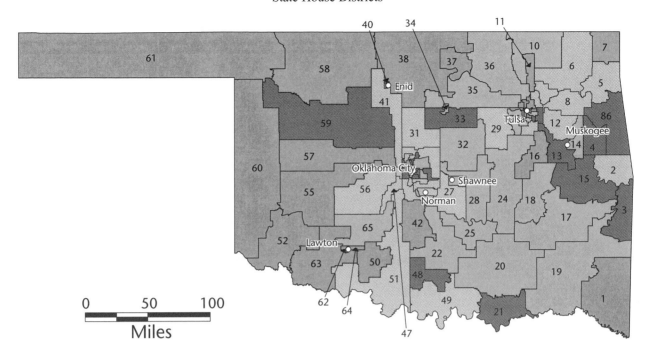

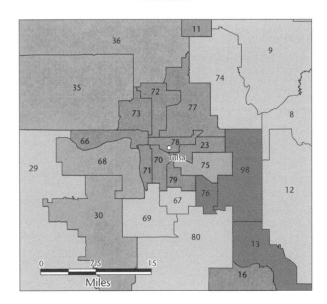

OKLAHOMA CITY

TULSA

Population Growth — -8% to 0% — 0% to 3% — 3% to 7% — 7% to 19%

Oklahoma State House Districts—Election and Demographic Data

House Districts	General Election Results Party, Percent of Vote							Population			Avg. HH Income	2006 Pop 25+ Some College +	2006 Pop 25+ 4-Yr Degree +	2006 Below Poverty Line	2006 White (Non-Hisp)	2006 African American	2006 American Indians, Alaska Natives	2006 Asians, Hawaiians, Pacific Islanders	2006 Hispanic Origin
Oklahoma	2000	2001	2002	2003	2004	2005	2006	2000	2006	% Change	($)	(%)	(%)	(%)	(%)	(%)	(%)	(%)	(%)
1	D, 59		D, 64					34,094	33,529	-2	38,355	23.3	7.9	30.5	67.0	8.7	13.2	0.3	4.0
2	D, 70							34,245	36,884	8	37,492	24.4	7.6	26.8	64.1	1.7	18.8	0.3	3.4
3								33,632	34,648	3	40,860	24.9	8.2	25.0	73.9	2.8	8.5	0.3	7.6
4	D, 65						D, 82	33,840	35,589	5	37,733	31.6	15.9	28.5	51.0	1.2	31.4	0.4	6.5
5			D, 60		R, 56			33,917	36,505	8	43,573	29.7	10.4	22.2	67.6	0.2	21.5	0.3	2.4
6	D, 61		D, 62				D, 61	34,817	38,204	10	46,800	28.2	8.6	19.0	72.5	1.2	13.1	0.3	1.9
7	D, 73							34,703	34,404	-1	39,933	28.5	8.6	23.9	70.1	0.6	15.9	0.5	4.0
8	D, 70				D, 62			34,075	36,952	8	46,185	27.1	9.0	19.9	72.4	0.4	15.9	0.4	2.2
9	R, 59		R, 67		R, 60			33,665	39,048	16	58,244	35.2	11.9	14.3	77.5	1.1	7.2	0.5	3.6
10	D, 70		D, 62		R, 52		R, 54	34,939	35,498	2	41,255	26.6	9.3	22.2	71.1	2.8	12.7	0.3	3.3
11					R, 72			33,581	33,530	0	62,608	42.8	22.5	13.6	80.2	1.5	6.7	1.2	3.6
12	D, 62				D, 51			32,763	38,314	17	50,268	28.4	9.3	17.9	73.2	4.4	11.2	0.4	3.1
13	R, 51		R, 55		D, 52			34,880	36,556	5	45,589	30.2	10.2	23.9	57.2	18.9	12.5	0.8	3.2
14	D, 69				D, 75		R, 54	34,292	34,970	2	44,359	32.0	12.7	21.5	65.5	3.7	16.4	0.7	5.0
15					D, 63		D, 77	34,176	35,291	3	40,015	25.7	8.4	27.9	71.9	1.5	16.1	0.3	2.1
16	D, 71				D, 73			33,108	32,765	-1	39,071	26.4	8.2	26.5	67.1	10.4	12.4	0.3	2.0
17					D, 63			34,061	34,581	2	39,445	27.6	8.8	25.9	74.2	1.0	15.3	0.3	2.0
18	D, 54		D, 62		D, 71			34,670	35,499	2	42,372	30.0	10.6	24.9	71.4	5.4	13.0	0.4	2.9
19	D, 85		D, 81		D, 79			34,180	34,818	2	34,002	24.3	8.5	30.9	70.4	4.9	16.1	0.2	2.1
20	D, 63		D, 66		D, 65		D, 60	34,304	35,028	2	36,177	24.3	9.0	29.8	72.8	3.0	13.7	0.3	2.6
21			D, 75					34,357	36,048	5	39,471	30.0	12.7	26.5	75.5	1.5	11.8	0.6	4.1
22					D, 57			34,922	35,541	2	42,930	26.7	9.2	21.9	75.7	3.7	9.0	0.3	5.1
23	R, 52				R, 62		R, 55	34,892	33,604	-4	48,571	37.5	14.1	15.0	57.1	9.3	5.0	3.3	16.7
24			D, 64					34,882	35,473	2	37,861	24.8	7.5	27.4	68.3	5.6	15.8	0.2	2.5
25	D, 77				D, 73		R, 50	33,857	34,579	2	40,279	31.7	15.2	23.5	72.8	1.9	14.7	0.6	2.9
26	R, 55				R, 69		R, 63	33,963	34,588	2	46,763	30.7	12.6	22.2	76.8	3.5	9.3	1.3	3.6
27	D, 57		D, 49		R, 55		R, 61	33,583	36,720	9	45,515	29.1	8.8	18.2	79.3	1.9	6.7	0.5	3.0
28			D, 65		D, 57		D, 64	34,068	34,284	1	41,360	26.4	8.6	26.2	69.5	6.1	14.8	0.4	2.7
29					R, 64		R, 51	33,848	36,444	8	43,685	25.3	7.9	19.8	80.0	2.3	8.8	0.3	2.1
30	D, 61		D, 64		R, 56		R, 55	35,238	35,518	1	52,104	29.1	10.0	18.8	76.4	3.0	9.1	0.6	3.5
31					R, 68		R, 57	34,485	38,173	11	59,379	34.8	16.0	16.0	83.0	5.4	3.0	0.6	3.2
32	R, 51		D, 52		D, 67		D, 72	33,939	34,381	1	42,168	24.7	8.4	21.0	83.2	2.5	6.7	0.3	2.1
33			D, 58		R, 61		R, 70	36,212	38,298	6	47,226	34.5	18.1	21.2	76.6	8.2	4.9	2.7	2.2
34								32,309	32,823	2	40,254	45.6	28.8	29.9	80.8	3.3	4.0	4.5	2.8
35					R, 58		R, 67	35,633	36,259	2	47,166	29.1	10.0	17.9	81.0	2.1	8.8	0.4	1.8
36	D, 68		D, 60				D, 53	33,557	33,749	1	45,322	28.1	9.3	20.6	65.9	4.7	16.9	0.3	2.6
37			R, 61				D, 56	34,253	34,178	0	48,973	34.6	14.5	19.6	78.4	2.3	7.9	0.7	4.4
38								34,579	33,942	-2	41,223	28.9	10.0	20.3	82.8	0.6	6.5	0.4	4.1
39			R, 82		R, 82			34,171	38,840	14	82,313	48.3	31.2	9.1	80.7	5.5	2.2	2.4	4.4
40	R, 52				R, 56		R, 73	33,612	32,464	-3	44,413	30.8	13.1	20.5	77.8	3.8	2.2	1.8	8.5
41							R, 71	35,602	38,427	8	62,677	39.8	18.1	10.8	85.3	2.5	2.3	2.4	3.6
42			D, 62		R, 57			33,312	33,024	-1	47,234	25.7	10.1	20.1	80.6	1.2	6.1	0.4	5.2
43	R, 67						R, 65	33,964	39,325	16	62,950	40.5	16.1	8.1	82.2	1.1	2.9	5.5	3.9
44	D, 49		D, 60		D, 59		D, 72	33,693	34,420	2	46,888	42.6	25.2	23.9	73.8	4.6	4.4	6.0	5.8
45	R, 52		R, 53		R, 57		D, 50	35,220	38,506	9	48,184	42.0	20.4	19.2	76.0	4.8	5.0	2.6	4.9
46	R, 56				R, 61		R, 61	35,173	38,329	9	65,167	47.0	26.3	13.1	81.7	1.9	3.9	2.7	4.3
47	R, 68		R, 62		R, 68			34,489	37,514	9	51,085	31.3	11.3	16.6	82.4	3.8	4.3	0.7	4.0
48	R, 56		R, 66		R, 59			33,925	35,067	3	41,547	28.9	11.7	25.3	71.7	9.1	8.0	1.0	4.1
49					D, 60		D, 63	33,864	36,496	8	43,779	26.1	8.8	21.5	74.0	1.6	8.2	0.3	7.7
50	D, 65						R, 52	34,027	32,863	-3	47,673	30.6	13.1	20.0	80.8	3.2	4.1	0.5	6.5

(continued)

Note: D=Democrat, R=Republican, R/D=Republican/Democrat (cross-filed), D/R=Democrat/Republican (cross-filed), I=Independent, C=Constitution, O=Other, GI=Green Independent, P=Progressive, P/D=Progressive/Democrat, P/D/R=Progressive/Democrat/Republican, HH=Households

Oklahoma State House Districts—Election and Demographic Data (cont.)

House Districts	General Election Results Party, Percent of Vote							Population			Avg. HH Income	Pop 25+ Some College +	4-Yr Degree +	Below Poverty Line	2006 White (Non-Hisp)	African American	American Indians, Alaska Natives	Asians, Hawaiians, Pacific Islanders	Hispanic Origin
Oklahoma	2000	2001	2002	2003	2004	2005	2006	2000	2006	% Change	($)	(%)	(%)	(%)	(%)	(%)	(%)	(%)	(%)
51					D, 57			34,420	37,530	9	40,665	26.5	9.7	22.3	83.9	0.4	6.0	0.4	4.1
52			D, 53		D, 55			34,378	32,844	-4	43,673	33.1	12.0	21.6	62.2	7.3	2.1	1.3	17.3
53			R, 64		R, 69		R, 64	34,165	37,588	10	65,814	40.4	16.5	8.4	80.4	2.1	4.7	2.1	4.8
54					R, 58			34,113	37,422	10	54,500	39.4	13.3	10.4	76.9	3.0	3.9	2.4	6.7
55					D, 51		D, 67	34,300	33,801	-1	42,819	28.6	10.6	22.0	75.4	5.0	5.9	0.5	8.3
56	D, 71		D, 51		R, 58			33,649	36,363	8	45,361	27.6	10.9	22.4	66.3	2.1	18.3	0.4	7.0
57	D, 55		D, 58		D, 56			34,971	34,738	-1	45,501	32.6	14.5	21.9	72.7	2.4	6.7	0.8	9.5
58					R, 65			34,547	33,474	-3	45,126	31.1	12.6	19.8	87.4	1.4	2.0	0.5	4.7
59	D, 70				R, 53		R, 53	33,338	34,670	4	47,596	28.5	11.6	18.2	77.3	2.9	4.4	0.9	7.8
60								33,958	31,413	-7	40,833	28.9	11.3	24.1	79.3	4.5	2.4	0.4	7.8
61	D, 59		R, 52		R, 69			34,226	33,676	-2	48,186	29.3	12.3	17.4	55.4	1.0	1.2	0.6	29.9
62			D, 57				R, 58	33,908	33,600	-1	51,279	37.4	14.7	14.6	55.3	21.6	3.0	4.3	8.8
63	D, 76		R, 56					33,504	32,200	-4	44,719	29.1	10.4	23.5	59.5	13.5	7.9	1.4	10.4
64	D, 72		D, 65		R, 51		R, 66	34,325	33,174	-3	40,632	33.5	12.2	24.6	58.4	16.1	4.7	3.0	10.2
65			D, 71		D, 61			36,186	36,337	0	43,758	29.5	10.1	19.5	68.5	9.5	7.1	1.5	7.2
66	D, 56		D, 70					31,573	30,802	-2	39,758	37.0	16.9	22.9	67.1	8.6	7.6	1.1	8.0
67								34,836	38,021	9	99,136	55.1	36.2	6.0	83.0	2.8	2.5	3.4	4.1
68	R, 61		R, 67					34,695	35,332	2	48,756	32.1	12.9	16.6	75.1	5.1	7.4	0.6	4.8
69			R, 76				R, 75	34,081	37,673	11	80,435	45.4	26.9	10.1	73.7	6.1	4.5	2.4	7.6
70							R, 66	34,784	33,548	-4	83,496	57.6	36.5	10.1	81.2	4.7	3.5	1.5	4.4
71			D, 69		R, 59			33,805	33,026	-2	62,003	50.1	30.4	15.1	67.2	11.3	4.4	1.7	9.4
72								34,213	33,618	-2	32,400	25.7	8.5	29.3	41.4	27.8	6.9	0.9	17.9
73	D, 85		D, 87		D, 87			34,430	33,474	-3	35,020	28.5	10.6	33.0	20.2	63.1	3.5	0.4	9.4
74	R, 50				R, 73		R, 57	34,864	40,005	15	63,559	39.7	16.7	9.6	80.5	1.3	6.2	0.9	4.7
75			R, 75					34,038	35,020	3	50,665	40.2	16.9	13.5	62.3	8.2	4.4	5.0	12.8
76								35,184	37,216	6	68,325	45.8	24.1	5.7	78.1	4.0	3.8	3.3	5.6
77	R, 52		R, 58				D, 52	34,072	34,018	0	41,137	30.0	10.3	17.4	63.0	7.3	7.7	1.2	12.0
78	D, 60		D, 68		D, 50		D, 53	34,550	33,158	-4	46,815	45.1	21.7	13.1	69.0	5.7	4.8	1.8	12.1
79								33,232	33,082	0	58,249	50.9	29.1	10.5	68.9	7.3	3.1	3.2	11.2
80	R, 69		R, 69				R, 71	33,181	35,829	8	68,617	43.8	20.8	9.3	80.2	2.4	5.5	0.8	5.1
81	R, 77		R, 77		R, 74			31,835	33,053	4	67,929	46.1	31.2	15.6	77.0	5.8	2.4	5.5	4.3
82	R, 88				R, 70			35,957	40,595	13	73,021	54.4	34.9	6.8	76.9	7.5	2.2	4.6	4.4
83							R, 66	35,356	39,602	12	69,125	51.3	31.7	10.8	71.2	13.4	2.1	3.7	5.0
84	R, 66		R, 66		R, 68			34,025	34,274	1	45,930	38.4	18.2	16.4	64.9	10.1	3.3	2.7	12.1
85			R, 62		R, 59		R, 51	34,509	34,358	0	63,735	55.4	35.1	11.4	75.4	6.9	2.7	3.7	6.0
86	D, 67				D, 62			33,959	36,039	6	35,913	19.9	7.4	28.3	50.3	0.2	37.0	0.2	3.2
87	R, 51		R, 61		R, 54		R, 52	34,445	34,141	-1	42,802	43.4	20.8	15.5	65.3	7.6	3.4	4.9	12.2
88	D, 60				D, 68			33,742	34,007	1	38,545	33.1	17.4	28.8	40.9	15.0	4.6	8.6	24.9
89								34,195	33,961	-1	30,590	17.4	5.6	33.3	26.4	6.2	5.9	1.1	53.0
90								34,237	35,509	4	44,036	31.8	12.3	19.2	61.6	10.8	4.2	4.9	12.1
91	R, 65				R, 73			33,385	39,444	18	66,075	44.1	19.5	8.4	76.0	3.4	3.3	6.2	5.7
92	D, 54		D, 58		D, 51		D, 62	35,810	37,105	4	37,852	27.6	9.4	22.5	52.4	13.0	4.8	3.5	17.8
93	D, 60		D, 56		D, 51		D, 51	33,435	33,586	0	35,798	23.6	7.9	25.4	45.4	5.6	5.2	2.0	30.4
94	R, 66				R, 60		D, 54	35,252	37,195	6	43,130	31.1	11.5	18.4	58.8	14.4	4.2	2.8	13.1
95							R, 56	34,481	35,433	3	46,088	37.4	15.1	13.5	68.9	10.9	3.7	3.2	7.0
96	R, 54		R, 76		R, 78		R, 68	36,180	40,133	11	71,053	40.4	21.6	10.9	81.7	3.5	4.2	1.5	3.7
97	D, 66				D, 67			35,106	35,970	2	49,048	34.5	15.5	22.3	38.7	50.1	2.1	1.2	3.7
98	R, 61		R, 57				R, 67	33,428	35,181	5	57,553	37.5	14.6	10.0	78.5	2.9	5.5	1.3	5.2
99	D, 73				D, 77		D, 77	32,685	34,022	4	36,196	31.5	14.4	29.6	30.3	53.7	2.1	2.1	9.3
100	R, 85		R, 74		R, 70			31,402	33,025	5	53,972	42.2	21.8	12.7	69.0	10.3	2.6	4.0	8.6
101			R, 55					33,987	35,597	5	54,714	36.4	14.3	13.2	69.1	14.9	3.5	1.7	4.9

Note: D=Democrat, R=Republican, R/D=Republican/Democrat (cross-filed), D/R=Democrat/Republican (cross-filed), I=Independent, C=Constitution, O=Other, GI=Green Independent, P=Progressive, P/D=Progressive/Democrat, P/D/R=Progressive/Democrat/Republican, HH=Households

OREGON

"Welcome to Oregon. While you're here, I want you to enjoy yourselves. Travel, visit, drink in the great beauty of our state. But for God's sake, don't move here," so declared then-governor Tom McCall to the national Jaycee convention in 1971. His attitude, conveying pride in the state's unappreciated beauty and a determination to keep it unappreciated, says a lot about Oregon and its development. People started moving to the Willamette Valley less than a decade after they started moving to Chicago, crossing the continent on the Oregon Trail in the 1840s with a vision of recreating an orderly New England society in the wilderness. (A delegation from Maine, who wanted to name the big city "Portland," won out over a contingent from Massachusetts who wanted to call it "Boston.") When gold was discovered in California a few years later, the nation's attention turned south, where it has stayed pretty much ever since.

Starting in the 1970s, though, people began to look again to Oregon. The state's unspoiled beauty and strict zoning laws to control development appealed to a nation growing more environmentally conscious. Harried suburbanites from Seattle and southern California found here a less crowded, less polluted way of life. International attention came a few years later after entrepreneur Phil Knight won a following at track meets selling a new brand of sneaker, called Nike for the Greek goddess of victory, out of the back of his car.

Oregon's population grew by 20 percent during the 1990s, and by another 5 percent since 2000, almost exactly the same pace as in Washington State. That is steady growth but not spectacular—sustainable, as environmentally conscious Oregonians might put it—faster than the national average but not enough to earn either state an additional congressional seat in the last round of reapportionment. Oregon was hurt by downturns in the lumber industry and the slowing of the dot-com boom and still has one of the ten highest rates of unemployment.

The Oregon in popular imagination is the state west of the Cascades, lush with trees and rain. To the east, however, the trees turn to sagebrush and the land is flat. Almost all of the state's big cities—Portland, Salem, Eugene, Corvallis, Medford—are located in a line along Interstate 5 at the western edge of the mountains, much like Colorado along the Front Range of the Rockies.

First among them, of course, is Portland, which has been described as an undeveloped Seattle although John Gunther once wrote that the two were as different as "tea and gin." Oregon and Washington are often lumped together in descriptions of the Pacific Northwest, but as Gunther points out they are different in many other ways, as is reflected in their place names. Oregon town names—Portland, Salem, Pendleton—are redolent of New England; Washington town names—Walla Walla, Yakima, Tacoma—have Native American roots.

Nevertheless, traditionally staid Portland has adopted some of Seattle's grunge, as well as some of its growth. Expansion has been fastest in the city's suburbs that, despite efforts to curtail it, have spread into Washington County northwest of the city and across the Columbia River into Vancouver, Washington. Bend, east of the Cascades, has also grown. The only parts of the state to have lost population, and not much, are in downtown Portland and rural areas near the Idaho border.

Lacking the diversity of California or the size of Seattle's port, Oregon is not an especially wealthy state; median household income is the lowest of the Pacific Rim states (Alaska included). There are a few wealthy districts, all in the Portland suburbs, but as much disparity as in most other parts of the country. The poorest districts are in the logging regions along the southern coast, and around Klamath Falls. What seems to be different about Oregon is that its wealthy districts have elected Democrats to the legislature, while the poor districts have all elected Republicans. Some of this, no doubt, reflects the cultural liberalism of the wealthy, especially on the West Coast.

Oregon's population is overwhelmingly white but it is becoming less so. The African American population has stayed the same at a minuscule 1.6 percent, but the Hispanic population doubled during the 1990s, from 4 to 8 percent. The 22nd assembly district, which runs along Interstate 5 north from the state capital of Salem, is now almost half Hispanic.

The state has a reputation for being politically liberal and has elected some distinguished senators in recent generations, including Wayne Morse, Mark Hatfield, and Bob Packwood. West of the Cascades, the state tends to vote Democratic; to the east, it is heavily Republican. The regions are well-balanced, so the state swings both ways politically, something that has been seen in the state legislature during this decade. Republicans controlled the state house by a ten-seat margin as recently as 2002, but Democrats regained control in 2006 for the first time in almost two decades. The state senate was tied, 15–15, after the 2002 elections but Democrats now hold an 18–11 majority, only the third time that body has changed hands in the last sixty-eight years.

Like Maine and Vermont, Oregon once held its statewide elections in September. Now it holds them over a two-week period. Voting in Oregon is done only by mail—there are no polling places—and as a consequence results are not definitely known until days after the rest of the country has voted. On the other hand, voter participation is said to be as high as 87 percent and, allaying concerns of fraud, mail-in ballots provide the ultimate paper trail. The practice is also gaining popularity in Washington State, though it is not yet used statewide. Perhaps true to its reputation for simplicity, Oregon is also one of only seven states (soon to be six) that does not have an office of lieutenant governor.

OREGON
State Senate Districts

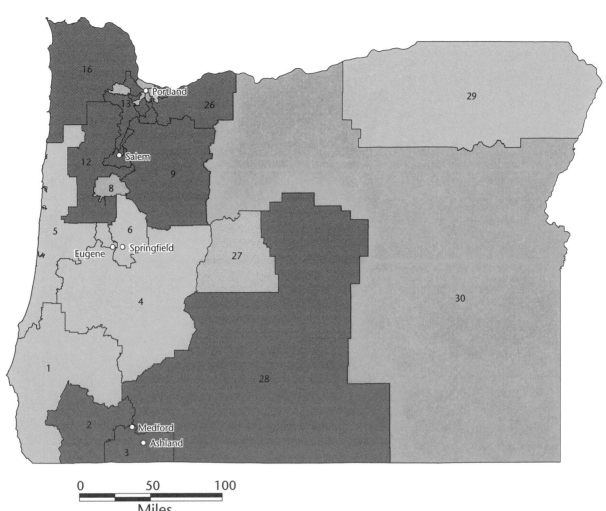

16
Portland
13
26
12
Salem
9
8
5
6
Eugene Springfield
27
4
30
1
28
2
Medford
Ashland
3
29

0   50   100
Miles

EUGENE

8
9
9
5   7
6
4
Eugene   Springfield
4
0   10   20
Miles

SALEM

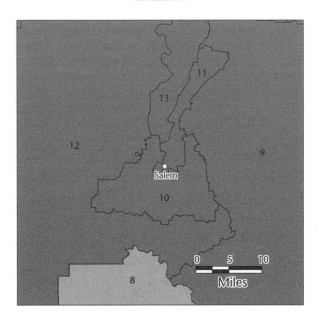

11
13
12
9
Salem
10
8
0   5   10
Miles

Population Growth   ☐ -1% to 3%   ☐ 3% to 7%   ☐ 7% to 20%   ☐ 20% to 26%

PORTLAND

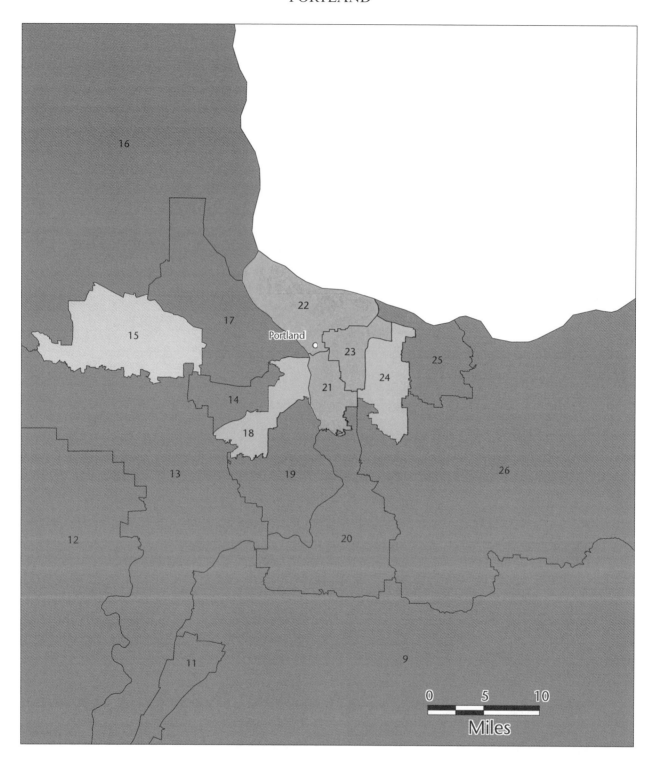

16

15

17

22

Portland

23

25

24

21

14

18

13

19

20

12

26

11

9

0   5   10

Miles

Population Growth   ☐ -1% to 3%   ☐ 3% to 7%   ☐ 7% to 20%   ☐ 20% to 26%

Oregon State Senate Districts—Election and Demographic Data

Senate Districts	General Election Results Party, Percent of Vote							Population			Avg. HH Income	2006 Pop 25+		Below Poverty Line	White (Non-Hisp)	African American	American Indians, Alaska Natives	Asians, Hawaiians, Pacific Islanders	Hispanic Origin
												Some College +	4-Yr Degree +						
Oregon	2000	2001	2002	2003	2004	2005	2006	2000	2006	% Change	($)	(%)	(%)	(%)	(%)	(%)	(%)	(%)	(%)
1					R, 66			113,553	118,943	5	45,763	34.0	10.6	18.6	90.8	0.2	1.2	0.9	4.1
2	R, 50				R, 96			116,414	128,987	11	47,141	35.7	10.8	17.7	89.6	0.3	0.8	0.9	5.5
3			R, 60		D, 52		D, 64	112,902	122,368	8	55,471	40.9	19.3	16.6	83.4	0.5	0.7	1.6	9.6
4	D, 52		D, 59		D, 61		D, 64	117,305	121,795	4	49,362	42.5	20.7	19.9	87.6	0.8	0.8	3.3	4.4
5					D, 51			114,735	119,707	4	45,952	39.6	14.1	18.0	88.1	0.3	2.0	1.3	5.3
6	D, 97		D, 99				D, 67	116,597	122,337	5	54,920	41.5	17.9	15.5	87.2	0.6	0.8	1.7	6.2
7	D, 90		D, 54				D, 52	113,233	119,950	6	53,355	45.1	20.6	14.7	84.4	1.1	0.8	2.9	6.9
8	D, 79		R, 55				R, 59	113,351	116,480	3	55,766	46.0	24.6	16.0	84.4	0.8	0.7	4.5	6.5
9					R, 83			114,380	126,374	10	55,605	32.9	11.2	14.4	82.9	0.3	0.9	0.9	10.4
10	D, 85		R, 54				R, 54	112,722	124,809	11	63,396	41.8	19.3	11.4	79.7	0.9	0.8	2.9	11.2
11	R, 55		D, 55				D, 57	112,624	123,262	9	45,214	29.6	10.1	18.4	49.4	1.4	1.3	3.5	35.5
12					R, 59			114,946	127,548	11	58,206	36.4	14.6	13.2	82.3	0.7	1.0	1.3	10.5
13			R, 60				R, 59	116,597	130,197	12	74,021	43.0	20.3	8.4	78.2	0.6	0.6	3.6	12.3
14					D, 64			113,493	125,550	11	73,404	49.1	27.0	8.5	72.1	1.5	0.4	9.0	12.9
15	R, 66		R, 62				R, 55	111,058	133,326	20	63,305	40.9	20.0	10.2	62.0	1.2	0.6	7.8	22.8
16			D, 56				D, 64	115,450	125,697	9	56,780	36.4	12.7	14.1	89.4	0.3	0.8	1.3	5.6
17			D, 55				D, 67	115,383	129,039	12	81,531	55.3	35.5	10.6	72.8	1.8	0.4	12.1	9.7
18					D, 62			114,661	121,840	6	72,808	57.2	36.5	12.3	79.3	2.1	0.5	6.8	8.1
19			D, 50				D, 61	111,886	123,001	10	103,783	56.6	37.8	5.9	84.8	0.8	0.3	4.8	6.6
20			D, 56				D, 96	113,718	127,809	12	62,024	40.1	16.6	10.0	84.3	0.7	0.5	2.1	8.8
21					D, 87			113,364	113,682	0	53,521	50.3	28.7	13.4	80.1	2.3	0.7	6.5	6.8
22					D, 97			114,443	116,541	2	48,622	42.5	22.4	16.0	53.7	21.7	1.0	6.0	14.3
23	R, 69				D, 88			114,665	114,189	0	59,022	48.4	27.1	11.8	72.4	4.1	0.6	11.7	7.9
24	R, 53		D, 57				D, 49	113,965	120,113	5	54,759	38.7	17.1	13.1	71.2	2.9	0.7	10.3	10.7
25	R, 96				D, 53			111,112	121,039	9	57,715	39.1	17.0	11.6	71.1	2.5	0.7	4.8	15.4
26			D, 54				D, 57	117,597	129,993	11	66,625	40.8	18.0	10.0	80.9	0.8	0.6	3.4	9.8
27	R, 70				R, 82			113,524	142,286	25	59,979	42.2	17.6	12.0	90.6	0.2	0.6	1.0	5.3
28	R, 65				R, 70			114,368	123,457	8	46,766	31.1	10.4	18.4	84.0	0.5	2.1	1.0	8.3
29	R, 72				R, 98			113,186	118,986	5	48,283	32.2	11.5	17.2	74.1	0.7	1.8	1.3	15.5
30	R, 71				R, 98			113,733	112,910	-1	46,160	30.6	10.1	18.3	73.6	0.6	3.1	1.4	15.0

Note: D=Democrat, R=Republican, R/D=Republican/Democrat (cross-filed), D/R=Democrat/Republican (cross-filed), I=Independent, C=Constitution, O=Other, GI=Green Independent, P=Progressive, P/D=Progressive/Democrat, P/D/R=Progressive/Democrat/Republican, HH=Households

OREGON
State House Districts

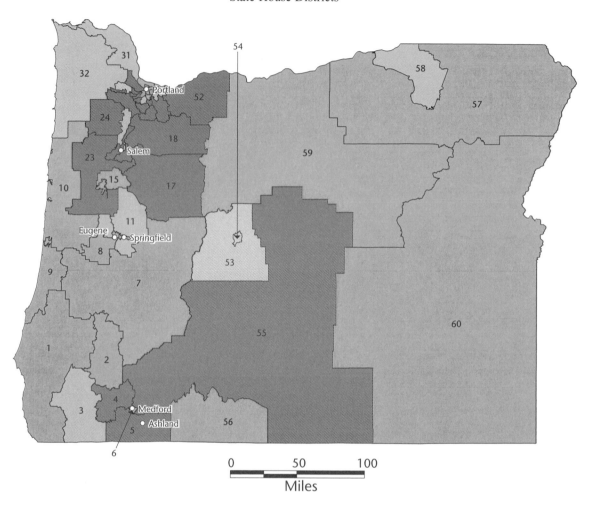

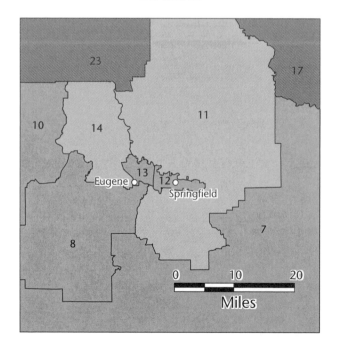

EUGENE

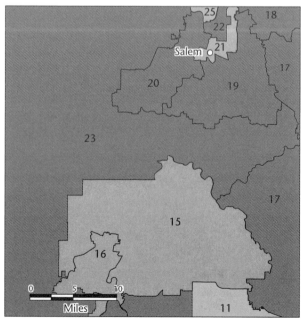

SALEM

Population Growth   ■ -3% to 5%   □ 5% to 9%   ■ 9% to 23%   □ 23% to 27%

PORTLAND

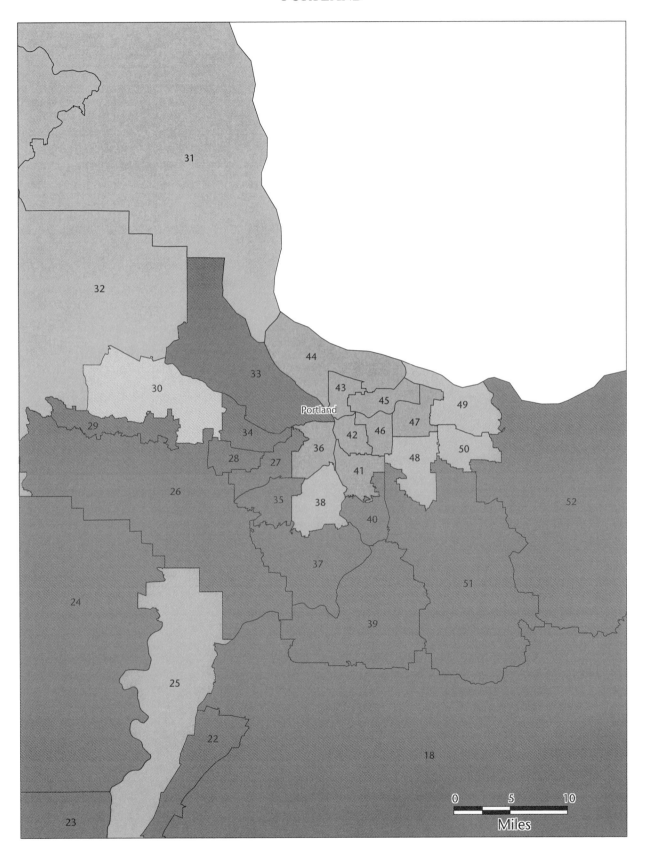

Population Growth   ▨ -3% to 5%   ▢ 5% to 9%   ▨ 9% to 23%   ▢ 23% to 27%

Oregon State House Districts—Election and Demographic Data

House Districts	General Election Results Party, Percent of Vote							Population			Avg. HH Income	Pop 25+ Some College +	Pop 25+ 4-Yr Degree +	2006 Below Poverty Line	2006 White (Non-Hisp)	African American	American Indians, Alaska Natives	Asians, Hawaiians, Pacific Islanders	Hispanic Origin
Oregon	2000	2001	2002	2003	2004	2005	2006	2000	2006	% Change	($)	(%)	(%)	(%)	(%)	(%)	(%)	(%)	(%)
1	D, 62		R, 66		R, 64		R, 73	56,289	59,014	5	45,175	36.1	11.4	18.8	90.8	0.2	1.4	0.8	4.0
2	D, 58		R, 74		R, 71		R, 97	55,880	57,980	4	46,392	32.0	9.7	18.3	90.8	0.2	1.1	1.1	4.2
3	R, 56		R, 70		R, 64		R, 62	55,583	60,369	9	42,101	35.4	9.9	20.6	89.5	0.3	0.9	0.9	5.5
4	R, 52		R, 60		R, 71		R, 70	59,243	66,308	12	52,033	36.0	11.5	14.8	89.7	0.2	0.8	0.9	5.5
5	R, 51		D, 96		D, 61		D, 97	55,731	61,259	10	54,666	44.1	22.7	16.7	85.5	0.5	0.7	1.5	7.8
6	D, 51		R, 63		R, 58		R, 52	55,411	58,643	6	56,322	37.4	15.8	16.5	81.2	0.6	0.7	1.8	11.5
7	R, 51		R, 66		R, 62		R, 96	55,531	58,278	5	46,696	36.6	12.1	17.0	90.9	0.2	1.0	0.9	4.2
8	D, 64		D, 73		D, 71		D, 77	54,665	55,779	2	54,297	48.3	29.4	21.5	85.4	1.2	0.6	5.4	4.4
9	R, 71		D, 75		D, 51		D, 58	56,400	58,684	4	43,641	38.9	12.8	19.8	89.6	0.3	1.5	1.4	4.5
10	R, 51		R, 51		R, 51		D, 51	56,666	58,756	4	48,297	40.3	15.4	16.3	86.7	0.3	2.5	1.2	6.1
11	D, 70		D, 62		D, 57		D, 62	60,846	64,308	6	65,332	46.2	22.4	12.8	90.3	0.5	0.8	1.7	4.0
12	D, 73		D, 53		D, 97		D, 64	56,100	57,731	3	43,753	36.5	13.4	18.6	83.6	0.8	0.9	1.9	8.5
13	D, 96		D, 73		D, 61		D, 72	55,042	57,190	4	54,661	49.3	25.6	15.6	83.7	1.2	0.8	3.5	6.8
14	D, 87		R, 53		R, 53		D, 52	56,552	60,548	7	51,611	41.3	16.0	13.9	85.0	1.0	0.8	2.3	7.0
15	D, 74		R, 52		R, 61		R, 68	56,698	59,152	4	56,285	40.3	15.7	13.7	87.6	0.5	0.8	1.7	6.2
16	D, 82		D, 68		D, 62		D, 67	55,157	55,264	0	55,213	52.1	34.2	18.4	81.1	1.1	0.6	7.5	6.7
17	D, 87		R, 69		R, 82		R, 59	55,741	61,065	10	51,109	32.0	9.1	16.1	89.7	0.2	1.0	0.9	5.4
18	D, 82		R, 82		R, 56		R, 53	58,088	64,222	11	60,383	33.7	13.2	12.4	76.2	0.4	0.8	1.0	15.3
19	D, 81		R, 64		R, 56		R, 57	56,585	62,247	10	63,659	41.3	17.6	8.9	80.9	1.1	0.9	2.8	10.1
20	R, 56		R, 63		R, 60		R, 59	55,327	61,162	11	63,288	42.2	20.8	13.7	78.3	0.7	0.8	2.9	12.4
21	D, 94		R, 53		R, 52		D, 61	56,136	60,038	7	48,418	34.6	12.6	15.9	62.8	1.8	1.3	4.4	23.2
22	D, 53		R, 50		D, 55		D, 51	54,176	60,096	11	41,592	24.7	7.8	21.4	37.6	1.0	1.3	2.6	47.6
23	D, 77		R, 68		R, 61		R, 58	56,822	63,044	11	56,939	39.0	15.2	13.2	87.4	0.7	1.1	1.2	6.3
24	D, 55		R, 59		R, 53		R, 49	56,346	62,005	10	59,455	33.7	14.0	13.1	77.3	0.8	0.9	1.4	14.8
25	D, 59		R, 74		R, 64		R, 57	54,696	59,031	8	59,962	37.3	14.3	10.7	76.3	0.6	0.7	1.9	14.9
26	D, 65		R, 64		R, 59		R, 59	58,553	66,666	14	85,976	47.7	25.3	6.5	79.7	0.6	0.4	4.8	10.4
27	R, 57		D, 99		D, 66		D, 60	57,231	62,612	9	81,980	55.0	33.5	7.4	78.0	1.4	0.3	8.6	8.4
28	R, 60		D, 48		D, 80		D, 65	54,393	59,720	10	64,249	43.5	20.5	9.6	67.5	1.7	0.6	9.5	16.3
29	R, 55		R, 52		D, 48		D, 52	49,940	55,581	11	55,803	32.5	13.3	15.1	48.5	0.9	0.7	2.7	38.6
30	R, 63		R, 49		R, 54		D, 56	59,204	74,760	26	67,867	47.0	24.9	7.3	72.1	1.4	0.5	11.5	11.2
31	R, 63		D, 67		D, 76		D, 59	56,448	61,380	9	57,537	34.7	10.9	14.0	90.0	0.4	0.9	1.2	4.8
32	R, 50		D, 51		D, 50		D, 62	57,554	62,213	8	56,080	38.1	14.5	14.1	88.7	0.2	0.7	1.3	6.4
33	R, 96		D, 58		D, 80		D, 70	60,426	66,983	11	90,228	60.0	41.4	12.6	79.5	1.8	0.5	10.7	5.2
34	R, 61		D, 53		D, 97		D, 62	54,714	62,151	14	69,904	49.2	28.2	8.1	64.4	1.7	0.4	13.5	16.1
35	D, 58		R, 60		D, 48		D, 56	56,188	62,489	11	70,525	51.9	28.2	7.5	77.2	1.4	0.4	7.3	10.3
36	R, 56		D, 96		D, 87		D, 85	57,085	57,304	0	75,186	63.2	45.7	16.3	81.8	2.9	0.5	6.3	5.6
37	R, 69		R, 64		R, 52		R, 53	56,976	63,755	12	96,926	51.9	31.0	6.4	82.4	0.7	0.4	4.1	9.3
38	R, 58		D, 54		D, 86		D, 69	54,692	58,631	7	109,761	61.5	44.9	5.4	87.2	1.0	0.2	5.6	3.7
39	D, 59		R, 51		R, 57		R, 55	55,503	62,892	13	65,588	39.5	16.2	9.7	85.2	0.5	0.6	1.3	9.0
40	D, 72		D, 54		D, 59		D, 97	55,996	61,776	10	58,933	40.7	17.0	10.1	83.4	0.8	0.5	3.0	8.6
41	D, 53		D, 80		D, 73		D, 97	56,201	56,806	1	58,278	44.8	23.1	11.5	82.5	1.3	0.7	5.3	6.6
42	D, 100		D, 82		D, 82		D, 83	52,855	52,106	-1	49,054	56.1	34.5	15.2	77.9	3.2	0.8	7.7	7.0
43	R, 58		D, 85		D, 88		D, 98	55,119	55,580	1	49,377	46.7	26.9	17.0	47.9	33.2	0.8	4.3	11.4
44	D, 53		D, 78		D, 79		D, 79	57,697	58,899	2	47,354	38.6	18.0	15.1	58.7	10.9	1.2	7.7	17.0
45	R, 68		D, 90		D, 90		D, 80	58,114	57,210	-2	64,559	50.2	29.1	10.2	71.9	5.5	0.6	10.3	8.4
46	R, 72		D, 80		D, 74		D, 77	58,106	57,946	0	53,841	47.0	25.7	13.4	73.1	2.7	0.6	12.9	7.4
47	D, 65		D, 93		D, 64		D, 64	57,025	58,770	3	51,650	39.6	17.5	13.7	70.0	3.6	0.7	10.6	11.0
48	R, 56		D, 54		D, 51		D, 74	55,450	59,299	7	58,444	38.1	16.9	12.1	72.7	2.2	0.6	10.2	10.2
49	R, 71		R, 60		R, 53		R, 52	57,603	62,740	9	56,126	38.5	15.9	12.0	68.4	3.0	0.7	4.9	17.0
50	R, 62		D, 61		R, 51		R, 63	53,095	57,285	8	59,172	39.7	18.2	11.4	73.8	1.9	0.6	4.7	13.9

(continued)

Note: D=Democrat, R=Republican, R/D=Republican/Democrat (cross-filed), D/R=Democrat/Republican (cross-filed), I=Independent, C=Constitution, O=Other, GI=Green Independent, P=Progressive, P/D=Progressive/Democrat, P/D/R=Progressive/Democrat/Republican, HH=Households

Oregon State House Districts—Election and Demographic Data (cont.)

House Districts	General Election Results Party, Percent of Vote							Population			Avg. HH Income	Pop 25+		Below Poverty Line	2006 White (Non-Hisp)	African American	American Indians, Alaska Natives	Asians, Hawaiians, Pacific Islanders	Hispanic Origin
												Some College +	4-Yr Degree +						
Oregon	2000	2001	2002	2003	2004	2005	2006	2000	2006	% Change	($)	(%)	(%)	(%)	(%)	(%)	(%)	(%)	(%)
51	R, 66		R, 58		R, 53		R, 58	57,139	63,488	11	69,124	41.8	18.9	9.1	82.4	1.1	0.5	5.2	7.4
52	D, 60		R, 64		R, 57		R, 56	59,444	64,933	9	63,942	39.7	17.1	11.0	79.6	0.5	0.7	1.6	12.1
53	R, 56		R, 66		R, 84		R, 59	112,014	139,795	25	59,963	42.2	17.6	12.0	90.6	0.2	0.6	1.0	5.3
54	R, 61		R, 62		R, 49		R, 55	53,723	66,339	23	56,862	43.5	19.3	12.1	88.9	0.3	0.6	1.3	6.3
55	R, 74		R, 64		R, 98		R, 98	56,868	63,910	12	47,443	30.3	9.4	17.4	86.7	0.2	1.8	0.7	6.9
56	R, 57		R, 97		R, 66		R, 67	56,373	57,818	3	46,071	32.1	11.4	19.4	91.9	0.8	4.7	1.3	9.6
57	R, 100		R, 67		R, 98		R, 70	56,752	58,028	2	46,439	32.9	12.0	18.6	78.1	0.4	0.7	1.2	13.3
58	R, 73		R, 97		R, 98		R, 69	55,080	59,020	7	50,262	31.5	11.0	15.6	70.2	1.1	2.9	1.3	17.7
59	R, 69		R, 55		R, 58		R, 51	55,807	56,017	0	48,930	32.2	11.2	16.5	82.9	0.3	7.4	1.1	12.8
60	R, 98		R, 72		R, 98		R, 74	56,450	54,956	-3	43,224	29.0	9.0	20.4	71.7	0.9	1.0	1.8	17.5

Note: D=Democrat, R=Republican, R/D=Republican/Democrat (cross-filed), D/R=Democrat/Republican (cross-filed), I=Independent, C=Constitution, O=Other, GI=Green Independent, P=Progressive, P/D=Progressive/Democrat, P/D/R=Progressive/Democrat/Republican, HH=Households

PENNSYLVANIA

Pennsylvania is a state that is often ignored by its great cities. Philadelphia scarcely admits it belongs there at all and faces toward New York. Pittsburgh looks down the Ohio River toward West Virginia and the Midwest. In between is a state of great natural beauty and once-great industrial might. Previous generations of Americans mastered the continent riding locomotives built in Philadelphia, made of steel forged in Pittsburgh, fired by coal mined in Scranton. Always more complacent than New York, Ohio, or Illinois and too insular to achieve the political influence its economic status accorded it, for more than a century Pennsylvania was, nevertheless, the nation's indispensable state.

It is much less indispensable today. Most of the mines, mills, and factories have closed. Pittsburgh residents no longer peer at the sun through a cloud of soot, but try to build a new reputation for the city as a medical center. Philadelphia struggles to lure shipbuilders and computer firms, though parts of its Center City are full of good restaurants and new condos.

As recently as the 1980s, Pennsylvania was the fourth-largest state but it has since fallen to sixth. Despite the well-publicized problems in rural coal country, most of its population loss is occurring in its cities, particularly Philadelphia and Pittsburgh. Repeating a pattern now decades old, families have moved in search of better schools, safer streets, and lower taxes. The outer suburbs, in more distant parts of Bucks and Chester Counties, are growing, sometimes by a lot.

The two fastest-growing state house districts, though— 189th and 176th—are in Pike and Monroe Counties, where Interstate 84 crosses the Delaware River. This has become the outer ring, not of Philadelphia, but of New York—the ultimate urban doughnut—where some residents now commute three hours into Manhattan while clinging to a more affordable suburban lifestyle.

What is left in the cities is often misery on a scale far exceeding the poorest parts of the rural South. Average household income in the heavily Hispanic 180th house district in North Philadelphia is less than $27,000, making it the second-poorest district in the country. Less than 14 percent have ever attended college, the fifth-lowest rate of any house district in the country. In the neighboring 190th district, which is 86 percent African American, average income is $30,000 and only 8 percent have finished college.

Still stocked with German, Irish, and Slavic immigrants, Pennsylvania is 85 percent white, considerably higher than either New York (68 percent) or New Jersey (73 percent). Five Philadelphia urban districts are more than 70 percent African American, and there are pockets of Koreans in Cheltenham, Vietnamese in South Philadelphia, and Mexicans in Reading and Lancaster. But most of the great rural middle of the state is white, poor, and conservative (it has the largest chapter of the National Rifle Association). Or, as Democratic strategist James Carville once said of the territory outside Pennsylvania's eastern and western suburbs, "Between Paoli and Penn Hills, it's just Alabama."

Another important factor in Pennsylvania politics is age. More than 15 percent of the state is older than sixty-five, a rate second only to Florida. In off-year elections, seniors can account for half the electorate, giving them political influence disproportionate to their numbers. Pennsylvania is, for example, one of the only states that devotes all of its lottery proceeds to senior citizen programs rather than to economic development or education.

Though it dates its origins to 1682, the state legislature has an undistinguished history. In the late nineteenth and early twentieth centuries it was in the pocket of the Pennsylvania Railroad and muckraker Henry Demarest Lloyd one remarked that the Standard Oil Company "did everything to the Pennsylvania legislature except refine it." In the 1990s house Democrats staged a coup against a speaker of their party who pushed reform too quickly.

The 2006 elections produced a startling upheaval in Harrisburg. The cause was a pay raise for legislators, state judges, and some executive officials that was slipped through at two in the morning. The raise was substantial— from 16 to 34 percent for legislators—but what really set the public off was that the state constitution prohibits legislators from accepting a pay raise in the same term that it was enacted. Lawmakers got around this and took their raises immediately by classifying them as "unvouchered expenses."

Public outcry was deafening and, unusual in these situations, sustained. The earliest casualty was a state supreme court justice who became the first in state history to lose his race for retention. That got attention in Harrisburg and the legislature quickly repealed the pay raise, but many members, who had already taken the extra money, refused to give it back. The Republican house speaker stubbornly insisted that lawmakers worked hard and deserved as much as they could get. Newspapers, meanwhile, ran articles for months exposing the many other lavish perks legislators received at a time when the state was losing jobs.

The following spring, seventeen legislators lost their primaries, including the top Republican leadership in the senate—an outcome unprecedented in Pennsylvania politics. Although both parties were complicit, voters blamed the GOP. Seven more legislators lost in the November general election and the Democrats emerged with a 102–101 majority in the state house, their first since 1994. (Republicans continue to control the senate.) Worried about the unpopularity of their leader and the possibility of a party switch, house Democrats made the highly unusual arrangement of nominating a Republican to be speaker, though they continue to control the legislative agenda.

Once a GOP stronghold, Pennsylvania has voted Democratic in recent presidential elections. Democratic strength lies not only in Pittsburgh, Philadelphia, and the Scranton area, but in the increasingly Democratic Philadelphia suburbs. The belt around Allegheny County, meanwhile, has grown more Republican.

PENNSYLVANIA
State Senate Districts

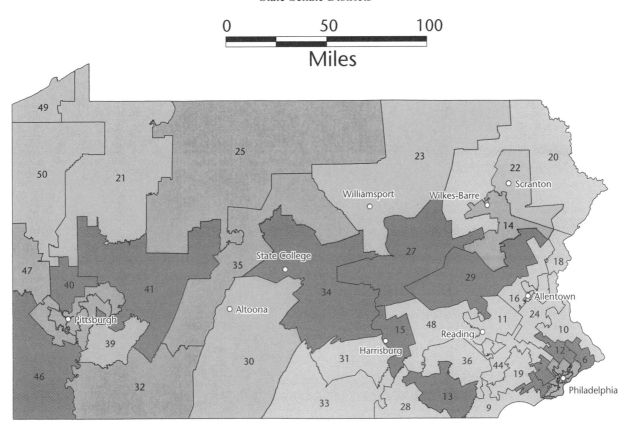

PITTSBURGH

PHILADELPHIA

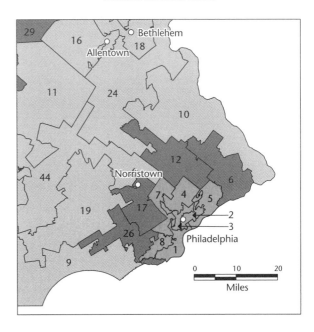

Population Growth ▢ -6% to -1% ▢ -1% to 0% ▢ 0% to 4% ▢ 4% to 10%

Pennsylvania State Senate Districts—Election and Demographic Data

Senate Districts	General Election Results Party, Percent of Vote							Population			Avg. HH Income	Pop 25+		Below Poverty Line	White (Non-Hisp)	African American	American Indians, Alaska Natives	Asians, Hawaiians, Pacific Islanders	Hispanic Origin
												Some College +	4-Yr Degree +						
																		2006	
Penn.	2000	2001	2002	2003	2004	2005	2006	2000	2006	% Change	($)	(%)	(%)	(%)	(%)	(%)	(%)	(%)	(%)
1	D, 81				D, 79			249,141	242,368	-3	52,447	33.8	22.5	23.5	50.0	30.7	0.2	9.5	7.3
2			D, 79				D, 84	244,086	229,634	-6	38,885	19.6	9.0	28.8	33.6	23.4	0.3	5.4	33.0
3	D, 100				D, 87			251,906	242,176	-4	40,874	23.6	11.6	29.5	25.2	57.5	0.2	6.4	10.9
4			D, 82				D, 84	250,054	242,704	-3	69,123	38.1	24.0	13.9	41.6	50.5	0.1	3.5	2.9
5	D, 53				D, 66			246,103	233,625	-5	50,767	27.5	14.4	16.5	67.7	17.0	0.1	5.3	6.6
6			R, 53				R, 53	247,856	253,404	2	73,538	37.5	19.7	8.7	85.1	4.8	0.1	4.0	3.9
7	D, 100				D, 84			252,658	244,586	-3	51,923	31.5	19.1	25.8	36.7	54.2	0.2	4.5	3.2
8			D, 79				D, 100	241,689	232,578	-4	42,321	24.7	11.8	25.0	38.3	52.7	0.1	4.6	2.8
9	R, 100				R, 59			252,335	269,112	7	80,085	37.9	23.8	11.4	74.0	16.1	0.1	2.1	5.7
10			R, 62				R, 52	249,006	265,757	7	97,030	46.3	29.4	6.9	90.6	2.8	0.1	2.7	2.4
11	R/D, 95				D, 71			248,073	259,825	5	56,133	30.0	16.2	14.7	68.0	5.0	0.1	1.4	18.1
12			R, 67				R, 57	250,303	258,965	3	85,322	45.4	30.1	6.5	85.7	4.1	0.1	6.1	2.5
13	R, 69				R, 66			246,956	256,631	4	60,856	31.9	16.9	11.7	76.7	4.7	0.1	2.1	11.0
14			D, 100				D, 100	250,503	245,373	-2	43,471	29.7	11.9	20.0	92.4	1.9	0.1	0.7	3.5
15	R, 67				R, 61			250,067	252,474	1	59,710	38.1	18.2	12.2	71.7	17.5	0.1	2.6	5.1
16			R, 65				R, 54	249,259	270,475	9	62,434	36.2	18.2	12.6	71.2	4.1	0.1	2.6	15.9
17	R, 50				D, 65			245,934	253,218	3	105,191	47.2	35.6	8.8	80.1	9.0	0.1	5.3	3.6
18			D, 62				D, 71	244,886	266,839	9	58,461	34.3	17.5	13.4	79.1	3.1	0.1	2.2	10.8
19	R, 63				R, 100			250,818	275,607	10	97,929	50.5	35.1	6.1	87.2	5.1	0.1	3.4	2.5
20			R, 70				R, 59	248,316	265,562	7	54,819	31.5	13.6	14.5	91.7	2.3	0.1	0.8	3.6
21	R, 88				R, 68			240,641	239,813	0	45,689	24.3	10.1	18.1	96.7	1.1	0.1	0.5	0.7
22			D, 69				D, 100	247,726	246,535	0	50,888	30.2	13.9	17.8	90.2	2.6	0.1	1.0	4.1
23	R, 100				R, 74			249,065	248,028	0	48,342	26.1	10.8	16.7	92.9	3.6	0.2	0.7	1.4
24			R, 55				R, 57	247,861	266,700	8	69,583	38.0	21.2	9.1	88.8	3.0	0.1	2.6	3.5
25	I, 33				R, 90			243,002	237,588	-2	45,385	24.2	9.7	17.6	97.2	0.7	0.1	0.5	0.7
26			R, 63				R, 52	247,699	249,983	1	76,434	38.8	24.4	10.1	82.7	8.3	0.1	5.9	1.5
27	R, 100				R, 70			248,568	248,753	0	47,204	23.5	10.4	16.9	95.5	1.4	0.1	0.6	1.4
28			R, 100				R, 66	247,092	264,511	7	57,424	35.5	16.0	11.7	85.5	5.2	0.1	1.2	5.2
29	R/D, 100				R, 66			248,401	255,990	3	50,261	26.1	10.9	15.7	93.2	2.0	0.1	0.6	2.7
30			R, 73				R, 63	241,356	239,903	-1	44,697	22.0	8.8	18.3	96.0	1.9	0.1	0.4	0.7
31	R, 66				R, 73			248,254	262,320	6	66,318	36.3	19.6	9.4	92.3	2.3	0.1	2.0	1.8
32			D, 100				D, 68	240,127	236,075	-2	41,596	21.4	8.7	23.1	95.0	3.1	0.1	0.3	0.6
33	R/D, 100				R, 76			246,106	265,884	8	54,539	25.2	11.0	11.6	91.7	1.9	0.1	0.7	3.5
34			R/D, 93				R, 56	245,292	249,523	2	50,368	29.4	17.4	17.0	92.1	1.8	0.1	3.1	1.6
35	D, 77				D/R, 100			237,736	231,863	-2	42,590	23.0	9.2	19.8	95.0	2.6	0.1	0.5	1.0
36			R, 95				R, 66	250,384	265,756	6	62,037	28.5	14.9	9.4	92.0	1.3	0.1	1.7	2.8
37	R, 64				R, 68			245,682	240,397	-2	78,489	47.0	30.5	8.5	93.3	2.8	0.0	2.1	0.9
38			D, 65				D, 84	238,976	228,216	-5	48,645	35.9	19.0	23.5	64.6	30.9	0.1	1.7	1.1
39	D, 58				R, 52			239,823	239,103	0	52,010	37.8	16.0	14.8	96.3	1.6	0.1	0.6	0.6
40			R, 71				R, 85	241,529	241,961	0	77,117	43.7	26.9	8.9	95.2	1.4	0.1	1.8	0.8
41	R, 54				D/R, 100			239,649	240,390	0	48,249	26.6	12.1	18.4	96.9	1.1	0.1	0.8	0.6
42			D, 72				D, 100	237,481	226,917	-4	48,873	35.9	18.7	17.2	83.2	11.7	0.1	2.2	1.2
43	D, 100				D, 100			244,429	232,889	-5	53,990	40.4	23.5	17.1	80.7	12.8	0.1	3.4	1.4
44			R, 59				R, 56	248,917	268,747	8	76,609	40.4	25.6	8.5	83.4	8.9	0.1	2.8	2.9
45	D, 61				D, 100			242,132	230,543	-5	46,624	35.8	16.4	17.7	85.5	11.0	0.1	1.2	0.9
46			R/D, 100				D, 100	237,650	239,305	1	48,697	26.7	11.4	17.1	93.7	4.0	0.1	0.4	0.8
47	R/D, 100				D/R, 100			237,039	228,514	-4	47,662	28.4	10.8	17.4	91.3	6.3	0.2	0.3	0.9
48			R, 70				R, 63	248,365	266,220	7	62,270	29.5	16.0	9.8	90.1	1.4	0.1	1.3	4.5
49	R, 58				R, 66			240,053	239,010	0	50,975	27.4	13.6	16.6	86.4	7.4	0.1	1.0	2.8
50			R, 65				R, 54	243,068	241,980	0	49,628	25.9	11.9	16.3	94.2	3.5	0.1	0.5	0.7

Note: D=Democrat, R=Republican, R/D=Republican/Democrat (cross-filed), D/R=Democrat/Republican (cross-filed), I=Independent, C=Constitution, O=Other, GI=Green Independent, P=Progressive, P/D=Progressive/Democrat, P/D/R=Progressive/Democrat/Republican, HH=Households

PENNSYLVANIA
State House Districts

HARRISBURG/YORK

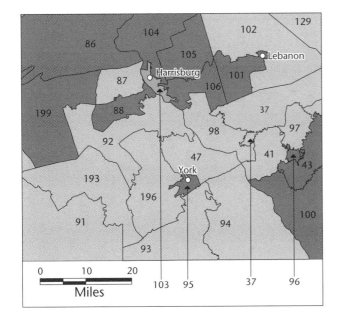

WILKES-BARRE/SCRANTON

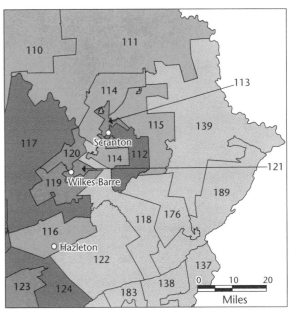

Population Growth ■ -7% to -4%   ■ -4% to 0%   ■ 0% to 5%   ■ 5% to 24%

ALLENTOWN-READING

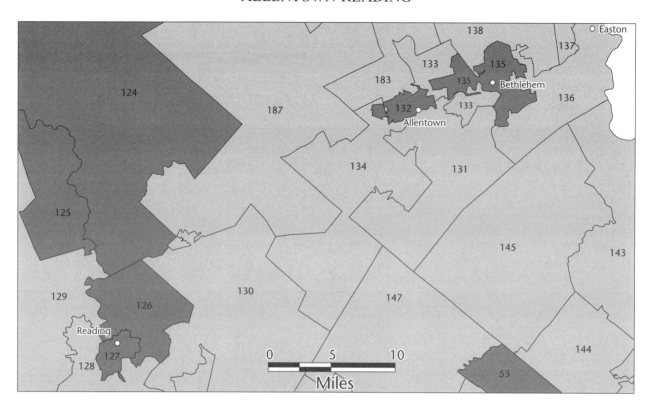

PITTSBURGH

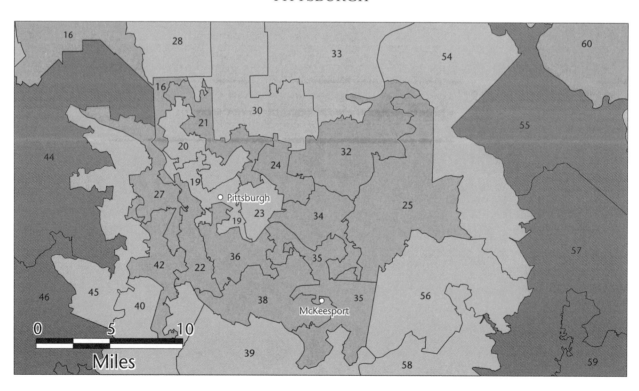

Population Growth   ■ -7% to -4%   ■ -4% to 0%   ■ 0% to 5%   □ 5% to 24%

PHILADELPHIA 1

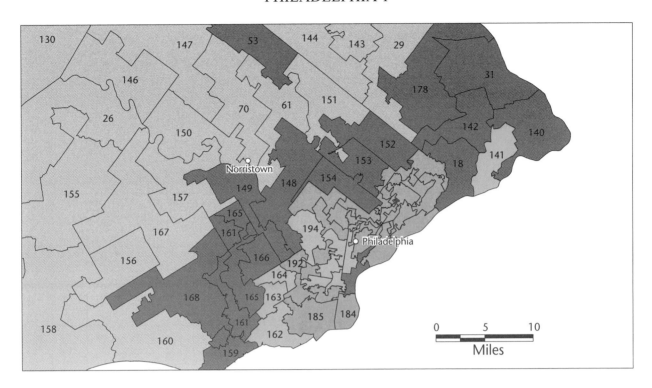

PHILADELPHIA 2

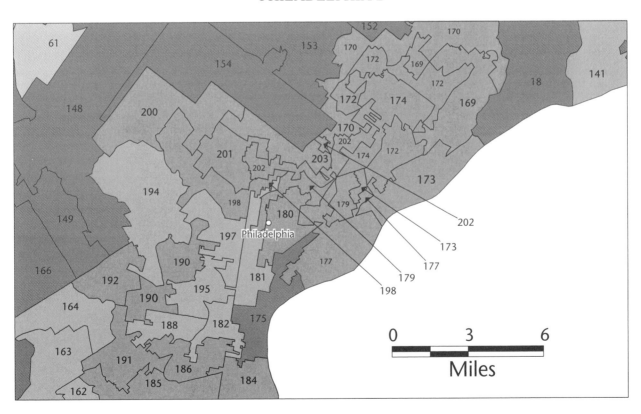

Population Growth   ▨ -7% to -4%   ▨ -4% to 0%   ▨ 0% to 5%   ▨ 5% to 24%

Pennsylvania State House Districts—Election and Demographic Data

House Districts	General Election Results Party, Percent of Vote							Population			Avg. HH Income	Pop 25+ Some College +	Pop 25+ 4-Yr Degree +	Below Poverty Line	2006 White (Non-Hisp)	African American	American Indians, Alaska Natives	Asians, Hawaiians, Pacific Islanders	Hispanic Origin
Penn.	2000	2001	2002	2003	2004	2005	2006	2000	2006	% Change	($)	(%)	(%)	(%)	(%)	(%)	(%)	(%)	(%)
1	D, 100		D, 73		D, 100		D, 75	58,515	56,758	-3	37,041	20.2	8.5	24.7	71.4	17.7	0.2	1.0	5.9
2	D, 100		D, 100		D, 100		D, 100	60,418	59,479	-2	45,947	28.3	13.7	18.0	85.0	7.9	0.1	1.0	3.3
3	R/D, 100		R, 77		D/R, 100		D, 49	59,672	60,769	2	64,351	33.8	18.5	10.5	94.9	1.5	0.1	1.4	1.1
4	D, 66		D, 64		R, 50		R, 100	58,166	58,458	1	49,280	22.7	9.4	14.9	96.2	1.2	0.1	0.5	0.9
5	R, 68		R, 100		R, 71		R, 51	58,327	59,447	2	52,642	25.5	12.6	15.4	94.4	2.8	0.1	0.6	1.1
6	R, 100		R, 60		R, 64		R, 61	58,846	57,704	-2	48,070	23.6	10.8	18.4	95.4	2.2	0.1	0.4	0.7
7	D, 61		D, 100		D, 100		D/R, 100	59,781	59,014	-1	49,497	28.3	12.7	17.5	87.8	9.3	0.1	0.5	0.9
8	R, 63		R, 67		R, 100		R, 100	61,240	63,742	4	53,355	29.3	13.5	13.7	96.5	1.5	0.0	0.5	0.7
9	D, 68		R/D, 100		D/R, 100		D/R, 100	59,028	56,236	-5	46,461	26.3	10.9	20.3	91.8	5.6	0.1	0.5	0.7
10	D, 100		R/D, 100		D, 100		D, 63	60,426	61,198	1	50,309	24.4	10.0	16.1	96.5	1.4	0.1	0.6	0.7
11	D, 68		D, 52		R, 56		R, 65	59,675	61,746	3	49,450	29.9	12.1	16.9	96.6	1.3	0.1	0.4	0.8
12	R, 86		R, 67		R, 100		R, 100	58,231	62,070	7	78,370	40.9	23.4	8.3	96.6	0.7	0.0	1.1	0.8
13	R, 100		R, 60		R, 59		R, 54	61,826	70,017	13	68,863	35.8	20.6	10.0	81.6	7.5	0.1	0.6	6.9
14	D, 73		D, 100		D, 100		R, 54	59,840	58,003	-3	46,075	27.6	9.6	17.5	89.2	7.6	0.1	0.4	1.0
15	D, 89		D, 53		D, 100		D, 51	59,716	58,195	-3	55,548	34.4	14.3	12.6	95.1	2.9	0.0	0.4	0.8
16	D, 70		D, 56		D, 60		D, 100	58,519	56,059	-4	50,139	34.4	16.1	17.6	87.1	9.7	0.1	0.8	1.1
17	R, 100		R, 100		R, 100		R, 53	60,020	60,220	0	47,451	23.9	10.6	15.2	97.2	0.9	0.1	0.4	0.6
18	R, 100		R, 66		R, 62		R, 62	61,317	62,282	2	59,371	37.0	18.5	10.9	76.8	7.0	0.1	8.0	5.6
19	D, 89		D, 100		D, 100		D, 100	64,430	62,787	-3	35,686	27.5	13.7	35.3	44.9	49.4	0.1	2.2	1.7
20	D, 95		D, 66		D, 100		D, 65	61,875	59,866	-3	42,493	34.0	16.6	20.8	81.7	14.5	0.1	1.1	1.0
21	D, 100		D, 67		D, 93		D, 100	61,054	58,273	-5	50,464	42.8	26.9	18.3	79.0	12.3	0.1	5.1	1.8
22	D, 78		D, 70		D, 100		D, 55	59,477	56,157	-6	51,902	37.7	19.3	14.3	90.6	5.9	0.1	1.0	1.1
23	D, 100		D, 100		D, 100		D, 100	57,460	55,600	-3	68,337	46.3	35.7	21.0	76.2	8.8	0.1	9.6	2.5
24	D, 100		D, 86		D, 100		D, 86	60,829	57,495	-5	43,294	38.6	20.6	25.7	29.0	66.4	0.2	1.2	1.4
25	D, 100		D, 70		D, 69		D, 62	61,054	58,100	-5	59,780	45.0	26.1	11.0	88.7	5.6	0.1	3.7	0.8
26	R, 58		R, 68		R, 100		R, 83	62,884	69,964	11	64,864	36.4	20.8	12.5	81.9	11.9	0.1	0.9	3.1
27	D, 88		D, 65		D, 100		D, 66	59,507	56,245	-5	45,637	36.1	17.7	17.0	85.0	10.6	0.1	1.5	1.1
28	R, 100		R, 100		R, 73		R, 71	61,140	60,515	-1	102,975	50.3	35.9	7.0	93.4	1.8	0.0	3.0	0.9
29	R/D, 100		R, 57		R, 62		R, 56	62,198	67,705	9	92,991	46.1	27.7	7.2	89.6	2.1	0.1	2.4	3.7
30	R/D, 100		R, 69		D/R, 100		R, 53	63,362	60,885	-4	91,139	46.4	30.2	8.0	94.4	1.6	0.0	2.5	0.8
31	R, 100		R, 59		R, 57		R, 52	60,564	62,556	3	128,773	56.2	41.3	3.5	90.1	2.3	0.0	4.4	1.9
32	D, 67		D, 100		D, 100		D, 100	61,511	58,712	-5	50,365	39.2	18.9	13.6	77.2	19.7	0.1	1.0	0.7
33	D, 59		D, 65		D, 100		D, 51	62,471	60,020	-4	56,554	36.9	19.5	13.5	95.0	2.6	0.1	0.9	0.6
34	D, 74		D, 90		D, 100		D, 100	61,192	57,973	-5	49,403	40.0	21.5	17.7	78.7	17.3	0.1	1.2	1.1
35	D, 100		D, 100		D, 92		D, 100	60,776	57,670	-5	38,712	31.5	13.5	23.8	76.7	19.5	0.1	0.7	1.1
36	D, 100		D, 100		D, 100		D, 100	62,237	58,826	-5	44,802	33.7	15.1	17.2	91.2	5.6	0.1	1.0	0.9
37	R, 74		R, 100		R, 100		R, 70	61,189	65,113	6	62,215	27.1	13.6	7.7	94.6	0.7	0.1	1.4	1.6
38	D, 100		D, 100		D, 100		D, 71	61,811	58,229	-6	46,657	35.2	15.9	15.4	90.1	7.0	0.1	0.7	0.9
39	D, 60		D, 59		D, 62		D, 100	61,847	60,266	-3	52,919	34.7	16.0	13.3	91.5	6.1	0.1	0.7	0.6
40	R, 100		R, 100		R, 100		R, 100	60,025	58,473	-3	100,983	50.5	35.1	6.1	94.3	1.6	0.0	2.6	0.8
41	D, 70		R, 67		R, 65		R, 82	60,399	63,686	5	70,767	39.3	23.0	7.4	88.3	2.2	0.1	2.6	4.2
42	R, 55		R, 62		R, 100		D, 58	63,773	61,201	-4	79,471	53.5	38.3	8.3	92.4	1.7	0.0	4.0	0.9
43	R, 100		R, 100		R, 75		R, 100	59,828	62,246	4	63,705	30.4	16.7	8.8	88.6	2.2	0.1	2.4	4.2
44	R/D, 100		R, 100		R, 59		R, 60	64,285	65,265	2	77,449	44.5	27.3	8.0	91.9	3.8	0.1	2.3	1.0
45	D, 100		D, 66		D, 100		D, 100	61,983	60,602	-2	55,082	38.9	21.1	13.0	91.2	5.3	0.1	1.4	0.9
46	D, 67		D, 55		D, 53		D, 54	62,368	64,511	3	50,926	26.5	11.3	14.1	95.7	2.4	0.1	0.2	0.6
47	D, 58		R, 92		R, 100		R, 100	61,668	66,384	8	62,215	38.7	19.1	7.9	90.2	3.0	0.1	1.9	2.9
48	D, 92		D, 64		D, 69		D, 83	59,202	60,102	2	52,759	29.8	13.6	17.5	91.3	5.8	0.1	0.6	0.7
49	D, 100		D, 100		D, 69		D, 63	60,285	59,447	-1	42,988	24.8	9.9	20.1	93.8	4.0	0.1	0.3	0.7
50	D, 62		D, 100		D, 100		D, 53	59,378	57,694	-3	42,032	20.8	9.0	23.6	93.4	4.6	0.1	0.2	0.8

(continued)

Note: D=Democrat, R=Republican, R/D=Republican/Democrat (cross-filed), D/R=Democrat/Republican (cross-filed), I=Independent, C=Constitution, O=Other, GI=Green Independent, P=Progressive, P/D=Progressive/Democrat, P/D/R=Progressive/Democrat/Republican, HH=Households

Pennsylvania State House Districts—Election and Demographic Data (cont.)

House Districts	General Election Results Party, Percent of Vote							Population			Avg. HH Income	Pop 25+		Below Poverty Line	2006 White (Non-Hisp)	African American	American Indians, Alaska Natives	Asians, Hawaiians, Pacific Islanders	Hispanic Origin
												Some College +	4-Yr Degree +						
Penn.	2000	2001	2002	2003	2004	2005	2006	2000	2006	% Change	($)	(%)	(%)	(%)	(%)	(%)	(%)	(%)	(%)
51	D, 100		D, 63		D, 35		D, 62	62,164	61,733	-1	42,719	20.9	8.8	25.1	94.1	4.0	0.1	0.4	0.5
52	D, 100		D, 100		D, 66		D, 68	63,243	61,351	-3	40,546	23.4	8.7	23.1	95.9	2.5	0.1	0.3	0.4
53	R, 70		R, 100		R, 100		R, 59	57,581	59,541	3	64,129	39.1	24.7	7.8	82.3	3.1	0.1	8.8	3.6
54	D, 100		D, 100		D, 60		D, 59	61,826	59,779	-3	54,990	38.2	17.2	15.5	92.9	4.3	0.0	1.0	0.7
55	D, 75		D, 100		D, 70		D, 100	61,110	61,155	0	45,614	33.6	12.0	16.6	97.3	1.2	0.1	0.3	0.5
56	D, 66		D, 62		D, 63		D, 63	60,751	59,153	-3	55,736	39.8	17.4	13.2	96.5	1.4	0.1	0.6	0.6
57	D, 68		D, 54		D, 60		D, 68	58,802	59,377	1	51,705	39.5	18.3	15.1	94.5	2.8	0.1	0.7	0.9
58	D, 100		D, 100		D, 100		D, 66	63,461	62,655	-1	46,928	35.0	13.5	16.9	95.0	3.0	0.1	0.4	0.6
59	R/D, 100		R/D, 100		D/R, 100		D/R,100	61,275	62,254	2	54,929	36.3	16.9	15.3	97.5	0.6	0.0	0.7	0.5
60	R, 52		R/D, 100		R, 62		R, 70	61,072	58,206	-5	43,889	22.5	8.8	18.8	97.6	0.8	0.1	0.2	0.6
61	R, 52		R, 63		R, 59		R, 55	62,670	67,912	8	97,840	50.1	36.0	6.2	83.5	4.9	0.1	8.2	2.0
62	D, 54		R, 57		R, 57		R, 63	59,800	57,829	-3	44,067	27.2	14.0	22.7	94.3	2.5	0.1	1.4	0.8
63	R/D, 100		R/D, 100		D/R, 93		R, 73	58,679	58,005	-1	41,732	20.4	9.1	20.7	97.7	0.8	0.1	0.3	0.5
64	R, 100		R, 68		R, 100		R, 66	62,131	60,551	-3	43,562	22.4	9.0	19.1	96.9	1.2	0.1	0.3	0.6
65	R, 100		R, 53		R, 63		D/R, 100	59,072	57,722	-2	46,236	24.9	9.5	15.4	95.5	1.8	0.2	0.4	1.0
66	R, 100		R, 73		R, 100		R, 56	58,671	60,581	3	42,491	19.7	7.6	19.4	98.3	0.2	0.1	0.3	0.5
67	R, 100		R, 100		R, 100		R, 100	59,090	57,247	-3	45,402	23.8	9.5	18.3	97.5	0.4	0.2	0.5	0.6
68	R/D, 100		R/D, 100		D/R, 100		D/R, 100	58,869	59,590	1	43,461	24.2	9.4	18.4	97.3	0.7	0.1	0.4	0.7
69	R, 100		R, 71		R, 70		R, 100	59,668	59,273	-1	42,411	19.9	8.1	19.6	95.3	2.3	0.1	0.4	1.1
70	R, 51		R, 61		R, 55		R, 49	59,899	63,135	5	77,048	42.6	28.0	9.4	75.3	13.7	0.1	4.4	4.6
71	D, 74		D, 57		D, 73		D, 78	56,284	52,454	-7	44,685	26.9	11.8	21.3	91.6	4.9	0.1	0.9	1.2
72	D, 78		D, 69		D, 77		D, 74	63,514	60,778	-4	42,445	24.4	9.8	18.5	97.4	1.2	0.0	0.3	0.6
73	D, 73		D, 66		D, 100		D, 71	58,317	58,106	0	40,708	20.3	7.8	20.1	95.6	2.0	0.1	0.3	1.3
74	D, 71		D, 68		D, 73		D, 63	59,204	58,386	-1	40,222	18.0	6.3	20.5	95.8	2.3	0.1	0.2	0.8
75	D, 74		D, 100		D, 100		D, 61	59,208	58,089	-2	49,789	25.6	10.6	15.0	98.1	0.3	0.1	0.6	0.5
76	D, 60		D, 69		D, 68		D, 100	59,720	59,114	-1	44,323	22.6	9.5	18.0	95.0	2.3	0.1	0.6	1.0
77	R, 62		R, 86		R, 58		D, 59	57,953	62,403	8	53,163	44.7	32.3	18.7	86.3	2.2	0.1	7.5	2.0
78	R/D, 100		R, 78		D/R, 100		R, 69	60,549	61,086	1	45,230	19.2	7.1	18.1	97.6	0.6	0.1	0.3	0.6
79	R/D, 100		R/D, 100		R, 69		R, 100	61,203	58,997	-4	40,673	23.0	9.2	21.2	95.2	2.4	0.1	0.5	0.8
80	R, 100		R, 82		D/R, 100		R, 100	62,975	62,572	-1	48,776	25.6	10.7	16.0	97.9	0.5	0.1	0.5	0.5
81	R, 71		R/D, 100		R, 100		R, 65	58,902	59,872	2	44,164	19.2	8.0	18.2	93.3	4.3	0.1	0.3	1.0
82	R, 100		R, 62		D/R, 100		R, 58	61,842	61,474	-1	43,682	17.4	7.0	18.0	96.8	0.5	0.1	0.4	1.3
83	R, 58		R, 100		R, 100		R, 60	60,399	58,446	-3	47,377	28.8	11.8	19.3	89.0	7.4	0.2	0.8	1.0
84	R, 81		R, 100		R, 100		R, 63	121,438	119,413	-2	47,239	27.1	10.4	17.1	91.6	5.2	0.1	0.6	1.2
85	R, 89		R, 90		R, 100		R, 68	58,644	60,440	3	53,246	22.8	11.8	15.0	90.4	4.3	0.1	1.1	2.8
86	R, 100		R, 100		R, 100		R, 100	61,327	63,767	4	53,417	21.0	8.3	12.6	96.5	1.0	0.1	0.4	1.1
87	R, 78		R, 78		R, 61		R, 66	62,759	66,535	6	73,952	42.9	24.9	7.3	91.1	1.5	0.1	3.9	1.9
88	R, 75		R, 77		R, 73		R, 69	58,685	60,735	3	65,964	40.2	21.6	7.9	90.9	3.4	0.1	1.9	2.4
89	D, 63		D, 51		R, 60		R, 70	61,061	65,657	8	51,185	23.9	11.7	14.4	89.0	3.8	0.1	1.0	3.9
90	R, 100		R, 100		R, 100		R, 54	60,595	64,077	6	54,725	23.9	9.1	11.8	95.3	1.4	0.1	0.6	1.5
91	R, 74		R, 75		R, 74		R, 52	59,541	65,320	10	55,573	26.5	12.9	12.0	90.7	1.8	0.1	0.8	4.0
92	R, 96		R, 77		R, 75		R, 71	63,100	68,594	9	70,139	37.4	17.3	8.0	95.0	1.0	0.1	1.0	1.6
93	R, 100		R, 100		R, 93		R, 100	59,581	65,270	10	66,909	39.9	19.2	8.7	95.1	1.3	0.1	1.0	1.3
94	R, 100		R, 100		R, 100		R, 73	60,076	65,994	10	58,596	33.5	13.9	9.6	95.8	1.0	0.1	0.6	1.3
95	D, 63		D, 100		D, 100		D, 58	60,832	62,054	2	46,770	30.7	13.3	20.2	59.2	17.6	0.2	1.5	16.5
96	D, 61		D, 61		D, 66		D, 63	59,802	60,256	1	43,240	23.5	11.5	21.0	38.7	13.5	0.3	3.2	37.0
97	R, 100		R, 94		R, 95		R, 62	56,571	59,940	6	74,409	42.9	25.7	6.7	91.2	1.2	0.1	2.7	2.8
98	R, 69		R, 71		R, 100		R, 100	59,196	62,443	5	53,476	28.8	13.7	10.8	91.0	2.2	0.1	0.9	3.4
99	R, 100		R, 78		R, 100		R, 74	60,597	63,985	6	58,616	23.1	11.2	9.9	93.2	0.8	0.1	1.6	2.5
100	R, 73		R, 74		R, 100		R, 100	59,487	62,355	5	60,691	22.4	10.5	11.5	96.0	0.9	0.1	0.5	1.2

(continued)

Note: D=Democrat, R=Republican, R/D=Republican/Democrat (cross-filed), D/R=Democrat/Republican (cross-filed), I=Independent, C=Constitution, O=Other, GI=Green Independent, P=Progressive, P/D=Progressive/Democrat, P/D/R=Progressive/Democrat/Republican, HH=Households

Pennsylvania State House Districts—Election and Demographic Data (cont.)

House Districts	General Election Results Party, Percent of Vote							Population			Avg. HH Income	2006 Pop 25+		Below Poverty Line	2006 White (Non-Hisp)	African American	American Indians, Alaska Natives	Asians, Hawaiians, Pacific Islanders	Hispanic Origin
Penn.	2000	2001	2002	2003	2004	2005	2006	2000	2006	% Change	($)	Some College + (%)	4-Yr Degree + (%)	(%)	(%)	(%)	(%)	(%)	(%)
101	R, 95		R, 65		R, 83		R, 84	59,402	61,245	3	52,256	24.8	11.8	13.7	82.0	1.9	0.1	1.5	9.9
102	R, 65		R, 76		R, 93		R, 80	60,481	64,184	6	57,558	21.2	10.2	10.0	93.5	0.9	0.1	0.9	2.9
103	D, 100		D, 61		D, 100		D, 72	61,164	60,464	-1	41,742	30.1	11.6	23.6	34.7	47.4	0.2	3.0	12.8
104	R, 66		R, 61		R, 100		R, 57	61,184	62,169	2	60,294	37.2	16.9	11.4	84.2	10.0	0.1	1.6	2.0
105	R, 76		R/D, 100		R, 87		R, 68	61,463	62,350	1	68,832	43.3	22.4	6.1	85.1	7.3	0.1	2.9	2.5
106	R, 90		R, 100		R, 60		R, 100	59,113	59,507	1	65,836	40.8	22.0	10.0	83.6	7.5	0.1	3.1	3.2
107	D, 71		D, 59		D, 61		D, 100	59,034	57,532	-3	42,862	22.8	10.1	20.1	94.8	2.2	0.1	0.7	1.3
108	R, 100		R, 85		R, 100		R, 74	62,199	62,390	0	47,773	22.3	9.6	15.2	95.9	0.8	0.1	0.4	1.4
109	D, 80		R, 78		R, 58		R, 58	59,101	59,214	0	47,396	24.5	11.4	17.3	95.6	1.0	0.1	0.8	1.5
110	R, 68		R, 100		R, 100		R, 73	58,853	58,063	-1	48,343	24.7	10.6	16.6	96.5	0.6	0.3	0.7	0.9
111	R, 77		R, 100		R, 90		R, 83	59,199	59,181	0	47,113	26.2	10.1	17.5	97.3	0.5	0.1	0.4	1.0
112	D, 97		D, 100		D, 100		D, 100	58,982	59,185	0	46,267	29.1	13.3	20.3	89.4	3.3	0.1	1.4	3.9
113	D, 100		D, 100		D, 100		D, 72	60,162	57,203	-5	49,466	29.2	13.8	18.6	93.8	1.2	0.1	1.1	2.5
114	D, 61		D, 67		D, 71		D/R, 100	55,545	55,415	0	57,562	33.0	16.3	14.4	97.0	0.5	0.0	0.8	1.0
115	D, 100		D, 100		D, 100		D, 100	59,935	59,134	-1	46,760	27.9	11.7	18.5	95.2	1.5	0.1	0.4	1.7
116	D, 66		D, 100		D, 69		D, 86	58,450	58,098	-1	49,885	30.1	12.6	18.6	89.8	1.3	0.1	0.8	6.1
117	R, 95		R, 100		R, 68		R, 67	60,104	62,507	4	54,113	32.5	14.4	14.1	95.9	1.1	0.1	0.6	1.5
118	D, 68		D, 100		D, 58		D, 67	57,413	65,256	14	53,350	30.6	13.0	15.1	88.1	2.9	0.1	0.9	6.2
119	D, 100		D, 100		D, 100		D, 80	59,530	56,268	-5	43,070	31.5	12.6	20.9	94.7	1.7	0.1	0.7	2.1
120	D, 64		D, 65		D, 100		D, 74	58,877	56,331	-4	50,312	37.8	18.1	16.0	95.1	1.8	0.0	0.7	1.7
121	D, 75		D, 100		D, 63		D, 65	59,903	56,292	-6	40,596	30.1	11.7	22.0	90.4	4.0	0.1	1.2	3.1
122	D, 100		D, 100		D, 100		D, 66	58,889	62,010	5	45,772	23.3	8.1	16.4	95.4	0.7	0.1	0.4	2.2
123	D, 72		D, 52		D, 73		D, 68	60,780	57,863	-5	40,062	21.6	8.0	22.1	91.1	5.0	0.1	0.5	2.5
124	R, 76		R, 74		R, 71		R, 62	60,699	62,233	3	53,536	29.4	14.5	13.3	95.3	0.6	0.1	0.7	2.0
125	R, 100		R, 72		R, 100		D, 54	60,588	60,674	0	51,919	25.4	10.9	14.6	96.5	0.7	0.0	0.5	1.2
126	D, 71		D, 73		D, 93		D, 64	60,611	63,064	4	54,640	29.4	15.2	14.0	65.1	6.4	0.1	1.4	19.4
127	D, 75		D, 72		D, 91		D, 100	60,743	61,744	2	37,519	22.4	10.6	27.3	30.2	10.7	0.3	2.0	48.7
128	R, 63		R, 65		R, 100		R, 55	61,716	66,307	7	77,440	40.8	25.2	7.8	90.9	1.7	0.1	1.8	3.3
129	R, 100		R, 71		R, 66		R, 53	62,520	69,826	12	65,118	34.0	19.9	8.4	88.9	2.3	0.1	1.4	5.1
130	R, 68		R, 68		R, 66		D, 57	61,121	66,095	8	69,134	34.4	19.0	7.6	93.2	1.8	0.1	0.9	2.4
131	R, 59		R, 62		R, 91		R, 53	62,230	66,384	7	64,960	37.9	18.9	10.3	74.5	3.6	0.1	2.8	13.4
132	D, 71		D, 100		D, 71		D, 79	61,387	63,237	3	44,252	30.9	13.9	21.0	43.2	8.7	0.2	2.5	37.3
133	D, 65		D, 68		D, 68		D, 66	59,377	63,481	7	46,507	29.6	12.4	18.2	61.8	4.5	0.2	2.6	23.1
134	R, 53		R, 63		R, 90		R, 60	60,523	65,780	9	75,736	43.2	24.6	7.3	91.6	0.9	0.1	3.1	2.7
135	D, 53		D, 64		D, 65		D, 100	61,959	64,943	5	54,724	36.8	19.8	14.8	69.2	3.4	0.1	2.4	17.5
136	D, 100		D, 100		D, 66		D, 100	57,622	61,854	7	54,949	30.4	15.0	13.9	79.8	6.5	0.1	1.9	8.1
137	D, 52		D, 100		D, 58		D, 100	57,584	64,519	12	66,815	36.4	18.9	10.3	93.5	1.5	0.1	1.3	2.3
138	R, 100		R, 100		R, 100		R, 100	63,579	70,152	10	71,533	38.1	21.2	8.0	93.1	1.1	0.1	1.9	2.3
139	R, 93		R, 100		R, 100		R, 100	59,361	67,139	13	54,576	31.1	13.1	15.1	92.4	1.6	0.1	0.8	3.6
140	D, 100		D, 100		D, 100		D, 71	58,169	59,150	2	58,524	31.6	13.5	11.6	81.1	8.0	0.1	2.5	5.7
141	D, 56		D, 73		D, 72		D, 77	60,016	59,347	-1	58,983	27.9	10.3	10.8	82.1	7.8	0.1	2.9	4.7
142	R, 100		R, 59		R, 59		D, 53	58,115	59,907	3	76,622	40.8	22.6	6.5	90.7	2.5	0.1	3.0	2.2
143	R, 55		R, 58		R, 61		R, 50	60,386	69,091	14	99,707	47.5	30.8	7.0	93.6	1.6	0.1	1.6	1.9
144	R, 57		R, 87		R, 66		R, 60	59,371	62,487	5	79,692	42.8	24.5	6.4	92.2	1.9	0.1	2.6	2.0
145	R, 100		R, 68		R, 65		R, 61	59,793	62,897	5	62,834	35.4	17.3	8.8	94.3	1.1	0.1	1.2	1.9
146	R, 55		R, 58		R, 52		R, 58	60,723	64,691	7	59,911	34.6	20.8	10.3	84.4	8.3	0.1	1.5	3.3
147	R, 100		R, 100		R, 100		R, 56	55,718	59,415	7	72,709	36.8	22.6	7.5	93.9	1.9	0.1	1.3	1.6
148	R, 100		R, 51		D, 50		D, 67	63,100	65,935	4	140,759	53.9	43.0	6.8	87.6	4.9	0.0	4.5	1.8
149	D, 62		D, 53		D, 62		D, 67	63,780	65,686	3	108,782	49.7	39.2	7.4	81.9	6.2	0.1	7.1	2.9
150	R, 100		R, 50		R, 55		R, 52	65,230	69,100	6	76,720	41.6	27.9	7.6	74.5	13.2	0.1	4.1	5.8

(continued)

Note: D=Democrat, R=Republican, R/D=Republican/Democrat (cross-filed), D/R=Democrat/Republican (cross-filed), I=Independent, C=Constitution, O=Other, GI=Green Independent, P=Progressive, P/D=Progressive/Democrat, P/D/R=Progressive/Democrat/Republican, HH=Households

Pennsylvania State House Districts—Election and Demographic Data (cont.)

House Districts	General Election Results Party, Percent of Vote							Population			Avg. HH Income ($)	2006 Pop 25+		Below Poverty Line (%)	White (Non-Hisp) (%)	African American (%)	American Indians, Alaska Natives (%)	Asians, Hawaiians, Pacific Islanders (%)	Hispanic Origin (%)
												Some College + (%)	4-Yr Degree + (%)						
Penn.	2000	2001	2002	2003	2004	2005	2006	2000	2006	% Change	($)	(%)	(%)	(%)	(%)	(%)	(%)	(%)	(%)
151	R, 56		R, 62		R, 58		D, 55	59,257	62,223	5	92,035	47.9	33.7	5.6	83.8	5.0	0.1	8.0	1.9
152	R, 100		R, 100		R, 56		R, 54	59,939	60,738	1	85,713	45.8	31.4	8.3	87.1	4.1	0.1	5.2	2.2
153	R, 62		R, 66		D, 54		D, 76	63,968	64,631	1	89,774	47.0	32.8	7.2	80.7	11.2	0.1	4.5	2.0
154	D, 74		D, 100		D, 75		D, 78	65,681	66,352	1	87,798	49.6	36.5	8.0	67.8	22.1	0.1	5.8	2.6
155	R, 100		R, 100		R, 100		R, 100	56,571	63,489	12	98,401	49.4	32.5	5.1	90.2	3.8	0.1	2.8	1.6
156	R, 60		R, 64		R, 55		D, 50	60,640	65,394	8	90,593	48.3	33.3	7.2	82.5	8.0	0.1	3.1	4.2
157	R, 100		R, 66		R, 89		R, 58	61,251	66,114	8	102,327	53.2	39.3	6.8	86.8	4.4	0.1	5.1	2.1
158	R, 68		R, 72		R, 65		R, 64	61,026	67,313	10	107,980	48.9	32.8	5.9	77.6	6.4	0.1	2.2	10.3
159	D, 64		D, 54		D, 69		D, 68	57,942	58,411	1	40,304	20.2	8.4	25.9	41.4	51.4	0.1	1.3	5.1
160	R, 66		R, 100		R, 66		R, 64	62,246	67,082	8	96,344	42.5	28.1	6.4	88.2	6.0	0.0	3.1	1.5
161	R, 95		R, 52		R, 100		D, 51	62,568	63,388	1	92,586	42.5	29.4	9.2	87.0	6.2	0.1	3.8	1.6
162	R, 64		R, 73		R, 64		R, 62	59,363	58,850	-1	52,815	26.6	11.9	11.9	87.9	7.1	0.1	2.3	1.2
163	R, 64		R, 68		R, 61		R, 57	58,301	58,092	0	56,869	34.5	18.4	10.9	85.1	8.0	0.1	4.1	1.3
164	R, 63		R, 68		R, 55		R, 57	60,827	59,985	-1	55,126	33.8	19.6	14.9	66.7	16.5	0.1	12.1	2.4
165	R, 66		R, 69		R, 65		R, 59	59,227	59,250	0	100,268	43.7	30.3	6.9	87.4	4.6	0.0	5.5	1.3
166	D, 69		D, 64		D, 60		D, 67	59,766	60,060	0	88,023	45.5	32.3	7.8	88.2	4.7	0.1	4.6	1.3
167	R, 67		R, 100		R, 100		R, 50	59,232	65,224	10	112,887	55.7	40.0	4.4	89.4	3.5	0.1	4.0	1.7
168	R, 67		R, 66		R, 100		R, 59	60,547	63,570	5	107,890	47.9	34.0	5.8	85.8	8.2	0.1	3.0	1.6
169	R, 100		R, 100		R, 100		R, 100	56,766	54,182	-5	57,566	27.8	13.6	11.5	72.8	15.4	0.1	4.4	4.6
170	R, 54		R, 65		R, 58		R, 54	59,430	56,522	-5	57,442	32.9	18.3	14.6	72.3	12.7	0.1	7.0	5.0
171	R, 93		R, 74		R, 67		R, 100	62,454	63,295	1	53,064	33.4	21.2	17.9	90.4	2.0	0.1	4.1	1.7
172	R, 50		R, 82		R, 75		R, 68	63,346	59,667	-6	51,452	29.0	15.3	14.6	75.1	13.7	0.1	3.7	4.5
173	D, 81		D, 83		D, 81		D, 76	54,093	51,265	-5	45,240	21.0	9.7	18.5	61.9	24.2	0.1	2.7	7.7
174	D, 100		D, 80		D, 76		D, 93	59,275	56,336	-5	47,281	30.4	16.5	17.3	62.9	16.1	0.1	8.8	8.6
175	D, 73		D, 100		D, 81		D, 84	57,270	57,656	1	62,153	33.0	22.9	23.6	50.5	20.6	0.2	10.6	14.2
176	R, 100		R, 65		R, 59		R, 62	58,114	68,470	18	58,634	30.7	14.3	13.6	70.5	8.8	0.2	1.8	14.4
177	R, 56		R, 78		R, 100		R, 66	56,396	52,787	-6	39,255	18.9	8.5	24.3	61.2	16.9	0.2	3.2	13.0
178	R, 56		R, 55		R, 62		R, 59	56,623	58,783	4	114,153	47.0	30.0	4.0	94.5	0.9	0.0	2.4	1.2
179	D, 100		D, 82		D, 84		D, 88	59,471	56,083	-6	38,059	18.9	8.2	31.6	23.6	36.9	0.3	7.4	32.4
180	D, 89		D, 86		D, 86		D, 92	60,155	57,068	-5	26,967	13.9	5.9	45.7	10.6	24.6	0.4	5.5	64.9
181	D, 100		D, 100		D, 100		D, 100	60,263	59,945	-1	31,076	17.8	8.2	43.2	12.9	56.6	0.3	2.7	34.0
182	D, 95		D, 79		D, 80		D, 82	58,184	57,347	-1	59,060	50.0	38.8	19.9	56.9	24.9	0.2	9.8	5.8
183	R, 68		R, 68		R, 100		R, 61	62,449	67,573	8	61,741	35.0	16.4	9.8	91.2	1.3	0.1	2.3	3.4
184	D, 100		D, 100		D, 79		D, 84	58,008	54,526	-6	39,052	21.1	10.3	27.5	56.8	20.2	0.1	13.7	6.4
185	D, 80		D, 80		D, 81		D, 84	57,920	55,169	-5	45,280	24.4	11.2	22.6	47.5	43.7	0.1	3.7	3.1
186	D, 91		D, 100		D, 93		D, 100	60,910	57,779	-5	34,221	22.6	10.9	34.4	21.5	66.6	0.2	7.2	3.8
187	R, 100		R, 67		R, 100		R, 51	61,910	67,006	8	73,785	36.9	20.0	8.8	92.7	1.1	0.1	1.7	2.7
188	D, 100		D, 100		D, 100		D, 86	58,566	57,457	-2	35,878	26.0	15.9	32.6	26.4	56.7	0.2	10.9	4.5
189	R, 51		R, 100		R, 100		D, 54	60,556	74,903	24	65,617	31.4	14.0	10.8	80.9	5.1	0.1	1.3	9.5
190	D, 94		D, 97		D, 95		D, 97	59,425	56,123	-6	30,256	20.5	8.3	38.0	8.7	86.3	0.2	1.7	2.8
191	D, 100		D, 100		D, 100		D, 100	61,396	58,076	-5	40,039	23.3	10.0	27.6	15.3	75.9	0.1	5.1	2.8
192	D, 100		D, 100		D, 100		D, 100	58,912	55,638	-6	45,084	28.2	13.8	22.9	20.6	71.8	0.2	3.0	3.4
193	R, 100		R, 72		R, 92		R, 67	61,565	67,134	9	53,797	27.8	11.6	10.9	91.3	0.7	0.1	0.8	4.8
194	D, 100		D, 80		D, 100		D, 81	59,732	58,818	-2	68,841	43.0	29.9	15.2	65.5	24.5	0.2	4.4	3.2
195	D, 100		D, 100		D, 100		D, 100	58,193	58,021	0	42,935	27.4	17.0	33.5	27.3	62.0	0.2	4.4	5.4
196	R, 64		R, 81		R, 96		R, 73	61,534	66,238	8	58,232	32.7	14.0	8.0	94.9	1.1	0.1	0.9	1.5
197	D, 97		D, 100		D, 94		D, 100	61,170	59,892	-2	33,876	20.7	10.1	39.4	16.7	76.7	0.2	2.5	3.5
198	D, 87		D, 100		D, 100		D, 96	58,653	55,398	-6	50,549	30.4	17.4	25.6	20.7	66.5	0.2	5.0	7.1
199	R, 63		R, 59		R, 58		R, 56	60,812	63,680	5	57,362	29.0	15.7	12.4	92.3	3.1	0.1	1.2	1.7
200	D, 84		D, 88		D, 100		D, 100	57,982	54,492	-6	68,463	39.6	24.8	12.4	30.5	61.9	0.2	2.6	3.3

(continued)

Note: D=Democrat, R=Republican, R/D=Republican/Democrat (cross-filed), D/R=Democrat/Republican (cross-filed), I=Independent, C=Constitution, O=Other, GI=Green Independent, P=Progressive, P/D=Progressive/Democrat, P/D/R=Progressive/Democrat/Republican, HH=Households

Pennsylvania State House Districts—Election and Demographic Data (cont.)

House Districts	General Election Results Party, Percent of Vote							Population			Avg. HH Income	Pop 25+		Below Poverty Line	White (Non-Hisp)	African American	American Indians, Alaska Natives	Asians, Hawaiians, Pacific Islanders	Hispanic Origin
												Some College +	4-Yr Degree +						
																		2006	
Penn.	2000	2001	2002	2003	2004	2005	2006	2000	2006	% Change	($)	(%)	(%)	(%)	(%)	(%)	(%)	(%)	(%)
201	D, 97		D, 97		D, 100		D, 97	60,463	57,213	-5	42,739	24.4	11.4	25.6	14.0	79.8	0.2	2.0	3.2
202	D, 100		D, 76		D, 79		D, 100	65,455	61,406	-6	45,859	24.2	11.7	21.3	39.8	37.1	0.2	10.1	11.2
203	D, 100		D, 90		D, 100		D, 100	56,495	53,118	-6	46,184	26.1	11.6	18.1	22.8	61.4	0.2	6.8	8.9

Note: D=Democrat, R=Republican, R/D=Republican/Democrat (cross-filed), D/R=Democrat/Republican (cross-filed), I=Independent, C=Constitution, O=Other, GI=Green Independent, P=Progressive, P/D=Progressive/Democrat, P/D/R=Progressive/Democrat/Republican, HH=Households

RHODE ISLAND

Rhode Island packs a lot of diversity into a small package. As everyone knows, it is the smallest state geographically, and it could fit into Texas 250 times with room to spare. For a more dramatic illustration of its size, consider this: the state of Rhode Island and Providence Plantations (its official name) is about the size of the territory covered by the Houston bus system. Yet only New Jersey crams in more people per square mile. Founded by people disgusted with Massachusetts Puritanism, it became a wide open colony known scornfully as "Rogue's Island," and later a wide open state. "Rhode Island," as one writer put it, "is separatism personified."

Ethnically, it is a hodgepodge of old family Yankees, Irish, French Canadians, Portuguese, and eastern and southern Europeans. Today, Rhode Island is also the fifth-largest destination for immigrants from the Dominican Republic and draws immigrants from other parts of Latin America, including Ecuador, Guatamala, and Peru. Already perhaps the most Catholic state, these immigrants will only make it more so.

The state can be divided into three broad regions. There are two urban pockets, one around Providence and Pawtucket along Interstate 95 and a second around Woonsocket. The lower half of the state along the ocean from Newport to the Connecticut border is rural. The rest, a broad band reaching from the Massachusetts border to Warwick, with a tongue pointing down to Narragansett, is suburban. Rhode Island is the third-most suburban state, after Maryland and Connecticut.

The recession in the early 1990s hurt Rhode Island's manufacturing plants, and in a state so small it is much less wrenching to move a few miles elsewhere, to Connecticut or Massachusetts, in search of work. Hence, having grown by almost 6 percent during the 1980s, Rhode Island lost population in the first half of the 1990s before recovering to post modest gains, thanks in part to its proximity to the booming Route 128 high-tech corridor in Massachusetts. Growth in this decade has been unspectacular but in line with the region: a little bit faster than in Massachusetts, a little bit slower than in Connecticut, but far short of New Hampshire. The 68th house district, near Bristol, has grown by 10 percent since 2000; the 73rd district, encompassing Newport, has shrunk by 5 percent. Everything else falls in between.

One hundred years ago Newport was summer home of wealthy Americans who built incredible mansions and vacation palaces. From 1930 to 1983, the America's Cup was raced every four years off its shores. The state still has areas of great wealth, but also of great poverty. It has three house districts where the average household income exceeds $100,000 (led by the 30th district—East Greenwich—where it is $124,000), but four districts where it is less than $35,000. The 56th district just north of Pawtucket, where average household income is just $29,000, is one of the ten poorest state house districts in the United States.

That extremely poor district is also almost 65 percent Hispanic, filling with the state's newest round of immigrants. Rhode Island's Hispanic population doubled, to nearly 9 percent, between 1990 and 2000, which is still a lower percentage than in Connecticut or Massachusetts. The 10th house district is almost 17 percent Asian. There are no black-majority districts or even districts in which African Americans make up a third of the population. Diversity in Rhode Island is more ethnic than racial.

Politically, Rhode Island is one of the most Democratic states in the country, one of six to support Jimmy Carter's reelection bid in 1980. Even its Republicans have tended to be liberals. But Rhode Island Republicans, liberal or conservative, are a rare lot. Democrats control the state house of representatives, 60–15, and the state senate, 33–5, making it one of the most politically imbalanced legislatures in the country.

Like many states, Rhode Island's legislature was long dominated by rural counties that preserved their power by refusing to reapportion seats to reflect the changing population. At the time of the U.S. Supreme Court's one-man, one-vote decision in 1964, Rhode Island house districts were still being drawn based on figures from the 1930 census. Reapportionment, however, brought its own headaches. Efforts to redraw the lines after the 1980 census were tied up in court so long that the 1982 state senate elections were not held until June 1983.

No doubt disgusted by such bickering, state voters in 1994 approved a constitutional amendment to cut the size of their legislature by a quarter—shrinking the state house from one hundred seats to seventy-five and the senate from fifty seats to thirty-eight. Those changes took effect with the 2002 election cycle. Even if it is smaller, Rhode Islanders can still feel connected to their government. Each member of the state house currently represents about 14,000 residents. Each member of the California assembly, by comparison, represents about 420,000.

RHODE ISLAND
State Senate Districts

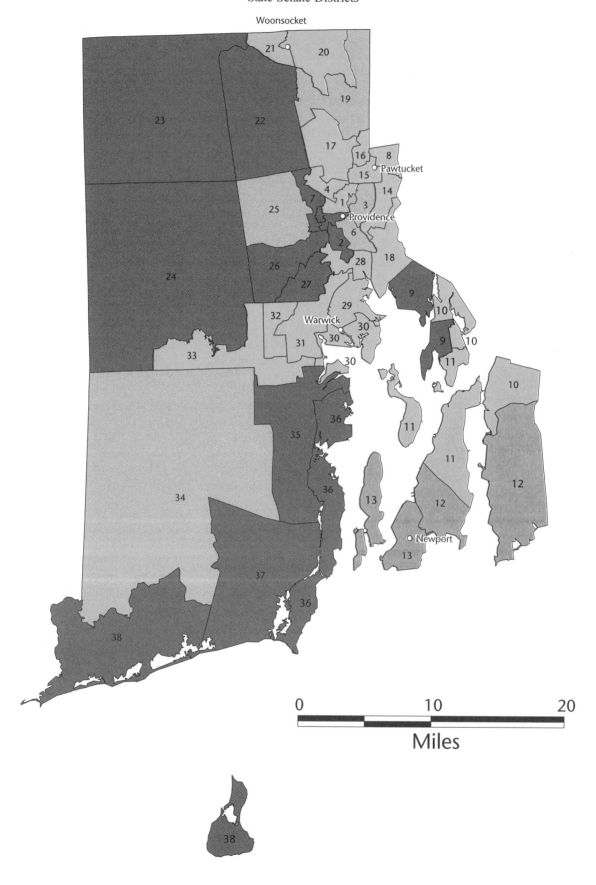

Woonsocket

21 20

19

23 22

17

16 8

15 Pawtucket

4 14

7 25 1 3

5 6

2 28 18

26 27 9

29 10

32 Warwick 30 10

31 30 9

33 30 11

35 36 10

11

36 13 11

34 12

37 13

36 Newport

38

0 10 20

Miles

38

Population Growth   ▨ -4% to -1%   ▨ -1% to 2%   ▣ 2% to 4%   ▨ 4% to 7%

Rhode Island State Senate Districts—Election and Demographic Data

Senate Districts	General Election Results Party, Percent of Vote							Population			Avg. HH Income ($)	Pop 25+ Some College + (%)	Pop 25+ 4-Yr Degree + (%)	Below Poverty Line (%)	White (Non-Hisp) (%)	African American (%)	American Indians, Alaska Natives (%)	Asians, Hawaiians, Pacific Islanders (%)	Hispanic Origin (%)
Rhode Island	2000	2001	2002	2003	2004	2005	2006	2000	2006	% Change	($)	(%)	(%)	(%)	(%)	(%)	(%)	(%)	(%)
1	D, 78		D, 82		D, 76		D, 83	27,178	27,584	1	39,625	27.4	15.0	30.6	35.9	17.3	0.9	7.5	37.1
2	D, 100		D, 74		D, 87		D, 88	27,897	28,929	4	41,277	23.1	11.1	33.9	13.8	21.3	1.3	14.9	61.6
3	D, 100		D, 86		D, 62		D, 100	27,735	28,910	4	94,913	46.4	38.7	18.0	73.8	6.1	0.3	9.2	5.8
4	D, 100		D, 100		D, 79		D, 79	28,929	29,324	1	53,668	34.5	18.2	17.8	69.7	9.0	0.4	3.4	12.7
5	D, 100		D, 77		D, 71		D, 64	27,344	28,243	3	33,504	23.5	11.7	37.7	24.4	15.0	1.1	8.7	54.5
6	D, 100		D, 79		D, 100		D, 100	28,546	29,764	4	37,386	25.6	14.2	38.1	22.6	29.3	1.5	6.2	44.9
7	D, 100		D, 80		D, 72		D, 82	28,222	28,952	3	48,970	31.8	16.4	21.6	56.7	7.6	0.7	4.9	24.5
8	D, 100		D, 100		D, 70		D, 100	26,223	26,073	-1	49,601	31.0	13.5	17.5	72.7	6.1	0.3	2.7	12.5
9	D, 100		R, 100		R, 55		D, 65	25,999	26,524	2	95,264	47.8	31.6	11.0	95.2	0.7	0.1	1.6	1.4
10	D, 91		D, 100		D, 100		D, 100	26,942	26,900	0	62,481	35.3	17.0	13.6	95.0	1.0	0.2	1.5	1.1
11	D, 77		R, 52		D, 54		D, 55	26,157	26,614	2	72,630	39.2	24.0	11.0	92.5	1.8	0.2	2.1	2.0
12	D, 70		R, 58		R, 59		R, 53	28,508	27,444	-4	71,962	46.7	27.6	8.8	87.5	4.5	0.3	2.9	2.5
13	D, 100		D, 74		D, 77		D, 100	28,436	27,570	-3	71,339	45.9	29.3	15.2	79.3	8.9	0.7	2.4	5.2
14	D, 75		D, 100		D, 100		D, 100	27,854	28,120	1	49,489	32.7	16.1	17.5	77.9	7.2	0.5	2.3	4.6
15	D, 71		D, 100		D, 100		D, 100	27,668	27,851	1	46,184	29.7	15.5	26.1	51.0	13.5	0.4	2.5	22.4
16	D, 77		D, 80		D, 100		D, 100	27,041	27,413	1	32,189	22.0	9.5	34.5	32.6	8.7	0.5	2.4	50.4
17	D, 100		D, 100		D, 67		D, 66	27,701	28,054	1	61,071	37.5	19.6	13.7	78.3	5.7	0.2	2.8	7.7
18	D, 100		D, 100		D, 51		D, 62	26,411	26,482	0	53,475	36.9	18.2	14.7	82.4	6.4	0.4	3.0	3.0
19	D, 65		D, 59		D, 47		D, 100	28,269	30,074	6	67,075	41.9	23.8	10.7	88.5	2.9	0.2	2.5	2.7
20	D, 100		D, 75		D, 100		D, 100	29,300	29,855	2	54,680	33.8	17.1	17.3	78.8	4.7	0.3	3.7	8.0
21	R, 44		D, 100		D, 79		R, 57	25,415	25,669	1	42,997	28.3	12.3	25.2	68.7	7.1	0.4	6.0	12.7
22	D, 64		D, 68		D, 54		D, 69	27,225	27,911	3	74,779	40.4	22.1	9.7	89.7	2.9	0.2	2.2	2.0
23	D, 56		D, 68		D, 69		D, 100	28,263	29,366	4	67,269	37.3	18.0	9.4	91.0	2.5	0.3	1.5	1.8
24	D, 60		R, 64		R, 61		D, 100	27,163	27,964	3	72,949	40.2	19.9	8.0	92.7	1.7	0.2	1.7	1.6
25	D, 57		D, 100		D, 100		D, 100	28,780	30,196	5	57,842	36.6	17.4	16.5	87.7	3.0	0.2	2.6	3.3
26	R, 100		D, 62		D, 62		D, 100	28,772	29,693	3	58,400	36.0	18.2	16.4	79.3	4.2	0.3	4.6	7.5
27	D, 73		D, 67		D, 55		D, 66	26,910	27,452	2	65,242	42.0	24.1	10.1	79.3	8.2	0.3	3.7	5.9
28	D, 100		D, 71		D, 68		D, 77	26,702	26,733	0	61,741	39.7	21.7	12.3	77.2	5.5	0.4	5.1	7.3
29	D, 51		D, 100		D, 100		D, 100	27,449	27,838	1	58,570	36.1	15.8	11.2	92.2	1.8	0.2	1.6	2.6
30	D, 61		D, 100		D, 70		D, 100	26,191	26,671	2	65,077	37.2	15.9	11.1	91.7	1.6	0.3	2.1	2.3
31	D, 100		D, 62		D, 63		D, 61	26,941	27,430	2	58,909	41.4	20.6	13.2	91.4	1.7	0.2	2.9	2.4
32	D, 100		D, 63		D, 61		R, 51	27,391	27,524	0	52,804	30.9	11.5	16.0	88.3	1.6	0.4	2.2	4.8
33	D, 67		D, 60		D, 100		D, 100	26,376	26,854	2	74,840	35.9	16.7	10.6	94.7	0.7	0.1	1.5	1.8
34	D, 63		R, 56		R, 60		R, 56	28,587	30,050	5	75,689	39.7	19.0	7.7	94.9	0.7	0.7	0.9	1.5
35	D, 100		D, 63		D, 51		D, 100	26,942	27,738	3	97,878	49.1	31.2	10.9	92.7	1.2	0.4	2.4	2.1
36	D, 100		D, 52		D, 62		D, 67	26,721	27,438	3	76,281	48.1	29.2	11.8	93.5	1.3	0.7	1.4	1.7
37	D, 100		D, 63		D, 67		D, 75	29,164	29,969	3	79,349	44.9	29.6	8.9	87.8	2.1	1.5	4.5	2.2
38	D, 100		R, 100		R, 100		R, 58	28,495	29,545	4	68,756	40.0	19.7	11.0	93.4	0.9	0.7	2.4	1.4
39	D, 80																		
40	D, 62																		
41	R, 100																		
42	D, 100																		
43	D, 100																		
44	R, 100																		
45	R, 69																		
46	D, 100																		
47	D, 70																		
48	R, 70																		
49	D, 100																		
50	D, 100																		

*After 2000, RI went from 50 to 38 districts due to redistricting.

Note: D=Democrat, R=Republican, R/D=Republican/Democrat (cross-filed), D/R=Democrat/Republican (cross-filed), I=Independent, C=Constitution, O=Other, GI=Green Independent, P=Progressive, P/D=Progressive/Democrat, P/D/R=Progressive/Democrat/Republican, HH=Households

RHODE ISLAND
State House Districts

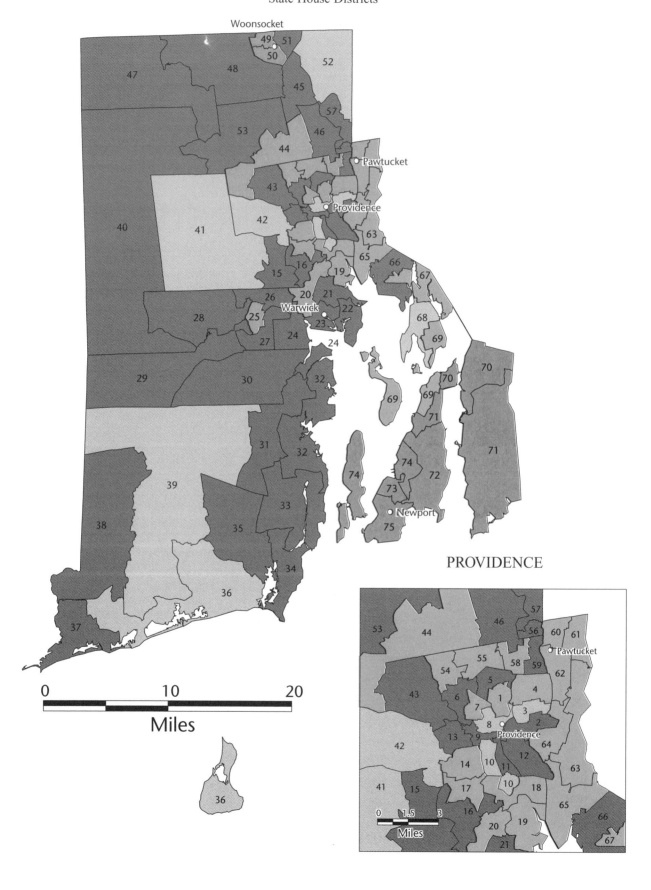

Woonsocket

Pawtucket

Providence

Warwick

Newport

PROVIDENCE

Pawtucket

Providence

0   10   20

Miles

0   1.5   3

Miles

Population Growth   ▨ -5% to -2%   ▨ -2% to 1%   ▨ 1% to 4%   ▨ 4% to 10%

Rhode Island State House Districts—Election and Demographic Data

House Districts	General Election Results Party, Percent of Vote							Population			Avg. HH Income ($)	Pop 25+ Some College + (%)	4-Yr Degree + (%)	Below Poverty Line (%)	White (Non-Hisp) (%)	African American (%)	American Indians, Alaska Natives (%)	Asians, Hawaiians, Pacific Islanders (%)	Hispanic Origin (%)
Rhode Island	2000	2001	2002	2003	2004	2005	2006	2000	2006	% Change					2006				
1	D, 81		D, 100		D, 81		D, 81	13,941	14,041	1	33,599	22.1	11.3	37.2	33.0	18.7	1.0	9.0	38.1
2	D, 100		D, 100		D, 82		D, 100	14,234	14,789	4	49,780	33.0	22.7	28.2	66.5	10.0	0.6	7.1	8.1
3	D, 100		D, 80		D, 78		D, 100	12,793	13,426	5	106,623	41.3	36.0	19.1	72.9	5.6	0.3	10.9	6.0
4	D, 100		D, 78		D, 77		D, 80	13,338	13,465	1	84,905	54.7	42.7	16.7	64.0	16.3	0.7	4.9	8.4
5	D, 87		D, 82		D, 78		D, 83	15,165	15,499	2	45,598	28.3	13.5	23.2	60.2	12.1	0.5	3.2	18.8
6	D, 100		D, 100		D, 73		D, 76	14,513	14,854	2	51,261	33.0	17.2	21.3	55.9	10.1	0.7	5.2	24.0
7	D, 100		D, 100		D, 67		D, 71	14,411	14,345	0	47,497	31.4	17.2	22.8	41.9	13.2	0.8	6.4	35.1
8	D, 100		D, 100		D, 84		D, 88	14,492	15,207	5	34,535	27.2	15.4	38.5	31.7	14.8	0.9	8.5	45.8
9	D, 100		D, 100		D, 82		D, 88	14,698	15,186	3	33,096	22.4	11.2	42.0	15.1	19.8	1.5	9.7	63.5
10	D, 100		D, 88		D, 87		D, 89	14,605	15,210	4	40,613	23.5	11.4	29.5	18.5	20.0	1.2	16.6	53.0
11	D, 100		D, 100		D, 89		D, 92	15,065	15,574	3	41,916	22.9	11.2	36.4	9.8	26.7	1.6	10.7	68.7
12	D, 100		D, 100		D, 100		D, 100	13,147	13,502	3	36,672	20.4	9.2	36.2	19.2	29.8	1.5	5.8	50.4
13	D, 85		D, 79		D, 100		D, 81	14,417	14,740	2	43,296	25.2	12.1	29.0	35.9	9.4	0.8	6.8	43.6
14	D, 100		D, 68		D, 100		D, 70	13,795	13,814	0	45,314	29.9	13.0	20.7	67.8	6.0	0.5	7.2	13.9
15	D, 52		D, 56		R, 52		D, 64	15,599	16,115	3	72,887	41.5	23.2	7.9	81.7	7.7	0.3	3.0	5.0
16	D, 68		D, 70		D, 58		D, 100	14,067	14,367	2	60,532	41.0	23.1	12.5	79.7	7.3	0.3	3.8	5.8
17	D, 91		D, 100		D, 60		D, 100	13,228	13,118	-1	60,875	40.9	21.7	12.3	83.0	3.6	0.3	5.2	4.2
18	D, 81		D, 53		D, 58		D, 74	13,982	13,948	0	63,107	39.4	22.2	13.8	71.7	7.4	0.5	5.4	10.0
19	D, 65		D, 56		D, 100		D, 100	13,308	13,273	0	66,770	43.0	24.1	9.5	92.0	1.8	0.2	1.6	2.6
20	D, 100		D, 100		D, 100		D, 100	15,141	15,011	-1	52,597	36.5	15.7	13.1	91.2	2.1	0.3	2.3	2.5
21	D, 60		D, 100		D, 61		D, 100	15,251	15,538	2	54,977	33.9	13.6	11.6	91.6	2.2	0.3	1.8	2.6
22	D, 100		D, 66		D, 100		D, 100	12,757	12,899	1	70,123	34.2	14.5	13.8	91.2	1.8	0.3	1.7	2.5
23	R, 100		D, 68		D, 100		D, 100	13,420	13,681	2	58,178	34.5	12.8	9.9	92.3	1.5	0.4	2.1	2.3
24	D, 100		R, 67		R, 100		R, 100	14,299	14,449	1	72,148	52.5	30.6	10.1	92.3	1.0	0.1	3.4	1.9
25	D, 100		D, 100		D, 68		D, 67	13,258	13,184	-1	48,982	26.0	8.0	17.1	88.1	1.1	0.5	1.5	5.7
26	D, 100		D, 100		D, 59		D, 100	13,285	13,502	2	56,419	30.6	11.5	17.2	90.5	1.4	0.3	2.1	3.5
27	D, 100		D, 65		D, 62		D, 58	13,797	14,284	4	62,318	38.0	17.0	11.3	91.8	1.5	0.1	2.6	2.4
28	D, 100		R, 51		R, 51		R, 52	15,135	15,506	2	67,850	36.6	14.9	10.3	94.9	0.8	0.2	1.1	1.7
29	D, 70		D, 67		D, 56		D, 100	13,208	13,353	1	67,473	36.7	16.8	10.6	95.8	0.4	0.2	0.9	1.6
30	D, 100		R, 100		R, 100		R, 57	13,719	14,057	2	124,555	52.6	36.9	9.6	93.4	1.0	0.1	3.1	1.4
31	D, 100		D, 100		D, 54		D, 59	12,386	12,793	3	81,475	43.9	24.0	14.3	91.3	1.6	0.7	1.9	2.8
32	D, 73		D, 50		R, 51		R, 52	13,685	13,903	2	79,511	52.0	31.8	8.7	93.7	1.2	0.4	1.4	1.8
33	D, 100		D, 58		D, 52		D, 52	13,763	14,080	2	79,185	49.9	32.5	9.0	92.1	1.3	1.0	2.8	1.4
34	D, 100		D, 100		D, 100		D, 100	13,113	13,364	2	70,906	42.9	26.2	14.0	91.7	1.5	1.6	1.6	1.8
35	D, 100		D, 54		D, 64		D, 59	13,756	13,941	1	81,374	38.4	26.3	7.4	83.3	2.8	1.6	6.7	3.1
36	R, 52		D, 51		D, 62		D, 100	13,344	14,179	6	81,404	49.9	28.6	7.5	95.5	0.5	0.7	1.1	1.1
37	D, 63		D, 60		D, 78		D, 54	14,482	14,915	3	68,382	41.1	21.1	12.7	93.2	0.8	0.4	3.3	1.2
38	D, 100		D, 64		D, 62		D, 100	14,442	14,608	1	68,818	33.8	14.4	10.6	93.8	1.2	0.8	1.0	1.8
39	D, 100		R, 100		R, 100		R, 100	14,232	15,221	7	73,202	40.3	19.3	6.1	94.5	0.8	1.0	1.0	1.5
40	R, 54		R, 63		R, 100		R, 53	14,783	15,327	4	69,623	40.2	20.2	7.3	91.4	2.2	0.2	1.7	1.6
41	D, 79		R, 100		R, 68		R, 53	13,934	14,569	5	83,990	42.5	24.3	6.3	90.4	2.5	0.1	2.2	1.8
42	D, 100		D, 100		D, 72		D, 100	13,498	14,393	7	54,182	36.6	17.6	18.0	88.0	2.7	0.2	2.7	3.1
43	R, 79		D, 100		D, 63		D, 100	14,639	15,009	3	57,445	36.3	17.0	15.3	87.7	3.0	0.2	2.5	3.4
44	D, 100		D, 65		D, 52		D, 65	14,073	14,172	1	76,921	43.6	23.9	10.4	89.2	3.1	0.2	2.5	2.1
45	D, 77		D, 100		D, 55		D, 100	13,716	14,126	3	65,570	44.1	25.2	10.1	87.8	3.0	0.1	3.1	2.6
46	D, 63		I, 60		R, 43		R, 50	15,191	15,517	2	54,946	36.1	19.7	15.7	74.6	5.5	0.2	2.4	10.3
47	D, 100		D, 54		D, 60		D, 100	13,713	14,212	4	64,938	34.1	15.2	10.5	90.8	2.5	0.3	1.6	2.0
48	D, 70		D, 51		D, 50		D, 52	13,570	14,097	4	71,601	40.8	20.3	10.6	90.8	2.7	0.2	1.7	1.6
49	D, 68		D, 64		D, 75		D, 100	14,599	14,576	0	39,487	26.9	11.4	28.0	67.8	7.3	0.4	6.3	13.2
50	D, 72		D, 100		D, 100		D, 82	14,136	14,096	0	42,963	27.0	11.2	21.2	68.8	7.0	0.4	6.2	12.3

(continued)

Note: D=Democrat, R=Republican, R/D=Republican/Democrat (cross-filed), D/R=Democrat/Republican (cross-filed), I=Independent, C=Constitution, O=Other, GI=Green Independent, P=Progressive, P/D=Progressive/Democrat, P/D/R=Progressive/Democrat/Republican, HH=Households

Rhode Island State House Districts—Election and Demographic Data (cont.)

House Districts	General Election Results Party, Percent of Vote							Population			Avg. HH Income ($)	Pop 25+ Some College + (%)	Pop 25+ 4-Yr Degree + (%)	Below Poverty Line (%)	2006 White (Non-Hisp) (%)	African American (%)	American Indians, Alaska Natives (%)	Asians, Hawaiians, Pacific Islanders (%)	Hispanic Origin (%)
Rhode Island	2000	2001	2002	2003	2004	2005	2006	2000	2006	% Change	($)	(%)	(%)	(%)	(%)	(%)	(%)	(%)	(%)
51	D, 100		D, 100		D, 100		D, 100	13,808	14,154	3	44,253	28.3	12.1	22.3	72.8	5.6	0.4	3.7	12.2
52	R, 56		D, 52		R, 53		R, 59	14,749	15,807	7	84,455	45.4	28.0	7.6	90.3	2.5	0.2	2.4	1.6
53	R, 61		D, 61		D, 61		D, 70	14,184	14,554	3	75,851	38.4	22.3	9.5	89.4	3.0	0.2	2.3	2.1
54	R, 69		D, 74		D, 100		D, 78	12,974	13,031	0	53,376	38.3	19.5	16.9	83.2	3.8	0.3	3.3	5.4
55	D, 100		D, 100		D, 100		D, 100	14,122	14,175	0	57,264	38.9	19.6	11.9	80.1	6.4	0.2	3.1	6.2
56	D, 100		D, 100		D, 70		D, 100	11,848	12,026	2	29,140	21.1	9.2	38.1	21.6	9.2	0.5	2.7	64.5
57	D, 68		D, 100		D, 70		D, 100	17,240	17,546	2	45,517	28.2	12.8	19.3	60.9	4.6	0.3	1.8	24.5
58	D, 100		D, 100		D, 100		D, 100	13,894	13,736	-1	41,766	27.6	12.7	25.6	50.9	13.1	0.3	2.0	22.0
59	D, 60		D, 100		D, 63		D, 82	13,397	13,546	1	49,713	32.1	18.7	31.2	51.8	14.1	0.6	2.5	22.4
60	R, 57		D, 100		D, 73		D, 73	14,449	14,334	-1	43,002	26.3	11.3	21.7	61.3	9.0	0.4	3.3	20.3
61	D, 100		D, 100		D, 100		D, 100	13,672	13,543	-1	55,261	36.2	16.3	14.3	83.7	3.7	0.2	2.2	5.3
62	D, 100		D, 85		D, 82		D, 85	14,982	14,853	-1	48,359	33.2	15.9	17.5	67.3	6.5	0.3	2.7	16.0
63	D, 82		D, 100		D, 53		D, 100	13,825	13,811	0	56,821	39.4	21.0	16.2	81.8	6.6	0.4	2.6	3.6
64	D, 100		D, 100		D, 70		D, 100	14,399	14,542	1	45,318	29.4	13.2	19.3	75.4	9.2	0.5	3.0	3.7
65	D, 68		R, 100		R, 59		R, 100	14,039	14,044	0	53,448	36.8	17.8	14.3	85.6	5.1	0.3	2.5	2.4
66	D, 100		R, 100		R, 100		R, 56	14,144	14,374	2	111,063	52.0	36.3	7.9	93.9	1.2	0.1	2.3	1.4
67	D, 100		D, 100		D, 64		D, 100	13,247	13,124	-1	67,626	37.8	20.4	14.2	94.8	1.0	0.3	1.3	1.3
68	D, 72		D, 59		D, 100		D, 52	16,141	17,715	10	67,931	35.1	19.7	13.7	94.9	0.9	0.2	1.3	1.7
69	D, 65		D, 61		D, 68		D, 57	11,116	10,925	-2	58,477	31.7	16.2	15.3	93.6	1.1	0.2	1.9	1.8
70	D, 100		R, 100		R, 61		R, 100	13,991	13,557	-3	65,447	38.4	18.9	12.3	95.2	1.1	0.2	1.4	1.0
71	D, 100		D, 56		R, 54		R, 100	13,320	12,928	-3	79,784	47.1	29.3	8.7	95.2	1.2	0.2	1.3	1.1
72	D, 100		R, 64		D, 57		D, 50	13,911	13,376	-4	87,030	51.2	34.5	7.2	92.2	2.1	0.1	2.7	1.5
73	D, 83		D, 100		D, 72		D, 100	13,288	12,656	-5	49,764	36.9	20.5	20.0	64.9	16.5	1.3	3.8	9.0
74	D, 100		R, 55		R, 61		R, 100	14,819	14,244	-4	76,872	47.9	27.2	8.8	85.6	5.6	0.4	3.1	2.9
75	D, 100		D, 52		D, 55		D, 100	14,159	13,649	-4	74,948	50.2	34.3	12.7	87.2	4.4	0.3	2.4	3.1
76	D, 100																		
77	D, 64																		
78	D, 100																		
79	D, 100																		
80	D, 100																		
81	D, 57																		
82	D, 100																		
83	D, 100																		
84	D, 100																		
85	D, 80																		
86	D, 74																		
87	R, 60																		
88	R, 60																		
89	D, 100																		
90	D, 56																		
91	D, 66																		
92	R, 70																		
93	D, 52																		
94	R, 54																		
95	R, 63																		
96	D, 100																		
97	D, 100																		
98	R, 51																		
99	R, 81																		
100	D, 100																		

*After 2000, RI went from 100 to 75 districts due to redistricting.

Note: D=Democrat, R=Republican, R/D=Republican/Democrat (cross-filed), D/R=Democrat/Republican (cross-filed), I=Independent, C=Constitution, O=Other, GI=Green Independent, P=Progressive, P/D=Progressive/Democrat, P/D/R=Progressive/Democrat/Republican, HH=Households

SOUTH CAROLINA

The English planters who first settled South Carolina, it has been written, thought they inhabited not the southern edge of America, but the northern edge of the West Indies. They came from Barbados and imported West Indian traditions, in particular an economy built on rice, indigo, and slaves. They established their society around Charleston ("where the Ashley and Cooper Rivers meet to form the Atlantic Ocean" in the marvelous old boast), never ventured far inland, and left the mountains to be explored not by South Carolinians moving west but by North Carolinians pushing south.

Theirs was the first of an unfortunate series of economic choices the state made. South Carolina produced turpentine for sailing ships until the age of steam, indigo until the development of synthetic dyes, cotton until the boll weevils came, and in our time, textiles until the mills moved overseas. It also benefited from the presence of a number of military bases, including Parris Island, long a recruiting center for the Marine Corps.

South Carolina's new economic base is tourism and recreation, and in this it has done quite well. Charleston remains one of the most charming cities in the United States but it is not a very big one. The Greenville metro area, in the western mountains, is larger but even so it is not as big as the metropolitan areas of Little Rock or Wichita. Development and growth are focused more on the coastal golf courses and tennis resorts from Myrtle Beach to Hilton Head that draw business conferences and vacationers year-round. But there is also a new industrial base, doing the sort of work that used to be done in the industrial north such as Detroit, Rochester, and Akron: manufacturing luxury cars for BMW, cameras for Fuji, and tires for Michelin.

Recreation and industry have energized the state's economy and helped it join the other surging states of the South. Growth here has been about 20 percent since 1990, not as robust as the emerging mega-states, Georgia and Florida, but consistent with Virginia, North Carolina, and Tennessee.

The distribution of growth perfectly mirrors its new economic base. The 118th state house district north of Hilton Head has grown by 39 percent since 2000 while the 104th district, around Myrtle Beach up the coast, has grown by 23 percent. The 20th district, in western Spartanburg County around the new manufacturing plants, has grown by 20 percent. There has been some modest population loss in rural areas away from both the coast and the Greenville area.

Long one of the nation's poorest states, South Carolina has much ground to make up. "Within living memory," Michael Barone has written, "this state looked like an underdeveloped country." Median household income today is about $39,000—below the national average but almost exactly in between North Carolina and Tennessee and hardly at a third world level. The poorest districts are sprinkled around the state, in downtown Spartanburg and North Charleston. The wealthy enclaves are along the Golf Coast, as it might be called, and in Spartanburg.

The first state to secede from the Union and the most implacable defender of slavery a century and a half ago, South Carolina today is 67 percent white and 29.5 percent African American. Yet the racial division still drives much of what goes on in the state. For example, nineteen of the twenty wealthiest state house districts vote Republican and in only two of them do blacks make up more than a quarter of the population. On the other hand, nineteen of the twenty poorest house districts vote Democratic and in only two of them do blacks make up less than 40 percent of the population. Looked at another way, every state house district in South Carolina that is more than 40 percent African American elected a Democrat in the 2006 elections. But sixty-seven of the seventy state house districts in which blacks make up less than a quarter of the population elected Republicans.

Building party strength around the racial group that makes up two-thirds of the state population has worked to the Republicans' advantage. When Strom Thurmond joined the GOP in 1964, he merely did what many white South Carolinians were growing inclined to do. It has taken a while for the rest of the state to follow, but in the 1990s it finally did so. As in so much of the country, 1994 was the breakthrough year, when a 71–52 Democratic majority in the state house became a 62–58 Republican majority, one they have since padded to 73–51. The GOP did not capture the state senate until 2002 but now holds a 26–20 majority there.

SOUTH CAROLINA
State Senate Districts

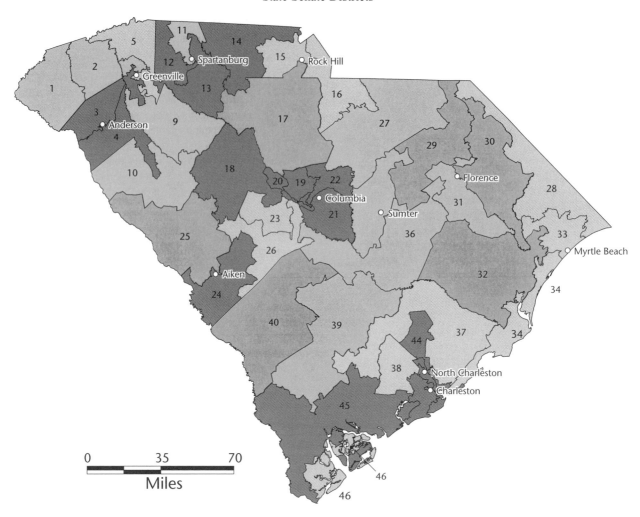

CHARLESTON

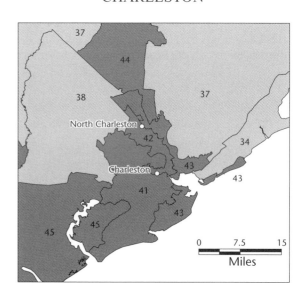

Population Growth   ▨ -1% to 3%   ▨ 3% to 6%   ▨ 6% to 10%   ▨ 10% to 21%

GREENVILLE

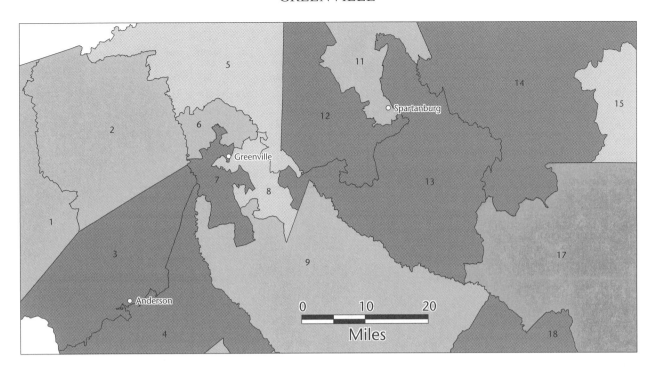

COLUMBIA

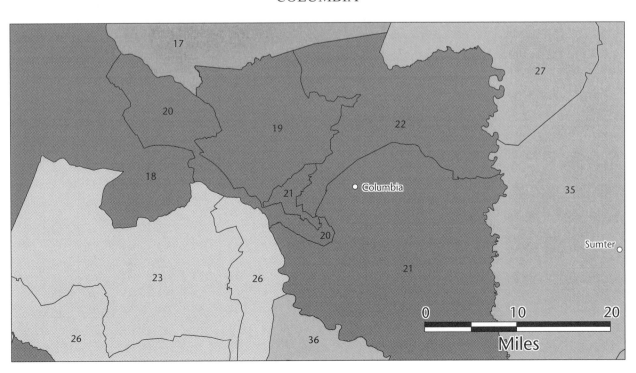

Population Growth ▨ -1% to 3% ▨ 3% to 6% ▨ 6% to 10% ▨ 10% to 21%

South Carolina State Senate Districts—Election and Demographic Data

Senate Districts	General Election Results Party, Percent of Vote							Population			Avg. HH Income	2006 Pop 25+		Below Poverty Line	White (Non-Hisp)	African American	American Indians, Alaska Natives	Asians, Hawaiians, Pacific Islanders	Hispanic Origin
												Some College +	4-Yr Degree +						
S. Carolina	2000	2001	2002	2003	2004	2005	2006	2000	2006	% Change	($)	(%)	(%)	(%)	(%)	(%)	(%)	(%)	(%)
1	R, 100				R, 100			86,517	90,798	5	49,988	32.7	17.4	18.8	85.1	8.7	0.1	1.8	3.2
2	R, 100				R, 100			89,904	94,033	5	50,344	31.2	12.9	16.6	90.5	5.5	0.1	0.5	2.3
3	R, 100				R, 63			90,952	97,914	8	56,717	36.7	17.5	14.6	84.2	12.5	0.1	0.8	1.7
4	D, 59				R, 62			87,266	93,823	8	45,223	26.2	9.7	20.7	77.5	19.6	0.1	0.3	1.7
5	D, 78				R, 90			88,035	97,849	11	67,371	39.7	21.6	12.6	84.3	8.2	0.1	1.8	4.5
6	R, 98				R, 99			90,866	95,039	5	55,191	38.9	20.8	14.2	72.0	9.4	0.3	2.5	10.6
7	D, 64				D, 99			81,930	87,191	6	46,267	32.2	15.6	24.2	44.0	47.4	0.2	0.7	6.8
8	R, 89				R, 99			91,072	101,393	11	75,165	50.5	31.5	8.4	79.7	12.1	0.1	2.3	4.9
9	R, 54				R, 60			90,067	94,628	5	47,391	28.3	11.4	17.6	74.6	21.2	0.1	0.3	3.1
10	D, 59				D, 66			82,524	85,171	3	45,549	28.9	12.5	20.9	61.9	33.6	0.1	0.7	3.7
11	D, 58				D, 56			89,033	93,760	5	44,985	30.9	13.0	20.2	63.6	28.7	0.1	1.9	5.3
12	R, 69				R, 70			88,411	95,474	8	55,703	35.1	16.9	14.1	75.9	15.8	0.1	1.9	5.0
13	R, 66				R, 100			84,201	90,565	8	60,163	37.6	19.7	14.9	78.9	15.7	0.1	1.9	2.6
14	R, 100				R, 69			91,456	99,256	9	49,748	25.9	10.8	18.5	78.5	17.4	0.1	0.5	2.5
15	R, 100				R, 99			91,178	105,578	16	63,466	37.0	17.9	12.9	77.0	16.4	0.2	1.4	3.9
16	R, 99				R, 65			84,907	95,134	12	53,781	31.7	13.0	15.4	76.4	18.6	0.4	0.7	2.9
17	D, 83				D, 100			87,029	89,033	2	44,109	24.8	9.2	23.2	48.5	49.8	0.1	0.3	1.1
18	R, 64				R, 100			82,616	88,785	7	64,359	37.8	20.6	14.9	74.9	19.0	0.1	0.8	4.9
19	D, 99				D, 86			93,423	100,554	8	49,374	45.3	26.9	16.4	33.5	60.6	0.3	1.8	2.2
20	R, 60				R, 98			84,896	92,439	9	64,472	50.8	34.2	13.1	72.7	20.7	0.1	3.1	2.5
21	D, 98				D, 98			92,148	98,097	6	53,202	43.4	25.5	20.3	37.0	55.8	0.4	1.3	3.6
22	R, 56				D, 56			89,848	98,476	10	73,265	49.8	31.5	8.8	63.9	26.2	0.5	2.9	4.1
23	R, 100				R, 99			84,132	93,432	11	60,221	35.4	14.6	11.1	86.2	8.1	0.1	1.0	3.4
24	R, 100				R, 100			86,541	92,801	7	58,981	38.2	19.3	14.4	74.0	20.3	0.1	1.1	3.6
25	D, 67				D, 68			89,870	92,415	3	45,622	27.8	10.9	22.4	58.7	37.0	0.1	0.4	3.6
26	D, 56				D, 89			83,126	93,455	12	45,241	30.7	12.9	18.7	72.5	21.6	0.2	1.0	4.0
27	D, 68				D, 56			85,154	89,232	5	44,912	25.7	10.3	22.7	64.9	31.7	0.1	0.4	2.4
28	D, 100				D, 53			85,246	95,564	12	46,893	30.6	12.0	19.8	68.6	26.6	0.7	0.4	3.1
29	D, 99				D, 58			82,400	81,689	-1	44,564	25.8	10.5	26.3	51.3	46.8	0.1	0.3	1.4
30	D, 99				D, 98			90,947	91,406	1	40,159	22.9	9.1	28.3	40.1	57.4	0.3	0.4	1.8
31	R, 56				R, 66			85,585	89,329	4	57,763	35.0	17.0	16.0	69.8	25.3	0.5	1.1	1.2
32	D, 100				D, 97			84,378	85,930	2	39,425	22.7	8.8	29.6	39.9	58.5	0.1	0.3	1.4
33	D, 54				R, 74			83,533	99,038	19	54,177	37.3	16.0	14.1	79.2	13.2	0.2	1.2	4.7
34	R, 100				R, 100			88,406	100,865	14	61,674	45.2	22.5	11.1	79.4	15.8	0.1	1.0	2.9
35	D, 60				D, 50			83,677	87,392	4	49,569	32.7	13.0	18.9	55.7	39.9	0.1	1.4	2.2
36	D, 74				D, 69			83,290	87,375	5	41,384	24.2	9.2	27.5	41.0	56.2	0.3	0.3	2.0
37	R, 51				R, 64			90,283	100,135	11	57,827	33.2	17.6	17.7	64.5	31.4	0.2	1.0	2.2
38	R, 100				R, 100			90,226	105,830	17	59,154	38.2	17.2	12.4	71.9	22.4	0.3	1.6	2.8
39	D, 99				D, 99			87,898	91,395	4	40,265	24.5	9.7	28.6	39.8	58.5	0.2	0.2	1.3
40	D, 91				D, 71			87,466	86,819	-1	44,703	28.8	12.7	27.3	44.4	53.1	0.1	0.7	1.3
41	R, 100				R, 64			86,198	92,719	8	60,158	49.8	32.6	12.2	73.8	21.5	0.3	1.6	3.0
42	D, 99				D, 69			81,156	86,656	7	38,189	34.8	19.9	27.8	36.1	57.9	0.1	1.8	4.3
43	D, 62				R, 62			91,466	99,365	9	65,117	46.1	31.0	16.5	71.1	23.0	0.1	1.4	3.4
44	R, 100				R, 66			84,742	90,119	6	54,360	34.2	11.8	12.3	71.2	19.7	0.3	3.4	3.5
45	D, 63				D, 99			90,637	96,775	7	46,674	25.5	10.9	25.8	39.2	54.5	0.1	0.6	6.9
46	R, 99				R, 99			88,117	106,226	21	79,555	51.2	29.8	8.4	72.4	15.4	0.1	1.0	9.5

Note: D=Democrat, R=Republican, R/D=Republican/Democrat (cross-filed), D/R=Democrat/Republican (cross-filed), I=Independent, C=Constitution, O=Other, GI=Green Independent, P=Progressive, P/D=Progressive/Democrat, P/D/R=Progressive/Democrat/Republican, HH=Households

SOUTH CAROLINA
State House Districts

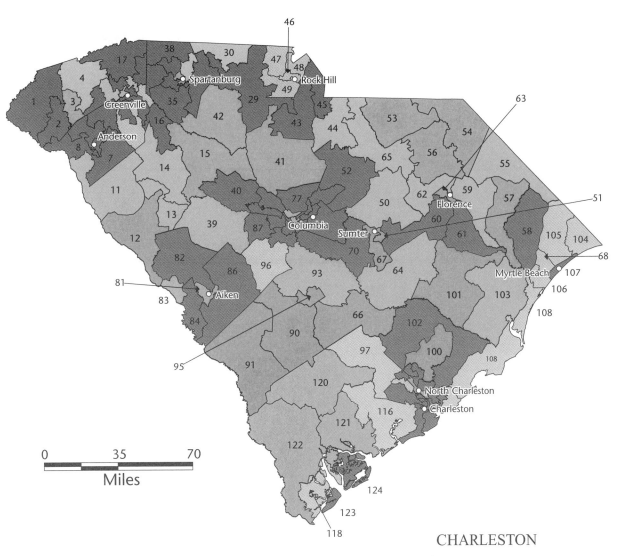

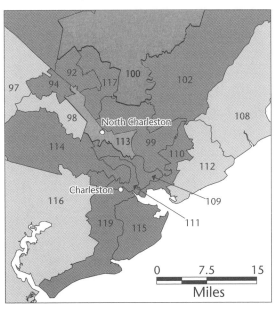

CHARLESTON

Population Growth   ▉ -6% to 2%   ▉ 2% to 5%   ▉ 5% to 13%   ▉ 13% to 40%

GREENVILLE

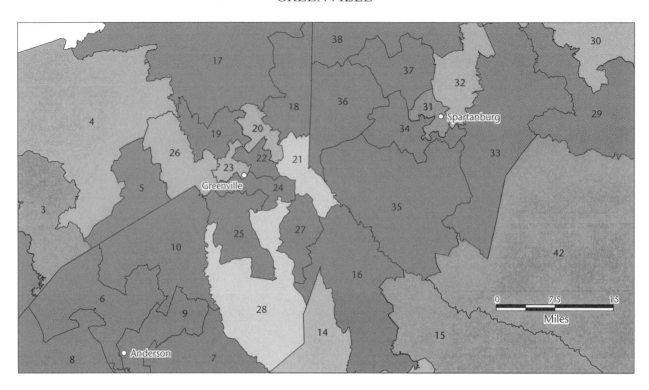

COLUMBIA

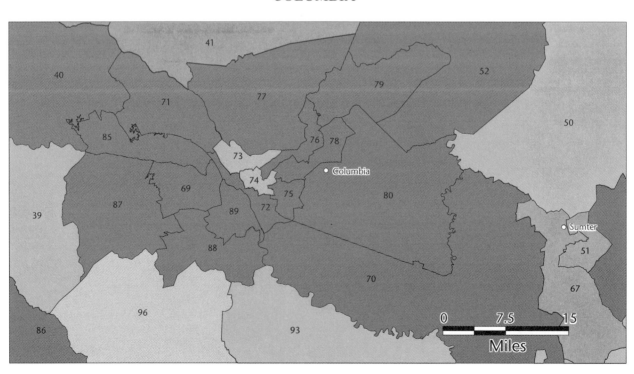

Population Growth ▢ -6% to 2% ▢ 2% to 5% ▢ 5% to 13% ▢ 13% to 40%

South Carolina State House Districts—Election and Demographic Data

House Districts	General Election Results Party, Percent of Vote							Population			Avg. HH Income	Pop 25+		Below Poverty Line	White (Non-Hisp)	African American	American Indians, Alaska Natives	Asians, Hawaiians, Pacific Islanders	Hispanic Origin
												Some College +	4-Yr Degree +						
S. Carolina	2000	2001	2002	2003	2004	2005	2006	2000	2006	% Change	($)	(%)	(%)	(%)	(%)	(%)	(%)	(%)	(%)
1	R, 100		R, 71		R, 66		R, 67	32,272	34,686	7	49,743	30.1	13.6	17.7	89.4	3.3	0.1	0.3	5.2
2	R, 100		R, 63		R, 100		R, 99	32,357	34,242	6	50,795	33.9	16.8	16.7	83.5	13.3	0.1	0.7	1.7
3	R, 99		R, 61		R, 99		R, 99	31,984	31,914	0	47,873	35.0	22.6	23.6	83.2	8.9	0.0	4.4	2.5
4	R, 99		R, 98		R, 100		R, 99	32,501	33,930	4	46,400	28.5	10.7	17.1	93.1	4.2	0.1	0.3	1.6
5	R, 100		R, 100		R, 100		R, 99	32,276	33,904	5	52,910	32.8	13.4	16.8	87.0	8.1	0.1	0.5	3.1
6	R, 52		R, 56		R, 99		R, 99	33,068	35,148	6	53,342	37.7	19.1	18.5	76.1	20.5	0.1	1.0	1.6
7	R, 100		R, 58		R, 100		R, 56	32,550	34,761	7	45,434	25.4	8.7	20.0	82.0	15.8	0.1	0.1	1.4
8	R, 56		R, 100		R, 85		R, 79	31,723	33,732	6	49,297	30.0	11.8	16.3	82.7	14.5	0.1	0.5	1.5
9	R, 50		R, 100		R, 64		R, 99	31,360	33,603	7	51,218	31.4	14.5	19.9	72.3	23.9	0.1	0.7	2.3
10	R, 100		R, 100		R, 100		R, 99	33,101	36,311	10	55,027	32.2	13.0	13.6	90.4	6.3	0.1	0.3	2.1
11	D, 100		R, 48		D, 52		D, 100	33,016	34,312	4	42,936	25.1	9.6	21.2	71.6	26.5	0.0	0.3	1.1
12	D, 99		D, 55		D, 56		D, 58	31,366	31,962	2	41,624	27.0	11.8	25.8	42.8	51.4	0.1	0.4	6.9
13	R, 65		R, 58		R, 99		R, 98	32,531	33,966	4	53,305	36.9	18.5	15.5	74.1	21.5	0.1	1.5	2.4
14	D, 60		R, 57		R, 99		R, 99	33,850	35,510	5	48,569	27.0	10.1	17.7	77.1	20.8	0.1	0.2	1.4
15	D, 100		R, 61		R, 95		R, 63	31,738	31,638	0	40,465	23.9	10.3	22.4	67.4	28.1	0.1	0.2	3.8
16	R, 53		R, 53		R, 98		R, 99	31,258	32,961	5	48,726	29.9	12.3	17.5	67.5	27.7	0.1	0.2	4.1
17	R, 98		R, 98		R, 99		R, 99	32,519	35,993	11	56,429	33.1	16.0	15.2	88.4	6.8	0.1	0.6	3.3
18	R, 89		R, 99		R, 99		R, 73	31,819	33,584	6	52,992	36.4	16.6	15.2	78.8	12.2	0.1	1.0	6.5
19	R, 66		R, 98		R, 72		R, 99	32,434	34,305	6	48,643	31.0	14.8	17.7	78.7	8.5	0.1	1.5	9.4
20	R, 99		R, 99		R, 99		R, 99	32,578	34,130	5	67,885	48.4	27.2	9.0	80.8	7.8	0.1	3.2	6.7
21	R, 99		R, 99		R, 99		R, 99	31,480	37,869	20	95,903	53.2	36.1	5.3	84.3	5.4	0.1	4.9	4.3
22	R, 99		R, 99		R, 99		R, 99	32,642	34,679	6	59,933	51.2	32.2	9.7	77.8	8.6	0.1	3.5	8.5
23	D, 69		D, 98		D, 99		D, 99	32,303	33,065	2	36,085	30.1	15.7	34.1	38.9	55.8	0.1	0.6	5.8
24	R, 73		R, 99		R, 99		R, 99	34,032	36,203	6	81,207	51.8	34.5	10.7	78.4	13.9	0.1	1.8	4.9
25	D, 98		D, 99		D, 99		D, 99	31,682	34,664	9	47,581	30.8	13.1	19.5	40.4	54.6	0.1	0.7	4.5
26	R, 99		R, 99		R, 100		R, 99	32,443	33,633	4	50,519	29.0	11.4	17.1	73.9	11.7	0.1	0.7	12.0
27	R, 73		R, 99		R, 88		R, 99	31,633	35,116	11	75,861	45.3	26.1	6.9	81.9	10.8	0.1	1.2	5.0
28	R, 98		R, 98		R, 99		R, 80	32,507	37,609	16	59,442	39.5	18.6	10.6	81.2	14.0	0.1	1.2	2.6
29	D, 100		D, 100		D, 99		D, 50	32,176	34,449	7	52,068	26.6	10.6	17.1	79.3	18.1	0.1	0.4	1.6
30	D, 100		D, 100		D, 57		D, 57	32,348	33,879	5	43,074	20.5	8.0	21.9	72.1	22.6	0.1	0.4	3.7
31	D, 100		D, 100		D, 100		D, 95	32,008	32,163	0	32,731	25.2	10.8	32.8	37.3	56.6	0.1	1.5	5.5
32	R, 100		R, 100		R, 66		R, 99	32,759	34,214	4	62,919	42.8	24.9	15.2	79.2	14.9	0.1	2.0	2.9
33	R, 100		R, 100		R, 72		R, 100	32,033	34,056	6	54,118	32.5	15.6	17.7	79.7	14.7	0.1	2.3	2.3
34	R, 100		R, 100		R, 65		R, 99	33,778	36,531	8	61,597	40.7	22.2	11.3	67.5	22.5	0.1	3.8	5.3
35	R, 68		R, 100		R, 100		R, 69	31,250	34,444	10	57,710	35.5	16.5	14.7	83.1	11.7	0.1	1.0	3.0
36	R, 100		R, 100		R, 100		R, 62	32,765	34,632	6	47,411	29.9	12.3	17.1	72.5	18.9	0.1	1.0	6.1
37	R, 100		R, 100		R, 99		R, 99	31,305	33,171	6	50,981	33.8	14.4	13.2	73.7	14.5	0.1	2.3	7.9
38	R, 99		R, 100		R, 99		R, 99	32,613	35,956	10	51,259	31.8	12.8	14.7	86.7	8.8	0.1	1.0	2.6
39	R, 100		R, 100		R, 100		R, 99	32,800	33,742	3	50,042	27.4	11.2	18.2	64.9	25.9	0.1	0.1	9.0
40	D, 63		D, 58		D, 100		D, 99	31,775	34,000	7	49,849	29.5	13.9	20.7	62.2	30.5	0.1	0.5	7.2
41	D, 100		D, 100		D, 100		D, 99	31,138	31,748	2	42,462	23.6	9.3	25.6	39.7	58.7	0.1	0.3	1.1
42	R, 48		D, 54		D, 99		D, 99	32,361	31,094	-4	43,049	24.7	9.0	21.4	69.7	28.8	0.0	0.3	0.9
43	D, 100		R, 66		R, 100		R, 99	33,560	36,140	8	49,412	28.2	10.4	17.6	73.7	23.4	0.4	0.5	1.3
44	D, 100		D, 100		D, 100		D, 100	32,621	34,156	5	44,856	23.8	6.9	18.6	70.7	26.0	0.1	0.2	2.6
45	D, 99		D, 57		D, 52		R, 51	33,183	36,770	11	53,561	33.1	14.5	17.3	71.4	22.5	0.8	0.7	3.9
46	R, 100		R, 64		R, 99		R, 99	33,775	38,968	15	64,452	39.9	21.3	12.5	77.9	14.7	0.3	2.0	4.3
47	D, 100		D, 100		D, 99		D, 99	31,904	37,994	19	58,524	30.6	12.2	14.2	81.0	13.5	0.3	0.8	3.3
48	R, 100		R, 100		R, 99		R, 69	32,635	38,939	19	72,519	47.8	25.6	8.2	87.3	6.0	0.2	1.9	3.3
49	D, 100		D, 100		D, 99		D, 99	31,999	36,534	14	52,704	26.7	9.8	19.8	45.9	51.3	0.2	0.5	2.2
50	D, 78		D, 81		D, 100		D, 99	33,041	34,436	4	43,283	24.2	8.7	26.3	36.8	60.6	0.1	0.5	2.4

(continued)

Note: D=Democrat, R=Republican, R/D=Republican/Democrat (cross-filed), D/R=Democrat/Republican (cross-filed), I=Independent, C=Constitution, O=Other, GI=Green Independent, P=Progressive, P/D=Progressive/Democrat, P/D/R=Progressive/Democrat/Republican, HH=Households

South Carolina State House Districts—Election and Demographic Data (cont.)

House Districts	General Election Results Party, Percent of Vote							Population			Avg. HH Income	Pop 25+		2006 Below Poverty Line	White (Non-Hisp)	African American	American Indians, Alaska Natives	Asians, Hawaiians, Pacific Islanders	Hispanic Origin
												Some College +	4-Yr Degree +						
S. Carolina	2000	2001	2002	2003	2004	2005	2006	2000	2006	% Change	($)	(%)	(%)	(%)	(%)	(%)	(%)	(%)	(%)
51	D, 100		D, 100		D, 100		D, 100	31,373	31,102	-1	41,183	28.9	10.6	26.1	33.0	64.0	0.1	0.7	2.0
52	D, 57		D, 99		D, 53		D, 99	32,389	34,595	7	51,261	29.3	13.8	19.1	65.4	31.5	0.1	0.4	2.2
53	D, 67		D, 99		D, 98		D, 99	31,521	31,755	1	39,648	24.1	8.8	25.9	61.9	33.9	0.1	0.4	3.1
54	D, 82		D, 100		D, 99		D, 100	32,128	31,533	-2	39,369	21.3	7.7	27.6	46.3	49.5	3.4	0.4	0.9
55	D, 99		D, 99		D, 99		D, 65	33,049	34,015	3	39,370	20.8	7.8	28.8	52.0	43.9	1.0	0.4	2.5
56	D, 100		D, 100		D, 100		D, 71	32,329	32,226	0	43,044	23.7	8.7	25.7	59.5	38.7	0.1	0.2	1.3
57	D, 100		D, 100		D, 100		D, 100	31,936	31,473	-1	40,516	22.3	8.9	28.7	41.2	55.9	0.1	0.4	2.9
58	R, 59		R, 58		R, 100		R, 99	32,709	35,108	7	43,476	26.2	9.1	21.5	71.4	24.8	0.2	0.2	2.8
59	D, 100		D, 99		D, 71		D, 99	32,436	33,363	3	39,860	24.8	9.6	25.3	42.3	55.7	0.1	0.4	1.2
60	R, 54		R, 52		R, 73		R, 60	33,934	37,540	11	48,379	27.9	11.7	20.6	58.7	39.0	0.1	0.5	1.4
61	D, 100		D, 96		D, 100		D, 100	32,004	33,719	5	44,445	23.9	9.4	25.7	57.9	39.9	0.1	0.4	1.4
62	D, 100		D, 99		D, 99		D, 67	33,506	34,935	4	42,767	26.5	10.5	25.1	40.3	58.2	0.1	0.3	1.0
63	R, 100		R, 99		R, 100		R, 68	31,335	31,569	1	69,961	47.1	26.7	11.0	80.6	15.2	0.1	2.3	1.1
64	D, 100		D, 100		D, 99		D, 100	31,978	33,449	5	41,257	23.9	9.6	29.0	44.0	53.3	0.1	0.4	2.3
65	R, 99		R, 99		R, 99		R, 100	31,483	32,648	4	49,673	28.8	11.8	21.7	71.5	25.5	0.1	0.3	1.9
66	D, 97		D, 94		D, 98		D, 73	33,155	33,195	0	39,397	25.5	9.6	30.9	34.4	64.0	0.2	0.1	1.2
67	R, 54		R, 100		R, 100		R, 100	31,685	31,860	1	58,162	37.4	17.4	14.2	72.5	22.8	0.1	1.6	1.9
68	R, 57		R, 70		R, 70		R, 91	31,017	36,798	19	53,955	37.4	14.5	11.8	83.5	8.0	0.1	1.8	5.0
69	R, 100		R, 100		R, 89		R, 99	34,458	38,357	11	66,796	48.5	26.5	8.1	83.9	9.5	0.1	2.5	3.0
70	D, 100		D, 91		D, 100		D, 100	32,083	33,886	6	44,557	32.3	13.0	21.2	37.4	58.3	0.1	1.3	2.1
71	R, 63		D, 98		R, 80		R, 99	36,288	39,674	9	75,584	52.0	34.1	7.0	70.8	25.0	0.1	1.7	1.7
72	D, 84		D, 99		D, 99		D, 99	33,819	36,421	8	47,105	46.5	31.7	19.5	59.5	33.7	0.1	3.5	2.3
73	D, 100		D, 100		D, 99		D, 100	28,334	29,178	3	41,203	42.5	24.5	20.1	25.4	70.8	0.1	1.6	2.1
74	D, 99		D, 99		D, 99		D, 99	32,688	33,970	4	43,803	42.0	27.1	30.7	35.9	60.6	0.1	1.3	2.1
75	R, 98		R, 99		R, 81		R, 55	30,838	32,746	6	80,326	56.5	41.5	10.2	73.6	17.1	0.2	2.4	4.8
76	D, 99		D, 96		D, 70		D, 87	31,411	34,263	9	62,116	47.8	29.3	15.3	35.4	57.5	0.1	3.0	4.2
77	D, 68		D, 66		D, 61		D, 63	34,439	38,148	11	57,652	45.8	26.4	13.1	40.3	55.8	0.1	1.6	1.9
78	D, 67		D, 69		R, 61		R, 99	31,148	33,061	6	76,980	54.4	35.9	10.6	62.9	26.5	0.2	3.6	5.6
79	R, 98		R, 98		R, 58		R, 46	33,713	37,682	12	67,132	43.2	25.1	8.0	69.5	24.4	0.1	2.0	3.0
80	D, 65		D, 99		D, 99		D, 70	33,327	35,776	7	51,382	42.9	22.5	13.3	45.4	46.8	0.1	1.7	4.8
81	R, 100		R, 100		R, 100		R, 99	33,726	34,750	3	64,957	45.6	27.2	13.1	79.2	16.2	0.1	1.5	2.1
82	D, 100		D, 100		D, 100		D, 99	32,437	34,117	5	42,126	25.1	9.7	25.4	43.2	53.9	0.1	0.2	2.7
83	R, 72		R, 100		R, 100		R, 99	32,690	33,759	3	55,989	38.4	18.1	14.3	76.3	18.2	0.1	1.1	3.4
84	R, 82		R, 100		R, 100		R, 99	32,908	35,398	8	46,779	27.4	8.9	19.4	71.6	23.8	0.2	0.5	3.0
85	R, 100		R, 100		R, 100		R, 99	32,674	35,909	10	84,001	54.2	34.3	5.6	83.8	11.2	0.1	2.2	2.0
86	R, 61		R, 65		R, 86		R, 99	32,372	36,388	12	51,546	29.5	12.2	19.2	69.8	24.3	0.2	0.5	4.1
87	R, 78		R, 100		R, 99		R, 99	32,368	35,333	9	70,541	40.5	19.7	10.2	87.0	7.0	0.1	0.8	4.0
88	R, 100		R, 100		R, 100		R, 99	31,569	34,712	10	53,553	31.4	10.4	12.8	81.3	13.0	0.2	1.0	3.6
89	R, 57		R, 100		R, 99		R, 99	33,334	35,139	5	45,875	37.2	17.8	17.0	73.6	18.6	0.2	1.9	4.7
90	D, 100		D, 73		D, 100		D, 97	32,789	33,282	2	41,042	25.4	10.0	27.3	50.4	47.9	0.2	0.3	1.0
91	D, 100		D, 100		D, 100		D, 100	32,154	31,626	-2	41,804	23.9	9.1	31.5	43.2	54.2	0.1	0.4	1.9
92	R, 99		R, 100		R, 100		R, 99	31,911	34,514	8	59,546	37.8	13.3	8.6	78.1	13.4	0.3	3.0	3.3
93	D, 97		D, 73		D, 73		D, 99	32,736	33,741	3	45,168	28.5	11.5	23.5	50.8	47.1	0.2	0.3	1.4
94	R, 100		R, 100		R, 100		R, 99	32,560	36,460	12	58,147	37.4	16.4	12.5	74.2	20.4	0.2	1.2	2.8
95	D, 98		D, 98		D, 98		D, 99	32,000	32,212	1	49,883	33.4	17.7	24.3	31.9	65.3	0.1	1.3	1.2
96	R, 99		R, 65		R, 95		R, 63	32,334	38,419	19	44,641	23.2	6.7	18.6	82.3	13.8	0.2	0.4	2.2
97	R, 51		D, 53		R, 52		D, 51	32,906	38,779	18	48,401	28.8	11.0	20.8	58.6	37.9	0.6	0.5	1.8
98	R, 100		R, 100		R, 100		R, 99	32,576	38,547	18	64,866	43.0	20.0	8.5	74.3	18.4	0.2	2.8	3.1
99	R, 67		R, 100		R, 100		R, 99	31,901	35,274	11	52,262	37.2	16.9	13.8	65.1	21.9	0.2	4.1	6.4
100	R, 100		R, 100		R, 100		R, 100	31,465	31,926	1	48,452	27.1	8.2	17.5	71.0	21.5	0.3	1.7	3.7

(continued)

Note: D=Democrat, R=Republican, R/D=Republican/Democrat (cross-filed), D/R=Democrat/Republican (cross-filed), I=Independent, C=Constitution, O=Other, GI=Green Independent, P=Progressive, P/D=Progressive/Democrat, P/D/R=Progressive/Democrat/Republican, HH=Households

South Carolina State House Districts—Election and Demographic Data (cont.)

House Districts	General Election Results Party, Percent of Vote							Population			Avg. HH Income	Pop 25+		Below Poverty Line	White (Non-Hisp)	African American	American Indians, Alaska Natives	Asians, Hawaiians, Pacific Islanders	Hispanic Origin
												Some College +	4-Yr Degree +						
															2006				
S. Carolina	2000	2001	2002	2003	2004	2005	2006	2000	2006	% Change	($)	(%)	(%)	(%)	(%)	(%)	(%)	(%)	(%)
101	D, 100		D, 67		D, 99		D, 99	33,037	31,369	-5	38,001	22.9	9.7	33.4	34.1	64.8	0.1	0.3	0.9
102	D, 100		D, 100		D, 61		D, 99	33,540	36,916	10	44,497	25.0	8.5	24.9	46.7	51.4	0.1	0.3	1.2
103	D, 100		D, 100		D, 60		D, 99	32,571	34,141	5	41,499	21.8	8.1	25.5	45.3	51.8	0.0	0.3	2.7
104	R, 53		R, 56		R, 63		R, 63	33,042	40,666	23	54,297	40.8	17.1	13.2	73.9	20.9	0.2	0.5	3.6
105	R, 100		R, 100		R, 100		R, 99	33,441	40,790	22	46,299	32.3	12.7	19.1	76.0	18.0	0.2	0.8	3.9
106	R, 65		R, 60		R, 66		R, 99	32,238	37,789	17	53,085	44.1	18.3	8.3	87.7	7.9	0.1	0.9	2.4
107	R, 100		R, 56		R, 99		R, 64	32,933	36,081	10	59,925	44.5	21.4	12.5	79.3	10.8	0.2	1.9	5.7
108	D, 54		D, 60		D, 55		D, 56	32,083	37,424	17	66,697	44.7	24.3	15.4	66.0	31.5	0.1	0.4	1.7
109	D, 100		D, 93		D, 100		D, 99	31,525	33,706	7	40,974	34.7	20.0	30.8	35.6	59.3	0.1	1.7	3.7
110	R, 66		R, 100		R, 100		R, 99	31,177	33,176	6	85,320	56.1	43.4	12.1	85.2	10.8	0.1	1.5	1.8
111	D, 100		D, 94		D, 100		D, 100	33,679	35,821	6	45,905	38.6	25.2	28.0	39.7	57.0	0.1	1.2	1.9
112	R, 100		R, 100		R, 100		R, 99	32,113	36,388	13	90,168	56.6	42.0	6.3	85.3	10.9	0.1	1.2	1.9
113	D, 53		D, 91		D, 65		D, 99	33,028	34,479	4	35,149	31.2	16.0	28.0	39.4	53.0	0.2	1.8	5.7
114	R, 65		R, 100		R, 100		R, 99	32,795	35,549	8	58,655	48.6	31.1	9.7	75.2	17.4	0.1	2.5	3.5
115	R, 64		R, 100		R, 63		R, 50	32,228	34,739	8	63,910	50.9	33.8	11.9	76.8	19.9	0.1	0.8	1.7
116	D, 59		D, 59		D, 100		D, 99	32,713	37,396	14	51,700	34.1	19.0	24.3	44.8	51.5	0.1	0.3	3.7
117	R, 100		R, 100		R, 100		R, 99	34,271	37,487	9	48,671	33.7	14.0	14.6	67.4	23.2	0.2	3.1	4.2
118	D, 100		R, 64		R, 99		R, 99	32,912	45,844	39	70,881	44.8	23.8	7.4	73.2	15.2	0.1	1.0	8.5
119	R, 55		R, 60		R, 54		D, 54	31,431	34,425	10	59,686	51.6	34.9	12.9	74.3	19.7	0.1	1.8	3.2
120	D, 72		D, 100		D, 100		D, 59	32,346	33,831	5	42,292	24.9	9.9	25.0	59.9	37.1	0.3	0.4	1.9
121	D, 99		D, 66		D, 99		D, 65	31,730	33,222	5	48,171	26.8	11.0	25.0	39.8	54.6	0.1	0.8	5.2
122	D, 55		D, 99		D, 100		D, 99	32,549	33,567	3	43,991	21.5	7.5	26.2	38.3	55.1	0.1	0.5	8.3
123	R, 99		R, 99		R, 68		R, 61	32,434	35,767	10	99,726	58.6	37.9	5.5	72.2	8.0	0.1	0.8	16.2
124	R, 53		R, 57		R, 68		R, 98	32,972	34,991	6	62,319	42.1	22.1	14.8	60.6	32.3	0.1	1.4	5.1

Note: D=Democrat, R=Republican, R/D=Republican/Democrat (cross-filed), D/R=Democrat/Republican (cross-filed), I=Independent, C=Constitution, O=Other, GI=Green Independent, P=Progressive, P/D=Progressive/Democrat, P/D/R=Progressive/Democrat/Republican, HH=Households

SOUTH DAKOTA

North and South Dakota entered the Union on the same day, November 2, 1889. Because it was impossible for President Benjamin Harrison to sign both statehood bills simultaneously, one of them was going to enter the Union first, albeit by a few seconds, creating a permanent source of pride for one and discontent for the other. In order to avoid the problem, both bills were covered so that only the signature lines showed. They were shuffled and then reshuffled after Harrison signed, so that no one would ever know which is rightfully the thirty-ninth and which the fortieth state.

Those who have never ventured west of the Alleghenies or east of the Sierras may joke that the states remain indistinguishable, but they are not. North Dakota grows wheat. South Dakota mines gold. North Dakota had the Nonpartisan League and socialist farmers. South Dakota had Native American leader Sitting Bull. North Dakota is in many ways an extension of the Minnesota grain fields; South Dakota is, too, but also includes the Black Hills and the Bad Lands, which George Armstrong Custer once described as "a part of hell with the fires burnt out." South Dakota has bigger cities, more Native Americans, and a more diversified economy, which includes meat packing. Most of Citicorp's credit card business is headquartered here, and until recently, so was Gateway Computers.

It is still a big state with few people, the forty-sixth most populous. South Dakota has the population of Delaware, but spread across a land area almost forty times bigger. But after having grown by less than 1 percent during the 1980s, when the farm crisis drove thousands of families out of state, it has grown by a stronger, although hardly robust 10.6 percent since 1990s, almost exactly the same rate as its southern neighbor, Nebraska. City work is becoming the basis of its economy. All the rapidly growing districts are located in and around Sioux Falls, the largest city, with a 2003 population of 133,834, while the farm districts along the Missouri River continue to lose people.

Given its reliance on agriculture and the large number of dependent Native American tribes, South Dakota has traditionally been a poor state. But with the development of a service economy, its median household income, although the lowest of the High Plains states, has grown substantially during the past fifteen years and is now equal to that in North Carolina. As might be expected, income levels are highest in and around Sioux Falls. They are low in the farm districts and on the reservations. Household income in the 27th house district, which includes the Rosebud Indian Reservation, is less than $34,000 a year.

It is impossible to write about South Dakota without writing about Native Americans, who still make up 8 percent of its population. The Sioux ruled the Plains until Custer, who discovered gold in the Black Hills and brought the settlers, drove them into Montana where they would take their revenge. Later, South Dakota saw the Ghost Dances, the tribes' late, futile turn towards mysticism before extinction. South Dakota also saw the massacre at Wounded Knee, the last shots fired in 1890 (at unarmed civilians) in the War for the West.

Settlers thoroughly filled the state after the Sioux were conquered, so much that whites make up more than three-quarters of the population in every state house district except the ones that included the reservations. In no district do Hispanic, Asian, or African Americans account for more than 4 percent of the population. There are still large concentrations of Sioux, just as there were more than a century ago, but they are much more politically aware than their great-grandfathers were.

This fact has led to lawsuits in this decade by those who claimed that South Dakota deliberately tried to minimize Native American voting strength. The first Indian-majority district in state history—the 27th district—was created during the 1980s on the Rosebud and Pine Ridge reservations. When state districts were redrawn again in the 1990s, the 27th was again created as an Indian-majority district, and Native Americans also made up a substantial part (though not a majority) of two more adjoining districts. (Like several other states, South Dakota is divided into legislative districts, each of which elects one senator and two representatives. In all but two districts, the representatives are elected at-large. In the districts covering the big reservations, representatives are elected from two separate subdistricts to maximize Native American voting strength.)

In 2001 the legislature redrew the lines again and fashioned the 27th district to be 90 percent Native American. Native Americans also made up 30 percent of the adjacent district, which included part of the Standing Rock reservation. Four Native Americans, however, challenged the plan on the grounds that by drawing too many Native Americans into the 27th district, the legislature had diluted their voting strength and deprived them of the opportunity to elect representatives of their race in the surrounding districts. A federal district judge agreed and substituted her own map, which created Native American majorities in three house districts: 26A, 27th, and 28A.

For a heavily Republican state, South Dakota has produced two prominent Democrats in former presidential nominee George McGovern and former Senate minority leader Tom Daschle. Yet the GOP controls both chambers of the legislature. In the house, their margin of 50–20 has not changed much in recent years notwithstanding the court fight. Their margin in the senate, though, now 20–15, has shrunk considerably over the last several years, making it conceivable that Democrats could someday win control.

SOUTH DAKOTA
State Legislative Districts

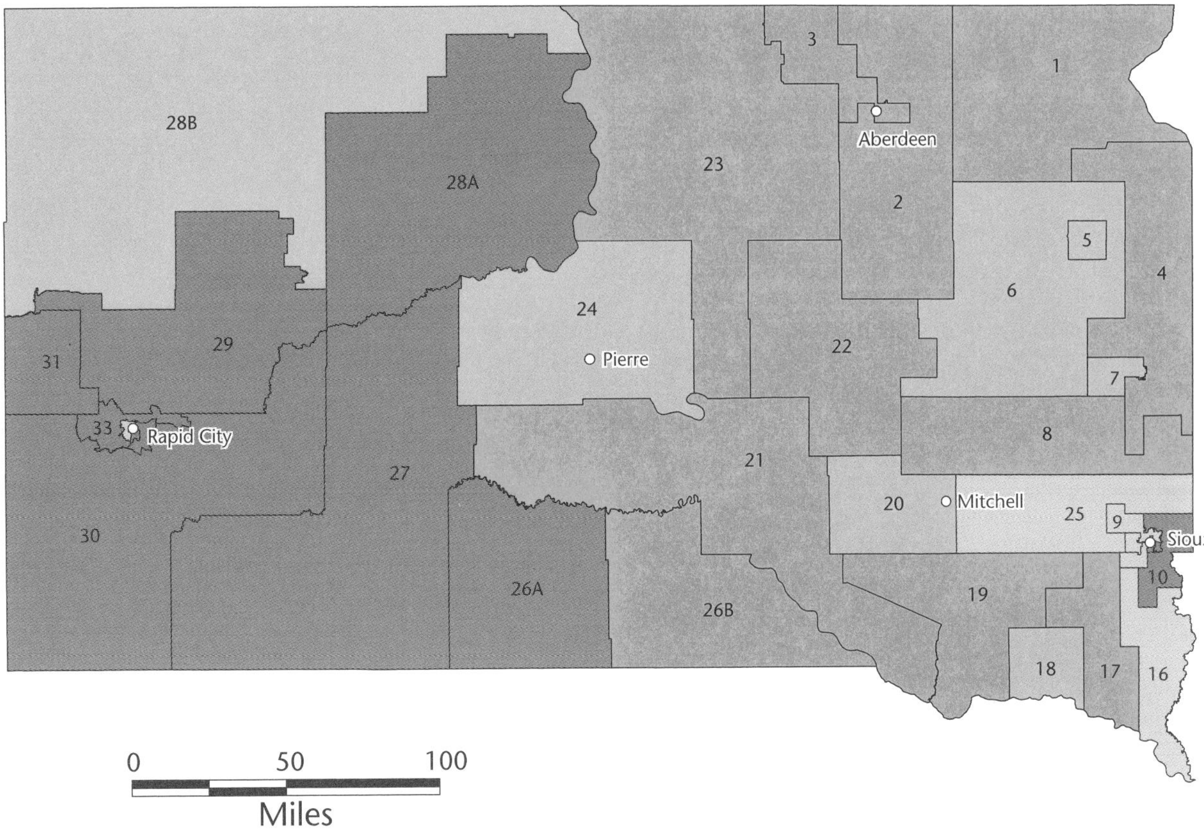
28B
28A
23
3
1
Aberdeen
2
5
4
6
24
Pierre
22
7
8
31
29
33
Rapid City
27
21
30
20
Mitchell
25
9
Sioux
10
26A
26B
19
18
17
16
0
50
100
Miles

RAPID CITY

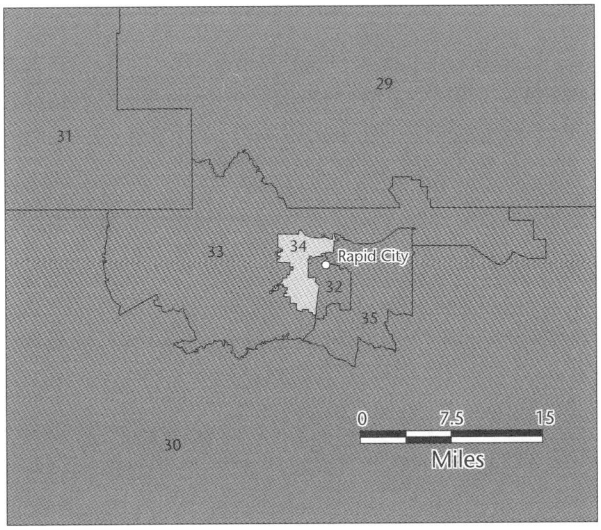
29
31
33
34
Rapid City
32
35
30
0
7.5
15
Miles

SIOUX FALLS

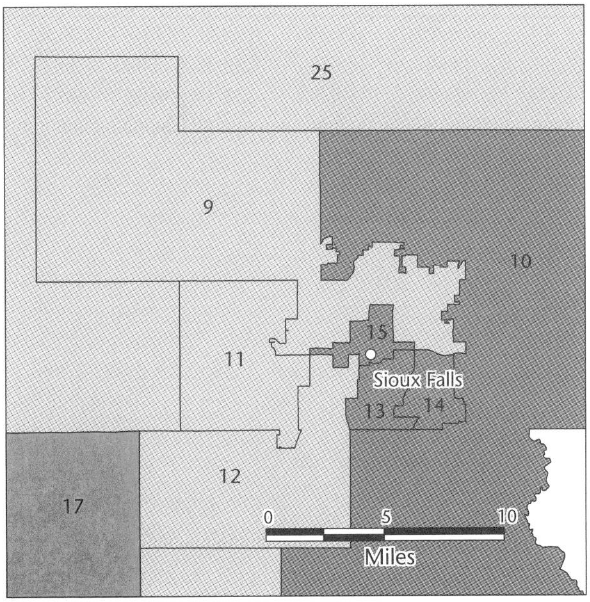
25
9
10
11
15
Sioux Falls
13
14
12
17
0
5
10
Miles

Population Growth ▢ -13% to -3% ▢ -3% to 7% ▢ 7% to 97% ▢ 97% to 98%

South Dakota Legislative Districts—Election and Demographic Data

Senate Districts	General Election Results Party, Percent of Vote							Population			Avg. HH Income	Pop 25+		Below Poverty Line	2006 White (Non-Hisp)	African American	American Indians, Alaska Natives	Asians, Hawaiians, Pacific Islanders	Hispanic Origin
												Some College +	4-Yr Degree +						
S. Dakota	2000	2001	2002	2003	2004	2005	2006	2000	2006	% Change	($)	(%)	(%)	(%)	(%)	(%)	(%)	(%)	(%)
1	D, 65		D, 70		D, 100		D, 100	20,859	20,121	-4	40,123	30.7	11.1	17.4	78.3	0.3	19.1	0.3	1.1
2	D, 77		D, 69		D, 52		D, 56	27,831	26,893	-3	46,843	38.1	14.8	14.9	95.1	0.3	2.7	0.3	0.8
3	R, 53		R, 73		R, 70		D, 50	15,083	14,303	-5	48,585	41.1	19.7	14.4	93.5	0.4	3.2	1.3	1.2
4	R, 59		D, 68		D, 61		D, 53	16,068	15,165	-6	44,968	31.4	11.8	15.5	96.6	0.1	1.0	0.3	1.1
5	R, 100		R, 100		R, 100		D, 52	23,617	23,619	0	50,576	34.7	14.1	13.8	94.4	0.2	2.1	0.4	1.4
6	R, 51		R, 56		R, 69		R, 61	43,491	42,703	-2	49,222	32.4	12.5	14.2	95.8	0.2	1.5	0.3	1.1
7	R, 100		R, 100		R, 57		R, 57	24,497	24,360	-1	49,181	43.7	23.1	14.2	94.4	0.5	1.5	2.0	0.9
8	D, 56		D, 100		D, 60		D, 57	23,430	22,589	-4	45,685	34.8	13.6	15.3	92.4	0.3	4.5	0.6	1.2
9	R, 67		R, 53		R, 57		R, 54	27,113	31,428	16	52,519	32.8	12.2	13.3	83.0	3.0	3.1	1.7	5.2
10	R, 70		R, 100		R, 100		R, 57	15,756	17,140	9	69,354	39.6	18.0	10.1	95.3	0.4	0.8	0.4	1.2
11	R, 100		R, 100		R, 60		R, 55	16,925	19,006	12	66,049	45.9	21.2	10.6	93.3	0.9	1.2	1.4	1.8
12	D, 52		R, 51		R, 56		D, 50	27,853	36,246	30	62,898	44.6	21.2	11.1	92.0	0.9	1.8	1.1	2.0
13	R, 65		R, 56		R, 57		D, 54	22,421	23,022	3	71,295	47.6	25.6	9.8	89.7	1.5	1.9	1.2	3.2
14	R, 67		R, 100		R, 83		R, 57	20,053	21,975	10	65,597	44.1	22.9	10.7	90.4	2.0	1.2	1.5	2.7
15	D, 65		R, 100		D, 61		D, 62	18,489	19,140	4	39,898	34.4	11.9	17.5	72.5	5.2	8.3	2.2	9.3
16	R, 58		R, 100		R, 100		R, 62	22,837	27,056	18	60,810	36.4	15.2	11.5	95.4	0.3	0.9	1.0	1.5
17	D, 51		D, 52		D, 52		D, 69	22,386	21,308	-5	43,821	40.7	20.5	15.9	93.5	0.9	2.3	1.6	0.9
18	D, 57		D, 72		D, 61		R, 55	21,652	21,893	1	47,737	38.2	16.6	14.6	91.8	1.5	2.1	0.6	2.9
19	R, 61		D, 54		D, 100		D, 56	18,793	17,792	-5	40,621	34.6	12.1	17.2	96.1	0.4	2.0	0.1	0.7
20	R, 59		R, 100		R, 100		R, 100	21,799	21,872	0	46,656	35.6	13.6	15.0	93.3	0.4	2.4	0.5	2.3
21	D, 72		D, 64		D, 71		R, 58	21,834	21,187	-3	37,663	29.1	10.8	18.6	72.3	0.4	24.5	0.5	1.6
22	D, 70		D, 69		R, 55		R, 54	20,963	18,965	-10	45,035	36.5	13.6	15.5	94.7	0.7	1.3	0.4	2.1
23	R, 100		R, 100		R, 100		R, 76	22,031	19,718	-10	40,696	32.8	12.1	17.2	93.6	0.1	4.8	0.2	0.5
24	R, 100		R, 100		R, 100		R, 100	20,809	21,177	2	55,926	42.6	21.1	12.5	87.8	0.3	8.1	0.5	1.8
25	D, 75		R, 100		R, 100		R, 52	19,219	21,511	12	52,220	34.0	12.3	13.4	97.2	0.1	0.9	0.2	0.8
26	R, 100		R, 57		R, 57		D, 59	22,355	22,280	0	33,911	27.3	8.6	20.6	66.1	0.4	30.4	0.5	1.3
27	D, 77		D, 81		D, 69		D, 54	21,166	22,008	4	33,735	25.8	7.7	20.7	8.7	0.7	89.2	0.7	3.2
28	R, 58		R, 100		R, 59		D, 54	20,331	20,606	1	33,982	28.1	8.9	20.6	53.1	0.5	43.3	0.5	2.6
29	R, 100		R, 100		R, 65		R, 66	20,860	21,350	2	48,971	36.0	11.3	14.3	91.4	0.6	2.6	0.5	2.9
30	R, 79		R, 79		R, 72		R, 61	23,278	24,822	7	47,483	40.6	16.5	14.7	89.4	0.4	4.3	0.5	2.7
31	R, 100		R, 100		R, 100		R, 62	21,802	22,610	4	45,573	40.6	17.4	15.3	92.7	0.3	2.6	0.5	2.6
32	R, 100		R, 100		R, 64		D, 53	21,707	22,921	6	51,169	43.3	19.3	13.7	85.2	1.4	3.9	1.1	3.2
33	R, 100		R, 68		R, 67		R, 55	29,167	30,953	6	59,034	41.0	17.4	11.8	82.1	1.8	4.5	1.1	4.6
34	R, 77		R, 72		R, 100		R, 100	14,195	15,845	12	62,288	45.6	21.9	11.2	86.9	1.1	4.6	1.2	2.2
35	R, 100		R, 58		R, 64		R, 53	24,490	25,808	5	37,905	32.7	9.5	18.4	77.8	1.7	8.4	2.0	4.3

Note: D=Democrat, R=Republican, R/D=Republican/Democrat (cross-filed), D/R=Democrat/Republican (cross-filed), I=Independent, C=Constitution, O=Other, GI=Green Independent, P=Progressive, P/D=Progressive/Democrat, P/D/R=Progressive/Democrat/Republican, HH=Households

South Dakota Legislative Districts—Election and Demographic Data

House Districts	General Election Results Party, Percent of Vote							Population			Avg. HH Income	Pop 25+		Below Poverty Line	2006 White (Non-Hisp)	African American	American Indians, Alaska Natives	Asians, Hawaiians, Pacific Islanders	Hispanic Origin
												Some College +	4-Yr Degree +						
S. Dakota	2000	2001	2002	2003	2004	2005	2006	2000	2006	% Change	($)	(%)	(%)	(%)	(%)	(%)	(%)	(%)	(%)
1A	D, 34		D, 34		D, 32		D, 44	20,859	20,121	-4	40,123	41.8	11.1	17.4	78.3	0.3	19.1	0.3	1.1
1B	D, 26		D, 30		D, 31		D, 36	20,859	20,121	-4	40,123	41.8	11.1	17.4	78.3	0.3	19.1	0.3	1.1
2A	R, 29		D, 32		D, 33		D, 35	27,831	26,893	-3	46,843	52.9	14.8	14.9	95.1	0.3	2.7	0.3	0.8
2B	D, 24		D, 30		D, 31		D, 32	27,831	26,893	-3	46,843	52.9	14.8	14.9	95.1	0.3	2.7	0.3	0.8
3A	D, 28		R, 31		R, 30		R, 27	15,083	14,303	-5	48,585	60.8	19.7	14.4	93.5	0.4	3.2	1.3	1.2
3B	R, 25		R, 30		R, 31		R, 28	15,083	14,303	-5	48,585	60.8	19.7	14.4	93.5	0.4	3.2	1.3	1.2
4A	D, 30		R, 33		D, 25		R, 35	16,068	15,165	-6	44,968	43.2	11.8	15.5	96.6	0.1	1.0	0.3	1.1
4B	R, 27		D, 29		R, 30		D, 35	16,068	15,165	-6	44,968	43.2	11.8	15.5	96.6	0.1	1.0	0.3	1.1
5A	R, 29		R, 56		R, 34		R, 34	23,617	23,619	0	50,576	48.8	14.1	13.8	94.4	0.2	2.1	0.4	1.4
5B	R, 27		R, 44		R, 28		R, 27	23,617	23,619	0	50,576	48.8	14.1	13.8	94.4	0.2	2.1	0.4	1.4
6A	R, 30		R, 32		R, 34		R, 38	43,491	42,703	-2	49,222	44.9	12.5	14.2	95.8	0.2	1.5	0.3	1.1
6B	R, 29		R, 32		R, 42		R, 39	43,491	42,703	-2	49,222	44.9	12.5	14.2	95.8	0.2	1.5	0.3	1.1
7A	R, 32		R, 50		R, 30		R, 32	24,497	24,360	-1	49,181	66.8	23.1	14.2	94.4	0.5	1.5	2.0	0.9
7B	R, 29		R, 50		R, 28		R, 32	24,497	24,360	-1	49,181	66.8	23.1	14.2	94.4	0.5	1.5	2.0	0.9
8A	D, 29		D, 30		D, 27		R, 36	23,430	22,589	-4	45,685	48.3	13.6	15.3	92.2	0.3	4.6	0.6	1.3
8B	R, 29		D, 25		D, 31		D, 34	23,430	22,589	-4	45,685	48.3	13.6	15.3	92.2	0.3	4.6	0.6	1.3
9A	R, 35		R, 25		D, 26		R, 26	27,113	31,428	16	52,519	45.0	12.2	13.3	83.0	3.0	3.1	1.7	5.2
9B	R, 34		D, 28		R, 26		D, 25	27,113	31,428	16	52,519	45.0	12.2	13.3	83.0	3.0	3.1	1.7	5.2
10A	R, 30		R, 53		R, 47		R, 32	15,756	17,140	9	69,354	57.6	18.0	10.1	95.3	0.4	0.8	0.4	1.2
10B	R, 26		R, 47		R, 53		R, 27	15,756	17,140	9	69,354	57.6	18.0	10.1	95.3	0.4	0.8	0.4	1.2
11A	R, 28		R, 58		R, 28		R, 29	16,925	19,006	12	66,049	67.1	21.2	10.6	93.3	0.9	1.2	1.4	1.8
11B	R, 31		R, 42		R, 34		R, 31	16,925	19,006	12	66,049	67.1	21.2	10.6	93.3	0.9	1.2	1.4	1.8
12A	R, 35		R, 30		R, 46		R, 33	27,853	36,246	30	62,898	65.7	21.2	11.1	92.0	0.9	1.8	1.1	2.0
12B	R, 35		R, 27		R, 54		R, 26	27,853	36,246	30	62,898	65.7	21.2	11.1	92.0	0.9	1.8	1.1	2.0
13A	R, 39		R, 33		D, 26		R, 26	22,421	23,022	3	71,295	73.2	25.6	9.8	89.7	1.5	1.9	1.2	3.2
13B	R, 31		D, 27		R, 29		D, 27	22,421	23,022	3	71,295	73.2	25.6	9.8	89.7	1.5	1.9	1.2	3.2
14A	R, 50		R, 55		R, 33		R, 29	20,053	21,975	10	65,597	67.0	22.9	10.7	90.4	2.0	1.2	1.5	2.7
14B	R, 50		R, 45		R, 35		D, 29	20,053	21,975	10	65,597	67.0	22.9	10.7	90.4	2.0	1.2	1.5	2.7
15A	D, 34		D, 32		D, 31		D, 41	18,489	19,140	4	39,898	46.3	11.9	17.5	72.5	5.2	8.3	2.2	9.3
15B	D, 27		D, 32		D, 30		D, 38	18,489	19,140	4	39,898	46.3	11.9	17.5	72.5	5.2	8.3	2.2	9.3
16A	R, 37		R, 29		D, 49		R, 31	22,837	27,056	18	60,810	51.6	15.2	11.5	95.4	0.3	0.9	1.0	1.5
16B	D, 32		D, 32		R, 51		D, 30	22,837	27,056	18	60,810	51.6	15.2	11.5	95.4	0.3	0.9	1.0	1.5
17A	R, 29		R, 28		R, 28		R, 28	22,386	21,308	-5	43,821	61.2	20.5	15.9	93.5	0.9	2.3	1.6	0.9
17B	D, 25		D, 30		R, 27		D, 27	22,386	21,308	-5	43,821	61.2	20.5	15.9	93.5	0.9	2.3	1.6	0.9
18A	R, 36		R, 29		R, 46		R, 24	21,652	21,893	1	47,737	54.9	16.6	14.6	91.8	1.5	2.1	0.6	2.9
18B	R, 26		R, 35		R, 53		D, 41	21,652	21,893	1	47,737	54.9	16.6	14.6	91.8	1.5	2.1	0.6	2.9
19A	D, 35		R, 35		R, 54		R, 35	18,793	17,792	-5	40,621	46.7	12.1	17.2	96.1	0.4	2.0	0.1	0.7
19B	R, 34		R, 41		R, 46		R, 32	18,793	17,792	-5	40,621	46.7	12.1	17.2	96.1	0.4	2.0	0.1	0.7
20A	R, 34		R, 33		R, 37		R, 29	21,799	21,872	0	46,656	49.3	13.6	15.0	93.3	0.4	2.4	0.5	2.3
20B	D, 32		D, 35		R, 26		R, 29	21,799	21,872	0	46,656	49.3	13.6	15.0	93.3	0.4	2.4	0.5	2.3
21A	D, 32		R, 32		D, 26		R, 27	21,834	21,187	-3	37,663	39.9	10.8	18.6	67.9	0.4	28.9	0.5	1.5
21B	R, 25		D, 45		R, 31		R, 29	21,834	21,187	-3	37,663	39.9	10.8	18.6	67.9	0.4	28.9	0.5	1.5
22A	D, 27		D, 29		D, 29		D, 28	20,963	18,965	-10	45,035	50.1	13.6	15.5	94.7	0.7	1.3	0.4	2.1
22B	D, 31		D, 29		D, 27		D, 26	20,963	18,965	-10	45,035	50.1	13.6	15.5	94.7	0.7	1.3	0.4	2.1
23A	R, 40		R, 42		R, 48		R, 44	22,031	19,718	-10	40,696	44.9	12.1	17.2	93.6	0.1	4.8	0.2	0.5
23B	R, 39		R, 38		R, 52		R, 35	22,031	19,718	-10	40,696	44.9	12.1	17.2	93.6	0.1	4.8	0.2	0.5
24A	R, 39		R, 30		R, 45		R, 52	20,809	21,177	2	55,926	63.7	21.1	12.5	87.8	0.3	8.1	0.5	1.8
24B	R, 43		R, 28		R, 55		R, 48	20,809	21,177	2	55,926	63.7	21.1	12.5	87.8	0.3	8.1	0.5	1.8
25A	D, 29		R, 32		D, 32		R, 32	19,219	21,511	12	52,220	46.3	12.3	13.4	97.1	0.1	0.9	0.2	0.8
25B	R, 25		D, 23		R, 37		D, 29	19,219	21,511	12	52,220	46.3	12.3	13.4	97.1	0.1	0.9	0.2	0.8

(continued)

Note: D=Democrat, R=Republican, R/D=Republican/Democrat (cross-filed), D/R=Democrat/Republican (cross-filed), I=Independent, C=Constitution, O=Other, GI=Green Independent, P=Progressive, P/D=Progressive/Democrat, P/D/R=Progressive/Democrat/Republican, HH=Households

South Dakota Legislative Districts—Election and Demographic Data (cont.)

House Districts	General Election Results Party, Percent of Vote							Population			Avg. HH Income	Pop 25+		Below Poverty Line	2006 White (Non-Hisp)	African American	American Indians, Alaska Natives	Asians, Hawaiians, Pacific Islanders	Hispanic Origin
												Some College +	4-Yr Degree +						
S. Dakota	2000	2001	2002	2003	2004	2005	2006	2000	2006	% Change	($)	(%)	(%)	(%)	(%)	(%)	(%)	(%)	(%)
26A	R, 41		R, 41		R, 37		D, 48	11,133	12,120	9	30,625	30.9	7.2	22.8	16.9	0.7	80.4	0.8	3.0
26B	R, 38		R, 40		R, 43		R, 51	11,222	10,160	-9	36,613	41.9	10.4	19.1	88.4	0.1	9.2	0.2	1.0
27A	D, 36		D, 43		D, 44		R, 25	21,166	22,008	4	33,735	33.6	7.7	20.7	22.9	0.7	74.0	0.7	2.7
27B	D, 30		D, 42		D, 40		D, 31	21,166	22,008	4	33,735	33.6	7.7	20.7	22.9	0.7	74.0	0.7	2.7
28A	D, 44		D, 64		D, 66		D, 60	10,267	10,715	4	31,558	31.0	6.8	22.1	23.0	0.6	74.7	0.7	2.8
28B	R, 100		R, 100		R, 100		R, 100	10,064	9,891	-2	36,048	43.5	11.2	19.4	83.4	0.3	11.8	0.4	2.4
29A	R, 36		R, 61		R, 40		R, 50	20,860	21,350	2	48,971	47.3	11.3	14.3	91.4	0.6	2.6	0.5	2.9
29B	R, 32		R, 39		R, 60		R, 50	20,860	21,350	2	48,971	47.3	11.3	14.3	91.4	0.6	2.6	0.5	2.9
30A	R, 39		R, 32		R, 32		R, 30	23,278	24,822	7	47,483	57.0	16.5	14.7	89.4	0.4	4.3	0.5	2.7
30B	R, 33		R, 34		R, 34		R, 29	23,278	24,822	7	47,483	57.0	16.5	14.7	89.4	0.4	4.3	0.5	2.7
31A	R, 42		R, 38		R, 32		R, 28	21,802	22,610	4	45,573	58.0	17.4	15.3	92.7	0.3	2.6	0.5	2.6
31B	R, 38		R, 36		R, 35		R, 28	21,802	22,610	4	45,573	58.0	17.4	15.3	92.7	0.3	2.6	0.5	2.6
32A	R, 33		R, 44		R, 32		R, 27	21,707	22,921	6	51,169	62.6	19.3	13.7	85.2	1.4	3.9	1.1	3.2
32B	R, 31		R, 36		R, 28		R, 29	21,707	22,921	6	51,169	62.6	19.3	13.7	85.2	1.4	3.9	1.1	3.2
33A	R, 37		R, 44		R, 38		R, 31	29,167	30,953	6	59,034	58.4	17.4	11.8	82.1	1.8	4.5	1.1	4.6
33B	R, 36		R, 32		R, 41		R, 27	29,167	30,953	6	59,034	58.4	17.4	11.8	82.1	1.8	4.5	1.1	4.6
34A	R, 53		R, 56		R, 37		R, 34	14,195	15,845	12	62,288	67.5	21.9	11.2	86.9	1.1	4.6	1.2	2.2
34B	R, 47		R, 44		R, 43		R, 32	14,195	15,845	12	62,288	67.5	21.9	11.2	86.9	1.1	4.6	1.2	2.2
35A	R, 31		R, 30		R, 29		R, 33	24,490	25,808	5	37,905	42.2	9.5	18.4	77.8	1.7	8.4	2.0	4.3
35B	R, 36		R, 25		R, 29		R, 32	24,490	25,808	5	37,905	42.2	9.5	18.4	77.8	1.7	8.4	2.0	4.3

Note: D=Democrat, R=Republican, R/D=Republican/Democrat (cross-filed), D/R=Democrat/Republican (cross-filed), I=Independent, C=Constitution, O=Other, GI=Green Independent, P=Progressive, P/D=Progressive/Democrat, P/D/R=Progressive/Democrat/Republican, HH=Households

TENNESSEE

Few states span such a great distance, psychologically as well as geographically, as Tennessee. Kingsport, at its eastern tip, is closer to Washington, D.C. than it is to Memphis, and Memphis is itself more a part of the Mississippi Delta than of the broad farms and tobacco fields in the middle of the state.

Rather like Ohio (which it resembles in practically no other way), Tennessee is three states, each with its representative city. The mountainous east, predominantly white and staunchly Unionist during the Civil War, is centered around Knoxville, though Chattanooga is also important. Early in the country's history, it was seriously proposed to break Tennessee into two states and name the eastern half after Benjamin Franklin.

In the middle of the state is bluegrass country (four times as much actual bluegrass as Kentucky), centered around Nashville, one of the country's rising cities. On the western edge is Memphis, more heavily black than the others and still Tennessee's largest city, but one being rapidly overtaken by Nashville (the Nashville metro area is now bigger than the Memphis metro area). Each region may also be said to have its distinctive style of music: bluegrass in the hills, country at the Grand Ol' Opry in Nashville, and the blues on Beale Street (as well as rock 'n roll at Graceland) in Memphis.

Tennessee is the sixteenth most-populous state, but it is projected to rise to fifteenth by 2030. It has been growing faster than some of its neighbors, such as Kentucky and Alabama, but not as fast as others, such as Georgia or North Carolina. It is the fulcrum of a region that calls itself the Mid-South.

There are no pockets of 40 or 50 percent growth in Tennessee, or even 30 percent, nor are there any pockets that have seen population fall by a great amount. High-growth areas in the 20–25 percent range form a ring around Nashville and Memphis, creating new suburbs ever further out from the city center. These are also the areas where Nissan and Saturn have built assembly plants that are turning out millions of cars and trucks, the sort of work that once made Detroit an economic giant.

To pick just one illustration of Nashville's growth, the 54th and 55th house districts downtown have not grown at all in this decade. The 56th district, home of Belle Mead, the old money suburb where former Senate majority leader Bill Frist lives, grew by 3 percent. But the 61st district just beyond it has grown by 22 percent and the 63rd district just beyond that, by 25 percent. Population has been falling a bit,

on the other hand, in Shelby County, but not so much downtown as in the older suburban areas just outside Interstates 240 and 40.

Income is rising quickly in Tennessee. That slowly growing Belle Mead district is the state's wealthiest (average income $117,000), but unlike some other states, the fast-growing outer suburbs are also among the wealthiest. The poorest districts, and the ones with the highest rates of unemployment, are in the big cities, as well, led by the 15th district in central Knoxville, where the median household income is just $30,000.

Although Tennessee borders several states with large African American populations—Mississippi, Alabama, Georgia, and North Carolina—it does not border heavily black sections of those states, hence the percentage of Tennessee residents who are African American is not particularly high. The districts with the greatest share of African Americans, the ones in which African Americans make up more than two-thirds of the population, are all located in and around Memphis, the one part of the state that does lie next to predominantly black areas in the Mississippi Delta and in Arkansas.

Tennessee's legislature was a constitutional footnote because it was the one successfully challenged in the landmark 1962 Supreme Court decision *Baker v. Carr,* the first to hold that redistricting cases can be brought in federal court. (At the time the decision was handed down, Tennessee still apportioned its legislature based on 1900 census figures). More than forty years later, Democrats still control the state house of representatives, 53–46, though Republicans have gained seats recently. In the state senate, the GOP won control in 2004 for the first time since Reconstruction. It is now a 16–16 tie, with one Independent. Although Tennessee has a lieutenant governor, the post is filled by the state senate and not by the voters. Hence the officeholder is known as the lieutenant governor and speaker of the senate and is currently a Republican. A Democrat holds the post of speaker pro tempore.

Once a state that produced such prominent Democrats as Cordell Hull, Estes Kefauver, and Albert Gore Sr. (not to mention Andrew Jackson and James K. Polk), Tennessee has more recently produced such well-known Republicans as Howard Baker, Lamar Alexander, Bill Frist, and Fred Thompson. The last time it last voted Democratic in a presidential election was in 1996. Had it done so in 2000, it would have given its own former senator, Al Gore Jr., the White House.

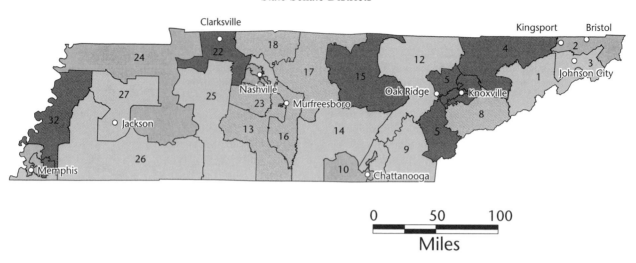

TENNESSEE
State Senate Districts

0   50   100
Miles

CHATTANOOGA

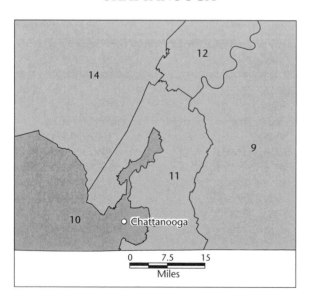

KNOXVILLE

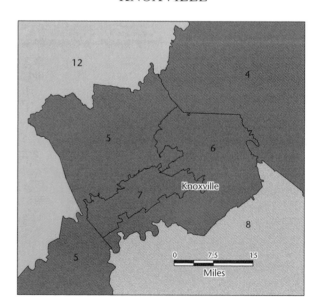

Population Growth   ▢ -2% to 2%   ▢ 2% to 7%   ▢ 7% to 11%   ▢ 11% to 21%

NASHVILLE

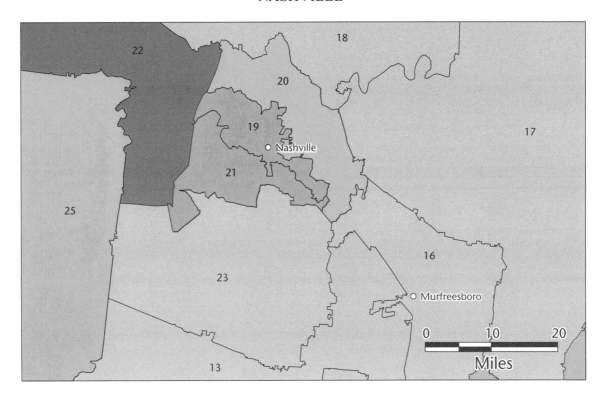

MEMPHIS

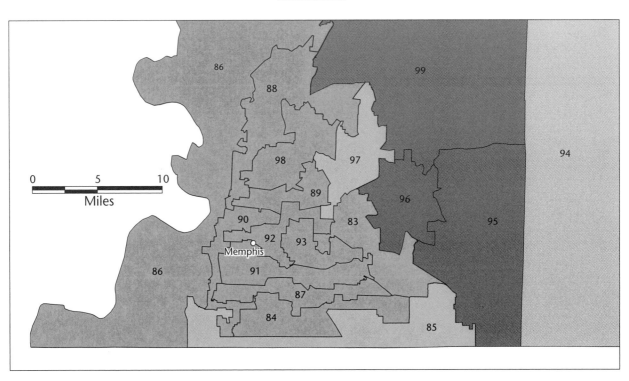

Population Growth   ▦ -2% to 2%   ▦ 2% to 7%   ▦ 7% to 11%   ▦ 11% to 21%

Tennessee State Senate Districts—Election and Demographic Data

Senate Districts	General Election Results Party, Percent of Vote							Population			Avg. HH Income	Pop 25+		Below Poverty Line	White (Non-Hisp)	African American	American Indians, Alaska Natives	Asians, Hawaiians, Pacific Islanders	Hispanic Origin
												Some College +	4-Yr Degree +						
Tennessee	2000	2001	2002	2003	2004	2005	2006	2000	2006	% Change	($)	(%)	(%)	(%)	(%)	(%)	(%)	(%)	(%)
1			R, 100				R, 69	172,197	179,671	4	42,820	24.9	9.5	21.9	90.0	2.7	0.2	0.6	4.6
2	R, 71				R, 66			168,033	169,267	1	48,888	32.0	13.8	20.2	95.5	2.0	0.2	0.6	0.9
3			R, 73				R, 100	163,916	173,605	6	46,176	33.8	15.5	21.0	93.0	2.9	0.2	0.8	1.7
4	R, 100				R, 100			172,857	186,838	8	41,707	23.0	8.3	24.3	95.8	1.4	0.2	0.4	1.3
5			R, 65				R, 100	180,888	195,173	8	50,834	33.1	14.5	17.1	92.5	2.6	0.3	0.8	2.1
6	D, 89				R, 73			175,545	191,244	9	62,264	45.6	24.2	14.9	90.2	5.5	0.2	1.3	1.5
7			R, 59				R, 100	174,926	187,429	7	52,699	45.2	24.0	20.6	79.9	13.2	0.2	2.7	2.3
8	R, 69				R, 67			176,509	198,132	12	51,204	33.5	13.0	15.9	93.9	2.0	0.3	1.0	1.6
9			R, 60				R, 100	164,228	173,457	6	47,907	28.5	10.3	19.9	91.0	3.7	0.3	0.8	2.5
10	D, 62				D, 72			164,063	163,326	0	47,681	31.6	14.9	22.8	61.4	33.2	0.3	1.4	2.6
11			R, 97				R, 64	170,475	176,993	4	66,536	41.5	22.6	10.4	88.1	5.9	0.3	2.2	2.1
12	D, 64				D, 54			177,540	185,199	4	41,248	22.7	8.1	25.3	95.5	1.6	0.2	0.4	1.1
13			R, 54				R, 58	176,761	201,831	14	56,489	29.5	11.2	14.6	83.5	9.8	0.3	1.3	3.5
14	D, 72				D, 100			168,656	179,305	6	46,628	24.9	10.1	22.0	90.4	3.4	0.2	0.7	3.3
15			D, 58				D, 100	168,061	181,334	8	43,248	26.2	11.5	22.4	94.0	1.0	0.2	0.8	2.5
16	D, 55				R, 52			176,658	212,042	20	57,200	31.7	15.0	15.0	78.3	10.2	0.3	2.2	7.0
17			R, 53				R, 58	176,334	196,282	11	57,730	27.5	11.5	16.6	90.7	4.5	0.3	0.6	2.5
18	D, 58				R, 52			181,121	205,763	14	60,475	31.1	12.0	13.1	87.2	6.8	0.3	0.8	3.5
19			D, 100				D, 100	161,374	161,471	0	40,793	37.6	18.5	26.1	33.5	55.9	0.3	2.8	7.7
20	D, 100				D, 100			177,287	182,568	3	54,157	44.8	22.0	11.2	72.0	17.4	0.3	2.0	6.0
21			D, 63				D, 66	178,822	180,556	1	76,365	51.9	33.3	10.6	70.7	12.1	0.2	5.2	8.5
22	D, 63				D, 57			179,347	194,087	8	52,569	32.8	12.3	14.2	74.5	15.2	0.4	2.5	4.2
23			R, 100				R, 59	179,980	212,604	18	95,220	50.5	32.7	6.9	84.7	7.0	0.2	2.5	3.9
24	D, 100				D, 65			181,000	181,684	0	43,389	22.7	8.5	22.2	88.1	7.9	0.2	0.8	1.8
25	D, 55		D, 63				D, 100	164,057	172,194	5	47,054	22.0	7.5	19.4	92.1	4.8	0.3	0.4	1.3
26	D, 55				D, 56			174,241	184,236	6	44,491	22.6	8.0	24.4	73.3	23.2	0.2	0.3	2.2
27			D, 55				D, 50	169,396	174,053	3	49,741	28.8	12.3	19.1	70.9	25.4	0.2	0.6	2.0
28	D, 66				D, 100			168,532	166,842	-1	49,566	29.6	14.3	19.0	42.2	50.0	0.2	2.1	5.6
29			D, 99				D, 72	167,137	168,210	1	40,366	27.0	13.2	31.7	26.1	69.7	0.2	1.7	2.4
30	D, 82				D, 67			170,516	168,147	-1	58,213	38.2	22.7	17.4	45.7	45.2	0.2	2.9	5.6
31			R, 68				R, 62	164,580	176,982	8	82,250	47.5	29.5	5.1	70.4	21.6	0.2	4.0	2.7
32	R, 100				R, 69			165,845	178,873	8	60,926	30.0	13.4	15.9	77.0	19.1	0.3	1.0	1.7
33			D, 100				D, 100	176,704	181,584	3	61,196	32.3	16.1	17.1	27.3	68.8	0.1	1.4	2.6

Note: D=Democrat, R=Republican, R/D=Republican/Democrat (cross-filed), D/R=Democrat/Republican (cross-filed), I=Independent, C=Constitution, O=Other, GI=Green Independent, P=Progressive, P/D=Progressive/Democrat, P/D/R=Progressive/Democrat/Republican, HH=Households

TENNESSEE
State House Districts

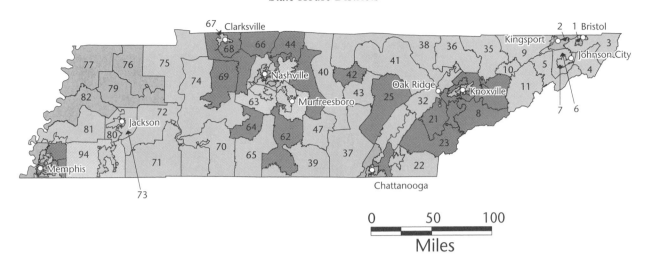

0   50   100

Miles

CHATTANOOGA

KNOXVILLE

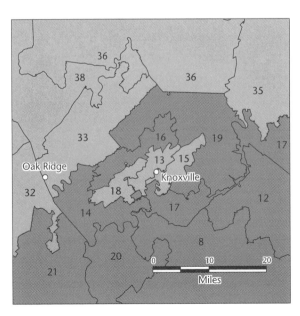

Population Growth   ▨ -3% to 1%   ▨ 1% to 7%   ▨ 7% to 16%   ▨ 16% to 26%

NASHVILLE

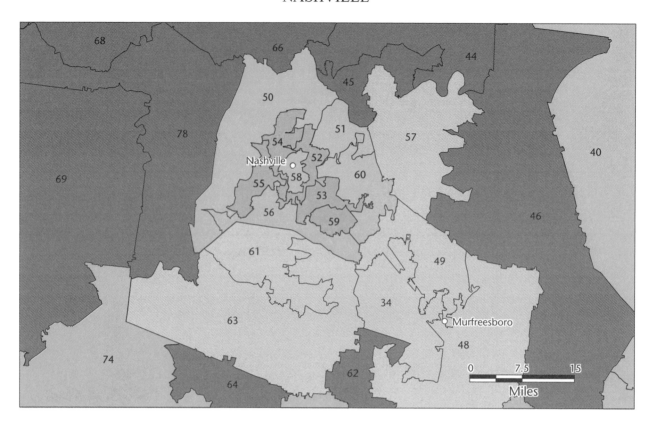

MEMPHIS

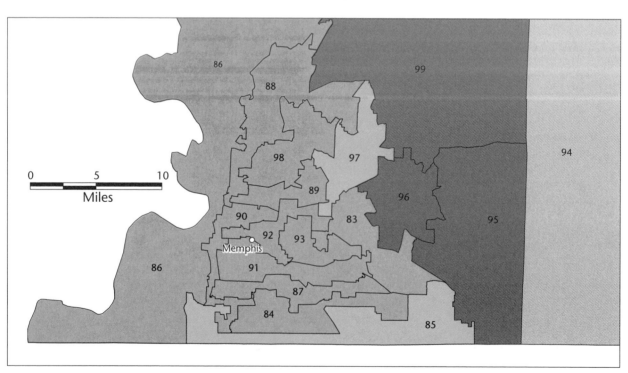

Population Growth   ■ -3% to 1%   □ 1% to 7%   ■ 7% to 16%   □ 16% to 26%

Tennessee State House Districts—Election and Demographic Data

House Districts	General Election Results Party, Percent of Vote							Population			Avg. HH Income ($)	Pop 25+ Some College + (%)	Pop 25+ 4-Yr Degree + (%)	Below Poverty Line (%)	2006 White (Non-Hisp) (%)	African American (%)	American Indians, Alaska Natives (%)	Asians, Hawaiians, Pacific Islanders (%)	Hispanic Origin (%)
Tennessee	2000	2001	2002	2003	2004	2005	2006	2000	2006	% Change	($)	(%)	(%)	(%)	(%)	(%)	(%)	(%)	(%)
1	R, 57		R, 97		R, 64		R, 61	54,462	53,805	-1	46,377	30.9	12.4	20.5	95.5	1.7	0.2	0.8	0.9
2	R, 82		D, 50		D, 58		D, 100	56,217	56,097	0	53,244	37.1	18.1	19.2	94.1	2.9	0.2	0.7	1.1
3	R, 86		R, 68		R, 64		R, 100	58,193	59,704	3	46,967	28.2	10.9	20.8	96.7	1.5	0.2	0.3	0.7
4	R, 100		R, 72		R, 100		R, 100	56,676	59,847	6	38,472	28.5	10.8	24.3	96.1	1.1	0.2	0.4	1.1
5	R, 100		R, 100		R, 68		R, 100	55,144	56,693	3	42,010	26.6	10.9	21.7	94.0	2.0	0.2	0.4	2.2
6	R, 98		R, 99		R, 100		R, 100	57,106	60,924	7	56,220	38.0	18.6	15.2	94.5	1.5	0.2	1.1	1.7
7	R, 100		R, 63		R, 59		R, 52	55,263	57,473	4	43,573	34.6	16.9	23.3	88.0	6.6	0.2	1.1	2.4
8	R, 100		R, 100		R, 100		R, 100	59,498	67,819	14	50,161	34.2	13.5	15.9	92.7	3.3	0.3	0.9	1.6
9	D, 59		R, 65		R, 100		R, 66	55,342	58,616	6	41,155	23.1	8.0	24.3	96.8	1.2	0.2	0.2	0.8
10	R, 58		D, 53		D, 54		D, 100	58,345	60,595	4	48,012	27.6	10.6	19.7	81.1	4.2	0.2	1.0	10.1
11	R, 72		D, 63		D, 50		D, 55	59,237	62,428	5	38,638	20.8	7.1	24.1	95.3	1.8	0.3	0.3	1.3
12	R, 100		R, 100		R, 100		R, 100	59,091	66,397	12	48,972	33.2	11.4	17.1	95.2	0.7	0.3	0.8	1.7
13	D, 61		D, 80		D, 55		D, 62	58,375	60,875	4	40,055	41.9	19.8	23.1	83.0	10.4	0.3	1.5	2.6
14	R, 100		R, 100		R, 64		R, 100	59,751	68,779	15	104,328	57.4	38.0	5.8	91.6	2.5	0.2	3.0	1.6
15	D, 100		D, 100		D, 87		D, 80	56,160	59,085	5	30,667	32.2	15.4	38.4	59.9	33.4	0.3	2.7	2.1
16	R, 71		R, 100		R, 100		R, 100	60,256	65,152	8	57,292	46.3	21.4	11.5	93.8	2.4	0.2	1.1	1.4
17	R, 100		R, 99		R, 61		R, 100	60,614	66,485	10	58,080	35.8	17.2	16.3	94.6	1.9	0.2	0.6	1.6
18	R, 100		R, 100		R, 65		R, 54	60,309	64,271	7	58,448	52.3	28.3	10.9	86.2	6.4	0.2	3.0	2.5
19	R, 100		R, 63		R, 100		R, 100	62,489	67,342	8	47,899	37.5	15.9	15.6	94.2	2.9	0.2	0.5	1.1
20	R, 64		R, 100		R, 100		R, 100	58,412	63,912	9	54,670	33.0	14.1	14.9	93.7	2.1	0.2	1.3	1.4
21	R, 100		R, 100		R, 86		R, 61	60,667	68,582	13	52,307	29.6	12.2	17.1	91.7	2.2	0.3	0.5	3.2
22	R, 83		R, 99		R, 100		R, 65	56,084	58,381	4	47,858	25.5	7.8	18.5	95.1	1.5	0.3	0.3	1.6
23	R, 77		R, 100		R, 100		R, 100	60,315	64,910	8	43,923	24.5	8.3	22.4	91.5	3.7	0.3	0.9	2.0
24	R, 100		R, 66		R, 100		R, 100	58,255	61,703	6	49,897	33.8	13.8	19.7	87.8	5.1	0.2	1.1	3.6
25	R, 77		R, 60		R, 58		R, 60	59,307	65,319	10	44,017	27.6	10.4	21.2	96.0	1.0	0.3	0.4	1.2
26	R, 97		R, 97		R, 68		R, 100	56,319	60,887	8	71,051	41.4	21.7	10.1	86.6	6.4	0.3	2.2	2.9
27	D, 63		R, 95		R, 99		R, 56	57,574	58,098	1	63,793	41.7	24.5	12.1	91.1	4.1	0.2	1.4	1.8
28	R, 97		D, 72		D, 100		D, 80	53,684	53,079	-1	40,187	28.2	14.5	33.0	35.0	59.4	0.2	1.4	4.0
29	D, 70		D, 60		D, 60		D, 100	55,856	54,774	-2	49,516	36.0	17.0	19.1	56.6	37.3	0.3	2.0	2.6
30	R, 98		R, 97		R, 62		R, 100	54,784	54,397	-1	64,259	42.9	22.6	10.2	85.0	8.0	0.3	3.1	2.1
31	R, 54		R, 60		R, 64		R, 65	59,324	63,159	6	52,744	29.6	12.6	16.9	93.2	2.6	0.3	1.0	1.7
32	D, 62		D, 61		D, 100		D, 100	58,239	60,328	4	48,770	29.3	11.4	20.2	93.4	2.6	0.2	0.6	1.5
33	D, 53		D, 50		D, 100		D, 61	57,797	58,648	1	52,315	37.3	17.9	16.1	90.6	4.7	0.3	1.4	1.4
34	R, 100		R, 62		R, 100		R, 55	62,510	78,533	26	66,121	36.9	17.2	7.9	84.4	6.3	0.2	3.1	4.4
35	R, 100		R, 58		R, 64		R, 69	60,477	64,478	7	39,070	22.0	8.8	27.2	95.4	1.3	0.2	0.5	1.5
36	R, 53		R, 100		R, 55		R, 57	57,675	60,704	5	36,924	18.8	6.1	28.3	97.1	0.3	0.2	0.3	1.0
37	D, 55		D, 67		D, 100		D, 72	58,983	60,825	3	42,731	21.0	7.6	23.9	95.6	2.1	0.3	0.3	0.8
38	D, 100		D, 99		D, 100		D, 69	59,158	61,159	3	37,630	19.9	7.5	27.8	97.1	0.6	0.2	0.2	0.9
39	D, 71		D, 49		D, 53		D, 60	58,273	62,005	6	51,034	28.0	11.1	19.0	91.0	4.7	0.3	0.6	1.9
40	D, 100		D, 98		D, 100		D, 57	55,863	59,763	7	46,287	19.7	7.2	22.7	93.2	1.5	0.3	0.3	3.1
41	D, 99		D, 100		D, 100		D, 100	56,736	58,477	3	36,732	18.0	6.8	27.2	97.1	1.0	0.2	0.2	0.9
42	D, 57		D, 98		D, 62		D, 77	57,035	62,324	9	46,085	30.8	16.1	21.4	90.4	1.8	0.2	1.7	3.9
43	D, 68		D, 99		D, 100		D, 100	55,001	57,606	5	40,990	19.9	6.4	23.5	87.8	2.5	0.2	0.5	5.9
44	D, 100		D, 66		D, 66		D, 65	59,583	68,228	15	54,754	26.7	9.1	14.9	89.2	6.3	0.3	0.4	2.2
45	R, 72		R, 68		R, 57		R, 64	59,297	65,240	10	64,324	38.2	16.1	11.5	87.6	5.9	0.2	1.4	3.1
46	D, 68		D, 60		D, 100		D, 67	60,805	68,400	12	52,029	24.3	9.4	17.3	86.8	8.1	0.3	0.6	2.9
47	D, 63		R, 54		R, 57		R, 53	59,010	63,016	7	50,329	29.2	12.9	19.7	89.7	3.4	0.3	1.1	3.6
48	D, 62		D, 65		D, 100		D, 56	57,290	71,649	25	56,231	31.6	16.1	17.3	76.3	12.8	0.3	3.6	5.2
49	R, 59		D, 50		D, 55		D, 56	59,616	70,833	19	58,387	34.4	15.8	12.4	80.1	10.3	0.3	1.8	5.5
50	D, 100		D, 100		D, 67		D, 100	57,007	59,299	4	56,428	44.9	22.8	10.4	73.1	19.2	0.3	2.0	3.6

(continued)

Note: D=Democrat, R=Republican, R/D=Republican/Democrat (cross-filed), D/R=Democrat/Republican (cross-filed), I=Independent, C=Constitution, O=Other, GI=Green Independent, P=Progressive, P/D=Progressive/Democrat, P/D/R=Progressive/Democrat/Republican, HH=Households

Tennessee State House Districts—Election and Demographic Data (cont.)

House Districts	General Election Results Party, Percent of Vote							Population			Avg. HH Income ($)	Pop 25+ Some College + (%)	Pop 25+ 4-Yr Degree + (%)	Below Poverty Line (%)	2006 White (Non-Hisp) (%)	African American (%)	American Indians, Alaska Natives (%)	Asians, Hawaiians, Pacific Islanders (%)	Hispanic Origin (%)
Tennessee	2000	2001	2002	2003	2004	2005	2006	2000	2006	% Change	($)	(%)	(%)	(%)	(%)	(%)	(%)	(%)	(%)
51	D, 74		D, 60		D, 60		D, 100	58,882	60,875	3	52,714	43.0	20.6	14.7	74.9	14.6	0.3	1.6	6.0
52	D, 100		D, 61		D, 61		D, 81	56,183	55,694	-1	49,757	40.4	21.6	19.0	54.4	30.9	0.3	2.4	10.0
53	D, 100		D, 67		D, 63		D, 100	55,996	55,487	-1	50,660	45.8	23.1	11.1	57.9	19.4	0.3	5.4	13.7
54	D, 65		D, 81		D, 100		D, 100	58,544	58,521	0	54,859	40.2	23.1	23.6	34.1	59.1	0.2	2.8	3.6
55	D, 100		D, 70		D, 100		D, 100	55,476	55,447	0	70,743	54.8	36.1	11.3	75.5	12.0	0.2	6.0	4.1
56	R, 74		R, 67		R, 73		R, 100	59,015	60,822	3	117,397	61.7	44.1	5.4	84.3	7.1	0.1	3.9	3.0
57	R, 65		R, 63		R, 100		R, 100	60,093	70,297	17	81,868	41.7	19.7	6.4	92.3	3.8	0.3	1.0	1.6
58	D, 100		D, 100		D, 100		D, 84	52,284	53,128	2	34,790	35.5	18.6	35.4	30.0	63.0	0.2	2.3	4.2
59	D, 100		D, 65		D, 100		D, 71	58,993	58,772	0	50,183	44.6	22.9	10.6	52.1	24.1	0.3	5.4	15.7
60	D, 73		D, 71		D, 100		D, 67	59,945	61,657	3	57,628	48.5	24.9	7.2	70.8	15.1	0.4	2.9	8.1
61	R, 100		R, 100		R, 100		R, 100	60,461	73,588	22	115,990	54.7	38.3	5.0	88.6	3.6	0.2	2.6	3.6
62	D, 99		D, 52		D, 100		D, 100	60,186	66,665	11	50,933	23.5	9.1	19.4	79.2	9.1	0.3	0.7	8.9
63	D, 53		R, 50		R, 100		R, 68	60,239	75,193	25	93,649	44.3	27.0	8.7	85.8	7.7	0.2	1.3	3.5
64	D, 65		R, 51		R, 53		R, 53	57,728	63,622	10	55,143	30.0	10.3	15.5	78.3	14.7	0.3	0.5	4.3
65	D, 99		D, 61		D, 52		D, 60	56,449	58,393	3	49,332	22.9	8.1	18.4	85.6	10.0	0.2	0.5	2.3
66	D, 59		D, 56		D, 54		D, 50	54,814	61,989	13	57,923	25.4	8.9	14.0	83.7	8.8	0.3	0.5	5.7
67	D, 100		D, 61		D, 61		D, 54	57,082	59,837	5	46,779	33.5	10.3	14.8	60.1	24.9	0.5	3.8	6.3
68	D, 58		D, 53		R, 55		R, 55	60,622	67,637	12	55,826	36.7	15.9	13.6	73.5	16.8	0.4	2.6	3.8
69	D, 63		D, 70		D, 100		D, 100	54,140	58,804	9	49,847	23.5	8.0	16.8	91.9	4.4	0.4	0.4	1.6
70	D, 59		R, 52		R, 55		R, 63	54,394	56,208	3	44,202	20.9	7.0	22.1	94.8	2.3	0.3	0.4	1.2
71	D, 99		D, 97		D, 100		D, 59	56,289	57,479	2	42,786	21.6	7.4	24.8	92.2	5.0	0.2	0.2	1.4
72	R, 100		R, 100		R, 72		R, 100	60,747	62,525	3	44,366	22.0	7.6	22.4	89.5	7.5	0.2	0.3	1.3
73	D, 52		R, 54		R, 72		R, 100	57,156	59,594	4	57,874	36.1	16.4	12.2	77.4	18.7	0.2	1.0	1.9
74	D, 100		D, 61		D, 100		D, 100	56,752	60,278	6	48,640	22.6	7.4	19.9	89.8	5.9	0.3	0.3	2.2
75	D, 99		D, 77		D, 69		D, 74	60,287	61,370	2	41,323	22.6	8.4	21.2	91.0	5.6	0.3	0.8	1.2
76	D, 100		D, 64		D, 100		D, 64	56,176	54,661	-3	43,886	24.8	11.0	23.0	87.3	8.6	0.1	1.2	1.5
77	D, 100		D, 58		D, 69		D, 73	59,821	60,150	1	45,524	22.8	8.0	20.6	84.2	11.4	0.2	0.4	2.8
78	D, 61		R, 51		R, 60		R, 52	61,034	67,941	11	57,434	29.4	11.2	12.3	89.2	4.3	0.4	1.1	2.7
79	D, 79		R, 52		R, 62		R, 57	56,505	56,428	0	43,375	23.3	7.9	20.4	78.7	18.3	0.2	0.3	1.4
80	D, 84		D, 100		D, 100		D, 68	51,864	53,229	3	46,630	27.1	11.6	26.7	41.0	55.4	0.2	0.7	2.6
81	D, 59		D, 53		D, 58		D, 100	56,690	59,113	4	49,242	23.2	7.7	22.5	63.2	33.2	0.3	0.5	2.1
82	D, 100		D, 58		D, 61		D, 100	59,447	59,181	0	42,038	20.9	8.0	25.3	69.5	25.6	0.3	0.4	3.2
83	R, 100		R, 80		R, 75		R, 100	55,026	55,402	1	113,359	54.9	39.0	5.7	77.7	14.8	0.1	3.9	2.4
84	D, 100		D, 86		D, 100		D, 100	56,636	56,758	0	52,962	33.4	15.4	13.5	23.4	71.8	0.1	1.6	3.3
85	D, 100		D, 100		D, 100		D, 100	59,081	61,783	5	61,140	35.1	16.8	10.7	28.4	67.3	0.1	1.6	2.7
86	D, 81		D, 80		D, 77		D, 77	54,058	54,483	1	45,863	27.4	14.1	26.4	32.7	63.9	0.2	1.1	1.9
87	D, 100		D, 100		D, 100		D, 100	51,820	51,936	0	44,376	30.5	14.4	16.3	18.4	72.5	0.2	3.0	7.4
88	D, 100		D, 100		D, 100		D, 100	57,592	57,536	0	38,876	23.1	9.6	27.5	25.7	70.8	0.2	1.0	2.5
89	D, 100		D, 74		D, 56		D, 67	53,461	52,064	-3	42,816	30.4	15.5	22.2	49.1	38.1	0.3	3.5	8.9
90	D, 100		D, 100		D, 100		D, 100	57,060	57,114	0	41,173	30.8	17.2	31.6	25.6	69.0	0.1	2.8	2.5
91	D, 100		D, 100		D, 100		D, 100	58,880	57,843	-2	43,725	27.8	12.9	24.4	19.7	73.6	0.1	2.1	5.9
92	D, 100		D, 100		D, 74		D, 100	55,606	54,567	-2	54,453	32.4	18.7	28.1	25.8	71.7	0.1	0.8	1.5
93	D, 80		D, 54		D, 55		D, 66	53,195	51,699	-3	50,209	36.2	20.1	18.9	52.4	39.9	0.2	2.4	4.6
94	R, 100		R, 68		R, 100		R, 64	54,055	64,236	19	53,749	26.2	9.0	19.5	69.3	27.3	0.2	0.5	1.9
95	R, 100		R, 100		R, 100		R, 100	57,418	65,368	14	117,334	48.3	32.4	4.1	81.4	12.6	0.2	2.9	1.9
96	R, 67		R, 100		R, 100		R, 100	58,824	64,775	10	77,636	48.8	31.4	5.0	74.3	15.7	0.2	5.0	3.5
97	R, 100		R, 82		R, 76		R, 100	59,514	60,378	1	60,605	38.3	19.6	8.2	72.3	19.5	0.3	2.7	3.8
98	D, 100		D, 81		D, 100		D, 100	59,114	57,938	-2	39,795	26.6	11.7	26.6	23.4	71.9	0.2	1.2	3.6
99	R, 100		R, 50		R, 100		R, 72	54,202	61,127	13	73,065	39.5	20.1	7.2	75.2	18.5	0.3	2.2	2.6

Note: D=Democrat, R=Republican, R/D=Republican/Democrat (cross-filed), D/R=Democrat/Republican (cross-filed), I=Independent, C=Constitution, O=Other, GI=Green Independent, P=Progressive, P/D=Progressive/Democrat, P/D/R=Progressive/Democrat/Republican, HH=Households

TEXAS

As John Gunther observed more than half a century ago, Texas does not properly belong either to the West, the South, or even the Southwest, although it spans all three regions. It is a region unto itself. The land area of Texas is bigger than New York, Pennsylvania, Massachusetts, Illinois, Ohio, and Wisconsin combined. Fifty-nine Texas counties are larger than the state of Rhode Island.

One dominating factor in state life, then, is distance. The town of Perryton, at the top of the Panhandle, is closer to Madison, Wisconsin, than it is to Brownsville on the Mexican border. Most towns in the Panhandle, in fact, are closer to six other state capitals than they are to Austin, fostering a sense of isolation and hostility to state, as well as to federal, government. Yet people there think of themselves as Texans, in a way difficult for non-Texans to appreciate. People in Ohio, for example, do not take strictly Ohio vacations, in which they set off not just for a specific destination, but to see the wonders of their state. Texans do.

The second-largest state is also the second most populous. Texas has twenty cities of more than 100,000 people and five of the country's twenty most populous: Houston (fourth), San Antonio (seventh), Dallas (ninth), Austin (sixteenth), and Ft. Worth (nineteenth). Population gains are widespread; seventy of the 150 state house districts have grown by 10 percent or more since 2000.

The Texas suburbs, as in many places around the country, are the fastest-growing areas of the state—such as the outer suburbs of Dallas, Houston, and Austin, in many cases far removed from the city center. At its most distant point, for example, the 15th state house district, which includes Montgomery County northeast of the Metroplex (and which has grown by 44 percent in the last seven years) is sixty-five miles from downtown Dallas. But of course few of the people who live there commute to downtown Dallas. Instead, they commute to jobs in other parts of the suburbs.

Dallas, Houston, San Antonio, and Austin are four prominent representatives of cities Michael Barone calls "Interior Boomtowns." Their shared characteristic, in addition to their location far from either coast, is that in most cases their rapid growth has been driven by domestic migration rather than immigration. San Antonio has more domestic immigration than foreign immigration even though it is only three hours from the Mexican border. (Dallas and Houston are exceptions in that they have enjoyed both significant domestic migration and a slightly larger degree of foreign immigration). The Interior Boomtowns are, Barone says, "the economic dynamos that are driving America's growth."

The few parts of Texas that are losing people are those lonely outposts up in the Panhandle and along the Red River that, no matter how fierce their state pride, are demographically and geographically more closely related to Kansas and the Dakotas than they are to the Gulf Coast or the Rio Grande valley.

As might be expected in such a wide open state, there are great disparities of wealth. In six Texas state house districts, median household income exceeds $100,000 (capped by the 66th district in Collin County north of Dallas, where it is $132,000). In seven state house districts, however, the median household income is less than $37,000. Texas is one of only a few states that has large numbers of both African Americans and Hispanics, but the number of Hispanics is rapidly growing while the number of blacks is not. Hispanics in Texas now outnumber African Americans by almost three-to-one and while Hispanics accounted for only a quarter of the state population in 1990, they account for almost a third of it now.

Hispanics are concentrated most heavily, though far from exclusively, along the Mexican border, where in some districts they make up more than 90 percent of the population. They are a majority in thirty-five state house districts; blacks in only one—the 22nd district, which includes Port Arthur on the Louisiana border. (Adding one more dimension to the racial mix, in two districts around Houston, Asians make up almost a fifth of the population, many of them former Vietnamese refugees).

African Americans and Hispanics live in close proximity to each other in major cities such as Houston but are divided politically thanks to skillful gerrymandering that can now use computers to sort neighborhoods down to the street level, placing Hispanics in one district and blacks in another. As a consequence, Dallas, Houston, and San Antonio have had some of the most tortuously drawn district boundaries in the country.

Those tortured districts helped Democrats hold on to control in the state house of representatives until 2002, though Republicans had previously captured the senate. Once the GOP was in charge of both houses of the legislature, and hence redistricting, they attempted to redraw the state's congressional boundaries in 2003, hoping to boost Republican control of the U.S. House and knock off several veteran Democratic incumbents. The mid-decade reapportionment fight drew national attention when fifty-one house Democrats fled to Oklahoma and refused to attend sessions of the legislature, thereby preventing a quorum. When the governor called a special session of the legislature later in the summer, the new congressional plan passed the state house but this time senate Democrats skipped to New Mexico. Ultimately, the new plan passed and survived court challenges. It had its intended effect, giving Republicans a majority of the state's congressional delegation.

TEXAS
State Senate Districts

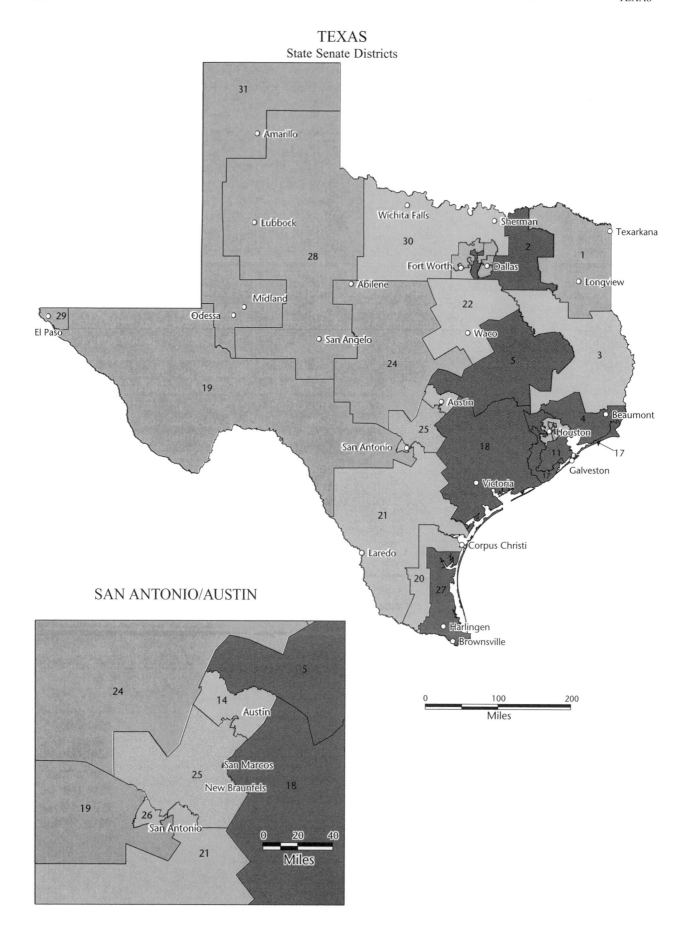

SAN ANTONIO/AUSTIN

Population Growth ▢ 0% to 9%   ▢ 9% to 14%   ■ 14% to 20%   ▢ 20% to 30%

DALLAS/FORT WORTH

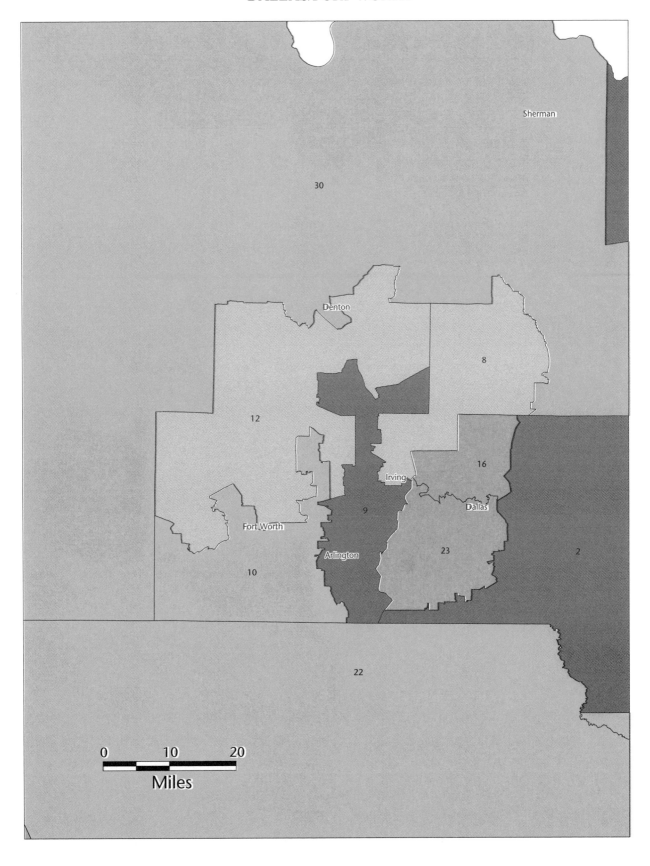

Population Growth   ▢ 0% to 9%   ▢ 9% to 14%   ▢ 14% to 20%   ▢ 20% to 30%

HOUSTON

Population Growth   ■ 0% to 9%   ■ 9% to 14%   ■ 14% to 20%   ■ 20% to 30%

Texas State Senate Districts—Election and Demographic Data

Senate Districts	General Election Results Party, Percent of Vote							Population			Avg. HH Income	Pop 25+		2006					
												Some College +	4-Yr Degree +	Below Poverty Line	White (Non-Hisp)	African American	American Indians, Alaska Natives	Asians, Hawaiians, Pacific Islanders	Hispanic Origin
Texas	2000	2001	2002	2003	2004	2005	2006	2000	2006	% Change	($)	(%)	(%)	(%)	(%)	(%)	(%)	(%)	(%)
1			R, 68				R, 83	674,791	712,836	6	49,234	30.7	11.2	20.8	72.3	15.7	0.3	0.7	9.3
2	D, 53		R, 54				R, 79	697,349	806,919	16	59,502	29.8	12.0	14.4	62.9	12.0	0.4	2.1	20.5
3	R, 61		R, 88				R, 100	705,698	784,313	11	50,847	29.2	11.9	20.6	72.5	11.4	0.3	0.6	12.8
4			R, 64		R, 100			654,312	749,523	15	68,695	35.9	17.2	14.6	72.5	11.3	0.2	1.9	12.6
5			R, 87				R, 61	660,805	782,559	18	59,958	36.8	19.3	17.6	65.4	10.5	0.2	2.7	18.5
6			D, 100		D, 92			639,809	683,991	7	42,783	16.2	6.2	25.6	16.5	11.7	0.4	2.8	72.7
7	R, 100		R, 91				R, 69	700,916	821,309	17	88,472	45.0	26.6	7.3	60.7	7.1	0.2	6.4	23.8
8	R, 100		R, 90				R, 100	674,642	874,801	30	100,298	50.3	32.8	5.4	65.3	5.2	0.2	9.4	18.1
9	R, 100		R, 87		R, 100			686,870	802,186	17	68,806	39.5	21.5	9.5	50.2	11.3	0.3	7.8	29.0
10	R, 100		R, 59		R, 59			705,277	799,183	13	69,084	37.6	20.4	13.5	51.6	15.3	0.3	3.5	27.8
11			R, 86		R, 100			671,509	769,604	15	67,523	36.5	16.9	11.6	59.0	9.2	0.3	4.3	24.7
12	D, 64		R, 90				R, 64	665,452	821,009	23	72,053	41.3	20.7	9.4	69.6	5.2	0.4	3.8	18.1
13			D, 100				D, 100	665,423	745,064	12	56,082	32.9	17.8	21.9	26.9	42.6	0.2	8.2	30.4
14	D, 82		D, 53				D, 80	698,575	774,227	11	71,552	46.7	29.8	12.9	47.1	9.8	0.3	5.8	33.7
15	D, 65		D, 60				D, 63	660,276	737,392	12	54,188	27.9	11.7	16.5	33.4	23.1	0.3	5.6	41.3
16			R, 64		R, 100			682,098	698,739	2	78,341	40.1	24.8	11.6	45.1	11.7	0.3	6.3	36.6
17			R, 61				R, 78	702,551	812,281	16	74,565	40.7	23.9	13.3	47.9	13.5	0.2	11.8	26.9
18			D, 53				R, 79	664,300	769,569	16	59,481	30.5	14.4	18.6	53.4	10.4	0.3	3.5	30.1
19			D, 100				D, 59	657,407	715,931	9	40,669	21.7	8.2	27.0	22.5	6.4	0.6	0.9	69.7
20			D, 100		D, 100			674,370	760,336	13	46,052	26.2	11.6	26.7	19.5	2.7	0.3	1.4	75.5
21	D, 66		D, 89		D, 100			638,084	718,606	13	45,229	22.9	8.6	26.5	24.8	4.5	0.3	1.2	69.6
22			R, 67				R, 81	687,644	775,720	13	54,221	29.8	10.5	17.7	67.0	10.1	0.3	1.1	18.2
23			D, 100		D, 100			682,224	728,464	7	50,147	24.1	11.1	22.4	23.9	36.5	0.3	2.1	45.7
24	R, 100		R, 90		R, 100			671,327	718,099	7	49,206	31.6	13.5	18.1	66.4	8.8	0.4	1.9	18.8
25	R, 87		R, 67				R, 58	701,161	846,355	21	73,394	44.1	25.0	10.1	59.4	3.8	0.3	2.2	30.3
26	D, 100		D, 100		D, 57			636,840	699,910	10	47,134	31.2	14.4	20.0	23.4	5.3	0.5	2.4	68.3
27	D, 100		D, 100		D, 100			641,991	761,016	19	38,640	21.3	9.3	34.7	10.5	1.0	0.3	0.8	87.6
28			R, 91		R, 100			674,557	677,448	0	46,450	29.4	13.8	22.3	53.8	6.0	0.4	1.1	33.4
29	D, 100		D, 100				D, 59	638,964	688,777	8	46,960	26.0	12.7	24.5	14.9	3.6	0.5	1.6	81.1
30			R, 68		R, 69			695,849	780,595	12	53,493	32.2	12.9	17.1	77.1	4.5	0.5	1.3	13.2
31			R, 100		R, 79			654,868	682,817	4	50,696	29.9	11.4	19.5	52.6	4.8	0.4	1.4	35.5

Note: D=Democrat, R=Republican, R/D=Republican/Democrat (cross-filed), D/R=Democrat/Republican (cross-filed), I=Independent, C=Constitution, O=Other, GI=Green Independent, P=Progressive, P/D=Progressive/Democrat, P/D/R=Progressive/Democrat/Republican, HH=Households

TEXAS
State House Districts

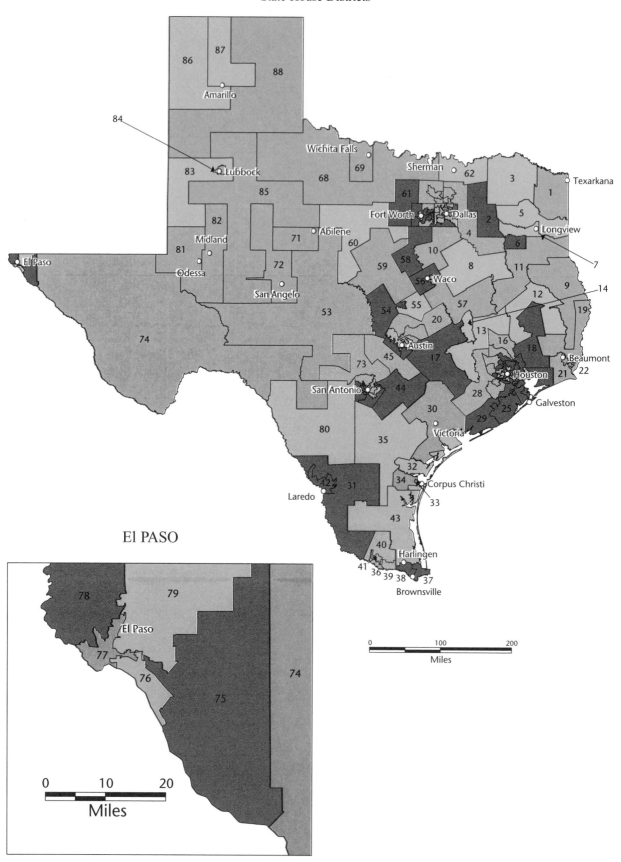

El PASO

Population Growth ▨ -4% to 4%   ▨ 4% to 9%   ▨ 9% to 21%   ▨ 21% to 61%

DALLAS/FORT WORTH

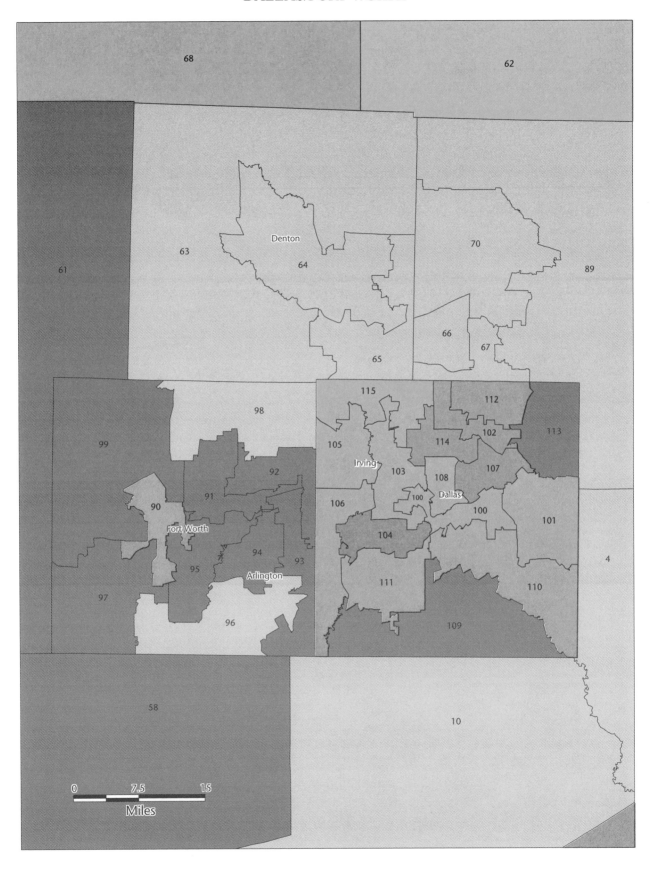

Population Growth   ▨ -4% to 4%   ▨ 4% to 9%   ▨ 9% to 21%   ▨ 21% to 61%

HOUSTON 1

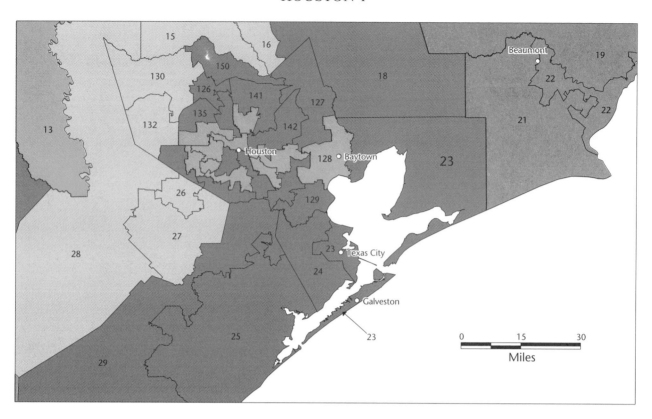

HOUSTON 2

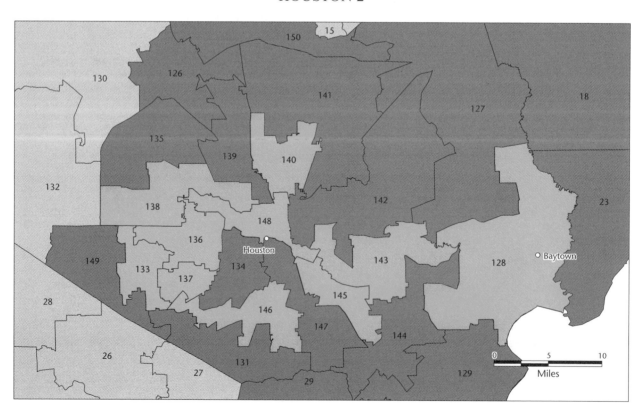

Population Growth   ▦ -4% to 4%   ▦ 4% to 9%   ▦ 9% to 21%   ▦ 21% to 61%

AUSTIN

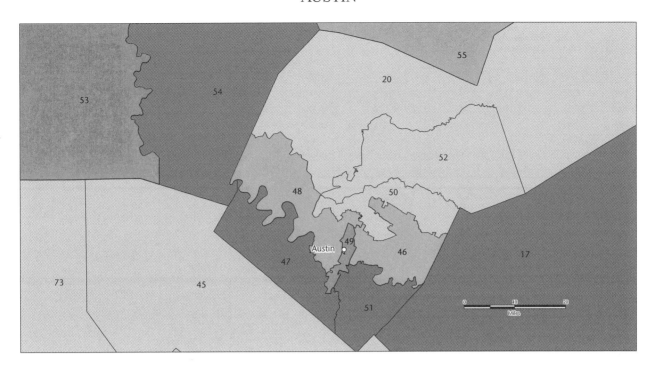

SAN ANTONIO

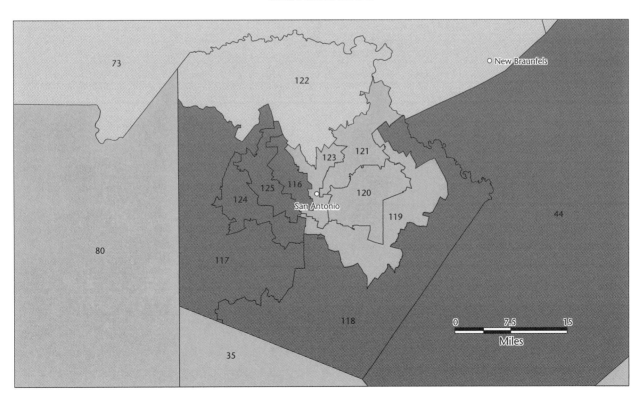

Population Growth   ▨ -4% to 4%   ▢ 4% to 9%   ▨ 9% to 21%   ▢ 21% to 61%

Texas State House Districts—Election and Demographic Data

House Districts	General Election Results Party, Percent of Vote							Population			Avg. HH Income	Pop 25+		Below Poverty Line	2006 White (Non-Hisp)	African American	American Indians, Alaska Natives	Asians, Hawaiians, Pacific Islanders	Hispanic Origin
												Some College +	4-Yr Degree +						
Texas	2000	2001	2002	2003	2004	2005	2006	2000	2006	% Change	($)	(%)	(%)	(%)	(%)	(%)	(%)	(%)	(%)
1	D, 100		D, 62		D, 53		D, 87	143,304	145,329	1	46,160	29.0	9.9	23.5	73.1	20.8	0.3	0.5	4.6
2	D, 100		R, 59		R, 100		R, 58	133,275	149,814	12	49,226	26.9	9.8	19.2	80.3	6.1	0.4	0.6	10.0
3	D, 100		D, 100		D, 50		D, 58	137,464	143,617	4	46,649	25.9	9.4	22.3	72.4	10.4	0.4	0.5	13.4
4	R, 64		R, 60		R, 100		R, 59	144,863	175,794	21	54,408	27.2	8.3	18.8	76.4	8.1	0.3	0.5	12.1
5	D, 53		R, 52		R, 62		R, 82	145,626	156,775	8	47,551	28.5	9.5	21.5	75.4	14.4	0.3	0.4	7.8
6	R, 74		R, 100		R, 100		R, 100	143,028	158,405	11	56,391	37.0	15.7	17.8	63.0	18.8	0.2	1.1	15.4
7	R, 100		R, 100		R, 100		R, 68	141,338	151,020	7	50,425	32.8	12.2	18.6	67.9	16.8	0.3	0.8	12.4
8	D, 100		R, 55		R, 100		R, 58	140,208	149,389	7	44,594	25.9	8.1	23.4	61.6	18.5	0.3	0.8	16.3
9	R, 55		R, 55		R, 57		R, 100	139,229	142,545	2	43,366	25.5	10.7	26.9	69.9	16.4	0.2	0.7	11.1
10	R, 100		R, 100		R, 73		R, 67	143,335	173,715	21	61,376	28.8	10.4	14.5	67.0	8.0	0.3	0.5	20.7
11	D, 53		D, 100		D, 53		D, 51	140,222	144,120	3	44,212	26.2	8.5	23.2	67.9	17.8	0.2	0.5	12.0
12	D, 100		D, 61		D, 51		D, 56	137,088	143,943	5	45,306	25.4	8.5	22.3	71.3	12.6	0.2	0.7	12.6
13	R, 100		R, 100		R, 100		R, 83	139,209	148,188	6	48,444	27.6	11.6	21.6	63.9	18.2	0.2	1.0	15.7
14	R, 87		R, 88		R, 100		R, 100	140,575	146,744	4	47,917	39.5	24.4	28.2	63.1	8.7	0.2	5.2	19.7
15	R, 88		R, 91		R, 91		R, 73	132,814	191,821	44	94,151	47.1	29.9	8.9	81.1	2.3	0.2	2.1	12.1
16	R, 100		R, 100		R, 100		R, 75	135,075	174,051	29	62,996	37.2	19.4	14.4	68.1	4.9	0.3	0.8	22.0
17	D, 100		D, 56		D, 54		D, 49	143,328	163,502	14	51,816	26.0	10.1	19.8	61.1	11.0	0.3	0.6	24.2
18	D, 51		D, 53		R, 55		R, 76	136,573	157,138	15	48,077	24.3	7.8	20.4	74.0	9.9	0.5	0.5	12.3
19	D, 100		R, 55		R, 55		R, 57	134,578	137,929	2	50,784	25.5	7.6	18.3	88.3	5.5	0.3	0.7	4.1
20	D, 54		R, 100		R, 69		R, 63	136,785	185,354	36	77,036	44.2	24.4	8.8	73.6	4.2	0.2	2.0	16.5
21	D, 56		D, 70		D, 100		D, 100	129,359	128,656	-1	59,660	36.5	15.1	14.0	72.8	11.8	0.2	3.4	10.8
22	D, 100		D, 100		D, 94		D, 91	135,323	131,714	-3	40,592	23.1	6.5	30.3	34.4	50.6	0.2	3.6	14.4
23	D, 57		D, 100		D, 100		D, 84	142,939	159,910	12	52,074	31.2	13.5	20.7	54.1	18.9	0.3	2.6	23.4
24	D, 59		R, 58		R, 100		R, 78	132,692	153,652	16	73,213	37.4	18.9	10.6	69.5	8.7	0.3	2.4	16.2
25	R, 100		R, 69		R, 66		R, 100	138,198	155,438	12	58,508	30.6	9.9	15.3	59.2	9.3	0.3	1.2	26.3
26	R, 70		R, 100		R, 100		R, 100	141,897	193,378	36	99,595	49.0	33.6	6.0	53.9	9.3	0.1	23.2	13.3
27	D, 64		D, 63		D, 100		D, 61	144,118	189,257	31	69,881	35.6	19.8	12.6	33.9	30.7	0.2	5.6	33.8
28	D, 63		R, 100		R, 64		R, 63	139,593	178,600	28	73,780	35.9	20.3	15.3	53.3	15.5	0.2	5.7	24.0
29	D, 100		R, 57		R, 100		R, 60	140,190	167,511	19	65,340	34.2	14.3	13.4	57.5	8.0	0.3	3.9	27.0
30	R, 100		R, 100		R, 87		R, 100	145,391	148,465	2	50,857	27.4	9.5	20.4	52.4	7.0	0.3	0.9	35.2
31	D, 100		D, 100		D, 100		D, 100	137,035	161,672	18	30,693	11.5	3.8	44.3	4.6	0.6	0.2	0.3	94.8
32	R, 100		R, 53		R, 100		D, 48	146,830	157,249	7	55,754	32.1	13.0	18.6	49.9	3.0	0.4	2.4	40.6
33	D, 100		D, 66		D, 100		D, 52	136,892	138,677	1	48,571	32.6	11.0	18.8	28.4	5.0	0.4	2.0	62.7
34	D, 100		D, 54		D, 55		D, 78	139,139	139,847	1	49,025	28.0	10.9	25.0	27.0	4.3	0.4	0.9	64.8
35	D, 100		D, 52		D, 51		D, 53	145,339	154,484	6	43,343	22.6	7.4	26.4	31.7	4.3	0.4	0.7	60.3
36	D, 100		D, 100		D, 100		D, 100	143,318	177,681	24	36,162	18.7	9.1	37.4	7.3	0.7	0.3	0.6	91.1
37	D, 100		D, 100		D, 100		D, 100	133,808	151,622	13	36,312	20.7	8.3	37.9	6.9	0.8	0.3	0.5	92.0
38	D, 64		D, 68		D, 100		D, 64	132,965	157,662	19	43,340	25.3	11.2	30.4	12.0	1.0	0.2	1.2	85.7
39	D, 100		D, 100		D, 100		D, 100	141,676	177,127	25	34,536	18.1	8.2	37.6	9.2	0.6	0.3	0.6	89.2
40	D, 100		D, 100		D, 100		D, 100	144,317	178,208	23	32,199	16.2	7.5	41.5	4.7	1.8	0.3	0.5	94.2
41	D, 100		D, 100		D, 100		D, 100	138,154	168,416	22	51,826	28.0	15.9	26.4	14.3	1.0	0.2	2.0	82.9
42	D, 100		D, 100		D, 100		D, 100	134,563	159,611	19	49,024	23.2	10.0	29.4	5.3	0.8	0.3	0.9	93.9
43	D, 100		D, 62		D, 59		D, 100	133,142	144,859	9	40,042	23.9	9.4	31.1	17.3	2.0	0.3	0.8	78.8
44	D, 55		R, 100		R, 100		R, 100	139,958	164,274	17	55,370	28.3	10.9	16.3	52.4	4.6	0.3	1.0	36.4
45	R, 100		D, 49		D, 55		D, 60	137,587	177,139	29	59,109	35.4	17.3	16.8	54.0	4.7	0.4	1.0	34.2
46	R, 57		D, 88		D, 100		D, 85	139,630	151,034	8	47,537	34.1	17.1	18.3	28.0	23.9	0.4	3.6	46.9
47	R, 83		R, 63		R, 100		R, 50	135,096	159,678	18	91,532	56.2	36.2	5.2	64.6	3.1	0.2	3.8	23.8
48	D, 59		R, 52		R, 50		D, 78	131,913	139,263	6	107,456	60.8	44.5	7.3	71.0	3.2	0.2	6.4	16.4
49	D, 59		D, 71		D, 86		D, 84	136,247	132,621	-3	53,145	51.7	35.2	16.9	58.1	3.7	0.4	5.9	27.3
50	D, 87		R, 56		D, 49		D, 62	133,763	169,573	27	78,231	54.6	34.8	5.1	59.3	8.7	0.2	9.6	20.6

(continued)

Note: D=Democrat, R=Republican, R/D=Republican/Democrat (cross-filed), D/R=Democrat/Republican (cross-filed), I=Independent, C=Constitution, O=Other, GI=Green Independent, P=Progressive, P/D=Progressive/Democrat, P/D/R=Progressive/Democrat/Republican, HH=Households

Texas State House Districts—Election and Demographic Data (cont.)

House Districts	General Election Results Party, Percent of Vote							Population			Avg. HH Income ($)	Pop 25+ Some College + (%)	Pop 25+ 4-Yr Degree + (%)	Below Poverty Line (%)	2006 White (Non-Hisp) (%)	African American (%)	American Indians, Alaska Natives (%)	Asians, Hawaiians, Pacific Islanders (%)	Hispanic Origin (%)
Texas	2000	2001	2002	2003	2004	2005	2006	2000	2006	% Change	($)	(%)	(%)	(%)	(%)	(%)	(%)	(%)	(%)
51	D, 100		D, 82		D, 100		D, 86	134,670	146,866	9	42,843	30.1	16.0	22.2	22.0	10.1	0.6	3.6	62.9
52	R, 84		R, 65		R, 94		R, 50	136,576	191,723	40	75,018	44.4	24.9	7.0	61.8	6.3	0.3	4.2	23.9
53	R, 100		R, 91		R, 100		R, 85	137,139	141,234	3	47,627	31.1	12.9	20.8	70.0	1.3	0.3	0.5	23.2
54	R, 62		R, 100		R, 61		R, 60	143,677	170,712	19	47,695	31.4	11.4	14.6	55.0	19.0	0.4	4.1	18.8
55	R, 100		R, 100		R, 100		R, 66	146,071	152,839	5	55,502	31.7	15.8	15.4	63.2	11.8	0.4	2.2	18.6
56	R, 100		D, 51		R, 53		R, 79	136,019	148,560	9	57,238	36.5	15.8	17.5	74.1	7.1	0.2	1.8	13.7
57	D, 100		D, 60		D, 58		D, 86	139,710	143,080	2	38,446	21.2	6.6	28.7	47.2	24.0	0.3	0.7	26.9
58	R, 100		R, 68		R, 70		R, 63	143,233	169,367	18	57,471	29.0	9.4	14.5	78.1	2.3	0.3	0.8	15.2
59	R, 54		R, 57		R, 64		R, 56	141,350	143,367	1	46,291	29.9	10.5	19.2	67.7	10.9	0.4	1.7	15.7
60	R, 100		R, 91		R, 70		R, 67	136,664	146,401	7	49,096	30.3	11.0	19.7	80.0	2.0	0.3	0.5	13.6
61	R, 100		R, 69		R, 100		R, 80	137,374	165,335	20	60,076	31.2	11.2	13.8	84.2	1.5	0.4	0.4	10.2
62	R, 100		R, 65		R, 100		R, 61	141,654	152,362	8	51,679	31.8	11.0	18.0	81.2	5.9	0.7	0.7	8.9
63	R, 88		R, 100		R, 100		R, 100	144,028	192,809	34	97,830	48.5	29.0	5.5	80.6	2.9	0.3	2.8	10.7
64	R, 100		R, 87		R, 100		R, 60	142,914	182,553	28	63,148	42.5	23.1	14.2	67.6	6.4	0.4	3.1	18.8
65	R, 100		R, 88		R, 86		R, 78	142,278	200,690	41	80,653	50.1	29.6	6.2	63.5	7.1	0.3	8.6	18.5
66	R, 100		R, 78		R, 100		R, 80	133,827	177,349	33	131,854	56.7	40.2	3.7	72.6	3.7	0.2	14.1	8.5
67	R, 88		R, 70		R, 100		R, 100	132,148	165,039	25	87,839	51.0	32.9	5.7	64.8	5.9	0.3	11.8	15.5
68	R, 58		R, 65		R, 100		R, 100	137,042	138,215	1	46,061	27.6	9.6	21.5	78.4	3.2	0.4	0.5	13.7
69	D, 100		D, 100		D, 53		D, 58	140,147	135,279	-3	48,217	31.8	12.7	17.9	71.2	8.9	0.5	2.2	13.9
70	D, 100		R, 78		R, 76		R, 69	132,513	213,153	61	99,779	46.9	28.9	4.8	74.2	4.5	0.3	3.7	14.3
71	R, 100		R, 91		R, 90		R, 58	142,034	139,801	-2	47,929	32.3	13.6	19.6	65.2	6.3	0.3	1.6	22.1
72	R, 74		R, 68		R, 57		R, 81	133,677	133,363	0	47,742	29.4	11.7	20.3	54.9	4.9	0.4	1.1	34.0
73	D, 54		R, 79		R, 100		R, 75	139,952	171,941	23	63,299	38.2	17.8	12.9	73.1	0.8	0.3	0.5	21.4
74	D, 100		D, 71		D, 100		D, 100	139,297	141,338	1	39,472	22.0	9.2	29.2	25.9	2.2	0.4	0.7	68.8
75	D, 100		D, 99		D, 100		D, 66	137,591	159,148	16	42,418	20.1	8.8	25.4	8.7	1.8	0.4	0.8	89.3
76	D, 100		D, 100		D, 100		D, 100	137,526	145,557	6	36,881	18.6	7.1	32.2	5.3	1.6	0.7	0.6	93.3
77	D, 100		D, 100		D, 100		D, 100	133,603	135,514	1	35,110	21.9	10.5	36.3	11.1	3.3	0.5	1.2	86.0
78	R, 100		R, 100		R, 100		R, 100	132,661	145,166	9	66,313	38.0	23.4	15.5	29.1	4.4	0.3	3.1	64.7
79	D, 100		D, 100		D, 67		D, 100	135,771	145,719	7	47,355	27.3	11.3	17.5	17.4	6.1	0.4	1.9	76.4
80	R, 100		D, 56		D, 100		D, 100	133,461	143,749	8	38,593	18.7	6.7	32.7	20.0	2.2	0.5	0.7	75.0
81	R, 100		R, 100		R, 75		R, 85	141,103	146,305	4	44,825	25.0	7.7	22.8	41.0	4.5	0.5	1.0	48.3
82	R, 78		R, 100		R, 100		R, 100	142,745	147,925	4	57,834	32.8	14.3	17.5	50.6	6.6	0.4	1.2	37.5
83	R, 87		R, 91		R, 79		R, 73	290,238	304,693	5	48,315	33.3	18.8	21.8	53.4	6.8	0.4	1.5	32.4
84	R, 88		R, 66		R, 68		R, 66	145,103	149,630	3	40,442	31.8	18.3	26.5	45.6	10.7	0.4	2.0	36.9
85	D, 100		D, 65		D, 59		D, 49	144,470	139,567	-3	43,850	23.1	7.9	24.1	47.0	5.5	0.4	0.6	41.3
86	R, 100		R, 100		R, 100		R, 86	137,169	144,359	5	57,595	39.1	16.8	14.7	71.4	1.8	0.4	1.1	20.6
87	R, 100		R, 66		R, 100		R, 100	142,902	151,243	6	45,474	25.8	8.6	22.0	49.0	8.0	0.5	2.8	34.3
88	R, 100		R, 100		R, 100		R, 85	144,005	138,450	-4	45,017	26.1	9.0	21.4	57.4	3.9	0.5	0.5	31.4
89	R, 63		R, 78		R, 76		R, 70	136,942	208,858	53	83,492	38.7	19.3	7.9	76.1	3.4	0.3	2.9	14.1
90	D, 100		D, 72		D, 65		D, 86	141,229	150,790	7	42,717	20.2	9.4	25.7	18.6	10.2	0.5	3.0	69.2
91	R, 100		R, 84		R, 100		R, 59	145,844	164,777	13	59,647	37.3	15.9	9.8	66.5	6.9	0.3	5.5	18.5
92	R, 100		R, 89		R, 100		R, 100	143,937	162,785	13	67,606	45.2	23.2	7.2	67.0	6.2	0.3	6.4	17.7
93	R, 100		R, 57		R, 56		D, 50	144,764	167,472	16	58,300	36.4	18.2	11.3	44.3	16.8	0.3	8.3	29.5
94	R, 100		R, 100		R, 63		R, 64	144,925	158,426	9	69,504	44.0	24.5	11.8	62.5	9.3	0.3	6.1	19.7
95	D, 100		R, 100		D, 100		D, 91	142,287	155,126	9	43,985	26.8	10.6	23.6	30.8	46.2	0.3	2.4	26.5
96	R, 87		R, 60		R, 60		R, 52	145,983	180,973	24	69,889	40.4	19.7	6.0	62.4	13.0	0.3	5.4	17.6
97	R, 88		R, 67		R, 63		R, 56	144,348	163,542	13	70,779	45.7	27.1	11.5	66.9	7.8	0.3	2.9	19.5
98	R, 73		R, 100		R, 100		R, 84	144,884	186,939	29	112,286	47.5	28.8	4.2	77.8	2.3	0.2	3.8	13.7
99	R, 100		R, 69		R, 70		R, 63	143,951	169,195	18	60,622	35.6	15.8	13.4	67.8	4.3	0.4	2.6	21.2
100	D, 100		D, 95		D, 100		D, 89	138,591	145,617	5	39,861	20.8	8.7	29.2	23.1	40.3	0.3	3.1	43.4

(continued)

Note: D=Democrat, R=Republican, R/D=Republican/Democrat (cross-filed), D/R=Democrat/Republican (cross-filed), I=Independent, C=Constitution, O=Other, GI=Green Independent, P=Progressive, P/D=Progressive/Democrat, P/D/R=Progressive/Democrat/Republican, HH=Households

Texas State House Districts—Election and Demographic Data (cont.)

House Districts	General Election Results Party, Percent of Vote							Population			Avg. HH Income	2006 Pop 25+ Some College +	2006 Pop 25+ 4-Yr Degree +	2006 Below Poverty Line	2006 White (Non-Hisp)	2006 African American	2006 American Indians, Alaska Natives	2006 Asians, Hawaiians, Pacific Islanders	2006 Hispanic Origin
Texas	2000	2001	2002	2003	2004	2005	2006	2000	2006	% Change	($)	(%)	(%)	(%)	(%)	(%)	(%)	(%)	(%)
101	R, 58		R, 100		R, 100		R, 76	144,063	154,711	7	61,147	31.1	12.5	9.5	55.1	13.4	0.4	4.3	26.2
102	R, 65		R, 100		R, 53		R, 52	138,325	139,080	1	75,640	40.6	25.3	11.3	42.3	14.9	0.3	8.9	35.2
103	D, 100		D, 69		D, 100		D, 83	128,216	134,741	5	50,582	19.1	9.7	21.0	15.9	10.9	0.4	3.5	74.4
104	D, 73		D, 74		D, 100		D, 85	134,922	139,500	3	43,770	15.1	6.5	24.8	11.2	10.2	0.6	1.7	80.1
105	D, 64		R, 76		R, 59		R, 55	139,902	146,647	5	68,892	41.2	24.8	8.3	42.8	11.4	0.3	11.2	35.5
106	R, 58		R, 100		R, 53		R, 49	134,124	142,105	6	57,845	28.0	12.0	13.5	39.2	10.8	0.5	5.5	43.2
107	D, 59		R, 58		R, 100		D, 50	142,914	141,177	-1	66,456	40.0	22.6	11.3	50.9	12.0	0.4	3.0	32.3
108	R, 100		R, 66		R, 63		R, 56	138,938	150,107	8	100,329	46.4	34.8	12.2	45.9	6.5	0.3	3.6	39.5
109	D, 100		D, 75		D, 100		D, 90	132,245	150,217	14	61,398	33.8	14.8	12.5	37.3	44.5	0.3	1.6	21.4
110	D, 100		D, 100		D, 100		D, 100	141,101	149,231	6	40,983	17.2	5.6	28.6	26.3	41.9	0.4	1.0	38.0
111	D, 100		D, 100		D, 100		D, 74	142,697	150,673	6	54,461	30.4	13.7	15.8	29.3	45.3	0.2	2.3	30.4
112	R, 100		R, 71		R, 66		R, 78	145,126	150,350	4	75,849	44.0	25.3	7.4	55.3	8.0	0.3	13.6	23.2
113	R, 100		R, 100		R, 65		R, 59	135,662	152,970	13	69,777	35.0	16.1	7.8	53.3	12.0	0.4	4.4	28.8
114	R, 68		R, 100		R, 100		R, 56	137,583	142,602	4	90,517	46.0	30.8	11.4	47.2	14.9	0.2	3.2	33.9
115	D, 100		R, 71		R, 100		R, 100	141,697	148,457	5	92,240	48.7	31.0	6.0	56.5	5.6	0.2	9.0	27.8
116	D, 100		D, 100		D, 64		D, 85	141,568	154,514	9	43,795	34.2	17.3	20.4	24.4	4.8	0.6	3.0	67.7
117	D, 100		R, 59		D, 51		D, 60	135,180	155,741	15	48,473	27.0	11.9	19.4	24.9	5.3	0.5	2.2	65.8
118	D, 100		D, 100		D, 57		D, 48	137,595	153,275	11	45,715	24.0	9.4	20.2	24.7	3.1	0.6	1.4	67.1
119	D, 100		D, 100		D, 62		D, 100	138,836	147,397	6	42,277	24.8	8.9	22.7	22.3	7.1	0.5	1.2	68.5
120	D, 100		D, 100		D, 100		D, 86	136,072	146,517	8	41,535	28.8	10.5	22.7	28.3	28.5	0.5	2.8	47.1
121	R, 68		R, 90		R, 100		R, 77	145,526	156,305	7	70,925	46.0	26.4	8.8	56.3	6.4	0.3	2.7	32.4
122	R, 86		R, 88		R, 100		R, 66	147,021	186,641	27	99,953	51.5	33.7	6.5	62.6	2.7	0.2	2.9	29.3
123	R, 85		D, 63		D, 62		D, 85	134,221	139,969	4	42,825	29.0	13.2	23.7	21.5	3.3	0.5	1.3	72.2
124	D, 100		D, 100		D, 100		D, 64	136,357	154,142	13	48,511	30.8	12.2	15.5	23.6	7.9	0.5	2.6	65.6
125	D, 59		D, 60		D, 100		D, 58	137,817	153,261	11	52,493	31.9	15.0	17.4	24.7	4.6	0.5	2.5	67.3
126	R, 100		R, 100		R, 69		R, 65	130,907	150,158	15	81,233	42.8	23.6	8.2	52.8	12.9	0.2	9.1	25.1
127	R, 100		R, 100		R, 70		R, 58	138,655	162,543	17	82,639	39.6	20.1	8.5	66.0	8.5	0.2	2.6	20.5
128	D, 100		R, 100		R, 65		R, 100	130,340	140,482	8	60,032	30.2	9.6	13.7	51.8	9.3	0.3	2.0	33.7
129	R, 88		R, 100		R, 100		R, 58	132,919	146,936	11	80,657	48.7	29.1	6.6	62.6	6.0	0.2	9.3	20.5
130	R, 74		R, 100		R, 92		R, 83	134,432	174,757	30	85,713	40.8	22.9	5.7	66.0	5.9	0.2	4.7	20.8
131	D, 100		D, 100		D, 100		D, 95	130,742	145,034	11	47,231	30.0	13.8	19.4	22.4	47.3	0.2	5.6	34.8
132	D, 100		R, 90		R, 100		R, 82	131,697	164,787	25	78,685	39.4	20.2	5.7	56.7	7.0	0.2	5.7	27.8
133	R, 88		R, 65		R, 78		R, 56	141,793	151,465	7	61,985	42.2	24.9	12.4	38.4	19.2	0.2	13.4	32.5
134	R, 59		R, 53		R, 54		D, 55	135,545	151,200	12	121,057	60.7	46.9	8.6	66.7	4.2	0.1	7.0	20.2
135	R, 100		R, 70		R, 100		R, 100	133,227	150,953	13	73,736	37.0	19.3	7.8	46.5	9.8	0.2	11.3	32.1
136	R, 100		R, 100		R, 90		R, 68	131,369	143,046	9	111,842	55.6	39.8	8.9	59.8	4.5	0.2	7.1	25.9
137	D, 62		D, 55		D, 57		D, 58	140,592	149,422	6	41,559	27.4	15.0	22.1	21.3	14.5	0.3	13.0	58.7
138	D, 62		R, 59		R, 64		R, 58	138,976	148,058	7	53,702	30.4	14.5	14.8	34.4	11.5	0.4	5.8	48.1
139	D, 100		D, 100		D, 100		D, 100	137,398	150,668	10	46,718	24.6	9.2	22.1	22.4	44.5	0.2	6.7	37.2
140	D, 100		D, 74		D, 67		D, 100	134,307	141,797	6	39,543	12.6	4.2	28.2	16.0	10.9	0.4	2.2	74.6
141	D, 100		D, 100		D, 100		D, 100	135,705	151,146	11	44,291	22.4	7.4	23.4	29.3	38.9	0.3	2.8	35.2
142	D, 100		D, 100		D, 80		D, 94	139,152	152,843	10	43,239	20.6	7.2	28.3	25.0	42.3	0.2	2.6	39.3
143	D, 69		D, 92		D, 93		D, 71	131,553	138,280	5	41,166	13.5	4.4	26.4	14.3	5.6	0.5	1.7	78.5
144	R, 62		R, 88		R, 100		R, 56	137,822	152,666	11	56,814	29.6	11.0	13.7	43.0	6.5	0.3	5.2	42.3
145	D, 71		D, 100		D, 100		D, 100	137,991	146,736	6	41,962	15.1	5.7	25.5	11.3	6.1	0.4	3.5	81.6
146	D, 100		D, 93		D, 100		D, 91	133,863	143,095	7	51,552	35.5	20.1	23.4	29.3	46.1	0.1	7.0	24.2
147	D, 93		D, 100		D, 100		D, 100	134,324	150,798	12	47,577	27.1	13.4	25.7	24.5	41.3	0.3	4.8	38.1
148	D, 100		D, 100		D, 100		D, 84	139,793	151,055	8	47,987	22.8	11.4	22.4	19.9	9.2	0.4	2.3	69.4
149	R, 100		R, 56		D, 50		D, 54	142,382	157,180	10	71,100	41.3	23.2	10.2	37.4	17.9	0.2	19.2	29.7
150	R, 100		R, 100		R, 100		R, 70	139,641	160,662	15	78,568	40.4	19.9	7.2	64.5	7.9	0.2	3.8	21.8

Note: D=Democrat, R=Republican, R/D=Republican/Democrat (cross-filed), D/R=Democrat/Republican (cross-filed), I=Independent, C=Constitution, O=Other, GI=Green Independent, P=Progressive, P/D=Progressive/Democrat, P/D/R=Progressive/Democrat/Republican, HH=Households

UTAH

Legend has it that in 1846, when Mormon settlers first looked over the crest of the Wasatch Mountains into the Valley of the Great Salt Lake, Brigham Young struck his cane on the ground and declared, "This is the place." Having endured a thousand-mile march across plains and mountains, Young and his band were nothing if not people who knew where they were going and who recognized where they were when they got there.

The Mormons raised orchards on the thin strip of land between the mountains and the lake, possibly the deadest body of water on the continent. Young wanted to name his state Deseret, the word from the Book of Mormon meaning "Land of the Honeybee," thus revealing much about his conception of the role his Latter Day Saints would play in their new society. The beehive symbol remains ubiquitous on state roadsigns and even the Salt Lake sidewalks.

Although Young sought safety in Utah, he did not seek isolation. Mormons were great traders and built their Zion as a distribution point for the vast territory beyond. Salt Lake City is not large (its metro area is smaller than Alabama's Birmingham), but it is strategically placed, almost exactly equidistant from Seattle, Portland, San Francisco, Los Angeles, and San Diego. In 2002, it hosted the Winter Olympics.

Mormonism may be a fundamentalist religion, but it is a peculiarly American kind of fundamentalism, embracing rather than resisting technology. The Golden Spike completing the Transcontinental Railroad was driven at Promontory Point, about fifty miles north of the Mormon Temple. Eventually, 70 percent of all east-west railroad traffic went through the state. Recently Utah has been one of the great high-tech areas of the West, home to Novell and WordPerfect, as well as Morton Thiokol, maker of rocket engines. In the rotunda of the state capitol is a statue of a young man holding a cylinder in his hand that he regards with a rather bemused expression—Philo T. Farnsworth, inventor of the image dissector tube and thus the "Father of Television."

Utah has grown by more than 37 percent during the past two decades, almost exactly as fast as neighboring Colorado and one of the faster rates in the country. The state is mostly rural except for a strip running along the edge of the Wasatch from Ogden to Provo where more than three-quarters of the state's population lives. That strip is filling up, pushing development northeast toward the Wyoming border, although the fastest growth has occurred in two places. One is a perfect ring of the outer counties around Salt Lake City. The other, surprisingly enough, has occurred in the far southwestern corner of the state, in Iron and Washington Counties, which are now a far-flung outer suburb of Las Vegas, nearly 150 miles away.

Utah's population is almost 90 percent white. There are hardly any African Americans in the state—Asians, who make up 1.7 percent of Utah's population, are nevertheless twice as numerous as blacks. Hispanics, though, now make up 9 percent of the state population, a figure that doubled during the 1990s. One state house district in Ogden now has a Hispanic majority and two more in Salt Lake County are close. Utah has the nation's highest literacy rate and, owing to the number of young Mormons who perform church service on foreign missions, one of the most multilingual.

About two-thirds of Utahns are Mormons, and Mormons believe in big families, giving Utah the largest average household size in the country. It is also the youngest state, with the lowest median age (twenty-eight years old versus nearly thirty-seven for the rest of the country) and the state with the greater share of its population under age eighteen, sparking the old joke that the most popular means of transportation here is the baby carriage. On the other hand, the percentage of residents over age sixty-five is low. Even so, when the number of elderly is combined with the number of children, it gives Utah the highest "dependency ratio" in the country; that is, the highest ratio of working people supporting persons either too young to work or in retirement age. In a state such as Pennsylvania, this might provoke intergenerational warfare, but Utah seems to bear it happily.

The number of Mormon missionaries Utah sends abroad each year has recently sparked a dispute that has reached Washington. Utah would have gained an additional congressional district after the 2000 census but for the fact that the Census Bureau did not include its 10,000 foreign missionaries when counting state population. The bureau did count soldiers serving overseas so North Carolina got the extra district instead. Utah politicians and national Republicans have been trying to gain that extra house seat and have agreed on a plan that would expand the size of the House of Representatives by two seats, giving one (presumably Republican) to Utah and one (certainly Democratic) to the District of Columbia. Legal scholars have questioned the constitutionality of giving voting representation to the district, because Article I explicitly states that representatives shall be chosen "by the people of the several states." If Congress ever does approve the plan, it will certainly be challenged in court.

Utah's legislature is overwhelmingly Republican and has remained so throughout the decade. At the start of 2007 Republicans outnumbered Democrats in the state house by 55–20, and in the senate by 21–8. Utah has voted for a Democratic presidential candidate just once since 1948. In 1992 Bill Clinton finished third here, behind Ross Perot.

UTAH
State Senate Districts

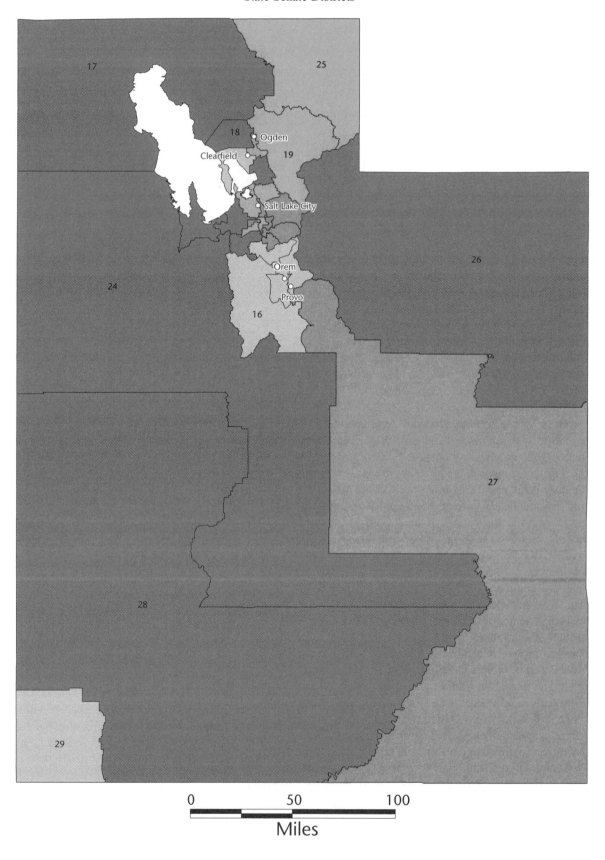

Population Growth   ▮ 2% to 7%   ▮ 7% to 12%   ▮ 12% to 22%   ▮ 22% to 39%

SALT LAKE CITY

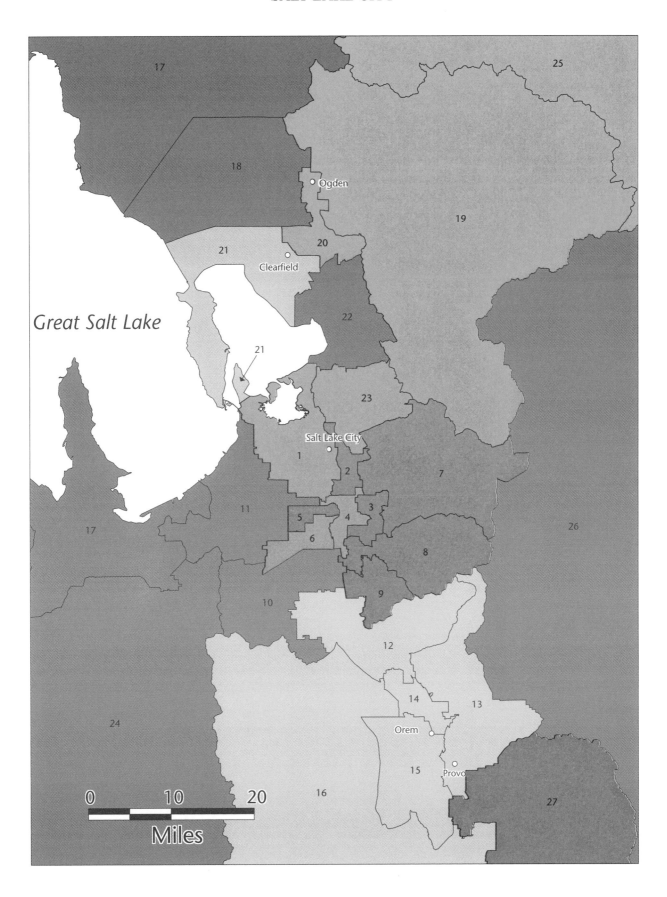

Great Salt Lake

Ogden

Clearfield

Salt Lake City

Orem

Provo

0 10 20
Miles

Population Growth   ▮ 2% to 7%   ▯ 7% to 12%   ▮ 12% to 22%   ▯ 22% to 39%

Utah State Senate Districts—Election and Demographic Data

Senate Districts	General Election Results Party, Percent of Vote							Population			Avg. HH Income	Pop 25+		Below Poverty Line	White (Non-Hisp)	African American	American Indians, Alaska Natives	Asians, Hawaiians, Pacific Islanders	Hispanic Origin
												Some College +	4-Yr Degree +						
															2006				
Utah	2000	2001	2002	2003	2004	2005	2006	2000	2006	% Change	($)	(%)	(%)	(%)	(%)	(%)	(%)	(%)	(%)
1			R, 48		D, 49			76,709	84,016	10	47,407	21.6	7.4	16.8	36.4	2.6	2.0	10.5	42.8
2	D, 76		D, 100				D, 69	79,522	81,579	3	47,618	37.8	19.7	19.7	58.5	2.3	2.0	4.8	25.3
3			D, 52				D, 55	75,517	77,262	2	77,110	46.5	26.0	7.9	86.7	0.9	0.5	2.8	5.8
4			D, 56				D, 56	79,338	85,594	8	53,622	36.0	15.8	11.8	68.7	1.7	1.5	4.5	17.6
5	R, 64		D, 64				D, 100	72,355	75,524	4	56,375	27.6	9.2	9.6	63.0	1.0	1.3	5.2	22.6
6	R, 59				R, 57			79,131	88,068	11	66,872	32.4	12.3	5.4	73.7	0.8	0.6	4.1	15.1
7			D, 67				D, 64	79,096	82,143	4	93,492	53.3	35.9	7.3	87.9	0.5	0.4	3.5	5.0
8	R, 53				R, 56			77,735	81,829	5	82,512	42.2	22.0	6.9	83.3	0.7	0.5	3.0	8.7
9			R, 80				R, 52	75,151	79,651	6	101,643	41.9	23.2	4.0	88.9	0.5	0.3	2.6	5.0
10					R, 65			75,390	86,869	15	74,105	33.0	14.3	6.0	80.7	0.6	0.6	2.3	10.6
11			R, 73				R, 66	80,853	93,096	15	59,209	27.2	8.7	7.4	67.8	0.8	0.9	4.7	18.8
12			D, 51				D, 49	77,453	94,632	22	87,423	38.1	19.1	4.1	89.8	0.6	0.4	1.1	5.5
13					R, 76			79,418	98,363	24	52,374	38.3	20.2	19.0	81.5	0.5	0.2	3.3	10.4
14	R, 79				R, 80			78,804	97,750	24	69,740	40.6	19.4	9.0	86.6	0.3	0.4	1.6	7.8
15			R, 90				R, 69	81,557	103,450	27	59,148	41.4	20.0	12.1	78.1	0.5	0.7	2.5	12.9
16	R, 64				R,77			76,584	106,288	39	65,206	36.6	14.7	9.1	90.6	0.2	0.1	0.7	5.8
17	R, 60		R, 100				R, 63	75,310	89,125	18	59,242	31.3	11.3	10.9	86.4	0.2	0.9	1.0	7.7
18			D, 59				R, 52	75,627	87,343	15	61,533	32.7	9.3	8.6	84.1	1.1	0.2	1.9	9.5
19	R, 50				R, 62			73,537	79,893	9	69,412	38.1	15.7	10.0	85.5	1.0	0.1	1.3	8.9
20	R, 51				R, 58			76,712	83,773	9	55,975	31.8	12.8	15.2	61.9	2.7	0.3	2.4	25.9
21			R, 75		R, 72			75,616	92,421	22	59,214	34.2	13.5	8.5	81.2	1.9	0.8	3.0	10.1
22			R, 87				R, 71	76,661	86,455	13	82,963	42.2	23.3	6.7	91.4	0.6	0.3	1.4	4.5
23	R, 69				R, 72			78,548	84,812	8	84,665	46.8	26.2	8.4	90.0	0.4	0.4	2.1	5.0
24					R, 69			78,525	89,077	13	50,192	28.5	8.5	16.4	85.2	0.9	1.6	0.8	7.5
25	R, 74				R, 77			74,453	82,567	11	53,046	37.7	18.3	16.0	84.5	0.5	0.6	3.2	8.1
26			R, 71				R, 58	75,958	87,913	16	66,827	32.2	13.9	13.8	83.7	0.2	4.0	0.7	8.1
27	D, 100				D, 53			73,281	76,876	5	49,707	32.8	11.8	19.0	78.3	0.3	10.7	0.7	7.2
28	R, 72		R, 100				R, 64	75,755	85,225	13	47,583	33.0	11.6	17.7	88.1	0.3	1.6	0.9	6.5
29	R, 74							77,810	104,863	35	53,464	36.4	12.8	13.2	87.3	0.2	1.3	1.0	7.2

Note: D=Democrat, R=Republican, R/D=Republican/Democrat (cross-filed), D/R=Democrat/Republican (cross-filed), I=Independent, C=Constitution, O=Other, GI=Green Independent, P=Progressive, P/D=Progressive/Democrat, P/D/R=Progressive/Democrat/Republican, HH=Households

UTAH
State House Districts

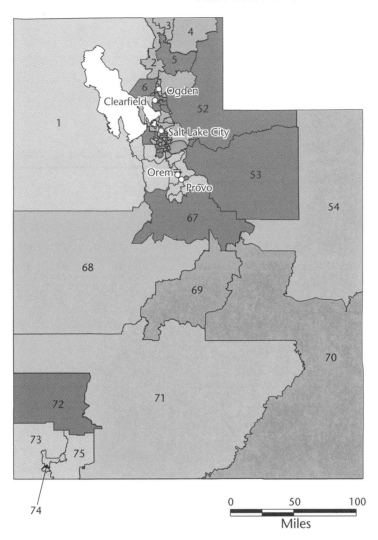

0   50   100
Miles

SALT LAKE CITY 1

0   5   10
Miles

PROVO/OREM

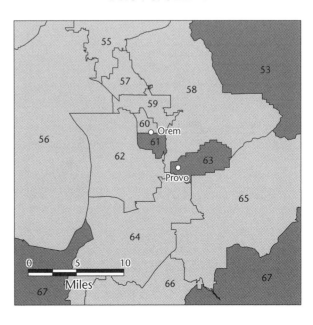

0   5   10
Miles

Population Growth   ▢ -2% to 5%   ▢ 5% to 12%   ▢ 12% to 21%   ▢ 21% to 47%

SALT LAKE CITY 2

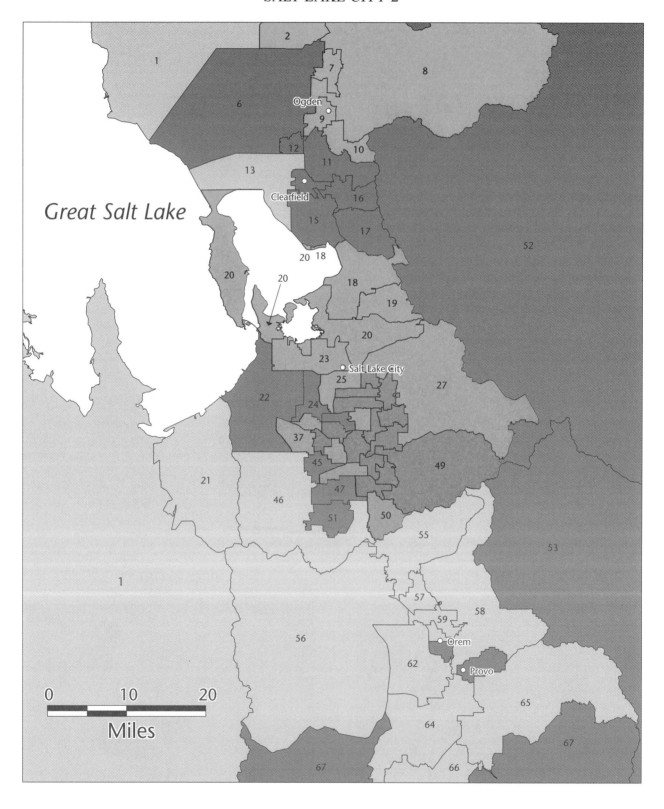

Population Growth   ■ -2% to 5%   ■ 5% to 12%   ■ 12% to 21%   □ 21% to 47%

Utah State House Districts—Election and Demographic Data

House Districts	General Election Results Party, Percent of Vote							Population			Avg. HH Income	Pop 25+		Below Poverty Line	White (Non-Hisp)	African American	American Indians, Alaska Natives	Asians, Hawaiians, Pacific Islanders	Hispanic Origin
												Some College +	4-Yr Degree +						
Utah	2000	2001	2002	2003	2004	2005	2006	2000	2006	% Change	($)	(%)	(%)	(%)	(%)	(%)	(%)	(%)	(%)
1	D, 86		D, 55		R, 55		R, 70	29,193	35,953	23	55,123	26.5	7.7	12.7	83.2	1.5	0.5	1.3	9.2
2	R, 87		R, 100		R, 87		R, 82	29,738	32,979	11	58,378	33.1	13.0	12.0	88.3	0.2	0.3	1.1	6.7
3	R, 71		R, 70		R, 75		R, 64	28,733	31,297	9	56,458	36.8	17.1	12.5	87.4	0.4	0.1	2.0	7.4
4	R, 61		R, 63		R, 69		R, 69	31,095	34,157	10	48,830	39.1	20.2	20.1	83.9	0.7	0.2	4.9	8.1
5	R, 53		R, 73		R, 78		R, 69	29,142	33,155	14	61,128	35.4	15.6	10.3	83.0	0.1	0.2	1.2	11.4
6	R, 70		R, 100		R, 76		R, 72	30,551	35,341	16	67,262	34.4	10.8	6.4	90.6	0.3	0.1	1.0	5.8
7	R, 56		R, 62		R, 68		R, 100	29,079	31,476	8	67,144	34.8	13.0	9.3	83.3	1.3	0.2	1.2	10.4
8	R, 50		R, 53		R, 62		R, 53	30,128	32,533	8	59,312	36.6	14.2	12.7	80.7	1.0	0.2	1.4	12.4
9	D, 60		D, 63		D, 56		D, 65	30,193	31,823	5	39,782	20.2	5.0	24.5	35.4	3.8	0.5	2.0	51.2
10	D, 58		D, 61		D, 56		D, 61	30,278	32,229	6	72,735	42.0	19.9	10.7	80.2	1.2	0.2	2.6	11.7
11	R, 52		D, 100		R, 65		R, 67	31,575	36,469	15	63,201	35.7	13.7	9.1	82.9	2.7	0.2	2.3	8.6
12	R, 63		R, 62		R, 100		R, 60	28,328	32,504	15	62,917	33.5	9.5	6.2	82.3	1.3	0.2	2.4	10.3
13	R, 65		R, 100		R, 86		R, 82	30,096	38,488	28	65,506	34.5	13.2	5.7	84.8	1.0	0.2	2.2	8.6
14	R, 61		R, 65		R, 80		R, 64	27,649	32,023	16	51,854	32.4	12.1	11.4	75.7	2.7	0.4	3.8	13.1
15	R, 61		R, 70		R, 86		R, 73	30,465	35,519	17	61,859	34.8	15.4	9.0	83.2	1.4	0.2	2.4	9.3
16	R, 87		D, 86		R, 70		R, 67	28,301	31,936	13	78,596	42.3	22.2	6.4	86.0	1.5	0.1	2.7	6.9
17	R, 75		R, 100		R, 81		R, 77	28,476	32,186	13	89,827	43.9	24.9	6.5	93.7	0.3	0.1	1.2	3.4
18	R, 73		R, 100		R, 72		R, 75	29,315	32,424	11	79,948	41.9	22.1	5.5	93.5	0.3	0.1	1.1	3.6
19	R, 74		R, 100		R, 76		R, 68	29,974	32,213	7	76,815	46.0	24.3	8.4	91.2	0.3	0.1	1.6	4.6
20	R, 68		R, 71		R, 67		R, 62	30,840	33,397	8	88,837	44.3	24.3	9.7	81.8	0.6	0.2	2.6	11.5
21	D, 59		D, 62		D, 57		D, 54	28,584	37,864	32	59,587	30.2	9.3	9.8	85.8	0.6	0.3	0.9	8.6
22	D, 56		D, 51		D, 56		D, 47	29,855	33,995	14	55,317	24.3	7.3	8.8	71.2	0.8	0.3	2.2	19.8
23	D, 59		D, 68		D, 68		D, 59	29,316	31,651	8	47,500	23.0	8.8	17.6	35.5	3.5	0.5	8.9	49.8
24	D, 59		D, 67		D, 69		D, 96	30,357	34,507	14	55,187	25.2	7.5	9.8	59.4	1.1	0.3	9.9	24.7
25	D, 67		D, 71		D, 65		D, 75	29,362	31,708	8	45,838	22.3	8.3	19.8	37.7	2.6	0.6	9.1	46.0
26	D, 61		D, 62		D, 59		D, 67	30,131	30,482	1	49,344	43.6	26.4	20.1	67.0	2.3	0.4	5.5	19.6
27	D, 64		R, 100		R, 100		R, 81	30,462	33,686	11	96,746	56.0	38.9	10.8	87.3	0.6	0.1	3.9	5.8
28	R, 100		R, 51		D, 51		D, 59	30,861	30,475	-1	87,529	52.6	35.6	7.6	89.6	0.6	0.1	4.2	4.0
29	D, 53		D, 57		D, 49		D, 47	31,998	32,399	1	49,153	39.2	22.1	15.5	65.8	1.8	0.5	5.8	21.1
30	D, 64		D, 73		D, 89		D, 77	28,246	28,576	1	51,285	34.3	15.7	14.6	67.5	1.7	0.5	3.9	21.0
31	D, 50		D, 62		D, 60		D, 65	29,831	29,677	-1	85,522	49.9	31.3	6.9	91.4	0.5	0.1	2.2	4.1
32	R, 55		R, 51		R, 51		R, 60	29,661	30,930	4	59,568	44.0	23.0	9.2	84.2	1.2	0.2	3.4	8.3
33	D, 58		D, 59		D, 57		D, 57	29,859	31,612	6	47,768	33.8	14.7	14.9	65.3	2.5	0.6	4.8	21.9
34	R, 49		R, 60		R, 59		R, 100	32,225	36,589	14	47,251	29.9	10.0	12.3	62.4	1.8	0.5	7.9	22.9
35	D, 59		D, 63		D, 51		D, 57	31,787	32,923	4	61,803	33.4	12.5	7.4	72.4	0.8	0.3	5.8	16.5
36	R, 54		R, 54		R, 55		D, 51	29,891	31,701	6	62,524	27.2	8.7	7.1	66.7	1.0	0.2	6.3	21.6
37	D, 56		D, 56		D, 67		D, 58	31,296	34,013	9	60,782	25.9	8.7	5.6	67.4	0.7	0.3	3.8	22.1
38	D, 95		R, 60		R, 59		R, 51	28,789	29,525	3	58,475	25.5	8.7	8.1	66.4	1.0	0.2	4.3	23.0
39	D, 51		R, 51		R, 92		R, 100	29,864	32,657	9	69,338	33.3	12.4	6.5	75.6	0.7	0.1	4.1	15.4
40	D, 55		D, 94		D, 60		D, 59	29,626	30,626	3	64,452	36.4	15.5	9.3	78.0	1.1	0.2	2.5	14.5
41	D, 59		R, 56		R, 100		R, 100	30,626	31,368	2	92,422	52.2	30.0	6.1	89.2	0.6	0.1	3.0	5.2
42	R, 53		R, 67		R, 100		R, 59	30,101	31,335	4	103,513	46.8	26.9	3.1	90.6	0.5	0.1	3.1	4.3
43	R, 59		R, 59		R, 79		R, 79	30,313	31,627	4	70,677	40.2	19.6	7.6	82.7	0.7	0.1	3.2	10.2
44	R, 54		R, 51		D, 55		D, 62	30,351	31,985	5	63,743	30.4	12.5	10.8	72.4	0.8	0.3	3.1	18.2
45	R, 53		R, 51		R, 51		R, 50	30,971	35,165	14	71,950	31.5	12.8	4.1	79.7	0.8	0.2	2.9	12.4
46	D, 54		D, 59		D, 100		D, 59	28,927	36,851	27	77,989	36.9	16.6	3.6	84.8	1.2	0.2	1.8	8.8
47	R, 51		R, 100		R, 60		R, 53	29,704	34,586	16	78,533	36.1	16.9	5.7	89.2	0.5	0.1	2.1	6.1
48	D, 53		R, 50		R, 63		R, 58	30,380	31,741	4	80,568	37.4	18.1	5.5	87.2	0.6	0.1	2.6	7.2
49	R, 57		R, 59		R, 52		R, 50	32,655	33,687	3	115,157	48.6	29.2	5.4	90.9	0.6	0.0	2.9	3.9
50	R, 67		D, 100		R, 66		R, 83	28,586	31,155	9	103,715	41.6	23.0	3.1	91.1	0.4	0.0	2.0	4.7

(continued)

Note: D=Democrat, R=Republican, R/D=Republican/Democrat (cross-filed), D/R=Democrat/Republican (cross-filed), I=Independent, C=Constitution, O=Other, GI=Green Independent, P=Progressive, P/D=Progressive/Democrat, P/D/R=Progressive/Democrat/Republican, HH=Households

Utah State House Districts—Election and Demographic Data (cont.)

House Districts	General Election Results Party, Percent of Vote							Population			Avg. HH Income	Pop 25+		Below Poverty Line	2006 White (Non-Hisp)	African American	American Indians, Alaska Natives	Asians, Hawaiians, Pacific Islanders	Hispanic Origin
												Some College +	4-Yr Degree +						
Utah	2000	2001	2002	2003	2004	2005	2006	2000	2006	% Change	($)	(%)	(%)	(%)	(%)	(%)	(%)	(%)	(%)
51	R, 65		R, 100		R, 69		R, 57	27,749	31,870	15	75,432	31.4	13.3	4.1	92.3	0.2	0.1	1.0	4.8
52	R, 100		R, 100		R, 85		R, 66	29,221	33,925	16	96,651	40.6	21.2	7.3	83.7	0.2	0.1	1.0	10.7
53	R, 52		R, 60		R, 62		R, 54	29,475	35,051	19	58,254	30.5	11.4	14.5	89.1	0.2	0.7	0.5	7.0
54	R, 82		R, 100		R, 86		R, 69	31,180	33,272	7	46,046	25.2	7.4	19.1	88.5	0.2	7.8	0.5	5.5
55	R, 100		R, 82		R, 81		R, 89	30,185	37,913	26	93,145	41.2	21.8	6.5	92.9	0.2	0.1	0.7	4.3
56	R, 73		R, 91		R, 69		R, 84	28,618	41,925	46	69,875	38.4	17.6	7.3	92.5	0.3	0.1	1.0	4.2
57	R, 72		R, 100		R, 100		R, 100	28,718	36,949	29	65,257	39.4	17.9	8.6	90.5	0.2	0.1	1.1	5.8
58	R, 85		R, 85		R, 85		R, 70	30,174	37,425	24	66,033	43.3	25.7	14.8	86.8	0.5	0.2	3.1	6.7
59	R, 77		R, 100		R, 84		R, 85	30,702	37,353	22	82,072	42.3	21.5	6.6	88.8	0.3	0.1	1.9	6.1
60	R, 66		R, 100		R, 100		R, 74	26,746	33,397	25	58,188	40.8	18.8	12.6	79.9	0.5	0.3	2.6	12.3
61	R, 69		R, 100		R, 75		R, 67	30,145	36,285	20	63,257	43.4	22.6	11.5	83.5	0.4	0.2	2.6	9.7
62	R, 82		R, 100		R, 100		R, 100	28,895	37,948	31	58,872	41.6	20.1	10.4	78.9	0.5	0.2	2.5	12.5
63	R, 100		R, 100		R, 100		R, 100	31,265	36,529	17	45,010	33.6	17.2	22.9	85.3	0.4	0.1	3.4	7.6
64	R, 76		R, 87		R, 89		R, 63	30,986	40,483	31	46,308	37.2	15.9	18.9	72.5	0.4	0.3	2.7	17.6
65	R, 68		R, 71		R, 100		R, 100	31,429	40,319	28	65,170	39.7	17.8	9.1	91.4	0.2	0.1	0.7	5.2
66	R, 65		R, 69		R, 100		R, 100	29,878	38,367	28	65,110	36.7	14.6	10.0	91.1	0.2	0.1	0.6	5.5
67	R, 58		R, 82		R, 68		R, 100	30,997	37,481	21	51,757	30.9	9.3	15.1	87.0	0.1	0.2	0.5	8.3
68	R, 86		R, 100		R, 87		R, 60	30,843	32,591	6	45,748	30.0	9.5	19.5	85.6	0.3	0.3	0.9	9.4
69	D, 76		D, 68		D, 100		D, 100	29,442	30,353	3	49,196	29.1	8.1	17.7	93.5	0.2	0.4	0.4	3.8
70	R, 100		R, 100		R, 89		R, 100	31,870	31,596	-1	44,352	29.5	9.8	24.5	70.6	0.4	25.4	0.9	5.7
71	D, 100		R, 75		R, 88		R, 71	29,441	31,008	5	45,583	30.3	10.1	17.5	92.0	0.2	0.4	0.6	4.6
72	R, 89		R, 100		R, 100		R, 68	29,017	33,188	14	48,140	36.0	13.4	18.9	89.9	0.4	0.6	1.3	5.3
73	R, 78		R, 100		R, 89		R, 82	29,342	38,065	30	61,509	39.2	14.5	10.3	91.8	0.1	0.4	1.0	4.6
74	R, 100		R, 74		R, 92		R, 72	30,166	39,432	31	50,485	34.6	12.2	15.2	84.3	0.4	0.5	1.1	10.1
75	R, 100		R, 100		R, 100		R, 77	29,242	41,272	41	47,902	34.8	11.5	14.6	90.5	0.2	0.4	0.7	5.8

Note: D=Democrat, R=Republican, R/D=Republican/Democrat (cross-filed), D/R=Democrat/Republican (cross-filed), I=Independent, C=Constitution, O=Other, GI=Green Independent, P=Progressive, P/D=Progressive/Democrat, P/D/R=Progressive/Democrat/Republican, HH=Households

VERMONT

The physical attributes of a state are immutable, but the characteristics, manners, and values of the people who live there change. So it is that Vermont, birthplace of Calvin Coolidge and long a state where Republican support was as solid as its granite hills, is now one of the most Democratic states, the home of Howard Dean.

As John Gunther points out in *Inside U.S.A.*, Vermont was also once one of the most belligerent states. It was a sovereign nation from 1777 until 1791, one of only three states ever to be so (Texas and Hawaii are the others), a place when Ethan Allen and the Green Mountain boys vowed to "make war on all mankind" rather than compromise their independence. Vermont sent more troops per capita to fight in the Civil War than any other northern state and had the highest percentage of volunteers for the army before World War II. The state legislature also did its part, passing a resolution two months before Pearl Harbor in which it declared its own "state of belligerency with Germany." During the 1980s, as it attracted more new residents from out of state, Vermont became a headquarters for Greenpeace and the nuclear freeze movement—belligerency of another kind, perhaps. One of its current U.S. senators is a socialist.

The state has grown faster during the past three decades than it ever had before. From 1880 until 1970, it gained fewer than 60,000 people, and twice during that period actually lost population. The state was appreciated anew for its clean environment during the 1970s, much as Oregon was, and population leapt by more than 15 percent, the biggest boom since the 1830s. It jumped another 10 percent during the 1980s. Growth has slowed since then, but in almost two decades since 1990, Vermont has grown faster than any other New England state except New Hampshire. But rapid growth is probably not the top priority in a state that engaged in a passionate debate recently over whether to welcome Wal-Mart superstores.

The state is entirely rural except for a small niche in the northwestern corner around Burlington. In what is almost a parody of a trend occurring across the country, Burlington is developing its own tiny metropolitan doughnut; districts in the center of town are stagnating while those on the outer edge of the suburbs, in Chittenden County, are growing fastest.

Vermont is usually regarded as quaint rather than poor, but average household income here is a shade below the national average and almost exactly the same as in Georgia. The inevitable comparison between Vermont and its neighbor, New Hampshire, is revealing. New Hampshire is considerably bigger (it ranks forty-first in size; Vermont is forty-ninth) and considerably wealthier. Lacking the mills or proximity to the growing Boston suburbs, Vermont has an average household income that is almost 25 percent lower than it is across the Connecticut River.

The Burlington suburbs include the wealthiest districts in the state (average household income peaks at just above $100,000) while the poorest districts are found in the center of that city (average income is $33,000), as well as on the mean streets of Barre, in the center of the state.

In large part because it has only one even moderate-sized city (39,000 people live in Burlington), Vermont has a high percentage of white residents (almost 97 percent); only Montana has fewer African Americans. In fact, Vermont has more Hispanic and Asian residents than black residents, probably the only thing it has in common with Hawaii.

Montpelier, with only 8,000 residents, is the smallest state capital (and the only one, it is said, without a McDonald's) yet Vermont has a 150-member house of representatives, each of whom represents about 4,100 people, a continuation of the New England town meeting tradition. It is one of only two states that still elect governors to two-year terms; the other is New Hampshire. In the state assembly, the speaker, majority, and minority leaders are all women.

The structure of Vermont's legislature is one of the more complicated in the country. Members of the state assembly are elected from legislative districts, some of which elect one member and some two. State senators are also elected from single and multimember districts, with the number varying according to the population of the district. District lines generally conform to county boundaries, although two small counties are combined. Third parties, usually on the left, are stronger here than in almost any other state. (Recently retired U.S. senator Jim Jeffords famously left the GOP in 2001 to become an independent.) Vermont was John Anderson's best state in the 1980 presidential election and Ralph Nader's best in 2000.

As strong as the Democratic trend has been in Vermont, Republicans held the state assembly from 2000 to 2004, when Democrats rode George W. Bush's unpopularity to pick up fourteen seats. In 2000 Republicans were within two seats of gaining control in the state senate but Democrats have made big gains in the last several election cycles and now control that chamber, 23–7. Vermont's transformation from the days when it was one of only two states to support Alf Landon against Franklin D. Roosevelt in 1936 seems complete.

VERMONT
State Senate Districts

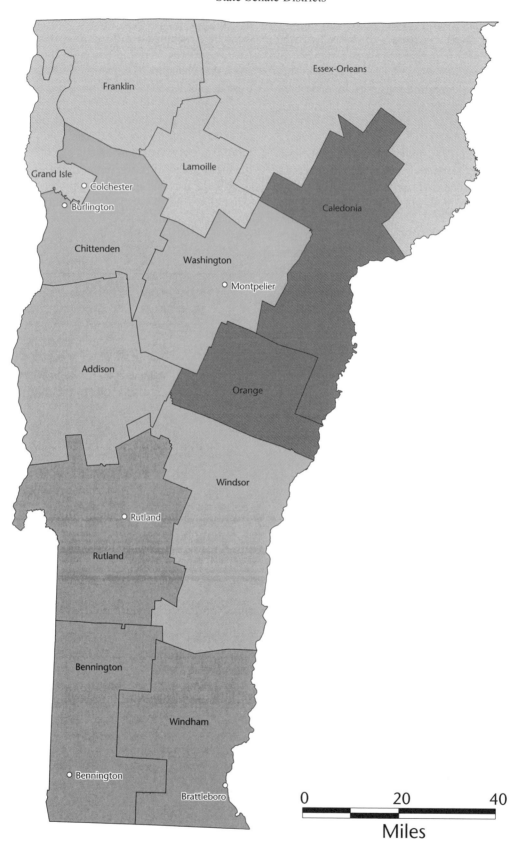

Essex-Orleans

Franklin

Grand Isle

○ Colchester

○ Burlington

Lamoille

Caledonia

Chittenden

Washington

○ Montpelier

Addison

Orange

Windsor

○ Rutland

Rutland

Bennington

Windham

○ Bennington

Brattleboro

0   20   40

Miles

Population Growth   ▨ -1% to 1%   ▨ 1% to 3%   ▨ 3% to 5%   ▨ 5% to 7%

Vermont State Senate Districts—Election and Demographic Data

Senate Districts	General Election Results Party, Percent of Vote							Population			Avg. HH Income	Pop 25+		Below Poverty Line	2006 White (Non-Hisp)	African American	American Indians, Alaska Natives	Asians, Hawaiians, Pacific Islanders	Hispanic Origin
Vermont	2000	2001	2002	2003	2004	2005	2006	2000	2006	% Change	($)	Some College + (%)	4-Yr Degree + (%)	Line (%)	(%)	(%)	(%)	(%)	(%)
Addison	R, 30		D, 31		D, 37		D/R, 55	39,663	40,754	3	59,036	36.2	21.3	13.1	95.8	0.5	0.1	0.8	1.0
Addison	D, 27		D, 28		D, 29		D/R, 45	39,663	40,754	3	59,036	36.2	21.3	13.1	95.8	0.5	0.1	0.8	1.0
Bennington	R, 36		D, 30		D, 32		D, 40	39,482	39,335	0	57,381	39.3	21.8	14.4	96.3	0.4	0.1	0.7	1.3
Bennington	D, 35		R, 27		R, 26		D, 28	39,482	39,335	0	57,381	39.3	21.8	14.4	96.3	0.4	0.1	0.7	1.3
Caledonia	R, 33		R/D, 52		D, 28		D, 33	37,948	39,261	3	48,089	32.3	16.9	17.2	96.7	0.3	0.2	0.4	0.9
Caledonia	R, 29		R/D, 48		R, 26		R, 27	37,948	39,261	3	48,089	32.3	16.9	17.2	96.7	0.3	0.2	0.4	0.9
Chittenden	D, 10		D, 10		D, 11		D, 13	129,444	132,207	2	67,384	48.5	31.6	10.6	93.2	1.0	0.1	2.3	1.3
Chittenden	D, 9		D, 10		D, 11		D, 12	129,444	132,207	2	67,384	48.5	31.6	10.6	93.2	1.0	0.1	2.3	1.3
Chittenden	R, 9		R, 9		D, 11		D, 11	129,444	132,207	2	67,384	48.5	31.6	10.6	93.2	1.0	0.1	2.3	1.3
Chittenden	D, 9		D, 9		D, 10		D, 11	129,444	132,207	2	67,384	48.5	31.6	10.6	93.2	1.0	0.1	2.3	1.3
Chittenden	D, 8		D, 9		D, 9		D, 10	129,444	132,207	2	67,384	48.5	31.6	10.6	93.2	1.0	0.1	2.3	1.3
Chittenden	D, 8		D, 9		D, 9		D, 9	129,444	132,207	2	67,384	48.5	31.6	10.6	93.2	1.0	0.1	2.3	1.3
Essex-Orleans	R/D, 44		R/D, 51		R, 34		D/R, 50	38,420	40,513	5	42,574	27.0	12.3	20.8	96.3	0.3	0.2	0.3	0.9
Essex-Orleans	R, 41		R/D, 49		D, 28		R/D, 50	38,420	40,513	5	42,574	27.0	12.3	20.8	96.3	0.3	0.2	0.3	0.9
Franklin	R, 29		D, 23		D, 30		D, 29	43,997	46,952	7	54,006	29.7	12.9	12.9	95.9	0.3	0.6	0.3	0.7
Franklin	D, 23		D, 22		D, 27		D, 28	43,997	46,952	7	54,006	29.7	12.9	12.9	95.9	0.3	0.6	0.3	0.7
Grand Isle	D, 60		D, 66		D, 100		D/R, 100	22,371	23,715	6	67,913	43.4	24.1	8.7	95.3	0.6	0.1	1.5	1.1
Lamoille	D, 51		D, 51		D, 63		D, 59	20,578	21,841	6	59,594	42.6	25.1	12.3	96.3	0.4	0.2	0.4	0.9
Orange	R, 49		D, 53		D, 58		D, 62	19,858	20,616	4	54,527	35.1	19.6	13.2	97.0	0.2	0.1	0.4	1.0
Rutland	R, 25		R, 24		R, 22		D, 22	59,110	59,038	0	50,582	36.6	18.8	15.3	97.2	0.3	0.1	0.4	0.9
Rutland	R, 22		R, 20		R, 19		R, 18	59,110	59,038	0	50,582	36.6	18.8	15.3	97.2	0.3	0.1	0.4	0.9
Rutland	R, 22		R, 20		R, 15		R, 16	59,110	59,038	0	50,582	36.6	18.8	15.3	97.2	0.3	0.1	0.4	0.9
Washington	R, 19		R, 20		R, 21		D, 20	58,104	59,445	2	56,527	41.8	24.9	13.2	95.4	0.5	0.1	0.6	1.5
Washington	R, 17		D, 17		D, 21		R, 18	58,104	59,445	2	56,527	41.8	24.9	13.2	95.4	0.5	0.1	0.6	1.5
Washington	D, 15		R, 17		R, 17		R, 18	58,104	59,445	2	56,527	41.8	24.9	13.2	95.4	0.5	0.1	0.6	1.5
Windham	D, 27		D, 30		D, 38		D, 46	41,330	41,181	0	54,758	40.4	24.0	14.3	95.1	0.5	0.1	0.9	1.3
Windham	D, 26		D, 29		D, 35		D, 42	41,330	41,181	0	54,758	40.4	24.0	14.3	95.1	0.5	0.1	0.9	1.3
Windsor	D, 18		D/R, 26		D, 24		D, 24	58,341	59,131	1	58,751	41.9	24.1	13.1	95.9	0.4	0.1	1.1	1.2
Windsor	D, 18		D, 24		D, 22		D, 22	58,341	59,131	1	58,751	41.9	24.1	13.1	95.9	0.4	0.1	1.1	1.2
Windsor	D, 16		D, 24		D, 21		D, 20	58,341	59,131	1	58,751	41.9	24.1	13.1	95.9	0.4	0.1	1.1	1.2

Note: D=Democrat, R=Republican, R/D=Republican/Democrat (cross-filed), D/R=Democrat/Republican (cross-filed), I=Independent, C=Constitution, O=Other, GI=Green Independent, P=Progressive, P/D=Progressive/Democrat, P/D/R=Progressive/Democrat/Republican, HH=Households

VERMONT
State House Districts

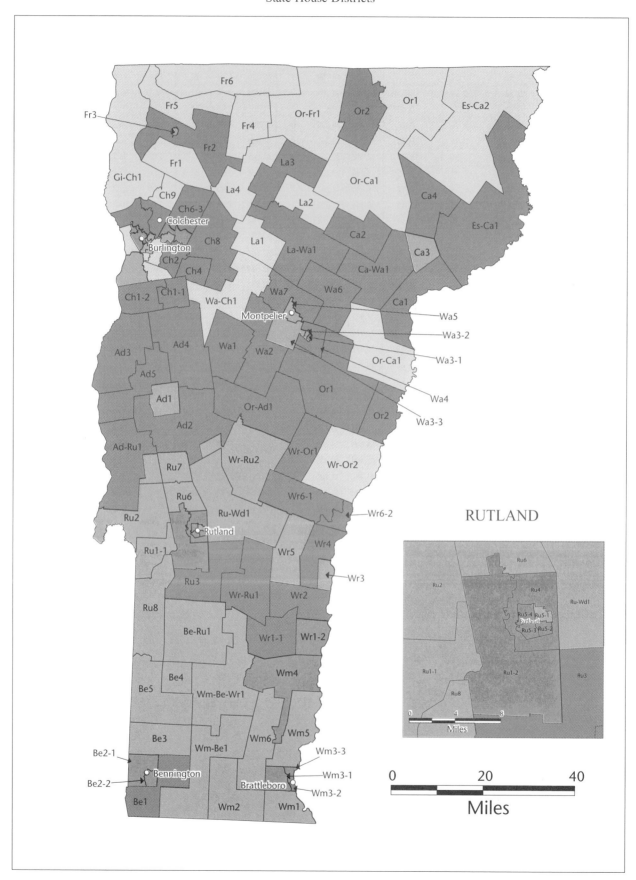

Population Growth   ■ -4% to -1%   ■ -1% to 1%   ■ 1% to 5%   □ 5% to 17%

BURLINGTON

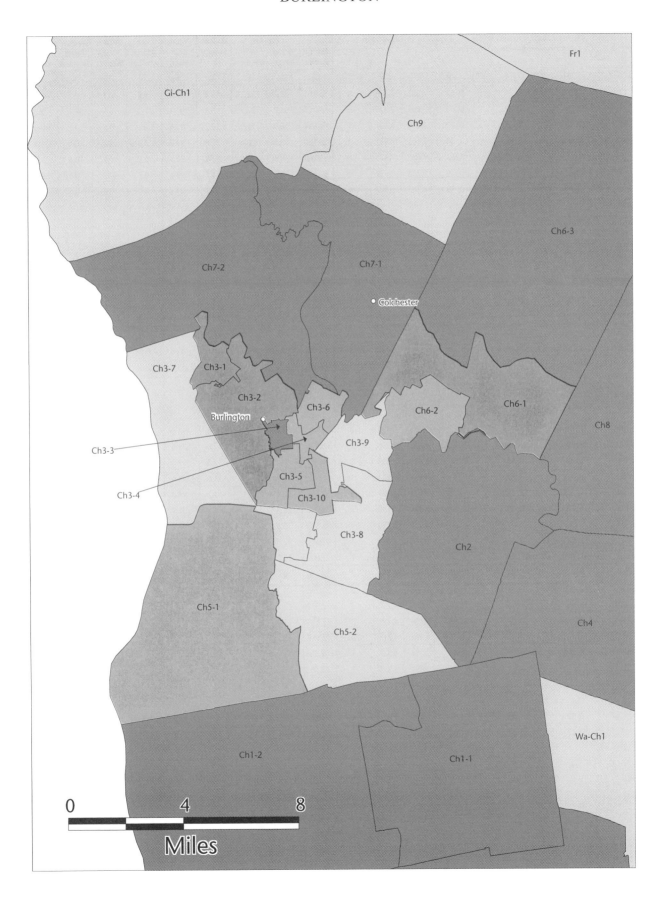

Gi-Ch1

Fr1

Ch9

Ch7-2

Ch7-1

Ch6-3

● Colchester

Ch3-7

Ch3-1

Ch3-2

Ch3-6

Ch6-2

Ch6-1

Ch8

Burlington ●

Ch3-3

Ch3-9

Ch3-4

Ch3-5

Ch3-10

Ch3-8

Ch2

Ch5-1

Ch5-2

Ch4

Ch1-2

Ch1-1

Wa-Ch1

0   4   8

Miles

Population Growth   ▧ -4% to -1%   ▧ -1% to 1%   ▧ 1% to 5%   ▢ 5% to 17%

Vermont State House Districts—Election and Demographic Data

House Districts	General Election Results Party, Percent of Vote							Population			Avg. HH Income	Pop 25+ Some College +	Pop 25+ 4-Yr Degree +	Below Poverty Line	White (Non-Hisp)	African American	American Indians, Alaska Natives	Asians, Hawaiians, Pacific Islanders	Hispanic Origin
Vermont	2000	2001	2002	2003	2004	2005	2006	2000	2006	% Change	($)	(%)	(%)	(%)	(%)	(%)	(%)	(%)	(%)
Add-1	R, 39		D, 30		D, 31		D, 51	7,893	7,926	0	55,103	33.2	22.2	16.3	91.4	1.2	0.1	2.1	2.3
Add-1	R, 29		D, 30		D, 30		D, 49	7,893	7,926	0	55,103	33.2	22.2	16.3	91.4	1.2	0.1	2.1	2.3
Add-2	D, 46		D, 51		D, 63		D, 100	4,245	4,302	1	61,354	36.9	21.9	13.2	97.6	0.1	0.0	0.5	0.4
Add-3	R, 54		R, 39		R, 30		R, 30	7,663	7,971	4	59,160	38.3	20.6	12.9	94.8	0.8	0.1	0.4	1.3
Add-3			R, 35		R, 29		R, 23	7,663	7,971	4	59,160	38.3	20.6	12.9	94.8	0.8	0.1	0.4	1.3
Add-4**			D, 31		D, 34		D, 35	8,296	8,632	4	61,696	36.9	22.6	11.1	97.3	0.2	0.0	0.6	0.5
Add-4**			D, 28		D, 31		D, 33	8,296	8,632	4	61,696	36.9	22.6	11.1	97.3	0.2	0.0	0.6	0.5
Add-4-1*	R, 55																		
Add-4-2*	D, 30																		
Add-4-2*	R, 25																		
Add-5**			R, 53		R, 51		D, 51	3,882	4,014	3	63,077	40.2	24.1	11.1	97.5	0.2	0.1	0.3	0.7
Add-Rut-1	R, 74		R, 100		R/D, 100		I, 64	3,762	3,882	3	53,389	34.3	18.2	13.1	97.5	0.4	0.0	0.3	0.8
Add-Rut-2*	R, 60																		
Ben-1	D, 56		D, 59		D, 80		D, 100	3,934	4,022	2	52,353	31.0	13.8	14.4	97.3	0.2	0.1	0.6	0.5
Ben-2-1	D/R, 53		D/R, 57		D, 58		D/R, 61	8,398	8,299	-1	49,683	33.8	17.9	17.1	94.9	1.0	0.1	1.1	1.4
Ben-2-1	D/R, 47		R, 43		R, 42		R, 39	8,398	8,299	-1	49,683	33.8	17.9	17.1	94.9	1.0	0.1	1.1	1.4
Ben-2-2	D/R, 81		R/D, 54		R, 37		R, 35	6,951	6,733	-3	44,456	32.2	14.9	19.8	95.8	0.3	0.1	1.1	1.4
Ben-2-2			D/R, 46		D, 26		D, 32	6,951	6,733	-3	44,456	32.2	14.9	19.8	95.8	0.3	0.1	1.1	1.4
Ben-2-3*	R, 41																		
Ben-2-3*	D, 34																		
Ben-2-4*	D, 52																		
Ben-3	R, 100		R, 52		D, 55		D/R, 100	3,756	3,759	0	65,412	42.9	22.8	11.8	97.4	0.3	0.0	0.3	1.2
Ben-4	R, 100		R, 100		R, 100		R, 100	3,976	3,998	1	66,227	50.3	33.5	10.8	95.4	0.4	0.0	0.3	2.4
Ben-5**			D, 53		D, 53		D, 57	3,639	3,639	0	64,172	42.3	24.0	12.3	97.4	0.3	0.0	0.6	0.7
Ben-Rut-1	R, 100		R, 100		R, 57		R, 61	4,055	4,083	1	71,168	45.1	29.2	11.0	98.0	0.2	0.1	0.2	0.7
Cal-1	R, 100		R, 100		R, 100		R, 100	3,735	3,907	5	52,552	36.4	19.1	13.2	97.4	0.3	0.2	0.5	0.4
Cal-2	R, 100		R, 63		D, 53		D, 81	3,961	4,130	4	45,512	25.6	12.0	18.5	97.7	0.1	0.2	0.0	0.5
Cal-2	R, 100							3,961	4,130	4	45,512	25.6	12.0	18.5	97.7	0.1	0.2	0.0	0.5
Cal-3	R, 67		R, 51		R, 100		R, 29	7,326	7,258	-1	41,666	32.8	16.6	20.9	95.0	0.5	0.2	0.7	1.5
Cal-3			R, 49		R, 100		R, 28	7,326	7,258	-1	41,666	32.8	16.6	20.9	95.0	0.5	0.2	0.7	1.5
Cal-4	R, 28		R, 51		R, 34		R, 40	7,867	8,013	2	51,378	30.7	17.3	17.9	96.8	0.3	0.2	0.6	0.7
Cal-4	R, 27		R, 49		R, 33		R, 34	7,867	8,013	2	51,378	30.7	17.3	17.9	96.8	0.3	0.2	0.6	0.7
Cal-Was-1	R, 100		R, 66		R, 56		R, 100	4,095	4,200	3	52,034	40.4	23.9	15.5	97.2	0.2	0.1	0.2	0.7
Chi-1-1	R, 29		D, 100		D, 62		D, 68	4,106	4,213	3	77,118	47.5	30.5	6.8	96.9	0.1	0.1	0.5	0.9
Chi-1-1	D, 28							4,106	4,213	3	77,118	47.5	30.5	6.8	96.9	0.1	0.1	0.5	0.9
Chi-1-2	D, 30		R, 55		D, 51		D, 47	3,884	3,923	1	102,955	55.9	40.8	6.9	96.8	0.2	0.0	0.7	0.7
Chi-1-2	R, 29							3,884	3,923	1	102,955	55.9	40.8	6.9	96.8	0.2	0.0	0.7	0.7
Chi-1-3*	D, 30																		
Chi-1-3*	D, 29																		
Chi-2**			D, 29		D, 43		D, 32	7,672	7,971	4	85,078	52.5	34.9	4.3	95.9	0.5	0.0	1.4	1.2
Chi-2**			D, 27		D, 38		D, 30	7,672	7,971	4	85,078	52.5	34.9	4.3	95.9	0.5	0.0	1.4	1.2
Chi-2-1*	R, 27																		
Chi-2-1*	R, 27																		
Chi-2-2*	R, 44																		
Chi-2-2*	R, 38																		
Chi-2-3*	D, 54																		
Chi-2-4*	R, 24																		
Chi-2-4*	R, 21																		
Chi-3*	D, 28																		
Chi-3*	D, 27																		

(continued)

Note: D=Democrat, R=Republican, R/D=Republican/Democrat (cross-filed), D/R=Democrat/Republican (cross-filed), I=Independent, C=Constitution, O=Other, GI=Green Independent, P=Progressive, P/D=Progressive/Democrat, P/D/R=Progressive/Democrat/Republican, HH=Households

Vermont State House Districts—Election and Demographic Data (cont.)

House Districts	General Election Results Party, Percent of Vote							Population			Avg. HH Income	Pop 25+		Below Poverty Line	2006 White (Non-Hisp)	African American	American Indians, Alaska Natives	Asians, Hawaiians, Pacific Islanders	Hispanic Origin
												Some College +	4-Yr Degree +						
Vermont	2000	2001	2002	2003	2004	2005	2006	2000	2006	% Change	($)	(%)	(%)	(%)	(%)	(%)	(%)	(%)	(%)
Chi-3-1**			R, 30		R, 30		R, 29	7,120	6,926	-3	56,020	46.5	28.3	9.5	91.8	1.4	0.1	2.4	1.6
Chi-3-1**			D, 28		D, 29		D, 28	7,120	6,926	-3	56,020	46.5	28.3	9.5	91.8	1.4	0.1	2.4	1.6
Chi-3-2**			D, 67		D, 100		D, 65	4,246	4,148	-2	50,408	47.4	30.1	14.4	90.2	2.3	0.3	2.5	1.3
Chi-3-3**			D, 34		D, 34		D, 33	9,947	10,068	1	33,671	41.6	27.2	24.4	86.3	2.5	0.2	4.7	1.8
Chi-3-3**			P, 24		D, 27		D, 32	9,947	10,068	1	33,671	41.6	27.2	24.4	86.3	2.5	0.2	4.7	1.8
Chi-3-4**			P, 32		P, 54		P, 57	6,426	6,404	0	42,552	31.5	22.8	19.2	90.7	1.6	0.2	2.8	2.0
Chi-3-4**			P, 27		P, 46		P, 43	6,426	6,404	0	42,552	31.5	22.8	19.2	90.7	1.6	0.2	2.8	2.0
Chi-3-5**			D, 51		D, 38		D, 51	8,478	8,434	-1	73,685	52.8	39.1	13.9	91.8	1.4	0.1	2.0	2.0
Chi-3-5**			D, 49		D, 33		D, 49	8,478	8,434	-1	73,685	52.8	39.1	13.9	91.8	1.4	0.1	2.0	2.0
Chi-3-6**			D, 50		D, 50		D, 35	7,416	7,409	0	41,835	40.4	22.4	20.3	88.4	1.7	0.2	5.5	1.6
Chi-3-6**			D, 50		D, 50		D, 32	7,416	7,409	0	41,835	40.4	22.4	20.3	88.4	1.7	0.2	5.5	1.6
Chi-3-7**			R, 100		D, 55		D, 69	3,285	3,573	9	82,435	61.2	43.5	6.2	90.4	1.1	0.1	3.3	1.5
Chi-3-8**			D, 53		D, 60		D, 84	4,300	5,028	17	88,993	60.5	42.4	3.2	91.8	0.4	0.0	5.0	1.2
Chi-3-9**			D, 60		D, 62		D, 53	3,610	3,910	8	57,584	47.2	24.7	9.3	92.5	0.9	0.1	3.0	1.6
Chi-3-10**			D, 58		D, 100		D, 100	3,981	3,961	-1	57,667	49.3	31.1	9.0	89.8	1.3	0.0	4.4	2.0
Chi-4	D, 52		R, 50		D, 57		D, 100	3,870	3,963	2	74,274	51.5	34.5	6.5	97.2	0.0	0.0	0.6	1.0
Chi-5-1	R, 57		R, 52		R/D, 100		R, 100	3,842	3,853	0	100,903	59.9	43.6	6.2	96.3	0.3	0.1	1.2	0.9
Chi-5-2	R, 54		R, 55		R, 51		D, 58	3,374	3,591	6	101,885	56.7	42.5	5.3	96.1	0.1	0.1	1.2	1.3
Chi-5-3*	R, 58																		
Chi-5-4*	R, 100																		
Chi-6*	D, 58																		
Chi-6-1**			R, 29		R, 30		D, 51	8,177	8,023	-2	81,366	52.7	35.9	4.9	93.4	1.1	0.1	2.8	0.8
Chi-6-1**			R, 27		D, 27		R, 49	8,177	8,023	-2	81,366	52.7	35.9	4.9	93.4	1.1	0.1	2.8	0.8
Chi-6-2**			D, 25		D, 30		D, 42	8,204	8,126	-1	70,551	52.4	30.1	5.6	94.0	0.8	0.1	2.5	1.4
Chi-6-2**			R, 22		D, 29		D, 40	8,204	8,126	-1	70,551	52.4	30.1	5.6	94.0	0.8	0.1	2.5	1.4
Chi-6-3**			D, 54		D, 58		D, 59	4,293	4,446	4	80,184	52.1	35.3	3.8	95.5	0.6	0.1	1.3	1.0
Chi-7-1	D, 26		R, 29		R, 30		D, 57	8,347	8,682	4	59,942	40.2	23.0	7.3	93.6	0.8	0.0	2.7	1.7
Chi-7-1	D, 22		R, 21		D, 26		D, 43	8,347	8,682	4	59,942	40.2	23.0	7.3	93.6	0.8	0.0	2.7	1.7
Chi-7-2	D, 57		R, 30		R, 59		R, 32	8,816	9,066	3	72,722	46.5	25.1	8.3	95.5	0.7	0.0	1.2	1.1
Chi-7-2	P, 43		D, 27		R, 41		D, 24	8,816	9,066	3	72,722	46.5	25.1	8.3	95.5	0.7	0.0	1.2	1.1
Chi-7-3*	P, 100																		
Chi-7-3*	P, 100																		
Chi-7-4*	P, 76																		
Chi-7-5*	D, 55																		
Chi-7-6*	R, 58																		
Chi-7-6*	D, 56																		
Chi-7-7*	D, 62																		
Chi-7-8*	R, 79																		
Chi-7-9*	D, 56																		
Chi-7-10*	D, 53																		
Chi-8**			D, 28		D, 30		D, 34	8,590	8,755	2	74,934	52.5	34.9	5.0	96.6	0.5	0.0	0.5	1.1
Chi-8**			D, 28		D, 25		D, 31	8,590	8,755	2	74,934	52.5	34.9	5.0	96.6	0.5	0.0	0.5	1.1
Chi-9**			R, 40		R, 35		R/D, 44	8,072	8,494	5	60,413	35.0	16.8	7.2	97.1	0.3	0.2	0.5	0.8
Chi-9**			R, 35		R, 35		D, 29	8,072	8,494	5	60,413	35.0	16.8	7.2	97.1	0.3	0.2	0.5	0.8
Es-Ca**			R, 64		R, 62		R, 57	3,786	3,897	3	41,814	24.5	10.7	19.3	95.8	0.1	0.2	0.2	1.2
Es-Ca-1*	R, 70																		
Es-Ca-2*	R, 56																		
Esx-Cal-Or**			R, 60		R, 64		R, 59	3,801	3,693	-3	44,731	20.3	6.3	19.1	100.0	0.0	0.0	0.0	0.0
Fra-1	R, 68		R, 28		R, 28		R, 27	7,771	8,485	9	67,099	36.5	16.1	6.7	97.4	0.3	0.1	0.3	0.7
Fra-1			R, 27		R, 27		D, 27	7,771	8,485	9	67,099	36.5	16.1	6.7	97.4	0.3	0.1	0.3	0.7

(continued)

Note: D=Democrat, R=Republican, R/D=Republican/Democrat (cross-filed), D/R=Democrat/Republican (cross-filed), I=Independent, C=Constitution, O=Other, GI=Green Independent, P=Progressive, P/D=Progressive/Democrat, P/D/R=Progressive/Democrat/Republican, HH=Households

Vermont State House Districts—Election and Demographic Data (cont.)

House Districts	General Election Results Party, Percent of Vote							Population			Avg. HH Income	Pop 25+		2006 Below Poverty Line	White (Non-Hisp)	African American	American Indians, Alaska Natives	Asians, Hawaiians, Pacific Islanders	Hispanic Origin
Vermont	2000	2001	2002	2003	2004	2005	2006	2000	2006	% Change	($)	Some College + (%)	4-Yr Degree + (%)	(%)	(%)	(%)	(%)	(%)	(%)
Fra-2	D, 40		D, 40		D/R, 52		D, 28	15,274	15,901	4	51,576	33.2	15.6	13.4	95.6	0.3	0.4	0.3	1.0
Fra-2	R, 26		D, 34		D/R, 48		D, 28	15,274	15,901	4	51,576	33.2	15.6	13.4	95.6	0.3	0.4	0.3	1.0
Fra-3**			D, 32		D, 33		D, 35	5,905	5,874	-1	46,500	34.4	15.8	14.7	94.8	0.5	0.5	0.4	1.1
Fra-3**			R, 27		R, 23		D, 30	5,905	5,874	-1	46,500	34.4	15.8	14.7	94.8	0.5	0.5	0.4	1.1
Fra-3-1*	D/R, 35																		
Fra-3-1*	D, 35																		
Fra-3-2*	D, 53																		
Fra-4	D, 100		D, 81		D, 100		D, 70	3,881	4,079	5	46,585	26.0	10.5	15.7	96.2	0.1	0.5	0.2	0.6
Fra-5**			R/D, 50		R/D, 47		R/D, 42	7,949	8,512	7	55,451	23.9	9.8	13.6	94.7	0.4	1.2	0.3	0.5
Fra-5**			R/D, 50		R, 40		D, 32	7,949	8,512	7	55,451	23.9	9.8	13.6	94.7	0.4	1.2	0.3	0.5
Fra-5-1*	R, 68																		
Fra-5-2*	D, 47																		
Fra-6**			D, 28		R, 52		R/D, 53	8,302	8,762	6	48,226	22.3	7.7	16.7	95.9	0.3	0.9	0.2	0.4
Fra-6**			R, 26		D, 48		D, 47	8,302	8,762	6	48,226	22.3	7.7	16.7	95.9	0.3	0.9	0.2	0.4
Fra-Gi-1*	R/D, 43																		
Fra-Gi-1*	R, 38																		
Gi-1*	R, 60																		
Gi-Chi-1**			D, 27		D, 30		D, 30	8,177	9,276	13	64,082	38.5	19.9	12.7	97.6	0.2	0.2	0.2	0.4
Gi-Chi-1**			D, 26		D, 30		D, 28	8,177	9,276	13	64,082	38.5	19.9	12.7	97.6	0.2	0.2	0.2	0.4
Lam-1	R, 69		R, 100		R, 100		R, 59	4,155	4,544	9	85,551	63.8	43.9	9.0	96.1	0.3	0.1	0.5	1.3
Lam-2**			R, 51		D, 55		D, 59	4,210	4,487	7	57,184	36.3	20.1	12.2	97.4	0.4	0.2	0.3	0.7
Lam-2-1*	R, 55																		
Lam-2-2*	R/D, 44																		
Lam-2-2*	R/D, 39																		
Lam-3	D/R, 61		D, 73		D, 68		D/R, 100	4,395	4,565	4	43,707	26.9	14.8	17.9	95.4	0.5	0.2	0.6	1.0
Lam-4**			R, 100		R, 68		R, 100	4,092	4,434	8	56,165	40.1	22.1	9.2	96.2	0.2	0.1	0.2	0.7
Lam-Was-1**			R, 30		D, 52		D, 41	7,599	7,917	4	48,330	39.3	21.0	13.9	96.1	0.3	0.1	0.4	0.9
Lam-Was-1**			D, 25		R, 48		D, 29	7,599	7,917	4	48,330	39.3	21.0	13.9	96.1	0.3	0.1	0.4	0.9
Ora-1	R, 29		R, 32		R, 30		P/D, 28	8,360	8,762	5	48,589	27.2	12.4	14.3	96.8	0.2	0.1	0.1	1.4
Ora-1	R, 28		R, 31		R, 30		R, 28	8,360	8,762	5	48,589	27.2	12.4	14.3	96.8	0.2	0.1	0.1	1.4
Ora-2	R, 34		D, 57		D, 71		D/R, 100	4,156	4,307	4	51,340	32.5	16.5	13.9	97.1	0.4	0.2	0.4	0.9
Ora-2	R, 33							4,156	4,307	4	51,340	32.5	16.5	13.9	97.1	0.4	0.2	0.4	0.9
Ora-3*	R, 53																		
Ora-4*	D, 60																		
Ora-Add 1**			D, 26		D, 33		D, 38	7,465	7,630	2	54,305	34.8	18.4	13.1	97.1	0.1	0.1	0.6	0.7
Ora-Add 1**			R, 23		D, 30		D, 35	7,465	7,630	2	54,305	34.8	18.4	13.1	97.1	0.1	0.1	0.6	0.7
Ora-Cal 1	R, 62		R, 62		R, 54		R, 53	3,880	4,143	7	49,296	32.6	16.3	15.4	97.2	0.3	0.2	0.3	0.5
Orl-1	R, 32		R, 29		R, 28		R, 29	7,298	7,737	6	44,840	29.8	13.4	19.2	97.0	0.3	0.3	0.3	0.7
Orl-1	R, 30		R, 27		P/D, 27		R, 28	7,298	7,737	6	44,840	29.8	13.4	19.2	97.0	0.3	0.3	0.3	0.7
Orl-2	R/D, 46		R, 31		R, 25		R/D, 53	8,473	8,839	4	42,759	26.7	11.4	21.6	95.7	0.5	0.2	0.5	1.3
Orl-2	R, 32		R, 28		R, 25		R/D, 47	8,473	8,839	4	42,759	26.7	11.4	21.6	95.7	0.5	0.2	0.5	1.3
Orl-Cal-1	R, 28		R, 28		D, 27		D, 32	7,504	7,986	6	42,919	30.5	16.1	21.9	96.3	0.2	0.2	0.2	0.7
Orl-Cal-1	R, 26		D, 25		R, 27		R, 27	7,504	7,986	6	42,919	30.5	16.1	21.9	96.3	0.2	0.2	0.2	0.7
Orl-Fra-1	D/R, 79		D/R, 100		P/D, 52		P/D/R, 67	4,132	4,442	8	40,396	26.0	12.1	21.2	96.7	0.3	0.1	0.2	0.9
Rut-1*	R, 37																		
Rut-1*	R, 31																		
Rut-1-1**			D, 64		R, 54		R, 100	3,320	3,321	0	42,500	29.4	15.6	18.0	97.0	0.5	0.2	0.8	0.6
Rut-1-2**			R, 41		R, 31		D, 51	7,274	7,162	-2	49,718	32.4	15.9	13.4	97.7	0.3	0.1	0.6	0.6
Rut-1-2**			R, 41		D, 29		R, 49	7,274	7,162	-2	49,718	32.4	15.9	13.4	97.7	0.3	0.1	0.6	0.6
Rut-2	R, 52		R, 41		R, 34		R, 52	8,061	8,053	0	51,907	31.8	15.2	15.4	96.4	0.3	0.1	0.5	1.3

(continued)

Note: D=Democrat, R=Republican, R/D=Republican/Democrat (cross-filed), D/R=Democrat/Republican (cross-filed), I=Independent, C=Constitution, O=Other, GI=Green Independent, P=Progressive, P/D=Progressive/Democrat, P/D/R=Progressive/Democrat/Republican, HH=Households

Vermont State House Districts—Election and Demographic Data (cont.)

House Districts	General Election Results Party, Percent of Vote							Population			Avg. HH Income	Pop 25+ Some College +	Pop 25+ 4-Yr Degree +	Below Poverty Line	2006 White (Non-Hisp)	African American	American Indians, Alaska Natives	Asians, Hawaiians, Pacific Islanders	Hispanic Origin
Vermont	2000	2001	2002	2003	2004	2005	2006	2000	2006	% Change	($)	(%)	(%)	(%)	(%)	(%)	(%)	(%)	(%)
Rut-2	R, 48		R, 33		R, 31		R, 48	8,061	8,053	0	51,907	31.8	15.2	15.4	96.4	0.3	0.1	0.5	1.3
Rut-3	R, 43		D, 55		D, 51		D, 52	3,895	3,941	1	52,879	39.6	21.0	11.9	97.5	0.2	0.1	0.2	0.9
Rut-4	R, 57		R, 100		R, 62		R, 100	20,878	20,631	-1	49,272	38.3	18.9	17.9	96.8	0.5	0.1	0.5	1.0
Rut-5*	R, 100																		
Rut-5-1**			R, 53		R, 63		D, 56	3,939	3,936	0	58,875	47.9	27.0	12.8	96.7	0.2	0.0	0.8	1.2
Rut-5-2**			R, 57		R, 62		D, 51	3,490	3,448	-1	48,065	37.7	17.4	15.4	97.1	0.6	0.1	0.3	0.9
Rut-5-3**			R, 100		D, 55		D, 100	4,153	4,091	-1	34,223	28.9	12.4	28.2	95.8	0.6	0.1	0.3	1.4
Rut-5-4**			R, 67		R, 58		D, 52	4,342	4,176	-4	42,332	31.9	14.7	20.6	97.0	0.4	0.0	0.6	0.7
Rut-6**			R, 100		R, 100		R, 100	3,781	3,797	0	50,294	37.3	19.2	11.7	98.5	0.2	0.1	0.2	0.5
Rut-6-1*	R, 54																		
Rut-6-2*	R, 64																		
Rut-6-3*	D, 24																		
Rut-6-3*	R, 23																		
Rut-6-4*	R, 53																		
Rut-7	R, 35		R, 100		R, 64		R, 55	3,688	3,704	0	56,570	33.3	16.2	14.2	98.4	0.1	0.1	0.2	0.3
Rut-7	R, 33							3,688	3,704	0	56,570	33.3	16.2	14.2	98.4	0.1	0.1	0.2	0.3
Rut-8**			D, 100		D, 53		D, 61	3,750	3,771	1	49,181	38.3	20.2	15.3	98.1	0.3	0.2	0.1	0.8
Rut-Ben-1*	D, 68																		
Rut-Wdr 1	R, 100		D, 58		D, 59		D, 58	4,134	4,162	1	65,618	49.5	29.2	9.7	97.9	0.2	0.0	0.5	0.5
Was-1	D, 28		D, 66		D, 62		D, 100	4,358	4,543	4	70,139	56.4	36.8	9.8	96.5	0.6	0.1	0.3	1.2
Was-1	R, 26							4,358	4,543	4	70,139	56.4	36.8	9.8	96.5	0.6	0.1	0.3	1.2
Was-2	D, 26		D, 35		D, 45		D, 38	7,560	7,717	2	52,676	32.8	20.2	11.6	93.4	0.8	0.1	1.3	2.2
Was-2	D, 26		R, 25		R, 43		R, 30	7,560	7,717	2	52,676	32.8	20.2	11.6	93.4	0.8	0.1	1.3	2.2
Was-3*	R, 32																		
Was-3*	R, 30																		
Was-3-1**			R, 55		R, 54		R, 51	3,710	3,670	-1	45,202	39.0	20.9	19.7	95.8	0.4	0.1	0.7	1.8
Was-3-2**			D, 100		D, 100		D, 100	3,896	3,896	0	37,928	28.7	11.8	21.5	94.9	0.5	0.2	0.4	2.1
Was-3-3**			R, 53		D, 52		R, 54	4,168	4,204	1	51,213	36.0	16.7	14.9	95.8	0.3	0.1	0.5	1.3
Was-4**			R/D, 37		R, 33		R/D, 40	7,885	7,987	1	63,390	36.0	16.7	10.6	96.4	0.2	0.0	0.4	1.7
Was-4**			R, 34		R, 29		R, 36	7,885	7,987	1	63,390	36.0	16.7	10.6	96.4	0.2	0.0	0.4	1.7
Was-4-1*	R, 54																		
Was-4-2*	D/R, 35																		
Was-4-2*	D, 34																		
Was-5	D, 37		D, 32		D, 51		D, 51	7,448	7,430	0	53,372	53.0	35.2	14.8	94.4	0.7	0.1	0.9	1.7
Was-5	D, 36		D, 27		D, 49		D, 49	7,448	7,430	0	53,372	53.0	35.2	14.8	94.4	0.7	0.1	0.9	1.7
Was-6**			I, 51		D, 55		D, 100	4,180	4,290	3	52,121	42.5	28.3	13.2	95.3	0.6	0.2	0.4	0.8
Was-7**			D, 60		D, 100		D, 100	4,491	4,682	4	61,615	47.2	32.0	9.7	96.0	0.6	0.2	0.4	1.0
Wasi-Add-1*	D, 55																		
Wasi-Ch 1	D, 30		D, 40		D, 33		D, 51	8,072	8,522	6	68,853	46.2	28.9	8.8	96.9	0.2	0.0	0.6	0.6
Wasi-Ch 1	D, 27		D, 36		D, 32		D, 49	8,072	8,522	6	68,853	46.2	28.9	8.8	96.9	0.2	0.0	0.6	0.6
Wasi-Lam-1-1*	D, 53																		
Wdm-1	D, 36		R, 62		R, 100		R, 100	4,011	4,026	0	62,263	37.8	18.9	9.9	96.7	0.1	0.0	0.4	0.9
Wdm-1	D, 33							4,011	4,026	0	62,263	37.8	18.9	9.9	96.7	0.1	0.0	0.4	0.9
Wdm-2**			D, 55		D, 100		D, 43	4,249	4,264	0	54,353	41.7	22.2	12.8	97.0	0.1	0.0	0.4	1.0
Wdm-2-1*	D, 100																		
Wdm-2-2*	I, 51																		
Wdm-2-3*	D, 42																		
Wdm-3*	D, 63																		
Wdm-3-1**			D, 100		D, 100		D, 100	4,793	4,711	-2	65,967	42.8	26.6	17.4	93.7	0.9	0.1	1.2	1.8

(continued)

Note: D=Democrat, R=Republican, R/D=Republican/Democrat (cross-filed), D/R=Democrat/Republican (cross-filed), I=Independent, C=Constitution, O=Other, GI=Green Independent, P=Progressive, P/D=Progressive/Democrat, P/D/R=Progressive/Democrat/Republican, HH=Households

Vermont State House Districts—Election and Demographic Data (cont.)

House Districts	General Election Results Party, Percent of Vote							Population			Avg. HH Income ($)	Pop 25+ Some College + (%)	4-Yr Degree + (%)	Below Poverty Line (%)	2006 White (Non-Hisp) (%)	African American (%)	American Indians, Alaska Natives (%)	Asians, Hawaiians, Pacific Islanders (%)	Hispanic Origin (%)
Vermont	2000	2001	2002	2003	2004	2005	2006	2000	2006	% Change									
Wdm-3-2**			I, 100		I, 100		I, 85	3,233	3,312	2	41,335	40.7	23.7	14.2	89.8	1.7	0.1	1.5	2.2
Wdm-3-3**			P/D, 54		P/D, 100		P/D/R, 100	3,441	3,347	-3	44,190	46.3	31.4	21.3	90.3	1.2	0.1	3.0	1.9
Wdm 4	R, 66		D, 44		D, 40		D, 53	6,709	6,578	-2	49,509	33.5	17.5	15.8	96.1	0.3	0.1	0.5	1.3
Wdm 4			D, 35		D, 30		D, 47	6,709	6,578	-2	49,509	33.5	17.5	15.8	96.1	0.3	0.1	0.5	1.3
Wdm-5	R, 52		D, 38		D, 100		D, 42	7,667	7,730	1	57,154	39.9	25.7	12.5	95.7	0.6	0.1	0.7	1.2
Wdm-5			D, 34		D, 100		D, 42	7,667	7,730	1	57,154	39.9	25.7	12.5	95.7	0.6	0.1	0.7	1.2
Wdm-6*			D, 50		D, 100		D, 100	3,791	3,793	0	56,524	45.3	28.6	10.8	96.5	0.1	0.1	0.5	1.0
Wdm-Ben-1	D, 58		R, 54		R, 51		D, 51	3,827	3,795	-1	53,350	41.1	23.3	12.3	97.5	0.1	0.1	0.5	0.8
Wdm-Ben-Wdr-1**			R/D, 100		R/D, 56		R, 56	1,433	1,427	0	73,717	45.3	28.6	12.9	97.0	0.1	0.0	0.4	1.3
Wdr-1*	D, 100																		
Wdr-1-1**			R, 58		D, 53		D, 65	3,760	3,826	2	50,066	37.8	20.5	13.5	97.9	0.3	0.1	0.3	0.8
Wdr-1-2**			D, 38		D, 32		D, 51	8,726	8,505	-3	46,369	34.6	14.3	15.5	96.4	0.2	0.0	0.9	0.9
Wdr-1-2**			D, 33		D, 29		D, 49	8,726	8,505	-3	46,369	34.6	14.3	15.5	96.4	0.2	0.0	0.9	0.9
Wdr-2**			D, 51		D, 54		D, 100	4,175	4,249	2	59,033	35.8	16.7	10.5	97.3	0.1	0.1	0.5	1.1
Wdr-2-1*	D, 51																		
Wdr-2-2*	R, 27																		
Wdr-2-2*	D, 27																		
Wdr-2-3*	D/R, 100																		
Wdr-3	R, 54		D, 100		D, 100		D, 100	3,545	3,530	0	42,837	36.7	15.4	14.1	96.2	0.2	0.2	0.3	1.4
Wdr-4	R, 48		R, 53		R, 54		R/D, 100	4,205	4,296	2	67,057	42.9	25.1	8.2	97.3	0.2	0.1	0.4	1.2
Wdr-5	R, 64		I, 67		D, 63		D, 100	3,758	3,752	0	73,557	53.5	34.7	10.9	96.9	0.4	0.1	0.6	1.1
Wdr-6*	R, 32																		
Wdr-6*	D, 28																		
Wdr-6-1**			D, 100		D, 61		D, 53	4,026	4,107	2	86,436	50.9	32.4	8.8	97.0	0.3	0.1	0.6	1.0
Wdr-6-2**			R/D, 51		D, 53		D, 32	7,877	8,032	2	53,890	42.2	24.0	14.1	95.2	0.6	0.1	1.1	1.3
Wdr-6-2**			D, 49		R, 47		R, 26	7,877	8,032	2	53,890	42.2	24.0	14.1	95.2	0.6	0.1	1.1	1.3
Wdr-Ora-1	D, 32		D, 55		D, 51		R, 53	3,775	3,861	2	45,122	39.7	24.2	20.6	96.4	0.7	0.1	0.7	1.4
Wdr-Ora-1	D, 32							3,775	3,861	2	45,122	39.7	24.2	20.6	96.4	0.7	0.1	0.7	1.4
Wdr-Ora-2**			D, 51		D, 50		D, 41	9,877	10,400	5	75,178	48.5	36.7	9.6	92.6	0.8	0.2	3.1	1.4
Wdr-Ora-2**			D/R, 49		D, 50		D, 40	9,877	10,400	5	75,178	48.5	36.7	9.6	92.6	0.8	0.2	3.1	1.4
Wdr-Rut-1	D, 53		D, 65		D, 53		R, 52	4,207	4,355	4	53,877	39.0	21.5	13.7	98.1	0.2	0.0	0.3	0.3
Wdr-Rut-2	R, 53		R, 64		P/D, 55		P/D, 57	4,115	4,127	0	53,146	43.1	23.6	15.0	96.6	0.3	0.0	0.3	1.4
Wdr-Wdm-1-1*	D, 33																		
Wdr-Wdm-1-1*	D, 23																		

* only applies to 2000 House

** only applies to 2002-2006 House

Note: D=Democrat, R=Republican, R/D=Republican/Democrat (cross-filed), D/R=Democrat/Republican (cross-filed), I=Independent, C=Constitution, O=Other, GI=Green Independent, P=Progressive, P/D=Progressive/Democrat, P/D/R=Progressive/Democrat/Republican, HH=Households

VIRGINIA

Though it left the Union reluctantly in 1861, no state suffered more during the Civil War than Virginia. Its capital was burned, its farms were looted, and a generation of its young men were killed. When the war ended, Douglas Southall Freeman wrote, Virginia "went straight from Appomattox to the old house that typified the civilization that had perished. She climbed to the second-story bedroom; she pulled down the blinds and through the darkness of reconstruction sat in her mourning."

There is great irony in the fact that Virginia owes much of its economic recovery in this century to the same federal government it once lost so much in fighting—to the branch of the Federal Reserve that made Richmond a banking center, to the naval base at Norfolk and Newport News, and to the swelling federal bureaucracy that has made the northern Virginia suburbs across the river from Washington the wealthiest part of the Commonwealth.

Virginia has ridden these developments back into a place of national prominence. It was the nineteenth-largest state as recently as the 1940s, and fourteenth in 1980, but it has since jumped over Indiana and Massachusetts (two Yankee states), to twelfth. Its 20 percent growth rate since 1990 is fast if one considers Virginia the southern edge of the northeast corridor, slow if one considers it the northern edge of the rising South. Virginia often seems to think of itself both ways.

Nowhere has growth been faster than in the Washington, D.C., suburbs. Few areas in the country better demonstrate the phenomenon of suburban growth called the metropolitan doughnut than northern Virginia. If one takes Washington as the declining city center (and it has lost more than a tenth of its residents since 1980), one finds population growth that is surging the further one pushes into what was only recently countryside, across the Beltway and out Interstate 66 past the last D.C. metro stop. Development that a decade ago threatened to engulf the Bull Run battlefield has rolled on into Prince William, Spotsylvania, and Stafford Counties. To pick just two examples, the 13th house district, which stretches out to Middleburg and beyond in Loudoun County, has grown by 81 percent since 2000, and the 33rd district, in the lower part of Loudoun near Leesburg, has grown by 53 percent. Parts of West Virginia have even been absorbed into the D.C. metro area.

A similar phenomenon has occurred in the sprawling Tidewater area that includes Norfolk, Chesapeake, Newport News, and Virginia Beach. With cutbacks in shipbuilding in the early 1990s, Norfolk was for a time the third-fastest shrinking city in the country after Hartford and New Haven. The downtown bleeding has been staunched and its suburbs, which are filling with young,

white, often military families, are rapidly growing, helping to make the metro area the nation's thirty-third largest, with more people than Indianapolis.

Growth has shifted the balance of economic power to the north, as well. Virginia's wealthiest districts are now all clustered around Washington in the older suburbs of McLean, Chesterbrook, and Falls Church. In the 34th house district, which contains Great Falls, average household income is $193,000, making it the wealthiest district outside of old money New England and the tenth wealthiest overall. Virginia Beach is prosperous but more middle class, while the old Richmond aristocracy has lost its economic prominence. Poverty is greatest, and unemployment highest, in the western mountains, which is the area of the state that is losing population.

Almost three out of every four Virginians is white but the races are unevenly distributed geographically. The western counties on the fringes of Appalachia are almost entirely white; the eastern Tidewater much less so. Urban house districts in Norfolk and Newport News are heavily African American, as are those in Richmond. But the demographic composition of Virginia is becoming more complex, especially in the Washington suburbs. There are now sizable pockets of Hispanic residents in Arlington and Manassas, and Asian neighborhoods in Springfield.

Two fast-growing sections—one in the northern part of the state, around Washington, and the other in the southern part, around Tidewater—have accentuated a growing political tension, as well. Virginia has voted Republican in every presidential election since 1976 but by closer margins than most other southern states. If the Virginia Beach area tends to be conservative, the D.C. suburbs are increasingly liberal, as are suburbs around Philadelphia and some other northern cities. This has helped Democrats elect the last two governors (who are limited to a single four-year term) and win a U.S. Senate seat in 2006.

Republicans, on the other hand, have held the general assembly. In 1999 they won the state house for the first in more than a century and have added to their majority since then. Republicans won control of the state senate in the 1990s, too, which they have maintained and increased in this decade.

Though Americans like to think of their country as young (and parts of it are), one should keep in mind that the lower house of the Virginia General Assembly, known as the House of Delegates, is a direct descendant of the House of Burgesses, which was founded at Jamestown in 1619. Past members include George Washington, Patrick Henry, Richard Henry Lee, Thomas Jefferson, James Madison, and James Monroe, a list that can be matched by few other legislative bodies in the world.

VIRGINIA
State Senate Districts

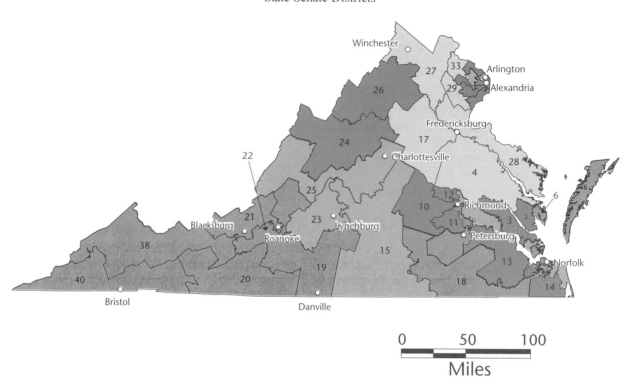

NORTHERN VIRGINIA

RICHMOND

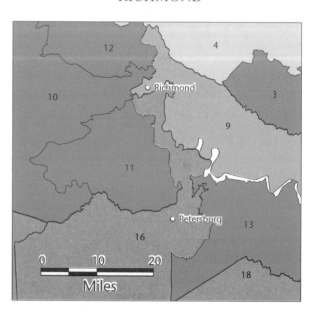

Population Growth ▨ -3% to 2%   ▨ 2% to 5%   ▨ 5% to 17%   ☐ 17% to 53%

NORFOLK

Population Growth ▨ -3% to 2% ▨ 2% to 5% ▨ 5% to 17% ▨ 17% to 53%

Virginia State Senate Districts—Election and Demographic Data

Senate Districts	General Election Results Party, Percent of Vote							Population			Avg. HH Income ($)	Pop 25+ Some College + (%)	Pop 25+ 4-Yr Degree + (%)	Below Poverty Line (%)	White (Non-Hisp) (%)	African American (%)	American Indians, Alaska Natives (%)	Asians, Hawaiians, Pacific Islanders (%)	Hispanic Origin (%)
Virginia	2000	2001	2002	2003	2004	2005	2006	2000	2006	% Change									
1				R, 95				175,692	180,390	3	60,538	42.9	19.9	10.0	67.6	22.1	0.3	4.0	4.5
2				D, 65				171,244	172,136	1	47,051	33.4	11.9	18.8	36.9	57.4	0.3	2.1	2.9
3				R, 66				177,958	197,276	11	69,263	41.9	21.2	9.8	75.0	17.3	0.3	2.7	3.4
4				R, 99				176,496	206,653	17	68,987	34.8	17.0	9.6	78.8	17.0	0.4	1.1	2.0
5				D, 98				175,044	177,272	1	46,666	32.0	14.7	22.5	35.6	58.1	0.2	2.9	2.8
6				R, 62				175,160	176,747	1	47,957	30.4	12.0	17.0	60.2	28.1	0.4	3.3	6.8
7				R, 59				174,714	180,627	3	65,162	45.2	24.7	7.6	67.1	18.4	0.3	8.0	4.8
8				R, 97				174,425	182,559	5	73,107	45.8	26.1	7.8	74.3	14.4	0.3	4.0	5.2
9				D, 99				180,606	185,597	3	48,520	35.2	17.8	18.6	37.7	57.8	0.5	1.7	2.1
10				R, 99				172,190	188,137	9	83,819	46.4	30.5	7.8	79.6	14.7	0.1	2.4	2.4
11				R, 97				172,469	193,021	12	69,646	38.9	20.2	6.2	71.0	20.7	0.2	2.8	4.5
12				R, 98				178,936	192,066	7	80,434	52.1	34.0	6.5	78.1	10.5	0.2	6.4	3.8
13				R, 76				177,006	197,596	12	59,611	35.4	14.5	12.9	68.7	26.7	0.2	1.6	2.1
14				R, 97				171,206	189,787	11	68,354	40.5	19.0	7.1	68.6	20.2	0.3	5.6	4.1
15				R, 100				180,174	185,040	3	46,718	26.3	11.0	20.9	64.5	33.0	0.1	0.5	1.6
16				D, 99				174,417	176,412	1	46,998	28.0	12.0	20.4	37.0	55.9	0.2	1.9	5.8
17				D, 59				177,483	218,740	23	63,215	31.7	14.6	11.4	77.6	15.6	0.2	1.3	4.3
18				D, 70				172,935	176,227	2	42,801	25.2	8.6	24.3	37.7	59.6	0.2	0.7	1.7
19				R, 100				180,122	180,503	0	47,515	27.6	10.3	19.5	73.1	24.3	0.1	0.5	1.7
20				D, 68				180,802	178,641	-1	43,780	26.3	9.6	20.8	82.3	12.6	0.1	0.5	3.9
21				D, 100				181,757	179,138	-1	47,179	36.3	19.2	20.1	78.0	15.3	0.1	3.3	2.0
22				R, 57				176,738	178,226	1	59,657	39.3	18.6	12.1	91.5	3.8	0.4	1.5	1.5
23				R, 64				180,288	186,970	4	53,040	33.8	15.6	15.4	79.9	16.8	0.2	1.2	1.1
24				R, 72				179,880	190,715	6	54,719	31.0	15.2	13.7	90.1	5.8	0.1	0.7	2.4
25				D, 98				180,301	186,613	4	61,392	40.8	25.9	15.3	80.7	12.1	0.1	3.4	2.6
26				R, 68				173,649	184,865	6	51,976	28.0	13.7	15.7	87.9	3.2	0.1	1.3	5.9
27				R, 58				177,501	215,261	21	79,091	38.1	20.4	9.4	87.0	5.7	0.1	1.1	4.8
28				R, 98				179,298	219,666	23	71,591	35.6	17.6	10.7	74.6	16.9	0.3	1.8	5.3
29				D, 55				174,473	235,219	35	87,545	37.4	21.7	5.0	60.1	14.6	0.3	4.6	19.7
30				D, 95				177,414	188,727	6	85,343	55.0	42.2	7.3	50.8	19.1	0.3	8.9	17.9
31				D, 69				177,620	184,648	4	96,653	58.7	47.5	7.1	57.7	6.6	0.2	13.0	18.6
32				D, 57				178,484	188,270	5	139,754	58.6	47.6	4.1	64.3	5.7	0.1	15.5	12.2
33				R, 97				177,800	270,297	52	110,434	49.3	33.7	2.7	70.1	7.0	0.1	10.7	10.5
34				R, 53				176,625	181,068	3	127,278	56.6	44.7	3.6	66.1	4.3	0.1	17.8	9.7
35				D, 82				176,977	186,721	6	81,093	53.0	38.0	6.5	46.9	13.8	0.2	19.6	18.6
36				D, 55				178,612	201,728	13	80,213	40.8	25.4	5.2	49.8	22.8	0.3	7.9	19.9
37				R, 53				174,296	183,923	6	106,520	53.3	39.9	2.7	64.0	6.4	0.2	18.7	9.3
38				D, 100				181,732	176,338	-3	40,361	26.6	9.2	24.0	95.6	2.8	0.1	0.4	0.7
39				R, 58				178,353	191,932	8	110,612	51.9	37.2	2.7	62.5	10.9	0.2	13.6	11.6
40				R, 100				177,717	177,790	0	42,608	28.4	11.1	22.8	96.0	2.1	0.1	0.4	0.8

Note: D=Democrat, R=Republican, R/D=Republican/Democrat (cross-filed), D/R=Democrat/Republican (cross-filed), I=Independent, C=Constitution, O=Other, GI=Green Independent, P=Progressive, P/D=Progressive/Democrat, P/D/R=Progressive/Democrat/Republican, HH=Households

VIRGINIA
State House Districts

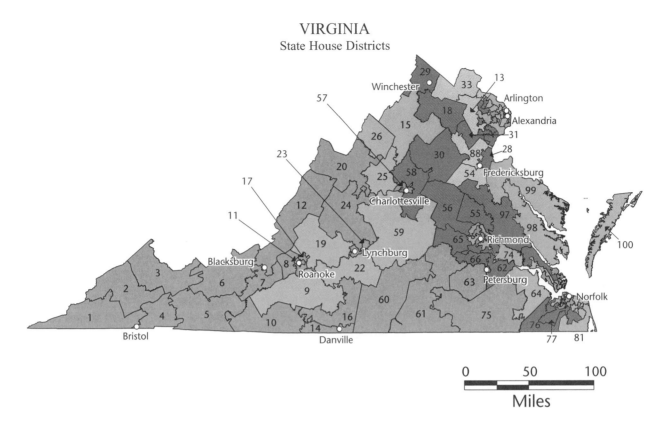

Winchester
29
33
13
Arlington
57
18
Alexandria
31
26
15
30
88
28
23
20
25
58
54
Fredericksburg
17
12
24
99
Charlottesville
56
55
97
11
19
59
65
98
Blacksburg
8
22
Richmond
100
3
7
Roanoke
66
74
2
6
9
62
1
4
5
10
16
60
63
Petersburg
64
14
61
75
Norfolk
Bristol
Danville
76
77
81

0   50   100
Miles

NORTHERN VIRGINIA

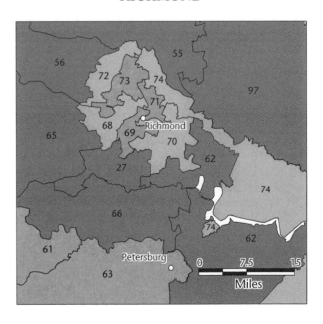

33
32
34
86
36
35
53
48
47
67
Arlington
49
18
13
37
39
38 46
Alexandria
40
41
50
43
45
42
44
51
50
31
52
88

0   7.5   15
Miles

RICHMOND

56
55
72
73
74
97
71
65
68
Richmond
69
70
27
62
66
74
61
62
63
Petersburg

0   7.5   15
Miles

Population Growth   ▢ -6% to 2%   ▢ 2% to 10%   ▢ 10% to 32%   ▢ 32% to 81%

NORFOLK

Population Growth   ▢ -6% to 2%   ▢ 2% to 10%   ▢ 10% to 32%   ▢ 32% to 81%

Virginia State House Districts—Election and Demographic Data

House Districts	General Election Results Party, Percent of Vote							Population			Avg. HH Income	2006 Pop 25+ Some College +	2006 Pop 25+ 4-Yr Degree +	2006 Below Poverty Line	2006 White (Non-Hisp)	2006 African American	2006 American Indians, Alaska Natives	2006 Asians, Hawaiians, Pacific Islanders	2006 Hispanic Origin
Virginia	2000	2001	2002	2003	2004	2005	2006	2000	2006	% Change	($)	(%)	(%)	(%)	(%)	(%)	(%)	(%)	(%)
1		R, 100		R, 100		R, 69		71,392	71,711	0	38,461	25.3	9.4	26.7	97.5	0.9	0.1	0.3	0.7
2		D, 100		D, 100		D, 64		70,189	68,889	-2	37,669	24.4	8.7	25.9	96.2	2.2	0.1	0.3	0.7
3		D, 100		D, 100		D, 100		70,042	66,368	-5	36,036	25.0	8.4	27.0	96.6	1.9	0.1	0.4	0.6
4		D, 100		D, 100		D, 99		70,722	70,795	0	46,354	32.8	13.6	19.8	95.4	2.6	0.1	0.5	0.9
5		R, 59		R, 55		R, 98		70,580	67,781	-4	42,747	25.5	8.5	21.2	93.1	3.2	0.1	0.3	2.4
6		D, 54		D, 50		R, 54		73,213	73,291	0	48,356	30.5	11.0	19.3	93.3	4.3	0.1	0.6	1.0
7		R, 52		R, 100		R, 62		65,538	63,206	-4	48,612	37.5	17.9	17.5	92.0	4.4	0.1	1.4	1.1
8		R, 70		R, 59		R, 98		70,408	71,045	1	66,123	42.5	21.4	8.7	91.7	4.1	0.1	1.9	1.4
9		R, 84		R, 59		R, 53		71,623	75,316	5	50,250	28.4	11.3	17.6	87.4	9.9	0.1	0.4	1.7
10		D, 53		D, 100		D, 63		73,141	71,692	-2	41,248	24.1	8.2	21.5	80.7	13.7	0.1	0.3	4.4
11		D, 100		D, 100		D, 99		71,514	68,964	-4	36,635	28.1	9.6	22.8	61.2	33.6	0.1	1.5	2.5
12		D, 78		D, 100		D, 79		76,218	75,625	-1	47,988	37.6	23.0	22.7	86.8	4.9	0.1	5.3	1.6
13		R, 63		R, 99		R, 55		68,939	124,778	81	103,890	43.3	28.1	4.4	74.0	8.4	0.2	4.5	11.7
14		R, 60		R, 100		R, 99		70,694	67,250	-5	45,845	28.1	10.5	21.8	59.8	36.9	0.1	0.7	2.5
15		R, 63		R, 63		R, 64		70,611	75,683	7	50,639	25.5	11.1	15.2	93.2	2.0	0.1	0.4	3.0
16		R, 65		R, 62		R, 99		71,260	69,865	-2	45,919	27.9	10.1	18.6	70.7	25.4	0.1	0.5	3.1
17		D, 100		R, 62		R, 99		70,022	69,829	0	63,288	42.8	21.5	10.7	91.6	3.9	0.1	2.0	1.6
18		R, 54		R, 99		R, 97		70,820	81,696	15	73,172	34.3	16.9	10.8	87.9	6.3	0.2	0.8	4.0
19		I, 100		I, 74		I, 100		72,506	76,558	6	60,026	34.6	15.5	12.8	91.4	6.5	0.1	0.6	0.8
20		R, 65		D, 99		R, 68		71,904	72,679	1	53,694	30.2	14.3	14.4	89.9	6.6	0.1	0.5	2.1
21		R, 97		R, 62		R, 96		72,691	75,666	4	58,911	41.5	20.6	8.1	58.9	22.9	0.3	11.0	5.7
22		R, 56		R, 100		R, 99		70,138	72,248	3	51,726	31.3	12.6	14.3	84.9	12.5	0.1	0.8	0.9
23		R, 98		D, 97		R, 97		69,973	71,180	2	49,252	33.9	17.3	19.3	66.6	29.0	0.2	1.7	1.4
24		R, 100		R, 69		R, 62		70,471	70,762	0	50,304	29.6	13.9	16.7	86.9	10.2	0.3	0.8	1.2
25		R, 99		R, 99		R, 98		70,824	76,903	9	54,788	31.9	15.8	12.9	90.2	5.1	0.1	0.7	2.9
26		R, 97		R, 54		R, 54		71,193	72,782	2	50,610	30.5	16.9	18.3	81.1	3.6	0.1	2.5	10.6
27		R, 98		R, 97		R, 96		71,749	80,214	12	68,112	39.5	20.3	4.4	69.7	21.4	0.3	3.2	4.6
28		R, 64		R, 96		R, 95		69,131	87,308	26	74,123	38.8	21.3	8.5	76.9	13.1	0.3	2.2	6.0
29		R, 78		R, 99		R, 98		70,301	80,721	15	59,493	31.9	15.3	11.5	86.3	5.1	0.1	1.3	5.7
30		R, 100		R, 86		R, 100		69,507	82,685	19	59,532	29.2	13.6	12.7	79.1	15.7	0.2	0.8	3.5
31		R, 56		R, 55		R, 96		72,431	87,853	21	81,781	36.3	18.7	4.4	56.5	22.5	0.3	5.3	15.6
32		R, 58		R, 52		D, 53		71,909	109,490	52	114,252	51.1	35.0	1.7	73.4	6.4	0.1	9.1	9.4
33		R, 98		R, 98		R, 92		71,889	109,957	53	97,992	45.3	27.7	6.1	82.4	6.4	0.2	2.9	6.5
34		R, 60		R, 98		R, 96		70,109	72,880	4	193,289	62.2	53.1	2.9	75.2	2.8	0.1	14.9	5.0
35		R, 59		D, 52		D, 60		71,067	74,280	5	139,107	60.1	49.2	3.4	70.6	3.9	0.1	15.9	7.6
36		D, 99		D, 98		D, 79		70,132	74,111	6	121,846	59.6	47.3	4.5	66.3	7.6	0.2	13.3	10.6
37		D, 52		D, 59		D, 53		72,048	72,016	0	102,897	52.7	39.4	4.4	61.0	5.5	0.2	19.2	12.4
38		D, 59		D, 99		D, 69		76,188	76,663	1	91,707	49.5	36.1	7.4	42.6	8.7	0.2	20.9	28.0
39		D, 54		D, 98		D, 63		71,656	74,403	4	92,286	51.7	37.1	5.2	51.2	5.5	0.2	25.6	17.1
40		R, 99		R, 98		R, 90		72,092	75,438	5	121,601	51.8	38.9	2.7	66.7	6.6	0.2	16.7	8.4
41		R, 84		R, 64		D, 59		70,549	71,025	1	118,912	54.7	41.8	2.6	64.4	5.1	0.1	19.1	9.7
42		R, 61		R, 99		R, 52		71,439	73,604	3	109,209	52.2	36.9	2.7	61.3	13.4	0.2	13.9	9.4
43		R, 51		D, 54		D, 64		72,661	77,262	6	92,932	54.0	39.2	3.1	59.1	13.5	0.2	14.2	11.4
44		D, 51		D, 56		D, 59		68,911	69,883	1	87,147	49.0	35.1	7.5	51.2	20.4	0.3	9.4	17.7
45		D, 97		D, 64		D, 68		72,258	73,836	2	105,128	65.2	53.9	5.6	69.8	14.3	0.2	4.8	8.3
46		D, 70		D, 94		D, 72		69,395	77,122	11	70,157	56.9	39.9	7.4	47.5	24.0	0.2	11.7	13.5
47		D, 66		D, 66		D, 97		70,601	73,390	4	89,542	61.4	49.4	6.8	62.3	6.9	0.2	12.1	14.2
48		D, 65		D, 61		D, 98		71,694	76,691	7	105,155	67.5	56.7	6.6	70.8	6.3	0.2	11.2	8.1
49		D, 69		D, 97		D, 98		69,481	75,894	9	65,741	41.4	29.0	9.6	30.4	20.8	0.4	12.0	35.9
50		R, 100		R, 100		R, 64		71,822	80,406	12	76,869	33.2	17.2	6.0	50.9	12.9	0.3	5.0	30.1

(continued)

Note: D=Democrat, R=Republican, R/D=Republican/Democrat (cross-filed), D/R=Democrat/Republican (cross-filed), I=Independent, C=Constitution, O=Other, GI=Green Independent, P=Progressive, P/D=Progressive/Democrat, P/D/R=Progressive/Democrat/Republican, HH=Households

Virginia State House Districts—Election and Demographic Data (cont.)

| House Districts | General Election Results Party, Percent of Vote | | | | | | | Population | | | Avg. HH Income | Pop 25+ | | Below Poverty Line | White (Non-Hisp) | African American | American Indians, Alaska Natives | Asians, Hawaiians, Pacific Islanders | Hispanic Origin |
| | | | | | | | | | | | | Some College + | 4-Yr Degree + | | | | | | 2006 |
Virginia	2000	2001	2002	2003	2004	2005	2006	2000	2006	% Change	($)	(%)	(%)	(%)	(%)	(%)	(%)	(%)	(%)
51		R, 64		R, 100		R, 54		68,461	77,480	13	83,458	40.9	24.7	3.8	53.5	19.7	0.2	6.5	20.5
52		R, 59		R, 56		R, 51		70,607	87,194	23	70,505	33.8	19.3	6.4	48.2	25.4	0.4	5.5	22.6
53		D, 60		D, 98		D, 97		70,714	74,328	5	107,899	57.0	45.2	4.3	59.7	4.1	0.2	21.1	13.9
54		R, 98		R, 98		R, 96		70,223	94,838	35	73,208	34.1	15.4	6.8	77.8	13.7	0.2	1.7	5.5
55		R, 100		R, 100		R, 99		70,837	82,201	16	78,184	40.5	22.1	6.9	86.1	10.2	0.2	1.3	1.5
56		R, 99		R, 58		R, 63		69,630	80,263	15	81,104	40.4	25.1	10.3	78.7	16.2	0.2	2.6	1.8
57		D, 98		D, 97		D, 75		69,364	69,251	0	60,235	48.0	35.1	17.3	71.6	17.3	0.1	6.6	3.3
58		R, 60		R, 99		R, 62		72,515	83,703	15	71,006	40.7	25.0	8.8	85.6	8.8	0.1	1.9	2.6
59		D, 37		D, 33		I, 99		72,154	76,834	6	52,071	27.2	13.1	18.0	69.0	27.7	0.1	0.6	2.0
60		R, 58		R, 67		R, 99		69,484	68,129	-2	43,342	24.7	9.9	23.8	60.8	36.9	0.1	0.5	1.5
61		R, 60		R, 100		R, 99		70,037	70,009	0	45,949	25.9	9.5	21.8	60.7	36.8	0.1	0.4	1.8
62		D, 98		R, 99		R, 97		72,731	80,042	10	60,999	32.7	13.7	11.5	66.8	25.3	0.3	2.1	4.4
63		D, 52		D, 99		D, 60		69,629	69,677	0	49,771	27.3	11.4	18.1	39.9	57.2	0.2	0.8	2.0
64		D, 61		D, 57		D, 54		70,524	77,124	9	63,485	39.1	20.4	13.3	72.4	23.1	0.2	1.9	1.8
65		R, 75		R, 75		R, 97		69,619	81,081	16	96,969	46.0	29.5	4.9	85.3	9.5	0.1	2.5	2.0
66		R, 98		R, 98		R, 97		70,064	78,691	12	75,020	39.4	20.8	7.4	80.4	12.0	0.2	3.1	3.4
67		R, 61		R, 98		D, 56		70,025	78,266	12	112,645	53.8	40.8	2.3	66.7	5.5	0.2	17.3	8.8
68		R, 41		R, 99		R, 50		70,291	71,942	2	86,248	54.2	38.0	6.7	80.3	12.4	0.2	3.0	3.0
69		D, 99		D, 99		D, 81		68,371	66,987	-2	44,467	33.4	16.5	19.3	31.7	59.9	0.2	2.4	7.1
70		D, 99		D, 99		D, 99		73,020	74,923	3	43,159	29.6	12.9	20.3	31.3	61.3	0.3	1.5	7.1
71		D, 76		D, 100		D, 99		68,393	67,883	-1	45,274	35.0	20.6	24.8	35.0	60.4	0.2	2.3	1.9
72		R, 99		R, 98		R, 97		71,155	77,129	8	83,193	55.0	36.7	5.3	80.0	8.3	0.2	7.4	3.1
73		R, 99		R, 98		R, 72		73,065	74,356	2	68,566	49.2	30.4	8.0	72.6	14.7	0.2	6.2	5.1
74		D, 61		D, 99		D, 75		69,571	72,603	4	49,585	35.0	16.5	15.4	36.7	58.6	0.8	1.4	2.3
75		D, 99		D, 71		D, 51		70,064	67,685	-3	43,989	24.2	9.9	24.4	41.5	56.6	0.1	0.5	1.7
76		R, 71		R, 99		R, 78		73,358	88,767	21	66,715	38.4	16.3	11.0	69.4	26.0	0.2	1.7	2.0
77		D, 99		D, 98		D, 99		71,005	80,056	13	46,035	28.6	10.1	20.9	38.0	58.4	0.2	1.3	1.9
78		R, 65		R, 98		R, 99		70,230	78,384	12	75,221	43.7	21.8	5.1	76.2	15.4	0.3	3.6	3.3
79		D, 68		D, 96		D, 97		70,432	73,948	5	56,381	36.6	15.8	13.7	57.2	36.1	0.3	2.7	2.8
80		D, 98		D, 97		D, 98		71,168	69,395	-2	46,215	31.9	13.2	21.3	38.6	57.6	0.3	1.3	1.7
81		R, 99		R, 70		R, 97		72,853	78,248	7	66,850	39.2	19.4	7.7	72.8	16.6	0.3	3.1	5.4
82		R, 99		R, 97		R, 71		71,559	73,731	3	88,548	54.9	36.2	7.8	82.8	8.6	0.2	2.8	4.1
83		R, 58		R, 97		R, 60		71,613	73,845	3	63,516	44.0	23.2	8.9	68.3	19.5	0.3	5.2	5.1
84		R, 98		R, 96		R, 55		70,756	74,762	6	61,171	41.6	20.5	6.9	63.8	20.3	0.3	7.9	6.1
85		R, 99		R, 73		R, 98		72,404	74,981	4	66,108	46.6	26.1	6.0	66.5	18.5	0.2	9.3	4.2
86		R, 62		R, 64		R, 92		71,847	84,164	17	95,150	45.4	31.3	3.8	52.5	8.4	0.2	17.8	20.1
87		R, 66		R, 97		D, 50		80,212	79,642	-1	44,956	29.6	9.7	15.2	59.2	27.1	0.5	4.6	6.7
88		R, 66		R, 71		R, 62		72,464	95,736	32	80,321	36.2	16.6	6.2	77.5	11.9	0.3	2.4	6.4
89		D, 98		D, 98		D, 77		71,386	69,387	-3	45,912	32.7	14.9	22.9	37.8	55.6	0.3	3.1	2.8
90		R, 53		D, 97		D, 99		73,290	73,595	0	43,882	27.5	10.1	22.6	37.6	55.5	0.2	3.0	3.4
91		R, 97		R, 95		R, 59		70,615	70,617	0	68,330	46.2	21.2	8.2	76.1	16.0	0.3	2.7	3.5
92		D, 68		D, 54		D, 78		71,241	69,541	-2	46,853	34.0	12.6	17.6	33.9	59.8	0.3	2.4	3.1
93		R, 97		R, 95		R, 95		69,158	72,538	5	55,682	38.5	16.7	11.4	56.5	31.8	0.3	4.2	5.8
94		R, 54		R, 93		R, 96		71,606	70,597	-1	59,271	39.8	16.9	10.8	63.8	25.2	0.3	3.9	5.0
95		D, 70		D, 65		D, 72		69,732	69,413	0	44,037	31.3	10.3	23.3	35.1	60.1	0.3	1.7	2.4
96		R, 46		R, 54		R, 92		72,540	84,283	16	74,096	47.4	26.7	8.0	76.0	15.3	0.2	3.7	3.5
97		R, 54		R, 99		R, 98		71,307	82,380	16	64,867	31.2	12.6	9.8	77.3	19.1	0.6	0.7	1.5
98		R, 75		R, 79		R, 99		70,849	75,206	6	57,350	34.2	13.8	13.4	79.3	17.1	0.3	0.8	1.7
99		D, 61		D, 65		R, 62		71,586	76,903	7	56,268	31.1	14.9	17.2	68.9	27.2	0.2	0.7	2.3
100		R, 100		D, 59		D, 99		65,185	67,108	3	45,214	27.2	11.4	21.5	56.2	33.1	0.3	1.7	8.4

Note: D=Democrat, R=Republican, R/D=Republican/Democrat (cross-filed), D/R=Democrat/Republican (cross-filed), I=Independent, C=Constitution, O=Other, GI=Green Independent, P=Progressive, P/D=Progressive/Democrat, P/D/R=Progressive/Democrat/Republican, HH=Households

WASHINGTON

Forty years ago, the corporation that best represented America to the world might have been Boeing. From its headquarters in Seattle and its assembly plant in nearby Everett, Boeing built the massive Saturn V rockets that took astronauts to the moon. Its sleek 747 jumbo jets epitomized both the wonder of travel and America's strength in what was then the cutting-edge industry, aerospace.

The most iconic American corporation today is also based near Seattle. To the pantheon of great inventors, like Thomas Edison at Menlo Park, New Jersey; Henry Ford in Dearborn, Michigan; and the Wright Brothers at Kitty Hawk, North Carolina; future generations will surely add Bill Gates and the birth of computer software in Redmond, Washington. More accurately, it should be Albuquerque, New Mexico, for that is where Micro-soft (it once had a hyphen) was founded in 1975 with three employees and $16,005 in revenues. But the company moved to Bellevue, Washington, in 1978 and up the road to Redmond in 1986, and will forever be associated with the Pacific Northwest.

To the list add yet another Seattle business—Starbucks—which, if not exactly iconic, is still one of the most ubiquitous American corporations today. Founded in 1971 by two school teachers and a writer, it became the perfect business for the postindustrial economy by making something simple, coffee, into a status symbol (the perfect place, also, from which to work on one's Microsoft-run computer). Starbucks now has more than 7,500 stores worldwide, gross sales of more than $7 billion and, proof that it has arrived as a major corporation, labor trouble and complaints from environmentalists.

The Sun Belt may be growing faster, but like San Francisco two generations ago, the Seattle area has become not only one of the hubs of the American economy but also the Place To Be. San Francisco, in fact, is an apt comparison. The Seattle-Tacoma metropolitan area has about the same population. Because both cities are hemmed in by water on two sides, they share exorbitant real estate prices. Both were built almost overnight on gold; Seattle burst into prominence in 1896 as the gateway to the Klondike. Both have seen radical politics, leading Postmaster General James Farley to joke in 1936 that "there are 47 states in the Union, and the Soviet of Washington."

The Seattle area has weathered rough times over the past several years. The dot-com bubble burst, though computers and the Internet continue to grow ever more widespread. Boeing, which was hard hit by the decline in air travel after the 2001 terrorist attacks and increased competition from Airbus, moved its corporate headquarters to Chicago and slashed jobs at its Washington plants. Nevertheless, Washington State has grown by more than 26 percent since 1990, the fastest rate of any state on the Pacific Coast.

The fastest-growing part of the state is actually the city of Vancouver, across the Columbia River from Portland, Oregon. Seattle's suburban growth is occurring far from the city center, on the San Juan Islands in the Strait of Georgia (which is closer to Victoria, British Columbia) and in Kittitas County, on the far side of the Cascades.

Fortunes have been made here recently, so Washington has some pockets of great wealth but none of deep poverty. The wealthiest state house district is the 41st, around Seattle's Mercer Island. (The 48th district, which includes the ritzy suburb of Medina on Lake Washington, where Bill Gates has built his 40,000 square foot mansion, is only the fourth-wealthiest district). The poorest district is located in Spokane, the self-proclaimed capital of the wheat-growing "Inland Empire," but it is the only one in the state in which average annual household income is less than $45,000.

Perhaps because it is a relatively new place, and because of its location on the Pacific Rim, Washington has been welcoming to racial and ethnic minorities. Only 3 percent of Washingtonians are African American, for example, yet Seattle has elected a black mayor, Norm Rice, and in 1986 the state rechristened King County, which includes Seattle, to honor Martin Luther King Jr., making it the only county in the country named for an African American. Only 5 percent of the state is of Asian ancestry, yet in 1996 the state elected the nation's first Chinese American governor.

Against the influence of large and powerful corporations, including the timber and paper companies, must be set Washington's strong environmentalism, an outgrowth of its historic liberalism. Those forces sometimes come into conflict, as in the labor unrest of the World War I era, the antiglobalization riots during the meeting of the World Trade Organization in 1999, or even the grunge craze, epitomized by the cool slacker in the lumberjack shirt.

Such diversity has made Washington politically unpredictable. It has elected Democratic governors, but the incumbent won in 2004 by 129 votes out of 2.7 million cast. It has flipped between Democratic and Republican U.S. senators, and though Democrats now dominate its congressional delegation, six of them lost their seats in the Republican landslide of 1994, including the Speaker of the House.

In the state house, Democrats who had gained seven seats in 1992, lost twenty-seven seats in 1994, then gained seven back again in 1996. The chamber was tied at the end of the decade, but Democrats then gained seats in four consecutive elections and now control the chamber by a two-to-one margin. Republicans, on the other hand, held the state senate in 1990, lost it in 1994, regained it in 1996, lost it in 1998, regained it in 2002, lost it again in 2004, and now trail Democrats there by fifteen seats, 32–17. It would be foolish to try to predict what will happen next.

WASHINGTON
State Legislative Districts

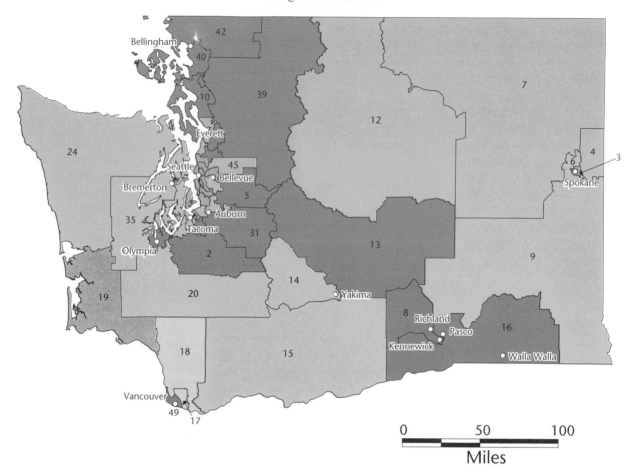

Population Growth   0% to 4%   4% to 10%   10% to 23%   23% to 25%

SEATTLE

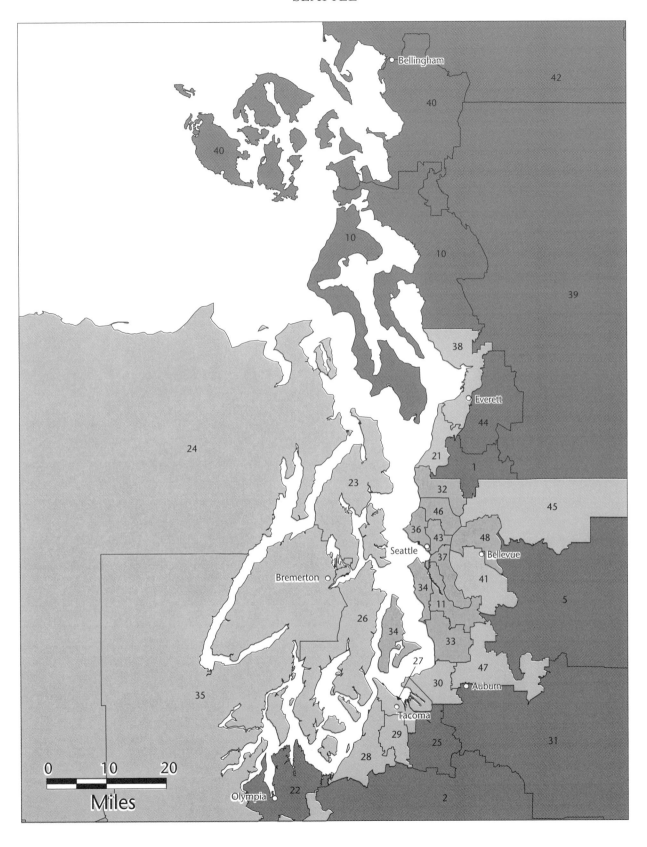

Population Growth   ▨ 0% to 4%   ▨ 4% to 10%   ▨ 10% to 23%   ▨ 23% to 25%

Washington State Legislative Districts—Election and Demographic Data

| Senate Districts | General Election Results Party, Percent of Vote | | | | | | | Population | | | Avg. HH Income | Pop 25+ | | 2006 Below Poverty Line | White (Non-Hisp) | African American | American Indians, Alaska Natives | Asians, Hawaiians, Pacific Islanders | Hispanic Origin |
| | | | | | | | | | | | | Some College + | 4-Yr Degree + | | | | | | |
Wash.	2000	2001	2002	2003	2004	2005	2006	2000	2006	% Change	($)	(%)	(%)	(%)	(%)	(%)	(%)	(%)	(%)
1	D, 55				D, 57			119,162	133,010	12	76,108	47.7	24.4	6.1	78.4	1.6	0.5	9.1	6.0
2	D, 57				D, 53			122,958	143,603	17	63,374	36.1	12.3	9.4	79.3	3.5	1.2	4.6	5.5
3	D, 100				D, 62			116,784	120,408	3	39,557	39.5	16.3	23.5	83.2	2.8	1.6	3.2	4.5
4	R, 62				R, 60			120,186	130,345	8	57,111	43.7	18.7	12.6	90.6	0.9	0.7	2.0	2.9
5	R, 70				R, 58			120,364	140,557	17	111,779	53.6	34.4	4.4	82.2	1.7	0.4	8.1	3.8
6			R, 51		R, 51		D, 55	121,956	130,040	7	63,823	49.9	27.1	11.2	89.6	1.2	0.7	2.5	2.9
7			R, 100				R, 68	119,902	126,888	6	46,585	34.6	11.9	20.0	84.5	1.0	3.9	1.1	4.6
8			R, 100		R, 71		R, 100	119,942	138,151	15	64,659	40.8	19.3	11.5	72.5	1.1	0.5	3.2	14.7
9	R, 84				R, 66			121,947	129,518	6	50,057	38.9	20.1	20.3	73.0	1.1	0.6	3.5	13.7
10	D, 51				D, 50			119,503	136,262	14	66,218	45.3	18.4	10.0	83.6	1.7	1.0	4.2	4.9
11	D, 100				D, 65			117,113	117,570	0	59,545	42.2	21.5	11.2	48.2	9.6	0.7	22.7	13.6
12	R, 100				R, 100			120,999	128,742	6	54,001	34.4	14.0	16.9	65.8	0.4	1.8	0.9	20.2
13			R, 100				R, 67	120,708	133,661	11	52,021	31.4	12.5	19.2	60.7	0.9	0.6	1.6	24.9
14	R, 71				R, 65			119,483	125,755	5	52,367	32.5	11.9	18.6	52.0	1.5	1.2	1.5	30.1
15			R, 100				R, 62	121,143	129,291	7	49,637	25.9	9.1	20.3	33.9	0.5	4.8	1.2	43.6
16	R, 52				R, 67			121,717	140,215	15	54,569	32.6	12.9	17.1	53.3	1.9	0.6	1.7	29.1
17	R, 53				R, 56			121,049	149,980	24	66,426	41.7	20.4	7.3	81.3	1.9	0.6	6.6	5.3
18	R, 59				R, 54			119,707	149,178	25	72,537	40.8	19.1	8.6	89.5	0.6	0.5	2.0	3.9
19	D, 66				D, 100			120,354	124,654	4	49,092	34.2	10.5	18.2	83.9	0.6	1.4	2.3	6.7
20	R, 62				R, 65			120,650	131,499	9	57,398	36.3	12.5	14.2	84.2	1.3	0.9	2.3	6.4
21			D, 62				D, 100	120,622	130,203	8	69,474	47.2	22.8	9.1	71.1	2.6	0.7	12.9	7.8
22	D, 78				D, 100			119,936	134,608	12	61,966	48.3	25.3	11.8	78.4	2.8	0.8	7.5	5.5
23	D, 56				D, 58			119,918	127,852	7	71,221	48.2	22.7	8.7	79.6	2.4	1.2	7.1	4.4
24	D, 82				D, 100			119,442	130,790	10	50,704	42.0	16.4	16.2	86.7	0.7	3.2	1.7	3.9
25	D, 49				D, 54			118,558	133,592	13	64,678	39.2	15.8	9.0	78.5	3.3	0.9	5.1	6.4
26			R, 50				D, 60	119,289	129,690	9	68,500	43.3	18.8	10.3	83.2	2.5	0.8	3.8	4.6
27	D, 100				D, 70			121,956	130,610	7	58,294	41.9	19.6	16.1	63.7	10.9	1.5	9.6	8.0
28	R, 68				R, 52			121,255	127,203	5	64,473	45.0	21.3	11.6	64.8	11.4	0.7	8.5	8.5
29			D, 100				D, 100	116,472	124,419	7	46,305	32.6	10.8	17.2	54.4	13.3	1.1	12.6	10.9
30			D, 54				D, 60	118,974	124,128	4	68,228	45.1	22.7	9.0	64.9	6.5	0.6	13.9	8.3
31			R, 52				R, 53	121,538	134,647	11	67,974	38.9	16.3	9.2	84.1	1.4	1.4	3.2	5.4
32			D, 62				D, 68	120,058	121,495	1	80,747	55.2	33.8	7.2	76.1	2.4	0.5	12.1	4.5
33			D, 63				D, 62	118,915	123,448	4	61,255	44.5	22.4	11.4	60.7	7.8	0.7	12.5	11.9
34	D, 73		D, 100				D, 80	120,031	121,196	1	74,902	52.8	31.8	10.6	65.3	5.6	0.8	13.2	9.2
35			D, 78				D, 72	121,741	133,066	9	58,418	38.8	13.8	13.3	82.6	2.0	1.8	3.2	5.2
36			D, 100				D, 100	120,851	123,027	2	77,596	64.6	45.8	8.5	79.0	3.0	0.6	7.7	5.1
37			D, 100				D, 87	119,010	122,832	3	66,005	45.2	27.0	18.1	33.6	24.0	0.7	29.3	9.1
38			D, 65		D, 65		D, 100	122,419	132,411	8	57,887	39.0	14.3	12.4	74.2	2.7	2.1	6.9	8.9
39	R, 55				R, 54			120,728	135,122	12	67,901	37.4	13.0	10.5	85.7	0.8	1.0	2.1	6.1
40	D, 61				D, 62			118,770	131,974	11	64,196	45.3	22.3	14.1	77.5	0.6	0.7	3.1	10.9
41	R, 100				D, 51			121,032	129,750	7	113,400	60.3	42.8	5.4	72.6	2.3	0.3	16.8	4.4
42			R, 49				R, 53	121,442	137,012	13	55,599	38.3	16.8	14.7	81.0	0.7	2.4	3.4	7.2
43			D, 79				D, 90	122,460	125,049	2	69,162	62.0	46.8	14.9	72.7	5.2	0.6	11.4	5.5
44			R, 53				D, 52	120,543	134,641	12	81,363	44.7	20.9	5.6	82.8	1.2	0.5	6.5	5.0
45			R, 100				D, 53	119,288	128,800	8	110,876	55.1	36.0	4.6	79.0	1.8	0.4	9.0	5.5
46			D, 100				D, 84	119,027	119,178	0	74,541	60.5	43.2	10.1	70.4	4.0	0.6	14.1	5.9
47			R, 56				D, 52	122,106	129,830	6	74,630	44.9	23.5	8.2	72.1	4.5	0.6	11.2	6.2
48			R, 78				D, 53	122,019	123,811	1	100,011	60.7	42.7	6.0	69.6	2.3	0.3	16.2	7.4
49	R, 53				D, 51			120,160	136,029	13	55,318	40.4	19.5	14.6	77.2	2.7	0.7	3.9	9.2

Note: D=Democrat, R=Republican, R/D=Republican/Democrat (cross-filed), D/R=Democrat/Republican (cross-filed), I=Independent, C=Constitution, O=Other, GI=Green Independent,
P=Progressive, P/D=Progressive/Democrat, P/D/R=Progressive/Democrat/Republican, HH=Households

Washington State Legislative Districts—Election and Demographic Data

House Districts	General Election Results Party, Percent of Vote							Population			Avg. HH Income	Pop 25+		Below Poverty Line	White (Non-Hisp)	African American	American Indians, Alaska Natives	Asians, Hawaiians, Pacific Islanders	Hispanic Origin
												Some College +	4-Yr Degree +						
Wash.	2000	2001	2002	2003	2004	2005	2006	2000	2006	% Change	($)	(%)	(%)	(%)	(%)	(%)	(%)	(%)	(%)
1	D, 62		D, 50		D, 54		D, 100	119,162	133,010	12	76,108	47.7	24.4	6.1	78.4	1.6	0.5	9.1	6.0
1	D, 57		D, 50		D, 51		D, 62	119,162	133,010	12	76,108	47.7	24.4	6.1	78.4	1.6	0.5	9.1	6.0
2	R, 56		R, 57		R, 52		R, 57	122,958	143,603	17	63,374	36.1	12.3	9.4	79.3	3.5	1.2	4.6	5.5
2	R, 57		R, 100		R, 57		R, 60	122,958	143,603	17	63,374	36.1	12.3	9.4	79.3	3.5	1.2	4.6	5.5
3	D, 68		D, 57		D, 62		D, 67	116,784	120,408	3	39,557	39.5	16.3	23.5	83.2	2.8	1.6	3.2	4.5
3	D, 69		D, 67		D, 59		D, 100	116,784	120,408	3	39,557	39.5	16.3	23.5	83.2	2.8	1.6	3.2	4.5
4	R, 63		R, 100		R, 62		R, 100	120,186	130,345	8	57,111	43.7	18.7	12.6	90.6	0.9	0.7	2.0	2.9
4	R, 60		R, 100		R, 66		R, 65	120,186	130,345	8	57,111	43.7	18.7	12.6	90.6	0.9	0.7	2.0	2.9
5	R, 54		R, 64		R, 52		R, 100	120,364	140,557	17	111,779	53.6	34.4	4.4	82.2	1.7	0.4	8.1	3.8
5	R, 62		R, 57		R, 54		R, 100	120,364	140,557	17	111,779	53.6	34.4	4.4	82.2	1.7	0.4	8.1	3.8
6	R, 56		R, 60		R, 52		D, 50	121,956	130,040	7	63,823	49.9	27.1	11.2	89.6	1.2	0.7	2.5	2.9
6	R, 49		R, 56		R, 61		R, 61	121,956	130,040	7	63,823	49.9	27.1	11.2	89.6	1.2	0.7	2.5	2.9
7	R, 68		R, 68		R, 64		R, 63	119,902	126,888	6	46,585	34.6	11.9	20.0	84.5	1.0	3.9	1.1	4.6
7	R, 70		R, 74		R, 65		R, 100	119,902	126,888	6	46,585	34.6	11.9	20.0	84.5	1.0	3.9	1.1	4.6
8	R, 100		R, 100		R, 73		R, 100	119,942	138,151	15	64,659	40.8	19.3	11.5	72.5	1.1	0.5	3.2	14.7
8	R, 66		R, 100		R, 70		R, 100	119,942	138,151	15	64,659	40.8	19.3	11.5	72.5	1.1	0.5	3.2	14.7
9	R, 65		R, 100		R, 67		R, 61	121,947	129,518	6	50,057	38.9	20.1	20.3	73.0	1.1	0.6	3.5	13.7
9	R, 80		R, 82		R, 62		R, 100	121,947	129,518	6	50,057	38.9	20.1	20.3	73.0	1.1	0.6	3.5	13.7
10	R, 51		R, 100		R, 50		R, 100	119,503	136,262	14	66,218	45.3	18.4	10.0	83.6	1.7	1.0	4.2	4.9
10	R, 58		R, 52		R, 58		R, 52	119,503	136,262	14	66,218	45.3	18.4	10.0	83.6	1.7	1.0	4.2	4.9
11	D, 76		D, 60		D, 68		D, 100	117,113	117,570	0	59,545	42.2	21.5	11.2	48.2	9.6	0.7	22.7	13.6
11	D, 76		D, 66		D, 66		D, 72	117,113	117,570	0	59,545	42.2	21.5	11.2	48.2	9.6	0.7	22.7	13.6
12	R, 100		R, 62		R, 66		R, 100	120,999	128,742	6	54,001	34.4	14.0	16.9	65.8	0.4	1.8	0.9	20.2
12	R, 69		R, 100		R, 67		R, 100	120,999	128,742	6	54,001	34.4	14.0	16.9	65.8	0.4	1.8	0.9	20.2
13	R, 73		R, 100		R, 67		R, 100	120,708	133,661	11	52,021	31.4	12.5	19.2	60.7	0.9	0.6	1.6	24.9
13	R, 70		R, 100		R, 67		R, 100	120,708	133,661	11	52,021	31.4	12.5	19.2	60.7	0.9	0.6	1.6	24.9
14	R, 67		R, 100		R, 65		R, 66	119,483	125,755	5	52,367	32.5	11.9	18.6	52.0	1.5	1.2	1.5	30.1
14	R, 73		R, 71		R, 67		R, 60	119,483	125,755	5	52,367	32.5	11.9	18.6	52.0	1.5	1.2	1.5	30.1
15	R, 65		R, 71		R, 100		R, 62	121,143	129,291	7	49,637	25.9	9.1	20.3	33.9	0.5	4.8	1.2	43.6
15	R, 64		R, 73		R, 68		R, 64	121,143	129,291	7	49,637	25.9	9.1	20.3	33.9	0.5	4.8	1.2	43.6
16	R, 70		R, 68		R, 64		R, 66	121,717	140,215	15	54,569	32.6	12.9	17.1	53.3	1.9	0.6	1.7	29.1
16	D, 76		D, 100		D, 58		D, 60	121,717	140,215	15	54,569	32.6	12.9	17.1	53.3	1.9	0.6	1.7	29.1
17	R, 53		R, 100		R, 55		R, 50	121,049	149,980	24	66,426	41.7	20.4	7.3	81.3	1.9	0.6	6.6	5.3
17	R, 55		D, 51		D, 53		D, 58	121,049	149,980	24	66,426	41.7	20.4	7.3	81.3	1.9	0.6	6.6	5.3
18	R, 61		R, 63		R, 57		R, 59	119,707	149,178	25	72,537	40.8	19.1	8.6	89.5	0.6	0.5	2.0	3.9
18	R, 64		R, 53		R, 60		R, 57	119,707	149,178	25	72,537	40.8	19.1	8.6	89.5	0.6	0.5	2.0	3.9
19	D, 64		D, 67		D, 100		D, 64	120,354	124,654	4	49,092	34.2	10.5	18.2	83.9	0.6	1.4	2.3	6.7
19	D, 68		D, 66		D, 100		D, 68	120,354	124,654	4	49,092	34.2	10.5	18.2	83.9	0.6	1.4	2.3	6.7
20	R, 80		R, 100		R, 62		R, 58	120,650	131,499	9	57,398	36.3	12.5	14.2	84.2	1.3	0.9	2.3	6.4
20	R, 81		R, 100		R, 100		R, 100	120,650	131,499	9	57,398	36.3	12.5	14.2	84.2	1.3	0.9	2.3	6.4
21	D, 59		D, 61		D, 65		D, 100	120,622	130,203	8	69,474	47.2	22.8	9.1	71.1	2.6	0.7	12.9	7.8
21	R, 52		D, 60		D, 66		D, 100	120,622	130,203	8	69,474	47.2	22.8	9.1	71.1	2.6	0.7	12.9	7.8
22	D, 64		D, 64		D, 60		D, 100	119,936	134,608	12	61,966	48.3	25.3	11.8	78.4	2.8	0.8	7.5	5.5
22	D, 68		D, 67		D, 100		D, 73	119,936	134,608	12	61,966	48.3	25.3	11.8	78.4	2.8	0.8	7.5	5.5
23	D, 55		D, 60		D, 56		D, 64	119,918	127,852	7	71,221	48.2	22.7	8.7	79.6	2.4	1.2	7.1	4.4
23	R, 49		R, 52		R, 57		D, 54	119,918	127,852	7	71,221	48.2	22.7	8.7	79.6	2.4	1.2	7.1	4.4
24	R, 61		R, 60		R, 51		D, 53	119,442	130,790	10	50,704	42.0	16.4	16.2	86.7	0.7	3.2	1.7	3.9
24	D, 66		D, 100		D, 100		D, 100	119,442	130,790	10	50,704	42.0	16.4	16.2	86.7	0.7	3.2	1.7	3.9
25	R, 54		D, 60		R, 56		R, 59	118,558	133,592	13	64,678	39.2	15.8	9.0	78.5	3.3	0.9	5.1	6.4
25	R, 51		D, 51		D, 54		D, 60	118,558	133,592	13	64,678	39.2	15.8	9.0	78.5	3.3	0.9	5.1	6.4

(continued)

Note: D=Democrat, R=Republican, R/D=Republican/Democrat (cross-filed), D/R=Democrat/Republican (cross-filed), I=Independent, C=Constitution, O=Other, GI=Green Independent, P=Progressive, P/D=Progressive/Democrat, P/D/R=Progressive/Democrat/Republican, HH=Households

Washington State Legislative Districts—Election and Demographic Data (cont.)

House Districts	General Election Results Party, Percent of Vote							Population			Avg. HH Income	Pop 25+ Some College +	Pop 25+ 4-Yr Degree +	Below Poverty Line	2006 White (Non-Hisp)	African American	American Indians, Alaska Natives	Asians, Hawaiians, Pacific Islanders	Hispanic Origin
Wash.	2000	2001	2002	2003	2004	2005	2006	2000	2006	% Change	($)	(%)	(%)	(%)	(%)	(%)	(%)	(%)	(%)
26	D, 54		D, 52		D, 49		D, 57	119,289	129,690	9	68,500	43.3	18.8	10.3	83.2	2.5	0.8	3.8	4.6
26	D, 51		R, 51		D, 50		D, 55	119,289	129,690	9	68,500	43.3	18.8	10.3	83.2	2.5	0.8	3.8	4.6
27	D, 100		D, 100		D, 100		D, 71	121,956	130,610	7	58,294	41.9	19.6	16.1	63.7	10.9	1.5	9.6	8.0
27	D, 67		D, 69		D, 70		D, 71	121,956	130,610	7	58,294	41.9	19.6	16.1	63.7	10.9	1.5	9.6	8.0
28	R, 100		R, 56		R, 54		D, 52	121,255	127,203	5	64,473	45.0	21.3	11.6	64.8	11.4	0.7	8.5	8.5
28	R, 52		R, 55		D, 50		D, 55	121,255	127,203	5	64,473	45.0	21.3	11.6	64.8	11.4	0.7	8.5	8.5
29	D, 100		D, 100		D, 100		D, 100	116,472	124,419	7	46,305	32.6	10.8	17.2	54.4	13.3	1.1	12.6	10.9
29	D, 69		D, 100		D, 100		D, 100	116,472	124,419	7	46,305	32.6	10.8	17.2	54.4	13.3	1.1	12.6	10.9
30	D, 58		D, 56		D, 56		D, 66	118,974	124,128	4	68,228	45.1	22.7	9.0	64.9	6.5	0.6	13.9	8.3
30	R, 61		R, 51		R, 52		R, 58	118,974	124,128	4	68,228	45.1	22.7	9.0	64.9	6.5	0.6	13.9	8.3
31	R, 50		R, 54		R, 100		R, 54	121,538	134,647	11	67,974	38.9	16.3	9.2	84.1	1.4	1.4	3.2	5.4
31	D, 55		R, 100		R, 100		D, 53	121,538	134,647	11	67,974	38.9	16.3	9.2	84.1	1.4	1.4	3.2	5.4
32	D, 100		D, 58		D, 100		D, 72	120,058	121,495	1	80,747	55.2	33.8	7.2	76.1	2.4	0.5	12.1	4.5
32	D, 83		D, 64		D, 63		D, 69	120,058	121,495	1	80,747	55.2	33.8	7.2	76.1	2.4	0.5	12.1	4.5
33	D, 65		D, 63		D, 65		D, 67	118,915	123,448	4	61,255	44.5	22.4	11.4	60.7	7.8	0.7	12.5	11.9
33	D, 64		D, 63		D, 100		D, 100	118,915	123,448	4	61,255	44.5	22.4	11.4	60.7	7.8	0.7	12.5	11.9
34	D, 81		D, 100		D, 75		D, 78	120,031	121,196	1	74,902	52.8	31.8	10.6	65.3	5.6	0.8	13.2	9.2
34	D, 75		D, 67		D, 74		D, 80	120,031	121,196	1	74,902	52.8	31.8	10.6	65.3	5.6	0.8	13.2	9.2
35	D, 59		D, 59		D, 100		D, 61	121,741	133,066	9	58,418	38.8	13.8	13.3	82.6	2.0	1.8	3.2	5.2
35	D, 58		D, 57		D, 59		D, 60	121,741	133,066	9	58,418	38.8	13.8	13.3	82.6	2.0	1.8	3.2	5.2
36	D, 77		D, 78		D, 79		D, 100	120,851	123,027	2	77,596	64.6	45.8	8.5	79.0	3.0	0.6	7.7	5.1
36	D, 78		D, 80		D, 90		D, 100	120,851	123,027	2	77,596	64.6	45.8	8.5	79.0	3.0	0.6	7.7	5.1
37	D, 88		D, 87		D, 88		D, 100	119,010	122,832	3	66,005	45.2	27.0	18.1	33.6	24.0	0.7	29.3	9.1
37	D, 100		D, 83		D, 86		D, 90	119,010	122,832	3	66,005	45.2	27.0	18.1	33.6	24.0	0.7	29.3	9.1
38	D, 62		D, 51		D, 54		D, 55	122,419	132,411	8	57,887	39.0	14.3	12.4	74.2	2.7	2.1	6.9	8.9
38	D, 71		D, 59		D, 58		D, 100	122,419	132,411	8	57,887	39.0	14.3	12.4	74.2	2.7	2.1	6.9	8.9
39	D, 51		R, 55		R, 56		R, 54	120,728	135,122	12	67,901	37.4	13.0	10.5	85.7	0.8	1.0	2.1	6.1
39	R, 48		R, 59		R, 60		R, 100	120,728	135,122	12	67,901	37.4	13.0	10.5	85.7	0.8	1.0	2.1	6.1
40	D, 78		D, 60		D, 100		D, 77	118,770	131,974	11	64,196	45.3	22.3	14.1	77.5	0.6	0.7	3.1	10.9
40	D, 58		D, 62		D, 100		D, 100	118,770	131,974	11	64,196	45.3	22.3	14.1	77.5	0.6	0.7	3.1	10.9
41	R, 100		R, 100		R, 55		R, 53	121,032	129,750	7	113,400	60.3	42.8	5.4	72.6	2.3	0.3	16.8	4.4
41	R, 82		D, 53		D, 56		D, 65	121,032	129,750	7	113,400	60.3	42.8	5.4	72.6	2.3	0.3	16.8	4.4
42	R, 57		R, 58		R, 58		R, 55	121,442	137,012	13	55,599	38.3	16.8	14.7	81.0	0.7	2.4	3.4	7.2
42	D, 49		D, 56		D, 58		D, 67	121,442	137,012	13	55,599	38.3	16.8	14.7	81.0	0.7	2.4	3.4	7.2
43	D, 100		D, 100		D, 87		D, 82	122,460	125,049	2	69,162	62.0	46.8	14.9	72.7	5.2	0.6	11.4	5.5
43	D, 100		D, 100		D, 85		D, 91	122,460	125,049	2	69,162	62.0	46.8	14.9	72.7	5.2	0.6	11.4	5.5
44	R, 55		D, 52		D, 54		D, 56	120,543	134,641	12	81,363	44.7	20.9	5.6	82.8	1.2	0.5	6.5	5.0
44	D, 54		D, 52		D, 59		D, 59	120,543	134,641	12	81,363	44.7	20.9	5.6	82.8	1.2	0.5	6.5	5.0
45	R, 69		R, 52		R, 59		D, 54	119,288	128,800	8	110,876	55.1	36.0	4.6	79.0	1.8	0.4	9.0	5.5
45	D, 54		D, 53		D, 51		D, 59	119,288	128,800	8	110,876	55.1	36.0	4.6	79.0	1.8	0.4	9.0	5.5
46	D, 86		D, 100		D, 72		D, 84	119,027	119,178	0	74,541	60.5	43.2	10.1	70.4	4.0	0.6	14.1	5.9
46	D, 79		D, 100		D, 88		D, 83	119,027	119,178	0	74,541	60.5	43.2	10.1	70.4	4.0	0.6	14.1	5.9
47	D, 50		D, 52		D, 52		D, 60	122,106	129,830	6	74,630	44.9	23.5	8.2	72.1	4.5	0.6	11.2	6.2
47	R, 50		R, 50		D, 52		D, 59	122,106	129,830	6	74,630	44.9	23.5	8.2	72.1	4.5	0.6	11.2	6.2
48	R, 59		D, 53		D, 57		D, 67	122,019	123,811	1	100,011	60.7	42.7	6.0	69.6	2.3	0.3	16.2	7.4
48	R, 57		R, 53		R, 52		D, 58	122,019	123,811	1	100,011	60.7	42.7	6.0	69.6	2.3	0.3	16.2	7.4
49	D, 55		D, 61		D, 62		D, 65	120,160	136,029	13	55,318	40.4	19.5	14.6	77.2	2.7	0.7	3.9	9.2
49	D, 60		D, 53		D, 60		D, 61	120,160	136,029	13	55,318	40.4	19.5	14.6	77.2	2.7	0.7	3.9	9.2

Note: D=Democrat, R=Republican, R/D=Republican/Democrat (cross-filed), D/R=Democrat/Republican (cross-filed), I=Independent, C=Constitution, O=Other, GI=Green Independent, P=Progressive, P/D=Progressive/Democrat, P/D/R=Progressive/Democrat/Republican, HH=Households

WEST VIRGINIA

Born in war, the scene of crushing poverty and brutal labor disputes, West Virginia has witnessed its share of trouble and lawlessness. It has been called, unfairly, the "Afghanistan of America," a place of fierce tribal loyalties and impenetrable communities hidden amid the mountains. In short, a state as often wild as it is wonderful.

Communication here has always been frustrated by topography (the mountains) and geography (the state's unusual shape). It has two panhandles and no direct, in-state route between Wheeling in the north and Harper's Ferry to the east. Although it never enjoyed the wealth its labor created, West Virginia took on some of the dirtiest, most hazardous work in industrial America—mining coal, forging steel, and developing a petrochemical industry along the Kanawha River that for a time produced almost all the nation's nylon and antifreeze.

"The State is a huge layer cake," wrote James M. Cain in *The Nation* in 1923, "hacked into grotesque slices by the elements; the slices are the mountains, the layers are rock, and the filling is coal." Yet coal did not become big here until the 1880s, when industrialization demanded it and the railroads were finally able to reach it. By the 1930s, after decades of violent struggle, the coal fields became the domain of the United Mine Workers Union and its flamboyant, beetle-browed leader, John L. Lewis. "To mine coal you had to mind John L.," John Dos Passos observed rather sourly in his novel, *Midcentury.*

No state fared worse during the 1980s, when declining oil prices hurt the chemical industry and the Clean Air Act made the state's bituminous coal uneconomical to mine. West Virginia lost 8 percent of its population during the 1980s, a cataclysm. It has grown by barely 1 percent since 1990, the slowest rate in the country except for North Dakota, which is losing people. The census bureau projects that it will lose 5 percent of its population by 2030, the only state that is predicted to shrink.

West Virginia's capital and largest city, Charleston, has only 51,000 people and is losing them rapidly—more than 4 percent since 2000. The suburban part of the state is growing rapidly but they are not the suburbs of Charleston, but of Washington, D.C. Antisprawl efforts in places such as Loudon County, Virginia, have simply pushed the sprawl further out, into Jefferson, Berkeley, and Frederick County, West Virginia, all of which have grown by more than 20 percent in the last seven years. Some residents commute all the way into Washington but many also work in the Virginia and Maryland suburbs.

Rural areas that are still dependent on extractive industry are faring poorly. The districts losing population fastest are still in coal country around the Kentucky and Virginia borders. The 23rd district, which includes McDowell County, has lost 27 percent of its population since 1990, double the rate anywhere else in the state, and is the poorest state house district in the country, with average household income less than $26,000 a year.

West Virginia is, by statistical measures, the county's least-educated and second-poorest state (annual household income is about $500 ahead of Mississippi, which ranks last). Unemployment, though, is currently about at the national average. Coal production is up, but it is now largely mechanized and a much less labor-intensive (and thankfully, less dangerous) job than it once was. Only 4 percent of West Virginia workers mine coal, down from a peak of 22 percent in 1950. Its lumber and poultry processing industries are doing well, and its long-serving U.S. Senator Robert Byrd has made good on his pledge to make himself "West Virginia's billion dollar industry" by forcing numerous federal agencies to move offices there. But because the state has attracted so few new jobs, most of its young people continue to move away. More than one out of every five people in West Virginia is age sixty-five or older and its population has the highest median age.

Statistically, West Virginia is one of the least racially diverse states in the Union; all but eight of its fifty-eight state house districts are at least 90 percent white. The 36th house district, in Webster County in the middle of the state, is 98.6 percent white, the second-highest percentage of any district in the country. The only part of the state that has any groups of African Americans is in downtown Charleston.

For a long time, West Virginia was one of the least diverse states politically, as well, but that may be changing. It voted twice for George W. Bush, the first time it backed a Republican since 1928. Democrats, however, control the legislature and have done so without interruption since 1930. Three-quarters of the members of the state house are Democrats, and they control the senate by a margin of 23–11. It was 33–1 as recently as 1990.

Members of West Virginia's House of Delegates (the name reflects the state's origins as a part of Virginia) are elected by a complicated system. The state is divided into fifty-eight legislative districts. Thirty-five of them are single-member districts but the remaining twenty-three are multimember districts that elect anywhere from two to seven delegates.

WEST VIRGINIA
State Senate Districts

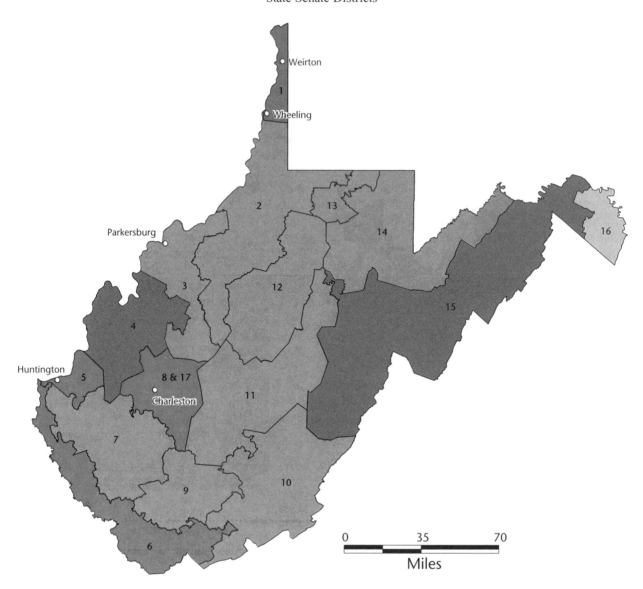

Population Growth   ■ -6% to -2%   ■ -2% to 3%   ■ 3% to 24%   ☐ 24% to 25%

West Virginia State Senate Districts—Election and Demographic Data

Senate Districts	General Election Results Party, Percent of Vote							Population			Avg. HH Income	Pop 25+		Below Poverty Line	2006 White (Non-Hisp)	African American	American Indians, Alaska Natives	Asians, Hawaiians, Pacific Islanders	Hispanic Origin
												Some College +	4-Yr Degree +						
W. Virginia	2000	2001	2002	2003	2004	2005	2006	2000	2006	% Change	($)	(%)	(%)	(%)	(%)	(%)	(%)	(%)	(%)
1	R, 54		D, 100		R, 53		D, 70	101,326	96,006	-5	47,059	31.4	13.6	18.9	95.4	2.4	0.0	0.4	0.7
2	D, 70		D, 100		D, 67		D, 65	106,664	106,033	-1	42,116	24.0	8.1	23.8	97.0	1.1	0.1	0.2	0.6
3	R, 71		R, 59		R, 100		R, 100	112,062	110,304	-2	46,526	29.9	10.7	19.5	97.1	0.9	0.1	0.3	0.5
4	R, 51		R, 52		R, 58		R, 52	111,244	115,326	4	49,973	28.8	11.7	19.3	97.7	0.4	0.1	0.3	0.6
5	D, 100		D, 50		D, 62		D, 64	103,933	100,214	-4	44,911	34.8	16.1	24.4	92.9	4.0	0.1	0.5	0.8
6	D, 100		D, 100		D, 72		D, 100	101,077	95,833	-5	34,687	20.0	6.8	32.8	94.3	4.0	0.1	0.1	0.5
7	D, 100		D, 69		D, 74		D, 77	101,274	100,281	-1	39,374	20.6	6.9	29.1	97.3	1.1	0.1	0.1	0.5
8	R, 53		R, 54		R, 56		D, 58	200,294	193,251	-4	52,179	33.8	16.3	18.9	89.8	6.9	0.1	0.6	0.7
9	D, 100		R, 52		D, 56		D, 56	101,786	100,428	-1	42,782	26.3	9.5	24.9	90.6	6.8	0.1	0.4	1.0
10	D, 100		R, 58		R, 51		R, 52	104,950	103,940	-1	41,352	26.0	10.9	25.9	92.5	5.1	0.1	0.2	0.6
11*	D, 100		D, 64		D, 65		D, 53	111,372	111,346	0	38,091	21.7	8.8	27.8	95.4	2.5	0.1	0.2	0.6
11*	D, 73							111,372	111,346	0	38,091	21.7	8.8	27.8	95.4	2.5	0.1	0.2	0.6
12	D, 100		D, 100		D, 65		D, 100	107,453	107,603	0	42,345	26.5	11.6	24.0	96.2	1.2	0.1	0.3	0.9
13	D, 100		D, 80		D, 68		D, 100	110,660	111,224	1	44,316	36.9	21.1	25.9	91.9	3.4	0.1	1.3	1.2
14	D, 54		R, 67		D, 51		R, 53	111,713	113,028	1	40,183	24.3	10.1	22.9	97.0	1.0	0.1	0.1	0.6
15	D, 100		D, 56		R, 50		D, 100	111,285	116,249	4	42,700	22.6	9.5	20.3	96.8	1.1	0.1	0.1	0.9
16	D, 51		D, 100		R, 58		D, 65	110,373	137,124	24	53,985	29.2	13.2	14.5	89.0	5.4	0.1	0.3	2.8

*In addition to the regular election in the 11th District in 2000, there was a second election for another Senate seat in the 11th District for an unexpired term.

Note: D=Democrat, R=Republican, R/D=Republican/Democrat (cross-filed), D/R=Democrat/Republican (cross-filed), I=Independent, C=Constitution, O=Other, GI=Green Independent, P=Progressive, P/D=Progressive/Democrat, P/D/R=Progressive/Democrat/Republican, HH=Households

WEST VIRGINIA
State House Districts

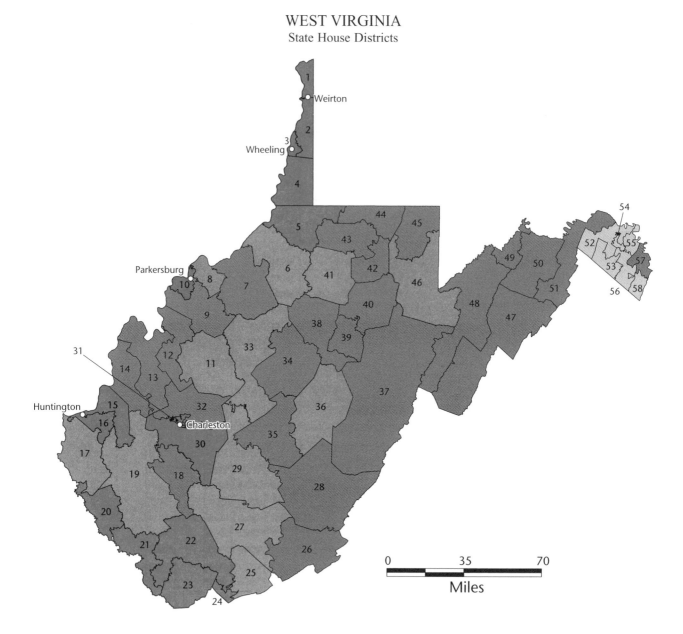

Population Growth   ▨ -15% to -3%   ▨ -3% to 0%   ▨ 0% to 21%   ▢ 21% to 28%

West Virginia State House Districts—Election and Demographic Data

House Districts	General Election Results Party, Percent of Vote							Population			Avg. HH Income	Pop 25+		Below Poverty Line	2006 White (Non-Hisp)	African American	American Indians, Alaska Natives	Asians, Hawaiians, Pacific Islanders	Hispanic Origin
												Some College +	4-Yr Degree +						
W. Virginia	2000	2001	2002	2003	2004	2005	2006	2000	2006	% Change	($)	(%)	(%)	(%)	(%)	(%)	(%)	(%)	(%)
1	D, 36		D, 50		D, 37		D, 50	35,064	33,006	-6	46,163	27.9	9.5	16.8	95.5	2.3	0.0	0.2	0.8
1	D, 33		D, 50				D, 50	35,064	33,006	-6	46,163	27.9	9.5	16.8	95.5	2.3	0.0	0.2	0.8
2	D, 40		D, 50		D, 34		D, 34	35,126	33,916	-3	47,473	29.2	11.9	17.3	97.2	1.0	0.0	0.2	0.6
2	D, 40		D, 50		D, 34		D, 33	35,126	33,916	-3	47,473	29.2	11.9	17.3	97.2	1.0	0.0	0.2	0.6
3	D, 38		R, 29		R, 31		D, 27	34,909	32,509	-7	45,623	36.5	19.0	23.6	92.8	4.4	0.0	0.6	0.6
3	R, 32		R, 27		R, 29		D, 26	34,909	32,509	-7	45,623	36.5	19.0	23.6	92.8	4.4	0.0	0.6	0.6
4	D, 36		D, 43		D, 37		D, 44	36,561	35,255	-4	45,076	25.8	8.6	21.4	97.6	0.4	0.1	0.2	0.7
4	D, 26		R, 33		D, 27		D, 28	36,561	35,255	-4	45,076	25.8	8.6	21.4	97.6	0.4	0.1	0.2	0.7
5	D, 61		D, 87		D, 67		D, 100	18,017	17,234	-4	47,002	22.7	8.2	23.0	98.3	0.1	0.0	0.2	0.5
6	R, 100		R, 100		R, 100		R, 100	17,927	17,577	-2	40,280	23.0	7.4	23.6	98.1	0.2	0.1	0.1	0.5
7	R, 100		R, 68		R, 62		R, 57	17,910	18,023	1	43,926	23.2	6.6	23.5	98.1	0.3	0.2	0.1	0.4
8	R, 67		R, 71		R, 100		R, 100	19,848	19,793	0	54,299	35.0	13.5	14.9	97.5	0.7	0.1	0.4	0.4
9	R, 57		R, 56		R, 57		R, 54	19,017	20,197	6	47,298	25.6	7.8	18.5	98.0	0.3	0.1	0.1	0.4
10	R, 21		D, 20		D, 21		D, 27	55,395	52,995	-4	45,443	32.9	12.2	19.6	96.3	1.3	0.1	0.4	0.6
10	D, 20		R, 19		R, 20		R, 25	55,395	52,995	-4	45,443	32.9	12.2	19.6	96.3	1.3	0.1	0.4	0.6
10	R,18		R, 18		R, 19		R, 25	55,395	52,995	-4	45,443	32.9	12.2	19.6	96.3	1.3	0.1	0.4	0.6
11	R, 57		R, 69		R, 100		R, 100	17,883	17,682	-1	37,105	20.1	7.1	27.9	97.9	0.2	0.1	0.1	0.8
12	R, 59		R, 66		R, 68		R, 63	18,706	19,656	5	45,649	29.1	10.7	19.5	98.1	0.1	0.1	0.1	0.5
13	D, 32		D, 37		D, 31		D, 38	38,937	40,074	3	45,302	24.7	8.2	19.7	98.1	0.4	0.1	0.1	0.5
13	D, 26		D, 32		D, 25			38,937	40,074	3	45,302	24.7	8.2	19.7	98.1	0.4	0.1	0.1	0.5
14	R, 34		R, 38		R, 34		R, 34	36,891	38,087	3	58,218	33.7	16.2	19.0	96.9	0.7	0.0	0.5	0.7
14	R, 30		R, 33		R, 27		R, 34	36,891	38,087	3	58,218	33.7	16.2	19.0	96.9	0.7	0.0	0.5	0.7
15	D, 23		D, 26		D, 22		D, 22	54,527	52,796	-3	41,788	31.1	13.4	27.9	90.8	6.0	0.1	0.4	0.8
15	D, 21		D, 22		D, 19		D, 18	54,527	52,796	-3	41,788	31.1	13.4	27.9	90.8	6.0	0.1	0.4	0.8
15	D, 20		R, 15		D, 18		R, 17	54,527	52,796	-3	41,788	31.1	13.4	27.9	90.8	6.0	0.1	0.4	0.8
16	R, 22		R, 19		R, 21		D, 21	51,142	49,141	-4	48,523	38.0	18.5	21.0	95.4	1.7	0.1	0.6	0.7
16	D, 22		R, 18		R, 20		D, 19	51,142	49,141	-4	48,523	38.0	18.5	21.0	95.4	1.7	0.1	0.6	0.7
16	D, 20		R, 18		D, 17		R, 18	51,142	49,141	-4	48,523	38.0	18.5	21.0	95.4	1.7	0.1	0.6	0.7
17	D, 100		D, 49		D, 34		D, 39	36,397	35,975	-1	41,800	24.8	9.5	26.0	98.3	0.1	0.1	0.1	0.5
17			D, 49		D, 34		D, 36	36,397	35,975	-1	41,800	24.8	9.5	26.0	98.3	0.1	0.1	0.1	0.5
18	D, 100		D, 100		D, 71		D, 84	16,878	17,030	1	40,392	19.1	6.5	27.6	97.7	0.9	0.1	0.1	0.5
19	D, 51		D, 18		D, 17		D, 20	73,762	73,200	-1	40,067	21.4	7.1	28.0	97.1	1.3	0.1	0.1	0.5
19	D, 49		D, 17		D, 16		D, 20	73,762	73,200	-1	40,067	21.4	7.1	28.0	97.1	1.3	0.1	0.1	0.5
19			D, 17		D, 15		D, 19	73,762	73,200	-1	40,067	21.4	7.1	28.0	97.1	1.3	0.1	0.1	0.5
19			D, 16		D, 14		D, 17	73,762	73,200	-1	40,067	21.4	7.1	28.0	97.1	1.3	0.1	0.1	0.5
20	D, 24		D, 100		D, 71		D, 100	16,604	16,034	-3	34,993	20.1	6.9	35.9	95.6	2.5	0.1	0.2	0.6
20	D, 24							16,604	16,034	-3	34,993	20.1	6.9	35.9	95.6	2.5	0.1	0.2	0.6
20	D, 22							16,604	16,034	-3	34,993	20.1	6.9	35.9	95.6	2.5	0.1	0.2	0.6
20	D, 22							16,604	16,034	-3	34,993	20.1	6.9	35.9	95.6	2.5	0.1	0.2	0.6
21	D, 100		D, 100		D, 80		D, 83	17,749	16,801	-5	30,419	15.5	4.7	38.0	97.5	1.0	0.1	0.1	0.5
22	D, 51		D, 52		D, 33		D, 41	35,998	33,782	-6	36,558	18.2	6.1	30.4	97.8	0.7	0.1	0.1	0.6
22	D, 49		D, 48		D, 27		D, 38	35,998	33,782	-6	36,558	18.2	6.1	30.4	97.8	0.7	0.1	0.1	0.6
23	D, 52		D,100		D, 76		D, 100	18,787	15,971	-15	26,752	17.1	6.0	39.4	81.1	16.9	0.1	0.0	0.6
23	D, 48							18,787	15,971	-15	26,752	17.1	6.0	39.4	81.1	16.9	0.1	0.0	0.6
24	D, 69		D, 66		D, 66		D, 71	17,267	16,393	-5	38,932	32.8	13.8	25.8	81.1	16.2	0.1	0.2	0.7
25	D, 39		D, 32		D, 31		D, 33	38,536	38,237	-1	42,113	27.2	10.9	25.2	95.4	2.4	0.1	0.4	0.6
25	D, 35		R, 28		R, 26		R, 29	38,536	38,237	-1	42,113	27.2	10.9	25.2	95.4	2.4	0.1	0.4	0.6
26	D, 77		D, 59		D, 53		D, 55	17,563	17,885	2	45,187	22.1	7.8	25.5	93.2	5.0	0.1	0.1	0.4
27	D, 18		D, 38		D, 12		R, 12	88,933	88,914	0	42,951	27.4	10.2	24.5	89.5	7.7	0.1	0.4	1.1
27	D, 18		D, 37		R, 12		D, 11	88,933	88,914	0	42,951	27.4	10.2	24.5	89.5	7.7	0.1	0.4	1.1

(continued)

Note: D=Democrat, R=Republican, R/D=Republican/Democrat (cross-filed), D/R=Democrat/Republican (cross-filed), I=Independent, C=Constitution, O=Other, GI=Green Independent, P=Progressive, P/D=Progressive/Democrat, P/D/R=Progressive/Democrat/Republican, HH=Households

West Virginia State House Districts—Election and Demographic Data (cont.)

House Districts	General Election Results Party, Percent of Vote							Population			Avg. HH Income	2006 Pop 25+ Some College+	2006 Pop 25+ 4-Yr Degree+	2006 Below Poverty Line	2006 White (Non-Hisp)	2006 African American	2006 American Indians, Alaska Natives	2006 Asians, Hawaiians, Pacific Islanders	2006 Hispanic Origin
W. Virginia	2000	2001	2002	2003	2004	2005	2006	2000	2006	% Change	($)	(%)	(%)	(%)	(%)	(%)	(%)	(%)	(%)
27	D, 18		D, 12		D, 11		D, 11	88,933	88,914	0	42,951	27.4	10.2	24.5	89.5	7.7	0.1	0.4	1.1
27	D, 17		D, 12		D, 11		D, 10	88,933	88,914	0	42,951	27.4	10.2	24.5	89.5	7.7	0.1	0.4	1.1
27	D, 15		D, 11		D, 11		D, 10	88,933	88,914	0	42,951	27.4	10.2	24.5	89.5	7.7	0.1	0.4	1.1
28	D, 38		D, 38		D, 33		D, 34	34,227	34,391	0	42,203	25.4	11.0	25.3	94.2	3.2	0.2	0.1	0.7
28	R, 31		D, 37		R, 31		R, 28	34,227	34,391	0	42,203	25.4	11.0	25.3	94.2	3.2	0.2	0.1	0.7
29	D, 31		D, 24		D, 24		D, 30	52,630	51,935	-1	37,453	22.0	8.5	28.1	92.6	5.0	0.2	0.2	0.7
29	D, 29		D, 24		D, 23		D, 29	52,630	51,935	-1	37,453	22.0	8.5	28.1	92.6	5.0	0.2	0.2	0.7
29	D, 26		D, 22		D, 23		D, 29	52,630	51,935	-1	37,453	22.0	8.5	28.1	92.6	5.0	0.2	0.2	0.7
30	D, 11		D, 10		D, 10		D, 10	128,130	121,884	-5	55,724	35.5	17.8	17.5	90.2	6.4	0.1	0.7	0.7
30	D, 9		D, 10		D, 9		D, 8	128,130	121,884	-5	55,724	35.5	17.8	17.5	90.2	6.4	0.1	0.7	0.7
30	D, 9		D, 9		D, 9		D, 8	128,130	121,884	-5	55,724	35.5	17.8	17.5	90.2	6.4	0.1	0.7	0.7
30	D, 8		D, 8		D, 9		D, 8	128,130	121,884	-5	55,724	35.5	17.8	17.5	90.2	6.4	0.1	0.7	0.7
30	D, 8		D, 8		D, 9		D, 8	128,130	121,884	-5	55,724	35.5	17.8	17.5	90.2	6.4	0.1	0.7	0.7
30	R, 6		D, 8		D, 8		D, 8	128,130	121,884	-5	55,724	35.5	17.8	17.5	90.2	6.4	0.1	0.7	0.7
30	R, 6		R, 7		D, 8		D, 7	128,130	121,884	-5	55,724	35.5	17.8	17.5	90.2	6.4	0.1	0.7	0.7
31	D, 63		D, 56		D, 65		D, 66	18,529	17,120	-8	40,599	34.1	16.5	31.9	66.1	28.1	0.1	0.6	1.0
32	R, 16		R, 22		R, 22		R, 20	53,693	54,275	1	48,295	29.9	12.9	17.0	96.6	1.4	0.1	0.3	0.5
32	R, 15		R, 22		R, 21		R, 19	53,693	54,275	1	48,295	29.9	12.9	17.0	96.6	1.4	0.1	0.3	0.5
32	R, 14		R, 21		R, 19		R, 18	53,693	54,275	1	48,295	29.9	12.9	17.0	96.6	1.4	0.1	0.3	0.5
32	R, 14							53,693	54,275	1	48,295	29.9	12.9	17.0	96.6	1.4	0.1	0.3	0.5
33	D, 67		D, 70		D, 71		D, 100	17,749	17,301	-3	33,109	19.9	8.9	32.7	97.8	0.3	0.2	0.1	0.6
34	D, 82		D, 100		D, 83		D, 100	17,627	17,929	2	36,753	21.1	8.7	29.4	97.4	0.7	0.2	0.1	0.5
35	D, 61		D, 83		D, 63		D, 58	18,334	18,395	0	43,212	22.1	8.5	23.6	98.3	0.0	0.1	0.1	0.5
36	D, 100		D, 66		D, 69		D, 61	17,360	17,299	0	34,188	18.6	7.5	32.5	98.6	0.0	0.1	0.1	0.4
37	D, 51		D, 35		D, 32		D, 28	37,422	37,520	0	40,369	23.8	10.8	22.6	97.1	1.0	0.1	0.2	0.7
37	D, 49		D, 30		D, 29		D, 27	37,422	37,520	0	40,369	23.8	10.8	22.6	97.1	1.0	0.1	0.2	0.7
38	R, 100		R, 73		D, 70		D, 62	17,930	18,318	2	36,977	22.6	8.9	26.2	98.0	0.1	0.1	0.2	0.6
39	R, 66		R, 100		R, 65		D, 74	18,946	19,467	3	38,281	23.8	11.6	25.3	97.1	0.7	0.1	0.2	0.8
40	D, 50		D, 53		D, 61		D, 72	18,866	18,907	0	35,148	20.4	9.1	27.7	97.2	0.4	0.3	0.2	0.6
41	D, 26		D, 26		D, 17		D, 20	70,716	70,394	0	45,794	29.0	13.0	21.5	95.5	1.6	0.1	0.4	1.1
41	D, 26		D, 26		D, 17		D, 18	70,716	70,394	0	45,794	29.0	13.0	21.5	95.5	1.6	0.1	0.4	1.1
41	D, 23		D, 25		D, 16		D, 17	70,716	70,394	0	45,794	29.0	13.0	21.5	95.5	1.6	0.1	0.4	1.1
41	D, 12		D, 23		D, 14		D, 17	70,716	70,394	0	45,794	29.0	13.0	21.5	95.5	1.6	0.1	0.4	1.1
42	D, 62		D, 62		R, 53		R, 54	18,331	18,628	2	38,462	25.3	10.1	24.3	97.5	0.8	0.1	0.1	0.7
43	D, 28		D, 25		D, 25		D, 23	57,013	57,221	0	42,275	30.6	12.7	22.3	94.2	3.2	0.1	0.3	0.9
43	D, 26		D, 22		D, 23		D, 23	57,013	57,221	0	42,275	30.6	12.7	22.3	94.2	3.2	0.1	0.3	0.9
43	D, 23		D, 19		D, 23		D, 22	57,013	57,221	0	42,275	30.6	12.7	22.3	94.2	3.2	0.1	0.3	0.9
44	D, 18		D, 18		D, 15		D, 16	75,828	78,924	4	45,399	39.2	24.6	26.9	90.9	3.5	0.1	1.8	1.4
44	D, 17		D, 18		D, 15		D, 16	75,828	78,924	4	45,399	39.2	24.6	26.9	90.9	3.5	0.1	1.8	1.4
44	D, 17		D, 16		D, 15		D, 15	75,828	78,924	4	45,399	39.2	24.6	26.9	90.9	3.5	0.1	1.8	1.4
44	D, 16		R, 15		D, 14		D, 15	75,828	78,924	4	45,399	39.2	24.6	26.9	90.9	3.5	0.1	1.8	1.4
45	D, 100		D, 74		D, 65		D, 100	18,206	18,973	4	39,295	22.0	9.3	22.9	98.1	0.4	0.0	0.1	0.5
46	D, 53		D, 55		R, 51		D, 54	18,532	18,191	-2	38,870	20.0	7.9	24.9	98.3	0.1	0.1	0.0	0.6
47	D, 100		D, 100		D, 76		D, 100	18,995	19,437	2	42,705	21.8	8.1	19.3	95.1	2.2	0.1	0.1	1.3
48	R, 61		R, 100		R, 73		R, 67	18,553	18,722	1	40,630	21.8	8.8	23.1	96.8	1.3	0.1	0.1	0.7
49	R, 57		D, 66		R, 66		R, 55	18,044	18,183	1	42,708	25.9	9.1	19.8	95.5	2.6	0.0	0.2	0.5
50	D, 100		D, 100		R, 55		R, 57	17,731	19,555	10	39,486	22.1	10.0	21.3	97.2	0.7	0.1	0.1	0.9
51	R, 72		R, 70		R, 100		R, 55	17,417	18,618	7	48,586	22.2	7.8	16.2	97.3	0.7	0.1	0.1	0.9
52	D, 54		R, 65		R, 63		R, 100	16,906	20,783	23	55,873	29.1	13.4	12.8	95.7	1.1	0.1	0.2	1.5
53	D, 57		R, 100		R, 54		R, 58	16,882	21,540	28	51,543	25.2	9.6	12.3	93.8	1.7	0.1	0.2	2.1

(continued)

Note: D=Democrat, R=Republican, R/D=Republican/Democrat (cross-filed), D/R=Democrat/Republican (cross-filed), I=Independent, C=Constitution, O=Other, GI=Green Independent, P=Progressive, P/D=Progressive/Democrat, P/D/R=Progressive/Democrat/Republican, HH=Households

West Virginia State House Districts—Election and Demographic Data (cont.)

House Districts	General Election Results Party, Percent of Vote							Population			Avg. HH Income	Pop 25+		Below Poverty Line	White (Non-Hisp)	African American	American Indians, Alaska Natives	Asians, Hawaiians, Pacific Islanders	Hispanic Origin
												Some College +	4-Yr Degree +						2006
W. Virginia	2000	2001	2002	2003	2004	2005	2006	2000	2006	% Change	($)	(%)	(%)	(%)	(%)	(%)	(%)	(%)	(%)
54	D, 60		R, 55		R, 100		R, 100	17,921	21,712	21	46,379	28.0	11.8	19.7	81.6	10.0	0.2	0.4	4.3
55	D, 56		R, 61		R, 100		R, 100	17,482	21,862	25	49,539	27.0	11.2	13.2	91.4	4.1	0.1	0.3	2.1
56	D, 61		D, 52		D, 52		D, 100	17,928	22,784	27	52,774	26.7	11.5	13.1	88.7	6.2	0.1	0.3	2.5
57*			D, 54		D, 58		D, 62	17,065	18,890	11	64,712	35.6	19.5	12.1	88.8	5.2	0.1	0.5	3.0
58*			D, 59		D/R, 100		D, 61	16,209	20,610	27	57,986	31.8	15.0	16.2	87.1	6.7	0.1	0.4	3.3

*Districts expand from 56 in 2000 to 58 in 2002 due to redistricting.

Note: D=Democrat, R=Republican, R/D=Republican/Democrat (cross-filed), D/R=Democrat/Republican (cross-filed), I=Independent, C=Constitution, O=Other, GI=Green Independent, P=Progressive, P/D=Progressive/Democrat, P/D/R=Progressive/Democrat/Republican, HH=Households

WISCONSIN

Blessed with a pleasant climate, rolling hills, orderly farms, and shores on two Great Lakes, Wisconsin begins the century still possessing many of the natural advantages with which it began the last one. No apology need ever be made on behalf of a state best known for cheese, sausages, and beer.

In the nineteenth and early-twentieth centuries, Wisconsin managed to balance the grasping capitalism of Chicago against the sometimes messianic collectivism of the Upper Plains. For years, Wisconsin was one of the country's leading producers of white pine and spruce, much of which was clear cut for boards with which to build houses. The stumps, branches, and debris left behind grew dry under the summer sun until a spark set them off. The Peshtigo Fire of 1871 killed as many as 2,400 people, destroyed a 2,000 square mile area, and remains one of the worst natural disasters in American history, though it is largely forgotten because of the great Chicago Fire, which started the same day 250 miles to the south.

Among the state's gifts to national politics have been Lincoln Republicanism (the GOP was born in Ripon in 1854) and Robert LaFollette's clear-eyed Progressivism, both of which shared a faith in the fundamental reasonableness of mankind. Wisconsin believed in innovation and participation—the direct primary, the referendum, and the recall. For many years, all state income tax returns were open for public inspection. There have been bitter strikes against the auto plants in Racine and Kenosha, but the huge government employees union, AFSCME, was also founded in Wisconsin, in 1935. Recently, Wisconsin's innovative welfare reforms lifted many out of poverty and became a model for the rest of the nation.

At times, Wisconsin politics have slid toward the ridiculous, like pro-German apologist Victor Berger, Milwaukee's avowedly Socialist U.S. representative in the 1910s, or the dangerous, like former senator Joe McCarthy in the 1950s. But a better exemplar might be former senator William Proxmire, who spent next to nothing on his campaigns and built a reputation exposing government waste. Another might be current U.S. Senator Russell Feingold, co-author of legislation that is supposed to get the money influence out of politics, perpetuating the old Progressive faith that if the right rules could only be written, and administered by the right people, human nature could be lifted to a higher level.

The state has steered a fairly steady course during the past few decades, at least relative to its neighbors. Wisconsin's 4 percent growth rate during the 1980s, a bad time for farmers, was unspectacular but best among the states in the region. The state grew by a little less than 10 percent during the 1990s, not as much as Minnesota but better than Illinois or Indiana. Wisconsin lost a congressional seat in 2002, as did Illinois, Indiana, and Michigan, but Minnesota did not.

It is startling to discover that Milwaukee is still the twenty-second largest city in the country, with about 200,000 more people than Minneapolis (which ranks forty-eighth). When one includes St. Paul, of course, the Twin Cities metro area becomes much larger than metro Milwaukee, and indeed all of Wisconsin's fastest growth is occurring just across the St. Croix River from Minnesota in the 29th and 30th state house districts. There has also been growth in suburbs of Madison, around Appleton, and along the Illinois border in what has become part of the Chicago metro area, but comparatively little around Milwaukee. Of the ten house districts that have lost population at the fastest rate, on the other hand, all are located in Milwaukee County.

Mansions overlook Lake Michigan but only a few miles away poverty approaches its national nadir. Wisconsin's wealthiest districts are found to the north and west of the city, in Waukesha County, which used to be full of dairy farms. According to Michael Barone, there were 105,000 dairy farms in Wisconsin in 1960, but only about 21,000 four decades later. Factories have closed, too, and so the 16th house district, on the north side of Milwaukee is the poorest in the state. Average household income there is about $32,000 a year.

Wisconsin as a whole is 89 percent white, slightly lower than Minnesota but considerably higher than Illinois. The state has five heavily black house districts, all in Milwaukee. A district in Madison is 9 percent Asian, as is one in suburban Waukesha County, home to a number of Filipinos, Koreans, and Laotians. The 8th district, in downtown Milwaukee, is three-quarters Hispanic. Mexican immigrants have also been drawn to work in the meat-packing plants in Green Bay and now make up almost 15 percent of the city's population.

Wisconsin has experienced more political volatility recently than either of its neighbors. Republicans have controlled the state house of representatives throughout the decade, although their current margin, 52–47, is the smallest it has been in recent years. The state senate has been almost evenly divided since 2000 and has swung back and forth between the parties. Democrats held it in 2000 and 2002, Republicans regained it in 2004, but Democrats took it back in 2006. In all, Democrats gained eleven seats in the 2006 elections while a Democratic governor won reelection. At the same time, a Republican was elected attorney general for the first time in sixteen years.

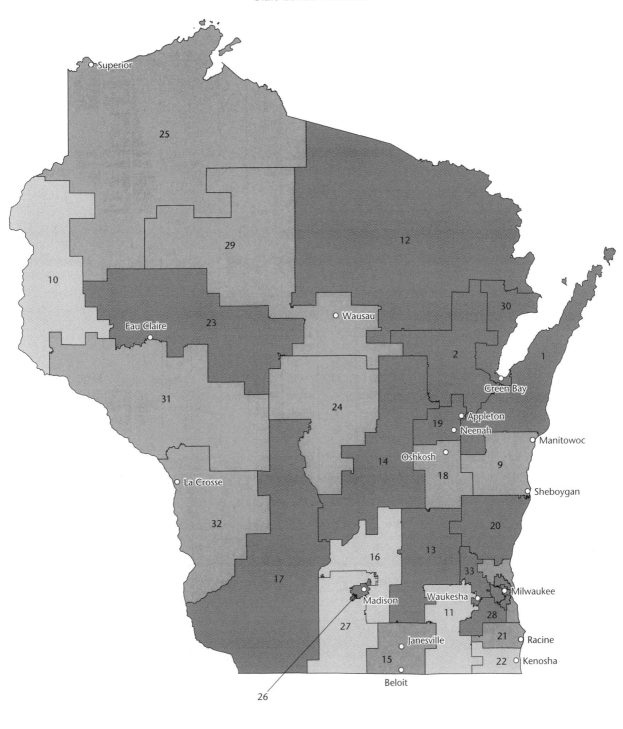

WISCONSIN
State Senate Districts

Superior

25

29

10

23

Eau Claire

Wausau

12

30

2

1

Green Bay

31

Appleton
Neenah

19

Manitowoc

24

Oshkosh

9

14

18

Sheboygan

La Crosse

32

20

17

16

13

33

Milwaukee

Madison

Waukesha

11

28

27

21

Racine

15

Janesville

22

Kenosha

Beloit

26

0   50   100

Miles

Population Growth   ▨ -4% to -1%   ▨ -1% to 3%   ▨ 3% to 8%   ▨ 8% to 14%

MILWAUKEE

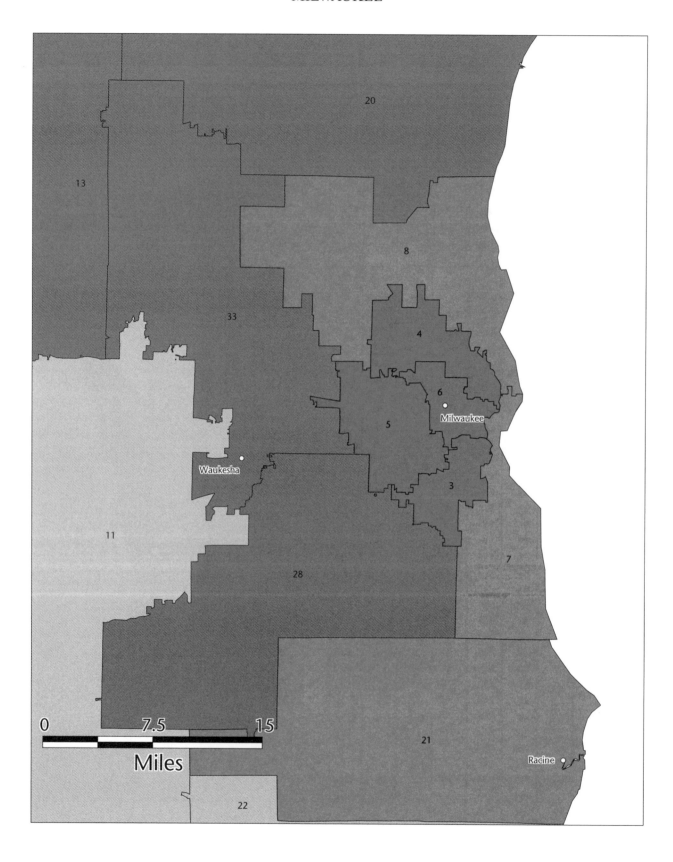

Population Growth   ■ -4% to -1%   ■ -1% to 3%   ■ 3% to 8%   □ 8% to 14%

Wisconsin State Senate Districts—Election and Demographic Data

Senate Districts	General Election Results Party, Percent of Vote							Population			Avg. HH Income ($)	Pop 25+ Some College + (%)	Pop 25+ 4-Yr Degree + (%)	Below Poverty Line (%)	White (Non-Hisp) (%)	African American (%)	American Indians, Alaska Natives (%)	Asians, Hawaiians, Pacific Islanders (%)	Hispanic Origin (%)
															2006				
Wisconsin	2000	2001	2002	2003	2004	2005	2006	2000	2006	% Change	($)	(%)	(%)	(%)	(%)	(%)	(%)	(%)	(%)
1			R, 63				R, 55	171,048	181,540	6	62,848	32.8	13.2	9.4	94.3	0.5	0.5	1.2	1.9
2	R, 100				R, 89			161,559	169,304	5	64,673	32.9	13.7	9.7	90.8	0.8	3.5	0.9	1.8
3			D, 98				D, 99	162,247	157,075	-3	45,613	30.8	11.1	17.2	38.9	7.0	1.4	3.0	39.1
4	D, 99				D, 99			164,863	159,482	-3	44,593	31.1	10.6	20.7	34.2	55.3	0.5	2.5	5.4
5			R, 53				D, 52	162,797	158,012	-3	63,388	47.6	23.6	9.2	82.8	6.3	0.5	2.1	4.6
6	D, 99				D, 99			159,872	153,691	-4	39,659	28.1	10.1	29.3	27.3	60.4	0.6	4.0	6.2
7			D, 79				D, 63	162,417	162,211	0	56,280	43.2	20.0	11.8	77.1	7.0	0.8	2.3	8.0
8	R, 66				R, 57			162,500	164,166	1	92,680	51.6	31.2	7.7	83.2	9.2	0.3	2.3	2.6
9			R, 50				R, 59	161,075	160,417	0	59,025	31.2	12.0	10.3	88.1	1.1	0.4	3.4	4.2
10	R, 50				R, 59			162,260	184,710	14	63,140	36.1	15.3	11.6	95.2	0.6	0.6	1.0	1.1
11			R, 69				R, 67	161,488	174,472	8	76,663	42.0	19.1	7.7	89.0	0.8	0.3	0.7	5.8
12	D, 88				D, 53			162,873	168,411	3	48,292	29.3	10.1	16.9	91.3	0.5	5.3	0.3	1.1
13			R, 69				R, 97	164,297	172,742	5	63,597	33.4	13.1	9.1	92.2	0.9	0.3	0.5	3.6
14	R, 66				R, 99			162,804	168,101	3	53,087	29.6	10.5	13.5	93.8	1.0	0.6	0.5	2.3
15			D, 65				D, 68	161,690	165,941	3	60,191	30.7	11.7	11.3	83.9	4.8	0.3	1.0	6.1
16	D, 58				D, 60			163,132	178,632	10	68,599	47.8	26.1	6.7	90.4	2.3	0.3	1.3	2.9
17			R, 67				R, 54	163,120	169,387	4	51,625	29.2	10.3	14.9	96.0	0.5	0.4	0.4	1.3
18	R, 68				R, 99			161,881	163,306	1	57,437	33.0	14.1	11.1	90.4	2.6	0.5	1.9	2.6
19			R, 99				R, 99	162,252	168,997	4	67,731	37.7	17.6	8.4	90.1	0.9	0.5	2.7	3.2
20	R, 73				R, 99			161,971	172,830	7	71,590	37.3	15.8	6.6	95.5	0.4	0.3	0.5	1.8
21			R, 51				D, 53	161,438	165,947	3	64,022	34.6	13.8	11.2	69.8	12.4	0.4	0.9	11.0
22	D, 56				D, 52			164,264	177,809	8	63,700	34.5	12.9	10.7	79.1	5.1	0.4	1.0	8.9
23			R, 63				D, 51	157,784	167,278	6	52,087	30.9	10.9	14.2	95.3	0.4	0.4	1.5	1.1
24	D, 99				D, 68			161,359	163,106	1	55,722	31.9	12.9	13.2	93.6	0.5	0.6	1.9	1.8
25			D, 62				D, 62	162,297	165,648	2	46,987	33.0	11.6	18.1	91.4	0.5	4.6	0.5	1.1
26	D, 99				D, 81			162,601	172,886	6	61,495	53.4	39.4	15.6	74.7	6.3	0.4	6.7	7.0
27			D, 99				D, 99	162,137	176,774	9	72,463	48.2	28.4	7.3	89.1	2.7	0.3	2.0	3.0
28	R, 67				R, 99			163,187	170,222	4	79,650	47.1	22.5	5.3	89.3	3.3	0.3	1.8	3.0
29			D, 68				D, 68	163,218	162,323	-1	56,747	30.9	11.6	13.5	92.7	0.5	0.4	3.9	1.0
30	D, 51				D, 55			163,414	169,279	4	53,370	31.7	12.0	12.9	82.8	1.2	1.9	2.7	7.1
31			R, 50				D, 52	168,998	172,313	2	52,837	32.4	12.7	14.9	94.0	0.8	1.2	0.9	1.4
32	D, 51				R, 52			163,073	165,862	2	52,677	35.6	14.4	15.0	93.4	1.0	0.4	2.4	1.2
33			R, 100				R, 67	164,199	173,980	6	84,084	47.4	24.2	6.6	88.9	1.1	0.2	2.0	4.8

Note: D=Democrat, R=Republican, R/D=Republican/Democrat (cross-filed), D/R=Democrat/Republican (cross-filed), I=Independent, C=Constitution, O=Other, GI=Green Independent, P=Progressive, P/D=Progressive/Democrat, P/D/R=Progressive/Democrat/Republican, HH=Households

WISCONSIN
State Assembly Districts

GREEN BAY

MADISON

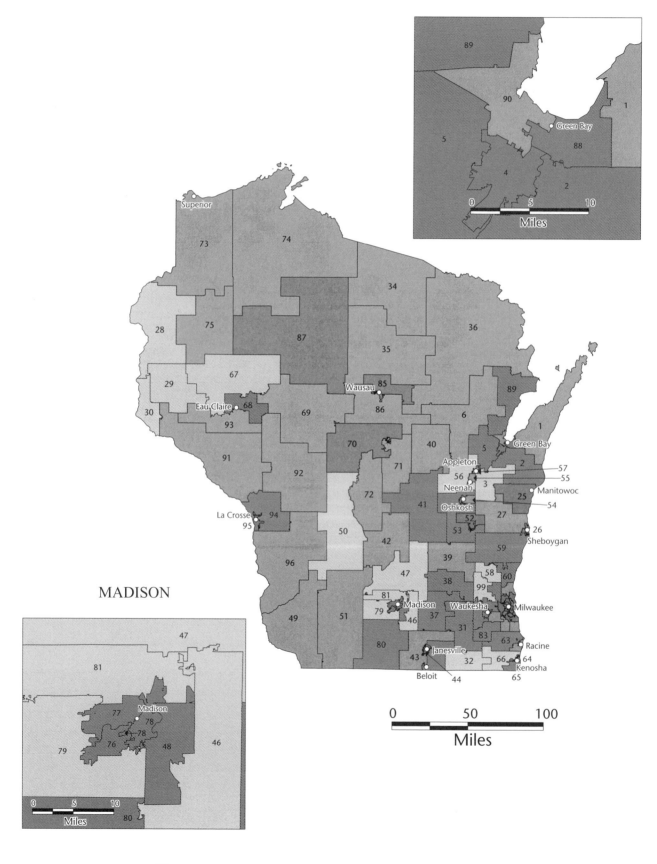

Population Growth   ■ -5% to 0%   ■ 0% to 4%   ■ 4% to 8%   □ 8% to 18%

MILWAUKEE

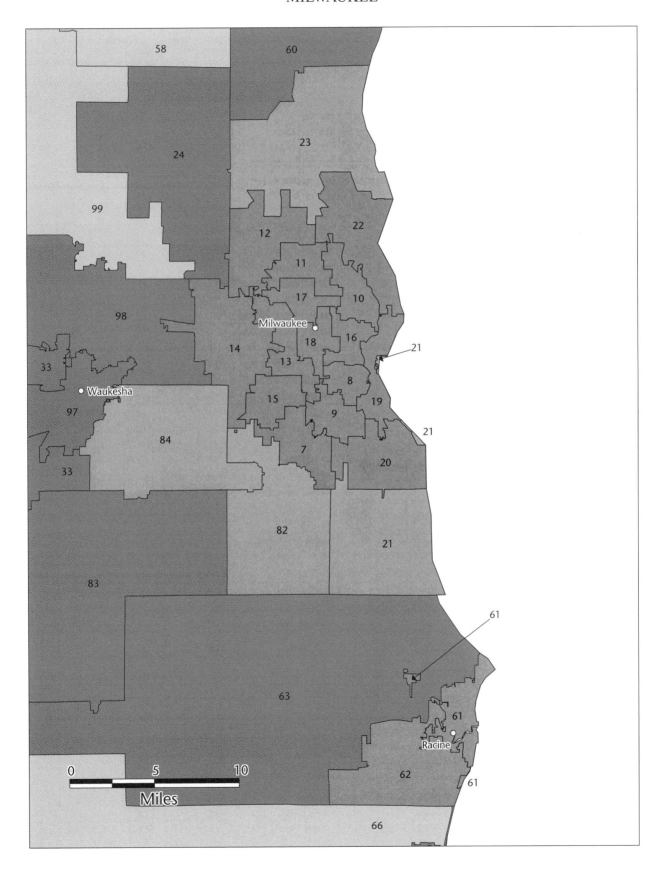

Population Growth ■ -5% to 0%   ■ 0% to 4%   ■ 4% to 8%   ■ 8% to 18%

Wisconsin State Assembly Districts—Election and Demographic Data

Assembly Districts	General Election Results Party, Percent of Vote							Population			Avg. HH Income ($)	2006 Pop 25+ Some College + (%)	2006 Pop 25+ 4-Yr Degree + (%)	2006 Below Poverty Line (%)	2006 White (Non-Hisp) (%)	2006 African American (%)	2006 American Indians, Alaska Natives (%)	2006 Asians, Hawaiians, Pacific Islanders (%)	2006 Hispanic Origin (%)
Wisconsin	2000	2001	2002	2003	2004	2005	2006	2000	2006	% Change	($)	(%)	(%)	(%)	(%)	(%)	(%)	(%)	(%)
1	R, 57		R, 66		R, 61		R, 54	53,605	54,998	3	56,767	33.3	12.9	12.4	95.9	0.5	0.5	0.4	1.3
2	R, 100		R, 63		R, 99		R, 89	54,631	57,627	5	63,657	31.5	11.9	8.6	93.4	0.4	0.6	1.3	2.4
3	R, 100		R, 100		R, 62		R, 59	54,532	60,336	11	67,416	33.2	14.6	7.0	94.3	0.5	0.5	1.5	1.8
4	R, 58		R, 63		R, 62		R, 56	53,560	56,510	6	74,733	41.4	20.5	7.1	91.5	1.9	1.4	1.4	1.9
5	D, 53		R, 52		D, 51		D, 62	53,867	57,933	8	67,705	31.3	12.3	8.1	88.5	0.3	6.1	1.1	1.8
6	R, 100		R, 99		R, 99		R, 60	54,048	54,768	1	51,543	25.8	8.2	13.6	92.5	0.3	3.0	0.3	1.8
7	D, 61		D, 99		D, 99		D, 99	53,670	52,522	-2	52,921	41.7	15.2	7.9	80.0	5.9	0.6	2.1	7.1
8	D, 98		D, 98		D, 99		D, 99	54,488	52,796	-3	34,668	20.1	7.2	32.0	10.5	8.5	1.9	3.7	74.0
9	D, 71		D, 98		D, 99		D, 98	54,185	51,823	-4	45,788	30.8	11.0	17.4	41.9	6.7	1.8	3.1	35.9
10	D, 99		D, 99		D, 93		D, 99	53,691	51,840	-3	38,984	29.8	10.3	27.3	23.7	66.8	0.5	1.1	7.0
11	D, 99		D, 99		D, 99		D, 99	55,182	52,874	-4	41,978	26.5	7.5	22.9	27.8	62.6	0.5	3.0	4.3
12	D, 99		D, 66		D, 91		D, 99	56,339	55,099	-2	52,280	36.8	14.1	12.6	50.4	37.6	0.5	3.3	5.0
13	D, 99		D, 51		D, 57		D, 64	54,338	52,455	-3	60,266	49.5	25.9	8.4	79.0	8.3	0.6	1.9	5.7
14	R, 98		R, 88		R, 99		R, 62	54,024	53,132	-2	82,583	53.9	31.3	7.5	86.7	4.7	0.3	2.7	2.9
15	D, 87		D, 58		D, 99		D, 97	54,666	52,642	-4	48,803	39.1	13.6	11.4	82.6	5.9	0.7	1.6	5.3
16	D, 99		D, 99		D, 99		D, 99	54,063	52,550	-3	32,207	24.0	8.9	40.1	26.3	61.7	0.5	3.1	7.7
17	D, 99		D, 99		D, 99		D, 91	52,834	50,280	-5	46,820	33.1	11.1	19.0	28.9	61.7	0.4	2.8	4.2
18	D, 99		D, 99		D, 99		D, 99	53,146	51,015	-4	39,675	27.2	10.4	28.8	26.9	57.8	0.7	6.1	6.7
19	D, 98		D, 98		D, 98		D, 98	54,160	53,932	0	57,036	50.4	31.1	15.5	72.9	9.0	0.9	3.0	9.1
20	D, 99		D, 98		D, 61		D, 98	54,098	53,013	-2	51,188	38.8	13.7	10.4	78.5	5.8	0.9	1.8	8.3
21	D, 63		D, 65		R, 99		R, 98	54,423	55,536	2	60,593	40.4	15.2	8.0	79.9	6.2	0.6	2.1	6.6
22	D, 63		D, 99		D, 65		D, 99	55,631	53,203	-4	102,185	57.5	40.4	8.2	78.7	11.2	0.3	3.1	3.5
23	D, 99		R, 62		R, 99		R, 56	52,430	53,057	1	101,711	51.9	31.6	8.9	76.1	15.1	0.3	2.7	3.1
24	R, 99		R, 100		R, 100		R, 99	54,434	57,898	6	74,906	46.1	22.4	5.9	94.1	1.8	0.2	1.2	1.4
25	D, 100		D, 100		D, 100		D, 54	53,511	52,250	-2	57,500	30.8	11.8	11.4	91.3	0.7	0.5	2.7	2.7
26	R, 58		D, 55		D, 99		D, 72	54,061	53,477	-1	54,904	30.8	12.2	11.6	79.0	1.0	0.5	6.6	8.2
27	R, 66		R, 100		R, 100		R, 100	54,258	55,451	2	64,806	31.8	12.1	7.7	94.0	1.7	0.3	0.9	1.8
28	R, 51		R, 52		R, 54		D, 51	54,404	59,347	9	54,221	31.0	10.5	14.6	95.6	0.4	1.3	0.3	0.9
29	D, 52		D, 61		R, 50		R, 52	54,484	64,133	18	59,010	33.8	13.4	12.8	94.8	0.7	0.3	1.7	1.0
30	R, 64		R, 69		R, 61		R, 57	53,464	61,332	15	76,950	43.6	21.8	7.0	95.4	0.6	0.3	0.8	1.4
31	R, 87		R, 87		R, 66		R, 64	54,212	58,214	7	71,254	39.7	16.5	7.9	92.1	0.5	0.3	0.6	3.8
32	R, 69		R, 52		R, 54		R, 54	54,224	59,730	10	63,243	36.5	14.7	10.6	81.7	1.0	0.2	0.7	11.1
33	R, 100		R, 100		R, 72		R, 72	53,279	56,763	7	97,941	50.2	26.5	4.0	93.7	1.0	0.3	1.0	2.2
34	R, 60		R, 60		R, 57		R, 56	54,340	55,976	3	50,234	35.5	14.0	15.8	92.9	0.5	4.1	0.3	0.9
35	R, 55		R, 66		R, 57		R, 99	53,908	55,945	4	48,981	27.8	9.0	16.1	96.1	0.5	0.5	0.4	1.1
36	R, 57		R, 61		R, 56		R, 54	54,506	56,397	3	45,523	24.8	7.2	18.7	85.0	0.6	11.4	0.3	1.3
37	R, 58		R, 63		R, 60		D, 50	54,617	58,802	8	64,209	35.9	15.0	8.6	90.9	0.7	0.3	0.7	4.6
38	R, 72		R, 58		R, 65		R, 67	54,924	57,868	5	68,230	35.7	14.7	8.8	93.3	0.4	0.3	0.5	3.3
39	R, 58		R, 99		R, 69		R, 62	54,980	56,289	2	58,262	28.2	9.5	10.0	92.5	1.5	0.3	0.4	3.1
40	R, 99		R, 99		R, 69		R, 53	53,646	54,785	2	53,892	28.6	10.8	13.0	95.0	0.4	0.4	0.5	2.1
41	R, 99		R, 100		R, 84		R, 65	54,397	57,675	6	51,515	28.2	9.7	14.6	93.9	0.5	0.3	0.4	2.8
42	R, 55		R, 99		R, 52		R, 53	54,936	55,811	2	53,917	32.0	11.1	13.0	92.4	2.2	1.0	0.5	2.1
43	R, 68		R, 51		R, 55		D, 50	56,872	58,721	3	62,767	30.0	11.5	10.9	89.5	2.3	0.3	0.7	4.3
44	D, 66		D, 99		D, 60		D, 69	50,629	50,444	0	58,544	32.3	12.0	10.4	89.2	2.0	0.3	1.0	4.3
45	D, 67		D, 100		D, 58		D, 99	54,442	57,030	5	59,129	30.0	11.5	12.6	74.0	10.0	0.3	1.1	9.5
46	D, 66		D, 61		D, 58		D, 99	53,838	59,269	10	72,392	49.9	28.8	6.5	91.5	2.1	0.3	1.3	2.4
47	R, 58		R, 57		R, 50		R, 50	56,157	62,576	11	68,424	40.8	18.9	7.6	93.9	0.8	0.3	0.7	2.1
48	D, 99		D, 84		D, 75		D, 76	53,762	57,476	7	65,218	53.5	31.3	6.1	85.5	4.2	0.4	1.9	4.3
49	R, 53		R, 57		R, 56		D, 51	53,997	54,027	0	48,606	29.4	11.1	16.1	96.9	0.7	0.2	0.6	0.7
50	R, 99		R, 99		R, 58		R, 57	54,282	58,956	9	50,742	27.4	8.4	15.4	95.0	0.4	1.0	0.4	1.7

(continued)

Note: D=Democrat, R=Republican, R/D=Republican/Democrat (cross-filed), D/R=Democrat/Republican (cross-filed), I=Independent, C=Constitution, O=Other, GI=Green Independent, P=Progressive, P/D=Progressive/Democrat, P/D/R=Progressive/Democrat/Republican, HH=Households

Wisconsin State Assembly Districts—Election and Demographic Data (cont.)

Assembly Districts	General Election Results Party, Percent of Vote							Population			Avg. HH Income ($)	Pop 25+ Some College + (%)	Pop 25+ 4-Yr Degree + (%)	Below Poverty Line (%)	2006 White (Non-Hisp) (%)	African American (%)	American Indians, Alaska Natives (%)	Asians, Hawaiians, Pacific Islanders (%)	Hispanic Origin (%)
Wisconsin	2000	2001	2002	2003	2004	2005	2006	2000	2006	% Change	($)	(%)	(%)	(%)	(%)	(%)	(%)	(%)	(%)
51	R, 62		R, 60		R, 57		D, 53	55,012	56,571	3	55,271	30.7	11.5	13.3	96.2	0.4	0.2	0.4	1.5
52	R, 54		R, 100		R, 66		R, 99	53,443	52,276	-2	56,162	33.3	12.8	11.7	89.8	1.9	0.5	1.4	3.7
53	R, 100		R, 99		R, 57		R, 98	56,073	58,631	5	64,626	32.9	14.0	8.8	90.2	4.8	0.6	1.0	2.2
54	R, 66		R, 58		R, 47		D, 62	53,779	53,894	0	52,133	33.0	15.6	12.7	91.1	1.0	0.4	3.4	2.2
55	R, 98		R, 99		R, 98		R, 52	51,943	52,005	0	63,847	35.6	15.8	8.5	90.1	0.7	0.6	1.5	4.1
56	R, 69		R, 100		R, 99		R, 59	55,182	60,833	10	74,726	38.9	17.8	6.7	93.3	0.6	0.4	1.3	2.2
57	R, 99		R, 99		R, 99		R, 53	55,584	56,648	2	64,380	38.4	19.2	9.8	86.7	1.4	0.7	5.1	3.3
58	R, 99		R, 99		R, 70		R, 99	51,439	56,157	9	70,883	37.6	15.2	7.0	95.7	0.4	0.3	0.4	1.7
59	R, 99		R, 79		R, 100		R, 100	56,547	59,474	5	66,708	30.9	10.8	6.5	95.5	0.3	0.3	0.5	1.9
60	R, 99		R, 99		R, 100		R, 99	54,169	57,386	6	77,045	43.6	21.5	6.3	95.4	0.5	0.3	0.7	1.7
61	D, 100		D, 98		D, 89		D, 99	54,038	54,588	1	56,607	29.7	11.8	16.3	51.5	22.1	0.4	0.7	18.9
62	D, 86		D, 85		D, 90		D, 52	54,375	55,228	2	58,667	34.9	13.3	11.0	70.8	12.2	0.4	1.0	10.5
63	R, 100		R, 99		R, 99		R, 58	53,368	56,471	6	77,676	39.1	16.3	5.7	88.8	3.3	0.4	0.9	3.7
64	D, 100		D, 100		D, 100		D, 99	53,459	57,253	7	54,371	30.2	10.1	14.7	66.1	9.5	0.5	0.9	15.2
65	D, 99		D, 99		D, 99		D, 97	55,151	59,027	7	69,515	38.3	15.9	8.9	81.2	4.2	0.4	1.3	7.8
66	R, 61		R, 99		R, 65		R, 78	56,300	62,280	11	67,001	34.9	12.8	8.4	89.8	1.9	0.2	0.8	4.1
67	R, 65		R, 61		R, 53		R, 54	53,465	58,438	9	50,912	30.9	10.3	15.2	97.1	0.2	0.3	0.5	0.8
68	D, 53		D, 51		R, 54		R, 51	52,023	54,665	5	53,816	38.9	15.0	10.3	92.2	0.7	0.5	3.7	1.1
69	R, 70		R, 69		R, 99		R, 64	55,063	56,843	3	51,737	23.7	7.8	16.9	96.2	0.3	0.3	0.6	1.4
70	R, 50		D, 54		D, 63		D, 67	53,831	53,495	-1	59,133	31.5	12.2	12.1	95.5	0.4	0.6	1.1	1.0
71	D, 70		D, 72		D, 99		D, 70	53,673	53,764	0	56,770	33.9	15.8	13.4	91.6	0.6	0.4	2.8	2.5
72	D, 68		D, 64		D, 61		D, 63	54,023	56,022	4	51,606	30.4	10.7	13.9	93.6	0.5	0.7	1.7	1.8
73	D, 60		D, 52		D, 64		D, 98	54,502	56,452	4	46,480	34.3	12.0	17.1	93.4	0.7	2.2	0.6	0.9
74	D, 62		D, 100		D, 53		D, 63	53,834	54,169	1	45,027	33.4	12.1	20.3	85.0	0.4	10.9	0.3	1.2
75	D, 62		D, 69		D, 59		D, 62	54,031	55,122	2	49,591	31.2	10.7	17.0	95.6	0.4	1.0	0.4	1.1
76	D, 68		D, 99		D, 99		D, 99	54,916	59,134	8	69,252	55.9	40.3	8.9	76.4	6.8	0.4	5.0	6.5
77	D, 99		D, 99		D, 99		D, 99	55,874	59,511	7	73,558	54.3	42.7	16.0	78.1	3.5	0.3	9.3	4.8
78	D, 81		D, 99		D, 83		D, 99	51,580	53,942	5	42,983	49.8	34.7	21.2	69.3	8.9	0.5	5.7	9.9
79	R, 56		D, 53		D, 60		D, 99	56,977	63,548	12	81,695	56.4	38.0	5.7	87.1	3.2	0.3	2.8	3.8
80	R, 61		R, 61		R, 49		R, 51	53,607	56,833	6	64,072	35.8	16.4	9.8	95.7	0.6	0.2	0.5	1.3
81	D, 68		D, 66		D, 99		D, 99	51,813	56,675	9	70,010	51.5	29.7	6.8	84.8	4.5	0.3	2.8	4.0
82	R, 62		R, 99		R, 99		R, 98	56,324	57,660	2	75,386	47.3	21.8	6.6	82.0	7.8	0.4	2.5	4.4
83	R, 76		R, 100		R, 100		R, 69	52,277	56,430	8	77,471	43.2	18.0	5.0	94.8	0.7	0.2	0.5	2.0
84	R, 100		R, 99		R, 100		R, 99	54,716	56,258	3	86,092	50.8	27.7	4.3	91.5	1.2	0.3	2.3	2.6
85	D, 62		D, 100		D, 57		D, 65	53,854	52,518	-2	58,231	33.9	14.0	12.6	86.4	0.8	0.6	9.3	1.3
86	R, 56		R, 67		R, 67		R, 64	55,631	56,775	2	65,217	33.8	13.1	8.9	95.0	0.3	0.3	2.4	0.8
87	D, 65		R, 51		R, 54		R, 51	54,272	53,659	-1	47,087	25.0	7.7	18.4	96.5	0.4	0.4	0.3	1.0
88	R, 50		R, 60		R, 54		D, 50	54,757	57,567	5	50,568	31.8	13.1	14.6	70.5	1.8	2.1	4.2	14.9
89	R, 73		R, 69		R, 64		R, 54	53,716	56,010	4	57,955	30.0	10.4	12.4	96.0	0.5	0.6	0.5	1.0
90	D, 50		R, 51		R, 52		R, 55	55,051	55,799	1	51,876	33.4	12.3	11.8	83.4	1.3	2.9	3.2	5.3
91	D, 100		D, 67		D, 65		D, 69	55,505	56,830	2	50,954	29.2	9.6	15.8	97.0	0.3	0.3	0.3	1.1
92	R, 100		R, 60		R, 58		R, 54	54,586	56,334	3	49,559	27.9	8.7	15.6	91.3	1.4	3.0	0.4	2.0
93	R, 63		R, 98		R, 52		D, 51	57,227	57,593	1	58,048	39.8	19.6	13.5	93.9	0.7	0.5	1.8	1.1
94	R, 68		R, 60		R, 58		R, 58	54,369	57,223	5	60,507	41.6	17.4	8.9	95.1	0.5	0.3	2.0	0.8
95	D, 54		D, 64		D, 99		D, 98	54,517	53,550	-2	51,040	38.2	16.8	16.8	89.2	1.9	0.5	4.9	1.3
96	R, 59		R, 62		R, 54		R, 51	54,352	55,246	2	46,475	26.7	8.8	18.7	95.6	0.7	0.2	0.3	1.5
97	D, 71		R, 62		R, 99		R, 56	54,246	56,465	4	63,601	44.6	22.0	9.2	78.8	1.6	0.4	2.1	11.5
98	R, 99		R, 83		R, 99		R, 71	55,429	58,480	6	105,186	54.6	32.2	4.2	92.5	1.0	0.1	3.2	1.5
99	R, 100		R, 84		R, 100		R, 100	54,670	59,169	8	83,502	43.1	18.5	6.2	95.2	0.6	0.2	0.8	1.6

Note: D=Democrat, R=Republican, R/D=Republican/Democrat (cross-filed), D/R=Democrat/Republican (cross-filed), I=Independent, C=Constitution, O=Other, GI=Green Independent, P=Progressive, P/D=Progressive/Democrat, P/D/R=Progressive/Democrat/Republican, HH=Households

WYOMING

Wyoming is the least populous state and one of the emptiest. Population density is five people per square mile, as compared with the District of Columbia, where it is 9,317. Just 507,000 people lived here in 2005, in a land area seventy-eight times as big as Rhode Island. Each of California's state senate districts, to make another comparison, contains 847,000 people.

One can drive for hundreds of miles across the middle of Wyoming without finding a gas station or picking up either an AM or FM radio station. Although real cowboys still work the cattle ranches (riding pickups instead of horses), vacationers from the Northeast still flock to the many dude ranches to experience the life they have read about in novels such as Owen Wister's *The Virginian*. The past is not far away. A visitor to the state sixty years ago could have still met living delegates to the statehood convention in 1889. (Like West Virginia and Nevada, Wyoming was admitted illegally, when it still lacked the requisite number of residents for statehood.) Stop by the side of the road to walk through the sage brush and it is still possible to see ruts made by covered wagons.

The state is more complicated than the old westerns suggest. Wyoming approved women's suffrage when it was still a territory, and when Congress insisted that suffrage be withdrawn as a condition of statehood, the territorial legislature replied that it would remain out of the Union for a hundred years before it would do so. (Congress backed down and Wyoming now calls itself the Equality State). In 1925 Wyoming became the first state to elect a woman governor. Nevertheless, it is still one of only six states in which men outnumber women. (The others are Alaska, Colorado, Idaho, Nevada, and Utah).

Much of what is now Jackson Hole National Monument once belonged to John D. Rockefeller Jr., who gave it to the United States in 1943. Although much of the state is devoted to sheep and cattle grazing (the two sets of ranchers once fought each other violently), Wyoming also grows sugar beets and alfalfa, and it is the nation's third-leading coal-mining state thanks to the Clean Air Act, which made its cleaner-burning, low-sulfur coal more economical. Wyoming also sits atop vast oil reserves. During the 1920s the nation shook with scandal when it was discovered that President Warren Harding's interior secretary, Albert Fall, had made sweetheart leases for cronies at the Naval Petroleum Reserve Number 3, better known for the name of a nearby rock formation called Teapot Dome.

An oil, gas, coal, and ranch-based economy was bound to suffer during the 1980s, and Wyoming did, losing more than 3 percent of its population. Since then, Wyoming has recovered, but it has not shared in the Mountain West boom. It has grown by just 11.5 percent since 1990, less than a third of the rate of its neighbors to the south and west, Idaho, Colorado, and Utah. But it is comparable to the rate of growth in South Dakota (10.6 percent) and Nebraska (10.5 percent).

The wealthiest part of the state is Jackson Hole, now a ritzy ski resort and gateway to Yellowstone National Park but as dissimilar from the rest of Wyoming as two sections of a state can be. Average household income in the state house district that includes Teton Village, where the Jackson ski slopes are located, is $118,000, which is $36,000 more than any other district in the state. This area is also the home of Vice President Dick Cheney. Soaring real estate prices have pushed most middle-class families over Teton Pass into Idaho or further out of town, so the fastest-growing parts of the state are in nearby Sublette and Lincoln Counties, the Jackson Hole suburbs, as it were. There has also been growth in and around the town of Gillette, which bills itself as the "Energy Capital of the World" and sits atop massive natural gas fields.

Whites make up 92 percent of Wyoming's citizenry, with the highest percentages in the isolated northeastern corner of the state. Most of the few African Americans (less than one percent of the population) live in Cheyenne and on the air force base that is located there. Another house district across town, however, is 27 percent Hispanic and one in Rawlins is 21 percent. Native Americans, 2 percent of the state's population, make up 35 percent of the population in the 33rd district, which includes the Wind River reservation.

The smallest of Wyoming's state house districts has about 8,000 people, making it possible for representatives to know many of their constituents personally, though they sometimes must travel great distances to see them. Republicans outnumber Democrats in the state house by more than two-to-one, and in the state senate by more than three-to-one. Voters adopted term limits for the legislature in 1992 but the state supreme court ruled them unconstitutional in 2004, just as they were to take effect.

Although Wyoming last elected a Democratic U.S. senator in 1970, three of its last four governors have been Democrats. Wyoming, finally, has one at-large U.S. representative, and in one hundred years of statehood has never had a second district. That explains why, delivering only three electoral votes, it had never placed anyone on a major-party political ticket until Dick Cheney.

WYOMING
State Senate Districts

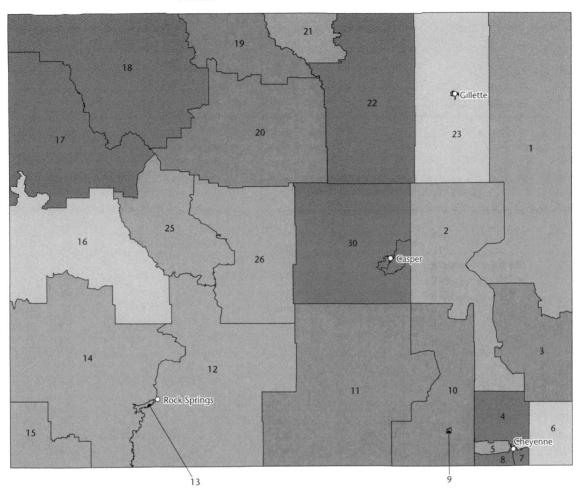

CASPER

GILLETTE

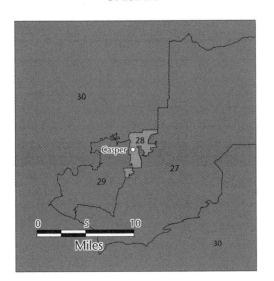

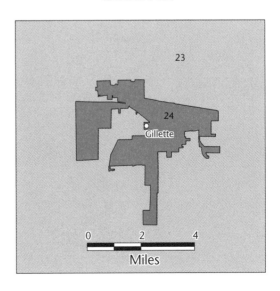

Population Growth   -17% to -6%   -6% to -1%   -1% to 6%   6% to 9%

Wyoming State Senate Districts—Election and Demographic Data

Senate Districts	General Election Results Party, Percent of Vote							Population			Avg. HH Income ($)	Pop 25+		Below Poverty Line (%)	2006 White (Non-Hisp) (%)	African American (%)	American Indians, Alaska Natives (%)	Asians, Hawaiians, Pacific Islanders (%)	Hispanic Origin (%)
												Some College + (%)	4-Yr Degree + (%)						
Wyoming	2000	2001	2002	2003	2004	2005	2006	2000	2006	% Change	($)	(%)	(%)	(%)	(%)	(%)	(%)	(%)	(%)
1			R, 100		R, 100		R, 100	16,136	15,400	-5	47,337	33.9	13.0	19.1	95.4	0.1	1.0	0.2	1.9
2	R, 62				R, 100			16,348	16,079	-2	50,649	35.1	12.1	17.2	91.4	0.2	0.9	0.3	4.7
3			R, 100				R, 58	15,811	14,650	-7	42,353	35.4	13.9	20.6	87.2	0.2	0.9	0.3	8.2
4	R, 65				R, 100			18,527	18,728	1	61,834	48.0	22.7	10.8	85.4	1.8	0.7	1.2	7.9
5			R, 100				R, 62	15,254	14,741	-3	67,381	51.1	25.9	7.9	84.1	3.9	0.6	1.8	6.7
6	D, 57				R, 58			15,503	16,554	7	55,784	42.5	16.5	11.0	85.3	2.0	0.7	1.1	7.9
7			D, 100				D, 100	16,103	16,249	1	42,267	40.2	14.6	14.9	78.5	2.3	1.0	0.9	12.6
8	D, 100				D, 100			16,050	15,991	0	39,701	33.9	10.6	17.6	64.6	4.6	1.6	0.9	22.2
9			D, 100				D, 100	14,799	13,523	-9	34,866	47.5	31.6	25.7	82.9	1.2	1.1	1.2	9.5
10	R, 57				R, 56			31,702	29,366	-7	43,206	49.8	33.3	24.3	85.1	1.2	1.0	2.1	7.3
11			D, 59				D, 59	15,955	14,765	-7	49,566	36.1	14.7	17.6	79.6	0.7	1.4	0.8	12.8
12	D, 56				D, 100			15,516	14,639	-6	49,688	35.5	13.5	13.3	81.6	1.3	1.0	1.0	11.2
13			D, 64				D, 100	16,544	15,903	-4	66,932	35.5	12.9	9.9	82.2	0.5	1.2	0.6	11.2
14	D, 100				R, 67			17,172	16,850	-2	56,098	32.1	10.9	12.0	91.6	0.2	0.6	0.4	5.1
15			D, 58				D, 100	15,062	14,272	-5	54,997	31.6	11.6	13.7	87.6	0.2	1.1	0.4	7.0
16	R, 100				R, 68			16,213	17,603	9	64,777	41.3	19.0	11.5	95.1	0.1	0.6	0.2	2.7
17			R, 100				R, 53	17,200	17,442	1	91,071	57.1	36.8	8.4	83.9	0.2	0.8	0.7	10.8
18	R, 100				R, 100			17,049	17,075	0	50,784	42.3	20.3	14.0	94.7	0.1	0.4	0.6	2.5
19			R, 100				R, 100	17,090	15,683	-8	44,513	36.3	14.1	18.4	89.4	0.1	0.7	0.4	6.5
20	R, 100				R, 100			16,298	14,996	-8	46,166	35.9	14.6	17.8	85.5	0.2	0.9	0.6	8.8
21			R, 57				R, 100	15,816	15,403	-3	50,242	43.5	18.6	15.7	93.6	0.2	1.3	0.6	2.6
22	R, 100				R, 100			17,820	18,264	2	49,711	42.4	17.6	17.5	94.6	0.2	1.1	0.3	2.3
23			R, 100				R, 72	33,701	36,126	7	61,453	34.5	11.6	11.0	92.1	0.2	1.0	0.4	4.5
24	R, 71				R, 84			16,585	13,891	-16	57,645	35.7	13.3	12.3	90.5	0.3	1.1	0.5	5.5
25			R, 100				R, 61	17,271	16,752	-3	47,110	35.3	15.6	21.4	60.0	0.1	35.2	0.3	3.9
26	R, 100				R, 100			16,729	16,029	-4	46,675	34.4	13.7	18.7	82.4	0.1	8.1	0.4	6.3
27			R, 100				R, 100	16,543	16,701	1	56,496	41.8	17.9	12.8	89.9	0.8	0.9	0.6	5.1
28	D, 51				R, 51			17,504	17,267	-1	45,748	39.3	15.6	17.8	87.6	1.2	1.4	0.8	6.3
29			R, 100				R, 51	16,851	16,866	0	56,668	42.8	17.6	12.1	93.3	0.4	0.7	0.3	3.4
30	R, 65				R, 67			15,604	15,908	2	46,957	35.4	10.9	15.0	88.5	1.0	1.4	0.3	5.6

Note: D=Democrat, R=Republican, R/D=Republican/Democrat (cross-filed), D/R=Democrat/Republican (cross-filed), I=Independent, C=Constitution, O=Other, GI=Green Independent, P=Progressive, P/D=Progressive/Democrat, P/D/R=Progressive/Democrat/Republican, HH=Households

WYOMING
State House Districts

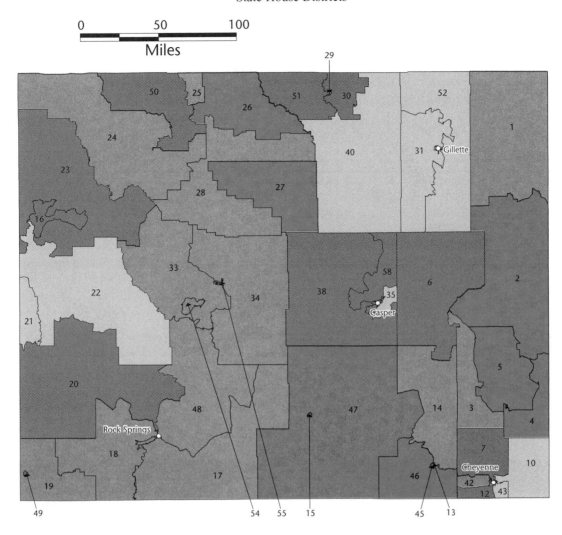

0   50   100

Miles

ROCK SPRINGS

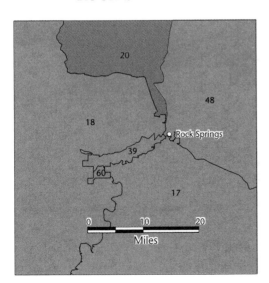

0   10   20

Miles

GILLETTE

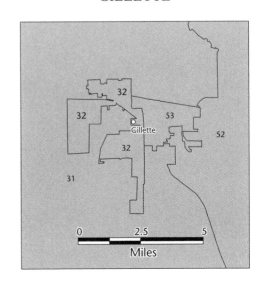

0   2.5   5

Miles

Population Growth   ▨ -7% to -1%   ▨ -1% to 4%   ▨ 4% to 10%   ▨ 10% to 16%

CASPER

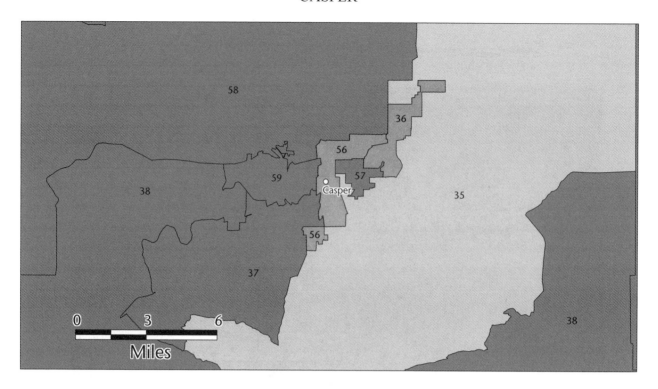

CHEYENNE

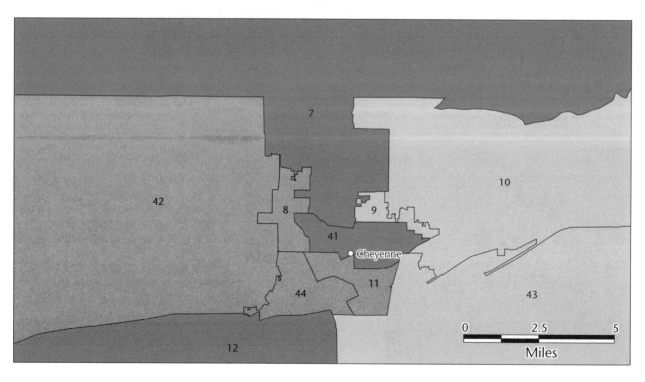

Population Growth   ■ -7% to -1%   ■ -1% to 4%   ■ 4% to 10%   □ 10% to 16%

Wyoming State House Districts—Election and Demographic Data

House Districts	General Election Results Party, Percent of Vote							Population			2006								
											Avg. HH Income	Pop 25+		Below Poverty Line	White (Non-Hisp)	African American	American Indians, Alaska Natives	Asians, Hawaiians, Pacific Islanders	Hispanic Origin
												Some College +	4-Yr Degree +						
Wyoming	2000	2001	2002	2003	2004	2005	2006	2000	2006	% Change	($)	(%)	(%)	(%)	(%)	(%)	(%)	(%)	(%)
1	R, 78		R, 100		R, 100		R, 100	7,757	8,051	4	48,846	34.3	13.8	20.1	96.6	0.0	1.1	0.1	1.4
2	D, 100		D, 53		D, 53		D, 100	7,773	7,613	-2	45,668	33.3	12.2	18.0	94.0	0.2	1.0	0.2	2.5
3	R, 100		R, 100		R, 100		R, 100	8,114	8,063	-1	50,605	35.8	12.9	16.7	91.8	0.2	0.6	0.3	5.0
4	R, 100		R, 100		R, 100		R, 100	7,885	7,697	-2	41,092	36.9	15.1	21.1	85.0	0.2	1.0	0.3	9.8
5	R, 82		R, 100		R, 100		R, 100	7,264	7,151	-2	43,722	33.8	12.6	20.0	89.6	0.1	0.7	0.3	6.5
6	R, 100		R, 100		R, 100		R, 100	7,491	8,174	9	50,671	34.5	11.3	17.8	91.0	0.2	1.1	0.3	4.4
7	R, 72		R, 100		R, 64		R, 100	8,517	9,130	7	82,758	53.8	27.8	7.2	89.8	1.2	0.5	1.5	5.2
8	R, 51		R, 55		R, 100		D, 50	6,695	6,801	2	64,231	55.0	29.6	9.0	87.7	1.8	0.5	1.5	6.1
9	R, 100		R, 100		R, 58		R, 57	6,130	6,801	11	55,572	43.5	16.6	9.3	80.4	3.0	0.6	1.7	10.4
10	R, 100		R, 100		R, 64		R, 100	8,808	10,067	14	55,937	41.8	16.4	12.1	88.6	1.3	0.8	0.7	6.2
11	D, 100		D, 55		D, 100		D, 61	8,011	8,112	1	40,107	41.4	16.4	16.3	77.8	2.3	0.9	1.2	13.2
12	D, 57		D, 57		D, 100		R, 50	8,112	8,754	8	42,605	33.3	9.0	14.1	70.4	3.6	1.1	0.8	17.8
13	D, 100		D, 66		D, 100		D, 100	7,514	7,077	-6	34,375	49.7	34.1	28.4	86.2	1.2	1.0	1.5	6.9
14	R, 56		R, 61		R, 57		R, 100	7,930	7,866	-1	43,960	51.6	37.0	26.2	86.6	1.6	0.8	4.2	4.7
15	R, 64		D, 50		D, 51		D, 61	6,961	6,830	-2	50,435	30.6	10.7	18.9	68.8	0.7	1.5	1.0	21.3
16	R, 52		D, 58		D, 100		D, 60	7,430	8,082	9	118,115	60.4	41.0	7.1	78.3	0.2	0.6	0.9	15.2
17	R, 55		R, 53		R, 51		D, 100	7,548	7,547	0	51,148	34.9	13.5	14.1	82.4	1.1	1.0	0.9	10.9
18	R, 51		R, 52		R, 100		R, 100	8,254	8,377	1	57,022	31.5	9.6	12.1	91.0	0.2	0.6	0.4	5.5
19	R, 54		R, 70		R, 100		R, 100	14,524	14,566	0	55,064	31.5	11.6	13.6	87.7	0.2	1.0	0.4	6.9
20	R, 60		R, 100		R, 100		R, 100	8,008	8,448	5	54,921	32.6	12.2	12.0	92.3	0.3	0.6	0.5	4.7
21	R, 100		R, 100		R, 100		R, 100	7,966	9,193	15	51,411	35.6	12.8	13.0	94.9	0.1	0.7	0.1	2.8
22	R, 100		R, 71		R, 100		R, 100	7,550	8,627	14	76,384	47.3	25.5	10.3	95.3	0.1	0.5	0.4	2.6
23	R, 100		R, 100		R, 52		R, 100	9,078	9,630	6	68,748	54.5	33.3	9.5	88.8	0.1	0.9	0.5	7.1
24	R, 100		R, 100		R, 100		R, 100	8,123	8,410	4	48,251	45.6	23.8	12.8	94.5	0.1	0.5	0.5	2.4
25	R, 100		R, 100		R, 100		R, 100	8,229	8,254	0	44,097	39.2	15.9	17.6	90.6	0.1	0.5	0.5	5.9
26	R, 66		R, 86		R, 100		R, 100	8,133	7,629	-6	44,951	33.2	12.0	19.2	88.1	0.2	0.9	0.3	7.0
27	R, 100		R, 100		D, 55		D, 100	7,944	7,432	-6	49,297	36.3	14.8	17.2	79.6	0.1	0.6	0.9	13.2
28	R, 100		R, 100		R, 100		R, 100	7,661	7,757	1	43,164	35.6	14.4	18.3	91.2	0.2	1.3	0.3	4.6
29	R, 80		R, 64		R, 100		R, 100	7,150	7,236	1	45,992	41.1	15.5	17.9	92.6	0.2	1.1	0.9	3.2
30	R, 63		R, 58		R, 62		R, 100	8,959	9,582	7	49,604	41.2	16.5	17.5	93.9	0.3	1.5	0.4	2.3
31	R, 68		R, 100		R, 100		R, 100	10,585	12,185	15	65,434	34.6	12.8	9.9	93.6	0.2	0.8	0.4	3.5
32	R, 83		R, 85		R, 82		R, 82	5,048	5,629	12	63,412	38.3	17.2	11.5	93.1	0.2	0.6	0.6	3.5
33	R, 100		R, 61		D, 56		D, 61	16,525	16,955	3	47,098	35.3	15.6	21.4	70.1	0.1	26.8	0.3	4.0
34	R, 100		R, 100		R, 100		R, 80	9,524	9,832	3	49,754	34.5	14.0	18.3	89.9	0.1	5.6	0.6	5.3
35	R, 100		R, 100		R, 100		R, 100	8,980	9,941	11	64,660	43.9	20.5	10.9	90.9	0.9	0.9	0.6	4.4
36	R, 52				R, 52		D, 55	7,215	7,306	1	45,613	38.9	14.4	15.4	88.7	0.7	0.9	0.7	6.0
37	R, 100		R, 62		R, 70		R, 70	7,955	8,376	5	74,367	50.8	24.5	7.2	95.1	0.3	0.5	0.2	2.5
38	R, 53		R, 56		R, 62		R, 67	6,848	7,354	7	55,997	40.4	13.7	8.1	92.2	0.4	1.0	0.3	4.0
39	D, 100		D, 100		D, 100		D, 100	7,837	8,009	2	67,531	36.6	13.8	10.7	83.0	0.7	0.9	0.9	10.4
40	R, 100		R, 100		R, 100		R, 57	8,107	8,918	10	49,803	43.6	18.7	17.6	95.4	0.1	0.6	0.2	2.2
41	D, 100		R, 51		R, 62		D, 56	9,247	9,823	6	45,017	42.8	18.3	13.2	81.8	2.3	1.0	1.1	10.2
42	R, 100		R, 75		R, 65		R, 100	7,730	7,946	3	72,387	47.8	22.6	5.7	81.1	5.7	0.6	2.0	7.1
43	R, 100		R, 52		R, 60		R, 100	7,569	8,545	13	44,584	38.7	12.7	13.3	78.6	2.4	1.1	0.6	12.4
44	D, 59		D, 65		D, 100		D, 66	7,139	7,321	3	36,914	34.6	12.6	20.8	57.9	5.7	2.1	1.1	27.4
45	D, 100		D, 100		R, 53		R, 50	6,521	6,499	0	35,159	44.8	28.5	22.7	79.3	1.3	1.3	0.8	12.5
46	R, 55		R, 100		R, 58		R, 55	8,383	8,295	-1	58,062	52.0	32.9	20.1	87.3	0.9	1.0	1.5	6.0
47	R, 61		R, 100		R, 100		R, 56	15,274	14,951	-2	49,566	36.1	14.7	17.6	79.6	0.7	1.4	0.8	12.8
48	D, 55		D, 55		D, 100		D, 100	7,452	7,433	0	48,246	36.1	13.4	12.6	80.8	1.5	1.0	1.1	11.4
49	D, 51		D, 64		R, 52		D, 64	6,468	6,216	-4	56,414	34.4	13.5	12.6	87.2	0.1	1.0	0.6	7.0
50	R, 65		R, 78		R, 100		R, 100	8,286	8,942	8	53,038	39.2	17.0	15.1	95.0	0.1	0.4	0.6	2.5

(continued)

Note: D=Democrat, R=Republican, R/D=Republican/Democrat (cross-filed), D/R=Democrat/Republican (cross-filed), I=Independent, C=Constitution, O=Other, GI=Green Independent, P=Progressive, P/D=Progressive/Democrat, P/D/R=Progressive/Democrat/Republican, HH=Households

Wyoming State House Districts—Election and Demographic Data (cont.)

House Districts	General Election Results Party, Percent of Vote							Population			Avg. HH Income	Pop 25+		Below Poverty Line	White (Non-Hisp)	African American	American Indians, Alaska Natives	Asians, Hawaiians, Pacific Islanders	Hispanic Origin
												Some College +	4-Yr Degree +						2006
Wyoming	2000	2001	2002	2003	2004	2005	2006	2000	2006	% Change	($)	(%)	(%)	(%)	(%)	(%)	(%)	(%)	(%)
51	R, 100		R, 64		R, 73		R, 100	7,983	8,358	5	54,310	45.7	21.3	13.4	94.4	0.1	1.4	0.3	2.1
52	R, 100		R, 100		R, 100		R, 100	9,270	10,666	15	62,425	32.8	8.1	9.9	92.6	0.1	1.1	0.3	4.3
53	D, 100		R, 61		R, 100		R, 68	7,360	8,100	10	53,955	34.1	10.7	12.8	88.5	0.3	1.5	0.4	7.0
54	R, 84		R, 100		R, 100		R, 100	8,047	8,200	2	52,385	43.0	22.3	14.1	87.3	0.2	6.5	0.5	3.7
55	R, 60		R, 100		R, 100		R, 100	6,527	6,437	-1	42,312	34.2	13.1	19.2	79.9	0.2	8.8	0.6	8.3
56	R, 59		R, 57		R, 66		R, 53	8,785	9,073	3	41,957	39.3	15.4	21.4	87.2	1.3	1.6	0.5	6.2
57	R, 55		R, 54		R, 65		R, 79	7,856	8,304	6	49,573	38.9	15.5	13.7	87.7	1.1	1.2	1.0	6.6
58	D, 51		D, 100		D, 100		R, 61	7,784	8,456	9	39,987	31.3	8.5	20.0	85.5	1.4	1.7	0.3	6.9
59	D, 61		D, 63		D, 53		D, 100	8,240	8,777	7	41,781	35.2	11.0	15.8	91.6	0.4	0.8	0.4	4.4
60	D, 63		D, 100		D, 100		D, 100	8,102	8,200	1	66,556	34.5	12.2	9.0	81.4	0.3	1.6	0.4	12.1

Note: D=Democrat, R=Republican, R/D=Republican/Democrat (cross-filed), D/R=Democrat/Republican (cross-filed), I=Independent, C=Constitution, O=Other, GI=Green Independent, P=Progressive, P/D=Progressive/Democrat, P/D/R=Progressive/Democrat/Republican, HH=Households